BREAKING TELEPRINTER CIPHERS AT BLETCHLEY PARK

IEEE Press
445 Hoes Lane
Piscataway, NJ 08854

BREAKING TELEPRINTER CIPHERS AT BLETCHLEY PARK

An edition of
I. J. Good, D. Michie and G. Timms

General Report on Tunny with emphasis on Statistical Methods (1945)

Edited and with introductions and notes by
James A. Reeds, Whitfield Diffie and J. V. Field

IEEE
IEEE Press

WILEY

Published by John Wiley & Sons, Inc., Hoboken, New Jersey.
Published simultaneously in Canada.

Library of Congress Cataloging-in-Publication is available.

ISBN 978-0-470-46589-9

10 9 8 7 6 5 4 3 2 1

Contents

31 - MR. NEWMAN'S SECTION

31A GROWTH

In December, 1942 Mr. M.H.A. Newman was given the job of developing machine methods of setting Tunny. In April, 1943 the first machines arrived, a Robinson and a Tunny, pilot models of somewhat uncertain behaviour. Mr. Newman formed his section with one cryptographer, two engineers and 16 Wrens. The section was founded and lived (for the most part) in a single room. After three months two or three messages were set each week.

By May, 1945 there were 26 Cryptographers, 28 Engineers, and 273 Wrens with 10 Colossi, 3 Robinsons, 3 Tunnies and 20 smaller electrical machines. The section moved into Block F in November, 1943, and expanded into a new and additional Block (H) in September, 1944, in which all chi-breaking was done. In the week ending March 31st, 358 messages were set on Chis, 151 on Motors and Psis and 23 sets of new wheels were broken.

The total number of log books used in 2 years was about 500.

31B STAFF REQUIREMENTS

The allocation of staff at 6 monthly intervals is shown in the following table.

		Apr.43	Sep.43	Apr.44	Sep.44	Apr.45
	Administration	–	–	1	2	2
	Cryptographers	2	5	6	20	22
Engineers	Maintenance	–	3	9	12	15
	Construction	–	4	9	11	13
	Wrens	16	16	68	180	273
	TOTAL	18	28	93	225	325

Finally the staff per shift was as follows:

7 Cryptographers : DO in charge of setting
1 Wheel-man in charge of wheel-breaking
1 in charge of Colossus and Robinson work
2 to supervise Colossus setting
2 to supervise Colossus wheel-breaking

67 Wrens : 7 Registrars
17 Tunny Operators
2 Robinson Operators
20 Colossus Operators

General Report on Tunny, **31**, TNA HW 25/5, p. 276; this edition, pp. 262–263.
(scale = .6)

Preface

This volume has its origins in a meeting of the British Society for the History of Mathematics held in Cambridge (UK) in 2000. The subject was the history of cryptography and one of the speakers, Prof. Donald Michie, used the occasion to announce that it had been agreed that the Report of the group of cryptographers to which he had belonged at Bletchley Park during the Second World War was to be declassified. This was the group that had designed and used the Colossus machines, so the planned declassification was of great interest to historians of computing as well as to historians of cryptography. The audience decided there and then that the book, which at the time no one present except Prof. Michie had seen, should be published. The present volume is the product of that resolution.

We are grateful to the Royal Society (London) for a grant that enabled us to pay for professional help in carrying out what proved to be an intricate task in typography. We are grateful to John Gilmore for providing additional financial support for the initial stage of the typesetting. We are grateful also to the Newcomen Society, which acted as our banker.

Many friends and colleagues have given us various forms of support and encouragement in our editorial work. Our greatest debts are to the late Prof. I. J. Good and the late Prof. Donald Michie, who were patient and generous in dealing with appeals for information and guidance. We are also grateful to the following: Prof. Richard Aldrich, Steve Boyack, A. O. Bauer, Prof. Colin Burke, Pam Camp, Ray Chase, Tom Collins, David DeGeorge, Gina Douglas and John Parmenter, Ralph Erskine, Frederika and Stephen Freer, David Goldschmidt, Ruth Greenstein, David Hamer, Barbara Hamilton, Mrs Vicki Hammond, Robert Hanyok, Jim Haynes, Ms Marit Hartveit, Grete Heinz, David Kahn, the late Hans-Georg Kampe, Joy MacCleary (née Timms), the late Dr Bera MacClement (née Timms), Bob McGwire, Marjorie McNinch, Alex Magoun, Ross Moore, Ned Neuburg, Selmer Norlund, Harris Nover, Sharon Olson, Jon D. Paul, John O'Rourke, H. N. Reeds, Karen Reeds, Randy Rezabek, the late Tony Sale, David Saltman, John N. Seaman, Jr, William Seaman, Betsy Rohaly Smoot, Christoph Steger, René Stein, Elaine Tennant, Frode Weierud, Tom Whitmore, Bill Williams, the late Shaun Wylie, Prof. Sandy Zabell, the current Departmental Historian of GCHQ, Tony Comer, and his predecessor, and *his* predecessor, the late Peter Freeman, and the staffs of the David Sarnoff Library, Princeton, New Jersey, the Hagley Museum and Library, Wilmington, Delaware, the Linda Hall Library, Kansas City, Missouri, the National Archives of the United Kingdom, the National Archives of the United States, and the National Cryptologic Museum, Ft. Meade, Maryland.

In addition, J. V. Field is grateful to Dr A. E. L. Davis, Dr J. Barrow-Green, Prof. Graeme Gooday, the late Prof. A. R. Hall, Prof. Frank A. J. L. James, Prof. Jonathan Michie, Alec Muffett, C. J. Reid and Dr K. C. Sugden for help on historical or technical points and occasional practical assistance. Thanks are also due to the archivists of various institutions: from Cambridge the archivists of Magdalene, Queens', St John's, Sidney Sussex and Trinity Colleges, and of Trinity Hall, from Oxford the archivists of New College, Balliol, Magdalen, Merton, Queen's and Wadham Colleges, and the university archivist; and the archivists of Imperial College, London, of the Royal Aeronautical Society, London, and of the former Beaumont College (Old Windsor).

J. A. Reeds, *Princeton*
W. Diffie, *Woodbridge*
J. V. Field, *London*

Editorial Notes

1. The essay 'Statistics at Bletchley Park', the editorial endnotes to the text of the *General Report on Tunny*, and the Appendices have been subject to review by the U.S. Department of Defense.

2. To avoid repetition in the introductory essays and editorial endnotes, we have provided a set of short biographies of people mentioned in the *General Report on Tunny* and other primary sources cited in this volume. In particular we have sought to include anyone we had occasion to refer to as having worked at Bletchley Park. There are also brief notes on a few famous people whose work was used at Bletchley Park, such as Bayes and Laplace. There are longer biographies of the three editors of the original *Report*.

3. The text of the *General Report on Tunny* used for our edition is held in the UK National Archives (TNA). Unless otherwise noted, material on pp. 1–258 is from TNA HW 25/4 and that on pp. 258–493 from TNA HW 25/5. The text, together with accompanying artwork, is Crown Copyright.

Notes on Vocabulary

In 2015, a cryptographer is the person making ciphers or encrypting texts, a cryptanalyst is the one breaking ciphers in order to read the original plain text. Obviously, each needs to know something of the craft practised by the other and at Bletchley Park it seems to have been usual to use the term 'cryptographer' in referring to both types of practitioner. The term 'cryptanalyst' was known at the time but seems to have been widely used in England only after the war. When engaging directly with texts of the 1940s we have generally adopted 'cryptographer' (using 'actors' categories') but on occasion the newer, narrower term has been used for the sake of clarity.

The authors of the *General Report on Tunny* worked in an institution whose title was 'Government Code and Cypher School'. This title implies that in formal usage, at least, there was a distinction between the terms 'code' and 'cipher'. In technical usage, a code is a system of some kind for conveying information, a cipher is a system for concealing information. However, the authors of the *General Report on Tunny* often use the term 'code' instead of 'cipher'. We have made no attempt to correct these technically incorrect uses of 'code'. No doubt in 1945, as in 2015, such usage was acceptable in a colloquial context. Our own text uses 'cipher' where appropriate.

The 'Glossary' of the *General Report on Tunny* (chapter **71**) makes its own usages clear by supplying the definition 'CRYPTOGRAPHY The science of breaking codes and ciphers. Usually applied specifically to hand processes.' It refers the reader to chapter **39** section **B** for details.

List of Abbreviations

We list here bibliographic abbreviations. Organisational abbreviations used in wartime sources, such as ‘GCCS’ for ‘Government Code and Cypher School’, will be found in one of the two glossaries below: the original ‘Glossary’ provided in 1945 (chapter **71** of the *General Report on Tunny*, pp. 400–446; this edition, pp. 387–434) or the ‘Supplementary Glossary’ provided by the present editors (pp. 542–546). Throughout this book we use a bold face to indicate chapter and section numbers in the original text of the *General Report on Tunny*. Throughout this book, URL visit dates are given in day/month/year format.

GRT *General Report on Tunny, with Emphasis on Statistical Methods*, TNA HW 25/4 and HW 25/5. See ‘*Report*’ below.

NARA United States National Archives and Records Administration; the College Park, Maryland branch holding the records we cite.

ODNB *Oxford Dictionary of National Biography* (*Oxford Dictionary of National Biography: In Association with the British Academy: From the Earliest Times to the Year 2000*, ed. by H.C.G. Matthew and Brian Harrison (London: Oxford University Press, 2004), URL: `http://www.oxforddnb.com/subscribed/` (visited on 07/06/2014)).

Report *General Report on Tunny, with Emphasis on Statistical Methods*. We use this term ambiguously, to refer both to the text of the *Report*, an edition of which we present in this volume, and to the physical artefact in the archives, items TNA HW 25/4 and 25/5: the ‘original *Report*’.

TNA The National Archives of the United Kingdom, located in Kew, Surrey.

Cryptanalytic Significance of the Analysis of Tunny

Whitfield Diffie

The analyses conducted at Bletchley Park of the higher-grade German cryptosystems — above the division-level Enigma system — are usually viewed in the military-historical context of their impact on the course of the Second World War. Also well known is the role this analysis played in the construction of Colossus, immediate ancestor of modern stored-program digital computers. What is less well known is the significance of the analytic process of which Colossus was but a part. The Lorenz SZ 40 and the Siemens and Halske T52 were given the cover names Tunny and Sturgeon by the British and collectively referred to as 'Fish'. Although these systems are crude by the standards of systems to follow within a decade, they look more like the binary systems that came to dominate cryptography than they do like the Enigma with its 26-letter rotors. The attack on Tunny can thus be seen as the first major 'modern' cryptanalysis.

The early part of the twentieth century saw a general mathematicization of cryptography and particularly of cryptanalysis. At the time of the First World War, cryptanalytic organisations sought their personnel primarily among linguists; by end of the Second, they sought them primarily among mathematicians.

Cryptography, despite a history leading back at least to ninth-century Baghdad and having enjoyed a burst of innovation in Europe during the Renaissance, entered the twentieth century as a sideshow in information security. Despite hundreds of years of interesting theoretical developments, cryptography at the beginning of the twentieth century was a minor aspect of information protection. The field we would now call information security was dominated by guards and locked doors and was just beginning to develop the distribution restriction markings and personnel vetting ubiquitous in government bureaucracies today. By and large, cryptography was a supplementary security measure applied to messages already protected by the careful handling of diplomatic pouches. The introduction of the telegraph in the mid-nineteenth century had stimulated cryptography but had fallen well short of bringing on a revolution. Most encryption was done with code books and was capable of encrypting at most a few words a minute and not very securely at that.

Marconi's transatlantic radio transmission on the 18th of January 1904 changed everything. Radio was an irresistible invention whose impact is most easily seen in naval warfare. Before radio, the First Sea Lord, who commanded the greatest fleet in the world, barely knew where it was. The Admiralty laid out a map of the world on a large table and pushed little models around to the estimated positions of ships. Actual contacts might come at intervals of days, weeks, or even months. Within a few years of the introduction of radio, it was possible to contact any ship in the fleet, at first within hours, then in minutes, now in seconds.

Radio, however, had a singular disadvantage from a security viewpoint: anyone could listen to the radio and often the people you did not want listening were getting better reception than the ones you did. Among all the information security techniques known at that time, only cryptography could address this problem. As the cryptography of the day was not up to the task, the development of systems that were became the major theme in information security and accounted for most of the activity in the field for the better part of a century.

A paradigm that dominated military cryptography from shortly after World War I until the 1950s and later is the rotor machine, of which Enigma — in its many varieties — is a perfect example. Systems of this general sort — which went under the name 'multiple Vigenère' — had been known for five hundred years. Each character of the plain text was encrypted by a different alphabet, selected by a character of key from a table of possibilities. In principle, the process could be repeated a number of times until the output was considered secure. In practice, it was not feasible to do more than one or two iterations by hand without suffering an unacceptable number of errors. The use of these 500-year-old polyalphabetic ciphers was made possible by electromechanical technology developed in the late nineteenth century, but this technology was not applied to cryptographic problems until World War I.

Expanding use of polyalphabetic ciphers led to improved tools for attacking them. In 1922, William Fredrick Friedman (1891–1969) of the Riverbank Laboratories in Illinois wrote a paper entitled 'The Index of Coincidence and its Applications in Cryptography', which is generally seen as heralding the introduction of statistics into cryptanalysis.[1]

The index of coincidence counts the number of agreements (or coincidences) between two sequences. Thus

'scurvy devils ride so high'

and

'meet me at the orange tree'

have index of coincidence 1; they only agree in the space before the last word, whereas

'body paint eventually washes off'

and

'there were no potatoes in stores'

agree in two, one space and one 'a'.

The index of coincidence exploits the most important principle in cryptanalysis, the consequence of functionality: if two plain text elements are identical and are enciphered in identical circumstances, the results will be the same. If we know that a cipher alphabet, like a rotor, transforms 'a' to 'q', we know very little about how it will translate 'b' (only that it will not translate it to 'q'). On the other hand, if we know that 'a' is translated to 'q' and we see a 'q', we know that the input must have been an 'a'.

The cryptanalytic utility of the index of coincidence is that it is preserved by polyalphabetic ciphers like rotor machines. If a rotor machine enciphers two messages using the same key and the same starting position, whenever the same plain text character appears in the same position in both plain texts, the same cipher text character will appear in that position in both cipher texts. This permits the cryptanalyst to detect when two rotor machines were started with the same key and at the same rotor setting.

In many large communication networks, crypto-machines across the network share the same key by design. They are meant to be initialized to a unique starting position for each message but errors in achieving this are common. Once the cryptanalysts have detected two messages encrypted by machines in identical states, they can often bypass most of the complexity of the machines themselves. This occurrence of two different views of the operation of the cryptographic devices is called a ̀dfdepth of two' problem.

The index-of-coincidence formulation is used by Solomon Kullback, as late as 1935, in a monograph called 'Statistical Methods in Cryptanalysis', written for the U.S. Army Signal Corps.[2]

[1] W. F. Friedman, *The Index of Coincidence and its Applications in Cryptography*, Riverbank Laboratories, 1922.
[2] Solomon Kullback, *Statistical Methods in Cryptanalysis*, United States Army Signal Corps, 1935.

As communications technology developed, it became more and more binary. Just as Morse code uses two types of symbols — dot and dash — from which it makes up a larger alphabet, teletype codes and others build large alphabets from strings of two symbols.

Binary sequences can be compared for coincidence exactly like sequences of letters. For example, the following two sequences of length 32:

```
0 0 1 1 0 1 0 0 0 0 1 0 1 1 1 0 1 0 1 1 0 1 1 1 1 0 0 0 1 0 1 0
1 1 1 0 1 0 0 0 1 0 1 0 1 0 1 1 1 0 1 0 0 0 1 0 0 1 1 0 1 0 1 1
    x         x x   x x x x   x   x x x   x   x         x x x x
```

agree in 17 places (as shown by the x) and therefore disagree in the remaining 15. Basing communication on the binary alphabet opens up a new possibility.

Regardless of the size of the alphabet, agreement between letters occurs in only one way: the letters are exactly the same. In alphabets that, like the Latin alphabet, have more than two characters, disagreements may occur in many different ways. In a binary alphabet, disagreements, like agreements, occur in only one way. This makes it possible to replace the index of coincidence by a different formulation: agreements minus disagreements. In statistics, this measure of the relationship of two binary sequences would be called correlation; in cryptanalysis, it is called the bulge.

In the case shown above, there are 17 agreements and 15 disagreements, so the bulge of the two sequences is 2. Two minor points about this measure are worth noting. First, changing one bit of either sequence will change the bulge by 2 because it will increase either agreements or disagreements by 1 and decrease the other one by 1. For this reason, it is often called the double bulge and equally often divided by 2. (Some people call this the half bulge.) The size of the number also depends on the length of the sequence and can reasonably be expected to be larger if the sequences are longer. This suggests normalising by dividing by the total number of bits. This is often called the proportional bulge. We will take our bulges to be proportioned but not halved.

$$\text{bulge} = \frac{\text{agreements} - \text{disagreements}}{\text{agreements} + \text{disagreements}} \quad .$$

At first appearance the index of coincidence and the bulge are not very different. If the number of agreements between two sequences of length n is a, then the number of disagreements is $n-a$ and the (unnormalised) bulge is $a-(n-a) = 2a-n$. The significance of the bulge is that it is in essence a Fourier transform, a relationship between time and frequency extensively studied by mathematicians and electrical engineers. This puts at the cryptanalyst's disposal a range of mathematical results from the fields called harmonic analysis and signal processing.

The most important tool in applied mathematics, and cryptanalysis is no exception, is linear approximation. In differential calculus, for example, curves are studied by approximating them by straight lines, their tangents. With the exception of the very limited class of constant functions, linear functions are the simplest. A linear function is a function with the property that for any two inputs, x and y, applying the function to the sum of the inputs is the same as taking the sum of the results of applying the function to each of the inputs individually

$$f(x+y) = f(x) + f(y).$$

In a sense, the inputs of a linear function do not interact in producing the output. Non-linear functions, such as the familiar cubing function that transforms an input x to $x \times x \times x = x^3$, do not have this property. In this case

$$(x+y)^3 = x^3 + 3x^2y + 3xy^2 + y^3$$

and the result is significantly more complicated than summing the cubes of the inputs which would give $x^3 + y^3$.

The non-interaction of the inputs makes computing with linear functions particularly simple. If cryptographic systems were built entirely with linear functions, cryptanalysis would be easy; for this reason, non-linearity is an essential element in cryptography. A major tool of cryptanalysis is to attempt to defeat the use of non-linear functions by approximating the non-linear functions with linear ones.

In order to compare binary functions, we simply write them as the sequence of outputs corresponding to the inputs in a standard order. For example, the majority function, which takes three inputs and has the value 0 or 1 depending on whether the majority of the inputs are 0 or 1, can be shown as a table.

x	y	z	majority(x, y, z)
0	0	0	0
0	0	1	0
0	1	0	0
0	1	1	1
1	0	0	0
1	0	1	1
1	1	0	1
1	1	1	1

and the function can be represented as its sequence of output values 0 0 0 1 0 1 1 1.

In order to compare two functions, we take the bulge of their output sequences. The object is to approximate non-linear functions with linear ones and we are therefore most interested in the bulge of an arbitrary function f with respect to a linear function ℓ.

There are eight linear functions of three variables; each linear function is the sum of a subset of the variables, and there are eight such subsets

Variables									Bulge wrt Majority
(none)	0	0	0	0	0	0	0	0	0
z	0	1	0	1	0	1	0	1	$\frac{1}{2}$
y	0	0	1	1	0	0	1	1	$\frac{1}{2}$
$y+z$	0	1	1	0	0	1	1	0	0
x	0	0	0	0	1	1	1	1	$\frac{1}{2}$
$x + z$	0	1	0	1	1	0	1	0	0
$x+y$	0	0	1	1	1	1	0	0	0
$x+y+z$	1	1	1	0	1	0	0	1	$-\frac{1}{2}$

The last column shows the bulge of the majority function with respect to each of the linear functions.

To see the bulge as a Fourier transform, we must write it in another form, a form that looks initially like nothing but a clever trick. The bulge of an arbitrary function f (with n inputs) with respect to a linear function ℓ (also with n inputs) is written

$$b_\ell(f) = \frac{1}{2^n} \sum_{i=0}^{2^n-1} (-1)^{f(i) \oplus \ell(i)} \quad .$$

If $f(i)$ and $\ell(i)$ agree, then the exponent $f(i) \oplus \ell(i)$ is 0 and the term $(-1)^{f(i)\oplus\ell(i)}$ will be 1, since anything to the power 0 is 1. Conversely, if $f(i)$ and $\ell(i)$ disagree, then the exponent $f(i) \oplus \ell(i)$ is 1 and the term $(-1)^{f(i)\oplus\ell(i)}$ will be -1, since anything to the power 1 is equal to itself.

If we replace -1 in the equation above by $e^{i\pi}$ (using $e^{i\pi} = -1$, a charming consequence of the fundamental relationship, $e^{i\theta} = \cos\theta + i\sin\theta$, between the sine, the cosine, and the exponent), we get

$$b_\ell(f) = \frac{1}{2^n}\sum_{i=0}^{2^n-1}(e^{i\pi})^{f(i)\oplus\ell(i)} = \frac{1}{2^n}\sum_{i=0}^{2^n-1}e^{i\pi[f(i)\oplus\ell(i)]}$$

a form closely resembling familiar Fourier series and transforms.

The analogy between the bulge and the Fourier transform cannot quite be pushed to make the bulge a special case of abstract harmonic analysis in the usual sense. That theory looks at functions on a variety of domains — the real numbers, the plane, the circle, the sphere, etc. — but looks at functions whose values lie in the fields of real or complex numbers. The values 0 and 1 of binary functions look like the usual numbers 0 and 1, but in an important sense they are not. They belong to the smallest of all fields, called the Galois field modulo 2, GF_2. In this field we have $1+1=0$, so their arithmetic is not the same as that of real numbers. Fortunately, despite the difference in the theories, the crucial result is true in both formulations.

A natural design goal for cryptography would be to avoid any possibility of linear approximation by designing cryptographic functions to have no correlation with any linear function — that is, $b_\ell(f) = 0$ for all ℓ.

Unfortunately for the cryptographer but fortunately for the cryptanalyst, this is not possible. The real payoff of the harmonic analysis viewpoint is Parseval's theorem:

$$\sum_\ell b_\ell(f)^2 = 1 \text{ for any } f$$

which states that the sum of the squares of the Fourier coefficients is 1. What this says for the binary functions is that the sum of the squares of the bulges of a function with respect to all the linear functions is 1. Note that in the case of the majority function for which the bulges are worked out above, four are non-zero with values $\frac{1}{2}$, $\frac{1}{2}$, $\frac{1}{2}$, and $-\frac{1}{2}$. Each of these squares to $\frac{1}{4}$, so the sum of the four squares is 1.

If the bulge (correlation) of a function f with every linear function ℓ were 0, the sum of the bulges would be 0, not 1, so Parseval's theorem tells us this cannot occur. Every binary function has some degree of correlation with a linear function and so it can be approximated by linear functions. After functionality, this may be the second most important fact in cryptanalysis.

Had I been asked, prior to reading the *General Report on Tunny*, when and where the bulge had first appeared, I would probably have said in the early 1950s as cryptography began the transition from rotor machines to shift registers, electronic devices in which every clock pulse causes the bits in the register to shift one place to the left (or right). By this period, the National Security Agency (NSA) and the Government Communications Headquarters (GCHQ) were in close collaboration and I would not have ventured to assign credit to one organisation versus the other. It was therefore an exciting discovery to find the term and concept of the bulge at Bletchley Park in the mid 1940s.[3]

The major vehicle by which the concept of the bulge made its way from Bletchley Park to Washington is the 'Small Report',[4] written by Albert W. Small (1910–1966), one of the Americans

[3]The term 'bulge' first appears on page 41 of the *Report* (*GRT*, **21(j)**, TNA HW 25/4, p. 41; this edition, p. 46) and thereafter it occurs frequently, appearing in chapters **21–27**, **53**, **71–72**, and **93**.

[4]Albert W. Small, 'Special Fish Report', December 1944. NARA, College Park, Maryland. Record Group 457 ('Records of the National Security Agency/Central Security Service') Historic Cryptographic Collection (Entry 9032), Box 1417, Item 4628 (on-line transcription at `http://www.codesandciphers.org.uk/documents/small/smallix.htm`, viewed on 9/6/2013).

seconded to Bletchley Park. (Curiously, according to Frank Rowlett (1908–1998), correlation calculations in his organisation (NSA) were called 'the Small sheets' because Small so frequently did them.[5]) Small' report contains several references to the bulge but no clear definition, which suggests that cryptanalysts on both sides of the Atlantic were familiar with the term, perhaps because of personnel exchanges.[6]

The bulge was to emerge as one of the central concepts of cryptanalysis in the postwar era. In the words of a former head of cryptanalysis at NSA, 'Doing cryptanalysis in the 70s, every other word out of your mouth was "bulge". '[7]

The attack on Tunny was the most ambitious analysis of a binary cryptosystem undertaken up to that time. In one direction, it pioneered techniques that dominated cryptanalysis for decades. In another, it was a milestone in the practice of building dedicated computing hardware to apply those techniques.

At the end of the war, most of the Colossi were scrapped.[8] To what use were the remaining ones put? The usual answer to this question is training, but it seems likely that the story is more complex. The Colossi were specifically designed for use against Tunny, but ciphers similar to Tunny were in use in the decade or so following the war, and machines similar to Colossus — or suitably modified Colossi — might have been used in solving them. Even if problems to which Colossus might have been applied continued through the 1950s, the scope of these problems (by comparison with the problem of the major opponent in the biggest war of all time) seems consistent with the reduction in the number of machines.

We have no solid evidence regarding postwar use of Colossi, but two problems suggest themselves.

One attractive possibility is Russian. A report on the Signal Intelligence activities of the Axis powers during the war years, written in 1946 for the U.S. security services, provides a hint of a possible use for operational Colossi during the Cold War. In the second volume ('Notes on German High Level Cryptography and Cryptanalysis') we read

> Russian teleprinter cryptographic apparatus may have been solved by Goering's "Research" Bureau in 1943, according to Dr. Buggisch of the Signal Intelligence Agency of the Army High Command (OKH/G d NA). [Ref 163: I 64 p. 2] Dr. Buggisch knew no more details. Traffic was supposed to have stopped soon after, and the machine evidently went out of use. He reported that the Army did some work on a Russian teleprinter cryptographic machine, read a few depths, obtained about 1400 letters of pure key, but went no farther. Corporal Karrenberg, mentioned above, said that Russian enciphered teleprinter messages, when sent in depth, were read by anagramming, and the corresponding keying characters recovered, but the machine itself was not solved. [Ref 164: I 169] Russian teleprinter links of which he had any knowledge were from Moscow to the Russian armies, and there were about eight in all. Reading of the depths indicated the messages contained operational and reconnaissance information. Examination of the sections of key obtained from the

[5] Author's conversation with Frank Rowlett circa 1990.

[6] The *Report*'s discussion of the cryptographic staff shows two and later three Americans (*GRT*, **31D**, TNA HW 25/5, p. 277; this edition, p. 263). Elsewhere it mentions the American visitor Walter Jacobs by name (*GRT*, **24W(d)**, TNA HW 25/5, p. 136; this edition, p. 127). A more extensive list of Americans working on Tunny at Bletchley Park is given in the 'Technical History of the 6813th Signal Security Detachment', 20 October 1945, NARA HCC 970:2941.

[7] Personal conversation circa 2005.

[8] See D. C. Horwood, *A technical description of COLOSSUS I*, August 1973, TNA HW 25/24. Horwood's text is discussed in section 2.2.1 of the Editors' Introduction, pp. xxv–lxxiv, esp. pp. xli–xliii. According to the sources cited by Simon Lavington, 'In the Footsteps of Colossus: A Description of Oedipus', *IEEE Annals of the History of Computing*, 28.2 (2006), pp. 44–55, esp. pp. 45, 46, exactly two Colossi were retained after the war.

> readings in Depth, led Karrenberg to the conclusion that the Russian enciphering device was similar in constructlon to the German teleprinter cipher attachment SZ-42 [i.e. 'Tunny'] with a "motor" wheel or "motor" wheels arranged somehow to give a cycle of 43. None of his surmises was investigated to ascertain its validity, it being claimed that the traffic was too scanty to effect a solution. [Ref 165: I 169][9]

In short, during the war the Russians were using cryptographic machines very like those the Colossi had been designed to attack.

It is, of course, not certain that the Russians did indeed continue to use Tunny-like machines. However, other Second World War cryptographic apparatus is known to have continued in use. A spectacular case is provided by the 'Sturgeon' machine (properly Siemens and Halske T52), which had not received much attention from GCCS during the war.[10]

According to Frode Weierud, from 1948 onwards the electromechanical firm Willi Reichert in Trier built SFM T52d and T52e machines from a large stock of T52 parts. From 1949 to 1953 Willi Reichert delivered more than 235 T52 machines to the French Foreign Office and other French military organisations.[11] Weierud's findings are confirmed by those of two other scholars.

Donald Davies (1924–2000), who made an intense study of the various Fish machines in the 1980s,[12] told me the same story in less detail, though he would not name the company.[13]

Georges-Henri Soutou gave a talk in 2008 in which he described how the French acquired Siemens and Halske machines shortly after the end of the war and continued to use them all the way through to 1960. The British and Americans warned France at a NATO conference in 1954 that they were capable of exploiting its communications and that the Soviet Union might have the same capability. Despite this warning and a forceful reiteration the following year, in which a tall stack of decrypted telegrams was delivered to the Quai d'Orsay, the French did not replace the vulnerable systems till the end of the decade.[14]

The utility of Colossus may not have been limited to electromechanical systems. Many of the early systems built with electronic shift registers are similar in basic principles to the Fish machines. Instead of using a number of wheels of relatively prime periods, they use a number of shift registers with relatively prime periods. (A more recent system of this kind is the A5 system used in GSM mobile phones.) It is possible that some of these systems — particularly early on when the cost of hardware was high and shift registers were often short — could be attacked with Colossus.

[9]United States Army Security Agency, *European Axis Signal Intelligence in World War II as Revealed by 'TICOM' Investigations and by other Prisoner of War Interrogations and Captured Material, Principally German*, FOIA release of 9-volume typescript report (Washington, D.C., 1946), URL: `http://www.nsa.gov/public_info/declass/european_axis_sigint.shtml` (visited on 07/06/2014), principally Vol. 2 ('Notes on German High Level Cryptography and Cryptanalysis'), paragraph d, pp. 75–76, transcription by J. V. Field. The references are presumably to transcripts of individual interrogations.

[10]For a discussion of why this was so, see Frode Weierud, 'Bletchley Park's Sturgeon — the Fish that Laid No Eggs' in B. Jack Copeland, ed., *Colossus: The Secrets of Bletchley Park's Codebreaking Computers* (Oxford: Oxford University Press, 2006), pp. 307–327.

[11]Frode Weierud, 'Bletchley Park's Sturgeon — The Fish that Laid No Eggs', *The Rutherford Journal: The New Zealand Journal for the History and Philosophy of Science and Technology*, 1 (Dec. 2005), URL: `http://www.rutherfordjournal.org/article010106.html` (visited on 07/06/2014), esp. p. 29.

[12]D. W. Davies, 'The Early Models of the Siemens and Halske T52 Cipher Machine', *Cryptologia*, 7.3 (1983), pp. 235–253, and D. W. Davies, 'New Information on the History of the Siemens and Halske T52 Cipher Machine', *Cryptologia*, 18.2 (1994), pp. 141–146.

[13]Donald Davies private communication with WD in the 1990s.

[14]Georges-Henri Soutou, 'French Intelligence about the East during the Fourth Republic: Pedestrian but Sensible', a paper given at a conference 'Keeping Secrets: How Important was Intelligence to the Conduct of International Relations from 1914 to 1989?' held at the German Historical Institute, London, Apr. 2008. A form of this talk had previously been published under the title 'La mécanisation du chiffre au Quai d'Orsay, ou les aléas d'un système technique (1948–1958)' in Michèle Merger and Dominique Barjot, eds., *Les entreprises et leurs réseaux: hommes, capitaux, techniques et pouvoirs XIXe – XXe siècles* (Paris: Presses de l'Université de Paris-Sorbonne, 1998), pp. 697–710.

The question of why some Colossi were kept after the end of the war goes hand in hand with the question of why the remaining machines were decommissioned when they were. On the face of it, the answer must take one of two forms: either the problems on which these machines were used went away or the machines were replaced by something else. As noted above, the problems did not go away and undoubtedly expanded. The question then is what replaced Colossus. This question surely has no single answer. Was Colossus replaced by programs running on general-purpose computers or was it replaced by newer special-purpose machines? This question merges with the question of what modifications may have been made to the Colossi in their later years. I have been told that in some or all of the surviving machines, the paper tapes were replaced by magnetic drums. For this claim, there is no evidence except that it makes eminently good sense. However glorious the engineering of the 5,000-character-per-second tape reader, it was a weak point in Colossus operations. Replacing the tape with a drum — readily available by the mid 1950s — would have improved reliability and probably increased speed.

A plausible explanation of the lifespans of the surviving machines is that they were replaced by programs running on general-purpose computers. The rising speed of computers in the 1950s suggests that 'Colossus programs' would have run as fast as the originals by about 1960, a date approximately consistent with their retirement in 1961.

Simon Lavington's interesting paper, however, reveals that both this question and that of the drums merge into a larger question of the course of cryptanalytic computation in the 1950s.[15]

Lavington names and describes — some in more detail, some in less — a variety of postwar machines with varying levels of specialization and flexibility. As machine cryptanalysis became the norm, the fate of the Colossi was to be subsumed in a flourishing environment that both spawned more specialized analytic machines and contributed to the evolving design of general-purpose computers.

[15]Lavington, 'In the Footsteps of Colossus: A Description of Oedipus' (see footnote 8, above).

Editors' Introduction

Whitfield Diffie and J. V. Field

Contents

It is not the purpose of an Introduction to an edition of a primary text to provide a definitive analysis of the history, content and historical significance of the document in question. Much of that must be left to our readers. In particular, since the text we are presenting here is concerned only with the breaking of ciphers and the reading of messages, not with the content of the messages, it is inappropriate for us to discuss the uses to which information derived from decrypted messages was put. That kind of assessment can only be made in the context of a military history.

The text of the *General Report on Tunny with Emphasis on Statistical Methods*, written at Bletchley Park in 1945 and declassified in 2000, has a history that makes our task as editors somewhat awkward. Even the authorship of the text is uncertain. No names are given on the original, but it has always been accepted that at the end of the war in Europe, between May and September 1945, three of the cryptanalysts who had worked on teleprinter ciphers, I. J. (Jack) Good (1916–2009), Donald Michie (1923–2007) and Geoffrey Timms (1903–1982), put together a detailed report on that work. The group whose work was described was led by Max Newman (1897–1984) and until it was declassified the *Report* was commonly known as *The History of the Newmanry* or *The Newmanry Report*. Internal evidence, and the recollections of the first two authors, indicate that much of the text is copied from other documents written by other members of Newman's team. Thus Good, Michie and Timms were largely editors rather than authors. However, as authors of particular passages cannot generally be identified, we shall normally refer to these three as the 'authors' of the *Report*, if only to distinguish them from the editors responsible for the present edition.

We, the present editors, need to supply not only some cryptographic and mathematical background but also a preliminary discussion of the historical significance of the document, though details will only become clear from a more thorough analysis of the contents of the *Report*. We provide some contextual material in the first section of our Introduction.

A difficulty at once becomes apparent. Ideally, an Introduction provides the background information that the writers of the primary text expected their original readers to have. In the present case that is impossible. The document was intended to be secret, that is, it was addressed to readers who had access to classified material, and from the very beginning there are references to documents that are not available to us at the time of writing (February 2015). At least some of these are known to be still extant, and in principle there is an intention that they will eventually be declassified and made available to the general public, as the *Report* itself has been. In the circumstances, a relatively substantial note on our sources seems to be required. The documentation, absent as well as present, will be discussed in our second section below.

We then consider the contents of the *Report* (section 3), give an account of the physical characteristics of the copy that we have used (section 4) and describe our editorial procedures (section 5).

1. Context and significance of the *General Report on Tunny*

1.1 Cryptography and Bletchley Park

The use of radio communications in warfare makes cryptography important. Anyone can receive the messages, but the sender wishes them to be understood only by the intended recipient. The importance of cryptography accordingly became apparent in World War I, and the British Government Code and Cypher School (GCCS) was set up in 1919.[1] In 1939 it was transferred to Bletchley Park, an undistinguished, moderately sized Victorian country house well situated for rail access from London, Oxford and Cambridge, and conveniently close to large telephone cables.

All the work was of course highly secret, but the choice of location suggests that the staff were not intended to work in complete isolation from the milieux from which most of the senior members were recruited. The gardens of the house were partly cleared and the space filled with rows of huts, used as office accommodation for staff and equipment. From the air the establishment appeared to be an ordinary army camp.

The volume of traffic that needed to be sent by radio also made it highly desirable — and thus in the longer run inevitable — that the processes of encryption and decryption of signals would use machines. When a radio operator could tap out a message in minutes it obviously made no sense for a cipher clerk to require several hours to work out what should be sent or what message had been received. The encryption and decryption machines that will concern us here are of two kinds. The first is the one the Germans called 'Enigma', which was introduced in the 1920s. Similar, though not identical, machines were used by the British and the Americans. The British one was called 'Typex'. The American one, 'Sigaba', was considerably more complicated, but employed the same basic principle as the other two. Machines that worked on a different principle were used for encrypting German teleprinter communications. It is the breaking of traffic from machines of this second kind that is the main subject of the *General Report on Tunny*. By the time the *Report* was written, the cipher used seems generally to have been known as 'Tunny', though at first specific names had been given not to ciphers but to links, that is pairs of enemy transmitting and receiving stations — see section 1.3 below.

The business of the staff at Bletchley Park was mainly signals intelligence, that is to read the encrypted radio messages picked up by an array of interception stations. A case can be made that the work done at Bletchley Park, initially by staff transferred there from intelligence services within the various parts of the Armed Forces and departments of government, eventually led to the recognition of Signals Intelligence as a specific branch of intelligence work.[2] There is, of course, no solid evidence for the assertion, sometimes made in histories of the work of GCCS, that its successful reading of enemy traffic — that is, of a proportion of enemy traffic — shortened

[1] [Francis Lyall Birch,] *The History of Britsh Sigint 1914–1945*, 2 vols, TNA HW 43/1 and 43/2; printed as Frank Birch, *The official history of British Sigint, 1914-1945 / by Frank Birch*, ed. by John Jackson (Milton Keynes: Military Press, 2004). See also Michael Smith, 'The Government Code and Cypher School and the First Cold War' in Ralph Erskine and Michael Smith, eds., *Action This Day* (London: Bantam Press, 2001), pp. 15–40, esp. p. 20.

[2] See Christopher Grey, *Decoding Organization: Bletchley Park, Codebreaking and Organization Studies* (Cambridge: Cambridge University Press, 2012), pp. 255–257.

the war. However, it appears from the historical record that the British Government thought that the intelligence gathered from reading German signals was valuable enough to warrant assigning considerable resources to the cryptanalysis. When, on 21 October 1941, four senior members of the staff of Huts 6 and 8 at Bletchley Park ignored the official channels of communication and sent a letter directly to the Prime Minister asking for additional resources, in particular additional staff, they got them.[3] That request was in connection with work on breaking Enigma traffic. Later, support for cryptanalysis had become a matter of course. In May 1943, when the Post Office was building machines for use against teleprinter ciphers, it was possible for a senior official to assure the Director of Telecommunications that the Prime Minister had authorized one of his staff 'to ask Departments for the necessary priorities when requested'.[4]

Like many later accounts, the *General Report on Tunny* concentrates its attention on the day to day work of cryptanalysts, and in so doing perhaps gives an exaggerated sense of their autonomy. In many respects Newman does indeed seem to have run his section like a university department, encouraging innovation and the democratic exchange of views. However, the work was narrowly focussed on a particular task. We are not looking at free research that forms its own objectives. The task was to break teleprinter traffic, and to do so in the least time possible. The priority governing which messages were attacked was in principle set by the staff of Hut 3. In some respects this does indeed seem to have been what happened. For instance, German Air Force messages, which used a teleprinter cipher that came to be known (by the cryptanalysts) as Sturgeon, proved harder to break than (Army) Tunny messages, so Sturgeon traffic was sent to the Research Section rather than to the Newmanry. All the same, it is clear, from the official reports of the various sections, that in practice the heads of other Huts had considerable autonomy.[5] It was in Hut 3 that decrypted Enigma and Tunny messages from Army and Air Force sources were translated and the information they contained was combined to form a larger picture of what was going on.[6] Thus the staff of Hut 3 were in a position to judge which links were likely to yield useful information, and they accordingly suggested which messages should receive attention from the cryptanalysts. The staff of Hut 3 could not give formal orders on the matter, since it was, for instance, up to the cryptanalysts to decide whether the quality of intercepts was good enough for an attack to stand a reasonable chance of success and, as the *General Report on Tunny* records, decisions might also be influenced by whether traffic had been broken for neighbouring days. Right to the end, the cryptanalysts in Newman's group were engaged in an art of the only just possible.

The work breaking the ciphers used in teleprinter messages, called 'Fish' ciphers by the cryptanalysts, seems to have benefited from the example of the success of the breaking of Enigma. The teleprinter traffic was routed through army headquarters, though there were some transmissions for other services (see endnote 2 to *General Report on Tunny*, **61**, p. 615, esp. paragraph 4, below.) Army teleprinter traffic carried very high-level communications, between generals in the highest

[3]The signatories of the letter were Alan Turing, Gordon Welchman, Hugh Alexander, and Stuart Milner-Barry. The letter and the reply are printed in Erskine and Smith, *Action This Day* (see footnote 1, above), pp. ix–xiii. For the context of this letter, see Grey, *Decoding Organization* (see footnote 2, above), pp. 91–92. For the background, see also Gordon Welchman, *The Hut Six Story* (New York: McGraw-Hill, 1982) and F. H. Hinsley and Alan Stripp, eds., *Codebreakers: The Inside Story of Bletchley Park* (Oxford: Oxford University Press, 1993; paperback repr. with corrections, 1994). On Welchman, and on the problems with the authorities regarding the publication of his book, see the work by Asa Briggs mentioned in note 6 below.

[4]Nigel de Grey to A. C. Taylor, Director of Telecommunications, GPO, 16 May 1943, TNA HW 62/5.

[5]See Grey, *Decoding Organization* (see footnote 2, above).

[6]For first-hand accounts, see William Millward, 'Life In and Out of Hut 3' in Hinsley and Stripp, *Codebreakers* (see footnote 3, above), pp. 17–29; Ralph Bennett, 'The Duty Officer, Hut 3' in Hinsley and Stripp, *Codebreakers* (see footnote 3, above), pp. 20–40; Edward Thomas, 'A Naval Officer in Hut 3' in Hinsley and Stripp, *Codebreakers* (see footnote 3, above), pp. 41–49. For a discussion of the relations between Hut 3 and other parts of the organisation at Bletchley Park, see Asa Briggs, *Secret Days: Code-Breaking in Bletchley Park* (London: Frontline Books, 2011). Briggs (b. 7 May 1921) worked in Hut 6; he later became a highly respected social historian.

military headquarters and those in command of field operations (occasionally from Hitler to a general). Reading it therefore yielded strategic rather than merely tactical information. The advantages obtained from reading Fish traffic doubtless helped to ensure that, as the cryptanalysis proceeded, resources were found for the construction of a number of electrical machines of unprecedented complexity.

Some of the machines built to help with work on the teleprinter ciphers are obviously part of the ancestry of the modern electronic computer, but whether one wishes to regard any of them as actually being a computer is essentially a matter of how one decides to define the term 'computer'. None of the Bletchley Park machines used a stored program in the present-day sense and none of them used 'branching', that is the machines did not make decisions between several possible logical paths.

The work at Bletchley Park seems also to have played a part in establishing an initial connection between computing (and what is now called 'computer science') and mathematics, because, as the *Report* records, there was an increasing use of mathematicians as cryptanalysts. Thus it was one of the effects of this wartime work that mathematics began to look a less rarefied academic discipline than before — but the later history of that change belongs to a much larger story than the one that concerns us here.

1.2 Enigma

In the early part of the war, most of the traffic intercepted and sent to Bletchley Park for analysis — it was carried by despatch riders on motorcycles — had been encrypted by the Enigma machine. The signals were in Morse code, which uses a series of dots and dashes (short and longer signals) to indicate letters of the alphabet and punctuation marks, spelling messages out letter by letter. The overall design of the machines that produced the enciphered messages was well known to the British cryptanalysts but as the war continued some variants were introduced. In the end, the difficulties the variants presented for the cryptanalysts did not prove to be insuperable, though there were periods when no traffic could be read.

A method for attacking the Enigma cipher had already been devised, before the war, by a team of Polish mathematicians led by Marian Rejewski (1905–1980). The Polish cryptanalysts passed their work on to the French and the British, so that by the time hostilities broke out, and the German army rapidly advanced to positions which made it necessary to use radio rather than landlines to carry its communications, the British were already well placed for reading German Enigma traffic. And by the spring of 1940 read it they did.[7] There were setbacks when the Germans increased the number of wheels used in their Enigma machines, but eventually the staff at Bletchley Park were able to mechanize the breaking of Enigma messages. The electromechanical machines that found the settings of the wheels used in an encrypted transmission were called 'bombes', after the name 'bomba' (plural 'bomby') that the Polish group had given to the similar, but simpler, apparatus used in their pre-war cryptanalysis. As their co-designer Alan Turing (1912–1954) put it, the bombes worked not by finding the correct solution but by eliminating those that were impossible. A copy of Turing's account of work on Enigma, known at Bletchley Park as 'The Prof's book' but properly called *A Treatise on Enigma*, is now held by the (UK) National Archives (pressmark HW 25/3), and there is another copy in the National Archives and Records Administration (NARA) in College Park, Maryland, USA.[8] Once the wheel settings had been found, a suitably set British

[7] Welchman, *Hut Six Story* (see footnote 3, above).

[8] NARA, College Park, Maryland. Record Group 457 ('Records of the National Security Agency/Central Security Service'), Historic Cryptographic Collection (Entry 9032), Box 201, Item Number 964. A transcription by Ralph Erskine, Philip Marks and Frode Weierud, dated February 1999, is available at `http://cryptocellar.org/Turing/index.html` (last accessed May 2014). On naval Enigma in the Battle of the Atlantic, see Arthur O. Bauer, Ralph Erskine and Klaus Herold, *Funkpeilung als alliierte Waffe gegen deutsche U-Boote 1939–1945: Wie Schwächen und Versäumnisse*

Typex machine could be used to produce decrypted text. We may note, however, that as one would need to type in the encrypted message, that is gibberish, a skilful typist was required. GCCS employed a large number of women, members of the WRNS ('Wrens', Women's Royal Naval Service) and ATS (Auxiliary Territorial Service) girls[9] to operate machines and carry out typing and other routine or administrative tasks. These ancillary staff far outnumbered the cryptanalysts whose work they supported.

The bombes were essentially a bank of Enigma simulators. It was thought that details of their design had been lost, but a set of engineering drawings was found to have been preserved at Bletchley Park's successor institution, the Government Communications Headquarters (GCHQ, situated on the outskirts of Cheltenham, Gloucestershire), and it has been possible to rebuild a bombe. The bombe used for attacking a 3-rotor Enigma machine was a substantial structure, the parts being assembled on a steel frame with base 2.21 m $\times$ 0.8 m, and height 1.78 m, mounted on heavy-duty castors. There were three sections, one above the other, each containing twelve columns of three wheels each (though in some of the earliest designs there were 30 columns). The three sections worked independently, each on a separate set of solutions, but if one stopped, on a possible solution, then all stopped. The wheels and a multitude of connection rods were driven by a direct-current (DC) electric motor, connected to the mains through a mercury-arc rectifier. The machines were manufactured in Letchworth (Hertfordshire) by the British Tabulating Machine Company (BTM, later to become ICL).

Rebuilding a bombe has shown that a significant effort must have gone into the original machines. Only 15% of the parts were standard items for BTM. It has become clear that the machines represented not only a considerable intellectual achievement on the part of the designers — Alan Turing and Gordon Welchman of Bletchley Park and Harold ('Doc') Keen of BTM — but also an important commitment of resources for manufacture.[10]

For reasons of security, work at Bletchley Park was divided between separate groups, whose members were strictly forbidden to discuss their work with anyone other than their immediate colleagues. However, a wider view was available from the higher levels in the organisation; the successful mechanization of the breaking of Enigma traffic made it seem reasonable to hope that machines could also be used against other ciphers. And as the project progressed, staff were transferred from working on Enigma to work on other ciphers.

1.3 'Fish' traffic

As we have already noted, messages encrypted in Enigma were received in Morse code.[11] British interception stations also received signals transmitted in the characteristic twittery tone used for teleprinters. The teleprinter had been widely used in the early 1920s and had been

bei der Funkführung der U-Boote zum Ausgang der 'Schlacht im Atlantik' beigetragen haben (Rheinberg: Liebig Funk, 1997). See also David Kahn, *Seizing the Enigma: The Race to Break the U-Boat Codes* (London: Arrow, 1996); and Hugh Sebag-Montefiori, *Enigma: The Battle for the Code* (London: Phoenix, 2004).

[9]Except for the highest officials, ATS staff were generally young women, from a lower social class than the Wrens. They were always known as 'girls'.

[10]The progress of the work of rebuilding a bombe is charted in a series of articles by the leader of the rebuild group, John Harper, in the magazine *Resurrection* (the newsletter of the Computer Conservation Society, which is a subgroup of the British Computer Society), between the years 1997 and 2007. See also J. V. Field, 'Sigint and Automation', *IEEE Annals of the History of Computing*, 25.1 (Jan. 2003), pp. 65–66 (which is an account of a lecture given by John Harper); John Harper, 'It's Complete', *Bletchley Park Times*, 4 (Autumn 2006), and Brian Runciman, 'It's a Bouncing Baby Bombe', *ITNOW, A Journal of the British Computer Society*, 49.1 (Jan. 2007), URL: `http://www.bcs.org/upload/pdf/jan07.pdf` (visited on 07/06/2014).

[11]Unlike the Tunny and Sturgeon, with their built-in relationship to the radio teletype transmission system (see below), Enigma is a pure cryptographic device, with input by hand and output to eye. It is therefore possible that some messages were encrypted with Enigma and then transmitted by other means such as radio teletype or being read over the telephone. We have, however, no evidence of any such traffic reaching Bletchley Park.

available for one customer to dial another since the 1930s. Foreign teleprinter signals were first intercepted in 1932, in the course of Metropolitan Police surveillance directed against unauthorized or suspect radio transmitters, following the General Strike of 1926. The police were alerted to the signal when Ivy Kenworthy, the wife of the director of the listening project, Harold Kenworthy (1892–1987), rang her husband to say that the undulator connected to the radio receiver at their home in Croydon (South London) was producing a strange trace consisting of 'long lines and little bumps'.[12]

Teleprinter messages were first subjected to cryptographic study at GCCS after the German invasion of the Soviet Union, in late June 1941(*GRT*, **41A(a)**, TNA HW 25/5, p. 297; this edition, p. 284). The various links over which these transmissions were made were given the names of fish: Whiting, Bream, Gurnard and suchlike, including (presumably humorously) Jellyfish. This system of naming has no obvious rationale and at the same time cryptanalysts in Hut 8 were using names of fish, and other aquatic creatures, to designate keys used on Enigma links carrying naval traffic. Names used for these Morse links included Shark (Atlantic U boats), Pike (surface craft), Plaice (Navy in the Baltic) and Seahorse (German Admiralty to Tokyo) as well as Dolphin (Naval Home Waters), Oyster (Naval Staff Key) and Turtle (U Boats in the Mediterranean).[13] Thus while all non-Morse links have fish names not all fish names indicate non-Morse links. The name system was, after all, designed to be used only by insiders.

Transmissions can be assigned to particular links once the call signs are identified, but the identification of a link with a specific pair of places is a separate matter. It involves having intercepted copies of the same message, or series of messages, from two different interception stations. Intercepts can be matched by time and call sign (thereby establishing that this is a single transmission) but, since the interception is by different stations, the directions will be different, and triangulation then gives the geographical position of the transmitting station. To get an accurate 'fix' on the position of a distant transmitting station, the angle between the lines of sight to it from the two interception stations must be as large as possible, which means that the interception stations must be widely separated. The British interception service (called the 'Y' service) made use of stations scattered across the length and breath of the island: such as Capel le Ferne (in Kent, between Dover and Folkestone) (H. C. Kenworthy, *The Interception of German Teleprinter Communications by Foreign Office Station Knockholt* (para 1.7, TNA HW 50/79, p. 2; this edition App. B, pp. 513–524 below), St Erth (near Penzance, Cornwall), Wymondham (near Norwich, Norfolk), Beverley (Yorkshire) and Thurso (Caithness, Scotland).[14]

Direction finding work, which does not involve attempting to read the messages, would be classed as 'traffic analysis'. In the early part of the war it was carried out by an Army group based at Beaumanor Hall (Woodhouse, Leicestershire), but in mid 1942 the operation was transferred to Bletchley Park. At GCCS it was carried out by a group in Hut 6, known as SIXTA (see section 2.1 below). The *General Report on Tunny* does not make it clear when precise geographical identifications of transmission stations were made; the maps and identifications it provides are a record of what was known by the end of the war. However, even rather imprecise identifications would have established that the teleprinter transmissions were from sites close to the Eastern Front. The strategic importance of events on the Eastern Front was widely recognised by political as well as military leaders, since it was obvious that if the Axis powers prevailed in the East they would be

[12] H. C. Kenworthy, *A Brief History of Events Relating to the Growth of the 'Y' Service*, 1957 (declassified 2004), Ch. IV, para 4.3, TNA HW 3/81, pp. 3–4.

[13] *Decoding German Enigma Machine Messages*, NARA, College Park, Maryland, Record Group 457 ('Records of the National Security Agency/Central Security Service'), Historic Cryptographic Collection (Entry 9032), Box 970, Item Number 2943, 15 June 1945, Chapter V, Job Meanings, p. 90. We have given the title of the text as it appears on the document itself. However, in the finding aid the document is identified as 'Operations of the 6312th Signal Security Detachment, ETOUSA' [*sic*, should be 6812th]. It is also sometimes referred to as 'The American Bombe Manual'. We are grateful to J. A. Reeds for information about this document.

[14] Kenworthy, *A Brief History...* (full ref in note 12 above), p. 10, paras 7.3 to 7.5.

free to move forces to other theatres. This was in the period during which Allied policy appeared to some to be 'to fight the war to the last Russian', an opinion for which historians have uncovered a fair amount of justification. Moreover, neither the British nor the American government was disposed to trust the Soviet Union overmuch, so an independent source of information about what was happening on the Eastern Front was very welcome.

The ciphers used in the teleprinter traffic took on the fish names of the links. It turned out that there were three distinct varieties of cipher machine, which were given the names of the corresponding links: Thrasher, Tunny and Sturgeon. The name 'Tunny' became attached to the cipher in the summer of 1942 (*GRT*, **41A(a)**, TNA HW 25/5, p. 297; this edition, p. 284); Thrasher, the cipher used in the German T43 machine, manufactured by Siemens, acquired its name towards the end of the war.[15]

The Tunny machine, with which the *General Report* is chiefly concerned, was manufactured by Lorenz. However, its origins were American. A machine of this kind was invented in 1930 by Parker Hitt (1878–1971), who patented it (US Patent No 1,848,291)[16] and assigned the rights to International Communications Laboratories Inc., of New York, a subsidiary of the International Telephone and Telegraph company (ITT). Hitt was on friendly terms with the founder of ITT Sosthenes Behn (1882–1957), who had served under his command in the Army. Lorenz was also a subsidiary of ITT, and it consequently seems highly likely that the German firm manufactured Hitt's machine and from 1937 supplied developed versions of it to the German military.[17] It seems that before 1941 the Lorenz machine was not used for encrypting radio signals, so that (as is clear from the text of the *General Report on Tunny*) British cryptanalysts knew nothing about it. They learned about the precise physical characteristics of the Lorenz machine (that is, the layout of its wheels and so on) only after the end of the war, when the US and British Chiefs of Staff sent a specially constituted Target Intelligence Committee (TICOM) to investigate Axis cryptography and cryptanalysis. Reports of this committee note the similarity between the Lorenz machines and the one designed by Hitt. Hitt's machine had been broken by the US intelligence service in the 1930s,[18] but information about their work was not (it appears) passed on to the British group attacking Tunny traffic. However, the matter was of no practical significance: the Tunny machine did not share the weakness that the US analysts had exploited in breaking messages from the Hitt machine.

The German name of the Lorenz machine was 'Schlüsselzusatz' ('cipher attachment'), which was shortened to SZ, the various developed forms being given numbers of years and sometimes letters to denote specific models, which resulted in names such as SZ 42 A. The device was attached to the teleprinter, so when sending or receiving messages the operators saw only plain text.

Whereas Enigma ciphers were used for traffic at field-command level, it turned out that, as we have already mentioned, the teleprinter traffic encrypted in Fish ciphers carried high-level communications (between generals and between Hitler and his generals). These high-level ciphers were much more secure, that is much more difficult to break, than Enigma. It did, however, prove possible to break them, though even by 1945 not all messages could be read and one of the cryptanalytic team said (in 2000) 'We were hanging on by our fingernails; if the Germans had changed two things at once instead of only one at a time they would have lost us'.[19]

[15] See Friedrich L. Bauer, 'Origins of the Fish Cypher Machines', Appendix 12 in B. Jack Copeland, ed., *Colossus: The Secrets of Bletchley Park's Codebreaking Computers* (Oxford: Oxford University Press, 2006), pp. 411–417, esp. p. 417.

[16] Hitt filed for the patent on 13 August 1930 and it was issued on 8 March 1932. The machine in question is a form of Tunny, lacking the motor wheels, and with wheels of sizes 96, 97, 98, 99, 100, 101, ... 105.

[17] We, and Dr Reeds, are grateful to Betsy Rohaly Smoot (NSA) for information about ITT's relations with Hitt and its ownership of Lorenz.

[18] Frank B. Rowlett, *The Story of Magic: Memoirs of an American Cryptologic Pioneer* (Laguna Hills, Calif.: Aegean Park Press, 1998).

[19] Donald Michie, 2000, in conversation with JVF.

1.4 Mr Newman's section

A Research Section had been set up in August 1941, reporting to the head of the military section, Colonel John Tiltman (1894–1982). In July 1942 some of its functions in regard to Tunny were taken over by a new section, run by Major Ralph Tester (1901–1998).[20] Its purpose was to apply the methods of attacking Tunny that had already been developed. In the same month, July 1942, current Tunny traffic was read for the first time. The style of nomenclature used at Bletchley Park owes much to British Public School slang — a characteristic that is indicative of the social origins of most of the senior staff — so the group run by Major Tester became known as 'The Testery'.

Max Newman was born in London, the son of a German immigrant (the family name had been Neumann)and an English mother. By the 1930s he was a successful mathematician, held in high regard by his professional colleagues. He was elected a Fellow of the Royal Society in 1939. At the outbreak of war he seems at first to have supposed that his German ancestry would make him ineligible for war work, but that turned out not to be so and in 1942 he temporarily laid aside his lectureship in mathematics at Cambridge University, and his fellowship of St John's College, to work at Bletchley Park, where he took up his appointment on 31 August.[21] Newman was employed in working on Tunny in the Research Section and, having an interest in automating mathematical and logical tasks, thought it would be possible to use machines for this one.[22]

Here it is relevant that we are considering not a general mathematical or logical task but specifically that of cryptanalysis: speed is important. The sooner one reads intercepted messages the more useful they are. The complicated nature of the Tunny machine made the cryptanalysis laborious, and — presumably thanks to the alertness of the German signals staff — procedures had been altered so that the traffic no longer supplied 'depths' — that is, the kind of multiple or repetitive transmission that had been exploited in making the initial crucial breaks and consequent 'diagnosis' of the structure of the machine. Alan Turing, whose position was that of a general consultant, joined in the Testery's work on Tunny and invented a method of finding the key stream by using differencing — that is subtracting successive bits one from another, thus finding the change from one bit to the next on the tape — but his method (known as 'Turingery') was slow. In November 1942, William Tutte (1917–2002), working in the Research Section, devised a statistical approach. It did not rely on depths and it could be used on a single message, provided it was long enough. The method involved counting characters (in today's terms bits), in each of the different possible cases. It was powerful but slow. Moreover, the cryptanalysts were looking for small effects, so the counting had to be done accurately. In this kind of procedure, omitting a letter can as it were push the cycles out of phase, making the pattern more difficult to see. As they put it in their *Report*:

> The standard of accuracy needed before there was any possibility of success was very much higher than would ordinarily be required of this kind of apparatus, or of operators. A single letter omitted in a tape destroyed the value of the run and the ordinary length of a tape was about 3000 letters. (*GRT*, **15B(b)**, TNA HW 25/4, p. 34; this edition, p. 40.)

[20]See *History of the Fish Section* (1945), TNA HW 50/63, 'June–October 1942', p. 1.

[21]Newman's papers are now preserved in the library of St John's College, Cambridge. Correspondence relating to his recruitment to GCCS is in box 3, folder 1. From this correspondence it appears that the person who initiated contacts between Newman and GCCS was P. M. S. Blackett. The letter giving the date of appointment, dated 19 August 1942, is 3/1/15.

[22]Newman had been the referee for Turing's paper 'On computable numbers', which describes the principles on which a computer works (A. M. Turing, 'On Computable Numbers, with an Application to the *Entscheidungsproblem*', *Proc. London Math. Soc.*, 42 (1936), pp. 230–265 and 'On Computable Numbers, with an Application to the *Entscheidungsproblem*: A Correction', *Proc. London Math. Soc.*, 44 (1937), pp. 544–546. See Andrew Hodges, *Alan Turing: The Enigma* (New York: Simon and Schuster, 1983; reprinted London: Vintage, 1992).

This was, of course, written when machines were in operation, long after the decision to mechanize had been taken. However, it carries echoes of why, a hundred years earlier, Charles Babbage (1792–1871) thought that machines should be used for calculating and printing mathematical tables. The idea of attempting a statistical attack on Tunny and that of using machines seem natural bedfellows. In November 1942 Newman suggested the use of electronic counting machines (*GRT*, **74**, 'Chronology', TNA HW 25/5, p. 458; this edition, p. 444). Such machines had been invented in Cambridge before the war (by Charles Eryl Wynn-Williams (1903–1979), see note 34 below), so Newman was in a good position to know of their existence and capabilities.

In December 1942 Newman was allowed to set up a new section, with the specific remit of mechanizing the breaking of Tunny. This group was known as 'The Newmanry'.[23] At first there were only two cryptographers: Newman himself and Donald Michie (who had recently left school and attended a course on cryptography in Bedford).[24] The next recruit was Jack Good, a Cambridge mathematician who had been working on Enigma, in Hut 8, since May 1941.[25] Probability theory was not an established research interest at Cambridge at this time: Alan Turing had been unconventional — and (it turned out) not properly familiar with the literature — in choosing to write on a topic in probability theory when submitting an original essay in support of his application for a fellowship at King's College in 1934. Nevertheless, he was elected a Fellow in 1935, and the essay was awarded the Smith's Prize in 1936.[26] Good had taken an interest in probability theory since his schooldays[27] and an examination of the first part of the *General Report on Tunny* shows that a considerable part of the statistical work carried out in the course of the attack on Tunny was later to find its place in his highly influential book *Probability and the Weighing of Evidence* (London: Griffin, 1950), though of course with no hint of its cryptanalytic origins. Turing, who as we have seen had done some work on Tunny in the Testery, also participated in the activities of Newman's group (or at least in the work described in the *General Report on Tunny*), and seems to have persisted in his habit of proving theorems for himself rather than finding them in the works of others: Good had to tell him that one result was a special case of Bayes' Theorem (named after the mathematician who had first proved it in the eighteenth century) (*GRT*, **21(f)**, last line, TNA HW 25/4, p. 39; this edition, p. 45).[28]

There is nothing in the known character of either man that allows one to decide which of them wrote the remark about Turing's failure to identify his result as a case of Bayes' theorem, though the balance of probabilities lies with Good, since he was formally attached to Newman's group. Turing did, however, write at least two short pieces on statistics while he was working for GCCS. They are *The applications of probability to cryptography* (45 pages) and a much shorter piece *Statistics of repetitions* (nine pages); both were declassified in April 2012.[29] Each of these texts identifies Turing as the author on its title page. Both documents seem to be conceived as introductions to the use of probability theory in cryptanalysis, perhaps addressed to staff newly recruited to GCCS (in which case they may have some affinity with the 'screeds' mentioned in chapter **31** of the *General Report on Tunny* and discussed in section 2.2 below). The longer piece

[23]Until the true title became public, when the document was declassified in 2000, the *General Report on Tunny* was usually known as 'The Newmanry History'. At the time of writing (February 2015) the corresponding report on the activities of the Testery, 'The Testery History', has not yet been declassified.

[24]For biographical details see Biographies of Authors, p. ciii below.

[25]For biographical details see Biographies of Authors, p. ciii below.

[26]Hodges, *Alan Turing: The Enigma* (see footnote 22, above), p. 114. For further details see S. L. Zabell, 'Alan Turing and the Central Limit Theorem', *American Mathematical Monthly*, 102 (1995), pp. 483–494, and *idem* 'Statistics at Bletchley Park', pp. lxxv–ci below, esp. p. lxxviii.

[27]I. J. Good, private communication to J. A. Reeds, 2006.

[28]The theorem is named after Thomas Bayes (1702–1761).

[29]TNA HW 25/37 (catalogued under the title *Report on the applications of probability to cryptography*), TNA HW 25/38 (catalogued under the title *Paper on statistics of repetitions*). We are grateful to J. A. Reeds for drawing our attention to these papers.

explicitly identifies what Turing prefers to call 'the factor principle' as also being known as Bayes' theorem (HW 25/37, p. 5), so if the testimony of the *General Report on Tunny* is to be taken at face value, this passage must have been written after Turing had discussed the material with Good. More precise evidence of the date of composition is provided by a reference to Hitler being of age 52 (HW 25/37, p. 1, passage quoted in section 3.4.1 below). Elsewhere, but not here, Turing remarks on figures being made up,[30] which suggests this particular number may be genuine, which, since Hitler was born in 1889, gives a date between April 1941 and April 1942. The first part of the longer text, in particular, is very general, and might have served as an introduction for work on Fish codes, but it might equally have been intended to introduce the method used to attack Enigma. In this connection we may note that Turing begins by stating

> The theory of probability may be used in cryptography with most effect when the type of cipher used is already fully understood, and it only remains to find the actual keys. It is of rather less value when one is trying to diagnose the type of cipher, ...[31]

In fact, neither of these two papers sheds any direct light on how, and how much, Turing contributed to the work described in the statistical part of the *General Report on Tunny*. Perhaps declassification of further documents will eventually help to decide the matter. At present the nearest approach to hard evidence is the fact that Turing's name appears in the Preface of Good's publication of 1950.[32] We may, also, see some effects of Turing's experience with Tunny in his work designing and constructing an encrypted radio telephone, called Delilah (see *Judges*, ch. 16), in early 1944.[33] The name Delilah was presumably chosen because it is commonly interpreted as meaning 'deceiver of men'.

1.5 The machines

Newman's idea of using electronic counting machines became reality: such a machine was designed, largely by the physicist and electrical engineer C. E. Wynn-Williams of the Telecommunications Research Establishment (TRE).[34] The first machine was ordered in January 1943. It arrived at Bletchley Park in June and acquired the name 'Heath Robinson' after the complicated mechanical contraptions depicted by the then well known cartoonist Heath Robinson (1872–1944). It seems that the names of machines were generally invented by the women who operated them (personnel of the WRNS, usually known as Wrens). In this case, the British habit of using only surnames led to the name becoming 'Robinson'. Later models were called Old Robinson and Super Rob.

The Robinson machines (by the end of hostilities there were three of them in operation) were designed to carry out some of the more laborious procedures involved in the breaking of Tunny traffic. The *Report* categorizes Robinsons as 'counting and stepping machines' (*GRT*, **13A(a)**, TNA HW 25/4, p. 25; this edition, p. 32). Various practical difficulties arose in using the Robinson, for instance that the machine did not print the numbers it found (*GRT*, **52(b)(i)**, TNA HW 25/5, p. 328; this edition, p. 312).

Even before the first Robinson was delivered, work had started on the design of faster machines. This work was a collaboration between GCCS and the Post Office Research Station. It was planned

[30]E.g. '(My facts are no doubt hopelessly inaccurate)': TNA HW 25/37, p. 5.

[31]TNA HW 25/37, p. 1. For a detailed consideration of these two papers by Turing see S. L. Zabell, 'Commentary on Alan M. Turing: The Applications of Probability to Cryptography', *Cryptologia*, 36.3 (2012), pp. 191–214.

[32]See S. L. Zabell, 'Statistics at Bletchley Park', this volume, pp. lxxv–ci below, esp. p. xcviii.

[33]See Hodges, *Alan Turing: The Enigma* (see footnote 22, above), pp. 285ff. Hodges' reference is to TNA FO 850/256. See also 'Report on speech secrecy system DELILAH, a technical description compiled by A M Turing and Lieutenant D Bayley REME', TNA HW 25/36; reproduced in *Cryptologia*, 36.4 (2012), pp. 295–340.

[34]Charles Eryl Wynn-Williams had worked at the Cavendish Laboratory in Cambridge in the 1930s. In 1931 he invented a device for counting alpha particles that used thyratrons, though it took the input from a conventional detector.

that the new machine should minimise repeated running of tapes (which sometimes damaged them). Although details are not known, it seems that an early version of the projected new machine stored information from a tape of key stream, but Newman seems to have had reservations about using so many valves, whose reliability was open to doubt (for Newman's comments on the earlier design see our Appendix D, 'Initial Conception of Colossus, pp. 535–539 below). In the end the new machine used about half the original number of valves. The data, which on Robinson was written on the key tape, was now recalculated as needed by what was, in effect, a Tunny simulator built into the new machine.

The authorities who had the power to approve the project did so — presumably despite remaining doubts whether a machine containing so many valves could be expected to be reliable — and the work went ahead at the Post Office Research Station (see Appendix D). Staff at the Research Station, at Dollis Hill, in north-west London, about forty miles (65 km) from Bletchley Park, had worked with TRE on the design and construction of the Robinsons. A team led by Thomas ('Tommy') Flowers (1905–1998) set to work on the design of the new machine in February 1943.[35] The fact is not recorded in the Chronology given in chapter **74** of the *General Report on Tunny*, though dates are given for the ordering of Robinsons. Nor does the Chronology record that the new machine was demonstrated successfully in an eight-hour run in December 1943. That proved the thyratron valves were sufficiently reliable. (It had turned out that valves failed much less often if the current was never switched off — which was how this machine was eventually used.)

In regard to the design and development processes for the new machine, the Chronology records only that the first operational machine was 'installed' at Bletchley Park in February 1944. The new machine had acquired the name Colossus several months before it was delivered to Bletchley Park; Newman refers to it by this name three times — twice in quotation marks and once without them — in a minute to Edward W. H. Travis (1888–1956), the head of GCCS, dated 28 November 1943 (the minute is mainly concerned with the possible usefulness of a different machine, called Dragon, on which see section 3.6 below).[36] And the machine is again called Colossus when Newman writes to Travis on 18 January 1944 to tell him it will be delivered that day.[37] Presumably the date in the Chronology refers to when Colossus was first put into operation. The machine consisted of multiple racks of apparatus. Allowing for circulation space for operators and engineers to move between the racks of components, the whole machine took up the floor space of a room measuring about four metres square.

The Colossus machine proved to be effective and by the end of the war there were ten Colossi in operation. The improved performance of Colossus compared with Robinson apparently made it easier to adapt to carrying out different procedures. This had a practical purpose, because changes were repeatedly made in the Tunny cipher and there always remained some traffic that was not broken, on which new techniques might be tried. Newman obviously recognised that Colossus came closer than any other machine had to being the 'universal machine' Turing had described in 1936 in his paper 'On computable numbers'.[38] And he realised his colleagues would have noticed the same. About sixty years later, Donald Michie still remembered the sternness with which he was told it was forbidden to play with Colossus.[39]

It was once usual to assert that all the Colossi were destroyed at the end of the war, but in view of the enthusiastic description of their performance in the *General Report on Tunny* such wholesale destruction seems exceedingly implausible (and reasons for the story being put about,

[35] See B. Jack Copeland et al., 'Dollis Hill at War' in Copeland, *Colossus* (see footnote 15, above), pp. 281–290.

[36] TNA HW 14/92.

[37] TNA HW 14/96. Further, Welchman used the name Colossus on 7 December 1943 (TNA HW 62/5): see Paul Gannon, *Colossus: Bletchley Park's Greatest Secret* (London: Atlantic Books, 2006), p. 269, note on p. 514.

[38] Reference in note 22 above.

[39] Donald Michie, 14 July 2004, private conversation with JVF.

or at least not contradicted by official sources, are not hard to guess). It is now believed that at least two Colossi were transferred to GCHQ (see subsection 2.2 below), where their users must surely have included Geoffrey Timms (who worked for GCHQ).[40] With Newman's help and the agreement of the proper authorities, parts from two Colossi were incorporated in the computer built in Manchester in 1948 ('Baby', properly SSEM) and perhaps also in later models.[41]

1.6 Staff

The increase in the number of machines went with an even steeper increase in the number of staff employed in Newman's group. In April 1943 there were two cryptographers and sixteen Wrens, making a total of eighteen. In April 1945 there were two administrators, 22 cryptographers, 28 engineers (fifteen for maintenance, thirteen for construction) and 273 Wrens, making a total of 325 (*GRT*, **31B**, TNA HW 25/5, p. 276; this edition, p. 262). It seems that mechanization had not brought about a reduction in the relative number of ancillary staff: the Wrens, who operated machines and carried out routine tasks such as calculations (that is acted as 'computers'), formed a roughly constant proportion of the staff.

Interestingly, the authors of the *General Report on Tunny* also considered it worth mentioning the backgrounds of the Newmanry cryptographers, dividing them into two groups, depending on whether they were recruited before or after July 1944. This analysis shows an increasing recruitment of men (they were all men) with mathematical training at university level.[42] Training in cryptanalysis was provided on arrival (for details see section 3 below), but some proven ability in mathematics seems to have been considered essential.

The usefulness of mathematics may seem obvious, and in the context of a statistical attack it perhaps is obvious: it was Tutte, employing mathematical techniques, who set such an attack in train. However, traditionally the background for cryptanalysts had been in languages. The two chief cryptanalysts at Bletchley Park in 1939 were the head of the civilian (Foreign Office) group, Oliver Strachey (1874–1960), who retired in December and was succeeded by Dillwyn Knox (1884–1943), well known as a classical scholar, and the head of the military division, John Tiltman, who had no university education but had long experience of cryptanalysis. Both Knox and Tiltman were greatly respected for the quality of their work. As it happened, Knox was responsible for recruiting the first mathematician to join the staff at Bletchley Park: an Oxford graduate, Peter Twinn (1916–2004). One Cambridge mathematician recruited by Gordon Welchman in 1940 was John Herivel (1918–2011), who was later to become a historian of science; he worked first in Hut 6 and then in the Newmanry.[43] Nevertheless, traditional recruitment continued. Linguists included John Chadwick (1920–1998), who worked on breaking Italian traffic while serving with the Navy in the Mediterranean and, after taking a course in Japanese at Bedford, joined GCCS as a translator of Japanese, having been recruited because he was trained in classical languages and spoke Modern Greek fluently.[44] Another linguist was Denys Page (1908–1978), who ran the section handling German intelligence services traffic (not a cryptanalytic task).[45] The first

[40] See Biographies of Authors, p. civ below.

[41] Newman's request for the parts, dated 8 August 1945, is in TNA HW 64/59; see David P. Anderson, 'Was the Manchester Baby Conceived at Bletchley Park?', British Computer Society: Electronic Workshops in Computing, Nov. 2007, URL: `http://www.bcs.org/upload/pdf/ewic_tur04_paper3.pdf` (visited on 07/06/2014) and *idem*, 'The Contribution of M. H. A. Newman and his Mathematicians to the Creation of the Manchester "Baby"', *BSHM Bulletin: Journal of the British Society for the History of Mathematics*, 24 (2009), pp. 27–39.

[42] On more general issues of recruitment to GCCS see Grey, *Decoding Organization* (see footnote 2, above), pp. 132ff.

[43] On Herivel see Briggs, *Secret Days: Code-Breaking in Bletchley Park* (see footnote 6, above).

[44] After the war, Chadwick taught in the Classics department at the University of Cambridge and became the leading expert on Mycenaean Greek.

[45] Page is mentioned in **39D** and his section in **14A(a)** of the *General Report on Tunny*. He was Regius Professor of Greek at Cambridge from 1950 to 1974.

recruit to the Nemanry, Donald Michie, who had taken the course in cryptography at Bedford (having arrived too late to join a course in Japanese), had specialized in classics at school and was intending to read classics at Oxford. Linguists in the Testery included Kevin O'Neill (1917–1986), recruited to GCCS in 1941, who went on to make a career in Signals Intelligence. On the literary side, one of the Cambridge friends who wrote to Newman from Bletchley Park before Newman arrived there was the English don, and well known literary critic, F. L. Lucas (1894–1967), who worked in Hut 3.[46]

Another traditional recruitment category was chess players, the game being seen as exemplifying logical reasoning. C. H. O'D. (Hugh) Alexander (1909–1974), of Hut 8, who had a degree in mathematics from Cambridge, was repeatedly Cambridge University chess champion and then British chess champion in 1938; Jack Good had merely been Cambridgeshire county chess champion. It seems likely that Alan Turing, who was not particularly good at chess, appeared suitable because he was a logician, rather than simply because of his mathematical abilities. In the event it was obviously not lost on his colleagues that his arguments regularly took mathematical form. From about late 1941 onwards, efforts were made to recruit mathematicians for all groups.[47] Elementary mathematics had always been seen as useful — there is a practical background to those schoolroom problems about how many men it takes to dig a ditch — but now advanced, cutting-edge university mathematics was also seen as useful, even if only in a tiny enclave of quasi-academic activity.

All members of the Newmanry who have written about their experiences agree that Newman was an immensely able and inspiring leader.

1.7 Significance of the *General Report on Tunny*

Primary documents tend to provide hard but limited evidence, leaving much room for interpretation. Future historians will doubtless find many uses for the *General Report on Tunny*. What follow here are our impressions as editors, based partly on the areas of investigation we found ourselves drawn into while trying to understand the text.

First, it is in the nature of things that properly technical accounts of major campaigns of cryptanalysis are rare. And this one is not only detailed but begins right at the beginning: the cryptanalysts initially knew very little about the cipher machines they were attacking. By the end, they could read a decent proportion of the traffic (on the quantity of traffic decrypted see endnote 1 to *GRT*, **61**, p. 611 below). Such an account is obviously of interest to cryptographers as well as cryptanalysts and is of considerable significance for the history of their subject.

Second, the large machines built at Bletchley Park are part of the lineage of the modern electronic computer, and it is notable that some of the participants in the work described in the *General Report on Tunny* are also associated with the immediate origins of the first stored-program machine, in Manchester in 1948. This connection, specifically in regard to Newman and Turing, makes the *Report* an important document for the history of computing.

Third, the statistical methods that the cryptanalysts used were notably innovative. Some of the theoretical work was later published by Jack Good in *Probability and the Weighing of Evidence*, and is recognised as an important component in the development of the field of theory of statistical inference. It presents a new understanding of what statistical reasoning is. The *General Report on Tunny* allows one to see this work in its original context, of which there is of course no trace in

[46] Newman papers, library of St John's College, Cambridge, 3/1/7, letter dated 27 July 1942. Lucas worked in Hut 3 (dealing with decrypts), see Millward, 'Life In and Out of Hut 3' (see footnote 6, above), pp. 24, 26. See also Grey, *Decoding Organization* (see footnote 2, above), p. 25 and fn. 14 (p. 43).

[47] See, for example, Peter Hilton, 'Living with Fish: Breaking Tunny in the Newmanry and Testery' in Copeland, *Colossus* (see footnote 15, above), pp. 189–203, esp. pp. 189–192.

the book published in 1950.[48]

Fourth, the *General Report on Tunny* shows us some beginnings of changes in the status of mathematics. Long seen as the archetypal inhabitants of an ivory tower, as cryptanalysts research mathematicians showed themselves to be useful in a practical way. The prominent Cambridge mathematician G. H. Hardy (1877–1947) who, as is made clear in his book *A Mathematician's Apology* (Cambridge: Cambridge University Press, 1941), was a strong advocate for the study of mathematics for its own sake, was (as it turned out) preparing many mathematicians for application-oriented work at Bletchley Park, among them Hardy's research student G. W. Morgan (1911–1989), who became head of the Research Section. The employment of mathematicians at Bletchley Park seems to have been important in associating computing machines, and eventually computer science, with mathematics rather than, say, logic or philosophy.

2. Documents available and not

Historians are accustomed to working with information that is less complete than they would wish. At a certain point a decision has to be taken that the information is now substantial enough to support the telling of a reasonably coherent and plausible story and that searching for further evidence is not likely to be sufficiently productive to justify the effort expended on it. The present case is unusual in one very important respect: while the normal processes of attrition have occurred, there is also a lack of evidence that is due to sources being deliberately withheld for security reasons.

For British sources, one usually learns of the existence of such documents only when they have reached the stage of bibliographic details being sent to the National Archives (UK) as a first step towards declassification, but leads are sometimes provided by references in other documents. Neither in the UK nor in the US is there a system whereby documents from the intelligence services are declassified after a fixed term, as some other state papers are. At any given time, preliminary guidance about possible release seems to be provided by a (secret) list of forbidden topics. For materials such as those that concern us here, one obvious impediment in the process of declassification is the need for a technical expert to look at the document and understand it well enough to be able to certify that it does not touch on the forbidden topics. Unfortunately the passage of time does not necessarily make this easier. And the British notoriously tend to err on the side of caution. For instance, during the First World War Beatrice Mabel Cave-Browne-Cave (1874–1947), who together with her sister Frances Evelyn (1876–1965) had studied mathematics at Girton College, Cambridge in the 1890s, was employed by the Admiralty air department, the Air Board of the Air Ministry, and the aircraft production department to work on fluid mechanics, in connection with a study of aeroplane wings. She wrote reports and two confidential information memoranda on these matters in 1917. The authorities took what proved to be a laughably pessimistic view of the speed of development of aircraft, and decided her work should remain secret for 50 years.[49] There may be an element of inadvertence in an even more spectacular example dating from the previous century. In 1854, in the course of the Crimean War, the Admiralty was considering using fumes from burning sulphur in an attack on Kronstadt (an island in the Gulf of Finland). Advice was sought from Michael Faraday (1791–1867), whose opinion was that the proposed method was almost certainly impractical. The attack was not made. All the same, the relevant papers were declassified only in 1946.[50]

[48]For a more detailed discussion, see S. L. Zabell, 'Statistics at Bletchley Park', pp. lxxv–ci below, esp. p. xcviii.

[49]We are grateful to A. E. L. Davis, who wrote on both the sisters Cave-Browne-Cave for the *Oxford Dictionary of National Biography* (2004), for drawing our attention to this story.

[50]They are now in the UK National Archives, ADM 1/5632. We are grateful to Frank A. J. L. James for telling us about this incident.

A list of the archival sources we used is given in our Bibliography (pp. 624–644). The present discussion is intended to supplement the Bibliography and will direct particular attention to what we were not able to use. This is to warn readers to exercise due caution in regard to what we have written.

2.1 Documents mentioned in the *General Report on Tunny*

All the cryptographers in Newman's team worked regular 'research shifts' in which they investigated problems whose solution seemed likely to have operational significance (*GRT*, **31D**, TNA HW 25/5, p. 278; this edition, p. 263). Their results were written up as 'Research Logs', which seem to have served as a kind of informal learned journal for the group. There are repeated detailed references to these Logs throughout the *General Report on Tunny*, though in an impersonal style that gives only the number of the piece and not an author's name. Some of the more technical passages of the *Report* seem to be more or less direct transcriptions from the Logs, and there is an occasional (probably revealing) use of the first person singular, for example 'I will discuss here . . . ' in the first paragraph of subsection **28A(e)** (*GRT*, **28A(e)**, TNA HW 25/4, p. 256; this edition, p. 239). We understand that the Research Logs have not been found at GCHQ but there is no record of their having been destroyed. In any case, they were not available to us. They would probably have helped us to decide on the authorship of various parts of the *Report*, a matter that, for lack of evidence, we have in general chosen not to address. The single exception is made for the section about the machines, where there is a tiny piece of specific evidence (see 3.6.1 below). As some members of the Newmanry published independent writings, it is possible that linguistic analysis could help to assign authorship of the more discursive parts of the *Report*.

The *General Report on Tunny* also sometimes refers the reader to the document now usually known in the secondary literature as *The Testery Report*. The names of the authors of this report are not known to us. A copy of the work is currently (February 2015) included in the catalogue of the National Archives (UK) with press-mark HW 25/28. The catalogue entry describes the volume as *Solution of German Teleprinter Cyphers (Testery) Linguistic Methods*. Since the Archives staff are not experts on the work of GCCS, one must assume that this description reflects either what is written on the book itself or what the cataloguers were told by a librarian at GCHQ. However, the given wording may not be the formal title of the work. The press-mark implies it is a single volume, so its length may be less than that of the *General Report on Tunny* (which is bound in two volumes). The catalogue entry for the *Testery Report* notes that the item is 'retained by Department', which is to say that it has not yet been declassified. The groups run by Tester and by Newman worked closely together, as is abundantly clear not only from the *General Report on Tunny* but also from the *History of the Fish Section* (1945, declassified 2004, TNA HW 50/63, described in 2.2.3 below) and in the multitude of personal reminiscences in such volumes as *Codebreakers: the inside story of Bletchley Park* (1993), *Action This Day* (2001) and *Colossus: The Secrets of Bletchley Park's Codebreaking Computers* (2006).[51] In particular, the activities of both groups stem from the work of Tiltman and Tutte described in Chapters **41** to **44** of the *General Report on Tunny* (see section 3 below).

As we have already noted (in section 1.3 above), the decision to start cryptanalytic work on teleprinter messages was presumably taken as a result of traffic analysis (a less glamorous part of signals intelligence than cryptanalysis). At Bletchley Park, traffic analysis, which was first carried out on Morse (Enigma) messages, was the province of a group in Hut 6, from which it took the name SIXTA. The Sixta group wrote a report at the end of the war, and it is referred to several times in the *General Report on Tunny*. The catalogue of the National Archives (UK) contains

[51] Hinsley and Stripp, *Codebreakers* (see footnote 3, above); Erskine and Smith, *Action This Day* (see footnote 1, above); Copeland, *Colossus* (see footnote 15, above).

entries for the *Sixta History*, with press-marks HW 43/63 and HW 43/82 to 43/93. However, at the time of writing (February 2015) the documents have not been declassified. Happily, a certain amount of information about Traffic Analysis, specifically about direction finding (usually called D/F) is provided in Harold Kenworthy's *The Interception of German Teleprinter Communications by Foreign Office Station Knockholt* (1946, declassified 2004) of which the National Archives has two copies: TNA HW 3/163 and HW 50/79 (see 2.2.4 below, printed in full in Appendix B, pp. 513–524 below), and his *A Brief History of Events Relating to the Growth of the 'Y' Service* (1957, declassified 2004), TNA HW 3/81. Both of Kenworthy's texts will be discussed in section 2.2.4 below. Neither of them tells us how the numerous individual links shown in *GRT*, **61** were identified.

The *General Report on Tunny* also contains a few references to the existence of a report written by the Post Office. This contained technical information about the electrical machines. Unfortunately, no copy of the Post Office report is known. In this case, however, good management on the part of GCHQ helped to provide a substitute, as will be described in our next paragraph.

2.2 Other relevant documents

2.2.1 Writings on Colossus (1973)

The substitute document in question, *A technical description of COLOSSUS I*, was written in August 1973, by D. C. Horwood, who had been a member of the Post Office team that built the first Colossus. This account, registration number P/0921/8193/16, was declassified in August 2003. The copy of it in the National Archives (UK) has press-mark HW 25/24. The story of how it came to be written is told in the first paragraph:

> This paper has been prepared to honour an undertaking given by GCHQ (reference a. [Z/1192/8612/24 of 24.7.72]) to prepare, and place in archives, a description of the early electronic computer-like equipment known as Colossus I. The decision to prepare this record followed representations, made by Professor B Randall [*sic*, should be Randell] of Newcastle University to the Prime Minister in January 1972, which sought the release of information on the machine so that it might be accorded an appropriate place in the history of the development of the modern electronic computer. After careful consideration it was decided that the information requested by Professor Randall [*sic*] could not be released at that time, but that a description of the machine should be prepared so that it would be available if it were to be decided, at some future date, that the information could be released.[52]

There is also a description of what documentation was available inside GCHQ in 1973:

> The decision to prepare the technical description having been taken, the next steps were to locate and assemble the available documents and diagrams and to produce a coherent record. This posed several problems. The design of the original machine was largely the work of Mr T H Flowers, at the time the senior Engineer in charge of what, in 1943, was known as the Signalling Group at the Post Office Research Station at Dollis Hill. Flowers, however, had retired and was no longer in any way associated with GCHQ. For security reasons all the official documents relating to the work at Dollis Hill had been handed over to GCHQ at the end of the War and unfortunately none of those relating to the original Colossus had been preserved.[53]

[52]D. C. Horwood, *A technical description of COLOSSUS I*, August 1973, TNA HW 25/24, p. 1 (section 1, paragraph 1). Transcription by JVF.

[53]D. C. Horwood, *A technical description of COLOSSUS I*, August 1973, TNA HW 25/24, p. 1 (section 1, paragraph 3). Transcription by JVF.

Horwood, who transferred to GCHQ in 1945, also gives us an insider account of what happened to the Colossi after the war:

> At the end of the War a number of the Colossus machines including the original were dismantled, but a small number of the more recent versions were moved to Eastcote and subsequently to Cheltenham. With the end of the war the particular purpose for which the machines were designed disappeared, but the nature and reliability of the machines was such that a number of attempts, some more successful than others, were made to make the remaining machines suitable for a number of other similar purposes, or, in effect, to generalise them. In the course of these successive changes, new drawings and documents were prepared and, probably to avoid confusion, most of the earlier drawings and documents were destroyed. Thus we have the paradoxical situation in which the success of the machine and the consequent attempts to adapt it to other applications contributed to the loss of much of the detailed information concerning its original form.[54]

This is essentially plausible, except for the statement that 'With the end of the War the particular purpose for which the machines were designed disappeared'. This is literally true, since wartime efforts had been directed against German signals, and Colossus was specifically designed to attack Tunny (the Lorenz SZ 40 series) but the statement is misleading: it seems highly likely that similar cipher machines continued in use elsewhere and UK intelligence services presumably continued to attempt to read the traffic, sometimes successfully.[55] We know of no direct evidence regarding Tunny, but the French secret service bought some Siemens T52 (Sturgeon) machines in 1949, and were warned off them by their US allies.[56]

Horwood's text also makes a comment that reflects on the *General Report on Tunny* and goes on to mention the existence of another text that might prove useful to readers of it:

> Historically, the significance of a particular machine is determined partly by its technical design and partly by the operations which it is or was capable of performing. This paper is concerned only with the technical design of Colossus, and while a fairly comprehensive description of the uses to which it was put is already on record (reference b. [The TUNNY report (unreferenced)]), that description is embedded in a document of considerable proportions covering a much broader subject. Shaun Wylie has therefore provided a companion paper describing the purpose and the mathematical logic of the machine. (reference c. [Colossus, its purpose and its facilities by Shaun Wylie P/0922/8103/16]).[57]

There is no mention of Wylie's paper in the catalogue of the National Archives (UK) and in June 2009 we were told there were no plans to declassify it.

[54] D. C. Horwood, *A technical description of COLOSSUS I*, August 1973, TNA HW 25/24, pp. 1–2 (section 1, paragraph 4). Transcription by JVF.

[55] This matter is discussed in more detail in Whitfield Diffie 'Cryptographic significance of the analysis of Tunny', above pp. xvii–xxiv.

[56] Frode Weierud, 'Bletchley Park's Sturgeon — the Fish that Laid No Eggs' in Copeland, *Colossus* (see footnote 15, above), pp. 307–327, esp. pp. 325–27; for material in French archives see Georges-Henri Soutou, 'La mécanisation du chiffre au Quai d'Orsay, ou les aléas d'un système technique (1948–1958)' in Michèle Merger and Dominique Barjot, eds., *Les entreprises et leurs réseaux: hommes, capitaux, techniques et pouvoirs XIXe – XXe siècles* (Paris: Presses de l'Université de Paris-Sorbonne, 1998), pp. 697–710 and Georges-Henri Soutou, 'French Intelligence about the East during the Fourth Republic: Pedestrian but Sensible', a paper given at a conference 'Keeping Secrets: How Important was Intelligence to the Conduct of International Relations from 1914 to 1989?' held at the German Historical Institute, London, Apr. 2008.

[57] D. C. Horwood, *A technical description of COLOSSUS I*, August 1973, TNA HW 25/24, p. 1 (section 1, paragraph 2). Transcription by JVF. On Wylie, see biographical notes, p. 559 below.

In accordance with his archival purpose, Horwood further provides a list of 'Technical Personalities', that is he gives brief biographical sketches of senior members of the staff who worked on Colossus I. The persons concerned are Mr T. H. Flowers, Mr S. Broadhurst ('Worked directly under Mr Flowers at Dollis Hill ... '), Mr Lynch ('concerned with the design of the tape reader assembly of Colossus'; this is Arnold Lynch (1914–2004), who worked for the Post Office Research Station from 1936 to 1974), Dr A. W. M. Coombs ('Assisted in the design and supervised the production of the second and subsequent models of Colossus.'), and Mr W. Chandler ('was involved under Flowers in the design and construction of all the Colossus machines ... Had previously worked under Dr Wyn [*sic*] Williams at Swanage.'). The remaining staff appear merely as names, without a biographical note: Mr T. Hauser, Mr H. Fensom, Mr B. Clayton, Mr Thompson, Mr J. Cane, Mr D. C. Horwood, 'and others'.[58]

2.2.2 Writings by Alan Turing

Alan Turing was never formally a member of the Newmanry. In 1942 he contributed to the mathematical work that is described in the *General Report on Tunny* (see *GRT*, **43B**, TNA HW 25/5, p. 313; this edition, p. 298; and *GRT*, **74** under July 1942, TNA HW 25/5, p. 458; this edition, p. 446). Earlier he had invented the factor in favour of a hypothesis and the 'ban'.[59]

Chapter **31** section **G** of the *General Report on Tunny* deals with the in-house education of new recruits to Newman's group. Its third paragraph reads

> The Education Committee co-ordinated this production of screeds and started a General Fish Series of papers which were duplicated and available in every room. (*GRT*, **31G**, TNA HW 25/5, p. 279; this edition, p. 265.)

Turing's two papers of 1941 or 1942, *The applications of probability to cryptography* (TNA HW 25/37) and *Statistics of repetitions* (TNA HW 25/38), discussed in section 1.4 above and 3.4.1 below, seem unlikely to have been addressed to Wrens, but they may be indicative of the content of screeds addressed to newly recruited mathematicians. However, neither appears in the list of screeds in the Bibliography in the *General Report on Tunny* (*GRT*, **73**, TNA HW 25/5, pp. 453–455; this edition, pp. 441–441).

2.2.3 *History of the Fish Section* (1945)

The National Archives (UK) contain a typescript *History of the Fish Section* (TNA HW 50/63) dated, on its last page, 20 August 1945. The document was declassified in 2004.

There is no mention of an author. Intenal evidence suggests that he was a member of the Testery (see entry for June and July 1943 discussed below) and from the general tenor of the writing it is hard to escape the feeling that he was an administrator or even (at some stage) an accountant. The text, whose main body is fifteen pages long, is written in the impersonal style appropriate to an official report. It may have been called a History to distinguish it from the Reports being written by the Newmanry and the Testery. Throughout the *History*, the Testery is presented as the dominant group within the Fish Section, in charge of relations with the interception stations and with the users of the decrypted traffic in Hut 3. The Testery had, of course, been the earliest group to work on Fish ciphers — except for the Research Section, which makes no appearance in the *History*.[60]

[58] D. C. Horwood, *A technical description of COLOSSUS I*, August 1973, TNA HW 25/24, Appendix A, p. 44. Transcription by JVF.

[59] See S. L. Zabell, 'Statistics at Bletchley Park', below, pp. lxxvi, lxxxi.

[60] It is possible that since, in the earlier days, the Testery was the Fish section, it may have retained this designation for administrative purposes, perhaps including the title in an essentially administrative report.

In some respects the *History* does take a wider view than the *General Report on Tunny*, as is made clear in the first two paragraphs of the brief Introduction:

> The following pages show the development of the section from the time it was started, presenting the principal changes in chronological order. Since our growth and organization depended on the Enemy, Knockholt, and later the Newmanry, certain facts regarding these have been commented on to explain the reasons behind the various changes.
>
> Technical terms have not been fully explained here, as these have been dealt with at length in the special cryptographic survey.[61]

It is not clear what is meant by 'the special cryptographic survey'. Since the author regards the Testery as the defining entity of the Fish Section, the phrase may refer to the *Testery Report*, although the wording does not echo the nearest we have to a formal title of the *Testery Report*, which is *Solution of German Teleprinter Cyphers (Testery) Linguistic Methods*. On the other hand, it might refer to the *General Report on Tunny*, though again there is no echo of the title. The *History of the Fish Section* shows us the work of the Testery and that of the Newmanry in context as complementary, parts of a single enterprise, and in consequence it sheds some light on the relations between the work of the two groups. Details, which the administration-oriented author of the *History* would doubtless have regarded as technical details, will presumably emerge with the declassification of further documents, notably the *Testery Report*.

True to the promise in the Introduction, the *History of the Fish Section* does indeed present its material in chronological order. However, the style resembles that of a calendar or a series of ledger entries. Events are presented in short sections, each with a title designating a specific period, usually a month or two months. The author — the uniformity of style suggests there was only one — obviously had access to detailed records of what was intercepted, which messages were attacked, what links were broken and so on. The story that emerges is, of course, largely one of success, but it also mentions difficulties and failings — probably with an eye to making improvements as SIS reorganises signals intelligence activity for peacetime operations. The Conclusion is

> Throughout the whole period of the section's history, all our requirements of staff and machinery were promptly met. Consequently, except for the necessary delay entailed in developing new techniques, we were always in a position to deal adequately with the material at our disposal, and were, in fact, prepared to cope with a great deal more, had the intercept station been able to provide this. Unfortunately, although adequate notice of our long-term requirements was given when the cryptographic solution of the various problems had been recognised, it was found impossible to organise and staff the intercept station to meet these and it was not until shortly before the close of hostilities, when traffic was falling off, that all current intercepts could be processed and supplied to us.
>
> We should like to place on record here our appreciation of the unstinted loyalty and efforts made by all sections of the staff. Every call made was more than willingly met and this was in no small degree due to the enthusiasm of the small body of men and women who had grown up with the section from its early years. Furthermore, we were fortunate in having chiefs to deal with who understood our problems and fully backed our efforts to solve them.[62]

In January 1945 there had been a serious attempt to improve the performance of Knockholt, the representative of the Fish Section being Major Tester:

[61] *History of the Fish Section*, Introduction, TNA HW 50/63, p. 1, transcription JVF.

[62] *History of the Fish Section*, Conclusion, TNA HW 50/63, pp. 14–15, transcription JVF.

> Major Tester spent some three weeks at Knockholt pending the arrival of Major King, the new O.C., Mr. Janes having resigned in December. Before going to Knockholt Major King spent some days in the section to learn what we did and required; Knockholt's figures began to improve and by April were maintained steadily at a 350,000 – 400,000 letter per day average.[63]

There are hints of this problem in the *General Report on Tunny*, but nothing as explicit as what is said in the *History of the Fish Section*.

The *History* also provides direct evidence of supervision by Hut 3. In the account of November and December 1942 we are told 'Outstanding Tunny traffic was decoded as a second priority task, until Hut 3 no longer required it.'[64]

The *General Report on Tunny* naturally puts the work of the Newmanry centre stage. In contrast, the *History of the Fsih Section* tends to refer to the Newmanry mainly in connection with its relations with other groups in the Fish Section. For instance, in the account of June and July 1943, we are told

> The Newmanry began operations, concentrating on Bream traffic, the Rome end being particularly favourable. Members of our staff helped in order to get experience and to provide a flexible pool of staff on which Newmanry could call. One cryptographer was transferred permanently to the Newmanry.[65]

This indicates that the writer was a member of the Testery and we may note that he seems to take it for granted that Testery staff could carry out Newmanry tasks. This cannot merely refer to ancillary staff, who are always explicitly identified as such. The references to the Newmanry are fairly numerous, but they all give the impression that Newman's staff were essentially back-room boys concerned only with specific narrow tasks for which they used machines. There is no hint of an awareness that the members of the group included some of the best mathematical minds of the time and that its recruits were the top mathematics graduates from Oxford, Cambridge and Imperial College, London. Unlike the authors of the passage about staffing in the *General Report on Tunny* (*GRT*, **31B**, TNA HW 25/5, p. 276; this edition, p. 262, see section 1.6 above), the writer of the *History* either had not noticed the increased employment of mathematicians or did not think it was worth remarking on. We are, however, occasionally told that a new recruit to the Fish Section had taken the cryptography course at Bedford.

The main text of the *History* is followed by three Annexes which present detailed information in tabular or semi-tabular form. The titles and contents of these Annexes are as follows:

Annex I 'Distribution of links by fronts with date link was first broken' (two pages), described at the end of the Introduction as 'List of Fish links broken, and date first broken'.

Annex II 'Links broken' (two pages), described at the end of the Introduction as 'List of Fish links broken from month to month'. The numbers are presented, month by month, starting in June 1942, running to August 1944 on the first page and from September 1944 to May 1945 on the second one. There is a note 'From July 1944 daily keys were gradually introduced on all links.'

Annex III 'Statistics (Nov 1942 – May 1945)' (a large fold-out page), described at the end of the Introduction as 'Statistics of transmissions intercepted, broken etc.'. This shows the total number of messages intercepted and broken per month and indicates which methods were used. A

[63] *History of the Fish Section*, 'January 1945', TNA HW 50/63, pp. 12–13, transcription JVF.
[64] *History of the Fish Section*, 'November and December 1942', TNA HW 50/63, p. 2, transcription JVF.
[65] *History of the Fish Section*, 'June-July 1943', TNA HW 50/63 p. 3, transcription JVF.

transcription of the table is printed in our endnote 1 to chapter **61** of the *General Report on Tunny*, p. 611, esp. p. 612 below.

2.2.4 Writings by Harold Kenworthy (1946, 1957)

The *General Report on Tunny* does not discuss the process of interception of enemy messages. The chapter devoted to the non-Morse interception station at Knockholt (*GRT*, **33**, TNA HW 25/5, p. 281; this edition, p. 268) is mainly concerned with the care taken in the checking of tapes (see section 3.5 below). A high level of accuracy in intercepts was crucial to the possibility of successful cryptanalysis. The importance of the interception programme is also emphasised in the *History of the Fish Section*, notably in its Conclusion (quoted in full in section 2.2.3 above). Operations at Knockholt were seen as integral to those at Bletchley Park, but as the tasks and the personnel were different, the activity of Knockholt was the subject of a separate report, written by its Chief, Harold Kenworthy. His report, *The Interception of German Teleprinter Communications by Foreign Office Station Knockholt*, dated March 1946, covers twenty foolscap pages. The National Archives (UK) holds two copies of the report, TNA HW 50/79 and HW 3/163. The full text of this report is printed below in Appendix B (pp. 513–524).

When he was called up in September 1916, Kenworthy, then aged 23, was placed in a Naval Wireless Telegraphy unit at Gibraltar. He went on to spend all of his life working on radio transmissions, largely on interception, for the Marconi Wireless Telegraph Company (in the engineering branch), the Metropolitan Police, GCCS, and after 1945 for GCHQ. A few weeks before his retirement from GCHQ, in June 1957, Kenworthy, who had been a protagonist in setting up interception stations in a wide vairiety of locations, wrote *A Brief History of Events Relating to the Growth of the 'Y' Service'* (TNA HW 3/81, declassified 2004, ten foolscap pages).[66] The period covered by the *Brief History* is from about 1920 to (probably) the mid 1950s — it is impossible to be precise because the later part of the work gives very few dates. As in his report on Knockholt, Kenworthy's writing style is that of a man whose job did not regularly require him to express himself on paper, except about purely technical matters. We are, in effect, warned about this in the Foreword, which reads

> Now that I am about to retire after many years in the 'Y' service I thought it would be a good idea to write a short history recalling the sequence of events or as many as I can remember which have led us to the present organisation.[67]

Kenworthy does indeed seem to have worked from memory, rather than from documents (except perhaps his appointments diary), and in most of the narrative there is an irritating lack of explicit dates, except for public events such as the General Strike (1926) and the outbreak of the Second World War (1939). However, the series of episodes and incidents preserves some information about the often unrecorded activities of technicians, for instance in the story of the first interception of teleprinter traffic (see section 1.3 above). Kenworthy mentions radio surveillance, ordered by the SIS, directed against the Italian embassy in the 1920s[68] and a whole chapter is devoted to the interception of messages from Moscow, starting in the period following the General Strike.[69] Stations were also set up overseas, for instance one in Hong Kong to intercept messages from the Italian embassy in Pekin (Beijing).[70] We are also told that 'during the Spanish Civil War there was a special station set up in Madrid', but no target is identified.[71] Kenworthy sketches the

[66] The *Brief History* is the last item in the file, which otherwise contains correspondence.
[67] *Brief History*, TNA HW 3/81, p. [ii].
[68] *Brief History* ch. 3, §3.4–6. TNA HW 3/81, pp. 2–3.
[69] *Brief History*, ch. 5 'Communist Activities', TNA HW 3/81 pp. 5–6.
[70] *Brief History*, ch. 6, §6.1, TNA HW 3/81, p. 6.
[71] *Brief History*, ch. 6, §6.1, TNA HW 3/81, p. 6.

events leading to the setting up of the Metropolitan Police interception station at Denmark Hill (South London), where reception was better than at Scotland Yard, and the work of the Denmark Hill station in the early part of the Second World War is described in some detail.[72]

The first part of chapter 7 is concerned with wartime work, at Denmark Hill, at a new station at Smallford (near St. Albans), and particularly with the work done at Knockholt.[73] In much of the *Brief History*, Kenworthy repeatedly refers to the various difficulties encountered in the interception process, and the variety of equipment he uses (which he seems sometimes to have had difficulty acquiring). For instance, we are told

> It must always be remembered that the signals required to be received are usually being transmitted between terminals far away and completely off our line of bearing and it is this that makes it essential that the operator should be given the best of apparatus and aerials to enable him to do his best for the "one chance" he has.[74]

This is a reminder that it was not only the cryptanalysts who were engaged in an art of the only just possible. And one may reasonably suspect that it echoes conversations that took place at the time.

We are told about the types of aerial that were used. And we are given short accounts of the activity at a number of small interception stations that worked alongside the main one at Knockholt. However, Kenworthy seems not to be interested in any details of the traffic. As in the Knockholt report, intercepted messages are conceived in terms of the total number of letters intercepted per day, not in terms of which link they correspond to. There are repeated references to various technical difficulties and the difficulty of finding adequate numbers of staff who can be trained to listen to the intercepted signals and read the trace made on the undulator tape (called 'slip reading'). Indeed, the very last word of the *Brief History* is 'difficulties' (though those difficulties are ones caused by the use of agricultural land for interception stations and they presumably refer to a period after 1945).

In some ways, the *Brief History* is a significant document, primarily as recording the voice of the technician. However, as this account was written in 1957, apparently with little or no reference to surviving documents, and sometimes strays from presenting events in chronological order, it is not clear how useful it might be in interpreting what Kenworthy himself wrote in 1946 (in the Knockholt report, TNA HW 50/79 and HW 3/163 and Appendix B below pp. 513–524) or what is said about the operation of Knockholt in the *History of the Fish Section* (1945, TNA HW 50/63, see 2.2.3 above) written by a representative of the cryptanalysts who used the material intercepted at Knockholt.

2.2.5 An official history

There is also another more general internal history that, in part, deals with work at GCCS: Francis (Frank) Birch (1889–1956), *The History of British Sigint 1914–1945* (2 vols, TNA HW 43/1 and 43/2, declassified 2004).[75] Unfortunately, when the author, who had been a history don at Cambridge, died in 1956, his *History* was still unfinished. This is stated in the Preface, but no details are given about the state in which Birch left the text or how the work was completed or by whom (though it must have been someone inside GCHQ since most of the references are to classified documents). If Birch himself assembled material for the part of the work that relates to the Second World War, this must have been done fairly shortly after the events it describes and, since Birch had been Head of the (German) Naval Section at GCCS throughout the war

[72] *Brief History*, ch. 6, §6.6–15, TNA HW 3/81, pp. 8–9.
[73] *Brief History*, ch. 7, §7.1, TNA HW 3/81, pp. 9–10.
[74] *Brief History*, ch. 7, §7.1, TNA HW 3/81, p. 10.
[75] The book has been published, full reference in footnote 1 above.

(having been in the naval cryptanalysis organisation, 'Room 40', during the First World War), it is obvious that he would have had access to secret documents and to information from protagonists. For instance, he presumably would have had access to documents such as the Testery report and the SIXTA report that at our time of writing (February 2015) remain classified. However, Birch cannot have been an expert on Tunny and on that subject his work, as (probably) completed after his death by an unidentified assistant, must rate merely as a high-grade secondary source.

3. The contents of the *General Report on Tunny*

This volume presents an edition of the *General Report on Tunny* as a historic document. If it had been submitted for publication as a book in its own right, the commissioning editor might have had much to say about the overall organisation of the text. (What a copy editor might have had to say will be dealt with in section 5 below.) As historians it is our business to deal with the text as it is, making the polite assumption that it was fit for purpose in 1945, trying to decide what that purpose was and how understanding it might help us to read the *General Report on Tunny* for what it is. The following account will slide over much technical detail; it is intended to give a non-specialist historian some idea of what may be found in the *Report*. For detailed navigation through the text, readers are recommended to use our index.

Although this is not immediately apparent from its contents pages, the scope of the *General Report on Tunny* is greater than was implied by its former title 'History of the Newmanry'. On the other hand, as can be seen from the *History of the Fish Section* (TNA HW 50/63 see section 2.2.3 above), the abbreviated title *General Report on Tunny* tends to exaggerate the scope of the text, so the reader sometimes needs to bear in mind that, as the remainder of the title says, the emphasis is on statistical methods. Nevertheless, the text occasionally touches on the activity of the interception station at Knckholt and repeatedly deals wth work done by the Testery (for example in *GRT*, **28**, 'Language methods', TNA HW 25/4, pp. 255–275; this edition, pp. 237–258, see section 3.3 below). Testery work is, however, usually treated rather briefly, since the authors of the *General Report on Tunny* expected their readers to have access to the Testery's own report. We cannot know how clear or how comprehensive a picture of Testery work might be obtained by detailed examination of these sketches of parts of it embedded in the report from the Newmanry. On the whole, it seems more prudent to await the declassification of the Testery's own report before analysing such passages. However, the fact that these accounts of Testery work are included in the Newmanry's report is an indication of the interactions between Newmanry and Testery work. As we have already noted (see 2.2.3 above), in the Testery perspective — or (as the author of the *History of the Fish Section* would probably have said) taking a wider view — the members of Newman's group appear as backroom boys, coming up with results by means of arcane procedures and complicated machines. By writing the *General Report on Tunny* the Newmanry staff avoided becoming another example of the 'invisible technicians' whose activities seem, with hindsight, to have been important but, being unrecorded, cannot easily be taken into account when writing the history of some particular technology. The Newmanry staff, other than the ancillary WRNS and ATS staff, avoided dropping out of the story largely because the senior members were university-educated and took it for granted that intellectual work should be written up.

3.1 The intended readership of the original

Government employees expect to write reports on particular projects. Indeed in the case of the Second World War the Prime Minister gave a report to Parliament and a much shortened and simplified version of it was printed under the title *What Britain has done, 1939–1945: A Selection of Outstanding Facts and Figures* and issued by the Ministry of Information.[76] The organisation of GCCS during the war was complicated by the diversity of origins of its personnel[77] but by 1945 Bletchley Park was, effectively, run by the Secret Intelligence Service, headed by Stewart Menzies (1890–1968) and was funded by the Foreign Office. In practice that meant that the Director at Bletchley Park had a considerable degree of autonomy. Formally, however, the staff of Newman's section were employed by the Foreign Office and were (doubtless) required to report on the success of the project on which they had been engaged and the use they had made of the resources assigned to it. Substantial references to the success of the project are not as prominent in the *General Report on Tunny* as one might perhaps have expected, but subsection **28B(j)** (*GRT*, **28B(j)**, TNA HW 25/4, pp. 260–261; this edition, pp. 243–243), headed 'Operational success', provides figures to show that an impressive proportion of traffic was broken in the last full month of the war, April 1945. We must note, however, that this refers only to the work of the Newmanry, which provided material for the Testery to work on. It was the Testery that completed the decryption and supplied plain text to Hut 3. Thus the success of the Newmanry in carrying out its part of the task is a necessary but not a sufficient condition for Tunny traffic to be read. Moreover, as appears very clearly from the *History of the Fish Section* (August 1945, TNA HW 50/63), adequate intercepts of the traffic were not always available. Thus the overall proportion of Tunny traffic that was read is somewhat less than the Newmanry account may at first sight seem to suggest (see section 2.2.3 above and our endnote 1 to *GRT*, **61**, p. 611 below).

The authors of the first chapter of the *General Report on Tunny*, '**01** Preface (should be read)', show an awareness of general Foreign Office readers — presumably including staff in other sections of GCCS — to the extent of including in their very brief summary of the contents of their report the sentence 'It is hoped that the Conclusions may be of value in other sections of the Foreign Office' (*GRT*, **01**, TNA HW 25/4, p. 1; this edition, p. 3). These Conclusions, chapter **81** (*GRT*, **81**, TNA HW 25/5, pp. 464–468; this edition, pp. 452–455), are divided into many subsections, each succinct. This part of the report, at least, seems to be designed for a busy administrator. It summarises results in a non-technical manner and effectively lists which, largely administrative, practices proved to be useful and which did not. It clearly does not expect the reader to have a background in science. For instance, subsection **81B(c)** 'Successive approximation' (*GRT*, **81B(c)**, TNA HW 25/5, p. 466; this edition, p. 454) consists of two sentences, the first stating that 'Several of our processes are examples of the method of successive approximation' and the second adding 'This is a well known part of ordinary scientific method.' Moreover, the reader of chapter **81** is not assumed to be an academic, since subsection **81A(i)** gives a banal defence of the usefulness of research, ending with the most familiar reflection of all: 'Incidentally the best ideas are often had outside working hours' (*GRT*, **81A(i)**, TNA HW 25/5, p. 466; this edition, p. 454). This seems to be addressed to a boss with little technical grasp of the work he is supervising. There is nothing wrong with the sentiments but a reader with experience of research would surely have expected something less naïve.

The chapter of Conclusions also gives technical comments on the performance of the machines used in decryption and on the German cipher machines that they were attacking. We shall return to some of these comments later. Their tone is often prescriptive, which suggests that the authors are addressing their successors, working in peacetime but engaged upon similar tasks and, initially at least, using similar equipment. In technical passages, which make up by far the greatest part of the *General Report on Tunny*, the vocabulary — whose style, like that of much other GCCS jargon, is (as already noted) often reminiscent of English Public School slang — would be opaque to outsiders. Indeed it proved to be so to an American visitor, George H. Vergine (1914–2001),

[76] Ministry of Information, *What Britain has done, 1939–1945: A Selection of Outstanding Facts and Figures*, reprinted, with an introduction by Richard Overy (London: Atlantic, 2007).

[77] See Grey, *Decoding Organization* (see footnote 2, above).

who joined Newman's team in March 1944.[78] The *General Report on Tunny* provides a glossary as chapter **71** (*GRT*, **71**, TNA HW 25/5, pp. 400–446; this edition, pp. 387–434). One element in the vocabulary, the term 'bulge', is discussed more fully by Diffie in 'Cryptanalytic Significance of the Analysis of Tunny', pp. xvii–xxiv above, esp. p. xix.

As that essay shows, there is good circumstantial evidence that the term 'bulge' originated at GCCS. The tenuous evidence in the *General Report on Tunny* suggests that the term did not originate in Newman's group. There is no entry for 'bulge' in the Glossary, but there is one for 'bulgy': 'Showing bulges not easily ascribed to random variation' (*GRT*, **71**, TNA HW 25/5, p. 403; this edition, p. 390). That is, the term 'bulge' appears as part of an explanation rather than as something that itself stands in need of an explanation, an *explicans* rather than an *explicandum*. The *Report* repeatedly uses terms that are defined only somewhat later — a natural consequence of the work being written in separate pieces, and perhaps a partial explanation for the provision of a glossary. So it would be unwise to put too much weight on the fact that when the term 'bulge' first appears, in **12C**, it is simply used, not defined, though a definition of a sort appears at one of its many later appearances, in **23C(a)** (*GRT*, **12C**, TNA HW 25/4, p. 21; this edition, p. 28; and *GRT*, **23C(a)**, TNA HW 25/4, p. 80; this edition, p. 82). However, this is in contrast to the treatment of 'proportional bulge', which first appears in **21(j)**, where it is introduced as new (*GRT*, **21(j)**, TNA HW 25/4, p. 41; this edition, p. 46). The contrast suggests that, unlike 'proportional bulge', the term 'bulge', unqualified, may not have originated in Newman's group. Perhaps the term was coined in the Research Section, or in the Testery, or (since Good was transferred from Enigma to Fish) perhaps 'bulge' originated in one of the groups working on Enigma.

3.2 Overall organisation of the text of the *General Report on Tunny*

The *General Report on Tunny* is supplied with an overall 'Table of Contents' that lists the names and numbers of sections of the work and within each section lists the numbers of chapters. Most chapters start with an individual analytical list of contents (not always perfectly reproducing the headings within the chapter itself). The initial list of parts and chapters shows that the scheme of organisation adopted is to divide the *Report* into ten parts, numbered **0** to **9**, and then number chapters within the parts, so that, for example, Part **1** contains five chapters, numbered **11** to **15**, but Parts **6** and **8** each consist of a single chapter, numbered **61** and **81** respectively. Only Part **3** runs to a full complement of nine chapters, and then chapter **39** is followed by chapter **41**. This scheme rather sets the tone: it is rational but can lead to confusion.

Part **0** has no title and consists only of a Preface. Part **1**, Introduction, has five chapters, which set out the problem that the cryptanalysts were confronting, but do so as one would in introducing the material for new recruits to the team. Everything is taken as known fact, from the Baudot code used for 5-hole teleprinter tapes to the structure of the German Tunny Machine (whose correct German name is given). The Baudot code was, of course, well known when work began in 1941, but the structure and mechanical details of the Tunny machine most certainly were not. The final chapter of Part **1**, '**15** Some Historical Notes', deals with the origins and early work of Newman's group, started in 1942, and not with what happened before then.

Giving an account of the German machine as a preliminary is to distort the story of what really happened. The cryptanalysts started out knowing only that the cipher system applied to teleprinter output. A much fuller story, dealing with what actually happened, is given in Part **4**, 'Early methods and History'. It seems as though the original plan of the *Report* was based on that for an induction manual, and was specifically for a 'History of the Newmanry', but that at some later stage it was decided that the story of the crucial initial breaks — which set everything in train, and make a cryptanalytic rattling good yarn — ought to be included in the story, thereby

[78] See endnote 5 to *General Report on Tunny*, **01**, p. 561 below.

making the *Report* into a 'General Report on Tunny'. Given their non-chronological placing, these historical chapters, numbered **41** to **44**, have an air of being interlopers. The work they describe uses linguistic rather than statistical methods, their English style seems to be different (which implies a different authorship) and they refer to work that was done before Newman's group was set up. They might be seen as belonging more properly in a history of the work of the Research Section or of Major Tester's group. The matter will perhaps be resolved when the *Testery Report* is declassified. Meanwhile, we may note that events in this period are covered, with a characteristic lack of cryptographic detail, in the part of the *History of the Fish Section* headed 'June to October 1941', whose last paragraph reads:

> During this period interception was at Denmark Hill and St. Albans, the signals being relayed to the Main Building, B.P. where the best possible intercept was prepared for the cryptographers. Decodes were being produced, when a month had been broken, a very few hours after interception — a position never again reached in the history of Fish.[79]

Apart from this apparent irregularity in the relationship of Parts **1** and **4**, the structure of the *General Report on Tunny* is straightforward, though within each part matters are generally presented in logical — or perhaps didactic — order, rather than chronologically. Moreover, the work described is not entirely that of Newman's group. For instance, in Part **2**, 'Methods of Solution', chi setting (described in chapter **23**) was carried out in the Newmanry, whereas wheel-breaking from key (chapter **26**) was carried out in the Testery before the Newmanry was set up. Part **3**, 'Organisation', deals with the way work was divided — partly a matter of specific techniques and partly one of different practical tasks being carried out by specialist groups. Part **5** concerns the machines, starting with a general introduction and ending with a valuable collection of photographs (alas mainly lacking formal indications of scale). Part **6** contains archival material. Part **7**, 'Reference', contains four chapters; chapter **71** is a glossary (which the present editors found now needed to be supplemented), chapter **72** is a list of notation, chapter **73** is a bibliography (apparently designed for a new recruit with access to the library of a state secret intelligence organisation), and chapter **74** is a chronological table that a historian will find extremely useful. Part **8** has a single chapter, which, as noted in our section 3.1 above, departs from the generally mathematical style of the report and concentrates upon operational and practical conclusions. Part **9** consists of five technical appendices.

In 2005 Jack Good recollected that 'Chapter **14** ['Organisation'] was written by Donald Michie, possibly with help from others, after I moved to Manchester'.[80] This is of interest as an indication that, as one might have suspected, the chapters of the *General Report on Tunny* were not written in the order in which they are presented. The involvement of multiple authors is confirmed by the recollections of Donald Michie in 2004.[81]

One consequence of this complicated authorship is that, when a new technical term appears, the Glossary sometimes refers the reader to a definition later in the text. As the original Preface breezily says, after the first Part, the others may be read in any order (*GRT*, **01**, TNA HW 25/4, p. 1; this edition, p. 3).

3.3 Preliminaries and organisational structures at Bletchley Park

The *General Report on Tunny* begins where a new recruit began, with the code, that is the series of patterns of holes, used on the paper tape for teleprinters. Teleprinters had been in

[79] *History of the Fish Section*, 'June to October 1941', TNA HW 50/79, p. 1, transcription JVF.
[80] I. J. Good, email to J. A. Reeds,9 February 2005.
[81] Donald Michie, 14 July 2004, private conversation with JVF.

common use since the 1920s, so the cryptanalysts knew they read and printed 5-hole punched tape which employed the Baudot code to indicate letters and symbols. The *General Report on Tunny* starts with the Baudot code, shown as a table (*GRT*, **11A**, 'Fish machines' **(a)**, TNA HW 25/4, p. 3; this edition, p. 7). This is presumably for the sake of completeness since the code could have been found in standard reference works such as the *Encyclopedia Britannica*. In using a teleprinter, the operator could either type directly into the machine using the typewriter keyboard or could feed in a pre-prepared punched tape. Output was as letters and symbols typed on paper or as a punched tape or (more usually, for the Germans using Tunny) letters and symbols typed on strips of gummed paper tape.

Having described the Baudot code, chapter **11** of the *Report* goes on to describe the cipher machine attached to the teleprinter. This description is clear when discussing the principles but less so in regard to physical details, which seem to have been derived from a manual and perhaps some photographs, rather than from an actual machine. In 1945 few British cryptanalysts had seen a Lorenz SZ (Tunny) machine.

As we noted in section 3.2 above, the account given in Part **1** of the *General Report on Tunny* represents the situation as it would have been for a new recruit in 1945. When cryptanalysis of Tunny traffic started, in mid 1941, the state of affairs was very different. We shall now turn to the story of the first break and what followed from it, as told in Part **4**, chapters **41** to **44**.

In June 1941, the cryptanalysts knew they were dealing with teleprinter ciphers, operating on Baudot code, but in other respects they started from zero: the encryption machine was unknown. In fact, it seems to have been relatively unfamiliar to the German operators also: the crucially important break was made because of an error by a teleprinter operator. By the time this occurred, the cryptanalysts already knew something of the Tunny cipher from occasional double transmissions (depths) sent by operators who were not following instructions sufficiently carefully, but such errors had ceased and progress was slow. Then, as the *Report* puts it: 'On 30th August, 1941, the German cipher operators came to the rescue' (*GRT*, **41C(b)**, 'The depth "HQIBPEXEZMUG" ', TNA HW 25/5, p. 298; this edition, p. 285). On that day, a clerk sent the same message twice, without altering the wheel settings (which meant that the key was exactly the same) but making many small changes in what was typed, for instance in the use of abbreviations, which produced small offsets in the relation between plain text and key. Once noticed and identified, both these errors could be exploited. The chief military cryptanalyst at Bletchley Park, John Tiltman, exploited them with spectacular success: he read the message (that is he found the original German plain text) and he isolated a stretch of nearly four thousand letters of pure key. Interpreting this piece of key was not easy, but in early 1942 the young Cambridge chemistry graduate (later mathematician) William Tutte succeeded in deducing the structure of the machine that produced the key.

The technical details of the machine are significant because they explain the choice of methods of attack used by the cryptanalysts. The five 'channels' (bit levels) of the Baudot code on the tape were encrypted separately. Each channel consisted of a stream of what the *Report* calls 'characters' (but are now called 'bits'), each of which was either a 0 or a 1, that is a blank or a hole in the tape, which the cryptanalysts signified by a dot (for 0) or a cross (for 1). It seems that the use of the term 'character' in the sense we find in the *Report* was restricted to GCCS, and there was no standard term in the engineering literature. Unfortunately, 'character' is the name that is now given to the row of five bits that make up the code for a symbol on the tape (a usage that was indeed current elsewhere in the 1940s, but not at Bletchley Park). In these introductory remarks we shall follow the usual historical practice of adopting the period vocabulary, confining our protest to employing it in quotation marks where that is necessary to avoid confusion. (See also section 5.1 below.) To this stream of 'characters' the Tunny machine added the key stream, a stream of 0s and 1s of its own devising. This key stream was generated by twelve wheels carrying elements that could be adjusted (by hand) to give either 0 or 1. The wheels were of three kinds, which the cryptanalysts called by the Greek letters chi, psi and mu. The five chi wheels turned on one place for every new 'character' (bit), the five psi wheels might or might not turn, depending on a complicated set of conditions involving the mu wheels, the previous chi and psi 'characters' (bits), the twice-previous plain text 'characters' and other conditions that could be set by the operator.

The numbers of adjustable elements on the wheels were as follows

chi wheels:	41, 31, 29, 26, 23
psi wheels:	43, 47, 51, 53, 59
mu wheels:	61, 37.

The numbers are all prime, except for the 26 on one of the chi wheels, and 51 on a psi, but as there is no 13 or 17 (and of course no 2 or 3), the numbers are all mutually prime, which is all that is required to maximise the length of the cycle (that is the number of 'characters' before the key pattern begins to repeat itself — ignoring irregularities in the motion of the psi wheels, which are intended to disrupt the cycle). As the numbers of adjustable elements have no common factors, the length of the period of the key stream, which is the lowest common multiple of these numbers, is simply their product, that is $41 \times 31 \times 29 \times 26 \times 23 \times 43 \times 47 \times 51 \times 53 \times 59 \times 61 \times 37$, which is about 1.6×10^{19}. The great length of the period presumably helped the designers and users to convince themselves (wrongly as it turned out) that the machine was adequately secure.[82]

The addition of the key stream does not permit carrying (that is one channel cannot affect another) so we have addition modulo 2, in which

$$0+0=0$$
$$0+1=1$$
$$1+0=1$$
$$1+1=0.$$[83]

This makes subtraction the same as addition (and this form of key is accordingly sometimes called a 'subtractor' key). So adding the key again is the same as subtracting it and the cipher attachment on the teleprinter can thus treat incoming and outgoing messages in exactly the same way. But there was one other form of adjustment to take into account: the initial starting positions of the wheels could be varied.

Thus to read a message the cryptanalysts needed to determine the pattern of 0s and 1s round each wheel (to 'break' the wheels) and to find their starting positions (to 'set' the wheels). This is in some respects similar to what was required for reading Enigma messages, but the form of encryption in the Tunny and Enigma ciphers is radically different. Whereas Enigma deals with characters (in today's sense), for instance turning an A into a Q, Tunny operates not on what we call characters but on bits. The ciphers used during the period of the Cold War were mainly of this bit-oriented type, which may go some way to explaining why the detailed report by Good, Michie and Timms remained classified for so long.

The use of part of the plain text to construct key, called 'autoclave' in the discussion of the psi wheels in the *General Report on Tunny* — it is now known as 'autokey' — was not new at the time.[84] Tutte's brief recollections on autoclave, written in 2000, seem to imply that the rather simple form used in the Tunny machines gave the cryptanalysts little trouble.[85] On closer

[82]The security of the Tunny machine is discussed in more detail in S. L. Zabell, 'Statistics at Bletchley Park', pp. lxxv–ci below, esp. pp. lxxxiv–lxxxvi.

[83]Because of its formal equivalence to the truth table for the exclusive 'or' this form of addition is now sometimes called 'xoring'.

[84]See endnote 18 to *GRT*, **11B(g)**, p. 566 below.

[85]William T. Tutte, 'My Work at Bletchley Park', Appendix 4 in Copeland, *Colossus* (see footnote 15, above), pp. 352–369, esp. p. 367.

inspection, Tutte's comment suggests he was out of touch with the day-to-day activities of the Testery and Newmanry teams, or that, by 2000, his recollections were inaccurate, see 'A note on autoclave' (3.3.1 below). On the other hand, since Tutte was a member of the Research Section, his recollection may perhaps be seen as confirming something that is implied by 1945 documents, namely that autoclave did not present a problem on which the Research Section was asked for assistance.

The Tunny machine is described in detail in sections **11A(c)** and **11B(j)–11C(c)** of the *Report* (*GRT*, **11A(c)** and **11B(j)–11C(c)**, TNA HW 25/4 pp. 4–5 and pp. 10–11, this edition pp. 8–9 and pp. 14–17). There follows a description of the cipher (chapter **12**) and of some of the early machines used in the cryptanalysis (chapter **13**). These are followed by a sketch of the organisation of various tasks (chapter **14**), which mentions that interception of Fish signals was carried out at a site at Knockholt (Kent) and decrypted messages were passed to Hut 3. It is only much later in the *Report* that we learn about the precautions taken to ensure that the intercepts were sufficiently accurate for it to be reasonable to attempt to break the messages.

3.3.1 A note on autoclave

An investigation into the effects of autoclave on the activities of the Testery and the Newmanry turns out to shed some light on the relations between the work of the two groups. The *History of the Fish Section* tends to present the Newmanry as a team of technicians who use machines (see 2.2.3 above), but the story of autoclave shows the work of the Newmanry becoming a crucial contribution in the work of cryptanalysis. It should, however, be borne in mind that what we are describing here are only methods of cryptanalysis that were tried; in any particular case, there was no guarantee they would succeed. Success rates are discussed in our endnote 1 to *GRT*, **61**, p. 611 below.

Tutte's suggestion that autoclave was not of much importance to the cryptanalysts was made in 2000.[86] In 1945, the writer of the *History of the Fish Section* took a very different view. Under the heading 'March 1943' we find

> On the 25th a more fundamental change in the cipher was made. This was the autoclave, whereby the fifth impulse of clear text was used to modify the action of the motor. Hence depths were no longer readable and work was almost at a standstill.[87]

Characteristically, we are given no technical details about how the form of autoclave was identified. But the fact that it is specified indicates that the cryptanalysts must eventually have worked out what was happening. The *General Report on Tunny* gives a fairly rapid account of what was done and describes the process as 'one of the triumphs of the hand methods of statistical analysis' (*GRT*, **44C**, 'Introduction of P_5 limitation', TNA HW 25/5, p. 323; this edition, p. 308). It is to be hoped that when the *Testery Report* is declassified it will tell us more.

It is clear from the repeated references to the presence or absence of autoclave throughout the *History of the Fish Section* that although the cryptanalysts learned how to deal with autoclave, they preferred not to have to do so. For example under the heading 'October 1944' we read

> The dropping of the autoclave continued and in two cases messages in depth were intercepted, wheels broken and messages decoded and issued, all within 24 hours. Bream continued to use autoclave for about 50% of its transmissions.[88]

And in the entry for the following month, November 1944, we are told that 'Apart from Bream, Codfish, and Gurnard, all links broken had dropped the use of the autoclave.'[89]

[86] See above and footnote 85.
[87] *History of the Fish Section*, 'March 1943', TNA HW 50/63, p. 2, transcription JVF.
[88] *History of the Fish Section*, 'October 1944', TNA HW 50/63, p. 11, transcription JVF.
[89] *History of the Fish Section*, 'November 1944', TNA HW 50/63, p. 11, transcription JVF.

To understand the impact of the use of autoclave we need to look briefly at the methods employed by the cryptanalysts. The *History of the Fish Section* tells us, in the entry for June–July 1943, that this was the period when 'the Newmanry began operations',[90] so in March 1943 we are concerned only with the methods used by the Testery. To break the wheels (that is to find the pattern of 0s and 1s on each wheel) the cryptanalysts used either depths, that is stretches of cipher text in which the key was repeated, or cribs, that is stretches of cipher text for which the plain text was known (or assumed to be known). Once the Newmanry was in operation, the Testery might be working not only on pure cipher text supplied by the interception station but also on cipher text from which the Newmary had removed the effects of the chi wheels ('de-chi'). When the Testery was operating on raw cipher text, both methods employed were in effect repeating the procedure followed by Tiltman and Tutte in their first break of a Tunny message in 1941, with the difference that as the overall architecture of the Tunny machine, and the number of adjustable elements on each wheel, were now known, there was less uncertainty about what to look for.[91]

In 1941, Tutte was working from pure key that Tiltman had isolated by exploiting a very long depth. As autoclave uses part of the plain text to construct the key, the key does not repeat (except in circumstances too unlikely to be worth thinking about). So when autoclave is in use there are no depths to exploit. Accordingly, the cryptanalysts had to use cribs, that is to use what one may call a 'long crib' consisting of the plain text of a complete message. For such a crib to be available, the message whose encrypted text was being attacked had to have been transmitted more than once, possibly to separate recipients (that is on different links), a practice mentioned in the chapter about cribs in the *General Report on Tunny* (*GRT*, **27C**, 'German TP operating practices', section **(b)** 'Use of the same plain text tape on different inks', TNA HW 25/4, p. 237; this edition, p. 221). The plain text of an earlier message is the 'long crib' that can be exploited to obtain a stretch of pure key from the encrypted message that is currently being attacked — the aim being not to read that particular message (whose plain text is assumed to be the same as that of the crib) but to find the wheel patterns and settings for the SZ machine at the time the message was sent so that other traffic sent in that month can be read (that is, if we are considering March 1943; after July 1944 keys were changed daily). To understand how this is done we need to go back to how the cipher works.

In the standard notation, in which Z indicates cipher text, P plain text and K is key, we have

$$Z = P + K,$$

where addition is modulo 2 with no carry between channels.

If we add P to each side we obtain

$$Z + P = (P + P) + K.$$

In addition modulo 2 with no carry between channels, adding anything to itself gives zero, so this becomes

$$K = Z + P. \qquad (1)$$

Thus we can find a stretch of pure key by adding the intercepted message, Z, to what (from the crib) we believe to be its plain text, P.

Once pure key is available, the cryptanalyst can repeat the process carried out by Tutte in 1941.

Expressed in algebraic terms, the procedure in equation (1) looks simple. But in practical terms it means adding together two streams of upwards of two thousand letters (in today's terms characters), each with five bits. Moreover, the task needs to be done with perfect accuracy.

[90] *History of the Fish Section*, 'June–July 1943', TNA HW 50/63, p. 2, transcription JVF.

[91] For a description of the method see *GRT*, **26**, TNA HW 25/4, pp. 195–233; this edition, pp. 185–218.

A cipher machine that carried out this kind of addition had been the subject of a US patent in 1919.[92] The machine, called a 'Telekrypton', was not a commercial success, but a few were used in SIS offices in New York (from late 1941) and Ottawa (from 1942). The person who set up the communications in Washington, the Canadian Benjamin de Forest (Pat) Bayly (1903–1994), was in effect a GCCS liaison officer in Washington, so someone at Bletchley Park must have known about the Telekrypton machine.[93] However, there is no evidence that any move was made to obtain such a machine for use in GCCS, or to ask anyone to design and build something similar. It seems that, when faced with adding long tapes together, in March 1943, Fish Section staff had recourse to the kind of 'hand method' that involved writing out very long sequences of dots and crosses on squared paper. Moreover, as perfect accuracy was required, it must have been necessary to check the results.

Later in 1943 a machine called Miles was used to carry out additions of tapes (*GRT*, **56F**, 'Miles', TNA HW 25/5, p. 370; this edition, p. 352; for the date of introduction of Miles see *GRT*, **15C(g)**, TNA HW 25/4, p. 36; this edition, p. 42). The *General Report on Tunny* does not say what task Miles was originally designed to carry out. It could, for instance, have been to make tapes for the Robinson (see section 3.6 below). In any case, all machines were deliberately designed to be adaptable and Miles was later developed to carry out several other tasks.

Once the stretch of key was obtained, wheel patterns could be found by repeating the procedures that Tutte had employed in 1941 when working on the pure key isolated by Tiltman.

The Newmanry developed and used a statistical procedure called 'rectangling' to attack raw cipher text. Rectangling had been invented by the Research Section in February 1943 (*GRT*, **74**, 'Chronology', TNA HW 25/5, p. 459; this edition, p. 447) and was then taken over by the Newmanry:

> Further investigation into Rectangling and other statistical chi-breaking methods was carried out by the Newmanry, but it was only after the general introduction of autoclave in Dec. 1943 that these methods were used operationally. (*GRT*, **44B(f)**, 'Statistical Chi-breaking', TNA HW 25/5, p. 323; this edition, p. 307.)[94]

As this passage of the *General Report on Tunny* makes clear, rectangling attacked only the chi wheels. It enabled the patterns of 0s and 1s on the chi wheels to be broken, and the wheels could then be set. After which, the Newmanry could provide the Testery with cipher text from which the effect of the chi wheels had been removed, ('de-chi'). Usually, what happened next was that the Testery then broke the psi and mu wheels (obtaining the patterns of 0s and 1s that would be used on that link for the month or, after July 1944, for the day) and then set the wheels so as to be able to read a particular message. The methods available for breaking the psi and mu wheels were based on those that were used against pure key but were more elaborate, involving repeated use of short cribs and making guesses that could then be checked for consistency with other guesses or things already known. We know from the *General Report on Tunny* that, given de-chi, the Testery could usually break the psi wheels (*GRT*, **28C(a)**, TNA HW 25/4, p. 261; this edition, p. 244). The process was not affected by the presence of autoclave. Somewhat confusingly, in view of the Newmanry use of the term 'rectangling' to describe the statistical procedure for breaking chi wheels, the *History of the Fish Section* uses 'rectangling' to describe the whole process of breaking a message for cases in which rectangling (by the Newmanry) is only the first stage.

So, from the point of view of the writer of the *History of the Fish Section*, there are three methods of breaking wheels (and thus eventually reading a message), abbreviated to 'depths',

[92] Gilbert Sandford Vernam (1890–1960), 'Secret Signaling System', US patent 1,310,719, issued 22 July 1919.

[93] John Ferris, 'The British Enigma: Britain, Signals Security and Cipher Machines, 1906–1953', Chapter 4 in *Intelligence and Strategy: Selected Essays* (London, 2005), pp. 138–180, esp. pp. 171–172.

[94] For technical details of rectangling, see *GRT*, **24**, TNA HW 25/4, pp. 113–151; this edition, pp. 110–138; see also S. L. Zabell, 'Statistics at Bletchley Park', below pp. lxxv–ci, esp. pp. xcii–xciv.

'cribs' and 'rectangling'. The three attacks are compared in the entry for February 1945 ('This again was a record month'), which provides a table showing the times taken from interception to decipherment by different methods, giving average times and best times.[95] 'By rectangles' has an average time of 3.8 days and a best time of 'less than 2 days'. For 'By depth' the figures are: average 2.0 days, best 'less than 1 day'. And for 'By crib' they are: average 7.1 days, best 'less than 5 days'. The overall average is given as 3.4 days. Similar comparisons for the following month (March 1945) show a similar pattern. These indications are enough for our present purposes and they have the advantage of showing what must have been noticeable at the time. Material for a solid overall assessment is given in a huge fold-out table in Annex III to the *History*. This provides data for every month throughout the war (see endnote 1 to **61**, p. 611 below).

It is clear from these various comparisons that if the cryptanalysts had been in a position to choose, their order of preference for the various methods would have been depths, 'rectangling' and cribs. Autoclave disrupted cycles in the motion of the psi wheels, so it eliminated depths, thus taking out the most expeditious method of breaking the wheels. Further, 'rectangling' (in the sense in which the term is used in the *History of the Fish Section*) involved the Newmanry using a statistical method to remove the effect of the chi wheels (a process unaffected by autoclave), and the next step would not be affected either: the usual Testery method of attacking de-chi to break and set psi and mu wheels did not depend upon depths (see *GRT*, **28C**, TNA HW 25/4, pp. 261–264; this edition, pp. 244–246 and *GRT*, **28B**, TNA HW 25/4, pp. 257–261; this edition, pp. 239–244). So autoclave would neither prevent nor slow down what the *History* calls 'rectangling'. The use of cribs is also unaffected by autoclave, but it is the slowest of the three methods of attack. The *General Report on Tunny* summarises what happened by saying that the introduction of autoclave led to the development of the use of cribs, because autoclave 'prevented the occurrence of depths, which had been the basis of all earlier wheel-breaking' (*GRT*, **27A**, TNA HW 25/4, p. 235; this edition, p. 219). The section about cribs is one of the passages in the *General Report on Tunny* that brings together the work of the Testery and that of the Newmanry and thus reminds us that, despite being for so long known as the 'History of the Newmanry', the scope of the *Report* is in fact more general. There was some sharing of personnel in regard to cribs, namely an arrangement for a 'Mr Y', that is one of the Testery staff transferred temporarily into the Newmanry to work on cribs (see *GRT*, **27H**, 'History of crib organisation', TNA HW 25/4, p. 249; this edition, p. 231).

There is also a disadvantage inherent in the nature of a crib. As the *General Report on Tunny* remarks:

> Crib setting can begin only after one transmission is decoded, a disadvantage when the value of traffic depends on its currency. (*GRT*, **27A**, TNA HW 25/4, p. 234; this edition, p. 219.)

In its account of Febrary 1945, the *History of the Fish Section* also supplies some numerical information about the distribution of tasks between the Testery and the Newmanry: of the 911 de-chi'd messages that were broken, 798 were broken by the Testery (that is the Testery broke the psi and mu wheels from de-chi provided by the Newmanry and then set the wheels before producing the plain text) and 113 were set entirely by the Newmanry (and the plain text would then have been produced by the Testery).[96]

The distribution of tasks between the Testery and the Newmanry was no doubt clear to participants at any given moment, but it obviously varied over time. Breaking psi wheels seems generally to have been the business of the Testery, but in March 1945 responsibility for setting psi wheels was transferred to the Newmanry (*GRT*, **74**, 'Chronology', TNA HW 25/5, p. 463; this

[95] *History of the Fish Section*, 'February 1945', TNA HW 50/63, p. 13.

[96] *History of the Fish Section*, 'February 1945', TNA HW 50/63, p. 13.

edition, p. 451). The Newmanry did not succeed in devising a statistical method for breaking psi wheels until mid May 1945:

> It should be mentioned finally that, about a week after VE-day, a method was successfully used for breaking Motor and ψ patterns by statistical methods. (Final sentence of *GRT*, **28C**, 'ψ'-breaking from de-χ', TNA HW 25/4, p. 264; this edition, p. 246.)

Despite the late date of its success, it seems unlikely that research on a statistical method for use against the psi wheels was simply an exercise in mathematical ingenuity. The motive may have been to find an alternative to cribs in dealing with traffic that used autoclave. Unfortunately, we do not know what this new statistical method was. From the delay in devising it, however, we may guess that rectangling, which the Newmanry had long been using to break the patterns on chi wheels, could not easily be adapted or extended for use against the psi wheels.

The effect of the German use of autoclave was to compel the cryptanalysts to rely on cribs and 'rectangling' in the sense in which the term is used in the *History of the Fish Section*, namely to mean the use of rectangling by the Newmanry against the chi wheels, followed by the Testery using hand methods against the psi and mu wheels. This latter procedure was unaffected by autoclave. If a suitable long crib was found to be available, it could be exploited, but this was much slower than it would have been to use depths between messages (had such depths been available). Thus, in the best case for the cryptanalysts, that is when a suitable crib was available, the enemy use of autoclave slowed down the process of breaking the traffic; in the worst case, when no suitable crib was available, traffic either had to be broken by 'rectangling' or it remained unbroken. So in these circumstances the Newmanry procedure of rectangling, which used machines, became an essential element in the cryptanalysis.

From the point of view of the Axis cipher-makers, the autoclave was a good idea. It reduced the options open to cryptanalysts. However, in high frequency radio transmissions it is common for there to be errors caused by interference, and if autoclave is in use such errors, even in a single bit, can make some of the message unreadable by its intended recipient. The receiving Tunny machine works through the message letter by letter, and when the letter it meets is not that intended by the sender, the decrypted letter will not be the one in the original plain text. If autoclave is in use, the motion of the psi wheels of the decrypting machine is controlled by earlier letters in the plain text (the autoclave employed in Tunny messages used the impulse in the fifth channel in the last but two plain text letter). So a fault in the text already derived, which the machine takes as plain text, can cause the psi wheels to move incorrectly, causing the remainder of the message to become unreadable. This disadvantage must have been apparent at the time.[97] However, the Germans continued to use autoclave.[98]

More elaborate autokey systems are still in use in the early twenty-first century.

3.4 Mathematics

The first part of the *General Report on Tunny* covers preliminaries and makes only occasional use of mathematics. The second part of the *Report*, 'Methods of Solution', is by far the longest (TNA HW 25/4, pp. 37–275; this edition, pp. 43–258). Almost all its content is mathematical and apparently addressed by experts to their peers. This is somewhat at variance with the assurance in the Preface (*GRT*, **01**, TNA HW 25/4, p. 1; this edition, p. 3) that 'The later section (**W**, **X**, **Y**, **Z**) of each chapter covers advanced theoretical aspects and involves a knowledge of mathematics of

[97] Tutte, 'My Work at Bletchley Park' (see footnote 85, above), p. 367.

[98] We are grateful to Dr J. A. Reeds for technical advice about the effects of the use of autoclave. Opinions expressed are, of course, our own.

at least sixth form standard.' For all sections of the chapters of Part **2**, readers are more likely to require the degree of confidence that comes with having studied mathematics at university level.

In their Conclusions (chapter **81**) the cryptanalysts offer advice which identifies what they perceived to be the weakness of the machine they were attacking. Subsection **81B(e)** is headed 'Cipher makers and cipher breakers' and its first paragraph reads

> With our experience of Tunny it would be easy to make suggestions for making Tunny unbreakable. Independent motorising of the ψ's would achieve this, except that depths could be read if an autoclave were not introduced also (see **R4**, 116). (*GRT*, **81B(e)**, TNA HW 25/5, p. 467; this edition, p. 455.)

The intention of the designers of the Tunny machine had been to make the key that it generated effectively random. But having the psi wheels all move or stay still together introduced a regularity, not in the individual channels (each produced by one of the five pairs of chi and psi wheels) but in the relationship between these channels. The cryptanalysts were able to use statistical methods to detect these regularities, which they then exploited to strip off the key and read the messages.[99]

3.4.1 Some definitions

The *General Report on Tunny* takes much for granted. However, in his essay *The Applications of Probability to Cryptography* (TNA HW 25/37, datable to 1941 or 1942, see section 1.4 above) Turing is more helpful. He first defines the basic notions, probability and odds:

> I shall not attempt to give a systematic account of the theory of probability, but it may be worth while to define shortly 'probability' and 'odds'. The probability of an event on certain evidence is the proportion of the cases in which that event may be expected to happen given the evidence. For instance if it is known that 20% of men live to the age of 70, then knowing of Hitler only 'Hitler is a man' we can say that the probability of Hitler living to the age of 70 is 0.2. Suppose however that we know that 'Hitler is now of age 52' the probability will be quite different, say 0.5, because 50% of men of 52 live to 70.
>
> The 'odds' of an event happening is the ratio $P/(1-P)$ where P is the probability of it happening. This terminology is connected with the common phraseology 'odds of 5:2 on' meaning in our terminology that the odds are 5/2.[100]

Turing then turns to the principle underlying a statistical analysis (under the heading 'Probabilities based on part of the evidence'):

> When the whole evidence about some event is taken into account it may be extremely difficult to estimate the probability of the event, even very approximately, and it may be better to form an estimate based on a part of the evidence, so that the probability may be more easily calculated. This happens in cryptography in a very obvious way. The whole evidence when we are trying to solve a cipher is the complete traffic, and the events in question are the different possible keys, and functions of the keys. Unless the traffic is very small indeed the theoretical answer to the problem 'what are the probabilities of the various keys?' will be of the form 'The key ... has a probability differing almost imperceptibly from 1 (certainty) and the other keys are virtually impossible.' But a direct attempt to determine these probabilities would obviously not be a practical method.[101]

[99] See S. L. Zabell, 'Statistics at Bletchley Park', pp. lxxv–ci below.

[100] A. M. Turing, *The Applications of Probability to Cryptography*, TNA HW 25/37, p. 1, transcription JVF.

[101] A. M. Turing, *The Applications of Probability to Cryptography*, TNA HW 25/37, p. 2, transcription JVF.

A detailed discussion of the statistical work described in the *General Report on Tunny* is given below in S. L. Zabell's essay 'Statistics at Bletchley Park' (pp. lxxv–ci, below).

3.5 Organisation of the teams and their activities

Part **3** of the *General Report on Tunny* is headed 'Organisation'. The first three of its chapters deal with individual groups: Newman's section (chapter **31**), the section run by Major Tester (chapter **32**) and then the interception station at Knockholt (chapter **33**).

Chapter **31**, 'Mr. Newman's section', is understandably upbeat in tone. Its first section, 'Growth', begins

> In December, 1942 Mr. M. H. A. Newman was given the job of developing machine methods of setting Tunny. In April, 1943 the first machines arrived, a Robinson and a Tunny, pilot models of somewhat uncertain behaviour. Mr. Newman formed his section with one cryptographer, two engineers and 16 Wrens. The section was founded and lived (for the most part) in a single room. After three months two or three messages were set each week.
>
> By May, 1945 there were 26 Cryptographers, 28 Engineers and 273 Wrens with 10 Colossi, 3 Robinsons, 3 Tunnies and 20 smaller electrical machines. The section moved into Block F in November, 1943, and expanded into a new and additional block (H) in September, 1944, in which all chi-breaking was done. In the week ending March 31st, 358 messages were set on Chis, 151 on Motors and Psis and 23 sets of new wheels were broken. (*GRT*, **31A**, TNA HW 25/5, p. 276; this edition, p. 262.)

In the following section, **31B**, there is a more detailed account of the numbers of staff, which are given for six-monthly intervals, starting in April 1943 and ending in April 1945, when there were two administrators, the 22 cryptographers already mentioned, 28 engineers (15 for maintenance, 13 for construction) and 273 Wrens, making a total of 325 (*GRT*, **31B**, TNA HW 25/5, p. 276; this edition, p. 262). It seems that mechanization had not brought about a reduction in the relative number of ancillary staff: the Wrens, who operated machines and carried out routine tasks such as calculations (that is acted as 'computers') formed a roughly constant proportion of the staff.

Interestingly, the *Report* also presents a discussion of the backgrounds, not to say the characters, of the Newmanry cryptographers. The text begins

> The first thirteen men to join the Section as cryptographers were drawn from other sections of GC&CS. In experience and infectious enthusiasm they preserved their lead to the end, and there were few in the section not affected by their keenness. After July 1944 they were joined by men from other war jobs and men straight from the universities. (*GRT*, **31D**, TNA HW 25/5, p. 277; this edition, p. 263.)

This is victors' history, written in the moment of victory, but it was objectively true that Newman's group had done what it was set up to do. Of the three authors of the *Report*, the first two, Jack Good and Donald Michie, belonged to the initial thirteen. The third author, Geoffrey Timms, reached Bletchley Park in September 1944, at the age of 41, after a university career in mathematics.[102]

The table introduced by the passage just quoted analyses the two groups of recruits in four ways. The first is by their level of mathematical education or expertise, in which the categories are 'Professional mathematicians etc and research students': 8 in the first group, 4 in the later one. The second category is 'Other university mathematicians': 3 in the first group, 11 in the later one.

[102] See biographical notes on the original authors, pp. ciii–cvi.

The dustbin category 'other' has 2 and 1. Recruits are also considered by age, and here the shift in the 'under 20' category, from 1 (that is Donald Michie) in the first group to 6 in the second suggests recruitment of undergraduate mathematicians or men who had taken a shortened degree course (as was, for instance, the case for L. N. Chown, mentioned in the Glossary). By mid 1944 it was presumably thought that some background in mathematics would be useful and the older hands in the Newmanry felt confident that they knew what they needed to teach new recruits. This latter is confirmed by the analysis according to previous cryptographic experience. In the pre-July 1944 group, 12 have some experience, 8 have experience in Enigma work (these include Jack Good and Shaun Wylie), 3 in Fish. These numbers need some thought to interpret, since the total number of cryptographers in the group is 13, but the numbers seem to imply that only one member of the group had no previous experience. In the later group the figures are 3, 2 and 1 — out of a total of 16, so presumably 13 had no previous experience. (The remaining analytical criterion in the table is nationality. The first group contained 11 British and 2 Americans, the second had 13 and 3.) It seems clear that the staff of the Newmanry had noticed that they were breaking away from the traditional habits of recruiting cryptanalysts among linguists and chess players (see section 1.6 above). After the end of hostilities in Europe, on 8 May 1945, and a few days' holiday, some of the Newmanry staff were transferred to other groups. For instance, L. N. Chown and at least three of his Newmanry colleagues were moved to the Japanese section.[103]

In discussing staff, mention is also made of the system of allowing time for research shifts:

> After the Section was fully staffed there were often two research men each week. Most of the important ideas were developed by men as a result of practical routine work and written up in the Research Logs. In a subsequent research period of a week or more they were at leisure to elaborate their ideas and to tackle any other problems of a pressing operational nature. (*GRT*, **31D**, TNA HW 25/5, p. 278; this edition, p. 263.)

There was, moreover, an established forum for discussion, the 'Tea Party' (at which tea was not served):

> Ideas for new methods, and routines for immediate instruction were discussed at the weekly "Tea Party" — a democratic assembly of cryptographic staff. (*GRT*, **31D**, TNA HW 25/5, p. 278; this edition, p. 263.)

Working conditions might sometimes be harsh (as many personal recollections record) but in other respects the style was like that of a university department. Indeed the 'Tea Party' itself may have been adapted from a somewhat similar series of mathematical discussion meetings held in Cambridge. The geometer Henry Frederick Baker (1866–1956), who, like Newman, was a Fellow of St John's College, held regular Saturday afternoon tea parties, followed by a mathematical discussion meeting at which papers were presented. These meetings were attended by Geoffrey Timms and perhaps also, on occasion, by Newman, who must certainly at least have known about the meetings. The Cambridge antecedents of Baker's meetings include the daily 'tea time' instituted by Lord Rayleigh (John William Strutt, 1842–1919) when he was director of the Cavendish Laboratory (1880–84). These gatherings, considered to be an innovation, were continued under his successor J. J. Thomson (1856–1940).[104]

The *General Report on Tunny* also gives accounts of the work of engineers (who were working 70 hours a week at the Post Office Research Station at Dollis Hill) (*GRT*, **31F**, TNA HW 25/5,

[103]L.N. Chown, telephone conversation with JVF, 1 September 2009.

[104]Dong-Won Kim, *Leadership and Creativity: A History of the Cavendish Laboratory, 1871–1919* (Dortrecht: Kluwer Academic Publishers, 2002). For further details, see our endnote 21 on the Glossary entry for 'Tea Party' (*GRT*, **71**), p. 620 below.

p. 279; this edition, p. 265) and of the education of new recruits (which sheds light on the skills they needed) (*GRT*, **31G**, TNA HW 25/5, p. 279; this edition, p. 265) and a statistics bureau (*GRT*, **31H**, TNA HW 25/5, p. 279; this edition, p. 266). L. N. Chown, one of the group who joined the Newmanry on 4 September 1944, recalled (in 2009) that the recruits were given lectures about statistics and probability, and about letter frequency, by Newman and others. Chown had not been taught statistics while reading mathematics at Oxford.[105]

The following chapter of the *General Report on Tunny*, 'Organisation of the Testery', consists of a single paragraph (*GRT*, **32**, TNA HW 25/5, p. 280; this edition, p. 267), which includes the comment that further details are to be found in the 'Report on Tunny (Major Tester's Section)', which at the time of writing (February 2015) is not available to us (see section 2.1 above). At the end of the paragraph the authors explain why they feel it is appropriate to be so terse: 'We do not go into further details here as they are of no great cryptographic interest and are not necessary for the understanding of the present report.' This remark tends to confirm that (as suggested in section 3.1 above) the *General Report on Tunny* was conceived more as an induction manual for cryptographers than as a history in the normal sense. This attitude may also partly reflect the prohibition on discussing one's work with anyone except immediate colleagues. It was, of course, true that Testery methods were distinct from those of the Newmanry. The *General Report on Tunny* described them in a chapter with the title 'Language methods' (*GRT*, **26**, TNA HW 25/5, pp. 255–275; this edition, pp. 237–258) pp. 237–258) but makes no attempt to justify this description, which perhaps refers to the use of cribs. Nevertheless, the *History of the Fish Section* naturally takes a wider view and makes it clear there was necessarily considerable interaction between the activities of Knockholt, the Newmanry and the Testery (see section 2.2.3 above).

The chapter on Knockholt, chapter **33**, is also terse, covering only a single page (*GRT*, **33**, TNA HW 25/5, p. 281; this edition, p. 268) and concerning itself only with the relationship between the interception station and the cryptanalysts at Bletchley Park. Stress is laid upon the requirement for accuracy in the intercepts. A much fuller account of the activities of this interception station is given in the formal report written by its Chief, Harold Kenworthy, in 1946, *The Interception of German Teleprinter Communications by Foreign Office Station Knockholt* (TNA HW 50/79 and HW 3/163, printed in Appendix B, pp. 513–524 below).

In the earlier part of the war, non-Morse traffic was initially intercepted at Denmark Hill (South London), a communication and interception station set up by the Metropolitan Police, with the support of the SIS, in the early 1930s.[106] Knockholt, which came into operation in mid 1942, was a specially built interception station, situated high on the North Downs, about 2 km northwest of Sevenoaks, Kent, in what was Ivy Farm.[107] The name of the farm no longer appears on Ordnance Survey maps but the site can be identified from the name of the adjoining building, which is still called The Grange. The site of Ivy Farm lies between Chevening Lane and Main Road, and is reached from the latter by Ivy Lane; the entrance beside The Grange in Chevening Lane is no longer in use. Houses have been built on some of the land, but (in 2014) the remainder is used by the local sports club, which has a bowling green, tennis courts and a large cricket field. During the war, the area covered by aerials eventually extended to about 160 acres (about 65 hectares) (see *Knockholt Report*, TNA HW 50/79 and HW 3/163, ch.1, para. 17; printed in Appendix B of this edition, p. 515 below). Sites nearby, notably in Halstead, appear to still be in use as interception stations.

The remaining five chapters of Part **3** are also short. Chapter **34**, 'Registration and circulation' (*GRT*, **34**, TNA HW 25/5, pp. 282–283; this edition, pp. 269–270), describes the procedures used to keep track of tapes of intercepted messages as they passed from place to place and from hand

[105] L.N. Chown, telephone conversation with JVF, 1 September 2009.

[106] Kenworthy, *A Brief History* … (full ref in note 12 above), p. 7, para 6.1, on SIS involvement, see pp. 5–6, Ch. V.

[107] See TNA HW 55/1, which includes a sketch map of the immediate vicinity; see also our endnote 5 to *GRT*, **28**, p. 595 and the reports printed in our Appendix B.

to hand along the stages of cryptanalysis. Chapter **35**, 'Tapemaking and checking' (*GRT*, **35**, TNA HW 25/5, pp. 284–287; this edition, pp. 271–274), describes the repeated checks of one tape against another, the making of multiple copies, and so on. This is one of the few passages in the *Report* from which one gets a clear idea of what the ancillary staff spent their time on. The remaining chapters of Part **3**, all short, deal with further stages of cryptanalysis, the last one, Chapter **39**, 'Language methods' (*GRT*, **39**, TNA HW 25/5, pp. 295–296; this edition, pp. 282–283), turning briefly to the work of the Testery.

3.6 Machines

The *General Report on Tunny* is concerned with machines for what they do and for how well they do it. There are no details of mechanical devices or electrical circuits. For instance, the first of the relatively large machines, the Robinsons, are categorized as 'counting and stepping machines' (a description that is also applied to the Colossi) and their action is described as follows:

> These machines are given two teleprinter patterns, combine them in some way and count the number of places of the combined pattern in which a certain condition is satisfied.
>
> An essential feature is that these counts must be made with the two patterns in all possible relative positions i.e. one pattern must 'step'. (*GRT*, **13A(a)**, TNA HW 25/4, p. 25; this edition, p. 32.)

An example is given and we are then told that 'at each setting the answer is, of course, a number.' The style of the *General Report on Tunny* marks it as written by specialists for their peers and their successors, so the simplicity of this last statement is a reminder that this kind of machine was not a familiar sight in the early 1940s.

The *General Report on Tunny* does sometimes consider matters historically (see section 3.7 below) but the Robinsons are treated rather condescendingly. The subsection devoted to them in a section entitled 'Machines' in the introductory part of the *Report* begins

> In pre-Colossus days the old Robinson did much of the work now assigned to Colossus, and, considering its primitive character, did so with remarkable success. (*GRT*, **13B(b)**, TNA HW 25/4, p. 26; this edition, p. 33.)

The design of the Robinsons allowed their operation to be flexible. This was necessary because the cryptanalysts knew from experience that their task might change if the Germans decided to modify the Tunny cipher. The design of successive Robinsons was also modified to take account of difficulties encountered in operating each model. Indeed the reasons for these changes bulk large in the fuller treatment of the machines in the chapters of the *Report* specifically dedicated to them, **52**, 'Development of Robinson and Colossus', and **54**, 'Robinson' (*GRT*, **52**, TNA HW 25/5, pp. 328–331; this edition, pp. 312–315; and *GRT*, **54**, TNA HW 25/5, pp. 353–362; this edition, pp. 336–345). Here again, the Robinson is subordinated to the Colossus, in chapter **52** by the Robinson being described almost entirely in terms of the features that proved inconvenient and led to the development of later models and eventually to Colossus, and in chapter **54** simply by the fact that the Colossus has been treated at much greater length in the previous chapter (*GRT*, **53**, 'Colossus', TNA HW 25/5, pp. 332–352; this edition, pp. 316–335).

The difficulties with the Robinson are largely practical ones, to do with the hardware. Nine 'handicaps' are listed. For example, the machine did not print the numbers it found (which had to be recorded quickly by operators, leading to errors) and the distance between the gate and the sprocket wheel that drove the tapes was too long (which caused stretching and thus misalignments) (*GRT*, **52(b)(i)** and **(ii)**, TNA HW 25/5, p. 328; this edition, p. 312). Details of hardware are precisely what was not to be supplied in the *Report*; section **51**, entitled 'Introductory', begins, under the heading 'Character of chapters **51** to **58**',

> This is a strictly functional and non-technical account of the machines used. A technical section is to be prepared by the post office engineers.
>
> Some attempt is made to avoid statements technically false, but none to avoid statements technically vague. (*GRT*, **51(a)**, TNA HW 25/5, p. 325; this edition, p. 309.)

As we have seen in section 2.2.1 above, the report by the Post Office engineers has not been found but a substitute for it, at least in regard to Colossus, has been supplied by one of the Post Office engineers who worked on the first Colossus machine.[108] This document is valuable, but historians are still left with a rather sketchy account of the passage from Robinson to Colossus. Nevertheless, it seems fairly clear that the details largely concern hardware, though from the first there was a sense that it should be possible to make something that worked faster than the Robinsons. The principles of the Robinson were, apparently, regarded as satisfactory, though the *Report* says so in a deterministic style that presumably owes something to hindsight from experience with Colossus:

> In the experimental stages of Tunny-breaking, though other forms of machine were considered, it was inevitable that one using Robinson principles should be chosen because
>
> (α) it is easy to make.
>
> (β) it can be adapted to any wheel length by preparing suitable tapes.
>
> (*GRT*, **52(b)**, TNA HW 25/5, p. 328; this edition, p. 312.)

We are then given a list of nine 'handicaps' of the early Robinson design that, with one exception, were remedied in the later models, Old Robinson and Super Robinson. The handicaps that were remedied include the non-printing of results already referred to and an inability to deal with tapes that had fewer than 2000 letters. The handicap that is mentioned as not having been overcome is the inability to carry out 'spanning' that is, to process only a set part of the tape, a procedure 'whose value was overlooked till later' (*GRT, loc. cit.*). These improvements were all incorporated in the first designs for Colossus. Tapes needed to be read repeatedly, so it was clear that speed could be improved if some way were found to store information from at least one of the tapes being compared. This would require the use of many more valves.

Moves towards designing and building Colossus started very soon after the construction of the first Robinson began (see section 1.5 above). The Robinson is dated to January 1943 (*GRT*, **74**, TNA HW 25/5, p. 459; this edition, p. 447) and work began on Colossus in February. As Newman first put forward his suggestion for an electronic counting machine only in the previous November (*GRT*, **74**, TNA HW 25/5, p. 458; this edition, p. 446), it hardly seems possible to regard the Colossus as anything other than a developed version of the Robinson; but the Robinson was not delivered until June, so experience of using Robinsons cannot have influenced the earlier stages of development work on the later machine. In any case, the intellectual thrust is already made with the Robinsons. Those machines already take the step of automating a mathematical task, that is an ordered series of operations, rather than merely a single mathematical procedure such as subtraction. In this sense the Colossus represents a practical rather than an intellectual development, simply using different electrical components to give a better performance. It is this better performance that ensures that Colossus takes precedence over Robinson in the *General*

[108] See section 2.2.1 above and D. C. Horwood, *A technical description of COLOSSUS I*, 1973 (declassified 2003), TNA HW 25/24.

Report on Tunny as it eventually did in the work the authors are describing: by the end of the war there were three Robinsons in operation and ten Colossi.

The unprecedented speed of the Colossus machines undoubtedly exercised a fascination. In the rather dry *General Report on Tunny* there are some passages that give a sense of intellectual drive, but few that give a sense of exhilaration. One such is the passage that captures the excitement of seeing an automatic machine at work, moving fast through calculations, in an unfamiliar kind of automation. The description, 'Impressions of Colossus', reads

> It is regretted that it is not possible to give an adequate idea of the fascination of a Colossus at work: its sheer bulk and apparent complexity; the fantastic speed of thin paper tape round the glittering pulleys; the childish pleasure of not-not, span, print main heading and other gadgets; the wizardry of purely mechanical decoding letter by letter (one novice thought she was being hoaxed); the uncanny action of the typewriter in printing the correct scores without and beyond human aid; the stepping of display; periods of eager expectation culminating in the sudden appearance of the longed-for score; and the strange rhythms characterizing every type of run: the stately break-in, the erratic short run, the regularity of wheel-breaking, the stolid rectangle interrupted by the wild leaps of the carriage-return, the frantic chatter of a motor run, even the ludicrous frenzy of hosts of bogus scores.
>
> Perhaps some Tunny-breaking poet could do justice to this theme; but although an ode to Colossus and various fragments appeared, all seemed to have been composed in times of distress and despondency, and consist almost wholly of imprecation or commination. (*GRT*, **51(j)**, TNA HW 25/5, p. 327; this edition, p. 310.)

(Although this passage cannot be ascribed to any particular author, it is perhaps significant that Donald Michie wrote poetry and that his younger brother James, in his teens when this passage was written, was to become a professional poet.)

The famous, and historically important, machines are the large ones, but right up to the end of the war there were also many smaller machines in use (and at least two being developed). Each was designed for a specialized task. For instance, the Dragon was used to set a 'crib' (a piece of text believed to occur within the plain text of a given message) in all possible positions against a tape of cipher text from which the chi wheel component of the key had been removed, a procedure that allowed the psi wheel component to be identified. The operation was called 'dragging' the crib, hence the name of the machine, which was used in the Testery (*GRT*, **55A**, TNA HW 25/5, p. 363; this edition, p. 346).[109] There was another machine, called Proteus, that handled depths (*GRT*, **28A(g)**, TNA HW 25/4, p. 257; this edition, p. 239; and **55B**, TNA HW 25/5, pp. 364–365; this edition, pp. 347–348). The machine probably took its name from its adaptability — a reference to Classical mythology is entirely in line with what we know of the education of many of the senior staff at Bletchley Park.[110] The Proteus machine is described as 'equally applicable to any mod-2-addition teleprinter cipher which has true depths' (*GRT*, **55B(d)**, TNA HW 25/5, p. 365; this edition, p. 348). It seems to somewhat resemble the Johnson and Oedipus machines that were designed and used at GCHQ after the war.[111]

The list of smaller machines in the *General Report on Tunny* is almost comically complete, as if it were intended as an inventory; it includes many entirely commonplace items, such as the slide rule, which attracts the acid comment 'Many of the slide rules used lack logarithms and have elaborate useless scales' (*GRT*, **57(a)**, TNA HW 25/5, p. 380; this edition, p. 361).

[109] A Dragon survives, see J. A. Reeds, 'American Dragon', *Cryptologia*, 35.1 (2011), pp. 22–41.

[110] Proteus appears several times in Ovid's *Metamorphoses* as well as at the beginning of Virgil's famous retelling of the story of Orpheus in *Georgics* book IV.

[111] On these machines see Simon Lavington, 'In the Footsteps of Colossus: A Description of Oedipus', *IEEE Annals of the History of Computing*, 28.2 (2006), pp. 44–55.

There is a table showing which machines were in use in various places in May 1943 and in May 1945. In May 1943 there was one Robinson, one Tunny machine, and one machine to help in sticking tapes together to make a loop to run on Robinson (or, later, on Colossus). By the end of the war there were many more machines. In May 1945 the Newmanry had 2 Robinsons and 10 Colossi; the Testery had 3 smaller machines (2 Dragons and a machine called Aquarius, described as 'on test') plus 13 Tunny machines (for decoding), while the Newmanry had 4 Tunny machines used for cryptanalysis, that is British Tunny machines.[112] There were also 33 minor items (*GRT*, **51(k)**, TNA HW 25/5, p. 327; this edition, p. 311).

It is clear that mechanization did not take place only in Newman's group. Smaller machines were used in the Testery, where hand methods were employed for wheel setting and for removing the effects of the psi wheels from messages from which the Newmanry cryptanalysts had removed the effects of chi wheels. Although it was recognised that, in principle, the whole task of breaking the cipher could be mechanized, allowing a Tunny machine to be set up so that messages could be decrypted, there seems to have been no attempt to actually carry out such a programme. Perhaps there would have been if the war had gone on longer. From the account Horwood gives of the use of Colossi after the war (see section 2.2 above) it seems that complete automation of cryptanalysis was probably put into operation at GCHQ.

At Bletchley Park, however, the machines, impressive as their performance was, seem always to have been seen as adjuncts to a process of cryptanalysis carried out by a skilled human being. There are many references throughout the *Report* to the need for personnel to have experience or specific skills in order to carry out particular cryptanalytic tasks. The human cryptanalyst makes many decisions along the way, the machines merely help to implement them. Here again chapter **81** (Conclusions), though concise, is informative.

First, it applauds the achievement of the accuracy that was one of the reasons for using machines (see section 1.5 above). It is of course Colossus that is singled out. We are told

> The most remarkable feature of our machines is the accuracy of Colossus, especially when doing ψ runs. (*GRT*, **81C(a)**, TNA HW 25/5, p. 467; this edition, p. 455.)

The next characteristic to be examined is adaptability, and here Robinson receives a commendation:

> For Tunny wheel setting and breaking Colossus is a much more powerful machine than Robinson, but Robinson is more adaptable to other problems. (*GRT*, **81C(b)**, TNA HW 25/5, p. 467; this edition, p. 455.)

However, the final sentence is revealing:

> The method of making a machine adaptable is first to think of a number of things required of it and then design the machine to cope with a general class of problem which includes all the special ones as particular cases. (*GRT*, *loc. cit.*)

This envisages adaptability like that of the Proteus machine. It is not envisaging adaptability like that of the stored-program electronic computer that was to be built in Manchester a few years later. Perhaps a suggestion of a 'universal' machine would have seemed too futuristic, given the problems of storing information inside the machine — which, as we have seen, deterred Newman from adopting Flowers' first plans for what was to become Colossus. But, for whatever reason, it seems that the writer of this part of the *Report* did not see Colossus as the immediate ancestor of

[112] The two types of Tunny machine are distinguished in *GRT*, **56J** (cryptanalytic use) and **56L** (decoding), TNA HW 25/5, pp. 376–379; this edition, pp. 358–360.

a 'universal' machine. And it seems that GCHQ also for some time preferred to have machines designed for specific purposes rather than taking to general purpose computers.[113]

The *General Report on Tunny* also makes a plea for recognising the usefulness of small machines: 'Our production increased considerably when we were able, in 1944, to present Knockholt with a few hand counters.' (*GRT*, **81C(d)**, TNA HW 25/5, p. 467; this edition, p. 455.)

As we have noted, there were practical reasons for not attempting to build a 'universal' machine to handle all the cryptanalytic tasks carried out in the Newmanry. Probably it was recognised that these difficulties could not be overcome sufficiently quickly to make the attempt worth while in operational terms. Despite its having some academic traits, the work of Newman's group was unlike that of a university department in many ways, one of them being that its research was very strongly directed to a specific end. The *General Report on Tunny* contains many references to things having 'operational' significance. Taking a wider view, we may also note that the breaking down of tasks into component parts, each assigned to a particular group, was characteristic of the organisation of GCCS (and was also reflected in a patchwork of management styles within the organisation).[114] This fragmentation was, of course, partly for reasons of security, and a similar spirit of limiting the 'need to know' may help to account for the continuing division of work on Tunny between Newman's section and Major Tester's. One effect of the division seems to have been that, on the whole, decrypted (plain text) messages were seen only by the latter group (which then forwarded them to Hut 3). Given this tendency to distribute tasks, it is perhaps not surprising to find the same attitude in the development not of one universal machine but rather of several specialized machines each for a specific task. In this respect, the machines mirror the institution from which they sprang. On the other hand, in its intimate combination of abstract theory with description of actual machines, the *General Report on Tunny* has something of the air of a team-work version of Turing's paper 'On computable numbers' of 1936.[115]

3.6.1 A note on authorship

There can be no reasonable doubt that Good, Michie and Timms should be regarded as the editors of the *General Report on Tunny* rather than its authors. But it is equally reasonable to suppose that each of them wrote some part or parts of the book. The heavily mathematical sections on statistics are presumably contributed by Good, though the work they describe almost certainly contains some input from Alan Turing — as is suggested by the fact that Good apparently waited to see whether Turing wanted to take the work further before deciding to do so himself.[116] As we see in the institution of the 'Tea Party', all work might contain a collaborative element. Nevertheless, despite the air of collegiality, we are not dealing with ordinary academic authorship in which the person who does the work writes it up and signs it. We have an anonymous official report.

Collaboration is particularly important in regard to the machines, where practical details of design, and the actual construction, were clearly the responsibility of the Post Office engineers at Dollis Hill (whose report seems not to have survived, see 2.1 and 2.2.1 above). The Newmanry's report on the machines seems to have been written, or at least put together, by Geoffrey Timms. The evidence for his authorship is provided by a short letter Good sent to Tiltman on 19 July 1945, while the Allies were still at war with Japan. The letter was written on behalf of John Herivel, who was away on leave, and its main purpose is to pass on suggestions for possible further uses of Robinson machines for breaking ciphers other than Tunny. This bears out the comment on

[113] See Lavington, 'In the Footsteps of Colossus: A Description of Oedipus' (see footnote 111, above).

[114] See Grey, *Decoding Organization* (see footnote 2, above).

[115] Reference in note 22 above.

[116] See S. L. Zabell, 'Statistics at Bletchley Park, this volume, pp. lxxv–ci.

the adaptability of the Robinson made in the *Report* (*GRT*, **81C(b)**, TNA HW 25/5, p. 467; this edition, p. 455, see 3.6 above). Good adds

> The cryptographer in our section who knows most about the machines is Dr. G. Timms, who is expected to join the Research Section on August 1st. He is at present engaged on writing the part of our report dealing with machines, as well as other parts of the report.[117]

This evidence is perhaps not as strong as it may at first appear. For instance, we may note that Good says Timms is writing this part of the report, not that he has finished it. However, the passage does suggest that Timms wrote at least part of the section of the *Report* that deals with machines.

3.7 History

The *General Report on Tunny* was written by people who, as far as we know, were either protagonists in the activity they describe or were in a position to base their account on very good second-hand information. The *Report* is thus indisputably a highly authoritative document. But it is not primarily written as a history. As we can see in its Conclusions, the *Report* is essentially interested in establishing where the cryptanalytic campaign now stands rather than in how it got there. On the other hand, there was a historical story to tell, and parts of it are given at various points, not necessarily in the order in which events occurred — the most flagrant example being the placing of the story of the first breaking of Tunny traffic, which is in Part **4** of the *Report*. Drastic reordering of material was clearly out of the question, so we can only reiterate that readers of the present edition are strongly advised to use the index if they are in search of information on any particular topic.

The original editors — who were also part-authors of the *Report*— were obviously aware that there was a historical narrative behind their *Report*, and to help the reader they provided an outline of it in chapter **74**. The outline takes the form of an eight-page month-by-month Chronology, running from June 1941 to June 1945 (*GRT*, **74**, 'Chronology', TNA HW 25/5, pp. 456–463; this edition, pp. 444–451). The information is presented in a table with five columns. The first gives the year and month, the second is headed 'Changes in Tunny' and its first entry is 'SZ40 first Tunny link' for June 1941, the third column is headed 'Organisation changes' and its first entry is 'Work in Research Section starts' for June 1941, the fourth column is headed 'Machines' and its first entry is 'Decoding machine ordered' for April 1942, the fifth column is headed 'Theoretical Discoveries and Achievements' and its first entry is 'Machine broken for Aug 1941' for February 1942. This entry refers to the completion of the process of understanding the overall design of the (German) Tunny machine, plus wheel patterns, from the work of Tiltman and Tutte on the message received in August 1941 (discussed above). The next break of a machine, that is the finding of wheel patterns, is recorded in April, and was for the traffic of the previous month.[118] The 'decoding machine' referred to in the entry for April 1942 is a Tunny machine simulator, designed to decrypt the traffic when the correct wheel patterns and wheel settings are known. The machine was delivered in June. As we have already noted, current Tunny traffic was read for the first time in the following month, July 1942, marking the beginning of the work of the Testery. After that, the machines considered worthy of mention in the Chronology are those for the Newmanry.

[117]Good to Tiltman, 19 July 1945, dated from 'Mr Herivel's Section, Blocks F and H'; TNA HW 62/6, transcription JVF. We are grateful to Ralph Erskine for drawing our attention to this letter.

[118]The text, Good, Michie and Timms, *GRT*, **74**, TNA HW 25/5, p. 457; this edition, p. 445, has 'March 1943' but this is presumably an error for 'March 1942'.

In contrast to the concise tabulated Chronology provided as one chapter of the *General Report on Tunny*, the complete 20-page text of the *History of the Fish Section* (1945, TNA HW 50/79, see section 2.2.3 above) is set out as a series of parts dealing with specified intervals, usually a calendar month. These record such details as which links were broken. At the end of the document there are three Annexes, the last of which is a table showing the number of messages decrypted month by month. This valuable supplement to the story told in the *General Report on Tunny* is printed below in our first endnote to chapter **61** of the *Report* (p. 612).

4. A physical description of the copy of the *General Report on Tunny* that we used

4.1 Summary

The *General Report on Tunny*, which carries no authors' names and has no title page, covers about five hundred typed pages. It was declassified and released to the Public Record Office (since renamed the National Archives) in September 2000. Its two volumes have press-marks HW 25/4 and 25/5. There is at least one further copy at GCHQ (Cheltenham).

4.2 Details

The copy of the *General Report on Tunny* held in the National Archives is bound in red buckram as two volumes. Each volume is about 5 cm thick, 32.5 cm tall and 25 cm wide (about 2 by 12.75 by 9.5 inches). That is, the format of the pages is foolscap, which was commonplace at the time the work was written.

Most of the leaves of both volumes are photostats, that is black and white photographic images of an original document, printed by a wet chemical process onto the front sides of sheets of stiff semi glossy photographic paper. There are plain paper pages at the front and back of each volume, and several pages on which ordinary photographs have been pasted onto the original pages and are now reproduced as photostats.

Most of the pages in the original document seem to have been made from foolscap pages typed on a manual machine, with a 'pica' typeface (that is; six horizontal lines per vertical inch and ten characters per horizontal inch); about half of the pages are single-spaced and about half double-spaced. The effect is more or less like pages printed in a 12-point 'Courier' typeface, with lines single spaced. Pages are generally full. Typing errors have been corrected in the usual ways, not always clearly.

On many leaves the image is slightly fuzzy and some pages have a scatter of black dots. These effects are merely artefacts of the photostat process, but can seriously impair legibility.

A few leaves are fold-outs of varying sizes. These are photostats of such items as large charts, building plans, and worksheets covered with calculations. Only the front sides of these leaves bear text or images.

The pages of the original document were numbered in manuscript at their upper right corners; these numbers are clearly visible in the photostats. The numbers run from 1 to 505, with three unnumbered interpolated leaves.

The foliation of Volume 1 is [i], [ii], 1–116, [116 bis], 117–273, and of Volume 2 is 274–505, where unnumbered leaves are given in brackets. Pages 186–188, 274 and 275 are foldouts. Pages 9, 332 and 381 to 393 included pasted-on photographs.

Volume 1 has a label on the spine reading 'GENERAL REPORT ON / TUNNY / VOL I' and a shelf mark sticker on the front cover reading 'RACK S.5/233'. The flyleaf has a red pencil notation 'COPY NO 4 / VOL. I'. The inside front cover and the flyleaf each bear a red-inked rubber stamp mark: 'TO BE RETURNED TO / G.C.H.Q. ARCHIVES / ROOM C/25404A / Priors Road / Oakley / CHELTENHAM, Glos. / Ext. 2134'. The back of the front flyleaf has a small pencil notation '£8' (perhaps the cost of the binding).

Pages i and ii are a table of contents for both volumes. There is no title page; the title of the work, *General Report on Tunny, with emphasis on statistical methods*, is stated formally only at the top of page i. There is no statement regarding authorship.

Volume 2 also has a shelf mark sticker saying 'RACK S.5 / 233', and a title on the front cover reading 'GENERAL REPORT ON / TUNNY / VOL II Copy No 1.' Its flyleaves are unmarked.

There is one defect. In HW 25/4, page 15 is a half-page, the bottom half having been excised. But a copy of the *Report* retained by GCHQ does not have this defect so, thanks to the generosity of the departmental historian, we have been able to supply the missing material.

Most of the text is typescript, but about a fifth of the pages are exhibits, to which the expository text makes repeated and detailed references. These exhibits include examples of Tunny intercepts, cryptanalysts' worksheets and many examples of Colossus output, as well as photographs and floor plans. Most of these exhibits predate the end of the war in Europe. Some pages are composites of exhibits and long expository captions.

From the evidence of the GCHQ copy numbers, it seems likely that the copy in the National Archives is from a small print run and that the photostat process was used (instead of a cheaper stencil process) in order to reproduce the exhibits. We do not know who received copies of the *Report* in 1945.

5. This edition

The overall organisation of the *General Report on Tunny*, discussed in section 3.2 above, would have made it easy for individual chapters to be written and typed separately and then slotted into place. Many details of the text make it seem likely that this is indeed what happened. Inconsistencies abound. For instance the lettering and numbering of sections and subsections is not the same in all chapters. The *Report* was not intended to be printed for publication and such inconsistencies, together with the various other eccentricities that we shall mention below, were probably acceptable in a typescript — even one intended for circulation — or at least not sufficiently unacceptable to justify the expense of retyping. We think that some of them would not be acceptable in a printed book. But since we are copy editing a primary source we have done so with as light a hand as possible.

We initially considered reproducing the text of the *Report* more or less as it might have been printed had it been published in England in 1945. That proved to be impossible, both on account of the idiosyncratic organisation (for instance in the numbering of chapters), which an editor would certainly have wished to 'tidy up', and because of the irregularities of style that a copy editor would certainly have insisted on 'ironing out'. In making a scholarly edition of an unpublished text, we were obliged to treat the text with much greater respect than a publisher would have done in 1945. The British spelling and grammatical usages of the original have, of course, been retained, as has the period style of punctuation, for instance a rather liberal employment of commas and the use of ':—' to introduce lists. That is, we have not tried to modernise the text. Our attempts to make particular passages more accessible take the form of endnotes. When decisions had to be made we sought conservative guidance from *New Hart's Rules: the Handbook of Style for Writers and Editors* (Oxford: Oxford University Press, 2005) and the *Shorter Oxford English Dictionary* (Oxford: Oxford University Press, 1944).

5.1 Vocabulary

Any technical text is likely to contain specialized terms that need to be explained. In this particular case, the authors were part of a small isolated group that had developed new terminology of its own, some of it jocular in the manner of English Public School slang.The *Report* includes a glossary (chapter **71**); we have added a supplementary glossary and, where appropriate, endnotes to catch lexical oddities.

Here it is worth remarking on a few usages that are more general, that is not merely characteristic of Bletchley Park. One striking difference from modern usage that might mislead the reader is the word 'character'. We have already had occasion to refer to this briefly in our account of the contents of the *Report* (see 3.3 above), but further comment seems appropriate here. The *Report* uses 'character' for what would now be called a 'bit' (a technical term which had not yet been coined). Unfortunately, the modern term 'character' denotes something that consists of several bits. The 1945 term for the row of 'characters' across a paper tape is 'letter'. So, whereas the modern version has five bits making a character, in the *Report* we have five characters making a letter. Since the cipher in question operates at character (bit) level, the vocabulary is disconcerting rather than a serious impediment to understanding.

As we have already remarked ('Note on vocabulary', p. xiv) readers familiar with modern terminology may also be surprised to find that the *General Report on Tunny* regularly refers to the people engaged in breaking the ciphers as 'cryptographers', the term that today would be used for people who make ciphers, though also more generally for anyone concerned with ciphers. The narrower term 'cryptanalysts' became current only later. Further, the *Report* regularly uses the word 'code' for 'cipher' — perhaps strangely since the title of the establishment in which the writers were working, the Government Code and Cypher School, apparently makes a point of distinguishing between the two. This particular imprecision is usual in informal speech and writing, but we have avoided it in our editorial contributions to this volume.

5.2 Corrections

We list here some of the more notable irregularities in the typescript text and our responses to them.

5.2.1 Spelling

We have corrected obvious spelling errors. For words with more than one correct spelling, typically ones ending in '-ise' or '-ize', we have been guided by the text. Where it shows a clear overall preference for one variant — as, for instance, it does for 'organise' — that has been taken as the norm. Where the preference is not clear, we have been guided by the *SOED* (1944).

All these changes are noted at the foot of the page, see below. We are, of course, aware that such variations in spellings may be a guide to the authorship of different passages. On the whole, GCCS typists were probably accustomed to reproducing exactly what they were given rather than imposing 'corrections' on it.

One word defeated us. The *Report* uses the words 'benzine' (**57(d)**, **71**, 'Fire') and 'benzene' (**23Z**, list item 23; **35D(b)**) as if they meant the same thing. As benzine is highly volatile and inflammable, it may seem more likely that the chemical regularly used as a solvent for glue was benzene, whose carcinogenic properties were not brought to the fore until the 1950s. However, there is evidence for widespread use of both chemicals as solvents in this period. No Tunny veteran we have found has remembered the smell, which would have allowed us to decide.

5.2.2 Words and symbols

Throughout the *General Report on Tunny*, even in formulae, words rather than symbols are sometimes used for dot, cross, chi, psi, mu, delta, sigma etc. We can see no reason behind this inconsistency, but have not attempted to remove it.

5.2.3 Punctuation

There are many trivial errors in punctuation, particularly in association with references given in parentheses. Sentences frequently lack a full stop, particularly when they end with an equation. There are also spaces lacking after commas in lists, or put in before other punctuation such as colons. We have silently corrected such errors.

We have not made changes to punctuation where the decision is essentially a matter of style, as in whether there should be a comma in referring to 'January, 1944'. The use of hyphens can also be a matter of style. The writers of the *Report* show a strong preference for the form 'wheel-breaking', which we have consequently adopted as a norm. But the forms 'chi-wheel' and 'chi wheel' occur with roughly equal frequency, so we have allowed both to stand.

Headings of sections and subsections, and figure captions, are variously punctuated and capitalised. We have silently imposed some degree of regularity. Headings appear in three forms: in upper case throughout, with nouns capitalised ('title case') and with only the first word capitalised ('sentence case'). The first form of heading appears in the edited text if and only if it appears in the corresponding position in the original typescript text. However, we have on occasion silently changed the second form into the third one (or vice versa).

It seems to have been a matter of choice in printed books of the time whether the decimal point appeared half way up the numbers or on the line like a full stop. As much of the mathematics in the *Report* is handwritten, raised decimal points occur there, although points on the line are normal in typing. We have imposed regularity: decimal points are raised, points to indicate multiplication are on the line.

5.2.4 Underlining

The typists of the *Report* used underlining for emphasis, we have interpreted it as indicating italic in prose and bold in headings. Taking a hint from I. J. Good, *Probability and the Weighing of Evidence* (London: Griffin, 1950), whose formatting style strikes us as being rather similar to that of the *Report*, we have also used bold in references.

5.2.5 Setting mathematics

We have set the formulae — which were largely handwritten — according to the usual conventions of mathematical typography, which have not changed appreciably since 1945. In setting the formulae we have sometimes slightly rearranged their format, breaking long formulae into several lines or changing their indentation, always with a view to making them easier to read. Major rearrangements of this kind (such as splitting lines) have been recorded in footnotes, minor ones (such as changing the spacing) have not.

5.2.6 Cryptographic notation

One example of the ambiguities to be found in the typewritten text of the *Report* is that of a typed lower case x. The x can, depending on context, mean (1) the multiplication sign, (2) an algebraic variable, or (3) the cross character (now known as the 'bit value 1'). If handwritten, x might also mean the Greek letter chi. Similarly, the possible meanings of a typed full stop include the cryptographic dot (corresponding to the modern 'bit value 0') as well as the decimal point and the multiplication point. In the case where the x and the full stop have their cryptographic meanings, we have set them as **×** and •. Similarly, we have followed modern (2015) cryptographic conventions for choices of typeface in examples, and so on.

5.2.7 Annotation

All notes on the text of the *General Report on Tunny* are marked in the margin and printed at the foot of the page or at the end of the book, as appropriate. No marks have been put into the body of the text.

The *General Report on Tunny* has a few 'native' footnotes, most of which are marked in the body of the text with the conventional footnote signs *, †, ‡. Such native footnotes have been printed at the foot of the page and a copy of the corresponding mark appears in the margin.

Textual notes have been marked in the margin and printed at the foot of the page. Simple corrections, the results of one-for-one replacements, are marked with lower case letters. Other textual notes are marked with lower case Roman numerals, the lettering and numbering starting afresh for each page.

Endnotes have been used for comments on the text such as identifications of persons or corrections of substantive errors. The endnotes are marked in the margin with an endnote number, in the style 'E.38'. Numbering begins afresh with each chapter.

We have also used the margins to indicate approximate locations of page breaks in the original copy of the *General Report on Tunny*, in the style 'p.123'.

Notes at the foot of our pages appear in this order: native footnotes, simple text corrections, other textual notes. A horizontal rule separates the body of the text from any footnotes, and another (if needed) separates native footnotes from textual notes.

5.2.8 Guide to marginal markings

*	means the *General Report on Tunny* has a footnote marked * here
p.123	means page 123 of the original starts about here
a	means a simple correction; original reading at foot of the page
i	means there is a textual note at the foot of the page
E.38	means see endnote 38 to this chapter

5.3 Illustrations and other artwork

The *General Report on Tunny* reproduces photographs, plans of the site at Bletchley Park and original worksheets. It also provides diagrams and tables.

Photographs presented no immediate difficulty: with a very few exceptions (on which see Appendix E, p. 540, below), the National Archives have original photographs, which we were able to reproduce. However, as the format of our book necessarily differs from that of the original copies of the *General Report on Tunny*, we have sometimes needed to rearrange pictures and to adjust their size. For details see Appendix E below.

Reproductions of plans and worksheets, many of which formed fold-out pages in the original, were also photographed, and are reproduced here at reduced size. Details of the changes are given in Appendix E.

When diagrams and tables were of suitable quality, they too were reproduced photographically, but in many cases we preferred to redraw or typeset such material. Our reworked versions are readily distinguished from originals. For artwork of this kind, as for photographs, the change in format has sometimes led to rearrangement or to the item appearing in a slightly different position in the text. Such alterations are, of course, a normal feature of the passage from typescript to print, but we have tried to keep them to a minimum.

6. In conclusion

The *General Report on Tunny* was probably never expected to be readable from end to end in the normal way, except by a very small number of people with a high degree of specialist knowledge. And the text has been locked away for a long time, so that by now even experts on the subject matter require explanations of parts of the content. As of course do historians. Against this obvious inaccessibility one must balance the historical importance of the story that the text has to tell. The origins of the Colossus machines are part of the origins of the modern electronic computer, a device which has made immense changes not only in the practice and development of the sciences but in almost every aspect of everyday life, since such machines began to become available, from the 1950s onwards, at first for military work and then for academic research projects and eventually as domestic appliances for use by the general public. Indeed the effects of the computer have been so pervasive that it is clear that any serious history of almost any aspect of life in the 'long' twenty-first century will need to begin with the story of the emergence of the computer. In that story, the *General Report on Tunny* is a key document. We hope our edition will have made it accessible to a relatively wide readership.

Statistics at Bletchley Park

S. L. Zabell

If the *General Report on Tunny*[1] had been declassified in 1950 rather than half a century later, two things would likely have surprised its contemporary readers. One of these would have been the vital role of machine computation in the attack on Tunny, the other, the central use of Bayesian statistics. Much has been written about the first of these;[2] this essay focuses on the second.

The use of Bayesian methods at Bletchley Park was recognised by its practitioners as flying in the face of the statistical orthodoxy of the time. This essay provides some historical background for this judgement; a summary of the statistical methods the cryptanalysts used, including the reason for their adoption and some of their more interesting aspects; and a discussion of the impact of this work on the outside statistical profession after the end of the war.

Before 1939

Bayesian statistics is so named because of its systematic use of *Bayes' theorem*, which takes its name from Thomas Bayes (1702–1761), an English Dissenting Minister who was a member of the Royal Society and a mathematician of no mean ability. Bayes wrote a celebrated paper, 'An essay towards solving a problem in the doctrine of chances' (published posthumously), that dealt with the problem of how to revise probabilities in the light of new information.[3] Despite its name, 'Bayes' theorem' in the form in which it was usually quoted in the 1940s, and still is today, was first stated only in a later paper of Pierre Simon Laplace (1749–1827).[4]

Bayes' theorem

In order to state Bayes' theorem, we need a few definitions. First, if $P(A)$ denotes the probability of an event A, and A and B are two events, then, using standard terminology, the *relative odds of A to B* are given by the ratio of their probabilities, $P(A)/P(B)$; the relative odds express how much more likely one event (here A) is compared to another event (here B). If, for example, $P(A) = 3/4$, and $\bar{A}$ represents the event 'not-A' (A does not occur), then $P(\bar{A}) = 1/4$, and the relative odds of A to $\bar{A}$ are 3 to 1.

The *conditional probability of A given B*, denoted $P(A \mid B)$, is the ratio of $P(A \text{ and } B)$ to $P(B)$:

$$P(A \mid B) = \frac{P(A \text{ and } B)}{P(B)}.$$

[1] *General Report on Tunny, with Emphasis on Statistical Methods*, The National Archives of the United Kingdom, HW 25/4 and 25/5. Hereafter abbreviated to '*GRT*'. References to particular places in it are given in the style '*GRT*, **23Z**, TNA HW 25/4, p. 109; this edition, p. 106'. This means chapter **23**, section **Z**, appearing at the indicated page numbers in the original copy and in this edition.

[2] For example, B. Jack Copeland, ed., *Colossus: The Secrets of Bletchley Park's Codebreaking Computers* (Oxford: Oxford University Press, 2006).

[3] Thomas Bayes, 'An Essay Towards Solving a Problem in the Doctrine of Chances', *Philosophical Transactions of the Royal Society of London*, 53 (1763), pp. 370–418.

[4] Pierre Simon Laplace, 'Mémoire sur la probabilité des causes par les évènemens', *Mémoires de mathématique et de physique, présentés à l'Académie royale des sciences, par divers sçavans, & lûs dans ses assemblées*, 6 (1774), pp. 621–656; translated in Stephen M. Stigler, 'Laplace's 1774 Memoir on Inverse Probability', *Statistical Science*, 1 (1986), pp. 359–378. For discussion of this and later papers on this subject by Laplace, see Anders Hald, *A History of Mathematical Statistics from 1750 to 1930* (New York: Wiley, 1995), Chapters 9–12.

As its name suggests, a conditional probability expresses the dependence of one chance outcome on another. It provides a formalism for quantifying such statements as 'if you are a heavy smoker, then you have a greater chance of developing lung cancer'. Now we can state the so-called 'odds ratio' version of Bayes' theorem: If H_0 and H_1 are two competing 'hypotheses' of interest (in the Tunny machine, for example, two possible wheel-settings), and E represents some form of evidence or data (in the analysis of Tunny traffic, for example, the letters observed in an encrypted message), then

$$\frac{P(H_1 \mid E)}{P(H_0 \mid E)} = \frac{P(E \mid H_1)}{P(E \mid H_0)} \cdot \frac{P(H_1)}{P(H_0)};$$

that is, the final or posterior odds ratio for H_1 versus H_0 given E (the expression on the left) equals the *likelihood ratio* (the first ratio on the right) times the initial or prior odds (the second ratio on the right). Put another way, the likelihood ratio is precisely the factor that transforms, by multiplying, the initial odds into the final odds.[5] Bayes' theorem is a simple consequence of the definition of conditional probability, one that can be derived in just a few lines of algebra. So from a purely mathematical perspective Bayes' theorem is a fact not subject to dispute. If the constituent probabilities in the equation are known, then the equation relating them is satisfied. What is controversial is the use of the theorem in an application; specifically, one may ask what the prior probabilities mean and where they come from. Understanding this controversial aspect of Bayes' theorem requires a brief detour into the history of probability, to trace the debate between 'Bayesians' and 'frequentists'.

The Laplacian synthesis

The birth of mathematical probability is conventionally situated in 1654, the year of an exchange of letters between Pierre de Fermat (c. 1601–1665) and Blaise Pascal (1623–1662).[6] Initially devoted largely to the analysis of games of chance using for the most part elementary mathematics, the subject was dramatically transformed in the nineteenth century by the profound work of Laplace. Not only did Laplace make mathematical contributions of great depth to its theory, but he also vastly extended the range of its practical application, summarising the work of a lifetime in his magisterial *Théorie analytique des probabilités* of 1812.[7]

The Laplacian viewpoint dominated studies of probability for nearly a century. Central to Laplace's approach was his embrace of what is today termed an 'epistemic' or subjective view of the nature of probability:

> The word 'chance' then expresses only our ignorance of the causes of the phenomena that we observe to occur and to succeed one another in no apparent order.
>
> Probability is relative in part to this ignorance, and in part to our knowledge.[8]

In the course of the nineteenth century, this approach was criticised by eminent philosophers and logicians such as Auguste Comte (1798–1857), John Stuart Mill (1806–1873), and John

[5] See I. J. Good, 'The Interface between Statistics and Philosophy of Science', *Statistical Science*, 3 (1988), pp. 386–397, esp. p. 390, and D. Wrinch and H. Jeffreys, 'On Certain Fundamental Principles of Scientific Inquiry', *Philosophical Magazine*, 6th ser., 42 (1921), pp. 369–390.

[6] See Ian Hacking, *The Emergence of Probability* (Cambridge: Cambridge University Press, 1975), Chapter 7 for discussion and further references.

[7] Pierre Simon Laplace, *Théorie analytique des probabilités* (Paris: Courcier, 1812).

[8] Pierre Simon Laplace, 'Mémoire sur les approximations des formules qui sont fonctions de très grands nombres', *Mémoires de mathématique et de physique, présentés à l'Académie royale des sciences, par divers sçavans, & lûs dans ses assemblées* (1783/1786), pp. 423–467, esp. p. 424, reprinted in Pierre Simon Laplace, *Œeuvres complètes de Laplace*, 14 vols. (Paris: Gauthier-Villars, 1878–1912), vol. 10, p. 295–338; see esp. p. 296. Translation, C. C. Gillispie, *Pierre-Simon Laplace 1749-1827: A Life in Exact Science* (Princeton: Princeton University Press, 1997), p. 91.

Venn (1834–1923).[9] For example, it was questioned whether one could attach precise numbers to degrees of belief; and on a more technical level, doubts were raised concerning the source of the prior probabilities that appear in Bayes' theorem.

In England the force and effect of such criticisms varied over time. On the whole, however, and despite endorsement by some eminent mathematicians, such as George Boole (1815–1864), critics of the Laplacian approach had only limited influence during the nineteenth century. The two most prominent British statisticians at the beginning of the twentieth century, Francis Ysidro Edgeworth (1845–1926) and Karl Pearson (1857–1936), belonged firmly in the Bayesian camp. The situation changed after the First World War with the rise to prominence of Ronald Aylmer Fisher (1890–1962), a prolific inventor and expositor of new techniques.

Fisher's career as a statistician began in 1919 when he went to work at the Rothamsted Agricultural Station (Harpenden, Herts., UK); during the following years he published many important and influential papers and books. Recognition quickly followed: he became a Fellow of the Royal Society in 1929, Galton Professor of Genetics at University College London in 1934, and Arthur Balfour Professor of Genetics at the University of Cambridge in 1943.[10] Fisher put forward a new foundation for theoretical statistics, incorporating novel elements such as his concepts of consistency, efficiency and sufficiency. These were presented not just as an alternative to, but as the remedy for, what Fisher perceived as the fatally flawed Bayesian approach.

In 1921 Fisher wrote that the Bayesian approach 'depended upon an arbitrary assumption, so that the whole method has been widely discredited'.[11] In particular, Fisher was critical of 'inverse probability, which like an impenetrable jungle arrests progress towards precision of statistical concepts'.[12] (Fisher's intense animus towards Karl Pearson may have played some role here: by discrediting Bayes, Fisher was attacking Pearson.)

In the mid 1930s Fisher's reforms were followed by those of Jerzy Neyman (1894–1981) and Egon Pearson (1895–1980).[13] Fisher had often worked on an intuitive rather than on a rigorous mathematical basis, basing his new ideas in many cases on clever insights about specific examples (fiducial inference being the most famous and controversial of these). The gist of Neyman's alternative to Fisher's programme was, in conjunction with Egon Pearson (Karl Pearson's son), to develop a purely frequency-based approach to statistical inference, using confidence intervals and tests of hypotheses. Fisher was its bitter enemy. But while they seemed to agree on little else, Fisher and Neyman certainly did agree on one thing: their complete and uncompromising rejection of the classical Bayesian approach.

This consensus between the two great rivals could not fail to make an impression, and it resulted in a virtually total eclipse of Bayesian statistics. I. J. Good gave some sense of the times when he related in 1993 that during his time at Cambridge in the years just before the war,

> [I] had been reading some of Harold Jeffreys [1891–1989, then the only active Bayesian at Cambridge], which, by the way, Maurice Bartlett [1910–2002, a young

[9]See John Stuart Mill, *A System of Logic, Ratiocinative and Inductive*, 4th ed. (London: John W. Parker, 1846), Vol. 2; John Venn, *The Logic of Chance*, 2nd ed. (London: Macmillan, 1876; reprinted New York: Chelsea, 1957) and Auguste Comte, *Cours de philosophie positive*, 4th ed., 4 vols. (Paris: Baillère, 1877), vol. 4, pp. 366–369.

[10]See R. A. Fisher, *Contributions to Mathematical Statistics* (New York: Chapman & Hall, 1950) and Joan Fisher Box, *R. A. Fisher: The Life of a Scientist* (New York: Wiley, 1978).

[11]R. A. Fisher, 'On the "Probable Error" of a Coefficient of Correlation Deduced from a Small Sample', *Metron*, 1 (1921), pp. 3–32, esp. p. 4.

[12]R. A. Fisher, 'On the Mathematical Foundations of Theoretical Statistics', *Philos. Trans. Roy. Soc. London A*, 222 (1922), pp. 309–368, esp. p. 311.

[13]Most notably Egon Pearson and Jerzy Neyman, 'On the Use and Interpretation of Certain Test Criteria for Purposes of Statistical Inference', *Biometrika*, 20 (1928), pp. 175–240, 263–294; Egon Pearson and Jerzy Neyman, 'On the Problem of the Most Efficient Tests of Statistical Hypotheses', *Philos. Trans. Roy. Soc. London A*, 231 (1933), pp. 289–337; and Jerzy Neyman, 'Outline of a Theory of Statistical Estimation Based on the Classical Theory of Probability', *Philos. Trans. Roy. Soc. London A*, 236 (1937), pp. 333–380.

> up-and-coming statistician then teaching at Cambridge] thought ought not to be taught at Cambridge at the same time as classical statistics. In other words, he wanted everybody to be brainwashed according to the 'orthodox' methods and not to be confused by a conflicting philosophy.[14]

Statistics comes to Bletchley Park

Thus by 1939 most leading statisticians had turned their backs on the Bayesian approach. So why were the cryptanalysts at Bletchley Park so receptive to it? The answer appears to lie in part with the relative lack of formal statistical training and experience on the part of its cryptanalysts.

Alan Mathison Turing (1912–1954) was an undergraduate at King's College Cambridge from 1931 to 1934. His formal training there in probability and statistics was limited to a few lectures by the famous astrophysicist Arthur Stanley Eddington (1882–1944). When Turing submitted a paper in support of his application for a Fellowship at King's, he wrote about what is now known as the 'central limit theorem' of mathematical probability,[15] a choice that reinforces rather than contradicts the impression that statistics was a relatively neglected area. In his lectures, Eddington had given a heuristic proof that the distributions of averages tend to follow closely the well known 'bell-shaped curve'. Turing attempted to make this work rigorous and to extend it, but in the process unwittingly reproduced results then largely already known.[16] The writing of this essay may nevertheless have had an important consequence (besides winning Turing a Fellowship at King's), sensitizing him to possible statistical approaches to problems.[17]

In many ways Bletchley Park was the ideal place for Turing. As Jack Good was to recollect in 1979:

> When [Turing] attacked a problem he liked to start from first principles, and he was rarely influenced by received opinion. This attitude gave depth and originality to his thinking, and also it helped him to choose important problems.[18]

Thus, coming to Bletchley Park (on 4 September 1939, the day after war was declared), Turing was both willing and able to attack a variety of problems essentially *de novo* (one of which, the Naval Enigma, was then generally regarded as being hopelessly resistant to practical solution), drawing upon his limited prior experience in statistics, but using it to very good effect.

Likewise, I. J. (Irving John, 'Jack') Good (1916–2009), who arrived at Bletchley Park on 27 May 1941, had essentially no formal background in probability and statistics. As he was to remember in 1993, 'In Cambridge I didn't attend any lectures on classical statistics ... and only a few by Jeffreys. He was an appalling lecturer in his regular course, so I soon gave up'.[19] At

[14]David L. Banks, 'A Conversation with I. J. Good', *Statistical Science*, 11 (1996), pp. 1–19. The interview itself took place on 23 December 1993.

[15]Alan Mathison Turing, 'On the Gaussian Error Function', King's College Archive Centre, Cambridge, The Papers of Alan Mathison Turing, AMT/C/28. On the Cambridge 'fellowship dissertation', see June Barrow-Green, ''A Corrective to the Spirit of Too Exclusively Pure Mathematics': Robert Smith (1689–1768) and his Prizes at Cambridge University', *Annals of Science*, 56 (1999), pp. 271–316, esp. pp. 295–296.

[16]This summarises S. L. Zabell, 'Alan Turing and the Central Limit Theorem', *American Mathematical Monthly*, 102 (1995), pp. 483–494.

[17]As suggested by Britton in A. M. Turing, *Collected Works of A. M. Turing*, 4 vols., ed. J. L. Britton (Amsterdam: Elsevier, 2001), vol. 2, p. ix.

[18]I. J. Good, 'Early Work on Computers at Bletchley', *Annals of the History of Computing*, 1.1 (1979), pp. 38–48, esp. p. 41. This is a republication of I. J. Good, *Early Work on Computers at Bletchley*, 82, National Physical Laboratory Report Com. Sci., Sept. 1976, which was again republished as I. J. Good, 'Pioneering Work on Computers at Bletchley' in N. Metropolis, J. Howlett and Gian-Carlo Rota, eds., *A History of Computing in the Twentieth Century: A Collection of Essays* (New York: Academic, 1980), pp. 31–45.

[19]Banks, 'Conversation' (see footnote 14, above), p. 17.

Cambridge, Good's main interests lay in analysis, a branch of pure mathematics that deals with continuous quantities and grew out of the effort to provide a rigorous basis for the infinitesimal calculus. As a graduate student his initial research was on simple continued fractions, work which won him the Smith's Prize in 1940, later formed the first part of his doctoral thesis (1941), and was published separately as a paper in 1941.[20] The thesis itself was written under the direction of the famous Cambridge mathematicians A. S. Besicovitch (1891–1970) and G. H. Hardy (1877–1947).[21]

This is not to say that Good had no background at all in statistics; but rather that, like Turing's, it was limited, informal, and unconventional. As Good noted later (in 1993 and 2007), he was familiar with William Allen Whitworth (1840–1905), *Choice and Chance* (Cambridge: Deighton, Bell, 1867), as well as John Maynard Keynes (1883–1946), *Treatise on Probability* (London: Macmillan and Co., 1921) and parts of Harold Jeffreys, *Theory of Probability* (Oxford: Oxford University Press, 1939).[22] These were all interesting and substantial works, but hardly the standard fare of the practising statistician of the day, who would more likely have read Karl Pearson, George Udny Yule (1871–1951), Fisher, and journals such as *Biometrika*.

Bayes comes to Bletchley

Their educational backgrounds mark Turing and Good as outsiders in the study of statistics. There was no obvious tradition into which they had been initiated. But that does not explain why they turned so readily to the Bayesian approach. The explanation seems to lie in the special nature of the problems that confronted the cryptanalysts at Bletchley Park: the problems were very different from those commonly encountered in standard scientific research. Objections to the use of prior subjective information on the grounds that one should instead attempt to collect further data of an objective nature lose their force in situations in which getting more data is not an option, or there is a substantial amount of prior information, or one must make a decision within a limited amount of time. All three circumstances were true of the applications that GCCS encountered in carrying out cryptanalysis under wartime conditions. So the Bayesian approach was indeed a natural one for the cryptanalysts, even if it went against the mainstream statistical orthodoxy. If, for example, you are trying to set the wheels in order to read a specific message, then you are necessarily constrained by the length of the message. That is, in principle you have no other material that uses the same settings so you have to work out what you can from what you have.

As time went on, a substantial body of information about likely message content, language characteristics, and operator usages became available. And reading a message as soon as possible is clearly essential for maximising its intelligence value. In addition, at Bletchley Park the range of alternatives was narrow, and consequently much more like that of a gambling game rather than that of a more general statistical analysis of scientific data, where the range of hypotheses is often ill defined. So people who might be unwilling to think about a prior probability for (say) the number of as-yet-undiscovered planets might be perfectly willing to put a prior probability on the set of possible wheel patterns. To borrow a frequently quoted characterization of statistics, this was indeed a paradigmatic case of 'decision-making in the face of uncertainty'.[23] The cryptanalysts

[20] I. J. Good, 'The Fractional Dimensional Theory of Continued Fractions', *Proc. Camb. Phil. Soc.*, 37 (1941), pp. 199–228.

[21] 'Some points in modern branches of analysis'. Recorded as Ph. D. 1163, 20 February 1941. Good's official Ph.D. supervisor is listed in the University records as John Charles Burkill, but this was likely purely pro forma. Good only mentions Burkill as someone whose lectures he attended (Banks, 'Conversation' (see footnote 14, above), pp. 6–7).

[22] See Banks, 'Conversation' (see footnote 14, above), p. 11 for Keynes and Jeffreys. Good's familiarity with Whitworth is a personal communication from Good to James A. Reeds, 10 December 2007.

[23] M. A. Girshick, Review of M. J. Moroney, *Facts from Figures* (Baltimore, 1951), *Journal of the American Statistical Association*, 58 (1953), pp. 645–647, esp. p. 646, has the earliest instance of this phrase that we are aware of.

at Bletchley Park, confronted with the daily necessity of deciding how to allocate their time in dealing with messages, were in effect forced to act like gamblers and play by the odds.

The Bayes factor

The statistical attack developed by Turing, first for use against Enigma traffic and then later used against Tunny, was based on what Turing called the *factor in favour of the hypothesis* (which in the early twenty-first century is usually called the 'Bayes factor' rather than simply the 'factor').[24] The definition of the factor in section **21(f)** of the *General Report on Tunny* (*GRT*, **21(f)**, TNA HW 25/4, p. 39; this edition, p. 45). The *General Report on Tunny* uses the factor, or its logarithm, on almost every page of its technical sections.

If $O(H)$ denotes the initial odds for an hypothesis H (relative to its negation, $\overline{H}$), and $O(H \mid E)$ denotes the odds after observing evidence E, then Turing's factor is the ratio of the two,

$$\frac{O(H \mid E)}{O(H)} = \frac{P(H \mid E)/P(\bar{H} \mid E)}{P(H)/P(\bar{H})}.$$

It is a measure of how strongly the evidence E supports H versus $\bar{H}$. (More generally, one can define the factor in favour of one hypothesis H_1 versus another H_2 as the ratio of the relative posterior and prior odds for the two, as defined in the first section of this essay.)

As I. J. Good noted in 1979,[25] 'It is an easy but important theorem' that this factor is the same as the likelihood ratio mentioned earlier:

$$\frac{O(H \mid E)}{O(H)} = \frac{P(E \mid H)}{P(E \mid \bar{H})}.$$

This can in fact be viewed as an equivalent form of Bayes' theorem. This was apparently unknown to Turing. In 1993 Good recollected:

> One morning I asked Turing 'Isn't this really Bayes' theorem?' and he said 'I suppose so'. He hadn't mentioned Bayes previously. Now, Harold Jeffreys with Dorothy Wrinch [1894–1976] had previously published the odds form of Bayes' theorem (without the odds terminology and without the sequential aspect), and Turing might have seen their work, but probably he thought of it independently.[26]

It is not hard to reconcile this recollection with the much simpler statement in the *General Report on Tunny* (in 1945) to the effect that 'Good had to tell Turing this was Bayes' Theorem' (*GRT*, **21(f)**, TNA HW 25/4, p. 39; this edition, p. 45).

We may note one very interesting consequence of Good's 'easy but important theorem'. In some circumstances (for example, when the H_i are so-called 'simple' statistical hypotheses), both $P(E \mid H_1)$ and $P(E \mid H_2)$ have agreed, 'objective' values. In this case, although the Bayes factor as defined on the left requires as its inputs 'subjective' probabilities, the likelihood ratio on the right involves only 'objective' ones and can therefore be viewed as an objective measure of support. This point of view is in fact the basis of a school of statistical inference.[27]

[24] See A. M. Turing, 'The Applications of Probability to Cryptography', Unpublished GCCS document. TNA HW 25/37, 1941; Good, 'Early Work on Computers' (see footnote 18, above); and S. L. Zabell, 'Commentary on Alan M. Turing: The Applications of Probability to Cryptography', *Cryptologia*, 36.3 (2012), pp. 191–214.

[25] I. J. Good, 'Studies in the History of Probability and Statistics. XXXVII: A. M. Turing's Statistical Work in World War II', *Biometrika*, 66 (1979), pp. 393–396, esp. p. 393.

[26] Banks, 'Conversation' (see footnote 14, above), p. 11. See also I. J. Good, 'The Contributions of Jeffreys to Bayesian Statistics' in A. Zellner, ed., *Bayesian Analysis in Econometrics and Statistics: Essays in Honor of Harold Jeffreys* (Amsterdam: North-Holland, 1980), pp. 21–34, esp. p. 26. For the work of Wrinch and Jeffreys, see footnote 5 to this essay, above.

[27] See, for example, Ian Hacking, *Logic of Statistical Inference* (Cambridge, 1965), and A. W. F. Edwards, *Likelihood;*

Decibans

One of Turing's basic contributions was his introduction of the *deciban*, which is defined as being ten times the common (or base 10) logarithm of the Bayes factor. (The term was a conscious borrowing of the term decibel (and its abbreviation "db"), as used in acoustics and electrical engineering (I. J. Good, *Probability and the Weighing of Evidence* (London: Griffin, 1950), p. 53).) The authors of the *General Report on Tunny* commented that 'Simple though this idea is, it makes an enormous simplification in practical work' (*GRT*, **21(g)**, TNA HW 25/4, p. 39; this edition, p. 45). The reason for the simplification is easily explained: given multiple independent items of information, the Bayes factor of their conjunction is the product of the individual Bayes factors, so its logarithm is the sum of the logarithms of the individual factors. The example given by the *General Report on Tunny* considers tossing a coin that is either two-headed (H) or fair ($\overline{H}$). If the coin comes up heads once, then the Bayes factor in favour of H is 2, i.e. 3 decibans. If the coin comes up heads 20 times, then this is $3 \times 20 = 60$ decibans. So if the odds were initially 10,000 to 1 against H (that is, -40 decibans), the decibans after are $60 - 40 = 20$ in favour, or odds of 100 to 1 (*GRT, loc. cit.*).[28]

The reason for the specific factor of 10 in the definition reflected an initial judgement regarding useful numerical precision. Curiously, the matter seems not to have been carefully thought through. In his interview with Banks in 1993, Good explained that when he arrived at Bletchley, he found

> They were using decibans (weights of evidence), with one decimal point. So I thought, why don't we drop the decimal point and call the unit a centiban, thus saving a lot of writing. And then I noticed that if we used a half deciban (hdb) [as the basic unit of measurement] we would save much more time in both writing and arithmetic because most of the individual scores would then be single digits...
>
> This must have saved half the time of the work on Banburismus. Of course, every numerical analyst knows that you shouldn't carry more decimal places than you need, in hand calculations, and it was essentially in that spirit that I made this suggestion, but here were these highly intelligent people, who for some weeks had been using the deciban with a decimal point.[29]

This episode reflects an interesting and characteristic aspect of Good's work at Bletchley Park. Despite his background in pure mathematics, he had a pragmatic streak that often proved extremely valuable. Another striking example of this was a contribution to the attack on the Naval Enigma, where Good noticed a practical shortcut to a sophisticated procedure developed by Turing. This shortcut was based on the fact that certain random choices of letters by German Enigma operators were not in fact random. It resulted in quicker solutions with less data.[30]

The statistician's fallacy

The 'statistician's fallacy' of the *General Report on Tunny* refers to confusing or improperly using one conditional probability in place of another. As a simple example, suppose a million lottery tickets are sold. If the lottery is fair (call this event A), then the probability that I will win the lottery (call this event B) is $P(B|A) = 1/1{,}000{,}000$. But this hardly means that if I do in fact win, then the probability of the lottery being fair ($P(A|B)$) is only 1/1,000,000. When it occurs in

An Account of the Statistical Concept of Likelihood and its Application to Scientific Inference, rev. ed. Baltimore, 1992 (London: Cambridge University Press, 1972).

[28] The example is similar to one in I. J. Good, *Probability and the Weighing of Evidence* (London: Griffin, 1950), p. 64.

[29] Banks, 'Conversation' (see footnote 14, above), p. 9.

[30] I. J. Good, 'Turing's Anticipation of Empirical Bayes in Connection with the Cryptanalysis of the Naval Enigma', *J. Statist. Comput. & Simul.*, 66 (2000): *Special Issue*, pp. 101–111, esp. pp. 109–110.

examples this simple, the fallacy seems like an unlikely mistake for someone to make, but in fact it often crops up.

From the statistical point of view, one of the most interesting passages in the *General Report on Tunny* discusses this fallacy and points out the contrast between the Bayesian and 'orthodox' approaches with respect to the Bayes factor $P(E \mid H_1)/P(E \mid H_0)$ (*GRT*, **21(o)**, TNA HW 25/4, p. 44; this edition, p. 48). (The chosen example is the evaluation of the effectiveness of a fertiliser, which suggests that one target of the criticism of the orthodox, non-Bayesian approach was R. A. Fisher, who had at one time worked at the agricultural research station at Rothamsted.)

In a classical test of significance, the hypothesis H_0 is called into question if the statistical evidence E is unlikely to arise under H_0 — that is, if $P(E \mid H_0)$ is small. It is apparent that this ignores the probability in the numerator of the Bayes factor, the probability of E under some competing hypothesis H_1 (or competing hypotheses $H_j, j \geq 1$). This would be particularly inappropriate if E is unlikely under *both* hypotheses, when what is really at issue is the balance of improbabilities. If one is deciding between two or more possibilities, the question is how good each is — relative to each other — in explaining or accounting for the evidence E, and this is precisely the task of the Bayes factor. Although the *General Report on Tunny* acknowledges the utility of conventional tests of significance, it emphasises their inadequacy as a means of estimating the posterior probability $P(H_0 \mid E)$. Using $P(E \mid H_0)$ as a proxy for $P(H_0 \mid E)$ is an instance of 'the statistician's fallacy'.

Initially doing so 'before the deciban had been brought over from Hut 8' sometimes resulted in a loss of valuable time and resources (*GRT*, **21(o)**, TNA HW 25/4, p. 44; this edition, p. 48).

Good moved from Hut 8 to the Newmanry in April 1943, that is, shortly before Heath Robinson became operational (June 1943). It seems likely that either Good or Turing was the person responsible for 'bringing over' the deciban (and more generally the considerable statistical expertise that had been developed by then in Hut 8). Presumably by this stage the statistical effort in Hut 8 had become sufficiently routine that it was thought Good's talents would be better deployed in the Newmanry. The *General Report on Tunny* noted that one of the insights gained after the introduction of Heath Robinson, mentioned as item six in a list of eight 'lessons learnt', was the 'value of using Bayes' theorem rather than [the] orthodox statistical outlook' (*GRT*, **23Z**, TNA HW 25/4, p. 109; this edition, p. 106). This too was presumably due to Good.

Perhaps more than a half of the contents of the technical chapters **22–28** in the *General Report on Tunny* on methods of solution are devoted to estimation of decibanage in various situations, for the purpose of deciding whether to abandon a particular avenue in the attack on a particular message, or even to abandon the message altogether. The entirety of section **24X** is devoted to this, as are many shorter passages scattered throughout these chapters. It is especially clear in the flow chart shown in Chapter **26** (*GRT*, fig. **26(VI)**, TNA HW 25/4, p. 205; this edition, p. 193).

The Operation of Tunny

To see how these ideas were used in Tunny breaking we must turn back to some of the terminology and notation found in the first two chapters of the *General Report on Tunny*, both for how the Tunny machine worked and (in the next section) for how it was broken.

As is explained at the beginning of the *General Report on Tunny*, Tunny enciphered the stream of letters produced by a conventional teleprinter machine. These letters were taken from a conventional alphabet (the *Baudot* or *ITA2* code), consisting of the 32 possible strings of five 0s and 1s. Strictly speaking the 0 and 1 refer to two different electric impulses; GCCS referred to these as *dot* and *cross*, but here we shall for the most part use 0 and 1 because of their use in the particular kind of arithmetic that is relevant here, namely arithmetic modulo two without carrying, in which 0 and 1 are the only numerals used and the rules are that

$$0+0=0$$
$$0+1=1$$
$$1+0=1$$
$$1+1=0.$$

A scheme of letter and figure modes allowed the 26 ordinary letters, the 10 digits, and a handful of punctuation marks to be represented. Details of the representation are supplied in a table near the beginning of the first section of the *General Report on Tunny* (*GRT*, **11**, TNA HW 25/4, p. 3; this edition, p. 7).

Tunny's mechanism produced a stream of key letters which were added to the letters in the plain text stream to produce the corresponding cipher text letters, which were transmitted over the air. In the *General Report on Tunny* the notation for this was $Z = P + K$, where Z, P, and K denote the corresponding cipher text, plain text, and key letters, or, somewhat ambiguously, the ongoing streams of such letters. The addition was bitwise — that is, each of the five channels of impulses that made up a letter was treated separately, the addition being modulo two (which follows the rules given above). So, for example, if P is 11000 (the letter A) and K is 10010 (the letter D), then Z is 01010 (the letter R):

$$P: 11000 \quad (\mathtt{A})$$
$$K: 10010 \quad (\mathtt{D})$$
$$Z: 01010 \quad (\mathtt{R}).$$

Note the reciprocal nature of such a key: since $X + X = 00000$ for any letter X, if $Z = P + K$, then $P = Z + K$. This feature means that the same key is used to both encrypt and decrypt; whatever setting the sender uses to encrypt plain text, the receiver also uses to decrypt the incoming cipher text.

The key stream in Tunny consisted of the sum of two parts, a *chi* key and an (extended) *psi* key:

$$K = \chi + \psi', \qquad Z = \chi + \psi' + P.$$

The five bits in both ψ' and χ were each generated by five wheels: the chi wheels, generating five bit streams $\chi_i (1 \leq i \leq 5)$, and the psi wheels, generating five bit streams $\psi'_j (1 \leq j \leq 5)$:

$$\chi = \chi_1\chi_2\chi_3\chi_4\chi_5, \qquad \psi' = \psi'_1\psi'_2\psi'_3\psi'_4\psi'_5.$$

Each of these wheels can be pictured as having a circular pattern of 0s and 1s (set by cams). At any given time on each wheel precisely one of these bits is in an *operative* position and is the bit used. After encryption (or decryption) of a letter, the wheels either advance one or not, so that the next cam is in the operative position, and a new letter of key ready to be used.

The chi wheels exhibited *regular* motion; that is, after encryption of a letter, all five of them advanced in unison. The *lengths* of the five chi wheels (that is, the number of cams or 0s and 1s along it) were

Wheel:	χ_1	χ_2	χ_3	χ_4	χ_5
Length:	41	31	29	26	23 .

Since the lengths are relatively prime, the overall period (number of letter encryptions until all five wheels are back to exactly the same setting) is very large: $41 \times 31 \times 29 \times 26 \times 23 = 22{,}041{,}682$.

By contrast, the five psi wheels stepped *irregularly*. Their lengths were

Wheel:	ψ_1	ψ_2	ψ_3	ψ_4	ψ_5
Length:	43	47	51	53	59 .

These lengths are also relatively prime to each other, and to those of the chi wheels as well. Unlike the chi wheels, the psi wheels sometimes did not step and sometimes did (but when they stepped, all five stepped), whenever a letter was enciphered. This irregular stepping was controlled by another part of Tunny's mechanism, called *total motor* by the cryptanalysts (*GRT*, **11B(f)–11B(j)**, TNA HW 25/4, p. 7; this edition, p. 12). The details of this mechanism, which are somewhat complicated, differed slightly with different models of the Tunny machine, and also depended on the method of use. (Two more wheels, the *motor wheels* μ_{37} and μ_{61}, were involved.)

Luckily, we do not need to know any of the details to understand the basic functioning of the machine, except to remark that the number of dots (0s) on the μ_{37} wheel (its *dottage*, d) affected the average rate of stepping: the bigger d was, the less often the ψ wheels stepped on average. The output of the psi wheels when irregularly stepped this way was termed the ψ' stream, the *extended psi*. Two successive letters in the ψ' stream might differ if the total motor had caused the psi wheels to step, but could not differ if the psi wheels did not step.

Taking all *twelve* wheels into consideration, because all twelve lengths are relatively prime, the overall period of the machine is a superficially impressive

$$22,041,682 \times 61 \times 37 \times 322,303,017 = 16,033,955,073,056,318,658.$$

Such large numbers appear to have played a major role in misleading the German cryptanalysts into thinking the machine was secure.

Security

The cryptographer's goal is to generate a cipher stream that completely disguises the underlying plain text; in the case of an additive cipher like Tunny this means making the key K appear as random as possible. The one-time pad in fact does precisely this: it consists of a randomly generated key to be used just once. Such a cipher, although in principle impregnable to even the most imaginative attack, suffers from a number of practical limitations, and usually some compromise with the dictates of complete security is made.

Cipher systems that use periodically generated key — sometimes called Vigenère ciphers after Blaise de Vigenère (1523–1596), author of a book on cryptography[31] — were known in the sixteenth century, and by the nineteenth century it was recognised that the security of such systems depended on their cycle being long (ideally, at least as long as the message being enciphered). This was the reason for not using just the chi wheels in Tunny. Although their overall period was 22,041,682, much longer than any intercepted message, the period of an individual chi wheel was much shorter (at most 41). Since the plain text showed statistical biases at the bit level as well as the letter level, bit encipherment by a single wheel was vulnerable for the same reason as the Vigènere cipher.

Suppose, for example, one had a machine that only added the output of the chi wheels, and one examines the first impulses of the cipher letters (that is, $Z_1 = P_1 + \chi_1$). If the output is written out on a *width* of 41, the length of χ_1 (that is, in a rectangular display where the first row consists of the first 41 impulses, the second row the next 41 impulses, and so on), then in each column *the same* χ_1 bit (0 or 1) is added to the initial bits of the plain text letters. As a result the output cipher bits will have either the same or the opposite bias as the plain text bits, depending on whether χ_1 is 0 or 1. Since Tunny messages were often thousands of letters long — a length presumably taken

[31] Blaise de Vigenère, *Traicté des chiffres, ou secretes manieres d'escrire* (Paris: Abel L'Angelier, 1586). Vigenère had not invented the form of cipher described; his name became attached to it in the nineteenth century.

into account by the German cryptographers — the direction of the bias would be evident and one could just read off the pattern of bits on a wheel. Such a machine would be completely useless.

Compound cyclic keys, such as in the Morehouse and Hitt teleprinter machines, were also known to be inadequate.[32] (The Hitt machine, for instance, which can be thought of as a Tunny machine with regularly stepping chi and psi wheels, was solved with ease by the SIS, the Signal Intelligence Service, a U.S. Army predecessor of the American NSA, in the 1930s.[33]) Suppose, for example, one has two regularly stepping wheels, α and β, having relatively prime lengths L and M, and these are added successively to a plain text impulse: $Z = P + \alpha + \beta$. The effect would be the same as adding the output of a single, virtual wheel of length LM. Although the task of *breaking* the wheels (determining the pattern of bits on them) would be much more challenging, it may still be relatively straightforward to set the wheels (determine the initial setting used to encrypt a message): one just tries (as discussed later) the LM different possible settings and scores for bias in either direction. In fact the prototype of the SZ 40 had just such a design: it consisted of five pairs of regularly stepping wheels with relatively prime lengths — in effect, five chi wheels and five regularly stepping psi wheels. But this design was rejected precisely because the Germans recognised the inherent weakness just discussed.[34]

The insecure prototype was modified to introduce an element of irregular motion. Two motor wheels, μ_{37} and μ_{61}, were introduced: μ_{61} induced irregular motion in μ_{37}, and μ_{37} induced irregular motion in the psi wheels. The μ_{61} stepped regularly; depending on whether its active bit was 1 or 0, μ_{37} did or did not advance. The output of the μ_{37} was termed the *basic motor*, and in the SZ 40 it determined whether or not the psi wheels advanced.

It is apparent that the German cryptographers regarded the element of irregular motion that the μ wheels introduced as key to the security of the entire device. First, Tunny messages were limited to being no more than 20,000 letters long, based in part on considerations regarding the overall period of the μ wheels.[35] Second, unlike the chi and psi wheels, whose patterns were only changed every month until late 1944, the patterns of the μ wheels were changed every day (*GRT*, **11D(e)**, TNA HW 25/4, p. 14; this edition, p. 19).[36] Finally, the security enhancements in the later models SZ 42 A and SZ 42 B added to the irregularity induced by the μ wheels (*GRT*, **11B(j)**, TNA HW 25/4, p. 10; this edition, p. 14, and generally **11B(g)–(j)**).[37]

[32]The Morehouse machine: 'Ciphering System', U.S. Patent 1,356,546, 26 October 1920; it used two loops of punched tape, of unequal length, to produce a key stream. The Hitt machine: 'Ciphering and Deciphering Apparatus', U.S. Patent 1,848,291, 8 March 1932.

[33]For a first-hand account, see Frank B. Rowlett, *The Story of Magic: Memoirs of an American Cryptologic Pioneer* (Laguna Hills, Calif.: Aegean Park Press, 1998), pp. 66–67, 70–74. On the historical connections between Hitt's machine and the Lorenz SZ 40 ('Tunny') machine see the Editors' Introduction, this volume, p. xxv above.

[34]The initial design and subsequent strengthening of the SZ 40 (to the SZ 42 A and SZ 42 B) is described in Dr. Erich Hüttenhain and Sonderführer Dr. Walther Fricke, 'OKW/Chi Cryptanalytic Research on Enigma, Hagelin and Cypher Teleprinter Machines', 1 Aug. 1945, URL: `https://sites.google.com/site/ticomarchive/the-targets/okw-chi/related-reports` (visited on 07/06/2014), FOIA release of TICOM document I-45, NSA DOCID: 3422500, pp. 16–19. (A photocopy of this report is in the library of the National Cryptologic Museum, Ft. Meade, Maryland.) Dr. Hüttenhain (1905–1990) was the chief cryptanalyst of OKW/Chi, *Oberkommando der Wehrmacht/Chiffrierabteilung*, the signals intelligence and communications security organisation of the German High Command, and Dr. Fricke (1915–1988) worked in OKW/Chi Referat IIb, the desk responsible for the production of German military codes, ciphers, and keys. After the war, Hüttenhain became chief cryptanalyst for the Gehlen Organization, and was later (1956–1970) head of the Federal Republic of Germany's *Zentralstelle für das Chiffrierwesen* ('German Cipher Board') in Bad Godesberg; see generally Friedrich L. Bauer, 'Erich Hüttenhain: Entzifferung 1939–1945', *Informatik Spektrum*, 31 (2008), pp. 249–261.

[35]Hüttenhain and Fricke, 'NSA TICOM I-45' (see footnote 34, above), p. 18. The 1 December 1942 *Wehrmacht* regulations covering the use of the SZ 40 machine specified maximum message length of 20,000; see the editorial endnote 30 to *GRT*, **11D(b)**, p. 571 below.

[36]Hüttenhain and Fricke, 'NSA TICOM I-45' (see footnote 34, above), p. 17; Copeland, *Colossus* (see footnote 2, above), p. 48.

[37]See also Hüttenhain and Fricke, 'NSA TICOM I-45' (see footnote 34, above), p. 19; I. J. Good, Donald Michie and Geoffrey Timms, 'The Motor-Wheels and Limitations', Appendix 10 in Copeland, *Colossus* (see footnote 2, above), pp. 406–408.

Nevertheless, even this final design adopted by the Germans remained fatally flawed. As the U.S. Army Security Agency noted in an internal report in 1946:

> None of these ruses succeeded in preventing Anglo-American cryptanalysis, since the attack was to ignore temporarily the irregularly-moving wheels, and to remove the effects of the regularly-moving wheels first. This made attack on the irregularly-moving wheels possible. The Germans had evolved elaborate protection for the *wrong end* of their machine.[38]

The issue of why the Germans never fully recognised the insecurity of their machines is discussed at length in this U.S. Army Security Agency document. It summarises the key findings of a long series of classified reports issued by TICOM, the 'Target Intelligence Committee', an Anglo-American organisation set up towards the end of the war, tasked with acquiring German cryptologic assets. This question is also addressed in a book published in 2006.[39] Both accounts point to serious dysfunctional elements in the organisation of the German signals intelligence and communications security agencies. Indeed, this was recognised by many of the German cryptologists themselves, some of whom voiced frustrations about this in their postwar TICOM interviews.

The attack on Tunny

As we have seen, the structure of Tunny encryption can be summarised as

$$P \to \chi + \psi' + P.$$

The decryption of Tunny at Bletchley Park proceeded in two stages: first χ was removed (the task of the Newmanry), then ψ' (the task of the Testery). This division of labour reflected a difference in the tasks. As the *General Report on Tunny* remarks: 'In general Testery methods were hand methods based on language properties, and Newmanry methods were statistical and needed machines' (*GRT*, **14A(c)**, TNA HW 25/4, p. 29; this edition, p. 36).

The basic flaw of Tunny was that, for reasons to be explained in detail shortly, ψ' was not unbiased, but in fact exhibited considerable statistical regularities. In principle, biases in plain text and key might cancel one another out, but in this case the nature of the ψ' bias meant that the sum $\psi' + P$ (termed *de-chi* or D) was still biased, although not as biased as the original plain text P, and therefore vulnerable to statistical attack.

Newmanry methods were inherently statistical because one was looking for the statistically biased D stream present but hidden in cipher; Testery methods were inherently linguistic because one was looking for the underlying plain text present but hidden in the D stream.

Turingery: The crack in the door

It was natural that the German cryptographers sought to ensure 'an equal number of dots and crosses in each impulse of the chi-stream and the extended psi-stream' (*GRT*, **11C(a)(2)**, TNA HW 25/4, p. 11; this edition, p. 16). But a balance of 0s and 1s in a bit stream does not ensure

[38] United States Army Security Agency, *European Axis Signal Intelligence in World War II as Revealed by 'TICOM' Investigations and by other Prisoner of War Interrogations and Captured Material, Principally German*, FOIA release of 9-volume typescript report (Washington, D.C., 1946), URL: `http://www.nsa.gov/public_info/declass/european_axis_sigint.shtml` (visited on 07/06/2014), vol. 2, 21–22. (A copy of this report is on deposit in the library of the National Cryptologic Museum, Ft. Meade, Maryland.)

[39] R. A. Ratcliff, *Delusions of Intelligence: Enigma, Ultra, and the End of Secure Ciphers* (Cambridge: Cambridge University Press, 2006).

equality in the bit stream that can be derived from it by taking successive first differences; that is, the differences (or equivalently in the case of mod two addition, sums) of two successive impulses in a stream. For example, consider the sequence 01010101 ... , whose successive pairwise sums form the sequence 1111111 ... . That is, the sum of the first two impulses, $0+1$, is 1; the sum of the second and third impulses, $1+0$, is 1, and so on.

The *General Report on Tunny* uses Δ to denote the result of taking the first difference of a stream. For the purpose of statistical analysis, one may also examine this difference stream Δ, so that as well as looking at χ and ψ' one can consider $\Delta\chi$ and $\Delta\psi'$. (For example, there are two (but only two) sequences that can have a given difference stream (Δ). If Δ at the first position is 0, one knows that the second bit is the same as the first. If Δ at the second position is 0, one knows that the third bit is the same as the second. If Δ at the third position is 1, one knows that the fourth bit is the complement of the third. Thus if the Δ stream is 001 there are two possibilities for the first four bits. If the first bit is 0, the first four bits are 0001; if the first bit is 1, they are 1110.) The realisation that working at the level of the derived Δ-stream (rather than the original bit stream) provides an extremely useful way of analysing Tunny output was an important insight of Turing; its use is referred to in the *General Report on Tunny* as *Turing's method*, or *Turingery* (*GRT*, **43B**, TNA HW 25/5, p. 313; this edition, p. 298).

The German cryptographers had specified that all four of the streams $\chi, \Delta\chi, \psi'$, and $\Delta\psi'$ should each appear to be as nearly random looking as was permitted by the overall design of the SZ machine. In practice this meant striving for equal numbers of 2-long patterns, 00, 01, 10 and 11 on each of the χ and ψ' streams individually. We shall see how well they fared when the streams are considered in combination.

Enforcing such an equality in the case of the $\Delta\psi'$ involves a constraint. Let a denote the proportion of crosses (1s) in the total motor stream (which determined whether or not the psi wheels advanced), and b the proportion of crosses in the $\Delta\psi$ stream. Then it is easy to see that the proportion of crosses in the $\Delta\psi'$ stream is ab. (The ψ stream must advance, which requires a cross, and the resulting advance in the $\Delta\psi$ — and therefore the $\Delta\psi'$ — stream must result in a cross.) Thus in order to have an equality of dots and crosses in the $\Delta\psi'$-stream requires 'the law' $ab = 1/2$ (*GRT*, **22D(a)**, TNA HW 25/4, p. 48; this edition, p. 53).

The initial failure of the German cryptographers to impose this constraint was a security flaw that meant that on an appropriate width (corresponding to the length of a chi wheel) the columns of cipher would display a non-uniform distribution of 0*s* and 1*s*, permitting an insight into the structure of the machine. But even after a belated security upgrade, the Germans left a serious defect in the machine: *because the* ψ *wheels advance in unison when they do advance*, the *joint* distribution of the five $\Delta\psi'$ impulses remained non-uniform. For example, one has

$$\begin{aligned}
P(\Delta\psi_i' = \bullet, \Delta\psi_j' = \bullet) &= (1-a) + a(1-b)^2,\\
P(\Delta\psi_i' = \bullet, \Delta\psi_j' = \times) &= ab(1-b),\\
P(\Delta\psi_i' = \times, \Delta\psi_j' = \bullet) &= ab(1-b),\\
P(\Delta\psi_i' = \times, \Delta\psi_j' = \times) &= ab^2.
\end{aligned}$$

It is easy to see that one cannot find values for a and b that make these four probabilities equal and still preserve irregular motion. (For uniformity we should require each of these to have probability $1/4$. But if $ab^2 = 1/4$ and $ab = 1/2$, then $b = 1/2$ and therefore $a = 1$; that is, the total motor is always cross and the ψ wheels always advance, which defeats the goal of irregular motion.)

The recognition and exploitation of such weaknesses in a cryptographic system was entirely standard at the time; the apparent complaisance of the German communications security experts must have reflected a judgement on their part that this insecurity could not be exploited.

Wheel setting

> The fundamental problem in chi-setting from a theoretical point of view is ... to estimate the decibanage in favour of the χ's being correct (*GRT*, **22Y**, TNA HW 25/4, p. 76; this edition, p. 78).

In wheel setting, the patterns of the twelve wheels are known, and the task is to find the particular settings of the wheels used to send a message. Although every individual impulse of the D stream was effectively random, combinations of two or more impulses were not, and this formed the basis of the attack, which was directed against *pairs* of wheels. The initial attack was on two χ wheels, usually χ_1 and χ_2, and was termed the *1+2–break-in*. This form of attack was discovered by William Tutte in November 1942 (*GRT*, **15A(a)**, TNA HW 25/4, p. 33; this edition, p. 39).[40] In 2002 Good pointed out that the 1 + 2 attack was successful despite the fact that these two wheels were the longest: although other pairs took less run time, they exhibited less bias — that is, departure from randomness — and were less likely to succeed.[41]

Using our earlier notation, the problem can be cast as follows: if E denotes the encrypted message, and $H_i, 1 \leq i \leq 1271$, the different settings of the first two chi wheels, then the problem is to determine the posterior probabilities

$$P(H_i \mid E),$$

that is, how likely each of the different possible settings is given the content of the encrypted message. In favourable situations one of these probabilities will be much larger than any of the others and the cryptanalyst will feel confident enough that the actual settings are known to proceed to the next stage in the attack. Once the settings for the first two chi wheels were determined, the three other chi wheels could then be attacked, bootstrapping off this, until finally the settings for all five were known.

The statistical vulnerability

Let $\Delta\chi_{12}$ denote the result of the mod two addition of the $\Delta\chi$-streams for χ_1 and χ_2:

$$\Delta\chi_{12} = \Delta\chi_1 + \Delta\chi_2.$$

Similarly, let ΔZ_{12} denote the result of mod two addition of Δ-cipher for the first two bits (that is, in the positions corresponding to χ_1 and χ_2), and similarly for $\Delta\psi'_{12}$ and ΔP_{12}. These quantities satisfy the relation

$$\Delta Z_{12} = \Delta\chi_{12} + \Delta\psi'_{12} + \Delta P_{12}.$$

The statistical vulnerability of Tunny resides entirely in the fact that the sum $\Delta\psi'_{12} + \Delta P_{12}$ *exhibits a bias* (or, more generally, that the sum $\Delta\psi'_{ij} + \Delta P_{ij}$ exhibits a bias).

To understand how chi wheel setting was done at Bletchley Park, consider the initially unobservable quantity

$$\Delta D_{12} = \Delta\psi'_{12} + \Delta P_{12}$$

(involving the de-chi, or D). We can then express the equation connecting Δ-cipher and Δ-plain text as

$$\Delta Z_{12} = \Delta\chi_{12} + \Delta D_{12}.$$

[40] See also William T. Tutte, 'Fish and I' in W. D. Joyner, ed., *Coding Theory and Cryptography: From Enigma and Geheimschreiber to Quantum Theory* (Berlin: Springer, 2000), pp. 9–17, URL: `http://math.uwaterloo.ca/combinatorics-and-optimization/sites/ca.combinatorics-and-optimization/files/uploads/files/corr98-39.pdf` (visited on 07/06/2014).

[41] I. J. Good, 'From Hut 8 to the Newmanry' in Copeland, *Colossus* (see footnote 2, above), pp. 204–222, esp. p. 216.

In principle, finding the settings of χ_1 and χ_2 is straightforward. There are a total of $31 \times 41 = 1271$ possible settings of the first two wheels, and one can try each of these in turn by adding the resulting $\Delta\chi_{12}$ to the cipher ΔZ_{12} to produce a candidate ΔD_{12} stream. In the single correct case the $\Delta\chi_{12}$ cancels out and the sum exhibits the bias characteristic of ΔD_{12}, but in the 1270 incorrect cases the candidate does not. The statistical problem is therefore: given a large number of sequences of 0s and 1s, to recognise the one sequence exhibiting a bias.

The frequentist approach

Whether it is possible to identify the bias successfully necessarily depends on the values of several quantities: the size of the bias, the length of the message, and the number of competing incorrect settings. For ΔD_{12}, the frequency of crosses in a favourable case might be around 55%. Since the length of a Tunny message could be (at least when using the SZ 40) up to 20,000 letters long (see editorial endnote 30 to section **11D(b)** of the *General Report on Tunny*, p. 571 below), and in any case was often several thousand, setting the chi wheels in favourable cases could be a simple matter. For example, if there are $n = 10,000$ letters in a message, one expects to see about 5,500 0s in the putative de-chi if one is using the correct setting, versus 5,000 if one is using an incorrect setting. If one takes the midpoint 5,250 as a threshold (if above, guess correct; if below, guess incorrect), then one is virtually certain to guess correctly: there is less than one chance in three and a half million of guessing wrong in either direction (i.e., misclassifying an incorrect setting as correct, or *vice versa*).

There is, however, an important complication here: what is at stake is not a comparison of just two settings, but of one correct and 1,270 incorrect ones. Consider a situation less favourable to the cryptanalyst than the one above, by assuming we see a message of length $n = 1,000$ letters. Now one expects approximately 500 0s if the two wheels are set incorrectly, and 550 if the two wheels are set correctly. If as before one takes the midpoint, here 525, to classify a setting as correct or incorrect, then approximately 5.3% of the 1270 incorrect settings will be tagged as correct. Thus almost inevitably some incorrect settings will pass the test; on average, we can expect about 60. Such considerations also enter in for wheel-breaking. For Tunny, message lengths in excess of 4,000 were necessary for wheel breaking to be successful (*GRT*, **12C(e)**, TNA HW 25/4, p. 20; this edition, p. 27).

This issue is addressed in the *General Report on Tunny* in the course of its discussion of the statistician's fallacy (*GRT*, **21(o)**, TNA HW 25/4, p. 43; this edition, p. 48), and the example given there illustrates the limitations of proceeding within a straight 'test of significance' framework. A more promising strategy would be to compute the 1271 likelihoods $P(E \mid H_i)$, where E denotes the text of the encrypted message, and $H_i, 1 \leq i \leq 1271$, the 1271 different hypotheses as to the setting of the first two chi wheels, using the resulting values to order the different possible settings in terms of decreasing likelihood. The problem with this approach is that although it gives an *ordering* of the settings (this is the most likely, try it first, this is the next most likely, try it next, and so on), it gives no sense as to *how likely* any given setting is to be right. This is a real problem in a situation — as here — where the correctness or incorrectness of a candidate is not immediately obvious: if one is wrong, then one spends a considerable amount of time trying to set the remaining chi wheels, as it were, spinning one's wheels, and even potentially sending on erroneous chi wheel settings to the Testery. What is needed instead is some assurance that a given setting is not merely the most likely to be correct in relative terms, but is indeed likely to be correct in absolute terms. There are, after all, many messages; why waste time on borderline cases?

The Bayesian approach

It is precisely at this point that the key role of Bayesian methods at Bletchley Park becomes apparent: it provides a means of incorporating information so as to obtain an estimate of how likely the top ranking setting is to be correct. Even if a cipher text E is most likely for a particular setting H (that is, H maximises $P(E \mid H)$), it may not make sense to pursue that setting if $P(H \mid E)$ is insufficiently large (especially if there are other, more promising messages in the queue).

In its pre-Good days the Newmanry ignored such Bayesian considerations, sometimes with unfortunate consequences. The *General Report on Tunny* describes an interesting instance of this:

> An example of this from our work is given by the score on a $1+2$ break-in. Suppose the best score is 4σ without serious rivals. 4σ or better occurs at random once in $30,000$ experiments so it would be natural to imagine that the odds of the setting given are $30,000$ divided by 1271 or $23:1$ on. In fact they are more like $3:1$ on, (that is, even after a factor has been set against all the other settings due to the existence of no serious rival), though the odds depend to a reasonable extent on the particular link and length of tape and d. In the very early days of the section there was a tendency to continue with a message for some time if it gave a 4σ, since it was not believed that the odds could be much below $20:1$ on. This was before the deciban had been brought over from Hut 8 (*GRT*, **21(o)**, TNA HW 25/4, p. 44; this edition, p. 48).

This brief paragraph, buried in a section containing a review of basic concepts in probability and some technical results, is vital to understanding the entire philosophy of the Bayesian attack on Tunny. Let N denote the message length and let p denote the fraction of 0s in de-chi corresponding to a given dottage and link. (Recall the 'dottage' is the number of dots (0s) on the μ_{37} wheel.) If X is the number of 0s (i.e., dots) in the resulting de-chi message when a putative setting H has been used to strip off chi, then the assumption is that X has a binomial distribution with parameters N, p (that is, as if you toss a coin with probability p of heads a total of N times) if H is correct, and parameters $N, 1/2$ if incorrect. That is, the probability that the random quantity X assumes a specific value k for a given messages is, in the two cases,

$$P(X=k) = \binom{N}{k} p^k (1-p)^{N-k}, \qquad P(X=k) = \binom{N}{k} \left(\frac{1}{2}\right)^N,$$

respectively.

The expected value of a quantity having a binomial distribution with parameters $N, 1/2$ is $N/2$; its standard deviation $\sigma = \sqrt{N/4}$. Thus the score X exceeds its expected value by at least 4σ if $X \geq N/2 + 4\sqrt{N/4}$; and using the normal approximation, one finds that such an outcome has, as indicated in the *General Report on Tunny*, a probability of approximately 0.003. Since there are 1270 incorrect settings, the overall chance that at least one of these will hit the 4σ threshold is about 1270×0.0032 or 0.04, or odds of approximately 23 to 1. Thus it is relatively uncommon for one of the incorrect settings to result in a 4σ result. So if precisely one of the 1271 candidates results in a 4σ score, it would seem natural not only to expect that it would represent the correct setting, but that in fact this would be fairly likely.

However, viewing the matter from a Bayesian perspective puts an entirely different light on the matter. The question is not just how unlikely it is for a random stream of 0s and 1s to result in a 4σ result, but how strong the evidence is in favour of a given setting. If $H_j, 1 \leq j \leq 1271$ are the 1271 possible settings, and X_j denotes the score for H_j (that is, the number of 0s using the H_j setting to strip off de-chi), and $q = 1 - p$, then it is not hard to see that the posterior probability in favour of a specific setting H_i is, assuming all settings are initially regarded as equally likely,

$$P(H_i \mid X_1, \ldots, X_{1271}) = \frac{(p/q)^{X_i}}{\sum_{j=1}^{1271} (p/q)^{X_j}}.$$

Note that this quantity depends not only explicitly on p but also on N via the values of the X_j.

To take a specific example: suppose $N = 1080$, and $p = 0.55$, this value for p representing a fairly favourable circumstance. (As in, for instance, the letter count data exhibited in *GRT*, fig. **12(II)**, TNA HW 25/4, p. 21; this edition, p. 28.) Then a 4σ result would be a score of 606 or greater. Suppose now that H_i is the true setting, and $X_i = 606$. Then the posterior probability will depend on the remaining 1270 values of X_j, and is therefore random, since these X_j are random. The expected value of the expression can be found in principle by computation, but on a twenty-first-century electronic computer it is relatively simple to determine its value by a brute-force Monte Carlo simulation: in an experiment involving 1,000 trials, on average the posterior odds in favour of H_i based on a score of $X_i = 606$ came out as 2.97.

This result lends support to the assertion in the passage quoted above (from *GRT*, **21(o)**, TNA HW 25/4, p. 44; this edition, p. 48) that the odds are about 3 to 1, rather than the 23 to 1 of the statistician's fallacy. Of course, as the *General Report on Tunny* indicates, 'the odds depend to a reasonable extent on the particular link and length of tape and *d*': the link affects the plain text (and hence ΔP_{ij}), the dottage affects $\Delta\psi'_{ij}$ (these being the two components of ΔD_{ij}), and the message length affects the separation between X_i, the score of the true setting, and X_j, the score of the incorrect settings. For example, if one retains the value $p = .55$, but cuts the message length down to $N = 500$ (too short a message to be useful for setting), then the average posterior odds in favour of a 4σ result are 2 to 1 *against*! This is not really paradoxical: the message is so short that a 4σ result is unlikely for either the correct or an incorrect setting. On the other hand, if the message length is $N = 2,542$ (two 1271 periods), then there is more than enough information and the average posterior odds are approximately 28 to 1.

The vulnerability of the SZ 40 prototype revisited

Now we can see in retrospect the vulnerability of *motorless Tunny* — that is, Tunny with chi and psi wheels but without irregular stepping. Consider the two cases of

$$\Delta Z_{ij} = \Delta\chi_{ij} + \Delta D_{ij} \qquad \text{and} \qquad Z_i = (\chi_i + \psi_i) + P_i;$$

these represent the two cases of standard and motorless Tunny, respectively. In both cases one has a key of roughly the same periodicity (ranging from 598 to 1271 in the case of $\Delta\chi_{ij}$ and 1357 to 1763 in the case of $\chi_i + \psi_i$, approximately an order of magnitude smaller than the longest messages that were sent) added to an input (ΔD_{ij} and P_i, respectively) exhibiting statistical bias. From a *qualitative* standpoint there is really no difference between the two. An attack on the one in principle can function just as well as an attack on the other. (Note that in the case of motorless Tunny there is no need to resort to Turingery and take the Δ differences, since these are designed to accentuate the zeros that occur in the irregularly stepping case.) Of course the specifics of the attack (which wheels to attack first, how long a message has to be in order to be vulnerable, and so on) will differ in the two cases. What, in retrospect, is both amusing and puzzling is that the Germans did not notice that the addition of irregular but synchronised stepping does not really change the nature of the vulnerability — it merely shifts it.

In view of how much historians of the work done at Bletchley Park have relied upon reminiscences, with greatest authority being ascribed to reminiscences by protagonists, it is of concern that the assessment of the SZ 40 machines given by Good and Michie in 2002 differs so markedly from that given here.[42] They state then that 'motorless Tunny would have been better than the actual Tunny'[43] and 'if the motor-wheels had been omitted from the German design, it is

[42] I. J. Good and Donald Michie, 'Motorless Tunny', Appendix 11 in Copeland, *Colossus* (see footnote 2, above), pp. 409–410.

[43] *Op. cit.*, p. 410 (words by Good).

overwhelmingly probable that Tunny would never have been broken'.[44] But for the reasons just discussed (as well as the ability of the SIS to break the Hitt machine and OKW/Chi's very justified concerns about the security of their prototype), these statements seem hard to justify. Perhaps after the passage of some sixty years both Good and Michie were remembering the vulnerability that the irregular but synchronised stepping introduced (which could have been eliminated by having each wheel step irregularly but asynchronously, as was the case for *T52 (Sturgeon)* — the Siemens *Geheimschreiber* — the other teleprinter encryption system used by the German military), and not the vulnerability its designers were all too aware of, and attempted to remove.[45]

Motorless Tunny would also have been vulnerable to the attacks used to *break* the wheels. Those attacks, as will be discussed shortly, depended on the fact that $\Delta\chi_{ij}$ is a sum of two wheel impulses ($\Delta\chi_i + \Delta\chi_j$), and the same is of course also the case for motorless Tunny, when $K_i = \chi_i + \psi_i$.

Breaking the chi wheels

> The general idea of convergence of a 1+2 rectangle is to find wheels χ_1, χ_2 which agree as well as possible with the entries in the cells of the rectangles (*GRT*, **24C(a)**, TNA HW 25/4, p. 120; this edition, p. 116).

In the much more challenging task of breaking the chi wheels (that is, determining the patterns of 0s and 1s on them), the initial attack was ordinarily on the two longest, χ_1 and χ_2 (*GRT*, **24A(b)**, TNA HW 25/4, p. 114; this edition, p. 110). Once these wheels were broken, the others could then also be attacked, until finally the pin patterns for all five chi wheels were found. The attack on χ_1 and χ_2 proceeded by first computing a *rectangle* based on the sequence of letters in a single message, a tedious process if done by hand; the wheel patterns were then found by an iterative process called *converging the rectangle*.

Rectangling

If the first wheel is in position i and the second wheel in position j, let us say the pair of wheels is in position ij. After a letter is enciphered, each wheel advances by one, so if the pair starts in position ij, then after t letters are enciphered, the pair is then in position $i+t, j+t$, addition being understood as modulo the length of each wheel. This can be shown in a diagram: given an 31×41 array of cells, if one starts out in cell ij, then as encipherment proceeds, one marches diagonally down the cells, the opposite edges of the rectangle being identified in torus-like fashion.

Consider a hypothetical pair of wheels of lengths 3 and 5, and suppose one has the following pattern (the sides denoting the two wheel patterns, the entries in the rectangle the sum of the side values):

	1	1	0	1	0
0	1	1	0	1	0
1	0	0	1	0	1
0	1	1	0	1	0

Note that in those rows where the first wheel is 0, one sees the pattern of the second wheel; and in those rows where the first wheel is 1, one sees the complement of the pattern. Thus there are just two possible rows, one the actual wheel pattern and the other its complement.

[44] *Op. cit.*, p. 409 (words by Michie).

[45] See Frode Weierud, 'Bletchley Park's Sturgeon — The Fish that Laid No Eggs', *The Rutherford Journal: The New Zealand Journal for the History and Philosophy of Science and Technology*, 1 (Dec. 2005), URL: `http://www.rutherfordjournal.org/article010106.html` (visited on 07/06/2014).

Suppose now that we did not know the two wheel patterns but only the entries in an empirical rectangle of actual counts in a message. Then the rows would provide precisely two complementary candidates for the pattern of the second wheel; and although we do not know which is in fact the correct pattern, each necessarily determines in turn the pattern of the other wheel (and the resulting two possibilities for the other wheel would themselves be complementary). Thus in this simple case the pair of wheel patterns is known up to complement. Furthermore, this is the best we can do: since χ_{12}, the sum of the first two impulses, equals both $\chi_1 + \chi_2$ and $\overline{\chi}_1 + \overline{\chi}_2$ (where $\overline{\chi}_i$ denotes the complement of χ_i), replacing the two wheels by their complementary wheels results in the same rectangle, so it is impossible to distinguish between the two possibilities on the basis of the rectangle.

In sum, if one saw the entries of the rectangle, one would know the two wheel patterns up to complement. The problem, of course, is that we do not get to see χ_{12} by itself, but rather Z_{12}, which is χ_{12} obscured by the addition of the corresponding de-chi stream D_{12} (which was discussed under 'The statistical vulnerability' above).

Exactly the same considerations apply if we work at the level of the Δ wheels $\Delta\chi_1, \Delta\chi_2$, and $\Delta\chi_{12}$; and exactly the same problem exists: we do not see $\Delta\chi_{12}$, since it is obscured by the addition of ΔD_{12}. The problem then is to come up with a *statistical* attack based on the likely nature of the underlying but *unobserved* $\Delta\chi_{12}$.

However, if one has a sufficiently long stream of text, then the hidden nature of the chi stream is unimportant. This is because whenever the wheels are in a given position ij, $\Delta\chi_{12}$ always takes on the same value, and the corresponding ΔD_{12} stream exhibits a bias in favour of 1s (this is just restating the design flaw of the machine), *a bias which will be apparent if one has a long enough stream of text.* For example, in the case of our hypothetical pair of (now Δ) wheels of lengths 3 and 5, suppose one observed a stream 9,000 letters long, 600 belonging to each of the 15 cells of the rectangle. If we were to record the difference between 1s and 0s in the ΔZ_{12}, which is observable, the entries in the rectangle might look something like the following, generated by a computer simulation:

	1	1	0	1	0
0	−80	−62	46	−68	70
1	86	82	−64	122	−70
0	−30	−32	62	−62	60

Obviously the pattern of pluses and minuses (positive and negative entries) exactly tracks the rows of 0s and 1s in the rectangle. The reason for this is that if the input stream of ΔD_{12} has a bias in favour of 1s versus 0s, then the output stream that results from adding mod two the fixed value of $\Delta\chi_{12}$ in a given cell either preserves the bias or reverses it depending on whether $\Delta\chi_{12}$ is 0 or 1, respectively.

This rectangle illustrates an extreme case, one in which the underlying bias of de-chi is apparent. If the stream is short enough, however, this might not be the case, for the same reason that if a coin is biased in favour of heads, but you only toss it a few times, then you might get more tails than heads. For example, suppose the stream is 900 letters long rather than 9,000, so that there are only 60 per cell in the rectangle. Then the simulation might come up with a result like

	1	1	0	1	0
0	−10	−2	6	−2	12
1	−2	−4	−16	4	−22
0	−8	−14	4	4	12

Here matters are no longer straightforward: in some cells the sign is the reverse of what it should be, the observed bias no longer reflecting the underlying bias of the stream; and there are no longer just two types of rows or columns. Dealing with even shorter messages and even more sign reversals is obviously going to be challenging. But the problem can be overcome in many cases. At Bletchley Park the method for doing this was to use a technique called *convergence* (see, for example, *GRT*, **12C(e)**, TNA HW 25/4, p. 20; this edition, p. 27).

Converging of rectangles

Given a message, let (a_{ij}) denote the kind of table discussed in the previous section, where a_{ij} is the difference between the number of 0's and the number of 1's in ΔZ_{12}, at places when wheel 1 is at i and wheel 2 is at j. Let $x = (x_i)$ and $y = (y_j)$ denote the patterns of the two Δ wheels, where (for reasons that will become apparent shortly), we will now denote the sequence of 0s and 1s (dots and crosses in the terminology of the *General Report on Tunny*) on each wheel by a sequence of $+1$s and -1s. The mission is to recover (x_i) and (y_j) from (a_{ij}).

Suppose that (x_i) represents a guess regarding the pattern of the first wheel, and we are trying to guess (y_j), the pattern of the second wheel. Then each position i on the first wheel has a 'vote' regarding the sign of y_j: namely $a_{ij}x_i$. For example, if $a_{ij} < 0$ and $x_i < 0$, then $a_{ij}x_i > 0$; so the vote is for $y_j > 0$, consistent with the expectation that x_i and y_j have opposite sign since $a_{ij} < 0$. It is then natural to add up the votes and decide on the basis of the sign of the sum:

$$y_j = \begin{cases} +1, & \sum_i a_{ij}x_i > 0; \\ 0, & \sum_i a_{ij}x_i = 0; \\ -1, & \sum_i a_{ij}x_i < 0. \end{cases}$$

Note the larger the magnitude of $|a_{ij}|$, the greater the impact of its vote, which is natural. In the special case when $y_j = 0$, obviously $\sum_i a_{ij}x_i$ is uninformative and neither setting is ascribed to the second wheel at position j.

At this stage one can iterate. Using the just computed values of y_j, one can in turn 'take them through the rectangle', to obtain new values for the x_i. And so on, until one reaches a set of x_i, y_j values that remain unchanged by a further iteration. This procedure was used to arrive at a pair of wheel patterns on the basis of an initial guess for one of them and was called 'converging the rectangle'. Although it can be shown that this procedure always converges to some pattern (as opposed to endlessly cycling through a succession of different ones), *what* it converges to depends on the initial guess. This was eventually recognised as well as the corollary that it was important to make a good initial guess in order to arrive at the correct pattern.

Such iterative procedures were not unknown in statistical practice in 1940, but they were certainly not common then.[46] A numerical analyst would see similarities with the so-called *power method* in linear algebra for finding the eigenvectors and eigenvalues of a matrix.[47] The technique used at Bletchley Park is in fact very close to a variant of the power method, based on the singular value decomposition, used to find the left and right singular vectors of a matrix. This variant was discussed by I. J. Good in his book *The Estimation of Probabilities: An Essay on Modern Bayesian Methods* (1965), one of many examples of his wartime experience informing his postwar publications.[48] (Successively multiplying a vector by a matrix A and its transpose A', mentioned by Good, is none other than taking a wheel pattern through the rectangle except that in the case of the latter one replaces $\sum a_{ij}x_i$ by ± 1 at each stage. This will of course substantially simplify the necessary calculations, albeit at the loss of some information.)

[46]For one example, see W. E. Deming and F. F. Stephan, 'On a Least Squares Adjustment of a Sampled Frequency Table when the Expected Marginal Totals Are Known', *Ann. Math. Statist.*, 11 (1940), pp. 427–444.

[47]See R. von Mises and H. Pollaczek-Geiringer, 'Praktische Verfahren der Gleichungsauflösung', *ZAMM — Zeitschrift für Angewandte Mathematik und Mechanik*, 9 (1929), pp. 152–164, for an early description.

[48]See I. J. Good, *The Estimation of Probabilities: An Essay on Modern Bayesian Methods* (Cambridge, Mass.: MIT Press, 1965), pp. 62–63.

Flagging

Thus wheel setting depends on wheel-breaking, wheel-breaking on converging a rectangle, and converging a rectangle on initially guessing at least part of a wheel pattern.

Flagging refers to the method used to guess the pattern of a wheel (*GRT*, **24D(b)**, TNA HW 25/4, p. 122; this edition, p. 117). It, like converging, exploits the fact that although one does not see the $\Delta\chi_{12}$ rectangle entries, one does see evidence for a 0 (no change in parity) or a 1 (change in parity) depending on the bias of the stream of 0s and 1s in each cell. Rows that have the same underlying pattern (whether the correct one or the complementary one) can then be detecting by their having a positive correlation; those with the opposite pattern show a negative correlation. So it is natural to construct a correlation matrix r_{ij} consisting of the dot products of the i-th and j-th rows. (The *dot product* of $x_1, x_2, \ldots, x_n$ and $y_1, y_2, \ldots, y_n$ is the sum $x_1y_1 + x_2y_2 + \cdots + x_ny_n$.) Because $r_{ij} = r_{ji}$, it is only necessary to compute the r_{ij} for $i \leq j$, hence the name *flag* (as in a triangular flag or pennant used to mark the corners of sports fields). Positive entries in the flag indicate a pair of x_i values that are likely to be the same, negative entries a pair of values likely to be the opposite.

In the convergence procedure it is not necessary to make an initial guess for every x_i; one can set some to zero if the evidence is not strong either way. Ordinarily the cryptanalysts at Bletchley Park took some subset; often a 9×9 flag was used (*GRT*, **24D(a)**, TNA HW 25/4, p. 122; this edition, p. 117).

ROMSing

'ROMSing' — using the Resources of Modern Science — was Hugh Alexander's humorous reference to a technical improvement by Jack Good in the attack on the Naval Enigma.[49] But in a setting where failing to do one's best might mean the difference between breaking a message and wasting a day's effort, technical improvements were no joke. The *General Report on Tunny* describes many technical refinements of the basic methodology sketched above; some of these were intended to streamline computation, others to make maximum use of information received. In the following we briefly note one example of each kind.

Proportional bulges

One interesting statistical novelty of the cryptanalytic work carried out at Bletchley Park was its introduction of what it termed the *proportional bulge* (*GRT*, **22E(a)**, TNA HW 25/4, p. 53; this edition, p. 56). Suppose one is observing whether or not an event occurs. If the probability the event occurs is p and the probability that it does not is $q = 1 - p$, then the associated proportional bulge was defined to be

$$\xi := p - q = p - (1 - p) = 2p - 1,$$

so that

$$p = \frac{1}{2}(1 + \xi), \qquad q = \frac{1}{2}(1 - \xi).$$

For example, suppose p is the probability of seeing a head when a biased coin is tossed. If $p = .6$ (so that $q = .4$), then the proportional bulge is $p - q = .2$. It measures the magnitude of the bias in terms of the difference in frequency of heads versus tails, rather than in terms of the absolute frequency of heads.

The 'real reason why 'proportional bulges' were introduced' was the 'theorem of the chain of witnesses' (*GRT*, **21(j)**, TNA HW 25/4, p. 41; this edition, p. 46). Suppose a proposition that can

[49] I. J. Good, 'Enigma and Fish' in F. H. Hinsley and Alan Stripp, eds., *Codebreakers: The Inside Story of Bletchley Park* (Oxford: Oxford University Press, 1993; paperback repr. with corrections, 1994), pp. 149–166, esp. p. 157.

be either true or false is transmitted in sequential fashion via a chain of n 'witnesses', each having a probability p_i of correctly transmitting the fact versus its negation. If ξ_i is the proportional bulge corresponding to p_i, then the probability P of correct transmission through the chain is complicated to express in terms of the p_i, but easy to state in terms of the bulges: if $\xi = \xi_1 \xi_2 \dots \xi_n$, then

$$P = \frac{1}{2}\left(1 + \prod_i^n (2p_i - 1)\right) = \frac{1}{2}\left(1 + \prod_i^n \xi_i\right) = \frac{1}{2}(1 + \xi);$$

that is, the proportional bulge of a chain is the product of the proportional bulges of the links in that chain. Expressed in terms of probabilities, this result had been known since the late eighteenth century.[50]

To see the reason for the formula, suppose there are just two witnesses. Then the overall transmission will be correct if the successive witnesses both tell the truth or if both lie: either $T \to T \to T$ or $T \to F \to T$. The chance of this is clearly $P = p_1 p_2 + q_1 q_2$, and it is easy to check that this is the same as $(1 + \xi_1 \xi_2)/2$. In general, if the formula has been established for a chain of length n, then it can be seen to hold for one of length $n+1$ by the above argument, letting p_1, ξ_1 denote the probability and bulge for the initial chain of length n and letting p_2, ξ_2 denote the corresponding quantities for the last link.[51]

Although the relevant subsection of the *General Report on Tunny*— only eleven lines of typescript in the original — does not examine the theorem itself in detail (*GRT*, **21(j)**, TNA HW 25/4, p. 41; this edition, p. 46), versions of this kind of calculation occur without comment throughout all the technical sections of the *General Report on Tunny*.

The 'chain of witnesses theorem' involves in effect the mod 2 addition of independent random quantities having values 0 or 1 (if the corresponding witness tells the truth or lies, respectively). The result then is that the proportional bulge of a sum of independent bit streams is the product of their individual bulges. (For example, the proportional bulge of ΔD_{12} is the product of those of ΔP_{12} and of $\Delta \psi'_{12}$.) The addition of such quantities can be studied by the *convolution* of their distributions, and by use of what the *General Report on Tunny* terms the *Faltung* theorem (*GRT*, **22E(b)**, TNA HW 25/4, p. 52; this edition, p. 57, and **22X(d)**, p. 74; this edition, p. 77). The *General Report on Tunny* does not mention the fact that the chain of witnesses result can be derived from the Faltung theorem.

The theorem of the weighted average of (partial) factors

In setting the chi wheels for a specific message, one knew both the *link* (the pair of communicating machines, such as Berlin-Paris) and the *end* (the machine sending the message) and sometimes the *dottage* (the number of dots in the pattern of μ_{37}). These all influenced the statistical characteristics of ΔD in a known way. In addition, from prior experience, one knew that a certain fraction of the time one of several different ΔD distributions occurred (depending, for example, on the operator and the type of message being sent) although one did not know which before the message was set. For example, two-thirds of the time ΔD might have one distribution and one-third of the time another. Such information was incorporated into the attack using the *theorem of the weighted average of (partial) factors*.

Good's 1950 book gives a clear statement and proof of this result.[52] Suppose $H = H_1 \cup \dots \cup H_n$ is a composite hypothesis (so that the H_i are mutually exclusive), $\overline{H}$ the negation of H, and E

[50] See P. Prevost and S. A. J. Lhuilier, 'Mémoire sur l'application du calcul des probabilités à la valeur du témoignage', *Mémoires de l'Académie Royale des sciences et belles-lettres* [Berlin] (1797), pp. 120–152, Pierre Simon Laplace, *Théorie analytique des probabilités*, 3rd ed. (Paris: Courcier, 1820), Book 2, chapter 11, § 58, and Siméon Denis Poisson, *Recherches sur la probabilité des jugements en matière criminelle et matière civile* (Paris, 1837), pp. 108–112.

[51] See editorial endnote 7 to *GRT*, section **21(j)**, p. 578 below.

[52] Good, *Probability and the Weighing of Evidence* (see footnote 27, above), p. 68.

evidence. Then if

$$p_i = P(H_i \mid H), \qquad f_i = \frac{P(E \mid H_i)}{P(E \mid \overline{H})},$$

the theorem states that the factor in favour of H given E is

$$\frac{P(E \mid H)}{P(E \mid \overline{H})} = \sum_i P(H_i \mid H) \frac{P(E \mid H_i)}{P(E \mid \overline{H})} = \sum_i p_i f_i.$$

The *General Report on Tunny* first states this in a somewhat garbled form (*GRT*, **21(i)**, TNA HW 25/4, p. 40; this edition, p. 46), but its meaning becomes clear when it is applied to message setting (**22Y**, p. 76; this edition, p. 79). To see the connection, let H denote the hypothesis that some specific setting is the correct one, E the ΔD count for the message being set assuming the putative H setting, T_i the hypothesis that the distribution $P^{(i)}$ is operative, and $H_i = H \cap T_i$. Then $P(H_i \mid H) = P(T_i \mid H) = P(T_i)$, because H and T_i are independent (whichever chi setting is being used, the operative ΔD distribution is the operative ΔD distribution). So if $P_j^{(i)}$ is the probability of the j-th letter in the $P^{(i)}$ distribution, if the letter j occurs n_j times in E, and if there are N letters in the message, then the theorem of weighted averages tells us that the Bayes factor in favour of H given E is

$$\frac{P(E \mid H)}{P(E \mid \overline{H})} = \sum_i P(T_i) \frac{P(E \mid H_i)}{P(E \mid \overline{H})} = \sum_i P(T_i) \frac{\Pi_j (P_j^{(i)})^{n_j}}{\left(\frac{1}{32}\right)^N}.$$

Aftermath

After the war was over, many scientific fields benefited from technical developments during the conflict. The study of statistics drew particular advantage from the wartime experiences of many previously ‘pure’ mathematicians: many prominent statisticians in the postwar period in both the US and UK became interested in the field because of their wartime experiences. Important examples in the U.S. include John Tukey (1915–2000), Herbert Robbins (1915–2001), and William Kruskal (1919–2005); in England George Barnard (1915–2002), David Kendall (1918–2002), and Dennis Lindley (1923–2013).. Many other statisticians of course did war work; what is being noted here are mathematicians who had little or no serious interest in statistics prior to the war, became involved in it during the war, and then remained permanently in the field after. Tukey, for example, was initially a topologist in the 1930s.

Bletchley Park, in particular, seems to have had a major impact on many of those who worked there. For example, Donald Michie (1923–2007), who went to Bletchley Park at the age of eighteen, said in 1995 that ‘my whole professional life really was fundamentally affected by those three years, and I am sure by the people’.[53] Another example would be Shaun Wylie (1913–2009), who — after initially returning to Trinity Hall, Cambridge — became Chief Mathematician at GCHQ in 1958 and remained with that organisation for the next fifteen years.

But although Bletchley Park had a transformative effect on the careers of many people who worked there during the war, a very different question is its outside technical impact (in the same sense, say, that the U.S. space programme had on science and engineering in the 1960s). Ordinarily signals intelligence organisations carefully guard their secrets, and GCHQ — GCCS’s peacetime successor — was no exception. For this reason it might seem futile to discuss the external impact of the applied statistical research done at Bletchley Park except for one reason: I. J. Good.

[53] John A. N. Lee and Golde Holtzman, ‘50 Years after Breaking the Codes: Interviews with two of the Bletchley Park Scientists’, *IEEE Annals of the History of Computing*, 17 (1995), pp. 32–43, esp. p. 39.

The postwar career of I. J. Good

Good left Bletchley (in September 1945) to join Max Newman (1897–1984) at Manchester and then moved to GCHQ in 1948, where he stayed for the next nine years.[54] Throughout this period Good published extensively in the 'outside' literature, becoming one of the most prolific and influential Bayesian statisticians of the time. Much of this work was in fact a natural outgrowth of his wartime efforts, although Good was careful to disguise its origins. A case in point is his book *Probability and the Weighing of Evidence*.[55] As Good tells us in its preface, although it was published in 1950, a draft of the book had been completed in 1946, the year after Good left Bletchley Park.[56] When read in conjunction with the *General Report on Tunny*, it is clear that the book represents a summing up of the Bayesian philosophy Good acquired during the war. It is no surprise to find that readers of the first draft were Turing, Newman and Michie.[57]

Good showed similar care in disguising the origins of many of his technical papers, such as the ones on the estimation of probabilities in large sparse contingency tables, a substantial body of work summarised in a later book.[58] In much of this, Good was heavily indebted to Turing. As he explained in 1979:

> Turing did not publish these wartime statistical ideas because, after the war, he was too busy working on the ground floor of computer science and artificial intelligence. I was impressed by the importance of his statistical ideas, for other applications, and developed and published some of them in various places. Much of my delay was caused by the wartime attitude that everything was classified, from Hollerith cards to sequential statistics, to empirical Bayes, to Markov chains, to decision theory, to electronic computers. These extreme standards of secrecy only gradually abated after the war.[59]

Instead, Good waited until it became 'clear that Turing's interests lay elsewhere', and 'statistics was no longer regarded as a classified topic'.[60] The resulting papers touched on a variety of topics: the sampling of species problem,[61] the variance of the weight of evidence (Turing had considered the case when the weight of evidence was normally distributed, and Good extended his results to the case when it is only approximately normal),[62] and the scoring method used in 'Banburismus' (a technique employed in breaking Naval Enigma messages).[63] (Banburismus is GCCS terminology and does not appear in Good's paper.)

But although many papers published by Good from the 1950s to the 1970s refer to statistical ideas of Turing, the origin of those ideas in work carried out at Bletchley Park was, of course,

[54] Banks, 'Conversation' (see footnote 14, above), pp. 12–13.

[55] Good, *Probability and the Weighing of Evidence* (see footnote 27, above).

[56] See Good, *Probability and the Weighing of Evidence* (see footnote 27, above), p. vi; Banks, 'Conversation' (see footnote 14, above), p. 12.

[57] Good, *Probability and the Weighing of Evidence* (see footnote 27, above), p. vi; passage dated December 1949.

[58] Good, *The Estimation of Probabilities* (see footnote 48, above).

[59] I. J. Good, 'Introductory Remarks for the Article in *Biometrika* 66 (1979), "A. M. Turing's Statistical Work in World War II"' in Turing, *Collected works* (see footnote 17, above), pp. 211–223, esp. p. 211. See also Banks, 'Conversation' (see footnote 14, above), pp. 10–11.

[60] Good, 'Turing's Anticipation of Empirical Bayes in Connection with the Cryptanalysis of the Naval Enigma' (see footnote 30, above), p. 107.

[61] I. J. Good, 'The Population Frequencies of Species and the Estimation of Population Parameters', *Biometrika*, 40 (1953), pp. 237–264; I. J. Good and G. H. Toulmin, 'The Number of new Species, and the Increase of Population Coverage, when a Sample is Increased', *Biometrika*, 43 (1956), pp. 45–63.

[62] I. J. Good, 'Weight of Evidence, Causality, and False-alarm Probabilities' in Colin Cherry, ed., *Papers read at a Symposium on 'Information Theory' held at the Royal Institution, London, August 29th to September 2nd 1960* (London: Butterworths, 1961), pp. 125–136.

[63] I. J. Good, 'The Joint Probability Generating Function for Run-Lengths in Regenerative Binary Markov Chains, with Applications', *Annals of Statistics*, 1 (1973), pp. 933–939, esp. p. 939; Good, 'Enigma and Fish' (see footnote 49, above); and Good, 'From Hut 8 to the Newmanry' (see footnote 41, above).

never mentioned. The cryptanalytic work in question had been, and still was, covered by the Official Secrets Act. It is natural to suppose that other papers by Good from this period also contain ideas of his own arising from his time at Bletchley Park, but for the present it is difficult to find documentary evidence of such connections. In the case of the Turing-via-Good papers, we know of Turing's role — and therefore the GCCS connection — because Good was always very careful to acknowledge 'Prof's' role. There is no mention of cryptanalysis, but the reference to Turing is the hint that (now) points us to it. However, in the case of papers containing results entirely due to Good, such hints are rarely evident, and it is only with the release of the *General Report on Tunny* that some of the connections become evident.

The discrete Fourier transform

A case in point is Good's long-standing interest in the discrete Fourier transform, on which he published a number of papers after the war. Good apparently first learned about the discrete Fourier transform (DFT) from Turing, who mentioned it to him in passing during the war.[64] The DFT has been of immense practical importance to all branches of applied mathematics and science since about 1960, especially in the analysis of periodic phenomena. But it plays a minor role in the *General Report on Tunny*, where it is only explicitly used a few times, in connection with the Faltung theorem. The DFT attracted Good's attention, and he returned to it repeatedly after the war.[65] One paper, dating from 1958,[66] was of particular importance in laying the groundwork for the creation of the modern Fast Fourier Transform (FFT) algorithm for efficiently computing the DFT, in a paper by Cooley and Tukey, published in 1965.[67] However, the history of the development of algorithms for computing the DFT is a complicated one.[68]

An acknowledgement in one of Good's papers, published in 1962 but presumably written the year before, is particularly noteworthy: 'I am indebted to Dr. S. Wylie, Professor D. Rees, and Professor M. H. A. Newman for stimulating discussions sixteen years ago'.[69] Thus such later work by Good seems naturally attributable, at least in part, to an atmosphere at Bletchley that fostered fruitful directions of research that continued after the war.

Such discreet hints about his wartime mathematical research can also be found from time to time in other papers written by Good. One instance illustrates Good's influence on others: the famous Kullback–Leibler paper on the generalization of Shannon information.[70] In his 1993 interview by Banks, Good reports 'Kullback told me his work was sparked by an unpublished paper of mine'.[71] This refers to Solomon Kullback (1907–1994), who worked for NSA and its predecessor organisations from 1930 to his retirement in 1962; he spent some time in the spring and summer of 1942 at Bletchley Park studying GCCS methods.[72]

[64] Banks, 'Conversation' (see footnote 14, above), p. 10.

[65] In such papers as I. J. Good, 'Random Motion on a Finite Abelian Group', *Proc. Camb. Phil. Soc.*, 47 (1951), pp. 756–762 and I. J. Good, 'Analogues of Poisson's Summation Formula', *Amer. Math. Monthly*, 69 (1962), pp. 259–266.

[66] I. J. Good, 'The Interaction Algorithm and Practical Fourier Analysis', *Jour. Roy. Statist. Soc. B*, 20 (1958), pp. 361–372.

[67] J. W. Cooley and J. Tukey, 'An Algorithm for the Machine Calculation of Complex Fourier Series', *Mathematics of Computation*, 19 (1965), pp. 297–301.

[68] See Michael T. Heidman, Don H. Johnson and C. Sidney Burrus, 'Gauss and the History of the Fast Fourier Transform', *IEEE ASSP Magazine*, 1.3 (1984), pp. 14–21 and James W. Cooley, 'How the FFT Gained Acceptance', *IEEE SP Magazine* (Jan. 1992), pp. 10–13.

[69] Good, 'Analogues of Poisson's Summation Formula' (see footnote 65, above), p. 259.

[70] S. Kullback and R. A. Leibler, 'On Information and Sufficiency', *Ann. Math. Statist.*, 22 (1951), pp. 79–86.

[71] Banks, 'Conversation' (see footnote 14, above), p. 14.

[72] R. D. Farley and H. F. Schorreck, 'Oral History Interview OH-17-82 with Dr. Solomon Kullback', interview transcript, 26 Aug. 1984, URL: `http://www.nsa.gov/public_info/_files/oral_history_interviews/nsa_oh_17_82_kullback.pdf` (visited on 07/06/2014), pp. 47, 64–65.

The revival of Bayesian statistics

However, in the longer run, Good's most important contribution was the part he played in the eventual revival of the Bayesian approach in statistical inference. Immediately after the war, opinion was largely against Bayesian methods; and since his wartime work had been secret, and remained classified, Good was not, of course, in a position to point to the recent spectacular success of Bayesian methods. A review of Good's book, *Probability and the Weighing of Evidence*, in the journal *Biometrika* provides an indication of the generally hostile climate. The reviewer, F. N. David (1909–1993), a well-known statistician of the Neyman–Pearson school, remarked: 'It is fair to say that statisticians in general will not accept Dr Good's approach to statistical problems'.[73] Later years saw the re-emergence of Bayesian statistics, driven by the influence of Good's book and others by L. J. Savage (1917–1971), Robert Schlaifer (1914–1994), and Howard Raiffa (b. 1924),[74] and the 'conversion' of other respected statisticians such as Dennis Lindley (1923–2013)).

Throughout this period, Good played an important role as an advocate for the Bayesian position, not only in the statistical literature, but in dozens of papers in the philosophical literature as well. These papers included not only expositions of and philosophical justifications for the theory of subjective probability and the use of Bayesian statistics, but also technical extensions of philosophical interest and resolutions of celebrated 'paradoxes' of probability from the Bayesian viewpoint.[75] This includes 22 papers in the *British Journal for the Philosophy of Science*, 7 papers in *Philosophy of Science* and 3 in *Synthese*, as well as multiple conference proceedings.

The lifting of the veil

Good necessarily remained silent about his wartime work at Bletchley Park for nearly three decades; his work there remained classified throughout this period, and not even the most limited discussion was possible until the ban on reference to 'Ultra', the code name for intelligence derived from cryptanalysis of high grade ciphers, was lifted in Spring 1974. Before then all one ordinarily said was that one had worked 'at the Foreign Office' during the war. The phrase is, of course, technically correct, as GCCS was formally part of the Foreign Office. Nevertheless, the reference to the Foreign Office is misleading. Unfortunately, its appearance in such biographical sources as *Who's Who* entries and the (British) *Dictionary of National Biography* means that it has found its way into many secondary sources. Reticence about his wartime work seems to have become second nature for Good in later years. For example, the biographical note attached to his paper of 1979, 'Early Work on Computers', which describes part of his work at Bletchley, tells the reader that 'I. J. Good was in the British Foreign Office during World War II'.[76]

Good first began to reveal his role at Bletchley Park shortly after the lifting of the comprehensive ban, in a lecture given at the (British) National Physical Laboratory (Teddington), on 28 April 1976, and published three years later.[77] This was followed in 1979 by a brief account of Turing's statistical work at Bletchley Park,[78] but little detail was given. For example, the deciban is described as being used as part of 'an important classified process called Banburismus' (but

[73]See Review of I. J. Good, *Probability and the Weighing of Evidence* (London, 1950), *Biometrika*, 38 (1951), p. 485.

[74]Good, *Probability and the Weighing of Evidence* (see footnote 27, above); Leonard J. Savage, *The Foundations of Statistics* (New York, 1954); and Howard Raiffa and Robert Schlaifer, *Applied Statistical Decision Theory* (Boston: Harvard Business School, 1961).

[75]Many of these reprinted in I. J. Good, *Good Thinking: The Foundations of Probability and Its Applications* (Minneapolis: University of Minnesota Press, 1983).

[76]Good, 'Early Work on Computers' (see footnote 18, above).

[77]Good, *Early Work on Computers at Bletchley* (see footnote 18, above).

[78]Good, 'Studies in the History of Probability and Statistics. XXXVII: A. M. Turing's Statistical Work in World War II' (see footnote 25, above).

we are not actually told what Banburismus is), and the main application of the deciban 'was to sequential analysis, not for quality control but for discriminating between hypotheses' (but we are not told what those hypotheses were).

In contrast, Gordon Welchman (1906–1985), the former head of Hut 6, was less careful and ran into difficulties. Welchman, who had moved to the U.S. and become a citizen, published a book on his wartime experiences, *The Hut Six Story* (1982) without first submitting it for technical review by the appropriate authorities.[79] This was a mistake: his U.S. security clearance was revoked and he was forbidden to talk to the media about his wartime work or about the book.

Over the next three decades, Good gradually disclosed further information about his Bletchley Park days,[80] but it seems likely that some secrets died with him on 5 April 2009.

[79]Gordon Welchman, *The Hut Six Story* (New York: McGraw-Hill, 1982).

[80]See, for instance, Good, 'Enigma and Fish' (see footnote 49, above) and Good, 'Turing's Anticipation of Empirical Bayes in Connection with the Cryptanalysis of the Naval Enigma' (see footnote 30, above).

Biographies of Authors

At the time the *General Report on Tunny* was written (or compiled), between May and September 1945, the three authors (or editors) to whom the text is ascribed by the library that originally held at least two of the copies, at GCHQ, were colleagues in the cryptanalytic campaign the *Report* describes. Good and Michie continued to be in regular contact until the latter's death in 2007, and Good and Timms were colleagues again after the war, when both were working at GCHQ. Later biographers may be in a position to take account of these continuing contacts. Here we merely propose to explain why our accounts of the first two authors, Good and Michie, are much briefer than that of Timms.

After 1945 Good and Michie went on to have distinguished university careers that are largely matters of public record through their own books and papers about their research work and through the writings of their academic colleagues and pupils. Both of them received substantial obituaries in newspapers and learned journals at the times of the their deaths and both now have entries in the *Oxford Dictionary of National Biography*. In contrast, it has proved rather difficult to learn about Timms, who had an academic career before he joined GCCS in 1944, but after 1945 worked for GCHQ until he retired. We have relied heavily upon personal enquiries and unpublished sources. In consequence — that is, as an aid to future historians who will lack some of the sources of personal reminiscence available to us — we have given a much longer account of Timms than of the other two authors.

Irving John ('Jack') Good, b. 9 December 1916, London, d. 5 April 2009, Radford, Virginia.

Good was born Isidore Jacob Gudak, the son of Polish immigrants. He went up to Jesus College, Cambridge in 1934, as a Major Scholar (in mathematics) and with the additional financial support of a State Scholarship. He graduated in 1938 and stayed on in Cambridge to do research. He won the Smith's Prize in 1940 and obtained a PhD in 1941. He was Cambridge County chess champion. With such qualifications he was a perfect example of the kind of Cambridge man GCCS was looking to recruit.

Good first worked on Enigma, with Alan Turing and Hugh Alexander, but was then transferred to Newman's group, becoming its third member (after Newman himself and Donald Michie). When the war ended, Good followed Newman to Manchester, but in 1948 took up the post of Chief Mathematician at GCHQ, where he remained until 1959. He then moved to the USA, working for various commercial concerns connected with computers and teaching at Princeton University and Virginia Polytechnic.

Good had been interested in probability since childhood, having taught himself about the subject by reading books, and he made use of his experience at GCCS to develop ideas that — shorn of any reference to their cryptanalytic connections — later found a place in a series of idiosyncratic books such as *Probability and the Weighing of Evidence* (London: Griffin, 1950) and *The Estimation of Probabilities: An Essay on Modern Bayesian Methods* (Cambridge, Mass.: MIT Press, 1965). These books exercised an important influence on the development of statistical work in the following half century.

Donald Michie, b. 11 November 1923, Rangoon, Burma, d. 7 July 2007, London.

Donald Michie was educated at Rugby School, where (according to his own account) being no good at sport he avoided bullying by being good enough at lessons to help his fellow pupils with their prep. He left Rugby in the summer of 1942, with a Classics scholarship to Balliol College,

Oxford, intending to defer his studies until after the war. Expecting call-up papers, he planned to spend the interim learning Japanese on a course in Bedford. As it happened, he had missed the beginning of the Japanese course, so he joined a course on cryptanalysis instead. These courses had been set up by Tiltman to provide recruits for GCCS, and Michie's joining the course was in line with the practice of employing linguists as cryptanalysts.

Working at Bletchley Park brought Michie into contact with some of the best mathematical minds of the day. While the experience seems to have convinced him he was not good enough at mathematics to make it his main subject when he went up to Oxford in October 1945, his interests shifted towards the scientific side, eventually to a subject that allowed him to make use of his understanding of statistics, namely genetics. However, his long-term intention was always to work on machine intelligence. In the 1960s, when computers had developed far enough, he was responsible for the first designs of prototype industrial robots. Late in life, and still not very good at chess, he found himself refereeing chess games that involved computers.

Michie wrote prolifically throughout his life. In the early 1950s he was science correspondent for the *Daily Worker*. His skill with language appears in his choice of names for robots, for instance MENACE ('Matchbox Educable Noughts and Crosses Engine', 1958) and the teachable FREDERICK ('Friendly Robot for Education, Discussion and Entertainment, the Retrieval of Information and the Collation of Knowledge', 1973). His younger brother, the poet and literary editor James Michie (1927–2007), dedicated his translation of Horace's Odes (London, 1964) 'to my brother Donald'.

Geoffrey Timms, b. 16 February 1903, Bradford (Yorkshire), England, d. 2 December 1982, Auckland, New Zealand.

Geoffrey Timms, the elder son of a Yorkshire rope-maker, was born in Bradford and educated there at Woodhouse Grove School. He went to Leeds University to study chemistry, but switched to mathematics after the first year and graduated with first class honours. His academic record resulted in an invitation to study geometry at Cambridge University, under H. F. Baker at St John's College. Although a rather shy man, Timms attended Baker's Saturday afternoon conferences, which were known as 'tea parties'. He became a member of the London Mathematical Society on 11 March 1926 (and retained membership for the rest of his life). In 1928 he was awarded a PhD, and his doctoral thesis became a major paper in *n*-dimensional projective geometry ['The Nodal Cubic Surfaces and the Surfaces from Which They Are Derived by Projection', *Proc. Roy. Soc. London A*, 119 (1928), pp. 213–248].

On leaving Cambridge, in 1928, Timms took up an assistant lectureship at St Andrews University, Scotland. Here he remained for sixteen years. He became a reader in mathematics, and was warden of Dean's Court. While at St Andrews he was elected a Fellow of the Royal Society of Edinburgh (6 March 1933). He was an active member of the Edinburgh Mathematical Society, which he joined in 1929. He gave talks at Society meetings in 1932, 1936 and 1939, served on the Society's committee (1938–40) and then as its President (1941–42). He published a paper in one of the Society's journals ('On the Highest Space in which a Non-ruled Surface of Given Order Can Lie', *Proceedings of the Edinburgh Mathematical Society*, 2nd ser., 6.3 (Aug. 1940), pp. 149–150) and was co-editor of its *Proceedings* (1940 – 43).

Timms was always interested in foreign places. In his youth he began a huge stamp collection, which included both a penny black and a two-penny blue. He liked to explore ancient monuments, the routes of old Roman roads, and every kind of railway. The Scottish highlands provided opportunities for rock-climbing with friends, but more often he preferred to be alone and travelled enormous distances on foot. Later he fell in love with Iceland, although his height — six feet three inches (191 cm) — made it hard to ride the small-sized local ponies.

For longer distances he used his motorcycle, with which he explored much of Europe. He became fully fluent in German, a little less so in French, Spanish and Icelandic, and had some knowledge of Russian, Lithuanian, Latvian, Estonian and Welsh. In 1936 he acquired a highly prized Leica camera. Also in the 1930s he visited Russia, where he met his future wife (Rhiannon Silyn Roberts, b. 16 July 1915, Barry, Glamorganshire, d. 2012), who was the only other British tourist on a boat trip down the Volga. They were married in 1939.

Another major interest was amateur radio. During the war he became a member of the Home Guard, and later boasted of how his skill in fixing electronic equipment enabled the post at St Andrews to maintain reliable wartime contact with headquarters. Later he volunteered for active service and arrived at Bletchley Park in September 1944, at the age of 41. There is an unconfirmed story (originating with Good in 1976 and repeated by Michie in 2002) that to celebrate the end of the war in Europe, on 8 May 1945, Timms demonstrated how a Colossus machine could be configured (at least in principle) to carry out multiplication in base-10 arithmetic [I. J. Good, 'Pioneering Work on Computers at Bletchley' in N. Metropolis, J. Howlett and Gian-Carlo Rota, eds., *A History of Computing in the Twentieth Century: A Collection of Essays* (New York: Academic, 1980), pp. 31–45, esp. p. 41; see also Donald Michie, 'Colossus and the Breaking of the Wartime "Fish" Codes', *Cryptologia*, 26.1 (2002), pp. 17–58, esp. p. 56].

On the practical level, Timms found a neat solution to the problem that at Bletchley Park his drinking mug sometimes went missing. He took to drinking from a flowerpot. When he used it, he stopped the drainage hole with a cork; when he had finished, he put the cork in his pocket. The pot stayed put.

After the war, Timms remained a civil servant in the newly formed GCHQ, first at Eastcote and later at Cheltenham. At GCHQ Timms was not employed as a specialist mathematician. His speciality was devising methods by which specific problems could be approached logically using existing or foreseeable tools; he has been described by former colleagues as a 'systems analyst', in the days before that description existed. He worked with the machines GCHQ then had (at first still Colossi and Robinsons). He created 'programmes' (implemented by plugging) for the extensive arrays of Hollerith machines which were used at GCHQ. He devised new machines (some of which were built) to meet new problems, though he was not a hands-on engineer. In the late 1940s, he participated in the design of GCHQ's main random number generator system (used for communications security purposes). He was responsible for the High Speed Checker which confirmed that the central system was indeed generating suitably random output. The patents had to be assigned to the government, but Timms received a monetary award under the terms of the Ministry of Defence's scheme for inventors.

Timms was awarded the Order of the British Empire (O. B. E.) in 1952. Details of such awards are never made public, and while this honour was presumably given in recognition of his work at GCHQ it seems very unlikely that the award was made specifically for Timms' work on the random number generator system, since the other designer concerned (who designed the part of the system that generated the random numbers) did not receive an award at that time.

Timms' colleagues at GCHQ recollect that Timms was tall, thin and reclusive; he never pushed his own views, finding more satisfaction in working by himself, but one or two who got close to him found him easy to like. He was considered eccentric.

Timms would officially have retired at age 60 in 1963, but he was retained, probably at the request of his long-term colleague Gerry Morgan, to work with the latter in the application of the techniques of Operational Research, and he continued to work on this until he finally left GCHQ in 1970.

In a letter to Timms' daughter, Bera MacClement (née Timms, 1941–2013), in 1983, the Chief Scientist at GCHQ told her that her father 'played a unique role in the early application of computer techniques'.

After his retirement, Timms returned for a while to Yorkshire, but his final years were spent with his daughter and her family, first in Canada and later in New Zealand. He was very fond of children, and he used to tell them the most wonderful stories, always freshly invented to suit the occasion. All those who knew him were struck by his immense intelligence and by the wide range of his knowledge.

Note An obituary of Geoffrey Timms appeared in W. L. Edge, 'Geoffrey Timms, O.B.E., Ph.D., F.R.S.E.', Obituary, *Proceedings of the Edinburgh Mathematical Society*, 26 (1983), pp. 393–394. This says nothing of his work at Bletchley Park or GCHQ. Timms' daughter commented (private communication to JVF 2007) that this obituary contains two errors of fact: her father did not travel by motorcycle in his journey to Moscow, and the year in which he was awarded the O. B. E. was not 1953 but 1952. The obituary omits Timms' promotion to Reader, which had taken place by 1944.

Acknowledgements

We are grateful to Ms Marit Hartveit (University of St Andrews Mathematical Institute) for information about Timms' involvement with the Edinburgh Mathematical Society, to Mrs Vicki Hammond for information about the Royal Society of Edinburgh, to Dr Bera MacClement (University of Auckland) for personal information about her father, and to the late Peter Freeman, the Historian at GCHQ, for answering questions about Timms' work there after the war. We are grateful to Joy MacCleary the daughter of Geoffrey Timms' brother Alan, for having checked our final text.

Notes on the Editors of the Present Volume

Whitfield Diffie, b. 1944, who is best known for his 1975 discovery of the concept of public key cryptography, worked for Sun Microsystems from 1991 to 2009. Prior to 1991, he was Manager of Secure Systems Research at Northern Telecom, a position he had held since 1978. Diffie is a 1965 graduate in mathematics of MIT and Dr. sc. techn. (hc), 1992, of the ETH in Zurich. Since 1993, Diffie has worked largely on public policy aspects of cryptography. His position — in opposition to limitations on the business and personal use of cryptography — has been the subject of articles in the *New York Times Magazine*, *Newsweek*, *Wired*, *Omni*, and *Discover* and has been the subject of programs on CNN, the Discovery Channel, Equinox TV in Britain, and the Japanese TV network NHK. Diffie is a fellow of the Marconi Foundation and author, jointly with Susan Landau, of the book *Privacy on the Line* (MIT Press, 1998, 2nd ed. 2007).

J. V. Field, b. 1943, an Honorary Visiting Research Fellow, Dept of History of Art, Birkbeck, University of London, is a historian of science, but in the 1960s was a computer programmer, using the Cambridge University Edsac II and Titan (Atlas Mk II) machines to help in designing the optical system of the Anglo-Australian telescope (now operational at Siding Spring Observatory, Coonabarabran, New South Wales).

James A. Reeds, b. 1947, is an applied mathematician. He has been assistant professor in statistics, University of California, Berkeley (1977-1982), member of the technical staff at Bell Labs and at AT&T Labs, (1981-2002), and is currently on the research staff at the Center for Communications Research, Princeton, New Jersey. He has worked on applied mathematics, statistics, applications of cryptography to cell telephones, and more recently, the history of cryptography.

List of Figures

This lists all numbered figures in the *Report*, and a few unnumbered ones. In cases where an illustration's caption does not give a title, we have supplied an explanatory description in square brackets. When the illustrations are scanned, we supply the exhibit number(s) of the scan in square brackets. We mark scans of photographs with a ϕ symbol. See our Appendix E (this volume, p. 540) for a list of all scanned exhibits.

As is explained in the *Report*'s preface, 'chapter **01**', starting at p. 3 in this edition, figures are numbered afresh in each chapter with Roman numerals and are referred to in the style fig. **22 (XI)** for the eleventh figure in chapter **22**.

GENERAL REPORT ON TUNNY p. i[i]

With Emphasis on Statistical Methods

TABLE OF CONTENTS [ii]

---

[i] The original *Report* begins here. The original *Report* ends on p. 505, corresponding to p. 493 in this edition.

[ii] This table of contents reproduces what is on the corresponding pages of the *Report*, pp. i-ii. The titles of chapters **32**, **37**, **38**, **51**, **73**, **91**, **92** and **94** given here differ from the titles used in the body of the *Report*.

[a] Specialised

[i] Note added by hand: '(See also p 332 / in section 53)'.

01 PREFACE (SHOULD BE READ) p. 1

The 'General Report on Tunny' is an account of machine and statistical methods for breaking Tunny ciphers. Language methods are briefly described so that the report may be understood without previous knowledge. For a fuller account of language methods the reader should consult the report of Major Tester's Section. E.1

This report is essentially cryptographic and is complementary to the electrical report prepared by Mr Flowers. Most of the book concerns cryptographic methods in their prime, but there is also E.2 a little historical perspective. The plan of the book is as follows:

Part **1** gives a broad outline of the entire subject. This part should be well understood by the reader before he proceeds to the other parts which may then be read in any order.

In Part **2** all methods are described in some detail. The later section (**W,X,Y,Z**) of each chapter covers advanced theoretical aspects and involves a knowledge of mathematics of at least [a] sixth form standard. These sections may be omitted on a first reading, but give valuable general E.3 examples of statistical cryptographic methods.

A description of the other parts is given in the table of contents. It is hoped that the 'Conclusions' may be of value in other sections of the Foreign Office. E.4

The report contains a number of references to the Research Logs of Mr Newman's Section, (labelled **R0**, **R1**, **R2**, **R3**, **R4**, **R5**) and that of Major Tester's Section (labelled **R41**). Those references which are not preceded by the word 'see' are intended to be of purely historical interest. The correlation of reference with date is given by the following list: E.5

R0	p 1	15th August, 1943
	26	September
	59	October
	92	November
R1	13	December
	34	January, 1944
	78	February
R2	5	March
	37	April
	60	May
	90	June
R3	5	July
	38	August
	62	September
	83	October
	106	November
R4	35	December
	77	January, 1945
R5	1	February
	33	March
	73	April
	111	May

References to the report itself are of the form **36F(b)** which means Part **3**, Chapter **6**, Section **F**, Paragraph **(b)**. Formulae are numbered in Arabic numerals by sections (e.g. (26F4) for the 4th formula of Part **2**, Chapter **6**, Section **F**), and tables and exhibits are numbered in Roman numerals E.6 by chapters (e.g. **26**(II)). Section headings are listed at the beginning of each chapter.

The authors wish to thank all who have helped them with the report, and in particular E.7

[a] involve a knowledge

to acknowledge the help they have received from the reports of the Research Section, Major
E.8, E.9 Tester's Section and Sixta which have in many places been quoted verbatim and without further acknowledgement.

p. 2

PART 1
INTRODUCTION

i

---

[i] This table of contents for Part 1 of the *Report* reproduces what is on the corresponding page of the *Report*, p. 2. The title given for section **15C** differs slightly from what is found in the body of the *Report*. None of the other Parts of the *Report* have such tables of contents.

p. 3 # 11 GERMAN TUNNY

[i]

11A FISH MACHINES

(a) The Teleprinter Alphabet

E.1 Two teleprinters in communication consist of two enlarged electromatic typewriters connected by cable, and constructed so that whatever is typed on either keyboard is printed on both typewriters. When a key is depressed by the sender, the enlarged typewriter sends along the cable one
E.2 of 32 electrical signals. These signals consist of five consecutive impulses, each of which may be
E.3 positive (known as DOT) or negative (known as CROSS) and they operate the appropriate key of the receiving typewriter. The 32 signals are known as 'LETTERS' and correspond to the keys on the teleprinter keyboard.

It is clear that the number of keys cannot be greater than 32, and it is in fact 31. However 29 out of 31 keys can have two meanings, one in figure shift and one in letter shift, the remaining two being used to operate the change to letter shift and the change to figure shift respectively.

The following table shows the construction and meanings of the letters in the teleprint alphabet
E.4 — as laid down by international convention. Figure shift meanings are liable to variation when they have a purely national significance (e.g. £). The order of the letters is specially devised for
E.5 cryptographic purposes and not conventional.

[i] In the original text of the *Report*, almost all chapters start with an analytical contents list. This one does not. We have accordingly supplied such a list, as a copy editor would have done, for uniformity and the convenience of readers.

CONVENTIONAL NAME	IMPULSE 1 2 3 4 5	MEANING IN LETTER SHIFT	IN FIGURE SHIFT	
/ occasionally 7	• • • • •	(no meaning)		i
9	• • × • •	space	space	
H	• • × • ×	H	£	
T	• • • • ×	T	5	
O	• • • × ×	O	9	
M	• • × × ×	M	full stop	
N	• • × × •	N	comma	
3	• • • × •	carriage-return	carriage-return	
R	• × • × •	R	4	
C	• × × × •	C	colon	
V	• × × × ×	V	equals	
G	• × • × ×	G	@	
L	• × • • ×	L	close bracket	
P	• × × • ×	P	0 (zero)	
I	• × × • •	I	8	ii
4	• × • • •	line feed	line feed	
A	× × • • •	A	dash	
U	× × × • •	U	7	
Q	× × × • ×	Q	1	
W	× × • • ×	W	2	
5 or +	× × • × ×	move to FIG shift	(none)	
8 or -	× × × × ×	(none)	move to LET. shift	
K	× × × × •	K	open bracket	
J	× × • × •	J	ring bell	
D	× • • × •	D	who are you?	
F	× • × × •	F	per cent	
X	× • × × ×	X	/	
B	× • • × ×	B	?	
Z	× • • • ×	Z	+	
Y	× • × • ×	Y	6	
S	× • × • •	S	apostrophe	
E	× • • • •	E	3	

It is worth noticing that the numerals 1, 2, 3, 4, 5, 6, 7, 8, 9, 0 are associated with the keys of the top row of the typewriter keyboard, taken in order from Q (on the left) to P (on the right). p. 4 E.6

The conventional names 3 4 5 8 9 / have no connection with the meaning or ordinary occurrence of numerals and punctuation on the typewriter keyboard in figure shift, but are just names given to those keys and electrical signals which do not correspond to any of the 26 letters of the ordinary alphabet. For example the transmission by teleprinter of the phrase 'PRICE 3/6' would involve the following electrical signals being sent in order 9PRICE95EXY89. Similarly a full stop is sent as 5M89 and a comma as 5N89. E.7 E.8

A teleprinter message can be thought of as a stream of "letters" corresponding to the keys depressed and the electrical signals sent during transmission. a

[a] stream of "Letters"

[i] Phrase 'occasionally 7' handwritten.

[ii] The code for letter 'I' is incorrectly given as • × × • ×.

(b) Five-impulse Tape

For speed and accuracy in transmission, long teleprinter messages can be 'perforated' in advance and transmitted automatically from five-impulse tape (AUTO) instead of by hand operation of the keyboard (HAND). The tape from which the transmission takes place is made of paper and
E.9 gives the sequence of signals to be sent, each signal being represented vertically as a set of five impulses with a blank for every dot and a hole for every cross. The tape for 'PRICE 3/6' would look like this

1st Impulse							o		o	o	o	o	o	
2nd Impulse			o	o	o	o			o				o	
Sprocket holes	(used to drive tape)	·	·	·	·	·	·	·	·	·	·	·	·	·
3rd Impulse		o	o		o	o		o			o	o	o	o
4th Impulse				o		o			o		o		o	
5th Impulse			o						o		o	o	o	
	(conventional name)	9	P	R	I	C	E	9	5	E	X	Y	8	9

Similarly the receiving teleprinter can be made to punch a tape, instead of, or in addition to, printing the message when it arrives.

(c) The German Ciphered Teleprinter

During the war in Europe in 1940–5 the Signals Units (FUNKTRUPPEN) attached to German
E.10 service authorities were issued with a novel type of WT and cipher equipment for communication
i with Berlin or other Headquarters stations. Receiving and sending teleprinter equipment were used but the electrical signals corresponding to the various teleprinter letters were not normally transmitted from sender to receiver by cable but sent out over the air in ciphered form. Cipher
E.11 machines (SZ or SCHLUESSELZUSATZGERAET) were therefore interposed between the sending teleprinter, which converted the message into a sequence of enciphered impulse-signals, and the transmitter which sent the ciphered sequences over the air, and similarly between the WT receiver and receiving teleprinter.

These cipher machines were given (by us) the general cover name of FISH and two particular features should be noticed

(i) the cipher was not directly applied to the message, which was reduced to teleprinter form before being enciphered.

(ii) the cipher text was never seen by sending or receiving operator, as no recording device was interposed between cipher machine and WT transmitter or receiver.

(iii) the receiving teleprinter printed on to continuous sticky tape, so that not only / but also 3 (carriage return) and 4 (line feed) did not occur in the unciphered stream. There was no bell.

---

[i] Word 'or' obscured in the photostat by a crumple in the original.

The equipment of a mobile FISH signal unit was housed in two trucks:

(a) The BETRIEBSWAGEN carried two cipher machines (for sending and for receiving) and teleprinter equipment for sending either from keyboard or from tape, and for receiving and printing. In addition, it carried a device for perforating five-impulse tape from a message by tapping it out on a keyboard.

(b) The SENDUNGSWAGEN carried the WT transmitter. E.12

The WT Receiver was independent of both trucks but carried by them when the unit was not p. 5 operating.

When in operation Sendungswagen and Receiver were usually placed about $\frac{1}{2}$ mile from the Betriebswagen and connected to it by cable. On occasions when the teleprinters were connected by land line, the Betriebswagen was connected up directly to an exchange board.

At the Berlin end of Fish links and in some other fairly firmly established places (e.g. Paris in 1943), equipment was not arranged on a mobile basis but in a central station or exchange.

Three types of Fish machines are known:

STURGEON	(used mainly by the German Air Force)
TUNNY	(used mainly by the German Army) which forms the subject of this report.
THRASHER	(which is dealt with in ch. **93**)

11B THE TUNNY CIPHER MACHINE

(a) Addition

	/ 9 H T	O M N 3	R C V G	L P I 4	A U Q W	5 8 K J	D F X B	Z Y S E	
/	/ 9 H T	O M N 3	R C V G	L P I 4	A U Q W	5 8 K J	D F X B	Z Y S E	/
9	9 / T H	M O 3 N	C R G V	P L 4 I	U A W Q	8 5 J K	F D B X	Y Z E S	9
H	H T / 9	N 3 O M	V G R C	I 4 L P	Q W A U	K J 5 8	X B D F	S E Z Y	H
T	T H 9 /	3 N M O	G V C R	4 I P L	W Q U A	J K 8 5	B X F D	E S Y Z	T
[i] O	O M N 3	/ 9 H T	L P I 4	R C V G	5 8 K J	A U Q W	Z Y S E	D F X B	O
M	M O 3 N	9 / T H	P L 4 I	C R G V	8 5 J K	U A W Q	Y Z E S	F D B X	M
N	N 3 O M	H T / 9	I 4 L P	V G R C	K J 5 8	Q W A U	S E Z Y	X B D F	N
3	3 N M O	T H 9 /	4 I P L	G V C R	J K 8 5	W Q U A	E S Y Z	B X F D	3
R	R C V G	L P I 4	/ 9 H T	O M N 3	D F X B	Z Y S E	A U Q W	5 8 K J	R
C	C R G V	P L 4 I	9 / T H	M O 3 N	F D B X	Y Z E S	U A W Q	8 5 J K	C
V	V G R C	I 4 L P	H T / 9	N 3 O M	X B D F	S E Z Y	Q W A U	K J 5 8	V
G	G V C R	4 I P L	T H 9 /	3 N M O	B X F D	E S Y Z	W Q U A	J K 8 5	G
L	L P I 4	R C V G	O M N 3	/ 9 H T	Z Y S E	D F X B	5 8 K J	A U Q W	L
P	P L 4 I	C R G V	M O 3 N	9 / T H	Y Z E S	F D B X	8 5 J K	U A W Q	P
I	I 4 L P	V G R C	N 3 O M	H T / 9	S E Z Y	X B D F	K J 5 8	Q W A U	I
4	4 I P L	G V C R	3 N M O	T H 9 /	E S Y Z	B X F D	J K 8 5	W Q U A	4
A	A U Q W	5 8 K J	D F X B	Z Y S E	/ 9 H T	O M N 3	R C V G	L P I 4	A
U	U A W Q	8 5 J K	F D B X	Y Z E S	9 / T H	M O 3 N	C R G V	P L 4 I	U
Q	Q W A U	K J 5 8	X B D F	S E Z Y	H T / 9	N 3 O M	V G R C	I 4 L P	Q
W	W Q U A	J K 8 5	B X F D	E S Y Z	T H 9 /	3 N M O	G V C R	4 I P L	W
5	5 8 K J	A U Q W	Z Y S E	D F X B	O M N 3	/ 9 H T	L P I 4	R C V G	5
8	8 5 J K	U A W Q	Y Z E S	F D B X	M O 3 N	9 / T H	P L 4 I	C R G V	8
K	K J 5 8	Q W A U	S E Z Y	X B D F	N 3 O M	H T / 9	I 4 L P	V G R C	K
J	J K 8 5	W Q U A	E S Y Z	B X F D	3 N M O	T H 9 /	4 I P L	G V C R	J
D	D F X B	Z Y S E	A U Q W	5 8 K J	R C V G	L P I 4	/ 9 H T	O M N 3	D
F	F D B X	Y Z E S	U A W Q	8 5 J K	C R G V	P L 4 I	9 / T H	M O 3 N	F
X	X B D F	S E Z Y	Q W A U	K J 5 8	V G R C	I 4 L P	H T / 9	N 3 O M	X
B	B X F D	E S Y Z	W Q U A	J K 8 5	G V C R	4 I P L	T H 9 /	3 N M O	B
Z	Z Y S E	D F X B	5 8 K J	A U Q W	L P I 4	R C V G	O M N 3	/ 9 H T	Z
Y	Y Z E S	F D B X	8 5 J K	U A W Q	P L 4 I	C R G V	M O 3 N	9 / T H	Y
S	S E Z Y	X B D F	K J 5 8	Q W A U	I 4 L P	V G R C	N 3 O M	H T / 9	S
E	E S Y Z	B X F D	J K 8 5	W Q U A	4 I P L	G V C R	3 N M O	T H 9 /	E
	/ 9 H T	O M N 3	R C V G	L P I 4	A U Q W	5 8 K J	D F X B	Z Y S E	

[ii] **Fig. 11 (I)** The addition square

p. 6 Before considering in detail the operations of the Tunny machine it is necessary to define the addition of two teleprinter letters.

Teleprinter letters are added by summing corresponding impulses according to the rules

• plus • equals •
× plus × equals •
• plus × equals ×
× plus • equals ×.

[i] The entry in row O, column D is incorrectly given as E.

[ii] Caption typed entirely in underlined capital letters, without final full stop. Caption moved from top of figure to bottom.

$$\text{Therefore } 9+\mathrm{Y} = \left\{\begin{array}{ccccc} \bullet & & \times & & \times \\ \bullet & & \bullet & & \bullet \\ \times & \text{plus} & \times & \text{equals} & \bullet \\ \bullet & & \bullet & & \bullet \\ \bullet & & \times & & \times \end{array}\right\} = \mathrm{Z}.$$

From this example it is clear that not only 9 + Y = Z but also that 9 + Z = Y and Y + Z = 9. This is an important result which may be stated in the form of the theorem: Addition and Subtraction of teleprinter letters (or characters) is the same thing. (A1) i, E.13

Any proof required is left to the reader.

Fig. **11 (I)** shows an addition square giving the sum of every pair of letters.

(b) Tunny Key

For each letter in turn of the unciphered stream of impulse signals, the Tunny machine makes up a key-letter (K) and adds it to the plain text (P) to get a ciphered letter (Z). E.14

The P-stream can contain any letter of the teleprint alphabet except /, 3, or 4. Of the letters that do occur 9 (space), 5, 8, and E are particularly common. The K-stream and therefore Z-stream, contains each letter of the teleprinter alphabet approximately an equal number of times.

Example		
	P-stream	9 D I E 9 S C H O E N E 9 J U N G F R A U 9
	K-stream	Y / R A V 8 B U J L / 3 K S H V 9 A I C D N
	Z-stream	Z D N 4 G G Q W W W N D J C W L V C N F C 3

(c) The Wheels

12 wheels are used to generate the key. Each wheel consists of a pattern of dots and crosses of a given length. Each character moves into the active position in turn, and when the wheel has gone round completely the pattern is repeated. The wheels are divided into three groups with the following names and lengths.

CHI (χ) Wheels	χ_1	length	41	characters
	χ_2		31	
	χ_3		29	
	χ_4		26	
	χ_5		23	
PSI (ψ) Wheels	ψ_1	length	43	characters
	ψ_2		47	
	ψ_3		51	
	ψ_4		53	
	ψ_5		59	
MOTOR or MU (μ) Wheels	μ_{61}	length	61	characters
	μ_{37}		37	

The key-letter is the sum of the letter of chi-key (χ) formed by the five characters in the active p. 7
positions of $\chi_1, \chi_2, \chi_3, \chi_4, \chi_5$, and the letter of psi-key (ψ') formed by the five characters in the E.15
active positions of $\psi_1, \psi_2, \psi_3, \psi_4, \psi_5$.

(d) Chi-key

After each letter of the P-stream has been enciphered each chi moves on once. The pattern of characters added to each impulse of the P-stream has a period equal to the length of the corresponding chi-wheel, and since the lengths of these wheels are prime to each other, the stream of letters generated by the chis has a period of $41 \times 31 \times 29 \times 26 \times 23$.

---

[i] Equation label '(A1)' handwritten.

(e) Psi-key

The motion of the psis is irregular and determined by the motor. After a letter has been enciphered either (i) each psi wheel moves on once and a new letter of the psi-key is used for ciphering the next letter or (ii) all five psis remain still and the same letter of psi-key is used again. When (ii) happens there is said to be an extension of the psi-stream. The term EXTENDED PSI
E.16 (or ψ') stream is used for the actual sequence of letters added by the Psis to the P-stream, and the
i term ψ-stream for the sequence of letters that the psis would generate if there were no extensions.

Example	P-stream	9 D I E 9 S C H O E N E 9 J U N
	ψ-stream	F L D E Q / K H B 4
	ψ'-stream	F L L D E E E Q / K K H B 4 4 4
	$(P+\psi')$-stream	D 5 H 3 S 9 K A O C A Y X D S C

(f) Motors

The dots and crosses arranged round the motor wheels do not mean the same as the symbols usually called dots and crosses.

E.17 A dot means STOP
A cross means GO.

Mu61 moves on once after each letter is enciphered. When mu61 has a cross in the active position (before moving) mu37 moves on once: when it has a dot in the active position (before moving) mu37 stays still. The character of mu37 in the earlier active position is the active character of the BASIC MOTOR (BM). In other words BM = Mu37 "extended by Mu61" = Mu37′.

Example of finding Basic Motor:

Mu61: × • × × × • × × • × × × × × • × ×
Mu37: × • • × • • × × • × • × • • × × •

(a) Number the characters of Mu61 repeating numbers whenever there is a dot:

× • × × × • × × • × × × × × • × ×
1 2 2 3 4 5 5 6 7 7 8 9 10 11 12 12 13

(b) Number the characters of Mu37 (without repeating)

× • • × • • × × • × • × • • × × •
1 2 3 4 5 6 7 8 9 10 11 12 13 14 15 16 17

(c) Replace the sequence of numbers given in (a) by their equivalents given by (b).

1 2 2 3 4 5 5 6 7 7 8 9 10 11 12 12 13
BM: × • • • × • • • × × × • × • × × •

The active character of the Basic Motor — in conjunction with the active character of the LIMITATION determines the character of the TOTAL MOTOR and this regulates the motion of the psis.

The limitation consists of a sequence of dots and crosses such that when there is a Basic Motor dot *and* a limitation cross in the active position there is a Total Motor dot and the psis do not move.
a At all other places (e.g. where there is a Basic Motor cross or a Basic Motor dot and a limitation dot) there is a Total Motor cross and every psi moves on once.

Example:	Basic Motor	× • • • × • • • × × × • × • × × •
	Limitation	• × • × × • • × × × • • × × • • ×
	Total Motor	× • × • × × × • × × × × × • × × •

[a] an limitation

[i] Handwritten 'the' inserted by caret in each of 'the actual sequence...' and in 'the sequence...'

(g) Limitations p. 8

The sequence of characters defined in paragraph **(f)** as the LIMITATION is a by-product of the other patterns on the machine or in the P-stream, and is not generated independently. Four different methods have been used to produce the limitation and the four different types are defined as follows: a

(i) $\overline{\chi}_2$ limitation (known for short as χ_2 lim. or chi 2 lim).
The active character of the limitation at any position is given by the character of χ_2 which was active in the previous position. This is called chi 2 ONE BACK and written $\overline{\chi}_2$.
(NB $\overline{\overline{\chi}}_2$ means χ_2 two back, $\underline{\chi}_2$ means χ_2 one forward etc.)

(ii) $\overline{\chi}_2 + \overline{\psi}'_1$ limitation (known for short as ψ_1 lim or Psi 1 lim).
The active character of the limitation is given by the sum of the characters of χ_2 and ψ'_1 which were active in the previous position. i

(iii) $\overline{\chi}_2 + \overline{\overline{P}}_5$ limitation (known for short as P_5 lim).
The active character of the limitation is given by the sum of the character of χ_2 which was active in the previous position and the character of P_5 which was active two positions previously. b

(iv) $\overline{\chi}_2 + \overline{\psi}'_1 + \overline{\overline{P}}_5$ limitation (known for short as $\psi_1 P_5$ lim).
The active character of the limitation is given by the sum of the characters of χ_2 and ψ'_1 which were active in the previous position and the character of P_5 which was active two positions previously.

Limitations involving P_5 constitute an "autoclave" since the key stream becomes dependent on the Plain Language. E.18

On the earliest model of the Tunny machine there was "No limitation". This was equivalent to a limitation stream consisting entirely of crosses, so that Total and Basic motors were the same.

(h) A General Example of Ciphering with $\overline{\chi}_2 + \overline{\psi}'_1$ limitation

(i)	P:	9 I M 9 K A M P F 9 G E G E N 9	(given)
(ii)	χ:	U O 8 X X R J Y W O R / E Q L 3	(given)
(iii)	ψ:	N L D E Q / K H B 4	(given)
(iv)	BM:	• • × × • • × • × • × × • • • ×	(given)
(v)	χ_2:	× • × • • × × • × • × • • × × •	(from ii)
(vi)	$\chi_2 + \psi'_1$:	× • × × × • • × × × • • × × × •	(from v and x)
(vii)	$\overline{\chi}_2 + \overline{\psi}'_1$:	• × • × × × • • × × × • • × × ×	(from vi)
(viii)	TM:	× $\underline{\bullet}$ × × $\underline{\bullet}$ $\underline{\bullet}$ × × × $\underline{\bullet}$ × × × $\underline{\bullet}$ $\underline{\bullet}$ ×	(from iv and vii)
(ix)	ψ':	N $\underline{L}$ $\underline{L}$ D $\underline{E}$ $\underline{E}$ $\underline{E}$ Q / $\underline{K}$ $\underline{K}$ H B $\underline{4}$ $\underline{4}$ $\underline{4}$	(from iii and viii)
(x)	ψ'_1:	• • • × × × × × • × × • × • • •	(from ix)
(xi)	$K = \chi + \psi'$:	J R F H M J R 4 W Q S H C Y T R	(from ii and ix)
(xii)	$Z = P + K$:	K N Z T W 3 P H V W 8 Y 4 H M C	(from i and xi)

Note that the ψ' (ix) depends on (vi) which depends on a character in ψ' at a previous place. ψ' therefore depends on its own recent past and can only be constructed letter by letter. Only

[a] byproduct [b] character of the lim tation

[i] Word 'were' handwritten.

when the 4th letter of ψ' is known can we tell if there is an extension in the ψ from the 5th letter to the 6th and so determine the 6th letter for certain. When this is known, and only then, can we start to find out if the ψ is extended from the 7th to the 8th letters, and so on.

The underlinings in the example show the relation between Total Motor dots and psi extensions.

(i) Functional Summary

The action of the Tunny machine at any given position is most easily expressed by the formula

$$\left.\begin{aligned} Z &= P + K \\ K &= \chi + \psi'. \end{aligned}\right\} \qquad \text{(A2)}$$

p. 10 It follows at once from (A1) that

$$K = P + Z$$

$$P = Z + K \qquad \text{(A3)}$$

$$\text{and} \quad Z + P + \chi + \psi' = /. \qquad \text{(A4)}$$

This shows that ciphering and deciphering both involve adding the key, and are in fact the same process as long as P_5 is not involved in the limitation. When P_5 is involved, the limitation must be taken from the output when enciphering and the input when deciphering.

(j) Mechanical Aspects

E.19 Three models of the Tunny machine are known:

SZ 40 (1940) with no limitation

SZ 42A (1942) with χ_2 or $\chi_2 P_5$ lim.

SZ 42B (1942) with $\chi_2 \psi_1$ or $\chi_2 \psi_1 P_5$ lim.

Apart from the limitation difference the models differ very little in construction.

i Fig. **11 (II)** shows a photograph of a German Tunny machine captured after the surrender. The machine is shown without its metal covering, stands on a metal base of dimensions 19 inches

E.20 × $15\frac{1}{2}$ inches, and has an overall height of 17 inches.

The 12 wheels appear in the picture with their German number painted above them. From left

E.21 to right these wheels are

German name	1	2	3	4	5	6	7	8	9	10	11	12
British name	ψ_1	ψ_2	ψ_3	ψ_4	ψ_5	μ_{37}	μ_{61}	χ_1	χ_2	χ_3	χ_4	χ_5

a The pattern of dots and crosses on each wheel is set up by means of a series of cams which may be either operative or non-operative, according to whether they are placed in a vertical position

E.22 (NOCKE) or an oblique position (KEINE).

Operative NOCKE

Non-operative KEINE

E.23

In the photograph, the cams are most easily seen on χ_2 (Wheel 9) and χ_4 (Wheel 11).

On the front of each wheel can be seen a series of numbers, one of which (seen through a window which is not shown) denotes the wheel position. German wheel numbering and British wheel numbering are arranged in opposite direction so that successive active positions are numbered by the Germans in reverse order.

b The addition of chis and psis is arranged electrically. The motorizing is mechanical.

[a] patterns [b] motorising

[i] Fig. **11 (II)**, which occupies all of p. 9 in the *Report*, has been moved to the following page, p. 15 below.

p. 9

11B/1: ×.95

Fig. 11 (II) i

[i] Caption moved from top of page to bottom of page.

i **(k) Switching on and Switching off**

The machine can be switched in and out of the circuit by moving the switch at the bottom to
E.24, a EIN or AUS. When the switch is at AUS, the teleprinter mechanism is wired direct to the W/T transmitter or receiver. When the machine is switched on, the wheels are reset at positions which are used for ciphering the first letter of the transmission. Before the second letter is ciphered all wheels move on once (irrespective of motor and limitation) and between the ciphering of the second and third letters the psis move normally but μ_{37} always moves. After that, the machine moves in the normal way.

When the machine is switched off, no further letters are enciphered and the wheels stop two places ahead of the last ciphering position.

p. 11 11C WHEEL PATTERNS

(a) German Precautions

Though the Germans never fully appreciated the weaknesses of the Tunny machine, they were alive to some of the more elementary pitfalls. In particular they took care to construct wheel patterns so that

(1) there were not too many extensions of the psis

(2) there was an equal number of dots and crosses in each impulse of the chi-stream and the extended psi-stream.

(3) the sum of consecutive characters in each impulse of the chi-stream and the extended psi-stream was dot and cross with equal frequency.

(b) Differenced and Undifferenced Wheels

The letter (or character) obtained by adding any letter (or character) to its successor is known
E.25 as the differenced or delta (Δ) letter (or character) e.g.

$$\Delta P = P + \underline{P}$$
$$\Delta \chi = \chi + \underline{\chi}$$
$$\Delta \psi_3' = \psi_3' + \underline{\psi_3'}.$$

A differenced wheel pattern is obtained by adding each character in a wheel pattern to its successor, and will clearly have the same period as the undifferenced pattern:

χ_4 pattern: • • × × • × • × × × • • × • • × × • • • × • • × × ×
$\Delta\chi_4$ pattern: • × • × × × × • • × • × × • × • × • • × × • × • • ×

It will be readily seen that the number of crosses in the differenced wheel pattern is equal to twice the number of 'groups' of crosses (or dots) in the undifferenced pattern and is therefore
E.26 even.

[a] teleprinter machanism

[i] The text of p. 10 resumes at this point.

(c) Constructions of Wheel Patterns

Conditions (2) and (3) above were fulfilled as far as the chi-stream was concerned by the rule that the number of crosses in each χ and $\Delta\chi$ pattern should be (as nearly as possible) half the length of the wheel.

The number of crosses in all undifferenced ψ patterns was also made (as nearly as possible) half the length of the wheel. When the psi was extended, the extension produced additional dots or crosses and the proportion was preserved.

The case of the differenced ψ patterns is different. At every extension, a letter of the ψ' stream is repeated and therefore there is a stroke in the $\Delta\psi'$ stream. A *dot* is therefore added to [a]
each impulse of the $\Delta\psi'$ stream at each extension, and therefore, in order to preserve an equal [i]
number of dots and crosses in each impulse of the $\Delta\psi'$ stream (after extension) there must be a preponderance of crosses in each $\Delta\psi$ pattern (before extension).

(d) The Law $ab = \frac{1}{2}$

The proportion of crosses in the TM stream is called a.

The proportion of crosses in each $\Delta\psi$ pattern is called b.

The Germans wished to ensure that the proportion of dots and crosses in each impulse of the $\Delta\psi'$ stream was (if possible) equal to $\frac{1}{2}$.

Now, at TM dots, there is an extension in the $\Delta\psi'$ and therefore a stroke. So a cross in any impulse of $\Delta\psi'$ must occur against a TM cross.

In each impulse, TM crosses occur a proportion a of the time, and at a proportion b of TM cross positions there is a $\Delta\psi$ cross. Therefore proportion of crosses in each impulse of $\Delta\psi'$ stream $= ab$.

By choosing suitable patterns for psis and motors it can always be arranged (and after March 1942 nearly always was arranged) that ab was as nearly as possible $\frac{1}{2}$ in each impulse. p. 12

(e) Dottage

The dottage (d) is defined as the number of dots in the pattern of μ_{37}.

Then proportion of dots in $\mu_{37} = d/37$. This proportion will be unchanged by the extension of μ_{37} by μ_{61}.

Therefore proportion of dots in BM $= d/37$.

But proportion of crosses in limitation $= \frac{1}{2}$ (approx).

Therefore proportion of dots in TM $= d/74$.

Therefore

$$a = \text{proportion of crosses in TM} = \frac{74-d}{74}$$

$$b = \frac{1}{2} \times \frac{74}{74-d} = \frac{37}{74-d}.$$

The $\Delta\psi_1$ pattern must therefore be constructed with the nearest even number to $\frac{43.37}{74-d}$ crosses (and so on).

For SZ 40 with no limitation the calculation is slightly different and left to the reader.

(f) Values of a, b, d

In known wheel patterns (for SZ 42A and SZ 42B)

d varies from 14 to 28

a varies from ·81 to ·62

b varies from ·62 to ·81 so that psi extensions occur from 2/5 to 4/5 of the time.

(Wheel characteristics are discussed more fully in Chapter **22**.)

---

[a] $\Delta\psi$

[i] Word 'equal' handwritten.

11D HOW TUNNY IS USED

(a) Fish Links

Tunny machines worked in pairs, and each pair formed a link which was given (by us) the name of a fish e.g. in May, 1944:

i, E.27 JELLYFISH connected STRAUSSBERG exchange (near BERLIN), with HEERESGRUPPE D and OBERBEFEHLSHABER WEST at PARIS.

E.28 WHITING connected KOENIGSBERG exchange with HEERESGRUPPE NORD at RIGA.

The units to which links were connected remained pretty stable, but the position first of the
E.29 army groups and later of the exchanges became increasingly mobile after the invasion. This aspect of Tunny is discussed in **11E**.

It is obvious that two Tunny machines transmitting to each other must generate identical key steams and must therefore

(i) have the same pattern of dots and crosses round their wheels

(ii) have the patterns set in the same position at the start of each transmission. After this the motors and limitation will act identically at both ends and the machines should always be in step, their motion being synchronised by electrical signals transmitted before and after each teleprinter letter.

p. 13 Different sets of wheel patterns (GRUNDSCHLUESSEL) and different books of settings (SPRUCHSCHLUESSELSAETZE) were used on each link.

a It was usual (though not invariable) for all four machines used on a given Fish link to be of the same type. The rule was broken particularly when spare machines were brought into use. For a long time for example on Gurnard

Berlin transmitted and Zagreb received on SZ 42B (psi 1 lim).
Zagreb transmitted and Berlin received on SZ 42A (chi 2 lim).

(b) Transmissions

b Tunny operators can transmit to each other either in cipher or in clear according to whether the Tunny machine is switched IN or OUT, and either in HAND or in AUTO. If sending and receiving machines were working simultaneously, transmission is described as DUPLEX, otherwise as SIMPLEX.

ii After October 1942 the normal routine was somewhat as follows: The operator sits at the keyboard of the sending teleprinter with the printer of the receiving teleprinter directly in front of him. He makes contact with the operator at the other end by hand transmission in clear, and may carry on a brief conversation in Q-code to ensure that conditions are satisfactory for cipher transmission.

Before the Tunny machine is switched in, the operator sets the wheels to the setting opposite the next number in the QEP book and transmits `QEP` followed by the last 2 figures of the number. Just before switching in he transmits `UMUM` in clear.

After the machine is switched in, all outgoing transmission is in cipher. Further chat by the operator may be answered in clear, or, if the receiving Tunny is also switched in, in cipher. The text of the operator's chat (clear or cipher) is received on the printer but not preserved.

As soon as the operator is ready to transmit his message (which should have been previously perforated) he switches in the auto transmitter and ceases to operate the keyboard. The message

---

[a] fish link [b] of in clear

[i] Mistakenly corrected by hand from 'STRAUSBERG' to 'STRAUSSBERG'; see endnote 27 to this chapter, p. 570 below.

[ii] Oct. 1942

starts with an address and serial number and as it is received it is stuck on a message form by the receiving operator.

The transmission of a complete tape is usually followed by operators' chat in hand and then mixed hand and auto transmission while the sender tries to discover if the message has arrived in comprehensible form, makes any necessary corrections, or retransmits any part of the tape. When the receiver is satisfied, he sends a receipt in clear or cipher according to whether his outgoing Tunny is switched in or not.

After the receipt, the sender may switch off or send another message before resetting. One transmission therefore may contain several serial messages. On the other hand, very long message tapes may be transmitted partly in one QEP and partly in the next, and resetting may also take place during a message if something goes wrong. E.30

(c) Repetition of *P*

Hand transmission is by no means continuous and a PAUSE implies that the operator has stopped to think or is waiting for the other operator to reply.

Pauses in an auto may also occur. Sometimes two tapes are transmitted without any intervening hand transmissions, and there is a pause while the new tape is inserted. More frequently, something goes wrong and auto transmission has to be stopped and restarted. When this happens the tape is moved back so that the last 100 letters are retransmitted. In the decode, therefore, 100 letters or so will be repeated. This repeat of *P* is known as a GO-BACK.

When the pause is accompanied by the resetting of the wheels and the transmission of a new QEP number, the tape is still set back so that the last 100 letters or so of the *P* of one transmission are reciphered at the beginning of its successor. This is known as an OVERLAP. [a]

(d) Depths

p. 14

Each QEP number, and each QEP list, should only be used once. However sometimes the same QEP number and settings are used for two (usually consecutive) transmissions. As long as a limitation involving P_5 is not being used the key generated will be the same for both transmissions and they will be in DEPTH.

If the Tunny machine is switched out and a new transmission started without resetting, there is said to be a FOLLOW-ON. **11B(k)** shows that the decodes of the two parts of a follow-on will be divided by two blanks for which nothing will have been transmitted.

(e) Change of keys

Once a day (usually between 0600 and 1200), some or all of the wheel patterns are changed. The sender sends out QZZ (usually in clear) and this tells the receiver that he is changing over to the new day's patterns, and that the receiver's incoming Tunny must also be changed.

Before Summer 1944 motor patterns were changed daily but chi patterns were changed monthly and psi patterns monthly or quarterly (see **11E(a)**). During the summer changes became more frequent, and after August 1st there was a daily change of all wheel patterns on all links.

Wheel patterns were issued for a month at a time. A day's wheel patterns — as issued — are shown in Fig. **11 (III)** where + = Nocke and 0 = Keine.

11E THE TUNNY NETWORK

(a) The period of experiment

The Tunny machine (SZ40 with no limitation) made a first and experimental appearance in June 1941 on the link Berlin–Athens–Saloniki. At first it was used crudely enough. E.31

(i) Wheel patterns were not chosen so that $ab = \frac{1}{2}$, and there was a regular excess of dots over crosses in the $\Delta\psi'$ stream.

[a] This is know as

(ii) The QEP indicating system had not been introduced and wheel settings were chosen by the sender, and sent out in a simple substitution of letters for settings which changed every month and was different for each wheel.

(iii) Motor patterns were changed daily, chi patterns monthly, and psi patterns every three months.

(iv) The machine was not wired to a tone transmitter, but the cipher text was recorded and sent
E.32 by facsimile (Hellschreiber).

E.33 Until October, 1942 there was still only one Tunny link, but the procedure gradually improved
E.34 with the introduction of $ab = \frac{1}{2}$ and of Tone Transmission before March, 1942.

The replacement of the single link by two links — Codfish from Berlin to Saloniki and Octopus from Koenigsberg to South Russia — using the QEP system and with monthly change of chi and psi patterns, signified the end of the German experimental period and the start of the general expansion of the Tunny system.

(b) The period of expansion

SZ42A was first introduced on Codfish in February 1943, and gradually replaced SZ40 on all links.

SZ42A was fitted with a P_5 attachment which was used experimentally on Herring (Rome–Tunis) in March 1943, but only made a general appearance after December 1943 on Western European links.

At the time of the allied invasion of the continent in 1944, Tunny had reached its most widespread and stable level of organisation. There were 26 links and two main central exchanges.
i STRAUSSBERG near Berlin — the terminus for the 9 Western links and
p. 15 KOENIGSBERG the terminus for the 10 Eastern links. The exchanges were connected by a further link (DACE) and there were 6 cross country links.

(c) The period of Flux

From July 1944 – May 1945, the organisation of the Tunny network became increasingly disorganised as German Army units and even German Headquarters stations moved to new
a positions. Nearly all links had their terminus moved to new exchanges at Zossen near Berlin between July 1944 and October 1944. When Berlin was threatened part of these exchanges moved
E.35 first to Erfurt then back to Berlin, and ultimately (by the end of the war) to Salzburg. Charts showing the Tunny network at various times in 1944–5 are given in Part **6**.

Cipher security was tightened in the summer of 1944 and by August 1st a daily change of all wheel patterns had been introduced on each link. SZ42B was first used on Codfish in June 1944
ii and about half the Tunny links were issued with this machine. At first it was used (as SZ42A was then used) with the P_5 limitation switched in (i.e. on $\psi_1 P_5$ lim) but later it was decided that the P_5 attachment on both machines gave more trouble than it was worth, and it dropped out of use from September 1944 onwards.

By May 1945 the German Army was in a state of complete disorganisation and the last Tunny
iii message was sent on 8th May, 1945.

---

[a] as Zossen

[i] See endnote 27 to this chapter, p. 570 below.
[ii] Word 'as' handwritten.
[iii] The words '8th May, 1945' handwritten.

Geheime Kommandosache!

Pr.-Nr. 1

SZ 42 Wehrmacht-Fernschreib-Grundschlüssel Nr. 863

(W. Fschr. Grd. Schl.)

Monatstag: 4

Rad	01 02 03 04 05	06 07 08 09 10	11 12 13 14 15	16 17 18 19 20	21 22 23 24 25	26 27 28 29 30	31 32 33 34 35	36 37 38 39 40	41 42 43 44 45	46 47 48 49 50	51 52 53 54 55	56 57 58 59 60	61
1	0+0+0	0+0++	0+0+0	+0+00	++000	++++0	0+0+0	+0++0	++0				
2	00+0+	0++0+	0+++0	0++0+	0+00+	+0000	+0+0+	++00+	0++0+	0+			
3	0+00+	++000	+0+00	0++00	+0+0+	+0+0+	++00+	0+00+	0+0++	+0+0+	+		
4	+0++0	0++0+	00+0+	0+00+	+0000	+++00	+0+++	+0+0+	0+0+0	+00+0	++0		
5	+0+00	+0+0+	0+00+	000++	000+0	+++0+	+0+0+	0+00+	++00+	0+++0	0+0++	0+0+	
6	++000	+0++0	++++0	+++00	++000	+0+0+	000++	+0					
7	+0+00	00+++	00+++	+0+++	+00++	++0++	++0++	++000	++++0	+++0+	++00+	+++0+	+
8	0++00	++00+	+00++	00++0	0++++	00++0	0+00+	+00++	0				
9	000+0	+00+0	++000	0+++0	0+0++	++0++	0						
10	+++00	+++00	+++00	+0000	+++0+	00+0							
11	00+0+	+++00	+00++	0000+	+++00	+							
12	++000	+++0+	00+++	0+000	++0								

11. 44. 30 000. L/0359

11E/1: ×.65

E.36

Fig. 11 (III) Specimen of captured Tunny wheel patterns [i]

[i] Caption moved from top of figure to bottom. Fig. **11 (II)** excised from TNA HW 25/4; this image scanned from the GCHQ copy of the *Report* by a 'discretionary release of retained material by GCHQ historian'. This image ©Crown Copyright. Used with permission of Director GCHQ.

p. 16 # 12 CRYPTOGRAPHIC ASPECTS

i

12A THE PROBLEM

(a) Formulae and Notation

In Chapter 11 we have defined P, K, χ, ψ', and Z as the letter of plain language, key, chi,
a extended psi and cipher streams in the active position, $\overline{P}$ and so on as their predecessors, $\underline{P}$ and so on as their successors and $\Delta P = P + \underline{P}$ etc.

Before discussing the cryptographic aspects of the Tunny machine it is necessary to restate the formula of the machine:

$$Z = P + K$$
$$K = \chi + \psi'$$

and to list the following relevant variants, D (or DE-CHI) being defined as the sum of Z and χ streams.

$$Z = P + K = D + \chi$$
$$K = P + Z = \chi + \psi'$$
$$D = Z + \chi = P + \psi'.$$

For practical, if not logical, simplicity it will be found that P, K, ψ', D and Z are sometimes used to refer not to any specific letter in the active position but to the whole of the stream concerned.

Further, now that the distinction between a message and a transmission has been carefully drawn, it will be convenient to refer to each of these as a message. This practice is in accordance with traditional usage and agrees with that found in the Research Logs and other contemporary
E.1 Tunny documents. The exact meaning will usually be clear from the context.

(b) Wheel-breaking and Setting

Cryptographic work on Tunny falls into two parts

(i) The recovery of wheel patterns or WHEEL-BREAKING

(ii) The recovery of message settings or SETTING.

The theoretical basis of wheel-breaking and setting is very similar, and for every method of setting there is a corresponding method of wheel-breaking which uses more traffic and more information.

---

[a] active position, P and so on

[i] In the original text of the *Report*, almost all chapters start with an analytical contents list. This one does not. We have accordingly supplied such a list, as a copy editor would have done, for uniformity and the convenience of readers.

Normal practice is therefore to select the most promising material enciphered on a given set of wheel patterns and to use this for wheel-breaking. When the wheel patterns are known, they can then be used for setting other messages enciphered on them.

It will be noticed that it is possible to determine

(i) relative but not absolute settings

(ii) wheel patterns of corresponding chis and psis (e.g. $\chi_4\psi_4$) only with the proviso that dots and crosses may be interchanged on both wheels. This does not apply if one of the wheels is involved in the limitation. E.2

(c) Weaknesses of Tunny

The fact that Tunny can be broken at all depends on the fact that P, χ, ψ', and hence K and D i have marked statistical, periodic or linguistic characteristics which distinguish them from random sequences of letters. p. 17

A typical operation in Tunny breaking consists in using these characteristics to separate out a stream of letters (such as a K-stream) into its component streams (e.g. χ and ψ'). This may be ii described as the solution of an equation; in the example quoted the equation is $K = \chi + \psi'$.

Several equations of this form are soluble given streams of sufficient length. In some cases the solution is a job for a linguist, in others for a statistician, and mechanical aid may or may not a be required.

(d) Early methods

In the early days comparatively simple hand methods of analysis were possible. Before the QEP system was introduced indicators could be used not only to set messages on one or more wheels (when the substitution equivalents were known) but also to recognise depths and near-depths (messages with common settings on nearly all wheels) and even to break wheel patterns. With depths, near depths and partly set messages, the plain language could sometimes be inferred and a stretch of key obtained.

This key could be easily analysed as long as $ab \neq \frac{1}{2}$

$$K = \chi + \psi'$$

$$\therefore \quad \Delta K = \Delta\chi + \Delta\psi'.$$

For when $ab \neq \frac{1}{2}$ there is a surplus of dots over crosses in each impulse of $\Delta\psi'$, and therefore it is immediately possible to deduce the pattern (or setting) of any $\Delta\chi$ from a long enough stretch of that impulse of Δkey.

These methods are described in some detail in Part **4**, but the bulk of this report is designed to show the more complex methods required when wheels and indicating system were constructed so as to invalidate the more simple-minded approaches. In the pages that follow it is assumed that $ab = \frac{1}{2}$, and that indicators give no information about the settings used. All methods described apply to the Tunny machine with limitation; the only simplifications which are possible for Tunny b with no limitation are trivial and easily deducible. c

12B MODERN STRATEGY

There are three main methods of Tunny analysis each of which can (in suitable circumstances) be used for wheel-breaking or setting. The stages by which Z is broken down into χ, ψ', P and Motors in each method are shown diagrammatically in fig. **12 (I)** and listed below. d

[a] for statistician [b] described, apply [c] easily deduceable [d] diagramatically

[i] Handwritten phrase 'and hence' inserted with a caret.
[ii] Parenthesis after 'K-stream' missing.

(a) 1st Method

a Stage I. Solution of $Z = \chi + D$. Various χ patterns (or settings) are tried mechanically and the correct one is distinguished by the statistical properties of ΔD.

Stage II. Solution of $D = P + \psi'$. This is a hand job for a cryptographer who can recognise
b, c plain language and extended psi stream. ψ patterns (or settings) follow at once from the ψ' stream.

Stage III. Solution of motor patterns (or settings), by hand from the extended psi-stream.

This method is the general method of wheel-breaking and setting when the motors are not known and Stage III is still in progress. The use of the method is limited by the minimum length
d required to obtain reliable chi patterns or settings in Stage I. For chi-breaking the minimum length
p. 18 is about 4000 and for chi setting about 1000 letters.

(b) 2nd Method

Stage I. Mechanical solution of $Z = \chi + D$ as in 1st method.

Stage II. Solution of motor patterns (or settings) from ΔD stream by statistical and mechanical means.

Stage III. Solution of $D = P + \psi'$. ψ' streams corresponding to the various possible ψ patterns (or settings) are tried mechanically, the correct one being distinguished by the statistical recognition of P. It will be noticed that this is only possible after the motors have been broken (or set).

This method is entirely mechanical and, as soon as there were sufficient machines available, it became the general method of setting as soon as the motor patterns were found. This method was used for wheel-breaking, but only experimentally. For this reason the statistical breaking of motor patterns from ΔD is discussed in the Appendix (**92**) and not in Part **2**. The minimum length required for wheel-breaking and setting is rather greater than that required in the first method.

(c) 3rd Method

Stage I. Solution of $Z = K + P$ by means of depth or crib. Plain language for two messages in depth found by hand or a predetermined stretch of P is mechanically tried in various positions of Z and the correct position distinguished by the statistical properties of ΔK.

e Stage II. Solution of $K = \chi + \psi'$. Various χ patterns (or settings) are tried by hand or mechanically and the correct one is distinguished by the statistical properties of $\Delta\psi'$.

Stage III. Solution of motor from ψ' as in 1st method.

This method (as far as depths are concerned) is the only method needing no machine help. Before the introduction of autoclave and the arrival of machines it was the general method of wheel-breaking and setting. Depths remained an important method of wheel-breaking on links without autoclave, though depths for setting became increasingly rare. Cribs provided a useful subsidiary method of wheel-breaking on all links. At least 100 letters of key were required for wheel-breaking.

---

[a] χ-patterns [b] ψ-patterns [c] follow a once [d] chi-patterns [e] χ-patterns

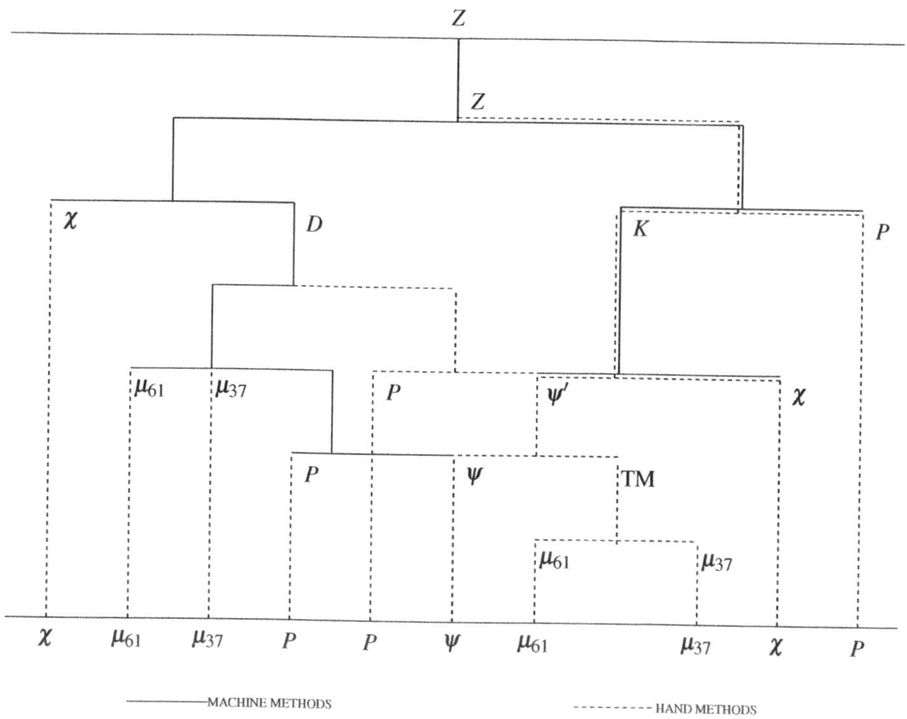

Fig. 12 (I)

12C CHI BREAKING AND SETTING Solution of $Z = \chi + D$

p. 19

(a) Frequency of letters in $\Delta\psi'$

The precautions taken by the Germans in the construction of wheel patterns produce χ, $\Delta\chi$, and ψ' streams in which each letter occurs an approximately equal number of times. But though the arrangements for $\Delta\psi'$ produce an even distribution of dots and crosses in each impulse separately, the fact that there is a dot on *every* impulse wherever there is an extension and a preponderance of crosses in other places, produces a $\Delta\psi'$ stream in which

> wherever there is a TM dot there is a stroke
>
> wherever there is a TM cross the frequency of the various letters in $\Delta\psi$ depend on the number of crosses in them.

It can easily be seen ... that the proportion of TM dots (which $= 1 - a$) and the frequency of crosses in each impulse at TM cross positions (which $= b$) both increase with the dottage. Fig. **12 (II)** gives a $\Delta\psi'$ count on a day with 26 dots in μ_{37}.

(b) Frequency of letters in ΔP

The number of occurrences of each letter in ΔP are by no means equal. The frequent repetition in P of groups of letters common in punctuation or German language like `55M889` or `5M89` (full stop) `EI`, `EN N9`, `SCH` and so on naturally implies the frequent repetition in ΔP of their differenced equivalents `/UA/5`, `UA5`, `U`, `F`, `3`, `JG`. Therefore letters like `5` and `U` which come from popular bigrams in P are frequent in ΔP. Typical P and ΔP counts are given in fig. **12 (II)**. E.3

(c) Frequency of letters in ΔD

We now consider what happens in $\Delta D = \Delta P + \Delta\psi'$. Wherever $\Delta\psi'$ is a stroke, ΔP will be reproduced in ΔD, since any letter added to stroke is unchanged. Therefore the shape of the ΔD [i] count at those places where there are TM dots is identical with the shape of the count of ΔP. In other places every letter in ΔD will occur an approximately equal number of times (though the combination of letters common in ΔP and in $\Delta\psi'$ against BM crosses will make some letters rather stronger than the others). A ΔD count can therefore be regarded as a watered down version of the ΔP count at the back of it.

Example		
	P:	`9 I M 9 K A M P F 9 G E G E N 9`
	ΔP:	`4 G O J N 8 R 5 D V 5 5 5 F 3`
	$\Delta\psi'$:	`8 / 5 3 / / P Q K / 5 / / V /`
	ΔD:	`X G A A N 8 M N I V / 5 5 W 3`

As the μ_{37} dottage increases and therefore also the proportion of strokes in $\Delta\psi'$, the proportion of ΔD count derived directly from ΔP count increases, and the ΔD count from a given ΔP count will be correspondingly stronger.

(d) Chi Setting

It has been shown that $\Delta D =$ not only $\Delta P + \Delta\psi'$ but also $\Delta Z + \Delta\chi$. If we know the wheel [a] patterns, we can (in theory) set the chi wheels to every possible combination of settings in turn and generate all the $\Delta\chi$ sequences corresponding to the χ streams with which the transmission could have been enciphered. These can be added to the ΔZ and all possible ΔD's obtained. The counts of letter frequency in all these possible de-chis will be more or less level, except the counts [b] of the correct de-chi which will follow the pattern described in the last paragraph. If the correct count shows the characteristics of a ΔD count strongly, it will be easily identified, and the chi [p. 20] settings will be found without any doubt even though the original chance that any particular set of settings is correct is as small as 1 in $41 \times 31 \times 29 \times 26 \times 23$, that is 1 in 22 million.

Fortunately it is not necessary to try out every combination of chi settings individually. We can count the combined frequency of `O` and `M` say, without knowing (or bothering) where chi 3 is [ii] set, by counting the number of positions where ΔD_1 is a dot, ΔD_2 a dot, ΔD_4 a cross, and ΔD_5 a cross. Therefore using the combined counts of `O` and `M` and of other pairs of letters differing from each other only on the third impulse we can set chi 1, chi 2, chi 4, and chi 5, and then go back later to chi 3.

When attempting to set a message we normally start with the '1+2 BREAK IN'. We count the $\Delta D_1 + \Delta D_2 =$ dot, that is the combined frequency of the letters `/9HT OMN3 AUQW 58KJ`, most of which occur frequently in ΔD. On a correct de-chi the count of these 16 letters should be well above the count of the other 16 letters, for which $\Delta D_1 + \Delta D_2 = \mathbf{x}$. On a de-chi at incorrect settings the combined frequency of any 16 letters should be about half the total number of letters counted. So by counting possible de-chis on the first two impulses only, at the $41 \times 31 = 1271$ possible settings for chi 1 and chi 2, we can probably set these wheels. Then, by counting the frequency of other suitably chosen sets of letters we can set the other chis in turn (either singly or in pairs). It is not necessary to set all chis simultaneously.

Even so, the counting of the 1271 possible Δ de-chis on the first two impulses and other similar operations are not jobs which could be undertaken by hand. The COLOSSUS is a machine which has been devised to do these jobs at high speeds. It can be made to record the answers only at

---

[a] wheel-patterns [b] dechis will be ... the correct dechi

[i] Handwritten 'TM' inserted with caret.

[ii] In this and the following paragraph, the *Report*'s $D1$ and $D2$, etc. have been rendered as D_1 and D_2, etc.

such settings as are likely to be correct. A ROBINSON is a more general machine which can be used for the same purpose. E.4

If a transmission is too short then the correct ΔD count will not stand out sufficiently from the others to make the settings certain. When the language is moderately good the minimum lengths required are very roughly as shown in the following table (d is the dottage of μ_{37}).

d	15	18	21	24	27
Rough minimum	6200	4000	2400	1700	1200

These figures have a very large probable error. E.5

(e) Chi Breaking

If there is a very strong ΔD count for a given transmission it is possible not only to select the settings used for making the correct $\Delta\chi$ stream if the wheel patterns are known, but to determine the patterns of the wheels themselves if they are not known. This is equivalent to selecting the correct ΔD count from the series of letter counts made with ALL POSSIBLE wheel patterns, and can often be done even though the original chance that any set of wheel patterns is correct is 1 in 2 to the power of $(41+31+29+26+23) = 1$ in $2^{150} = 1$ in 10^{45}. (In fact the figure 10^{45} is an a overstatement, as the Germans impose restrictions on themselves in the choice of wheel patterns which reduce the figure to about 10^{38}.) (See **25X**.)

The $1+2$ RECTANGLE which is made on Colossus or Garbo and CONVERGED by hand is E.6, E.7 a means of finding the patterns of $\Delta\chi_1$ and $\Delta\chi_2$ which maximise the number of letters of ΔD in which $\Delta D_1 + \Delta D_2 =$ dot. The extent to which this frequency can be made to exceed $\frac{1}{2}$ when the b optimum patterns have been chosen, determines (a) how much relation the optimum patterns are likely to have to those really used and (b) whether it is worth while to attempt to use the most reliable characters in the optimum pattern for setting other messages enciphered on the same wheel patterns or as a start for COLOSSUS WHEEL-BREAKING. In Colossus wheel-breaking E.8, c attempts are made to find the deltaed patterns of all the chis which will lead to the strongest ΔD count.

Unless there is a transmission of over 4000 letters it is unlikely that the optimum $\Delta\chi_1$ and $\Delta\chi_2$ will be strong enough to be in any way significant and therefore chi-breaking by means of the rectangle will be impossible.

---

[a] in fact [b] $\Delta D1 + \Delta D2 =$ dot. [c] Colossus-wheelbreaking

p. 21

	P		ΔP	ψ'	$\Delta\psi'$	ΔD	χ	Z	
/	4	(a)	91	118	1159	128	98	110	/
9	544		78	107	4	127	99	81	9
H	67		82	97	17	128	99	94	H
T	123		56	108	4	98	101	124	T
O	89		121	107	18	128	101	108	O
M	180		69	100	47	105	106	89	M
N	212		66	98	7	78	95	95	N
3	1	(a)	157	99	2	118	101	114	3
R	159		77	87	11	87	105	110	R
C	44		73	84	53	84	98	105	C
V	21		64	100	153	80	99	89	V
G	94		127	109	32	125	114	93	G
L	87		76	85	17	98	118	104	L
P	51		90	116	47	99	110	123	P
I	137		50	121	10	94	89	87	I
4	3	(a)	52	79	5	71	105	93	4
A	161		136	96	13	96	90	82	A
U	81		224	109	52	148	103	99	U
Q	23	(b)	79	103	186	92	97	88	Q
W	38		67	108	52	70	114	104	W
5	200		326	106	160	170	108	106	5
8	197		144	75	572	101	107	112	8
K	60		45	106	154	66	99	95	K
J	6		194	96	46	115	96	77	J
D	71		83	91	14	71	91	85	D
F	42		156	103	56	107	83	104	F
X	1		83	79	168	87	93	106	X
B	57		32	111	47	55	104	101	B
Z	26		65	81	13	81	103	108	Z
Y	7		84	94	62	88	95	106	Y
S	110		90	121	14	109	75	110	S
E	304		63	106	5	96	104	98	E
Total	3200		3200	3200	3200	3200	3200	3200	

i **Fig. 12 (II)** Some Typical letter counts

Notes

E.9 All counts are taken from the same message ciphered on the keys of Grilse Jan. 10th 1945. (26 dots in μ_{37}.)

E.10 The bulges in the counts of P, ΔP, $\Delta\psi'$, ΔD have been explained. ψ', χ, Z show (for all practical purposes) typical random count in which every letter occurs an approximately equal number of times. The counts of D, K, $\Delta\chi$, ΔZ must also be flat.

a (a) /, 3, and 4 should not occur in P. Their occurrence is due to corruption.

(b) Q rarely occurs in 'letter-shift', but is quite frequent in figure-shift, where it corresponds to 1 (one).

(c) Note how the frequency of letters other than / depends on the number of crosses in them. For 26 dots in μ_{37} $a = \cdot 65$ $b = \cdot 77$.

[a] /34 should not

[i] Caption moved from top of figure to bottom.

12D MOTOR AND PSI BREAKING AND SETTING Solution of $D = P + \psi'$

p. 22

(a) Psi-breaking and setting by hand

When chi-wheels and settings for a message are known the chi stream and *Z* stream can be added together and de-chi stream found. A stretch of de-chi can be converted by eye into the sum of *P* and psi by a skilled cryptographer with knowledge of "Tunny-German" and the power of instantaneous mental addition of letters of the Teleprint alphabet.

A start can be made as follows: it is very likely that somewhere in every message a full-stop (say 5M89) in *P* will occur at the same place as a long extension of the psis (say TTTT). Experienced men know at sight that

JNKH = 5M89 + TTTT

NJ3W = 5M89 + QQQQ [i]

and so on, so that the identification of a 'stop' often provides an initial break from which further *P* and ψ' can be determined.

Example		
	Part of de-chi stream (data):	C Q P Q V B G Q F F Y J E B 4 L T
	P stream (inferred):	9 I N F 5 M 8 9 D I V 5 M 8 9
	ψ' stream (inferred):	R Z G G S S S W 9 J J T X I I

From ψ' obtained in this way the unextended psi is easily found. If there are 59 letters of it, the sequence will give us the complete pattern of dots and crosses on psi 5 (unconfirmed) and a complete pattern (partly confirmed) on the other psis. Fewer letters of psi (about 10) are required to find the *settings* of wheels whose patterns are already known.

As the dottage and number of extensions increases, reading a de-chi becomes correspondingly easier although more letters of ψ' are required to give an adequate stretch of psi.

(b) Motor-breaking and setting given $\Delta\psi'$

When the psi patterns (or settings) for some point in a message have been found, it is necessary

(i) To find the psi settings for the start of the message.

(ii) To recover a sufficiently long stretch of ψ' to enable the motor patterns (or settings) to be determined.

In order that motor settings for the beginning of the message may be found directly, these two jobs are usually done in unison. The approximate psi settings for the start of the message may be calculated and the psi stream generated. This can be fitted on to the de-chi stream and used to separate into *P* and ψ' a longish stretch of de-chi near the start — the psi being extended wherever this is required to make sense of the *P*.

When a longish stretch has been read the motor can be worked out. The ψ' shows where the TM dots occur. There is a BM dot at all these places and a BM cross at every other place which has a limitation cross, the character of the limitation being determined since chi, psi and *P* are known.

Consequently, certain dots and crosses in the BM stream can be placed: when enough have been placed it is possible to find a unique pattern of motor wheels (or a unique position of motor wheels) which will fit these BM dots and crosses without contradiction.

The length of ψ' required depends on the dottage; the normal minima are 300 letters for motor breaking and 120 letters for motor setting.

---

[i] No line break after 'QQQQ'.

(c) Motor and psi-settings by machine

It has already been shown that a ΔD count consists of the sum of the count against TM dots, where $\Delta D = \Delta P$, and the count against TM crosses which is nearly random. The strong letters in ΔD therefore derive a proportion of their strength from BM dots which is greater than the
p. 23 proportion of BM dots in the whole message. We can therefore — in favourable circumstances — select the correct motor settings by trying each pair of settings in turn and choosing those at which the frequency of the strongest ΔD letters against BM dots is a maximum.

a With $\overline{\chi}_2$ limitation, the extended psi pattern corresponding to each possible setting of each psi is known as soon as the motors have been set, and the correct setting of each psi can be recognised by the marked characteristics $D + \psi' = P$ in each impulse. For unlike ΔD, which has an equal number of dots and crosses in each impulse as long as $ab = \frac{1}{2}, P_1, P_2, P_4, P_5$ normally have an excess of dots and P_3 an excess of crosses sufficient for it to be possible to set at least one psi wheel independently of the others.

b For psi 1 (or P_5) limitation a similar method can be used, provided psi 1 (or psi 5) is set first and no effort is made to set the other psis until the pattern of the Total Motor has been completely determined.

Colossus is designed to carry out both these jobs.

12E METHODS INVOLVING KEY Solution of $Z = K + P$, and $K = \chi + \psi'$

(a) Obtaining of key from depths

As the key stream is the same for both messages (a and b) of a depth, we get

$$Z_a + P_a = K = Z_b + P_b$$
$$\therefore \quad Z_a + Z_b = P_a + P_b.$$

Z_a and Z_b are known. $Z_a + Z_b$ can be found by addition and a skilled cryptographer can separate this out into the sum of two stretches of plain language.

Example: Z_a	=	A O 9 V Y P B 8 S L K N 9 I I / P R 8 Y Q A H V 8
Z_b	=	N N R Z Y A P Q U F G L I N C 3 A 4 L P 8 / K 9 Z
$Z_a + Z_b$	=	K H C K / Y K 3 4 8 Y V 4 R 3 3 Y 3 F A 3 A 5 G C
P_a	=	5 Q M 8 9 E N G L 5 M 8 9 I N F 5 M 8 9 D I V 5 M
P_b	=	H A L T 9 H A L T 9 D E I N 9 S C H L U E S S E L

from Z_a and P_a the stretch of key is found by addition.

(b) Obtaining of key from cribs

At certain times in the history of Tunny certain routine reports were sent out from the "Berlin" end of two or more different links from the same P-tape. It may be possible to identify retransmission of this type from serial receipts and other forms of unciphered operators' chat before either version has been decoded, and as soon as one version has been decoded it is comparatively easy to do so.

When the report has been decoded on one link it is possible to find the point in the Z of the undeciphered link at which the P from the known decode starts. This is done by trying the various possible positions (on a Robinson) and testing $P + Z$ at each position for the statistical characteristics of ΔK.

[a] settings [b] are

(c) Wheel-breaking from key

Chi-breaking from key is analogous to chi-breaking from Z, the method being to select the [a] patterns of $\Delta\chi$ wheels which will give the strongest count for $\Delta\psi'$. It is, in fact, equivalent to chi-breaking from Z when the P-stream consists entirely of strokes. p. 24

The comparative strength of a $\Delta\psi'$ and a ΔD count can be seen in fig. **12 (II)** and is such that whereas chis are rarely broken from under 4000 letters of $Z = \chi + D$, they can sometimes be broken from 100 letters of $K = \chi + \psi'$. This means that the dimensions of the job make it quite practicable by hand though a Colossus may profitably be used if the stretch of key is sufficiently long.

Wheel-breaking from key on χ_2 limitation normally starts with a $\widehat{\chi}_2$ count or run. Wheel- [b] breaking from other kinds of key normally starts with KEY RECTANGLES and a COMBINED ($\Delta\chi_5$) FLAG. If this is significant the chi patterns obtained are used to complete the wheels by an improved form of TURINGERY (Turing's Method), or alternatively by Colossus wheel-breaking methods, if the key has more than about 300 letters.

Once the chi patterns have been found and the $\Delta\psi'$ stream obtained, the recovery of the psi patterns is trivial.

---

[a] analagous [b] Wheelbreaking

p. 25 # 13 MACHINES

i

13A Explanation of the categories
13B Counting and stepping machines
13C Copying machines
13D Miscellaneous simple machines

E.1 The machines used in Tunny-breaking may be classified as:—

(1) Counting and Stepping Machines.

(2) Copying Machines.

(3) Miscellaneous simple machines.

13A EXPLANATION OF THE CATEGORIES

(a) Counting and stepping machines

These machines are given two teleprinter patterns, combine them in some way and count the number of places of the combined pattern in which a certain condition is satisfied.

An essential feature is that these counts must be made with the two patterns in all possible relative positions i.e. one pattern must "step".

For example, chi-setting consists of adding $\Delta\chi + \Delta Z$ in all possible relative positions, and counting for each position the number of places in which a condition such as $\Delta\chi_1 + \Delta\chi_2 + \Delta Z_1 + \Delta Z_2 = \text{dot}$ is satisfied.

At each setting the answer is, of course, a number.

(b) Copying Machines

These combine one or more teleprinter patterns. They differ from "Counting and Stepping" machines in that

(i) there is no stepping.

(ii) the result is not a number, but a sequence of letters.

The sequence of letters may be either a punched tape or a print-out.

These machines vary greatly in complexity, from the hand-perforator in which a pattern tapped out on a keyboard letter by letter is reproduced on a tape, to the decoding machine in which Chi, Mu, Psi set up electrically are combined with Z to produce P.

Of all machines "Counting and Stepping" machines are by far the most spectacular: both cryptographically and electrically they are notable achievements. For producing results they are dependent on humbler machines, especially tape-making machines.

[i] In the original text of the *Report*, almost all chapters start with an analytical contents list. This one does not. We have accordingly supplied such a list, as a copy editor would have done, for uniformity and the convenience of readers.

13B COUNTING AND STEPPING MACHINES

There are three versatile machines:—

Colossus

Robinson

5202

The fundamental difference between Colossus and Robinson is that on Robinson all patterns are punched on tapes, whereas on Colossus only one pattern is on a tape, the other being represented electrically.

5202, the photographic machine, is essentially a Robinson, using film instead of tape, but working many times faster, first making an approximate count. For details see **91**. p. 26

(a) Colossus

Colossus has a "bedstead" round which the Z tape is driven by pulleys so as to be scanned at 5000 letters per second; and "triggers" in which chi, Mu, Psi patterns may be set up. E.2

The counts most commonly required are of $\Delta D = \Delta Z + \Delta\chi$ and $P = Z + \chi + \psi'$. For these there is a switch panel which imposes conditions on Q, where Q is, at choice, any sum, with or without deltaing, of Z, Chi, Psi.

The Q panel suffices to select almost any arbitrary group of letters, but is kept reasonably small by 'not' switches: "either A or B or C" is replaced by the equivalent "Not(not A, not B, not [a]
C)".

There is a plugboard for conditions not expressible in terms of Q. It has no "not".

The effective speed is increased fivefold by five separate counters which, in particular, can be used for counting at five different settings simultaneously (multiple test).

Specialized facilities include "not 99", for ignoring the 9's used to replace corruption; "spanning", for selecting a part of the text; "set total", for cancelling scores too small to be of interest. [b]

On some Colossi there is an elaborate rectangling gadget; on others a wheel-breaking panel.

Scores are displayed and printed.

Colossus is the standard machine for wheel-setting and breaking: it is too large to replace hand work economically in all cases.

On Colossus only one pattern is arbitrary viz. the tape, the others being restricted by wheel periodicities. If two arbitrary patterns are to be compared Robinson is used.

(b) Robinson

In pre-Colossus days the old Robinson did much of the work now assigned to Colossus, and, considering its primitive character, did so with remarkable success.

The present 'Super Rob.' has four bedsteads, a plugboard rather more flexible than that of Colossus, a very meagre switchboard, "span" and "set total". It lacks the immense elaboration of facilities provided by Colossus.

Its advantage is that patterns punched on a tape are completely arbitrary; its disadvantage that they are difficult to change.

Since Colossus became generally available, Robinsons have been used mostly for cribs and [c]
for experimental work, occasionally for rectangling.

(c) Specialized Counting and Stepping Machines

These are Dragon, for setting short cribs in de-chis; and two machines which arrived too late for operational use: Aquarius, for go-backs and Proteus for depths.

---

[a] not*B* [b] Specialised [c] Robinsons has

p. 27 13C COPYING MACHINES

These machines are fed with tape, keyboard operation or electrically plugged patterns. They produce either tape or printed letters.

E.3 It is convenient to describe them in tabular form.

INPUT		OUTPUT	NAME OF MACHINE	REMARKS
Keyboard	→	tape	Hand perforator	
Tape	→	tape	Angel	
			Insert machine (or I.B.M):	Special facilities for making corrections by hand.
Tape	→	print	Junior:	Has comprehensive steckering
			Garbo:	A Junior with Δ'ing.
Tape	→	tape	Miles:	Can add five tapes with impulse permutation, etc.
			Miles A:	Has also Δ'ing and is more flexible.
Plugged pattern and tape or keyboard	→	tape or print	Tunny:	The plugged patterns are arbitrary Tunny key.
			Decoding machine:	These two machines differ principally in application.

All these machines make use of certain standard units: the simpler ones consist of little else:

1. Tape *Readers* (or transmitters, or auto-transmitters).
2. *Reperforators* (or punches).
3. Electromatic *Typewriters*.

[a] The varieties named in brackets differ technically, not functionally.

13D MISCELLANEOUS SIMPLE MACHINES

These include:—

Slide-rules.

Adding machines.

Hand counters for measuring the length of tapes in terms of sprocket-holes.

E.4 "Stop and Start" for punching stop and start signs.

Stickers (h and c): a device used in joining tapes.

[a] names in brackets

14 ORGANISATION p. 28

i

14A EXPANSION AND GROWTH

(a) General position

In order that information sent out by the Germans in Tunny messages might become available to Allied authorities, four types of organisation had to be built up. These were all under the direction of G.C. and C.S. and concerned Interception, Cryptography, Traffic Analysis and Intelligence.

This report is concerned only with Cryptographic work on Tunny, and the sections at Station X concerned with this occupied an intermediate position between E.1

> GCWS KNOCKHOLT and ancillary non-morse interception stations working on Fish Traffic, and E.2, a

> Intelligence sections at Station X to which Tunny decodes passed (Hut 3, Naval Section, ISOS). ii b, E.3

Traffic Analysis — undertaken by Sixta (Non-morse) — was often of cryptographic value, and several references to Sixta's work will be found in the chapters that follow.

(b) Three periods

The history of cryptographic work on Tunny can be suitably divided into three periods — the Research period, the Testery period, and the combined period.

Tunny traffic was tackled by the Research section shortly after the first link was set up in June 1941. The Research period lasted until July, 1942, by which time a stretch of key had been obtained from a depth (August, 1941), the workings of the machine deduced (January, 1942), and various hand methods of wheel-breaking and setting on the basis of the indicating system, depths, near depths and short cribs devised and used with success on the traffic of March to July, 1942. In July, current traffic was read for the first time.

In July, 1942 Major R.P. Tester formed a Tunny section (the "Testery" — consisting mainly of ex-members of the Research section) to tackle Tunny on an operational basis, and from July to October, 1942 nearly every message was read. In October, 1942, the expansion of the Tunny system started and the QEP system was introduced. After this, operational activity was restricted to wheel-breaking and setting from depths. Depths were frequent and produced many sets of wheels but covered only a fringe of the setting problem.

The Research section again set to work on Tunny and devised statistical and mechanical methods of setting which did not depend on depth. Mr M.H.A. Newman was given the job of developing these operationally in December, 1942, and his section (the "Newmanry") with its first two machines was founded in June, 1943. The section was at first regarded by members of Major E.4

---

[a] ancilliary [b] 180S

[i] In the original text of the *Report*, almost all chapters start with an analytical contents list. This one does not. We have accordingly supplied such a list, as a copy editor would have done, for uniformity and the convenience of readers.
[ii] Word 'Station' handwritten.

Tester's section with some amusement, but by October, techniques were improved and operational work had started.

With the introduction of P_5 limitation in December, 1943, depths disappeared. Mr Newman's section became essential to all Tunny work and a new division of labour was effected. The section became responsible for chi-breaking and setting (which had to be done mechanically), and Major Tester's section for psis and motors which could be broken or set by hand. More and better
p. 29 machines were ordered, so that, when the daily wheel change was introduced in the summer of 1944, the combined sections took it in their stride. The main division of work remained unchanged to the end, though an increasing amount of wheel-breaking was done by Major Tester's section as P_5 was dropped and depths became more frequent, and an increasing amount of motor and psi setting was done by machine as soon as the number of Colossi made this possible.

(c) Combined operations

In general Testery methods were hand methods based on language properties, and Newmanry methods were statistical and needed machines. But there were many contradictions. The computing of Rectangles is a statistical hand job undertaken by the Newmanry, and on the other hand
E.5 Dragon is a machine designed to do a language job in the Testery. Hand analysis of key (by methods elaborated from that devised by TURING in 1942) is a statistical hand job involving probability techniques which was done by the Testery before (and after) the Newmanry was founded.

The decoding room grew up as part of Major Tester's section and remained so. A joint Registry was founded in January, 1944.

14B THE TWO SECTIONS IN 1945

The following brief notes show the general set up of the operational organisation in its final stage of development. Every department was staffed 24 hours a day.

(a) Control and registration

The Control Officer maintained all contacts with Knockholt and Hut 3. In particular he was responsible for informing Knockholt which links were to be covered and which messages were required for wheel-breaking or setting.

Z-tapes for all messages required were prepared at Knockholt and teleprinted in the case of wheel-breaking tapes to Block H, and in the case of setting tapes to Room 11, Block F. Red forms were sent by bag.

The joint registry in Room 12 was responsible for arranging the circulation of these tapes and relevant documents to the Newmanry, the Testery cryptographic departments, and to the decoding room. The registry itself kept all material not in direct operational use, and arranged the disposal and storage of materials relevant to decoded and abandoned messages on which further work was unlikely. This arrangement was of great value in keeping the number of tapes and papers in operational rooms to a minimum. "Room 12" had two branches: the T-Registry in Block H for dealing with wheel-breaking tapes and the Main Registry in Room 12 itself for dealing with setting tapes.

(b) Mr Newman's section

Wheel-breaking activities took place in Block H under the direction of the Wheel Man, setting activities in Block F under the direction of the Duty Officer who also had general charge of the section's activities on his shift. Each Block contained a Registry, Tunny Room and Colossus
p. 30 Rooms.

The TUNNY ROOMS housed copying machines as described in the last chapter. Tunny Room (Block F) undertook the preparation and copying of tapes for setting and the making of printed de-chis (i.e. printed copies of the *D*-stream for sending to the Testery). Room D (Block H) undertook the preparation and copying of wheel-breaking and crib tapes and the making of printed rectangles.

COLOSSI in Block F were used for setting, those in Block H primarily for wheel-breaking and Rectangle-making and the residue for setting. When ROBINSONS were used for setting [i] these were housed in Block F but improved ("super") Robinsons — used mainly for cribs — were [a] installed in Block H.

Details of Tunny Room and Colossus jobs were left to the operators concerned but the jobs were ordered by the REGISTRARS and returned to them on completion. The OPS REGISTRY [ii] in Block F (Ops.) consisted of the RUNS REGISTRARS who issued setting jobs to Colossi (previously to Robinsons), the TAPES REGISTRARS who issued jobs to the Tunny Room (Block F), and the LOGS REGISTRAR who kept in touch with Room 12 and kept track of all tapes sent up by them for setting. In Block H there was a single H-REGISTRY which kept track of all wheel-breaking tapes and ordered any Tunny Room or Colossus jobs.

In addition to these departments, Block H housed the computers and (Newmanry) Cribs section.

COMPUTERS, under the direction of the RECTANGLES REGISTRAR converged rectangles E.6 and did other paper work on Key Rectangles and Flags.

The (Newmanry) CRIBS man and Registrar selected suitable messages for crib jobs with the help of Sixta and (Testery) Cribs Watch and itself organised and ordered the necessary tape-making and Robinson Runs. In addition to this, they were responsible for any other (routine or experimental) Robinson jobs.

Maintenance of machines was the responsibility of the engineer in charge.

(c) Major Tester's Section

ROOM 41 contained 2 registrars and cryptographers for psi-breaking and setting (by hand) from de-chis, reading of depths, and wheel-breaking from Key (by hand). DRAGON — though in a different room — was fed and operated by members of Room 41. The head of Room 41 was in general charge of all work in Major Tester's section on his shift.

De-chis on which psis were broken or set at some point in the message were passed to ROOM 40. ROOM 40 were responsible for Motor breaking and setting, and for finding settings for all wheels as near the start of the message as possible. It also dealt with decoding breakdowns.

Messages set on all wheels were passed to the supervisor of the Decoding Room who issued them to decoding machines as soon as possible, and checked them on return.

Decodes were read by the (Testery) CRIBS watch who routed them to the correct intelligence section and looked out for items of cryptographic importance or of wireless importance (for Sixta) and in particular for possible retransmissions which might serve as cribs.

(d) Sixta p. 31

SIXTA (non-morse) — Mr Uzielli's section — read the unciphered chat between German Operators (which was intercepted at Knockholt), and studied Fish wireless procedure from the Logs of intercept stations and decodes. In particular Sixta supplied information about Retransmissions, daily times of QZZ, and any changes of machine (and limitation) used. E.7

14C CIRCULATION

This section gives four examples of the passage of a message through the two sections in various circumstances. The examples are typical but clearly not exhaustive. The methods referred to are defined in Section **12B**.

[a] mainly for Cribs

[i] Word 'ROBINSONS' handwritten.

[ii] First 'REGISTRARS' and words 'OPS REGISTRY' handwritten.

(a) 1st method. Setting

The Tape arrives in Room 11; is passed on to the Ops. Registry; sent by the Tapes Registrar to Tunny Room to be prepared for Colossus and returned; sent by the Runs Registrar to Colossus for chi-setting and returned. If set, a de-chi is ordered by the Tapes Registrar and returned. Tapes, de-chi, and chi-settings are then sent from the Ops. Registry to Room 12.

E.8 De-chi with RF and chi-settings is sent by Room 12 to Room 41 for psi setting, passed on to Room 40 for motor settings, and on to the Decoding Room. The decode is passed to the Cribs Watch who route it to the appropriate intelligence section via Room 12.

(b) 2nd method. Setting

The tape arrives in Room 11; is passed on to the Ops. Registry; sent by the Tapes Registrar to Tunny Room to be prepared for Colossus and returned. Sent by the Runs Registrar to Colossus for setting on all wheels and returned. If set, tapes and settings are sent to Room 12.

RF and settings are sent from Room 12 to the Decoding Room — then as in **(a)**.

(c) 1st method. Wheel-breaking

The tape arrives in Block H; it is passed to H-Registry; thence it is EITHER sent to Room D for Rectangling on Garbo and returned, OR sent to Room D to be prepared for Colossus and then to Colossus for rectangling and returned. The rectangle is sent to the computers for convergence.

If significant, Tapes and Rectangle go to Colossus for chi-breaking and, if successful, tapes and chi patterns are sent to the Ops. Registry via the H-Registry. A de-chi is ordered from Tunny
a Room (F) by the Tapes Registrar and returned, and tapes, de-chi and chi patterns sent from the Ops. Registry to Room 12.

De-chi with RF and chi patterns is sent by Room 12 to Room 41 for psi-breaking, passed on to Room 40 for motor-breaking, and on to the Decoding Room — then as in **(a)**.

p. 32 **(d) 3rd method. Wheel-breaking from Depth**

Printed texts of the alleged depth are teleprinted to Room 11 and passed to Room 41. If the alleged depth is read successfully, wheel-breaking from Key starts at once by hand in Room 41, but the key is also sent to Block H where it is perforated and rectangled in Room D, a combined flag being then made by the computers. If significant the partial chis from the flag are passed to the key-breaker in Room 41.

b, c If chi and psi patterns are broken successfully they are passed with Key and RF to Room 40 for Motor-breaking, then on to the Decoding Room and as in **(a)**.

Tapes on which setting and wheel-breaking are abandoned are returned to Room 12 and T-Registry respectively.

---

[a] dechi [b] chis [c] patterns ar e broken

15 SOME HISTORICAL NOTES p. 33

i

15A FIRST STAGES IN MACHINE DEVELOPMENT

(a) Early development of Statistical methods

The idea of breaking single Tunny messages without depth by statistical methods was first propounded in the autumn of 1942. The '1+2–Break-in' was invented by W. Tutte in November, 1942 and tested out with success by paper stencils. He also suggested at this time the breaking of chi-wheel patterns by means of the rectangle, and succeeded in finding the chis from a message 15,000 letters long.

Methods for setting motors and psi-wheels (by 'contracting' de-chis) and the rectangle-method for breaking motors, were suggested by others working in the Research section at that time.

(b) Proposals for the use of machinery

The idea of using electronic counters to carry out these processes at a practically useful speed a
was put forward by M.H.A. Newman and in December, 1942 he was given the task of developing machine methods of setting TUNNY.

A number of schemes were considered, including that of sliding photographic plates over E.1
each other, a method later perfected in U.S. It was soon settled that the best machine for the early experimental stages was one which read a 'message-tape' and a 'wheel-tape' photo-electrically, and combined them electrically before counting. Emphasis was laid from the start on the need for flexibility, in order that the routines designed *in abstracto* might be able to be modified in the light of experience without changing the machine.

(c) Heath Robinson

The result of many discussions was the two-tape machine later called 'Robinson'. It consisted E.2
of a valve and relay counter, designed by Dr Wynn-Williams, coupled to a tape-rack ('bedstead') E.3
and a "combining" unit, designed by Mr Flowers of the Post Office Research Station, Dollis Hill. The Pilot model, Heath Robinson, was commissioned in January, 1943 and began working in June of the same year.

'Heath Robinson' amply satisfied the demands for flexibility, and there can be little doubt that the opportunities it gave for trying new techniques at this crucial stage played a decisive part in the later successes of Colossus.

(d) The first 'Tunny'

The 'Robinson' machine for makings counts was accompanied by what was called in the section the 'Tunny' machine, for preparing tapes. This was essentially a reproduction of the German machine in terms of relays and uniselectors, but with facilities for switching in only a section of the wheels and impulses.

It is an important feature of all apparatus used in the section that it uses standard five impulse tape, without any special preliminary processing. Although this led to a good deal of trouble both in designing the apparatus and in the early days of operation, through stretching tapes, it was well

[a] practiclly

[i] In the original text of the *Report*, almost all chapters start with an analytical contents list. This one does not. We have accordingly supplied such a list, as a copy editor would have done, for uniformity and the convenience of readers.

worth while surmounting these troubles in order to be able to use ordinary commercially produced tapes and tape-making plants, (later including American (I.B.M.) Machinery).

p. 34 **(e) Automatic Recording**

In the Robinson as originally designed the selected readings (those above the 'set-total') were shown on a screen, to be copied down by operators, who were then to cancel the reading by a
E.4 switch. Shortly before the machine was finished Mr Gifford, of TRE, suggested that he should design a printer which would print the settings and totals. The automatic recording to which this led proved to be an indispensable part of the process. For operations in which certain initial scores form the basis of complicated later runs, the extra hazards introduced by mistakes and fatigue of copying, and lack of uniformity in hand written dossiers, are great enough to reduce the proportion of success substantially. A rack for automatic recording was therefore made part of
a, E.5 Colossus, even though this entailed some weeks' delay in the arrival of Colossus 1.

15B EARLY ORGANISATION AND DIFFICULTIES

(a) The Initial Staff

The initial staff of Mr Newman's section consisted of M.H.A. Newman, soon joined by
E.6, E.7 D. Michie, with 16 Wren operators and two engineers, working first two shifts and then three, in a two-roomed hut (Hut 11).

(b) Development of the system of checks

The early difficulties were sufficiently severe to prevent more than three messages from being set in any week in the first three months of operation. They arose partly from machine faults, (incorrect tapes from Tunny and incorrect counts on Robinson), partly from operator's errors. The standard of accuracy needed before there was any possibility of success was very much higher than would ordinarily be required of this kind of apparatus, or of operators. A single letter omitted in a tape destroyed the value of the run and the ordinary length of a tape was about 3000 letters. A count missed at the beginning of a run on Robinson gave wheel settings bearing no simple relations to the true ones. In addition there were numerous opportunities for wrong plugging, switching, and tape-setting on both machines. An error which passed undetected through several stages of the work could take hours or even days to track down.

To remedy this state of affairs a system of checks was gradually evolved which made it a rare
b occurrence for a mistake to persist through several operations. To achieve this very elaborate checks were necessary, and about half the operational time was occupied in carrying them out. It was made a principle that the design of a new routine must include all the checks required, and in estimating the merits of a proposed routine the nature of the checks required had always to be taken into account. It is for this reason that checks are described so fully in the chapters that follow.

15C PERIOD OF EXPANSION

(a) Mass production of Robinsons

Towards the end of 1943 the pressure for a large production by machine methods had grown, for two main reasons. The Tunny network had grown, the value of the contents had raised the traffic to the highest level, and the tightening up of German precautions against 'depths' had caused production by 'hand' setting methods to sink almost to zero. The introduction of the P_5 limitation of the end of 1943 made depth-reading impossible. A large programme of machine construction was therefore embarked on. Twelve Robinsons were ordered in the late summer of
p. 35 1943, and the first factory model arrived in November, just in time for the move to more adequate quarters in Block F. The original Pilot model, which was by this time completely worn out, was thereupon abandoned. Some of the later Robinsons had four 'bedsteads' enabling complicated runs to be done without special tape-making.

[a] Colossus I [b] occurence

(b) Colossus

Meanwhile Colossus 1 was delivered in February, 1944, and immediately sent up the output [a] to more than twice its previous level. Colossus was entirely the idea of Mr Flowers of Dollis Hill. His original scheme was to set up the message, as well as the wheels, on valves but this was given up when it was realised that messages of 5000 or more would be wanted. The combination of one tape, carrying the message, with wheel patterns set up electrically, gave nearly all the advantages of the pure valve machine with a great saving in valves and in setting time. The advantages of this machine over Robinson were (1) Its speed, a factor of $25/2$ when 5 counters were available on all chi-runs: (2) The absence of inertia which enabled a run to be stopped at any moment and the wheels switched to assigned settings. (3) The great reliability resulting from the use of valves throughout, instead of relays and the abolition of synchronised tapes. A preliminary order for four further Colossi was placed in March, 1944, increased to twelve at the end of April. The order for Robinsons was curtailed. Great pressure was put on Dollis Hill to deliver the Colossi quickly and they promised on the 14th March to have Colossus 2 (i.e. the first production model) working by 1st June. This promise they fulfilled. Colossus 2 came into action on 1st June at 0800. The remaining Colossi followed at the rate of about 1 a month. A new building (Block H) was erected to house Colossi 5 to 11. Its plans were approved on 25th May, 1944 and it was ready for occupation on 17th September. Work on assembly of Colossus 11 had started on 8th May, 1945 and was stopped (before completion) a few days later.

(c) Staff expansion

The machine expansion was accompanied by an expansion of Newmanry staff which finally amounted to 272 Wrens and 27 men. The organisation had to be correspondingly elaborated, mainly by the multiplication of Registrars to keep track of tapes and jobs in their travels round the Newmanry, and to keep in touch with Major Tester's Section.

(d) Reallocation of work between the two sections

The original paper schemes for machines processes proposed the setting of all 12 wheels by statistical methods carried out on Robinson. The Motor was to be set by running the motor pattern [b] against strokes of ΔD, and psi wheels could then be run against ΔD, 'contracted' by missing out letters opposite motor dots. The Tunny machine had a special contrivance for making the [c] contracted version.

This programme was actually carried out for some months, until it was realised that, given a de-chi, it is possible to set the motor and psis by 'language' methods. This work was done in Major Tester's section, and a convenient division of work and utilization of available resources [d] resulted. With the introduction of the P_5 limitation this division became a necessity, since, on the one hand, chis could no longer be set on depths, and on the other, de-chis could no longer be 'contracted' on Tunny. The division of work on chis and psis necessitated a close co-operation between the two sections, and an important step was the setting up of the joint registry. With the switch over to Colossus, complete setting on all 12 wheels by machine again became possible, and when at the end of 1944 Colossi began to be plentiful a large proportion of messages were completely set by machine methods.

(e) Wheel-breaking [e]

With the introduction of the P_5 limitation it became necessary to break the chi-wheel pattern [f] statistically from ΔD. As long as the wheels changed only once a month this could be done without seriously interfering with the normal setting organisation, and with the use of only about two Wrens a shift for computing. When a daily wheel change was introduced in July, 1944, p. 36 wheel-breaking became a normal part of the Newmanry's work, and about 18 Wrens a shift were employed in computing and (eventually) 3 Colossi on the later wheel-breaking processes.

---

[a] Colossus I [b] motor-pattern [c] tunny machine [d] utilisation [e] Wheel breaking [f] chi-wheel-pattern

'Key-breaking', i.e. finding the wheels by statistical methods from key found from depths, was closely allied to ordinary wheel-breaking, and undertaken in collaboration with the Testery.

(f) Super-Robinson

'Cribbing' as a method of obtaining wheels, was begun in June, 1944. Since this required two message tapes to be run against each other, the use of Robinson was essential, and in view of the [a] troubles on the old Robinson a new model was designed by DR. COOMBS and MR. CHANDLER of Dollis Hill; two of them had been completed by 8th May, 1945.

(g) Tape-making machinery

The prototypes of Garbo and Miles were introduced towards the end of 1943.

[a] DR. COOMBES

21 SOME PROBABILITY TECHNIQUES p. 37

[i]

(a) Symbols used in symbolic logic
(b) Simple probability notations
(c) Special values of p
(d) Relationship of events
(e) The laws of probability
(f) Some theorems — (including Bayes' theorem)
(g) The deciban
(h) Methods of applying the above axioms
(i) Theorem of the weighted average of factors
(j) Theorem of the chain of witnesses
(k) Expected value, standard deviation, variance, distributions
(l) Some special distributions
(m) Some simple formulae of a non-analytic type, concerning proportional bulges
(n) The general formula for sigma in Tunny work
(o) The statistician's fallacy
(p) The principle of maximum likelihood

E.1

It is assumed that the reader has at any rate an elementary knowledge of probability theory. Therefore the account presented here does not contain many examples but is mainly a list of definitions, notations and theorems. Rigour is *deliberately* avoided when it would make the account more difficult to read.

(a) Symbols used in symbolic logic

$\vee$ means 'or'. E.2

. means 'and', but the symbol . is often omitted, thus $E.F$ can be written EF (E and F being propositions).

$\sim$ means 'not' but we shall write '$\widetilde{X}$' instead of the usual '$\sim X$'.

(b) Simple probability notations

$P(E|H)$ means the probability of an event E given a hypothesis H. When H is taken for granted we write $P(E)$ simply.

The letter p represents a probability.

The letter o represents odds and is defined by the equation $o = \frac{p}{1-p}$. The odds of an event E p. 38
given an hypothesis H are written as $O(E|H)$. Sometimes odds are expressed as a ratio such as '3 : 2' or '3 to 2'. This means $o = 3/2$. The following phrases are equivalent.

'$a : b$', '$a : b$ on', '$o = a/b$', 'a to b', 'b to a against' etc.

(c) Special values of p

'Certainty'	$p = 1$ or $o = \infty$
'Impossibility'	$p = 0$ or $o = 0$
'Evens'	$p = \frac{1}{2}$ or $o = 1$.

---

[i] Chapters **21** through **27** are typed double space.

(d) Relationships of events

Two events are 'mutually exclusive' if they cannot both happen. Two events are 'independent' if a knowledge that one is true does not affect the probability of the other one. A number of events is 'exhaustive' if it is certain that one or the other of them will happen.

(e) The laws of probability

(i) the law of addition of probability

$$P(E_1 \vee E_2|H) = P(E_1|H) + P(E_2|H)$$

if E_1 and E_2 are mutually exclusive.

(ii) the law of multiplication of probabilities

$$P(E_1E_2|H) = P(E_1|H)P(E_2|E_1H).$$

In particular, if E_1 and E_2 are independent

$$P(E_1E_2|H) = P(E_1|H)P(E_2|H).$$

(f) Some theorems

(i)

$$\begin{aligned}&P(E_1E_2\ldots E_n|H)\\&= P(E_1|H)\,P(E_2|E_1H)\,P(E_3|E_1E_2H)\cdots P(E_n|E_1\ldots E_{n-1}H).\end{aligned}$$

(ii)

$$\begin{aligned}&P(E_1 \vee E_2 \vee \cdots \vee E_n|H)\\&= \sum_r P(E_r|H) - \sum_{r,s} P(E_rE_s|H) + \sum_{r,s,t} P(E_rE_sE_t|H) - \cdots \text{etc.},\end{aligned}$$

and in particular if $E_1, E_2, \ldots E_n$ are all mutually exclusive, the right hand side can be replaced by
a $\sum P(E_r|H)$. If $E_1 \vee \cdots \vee E_r$ is exhaustive the left-hand side is 1. Therefore $P(\widetilde{E}) = 1 - P(E)$.

E.3 **(iii) Bayes' theorem**

For various hypotheses H_i $\quad (i = 1, 2, \ldots)$

$$\frac{P(H_i|E)}{P(H_i)} \propto P(E|H_i).$$

p. 39 The proof of this is simple. For by the law of multiplication of probabilities,

$$\begin{aligned}P(H_i|E)\,P(E) &= P(EH_i) = P(E|H_i)\,P(H_i)\\ \therefore \quad \frac{P(H_i|E)}{P(H_i)} &= \frac{P(E|H_i)}{P(E)} \propto P(E|H_i).\end{aligned}$$

A special case of Bayes' theorem, itself often referred to in the research logs as Bayes' theorem, is particularly important in cryptographic problems. Suppose we consider the hypotheses H and $\widetilde{H}$. Then, by the theorem above

$$\frac{P(H|E)}{P(H)} \Big/ \frac{P(\widetilde{H}|E)}{P(\widetilde{H})} = \frac{P(E|H)}{P(E|\widetilde{H})}$$

[a] left hand

$$\frac{O(H|E)}{O(H)} = \frac{P(E|H)}{P(E|\widetilde{H})}.$$

$P(E|H)/P(E|\widetilde{H})$ is called the factor in favour of H given E, and is seen to be the factor by which the 'prior *odds*' $O(H)$ must be multiplied in order to get the 'posterior odds' $O(H|E)$. In the more general form of Bayes' theorem any set of numbers proportional to $P(E|H_i)$ can be called the 'relative factors' in favour of the various hypotheses H_i and they are the ratios by which the prior probabilities may be multiplied, in order to get the correct ratios for the posterior probabilities. The special case of Bayes' theorem was first used in B.P. by A.M. Turing. (The fact that it was a special case of Bayes' theorem was pointed out by I.J. Good.) i

(g) The deciban

But Turing's great advance consisted in the invention and application of the 'deciban' (in Hut 8). (Deciban is abbreviated to 'db'.) E.4, ii

This is defined simply as $10\log_{10} f$, where f is the factor as defined above. Simple though this idea is, it makes an enormous simplification in practical work. As an example let us suppose that a penny is tossed 20 times and that each time it comes down heads. Suppose that we have two theories (i) that the penny is unbiassed, (ii) that it is double headed, and suppose that the second hypothesis (H) has prior odds of one in ten thousand. If we call E the event that the coin comes down heads then

$$P(E|H) = 1$$
$$P(E|\widetilde{H}) = \frac{1}{2}.$$

Therefore the factor in favour of H given E is 2, i.e. 3 decibans. So we gain $3 \times 20 = 60$ decibans from the whole series of experiments. The prior odds were $1/10^4$ i.e. 40 db down and so the posterior odds are $60 - 40 = 20$ db or $100:1$ on. (Observe that we talk about the decibanage of 'Odds', meaning of course, $10\log_{10} o$). E.5

(h) Methods of applying the above axioms p. 40

We assume that probability is a measure of the degree of belief that one *ought* to have, given certain evidence about an event, and that it satisfies the axioms given above. In order to apply the theory one must be able to judge that two events are equally probable, or at least sufficiently nearly so for all practical purposes. For example, if there was a barrel containing 10,000 ordinary pennies and one double-headed one, all thoroughly mixed up, we should judge that a coin chosen at random would have an equal probability of being any of the coins. Therefore by the law of addition it follows that the probability of drawing the double-headed coin is $1/(10{,}001)$, or odds of $10{,}000:1$ against, i.e. 10^{-4}. In the example of decibanning given above the coin might have been chosen in this way. This is quite a good analogue of the sort of thing done in cryptographic problems, namely one looks for needles in haystacks and the object chosen has to have a large factor in favour of being a needle in order to overcome its prior odds. (It will be observed that one would take a long time to find the needle if one could not estimate the factor very quickly — hence the necessity of machines in such problems.) a

Another thing that is often necessary in practice is to make a probability judgement of the type that a certain probability lies in a rather large interval. For example if a man produced a coin and began to toss it, you may be able to judge by his manner and some half-remembered facts that the probability of its being a double-headed coin must lie between $1/(\text{million})$ and

[a] problem

[i] Word 'and' handwritten.

[ii] In this chapter 'deciban' is consistently abbreviated 'd.b.'

$1/(100)$. If no such judgement were possible you could never assert that you believed the coin to be double-headed, even if it came down heads 100 times running.

(i) Theorem of the weighted average of factors

Suppose that a number of unreliable witnesses each says that a certain event E has happened but it is known that one and only one of them has in fact seen the evidence. Let the probabilities that the witnesses have seen the evidence be $p_1, p_2 \ldots$ and the factors in favour of an hypothesis
E.6 H be $f_1, f_2, \ldots$ respectively. Then the resulting factor is $\sum p_i f_i$.

As a special case suppose that an experiment is done and it has a probability p of having been done correctly, in which case it contributes a factor f to a certain hypothesis. If it is done incorrectly it supplies no evidence, i.e. a factor of 1. Then the resulting factor is $pf + 1 - p$. This
p. 41 special case is sometimes referred to as the theorem of corrected excess.

(j) Theorem of the chain of witnesses (and 'proportional bulges')

A proposition which can either be true or false is handed on through a chain of witnesses of 'reliabilities' $\frac{1}{2}(1+\xi_i)$ $(i = 1, 2, 3, \ldots)$. (By reliability we mean here the probability of repeating
E.7 what is heard instead of negating it.) Then the reliability of the chain as a whole is $\frac{1}{2}(1 + \prod_i \xi_i)$.

This theorem is the real reason why 'proportional bulges' were introduced. The '*Proportional bulge*' or P.B., ξ, of a proposition is defined by saying that its probability is $p(1+\xi)$ where p is the probability that the proposition would have in certain conditions which in the applications can be described as a 'wrong case' or 'random case'. The theorem of multiplication of proportional bulges, given above, is true only when $p = \frac{1}{2}$. There is a tendency for P.B.'s to lead to a slight algebraic simplification even if $p \neq \frac{1}{2}$.

(k) Expected value, standard deviation, variance, distributions

Let a variable or 'variate' x have probability $f(x_i)$ of being equal to x_i. Then its expected value is defined as $E(x) = \sum x_i f(x_i)$. This is also called the mean (value) of x or the mathematical expectation of x or the average (value) of x. The average of the sum of two independent variables is equal to the sum of the averages, and similarly for the product.

The 'variance' of a variable is defined as the mean value of the square of the deviation of x
a from its mean. The positive square root of the variance is called the 'standard deviation' (S.D.) of x and is usually denoted by σ. Thus, if $\bar{x}$ is the mean value of x, then

$$\sigma^2 = E\left\{(x-\bar{x})^2\right\}.$$

When we write $x = \bar{x} \pm \sigma$ we mean $E(x) = \bar{x}$ and S.D. of x is σ. There is no difficulty in extending the definition of an average to the case of a continuous variable.

If

$$P(x_i < x < x_i + dx_i) = f(x_i)\, dx_i,$$

then

$$E(x) = \int t f(t)\, dt.$$

$f(x)$ is called the distribution function of x.

(l) Some special distributions

p. 42 Let n experiments be performed each with the probability p of success. Then the probability
i of exactly r successes is

$$\binom{n}{r} p^r (1-p)^{n-r}.$$

---

[a] root of the variants

[i] Word 'successes' handwritten.

This is the so-called binomial distribution.

If

$$f(x) = \frac{1}{\sigma\sqrt{2\pi}} e^{-(x-\bar{x})^2/2\sigma^2}$$

we say that x has a normal (or Gaussian) distribution. It is easy to see that the mean of x is $\bar{x}$ and its S.D. is σ. The factor $1/\sigma\sqrt{2\pi}$ is the so called normalising factor which makes $\int f(x)\,dx = 1$.

The integral of $f(x)$ is called the error function. A convenient way of tabulating this is in a deciban form. A table of $\psi(x)$ is given in **R1**, p. 109 where a, E.8

$$\psi(x) = -10\log_{10}\left(\frac{1}{\sqrt{2\pi}}\int_x^\infty e^{-\frac{1}{2}t^2}\,dt\right).$$

The binomial distribution is closely approximated by the normal one for quite small values of n, if we take $\bar{x} = pn$ and $\sigma = \sqrt{np(1-p)}$. In Tunny theory this is the most frequent form for σ. The normal distribution is also a good approximation when a variable is the sum of a lot of small independent contributions.

If the probability of exactly n successes is $e^{-a}a^n/n!$, n is said to have a 'Poisson distribution'. The formula is easy to remember since $a^n/n!$ is a typical term of the expansion of e^a, so that

$$\sum_n e^{-a}a^n/n! = 1.$$

The average and variance of the distribution are both equal to a.

The binomial distribution is approximated by the Poisson distribution if n is fairly large but p b
is small, so that the average is much less than n. The Poisson distribution is approximated by the i
normal distribution when the number of successes minus a is small compared with a. E.9

There is one other distribution used in the research logs, namely the 'χ^2 distribution'. Given n independent variables each with a normal distribution of mean 0 and S.D. 1, let χ^2 be the sum of the squares of these variables.

Writing ii

$$\phi(n) = P(\chi^2 > t)$$

we have

$$\phi(n) = \frac{e^{-t/2}(t/2)^{(n/2)-1}}{(\frac{n}{2}-1)!} + \phi(n-2)$$

where

$$\phi(2) = e^{-t/2}, \quad \phi(1) = \sqrt{\frac{2}{\pi}}\int_{\sqrt{t}}^\infty e^{-\frac{1}{2}x^2}\,dx, \quad \frac{1}{2}! = \frac{1}{2}\sqrt{\pi}.$$

This is the most convenient formula when t is a good deal larger than n, as it is in all our applications. E.10

This distribution applies also to the sum of the squares of $(n+1)$ such variables whose sum is fixed. p. 43

[a] **R1**,109 [b] app oximated

[i] Word 'much' handwritten.

[ii] Words 'we have' in following equation handwritten.

(m) Some simple formulae of a non-analytic type concerning proportional bulges

If P and Q are independent propositions

a, E.11 $$\text{P.B.}(P.Q) = \text{P.B.}(P)\,\text{P.B.}(Q) + \text{P.B.}(P) + \text{P.B.}(Q)$$

If P_i $(i = 1, 2, \ldots)$ are mutually exclusive and exhaustive propositions each with the same 'random probability' then

$$\sum \text{P.B.}(P_i) = 0.$$

E.12 If P_i $(i = 1, 2, \ldots)$ are mutually exclusive propositions with the same random probability,

$$\text{P.B.}(P_1 \vee P_2 \vee P_3 \vee \cdots) = \text{Average}_i\,\{\text{P.B.}(P_i)\}$$

If P, Q, Φ, Θ are teleprinter letters which have the same number of components, then

$$\text{P.B.}(P + Q = \Phi) = \text{Average}_\Theta\,\{\text{P.B.}(P = \Theta)\,\text{P.B.}(Q = \Phi + \Theta)\}.$$

Here Φ is a fixed teleprinter letter, P and Q are letters belonging to certain classes.

(n) The general formula for sigma in Tunny work

Let two tapes be compared, one with a proportion p_i of letters A_i and the other with a
i proportion q_i of letters B_i $(i = 1, 2, \ldots r)$. Let the overlap of the two tapes be N. Let the number
ii of times A_i comes opposite B_i be ν_i. Let $\nu = \sum_{i=1} \nu_i$. Then the average of ν is $A = N\sum p_i q_i$ and
b, E.13 $(N-1)\sigma^2 = A^2 + NA - N^2 \sum p_i q_i (p_i + q_i)$.

In particular, if $r = 1$

c $$\sigma^2 = \frac{N^2}{N-1}(1-p)q(1-q).$$

The proof of the general formula is best done by the method of characteristic functions. We do not describe this method here, but instead refer the reader to **R4**, 105–108.

(o) The statistician's fallacy

A standard type of statistical experiment is exemplified by the following. A new fertiliser is tried and the amount of the crop produced is increased by 2σ. A deviation 2σ above the mean occurs about once in 40 experiments at random, assuming a normal distribution, and the result would probably be regarded as significantly good. As a conventional test of significance this is a useful method and one which is used in Tunny breaking also (as in the significance test for a short
d, p. 44 wheel-breaking run). On the other hand it would be quite wrong to assume that it was 40:1 on that the new fertiliser was better than the usual type. This would be equivalent to neglecting the
e numerator in the special form of Bayes' theorem, namely the probability of obtaining as good a result as the one obtained with a fertiliser known to be better than before. This may be hard to estimate but it is at any rate less than one. Another equally important criticism is that we are throwing away a lot of evidence if we say only that the result of the experiment is that a deviation of at least 2σ above the mean is obtained. The result is likely to be known more exactly, say that the deviation is between $2{\cdot}0\sigma$ and $2{\cdot}1\sigma$, and in this case the factor in favour of the hypothesis would be less (with a normal distribution). These points are stressed because there is a prominent
f, E.14 school of Statisticians who do not even accept Bayes' theorem.

---

[a] P.B.$(P.Q.)$ [b] $N^2\sigma^2 = A^2 + NA - N^2\sum p_i q_i (p_i + q_i)$ [c] $\sigma^2 = Np(1-p)q(1-q)$. [d] wheelbreaking [e] Bayes [f] Bayes

[i] r, the upper limit of subscript range, is unclear.

[ii] Handwritten 'of' inserted in 'number of times' with a caret.

An example of this from our work is given by the score on a 1+2 break-in. Suppose the best score is 4σ without serious rivals. 4σ or better occurs at random once in 30,000 experiments so it would be natural to imagine that the odds of the setting given are 30,000 divided by 1271 or 23 : 1 on. In fact they are more like 3 : 1 on, (that is, even after a factor has been set against all the [a] other settings due to the existence of no serious rival), though the odds depend to a reasonable extent on the particular link and length of tape and d. In the very early days of the section there was a tendency to continue with a message for some time if it gave a 4σ, since it was not believed that the odds could be much below 20 : 1 on. This was before the deciban had been brought over from Hut 8. (Later on the deciban exerted an influence on the work of the Testery also, due to the liaison between the two sections.) E.15

(p) The principle of maximum likelihood

If one has a continuous sequence of possible theories depending on a parameter x, it often happens that one has very little knowledge about the prior probabilities of the theories. If an experiment is done whose result has probability $f(x)$, then the numbers $f(x)$ are the relative factors of the various theories concerning the magnitude of x. $f(x)$ often has a maximum value at say $x = x_0$. Then x_0 is called the maximum likelihood solution for x. For a given value of ε it is more probable that x will lie in the interval $(x_0 - \varepsilon, x_0 + \varepsilon)$ than in any other interval of the same size, provided that the prior distribution is uniform. In this special case the maximum likelihood solution is equal to the 'most probable value'. Neither of these should be confused with the expected value.

[a] or 23·1 on.

p. 45

22 STATISTICAL FOUNDATIONS

E.2

22A INTRODUCTORY

Statistical methods of Tunny breaking are possible because (and only because) cipher, plain, key, chi, extended psi, de-chi and motor streams can — with suitable treatment — be made to exhibit marked characteristics which will distinguish them from a random sequence of letters. In this chapter we analyse these characteristics, and in subsequent chapters we show how they are exploited.

(a) Notation

The letters Z, P, K, χ, ψ', D are used to denote the operative letters of the Cipher, Plain, Key, Chi, Extended psi and de-chi Streams at any given ciphering position. They are connected by the equations:

$$Z = P + K$$
$$K = \chi + \psi'$$
$$D = Z + \chi = P + \psi'.$$

The suffixes 1, 2, 3, 4, 5 are used when a particular impulse is specified so that (using a generalized
a, p. 46 form) U_i denotes the operative character of the i-th impulse of the U-stream at a given ciphering position.

L is used to denote the operative character of the limitation.

(b) Some further definitions

The following symbols are generally used in Tunny-analysis and must be defined here:

[a] generalised

$\overline{U}$ = letter preceding U
$\overline{U_i}$ = character preceding U_i
$\overline{\overline{U}}$ = letter preceding $\overline{U}$
$\underline{U}$ = letter following U
$\underline{\underline{U}}$ = letter following $\underline{U}$ and so on.

$$\Delta U = U + \underline{U}$$ E.3
$$\Delta^2 U = \Delta(\Delta U)$$
$$\Delta^n U = \Delta(\Delta^{n-1} U)$$
$$\Delta_2 U = U + \underline{\underline{U}}$$
$$\Delta_3 U = U + \underline{\underline{\underline{U}}}$$ and so on.

$$\widehat{U} = \overline{U} + U + \underline{U} = \overline{U} + \Delta U$$
$$U_{ij} = U_i + U_j$$
$$\widetilde{U_i} = U_i + \text{a cross}$$

$U_i \longrightarrow \times$: $P(U_i = \times) > 1/2$
$U_i \longrightarrow \bullet$: $P(U_i = \bullet) > 1/2$
$U_i \underset{p}{\longrightarrow} \times$: $P(U_i = \times) = p$ where $p > 1/2$
$U_i \underset{p}{\longrightarrow} \bullet$: $P(U_i = \bullet) = p$ where $p > 1/2$.

(c) Two general theorems

Theorem I: $\Delta(U+V) = \Delta U + \Delta V$ (A1) i
Theorem II: $\Delta^2 U = \Delta_2 U$ (A2)
Proof : $\Delta^2 U = \Delta(\Delta U) = (U + \underline{U}) + (\underline{U} + \underline{\underline{U}}) = U + \underline{\underline{U}} = \Delta_2 U$
Theorem II is a special case of the general theorem: $\Delta^n U = \Delta_n U$ if and only if $n = 2^r$. (See **R5**, p. 114.) E.4 ii

22B THE CHI-STREAM

The chi-stream differs from a random sequence of letters in its periodicity in each impulse taken separately and in the deliberately arranged equality of dots and crosses in each impulse. p. 47

In order to prevent simple statistical recognition of the chi-stream each individual chi pattern is constructed with

(i) As nearly as possible an equal number of dots and crosses in the undifferenced and in the differenced wheel,

(ii) No stretch of 5 or more identical consecutive characters in the undifferenced wheel. (See **R5**, p. 4.)

Alleged chi patterns fulfilling these conditions are said to be 'legal'.

The conditions of legality are most obviously fulfilled by the pattern:

$$\chi: \quad \bullet\ \bullet\ \times\ \times\ \bullet\ \bullet\ \times\ \times\ \bullet\ \bullet$$
$$\Delta\chi: \quad \bullet\ \times\ \bullet\ \times\ \bullet\ \times\ \bullet\ \times\ \bullet\ \times.$$

A few of the patterns recovered consisted entirely of this pattern and were known at 'perfect wheels', e.g.

---

i Statements of Theorems I and II underlined.
ii Reference handwritten.

χ_5: • • × × • • × × • • × × • • × × • • × × • • ×
i $\Delta\chi_5$: • × • × • × • × • × • × • × • × • × • × • × ×.

In other cases the pattern was used over shorter stretches.

In the construction of chi patterns no attention was paid to the distribution of dots and crosses in the Δ^2 wheel. However, empirical evidence (see **R3**, p. 18) shows that $\Delta^2\chi_i \underset{\cdot 63}{\longrightarrow} \times$. (B1)

The fact that $\Delta^2\chi_i \rightarrow \times$ can be seen to be a natural result of the conditions of legality and the popularity of the pattern • • × × • • × ×.

E.5 The following table give the conditions of legality in numerical terms:

Wheel	Length	No. of crosses in χ	No. of crosses in $\Delta\chi$	Av. no. of crosses in $\Delta^2\chi$
1	41	20 or 21	20	26
2	31	15 or 16	16	$19\frac{1}{2}$
3	29	14 or 15	14	19
4	26	13	12 or 14	$16\frac{1}{2}$
5	23	11 or 12	12	14

Fig. 22 (I)

ii The number of legal chis is discussed in **25X**, and the frequency of various patterns of 5 and 10 consecutive characters in **R3**, pp. 125, 126.

p. 48 22C THE MOTOR STREAM

(a) Definitions

For a given set of wheel patterns we define

Number of dots in μ_{37} as	d
Proportion of dots in μ_{37} as	$D \equiv d/37$
Proportion of crosses in μ_{37} as	$a' \equiv 1 - D$
Proportion of crosses in TM as	a
Number of crosses in μ_{61} as	k.

(b) The motor wheels

μ_{61} is constructed so that $30 \leqslant k \leqslant 50$ and $k \neq 37$ without more than so far as is known 5 consecutive dots or 15 consecutive crosses.

μ_{37} is constructed so that $14 \leqslant d \leqslant 28$ without more than, so far as is known, 5 consecutive dots or 6 consecutive crosses.

(c) The basic motor

Theorem I. The BM has a period of $61 \times 37 = 2257$. (C1)

Proof After n complete revolutions of μ_{61}, μ_{37} has moved nk places. The initial position is reached when

$$nk \equiv 0 \pmod{37}.$$

Since $k \neq 37$, n must be a multiple of 37, and the motor returns to its original position after 37 revolutions of μ_{61}.

Theorem II. Proportion of crosses in BM $= a'$. (C2)

Proof Since the period of the BM = 2257, each position of μ_{37} occurs with each position of μ_{61} once in each cycle. As each character of μ_{37} occurs 61 times per cycle, the proportion of crosses in μ_{37} is not changed by the extension.

---

i Final × in $\Delta\chi_5$ row is a hand-correction of typed •.

ii Handwritten 'of' inserted with a caret.

(d) The total motor

Assuming that the proportion of crosses in the limitation is $\frac{1}{2}$ — which is not strictly true for $\overline{\chi}_2$ or $\overline{\chi}_2\overline{\overline{P}}_5$ limitation — we have:

Proportion of dots in TM = $\frac{1}{2}$ × proportion of dots in BM

$$\text{i.e.}\quad 1-a=\tfrac{1}{2}(1-a').$$

Proportion of crosses in TM is composed of: a, E.6

$$\left.\begin{array}{ll} \text{Proportion of BM dot lim dot} & \tfrac{1}{2}(1-a') \\ \text{BM cross lim dot} & \tfrac{1}{2}a' \\ \text{BM cross lim cross} & \tfrac{1}{2}a'. \end{array}\right\} \qquad \text{(C3)}$$

Summary

$$d/37=D=1-a'=2(1-a). \qquad \text{(C4)}$$

(e) Double dots in BM

The proportion of double dots in the BM is empirically $1{\cdot}1(1-a')^2$ (see **R3**, pp. 50, 51).

22D THE PSI STREAM p. 49

(a) Construction of psi patterns

The psi patterns are constructed so that there are as nearly as possible an equal number of dots and crosses in each impulse of the ψ' (extended psi) and $\Delta\psi'$ streams. This implies that each ψ wheel has

(1) as nearly as possible an equal number of crosses and dots in the undifferenced wheel (actually one more cross than dot).

(2) a proportion b of crosses in each differenced (unextended ψ) where $b=1/2a=\frac{1}{2}(1+\beta)$.

(b) A few identities

$$\beta\equiv 2b-1 \qquad \text{(D1)}$$

$$a\equiv\frac{1}{2b}\equiv\frac{1}{1+\beta} \qquad \text{(D2)}$$

$$1-a\equiv\frac{2b-1}{2b}\equiv\frac{\beta}{1+\beta} \qquad \text{(D3)}$$

$$1-a'\equiv\frac{2b-1}{b}\equiv\frac{2\beta}{1+\beta}\equiv D\equiv\frac{d}{37} \qquad \text{(D4)}$$

$$a'\equiv\frac{1-b}{b}\equiv\frac{1-\beta}{1+\beta}. \qquad \text{(D5)}$$

---

[a] is comprised of

(c) Corresponding values of d, a, b, β, and the number of crosses in each $\Delta\psi$

For all values of d:				ψ_1	ψ_2	ψ_3	ψ_4	ψ_5	
Length				43	47	51	53	59	
No. of crosses in ψ				22	24	26	27	30	
				Number of crosses in					
d	a	b	β	$\Delta\psi_1$	$\Delta\psi_2$	$\Delta\psi_3$	$\Delta\psi_4$	$\Delta\psi_5$	d
14	·81	·62	·24	26	28	32	32	36	14
15	·80	·63	·26	26	30	32	34	38	15
16	·78	·64	·28	28	30	32	34	38	16
17	·77	·65	·30	28	30	32 or 34	34	38	17
18	·76	·66	·32	28	32	34	36	38	18
19	·74	·68	·35	28	32	34	36	40	19
20	·73	·69	·37	30	32	34 or 36	36	40	20
21	·72	·70	·40	30	32	36	38	42	21
22	·70	·71	·42	30	34	36	38	42	22
23	·69	·73	·45	32	34	38	38	42	23
24	·67	·75	·49	32	34	38	40	44	24
25	·66	·76	·51	32	36	38	40	44	25
26	·65	·77	·54	34	36	40	40	46	26
27	·64	·79	·58	34	36 or 38	40	42	46	27
28	·62	·81	·61	34	38	42	42	48	28

[i] **Fig. 22 (II)**

p. 50 **(d) Frequency of letters in ψ'**

The number of dots and crosses in each impulse of the ψ' stream are equal and their positions relatively independent. Therefore the frequency of every letter in the ψ' stream is approximately equal. E.7

(e) Frequency of letters in $\Delta\psi'$

In the $\Delta\psi'$ stream, though there are an equal number of dots and crosses in each impulse, they are so placed that there is a dot in every impulse at each extension.

TM dot positions occur $(1-a)$ of the time and at each of these there is a stroke in $\Delta\psi'$.

The $\Delta\psi'$ stream at TM cross positions is in fact the $\Delta\psi$ stream (unextended) and the chance of a cross in any impulse is b. Therefore the frequency of various letters is as follows

/	0 crosses	$(1-a)+a \quad (1-b)^5$
9T34E	1 cross	$ab \ (1-b)^4$
HONRLIADZS	2 crosses	$ab^2 \ (1-b)^3$
MCGPUWJFBY	3 crosses	$ab^3 \ (1-b)^2$
VQ5KX	4 crosses	$ab^4 \ (1-b)$
8	5 crosses	ab^5.

(D6)

(f) $\Delta\psi'_{ij}$

$\Delta\psi'_{ij}$ = dot, when TM = dot.

[i] Caption moved from right-hand side of figure to bottom.

When TM = cross

$$P(\Delta\psi_{ij} = \text{dot}) = b^2 + (1-b)^2$$
$$= 2b^2 - 2b + 1.$$

$$\therefore \quad \Delta\psi'_{ij} \longrightarrow \bullet \text{ with probability } (1-a) + a(2b^2 - 2b + 1)$$
$$= 1 - a + b - 1 + a = b.$$

$$\therefore \quad \Delta\psi'_{ij} \underset{b}{\longrightarrow} \bullet. \qquad \text{(D7)}$$

(g) $\Delta\psi'$ stream and limitation

In each impulse of $\Delta\psi'$ stream and in limitation stream there are an equal number of dots and crosses.

Now at TM dot positions,

$$\Delta\psi'_i = \text{dot}$$
$$L = \text{cross}.$$

Therefore the remaining $\Delta\psi'_i$ dots, and the remaining lim **x**'s form the same proportion of the TM cross positions.

Therefore at TM cross positions

$$\Delta\psi'_i \underset{b}{\longrightarrow} \text{cross}$$
$$L \underset{b}{\longrightarrow} \text{dot}.$$

Consequently in any position,

$$P(\Delta\psi'_i = \text{dot}) = P(L + \mathbf{x} = \text{dot})$$

and for calculating the frequency of various letters in combination with limitation, $(L + \mathbf{x})$ can be treated as $\Delta\psi'_6$ — a stream of characters with a period of 31 for χ_2 imitation, and virtually non-periodic for other limitations. E.8, a p. 51

The following table gives the frequency in $\Delta\psi'$ of each '6-impulse letter'.

'letters' with	Prop: ag: TM •	Prop: ag: TM **x**	Prop: in $\Delta\psi'$
0 crosses	1	$(1-b)^6$	$(1-a) + a(1-b)^6$
1 crosses	—	$b(1-b)^5$	$ab(1-b)^5$
2 crosses	—	$b^2(1-b)^4$	$ab^2(1-b)^4$
3 crosses	—	$b^3(1-b)^3$	$ab^3(1-b)^3$
4 crosses	—	$b^4(1-b)^2$	$ab^4(1-b)^2$
5 crosses	—	$b^5(1-b)$	$ab^5(1-b)$
6 crosses	—	b^6	ab^6

Fig. 22 (III) i

[a] a stream of letters

[i] Caption moved from right-hand side of figure to bottom.

From this table we see that $P(\Delta\psi' = 9, L = \bullet)$

$$= P(\Delta\psi' = \mathtt{N}, L = \times) = ab^2(1-b)^4.$$

i Fig. **22 (V)** shows $\Delta\psi'$ letter counts for ψ' streams corresponding to $d = 27, 24, 21, 18, 15$. $\Delta\psi'$
ii counts are given separately for $\overline{\chi}_2$ lim and $\overline{\chi}_2\overline{\psi}'_1$ lim, and in the case of $\overline{\chi}_2$ lim the counts of $\Delta\psi'$ against $L = \times$ and $L = \bullet$ are given separately.

An immediate application of the $\Delta\psi'_6$ principle to (7) gives

$$\Delta\psi'_i + L \underset{b}{\longrightarrow} \times. \qquad \text{(D8)}$$

(h) Proportional bulges of letters in $\Delta\psi'$ stream

The proportional bulges of $(\Delta\psi = \Theta)$, $(\Delta\psi' = \Theta)$ where Θ is any letter, are denoted by β_Θ, β'_Θ and PB's $(\Delta\psi_{ij} = \text{dot})$ and $(\Delta\psi'_{ij} = \text{dot})$ by β_{ij}, β'_{ij}.

iii A table similar to fig. **22 (III)** showing P.B.$(\Delta\psi' = \Theta)$ for all values of Θ in terms of β is given in **R5**, p. 27.

$P(\Delta\psi'_{ij} = \text{dot}) = \frac{1}{2}(1 + \beta'_{ij}) = b = \frac{1}{2}(1+\beta)$

$$\therefore \quad \beta'_{ij} = \beta. \qquad \text{(D9)}$$

The idea of a PB and the introduction of β first occurs on **R1**, p. 20.

(i) Δ^2 characteristics

It is a fairly good approximation to accept the simple minded results

$$\Delta^2\psi_i \longrightarrow \bullet \text{ with probability } b^2 + (1-b)^2 = 2b^2 - 2b + 1$$

$$\Delta^2\psi'_i \longrightarrow \bullet \text{ with probability } \frac{1}{2}$$

$$\Delta^2\psi'_{ij} \longrightarrow \bullet \text{ (See \textbf{R3}, p. 22.)}$$

(j) The sum of psi streams

p. 52 It is sometimes useful to be able to recognise statistically the sum of 2 psi streams. This problem is dealt with in **22W(a)**.

22E THE SUM OF TWO STREAMS

(a) The Proportional Bulge

In calculating the frequency of various letters or groups of letters in the sum of two streams whose letter frequencies are known, it is sometimes more convenient to consider the proportional bulges of the letters concerned and not their frequencies. The PB has been introduced in **21(j)** and is normally designated by a small Greek letter.

Consider a stream of letters (U) drawn from an alphabet of r letters, then P.B.$(U = \Theta) = \xi^U_\Theta$ where

$$P(U = \Theta) = \frac{1}{r}(1 + \xi^U_\Theta).$$

Summing over the r letters of the alphabet we get

$$\sum_\Theta P(U = \Theta) = 1$$

$$\sum_\Theta \xi^U_\Theta = 0.$$

---

[i] Fig. **22 (V)** relocated to p. 63 below.

[ii] Word 'for' handwritten.

[iii] In formulae the notation PB instead of P.B. is used consistently throughout **22**, except in **22X**, where it is never used.

(b) The Faltung theorem (a special form of a result stated in **21(m)**)

In a stream of letters $(U+V)$ which is the sum of two streams U and V it is clear that E.9

$$P(U+V=\Theta)=\sum_{\Phi}\{P(U=\Phi)\,.\,P(V=\Theta+\Phi)\} \tag{E1}$$

$$\therefore\quad \frac{1}{r}(1+\xi_{\Theta}^{U+V})=\frac{1}{r^2}\sum_{\Phi}\{(1+\xi_{\Phi}^{U})(1+\xi_{\Theta+\Phi}^{V})\}$$

$$=\frac{1}{r^2}\sum_{\Phi}\{1+\xi_{\Phi}^{U}.\xi_{\Theta+\Phi}^{V}\}$$

$$=\frac{1}{r^2}\left\{r+\sum_{\Phi}\xi_{\Phi}^{U}.\xi_{\Theta+\Phi}^{V}\right\}$$

$$\therefore\quad \xi_{\Theta}^{U+V}=\frac{1}{r}\sum_{\Phi}\{\xi_{\Phi}^{U}.\xi_{\Theta+\Phi}^{V}\}. \tag{E2}$$

If every $\xi_{\Phi}^{U}=0$, then $\xi_{\Theta}^{U+V}=0$. (E3)

Therefore if two streams, one of which is random, are added together the resulting stream is random.

(c) Multiplication of PB's

If we put $r=2$ and consider the sum of two streams each consisting of dots and crosses, we get

$$\xi_{\bullet}^{U+V}=\frac{1}{2}\{\xi_{\bullet}^{U}\xi_{\bullet}^{V}+\xi_{\times}^{U}\xi_{\times}^{V}\}.$$

But $\xi_{\bullet}+\xi_{\times}=0$

$$\therefore\quad \xi_{\bullet}^{U+V}=\xi_{\bullet}^{U}\xi_{\bullet}^{V}.$$

This multiplication property is first mentioned in **R1**, p. 20. p. 53

22F THE KEY STREAM

$$K=\chi+\psi'$$

$$\therefore\quad \Delta K=\Delta\chi+\Delta\psi'.$$

The undifferenced ψ' stream is flat, therefore the undifferenced K stream is random and [i] unrecognisable statistically. ((E3).)

(a) Recognising key on any limitation

$$\Delta\psi'_{ij}\xrightarrow[\frac{1}{2}(1+\beta)]{}\text{dot}$$

$$\therefore\quad \Delta\chi_{ij}+\Delta\psi'_{ij}\xrightarrow[\frac{1}{2}(1+\beta)]{}\Delta\chi_{ij}$$

$$\therefore\quad \Delta K_{ij}\xrightarrow[\frac{1}{2}(1+\beta)]{}\Delta\chi_{ij}. \tag{F1}$$

Differencing at distance w_i where w_i is the length of χ_i (**R3**, p. 62)

$$\Delta_{w_i}(\Delta K_{ij})\xrightarrow[\frac{1}{2}(1+\beta^2)]{}\Delta_{w_i}(\Delta\chi_{ij})$$

---

[i] Word 'random' handwritten.

[i] since we are in effect adding two streams in which $\Delta K_{ij} \longrightarrow \Delta\chi_{ij}$ with proportional bulge β.

Now $\Delta_{w_i}(\Delta\chi_i) = \text{dot}$

$$\therefore \quad \Delta_{w_i}(\Delta K_{ij}) \xrightarrow[\frac{1}{2}(1+\beta^2)]{} \Delta_{w_i}(\Delta\chi_j). \qquad \text{(F2)}$$

Similarly, differencing at $w_i w_j$ (e.g. 26×23 for χ_4 and χ_5)

$$\Delta_{w_i w_j}(\Delta K_{ij}) \xrightarrow[\frac{1}{2}(1+\beta^2)]{} \text{dot}. \qquad \text{(F3)}$$

This result shows that all key may be recognised by an excess of dots over crosses in $\Delta_{598}(\Delta K_{45})$. (**R2**, p. 90.)

(b) Recognising key on $\overline{\chi}_2$ limitation

$$\Delta\psi_i' + \lim \xrightarrow[\frac{1}{2}(1+\beta)]{} \times$$

$$\therefore \quad \Delta K_i \xrightarrow[\frac{1}{2}(1+\beta)]{} \Delta\chi_i + \lim + \times$$

$$\therefore \quad \Delta K_2 \xrightarrow[\frac{1}{2}(1+\beta)]{} \Delta\chi_2 + \overline{\chi}_2 + \times$$

$$\therefore \quad \Delta K_2 \xrightarrow[\frac{1}{2}(1+\beta)]{} \widehat{\chi}_2 + \times \qquad \text{(F4)}$$

[ii] and differencing at 31 (**R2**, p. 70) we get

$$\Delta_{31}(\Delta K_2) \xrightarrow[\frac{1}{2}(1+\beta^2)]{} \text{dot}. \qquad \text{(F5)}$$

(c) $\Delta^2 K$

In cases where $\Delta^2\chi_i$ and $\Delta^2\chi_j$ each $\rightarrow \times$ with high probability

$$\Delta^2\chi_{ij} \longrightarrow \text{dot}.$$

Now

$$\Delta^2\psi_{ij}' \longrightarrow \text{dot}$$

[iii] and therefore

$$\Delta^2 K_{ij} \longrightarrow \text{dot}. \qquad \text{(F6)}$$

Key has once been recognised by this method (see **R3**, p. 22) (**R3**, pp. 15, 76). Further

$$\Delta^2\psi' = \text{ stroke at double dots in the TM}$$

$$\Delta^2\chi \xrightarrow[\cdot 1]{} 8 \ \text{ since } \ \Delta^2\chi_i \xrightarrow[\cdot 63]{} \times$$

$$\Delta^2 K \xrightarrow[\cdot 1]{} 8 \ \text{ at double dots in the TM}. \quad (\mathbf{R0}, \text{p. } 53) \qquad \text{(F7)}$$

(d) The sum of key streams

There are a few words on this topic in **22W(b)**.

---

[i] Word 'with' handwritten.

[ii] Phrase 'and differencing ... we get' handwritten.

[iii] Both equations in this sentence written in-line, but clause 'and therefore...' started on fresh indented line.

22G THE PLAIN LANGUAGE STREAM

(a) *P* and ΔP

Machine methods of work on Tunny make it important that we should be able to recognise plain language not only by its linguistic, but also by its statistical properties.

The statistical properties of the *P* steam are obvious enough, the frequency of the various letters ranging from that of 9 (space) which normally occurs once in every 6 or 7 letters to that of stroke, 3, and 4 which should not occur at all.

In ΔP the frequency of each letter depends on the frequency of the 32 bigrams which add up to it. The letter count is not as bulgy as that of *P*, but is of greater basic importance in view of its contribution to the count of ΔD.

Fig. **22 (IV)** shows bigram frequencies and their contribution to the various letters of ΔP in a sample of 25,600 letters of Jellyfish June 1944.

The first references to ΔP counts are on **R0**, pp. 21, 45–47 and to *P* counts on **R2**, pp. 83, 110–2.

(b) Heterogeneous nature of *P* and ΔP a

Fish messages consist of a mixture of three component types of *P*: German language (in letter shift), numerals (in figure shift), and punctuation (involving frequent shift changes). The *P* and ΔP counts for these components are strikingly different and, even within each type the form of the count depended on the operators' spacing and punctuation habits. b, i, p. 62

Some messages consist entirely of German, of abbreviations and punctuation, or even of numerals, but in most messages there is a heterogeneous mixture of

Hand patches (German language with irregular spacing) E.10

Addresses (Abbreviations and punctuation)

Message content (Language usually with some abbreviations and numerals)

and occasional places where the tape sticks and the same letter of *P* is transmitted until the tape is adjusted. (**R0**, p. 67.)

(c) Component types of language

(1) German Language (Type C) ii

The *P* and ΔP counts for German Language with single 9 spacing vary little in shape, those given in fig. **22 (VI)** being a good example. In *P*, it will be noticed that the most popular language letter E is almost as frequent as 9, and that other good language letters N, R, I, A, S occur with frequency well above random. The message being largely in lettershift (except for incidental punctuation) the shift change letters 5 and 8 are both below random. Q, J, X, Y are rare.

In ΔP, the most significant letters are: F (= E + N), 3 (= N + 9), E.11
J (= E + R = U + N), U (= 5 + M = I + E), 5 (= 9 + 8), G and S which are all high, and B whose 13 contributing bigrams are all feeble. (**R2**, pp. 97–100.)

(2) Single Punctuation (Type B)

All punctuation signs are sent in figure shift, and unless punctuation follows or precedes numerals each sign must be preceded by a 5 and followed by an 8. The most common form of punctuation is the full stop, which occurs extensively in abbreviations and addresses, and has the basic form 5M89 or 5MA89.

Fig. **22 (VII)** shows *P* and ΔP for a standard type of message consisting largely of German language abbreviated with 5M89. 9 which is frequent (in *P*) both for punctuation and for language

[a] Heterogenous [b] operators

[i] Figs. **28 (IV)** through **(IX)**, which occupy pp. 55–61 of the *Report*, break the sentence between the words 'punctuation' and 'habits'.

[ii] Of the seven numbered sub-subsections in **22G(c)**, only **(2)**'s head underlined.

is well ahead of any other letter. It is followed (at a distance) by the punctuation letters 5M8, and E at the head of the language group.

In ΔP, the German language letters are still strong (but in a part of the message only), and the lead is taken by 5 (= 9 + 8), U (= 5 + M = I + E), A (= M + 8) and 8 (= M + A = 5 + 9), 5 and U
a, p. 63 being especially strong in most cases.

(3) Double Punctuation (Type A)

In practice punctuation is often modified according to the habits of the operator perforating the tape. Many operators were trained to change from figure to letter shift and vice versa by depressing the shift keys twice (or more) to ensure that the shift change actually took place. These operators were mostly employed at the Königsberg exchange or on Rome Bream, but after the Königsberg exchange had moved to Berlin double punctuation made a general appearance in the West (see also **R4**, p. 5).

Fig. **22 (VIII)** shows *P* and ΔP counts for a message with double punctuation. In the *P* count 5 and 8 are almost twice as frequent as they are in the single punctuation count (fig. **22 (VIII)**), and are almost as high as 9. Language naturally forms a small proportion of the message and the strength of language letters is reduced.

The main significance of double punctuation lies in the inflation of stroke in ΔP, so that strokes may occur with 3–6 times random frequency.

(4) Other operators habits (auto)

Certain other forms of punctuation are popular on particular links or with particular operators: they are given differenced and undifferenced so that their contribution to ΔP can be estimated

P:	5M98	ΔP:	U05
	5M989		U055
	5MMA89		U/8M5
	55KK889, 55LL889 (Brackets)		/H/T/5, /D/P/5 and so on.

In some messages 9 is inserted before all punctuation and 8 is the highest letter in ΔP. A few operators divide words with 89 or even 989 and this inflates 5 to a high level in ΔP even in German language messages with little punctuation.

(5) Operators habits (hand)

Spacing and punctuation in hand is erratic, and even the most improbable letters may be inflated by operators who tap out some pair of letters in turn while thinking, e.g. LALALALA.

(6) Numerals

The most common letters in undifferenced numerals are P, Q, and W. In general, numerals are rarely sufficiently frequent to make much difference to the shape of *P* or ΔP counts.

p. 64 Occasional examples of messages consisting entirely of numerals have occurred. A good example is a message giving a sheet of QEP numbers whose letter count is given in fig. **22 (IX)**. (**R4**, p. 16.)

(7) Freaks

It is unreliable to reject any letter count with significant bulges however oddly arranged these
E.12 bulges appear to be. A few of the last German messages ever sent on Tunny gave some new wheel patterns and consisted almost entirely of the words NOCKE and KEINE separated by commas e.g.

P NOCKE5N89NOCKE5N89KEINE5N89

ΔP HPECGQW53HPECGQW5JCURFGQW5.

[a] 5+U being especially

//	-	/9	-	/H	-	/T	-	/O	-	/M	-	/N	-	/3	-	/R	-	/C	-	/V	-	/G	-	/L	-	/P	-	/I	-	/4	-
99	253	9/	-	9T	57	9H	59	9M	106	9O	61	93	-	9N	154	9C	41	9R	101	9G	90	9V	108	9P	54	9L	58	94	-	9I	136
HH	-	HT	51	H/	-	H9	96	HN	21	H3	-	HO	23	HM	20	HV	-	HG	-	HR	50	HC	-	HI	22	H4	-	HL	16	HP	2
TT	45	TH	7	T9	179	T/	-	T3	-	TN	2	TM	14	TO	24	TG	2	TV	-	TC	-	TR	28	T4	-	TI	47	TP	3	TL	29
OO	16	OM	43	ON	61	O3	-	O/	-	O9	76	OH	2	OT	25	OL	31	OP	12	OI	4	O4	-	OR	76	OC	17	OV	-	OG	7
MM	27	MO	26	M3	-	MN	-	M9	284	M/	-	MT	17	MH	-	MP	8	ML	10	M4	-	MI	44	MC	-	MR	14	MG	-	MV	22
NN	69	N3	-	NO	44	NM	2	NH	4	NT	47	N/	-	N9	346	NI	47	N4	-	NL	2	NP	-	NV	2	NG	153	NR	7	NC	4
33	-	3N	-	3M	-	3O	-	3T	-	3H	-	39	-	3/	-	34	-	3I	-	3P	-	3L	-	3G	-	3V	-	3C	-	3R	-
RR	30	RC	15	RV	2	RG	34	RL	19	RP	8	RI	81	R4	-	R/	-	R9	201	RH	5	RT	48	RO	78	RM	33	RN	25	R3	-
CC	7	CR	-	CG	-	CV	-	CP	-	CL	-	C4	-	CI	15	C9	24	C/	-	CT	-	CH	268	CM	-	CO	13	C3	-	CN	4
VV	7	VG	10	VR	3	VC	-	VI	23	V4	-	VL	-	VP	-	VH	-	VT	-	V/	-	V9	28	VN	-	V3	-	VO	55	VM	-
GG	4	GV	-	GC	-	GR	53	G4	-	GI	5	GP	-	GL	48	GT	30	GH	7	G9	87	G/	-	G3	-	GN	4	GM	-	GO	-
LL	52	LP	2	LI	40	L4	-	LR	5	LC	-	LV	3	LG	17	LO	7	LM	9	LN	2	L3	-	L/	-	L9	107	LH	-	LT	23
PP	19	PL	4	P4	-	PI	12	PC	-	PR	16	PG	-	PV	-	PM	2	PO	10	P3	-	PN	-	P9	28	P/	-	PT	2	PH	-
II	11	I4	-	IL	29	IP	-	IV	17	IG	56	IR	18	IC	99	IN	163	I3	-	IO	16	IM	49	IH	4	IT	104	I/	-	I9	38
44	-	4I	-	4P	-	4L	-	4G	-	4V	-	4C	-	4R	-	43	-	4N	-	4M	-	4O	-	4T	-	4H	-	49	-	4/	-
AA	223	AU	98	AQ	-	AW	-	A5	48	A8	373	AK	15	AJ	5	AD	10	AF	15	AX	-	AB	65	AZ	9	AY	2	AS	42	AE	61
UU	4	UA	-	UW	-	UQ	-	U8	8	U5	10	UJ	-	UK	-	UF	50	UD	-	UB	3	UX	2	UY	-	UZ	-	UE	97	US	34
QQ	11	QW	9	QA	-	QU	17	QK	-	QJ	-	Q5	-	Q8	18	QX	6	QB	-	QD	-	QF	-	QS	3	QE	7	QZ	-	QY	2
WW	4	WQ	5	WU	19	WA	24	WJ	-	WK	-	W8	25	W5	18	WB	-	WX	5	WF	-	WD	-	WE	94	WS	-	WY	-	WZ	-
55	43	58	18	5K	43	5J	-	5A	284	5U	2	5Q	77	5W	70	5Z	24	5Y	14	5S	22	5E	17	5D	-	5F	-	5X	42	5B	5
88	156	85	17	8J	-	8K	46	8U	9	8A	82	8W	18	8Q	4	8Y	-	8Z	27	8E	24	8S	19	8F	38	8D	29	8B	25	8X	-
KK	-	KJ	-	K5	46	K8	29	KQ	-	KW	5	KA	27	KU	5	KS	-	KE	41	KZ	-	KY	-	KX	-	KB	-	KD	18	KF	-
JJ	-	JK	-	J8	-	J5	3	JW	-	JQ	-	JU	-	JA	9	JE	2	JS	-	JY	-	JZ	-	JB	-	JX	-	JF	-	JD	-
DD	2	DF	4	DX	-	DB	-	DZ	-	DY	-	DS	7	DE	170	DA	42	DU	37	DQ	-	DW	2	D5	49	D8	4	DK	2	DJ	2
FF	64	FD	6	FB	-	FX	-	FY	-	FZ	9	FE	85	FS	5	FU	25	FA	34	FW	-	FQ	-	F8	6	F5	15	FJ	-	FK	7
XX	-	XB	-	XD	-	XF	-	XS	-	XE	-	XZ	-	XY	16	XQ	-	XW	2	XA	-	XU	-	XK	-	XJ	-	X5	19	X8	37
BB	-	BX	-	BF	2	BD	3	BE	137	BS	17	BY	-	BZ	-	BW	8	BQ	-	BU	8	BA	22	BJ	-	BK	2	B8	7	B5	21
ZZ	8	ZY	-	ZS	-	ZE	43	ZD	-	ZF	-	ZX	-	ZB	5	Z5	43	Z8	16	ZK	-	ZJ	-	ZA	9	ZU	47	ZQ	-	ZW	13
YY	-	YZ	-	YE	-	YS	-	YF	-	YD	-	YB	-	YX	6	Y8	10	Y5	2	YJ	-	YK	-	YU	2	YA	-	YW	-	YQ	-
SS	79	SE	85	SZ	12	SY	-	SX	-	SB	-	SD	6	SF	7	SK	2	SJ	-	S5	41	S8	21	SQ	-	SW	9	SA	18	SU	32
EE	22	ES	166	EY	5	EZ	11	EB	36	EX	17	EF	33	ED	45	EJ	-	EK	6	E8	26	E5	34	EW	16	EQ	-	EU	42	EA	-
/	1156	9	566	H	542	T	432	O	1001	M	786	N	451	3	1131	R	577	C	549	V	380	G	755	L	490	P	665	I	420	4	479

Fig. 22 (IV) Frequency of Bigrams in 25,600 letters of Jellyfish traffic of June, 1944
The bigrams are sorted by their differences and the no. of occurrences of each ΔP letter occurs at the foot of each column.

p. 55, i

a

[a] occurences

[i] Pages 55–61 of the original *Report* constitute a block of figures, figs. **22 (IV)–(IX)**, interrupting a sentence in **22G(b)** (on p. 59 of this edition). They are relocated to here, pp. 61–67. All the captions have been moved from the tops of the figures to the bottoms. The explanatory sentence for fig. **22 (IV)** continues on the same line of typing as the caption.

p. 56

/A	-	/U	-	/Q	-	/W	-	/5	-	/8	-	/K	-	/J	-
9U	103	9A	218	9W	121	9Q	38	98	813	95	723	9J	7	9K	95
HQ	-	HW	10	HA	24	HU	10	HK	-	HJ	-	H5	31	H8	2
TW	13	TQ	-	TU	18	TA	75	TJ	-	TK	3	T8	21	T5	96
O5	19	O8	6	OK	15	OJ	-	OA	-	OU	2	OQ	2	OW	2
M8	382	M5	38	MJ	-	MK	-	MU	6	MA	208	MW	2	MQ	-
NK	17	NJ	-	N5	78	N8	79	NQ	-	NW	17	NA	75	NU	11
3J	-	3K	-	38	-	35	-	3W	-	3Q	-	3U	-	3A	-
RD	43	RF	21	RX	4	RB	12	RZ	8	RY	-	RS	51	RE	98
CF	-	CD	-	CB	-	CX	-	CY	-	CZ	-	CE	2	CS	-
VX	-	VB	-	VD	-	VF	-	VS	-	VE	40	VZ	-	VY	-
GB	-	GX	-	GF	-	GD	-	GE	190	GS	8	GY	-	GZ	-
LZ	2	LY	-	LS	17	LE	68	LD	28	LF	-	LX	-	LB	3
PY	-	PZ	4	PE	17	PS	-	PF	10	PD	-	PB	-	PX	-
IS	66	IE	107	IZ	-	IY	-	IX	2	IB	6	ID	5	IF	27
4E	-	4S	-	4Y	-	4Z	-	4B	-	4X	-	4F	-	4D	-
A/	-	A9	185	AH	22	AT	14	AO	3	AM	52	AN	202	A3	-
U9	31	U/	-	UT	15	UH	8	UM	53	UO	-	U3	-	UN	153
QH	-	QT	-	Q/	-	Q9	19	QN	-	Q3	-	QO	6	QM	8
WT	11	WH	-	W9	63	W/	-	W3	-	WN	8	WM	18	WO	13
5O	9	5M	617	5N	62	53	-	5/	-	59	36	5H	-	5T	10
8M	20	8O	34	83	-	8N	21	89	1491	8/	-	8T	5	8H	7
KN	3	K3	-	KO	16	KM	25	KH	13	KT	6	K/	-	K9	38
J3	-	JN	-	JM	3	JO	3	JT	-	JH	-	J9	-	J/	-
DR	8	DC	-	DV	-	DG	7	DL	26	DP	-	DI	55	D4	-
FC	-	FR	16	FG	6	FV	-	FP	3	FL	14	F4	-	FI	6
XV	-	XG	-	XR	4	XC	-	XI	-	X4	-	XL	-	XP	-
BG	4	BV	-	BC	-	BR	31	B4	-	BI	34	BP	-	BL	7
ZL	-	ZP	-	ZI	-	Z4	-	ZR	2	ZC	-	ZV	-	ZG	-
YP	-	YL	2	Y4	-	YI	-	YC	-	YR	-	YG	-	YV	-
SI	36	S4	-	SL	5	SP	4	SV	-	SG	6	SR	-	SC	90
E4	-	EI	214	EP	8	EL	90	EG	50	EV	5	EC	23	ER	383
A	767	U	1472	Q	498	W	504	5	2698	8	1168	K	505	J	1049

/D	-	/F	-	/X	-	/B	-	/Z	-	/Y	-	/S	-	/E	-
9F	96	9D	194	9B	162	9X	-	9Y	8	9Z	56	9E	124	9S	198
HX	-	HB	-	HD	2	HF	-	HS	-	HE	94	HZ	2	HY	-
TB	-	TX	-	TF	-	TD	4	TE	188	TS	16	TY	-	TZ	51
OZ	-	OY	-	OS	38	OE	66	OD	2	OF	12	OX	-	OB	32
MY	31	MZ	-	ME	92	MS	7	MF	5	MD	-	MB	-	MX	-
NS	28	NE	84	NZ	18	NY	-	NX	-	NB	10	ND	151	NF	22
3E	-	3S	-	3Y	-	3Z	-	3B	-	3X	-	3F	-	3D	-
RA	78	RU	36	RQ	10	RW	13	R5	52	R8	22	RK	26	RJ	-
CU	3	CA	28	CW	-	CQ	-	C8	19	C5	27	CJ	-	CK	15
VQ	-	VW	-	VA	7	VU	-	VK	-	VJ	-	V5	19	V8	41
GW	2	GQ	-	GU	21	GA	6	GJ	-	GK	8	G8	11	G5	30
L5	42	L8	50	LK	-	LJ	-	LA	84	LU	22	LQ	-	LW	4
P8	17	P5	16	PJ	-	PK	3	PU	6	PA	21	PW	2	PQ	2
IK	24	IJ	-	I5	23	I8	5	IQ	2	IW	-	IA	17	IU	4
4J	-	4K	-	48	-	45	-	4W	-	4Q	-	4U	-	4A	-
AR	47	AC	47	AV	10	AG	33	AL	55	AP	-	AI	4	A4	-
UC	18	UR	58	UG	19	UV	2	UP	9	UL	3	U4	-	UI	10
QV	-	QG	-	QR	9	QC	-	QI	2	Q4	-	QL	5	QP	4
WG	-	WV	-	WC	-	WR	2	W4	-	WI	19	WP	12	WL	4
5L	63	5P	10	5I	11	54	-	5R	27	5C	61	5V	38	5G	-
8P	12	8L	4	84	-	8I	2	8C	7	8R	45	8G	31	8V	19
KI	-	K4	-	KL	17	KP	7	KV	2	KG	3	KR	25	KC	-
J4	-	JI	-	JP	-	JL	2	JG	-	JV	-	JC	-	JR	-
D/	-	D9	85	DH	-	DT	6	DO	29	DM	2	DN	-	D3	-
F9	65	F/	-	FT	16	FH	17	FM	-	FO	19	F3	-	FN	4
XH	-	XT	-	X/	-	X9	-	XN	-	X3	-	XO	-	XM	-
BT	21	BH	5	B9	18	B/	-	B3	-	BN	-	BM	-	BO	22
ZO	3	ZM	-	ZN	-	Z3	-	Z/	-	Z9	33	ZH	-	ZT	16
YM	42	YO	-	Y3	-	YN	-	Y9	19	Y/	-	YT	4	YH	-
SN	2	S3	-	SO	23	SM	-	SH	9	ST	188	S/	-	S9	134
E3	-	EN	374	EM	80	EO	-	ET	96	EH	51	E9	224	E/	-
D	594	F	991	X	57	B	175	Z	621	Y	712	S	695	E	612

Fig. 22 (IV) (cont)

p. 57, i

	DELTA ψ' ($\overline{\chi}_2$ Lim.)									
	27		24		21		18		15	
	$L_\times$	$L_\bullet$	$L_\times$	$L_\bullet$	$L_\times$	$L_\bullet$	$L_\times$	$L_\bullet$	$L_\times$	$L_\bullet$
/	1155	0000	1017	0002	0867	0004	0746	0006	0646	0012
9	0000	0003	0003	0010	0007	0012	0009	0015	0010	0024
H	0005	0007	0007	0017	0015	0023	0010	0022	0014	0041
T	0000	0003	0001	0003	0007	0005	0005	0017	0009	0018
O	0004	0009	0002	0014	0009	0021	0014	0023	0017	0033
M	0006	0043	0012	0058	0022	0061	0032	0054	0040	0066
N	0002	0012	0003	0013	0012	0015	0010	0035	0021	0031
3	0000	0006	0001	0007	0005	0009	0007	0016	0011	0014
R	0002	0016	0008	0020	0011	0025	0017	0035	0024	0033
C	0016	0040	0014	0039	0018	0056	0030	0059	0036	0058
V	0037	0170	0041	0128	0040	0121	0065	0102	0054	0104
G	0011	0045	0016	0046	0019	0060	0020	0061	0041	0064
L	0003	0008	0003	0013	0008	0019	0013	0028	0027	0034
P	0012	0043	0016	0036	0019	0053	0021	0068	0041	0051
I	0001	0013	0006	0010	0003	0017	0013	0026	0019	0031
4	0001	0005	0002	0004	0000	0008	0009	0011	0010	0017
A	0002	0013	0003	0013	0005	0024	0016	0032	0015	0025
U	0006	0041	0011	0041	0019	0041	0033	0061	0023	0059
Q	0030	0128	0053	0115	0048	0115	0045	0085	0048	0099
W	0013	0029	0015	0039	0024	0041	0027	0048	0030	0059
5	0030	0141	0048	0117	0045	0117	0056	0098	0051	0098
8	0105	0486	0106	0386	0122	0274	0108	0228	0090	0165
K	0035	0129	0040	0139	0057	0118	0057	0115	0050	0099
J	0012	0030	0009	0041	0015	0043	0029	0056	0029	0050
D	0001	0008	0007	0021	0015	0018	0012	0032	0020	0040
F	0007	0037	0012	0048	0016	0053	0018	0057	0021	0049
X	0032	0110	0038	0140	0046	0142	0043	0102	0050	0094
B	0007	0032	0023	0052	0024	0064	0033	0045	0031	0056
Z	0002	0009	0004	0018	0005	0025	0010	0029	0019	0026
Y	0009	0026	0017	0044	0029	0038	0023	0048	0024	0059
S	0002	0010	0009	0013	0010	0024	0015	0028	0019	0018
E	0000	0000	0001	0005	0006	0006	0002	0010	0008	0025
	1548	1652	1548	1652	1548	1652	1548	1652	1548	1652
$\Delta\psi' = \bullet$	1405	1077	1331	1015	1279	0923	1204	0911	1104	0893

	DELTA ψ'					
	27	24	21	18	15	
/	1120	1032	0871	0787	0678	/
9	0003	0009	0017	0021	0024	9
H	0008	0021	0032	0039	0060	H
T	0002	0007	0013	0020	0032	T
O	0016	0020	0030	0038	0057	O
M	0048	0066	0079	0086	0098	M
N	0017	0018	0032	0041	0046	N
3	0005	0012	0016	0020	0031	3
R	0011	0025	0032	0046	0053	R
C	0053	0056	0069	0098	0106	C
V	0209	0174	0183	0167	0153	V
G	0059	0049	0065	0076	0099	G
L	0013	0020	0032	0047	0060	L
P	0060	0054	0068	0067	0088	P
I	0020	0015	0018	0045	0050	I
4	0007	0006	0013	0025	0027	4
A	0014	0016	0024	0043	0040	A
U	0044	0053	0062	0088	0081	U
Q	0157	0164	0168	0149	0145	Q
W	0040	0048	0060	0067	0090	W
5	0172	0177	0176	0156	0151	5
8	0600	0487	0375	0327	0259	8
K	0171	0173	0180	0158	0137	K
J	0051	0053	0063	0089	0083	J
D	0010	0024	0031	0044	0054	D
F	0042	0055	0064	0077	0075	F
X	0147	0181	0192	0145	0150	X
B	0037	0070	0088	0074	0079	B
Z	0013	0019	0029	0040	0039	Z
Y	0039	0064	0073	0062	0077	Y
S	0012	0026	0036	0045	0046	S
E	0000	0006	0009	0013	0032	E
	3200	3200	3200	3200	3200	
	2458	2356	2198	2129	2012	•

Fig. 22 (V) The ψ' stream

[i] Figure title entirely in underlined capital letters.

p. 58, i

	P	ΔP		DELTA ψ' ($\bar{\chi}_2$ Lim.)											DELTA ψ'					
				27		24		21		18		15			27	24	21	18	15	Dottage
				$L_\times$	$L_\bullet$	$L_\times$	$L_\bullet$	$L_\times$	$L_\bullet$	$L_\times$	$L_\bullet$	$L_\times$	$L_\bullet$							
/	0002	0560	/	0205	0063	0189	0049	0165	0043	0141	0052	0124	0046	/	0265	0259	0234	0208	0186	/
9	0529	0051	9	0039	0072	0042	0063	0050	0066	0039	0063	0045	0067	9	0104	0116	0094	0103	0102	9
H	0054	0061	H	0036	0045	0042	0059	0045	0059	0029	0069	0028	0063	H	0088	0091	0084	0085	0101	H
T	0096	0063	T	0040	0058	0045	0049	0035	0043	0038	0048	0045	0060	T	0081	0079	0098	0105	0093	T
O	0076	0096	O	0044	0072	0053	0060	0051	0051	0040	0054	0051	0051	O	0090	0106	0102	0110	0089	O
M	0210	0083	M	0035	0057	0038	0046	0049	0061	0052	0072	0050	0060	M	0096	0106	0105	0104	0092	M
N	0117	0051	N	0033	0045	0031	0058	0032	0050	0039	0054	0038	0038	N	0080	0077	0080	0087	0087	N
3	0002	0109	3	0061	0042	0064	0051	0063	0048	0050	0053	0046	0054	3	0100	0108	0089	0100	0098	3
R	0116	0068	R	0034	0043	0030	0041	0038	0044	0038	0055	0038	0047	R	0070	0065	0077	0084	0091	R
C	0037	0084	C	0051	0040	0045	0059	0041	0049	0057	0046	0045	0048	C	0085	0092	0105	0089	0094	C
V	0048	0044	V	0031	0076	0028	0075	0029	0069	0053	0065	0043	0048	V	0081	0105	0107	0101	0110	V
G	0066	0060	G	0036	0041	0033	0047	0033	0051	0036	0060	0042	0062	G	0070	0072	0069	0098	0097	G
L	0073	0052	L	0035	0036	0029	0037	0032	0041	0032	0055	0030	0056	L	0075	0075	0085	0093	0083	L
P	0046	0065	P	0029	0043	0048	0055	0038	0054	0044	0059	0057	0058	P	0072	0094	0086	0077	0101	P
I	0070	0064	I	0032	0045	0040	0053	0031	0045	0045	0060	0049	0056	I	0097	0078	0086	0094	0098	I
4	0001	0067	4	0042	0053	0039	0046	0036	0047	0034	0051	0041	0041	4	0083	0093	0075	0083	0094	4
A	0145	0125	A	0055	0044	0055	0042	0069	0041	0054	0048	0054	0045	A	0089	0080	0107	0098	0117	A
U	0074	0191	U	0081	0054	0088	0053	0078	0042	0084	0043	0070	0048	U	0133	0139	0108	0115	0119	U
Q	0027	0069	Q	0041	0055	0041	0053	0046	0066	0042	0045	0049	0056	Q	0103	0103	0105	0106	0099	Q
W	0043	0081	W	0038	0048	0035	0033	0046	0045	0044	0044	0049	0048	W	0084	0083	0076	0095	0082	W
5	0425	0275	5	0102	0057	0105	0048	0090	0063	0073	0041	0073	0051	5	0166	0165	0166	0119	0134	5
8	0465	0171	8	0087	0108	0073	0096	0086	0091	0088	0075	0065	0075	8	0212	0181	0157	0135	0132	8
K	0026	0065	K	0036	0055	0041	0066	0045	0058	0055	0035	0042	0044	K	0095	0078	0096	0088	0104	K
J	0008	0084	J	0040	0038	0031	0030	0037	0033	0034	0052	0037	0050	J	0103	0090	0074	0104	0088	J
D	0053	0084	D	0037	0043	0042	0049	0040	0039	0029	0034	0043	0058	D	0081	0077	0084	0087	0096	D
F	0042	0091	F	0042	0056	0047	0049	0039	0045	0052	0045	0048	0055	F	0096	0085	0099	0103	0102	F
X	0023	0074	X	0044	0064	0045	0055	0035	0073	0052	0051	0043	0051	X	0093	0110	0124	0100	0101	X
B	0031	0046	B	0029	0033	0037	0043	0031	0042	0038	0052	0041	0038	B	0073	0066	0076	0108	0093	B
Z	0030	0069	Z	0037	0044	0024	0046	0030	0049	0037	0043	0040	0043	Z	0077	0088	0082	0087	0087	Z
Y	0022	0079	Y	0036	0040	0034	0052	0042	0045	0035	0053	0042	0049	Y	0095	0093	0097	0091	0095	Y
S	0067	0059	S	0027	0042	0030	0046	0040	0057	0031	0041	0041	0047	S	0082	0078	0103	0069	0072	S
E	0176	0059	E	0033	0040	0024	0043	0026	0042	0033	0034	0039	0039	E	0081	0068	0070	0074	0063	E
	3200	3200		1548	1652	1548	1652	1548	1652	1548	1652	1548	1652		3200	3200	3200	3200	3200	
$\Delta D_{12}=\bullet$		2135		0973	0913	0973	0896	0987	0859	0902	0848	0866	0796		1889	1861	1775	1762	1723	

Fig. 22 (VI) The *D* stream type A (Gdz 3110 8.4.45)

[i] In the original the side label 'Dottage' stands opposite the line labelled /. We have moved it to its correct location. Figure title entirely in underlined capital letters.

p. 59, i

	P	ΔP		27		24		21		18		15			27	24	21	18	15	
				$L_\times$	$L_\bullet$	$L_\times$	$L_\bullet$	$L_\times$	$L_\bullet$	$L_\times$	$L_\bullet$	$L_\times$	$L_\bullet$							
/	0008	0074	/	0050	0060	0046	0075	0046	0048	0052	0067	0045	0058	/	0089	0122	0110	0119	0101	/
9	0468	0069	9	0045	0083	0041	0085	0054	0055	0047	0065	0046	0057	9	0107	0130	0096	0106	0109	9
H	0056	0094	H	0054	0092	0058	0076	0045	0065	0062	0049	0051	0074	H	0104	0092	0127	0113	0104	H
T	0087	0056	T	0039	0042	0035	0060	0047	0058	0038	0056	0042	0057	T	0103	0089	0095	0101	0095	T
O	0061	0140	O	0057	0070	0056	0073	0070	0058	0048	0044	0044	0052	O	0133	0135	0144	0114	0129	O
M	0280	0098	M	0050	0066	0052	0060	0048	0052	0045	0045	0052	0063	M	0105	0105	0104	0100	0114	M
N	0167	0077	N	0039	0043	0030	0042	0038	0053	0033	0056	0037	0064	N	0092	0094	0098	0092	0106	N
3	0001	0105	3	0053	0052	0055	0049	0056	0046	0056	0045	0060	0051	3	0101	0083	0106	0114	0115	3
R	0155	0088	R	0044	0035	0032	0042	0048	0048	0045	0050	0047	0034	R	0081	0086	0087	0086	0092	R
C	0041	0082	C	0043	0042	0038	0035	0037	0037	0043	0041	0034	0047	C	0069	0082	0068	0077	0074	C
V	0042	0051	V	0031	0047	0031	0045	0026	0061	0043	0059	0037	0042	V	0076	0077	0084	0078	0076	V
G	0074	0111	G	0048	0050	0040	0059	0047	0059	0045	0049	0055	0046	G	0104	0095	0095	0097	0109	G
L	0086	0069	L	0033	0068	0044	0053	0040	0052	0055	0058	0051	0051	L	0102	0100	0106	0088	0091	L
P	0041	0086	P	0041	0067	0042	0052	0048	0060	0046	0051	0043	0052	P	0096	0112	0106	0110	0111	P
I	0177	0048	I	0021	0033	0032	0048	0038	0061	0040	0062	0038	0067	I	0089	0086	0094	0094	0103	I
4	0003	0069	4	0031	0040	0036	0045	0038	0055	0045	0062	0040	0049	4	0075	0077	0087	0083	0088	4
A	0164	0172	A	0069	0050	0074	0042	0064	0043	0059	0055	0066	0055	A	0139	0115	0131	0124	0114	A
U	0080	0246	U	0109	0050	0094	0053	0090	0063	0081	0067	0084	0055	U	0148	0178	0134	0129	0161	U
Q	0014	0069	Q	0037	0042	0051	0055	0039	0066	0046	0037	0037	0054	Q	0097	0095	0070	0101	0096	Q
W	0033	0058	W	0030	0052	0037	0042	0030	0060	0034	0044	0043	0039	W	0071	0089	0099	0095	0072	W
5	0260	0321	5	0128	0040	0122	0041	0099	0040	0103	0047	0074	0054	5	0171	0169	0156	0144	0113	5
8	0266	0174	8	0073	0038	0078	0041	0067	0055	0060	0056	0058	0055	8	0131	0112	0103	0098	0103	8
K	0068	0066	K	0033	0037	0034	0048	0036	0036	0037	0049	0042	0058	K	0078	0064	0089	0075	0074	K
J	0009	0153	J	0077	0039	0064	0035	0070	0037	0059	0047	0063	0047	J	0125	0110	0106	0098	0108	J
D	0083	0115	D	0057	0036	0056	0037	0045	0049	0047	0037	0046	0050	D	0109	0091	0087	0100	0097	D
F	0046	0121	F	0055	0040	0054	0045	0053	0046	0049	0055	0048	0049	F	0098	0096	0095	0102	0101	F
X	0014	0095	X	0040	0041	0049	0061	0045	0040	0052	0044	0052	0044	X	0098	0093	0096	0102	0100	X
B	0039	0030	B	0019	0053	0023	0037	0029	0047	0032	0055	0037	0045	B	0068	0069	0060	0078	0071	B
Z	0036	0053	Z	0025	0053	0038	0040	0034	0055	0026	0048	0046	0065	Z	0095	0081	0084	0086	0082	Z
Y	0005	0056	Y	0045	0067	0036	0074	0044	0042	0040	0049	0052	0031	Y	0067	0077	0079	0091	0098	Y
S	0074	0098	S	0045	0060	0036	0065	0041	0057	0050	0050	0041	0042	S	0111	0111	0121	0111	0097	S
E	0262	0056	E	0027	0064	0034	0037	0036	0048	0030	0053	0037	0045	E	0068	0085	0083	0094	0096	E
	3200	3200		1548	1652	1548	1652	1548	1652	1548	1652	1548	1652		3200	3200	3200	3200	3200	
$\Delta D_{12} = \bullet$		1972		0943	0856	0927	0877	0899	0835	0860	0829	0844	0893		1794	1782	1768	1723	1714	

Fig. 22 (VII) The D-stream type B (GEP 5717 9.4.45)
Delta D ($\overline{\chi_2}$ lim.) Delta D ($\overline{\chi_2 \psi_1}$ lim.)

[i] Figure title entirely in underlined capital letters.

p. 60

i, E.13

	P	ΔP		DELTA D ($\bar{\chi}_2$ Lim.)												DELTA D ($\chi_2 + \bar{\Psi}_1$ Lim.)			
				27		24		21		18		15			27	24	21	18	15
				$L_\times$	$L_\bullet$	$L_\times$	$L_\bullet$	$L_\times$	$L_\bullet$	$L_\times$	$L_\bullet$	$L_\times$	$L_\bullet$						
/	0002	0100	/	0054	0043	0054	0055	0056	0061	0051	0049	0060	0057	/	0100	0095	0111	0090	0097
9	0428	0073	9	0035	0067	0035	0088	0050	0055	0041	0067	0043	0054	9	0082	0104	0078	0092	0105
H	0092	0088	H	0052	0053	0043	0058	0053	0060	0054	0046	0042	0068	H	0118	0102	0091	0099	0082
T	0173	0073	T	0044	0061	0042	0061	0042	0063	0048	0064	0041	0054	T	0101	0092	0093	0110	0099
O	0055	0093	O	0046	0048	0043	0060	0049	0032	0059	0050	0050	0054	O	0104	0098	0096	0105	0101
M	0094	0060	M	0041	0052	0039	0045	0036	0065	0035	0049	0042	0042	M	0087	0075	0102	0085	0117
N	0298	0080	N	0038	0049	0048	0045	0045	0074	0038	0052	0042	0063	N	0078	0083	0083	0088	0072
3	0003	0218	3	0088	0070	0075	0059	0075	0055	0088	0053	0067	0053	3	0130	0131	0126	0123	0135
R	0172	0091	R	0034	0059	0040	0043	0047	0046	0034	0053	0039	0045	R	0099	0113	0099	0101	0095
C	0074	0072	C	0042	0046	0032	0057	0041	0041	0041	0039	0042	0043	C	0075	0085	0080	0085	0095
V	0032	0053	V	0034	0052	0047	0046	0039	0049	0041	0063	0040	0045	V	0088	0102	0080	0092	0084
G	0083	0147	G	0068	0051	0068	0059	0076	0055	0055	0050	0070	0059	G	0128	0116	0132	0117	0113
L	0073	0066	L	0048	0080	0050	0059	0057	0056	0040	0055	0047	0051	L	0108	0105	0111	0107	0101
P	0045	0107	P	0044	0060	0053	0057	0048	0068	0055	0054	0053	0051	P	0104	0097	0107	0103	0110
I	0172	0076	I	0029	0034	0038	0054	0040	0051	0042	0043	0057	0043	I	0080	0087	0103	0071	0107
4	0001	0075	4	0034	0042	0035	0060	0038	0036	0049	0055	0043	0055	4	0081	0111	0084	0103	0093
A	0156	0072	A	0039	0040	0055	0038	0028	0043	0048	0051	0043	0041	A	0095	0090	0091	0094	0102
U	0107	0158	U	0091	0045	0084	0062	0076	0045	0073	0050	0072	0052	U	0108	0130	0128	0098	0099
Q	0014	0095	Q	0049	0073	0051	0057	0046	0060	0042	0063	0029	0058	Q	0129	0117	0120	0127	0103
W	0045	0074	W	0029	0042	0040	0053	0040	0052	0045	0044	0034	0060	W	0100	0112	0083	0104	0096
5	0086	0149	5	0055	0038	0044	0044	0052	0047	0052	0048	0050	0050	5	0119	0108	0103	0114	0112
8	0085	0095	8	0046	0048	0048	0051	0036	0059	0038	0057	0055	0055	8	0106	0095	0094	0098	0103
K	0042	0075	K	0033	0048	0036	0047	0042	0058	0033	0041	0036	0050	K	0076	0082	0078	0084	0100
J	0004	0167	J	0069	0053	0074	0046	0065	0042	0063	0049	0060	0066	J	0113	0096	0107	0122	0107
D	0105	0066	D	0034	0040	0026	0038	0043	0048	0043	0055	0049	0049	D	0092	0087	0099	0075	0104
F	0083	0220	F	0083	0042	0084	0046	0068	0037	0067	0039	0070	0040	F	0134	0134	0121	0120	0116
X	0008	0078	X	0049	0046	0041	0039	0050	0048	0040	0052	0038	0037	X	0071	0089	0098	0103	0091
B	0057	0026	B	0019	0060	0023	0046	0018	0045	0032	0052	0032	0049	B	0080	0068	0085	0078	0078
Z	0053	0112	Z	0049	0049	0043	0047	0047	0046	0033	0045	0031	0048	Z	0092	0095	0101	0081	0100
Y	0008	0118	Y	0067	0056	0051	0048	0047	0062	0064	0066	0062	0054	Y	0113	0110	0119	0115	0099
S	0126	0119	S	0060	0058	0050	0036	0054	0050	0066	0055	0053	0046	S	0118	0109	0111	0132	0091
E	0424	0104	E	0045	0047	0056	0048	0044	0043	0038	0043	0056	0060	E	0091	0082	0086	0084	0093
	3200	3200		1548	1652	1548	1652	1548	1652	1548	1652	1548	1652		3200	3200	3200	3200	3200
$\Delta D_{34} = \times$	1791			These figures are not entered as $\Delta D_{3+4} \times \Delta D_{1+2}$ are normally counted before χ_2 is set and limitation positions determined. (See **23**)											1717	1673	1704	1672	1641
$\Delta D_{12} = \bullet$	1821														1706	1727	1721	1733	1636

Fig. 22 (VIII) The D-stream type C (JB 8347 20.3.45)

[i] Figure title entirely in underlined capital letters.

p. 61

E.14

	1	2	3	4	5	6
	ΔP	ΔD 26 dots JB	ΔD 28 dots JB	ΔD 26 dots GDB	ΔD 26 dots C2Z	ΔD 20 dots JP
/	149	175	213	117	188	164
9	46	95	166	148	189	111
H	142	119	102	94	123	102
T	40	83	79	69	86	87
O	71	116	88	176	114	97
M	115	98	88	120	73	116
N	13	90	101	78	85	82
3	23	96	122	111	98	119
R	4	88	86	98	92	82
C	224	85	80	62	86	93
V	4	72	79	80	73	109
G	13	103	110	138	77	97
L	346	93	72	96	72	89
P	44	60	78	96	82	87
I	72	108	79	64	89	87
4	93	72	80	76	77	89
A	147	106	65	85	79	84
U	230	119	95	168	102	118
Q	324	129	96	95	77	108
W	275	57	90	95	88	93
5	32	183	161	126	224	136
8	112	132	255	110	189	106
K	15	70	63	80	92	93
J	41	134	110	130	92	120
D	1	80	71	86	73	72
F	26	116	92	114	76	121
X	27	101	70	94	68	103
B	52	72	60	55	66	70
Z	158	75	71	86	105	99
Y	13	111	82	86	76	116
S	286	108	90	94	98	72
E	62	54	106	73	91	89
COUNTS ARE NORMALISED TO	3200	3200	3200	3200	3200	3200
LENGTH OF SAMPLE	2480	1240	5249	1848	2191	5003
STANDARD DEVIATION (FOR THE RANDOM CASE) OF EACH ENTRY $100\sqrt{31/N}$	11·2	15·7	7·7	12·9	11·9	6·2

E.15

Fig. 22 (IX)

Some further $\Delta P + \Delta D$ counts showing the main types combined in various proportions, and the characteristic features of some well defined but less frequent types. Should be read in conjunction with more typical counts given in figs. **12 (II)** and **22 (VI–VIII)**. i

1. ΔP count described in **22G(c)**(6). Numerals interspersed with 99. No letter shift at all.
2. Strong in / and 5 and in some language letters I is surprisingly high, P surprisingly low, and W and E lower than would be normally expected.
3. See **22G(c)**(4). 8 is strong enough in ΔP to dominate ΔD and to increase the frequency in ΔD of 9 and E to a higher level than usual.
4. Count dominated by U and O. A combination of strong language and 5M98 punctuation.
5. A typical Codfish Zagreb in which letters differing in the third impulse differ little in frequency. Hard to set on χ_3 for this reason.

i Caption, including the two sentences starting ‘Some further…’ moved from above figure to below.

(d) P counts on 1–2 impulses

The best P_i bulge is on $P_3 = \times$ for punctuation (single or double) and on $P_5 =$ dot for language. Normally $P_1, P_2, P_4, P_5 \longrightarrow$ dot and $P_3 \longrightarrow \times$ but if 5's and 8's in P are very strong, they may be sufficient to negative the bulges on P_1, P_2, P_4 and P_5.

E.16 Fig. **22 (X)** shows the one and two impulse bulges for the 3 messages (type A, type B, type C) whose full counts are given in figs. **22 (VI)**, **22 (VII)**, **22 (VIII)**, and average bulges for a set of messages described in **R5**, p. 86.

	A	B	C	Crude av. of 57 Messages
$P_1 = \bullet$	1543	1747	1797	1660
$P_2 = \bullet$	1530	1687	2009	1720
$P_3 = \times$	1857	1837	1708	1800
$P_4 = \bullet$	1455	1594	1919	1660
$P_5 = \bullet$	1465	1806	2197	1720
$P_{45} = \bullet$	2408	2272	1916	2240
$P_{12} = \bullet$	2299	2022	1684	2100
$P_{13} = \times$	1951	2074	2116	2080
$P_{25} = \bullet$	2181	1925	1932	2060
$P_{24} = \bullet$	2167	1881	1884	2040
$\Delta P_2 = \bullet$	1565	1863	1572	
$\Delta P_{12} = \bullet$	2135	1972	1670	
$\Delta P_{13} = \bullet$	1874	1637	1821	
$\Delta P_{34} = \times$	1461	1829	1791	
$\Delta P_{25} = \bullet$	1881	1654	1766	
$\Delta P_{45} = \bullet$	2025	1852	1478	

i **Fig. 22 (X)**

(e) ΔP counts on 1 and 2 impulses

Bulges on ΔP_i are of interest only in case of ΔP_2 on messages with $\overline{\chi}_2$ limitation. $\Delta P_2 \longrightarrow$ cross in messages strong in single punctuation. Double punctuation will normally cancel out the tendency for $\Delta P_2 \longrightarrow \times$, but only rarely produces a comparable bulge on $\Delta P_2 =$ dot.

p. 65 Except when a message consists almost exclusively of German language, the best ΔP_{ij} bulge is on $\Delta P_{12} \longrightarrow$ dot. On German language, the bulge on $\Delta P_{12} \longrightarrow$ dot is weak (though usually positive) and the best bulges are on $\Delta P_{34} \longrightarrow \times$ and $\Delta P_{13} \longrightarrow$ dot. See fig. **22 (X)**.

$$\text{P.B.}(\Delta P_i = \text{dot}) \text{ is defined as } \pi_i$$
$$\text{P.B.}(\Delta P = \Theta) \text{ is defined as } \pi_\Theta.$$

(f) $\Delta^2 P$

A $\Delta^2 P$ letter count and the corresponding ΔP count is given in **R3**, p. 86. The bulginess of $\Delta^2 P$ is the more marked, the frequency of `U` being about 8% and `0 S M 3 4` all occurring 5% of the time. (**R0**, p. 50.)

(g) Bigrams in P and ΔP

Fig. **22 (IV)**gives a table of Bigram frequency in P.

No statistics of ΔP bigrams were taken.

[i] Caption moved from right-hand side of figure to bottom.

(h) The sum of two P streams

By considering the frequency of letters in $Z_a + Z_b$ for two messages (a, b) alleged to be in depth it is sometimes possible to decide whether $Z_a + Z_b = P_a + P_b$ and the messages are in fact in depth or not. A Scoring table for alleged depths is given in **22W(c)**. a

22H THE DE-CHI STREAM b

$$D = P + \psi' \qquad \therefore \quad \Delta D = \Delta P + \Delta\psi'.$$

The undifferenced ψ' stream is flat, therefore the undifferenced D stream is flat and unrecognisable statistically. ((E3).)

(a) Frequency of letters in ΔD

Applying (E1) and (E2) we get

$$P(\Delta D = \Theta) = \sum_{\Phi} \{P(\Delta\psi' = \Phi) \,.\, P(\Delta P = \overline{\Theta + \Phi})\} \qquad \text{(H1)}$$

$$\delta_\Theta = \text{P.B.}(\Delta D = \Theta) = \frac{1}{32} \sum_{\Phi} \{\beta'_\Phi . \pi_{\Theta+\Phi}\}. \qquad \text{(H2)}$$

The most important contribution to the frequency of any letter Θ in ΔD comes from the proportion of places in which there is a Θ in ΔP and a stroke in $\Delta\psi'$. Now $P(\Delta\psi' = /) = (1-a) + a(1-b)^5 =$ approx. $(1-a)$, and $(1-a)$ varies in value from ·18 when there are 14 dots to ·38 when there are 28 dots. i

As a result, $1/5$–$2/5$ of the ΔP stream is reproduced exactly in the ΔD stream, and, assuming (as a first approximation) that ΔD is flat when $\Delta\psi' \neq /$, we can see how ΔD count can be thought of as a ΔP count "watered down" by the addition of random material from the places where there is a TM **×** and no extension of the psis. As the dottage increases more and more of the ΔP stream is reproduced in ΔD, and the stronger is the ΔD count for a given ΔP count. p. 66

In fact, ΔD is not flat when $\Delta\psi' \neq /$, for the frequency of 8 in $\Delta\psi'$ (and even the frequency of V, X, 5, Q, K) is sufficiently high to ensure that a high letter (Θ) in ΔP will make a considerable contribution to the frequency of $(\Theta + 8)$ and of $(\Theta + \text{V})$ etc. in ΔD. Letters whose frequency in ΔD gets a substantial contribution in this way are known as "Good TM**×** letters" (**R0**, p. 57).

The relative importance of TM**×** contributions can be seen from the fact that $P(\Delta\psi' = 8) = ab^5 = \frac{1}{2}b^4$ which equals ·07 when there are 14 dots and ·22 when there are 28 dots. It will be noticed that as the dottage increases, not only does the strength of the TM dot and TM cross components of $\Delta\psi'$ increase, but that relative importance of TM cross components gradually increases.

To summarise we may say

$$P(\Delta D = \Theta) = (1-a) \,.\, P(\Delta P = \Theta) + aP(\Delta D = \Theta | \text{TM}\boldsymbol{\times}) \qquad \text{(H3)}$$ ii

where the great part of the "bulginess" comes from the first term on the right-hand side. c

[a] infact [b] DECHI STREAM [c] right hand

[i] Word 'in' handwritten.
[ii] Equation (H3) underlined.

(b) ΔD, with limitation

The TM dot positions are concentrated at places where there is a limitation cross, and using (H3) we may say

$$P(\Delta D{=}\Theta) = \left[(1-a)P(\Delta P{=}\Theta) + \tfrac{1}{2}a'P(\Delta D{=}\Theta|\,\mathrm{TM}\boldsymbol{\times})\right] + \left[\tfrac{1}{2}P(\Delta D{=}\Theta|\,\mathrm{TM}\boldsymbol{\times})\right]$$

where the square brackets cover lim cross and lim dot positions.

$$\therefore \quad P(\Delta D = \Theta|L = \bullet) = P(\Delta D = \Theta|\,\mathrm{TM}\boldsymbol{\times}) \qquad \text{(H4)}$$

i
$$P(\Delta D = \Theta|L = \boldsymbol{\times}) = \left\{(1-a')P(\Delta P = \Theta) + a'P(\Delta D = \Theta|\,\mathrm{TM}\boldsymbol{\times})\right\} \qquad \text{(H5)}$$

since $(1-a') = 2(1-a)$.

This result demonstrates symbolically that the bulginess of a ΔD count against limitation cross is essentially greater than the bulginess of the total ΔD count, since what has been left out consists entirely of count against TM**×**, and the proportion of ΔP in the remainder has been doubled.

p. 67 It might be noticed that the frequency of ΔD letters against limitation can be derived directly
E.17 from (H1) by treating the limitation as $\Delta\psi_6'$. Since $\Delta D_6 = \Delta\psi_6'$, ΔP_6 must be regarded as a dot, and $P(\Delta P = \Theta)$ put equal to zero, where Θ is a "letter" whose 6th impulse is a cross.

ii As a de-chi is usually counted when Z and chis only are known, it is only possible to count against limitation dots and crosses when $\overline{\chi}_2$ lim is being used.

(c) Some ΔD counts

E.18 In practice it is arduous to obtain information about the frequency of letters in ΔD by means of ΔP counts and the relation (H2). The simplest way of obtaining information is by collecting ΔD counts from chi-setting messages or by combining ΔP and $\Delta\psi'$ on a Robinson or Colossus.
a This was not at first realised (**R1**, pp. 31, 79; **R2**, pp. 37, 51).

In figs. **22 (VI)(VII)(VIII)** are shown ΔD counts corresponding to three different ΔP counts (Types A, B, C) and the $\Delta\psi'$ counts given in fig. **22 (V)**. As with $\Delta\psi'$, ΔD counts are given separately for $\overline{\chi}_2$ lim. and $\overline{\chi}_2\overline{\psi}_1'$ lim, and in the case of $\overline{\chi}_2$ lim the counts of ΔD against $L = \boldsymbol{\times}$ and $L = \bullet$ are given separately.

The counts show the gradual flattening of $\Delta\psi'$ and ΔD as the dottage decreases, and also how this flattening is to some extent masked by random variations. The importance of good TM**×** letters is shown particularly by the Type A figures. Here the ΔP (and ΔD) counts are dominated by one very powerful letter (/), with the result that 8 = (/ + 8) is the second highest letter in ΔD. The importance of 8, V, X, 5, Q, K etc. is even more marked in the counts of ΔD against $L = \bullet$ as given for $\overline{\chi}_2$ limitation.

(d) ΔD counts with $\overline{\chi}_2\overline{\overline{P}}_5$ limitation

With $\overline{\chi}_2\overline{\overline{P}}_5$ limitation it is not possible (in practice) to count ΔD against lim dot and lim cross, but it is possible to count ΔD against $\overline{\chi}_2$ dot and $\overline{\chi}_2$ cross (**R3**, p. 56.)

When P consists of German language $P_5 \longrightarrow$ dot (see **22G**) and therefore $L = \overline{\chi}_2 + \overline{\overline{P}}_5 \longrightarrow \overline{\chi}_2$. Therefore rather more than half the bulge on good language letters (3, U, F, J etc) in ΔD comes against $\overline{\chi}_2$ crosses.

The strength of 5 in ΔP is largely derived from P = 5M89, with ΔP = UA5. Now when 5
p. 68 occurs in this way in ΔP, $\overline{\overline{P}} = 5$ and $\overline{\overline{P}}_5 \longrightarrow \boldsymbol{\times}$. Therefore lim $\longrightarrow \overline{\chi}_2 + \boldsymbol{\times}$, and most of the bulge of 5 in ΔD comes against $\overline{\chi}_2$ DOTS. These two facts are shown by the following count of a Gurnard message.

---

[a] (**R1**, 31, 79; **R2** 37,51)

[i] Equations (H4) and (H5) underlined; equation number '(H4)' handwritten.
[ii] dechi

p. 68, i

	$\overline{\chi}_2 = \times$	$\overline{\chi}_2 = \bullet$
/	151	157
9	168	121
H	157	166
T	183	161
O	172	167
M	146	142
N	166	136
3	169	154
R	157	157
C	139	122
V	170	130
G	176	156
L	126	138
P	140	154
I	128	145
4	141	125
A	165	144
U	187	173
Q	137	130
W	135	142
5	155	239
8	163	149
K	127	126
J	181	142
D	126	140
F	176	149
X	129	138
B	134	107
Z	162	131
Y	186	137
S	172	134
E	126	131
Total	4950	4643

Fig. 22 (XI) ii

For Statistics on a longish sample of language type messages see **R3**, p. 87. a

(e) ΔD against BM

By an argument similar to that in **(b)** it can be seen that

$$P(\Delta D = \Theta | \text{BM} = \times) = P(\Delta D = \Theta | \text{TM}\times) \tag{H6}$$

$$P(\Delta D = \Theta | \text{BM} = \bullet) = \left\{\tfrac{1}{2}P(\Delta P = \Theta) + \tfrac{1}{2}P(\Delta D = \Theta | \text{TM}\times)\right\} \tag{H7}$$

and that the bulginess of a ΔD count against BM is essentially greater than the bulginess of the total ΔD count.

[a] for Statistics

[i] Fig. **22 (XI)** moved here from **22H(d)**, p. 68 in the *Report*.
[ii] Caption moved from right-hand side of figure to bottom.

(f) ΔD counts on 1 and 2 impulses

i, E.19 From (E4) we get $\delta_{ij} \equiv \text{P.B.}(\Delta D_{ij} = \text{dot}) = \beta'_{ij}.\pi_{ij}$.

But $\beta'_{ij} = \beta$

ii $$\therefore \quad \delta_{ij} = \pi_{ij}.\beta. \qquad \text{(H8)}$$

p. 69 Putting $j = 6$ $\quad \delta_{i6} = \pi_{i6}\,.\,\beta$

$$\therefore \quad \text{P.B.}(\Delta D_i + \text{lim} = \text{cross}) = \pi_i\beta$$

iii $$\therefore \quad (\text{for } \chi_2 \text{ lim})\ \text{P.B.}(\Delta D_2 + \widehat{\chi}_2 \longrightarrow \times) = \pi_2\beta. \qquad \text{(H9)}$$

$$\text{Now} \begin{cases} \Delta P_{12} \longrightarrow \text{dot} & \text{(nearly always)} \\ \Delta P_2 \longrightarrow \text{cross} & \text{(for punctuation)} \end{cases}$$

$$\therefore \quad \Delta D_{12} \longrightarrow \text{dot}$$

$$\Delta D_2 + \text{Lim} \longrightarrow \text{dot}\,. \qquad (\textbf{R1}, \text{p. } 9) \qquad \text{(H10)}$$

Figs. **22 (VI)(VII)(VIII)** give scores of ΔD_{12} etc. for the various ΔD counts shown.

The following table gives values for two impulse ΔD proportional bulges against limitation

E.20 dots and crosses.

$$\underline{\delta}_{\bullet\bullet} \equiv \text{P.B.}(\Delta D_i = \bullet \quad \Delta D_j = \bullet \mid \quad L = \bullet)$$

$$\overline{\delta}_{\bullet\bullet} \equiv \text{P.B.}(\Delta D_i = \bullet \quad \Delta D_j = \bullet \mid \quad L = \times)$$

$$\delta_{\bullet\bullet} \equiv \text{P.B.}(\Delta D_i = \bullet \quad \Delta D_j = \bullet) \text{ and so on.}$$

	$\underline{\delta}_{\bullet\bullet}$	$\frac{\beta}{2}\{\beta(\pi_{\bullet\bullet} + \pi_{\times\times}) - (\pi_{\bullet\bullet} - \pi_{\times\times})\}$
	$\underline{\delta}_{\times\times}$	$\frac{\beta}{2}\{\beta(\pi_{\bullet\bullet} + \pi_{\times\times}) + (\pi_{\bullet\bullet} - \pi_{\times\times})\}$
	$\underline{\delta}_{\times\bullet}$	$\frac{\beta}{2}\{-\beta(\pi_{\bullet\bullet} + \pi_{\times\times}) - (\pi_{\times\bullet} - \pi_{\bullet\times})\}$
	$\underline{\delta}_{\bullet\times}$	$\frac{\beta}{2}\{-\beta(\pi_{\bullet\bullet} + \pi_{\times\times}) + (\pi_{\times\bullet} - \pi_{\bullet\times})\}$
	$\overline{\delta}_{\bullet\bullet}$	$\frac{\beta}{2}(1+\beta)\{-\beta^2(\pi_{\bullet\bullet} + \pi_{\times\times}) + 2\beta\pi_{\bullet\bullet} + (3\pi_{\bullet\bullet} + \pi_{\times\times})\}$
	$\overline{\delta}_{\times\times}$	$\frac{\beta}{2}(1+\beta)\{-\beta^2(\pi_{\bullet\bullet} + \pi_{\times\times}) + 2\beta\pi_{\times\times} + (3\pi_{\times\times} + \pi_{\bullet\bullet})\}$
	$\overline{\delta}_{\times\bullet}$	$\frac{\beta}{2}(1+\beta)\{+\beta^2(\pi_{\bullet\bullet} + \pi_{\times\times}) + 2\beta\pi_{\times\bullet} + (3\pi_{\times\bullet} + \pi_{\bullet\times})\}$
E.21	$\overline{\delta}_{\bullet\times}$	$\frac{\beta}{2}(1+\beta)\{+\beta^2(\pi_{\bullet\bullet} + \pi_{\times\times}) + 2\beta\pi_{\bullet\times} + (3\pi_{\bullet\times} + \pi_{\times\bullet})\}$
	$\delta_{\bullet\bullet}$	$+\frac{1}{2}\beta(\pi_{\bullet\bullet} + \pi_{\times\times})$
	$\delta_{\times\times}$	$+\frac{1}{2}\beta(\pi_{\bullet\bullet} + \pi_{\times\times})$
	$\delta_{\times\bullet}$	$-\frac{1}{2}\beta(\pi_{\bullet\bullet} + \pi_{\times\times})$
	$\delta_{\bullet\times}$	$-\frac{1}{2}\beta(\pi_{\bullet\bullet} + \pi_{\times\times})$

Fig. 22 (XII)

The workings are left to the reader (similar workings are given on **R4**, p. 80).

Two results should be noticed.

[i] The 'PB' seems to have an illegible subscript.

[ii] Equation number '(H8)' handwritten.

[iii] Equation number '(H9)' handwritten.

(i) $\delta_{\bullet\bullet} = \delta_{\times\times}$ and $\delta_{\bullet\times} = \delta_{\times\bullet}$, whatever the relative values of $\pi_{\bullet\bullet}$ and $\pi_{\times\times}$. This shows that the benefits of counting against χ_2 limitation increases as $|\pi_{\bullet\bullet} - \pi_{\times\times}|$ increases (**R2**, p. 96). (H11) a p. 70

(ii) $\underline{\delta}_{ij} = \frac{1}{2}\{\underline{\delta}_{\bullet\bullet} + \underline{\delta}_{\times\times}\} = \frac{1}{2}\beta^2(\pi_{\bullet\bullet} + \pi_{\times\times}) = \beta^2\pi_{ij}$. b, E.22

But $\delta_{ij} = \frac{1}{2}\left\{\underline{\delta}_{ij} + \overline{\delta}_{ij}\right\} = \beta\pi_{ij}$ (from H6).

$$\therefore \quad \overline{\delta}_{ij} = \pi_{ij}(2\beta - \beta^2) = \beta(2-\beta)\pi_{ij}$$

$$\therefore \quad \overline{\delta}_{ij} / \underline{\delta}_{ij} = \frac{2-\beta}{\beta}. \qquad \text{(H12)}$$

The following table gives values for $\Delta D_1 = \Delta D_2 = \text{dot}, L = \times$ etc. for the messages considered in figs. **22 (VI)(VII)(VIII)**. c

ΔD_1	ΔD_2	L	Type A	Type B	Type C
•	•	×	490	404	406
•	×	×	278	322	386
×	×	×	497	495	385
×	•	×	283	327	371
•	•	•	421	435	465
•	×	•	400	433	402
×	×	•	439	400	406
×	•	•	392	384	379

ii

Fig. 22 (XIII) i

(g) $\Delta^2 D$

$$\Delta^2 D = \Delta^2 P + \Delta^2 \psi'.$$

It was several times suggested that methods involving use of $\Delta^2 D$ frequencies should be used. However counts taken showed that although the count of $\Delta^2 D$ was more bulgy than that of ΔP nevertheless the count of $\Delta^2\psi'$ was feeble compared with that of $\Delta\psi'$. As a result the count of $\Delta^2 D$ has no statistical (or other) advantages over that of ΔD. (See **R3**, pp. 44–5, 52–3 and **R4**, pp. 131–3 for example of $\Delta^2 D$ counts) (First $\Delta^2 D$ count **R1**, p. 82.)

(h) Bigrams in ΔD

Little work was done on bigram frequencies. Some experiments, however showed that the frequency of $\Delta D_1 + \Delta D_2$ bigrams ••, •×, ××, ×• did not differ significantly from the estimated frequency assuming random juxtaposition (**R3**, p. 63).

[a] Whatever [b] $\cdots = \beta^2(\pi_{\bullet\bullet} + \pi_{\times\times}) = \beta^2\pi_{ij}$ [c] value

[i] Caption moved from right-hand side of figure to bottom.
[ii] Column headings in fig. **22 (XIII)** are $\Delta D1$ and $\Delta D2$

p. 71 22J THE CIPHER STREAM

$$Z = \chi + D$$
$$\therefore \quad \Delta Z = \Delta\chi + \Delta D.$$

a, E.23 $\therefore$ Adapting (F1) and (F3) we get

$$\Delta Z_{ij} \xrightarrow[\frac{1}{2}(1+\delta_{ij})]{} \Delta\chi_{ij} \tag{J1}$$

$$\Delta_{w_i w_j}(\Delta Z_{ij}) \xrightarrow[\frac{1}{2}(1+\delta_{ij}^2)]{} \text{dot}, \tag{J2}$$

i and in particular

$$\Delta_{1271}(\Delta Z_{12}) \xrightarrow[\frac{1}{2}(1+\delta_{12}^2)]{} \text{dot}. \tag{J3}$$

This formula has been used as the basis of a formula for determining whether unidentified traffic is on Tunny, (see **R3**, p. 77) and the discussion on Significance test 0 in Ch. **24**.

22K SAMPLING ERRORS IN ALPHABETICAL COUNTS

Our knowledge of alphabetical counts of ΔP and ΔD is essentially empirical. There is no very exact knowledge of what a ΔP count should look like, even for a given end of a given link, since the count depends on the particular operator and the content of the message. The factor which a supposed ΔD count gives, in favour of the de-chi being correct, is discussed in **22Y**. Here we discuss shortly the method of obtaining typical counts.

Suppose we have r samples, all of length 3200, of ΔD for a particular link end and value of d. It is so convenient to be able to work with the average of these counts that we normally do so unless there is too obviously more than one type of language represented. Suppose the numbers of occurrences of Θ in the samples are

$$n_\Theta^{(1)}, n_\Theta^{(2)}, \ldots, n_\Theta^{(r)}.$$

The obvious thing to do is to take the number of occurrences in a typical example as

$$n_\Theta \pm \sigma_\Theta,$$

where

$$rn_\Theta = \sum_{s=1}^{r} n_\Theta^{(s)}$$

$$r\sigma_\Theta^2 = \sum_{s=1}^{r} \left(n_\Theta^{(s)} - n_\Theta\right)^2. \tag{K1}$$

In order to estimate σ_Θ it is easier to calculate $\sum_{s=1}^{r} \left|n_\Theta^{(s)} - n_\Theta\right|$, which can be done in a self-checking way, and to write

$$\cdot 8\,\sigma_\Theta = \sum_{s=1}^{r} \left|n_\Theta^{(s)} - n_\Theta\right|, \tag{K2}$$

[a] Adapting (6a) and (6c)

[i] Words 'and in particular' handwritten. The expression under the arrow in following equation (J3) reads $\frac{1}{2}(1+\delta_{ij}^2)$, that is, the specialization to the case $i = 1, j = 2$ is imperfectly carried out.

since the expected value of the modulus of the deviation from the mean is $\sigma\sqrt{2/\pi} \doteqdot \cdot 80\sigma$ in the case of a normal variate. Of course this is not accurate, but accuracy is not the point. p. 72

The expected sigma-age of a chi run (see **23C(d)**) can be worked out sufficiently accurately from the average letter count, i.e. the 32 numbers n_Θ. Some estimate of the S.D. of this sigma-age can be obtained from the numbers σ_Θ. A very crude method of doing this is given in **R2**, 56, 60, 61 and pp. 17, 21 of the note-book 'Alphabetical counts and runs statistics'.

22W SOME FURTHER STREAMS

(a) The Sum of two *P*-Streams

The frequency of letters in $P_a + P_b$ is deducible from the frequency of letters in P_a by means of the Faltung Theorem (**22E**).

We can score a stream of letters suspected of being $P_a + P_b$. For each occurrence of Θ in the stream we get a factor

$$\frac{P(P_a + P_b = \Theta)}{1/32},$$

that is, decibanage of $10\log_{10}\{32P(P_a + P_b = \Theta)\}$. (W1) i, a

The following table gives the *centiban* scores actually used in Room 41 for scoring suspected depths. E.24

Θ	score	Θ	score	Θ	score	Θ	score
/	+31	R	−15	A	−2	D	−2
9	−1	C	−1	U	+11	F	+2
H	−12	V	+7	Q	−12	X	−2
T	−16	G	+2	W	−1	B	−14
0	+7	L	−24	5	+3	Z	−4
M	+1	P	−4	8	+2	Y	−3
N	−17	I	−1	K	−3	S	+17
3	+4	4	+10	J	+6	E	−12

Fig. 22 (XIV)

(b) The sum of two extended psi-streams

Given two stretches of de-chi (a,b) which are known to have the same decode (as in an overlap) it is often possible to find the relative position of the *P* in the two stretches. For when set correctly b

$$\begin{aligned}\Delta D_a + \Delta D_b &= \Delta\psi'_a + \Delta P_a + \Delta\psi'_b + \Delta P_b\\ &= \Delta\psi'_a + \Delta\psi'_b \qquad (\text{since } \Delta P_a = \Delta P_b).\end{aligned}$$

If Θ_n^m is a letter of n dots and m crosses p. 73

$$P(\Delta\psi'_a + \Delta\psi'_b = \Theta_n^m \mid \mathrm{TM}_a = \bullet,\ \mathrm{TM}_b = \bullet) = X_n^m = \begin{cases} 1, & m = 0\\ 0, & m \neq 0\end{cases} \qquad \text{(W1)}$$ ii

$$P(\Delta\psi'_a + \Delta\psi'_b = \Theta_n^m \mid \mathrm{TM}_a = \bullet,\ \mathrm{TM}_b = \times) = Y_n^m = \left(\frac{1+\beta}{2}\right)^m \left(\frac{1-\beta}{2}\right)^n \qquad \text{(W2)}$$

$$P(\Delta\psi'_a + \Delta\psi'_b = \Theta_n^m \mid \mathrm{TM}_a = \times,\ \mathrm{TM}_b = \times) = Z_n^m = \left(\frac{1-\beta^2}{2}\right)^m \left(\frac{1+\beta^2}{2}\right)^n \qquad \text{(W3)}$$

[a] $10\log_{10}\{32P(P_a + P_b) = \Theta\}$ [b] overlape

[i] Commas supplied for clause 'that is'. Note that equation label (W4) is reused in **22W(b)** below.
[ii] Note equation label (W1) already used in **22W(a)** above.

and

$$P(\Delta\psi_a' + \Delta\psi_b' = \Theta_n^m) = (1-a)^2 X_n^m + 2a(1-a)Y_n^m + a^2 Z_n^m$$
$$= \frac{\beta^2 X_n^m + 2\beta Y_n^m + Z_n^m}{(1+\beta)^2}. \quad \text{(W4)}$$

E.25 Because limitation (L) is equivalent to $\Delta\psi_6' + \boldsymbol{\times}$,

$$P(\Delta\psi_a' + \Delta\psi_b' = \Theta_n^m \,|\, L_a + L_b = \bullet) = P(\Delta\psi_a' + \Delta\psi_b' = \Theta_{n+1}^m \,|\, \Delta\psi_a' + \Delta\psi_b' = \Theta_1^0)$$
$$= \frac{P(\Delta\psi_a' + \Delta\psi_b' = \Theta_{n+1}^m)}{P(\Delta\psi_a' + \Delta\psi_b' = \Theta_1^0)}$$
$$= 2P(\Delta\psi_a' + \Delta\psi_b' = \Theta_{n+1}^m). \quad \text{(W5)}$$

Similarly

$$P(\Delta\psi_a' + \Delta\psi_b' = \Theta_n^m \,|\, L_a + L_b = \boldsymbol{\times}) = 2P(\Delta\psi_a' + \Delta\psi_b' = \Theta_n^{m+1}). \quad \text{(W6)}$$

The following table (for $m+n=5$) is constructed, with the aid of W1, 2, 3, 4, 5, 6, in the same way as the table in the last section and gives deciban scores per letter and is used for scoring possible positions for go-backs. Scores for intermediate dottages can be interpolated.

	$L_a + L_b$ = dot	$L_a + L_b$ = cross	Dottages				
			15	18	21	24	27
Number of dots (n)	5	–	$+5\frac{1}{2}$	+7	+8	+9	$+10\frac{1}{2}$
	4	5	−1	−1	–	–	$+\frac{1}{2}$
	3	4	−1	−1	−1	−2	−2
	2	3	−1	−1	−2	−2	−5
	1	2	0	0	–	−1	−2
	0	1	$+\frac{1}{2}$	+1	+2	$+2\frac{1}{2}$	+3
	–	0	+2	$+3\frac{1}{2}$	+5	+7	$+8\frac{1}{2}$

Fig. 22 (XV)

(c) The sum of two key streams

It has been suggested that in cases where there are two stretches of Z with the same P it might
a be possible to find the relative positions of the P, even if neither message has been decoded, for $\Delta Z_a + \Delta Z_b = \Delta K_a + \Delta K_b$

$$\therefore \quad \underset{w_i w_j}{\Delta}\left\{\Delta \underset{a}{Z_{ij}} + \Delta \underset{b}{Z_{ij}}\right\} = \underset{w_i w_j}{\Delta}\left\{\Delta \underset{a}{K_{ij}} + \Delta \underset{b}{K_{ij}}\right\} \xrightarrow[\frac{1}{2}(1+\beta^2)]{} \text{dot}. \quad \text{(W8)}$$

p. 74 22X THE ALGEBRA OF PROPORTIONAL BULGES

E.26 **(a) The Problem: Recovery of ΔP from ΔD**

It has been pointed out in **22H** that the expected letter count of ΔD can be obtained from that of ΔP by means of the equations

$$\text{P.B.}(\Delta D = \Theta) = \frac{1}{32}\sum_{\Phi} \text{P.B.}(\Delta P = \Phi)\,\text{P.B.}(\Delta\psi' = \Theta + \Phi). \quad \text{(X1)}$$

---

[a] messages

The problem of solving these equations for P.B.(ΔP) given P.B.(ΔD) led to the 'algebra of proportional bulges'. Even theoretically the problem is not simple, since the determinant of the coefficients vanishes. The advantage of using P.B.'s rather than probabilities is not great, but it does help a little. The reasons why proportional bulges were first introduced are mentioned in **21(j)** (**R1**, p. 20). a, b

(b) Application to Motor Runs

The problem we are considering here has an application to the question of the expected score on a motor run **R5**, pp. 32, 32. For we know that c

$$\text{P.B.}(\Delta D|\,\text{BM} = \bullet) = \frac{1}{2}\text{P.B.}(\Delta P) + \frac{1}{2}\text{P.B.}(\Delta P + \Delta\psi),$$

and the second term can be written as a 'Faltung', i.e. in a form similar to (X1) above. When the limitation is $\overline{\chi}_2$ the count of ΔD against $\overline{\chi}_2 =$ dot provides a sample of ΔD against motor crosses and we can therefore obtain a good idea of the L.C. of ΔP and of the expected score in a motor run (**R0** 47–50). For limitations other than $\overline{\chi}_2$, the usual method was to assume 'flatness' of $\Delta P + \Delta\psi$ in order to obtain a quick estimate (see chapter **23**). d E.27

(c) Efforts at Solution

The problem of solving equations (X1) for P.B.(ΔP) was first attacked in **R2**, p. 69 where an erroneous connection with 'Fourier Transforms' was suggested. The theoretical aspects of the problem were pursued in **R2**, p. 87, 104; **R3**, pp. 24, 28, 32, 34, 37, 38, 48; **R5**, pp. 23, 32; and a practical experiment in the solution of ΔP from ΔD is described in **R3**, pp. 71–3. Finally a relatively simple exposition of the whole subject was given in **R5**, pp. 59. In this chapter we give a still simpler account which contains all the essential ideas, with the introduction of the minimum of new notation. It will be observed that 'Fourier Transforms' are after all the simplest way of treating the problem. e, f g h E.28

(d) Exposition of the algebra

Denote an arbitrary teleprinter letter by Θ or Φ. Let $F(\Theta)$ be an arbitrary numerical function of teleprinter letters. The Fourier Transform (F.T.) of F is defined as the function F^* where p. 75

$$F^*(\Phi) = \frac{1}{\sqrt{32}}\sum_{\Theta} F(\Theta)(-1)^{\Theta.\Phi} \qquad \text{(X2)}$$

where $\Theta.\Phi$ is the scalar product of Θ and Φ when they are considered as vectors with 0 for dot and 1 for cross. For example $(\texttt{U.N}) = 1.0 + 1.0 + 1.1 + 0.1 + 0.0 = 1$. It can easily be shown that $F^{**} = F$, i.e. that F is the F.T. of F^*, so the relation between F and F^* is symmetrical. E.29 i

---

[a] in **21(J)** [b] (**R1**,20) [c] (**R5** 23,32) [d] similar to (1) above [e] equations (XI) [f] **R2**,69 [g] **R5** 23 32 [h] **R5** 59
[i] (U.N.)

The "Faltung", F, of two functions F_1 and F_2 is defined by the equation

$$F(\Theta) = \sum_{\Phi} F_1(\Phi) F_2(\Theta + \Phi), \tag{X3}$$

which is clearly also equal to $\sum_\Phi F_2(\Phi)F_1(\Theta+\Phi)$.
It is easy to see that if F is the Faltung of F_1 and F_2 then $F^* = \sqrt{32}F_1^*.F_2^*$. In other words the F.T. of a Faltung is $\sqrt{32}$ times the product of the F.T.'s. Therefore, by equation (X1)

$$\sqrt{32}\,\mathrm{P.B.}^*(\Delta D) = \mathrm{P.B.}^*(\Delta P)\,\mathrm{P.B.}^*(\Delta\psi') \tag{X4}$$

i (see foot-note).

where P. B.* means the Fourier Transform of the Proportional Bulge.

This gives $\mathrm{P.B.}^*(\Delta P)$ in terms of $\mathrm{P.B.}^*(\Delta D)$ and $\mathrm{P.B.}^*(\Delta\psi')$ and hence $\mathrm{P.B.}(\Delta P)$ in terms of $\mathrm{P.B.}(\Delta D)$ and $\mathrm{P.B.}(\Delta\psi')$. The process is not as laborious as it sounds in virtue of the rather simple interpretation of an F.T. For example if Θ is the T.P. letter J or vector $(1,1,0,1,0)$ and if F is a P. B. function, taken as $\mathrm{P.B.}(\Delta D)$ for definiteness, we have

$$\begin{aligned} F^*(\mathrm{J}) &= \frac{1}{\sqrt{32}}\left\{\sum_{\Phi_1+\Phi_2+\Phi_4=\bullet} F(\Phi) - \sum_{\Phi_1+\Phi_2+\Phi_4=\times} F(\Phi)\right\} \\ &= \frac{2}{\sqrt{32}} \sum_{\Phi_1+\Phi_2+\Phi_4=\bullet} F(\Phi) \end{aligned}$$

since F is assumed to be a P. B. function.

Thus

$$\mathrm{P.B.}^*(\mathrm{J}) = \sqrt{32}\,\mathrm{P.B.}(\Delta D_{1+2+4} = \bullet) \tag{X5}$$

so we see that the F.T. of a P. B. is $\sqrt{32}$ times the P. B. of the so-called "32-combination count" (**R3**, p. 49; **R5**, p. 55), for which the lower half of the Colossus switchboard is well adapted. The equation (X4) is now seen to express the well known and elementary property of the multiplication of P. B.'s.

Observe that $\mathrm{P.B.}(\Delta P)$ is not quite determinate since

E.30
$$\mathrm{P.B.}^* P(\mathrm{E}) = \sqrt{32}\,\frac{\mathrm{P.B.}^*\,\Delta D(\mathrm{E})}{\mathrm{P.B.}^*\,\Delta\psi'(\mathrm{E})}$$

and the expected values of both numerator and denominator of this are zero, if $ab = \frac{1}{2}$. The same applies to the arguments 4, 9, 3, T.

p. 76 22Y THE AMOUNT OF EVIDENCE DERIVED FROM A LETTER COUNT

The fundamental problem in chi-setting from a theoretical point of view is of the following type: given a ΔD letter count in which Θ occurs n_Θ times, with $\sum_\Theta n_\Theta = N$, to estimate the decibanage in favour of the χ's being correct. The link and end being dealt with will be known always, the dottage (d) possibly. We will also have some prior knowledge of expected ΔD characteristics.

Note: $\mathrm{P.B.}(\Delta P)$ is a function of Θ and should strictly be written as $\mathrm{P.B.}(\Delta P = \Theta)$.

---

[i] Native footnote untagged with a footnote mark.

This knowledge can be expressed by saying that there is a probability P_i ($\sum P_i = 1$) for the theory, T_i, that the frequency of letter Θ in ΔD is $P_\Theta^{(i)}$; ($\Theta = /, 9, \mathrm{H}, \ldots, i = 1, 2, 3, \ldots$).

If theory T_i is true then the factor in favour of the χ's being correctly set rather than random is f_i, where

$$f_i = \prod_\Theta (32 P_\Theta^{(i)})^{n_\Theta}. \tag{Y1}$$

This factor can be conveniently expressed in decibans of course.

Now, by the theorem of the weighted average of factors (see **21(i)**), the factor in favour of the χ's being correct is E.31

$$\sum P_i f_i. \tag{Y2}$$

So we have a complete theoretical solution of the problem. The method could be made practicable for letter counts which are of a more or less standard type, but even for these, a great deal of preliminary statistical work would have to be done (**R2**, pp. 1, 59). If the letter count is not of a standard type it is tempting to use the χ^2 test. This has the disadvantage that the χ^2 test takes E.32 no account of which are the high-scoring letters and which the low-scoring ones. An attempt to overcome this objection is made in **R5**, pp. 1–4. This attempt is a theoretical formulation of what is really done in practice — namely the count is looked at to see if it is sufficiently 'bulgy' and then (slightly less important) to see if the bulges come at the right letters.

An alternative test, which is quicker to apply, is the method of 'decibanning a letter count using the message as its own sample' (**R4**, pp. 56, 121). This method is obtained by writing, in (Y1), $P_\Theta^{(i)} = n_\Theta / N$. The decibanage given by this is

$$\sum_\Theta n_\Theta \log n_\Theta - N\{\log N - \log 32\}, \tag{Y3}$$

when the logarithms are to base $\sqrt[10]{10}$ of course. It can be proved easily that this is equivalent to E.33 taking the maximum possible value of f_i and therefore, by (Y2), the method is optimistic. It was designed originally as a method of rejecting seedy wheel-breaking stories. It is shown in **R4**, 121 E.34 that the decibanage will not be more than 80 db too high. [a]

[a] will not be more the

p. 77 # 23 MACHINE SETTING

p. 78 ## 23A INTRODUCTION

(a) The problem of chi-setting

c The problem of chi-setting is: given the cipher Z and the chi patterns, to find the settings of the chis relative to Z and so obtain

$$D \equiv Z + \chi.$$

E.1

(b) The evidence available

The evidence available is that of the ΔD letter count, which has non-random bulges: the method is to find settings which make these bulges as large as is possible, discriminating in favour of settings whose bulges are on the right letters. Unless the bulges are so large as to be unlikely to have occurred at random, the chis cannot be regarded as set.

(c) The ideal method

The ideal method would be to examine the 32 letter count at all possible settings, but this
E.2 means $41 \times 31 \times 29 \times 26 \times 23 = 23{,}561{,}898$ letter counts.

(d) Practical chi-setting

Practical chi-setting must be completed in a reasonable time, so that it will be necessary at each stage to set a smaller number of chis and to examine not the whole letter count, but only its strongest feature. Runs are classified as one-wheel or short, 2-wheel or long, 3-wheel, and 4-wheel.

---

[a] INtroduction [b] Annotated Exhibits [c] chi-patterns

(e) The art of chi-setting

The art of chi-setting consists of:

(i) choosing runs so as to obtain significant scores as quickly as possible.

(ii) knowing how significant the scores obtained are; in particular, knowing when they are "good" or "certain".

23B THE CHOICE OF RUNS p. 79

(a) ΔD Statistics

The choice is based on the statistics of Δ*D* letter counts for messages already set (**22H**). Some Δ*D* characteristics are permanent and common to all links, others are peculiar to a particular link, or to one end of a link, or to particular messages.

In almost all messages /, 5, U, 8 are common; B is rare;
In Type A (stroky) messages / is very common;
In Type B (language) messages 3, J, F, G are common.

Originally the Berlin ends of Western links were type B, the outer ends of most Western links and both ends of Eastern links were type A. Later the situation became confused and so did the notation A, B, C... (cf. **22G(c)**).

(b) Practical Runs

E.3

For rapid setting it is insufficient to remember the frequencies of the 32 individual letters: it is necessary to know explicitly what are the best runs for direct application; e.g. to know that 1+2=• is the best run involving only two wheels. This is of course deducible from the 32 letter count, largely because 1+2/ is satisfied by all the letters /, 5, U, 8, 3, J, and not by B. Succinct rules are given in "trees". a

(c) A simple tree

E.4, i

TYPE A

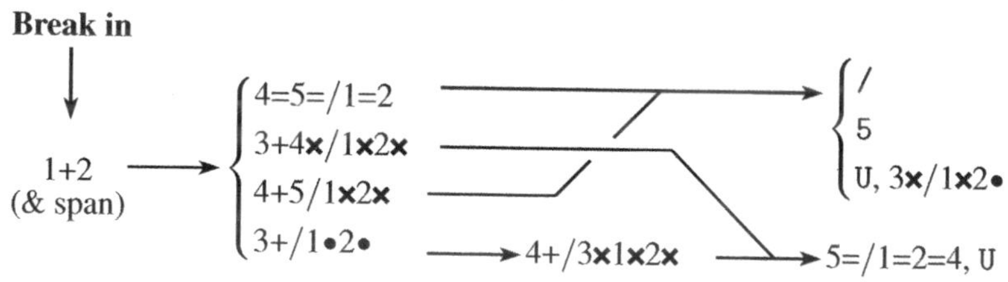

[a] Succint

[i] Original drawings in *Report* have curved arrows.

TYPE B

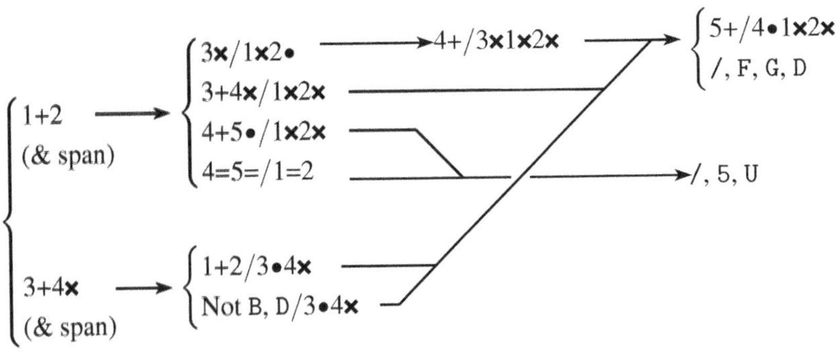

p. 80 (i) Runs bracketed are to be tried, in order, till one of them gives a "certain" or "good" setting. See **23C(a)**. The runs for the last wheel should be "certain". If all these fail, the message is abandoned, unless it is to be flogged (**23J**).

(ii) ΔD is omitted and only the suffixes denoting the impulses are written: this is the invariable custom. (**R0**, p. 110.)

(iii) Impulses to the right of the oblique stroke are supposed already set.

(iv) The Break In is the initial run used when setting a message (which has nothing to the right of the oblique stroke).

(v) "Span" is in the diagram, because, as soon as the first wheels are set, the message is invariably spanned for possible message slides. (See **23F**.) (See also **R3**, p. 134; **R4**, p. 7; **R1**, p. 99; **R2**, pp. 42, 44, 48.)

(d) More powerful methods

Though the above tree will suffice to set a large proportion of messages, it is rather crude. Having already set several recent messages on the same link, one would probably introduce a few modifications.

For the best results messages on $\overline{\chi}_2$ limitation may require a quite different break-in. (**23E**)

Other runs are mentioned in **23J**: **R1** is full of such references; recent notes include **R3**, p. 131, **R5**, p. 106.

23C WEIGHING THE EVIDENCE

(a) Sigma-age

The bulge of a score is its excess over random.

The sigma-age is the ratio of the bulge to the standard deviation for random scores: it is a measure of the improbability that the sum will occur at random in a single trial, i.e. at a particular setting. If many settings are tried, the improbability will be proportionally reduced. In a one-wheel run the number of settings tried lies between 23 and 41, in a two-wheel run between 598 and 1271 and so on.

This improbability that a score will have occurred at random is clearly some indication of the degree of certainty that the corresponding setting is correct. Unless there are rival settings the following table is used.

		1	2	3	4	5
	Number of wheels set by the run	1	2	3	4	5
Sigma-age	for a “certain” setting i.e. odds 50:1 on	3·8	4·5	5·2	5·8	6·4
	for a “good” setting i.e. odds 6:1 on	3·2	4·0	4·7	5·4	6·0

a

The formula for sigma is $\sigma = \sqrt{p(1-p)N}$, where p is the random proportional frequency (**21(k)**). In χ-setting p is almost always $\frac{1}{2}$, $\frac{1}{4}$ or $\frac{1}{8}$, giving $\sigma = \frac{1}{2}\sqrt{N}$, $\frac{1}{4}\sqrt{3N}$, $\frac{1}{8}\sqrt{7N}$. b, i

(b) Pick-ups p. 81

If two independent runs contain the same wheel, their evidence may be combined. A table has been compiled which is sufficient for elementary setting. (For the basis of the table see **23J(b)** and **23X**.) E.5

CERTAIN						GOOD					
Long	**Long**	**Long**	**Short**	**Short**	**Short**	**Long**	**Long**	**Long**	**Short**	**Short**	**Short**
4·5	—	4·5	—	3·8	—	4·0	—	4·0	—	3·2	—
4·4	2·7	4·4	1·0	3·7	1·0	3·9	2·7	3·9	1·0	3·1	1·0
4·3	2·8	4·3	1·2	3·6	1·1	3·8	2·9	3·8	1·3	3·0	1·2
4·2	3·0	4·2	1·6	3·5	1·3	3·7	3·0	3·7	1·5	2·9	1·5
4·1	3·1	4·1	1·8	3·4	1·6	3·6	3·1	3·6	1·7	2·8	1·7
4·0	3·2	4·0	2·0	3·3	1·8	3·5	3·2	3·5	1·9	2·7	1·8
3·9	3·4	3·9	2·3	3·2	2·0	3·4	3·3	3·4	2·1	2·6	2·0
3·8	3·5	3·8	2·5	3·1	2·1			3·3	2·3	2·5	2·1
3·7	3·7			3·0	2·3			3·2	2·5	2·4	2·2
				2·9	2·5						
				2·8	2·6						
				2·7	2·7						

As an example of the use of the table, suppose that with the same setting of χ_3 the sigma-age

of 3**x**/1**x**2• is 2·4σ
and of 3+4**x**/1**x**2**x** is 3·9σ.

According to the table, the settings of χ_3, χ_4 are both “certain”, though neither run separately would give even a “good” setting. E.6

(c) Rival Settings

In this section the effects of competing scores have been ignored. (See **23J**, **23X**.)

(d) Expected Sigma-age

The expected sigma-age is

$$\frac{\text{expected bulge}}{\sigma} = \frac{p\xi N}{\sqrt{p(1-p)}} = \xi\sqrt{N\frac{p}{1-p}}, \qquad \text{E.7}$$

where ξ is the proportional bulge. For $p = \frac{1}{2}$, $\frac{1}{4}$, $\frac{1}{8}$ this is $\xi\sqrt{N}$, $\xi\sqrt{N/3}$, $\xi\sqrt{N/7}$.

[a] odd 6:1 on [b] **(21(K))**

[i] Handwritten phrase ‘almost always’ inserted with a caret.

23D ANNOTATED EXHIBITS

E.8 This is rather illogically included here to exhibit the practice of chi-setting as concretely as possible: its perusal is recommended. Inevitably it includes much which is explained only in the later sections of the chapter but this is always indicated by reference. The message shown is on $\bar{\chi}_2$ limitation, but no special method is used except that all runs are made against $\bar{\chi}_2$ crosses only. (The operator neglects the four letter count on $\Delta D_1 \Delta D_2$: it may be repeated that on the whole text there can be only a random bulge of **××** over ••.)

p. 82

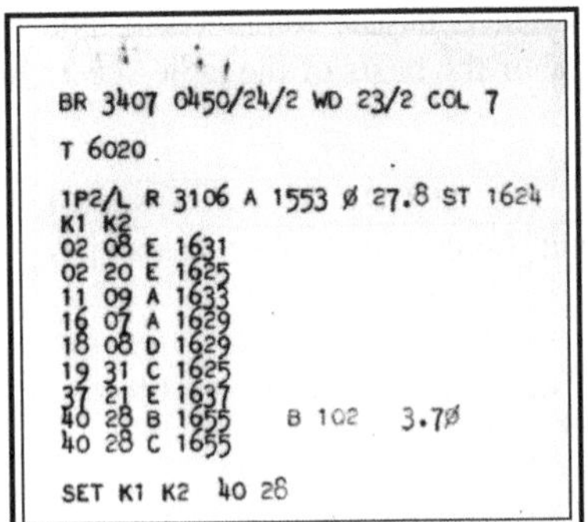

```
BR 3407 0450/24/2 WD 23/2 COL 7
T 6020
1P2/L R 3106 A 1553 ø 27.8 ST 1624
K1 K2
02 08 E 1631
02 20 E 1625
11 09 A 1633
16 07 A 1629
18 08 D 1629
19 31 C 1625
37 21 E 1637
40 28 B 1655        B 102   3.7ø
40 28 C 1655
SET K1 K2 40 28
```

23D/1.1: ×.5

The items in the first line are message number, time and date sent, wheel day and Colossus number.

T 6020 is the text length, measured as a check, as soon as the tape is on Colossus.

1P2/L is typewriterese for $1{+}2/\bar{\chi}_2$×; this run is chosen because the chit (not preserved) was so marked (**23E**).

R 3106 is the number of places looked at, i.e. the number of places where $\bar{\chi}_2$=×.

At random the expected number (A) of these when 1+2=• is $\frac{1}{2} \times 3106 = 1553$.

ø (typewriterese for σ) 27·8 is the standard deviation of 1+2=• viz. $\frac{1}{2}\sqrt{R} = \frac{1}{2}\sqrt{3106}$. This is of course an application of the formula quoted in **21(b)**, that if random proportional frequency in a normal distribution is p, the standard deviation is $\sqrt{Rp(1-p)}$. A table of $\frac{1}{2}\sqrt{R}$ and $\frac{1}{4}\sqrt{3R}$ is provided at each Colossus.

```
SPAN IN 1000'S

0271
0245

0268
0249

0301
0214

0280
0237

0268
0247

0261
0257

SPAN 4000-END IN 500'S

0139
0119

0129
0128

0131
•0128

0130
0129

▸ SPAN 01-4500

1259
1064    2B 195 B 98   4.1Ø

SPANNING 01-4500

SET K1 K2 40 28 GOOD
```

23D/1.2: ×.5

ST 1624 is the set total, i.e. Colossus is set so as not to display or print any smaller score. Because this is a two-wheel run, ST is taken as $A+2\frac{1}{2}\sigma$.

The best score is $3{\cdot}7\sigma$, not even "good" (**23C(a)**) but worth spanning (**23F(c)**). In each pair of span scores the upper is 1+2=•, the lower 1+2=**x**: this makes it easy to see where a slide occurs, evidently between 4000 and 5000, for 5000–6000 shows almost no bulge and 4000–5000 only a small bulge. 4000–5000 is therefore spanned in 500's and the bulge of 1+2=• is seen to cease at about the 4500th letter: it is therefore believed that there is a message slide here and the subsequent runs are done spanning 1–4500: the sigma-age is now 4·1 instead of 3·7; the setting is therefore "good".

Here the operator makes the mistake of neglecting a 4-letter count for ΔD_1, ΔD_2 (**23E(h)**). This is easily reconstructed and would read a

••	592
•**x**	498
xx	667
x•	567.

Because **xx** is so strong, this would have suggested the run 3+4**x**/1**x**2**x** which would in fact yield a score of $7{\cdot}9\sigma$.

```
C3 R 1259 A 315 Ø 15.4 ST 353
K4 K5
05 06 B 0369
05 13 B 0356
05 22 B 0379        B 64  4.15Ø
17 06 E 0357
18 11 D 0363
26 11 A 0357
26 11 B 0358

SET K4 K5 05 22 GOOD
```

23D/2.1: ×.5

Instead the operator uses C3, i.e. 4=5=/1=2. p. 83, E.9 R 1259 is the number of places looked at, i.e. of places where 1=2. *A*, the expected random number of places where 4=5=/1=2 is a *quarter* of this, because *two* more conditions are imposed, and $\sigma=\frac{1}{4}\sqrt{3R}=\frac{1}{4}\sqrt{3\times1259}=15{\cdot}4$.

ST as above.

The best score is $4{\cdot}15\sigma$. It should be noticed that three scores above the set total have χ_4 at 05; and that the χ_5 settings are 22, $22+7$, $22+14$, suggesting a wheel slide (**23G**) of 7 on χ_4, but b fortunately one too weak to make the setting really doubtful.

The most likely letters to set χ_3 are /, 5, U: to decide which the operator counts / & 9, 5 & 8, U & K; and because 5 & 8 are most numerous (212) chooses 5.

[a] this is easily [b] wheel-slide

i

```
///   555   UUU
168   212   177

555 A 106 Ø 7.2 ST 115
K3
02 A 0125
08 A 0146        B 40   5.6Ø
 10 A 0116
 12 A 0116
14 A 0118
16 A 0125

K1 K2 K3 K4 K5
40 28 08 05 22        SPAN 01-4500
```

23D/2.2: ×.5

```
     AG X2 XX .          AG X2 ...
/    0086                0092
9    0082                0084
H    0063                0067
T    0052                0064

O    0084                0055
M    0086                0078
N    0044                0063
3    0095                0057

R    0058                0059
C    0053                0053
V    0042                0073
G    0075                0082

L    0053                0094
P    0088                0067
i    0072                0055
+    0057                0065

A    0066                0078
U    0111                0067
Q    0067                0066
W    0058                0047

5    0146                0074
8    0066                0060
K    0057                0060
J    0096                0058

D    0049                0064
F    0120                0074
X    0064                0082
B    0054                0067

Z    0055                0071
Y    0087                0068
S    0081                0066
E    0056                0067

             ALL CERTAIN  SPAN 01-4500
                      E.M.LEWIS
```

23D/2.3: ×.5

A and σ are as before, but ST is now only $A+\sigma$, because this is a one-wheel run.

The setting obtained is "certain".

$$\left.\begin{matrix} \texttt{K1} & \texttt{K2} & \texttt{K3} & \texttt{K4} & \texttt{K5} \\ 40 & 28 & 08 & 05 & 22 \end{matrix}\right\} \text{ is printed}$$

by means of P.M.H. so that errors in Colossus setting will be manifest.

E.10 AG X2 XX means against $\overline{\chi}_2$=**x**.

The settings for χ_1 χ_2 χ_3 χ_4 χ_5 were not *very* strong, so that although the final χ_3 score makes them "certain", it is just as well to inspect the letter count.

This resolves all doubts as to the correctness of the settings, e.g. χ_5 is made very certain by the scores for U>Q, 5>J, F>X. The count is in fact much better than average; the worst contradictions with the pairs in **23H(e)** are OM, DB, ZE.

The dossier is therefore marked all certain.

The letters have been inserted in the letter count for the purpose of this report: Colossus operators knew them too well to need this.

E.11 The pen entries at the right of the letter count are the DO's order for a motor run [which appears on the next page but one].

The part 4500–end is not yet set: it is believed that there is a message slide so that the settings for all chi's in the part of the message will be increased, or decreased, equally.

p. 84

```
33QQUU55FF

SPAN 4500-END
K1 K2 K3 K4 K5
30 18 27 21 12 A 0108
31 19 28 22 13 A 0129
32 20 29 23 14 A 0138
34 22 02 25 16 A 0125
35 23 03 26 17 A 0129
36 24 04 01 18 A 0123
37 25 05 02 19 A 0121
39 27 07 04 21 A 0134
40 28 08 05 22 A 0123
41 29 09 06 23 A 0170
01 30 10 07 01 A 0139
```

23D/3: ×.5

The chis are therefore set back equally and stepped together, counting 3GU5F (G evidently in mistake for J).

For this run R is $\frac{16}{31} \times 1520$ (There are 16 **x**'s in χ_2).

$A = \frac{5}{32} \times \frac{31}{16} \times 1520$ (3GU5F are five letters out of 32).

$\sigma = \sqrt{\frac{16}{31} \times 1520 \times \frac{5}{32} \times \frac{27}{32}}$ (using $\sqrt{Rp(1-p)}$).

[i] Displays 23D/2.2 and 2.3, shown here separately, occur as one long display in the *Report*.

The sigma-age obtained is $4{\cdot}3\sigma$ which is ample, for the slide is of one place only. Note: in most cases, as here, the calculation of σ for a slide run is unnecessary.

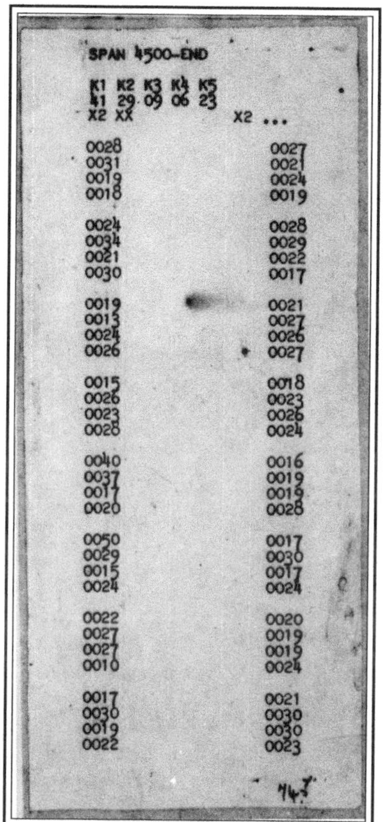
SPAN 4500-END
K1 K2 K3 K4 K5
41 29 09 06 23
X2 XX X2 ...

0028 0027
0031 0021
0019 0024
0018 0019

0024 0028
0034 0029
0021 0022
0030 0017

0019 0021
0013 0027
0024 0026
0026 0027

0015 0018
0026 0023
0023 0026
0028 0024

0040 0016
0037 0019
0017 0019
0020 0028

0050 0017
0029 0030
0015 0017
0024 0024

0022 0020
0027 0019
0027 0019
0010 0024

0017 0021
0030 0030
0019 0030
0022 0023

23D/4: ×.5

A letter count is done on the newly set part. It looks much worse: this is due in part to the shorter text which makes random effects larger, relative to systematic effects: it is possible that a small part should be set at 01, 30, 10, 07, 01. An excellent feature of this count is low B's. This part could just have been set by itself.

The de-chi check (**23K(f)**) is made by switching $Q = Z + \chi$ and counting 1**×**, 2**×**, 3**×**, 4**×**, 5**×**, simultaneously on the five counters, spanning 01–02. The scores obtained are 1, 1, 1, 0, 0, showing that the second letter of $Z + \chi$ is U; similarly GYN..... [01–08 is a mistake for 02–09].

Four letters are found at intervals of 620 up to 3100, thereafter only the last five. a

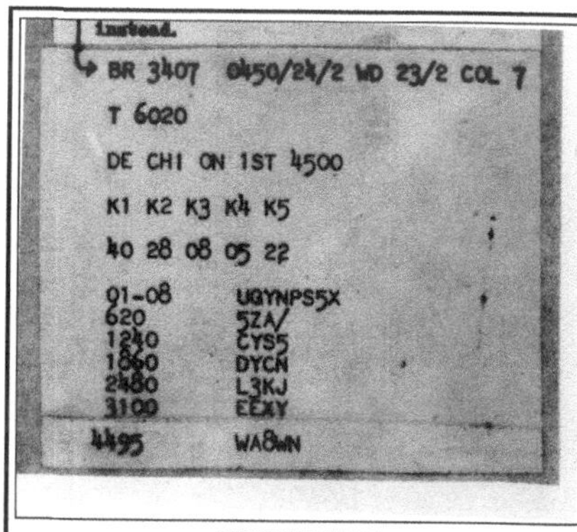
Instead.
BR 3407 0450/24/2 WD 23/2 COL 7
T 6020
DE CHI ON 1ST 4500
K1 K2 K3 K4 K5
40 28 08 05 22
01-08 UGYNPS5X
620 5ZA/
1240 CYS5
1860 DYCN
2480 L3KJ
3100 EEXY
4495 WA8WN

23D/5: ×.5

Message particulars are repeated here because the de-chi check is sent to the Tunny room for i
making the de-chi tape: it is left here only because a motor run was ordered instead.

For completeness the remainder of the Colossus record, showing the setting of motors and p. 85
psis is included here: for such further explanation as is needed see **23L, M**. It will be noted that several runs are done simultaneously on different counters, e.g. 1•, 2•, 3**×**, 4•, 5•.

---

[a] similiarly

[i] An arrow leads from 'here because...' to the 23D/5 exhibit.

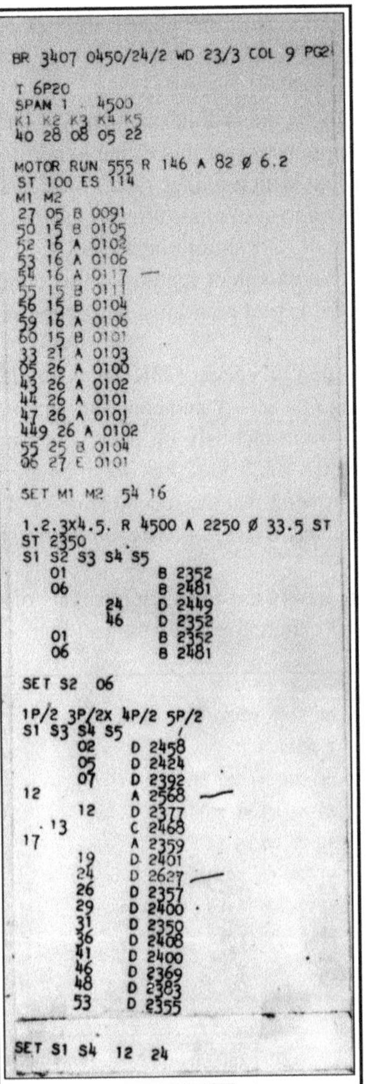

```
BR 3407 0450/24/2 WD 23/3 COL 9 PG2

T 6P20
SPAN 1 . 4500
K1 K2 K3 K4 K5
40 28 08 05 22

MOTOR RUN 555 R 146 A 82 Ø 6.2
ST 100 ES 114
M1 M2
27 05 B 0091
50 15 B 0105
52 16 A 0102
53 16 A 0106
54 16 A 0117 —
55 15 B 0111
56 15 B 0104
59 16 A 0106
60 15 B 0101
33 21 A 0103
05 26 A 0100
43 26 A 0102
44 26 A 0101
47 26 A 0101
449 26 A 0102
55 25 B 0104
06 27 E 0101

SET M1 M2  54 16

1.2.3X4.5. R 4500 A 2250 Ø 33.5 ST
ST 2350
S1 S2 S3 S4 S5
   01            B 2352
   06            B 2481
         24      D 2449
         46      D 2352
   01            B 2352
   06            B 2481

SET S2  06

1P/2 3P/2X 4P/2 5P/2
S1 S3 S4 S5
      02      D 2458
      05      D 2424
      07      D 2392
12            A 2568 —
      12      D 2377
   13         C 2468
17            A 2359
      19      D 2401
      24      D 2627 —
      26      D 2357
      29      D 2400
      31      D 2350
      36      D 2408
      41      D 2400
      46      D 2369
      48      D 2383
      53      D 2355

SET S1 S4  12  24
```

23D/6: ×.5

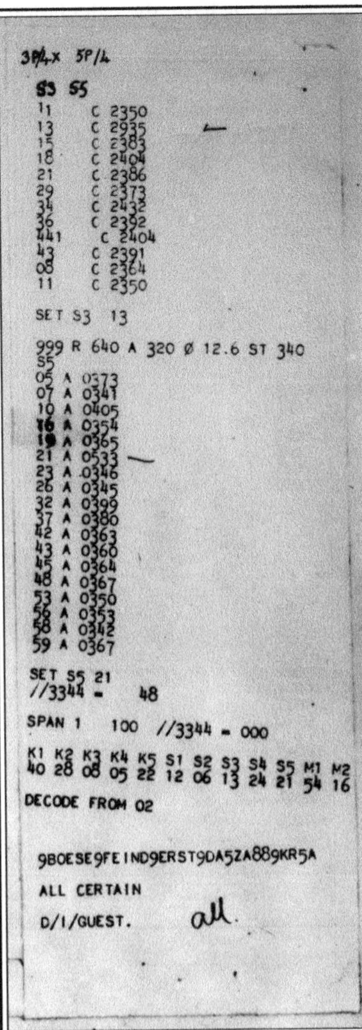

```
3P/4X 5P/4

S3 S5
11      C 2350
13      C 2935  —
15      C 2383
18      C 2404
21      C 2386
29      C 2373
34      C 2432
36      C 2392
441      C 2404
43      C 2391
08      C 2364
11      C 2350

SET S3  13

999 R 640 A 320 Ø 12.6 ST 340
S5
05 A 0373
07 A 0341
10 A 0405
16 A 0354
19 A 0365
21 A 0533 —
23 A 0346
26 A 0345
32 A 0399
37 A 0380
42 A 0363
43 A 0360
45 A 0364
48 A 0367
53 A 0350
56 A 0353
58 A 0342
59 A 0367

SET S5 21
//3344 -    48

SPAN 1   100  //3344 - 000

K1 K2 K3 K4 K5 S1 S2 S3 S4 S5 M1 M2
40 28 08 05 22 12 06 13 24 21 54 16
DECODE FROM 02

9BOESE9FEIND9ERST9DA5ZA889KR5A

ALL CERTAIN

D/I/GUEST.      all.
```

23D/7: ×.5

E.12

23E χ-SETTING WITH $\overline{\chi}_2$ LIMITATION

p. 86

(a) Runs against $\overline{\chi}_2$=×

Bulges are greater when $\overline{\chi}_2 =$ × than when $\overline{\chi}_2 = \bullet$.

To run against $\overline{\chi}_2 =$ ×, instead of on the whole text, approximately halves the effective text, so that it will not increase the sigma-age unless the proportional bulge is greater in the ratio $\sqrt{2}$ to 1 at least; but this is usually so.

It is shown below that 1+2, $\overline{\chi}_2$× will have a greater sigma-age than 1+2 if d, the number of dots in μ_{37} is less than 28, so that a break-in against $\overline{\chi}_2$ crosses is preferable unless the dottage is very high. It is fairly obvious that the effect will be greater in subsequent runs, which involve altogether three or more χ-wheels; in fact, whenever it appears that a message is on $\overline{\chi}_2$ limitation, all subsequent runs are done against $\overline{\chi}_2 =$ ×.

(b) Break-in runs for $\overline{\chi}_2$ limitation

There is often a better break-in than either 1+2 $\overline{\chi}_2$×, or 1+2. On the whole text, excluding random effects, 1=•, 2=•, are flat, and 1×2× has the same bulge as 1•2•. Against $\overline{\chi}_2$=× this is not so, the bulges having the same direction as in ΔP. Against $\overline{\chi}_2$=•, ΔP tends to appear reversed.

This suggests, if U58 are very numerous, the one-wheel break-in 2=$\overline{\chi}_2$ (since 2×$\overline{\chi}_2$×, 2•$\overline{\chi}_2$• are equally strong, there is no point in running them separately); if /'s are very numerous (this is now rare) 2≠$\overline{\chi}_2$.

It suggests further, the runs 1×2×$\overline{\chi}_2$×, 1•2•$\overline{\chi}_2$• or the combined run 1=2=$\overline{\chi}_2$ (for plugging and switching see **53J(k)**).

Note: the more consistently good run "1×2×$\overline{\chi}_2$× OR 1•2•$\overline{\chi}_2$•" cannot be done on existing Colossi: it could be done on Super Rob. See **R5**, p. 100, **R0**, pp. 42, 43. E.13

The following table is a useful practical guide: its theoretical basis is indicated in **23E(d)** below.

	$d \leq 19$	$20 \leq d \leq 27$	$d \geq 28$
First choice	1+2•$\overline{\chi}_2$×	1=2=$\overline{\chi}_2$	1=2=$\overline{\chi}_2$
Second choice	1=2=$\overline{\chi}_2$	1+2•$\overline{\chi}_2$×	1+2

(c) Theoretical note on A, σ, θ, ϕ [a]

With negligible error A and σ for the runs 2=$\overline{\chi}_2$, 1=2=$\overline{\chi}_2$ may be taken as

$$2{=}\overline{\chi}_2: \quad A = N/2, \quad \sigma = 1/2\sqrt{N(1-\theta^2)},$$

$$1{=}2{=}\overline{\chi}_2: \quad A = N/4; \quad \sigma = 1/4\sqrt{3N(1-\theta^2/3)},$$

where θ is the proportional bulge of $\Delta\chi_2 + \overline{\chi}_2 = \bullet$. p. 87, i

In practice σ is calculated by supposing $\theta = 0$, though because θ may be as great as $\frac{1}{2}$, the error is not always negligible (**R5**, p. 93).

The exact expressions for A and σ are

$$2{=}\overline{\chi}_2: \quad A = \frac{N}{2}(1+\theta\phi); \quad \sigma^2 = \frac{N^2}{4(N-1)}\left\{1-(\theta^2-2\theta\phi+\phi^2-\theta^2\phi^2)\right\}$$

$$1{=}2{=}\overline{\chi}_2: \quad A = \frac{N}{4}(1+\theta\phi); \quad \sigma^2 = \frac{3N^2}{16(N-1)}\left\{1-\tfrac{1}{3}(\theta^2-4\theta\phi+\phi^2-\theta^2\phi^2)\right\}$$

where ϕ is the proportional bulge of $\Delta Z_2 = \bullet$, its expected value being $\theta\beta\pi_{\times}$.

[a] Theoretical not

[i] 'Where θ is...', indented.

(d) Expected sigma-age of $\overline{\chi}_2$ limitation break-ins

i The above table para. **(b)** is constructed by finding the expected sigma-ages, viz. (for the last three it is supposed that $\theta = 0$)

$$1{+}2\bullet: \quad \frac{\beta\sqrt{N}}{2\sqrt{6}}\pi_{\times\times}\,.\,\sqrt{6}\left(1+\frac{\pi_{\bullet\bullet}}{\pi_{\times\times}}\right)$$

$$1{+}2{=}\overline{\chi}_2\times: \quad \frac{\beta\sqrt{N}}{2\sqrt{6}}\pi_{\times\times}\,.\,\sqrt{3}(2-\beta)\left(1+\frac{\pi_{\bullet\bullet}}{\pi_{\times\times}}\right)$$

$$1{=}2{=}\overline{\chi}_2: \quad \frac{\beta\sqrt{N}}{2\sqrt{6}}\pi_{\times\times}\,.\,2\sqrt{2}$$

$$2{=}\overline{\chi}_2: \quad \frac{\beta\sqrt{N}}{2\sqrt{6}}\pi_{\times\times}\,.\,\sqrt{6}\left(1+\frac{\pi_{\bullet\times}}{\pi_{\times\times}}\right)$$

$$\left.\begin{array}{r} 1{\times}2{\times}\overline{\chi}_2{\times} \\ \text{or } 1{\bullet}2{\bullet}\overline{\chi}_2{\times} \\ \text{or } 1{\bullet}2{\bullet}\overline{\chi}_2{\bullet} \end{array}\right\}: \quad \frac{\beta\sqrt{N}}{2\sqrt{6}}\pi_{\times\times}\,.\,\sqrt{\frac{2}{5}}\left\{(5-\beta)+(3-\beta)\frac{\pi_{\bullet\bullet}}{\pi_{\times\times}}\right\}.$$

Comparing these

$1{+}2\bullet$ is better than $1{+}2{\bullet}\overline{\chi}_2{\times}$ if $\sqrt{2} > 2-\beta$, i.e. to the nearest integer $d \geq 28$;

$1{=}2{=}\overline{\chi}_2$ is better than $1{+}2\bullet$ if $\pi_{\bullet\bullet}/\pi_{\times\times} < 2/\sqrt{3}-1$;

$1{=}2{=}\overline{\chi}_2$ is better than $1{+}2{\bullet}\overline{\chi}_2{\times}$ if $\pi_{\bullet\bullet}/\pi_{\times\times} < \sqrt{\frac{2}{3}}\,\frac{2}{2-\beta} - 1$.

$\pi_{\bullet\bullet}/\pi_{\times\times}$ is usually small and often negative. The table is devised by supposing it to be 0·1

When θ is large, the above formulae are unfair to the last three runs, especially to $2{=}\overline{\chi}_2$.

It may be shown, similarly, but with more algebra, that neither component of $1{=}2{=}\overline{\chi}_2$, i.e. $1{\bullet}2{\bullet}\overline{\chi}_2{\bullet}$ or $1{\times}2{\times}\overline{\chi}_2{\times}$, can ever be the best run to use. (**R0**, pp. 40, 44, 107; **R1**, pp. 5, 9, 27; **R5**, p. 38; See **R5**, pp. 13, 29.)

(e) $2{=}\overline{\chi}_2$

This is better than its sigma-age would indicate, for it is a one-wheel run. It is at its best for large values of θ (which may be as great as $1/2$), but will never be the strongest run unless $\pi_{\bullet\times}/\pi_{\times\times} > -1/6$.

It takes very little time to run. (**R1**, pp. 5, 9; see **R4**, pp. 70, 92.)

E.14 **(f) QTQ**

It is not always known beforehand whether $\overline{\chi}_2$ limitation is in use. A few links change the

p. 88 limitation frequently (this was common in the days of $\overline{\overline{P}}_5$): Sixta is sometimes able to give log information about this (QTQ information).

(g) Tests for $\overline{\chi}_2$ limitation

If there is any doubt, the initial run is chosen according to whichever limitation is the more probable, and when the message is set on χ_1 and χ_2, $1{+}2{=}\bullet$ is counted against $\overline{\chi}_2{=}\times$ and against

a $\overline{\chi}_2{=}\bullet$. There is an exact formula for the decibanage which this gives in favour of $\overline{\chi}_2$ limitation, in

ii terms of motor dottage; but commonly a simpler inexact rule is used, namely: for $\overline{\chi}_2$ limitation, the bulge against $\overline{\chi}_2{\times}$ is at least twice the bulge against $\overline{\chi}_2{\bullet}$.

The earlier rule, that for $\overline{\chi}_2$ limitation the sigma-age against $\overline{\chi}_2{=}\times$ should be greater than the

iii sigma-age on the whole text, is grossly biased against $\overline{\chi}_2$ limitation. (See **R4**, p. 89. **R4**, pp. 7, 50,

---

[a] decibannage

[i] Handwritten words 'para **(b)**' inserted with a caret.
[ii] Handwritten 'namely' inserted with a caret.
[iii] It is not clear if both instances of '**R4**' are correct.

55, 72.) If the motor dottage is high it may be impossible to decide whether the limitation is χ_2 until more wheels are set.

(h) 4-letter counts

When a $\overline{\chi}_2$ limitation message is set on 1+2, four counts are made against $\overline{\chi}_2$=**x**: 1•2•, 1•2**x**, 1**x**2**x**, 1**x**2•. These confirm that $\overline{\chi}_2$ is in use and indicate which letter to run for, in particular i
whether to run for 58U or for / (**R5**, pp. 38, 71, 80).

(i) C3 = $\overline{\chi}_2$ E.15

In **R5**, p. 94 the run 5=4/=1=2=$\overline{\chi}_2$ is suggested, but the evidence is not unbiassed.

(j) $\overline{\chi}_2 + \overline{\overline{P}}_5$ limitation

Since $P_5 \to \bullet$, this shows the characteristics of $\overline{\chi}_2$ limitation weakly; the letter 5 is anomalous, being stronger against $\overline{\chi}_2$ dots. (**22H(a) R3**, pp. 54, 58, 74, 87.)

(k) The effect of corruption on 2=$\overline{\chi}_2$, 1=2=$\overline{\chi}_2$

If there are many corrupt letters replaced by 9's, the not 99 gadget should be used to ignore these; otherwise, except when $\theta = 0$, the score may be spuriously enhanced.

It is easy to show that, if a proportion λ of the message consists of corruption 9's, and the sigma-age of these runs on the incorrupt text is S, then the apparent sigma-age is approximately

$$\begin{array}{lcl} \text{for } 2=\overline{\chi}_2 & : & S\sqrt{1-\lambda}+\lambda\theta\sqrt{N}; \\ \text{for } 1=2=\overline{\chi}_2 & : & S\sqrt{1-\lambda}+\lambda\theta\sqrt{N/3}. \end{array}$$

23F MESSAGE SLIDES p. 89

(a) Definition of Message Slides a

In statistical setting, a few wrong letters of cipher do not matter much, but a single omitted letter or inserted letter makes it impossible to find any setting for the χ's which is correct for the whole message. The effect of one (or more) omitted or inserted letters is called a Message Slide. It does not necessarily make it impossible to find settings, for, with the χ's set correctly for one part of the message ΔD will have systematic bulges on this part, which will not be greatly changed by the addition of the merely random bulges on the rest of the message: the sigma-ages will of course be reduced, because the text length is that of the whole message, the score that of a part only.

(b) Rival Settings

A message slide can sometimes be detected by inspection of the 1+2 scores. If several (say 3) letters are omitted, the settings of all χ-wheels will be increased by three. b

A pair of scores such as $\begin{array}{cccc} 26 & 17 & 1398 & 5{\cdot}9\sigma \\ 29 & 20 & 1253 & 4{\cdot}1\sigma \end{array}$ suggests very strongly that there is a slide of 3 at a place dividing the tape roughly in the ratio 3:2; but see Antislides (**23G(d)**).

---

[a] Definition. of Message Slides [b] ommitted

[i] Handwritten phrase 'confirm that $\overline{\chi}_2$is in use and' inserted with caret.

(c) Spanning

In *any* case, as soon as a message is set on any wheels, the relevant score is spanned, in thousands or in thirds whichever is the less. If some parts show no bulge there is probably a slide: this will increase the sigma-age on the remainder; it is worth while to span scores down to $3{\cdot}7\sigma$ unless a certain setting has already been obtained. Subsequent runs are done on a slide-free portion.

(d) Slide Runs

When the parts of a message at slide settings are of considerable length, it is usual, after
i setting all wheels or even before to set the other parts by means of a Slide Run. The χ's are all set
E.16 back a few places and are stepped together (upper switches on Colossus) counting those letters which are most numerous in the part already set, e.g. /U58, spanning a part not set. Because this
p. 90 is a short run (usually 50 positions at most) it is not necessary to have a very high sigma-age, especially if the slide between the two parts is found to be small.

(e) Doctoring of tapes

If it is difficult to set the other wheels, it may be worth while to do a slide run on 1+2•, for when the settings of the various parts have been found it is possible to "doctor" the tape, i.e. to put the parts in their correct relative positions by inserting or removing letters: this is in fact rarely done except during wheel-breaking (**25D(c)**).

(f) Break-ins with spanning

If it is thought likely that a message contains a slide, especially when it is to be "flogged" (**23J(b)**), the break-in runs may be done whilst spanning a suitable part of the text. Suitable spans are first two-thirds and last two-thirds.

Alternatively, since slides are more probable when interception fails to identify letters, which
ii are then represented by 9's, count 99's with spanning, and select a stretch with as few as possible.

Raw tapes are spanned over the first 2500 letters, and, if long enough (> 4000) over the last 2500.

(g) Message slides and wheel slides

It is important not to confuse message slides with wheel slides (**23G**) whose only common feature is that they give rise to rival settings.

(h) N Procedure

Occasionally two messages are sent without resetting wheels: switching the Tunny machine out and in automatically inserts exactly two letters of key between them; the two messages are therefore punched on the same tape with two letters inserted, and become a single message so far as χ-setting is concerned. (cf. **11B(k)**, **11D(d)**.)

Note: The interruption disturbs the stepping of the ψ's so that when setting ψ's the two cannot always be treated as a single message.

23G WHEEL SLIDES

(a) Definition

p. 91 Consider a wheel which has a large number of agreements with itself at a different setting; for example, the extreme case of a "perfect" wheel such as

$\Delta\chi_5$	× × • × • × • × • × • × • × • × • × • × • × •
$\Delta\chi_5$ 2 back	× • × × • × • × • × • × • × • × • × • × • × •

where there are only two disagreements between the wheel and the same wheel two back. The two settings are said to be slides of one another.

---

i Handwritten phrase 'or even before' inserted with a caret.

ii Handwritten 'then' inserted with a caret.

(b) Rival settings

At characters where two settings of a wheel agree, each setting will gain the same contribution [i] for its ΔD count: if one of them is the right setting then at these characters the wrong ("slide") setting will have a systematically good ΔD count, elsewhere a systematically bad count. If the agreements are sufficiently numerous, this slide setting will have a score almost as large as the right setting, and may by random chance have a higher score.

With perfect wheels it is in fact often difficult to distinguish between the right setting and its slides.

(c) Length of slides

Owing to the absence of long stretches of dots or crosses in $\Delta\chi$ wheels, slides at interval 1 do not occur: a slide at interval 2 is by far the most common: it tends to produce consequent slides of 4, 6, . . .

(d) Antislides

When setting messages on wheels known to have strong slides, the most rapid method is to accept, provisionally, the highest score for a slidy wheel, even though there are others almost equally good, for on this basis it will generally be possible to set the other wheels. When all wheels are "set", at settings which are either correct or good slides, all the evidence of the 32 letter count will be available to discriminate between a correct setting and its slides. The evidence from, say, /, 5, U, may be adequate to set χ_1 uniquely, when the evidence of 1+2• is not.

Even in cases where the slides are only moderately strong, it is often worth while, at the end p. 92 of setting, to "run back to confirm" a setting which has possible competitors.

(f) Random setting of perfect wheels [ii]

When some wheels are perfect or nearly perfect it should be possible to set messages by taking each such wheel at two (odd and even) random settings, and using these to set the other wheels. Perhaps the simplest method is to allow the perfect wheels to step while the other wheels are run round a few times. In this way it is feasible to do what are in effect 3- or 4- wheel break-ins. (**R1**, pp. 19, 22–25, 29; **R2**, pp. 19, 21; **R4**, pp. 24, 28.)

23H FLOGGING RUNS

(a) Flogging

Flogging is trying all methods which may possibly help to set a message. This may be done

(i) because of intelligence or cryptographic priority.

(ii) because of lack of work.

(iii) for ostentatious display (towards D.O. or Wrens).

(b) Flogging Break-ins

The usual runs are 1+2• and 3+4**×**. If these fail on a message which is to be flogged, 2+5, 4+5, 1+3, 2+4 are all reasonable; but see **R4**, p. 15. Note: except with $\bar{\chi}_2$ limitation the *only* 2-wheel break-ins are $i + j$=• or **×**.

If there is any doubt about $\bar{\chi}_2$ limitation, break-ins can be done on both assumptions.

Break-ins with spanning can be used on a generous scale. (cf. **23F(f)**.)

(c) 3- and 4- wheel runs

A more powerful method is to do a break-in on more than two wheels. It might be possible to do a complete 3-wheel run in ten hours or so, but ΔD characteristics happen to be such that no 3-wheel run is very advantageous. 4-wheel runs, in particular 1=2=4=5/ are powerful, but run completely they are intolerably long (but see **91C**).

[i] Handwritten 'setting' inserted with a caret.

[ii] There is no subsection **23G(e)**: the series skips from **23G(d)** to **23G(f)**.

A compromise is to do a 1+2 break-in followed by 4=5=/1=2 at all χ_1 χ_2 settings which score more than 2σ, naturally taking the higher scores first. This has sometimes succeeded, but it is
p. 93 long and laborious. So little evidence is obtained from the 2σ score that the full sigma-age for a four-wheel run is needed (**23C(a)**) (**R2**, p. 76; **R5**, pp. 35, 54, 97).

(d) Subsequent Runs

The number of theoretically possible runs is large. If there are two possible runs for the same
a wheels there is clearly some advantage in combining them: it saves time; the text is longer and if the runs are of similar strength the expected sigma-age is higher; but if, contrary to expectation, one of them is weak, or goes the wrong way, a great deal of evidence is lost. When flogging very hard it is better to keep runs separate and to combine their evidence by the methods of **23J**. Note: if two runs whose texts and proportional bulges are n_1, δ_1; n_2, δ_2, are run together the sigma-age is greater than that of the run n_1, δ_1, if

$$\frac{\delta_2}{\delta_1} > \sqrt{\left(\frac{n_1}{n_2}\right)^2 + \frac{n_1}{n_2}} - \frac{n_1}{n_2};$$

if $n_2 \ll n_1$, this is $1/2$; if $n_2 = n_1$, this is $\sqrt{2} - 1$. (**R1**, p. 62.)

(e) Construction of useful runs

It is unnecessary to enumerate all runs: consider how such runs may be devised. Suppose that χ_1 χ_2 are set, and that it is desired to set χ_3 χ_4. Clearly two letters differing only in the fifth impulse will be indistinguishable. Moreover when counting, for example, /T i.e. 1•2•3•4•, it
b will be necessary to look at all places where 1=• 2=•. It is convenient to set forth the 32 letter alphabet thus:

/T,9H,03,MN	RG, CV,L4,IP	AW,UQ,5J,8K	DB,FX,ZE,YS
1•2•	1•2×	1×2×	1×2•

Where 1•2• a good run is $\frac{\text{/T 03}}{\text{9H MN}}$ i.e. 3•/1•2•

c 1•2× a weak but usable run is $\frac{\text{RG IP}}{\text{L4 CV}}$ i.e. 3+4×/1•2×

1×2× a good run is $\frac{\text{UQ 5J}}{\text{AW 8K}}$ i.e. 3+4×/1×2×

d or if 8's are numerous $\frac{\text{UQ 5J 8K}}{\text{AW}}$ i.e. not 3•4•/1×2×

1×2• a good run is $\frac{\text{FX YS}}{\text{DB ZE}}$ i.e. 3×/1×2•

e a sometimes usable run is $\frac{\text{FX YS ZE}}{\text{DB}}$ i.e. not 3•4×/1×2•.

3+4×/1•2× and 3+4×/1×2× could be combined into 3+4×/2×, but the run 3+4×/1•2× is so much weaker than the other that this would be unwise.

Not infrequently 3×/1×2• and 3•/1•2• can profitably be combined as 3+/1•2•.

p. 94 To set χ_4 χ_5, having set χ_1 χ_2 the useful runs (not all independent) are

---

[a] times [b] it is convenient [c] useable [d] or if 8' are numerous [e] useable

$$\frac{\texttt{/9}}{\texttt{HT OM N3}} \quad \text{i.e.} \quad 4\bullet 5\bullet/1\bullet 2\bullet$$

$$\frac{\texttt{58}}{\texttt{AU QW KJ}} \quad \text{i.e.} \quad 4\times 5\times/1\times 2\times$$

$$\frac{\texttt{/9 58}}{\texttt{HT OM N3 AU QW KJ}} \quad \text{i.e.} \quad 4{=}5{=}/1{=}2$$

$$\frac{\texttt{58 AU}}{\texttt{QW KJ}} \quad \text{i.e.} \quad 4{+}5/1\times 2\times$$

$$\frac{\texttt{/9 58 AU}}{\texttt{HT OM N3 QW KJ}} \quad \text{i.e.} \quad \begin{cases} 4{+}5/1\times 2\times \\ \text{or } 4\bullet 5\bullet/1\bullet 2\bullet\,. \end{cases}$$ [a]

All these can easily be run using multiple testing.

To set χ_3 χ_5 having set χ_1 χ_2 the only new useful run is $3\bullet 5\bullet/1\bullet 2\bullet$.

The reader may be interested to work out all possible runs supposing that χ_3 χ_4 are set first (**R3**, pp. 95, 124; **R5**, p. 106).

(f) Runs for the last wheel

These may be expressed compactly

For χ_3

U	/	5	J	3	F	X	O	G	P	Q	Y	S	H	I	R
A	9	8	K	N	D	B	M	V	L	W	Z	E	T	4	C

For χ_5

/	U	5	8	D	F	G	Z	9	P	3	A	Y	M
T	Q	J	K	B	X	R	E	H	I	O	W	S	N

The letters above are good letters in order of merit, the letter below is that which differs from it on the impulse to be set.

For hard flogging the letters may be run separately but simultaneously on the five counters of Colossus.

Otherwise the letters may be run in batches e.g. for χ_3 `U/5` ; `J3FXOG` ; `PQYSH`. (**R4**, pp. 42, 82.)

(g) ΔD Bigram Runs

Because Colossus looks only at one place and remembers one other, the use of these is limited. The multiple test memory circuits are unsuitable because they remember only a single wheel.

The ΔD bigram `U5`, since Colossus Δ's backwards, is equivalent to $\Delta D = 5$ $\Delta^2 D = \texttt{M}$. If a ΔZ tape and $\Delta\chi$ wheels are used the Colossus plugging and switching required is

$$Z_1+\chi_1=\times,\quad Z_2+\chi_2=\times,\quad Z_3+\chi_3=\bullet,\quad Z_4+\chi_4=\times,\quad Z_5+\chi_5=\times,$$
$$\Delta Z_1+\Delta\chi_1=\bullet,\quad \Delta Z_2+\Delta\chi_2=\bullet,\quad \Delta Z_3+\Delta\chi_3=\times,\quad \Delta Z_4+\Delta\chi_4=\times,\quad \Delta Z_5+\Delta\chi_5=\times.$$

(h) Use of evidence other than ΔD

If a message can be set on some but not all χ's it may yet be possible to

(i) set the motors (**23L**)

(ii) send a de-chi on fewer than 5 wheels to the Testery, where language methods can be applied.

---

[a] i.e. or {

p. 95 23J FLOGGING THE EVIDENCE

(a) Impracticability of an exact formula

No simple formula for weighing the evidence of a run can be exact. Evidence is derivable not only from the sheer magnitude of the bulges but also from having bulges on the right letters, or on a consistent group of letters (e.g. on all language letters); in other words it is unjust to take the message as a fair sample of itself, and necessary to include other messages.

This section gives only a brief crude account with a minimum of mathematics. For a more refined treatment see **23X**.

(b) A primitive formula

If it is assumed that the message is a fair sample of itself, the factor in favour of a setting due to a sigma-age is proportional to $e^{s^2/2}$ (cf. **24X**).

It follows that the odds in favour of a setting with sigma-age s_1 is about

$$\frac{e^{s_1^2/2}}{2w + \sum e^{s^2/2}}$$

where $\sum$ refers to rival settings and $2w$ allows for random settings.

The decibanage is $10 \log_{10}$ of this (**21(g)**). This is, essentially, the formula used to construct the table for decibanning wheel-setting runs.

(c) Combining the evidence of several runs

If several runs are used to set the same wheel or wheels.

i
$$\text{odds} = \frac{e^{\sum_{\text{runs}} s_1^2/2}}{wf + \sum_{\text{competitors}} e^{\sum_{\text{runs}} s_1^2/2}}.$$

If there is no competition the decibanage is

$$\sum_{\text{runs}} 2{\cdot}17 s_1^2 - 10 \log_{10} w - 3$$

p. 96 from which the "Certain, Good" tables (**23C(b)**) may be derived.

If there is competition, $\sum 2{\cdot}17\, s_1^2$ can be found for each competitor and the results compared. (**R3**, p. 134; **R4**, p. 1, 70; **R5**, p. 1, 3, 7, 113.)

23K CHECKS ON SETTING

(a) General

This does not deal with the complete system of checks (**35D, E**), but only with checks applied during setting on Colossus.

Setting yields $D = \chi + Z$.

Both χ and Z are checked beforehand; D is checked afterwards. Each score used is checked as it occurs (see **23D**).

(b) χ Tests

E.17 The χ to be tested is the pattern set up on the triggers: this is not checked for each message, but only when patterns are set up afresh or are subject to suspicion.

---

[i] The numerator of the right-hand side of the equation has an extraneous exponentiation, reading

$$\text{odds} = \frac{e^{\sum_{\text{runs}} e^{s_1^2/2}}}{wf + \sum_{\text{competitors}} e^{\sum_{\text{runs}} s_1^2/2}}.$$

(c) χ Test Tapes

The obvious method of checking χ triggers is to make a tape $Z \equiv \chi$ at some definite settings, and count /'s in $Z+\chi = \chi+\chi = /$. The correct score is of course the text length, or span length. It is better to count /'s in $\Delta Z + \Delta\chi$ which checks Colossus Δ'ing simultaneously: this of course reduces the score by 1.

Such a tape not only checks the trigger; but, by being spanned, enables a fault to be located either on the trigger or on the tape itself.

χ test tapes are made to a standard length of 2002 and spanned 0001–2001.

(d) χ Test Runs

To avoid the need for putting on the special χ test tape, counts are made depending only on the χ trigger and the span, so that any sufficiently long tape which happens to be on Colossus can be used. The χ test tape is required once only, as early as possible: if it checks, χ test runs are done at once and the scores recorded. Thereafter the trigger can be checked by repeating these runs and seeing that the same scores are obtained.

The actual form of the test is to count $\Delta\chi_1+\Delta\chi_2+\Delta\chi_3+\Delta\chi_4+\Delta\chi_5 = \bullet$ spanning 0001–2002, p. 97
starting with settings 01, 01, 01, 01, 01 and stepping χ_1, χ_2 together through ten places.

(e) *Z* **Check**

The preliminary checks are described in **35**. The text length is measured by hand counter: as soon as the tape is put on Colossus the text length is counted: the score should be one less because of Δ'ing.

(f) *D* **Checks** (i.e. check of the *D* tape made by Tunny)

Two different methods are used

(i) Comparison of $\left\{\begin{array}{l}\Delta D \text{ 32 letter count using } Z\text{-tape and } \chi \text{ wheels.}\\ \Delta D \text{ 32 letter count using } D\text{-tape.}\end{array}\right.$

(ii) On Colossus, using a slide-free portion of text, find the 2nd, 3rd, ... 9th letters (by spanning 01–02, 02–03 etc.) and similarly 4 letters at the beginning of each stretch of 620 letters, and the last 4 letters.

Compare this with a print-out, on Junior, of *D* in widths of 31 ($620 = 20 \times 31$) (For an early form of the test **R4**, p. 65).

(g) Theory of χ Test Runs

Suppose there is one erroneous character in $\Delta\chi_i$, (in fact, if there is one there must be two, because χ_i is Δ'd by Colossus). As usual let the text length be N, the wheel length w.

This one error will cause the score of $\Delta\chi_i + U = \bullet$ to be changed by the excess of dots over crosses in U at the N/w places against the erroneous character of $\Delta\chi_i$.

This excess has expected value 0 and standard deviation $\sqrt{N/w}$.

The change will be numerically less than 4 if

$$|\text{sigma-age}| \times \sqrt{\frac{N}{w}} < 4.$$

If $w = 41, N = 2000$, then $|\text{sigma-age}| < \cdot 57$, whose probability is 0·43.

To exclude the possibility of having all changes less than 4 (smaller changes being liable to confusion with unsteady counting by Colossus) a considerable number of readings is required. E.18
Ten readings reduce the probability to $(0{\cdot}43)^{10} = 1/7{,}000$.

It is clearly wasteful not to include every $\Delta\chi_i$ in every reading taken.

In an archaic version $\Delta\chi_1 + \Delta\chi_i$ was counted in four positions only: the chance of nearly correct scores with a wrong wheel in the trigger was considerable and is believed to have occurred. (**R3**, p. 60, 127, 128, 129.)

p. 98 ## 23L STATISTICAL SETTING OF THE MOTOR

(a) Rough Method

When the motor is set by hand it is done after the ψ's have been set on the de-chi. In statistical setting the motor is set before the ψ's. The usual method of doing this is by consideration of the number of occurrences of various ΔD letters occurring opposite BM dots, though it is occasionally convenient to make use of the BM crosses also. For example if / is a very good letter in ΔD this will mean that it is even better, relatively, in ΔD opposite BM=$\bullet$. If the limitation is $\overline{\chi}_2$ one would naturally 'look' at places on the tape where $\overline{\chi}_2$=$\times$, in order not to water down the run. In this case the run for the BM may be regarded as a run for the TM and therefore the ΔD frequencies
a opposite motor dots will be ΔP frequencies.

(b) Expected sigma-ages

Suppose that the limitation is $\overline{\chi}_2$ and that there are $r_{\times}$, $r_{\bullet}$ /'s opposite $\overline{\chi}_2 = \times, \bullet$ in ΔD. Let the text length be N of which $N_{\times}$, $N_{\bullet}$ letters occur opposite $\overline{\chi}_2 = \times, \bullet$. Let the number of dots in μ_{37} be $37D$. Let the proportion of /'s in ΔP be p, and let the proportion of /'s in ΔD at motor crosses be q. The expected proportion of /'s in ΔD at TM dots is p and the expected value of q is $r_{\bullet}/N_{\bullet}$. (This idea of using the count of ΔD at $\overline{\chi}_2 = \bullet$ as a means of sampling what happens at motor crosses was first suggested in **R0**, p. 49.) The expected number of /'s in ΔD at $\overline{\chi}_2 = \times$ is

$$N_{\times}\{Dp + (1-D)q\}$$

and the expected no. of /'s opposite TM dots is $N_{\times}Dp$. Thus

$$r_{\times} = N_{\times}\left\{Dp + (1-D)\frac{r_{\bullet}}{N_{\bullet}}\right\}$$

and

$$\text{E.S.} = N_{\times}Dp = r_{\times} - (1-D)r_{\bullet}\frac{N_{\times}}{N_{\bullet}}$$

where E.S. means expected score. If the motor is incorrectly set the expected score or average, a, is given by $a = Dr_{\times}$ and

$$\sigma = \sqrt{r_{\times}D(1-D)(a - r_{\times}/N_{\times})} \qquad \text{(see } \mathbf{21(n)}\text{)}$$
$$\doteqdot \sqrt{r_{\times}D(1-D)}$$

in most cases.

Therefore expected bulge is

$$(1-D)\,(r_{\times} - r_{\bullet}N_{\times}/N_{\bullet})$$

and this is fairly close to $(1-D)(r_{\times} - r_{\bullet})$. The expected sigma-age is

$$(r_{\times} - r_{\bullet})\sqrt{\frac{1-D}{Dr_{\times}}}.$$

p. 99 For example if $D = \frac{1}{2}$, $r_{\times} = 169$, $r_{\bullet} = 100$, the expected sigma-age would be 5·3. This would be more than sufficient to distinguish between the 2257 ($= 37 \times 61$) different possible hypotheses about the possible motor settings. With $D = 3/4$ and the same values of $r_{\times}$ and $r_{\bullet}$ the expected sigma-age would be only 3·7.

The argument and formula for the expected sigma-age would be equally valid for any other letter or group of letters, instead of /'s. In particular it can be used for groups of weak letters instead of strong ones. The expected sigma-age is then negative and one has to look for low scores instead of high ones. The formula is not so reliable in this case, since the sampling numbers $r_{\times}$ and $r_{\bullet}$ are smaller.

[a] frquencies

(c) Expected sigma-age with limitation not $\overline{\chi}_2$

When the limitation is not $\overline{\chi}_2$, a similar formula can be obtained equally easily if ΔD is assumed to be 'flat' against motor crosses.

If r is the number of occurrences of the letters in ΔD and if p, q, N, D have the same meanings as before, then, by equating the expected value of r to the observed value we have

$$r = N\frac{D}{2}p + N\left(1 - \frac{D}{2}\right)q$$

and

$$\begin{aligned}\text{E.S.} &= N\frac{D}{2}p + N\frac{D}{2}q \\ &= r - (1-D)Nq.\end{aligned}$$

Expected bulge

$$\begin{aligned}&= (1-D)(r-Nq) \\ &= (1-D)(r-N\nu)\end{aligned}$$

where ν is the number of letters of the alphabet being looked for. Expected sigma-age is

$$\left(r - \frac{N\nu}{32}\right)\sqrt{\frac{1-D}{Dr(1-\frac{r}{N})}}$$

$$\simeq \left(r - \frac{N\nu}{32}\right)\sqrt{\frac{1-D}{Dr}}.$$

Sometimes the assumption of 'flatness' opposite motor crosses is quite wrong. For example, if / is a common P letter then 8 is a good motor cross (ΔD) letter and a motor run for 8's may be far less powerful than the preceding formula suggests.
(See operational log **O1**, pp. 32, 37, and **R5**, p. 32 etc.)

This difficulty does not arise when the limitation is $\overline{\chi}_2$.

(d) Complementary nature of machine and hand methods

It is interesting to observe that, for given ΔD count, the expected sigma-age on any motor run is larger for smaller μ_{37} dottages d. This is what has been described as a 'swings and roundabouts' effect. When d is lower it is harder to set the χ's, but if they can be set then it is easier to set the p. 100 motor. Fortunately machine and hand methods are complementary in this respect. When d is high, the psis are easy to set by hand and then the setting of the motor is a routine job.

(e) Pick-ups

The formula of the expected sigma-age can be used for deciding between alternative motor runs, but of course, it is possible to do more than one independent motor run and look for pick-ups between the runs. (This is a reason for using a set total of not more than $2\frac{1}{2}$ sigma in motor runs.)

(f) Switching of a motor run on Colossus

The motor run is usually of the form

$$\text{BM} = \bullet \mid \Delta D \in \mathscr{C}$$

or

$$\text{BM} = \bullet \mid \Delta D \in \mathscr{C}; \overline{\chi}_2 = \times$$

E.19 where $\mathscr{C}$ is a class of teleprinter letters. When the conditions to the right of the vertical line are switched by themselves the score obtained, which is called r, provides a check of the χ settings and patterns and of the correctness of the tape etc. The routine of counting r before doing the run
E.20 is the same as in the case of χ setting. The run is done quintuple testing on μ_{37} and takes under 10 minutes for a tape of length 5000. For further details as to switching see **53L(h)**, **(l)**. The best score on the motor run is always checked even if it is not good enough to use.

(g) Good slides of the motor

Quite often a top score of as much as 5σ on a motor run may not be certain due to strong competition arising from good slides of the basic motor against itself. These good slide settings do not at all agree with one or other of the settings corresponding to the top score. See for example
a, b **R0**, p. 58 and **R3**, p. 9. In this way good slides of the motor are rather different from those of the χ's and ψ's. In particular it is not a good policy to stop motor runs in the middle when a good score comes up and then cross run for μ_{37} and μ_{61} as short runs.

(h) Motor runs with not all the χ's set

Suppose $\chi_{1,2,3,4}$ are set but χ_5 has given difficulty. Then we may sometimes be able to set the motor and to use the new information for setting χ_5. The expected score for a motor run with not all the χ's set can be obtained in the same way as in the case when all five χ's are set, but it
p. 101 so happens that we are more likely to run into trouble due to the use of good motor cross letters. For example, the expected score for the motor run on C3 (not χ_2 limitation) has been found by a semi-empirical method to be about $(1-d/60)$ times the value obtained by the crude method of assuming flatness against motor crosses. (See **R5**, pp. 26, 32.)
c We should perhaps emphasise here that with χ_2 limitation there is always the sample of $\overline{\chi}_2 = \bullet$ and complicated formulae can be avoided.

(i) Motor run with only χ_1 and χ_2 set

The last remark applies even in the extreme case in which the only wheels set are χ_1 and χ_2, when the 4 letter counts against $\overline{\chi}_2 = \times$ and $\bullet$ may both be done and the best run or combination of runs may be deduced. There is a single exception to this, namely in the run BM=$\bullet$/1+2$\bullet$. In this case the behaviour of ΔD_{12} at motor crosses can be calculated easily from the score of /1+2 at $\overline{\chi}_2$=$\times$ and the result obtained in this way is subject to a much smaller S.D. than the result obtained from the sample opposite $\overline{\chi}_2$=$\bullet$. In theory a similar remark applies however many χ's are set, but the calculations are usually too complicated.

It was first realised that motor runs of the type BM=$\bullet$/1+2 may be frequently practicable when the formula for σ of the type $\sqrt{Np(1-p)q(1-q)}$ was found to apply to motor runs (see **21(n)** and **R4**, pp. 4, 44, 88). The earlier assumption was that σ was $\sqrt{2}$ times as large as it really is. It is found (**R4**, p. 44) that the expected sigma-age of the run BM=$\bullet$/1+2 divided by the sigma-age of /1+2 is

$$\sqrt{\frac{1-D}{D}\cdot\frac{1-D}{1-\frac{1}{2}D}}.$$

The corresponding formula in the case of χ_2 limitation is (**R4**, p. 91)

$$\frac{8(1-D)}{4-3D}\sqrt{\frac{1-D}{6D}}.$$

These expressions are sensitive functions of d. (See **R4**, p. 88.)

A peculiar feature of the run BM=$\bullet$/1+2 is that the top score is not necessarily the most probable, if the additional evidence of the number of BM dots in the whole text is taken into

[a] **R0**,58 [b] **R3**,9 [c] these is always

account (**R4**, p. 47). (This type of difficulty occurs also in runs against partial wheels—see a
25D(b).) A method of getting round the difficulty is to run BM+/1+2 (see **R4**, pp. 50, 55, 56, 58, b
105). In theory the same difficulty arises in all motor runs, but the effect is usually negligible.

(j) Spanning

It is sometimes possible to do a more powerful motor run by using only part of the message
tape, even if there is no slide, because the message may contain patches which are rich in particular p. 102
properties. Such spanning can be done in conjunction with an examination of the Red Form, by correlating the spanning with pauses, but in practice it is found too much trouble to get the Red Form as a rule.

(k) Proving the motor settings

When the limitation does not involve P_5, that is when there is no autoclave it is easy to set the ψ's. However, for this purpose it is nearly always necessary for the motor to be correctly set (not merely a good slide). In this sense the setting of the ψ's is the most conclusive way of testing the motor settings. If, however, there are many different settings to choose between, it may be quicker to do a corroborative motor run and look for pick-ups; or simply to count a group of good (or bad) ΔD letters against motor dots at the rival settings of the motor.

Suppose, however, that there is still some uncertainty about the χ's. Then a motor setting
which is known to be at least a good slide of the correct motor may be used for setting or resetting c
the χ's, by means of runs against motor dots, just as if the motor were correctly set (**R3**, p. 66). If in this way a new χ setting is found it may be used to reset the motor. This is an example of a method of successive approximation (**R3**, p. 56). A motor setting can be identified as probably a good slide of the right setting by its sigma-age and by comparison of the relations between the settings that have turned up in the run. Observe that if a particular day's motor has a lot of good slides against itself, then there are effectively a lot less than 2257 independent settings possible and therefore a lower sigma-age may be significant. Thus the effect of the motor having good slides is double-edged.

(l) Proving mu 61

Sometimes a motor run is done with a provisional μ_{61} and the result used to clear up ambiguities in μ_{61}.

23M ψ-SETTING

(a) Setting ψ_1 as a motor run

Suppose that the limitation is $\overline{\chi}_2 + \overline{\psi}'_1$. Then the correct TM depends on the setting of ψ_1. Therefore it is possible to do a run for ψ_1 as a motor run, provided the BM and χ_2 are set correctly. Observe that the ψ_1 wheel is driven by a motor on which it itself has an influence, and in this respect the run differs from a BM run. A similar method can be used for ψ_5 when the limitation is
$\overline{\chi}_2 + \overline{\overline{P}}_5$ (**R2**, p. 32) but in this case the dangers of corruption are greater and the usual practice is d
to use stretches of 800 letters of the message for all ψ runs with an autoclave limitation.

In these runs for ψ_1 or ψ_5 as motor runs there is a tendency for the settings to bunch together. p. 103
This is due to an effect from a coalescence which is described below. As a consequence a given sigma-age is more significant than it would otherwise be.

(b) Statistical ψ-setting with χ_2 limitation

Once the TM is known, the most powerful ψ runs are usually those which depend on undifferenced plain language properties. Easily the best letter in undifferenced plain language is 9, so it is not very surprising that one of the five short runs P_1=•, P_2=•, P_3=**x**, P_4=•, P_5=• is usually successful. Those runs are done simultaneously on the five counters with S.T. of 3 or 4 sigma.

---

[a] (**R4**,47) [b] See **R4** [c] know [d] (**R2**,32)

If one of the psis sets there are good runs like 4+5, 1+3**×**, 1+2, 2+5, and if more than one psi sets there are even more powerful runs. For example 3**×**/1245 should give a nearly 100% score. However for convenience one may use runs of the form $P_{ij...k}$ = • or **×** throughout, since the switching is simple and no change in S.T. is required. For statistics of these runs see **R5**, p. 86. If all five of the short runs fail, the best long runs to try are 1+3**×**/, 4+5/, and 1+2/. The time taken for a long psi run can be cut down by a method called the 'dottery'. This method depends on the fact that the psis usually have good slides on themselves and also the expected sigma-age in
a the right place is so large (see **R0**, p. 41). However if the short runs all fail one should seriously consider the possibility of some of the previous settings being wrong.

A possible effect of a wrong chi setting which is only a good slide for the differenced chi and an antislide for the undifferenced chi is that the corresponding psi may set as an antislide.

When all the wheels have been set the acid test of their correctness is a count of /34 in
E.21 undifferenced plain language. There should be a patch of about 200 letters with no /34. This test can be used as a method of detecting slides, in order to make the decoding easier. It can also be used for resetting any wheels that have been incorrectly set. Another test of the correctness of the settings is to do some Colossus decoding—the first 9 letters is usual. This helps with the decoding on Tunny later on. The method is to span $(n-1)$ to n $(n = 2, 3\ldots)$ and count P_1 = **×**, P_2 = **×** etc. on the five counters. If the scores are say 00100 then the nth letter is 9. The possibility of decoding in this way on Colossus was not foreseen and is a good example of the flexibility of the machine.

Sometimes the '/34' test fails because all the psis are antislides. When this happens it is easy
p. 104 to put it right. It can also fail due to a 'smooth motor' effect. (This happened about 5 times.) This means that the motor settings are wrong, but happen to give long patches in which the ψ's are correctly set. It is not easy to put this right on Colossus and the best thing to do is to give the hand cryptographer a de-chi and 'pseudo-psi' stream. This will enable him to get a 'break' and thus to set the psis correctly and reset the motor. Finally the /34 test could fail due to the machine being out of order. The easiest way of deciding the cause of failure is, as ever, to do a letter count, in this case on undifferenced plain language.

(c) Setting ψ's when not all the χ's are set

If not all the χ's are set but the motor is set, then this motor can be used for more powerful χ runs, as already pointed out. However a more powerful method is to set the χ's and ψ's simultaneously.

For example if χ_1, χ_2, μ_{61}, μ_{37} are set the most powerful procedure is to set ψ_1 and ψ_2 and
b then set χ_3 and ψ_3 together (**R4**, p. 46).

(d) Testing the machine

When ψ runs are done the machine is fully extended and test runs become particularly
c important. The test runs done are similar to those in the case of χ's and motorized ψ tapes are made available for each day's keys.

23N COALESCENCE

Suppose that the limitation is $\overline{\chi}_2 + \overline{\psi}'_1$. Then the ψ_1 character at any letter of the message may have an influence on the setting of ψ_1 at the next letter. This gives rise to a remarkable phenomenon known as coalescence. For example two different hypotheses about the initial setting of ψ_1 with χ_2 and basic motor settings fixed, may give rise to the same ψ_1 setting at the nth letter and all succeeding letters. The two initial settings are then said to have coalesced by the nth letter.
E.22 Two theories coalesce by the nth letter if and only if they give rise to the same setting at both the nth letter and the $(n+1)$th letter. It is shown in (**23X**) that the chance of the right setting not being

[a] **R0**,41) [b] and then say [c] motorised

coalesced with a good proportion of the 42 other hypotheses after n basic motor dots is about $1{\cdot}3e^{-n/750}$.

There are several ways of taking advantage of the phenomenon of coalescence. If a message is sufficiently long, there is no need to run for ψ_1 if χ_2 and the basic motor are set. We can simply assume a conventional setting (say 01) for ψ_1 and span from about 2000 to the end, and the wheel will probably be correctly set for the part of the message used. Long runs can be replaced by short runs and 3-wheel runs by ordinary long runs. For example the run $P_3 + P_1 = \times$ can be done as a p. 105
short run (with multiple testing). Or a total motor run can be done instead of a basic motor run (but this cannot be done without multiple testing).

If χ_1 and χ_2 are set a total motor run can be done with a set total of 2σ and then all the results tested out by running $P_2 + /P_1$ multiple testing at each motor setting. If ψ_2 has very good slides against itself it is not even necessary to finish the short runs and 20 or 30 different motor settings can be tried out in a few minutes. Another method of doing the total motor run is to do the basic motor run with a set total of 2σ and then run for ψ_1 quintuple testing, but using only counter 1 (the ψ's corresponding to the other counters are not correctly motorized). a

The phenomenon of coalescence occurs with $\overline{\chi}_2\,\overline{\overline{P}}_5$ limitation; this time ψ_5 corruption is liable to interfere in this case. For further suggestions related to coalescence, see **R4**, pp. 74, 75, 87, 91, b, E.23, c
97. **R5**, pp. 36, 57, 112.

23P EXAMPLE

For a dossier showing a simple example of a motor and psi run see **23D**. For an example showing coalescence see fig. **23 (I)** at the end of this chapter (**23**).

23W CALCULATION OF THE ODDS OF THE BEST SCORE IN A χ-SETTING RUN

Suppose we have a message of length N and the score of $\Delta D_1 + \Delta D_2 = \bullet$ is $\frac{1}{2}(N+x)$ for particular settings of χ_1 and χ_2. Then, as in **24X(e)**, the factor in favour of these settings is roughly

$$\frac{25}{\sqrt{N}}e^{x^2/2N}$$

provided that nothing is known about the scores at other settings. In practice however we do possess additional information. In fact the knowledge which we are usually willing to use in practice is as follows. The bulge of the top score is B_1, the bulge of the second best score is B_2 and the bulges at all the other settings are (of course) less than B_2. Let T_1, T_2 be the theories that the top score is right or that the second best score is right, respectively, and let T_3 be the theory that one of the others is right. The prior probabilities of these theories are respectively, $1/1271$, $1/1271$, $1269/1271$. The factors in favour of the first two, not allowing for competition are

$$\frac{25}{\sqrt{N}}e^{2B_1^2/N}, \qquad \frac{25}{\sqrt{N}}e^{2B_2^2/N}.$$

In order to obtain the corresponding factor in favour of T_3 it is necessary to introduce a new symbol. Let q be the probability that the correct setting will have a bulge less than B_2. The probability that 1269 *wrong* settings will all have bulges less than B_2 is obviously a number fairly close to 1 (e.g. at least $3/4$), unless B_2 is unusually small. Therefore, in most cases, the factor in p. 106
favour of T_3 not allowing for competition is approximately q. It follows now by the general form

[a] motorised [b] limitation, this time ψ_5 Corruption is liable [c] suggestion

of Bayes' Theorem (**21(f)**) that the odds of theory T_1 allowing for all the evidence mentioned is usually approximated by

$$\frac{\frac{1}{1271}\cdot\frac{25}{\sqrt{N}}e^{2B_1^2/N}}{\frac{1}{1271}\cdot\frac{25}{\sqrt{N}}e^{2B_2{}^2/N}+\frac{1269}{1271}\cdot q}$$

$$\simeq \frac{e^{S_1^2/2}}{e^{S_2^2/2}+\frac{1269\sqrt{N}}{25}\cdot q}$$

where S_1 S_2 are the best and second best sigma-ages. The estimate of q must be based on statistics. It depends on the link and end and on N, d, quality of interception and B_2. However it is a
a reasonable approximation to assume $q\sqrt{N}$ to be independent of N and this enables the decibanage of the odds to be calculated easily, with the help of tables of

$$10\log_{10}e^{S^2/2}=2{\cdot}17\,S^2 \qquad \text{and} \qquad 10\log_{10}\left\{e^{S^2/2}+\frac{1269\sqrt{N}}{25}q\right\}.$$

This is how the 'χ-setting scoring charts' were constructed. The tables required for all types of runs are of the form

$$10\ \log_{10}\left\{e^{S^2/2}+\text{constant}\right\}.$$

Discussion of the subject may be found in **R2**, pp. 7, 27, 30 and **R5**, pp. 66, 73, 74, 83, 89.

23X THEORY OF COALESCENCE (R4, pp. 83–85)

Suppose that we know the settings of χ_2, μ_{61}, μ_{37} for a particular message on $\overline{\chi}_2+\overline{\psi}'_1$ limitation. Consider two different hypotheses about the ψ_1 setting at a particular letter of the message. If these two ψ_1 settings differ by s ($s=2,3,\ldots$) it is a reasonable approximation to suppose that at the next BM dot there is a chance $1/2$ that they will remain s apart, a chance $1/4$ that they will become $(s+1)$ apart and a chance $1/4$ that they will become $(s-1)$ apart. The probabilities in the case of $s=0$ and 1 (when the streams can even cross over) are more complicated. It is worth making the assumption that for $s=1$ the probabilities are the same as for $s>1$ and that coalescence is complete if $s=0$. These assumptions simplify the problem and are unlikely to produce any serious error.

p. 107 We now ask "What is the probability that a setting S which is s positions behind a setting T, of ψ_1, will have coalesced with it after m BM dots?" The question can be tied up with a problem
i which was stated by Lagrange. (See Uspensky "Mathematical Theory of Probability", Ch. 8, pp. 154, 158).

"Players A and B agree to play not more than n games, the probabilities of winning being p and q respectively. Assuming that the fortunes of A and B amount to a and b single stakes, find the probability for A to be ruined in the course of n games.

"The chance of A being ruined is

$$\frac{q^a(p^b-q^b)}{p^{a+b}-q^{a+b}}$$

$$-\frac{(2\sqrt{pq})^{n+1}(qp^{-1})^{\frac{1}{2}a}}{a+b}\cdot\sum_{r=1}^{a+b-1}\frac{\sin\frac{\pi r}{a+b}}{1-2\sqrt{pq}\cos.\frac{\pi r}{a+b}}\sin\frac{\pi ar}{a+b}\left(\cos\frac{\pi r}{a+b}\right)^n.$$

[a] decibannage

[i] ch8

The first term should be replaced by $\frac{b}{a+b}$ if $p=q=\frac{1}{2}$". E.24

If we imagine two games played corresponding to every motor dot and equate a difference of 1 in the ψ_1 setting to two units of the stake we can apply Lagrange's result with $n=2m$, $p=q=1/2$ and $a=2s$, $a+b=2\times 43=86$. We see then that the chance that a particular ψ_1 setting will have caught up with the setting s places ahead on the ψ_1 wheel, after m BM dots is (if $t=s/43$),

$$1-t-\frac{1}{86}\sum_{r=1}^{85}\cot\frac{\pi r}{172}\sin\pi t r\left(\cos\frac{\pi r}{86}\right)^{2m}$$

$$\doteqdot 1-t-\frac{2}{\pi}e^{-m/750}\sin\pi t.$$

If $m>500$ the error involved here is very small. Thus the probability that the correct setting will have coalesced with a proportion t of the ψ_1 settings following it, or else a proportion $1-t$ behind it is

$$1-\frac{2}{\pi}e^{-m/750}(\sin\,\pi t+\sin\,\pi\,\overline{1-t}),$$

so the chance of not doing this is

$$\frac{4}{\pi}\,e^{-m/750}\,\sin\,\pi t.$$

If m is at all large this probability is surprisingly insensitive to the size of t. Our result can be stated in the crude form:

The chance that the right setting will not have collected a high proportion of the ψ_1 wheel, after m BM dots is roughly $1{\cdot}3e^{-m/750}$.

For a more elementary and less rigorous approach to the problem of coalescence see **R4**, 102. There is an interesting exposition in terms of Quantum Theory methods in **R5**, 71.

23Z HISTORY OF MACHINE SETTING

p. 108

The original machine methods of setting were naturally the same as the hand statistical method (see ch. **44**). That is to say the χ runs were of the form $i{+}j/$.

The motor runs were all of the form motor = • given $\Delta D = /$. The ψ runs were of the form $P_i+P_j=\bullet$, using a contracted de-chi (see part **4**).

The statistics for all this were at first very scanty. Consider for example the surprise expressed in **R0**, p. 25 at the failure of a 1+3/ run. (See also **R0**, p. 72.) a, b

When the χ_2 limitation was introduced it was seen that this was no serious matter and the B.I.'s involving χ_2 were done making use of the limitation by having $\overline{\chi}_2$ put in the third impulse of the $\chi_{1,2}$ tape.

After this it was realised that /'s in ΔD were a good thing to look for, so that χ_4 and χ_5, for example, could be set by the long run 45/123, instead of 4+5, 5+2 etc. This was done by a de-chi of the first three impulses only (**R0**, p. 1). Anti-repeats in D were suggested too, as being due to c /'s in ΔP at motor crosses. It was only later realised that anti-repeats in P were quite likely to be good (**R0**, pp. 44, 45). d

The idea of making simultaneous use of repeats and anti-repeats occurred first in connection with motor setting (**R0**, p. 77). e

The run repeats or anti-repeats was an example of the value of being able to use the same E.25 electrical impulse more than once. This facility was advocated first in **R0**, p. 41. At the same f time the 'and/or' machine was advocated. The fact that 'not' can be used as a method of saying 'or' was implied in **R0**, p. 23. All this can be regarded as the germ of the idea of the Colossus g

[a] **R0**.25 [b] **R0**,72 [c] (**R0**,1) [d] (**R0**, 44, 45) [e] (**R0**,77) [f] **R0**,41 [g] **R0**, 23

switchboard. Other suggestions for machine improvements that were suggested in those days but
i which were adopted only in the sense that they had some slight influence on future methods were

(i) Possible use of Δ^2 properties for χ-setting (August, 1943).

a (ii) Decibanning machine (**R0**, p. 43)

b (iii) Square-summing method for using heterogeneity (**R0**, p. 29).

The tendency to think in terms of repeats instead of in terms of the 32 letter count of ΔD is the origin of the use of the symbol r to denote the 'number of places looked at'. r at first was always a number of repeats. This attitude was changed overnight by a single ΔP letter count that was
p. 109, c done in connection with a motor rectangle (**R0**, pp. 45, 48). Effects of this were

(i) General method of setting motor (instead of by using strokes) and calculation of expected
d score in case of χ_2 limitation (**R0**, pp. 47–49).

e (ii) Tendency to use ΔP statistics for finding the best runs (e.g. **R0**, pp. 103, 105).

But when we had set enough messages we felt that ΔD letter counts of messages set by us would not be misleading for run statistics (Dec.1943).

Other lessons learnt at the time of Heath Robinson setting were

(i) The importance of checks at every stage, including two makes, hand checks and exact
E.26 numerical checks.

(ii) Ability of Wrens to compute and use simple formulae for set totals etc.

(iii) Possibility of good slides on $\Delta\chi$'s.

(iv) Value of having sprocket guide near lamp on a Robinson to minimise the effect of the sprockets of two tapes not matching exactly.

f (v) Importance of careful labelling of all work and of pigeon-holes for tapes. (Tapes were originally hung up on hot water pipes.)

(vi) Value of using Bayes' theorem rather than orthodox statistical outlook.

(vii) 'Dottery' method for setting ψ's.

(viii) Use of Δ wheel tape to save plugging.

When the first 'Robinson' arrived we had not yet adopted the method of checking the result of every run before accepting it. This was done by using various standard lengths of tape. For example the 1+2 run was usually done with tape length of 3814, even if this meant putting in a thousand blanks. The object was first to make the Robinson 'readings' equal to the settings, and second so that the tape could have one letter removed and then be used for checking the result of the run. This idea of using a message tape of length a multiple of a wheel length was first devised for Heath Robinson and enabled Robinson de-chis to be done. The method really came into its own with the double Robinsons which could take four tapes. It then became possible to set all five χ's without ever making a de-chi tape. For example, when setting χ_3 given the setting of χ's 1, 2, 4, 5, a message tape of length 3813 was used with a $\Delta\chi_{1,2}$ tape and a special $\Delta\chi_{4,5}$ tape of length 3813 (and therefore non-periodic). It was necessary to have four distinct types of $\Delta\chi_{4,5}$ tape (**R1**,
g p. 8).

In the Robinson period a large variety of new setting runs were discovered and routines were improved to a point at which not many mistakes were made. However when Colossus 1 arrived it was found that it could cope with more material than all the three Robinsons then operating. This
p. 110 applied to wheel-breaking as well as setting.

For the history of setting in the Colossus period the reader is referred to the references in the earlier part of the chapter and to the index of the Research logs.

In conclusion we give a list of some difficulties that occurred in the early days, particularly in the Heath Robinson period:—

---

[a] (**R0**,43) [b] (**R0**,29) [c] (**R0**,45, 48) [d] (**R0**,47–49) [e] **R0**, 103, 105 [f] pigeon holes [g] (**R1**,58)

[i] Handwritten phrase 'some slight influence on' inserted with a caret.

(1) Sprockets tearing and stretching.

(2) Tapes breaking and coming unstuck.

(3) Failure of experiments with oiled tape.

(4) Incorrect setting up of wheel settings and wheel patterns on Tunny.

(5) Blurred figures on Robinson printer and running out of printing ink.

(6) Putting tape on Robinson back to front.

(7) Inaccurate punching of start and stop signals—high standard required by Heath Robinson. E.27

(8) Incorrect setting of repeat dials.

(9) Difficulty in calculation of wheel settings from readings, especially motor settings.

(10) Incorrect setting of χ_2 when contracting a tape on Tunny.

(11) Mysteriously long time taken for production of de-chi tapes and contractions.

(12) Prevalence of transient faults on machines which were therefore difficult to diagnose.

(13) Badly written figures and figures incorrectly written down.

(14) Runs not checking with de-chi tape and other mysteries.

(15) Insufficient handing over from one shift to the next.

(16) Print-outs with letters erroneously inserted or omitted by the machine.

(17) Habit of guessing the average from readings in the run, instead of calculating it in advance.

(18) Using even length of tape for runs involving χ_4. [a]

(19) Inaccurate counting by Heath Robinson.

(20) Damaging tapes by maltreatment.

(21) Numerous slides in tapes provided at that time by Knockholt.

(22) Presumed certainty of 4σ on a long run.

(23) Running out of benzene, squared paper, and method of obtaining benzene, paint brushes and rubbers from local sources. E.28

(24) Difficulty of getting supplied with the small machines like hand counters and stickers.

(25) Setting tape in wrong place (on any machine). Forgetting χ_2 lim for Tunny contraction. Forgetting to reset a tape when restarting a job.

(26) Sickness due to intolerable working conditions.

p. 111

(27) Knockholt perforating the wrong tapes (e.g. **R0**, p. 95). [b]

(28) Mechanical relays developing ‘pips’.

[a] unvolving [b] R.O. 95

(29) Over emphasis on (necessarily meagre) operational results at the expense of research work.

Suffice it to say that most of these difficulties and troubles were eventually almost entirely eliminated.

p. 111

GEB 9904 WD 29/3 COL 3 Page 2

FIG 23 (I)

EXAMPLE OF MOTOR AND PSI RUNS SHOWING COALESCENCE.

```
SETTINGS on 29 th wheels
k1 k2 k3 k4 k5
20 01 12 12 18

Motor run
///
r 183 a 139 eb 26 ee165 & 5.8 st 156
kkrk
2m1 m2
20 05 b 0156
32 05 b 0156
37 04 c 0156
38 04 c 0156
39 04 c 0156
43 04 c 0160
44 04 c 0163
45 04 c 0162
46 04 c 0156
31 09 c 0160
32 09 c 0161
33 08 d 015
36 08 d 0157
37 08 d 0157
38 08 d 0157
39 08 d 0157
41 08 d 015
42 08 d 0163
43 08 d 016
44 08 d 0170
45 08 d 0167
46 08 d 0160
48 08 d 0156
49 08 d 0156
53 09 e 0158
54 09 e 0160
55 09 e 0161
56 08 d 0157
02 13 d 0156
03 13 d 0157
31 13 d 0161
42 16 a 0162
42 12 e 0162
43 16 a 0171
43 12 e 016
44 16 a 0172
---------------------
44 12 e 016
45 16 a 0168
45 12 e 0165
53 13 d 0160
54 13 d 0161
55 13 d 0160
43 20 b 0162
44 20 b 0163
53 17 e 0160
54 17 e 0162
43 28 d 0162
```

The χ's have already been set.

The motor run is BM = ./ΔD = /

The S1 (typewriterese for ψ_1) run is the ψ_1 motor run TM = ./ΔD ≐ /

It will be seen that the basic motor run was insufficiently powerful to produce the best score at the correct setting; but that the scores on the ψ_1 motor run make it obvious that the second highest BM score is at the correct setting.

One effect of coalescence is that settings 26,31,36 for ψ_1 all score alike.

```
set m1 44 m2 16

s1 run

s1
01 a 0097
06 a 0088
11 a 0086
16 a 0086
21 a 0101
26 a 0093
31 a 0093
36 a 0093
41 a 0093
01 a 0093

set m1 43 m2 16

s1
s1
01 a 0101
06 a 0102
11 a 0103
16 a 0101
21 a 0123
26 a 0137
31 a 0137
36 a 0137
41 a 0099
```

23Z/1.1: ×.7

Fig. 23 (I) Example of motor and psi runs showing coalescence.

p. 112

23Z Page 112

```
set s1 26      1     2    3x    4  5
r2281      a  11 40       & 24      st 1215
s2 s3 s4 s5
         o1       d 1226
o2                b 1250
         o3       d 1232
12                b 1244
14                b 1279
   14             c 1265
   16             c 1268
19                b 1268
            19    e 1346          s5
21                b 1257
         26       d 1251
28                b 1249
         28       d 122
   29             e 1313
   31             c 1456        s3
33                b 1306
   33             c 1295
         41       d 1385      s4
   44             c 1256
45                b 1292
   46             c 1308
47                b 1518     s2
```

```
k1 k2 k3 k4 k5 s1 s2 s3 s4 s5 m1 m2
20 01 12 12 18 26 47 31 41 19 43 16
```

```
///333444  10
```

```
psis 10 back
step  ///333444
```

```
s1 s2 s3 s4 s5
30 04 35 45 23   a 0008
31 05 36 46 24   a 0004
35 09 40 50 28   a 0002
36 10 41 51 29   a 0004
37 11 42 52 30   a 0002

on 1st 200

s1 s2 s3 s4 s5
31 05 36 46 24   a 0002
35 09 40 50 28   a 0000
36 10 41 51 29   a 0002
37 11 42 52 30   a 0000
```

```
k1 k2 k3 k4 k5 s1 s2 s3 s4 s5 m1 m2
20 01 12 12 18 35 09 40 50 28 43 16
```

FIG 23(I) (continued)

Ψ_1 is set provisionally at 26, (later found to be incorrect) but coalescence enables the other Ψ settings to be found easily using 2.3 x 4.5., the weakest setting having an 8.6 σ bulge.

The Ψ's are set back and stepped together looking for the least number of /'s,3's and 4's. Settings 35,37 both yield only 2 (the provisional setting yields 10) and neither yields any /,3,or 4 in the first 200 letters of text.

A decode at each of these settings shows that 37 is correct, and that setting 35 coalesces with it at the tenth letter.

SETTINGS

```
k1 k2 k3 k4 k5 s1 s2 s3 s4 s5 m1 m2
20 01 12 12 18 35 09 40 50 28 43 16
```

///333444 0000 on 1st 200

DECODE from o2

qnoqakqste9kmabem9

```
k1 k2 k3 k4 k5 s1 s2 s3 s4 s5 m1 m2
20 01 12 12 18 37 11 42 52 30 43 16
```

///333444 0000 on 1st 200

DECODE from o2

9fuchsrote9kmabem95ww9899kr9b E.29

A.S. HICKEY.

23Z/1.2: ×.7

p. 113 24 RECTANGLING

24A INTRODUCTORY

(a) General remarks on Chi-breaking

b The ultimate criterion in chi-breaking, as in chi-setting, is the ΔD count.

As in setting, and for like reasons, runs are limited to:

1-wheel runs, known as short wheel-breaking runs;

2-wheel runs known as rectangles.

Even these are impracticable to run by actually trying all possible wheels, involving millions
E.1 of trials (**25X**).

Instead methods are used which, in effect, count ΔD against *each character* supposing it to be a dot: a good count is evidence that it is a dot; a bad count that it is a cross.

This applies equally to short wheel-breaking runs (**25A**) and to rectangles: a rectangle could be treated as a short wheel-breaking run whose wheel is composite, e.g. in a 1+2 rectangle the "wheel" is $\Delta\chi_1 + \Delta\chi_2$ which is $41 \times 31 = 1271$ long.

p. 114 (b) The 1+2 rectangle

ii It will be convenient to describe a rectangle for two particular wheels. In fact in chi-breaking from cipher the 1+2 rectangle was used almost exclusively. (For other rectangles see **24F**, **24G**.)

$$\Delta Z_1 + \Delta Z_2 + \Delta\chi_1 + \Delta\chi_2 = \Delta D_1 + \Delta D_2 \text{ which } \rightarrow \bullet.$$

Thus any place of Z would contribute favourably to the ΔD count if $\Delta\chi_1 + \Delta\chi_2$ had the same sign as $\Delta Z_1 + \Delta Z_2$, which is evidence that it has the same sign as $\Delta Z_1 + \Delta Z_2$ has: the magnitude of this evidence is called a pip.

Consider all the places of the cipher which are opposite the ith character of $\Delta\chi_1$ and the jth character of $\Delta\chi_2$: if there are u of these where $\Delta Z_1 + \Delta Z_2 = \bullet$, and v where $\Delta Z_1 + \Delta Z_2 = \times$ the net evidence that $\Delta\chi_1^i + \Delta\chi_2^j$ is a dot is $u - v$ pips.

E.2 This score is entered in the ith column and jth row of a 41×31 rectangle ($+x$ as $\textcircled{x}$, $-x$ as x).

---

[a] generalised [b] in the ΔD count

[i] The *Report* has a horizontal rule marking the gap between **24G** and **24W**.

[ii] Handwritten 'in' inserted with a caret.

The substance of the foregoing is that the 41 columns of the rectangle correspond to the characters of $\Delta\chi_1$, the 31 rows to the characters of $\Delta\chi_2$. The entry in any cell (i,j) is the excess of[a] contributory places where $\Delta Z_1 + \Delta Z_2 = \bullet$ over places where $\Delta Z_1 + \Delta Z_2 = \times$, and measures the evidence that $\Delta\chi_1 + \Delta\chi_2$ is a dot. i

The rectangle so constructed is afterward converged, i.e. wheels $\Delta\chi_1$, $\Delta\chi_2$ are found, to agree as well as possible with the evidence for $\Delta\chi_1 + \Delta\chi_2$.

24B MAKING AND ENTERING RECTANGLES ii

(a)

The entry in each cell of the rectangle is found by determining which places of Z correspond to it, and then taking the excess of such places where $\Delta Z_1 + \Delta Z_2 = \bullet$ over those where $\Delta Z_1 + \Delta Z_2 = \times$.

To find which places correspond to any cell remember that Z and the chis move together. If all the places of Z are numbered successively 1, 2, 3 ..., these will appear on the diagonal.

p. 115

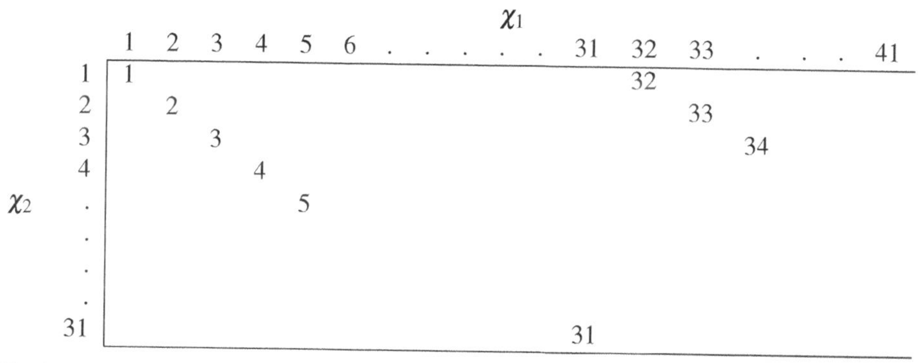

The 32nd place will clearly be in the cell (32,1); similarly whenever a side of the rectangle is reached.

The first 1271 places will just fill the rectangle.

Evidently the first cell will contain not only the first place but also the $(1271+1)$th, $(2 \times 1271+1)$th, etc. places, and similarly for every cell.

(b) iii

Two methods for entering have been used:

(i) Find the score for all places spaced at interval 1271 beginning with the 1st place of Z, then for all places spaced at interval 1271 beginning with the 2nd place of the cipher, and so on; iv afterwards enter diagonally.

(ii) Look for the scores in the various cells of the rectangle arranged by rows and columns, entering directly in the correct position.

Method (i) was normally used for Garbo, Thurlow and Robinson rectangles.

Method (ii) was used normally for Colossus rectangles.

The mechanical difficulty in method (ii) is the irregular stepping at the end of a row: this was found to make it not worth while except on Colossus, which can step irregularly (**53C(b)**): even Colossus requires a gadget to do this properly (Colossus rectangling gadgets do much more besides); with the gadgets this method is preferred.

---

[a] in the excess

[i] Word 'contributory' handwritten.

[ii] Subsection unnamed in *Report*. Text runs in on same line after the **(a)** head.

[iii] Subsection unnamed in *Report*. Text runs in on same line after the **(b)** head.

[iv] Handwritten 'beginning' inserted with a caret.

Note: prior to the introduction of the gadget, Colossus rectangling used method (i). Method (ii) was attempted on Super-Robinson, but abandoned (**R5**, p. 81).

p. 116 **(c) Garbo rectangles**

By means of the special switches (**56E**), Garbo is made to print $\Delta Z_1 + \Delta Z_2$, as • or ×, in widths of 41, with plenty of spacing.

After 31 rows, i.e. after 1271 places, a dot or cross will have been printed for each cell of the rectangle. The 1272nd entry is printed immediately below the 1st, the 1273rd below the 2nd, and so on. Finally the scores for a particular cell of the rectangle will be a short column of dots and crosses: the excess of dot over cross for each cell is entered by hand on the Garbage, and afterwards transferred diagonally to a rectangle.

Because Garbo deltas backwards it is necessary to start at the second place of the cipher tape and correct the first entry by hand.

The method is very convenient for short texts, such as key. Its disadvantage is that if the depth, i.e. the number of places per cell, is large, adding the scores for each individual cell is laborious.

In diagonal entering each row of Garbage must obviously end in the last column of the rectangle: to aid and check entering, it is labelled with the row of the rectangle in which it should start, viz., in order, 1, 11, 21, 31, 10, 20, 30, 9, 19, 29, 8, 18, 28, 7, 17, 27, 6, 16, 26, 5, 15, 25, 4, 14, 24, 3, 13, 23, 2, 12, 22. A better plan would be to write (or have printed) Garbage row numbers against the rectangle: this has been done spasmodically for key rectangles.

For the complete system of checks see **36G**.

(d) Thurlow rectangles

A modification of Garbo rectangles, devised for long texts to reduce the labour in finding the scores for individual cells: the idea is to represent 5 dots and crosses by a single figure.

The first step is to produce a tape on Miles, on which is punched nothing but $Z_1 + Z_2$, as dot or cross, arranged thus

1st	1271	places	2nd	1271	places	3rd	1271	places
4th	”	”	5th	”	”	6th	”	”
7th	”	”	8th	”	”	9th	”	”
10th	”	”	11th	”	”	12th	”	”
13th	”	”	—			—		

Thurlow tapes of the first kind.

p. 116 bis

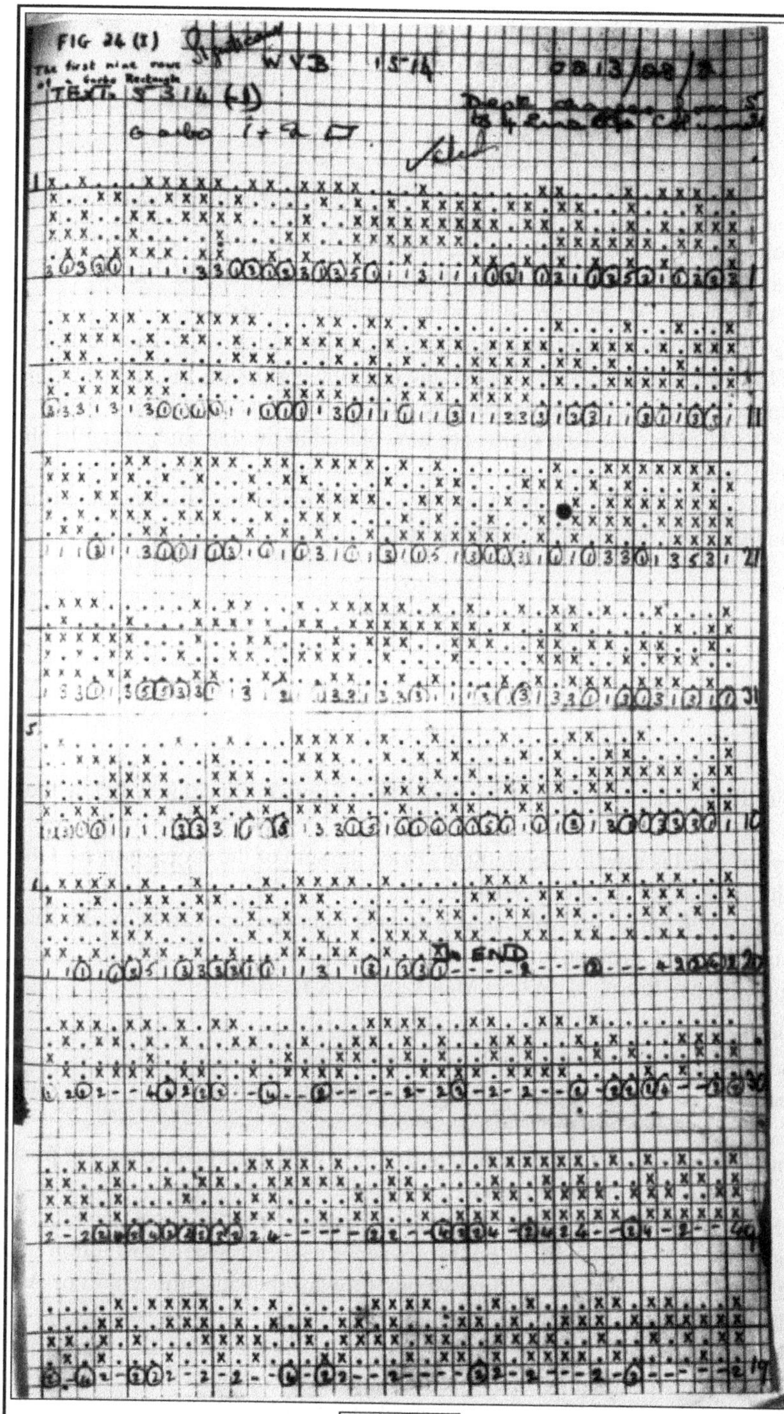

24B/1: ×.55

Fig. 24 (I) The first nine rows of a Garbo rectangle [i]

[i] Caption moved from to of figure to bottom.

p. 117

1st	1271	places	6th	1271	places	11th	1271	places
2nd	"	"	7th	"	"	12th	"	"
3rd	"	"	8th	"	"	13th	"	"
4th	"	"	9th	"	"	—		
5th	"	"	10th	"	"	—		

Thurlow tapes of the second kind.

Such tapes are easily made on Miles: the first character of each batch of 1271 places on the cipher tape is marked. For a Thurlow tape of the second kind 1st, 2nd, 3rd, 4th, 5th marks are placed in the eyes of the 1st, 2nd, 3rd, 4th, 5th transmitters of Miles.

Z_1 and Z_2 from the nth transmitter are added into the nth impulse of the distributor.

When 1271 characters have been punched the machine is stopped, the 2nd mark on the cipher tape will be in the 1st eye, the 3rd in the 2nd eye and so on (if not, something is wrong — a useful check). The 6th, 7th, 8th, 9th, 10th marks are now placed in the 1st, 2nd, 3rd, 4th, 5th eyes, the machine restarted and so on.

The second step is to difference the Thurlow tape just made on Garbo (with normal deltaing, not the special rectangle device) and print out, steckering

/ to 0

all	1	cross	letters	to	1
"	2	"	"	"	2
"	3	"	"	"	3
"	4	"	"	"	4
"	5	"	"	"	5

i As in an ordinary Garbo rectangle the 32nd row is printed immediately below the 1st and so on.

The entry for a cell is now the depth minus twice the sum of the scores printed. Otherwise the entering is the same as for a Garbo rectangle.

Note: Alternatively, if Miles A is available, a deltaed Thurlow tape can be made: this is printed out without deltaing on Garbo or Junior.

(For Thurlow tapes **R4**, p. 71, Wheel Man's log book **II**, 103.)

p. 118 **(e) Robinson rectangles**

Two tapes are used, viz.

(i) cipher tape, on bedstead A, tape length one less than a multiple of 1271, with start and stop.

(ii) control tape, on bedstead B, tape length 1271, with a start (for counting position only) and a single "E" in the first place of the tape.

Switch B = "E": this selects those places on A opposite the "E" on B, which are of course spaced at intervals 1271 (the length of B). Moreover in each successive revolution of the cipher tape A, all the places opposite "E" will move one forward (because the length of A is one less than a multiple of 1271), so that the 1271 cells are selected in "diagonal" order.

The score counter is split; one half counts $\Delta Z_1 + \Delta Z_2 = \bullet$ the other $\Delta Z_1 + \Delta Z_2 = \times$.

The difference between them is the score for the corresponding cell.

Their sum is the depth, which serves as a check, for there can be only one change of depth.

E.3 The position counter is split to repeat after 41, 31. Since the start on A is used, it necessarily records how much A is ahead of B and so runs backwards, 0000, 4030, 3929, ... These figures are written along the sides of the rectangle to check the entering.

[i] Handwritten 'an' inserted with a caret.

As a check on Robinson scores the machine is allowed to run round a few times after the rectangle is finished; it immediately begins to repeat the rectangle.

In fact, the B tape contains also 41 “4”s at intervals 31, which are used analogously for $\widehat{\chi}_2$ runs. The first “4” is one place back from the “E”: this is merely a trick to make the position counter readings tally with those of a $\widehat{\chi}_2$ run on Colossus.

For the details of plugging and switching see Synopsis of Robinson plugging (**54J**). It will be noticed that some unnecessary cords are used: this is to minimise changes between 1+2 rectangles, E.4
$\widehat{\chi}_2$, and counting “9”s.
(For early versions see **R1**, p. 32.)

(f) Colossus Rectangling p. 119

Colossus rectangling is the most highly developed method in use.

The necessary rectangle gadgets have been fitted to Colossi 2, 4, 6, 7, 9. Colossus 6 has a bedstead for tapes 26,000 long, and is used almost continuously for rectangling.

The basis of Colossus rectangling is as follows: put one cross in chi 1, one cross in chi 2 [i]
and switch the condition $\chi_1 = \mathbf{\times}$, $\chi_2 = \mathbf{\times}$: This will select a set of places on the cipher spaced at intervals 1271, i.e. the places in a cell of the rectangle. If these wheels step through all settings, E.5
they will select all cells of the rectangle in turn. Chi wheels move backwards when their settings increase, and therefore the rectangle is made backwards. If the wheels were to step uniformly the rectangle would be made backwards diagonally.

On Colossus, however, it is possible to produce the rectangle row by row. Step chi 1 fast, chi 2 slow (i.e. chi 2 steps only when chi 1 reaches the setting plug in χ_1): chi 1 steps and a row of the rectangle is produced; when chi 1 reaches its setting plug, chi 2 steps and another row is produced and so on.

It is impossible to make Colossus rectangling fully intelligible without a detailed account of the operations performed by the machine. For this reason the instructions are given here baldly, the explanation being postponed to **53M**.

It may be remarked at once that the “rectangling gadget” modifies the operation of Colossus in many ways. Optionally, if the depth is constant, it can be made to perform the subtraction pippage $= 2 \times (\text{ score of } \Delta Z_{12} = \bullet) - \text{depth}$: rectangling which uses this facility is known as “Normal” as opposed to “Print Scores”. This reduction of the length to a multiple of 1271 may cause a serious loss of evidence on a short text.

The instructions for a 1+2 rectangle are: E.6

---

[i] ‘put one…’ starts on a fresh line.

	Spanning.	Span 04 to (04 + 1271 × depth) Count text.
a	**Chi patterns.**	(triggers) Crosses in 02, 02 of χ_1, χ_2: on rectangling Colossi one trigger has this permanently set up.
	Selection switches.	$Q = \chi$
	Q Panel.	$\chi_2 = \times$ in all counters. Multiple test impulses $R_1, R_2, R_3, R_4, R_5 = \times$ in counters 5, 4, 3, 2, 1 respectively.
p. 120	**Control Panel**	Multiple test switch to χ_1 Check depth, i.e. $\chi_1 = \times$, $\chi_2 = \times$ Rectangle switch to "Normal".
	Rectangling gadget	Carriage return on χ_1 Switch in appropriate depth.
	Plug Panel	$\Delta Z_1 + \Delta Z_2 = \bullet$ in all counters.
	Settings	$\chi_1 = 06$, $\chi_2 = 02$ After setting wheels return plugs to 01, 01, *without resetting.*
	Step	χ_1 (lower switch down) fast to control χ_2 slow (lower switch up).
	Printer	Paper of sufficient width, start at extreme left.
	Final Checks.	Repeat first and last rows.

Unfortunately, although the rectangle is produced in its final form, it was in practice found necessary to transfer it by hand to squared paper in order to converge it, so that the advantages of this method are less than would be supposed.

24C CRUDE CONVERGENCE

i **(a)**

The general idea of convergence of a 1+2 rectangle is to find wheels $\Delta\chi_1$, $\Delta\chi_2$ which agree as well as possible with the entries in the cells of the rectangles.

The interpretation of 'agreeing as well as possible' is not obvious nor is Crude Convergence the only convergence which has been contemplated.

In a sense the evidence would be better represented, not by ordinary wheels of dots and crosses, or say ± 1, but by generalized wheels in which the magnitude of a character is proportional to the evidence in its favour. It would be possible to work in terms of generalized wheels and finally convert into ordinary wheels by taking each character as dot or cross according to its sign. There is some evidence that the particular method known as 'accurate convergence' is more reliable than crude convergence. For references to other proposed methods see **24W**.

ii **(b) Crude Convergence**

The only form of convergence used operationally is crude convergence which uses only ordinary wheels of dots, crosses, and doubts to make the bulge of $\Delta D_{12} = \bullet$ a maximum.

p. 121, iii It is not easy to find which $\Delta\chi_1$ and $\Delta\chi_2$ do make this bulge a maximum.

It is however, very easy, if one is given, to find the other, viz. by 'taking the known wheel through the rectangle' (details below).

---

[a] **Chi-patterns**

[i] Subsection unnamed in *Report*. Text runs in on same line after the **(a)** mark.

[ii] Text runs in on same line as subsection heading.

[iii] Handwritten 'do' inserted with a caret.

Accordingly the method used is to find somehow a crude approximation (a start) to one wheel, say $\Delta\chi_2$, take it through the rectangle to get $\Delta\chi_1$, take this through to get a new $\Delta\chi_2$ and so on till $\Delta D_{12} = \bullet$ is a maximum. The rectangle is then said to be crudely converged.

Unfortunately this maximum may be only a relative maximum (false convergence) in the sense that though the score cannot be increased by changing either wheel separately, it can be increased by changing both wheels at once (**24W(c)**). For this reason the most important item in convergence is finding a correct start.

(c) To take the wheel through the rectangle i

Place the given wheel (say $\Delta\chi_1$) against the first row of the rectangle and add all the entries therein, changing their signs wherever $\Delta\chi_1$ is a cross (and counting 0 where $\Delta\chi_1$ is 'doubted'). According to whether this sum is positive or negative, the first character of $\Delta\chi_2$ is taken to be a dot or cross. Likewise for all rows.

It is easy to see why. The rectangle entries are bulges of $\Delta Z_{12} = \bullet$ and if their signs are changed where $\Delta\chi_1 = \times$ they become bulges of $\Delta Z_{12} + \Delta\chi_1 = \bullet$, i.e. of $\Delta D_{12} + \Delta\chi_2 = \bullet$. The sum of these for a particular row is the total $\Delta D_{12} + \Delta\chi_2$ bulge against the corresponding character of $\Delta\chi_2$ (the 'score for this character'). By giving each character of $\Delta\chi_2$ the same sign as this bulge, each is made to contribute positively to the bulge of $\Delta D_{12} = \bullet$. With the given $\Delta\chi_1$ and this $\Delta\chi_2$ the ΔD_{12} bulge for the whole rectangle is the sum of the moduli of the scores for $\Delta\chi_2$ characters.

When the rectangle is converged, the bulge is, by definition, a maximum (possibly only relative). If a wheel is taken through again, the score (which will certainly not diminish) must remain constant. In other words the sum of the moduli is the same for $\Delta\chi_1$ and $\Delta\chi_2$. It is easy to see that, conversely, when two consecutive scores are equal, the rectangle is converged. This is a E.7
useful check.

It is found better not to take all characters of a wheel when converging, but only those which p. 122
score reasonably well, say more than 10 pips. The others are 'doubted', i.e. ignored. The start is usually made from very few characters, more being added at each stage: towards the end, the standard of 10 pips may need to be lowered, and finally all characters are taken. While doubting is in use, the score does not necessarily increase at each stage.

Note 1: To take a wheel through write out $\Delta\chi_1$ (say) on a strip of paper which can be placed against each row in turn. It will suffice to include only new or changed characters, the earlier score for $\Delta\chi_2$ being added in.

Note 2: Taking a wheel through is in fact a short wheel-breaking run (**25A**: **R1**, pp. 92, 94) and can be done on Colossus (**25A**) but computer time is often cheaper than Colossus time. E.8

Note 3: For a suggested automatic converging machine **R1**, p. 91.

Note 4: For the standard in taking characters during convergence **R2**, pp. 9, 11, 15.

24D STARTS FOR CONVERGING RECTANGLES

(a) ii

In the following paragraphs several methods will be described. All have been used operationally: the 9×9 flag and "E2" are probably the most popular with computers, who are normally allowed considerable freedom of choice. The skeleton was rather neglected, probably because it E.9
is unsuitable for depth 8, at one time the maximum for a Colossus rectangle. (**R2**, pp. 4, 14, 17, 19. **R3**, p. 21. **R4**, p. 23.)

---

[i] Text runs in on same line as subsection heading, continuing the sentence: '**To take the wheel through the rectangle** place the given…'.

[ii] Subsection unnamed in *Report*. Text runs in on the same line after the **(a)** mark.

(b) Flagging

In **24W(a)** an "accurate" system of scoring the evidence that two wheels are alike (or opposite) is given. This may be applied to two rows of a rectangle to find whether the corresponding characters of $\Delta\chi_2$ are alike or unlike. The calculation is too long for starting rectangles quickly, but there are two simple approximations

(i) the sum of products of corresponding entries (Scalar product)

i (ii) the sum of the smaller of every two corresponding entries, with a positive or negative sign
a, E.10 according to whether the two entries are alike or unlike (Jacobs flagging).
p. 123 (i), (ii) are exact in the limiting cases $\delta = 0$, $\delta = 1$ respectively.

Using either method the scores for each pair of rows can be entered in a square, which however is symmetrical, so that half of it suffices. This is the flag.

The score in the cell (i, j) measures the evidence that $\Delta\chi_2^{(i)} + \Delta\chi_2^{(j)}$ is a dot: thus the flag square behaves like a rectangle. In particular it may be converged: a correct convergence should give the same wheel along both sides.

A flag may be tested for significance (**R2**, p. 92. **R3**, pp. 8, 79, 81, 82).

E.11 To flag all of the 31 scores of the rectangle by hand would take too much time. A special machine is feasible; for the attempted flagging on Miles and Robinson see Appendix **95**.

Three abbreviated methods of flagging are described in the ensuing paragraphs **(b)**, **(c)**, **(d)**.

(c) 9×9 **flag**

For each row find the sum of the entries ignoring their signs (sum of moduli).

Take the 9 best rows and flag them (by Scalar products).

There may be an obvious start: if not, converge the flag. To save time divide by 10 and ignore fractions.

Note: If chi 2 lim is expected, flagging is applied, not to 9 rows, but to 11 columns.

(d) Skeleton (See **R2**, p. 4)

Make a skeleton of the rectangle; if, for example, the depth is 7 this means: take sums of ± 7 as ± 2, ± 5 and ± 3 as ± 1, ± 1 as 0. This reduces the arithmetic substantially: it is practicable to flag many more rows.

Note: These are written in the rectangle as dots and crosses with 2 entries in a cell for ± 7.

ii A skeleton is unsatisfactory if the depth is even, e.g. if it is 6 the possible sums are ± 6, ± 4, ± 2, 0, which cannot effectively be simplified without taking ± 2 as 0, and this throws away too much evidence.

p. 124 **(e) E 2** (**R2**, p. 82, **R3**, p. 74, **R4**, pp. 4, 20)

Select the five best rows, as for 9×9 flag: A, B, C, D, E.

In A take all scores above the standard (see below) to form a rudimentary $\Delta\chi_1$ wheel.

Take this through the rectangle, getting $\Delta\chi_2 A$, similarly $\Delta\chi_2 B$, $\Delta\chi_2 C$, $\Delta\chi_2 D$, $\Delta\chi_2 E$, each a column of scores, not merely dots and crosses.

b Make a flag of these five $\Delta\chi_2$'s by Jacobs's method.

Choose 2, 3, 4 or 5 of these, and, with the appropriate $\pm$ signs add them. The high scoring characters can be used as a start.

Depth	4–6	6–8	8–10	10–12	12–14	14–16
Standard	4	5	6	7	8	9

[a] Jacob flagging [b] Jacob's

[i] Word 'smaller' handwritten.
[ii] Word 'possible' handwritten.

(f) Restarts

At the end of a convergence the characters used in the start are liable to score unduly well; but even if the start is a poor one, some of the characters for which the rectangle really does provide strong evidence should also score well (**R3**, p. 16). If high scoring characters which appeared late in the convergence are taken as a new start, a better convergence may be obtained. (**R2**, p. 101, **R3**, p. 98.)

(g) E 1

An elaborate variation on restarts is E 1 for which the instructions are:—

Make a start by eye

Purge

Take 5 characters as a new start

Purge again

Each purge involves the following:—

Suppose the eye-start is $\Delta\chi_2\alpha$ of 3 to 5 characters. Take $\Delta\chi_2\alpha$ through the rectangle getting $\Delta\chi_1 A$ of 6–10 characters. Take $\Delta\chi_1 A$ through the rectangle getting $\Delta\chi_2\beta$ of 8–12 characters, in choosing which, reduce the score of any character which was in $\Delta\chi_2\alpha$ by one-third. Take $\Delta\chi_2\beta$ i
through the rectangle getting $\Delta\chi_1 B$ of 5–10 characters, excluding all characters which were in $\Delta\chi_1 A$. (**R4**, p. 3; for random starts **R1**, p. 93.)

24E RECTANGLE SIGNIFICANCE TESTS p. 125

(a) ii

In view of the account given in **24X** this deals only with tests in practical use.

It is perhaps desirable to stress the distinction between tests for rectangles not converged, i.e. treating the rectangle simply as a run for a wheel 1271 long; and tests for converged rectangles, i.e. using the additional knowledge that the 1271 cells of the rectangle are derived from two wheels 41 and 31 long. The latter are naturally more powerful.

Essentially only one test of each type is used operationally; this excludes tests which involve a
the use of additional evidence.

For rectangles not converged: the square-summing test, or its equivalent the Δ_{1271} test.

For converged rectangles: Significance Test IV and several simple approximations to it.

(b) Test for rectangle not converged

If θ_{ij} is the entry in a cell of a 1+2 rectangle of length N and depth k (so that $N = 1271k$) the random value of $\sum_1^{1271} \theta_{ij}^2$ is N and its variance is

$$2N(k-1) \qquad (\mathbf{24X(d)}).$$

$\sum\theta_{ij}^2$ is evaluated when making a rectangle on Colossus, by means of a series of cyclometers which record the number, $n(\theta)$, of occurrences of each possible score. Then $\sum\theta_{ij}^2 = \sum\theta^2{\cdot}n(\theta)$: the calculation is made foolproof by means of a printed form.

The analogous hand process is possible for a non-Colossus rectangle.

The test is not ordinarily a very powerful one (**24X(d)**), but the following statistics are of b
some interest.

---

[a] type used [b] **(24)**

[i] Handwritten 'in' inserted with a caret.

[ii] Subsection unnamed in *Report*; text 'In view of...' begins on same line as **(a)**.

Depth		3	4	5	6	7	8	9	10	11	12	13	14	15	16
Significant Rectangles	Number	8	30	9	12	9	4	1	3	1	2	3	1	–	–
	Average sigma-ages.	2·13	1·54	1·63	1·93	2·3	1·55	1·8	1·85	3·5	2·62	3·3	3·4	–	–
Abandoned Rectangles	Average sigma-ages.	·14	·58	·51	·55	·19	1·13	·15	1·23	1·06	—·45	·58	·07	·89	·83
	Number	41	295	88	112	18	28	11	8	9	2	7	5	8	1

(**R1**, pp. 32, 34, 38. **R3**, pp. 37, 77.)

p. 126 **(c) Δ1271 Test**

Since

i
$$\Delta_{1271}\Delta Z_{12} = \Delta_{1271}(\Delta D_{12} + \Delta\chi_{12}) = \Delta_{1271}\Delta D_{12} \xrightarrow[\frac{1+\delta^2}{2}]{} \bullet$$

a count of $\Delta_{1271}\Delta Z_{12} = \bullet$ is a possible test. It is strengthened if differencing at every multiple of 1271 is included, when it becomes equivalent to the $\sum\theta_{ij}^2$ test (**24X(b)** cf. **R2**, p. 102), for which reason it was discontinued when the cyclometers came into use.

It is however more easily adaptable to the detection of slides. A (half) square is made in which the entry in the cell (*m*,*n*) is the number of agreements between the *m*th and *n*th stretches of 1271 in ΔZ_{12}. Two stretches in the correct relative positions will show a bulge: two between which there is a slide will show no bulge.

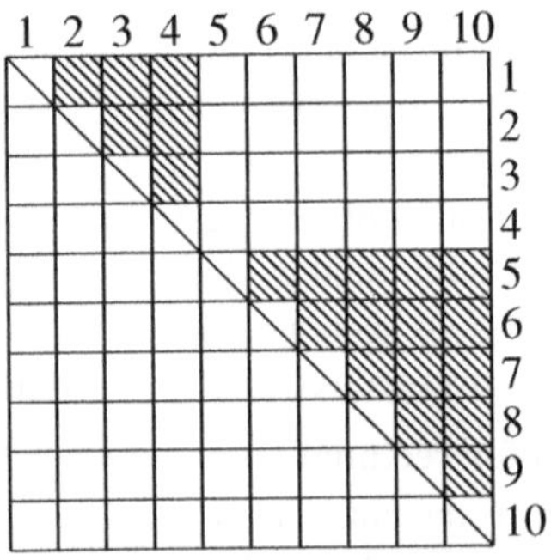

In the example depicted there is a slide between the fourth and fifth stretches of 1271 letters. Only the entries in the shaded positions show a bulge. If the slide is near the middle of the fifth stretch, the entries in the fifth row will also show no bulge.

In fact the expected bulge in a single cell is only about $\frac{1}{3}\sigma$, so that long texts are required: the method is not in current use.

The counts can easily be made on Robinson using a cipher tape or any kind of Thurlow Tape. Two copies are required; if their lengths are consecutive multiples of 1271, the whole test can be made very quickly without stopping the machine.

If a slide is suspected, it may be investigated by similar runs with an artificial slide between stretches from different parts. (See **R3**, pp. 77, 82, 92. **R4**, pp. 71, 82, 122.)

(d) Significance test for converged rectangles

The standard test for a 1+2 rectangle is

ii
$$2{\cdot}17\frac{x^2}{N} + \sum\vartheta\left(\frac{2Y_i(x-k)}{N}\right) - 219 > 0;$$

p. 127, a left-hand the side being the decibanage in favour of significance, where Y_i is the modulus of

[a] left hand

[i] This equation, partly typed and partly hand written, occurs in-line in the *Report*, with $\frac{1+\delta^2}{2}$ bulging under the arrow.
[ii] Formula lacks a parenthesis; parentheses do not enclose fraction: $2{\cdot}17\frac{x^2}{N} + \sum\vartheta\frac{(2Y_i(x-k)}{N} - 219 > 0$.

the score of a character and $\sum$ is extended over both wheels, $\vartheta(u) \equiv 10\log_{10}(1+e^{-u})$ and is tabulated, k is controversial (see **24X(e)**).

For other rectangles 219 should be replaced by $3{\cdot}01(w_1+w_2-1)+5$, where w_1,w_2 are the two wheel lengths.

The formula is believed to provide a normally reliable condition for the essential correctness of the rectangle wheels. Ordinarily, though not always on all links, this implies that wheel-breaking can be completed, though it cannot be guaranteed, for it depends on supporting messages and on ΔP characteristics in impulses not used for the rectangle.

The formula has been criticised because $\sum\vartheta$ is tedious to calculate and varies but little. Approximations have been suggested:

$$\sum\vartheta = \frac{2{\cdot}4\times10^{10}}{x^2}\pm3{\cdot}6$$ (for messages 10168 long: **R3**, p 5).

$$\sum\vartheta = 23 \text{ i.e. } \frac{x}{\sqrt{N}} > 9{\cdot}5$$ (based on a perverse attitude to decibans:

R4, pp 111, 115) i

$$\sum\vartheta = 2+\frac{217{,}000}{N}-\frac{54{,}250{,}000}{N^2} \quad \text{i.e. } \frac{x}{\sqrt{N}} > 10\left(1-\frac{5000}{N}\right)$$

(Too optimistic for small N: used by

the computers).

An empirical formula for $\sum\vartheta$ as a function of N in a marginally significant rectangle would have been preferable.

In practice everyone assumes that $\sum\vartheta$ is about 20–30, being greater for short messages and that if $2{\cdot}17x^2/N$, the LEADING TERM, is more than 200 or much less than 180 it is unnecessary to calculate the ϑ terms. (See **R2**, p. 15, **R4**, pp. 40, 111, 117.) ii

24F CONDITIONAL RECTANGLE

This means a rectangle in which scores are counted only at places of Z where some fixed condition is satisfied.

E.g. in a cell of the 3+4**x**/1**x**2**x** rectangles the entry is a

(the number of places where $\Delta Z_3+\Delta Z_4=\times, \Delta D_1=\times, \Delta D_2=\times$) minus iii

(the number of places where $\Delta Z_3+\Delta Z_4=\bullet, \Delta D_1=\times, \Delta D_2=\times$).

The convergence is identical with that of an ordinary rectangle.

Almost the only conditional rectangles used are 3+4**x**/1**x**2**x**, 4+5/1+2, 4+5/1**x**2**x** (see next section **24G**).

Because the number of places where $\Delta D_1=\times$, $\Delta D_2=\times$ varies from cell to cell (and in p. 128 addition $\Delta\chi_1$, $\Delta\chi_2$ may be 'doubted') the depth cannot be made constant, so that even if Colossus is used 3+4**x**/1**x**2**x** and 3+4•/1**x**2**x** must be printed separately, preferably in alternate lines and distinctive colours, and the differences found by hand. Although the other methods can be applied Colossus is preferred because it avoids auxiliary tapes. b

[a] e.g. [b] Colossus preferred

[i] Text 'based on ... decibans: **R4**, pp. 111, 115' appears on one line, as does 'Too optimistic ... the computers'.
[ii] see **R2**, p. 15
[iii] Displayed equation unindented.

Colossus switching. (cf. 1+2 rectangle)
Count text, and check 1+2=•

a **Chi patterns**	(triggers) Cross in 02, 02 of χ_3, χ_4.
	$\Delta\chi_1$, $\Delta\chi_2$ in χ_1, χ_2 triggers.
	Doubts in special patterns χ_1, χ_2 triggers.
Plugging	(everything plugged goes to all counters)
	Special pattern χ_1 = • } It is improbable that there will
	Special pattern χ_2 = • } be no doubting.

Check effective text
$\Delta Z_1 + \chi_1 =$ ×
$\Delta Z_2 + \chi_2 =$ ×

Check "R"
$\Delta Z_3 + \Delta Z_4 =$ ×.

Selection switches	$Q = \chi$
Q Panel	$\chi_3 =$ × in all counters
	Multiple test impulses R_1 R_2 R_3 R_4 R_5 into counters 5, 4, 3, 2, 1, respectively
Control panel	Multiple test switch to χ_4
	Rectangle switch to "Print Scores"
Rectangling gadget	Carriage return on χ_4
	Do *not* switch a depth
Settings	$\chi_1 = 41$, $\chi_2 = 31$, $\chi_3 = 02$, $\chi_4 = 02$
	After setting wheels replace χ_3, χ_4 plugs in 01, 01, *without resetting*
Step	χ_4 fast (lower switch down) to control χ_3 (lower switch up)
Printer	Triple line feed
Final checks	Repeat first and last rows

Re-run with $\Delta Z_3 + \Delta Z_4 =$ • instead of ×
(For an attempt to avoid the separate printing of × and • see **R3**, p. 11.)

p. 129, b 24G SOME GENERALIZED RECTANGLES

In order that the entry in each cell of a rectangle shall be a single number only a single condition can be imposed on the two impulses involved. The condition must therefore be of the form $i + j/(\text{known } \Delta D) = \genfrac{}{}{0pt}{}{\times}{\bullet}$, with or without fixed conditions.

Among the plain $i + j$ rectangles 4+5, 2+5, 1+3, 3+4**×**, 2+4 have all been tried: indeed at one time it was erroneously supposed that 4+5 would be better than 1+2 (see **24Y(a)**).

E.12 A peculiar class of i+j rectangle is that of i+6 rectangles in which each entry is the score for $\Delta Z_i + \Delta Z_6 =$ • i.e. $\Delta Z_i =$ •, entered in a $31 \times w_i$ rectangle. In particular if $i = 2$ all entries lie on the principal diagonal and the rectangle degenerates into $\widehat{\chi}_2$.

A rectangle which makes full use of the run 4=5•/1=2 requires 4 entries (3 independent) in each cell (cf. **25C(e) R1**, p. 62).

Several members of the section have contemplated "Rectangular parallelepipeds": probably the most favourable is i+j+6/, ΔZ_6 being always dot.

Rectangles may be combined, thus

---

[a] **Chi-patterns** [b] GENERALISED

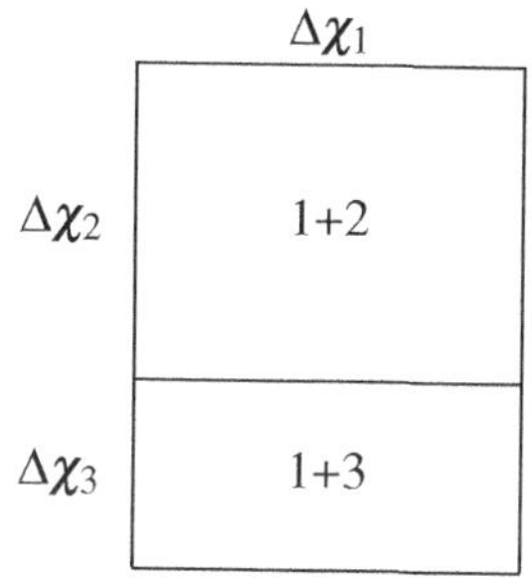

but in practice this is done only for key (**26C**), because in cipher, pips in different rectangles are of unequal value.
(For Motor Rectangles see Appendix **92**.)

24W THEORY OF CONVERGENCE p. 130

(a) Elementary properties of the convergence of a rectangle

Let the length of message be N.

Let the entry in the cell which is the ith row and jth column be θ_{ij} .

If some value of δ is assumed then the odds that $\Delta\chi_{12}$ = dot in all (i,j) are $\zeta^{\theta_{ij}}$ where $\zeta = \frac{1+\delta}{1-\delta}$. This is a trivial consequence of Bayes' theorem *if the message is assumed to contain no slide* (see **R3**, p. 130). Another way of stating the result is that the hypothesis $\Delta\chi_{12}$ = dot is θ_{ij} pips up, where a pip is $10\log_{10}\zeta$ decibans. This enables one to regard the rectangle as an array of 1271 pieces of probability information, arranged in a convenient form for attempting to find the $\Delta\chi_1$ and $\Delta\chi_2$ patterns. We now give a description of methods used for doing this.

A partial wheel pattern can be regarded as a sequence of numbers, $\varepsilon_1, \varepsilon_2, \ldots$ each equal to ± 1 or 0, where $+1$ stands for a dot and -1 for a cross and 0 for a doubt. The process of taking the pattern through the rectangle consists in forming scalar products

$$y_i = \sum_j \theta_{ij}\varepsilon_j.$$ [i]

The numbers y_i are then called the scores in pips of the characters of the other wheel.

In the original form of convergence one would take $\varepsilon_{j'} = \text{sign } y_j$, i.e. E.13

$$\begin{aligned} \varepsilon_{j'} &= +1 && \text{if } y_j > 0 \\ \varepsilon_{j'} &= -1 && \text{if } y_j < 0 \\ \varepsilon_{j'} &= 0 && \text{if } y_j = 0 \end{aligned}$$

and take this wheel pattern back through the rectangles giving pippages

$$x_i = \sum \theta_{ij}\varepsilon_{j'}.$$

The resulting pattern is then taken back in a similar way, giving new values for y_i and so on until the pattern on one side of the rectangle is the same twice running. The rectangle is then said to be converged (crudely). The result of the convergence may depend on the particular pattern with which the convergence is started. The sum of the moduli of the scores of one wheel is called X, $X = \sum |x_i|$. This score is independent of which of the two wheels is used, when the convergence is completed, for

$$X = \sum_i \varepsilon_i x_i = \sum_{ij} \varepsilon_i \theta_{ij} \varepsilon_{j'}$$

[i] Displayed equation reads $y_i = \sum_i \theta_{ij}\varepsilon_i$.

p. 131 and this is symmetrical with respect to the two wheels. If the message were de-chied with the
E.14 wheels consisting of the final patterns then $X =$ the double bulge of the 1p2 score (provided that places where the differenced wheels are doubted are not included in the count).

i The formula $X = \sum_{ij} \varepsilon_i \, \theta_{ij} \, \varepsilon_{j'}$ is true at all stages of the convergence and the effect on the wheel patterns of the progress of convergence is the same as first choosing the numbers $\varepsilon_{1'}, \varepsilon_{2'}, \ldots$ so as to maximise $\sum \varepsilon_i \theta_{ij} \varepsilon_{j'}$ (leaving $\varepsilon_1, \varepsilon_2, \ldots$ unchanged) and then changing $\varepsilon_1, \varepsilon_2, \ldots$ so as to maximise X (leaving $\varepsilon_{1'}, \varepsilon_{2'}$ unchanged) and so on. Clearly X must keep on becoming larger and
E.15 larger until it reaches a maximum value, when the rectangle is converged.

If the phrase 'crude convergence' is interpreted in a more up to date sense, in which characters may be doubted if their scores in pips are low (or on grounds of unfavourable wheel characteristics), then it is no longer essential that X should continually grow (see **R2**, pp. 9, 11). However it was always the practice to complete the convergence (i.e. to get complete patterns) in order to get a check on the sum of the moduli of the pippages of the two wheels.

The mathematical description given above applies to the hand process of crude convergence and to the Colossus process of convergence of a rectangle. The two processes are of course equivalent.

The reason for the adjective 'crude' is that there is another method called 'accurate convergence', in which

ii
$$y_j = \sum_i f(\theta_{ij}, x_i)$$
$$x_i = \sum_j f(\theta_{ij}, y_j)$$

where $f(k,l)$ is a symmetrical function of k and l. It will be seen that the exact magnitude of the pippages of the wheel taken through are used, instead of their sign. The function $f(k,l)$ is defined as

$$f(k,l) = \log_\zeta \left(\frac{\zeta^{k+l} + 1}{\zeta^k + \zeta^l} \right)$$

where

$$\zeta = \frac{1+\delta}{1-\delta}$$

and (see **R1**, pp. 37, 43, 45, 49) a conventional value of δ is assumed. A table of $f(k,l)$ can be conveniently constructed by means of a specially made cardboard slide-rule, in view of the identity $\phi(k) + \phi(l) = \phi[f(k,l)]$ where $\phi(k) = \log \frac{\zeta^k+1}{\zeta^k-1}$.

p. 132 It is found that the entries in the table are not sensitive to the exact value of ζ assumed. (**R1**, p. 49, **R2**, p. 1.)

The sense in which this type of convergence is accurate is that if the x_i's are a correct measure of the odds of the characters of one wheel (measured in 'pips' of $10 \log_{10} \zeta$ decibans each), then the formula gives the odds of the characters of the other wheel accurately, if the numbers θ_{ij} are regarded as evidence which is independent of the x_i's. Clearly the last assumption is not really accurate, but this does not prevent accurate convergence from being theoretically more satisfactory than crude convergence. In fact crude convergence is the limiting case of accurate scoring when

---

[i] Formula half-displayed, with 'is true' starting on a fresh line.

[ii] The equations read

$$y_i = \sum_i f(\theta_{ij}, x_i)$$
$$x_i = \sum_j f(\theta_{ij}, y_i).$$

$\zeta \to \infty$, if the pippages of the characters of the wheel taken through exceed those in the cells of the rectangle.

The precise interpretation of the pippages of the characters of a wheel, as the result of a crude convergence is that they are proportioned to the decibanages assuming the pattern of the other wheel to be certain. In practice the relationship between the pippages and the true decibanage (assuming the patterns to be substantially correct) is not linear (see **R3**, p. 132).

When a message contains a lot of 9's (representing letters missed) there is a modification that can be made to crude convergence. The modification was given in **R4**, p. 39, but it was seldom used.

(b) Proof of accurate scoring formula

The formula for accurate scoring is of exactly the same form as that for 'scoring one column of the rectangle against another'. Given two columns of the rectangle we may be interested in the question of whether the two corresponding characters of the wheel are the same or different. Let us suppose that the pippages of the two columns are respectively

$$\theta_1, \theta_2 \ldots$$
$$\theta'_1, \theta'_2 \ldots$$

Then the factor in favour of the two columns being the same (i.e. the two corresponding characters of the wheel being the same) is

$$\prod_i f_0(\theta_i, \theta'_i)$$

where $f_0(\theta_i, \theta'_i)$ is the factor accruing from one pair of corresponding cells. Let us then consider the following problem: Given two characters where odds of being dots are ζ^{θ}, $\zeta^{\theta'}$, what are the odds ζ^{π} that the two characters are the same? The proportional bulge corresponding to odds ζ^{θ} is $\frac{\zeta^{\theta}-1}{\zeta^{\theta}+1}$. Therefore, by the theorem of the chain of witnesses, p. 133

$$\frac{\zeta^{\pi}-1}{\zeta^{\pi}+1} = \frac{\zeta^{\theta}-1}{\zeta^{\theta}+1} \cdot \frac{\zeta^{\theta'}-1}{\zeta^{\theta'}+1}$$

and this gives the relation between π, θ, θ' in the slide-rule form.

(c) Wrong convergences of a rectangle and methods of starting

A rigorous solution of the problem of the number of different crude convergences of a (1+2) rectangle seems to be very hard to find. However, two quite distinct attempts to solve the problem have been made. The first one (**R1**, pp. 56, 57) tends to show that there are not more than 31 possible convergences.* The second one (**R2**, p. 10, etc.) shows that for a rectangle of length 1271 probably at least 20 convergences are to be expected. *, i

A very striking example of a wrong convergence occurred in about February, 1944. A message was converged twice on Colossus from two different random starts (**R1**, p. 93, **R2**, p. 14) and the same result was obtained each time. The rectangle was then converged by hand, using intelligence in the selection of a start and a very much better convergence was obtained (which was then checked on Colossus when the other wheels were broken). As an experiment, accurate convergence was applied to the original convergence and after a few steps it began to improve and became the same as the better convergence (**R2**, pp. 21 etc.). Since that time more care was used in starting the convergence, but the accurate method was used only at first, and when there was not a flood of work.

*In fact there are exactly 31 convergences for 'scalar product' convergence.

[i] Text of native footnote * handwritten.

One method of starting convergence is by the use of a skeleton (see e.g. **R2**, p. 82, **R4**, p. 20). This has the advantage that most of the arithmetic is avoided and a flag 16 by 16 can be made in the same time as a much smaller flag of the ordinary type. This method is not suitable for rectangles of length $2n \times 1271$ ($n = 2,3,4$) and since so many of the rectangles were of length 8×1271 the method was not generally adopted (**R3**, p. 74). The method is a special case of throwing away a lot of the smaller pieces of evidence in order to be able to work more quickly with the larger pieces (see **R2**, p. 94).

p. 134 Here is a list of references to methods of starting the convergence of a rectangle:

Techniques for starting convergence on Colossus **R1**, p. 93.

Necessity of a good start. Suggestion of starting from eleven selected rows, trying all possible signs **R2**, p. 4 (see also **R2**, pp 18, 22, **R3**, p. 21).

Eye starts **R3**, p. 108.

Random starts, with purging **R4**, p. 3.

Methods of starting and suggestion that the choice amongst certain standard methods should be optional **R4**, p. 23.

Statistics for various methods of starting **R4**, p. 68.

Here are some references to methods of analysis of a rectangle, not connected with methods of starting.

Solving rectangle by linear equations. Crude convergence. Solving a rectangle by minimising a quadratic form **R1**, pp. 40, 56.

Maximum likelihood solution of a rectangle **R2**, pp. 16, 29, 32, 34, 35, 37, 39, 40.

There are other consequences of the knowledge that more than one convergence is possible, besides the importance of a good start. One is that the convergence must be done with care. The standard of acceptance of a character should be lowered gradually and arithmetical mistakes should be avoided. There were several examples of a wrong convergence being reached due to mistakes of various kinds. Another consequence is that a better convergence than the first one can often be obtained by a 'restart' in which the highest scoring characters of the first convergence are taken for the restart of another convergence (see **R3**, p. 98). The validity of this method (apart from the successes attained) (see e.g. **R2**, p. 101) depends on the empirical observation that the high-scoring characters tend to have the right sign even if the rectangle has not reached 'significance' (**R3**, pp. 16, 17, 36). (For the meaning of the term significance see below — significance test IV.)

(d) Flags

It has been found that crude convergence of a rectangle from a random start is liable to lead to
p. 135 a convergence which is not the best one. Therefore various methods of starting the convergence have been suggested. One of these is the method of 'flags'. This consists in comparing every pair of a certain number of rows of the rectangle and scoring these pairs by some scoring system.
E.16 The resulting scores are entered into a triangle like an American Tournament table and the result examined in order to get a starting pattern for $\Delta\chi_2$. This method using scalar products was started
E.17 by Vergine who had used the method in connection with the Hagelin machine. Later we began entering the flag double entry, making it square and then crudely converging the flag, (**R2**, p. 79). The number of rows used varied from 6 to 16 depending to some extent on the type of scoring system used.

The correct scoring system for an assumed value of δ is given by the function $f(\theta, \theta')$ above. This is troublesome to use in practice and an approximate formula must be used. The usual formula was $\theta\theta'$, so the entries in the flag were simply the scalar products of the pairs of rows. This method is a good approximation if δ is small. (It is the sort of method that a statistician would think of naturally.) When this method is used it is often convenient to divide all entries in the flag by 10 before converging it (giving the results to the nearest whole number).

It might be thought that the scalar product method could be used as a substitute for accurate convergence. However the degree of approximation would be very bad in this case since the pippages involved are much larger. In fact the accurate score of x pips compared with y pips is i
easily seen to be

$$(\log\cosh\frac{1}{2}(x+y)p - \log\cosh\frac{1}{2}(x-y)p)$$

natural bans where $p = \log\frac{1+\delta}{1-\delta}$ (i.e. approximately 2δ), and this is sufficiently close to ii, E.18

$$\begin{aligned}
&\log\cosh(x+y)\delta - \log\cosh(x-y)\delta \\
&\quad = \frac{\delta^2}{2}\{(x+y)^2-(x-y)^2\} - \frac{\delta^4}{12}\{(x+y)^4-(x-y)^4\} \\
&\qquad + \frac{\delta^6}{45}\{(x+y)^6-(x-y)^6\}\cdots \\
&\quad = 2\delta^2 xy - \frac{2}{3}xy(x^2+y^2)\delta^4 + \cdots
\end{aligned}$$

The first two terms can be written

$$2xy\delta^2\left\{1-\frac{(x^2+y^2)\delta^2}{3}\right\}.$$

As a rather extreme case, if $x=8$, $y=6$ and $\delta = 1/10$, the term $2xy\delta^2$ would be 50% too large. So for flag making xy is quite a good approximation (**R3**, pp. 4, 5, 29) if the unit (or 'pippette') is taken as $2\delta^2$ natural bans, i.e. 1 pippette $\doteqdot \delta$ pips. On the other hand, in accurate p. 136
convergence one of the numbers x, y is generally far too large for the approximation to be valid. In this case the formula

$$\log\cosh(x+y)\delta - \log\cosh(x-y)\delta$$

can naturally be used to justify crude convergence.

There is another type of flag, called the Jacobs flag (see **R2**, p. 101) in which the function xy E.19
is replaced by

$$\operatorname{sign}(xy)\min(|x|,|y|).$$

This type of flag was used for one of the methods of starting the convergence of a rectangle, because it is quicker than multiplication, though much less accurate. It would be a good approximation for large values of δ. If all the entries in the rectangle are ± 1 or 0 then Jacobs flag and the ordinary (scalar product) flag are the same thing. This remark applies in the case of most key rectangles.

For mechanical flag-making for cipher tapes see **R3**, pp. 63, 78, 82, 106, **R2**, p. 101 and ch. **91**.

24X SIGNIFICANCE TESTS

(a) Introductory remarks

We are about to discuss a number of significance tests for rectangles. The first one, 'significance test 0' is designed for rectangles not converged. Tests I to IV are for converged rectangles. The standard one is significance test IV, and is the most difficult to understand.

---

[i] Handwritten 'score' inserted with a caret.

[ii] Sentence broken at '(i.e. approximately 2δ).' with full stop, and continues on next line with 'and this is…'

(b) Tests for unconverged rectangles (historical)

No rectangle was made with mechanical aid of any sort until after the autoclave had been
E.20 generally introduced (January 1944). It was then suggested (**R1**, p. 32) that if the rectangles were made on a Robinson, with a set total, the number of readings that came up would be an indication of how good the rectangle was likely to be. Such a test was particularly important at a time when it was troublesome to make rectangles. It was thought at first that such a test would be quite powerful and that it might even be possible to stop Robinson in the middle of the run. However some figures were then produced (**R1**, pp. 34, 38) depending on a single message
p. 137 that had been rectangled by hand a long time before, and these figures tended to show that the method would not be very powerful. Soon after this the square-summing test was suggested,
E.21 emerging from some calculations which appear in the black file. These calculations contain an error (corrected below) but the order of the answer was right and agreed with the indications of the message just mentioned. It was not until September 1944 that the slide and significance test was invented (**R3**, pp. 77, 83). It was not realised absolutely at once that this test is equivalent to the square-summing test. The original object of the slide and significance test was for putting rectangles in a priority order and even for rejecting them. Unfortunately the tapes took some time to make and the earlier Robinsons were rather hard on long tapes, so the rectangle was often converged before the sigma-age of the test had been worked out. It was suggested further that a slight modification of the test could be used for attempting to detect slides of ± 1 (**R3**, p. 92). This was tried only a few times and would probably have had an occasional success. The slide and significance test was made more practicable by the introduction of 'Thurlow tapes of the second kind' as the standard non-Colossus method of producing a rectangle (**R4**, pp. 71, 82). However, the Robinson routine was dropped when the Colossus gadget, which counts the frequencies of occurrence of the different values of $\boldsymbol{\theta}_{ij}$ was brought in.

For another test for unconverged rectangles see **R1**, p. 36. This test in effect is equivalent to a crude form of flagging a skeleton. Significance tests for flags are suggested in **R2**, p. 92, and **R3**, p. 8, and these can be regarded as tests for a rectangle on which no convergence has been done. But these tests would not be expected to do very well unless the rectangle is an exceptionally good one. On p. 92, **R2** there is also a suggestion which is a test rather of the start of a convergence.

An entirely different way of possibly obtaining evidence about the wheels without rectangling is by doing a $\Delta^2 Z$ alphabetical count (**R3**, p. 64). This can be of value only if at least one of the χ's has good Δ^2 properties, i.e. $\Delta^2\chi_i$ nearly all crosses. (See also **25E(e)** for $\widehat{\chi}_2$ runs and chapter **25F** for one wheel break-ins if $ab \neq \frac{1}{2}$.)

(c) Tests for converged rectangles (historical)

E.22 The first rectangle ever done for wheel-breaking purposes is mentioned in Part **4**. The first
p. 138 10,000 letters of a message were used and the result of the convergence enabled the rest of the message to be set convincingly at a slide. This enabled the worker to feel that things were going well, and can be regarded as a form of significance test. It is a special case of setting another message against the (partial) wheels obtained from a rectangle. In the early days of mechanical wheel-breaking there was a tendency to rely rather too much on this method. At first the allied method of wheel-sliding was used, as it was believed to be more accurate in some ways, and it avoided the use of machine time.

Another test for significance, easy to apply with our improved machines, is to span the message using partial wheels from the rectangle and see if there is an obvious slide. Yet another test is to see if the wheels obtained from the rectangle have outstandingly good Δ^2 properties (**R3**, p. 63). This method was most successful when the Δ^2 properties were so good that perfect wheels were assumed for both χ_1 and χ_2 and the wheels were broken although the rectangle was considerably below significance.

Useful as all these methods have been, none of them has ever been successful for rectangles falling short of significance by more than 15 decibans, on significance test IV. This test was introduced about the 1st March, 1944. Up to about a fortnight before that time it was thought likely that the result of an accurately converged rectangle really did give the correct pippages of the characters of $\Delta\chi_1$ and $\Delta\chi_2$. The only important theoretical problem seemed to be to find an estimate of δ.

It was the failure of the wheel-sliding attempts on Jellyfish which made us suspect that a significance test was necessary. The tests I, II, III, IV were all put forward within about two weeks.

A crude form of significance test IV was designed in July, 1944 for the benefit of the computers (**R3**, p. 23). The idea of this test was that the wheel man should be informed as soon as possible when a rectangle was likely to be quite good. It was observed empirically that the ϑ terms hardly ever added up to more than 30 decibans for the usual length of text, namely 10168. (See below for the definition of the ϑ terms.) Further it was assumed somewhat arbitrarily that $\sum\vartheta$ was inversely proportional* to N. The significance test can be written *, i

$$\frac{2{\cdot}17x^2}{N} > 219 - \frac{300{,}000}{N}.$$ p. 139

This gives, to a sufficient approximation,

$$x > 10\sqrt{N-1500}$$

and the function $10\sqrt{N-1500}$ was therefore tabulated.

Some time later (**R4**, pp. 111, 117) another alternative was suggested, also based on an empirical consideration of ϑ terms. Unfortunately it was not based on a careful study of the statistics about ϑ terms available by that time. The sum of the ϑ terms for $N = 8\times 1271$ were examined empirically, since the sample for this text length was considerable (**R3**, p. 95). It was found that this sum could be approximated by the expression

$$\frac{24{,}000{,}000{,}000}{x^3} \pm 3{\cdot}6 \text{ decibans.}$$ ii

This enabled one to say (with only a small probable error) how many decibans up or down any rectangle of this length would be, given x. By 1945 there were probably sufficient statistics to obtain an empirical simplification for all values of N, but this was never done.

(d) Significance test for a rectangle not worked on — the square summing test

By a 'significance test for a rectangle not worked on' we mean a test which depends only on the numbers in the 1271 cells of the rectangle and not on any convergence of the rectangle for comparison of the rows. Such a test is the one referred to as significance test 0, which amounts roughly to summing the squares of all the 1271 entries in the rectangle. (This test appeared in the 'Black File' at an early date.) Naturally such a test cannot be as powerful as tests which can be applied after the rectangle is converged but occasionally a result is obtained enabling one to forecast that the rectangle will be significant when converged.

Let the entry in the cell (i, j) of the rectangle be θ_{ij}. Then the function required is $s_2 = \sum_{ij}\theta_{ij}{}^2$. There is a gadget on Colossus which counts the number of occurrences of each value of $|\theta_{ij}|$ when producing a rectangle, so that s_2 can be calculated without difficulty.

A test that can be applied even before the rectangle is made is the so-called 'slide and significance test'. Leaving aside the part of this test that deals with the detecting of slides

*Perhaps inversely proportional to $\sqrt{N}$ would have been a better assumption.

[i] Text of native footnote * on p. 133 of *Report* handwritten.

[ii] Capital X used instead of x in displayed formula and in following sentence.

it can be shown that this test is equivalent to square summing. The test consists in counting
p. 140 $\Delta_{1271\nu}(\Delta Z_{12}) = \bullet$ for $\nu = 1, 2, \ldots, k-1$, using a message of length $N = 1271k$ stuck with the end running straight on to the beginning. This method of sticking enables the text length used for each of the $(k-1)$ counts to be equal to N. The result is that if the scores for $\nu = 1, 2, \ldots (k-1)$ are added together and the result is called X then every pair of letters in ΔD at a distance which is a multiple of 1271 will have an opportunity of contributing either 2 or 0 to N. The total number of such distinct pairs of letters is $1271 \times k(k-1)/2$ so that $\frac{1}{2}X - \frac{1}{2}(1271 \times k(k-1)/2)$ is defined as the bulge B of the test. It is reasonable to suppose that the value of B (if $\delta = 0$) is 0 and that its S.D. is $\frac{1}{2}\sqrt{\{1271k(k-1)/2\}}$. Both of these assertions are true, though the proofs are not entirely trivial. Further it is clear that

$$X = \sum\{r(r-1) + s(s-1)\}$$

summed over all cells of the rectangle, where r is the number of dots and s is the number of crosses in a typical cell. If we now remember that $r + s = k$, $r - s = \theta_{ij}$,

$$s_2 = \sum\theta_{ij}^2, \qquad B = \frac{1}{2}X - \frac{1}{2}\left(1271\frac{k(k-1)}{2}\right)$$

it follows that

$$B = \frac{1}{4}(s_2 - N).$$

This is the connection between the square-summing test and the 'Slide and significance test'. It is implicit in all this that the expected value of s_2 is N and that its S.D. is $\sqrt{2N(k-1)}$.

E.23 The distribution of s_2 or B is really of χ^2 type but it is near enough to a normal distribution for most practical purposes.

In order to see how strong the test is we may argue as follows: The number of comparisons is $N_0 = 1271k(k-1)/2$ and the P.B. for a given value of δ, in each comparison is δ^2. Thus the expected sigma-age is $\delta^2\sqrt{1271k(k-1)/2}$. For example if $k = 8$ the expected sigma-age is $187\delta^2$. If $\delta = \cdot 1$, which is sufficient for the significance of the *converged* rectangle, the expected sigma-age would be 1·9. If $\delta = \cdot 15$ the expected sigma-age is 4·2, so highly significant rectangles are liable to be picked out quite well. One might be tempted to reject all rectangles whose sigma-age on the test was negative, but although this should not often happen if the rectangle is a good one, it also does not often happen anyway and the factor against the rectangle being significant is not at all large

p. 141 In order to estimate this factor, the simplest method is as follows:
Let sigma-age observed be s.
Let sigma-age expected for a given value of δ be s_1.
Then

$$s_1 = \delta^2\sqrt{1271\frac{k(k-1)}{2}}$$

and the factor in favour of a particular value of δ rather than $\delta = 0$ is, if we assume σ independent of δ,

$$e^{-1/2(s_1-s)^2} \Big/ e^{-\frac{1}{2}s^2}$$

$$= e^{ss_1 - \frac{1}{2}s^2}$$

or, in natural bans, $ss_1 - \frac{1}{2}s^2$.

$$s = \frac{B}{\frac{1}{2}\sqrt{\frac{k(k-1)1271}{2}}}.$$

Therefore natural banage is

$$
\begin{aligned}
&2B\delta^2 - \frac{N(k-1)}{4}\delta^4 \\
&= \frac{1}{2}(s_2 - N)\delta^2 - \frac{(k-1)N}{4}\delta^4 \\
&= \lambda\delta^2 - \mu\delta^4, \text{ say.}
\end{aligned}
$$

The factor in favour of $\delta > \delta_0$, rather than $\delta < \delta_0$, assuming a uniform prior distribution for δ for positive δ (and no chance of $\delta < 0$), is

$$
\int_{\delta_0}^{\infty} e^{\lambda\delta^2 - \mu\delta^4} d\delta \bigg/ \int_{-\infty}^{\delta_0} e^{\lambda\delta^2 - \mu\delta^4} d\delta.
$$

If $s_2 = N$, $k = 8$, $\delta = {\cdot}08$ this reduces to

$$
\int_{\cdot 08}^{\infty} e^{-17{,}800\,\delta^4} d\delta \bigg/ \int_{0}^{\cdot 08} e^{-17{,}800\,\delta^4} d\delta
$$
$$
= {\cdot}15.
$$

Thus with $N = 10168$ a zero score on the significance test implies a factor of about 6 against the rectangle being significant.

The original discussion of 'significance test 0', given in the black file, makes no assumptions about distributions and is a direct application of Bayes' theorem. We proceed now to give an account of this with simplification and correction of the original argument. It is not assumed that the length N of the message is necessarily a multiple of 1271.

Let us assume some definite value of δ and suppose that the depth of the rectangle in a particular cell is k. Then the probability that there will be an entry of θ in the cell (where θ and k are integers of like parity) is p. 142

$$
\binom{k}{\frac{k}{2}+\frac{\theta}{2}} \times \frac{1}{2^k}\left\{(1+\delta)^{k/2+\theta/2}(1-\delta)^{k/2-\theta/2} + (1+\delta)^{k/2-\theta/2}(1-\delta)^{k/2+\theta/2}\right\}
$$

and therefore the factor in favour of this value of δ rather than $\delta = 0$ is

$$
\begin{aligned}
&(1-\delta^2)^{k/2} \times \frac{1}{2}\left\{\left(\frac{1+\delta}{1-\delta}\right)^{\theta/2} + \left(\frac{1+\delta}{1-\delta}\right)^{-\theta/2}\right\} \\
&= \operatorname{sech}^k \delta' \,.\, \cosh(\theta\delta'),
\end{aligned}
$$

where

$$
\delta' = \frac{1}{2}\log\frac{1+\delta}{1-\delta} = \delta + \frac{1}{3}\delta^3 + \cdots,
$$

and is very close to δ in all practical cases. The natural banage from all the cells together is thus

$$
\begin{aligned}
&\sum_{ij} \log\cosh\,(\delta'\theta_{ij}) - N\log\cosh\,\delta' \\
&= \frac{\delta'^2}{2}(s_2 - N) - \frac{\delta'^4}{12}(s_4 - N) + \frac{\delta'^6}{45}(s_6 - N)\cdots \\
&\qquad \text{where } s_n = \sum \theta_{ij}{}^n.
\end{aligned}
$$

Now $E(s_2) = N$, $E(s_4) = 3kn$, $E(s_6) = 15k^2n$, ... if $\delta = 0$ and $N = 1271k$ so, if $\delta^2 N < 200$, a sufficiently good approximation is

$$\frac{\delta^2}{2}(s_2 - N) - \frac{\delta^4(s_4 - N)}{12}.$$

Observe that we cannot neglect the term in δ^4 since $E(s_2 - N) = Nk\,\delta^2$, so the expected value of the second term is about half of that of the first term if δ is small. If we write $s_4 = 3kN$ there is still a small discrepancy between the natural banage obtained here and that obtained before. This discrepancy is due to the assumption (see **R4**, p. 122) that σ is independent of δ. A more interesting remark is that the present method shows that the evidence of the value of s_4 should be taken into account. The 'maximum likelihood' value of δ is

$$\sqrt{\frac{3(s_2 - N)}{s_4 - N}}$$

[a] though this is itself liable to a large S.D. which can be estimated. Larger values of s_4 give smaller values of δ so the previous formula lays too much stress on the higher entries in the rectangle.

(e) Significance tests for rectangles which have been crudely converged

Let the double bulge on $/1{+}2$ on a message of length N, against the correct wheels be x^*. (We assume no slide — otherwise the phrase 'correct wheels' becomes ambiguous.) If a crude convergence is done, starting with one of the correct wheels (say $\Delta\chi_1$), then a result will be
p. 143 obtained in which the double bulge x is greater than or equal to x^*. The true value of δ is approximately x^*/N (see **R5**, pp. 68, 87). The difference $x - x^*$ is something like $\sqrt{N}$ (**R3**, pp. 117, etc.). This estimate depends on the assumption that the final convergence gives wheels that are substantially correct and this is the question we are going to consider here. We begin with three significance tests which have a certain weakness in common and then describe a fourth test which is *relatively* free from this weakness.

I. We may try to use the value of a pip to estimate the factor in favour of the wheel patterns being substantially right. If we say that the rectangle is x half pips up we get a decibanage of roughly $2{\cdot}17xx^*/N$.

This expression is very sensitive to the exact estimate of x^*.

II. Suppose we imagine $\delta = 0$ and assume the distribution of x is normal. Then the probability that x will reach a specified value is roughly

$$\frac{1}{x}\sqrt{\frac{N}{2\pi}}e^{-x^2/2N}.$$

We should like this to be less than 2^{-71}, since 2^{-71} represents the prior probability of the wheel patterns assumed ($71 = 41 + 31 - 1$). (One is subtracted because two theories for which the wheels are relatively inside out are equivalent.)

III. There is a method called the square summing of columns, described in **R1**, p. 95, which is more rigorously provable than II but is more trouble to apply. (Also it sacrifices some of the evidence, unless the rectangle is exactly 1271 long.) (See **R2**, p. 15.)

In the three methods described above it is implicit that there is a prior probability of 2^{-71} to be offset, or a decibanage of 214. But really it is not as bad as this, because we are interested only in the wheels being substantially right, and the number of wheel patterns which can be regarded as substantially the same as the converged rectangle wheels may be quite large. In this sense

[a] given

the tests II and III are too harsh, but in another sense they are too lenient, namely in the sort of way that the glib use of the error function is too lenient when setting chi's. (See chapter **21(o)** 'Statisticians' Fallacy'.) On the whole it seems best to make a direct appeal to Bayes' theorem. i

IV. Consider first the two theories p. 144

(i) Two definite wheel patterns and a definite value of δ

(ii) $\delta = 0$ (i.e. rectangle is random).

The probability of an excess θ of dots over crosses in a cell of the rectangle containing k entries (where θ and k have the same parity) is

$$\frac{1}{2^k}\binom{k}{\frac{k}{2}+\frac{\theta}{2}}(1+\delta)^{k/2+\theta/2}(1-\delta)^{k/2-\theta/2}$$

if $\Delta\chi_{12}$ is assumed to be a dot in the cell. Therefore the factor for theory (i) rather than (ii) is

$$\left(\frac{1+\delta}{1-\delta}\right)^{\theta/2}(1-\delta^2)^{k/2}.$$ ii

Therefore, using all of the cells of the rectangle, the total factor in favour of theory (i) rather than (ii) is

$$\left(\frac{1+\delta}{1-\delta}\right)^{x/2}(1-\delta^2)^{N/2},$$

where x is the double bulge of $/1{+}2$ using the wheel patterns of theory (i). Denote by $\varphi(\delta)$ the prior probability distribution of δ. Then the factor in favour of the particular wheel patterns, not allowing for competition is a number f where

$$\begin{aligned} f &= \int_{-1}^{1}\varphi(\delta)\left(\frac{1+\delta}{1-\delta}\right)^{x/2}\left(1-\delta^2\right)^{N/2}d\delta \\ &= \int_{-1-x/N}^{+1-x/N}\varphi\left(\frac{x}{N}+\varepsilon\right)\exp.\left\{\lambda-\frac{N}{1-(x/N)^2}\cdot\frac{\varepsilon^2}{2}+\cdots\right\}d\varepsilon \end{aligned}$$

where

$$\begin{aligned} \lambda &= \log\left\{\left(\frac{1+\delta}{1-\delta}\right)^{x/2}\left(1-\delta^2\right)^{1/2N}\right\}\Bigg|_{\delta=x/N} \\ &= \frac{x^2}{2N}+\frac{x^4}{12N^3}+\cdots \end{aligned}$$

Therefore iii

$$f \risingdotseq e^{x^2/2N+x^4/12N^3+\cdots}\cdot\sqrt{\frac{2\pi}{N}}\,\varphi\left(\frac{x}{N}\right).$$

---

i Handwritten 'the' inserted with a caret.

ii The displayed equation reads $\left(\frac{1+\delta}{1+\delta}\right)^{\theta/2}(1-\delta^2)^{k/2}$.

iii 'Therefore' handwritten.

i, † If[†] $x^2 < 120N$, the term $x^4/(12N^3)$ is less than $10(x/N)^2$ (natural bans) which is nearly always
‡ negligible. If we assume δ has a uniform distribution in an interval[‡] of length ·1, and has no
p. 145 chance of lying outside this interval, then $\varphi(x/N) = 10$ and the natural banage is

$$\frac{x^2}{2N} - \log \frac{\sqrt{N}}{25}$$

or roughly $(2{\cdot}17x^2/N - 5)$ decibans with an error of less than two decibans for the usual values of N.

The prior probability of any particular (differenced) wheel patterns (for a 1+2 rectangle) is 2^{-71} if the patterns obtained by reversing dots and crosses are regarded as equivalent to the original patterns. (This neglects wheel characteristics.) So particular wheel patterns are evens not allowing for competition, if

$$\frac{2{\cdot}17x^2}{N} - 219 = 0.$$

(Compare the argument this far with **R3**, p. 40.)

If $x^2/N = 120$ the wheel patterns are 41 decibans up, not allowing for competition. This is the justification for assuming $x^2 < N.120$ in the argument above. If $x^2 \geq 120N$ it is certain that the wheels are substantially right and inaccuracy in the odds does not matter.

We now go on to the problem of finding the odds that the wheels are substantially right. Clearly the result must depend on what is meant by wheel patterns being substantially correct, but it may not be very sensitive to variations in the definition, provided that the definition is a reasonable one.

Let x' be the double bulge on a typical pair of wheel patterns. Then whatever the definition of substantially correct, the factor in favour of the wheel patterns, obtained from the rectangle, being substantially correct is

$$\frac{1}{3}\sum_{x'} \exp.\frac{x'^2}{2N}$$

summed over all wheel patterns which are regarded as substantially equivalent to those of the rectangle. (The factor $1/3$ corresponds to the -5 db referred to above.)

If, for a typical pair of wheel patterns, y is the sum of the moduli of the scores of the characters that are changed in the rectangle patterns in order to get the new ones, then a good approximation is $x' = x - 2y$ if the new patterns are not too different from the old ones. Therefore the factor above is approximately equal to

$$\frac{1}{3}\sum_{y} \exp.\frac{(x-2y)^2}{2N}$$
$$= \frac{1}{3}e^{x^2/2N}\sum_{y} \exp.\{-\frac{2y}{N}(x-y)\}$$

p. 146 where the summation is over all wheel patterns defined as substantially the same as those of the rectangle. This formula is equal to

$$\frac{1}{3}e^{x^2/2N}\sum_{y} \exp.\{-\frac{2y}{N}(x-K)\}$$

[†]See below.

[‡]This estimate was originally a guess, but it was borne out quite well by statistics of set messages. In any case the result is not sensitive to variations in the assumption of the precise distribution of δ.

[i]Native footnotes marked with typed plus sign and what seems to be an overstrike of a lowercase 'x' and an equals sign, which we have taken to be the typist's approximation to † and ‡, respectively.

where K is some sort of mean value of y for substantially equivalent patterns. We assume further that y is the sum of any number of terms $y_1, y_2, \ldots$ which are the moduli of the x's. It might be objected that this includes values of y that are too large to be permitted for substantially equivalent patterns, but then the terms with large values of y are negligible anyway.

This makes the factor

$$\frac{1}{3}\, e^{x^2/2N} \sum_{i,j,\ldots} \exp.\left\{-\frac{2(y_i+y_j+\ldots)}{N}(x-K)\right\}$$
$$= \frac{1}{3}\, e^{x^2/2N} \prod_i \left\{1+e^{-2(x-k)y_i/N}\right\}.$$

Expressed in decibans, this gives, allowing for the prior odds

$$\frac{2{\cdot}17x^2}{N} + \sum \vartheta\left(\frac{2(x-K)y_i}{N}\right) - 219$$

where

$$\vartheta(a) = 10\log_{10}(1+e^{-a}).$$

The formula is now suitable for numerical calculation provided some value of K can be decided upon. It is just this part of the problem which is the least important though it is the most E.24 difficult. Let the pippages of the $\Delta\chi_1$ on the rectangle be $a_1, a_2, \ldots, a_{41}$ and let any other pattern be put into correspondence with pippages which are the same as the a_i's at places where the wheels are the same and are $-a_i$ at places where they are different. We can then say that the wheel patterns are substantially equivalent if these two sets of pippages score positively against each other when scored on the wheel-sliding table. It can be shown (see Black File) that if the message is not too short this definition leads to a maximum value of y of about 432. This is the origin of the usual value of K, namely 216. A rival value for K is $\sqrt{N}$ (see **R3**, pp. 117, 118, **R4**, p. 38) and in any case K must be taken as a function of N in order to cope with key rectangles. As a rough judgement based on experience, $K = 1{\cdot}5\sqrt{N}$ seems fairly good. Observe that every zero scoring character contributes a factor of 2. This is exactly right because the character can be taken as a dot or a cross without affecting the double bulge, so the prior probability of the wheel patterns permitting the double bulge of x is 2×2^{-71} instead of 2^{-71}.

When a rectangle has a positive decibanage on significance test IV it is usually said to be p. 147 'significant'.

(f) Significance test for flags

When a flag is entered double (in the form of a square) and is crudely converged, the convergence differs from ordinary crude convergence in that it is one-sided instead of two-sided. That is to say the 'pattern' which is taken through the flag gives rise to another pattern which is written down on the same side of the flag. It is not necessarily possible to reach a complete convergence — it may be necessary to doubt some characters in order to avoid an oscillation of the pattern. For example consider

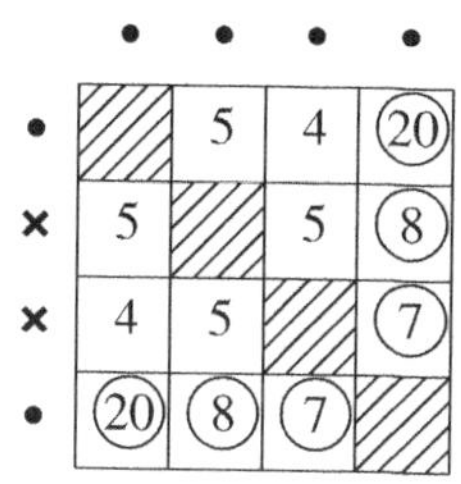

the flag shown in the diagram. The pattern inevitably oscillates between **••••** and **•××•** or else between **××××** and **×••×**. Observe that a pattern is equivalent to itself inside out just as in the case of an ordinary rectangle. If the effect of oscillation is ignored we may say that there are 2^{n-1} different possible patterns to choose between, so the prior probability of any particular pattern is 2^{-n+1}. The sum of the moduli of the pippages is still denoted by X, and the sigma-age of a convergence is $X/(2\sigma)$ where σ^2 = sum of square of entries in triangular flag. The presence of the factor 2 in the denominator is due to all the evidence being counted twice in virtue of the double-entering of the flag. The flag can be regarded as significant if the function $\psi(x/2\sigma)$ is greater than $3(n-1)$ decibans (where ψ is the function defined in chapter **21**). (See **R2**, p. 92, **R3**, p. 8.) This test is the analogue of significance test II for rectangles. It can be improved by making a mental allowance for ϑ terms (as in significance test IV). Thus every very small pippage of a character is worth 3 decibans.

This test assumes a flag to be a random collection of numbers and this assumption is not strictly true even if the rectangle from which it is derived is random.

It is rare that a 9 by 9 flag has a significant convergence except for a very significant rectangle
p. 148 (**R3**, p. 82). The main application of the test was to key flags (see Chapter **26**). For another form of significance test, based on Bayes' theorem, see **R3**, pp. 77, 79. This latter test was applied to 'flag rectangles' (**R3**, pp. 81, 85).

For a theory which connects the score and significance of a complete flag with those of its rectangle, see **R4**, p. 112, **R5**, pp. 17, 21, 90.

24Y OTHER THEORY OF RECTANGLES

(a) Length required to break wheels and rectangles other than 1+2

The message length required to break all the wheels is about the same as that required for a significant rectangle. Roughly, the score (or double bulge) x of the rectangle (assumed to be 1+2) must satisfy the inequality

$$\frac{2{\cdot}17x^2}{N}+30 > 219$$

a assuming the ϑ terms do not amount to more than 30 decibans,

$$\text{i.e. } x > 9{\cdot}4\sqrt{N}$$

i.e. since the score on correct wheels is approximately $x-\sqrt{N}$

$$\delta N+\sqrt{N} > 9{\cdot}4\sqrt{N}$$

$$\text{or } N > \frac{71}{82} \text{ or } N > \frac{71}{\beta^2\pi_{12}^2}.$$

E.25 Observe how sensitive the minimum value of N is to the value of d. The conclusion that the minimum text length required was proportional to $(\beta^2\pi^2)^{-1}$ was reached by an entirely different method in **R1**, pp. 51, 53. With $d=21$ and $\pi=\cdot2$ the minimum N is about 11,000; with $d=28$, $\pi=\cdot2$ the minimum is about 3000.

For a 4+5 rectangle the condition would be roughly

$$\frac{2{\cdot}17x^2}{N}+20 > 149$$

$$\therefore \quad \delta N+\frac{1}{2}\sqrt{N} > 7{\cdot}8N \qquad \left(x \risingdotseq \delta N+\frac{1}{2}\sqrt{N} : \text{see } \mathbf{R3}\text{, p. 117}\right)$$

$$\text{i.e. } N > \frac{53}{\beta^2}\pi_{45}^2.$$

---

[a] decibans.

Incidentally this shows that a 4+5 rectangle would probably be just significant on a shorter text than a 1+2 rectangle if E.26

$$\left(\frac{\pi_{45}}{\pi_{12}}\right)^2 > \frac{53}{71} \text{ i.e. } \pi_{45} > \cdot 86\pi_{12}.$$

This condition was seldom likely to be satisfied and 4+5 rectangles were seldom made. The condition for a 4+5 rectangle to be more decibans up than a 1+2 rectangle is not the same (see **R2**, p. 82).

It was thought at first that the 4+5 rectangle would be better, especially allowing for the greater time taken to make a 1+2 rectangle (**R1**, pp. 35, 36). A 2+5 and a 4+5 rectangle could both be made, so as to obtain independent evidence for χ_5 (**R1**, p. 48). In this case one would naturally have a 1+2 rectangle also, but it was decided that the extra trouble was not compensated for by the slightly increased power. For references to 3+4**x** rectangles see **R3**, p. 7. p. 149

For a 'pseudo 2+5 rectangle' see **R3**, pp. 81, 86. The method may be suitable for the case of $\overline{\chi}_2$ and $\overline{\overline{P}}_5$ limitations, but limited statistics tended to show that an ordinary 2+5 rectangle would be better. Another idea that was put forward was a Δ^2 rectangle or a 2-impulse bigram rectangle. This also was not encouraged by the statistics. (**R3**, pp. 44, 52, 58.) a

(b) Rectangles with χ_2 limitation

As early as **R1**, p. 59 it was thought that the χ_2 limitation might have a characteristic effect on rectangles. On p. 62, **R1** there was a reference to a suggestion for a 'repeats' rectangle in which ••, •**x**, **x**• and **xx** would be treated separately. This makes sense for χ_2 limitation but not for other limitations (see **R2**, p. 96).

The difference $x - x^*$ between the score of a converged rectangle and the score on the correct wheels tends to be greater when the limitation is χ_2.

Methods for diagnosing χ_2 limitation from a converged rectangle were suggested and discussed in **R3**, pp. 59, 101, 119, 122, 123, 126, 128, **R4**, pp. 31, 35, 38. More to the point is a note in **R4**, p. 71 (see also **R4**, p. 80, **R5**, p. 38). It is pointed out here that a 4 l.c. provides evidence about the limitation and that this is so even if a complete χ_2 is assumed, because it will tend to be wrong at $\overline{\chi}_2$ dots rather than crosses.

(c) Wheel-sliding

In the very early unsuccessful attempts on Jellyfish the following method was used. Several rectangles of messages on the same month were accurately converged. Then the relative positions of say χ_2 were looked for by sliding the pippages from one rectangle against those of another. The crudest method of wheel-sliding is to express the wheels in dots, crosses and doubts and to insist on an excess of say 6 or more agreements than disagreements, or vice versa. (Remember that it would not usually be known whether the Δ wheels were relatively inside out.) The rival good positions can then be scored by a more accurate method. Before we had time to work out the correct wheel-sliding table a cruder method was used. This cruder method is to evaluate p. 150 i

$$\sum_i \frac{1}{2}\{1 \pm \text{sign}\, a_i \text{ sign}\, a_i'\} \min\left(|a_i|, |a_i'|\right)$$

where the lower sign is taken if the patterns $a_1, a_2, \ldots$ and $a_1', a_2', \ldots$ are assumed to be relatively the right way round. This method is easy to apply in practice and is a reasonable approximation (in a sense) to the accurate method which we now prove.

Denote the decibanage of a typical character of one wheel by x, so that its odds of being a dot are $o = 10^{x/10}$ and probability $p = o/(1+o)$ Let $p = \frac{1}{2}(1+\pi)$. Let the probability of having an x ii

[a] than

[i] Word 'method' handwritten.

[ii] Handwritten 'an' inserted with a caret.

in a cell of the first wheel be p_x if the character is a cross. Then the probability of having an x if the character is a dot is op_x. Denote by x', o', $p'_{x'}$ the corresponding functions for the second wheel. Then the probability of seeing an x opposite an x' if the relative position of the two wheels
i is correct and they are not relatively inside out, is

$$\frac{1}{2}(p_x p'_{x'} + op_x o' p'_{x'})$$

and if it is wrong

$$\frac{1}{2}p_x(1+o)\cdot\frac{1}{2}\,p'_{x'}(1+o').$$

Therefore the factor obtained from one pair of entries in favour of the slide being correct is

$$2\cdot\frac{1+oo'}{(1+o)(1+o')} = \frac{1}{2}(1+\pi\pi').$$

The factor obtained from the complete comparison is

$$\prod\left\{\frac{1}{2}(1+\pi\pi')\right\}.$$

In order that this formula should not be misleading, it is necessary to allow for competition, because the correct wheel may have very good slides against itself. A table exists for accurate
a wheel-sliding with pip value $2/3$ deciban (see **R1**, p. 97).

(d) Setting two messages in depth on Chi 1 and Chi 2

Closely related to significance test 0 is the problem of attempting to set two messages in depth
b on chi 1 and chi 2 before either rectangle is converged: (**R1**, p. 75; **R3**, pp. 28, 35). In order to show how close the relationship is, the problem can be attacked in the following way. Let
p. 151 each of the 1271 different relative settings of chi 1 and chi 2 be tried out. For each of these let significance test 0 be applied. Let θ, θ' denote typical entries in the separate rectangles, then the expression considered is $\Sigma(\theta+\theta')^2$. This is equal to $\Sigma\theta^2 + \Sigma\theta'^2 + 2\Sigma\theta\theta'$. The first two terms are independent of the particular selection amongst the 1271 theories. Thus the method is equivalent to scalar multiplication. If the lengths of the messages are $1271k$ and $1271k'$ with
c P.B. of ΔD_{12} = dot of δ and δ', then the proportional bulge of ΔZ_{12} and $\Delta Z'_{12}$, in a particular cell, is $\delta\delta'$ if the rectangles are correctly set relatively. The number of comparison is $1271kk'$ so the expected sigma-age is $\delta\delta'\sqrt{1271kk'}$. In order that this should exceed 3 it is necessary that either $\delta\sqrt{1271k}$ or $\delta'\sqrt{1271k'}$ should exceed 10. Thus it is impossible for two rectangles to be set by Significance Test *0* (i.e. when unconverged), unless at least one of them would be significant according to Significance Test *IV* (i.e. when converged). The sum may nevertheless, of course, be significant according to Significance Test IV, but 1271 separate convergences are impracticable. This scalar product method is an approximation to the theoretically correct method of comparing the two rectangles by means of the wheel-sliding table treating them as wheels 1271 long. (**R3**, 35.)

---

[a] (See **R1**, 97) [b] (**R1**,75;**R3**,28,35) [c] proportionate

[i] Words 'and they ... is' handwritten.

25 CHI-BREAKING FROM CIPHER p. 152

This chapter describes all aspects of chi-breaking from cipher except the details of rectangles and flags (**24**). The special case of chi-breaking from key is treated separately (**26**).

25A THE SHORT WHEEL-BREAKING RUN

(a) General description

The basic method is the short (i.e. one-wheel) wheel-breaking run which consists essentially of choosing each character of a wheel to make the ΔD letter count, against that character, as good as possible.

Suppose for example that $\chi_1, \chi_2, \chi_3, \chi_4$, are known: then ΔD_1 ($= \Delta Z_1 + \Delta\chi_1$), ΔD_2, ΔD_3, ΔD_4 can be found.

$\Delta D_1, \Delta D_2, \Delta D_3, \Delta D_4, \Delta Z_5$ (a partial de-chi) represented at each place by a single letter, may be written out in widths of 23 so that all entries in a column are against the same character of $\Delta\chi_5$.

Itis expected that in ΔD /'s will be more numerous than T's. Suppose that in the first column of the partial de-chi there are 6 /'s and 10 T's: then if the first character of $\Delta\chi_5$ is a dot the contribution to ΔD is 6 /'s and 10 T's; but if the first character of $\Delta\chi_5$ is a cross the contribution to ΔD is 10 /'s and 6 T's wherefore the character is more likely to be a cross than a dot. p. 153, a

Each character of $\Delta\chi_5$ can thus be estimated, though some may be doubtful because the numbers of /'s and T's in a column are too nearly equal. Similarly evidence is obtainable from other pairs of ΔD letters differing only in ΔD_5, e.g. it is expected that there will be more 5's than J's, more U's than Q's.

[a] numerous T's

[i] This chapter's analytical contents reproduces what is on the corresponding page of the *Report*, p. 152. The title for section **25D(c)** given here does not exactly match what is in the body of the chapter.

[ii] Blank line separating **25G** and **25W** not present in *Report*.

The method does not, of course, require that four χ's shall be known e.g. if only χ_1, χ_2 are known, $\Delta\chi_4$ may be found using the ΔD characteristic: 4=1=2 is commoner than 4≠1=2.

Nor does it require of a $\Delta\chi_i$, regarded as known, and used to find ΔD_i, that all its characters shall be known; places on Z against unknown ('doubted') $\Delta\chi$ characters are simply ignored.

The evidence for a particular character is derived only from places against that character; and, very crudely, the evidence for a dot may be described as 'excess of good letters over bad letters' measured in the first place as so many 'pips'.

Clearly refinements are needed. Even at random ΔD letters will not all be exactly equally numerous, so that it will be necessary to have a criterion to determine whether the bulges are significantly large; and, when they are, to have a method for evaluating the evidence with some precision (**25B**). Further, the evidence of a wheel-breaking run may conflict with known $\Delta\chi$ characteristics, and require adjustment.

A special instance of this is that wheels must have approximately equal numbers of dots and crosses: it might seem reasonable to take as dots and crosses not those characters where 'pippages' are positive and negative, but those whose 'pippages', having regard to sign, are above and below average. The two methods should however agree, just because wheels do contain approximately equal numbers of dots and crosses. Discrepancies are due to

p. 154 (1) $\overline{\chi}_2$ limitation phenomena

(2) Corruption represented by 9's

(3) Random variations.

These are the origins of the "R minus twice norm" controversy. (**R4**, pp. 44, 54, 73, 86.)

Before considering these necessary refinements, the adaptation of 'excess of good over bad' to Colossus counting will be described. The outlines of this are desirable for understanding the sequel.

(b) Adaptation to Colossus counting

To save Colossus time the excess (to revert to the earlier example) of /'s over T's is found from a single run, not by counting /'s and T's separately.

$$\begin{aligned}
x_i &= \text{pippage of evidence that } \Delta\chi_5^i \text{, the } i\text{th character of } \Delta\chi_5 \text{ is a dot} \\
&= \text{/'s against } \Delta\chi_5^i - \text{T's against } \Delta\chi_5^i \\
&= \left.\begin{array}{l} \text{/'s against } \Delta\chi_5^i + \text{T's against other characters} \\ \qquad\qquad - \text{T's against other characters} \\ \qquad\qquad - \text{T's against } \Delta\chi_5^i \end{array}\right\} \Delta\chi_5 \text{ supposed all dots} \\
&= (\text{ /'s against all characters, if } \Delta\chi_5^i \text{ is a dot, all other characters crosses}) \\
&\qquad - (\text{ /'s against all characters, if all are crosses}) \qquad\qquad (A1) \\
&= (\text{T's against all characters, if } \Delta\chi_5^i \text{ is a cross, all other characters dots}) \\
&\qquad - (\text{T's against all characters, if all are dots}). \qquad\qquad (A2)
\end{aligned}$$

i In either (A1) or (A2) the first term can be found on Colossus in one run, stepping chi 5; the second term (known as the NORM) can be found on Colossus as a single count without stepping.

The two descriptions (A1), (A2) are equivalent. Because it seems more natural to run for good letters, the theory, including the naming of runs, is in terms of the former.

Because it is better and easier to have strings of dots on Colossus than to have strings of crosses, the actual Colossus runs are those of the latter description.

a Thus it is said "Wheel-breaking runs are always run inside out on the impulse being run for".

[a] Wheelbreaking

[i] Displayed equations (A1) and (A2) marked, and in following two paragraphs referred to, as (A1) and (A2).

A simple check can be applied p. 155

$$\left.\begin{aligned}\sum_i x_i &= \sum_i \text{/'s against } \chi_5^i - \sum_i \text{T's against } \chi_5^i\\ &= \text{all /'s} - \text{all T's}\\ &= (\text{all /'s} + \text{all T's}) - 2(\text{all T's})\\ &= R - 2\text{ norm}\end{aligned}\right\}\ \Delta\chi_5 \text{ supposed all dots.}$$

R is easily measured, being independent of $\Delta\chi_5$. The check tests not only the Colossus readings, but, also the subtractions of the norm to find the x_i.

Counting T's in ΔD with each character of $\Delta\chi_5$ taken in turn to be a cross, all the others being dots, could be done, and in fact originally was done, by actually placing a cross in each position of the trigger in turn; but it is much easier to insert a cross in a fixed position (in practice the last) and allow the wheel to step.

The characters of the wheel are produced in reverse order: **(c)** shows in detail why this happens.

(c) Why the wheel is obtained backwards

In such a use of the Colossus wheel trigger it is necessary not to confuse the true wheel, which is of course fixed relative to the cipher, with the wheel trigger, which is deliberately stepped relative to the cipher.

Suppose that the setting of the true wheel relative to the cipher is i.[†] Consider firstly that particular position of the trigger in which its setting is also i (so that display and printer read i): true wheel and trigger now begin in the same place, thus: †

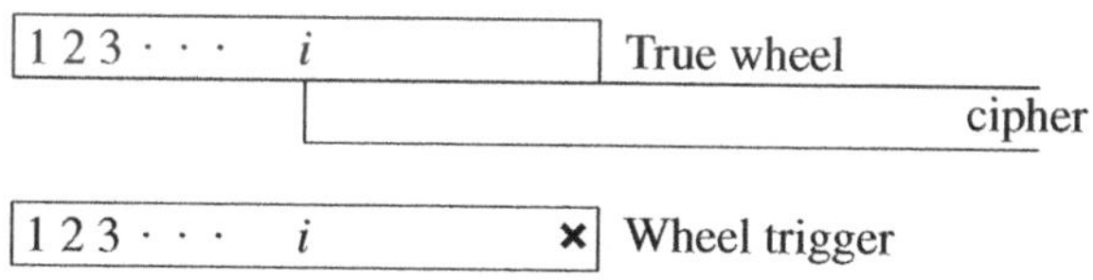

The score measured in any position is for that character of the true wheel which is against the cross in the wheel trigger; in this position the last character of the true wheel.

When the reading is $i+j$, the cipher, and therefore the true wheel also, has moved forward j places relative to the trigger, i.e. the trigger with its cross has moved backwards j places relative to the true wheel, and the score is that for the $w-j$th character of the wheel. p. 156

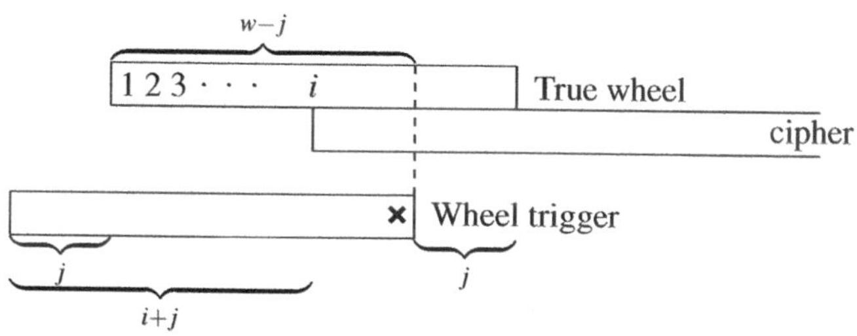

This argument depends only on relative settings and is not invalidated by the fact that deltaed wheels are set up on Colossus. Because Colossus deltas the cipher backwards, the settings recorded must be increased by one to obtain true settings, (**53E**). To avoid confusion, settings appropriate to deltaed wheels are used throughout wheel-breaking, and converted only when sending messages to Ops.

[†] i is not necessarily 01, for several messages may be used in a wheel-breaking job. The setting for the first message is naturally taken to be 01, though custom sanctions a curious inconsistency, viz. that for χ_1, χ_2 this refers to true settings; for χ_3, χ_4, χ_5, to Δ'd wheels set up on Colossus, whence the (Δ'd wheels) settings 41, 31, 01, 01, 01.

(d) Practical Procedure on Colossus

Count R the number of places looked at: i.e. /'s and T's.

Count Norm: i.e. /'s assuming that $\Delta\chi_5$ is all crosses, measured on Colossus as T's with $\Delta\chi_5$ all dots.

Both R and norm are unaffected by stepping χ_5, and as a check are each measured at least twice, whilst $\Delta\chi_5$ steps.

Reset to the correct message setting: insert a cross in the last position of the $\Delta\chi_5$ trigger, step $\Delta\chi_5$ and start.

The frequent changes in the trigger were originally effected by pushing pins into the back of Colossus, but finally all machines used seriously for wheel-breaking were equipped with a wheel-breaking panel, on which each has a three-way switch, the three switch positions being

(i) single cross in last position
(ii) all dots
(iii) patterns as set up on panel.

(Early wheel-breaking on Robinson see **R1**, pp. 51, 56, 86; On Colossus **R1** p. 96. Some suggestions not adopted **R2**, p. 84, **R4**, p. 26.)

25B WEIGHING THE EVIDENCE

(a) Significance test

p. 157 After a wheel-breaking run has been completed it is necessary to know whether it has any significance, and if so, to evaluate its evidence.

When no evidence other than that provided by the run itself is adduced, a condition for significance is

$$\frac{x}{\sqrt{R}} > 0{\cdot}8\sqrt{w} + 1{\cdot}2$$

[i] where R is the number of places looked at, w is the wheel length, x is the sum of the moduli of the scores x_i, i.e. the sum of the scores x_i ignoring their signs.

x is said to be the "score of the run on its own wheel", for if the run is so completely believed [ii] that each positive score is taken as a dot, and each negative score as a cross, the ΔD double bulge is the sum of the moduli.

The test is invariably used when making the initial runs for a new chi wheel.

The run is not necessarily a single run on Colossus, e.g. in attempting to obtain a $\Delta\chi_3$ knowing $\Delta\chi_1$, $\Delta\chi_2$ only, one can do all the runs,

$$3\bullet/1\bullet2\bullet,\ 3\times/1\times2\bullet,\ 3\times/1\times2\bullet,\ 3\bullet/1\bullet2\times$$

and find that all fail to satisfy the test, but that if the scores, for each character, of $3\bullet/1\bullet2\bullet$ and $3\times/1\times2\bullet$ are added, the resulting run $3{+}/1\bullet2\bullet$ is significant. It might otherwise be necessary to combine the three runs $3\bullet/1\bullet2\bullet$, $3\times/1\times2\bullet$, $3\times/1\times2\times$. Obviously the sum of the two runs will not be more significant unless there is some measure of agreement between them; and in fact it would be bad policy not to do the runs separately.

Note. It is not of course possible to add the x's of two runs to get the x of the combined run.

---

[i] The sequence of clauses starting 'where R...' are formatted in the *Report* as three separate displayed equations, without commas.

[ii] Words 'double bulge' handwritten, with 'bulge' inserted with a caret.

(b) Fundamental decibanning formula

The formula for calculating the evidence of a significant short wheel-breaking run is

$$\text{decibans per pip} = 10 \log_{10} \frac{R+x^*}{R-x^*}$$

where x^* is the ΔD score on the *correct* wheels (**25W(b)** and (**d**)). When the scores of two or more *independent* runs are expressed in decibans, they can be added directly.

(c) Decibanning a run on its own wheel

The score of a run on its own wheel, is generally greater than on the correct wheel, of para. (**b**) for wherever the score against an individual character has the wrong sign, and should diminish the total score, $\Delta\chi$ has its sign incorrectly adjusted, so that it actually increases the score. Accordingly p. 158
a table is used for the ratio

$$q = \frac{\text{expected score on the correct wheel}}{\text{score on the run's own wheel}}$$

so that decibans per pip $= 10 \log_{10} \dfrac{R+q^x}{R-q^x}$.

The table, whose construction is explained in **25X(e)**, is

$x/\sqrt{Rw}$	·798	·9	1·0	1·1	1·2	1·3	1·4	1·5	1·6	1·7	1·8	1·9	2·0	2·1
q	0	·57	·72	·82	·87	·91	·93	·95	·96	·97	·98	·98	·99	1·00

Crude decibanning is the result of taking $q = 1$.

A different rule is required for wheels obtained from a rectangle (**24X(e)**IV).

(d) Decibanning a run on the wheel from another run

Suppose, now, that a wheel has been obtained from a single run, say $\Delta\chi_3$ from /'s and that additional evidence is desired, say from 5's. The crude decibanning formula can be used, x being a
the score on the wheel obtained from /'s, for although this wheel is not necessarily the correct wheel, its wrong signs are unrelated to the scores for 5's, and there is no reason to suppose that the wrong signs will enhance the score. b

The same remark applies to runs on another message set on these wheels, even runs for the letters used, on the first message, to make the wheel.

Moreover it is unnecessary to apply a significance test, the significance of the original run being sufficient.

The statements in this paragraph are not strictly exact (**25W(f)**).

(e) Decibanning from a letter count

When a previous approximation to a wheel is available, the usual method of decibanning for the next runs is to make a letter count (4, 8, 16 or 32) on the previous approximation. This is compact and helps one to see beforehand which runs are likely to be worth while (allowance being made for general Fish characteristics): moreover runs having approximately the same decibanage c
per pip can be run together.

These runs, which may be numerous, will have contributed in varying degrees to the previous wheel. A table generalizing that in para. (**c**), would be unwieldy: moreover it would necessarily d, i
use only the evidence of such messages as were set on these wheels. In fact general Fish evidence e
cannot be ignored; for example very strong evidence would be required to justify running B's for p. 159
any $\Delta\chi$. This remark about B's assumes that B's really are B's and would be invalid if it were

[a] can be use [b] willenhance [c] fish characteristics [d] generalising [e] fish evidence

[i] Words 'in para (c)' handwritten.

not known which way round the wheels were (**25D(f)**); or if (e.g.) $\Delta\chi_2$ were very uncertain, B's (against D's) for $\Delta\chi_5$ would not be unreasonable, because many apparent B's would in fact be 5's.

It is accordingly necessary to use judgement in choosing and decibanning runs, ignoring
i improbable runs, 'knocking off something' from the crude decibanage of runs already used in making the wheel, and generally exercising discretion.

E.1 'Knocking off' is needed till the wheels are almost complete and correct, when the effect becomes negligible.

ii Note: in decibanning U's for χ_3, for example $\dfrac{R+x}{R-x}$ is simply $\dfrac{\text{number of U's}}{\text{number of A's}}$.

25C GENERAL PLAN OF WHEEL-BREAKING

(a) Typical description

A complete wheel is comparatively rarely obtained from a single wheel-breaking run. The sort of thing to expect is more like the following. A rectangle provides incomplete $\Delta\chi_1$, $\Delta\chi_2$
a wheels. Runs for $\Delta\chi_3$, $\Delta\chi_4$, $\Delta\chi_5$ are made, in an order depending on the particular Fish link, until a significant one is found, say 5=/1=2: this gives an incomplete $\Delta\chi_5$, using which 4=/1=2=5 is significant for $\Delta\chi_4$. A 16 letter count indicates the most suitable runs for improving $\Delta\chi_1$, $\Delta\chi_2$, $\Delta\chi_5$, $\Delta\chi_4$ all of which are used, a fresh letter count being made whenever a wheel changes considerably. It is now possible to obtain a significant run for $\Delta\chi_3$. A 32 letter count indicates suitable runs for strengthening $\Delta\chi_3$, and another count indicates runs for improving $\Delta\chi_1$, $\Delta\chi_2$, $\Delta\chi_5$, $\Delta\chi_4$, $\Delta\chi_3$ in turn (unless there are contradictions, it is preferable to treat wheels cyclically), and finally, perhaps after going round all wheels several times, and with the aid of methods yet to be described, all wheels are made certain.

(b) Wheel sheets

The whole process is unmanageable unless the results at each stage are recorded systematically. This is done on five appropriately headed wheel-sheets, each containing the runs for one chi wheel.

p. 160 For each run the following particulars are entered (horizontally: see exhibits).

Number of run (corresponding to that on the Colossus run sheet).

Number of messages used.

Wheels used (the various incomplete wheels are named systematically, $\Delta\chi_1 A$, $\Delta\chi_1 B$, $\Delta\chi_1 C$
E.2 e.g. on the chi 4 sheet. BB – – A means that $\Delta\chi_1 B$, $\Delta\chi_2 B$, $\Delta\chi_5 A$ were used, $\Delta\chi_3$ being as yet unknown).

Spanning, limitation, doubting, etc. (if needed).

The run used.

Decibans per pip, and/or a statement (simply PIPS) that results are entered in pips.

The score for each character (in pips or decibans).

$$\left.\begin{array}{c} R \\ x \\ x/\sqrt{R} \\ q \end{array}\right\} \text{generally omitted when the wheels are complete enough to use letter counts for decibanning.}$$

Other particulars are recorded in a log book (cf. **R4**, p. 19).

---

[a] fish link

[i] Handwritten 'crude' inserted with a caret.

[ii] Sentence beginning 'Note . . . ' handwritten.

(c) Choosing wheel-breaking runs

In setting, the break-in is usually followed by another two-wheel run. In breaking, the rectangle is NOT usually followed by another two-wheel run, i.e. a conditional rectangle, because of the time required: the neglect of conditional rectangles has perhaps been excessive. (See **24F**.)

It is very easy to see that the conditions for the success of a given short run in setting and breaking are similar but not identical, for the criterion in setting is sigma-age.

The sigma-age of a wheel-breaking run on its own wheel is $x/\sqrt{R}$.

$$\text{Significance depends on } \frac{x/\sqrt{R}}{0{\cdot}8\sqrt{w}+1{\cdot}2}.$$

$$\text{Decibanage per pip depends on } \frac{x/\sqrt{R}}{\sqrt{w}}.$$

The average number of pips per character is x/w.

Evidently, when there is a choice of the wheel to be run for, a weaker run for a shorter wheel may be preferable.

Because of different decibanages per pip, and the possibility that one of the component runs may be very weak there is rather more advantage than when setting in keeping runs separate e.g. a
5•1•2• and 5×1×2× rather than 5=1=2. If the two runs can profitably be added this is evident to the eye. (**R2**, p. 14, but see **R2**, p. 62.)

Once a wheel is obtained, runs to improve it are chosen with the aid of the letter count. p. 161

At all stages, resourcefulness and experience are needed to deal with abnormal cases.

(d) Some particular runs

Wheel-breaking almost always starts from $\Delta\chi_1$, $\Delta\chi_2$: even if it starts from $\widehat{\chi}_2$, the second wheel obtained is usually $\Delta\chi_1$.

The short runs then available are

3•/1•2•	3×/1×2•	3×/1×2×	3•/1•2×
4•/1•2•		4×/1×2×	
5•/1•2•		5×/1×2×.	

i

The remaining four theoretically possible runs are generally useless.

On a particular link at a particular period some of these are better than others, but strong preferences, applied universally, seem difficult to justify, especially when, as ordinarily, the wheels may be inside out.

It is not unusual to do these runs more or less blindly till one of them is found to be significant.

The best run is generally the result of combining two of the above runs, thus obtaining 5=/1=2, b
4=/1=2, 3+/1•2• (or 3+/1•2× if the wheels are inside out); indeed if the rectangle is highly significant it may save time to run them thus combined.

If χ_4 or χ_5 is obtained first, the next run is 4=5=1=2 or 4+5•1×2×.

If χ_3 is obtained first, the next run is 4+/3×1×2×.

For the fifth wheel the best letters are as in setting: to attain significance it may be necessary to combine runs. (See **R3**, p. 131, **R5**, p. 106.)

---

[a] keeping run separate [b] containing two of the above

[i] In the *Report*, the second runs in each line are all vertically aligned. We have shifted the second runs in lines 2 and 3 for clarity.

(e) Two-wheel convergence

If all short wheel-breaking runs fail, a conditional rectangle, which is a 2-wheel wheel-breaking run, may be used.

Alternatively it is possible to use a two-wheel convergence i.e. an alternating sequence of short wheel-breaking runs involving two unknown wheels.

Suppose that a $\Delta\chi_1$ and $\Delta\chi_2$ have been obtained, and that although there is no significant run for $\Delta\chi_3$, a few characters can be guessed. With this rudimentary $\Delta\chi_3$ a short wheel-breaking run
p. 162 e.g. `5JUQ` may produce a $\Delta\chi_4$ wherewith a run, say `5JUQ03`, produces a new $\Delta\chi_3$, whence a new $\Delta\chi_4$ and so on.

Because the characters of both $\Delta\chi_3$ and $\Delta\chi_4$ are arbitrary the significance value of $x/\sqrt{R}$ is not 5·3 or 5·5 but approximately 8·4, as for a 3+4×/ rectangle (**24X**, **24Y**).

This is easily overlooked, because the individual runs are short.

In particular if the runs are 4+/3×1×2× and 3+/4×1×2×, the two wheel convergence is identical with the convergence of a 3+4×/1×2× conditional rectangle. Indeed every rectangle convergence is a two-wheel convergence, for, as is easily seen, "taking a wheel through a rectangle" is really a short wheel-breaking run. The only advantage of an actual rectangle, apart from the fact that computer time may be cheaper than Colossus time, is that it provides powerful methods, e.g. flagging, for starting the convergence. In a two wheel convergence a good start is often available from the high scoring characters of a not quite significant short run.

A popular run for two wheel convergence is 4=5=/1=2. The rectangle which fully corresponds to this is not an ordinary rectangle, but has four entries in each cell viz.

$$(\bullet\bullet)-(\times\bullet),\quad (\bullet\times)-(\times\times),\quad (\bullet\bullet)-(\bullet\times),\quad (\times\bullet)-(\times\times)$$

where, e.g. $(\bullet\times)$ means $\left.\begin{array}{l}\Delta Z_4 = \\ \Delta Z_5 \neq\end{array}\right\}\Delta D_1 = \Delta D_2$.

(**R5**, pp. 35, 95, 96 (but the method is of course much older).)

25D PARTICULAR METHODS

(a) Doubts

The use of incomplete wheels is unavoidable; indeed it is rarely wise to use any character, the evidence for which is less than 10 decibans. A character not assumed to be either dot or cross is said to be 'doubted': the evidence of letters of cipher against such characters is ignored ('running on doubted wheels'). This is effected on Colossus by means of the special pattern trigger of the wheel-breaking panel (formerly by means of trigger e′); the doubted characters are made crosses in the special pattern, and the condition imposed: special pattern = dot (or vice versa if the doubts are very numerous).

p. 163 Evidence using letters against doubted characters is obtainable from runs not involving the chi-wheel to which the doubts belong ('running against doubts'); and may be worth while; e.g. if chi 5 is heavily doubted 4=/5=1=2 against the known characters of $\Delta\chi_5$, and 4=/1=2 against the doubted characters of $\Delta\chi_5$ are independent, and the latter is likely to be useful.

N.B. It should NOT be decibanned from the letter count against known characters.

In difficult wheel-breaking this device is used extensively. (**R3**, pp. 13, 25.)

Doubting reduces the effective text: for example if one third of each of the four wheels is doubted, the remaining text is $(2/3)^4$, i.e. less than one fifth of the whole.

When deciding how many characters to doubt, it is necessary to judge between the conflicting considerations of not losing too much text, and of not including too many wrong characters. 10 decibans is usually reasonable evidence for inclusion.

(b) Setting other messages (on Colossus)

That the evidence from a single message should suffice to make all wheels complete and certain is exceptional, but it will commonly make them sufficiently complete to set other messages, the addition of whose evidence, which is independent, will suffice. The addition of so much independent evidence is most effective; but rather prosaic, and apt to be unjustly neglected in favour of 'squeezing' a single message.

When there are more than a very few doubts, setting is complicated by 'variable R' e.g. if χ_3 is being set by means of $3\mathbf{x}/1\mathbf{x}2\bullet$, χ_1, χ_2 are fixed in the cipher, whilst χ_3 is tried in all possible 29 positions. Of the places where $1\mathbf{x}2\bullet$, the only ones looked at are those where $\Delta\chi_3$ is known and this may vary considerably when χ_3 steps. Thus a large $3\mathbf{x}1\mathbf{x}2\bullet$ may be due to a large $1\mathbf{x}2\bullet$, which is not relevant to setting χ_3.

This is commonly circumvented by printing R, i.e. $(1\mathbf{x}2\bullet)$ and the score, $(3\mathbf{x}1\mathbf{x}2\bullet)$, for all positions of χ_3, afterwards finding the sigma-age $\frac{x-R/2}{\frac{1}{2}\sqrt{R}}$ for promising scores. a

A preferred modification which reduces useless printing is to run simultaneously on two counters: $3\mathbf{x}/1\mathbf{x}2\bullet$ with a high set total; $3\bullet/1\mathbf{x}2\bullet$ with a low set total, (with SIP if available). If the bulge of $3\mathbf{x}/1\mathbf{x}2\bullet$ over $3\bullet/1\mathbf{x}2\bullet$ is significant, one score or the other must be printed. To consider only scores too large to be explained by random variations in R[†] throws away evidence, p. 164, † for in fact R can be found at each setting; but in long subsequent runs such as 4=5=/1=2 it may be necessary to consider only scores which are reasonably good on this basis. In a break-in run, as a little consideration will show, the variation of R is usually negligible.

When two messages have each produced a wheel (generally from a rectangle, or especially, $\widehat{\chi}_2$) these can be set by a direct comparison of the (incomplete) wheels. See **24Y(c) R1**, pp. 53, 76, 79, 83, 97; **R2**, p. 29. For application of corrected excess to wrongly set messages (never used) **R3**, p. 91.

(c) Spanning for message slides

This is particularly important in wheel-breaking: as soon as the rectangle message is on Colossus the 1+2/ score is checked and spanned. If a message slide is found, the remainder of the message is set by slide runs (**23F(d)**) after which the tape may be doctored so that its parts are in the correct relative position.

Every supporting message set should at once be spanned and possibly doctored.

Doctoring requires only the removal or insertion of sprocket holes. A hole is quickly removed by covering it with opaque paper. Inserting a hole is done by copying and takes time; meanwhile wheel-breaking should proceed on a slide-free portion: if this portion is most of the message, doctoring may be not worth while.

Note. To decide whether to remove or insert a hole imagine that each place on the tape is marked with the corresponding position of (say) chi 1

04	05	06	07	08	09	10	setting before slide 04
06	07	08	09	10	11	12	setting before slide 06

slide here

07, 08 are missing, wherefore two holes must be *inserted.*

[†]The standard deviation for this is $\sqrt{Np(1-p)q(1-q)}$, for the meaning of which **21(n)**; **R4**, p. 4, 11, 12, 17.

[a] sigmaa-age

(d) Spanning for changes in ΔP characteristics

The character of P and hence of ΔP may change considerably during the same ‘message’ (meaning transmission or QEP), for it may contain several messages, possibly from different
a originators; hand passages, tables of figures, lists of names, etc. will have abnormal characteristics.
p. 165 It may well happen for example, that in one part of a message 8’s are more numerous than 5’s, whilst in the rest 5’s are more numerous than 8’s. Evidently more evidence is obtained by
b spanning the parts separately. This however takes twice the time and is not done unless there is difficulty in completing the wheels, or in making them certain. (**R5**, p. 11.)

(e) Wheel characteristics

Restrictions on permissible chi wheels have been mentioned (**11C**). Wheels which conform
E.3 are said to be legal. Any deltaed wheels must have an even number of crosses, and for legality both Δ’d and un-Δ’d wheels must have, as nearly as possible, equal numbers of dots and crosses. For the five wheels the number of crosses is:

Δ	20	16	14	12 or 14	12
un-Δ	20 or 21	15 or 16	14 or 15	13	11 or 12

The final form of legality forbade more than four consecutive like characters in the un-Δ wheel, i.e. more than three consecutive dots in the Δ’d wheel.

If most characters are certain on the evidence from wheel-breaking runs, the requirement of legality may suffice to complete the wheels: various tricks have been devised for doing this easily.

$\Delta\chi_5$	•	×	•	×	•	×	•	•	×	•	$\underline{\bullet}$	×	•	×	$\underline{\times}$	×	×	•	•	×	$\underline{\times}$	×	•

is legal because (i) it has 12 crosses

(ii) if the 12 crosses are paired as indicated there are 6 dots inside the pairs, as nearly as possible half the 11 dots.

E.4 Integrating,

$\Delta\chi_5$	•	×	•	×	•	×	•	•	×	$\underline{\bullet}$	•	×	•	×	$\underline{\times}$	×	×	•	•	×	$\underline{\times}$	×	•	
χ_5	•	•	×	×	•	•	×	×	×	•	•	•	×	×	•	×	•	×	×	×	•	×	•	12 crosses.

The underlining of three characters indicates, conventionally, that they are doubtful; the first and second of these cannot be interchanged, for if they were, the characters of chi 5 between them would be changed in sign, increasing the number of crosses to 13. Similarly the first and third of these *can* be interchanged.

At an early stage in wheel-breaking it may be justifiable to accept rather weak scoring characters which interrupt what would otherwise be long strings of dots. Of course until it is
c, p. 166 known which way round (**25D(f)**) the wheels are, these may be really long strings of crosses.
E.5 There are other less definite characteristics. With the aid of Freeborn counts, a table has been constructed for decibanning their evidence, but most wheel-breakers prefer to use their judgement. (**R3**, pp. 125, 133.)

Even three consecutive dots is some evidence against a Δ’d wheel. There is a tendency to favour a pattern of alternate dots and crosses in the Δ’d wheels. In the extreme case when there is only one break in the alternating pattern, the wheel is said to be perfect. A guess that the wheels of

[a] list of [b] take [c] **25D(F)**

a non-significant rectangle are perfect has been known to succeed. Perfect wheels can be tiresome because the numerous wheel slides make it difficult to set messages: fortunately a slide setting a
will suffice for chi-breaking except when running for the perfect wheel.

In the early days the rules of legality were apparently less stringent: un-Δ wheels with the wrong number of crosses are known.

(f) Inside out

The 1+2/ rectangle is based on $\Delta Z_1 + \Delta Z_2 + \Delta\chi_1 + \Delta\chi_2 = \bullet$ which is unchanged if, in both $\Delta\chi_1$ and $\Delta\chi_2$, dot and cross are interchanged: the wheels are then said to be inside out.

Wheel characteristics often determine unambiguously whether wheels are inside out or not; b
e.g. $\Delta\chi_1$ is inside out if it has 21 crosses or 4 consecutive dots.

Otherwise the problem may be tiresome and it is not impossible to have considerable $\Delta\chi_1$, $\Delta\chi_2$, $\Delta\chi_3$, $\Delta\chi_4$ wheels and yet remain uncertain; but generally the 16-letter count will solve it: `U`'s and `A`'s, for example, should be more numerous than `O`'s and `M`'s. In practice it can safely be assumed that these four wheels are not relatively inside out.

When there is a 32-letter count, it should be conclusive though it is possible to be momentarily puzzled by a $\Delta\chi_3$ which is inside out relative to the other wheels.

(g) Flogging

Statistical methods cannot achieve certainty: the standard of 'certainty' is taken to be that no character of a wheel can be changed legally without losing 40 decibans (formerly 50 decibans), i.e. the odds are 10,000 to 1. The ostensible rule that each character must score 20 decibans is ignored, though of course a wheel-breaker would not trust to wheel characteristics if there were p. 167
many weak characters.

The following paragraphs enumerate methods which can be used in difficult cases to make wheels complete and certain.

1. Set all messages, with flogging.
2. Make sure that all wheel-breaking runs for each chi not yet certain have been done using the latest wheels for the other four chis, and that the decibanning is on the basis of these wheels: if the wheels are nearly correct, crude decibanning is permissible.
3. Do a 32-letter count against each doubtful character, and deciban it on the 32-letter count for the whole wheel. This is equivalent to doing every possible short wheel-breaking run separately, but saves time by considering only uncertain characters. It is done easily on Colossus by putting a single pin in the special pattern trigger, and plugging special pattern = cross.
4. Span all messages, looking for slides (**25D(c)**) and changes in ΔP characteristics (**25D(d)**).
5. Make a temperate use of wheel characteristics.
6. Make a provisional de-chi on uncertain wheels for Room 41 where it can be treated by E.6
non-statistical methods. In an extreme case de-chi on four wheels only.
7. Span /'s on ΔD on a hundred letters immediately before each autopause with the faint c
hope that ΔZ is really Δ key, the P tape of the German Tunny machine having broken. (**R5**, d
pp. 70, 80.)
8. In one instance wheel-breaking was completed because there was a crib into a message already set on four chis: the ordinary crib run failed because of a slide, but running $\Delta P_{1,2,4,5}$ against $\Delta D_{1,2,4,5}$, and looking for /'s in $\Delta\psi'_{1,2,4,5}$ succeeded.

---

[a] wheel-slides [b] unambigously [c] immedately [d] with faint hope

25E SPECIAL METHODS FOR $\overline{\chi}_2$ LIMITATION

(a) Running against $\overline{\chi}_2$ crosses

Because the bulges of runs against $\overline{\chi}_2 = \times$ are so much greater than against $\overline{\chi}_2 = \bullet$, these are made separately (as in setting), and indeed it is rarely worth while to do runs against $\overline{\chi}_2 = \bullet$, and
E.7 then only for good motor cross letters (**R3**, p. 101).

p. 168
(b) Runs for $\Delta\chi_2$ and $\overline{\chi}_2$

In a run for $\Delta\chi_2$ however, the scores for all characters of $\Delta\chi_2$ will appear, those where $\overline{\chi}_2 = \times$ scoring strongly, those where $\overline{\chi}_2 = \bullet$ weakly, so that the run provides two types of evidence:

(i) high and low scores indicate $\overline{\chi}_2 = \times$ and $\bullet$,

(ii) positive and negative scores indicate $\Delta\chi_2 = \bullet$ and $\times$, moreover the $\overline{\chi}_2$, and $\Delta\chi_2$ obtained by differencing, must be consistent.

Scores against $\overline{\chi}_2 = \times$ and $\overline{\chi}_2 = \bullet$ must be decibanned separately, the result of which is usually that scores against $\overline{\chi}_2 = \bullet$ are found to be negligible. Until a complete χ_2 can be found the best plan is to ignore all but strong characters.

[i] (c) Working out the limitation

It is often possible to find a complete or nearly complete χ_2 at an early stage, even straight from the rectangle. It is justifiable to assume $\overline{\chi}_2$ limitation if there are many high scores and many low scores for $\Delta\chi_2$ characters, but few moderate ones.

An easy example of this is:

Scores for part of $\Delta\chi_2$												
		⑨	㉗	12	⑤	⑮	㉚	①	㊶	36	–	2

E.8 It is reasonable to suppose that ㉗, ㉚, ㊶, 36, 51 are $\overline{\chi}_2$ crosses and here $\Delta\chi_2$ is reliable. It is reasonable to suppose that ⑨, ⑤, ①, – , ② are $\overline{\chi}_2$ dots, and here $\Delta\chi_2$ is uncertain.

$\Delta\chi_2$			•				•		•	×		
χ_2	•	×		•		×		×	×	•	•	

It will be seen that the differencing is always wrong so that $\Delta\chi_2$ must be inside out. For clarity the scores will be written with the signs changed.

		9	27	⑫	5	15	30	1	41	㊱	–	②
$\Delta\chi_2$			×				×		×	•		
χ_2	•	×		•		×		×	×	•	•	

Here differencing enables additional characters to be inserted.

$\Delta\chi_2$	×	•	×			×	×	•	×	•		
χ_2	•	×	×	•		×	•	×	×	•	•	

Because ⑫ is a $\overline{\chi}_2$ cross, it probably gives the right sign for $\Delta\chi_2$ whence

$\Delta\chi_2$	×	•	×	•	×	×	×	•	×	•		
χ_2	•	×	×	•	•	×	•	×	×	•	•	

[i] Section head surrounded in quotation marks: "Working out the limitation".

If such methods leave only a few doubts, wheel characteristics may solve them. p. 169

In marginal cases the difficulty is that the highest $\overline{\chi}_2$ dot scores and the lowest $\overline{\chi}_2$ cross scores may be confused, so that the evidence appears to be conflicting.

The same methods can be used when making chi 2 certain but moderately scoring characters can be tricky because the decibanage for a character depends on whether it is taken as a $\overline{\chi}_2$ cross [a] or a $\overline{\chi}_2$ dot. A more precise formulation is given in **R4**, p. 57 sqq. Whilst the wheel-breaker is cerebrating, all available runs should be done, for if each supposed $\overline{\chi}_2$ cross scores 40 decibans more than any supposed $\overline{\chi}_2$ dot, even when the latter is decibanned as though it were a $\overline{\chi}_2$ cross, the wheel is certain. For decibanning **R3**, p. 42, **R4**, pp. 57, 104, **R5**, p. 65.

(d) The four-letter count

As in setting, (**23E(h)**) a 4-letter count for ΔD_1, ΔD_2 against $\overline{\chi}_2$ crosses, provides some evidence for the sort of ΔP to be expected. On the whole text there is no bulge of × × over • •, or vice versa (**22H(f)**), the bulge against $\overline{\chi}_2$ dots being equal and opposite to that against $\overline{\chi}_2$ crosses; but at an early stage in wheel-breaking, so many of the $\Delta\chi_2$ characters against $\overline{\chi}_2$ dots may be wrong that even on the whole text a significant bulge will appear. This will not occur with other limitations, and provides additional evidence that the limitation is $\overline{\chi}_2$.

(e) $\widehat{\chi}_2$

From a $\overline{\chi}_2$ limitation message, it is sometimes possible to break wheels without a rectangle. This depends on $\Delta\chi_2 + \overline{\chi}_2$, usually written $\widehat{\chi}_2$, (**22A(b)**, **22D(g)**), which has of course a definite value at each position of the chi 2 wheel.

Proportional bulge of $(\Delta Z_2 + \widehat{\chi}_2 = \bullet) = \beta\pi_{\times}$ where $\pi_{\times}$ is the P.B. of $\Delta P_2 = \times$. (**22H9**) E.9

So that if $\pi_{\times}$ is great enough $\widehat{\chi}_2$may be found from the short wheel-breaking run $\widehat{\chi}_2 + \Delta Z_2 = \times$, the condition for significance being as usual $x/\sqrt{R} > 5{\cdot}7$. (**R1**, p. 11, **R4**, pp. 70, 92, **R5**, p. 9.)

This run is made systematically on A-tapes (**33A(c)**) of links likely to use $\overline{\chi}_2$ limitation, both on the whole text; and also, in order to detect slides, on thirds. Corruption 9's spuriously enhance the score, so that NOT 99 must be used.

(f) Runs to follow $\widehat{\chi}_2$ p. 170

Unfortunately it commonly happens that although the $\widehat{\chi}_2$run is genuinely significant it is impossible to proceed further.

The strongest run to follow $\widehat{\chi}_2$ is usually (**R5**, pp. 8, 11, 17, 28; **25Y4**) $\Delta\chi_1 + /\Delta Z_1 + \Delta Z_2 +$ E.10
$\widehat{\chi}_2 = \bullet$ whose proportional bulge is

$$\beta(1-\beta)\frac{\pi_{\bullet\bullet} + \pi_{\times\times}}{2}.$$

The ratio of this to the proportional bulge of $\widehat{\chi}_2$ is

$$(1-\beta)\frac{\pi_{\bullet\bullet} + \pi_{\times\times}}{2\pi_{\times}}$$

which is often considerably less than unity (**R5**, p. 108).

Statistics (**R5**, pp. 98, 105, 106) show that wheel-breaking from a $\widehat{\chi}_2$ start rarely succeeds unless $x/\sqrt{R} > 7$.

Having a significant $\widehat{\chi}_2$ the best policy seems to be to set all available messages on $\widehat{\chi}_2$ (a one-wheel run), not forgetting to span for message slides, strengthening $\widehat{\chi}_2$, and then trying the wheel-breaking run $\Delta\chi_1 + /\Delta Z_1 + \Delta Z_2 + \widehat{\chi}_2 = \bullet$ on each message set. When a $\Delta\chi_1$ is obtained the next run 2+/1 is $\Delta\chi_2 + \Delta Z_2 + \Delta\chi_1 + \Delta\chi_2 = \bullet$ after which ordinary runs are possible.

---

[a] decibannage

It is sometimes possible to integrate $\widehat{\chi}_2$ i.e. to find χ_2 directly from $\widehat{\chi}_2$, either as a whole, if $\widehat{\chi}_2$ is nearly complete, otherwise in stretches: in the latter case the ambiguities are apt to make the method of doubtful value. (See also **26**.)

It is believed that Jellyfish 4/3/45, broken on $\widehat{\chi}_2$, could not have been broken otherwise, (**R5**, p. 52) but ordinarily the advantage of $\widehat{\chi}_2$ over a rectangle is speed. $\widehat{\chi}_2$ is perhaps most useful as an ancillary method, detecting slides in rectangles, setting rectangles on χ_2, providing a start for convergence, strengthening marginally significant rectangles, acting as a check on dubious characters in χ_2, ($\overline{\chi}_2, \Delta\chi_2$ must satisfy $\overline{\chi}_2 + \Delta\chi_2 = \widehat{\chi}_2$).

(g) Excess of dot or cross in $\widehat{\chi}_2$

The number of dots and crosses in $\widehat{\chi}_2$ may be very far from equal: if the proportional bulge of dots is θ, then $\Delta Z_2 = \bullet$, which can be counted in one operation, has a proportional bulge $\theta\beta\pi_{\times}$
E.11 (**25Y1**): this has been suggested as a significance test; but it is really more profitable to do $\widehat{\chi}_2$ properly, for it takes very little time.

(h) $\overline{\chi}_2 + \overline{\overline{P}}_5$ limitation

p. 171 Because P_5 tends to be dot, this exhibits weakly the characteristics of $\overline{\chi}_2$ limitation; but insufficiently to do more than justify separate decibanning against $\overline{\chi}_2$ cross and $\overline{\chi}_2$ dot, both being used. The ΔD letter 5 is peculiar in scoring better against $\overline{\chi}_2$ dot than against $\overline{\chi}_2$ cross. (**22E(d)**.) (**R3**, pp. 10, 39.)

25F SPECIAL METHOD FOR $ab \neq 1/2$

i
$$\text{P.B.}(\Delta D_i = \bullet) = \text{P.B.}(\Delta\psi_i' + \Delta P_i = \bullet)$$
$$= \beta_i'\pi_i$$

where β_i' is the proportional bulge of $\Delta\psi' = \bullet$, so that if $ab \neq 1/2$, single wheel initial χ-breaking runs are possible.

The resultant wheel is of course a true $\Delta\chi$ wheel and not a horrid hybrid like $\widehat{\chi}_2$.

The rule $ab = 1/2$ was introduced in March 1942. In one later instance the limitation on a machine used by the Stickleback link became inoperative; this in effect doubled the motor dottage, making $ab \neq \frac{1}{2}$ and $\beta_i' = \beta$.

p. 172 25G WHEEL-BREAKING EXHIBITS

These consist of the wheel-sheets and most of the Colossus sheets of Mullet 25/4; and some miscellaneous exhibits. Mullet 25/4 is rather easier and more straight-forward than the average wheel-breaking job. The margins of Colossus sheets have been drastically reduced.

E.12 **(a) The rectangle** (ch **24**)

This was evidently a Garbo rectangle (**24B(c)**), but the Garbage is not preserved. At bottom right is the 9×9 flag and its convergence, used as a start for converging the rectangle (**24D(c)**). When converged the rectangle is easily significant; the 1+2 double bulge is 758 (or 759), 615
a being sufficient according to the crude computery test; the leading term of significance test IV (**24E(d)**) is 258, so that it is unnecessary to calculate the ϑ terms. Raw means made from a raw tape. (**33B**)

(b) Checks on Colossus

The rectangle wheels, $\Delta\chi_1\ \Delta\chi_2$ with low-scoring characters doubted (**25D(a)**), are set up on
b, ii Colossus (wheels AA – – –, figs. **25 (II)**, **(III)**) and the score is checked: doubting reduces the double bulge to 705. The message is spanned (run ①) in 200's for possible message slides: none is found. The two readings in each pair are 1+2=•, 1+2=**×**.

---

[a] text [b] Figs II, III

[i] Throughout **25** the notation PB is used instead of P.B. in formulae.
[ii] Figs. **25 (I)–(IX)** appear at the end of **25G**, pp. 166–178 in this edition.

(c) Initial runs for $\Delta\chi_5$, $\Delta\chi_4$

The first short run is C2, 5=/1=2. It is just significant (**25B(a)**): $x/\sqrt{R} = 5{\cdot}1$. Note the check $\sum x_i = r - 2 \times$ norm with a discrepancy of 2. The pencilled figures are the pippages (**25A**) for the various characters, i.e. score minus norm. The wheel $\Delta\chi_5 A$, heavily doubted, is set up (fig. **VI**). A bold run, 4=/5=1=2, for $\Delta\chi_4$ is comfortably significant producing wheel $\Delta\chi_4 A$. (Fig. **V**).

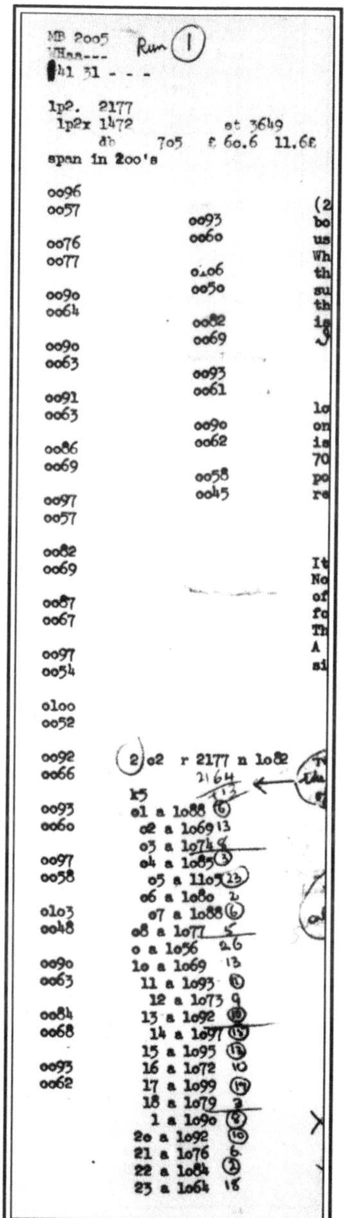

MB 2005 Run (1)
41 31 - - -
1p2. 2177
1p2x 1472 et 3649
db 705 £ 60.6 11.6£
span in 200's

0096 0057 0076 0077 0090 0064 0090 0063 0091 0063 0086 0069 0097 0057 0082 0069 0087 0067 0097 0054 0100 0052 0092 0066 0093 0060 0097 0058 0103 0048 0090 0063 0084 0068 0093 0062

0093 0060 0106 0050 0082 0069 0093 0061 0090 0062 0058 0045

(2) o2 r 2177 n 1082
2164
13
k5
o1 a 1088 ⑥
o2 a 1069 13
o3 a 1074 8
o4 a 1085 ③
o5 a 1105 ㉓
o6 a 1080 2
o7 a 1088 ⑥
o8 a 1077 5
o a 1056 26
1o a 1069 13
11 a 1093 ⑪
12 a 1073 9
13 a 1092 ⑩
14 a 1097 ⑮
15 a 1095 ⑬
16 a 1072 10
17 a 1099 ⑰
18 a 1079 3
1 a 1090 ⑧
2o a 1092 ⑩
21 a 1076 6
22 a 1084 ②
23 a 1064 18

25G/1: ×.55

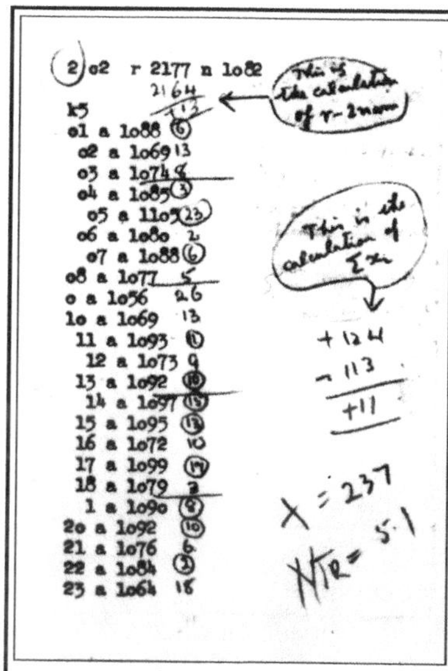

(2) o2 r 2177 n 1082
2164
13
k5
o1 a 1088 ⑥
o2 a 1069 13
o3 a 1074 8
o4 a 1085 ③
o5 a 1105 ㉓
o6 a 1080 2
o7 a 1088 ⑥
o8 a 1077 5
o a 1056 26
1o a 1069 13
11 a 1093 ⑪
12 a 1073 9
13 a 1092 ⑩
14 a 1097 ⑮
15 a 1095 ⑬
16 a 1072 10
17 a 1099 ⑰
18 a 1079 3
1 a 1090 ⑧
2o a 1092 ⑩
21 a 1076 6
22 a 1084 ②
23 a 1064 18

This is the calculation of r-2norm
This is the calculation of Σxi
+124
-113
+11
X = 237
X/√R = 5·1

25G/2: ×.55

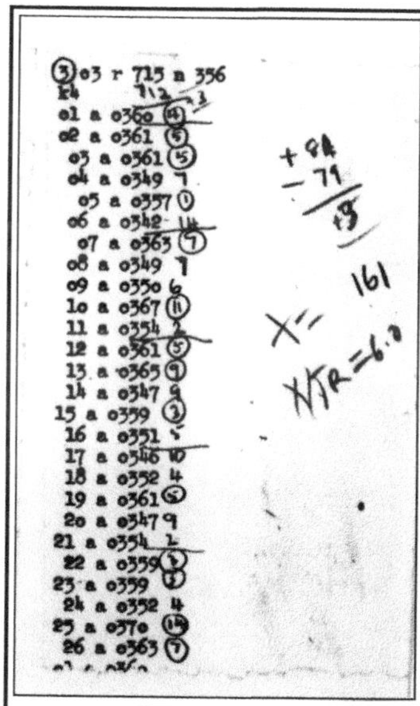

(3) o3 r 715 n 356
712
3
k4
o1 a 0360 ④
o2 a 0361 ⑤
o3 a 0361 ⑤
o4 a 0349 7
o5 a 0357 ①
o6 a 0342 14
o7 a 0363 ⑦
o8 a 0349 7
o9 a 0350 6
1o a 0367 ⑪
11 a 0354 2
12 a 0361 ⑤
13 a 0365 ⑨
14 a 0347 9
15 a 0359 ③
16 a 0351 5
17 a 0346 10
18 a 0352 4
19 a 0361 ⑤
2o a 0347 9
21 a 0354 2
22 a 0359 ③
23 a 0359 ③
24 a 0352 4
25 a 0370 ⑭
26 a 0363 ⑦

+94
-79
+15
X = 161
X/√R = 6·0

25G/3: ×.55

p. 173

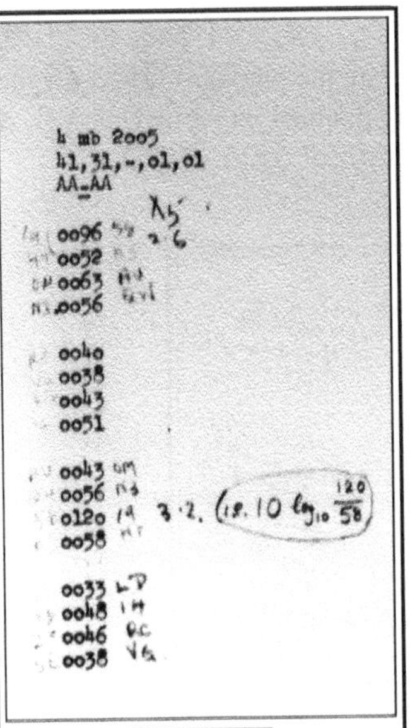

25G/4: ×.6

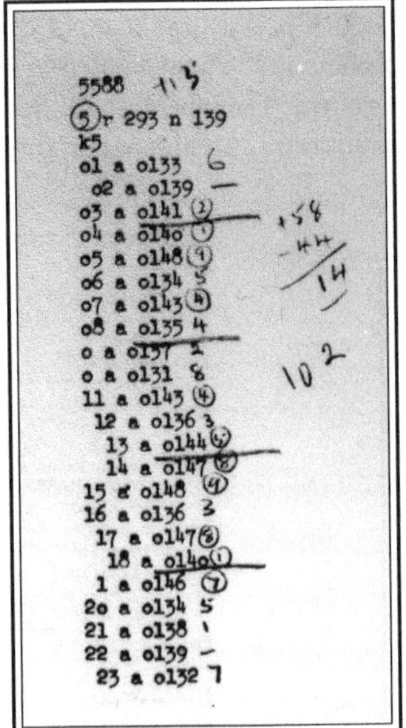

25G/5: ×.6

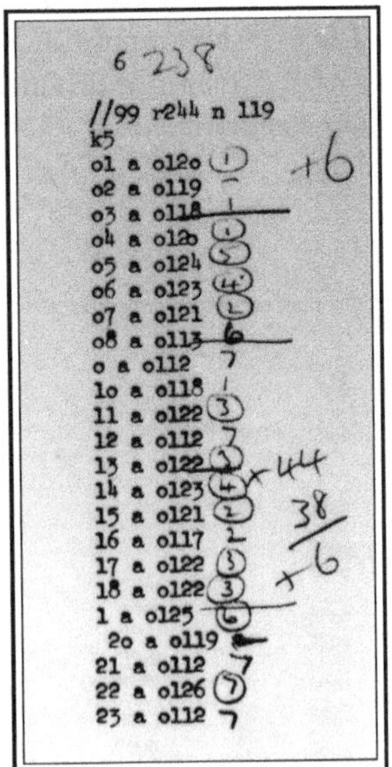

25G/6: ×.6

(d) Sixteen-letter counts

A 16-letter count is made on wheels AA–AA, primarily in order to choose and deciban runs to improve $\Delta\chi_5$ (**25B(d)**, **(e)**). Only /9 and 58 seem to be worth while. The pencilled letters at the right indicate a justifiable suspicion that the wheels are inside out (**25D(f)**); but it is decided that reversal would be premature.

Runs (5)(6) are entered in pips on the run sheets, but in decibans on the wheel sheet (fig. **VI**).

$\Delta\chi_5 B$ is a great improvement. A fourth 16-letter count is made before doing runs for $\Delta\chi_4$. The suspicion that the wheels are inside out grows.

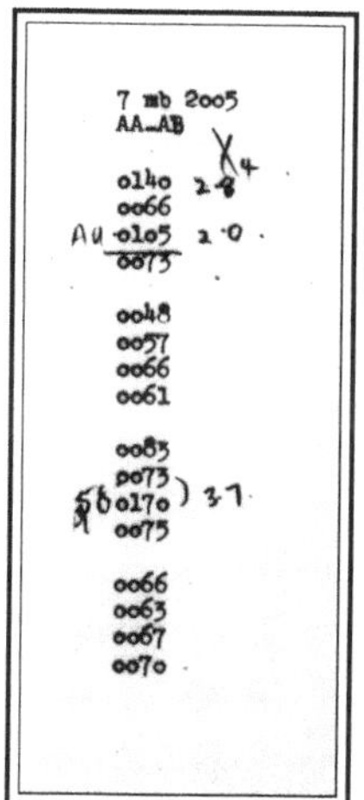
25G/7: ×.5

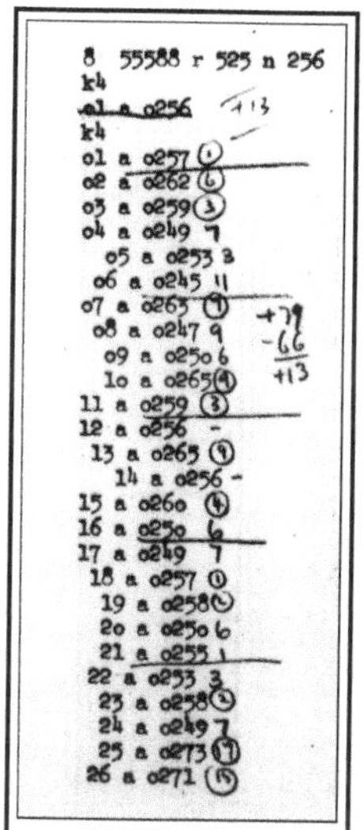
25G/8: ×.5

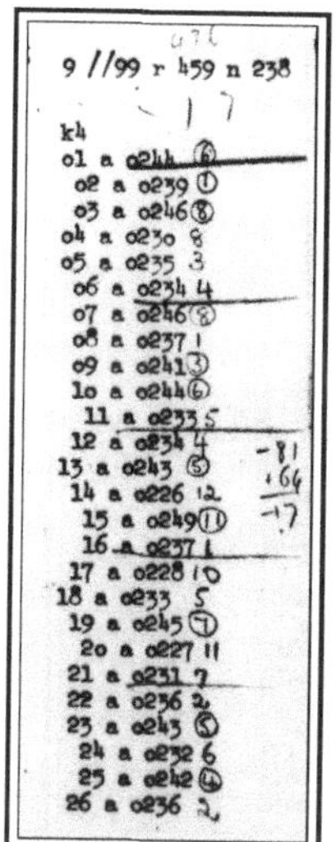
25G/9: ×.5

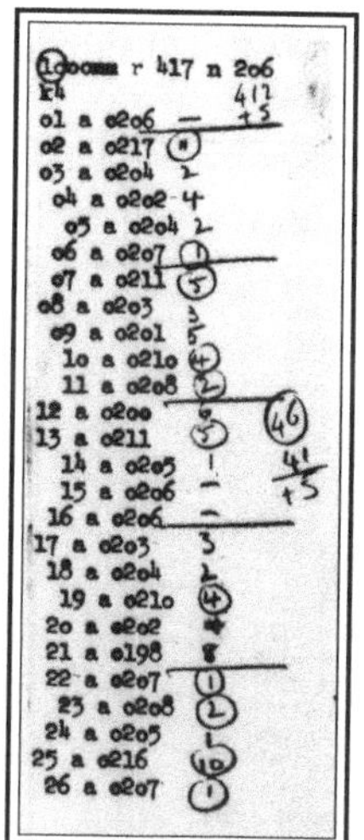
25G/10: ×.5

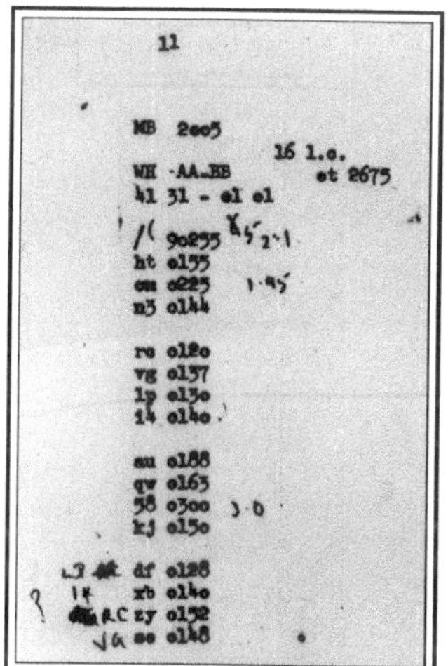
25G/11: ×.5

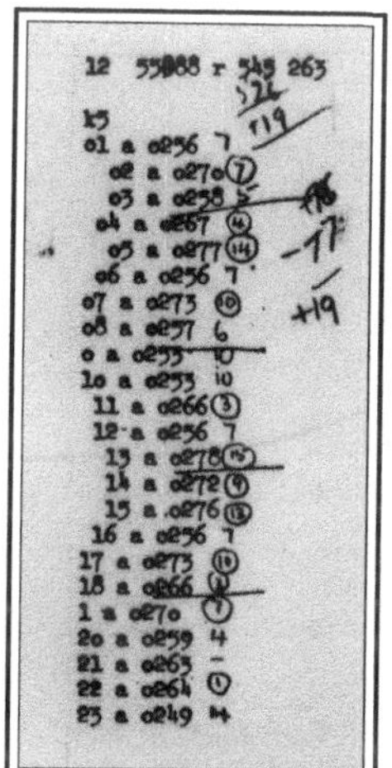
25G/12: ×.5

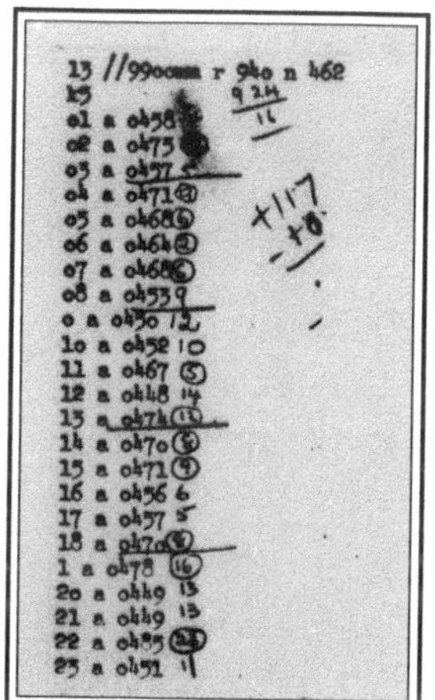
25G/13: ×.5

p. 174

(e) $\Delta\chi_5$ made certain

Run (11) is yet another 16-letter count, followed by runs (12)(13) for $\Delta\chi_5$ yielding a nameless wheel having 12 dots (instead of 11), the weakest character being 19 decibans up, so that in view of other evidence, reversal seems inevitable, and on this assumption $\Delta\chi_5 C$ is 47 decibans up and therefore "certain" (**25D(g)**). Characters 13, 18 cannot be interchanged (cf. **25D(c)**).

(f) Unsuccessful attempt to get a $\Delta\chi_3$

i Run (14) evidently made on reversed wheels.

ii

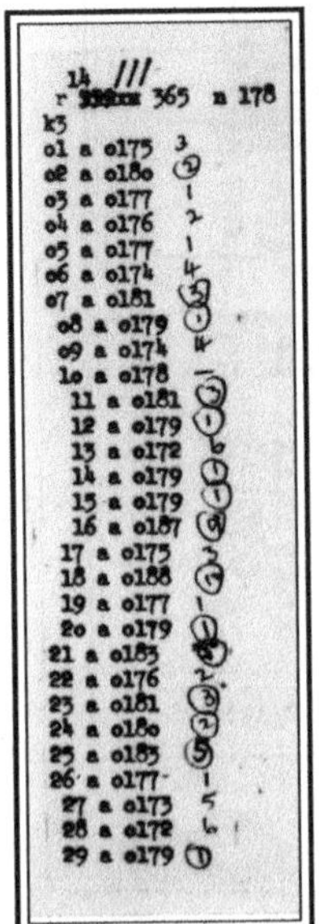

25G/14: ×.5

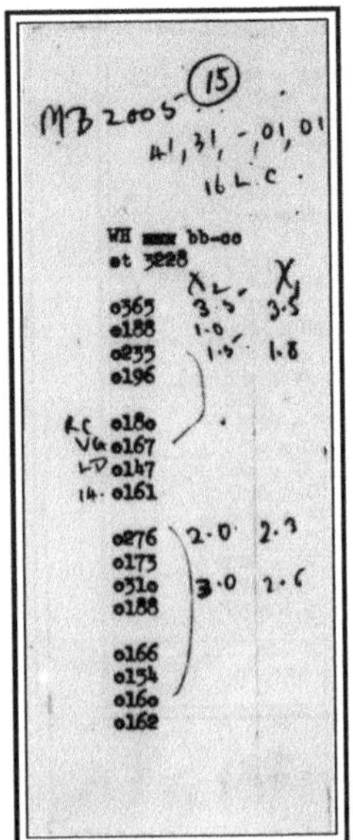

25G/15: ×.5

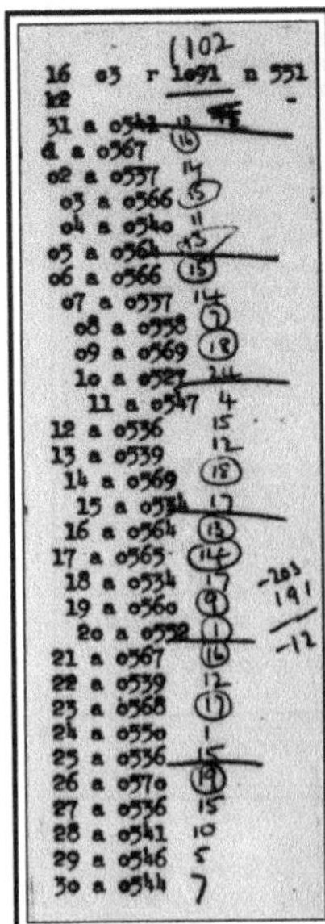

25G/16: ×.5

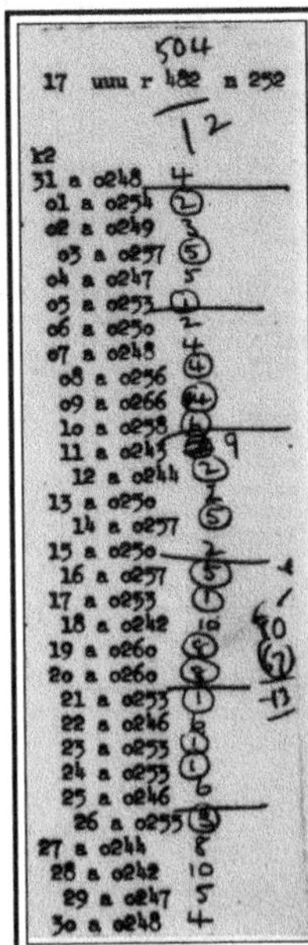

25G/17: ×.5

---

[i] Head for **25G(f)** on same line as text 'Run…'.

[ii] Displays 22G/14 through 22G/17 moved to come before paragraph **(g)**, instead of after as in the *Report*.

(g) Wheels reversed

After reversing the wheels a letter count is made to select runs for improving $\Delta\chi_2$ and $\Delta\chi_1$, viz ⑯ – ㉑.

p. 175

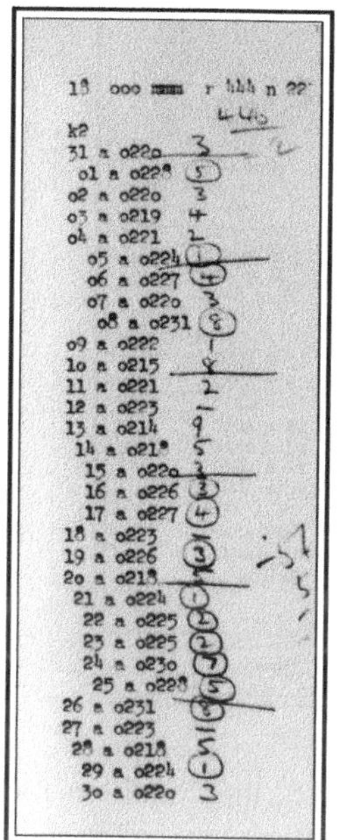

25G/18: ×.5

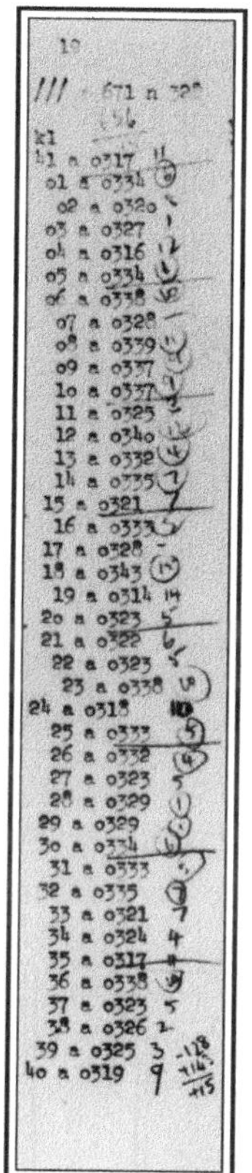

25G/19: ×.5

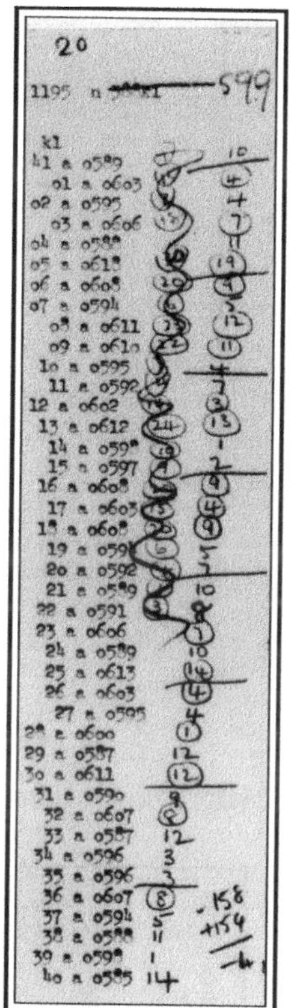

25G/20: ×.5

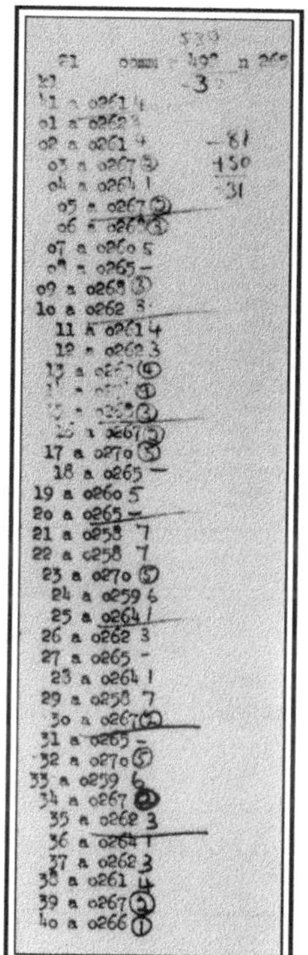

25G/21: ×.5

(h) $\Delta\chi_4$ made certain

Run ㉒ is used to deciban runs for $\Delta\chi_4$ viz ㉓, ㉔, ㉕, which suffice to make $\Delta\chi_4$ certain.

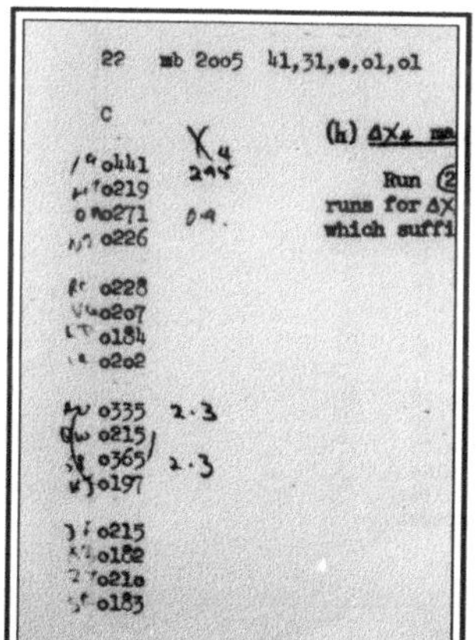

25G/22: ×.5

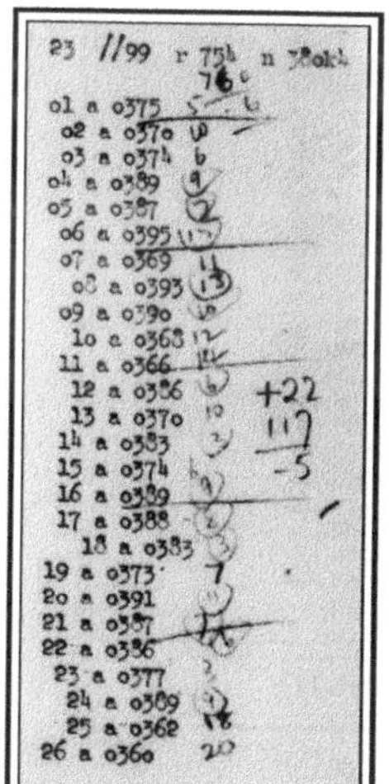

25G/23: ×.5

p. 176

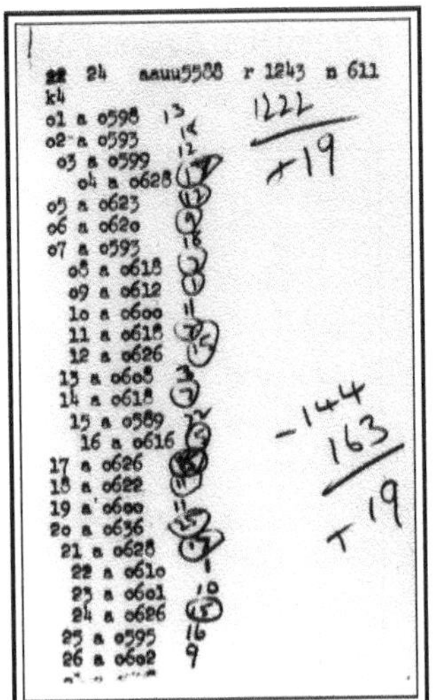

25G/24: ×.5

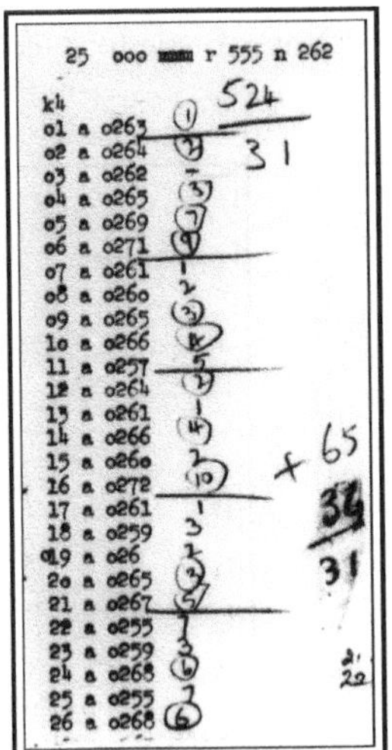

25G/25: ×.5

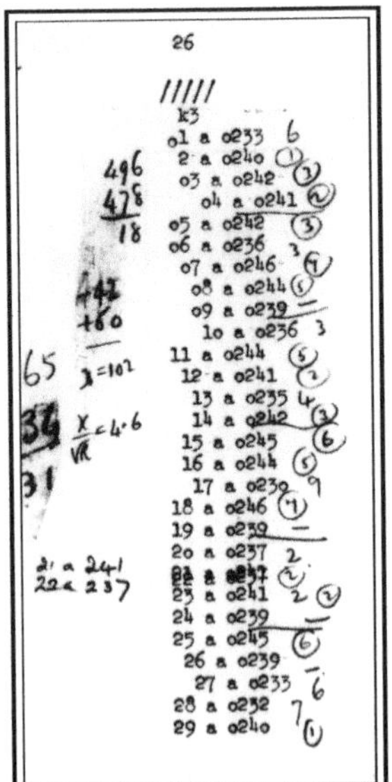

25G/26: ×.5

(i) A partial $\Delta\chi_3$ obtained

Runs ㉖, ㉗, ㉘, ㉙ are made for $\Delta\chi_3$; only ㉘ has $x/\sqrt{R} > 5{\cdot}5$, the condition for significance. From the table in **25B(c)**, this is found to be worth 2·5 decibans per pip; and from it wheel $\Delta\chi_3 A$ is constructed.

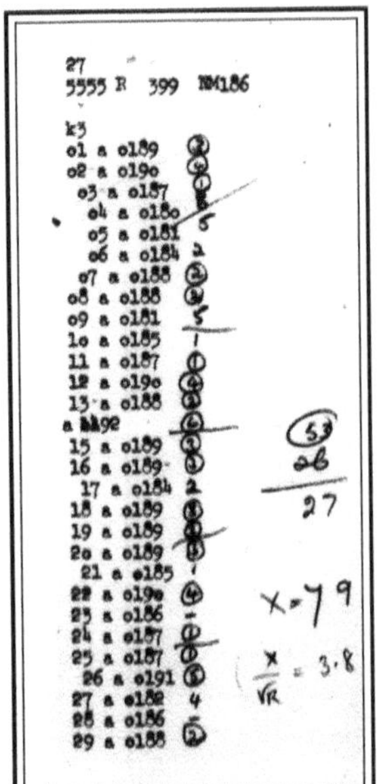

25G/27: ×.5

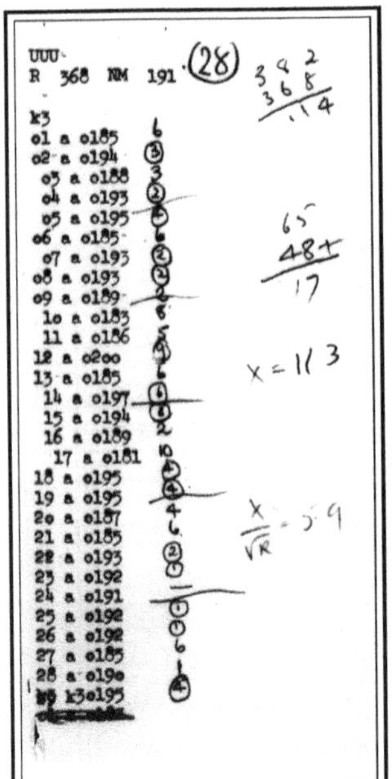

25G/28: ×.5

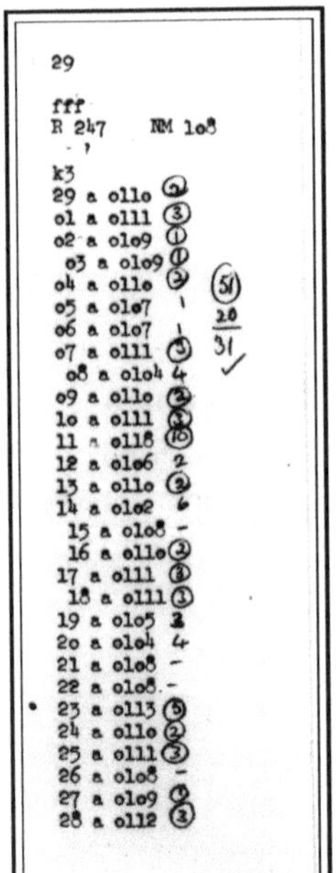

25G/29: ×.5

p. 177

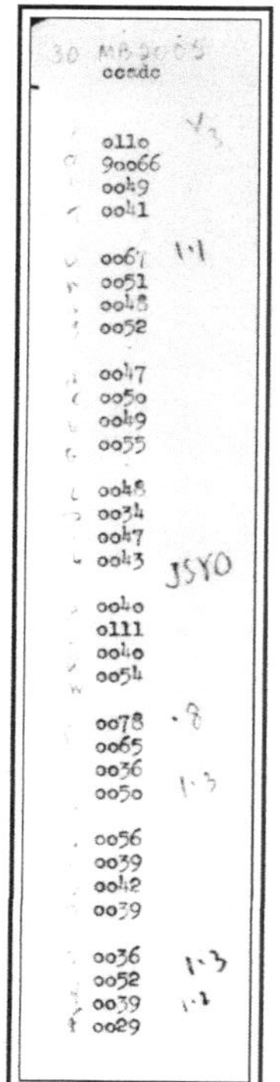

25G/30: ×.5

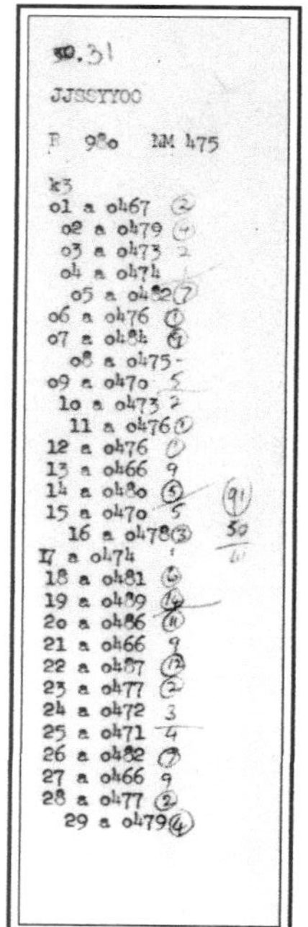

25G/31: ×.5

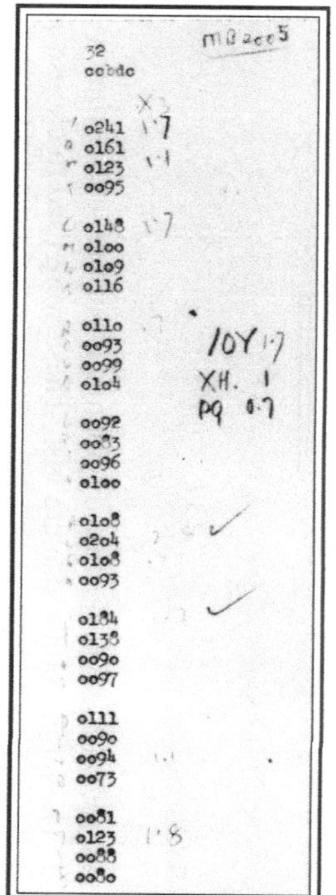

25G/32: ×.5

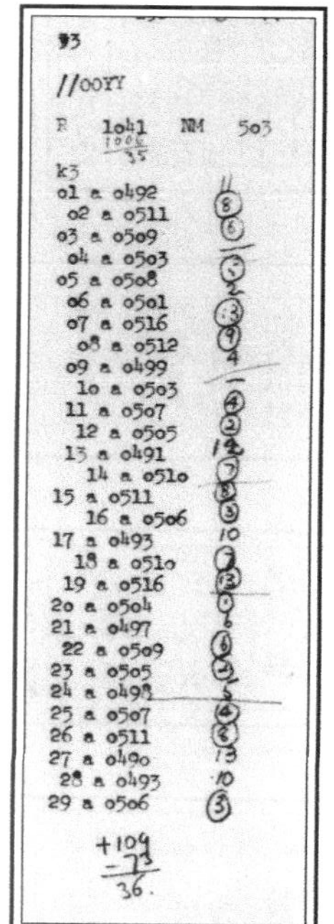

25G/33: ×.5

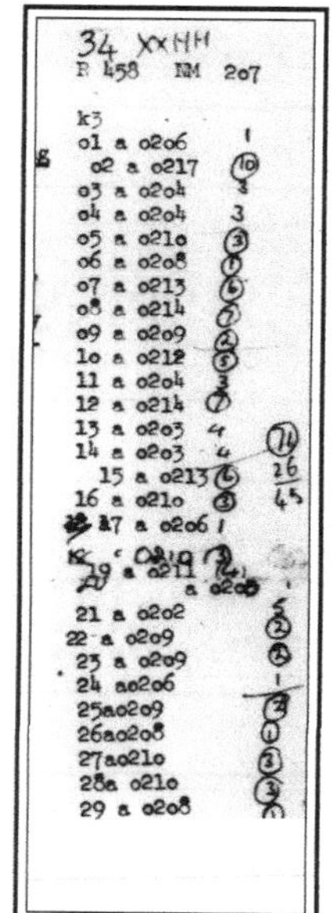

25G/34: ×.5

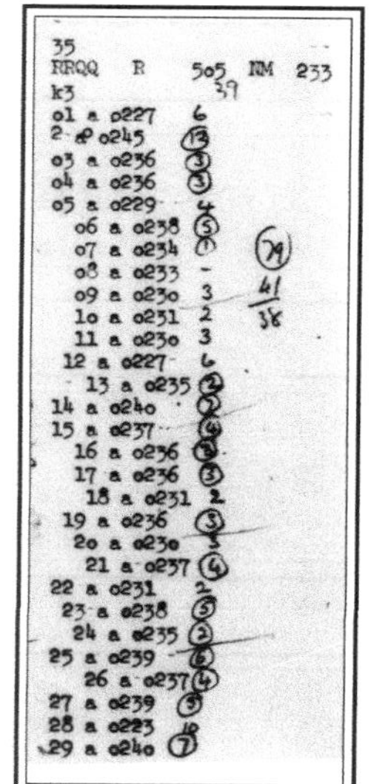

25G/35: ×.5

(j) Runs to improve $\Delta\chi_3$: redecibanning

A 32-letter count is used to choose runs to improve $\Delta\chi_3$, and, more especially, to deciban the runs (26), (27), (29) already made, so that they appear twice on the wheel-sheet, entered firstly in pips, and then in decibans. Actually JSYO is the only new run, but $\Delta\chi_3 B$ is a great improvement on $\Delta\chi_3 A$, and a further letter count, numbered (32), suggests additional runs as well as redecibanning (27) a second time.

p. 178

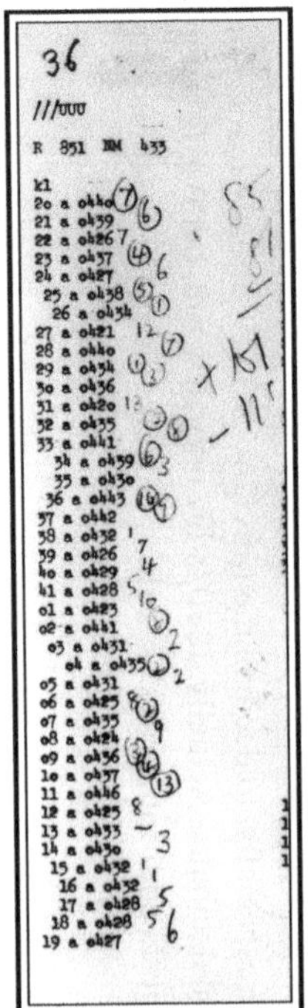

25G/36: ×.4

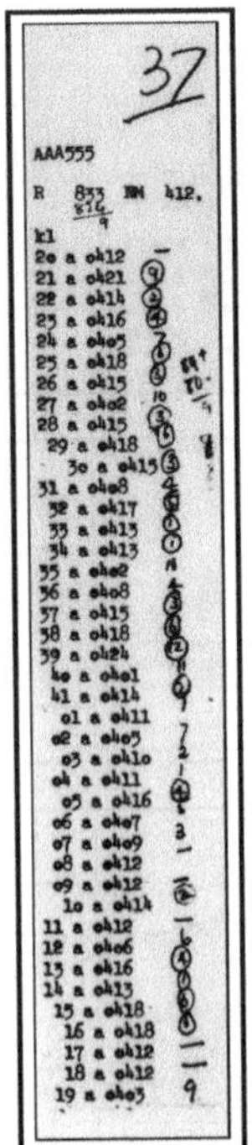

25G/37: ×.4

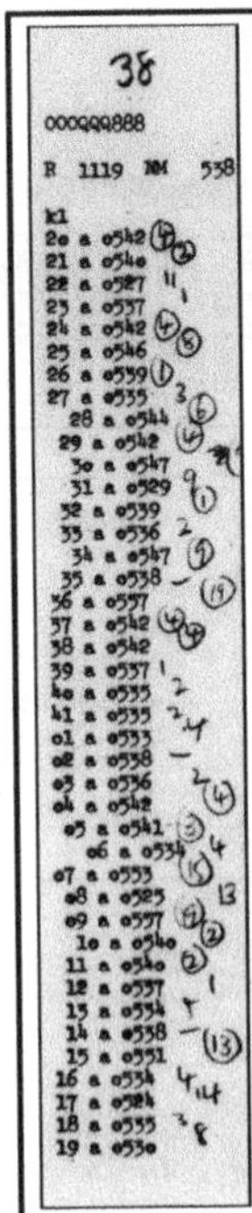

25G/38: ×.4

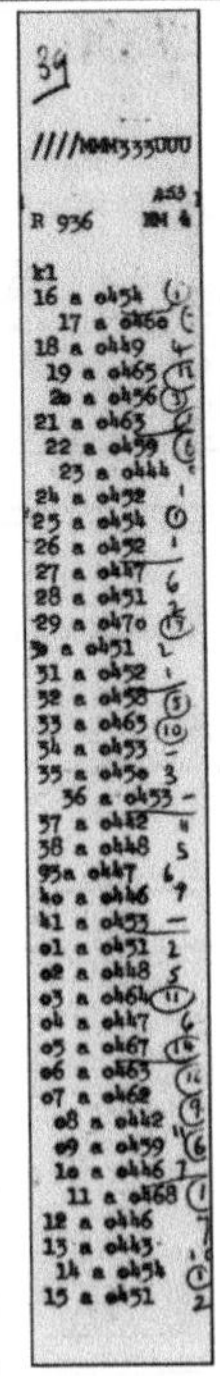

25G/39: ×.4

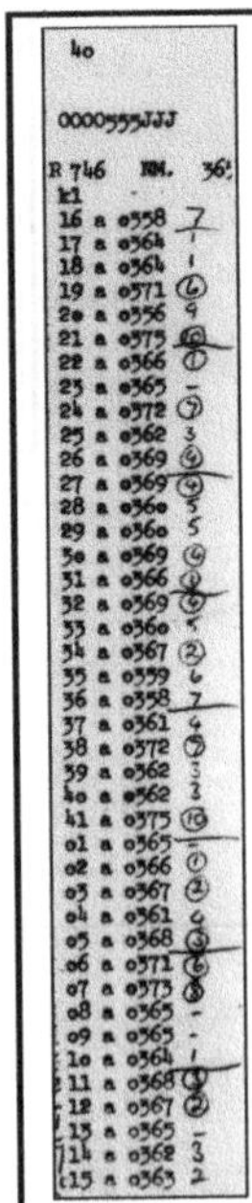

25G/40: ×.4

(k) Setting other messages

MB2004, MB2003 are now set on the wheels already obtained, but the setting runs were sent to Ops and not preserved. The letter counts also are lost. These were used to choose and deciban runs 36 to 40, yielding $\Delta\chi_1 D$ complete and nearly, but not quite, certain; the 7th and 10th characters can be interchanged with a loss of only 38 decibans.

p. 179

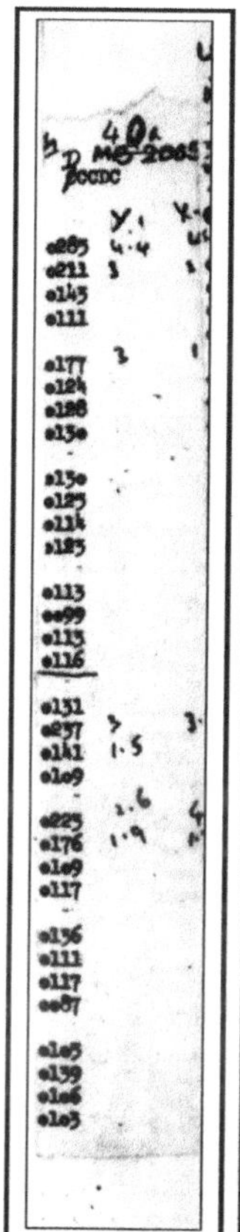

25G/40a: ×.5

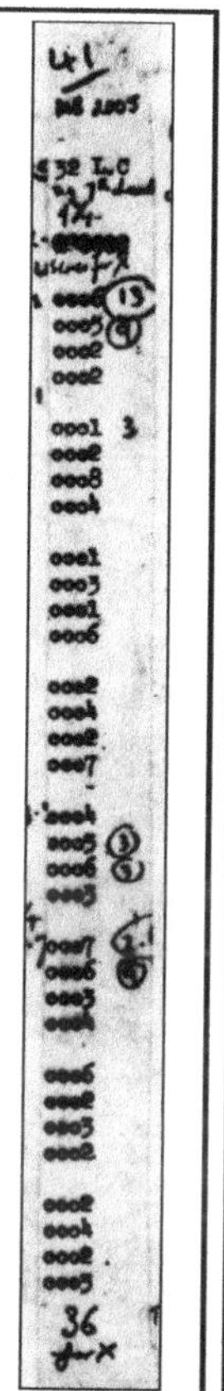

25G/41: ×.5

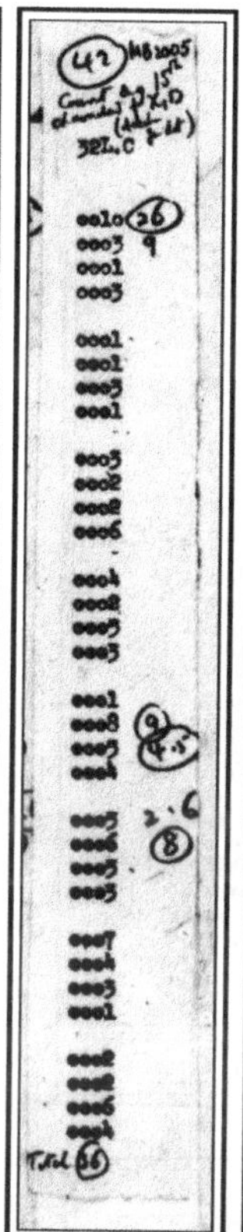

25G/42: ×.5

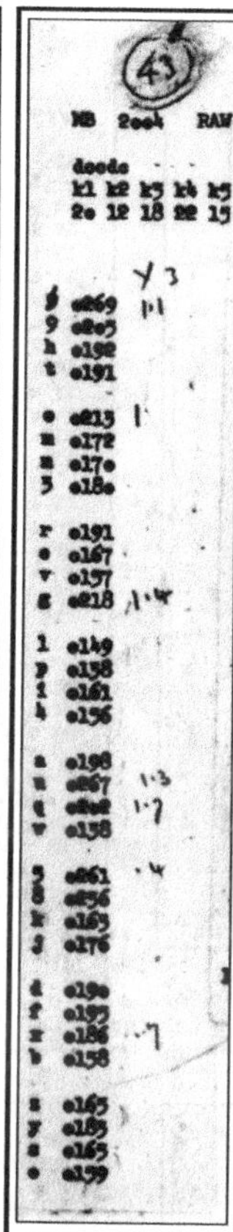

25G/43: ×.5

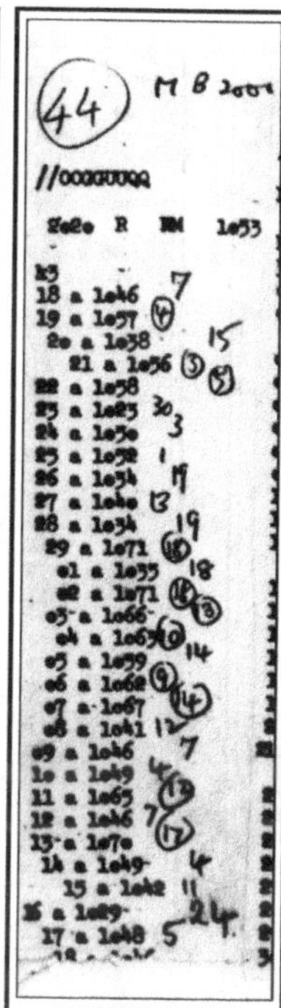

25G/44: ×.5

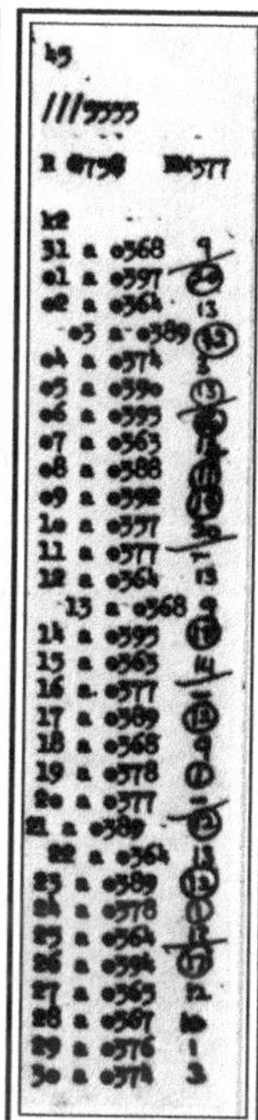

25G/45: ×.5

(l) Letter counts against doubtful characters

To make $\Delta\chi_1$ certain a new ordinary 32-letter count (40a) is made on the rectangle message MB2005, and also a 32-letter count against the doubtful 7th character, supposing it to be a cross. The letter count against the 7th character is decibanned from the complete letter count, for example for /'s the decibanage[a] is $(6-3) \times 10\log_{10}\frac{285}{103} = 3 \times 4{\cdot}4 = 13$.

In effect 7 runs are used; they make $\Delta\chi_1$ certain (cf. **25D(g)**3).

(m) Making $\Delta\chi_2$ certain

The letter count (43) on MB2004 suggests a slightly odd run (44) for $\Delta\chi_3$, and also run (48) for $\Delta\chi_2$. The previous letter count (40a) is used to deciban runs (45), (46), (47) for $\Delta\chi_2$; $\Delta\chi_2 C$ becomes certain.

[a] decibannage

p. 180

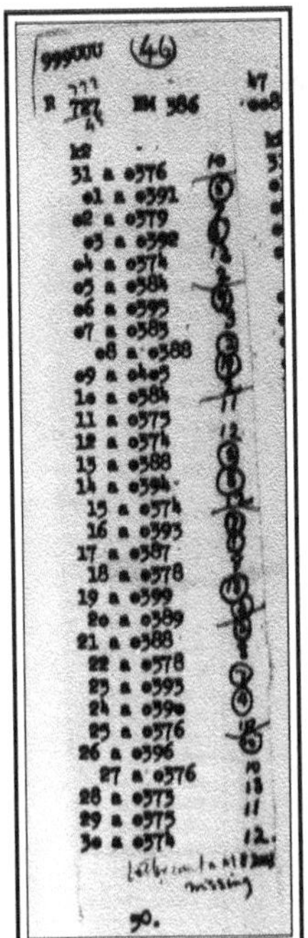

25G/46: ×.5

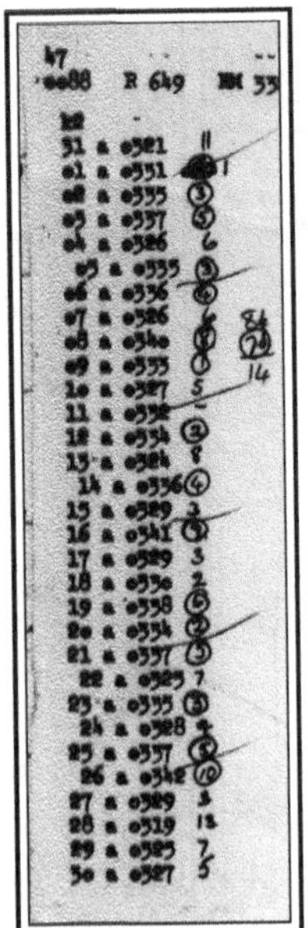

25G/47: ×.5

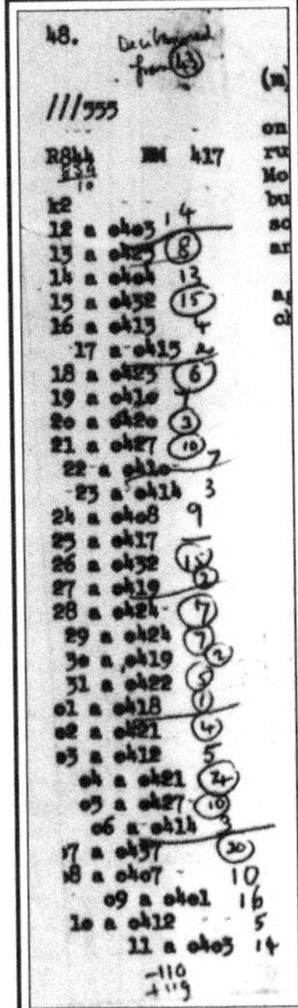

25G/48: ×.5

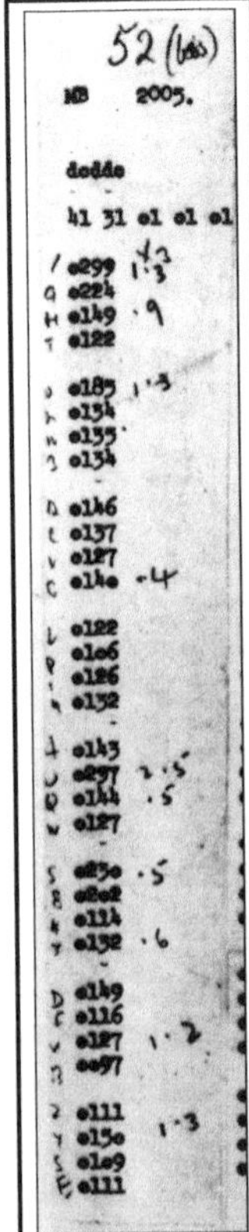

25G/52bis: ×.5

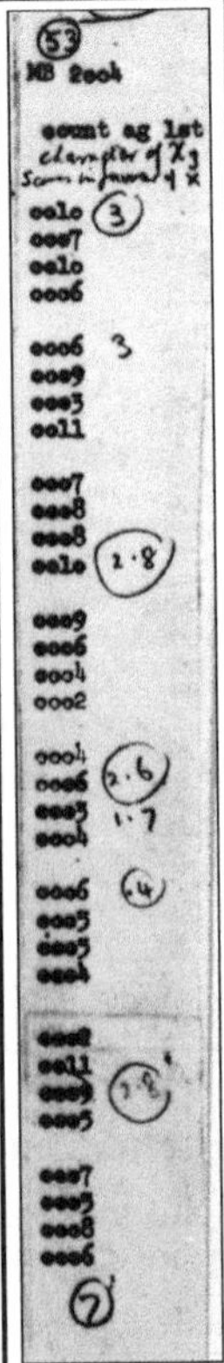

25G/53: ×.5

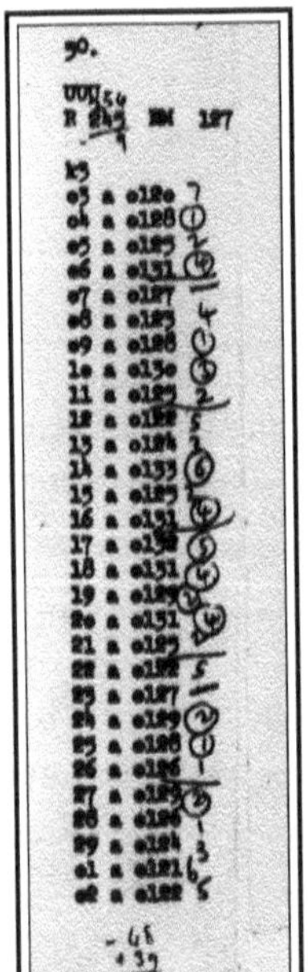

25G/50: ×.5

25G/51: ×.5

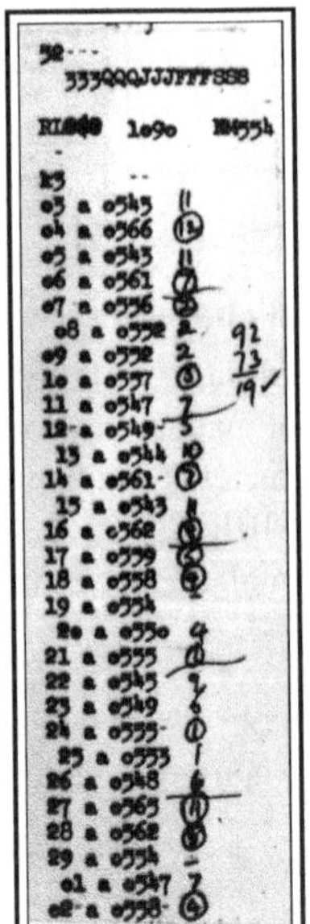

25G/52: ×.5

(n) Making $\Delta\chi_3$ certain

A (lost) letter count on MB2003 is used to deciban runs (50), (51), (52) for $\Delta\chi_3$. Most characters score well, but the 1st character has a score with the wrong sign, and the wheel is not certain.

p. 181

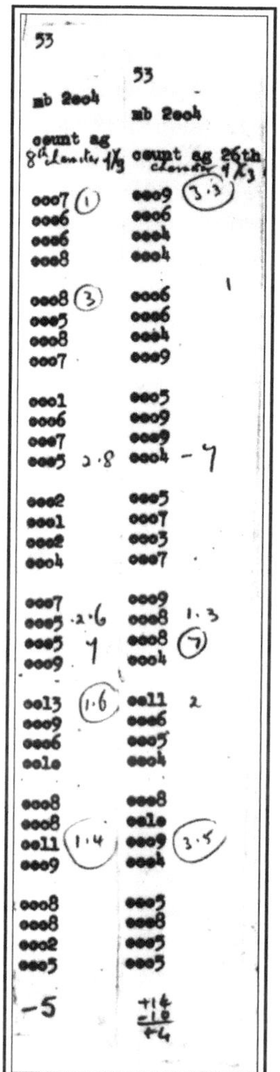

25G/53a: ×.6

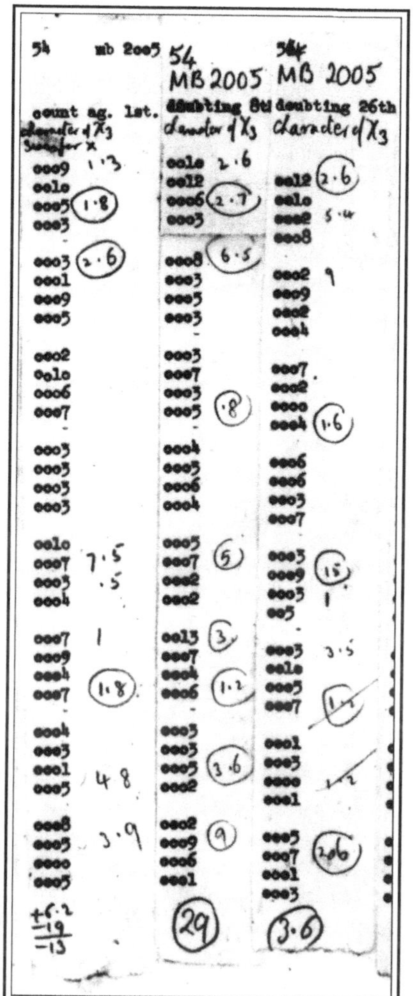

25G/54: ×.6

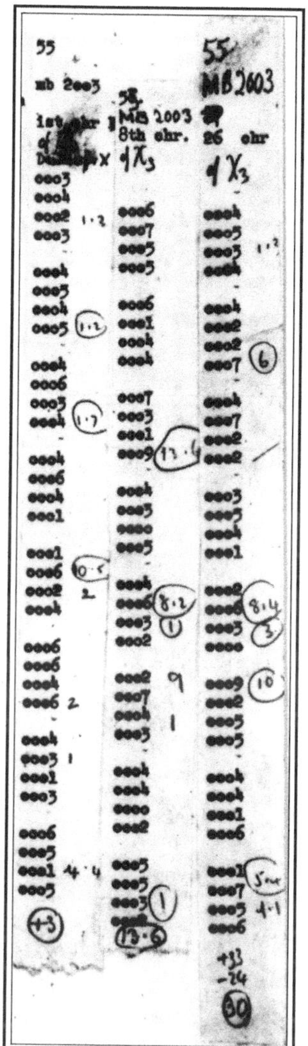

25G/55: ×.6

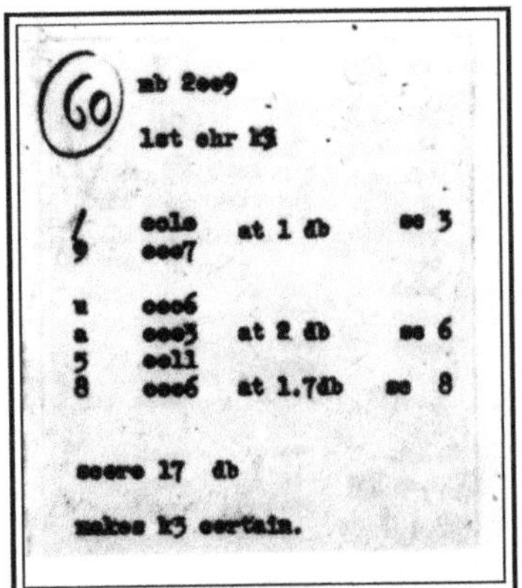

60

mb 2oo9

1st chr k3

/ colo at 1 db sc 3
9 ooo7

u ooo6
a ooo3 at 2 db sc 6
5 ooll
8 ooo6 at 1.7db sc 8

score 17 db

makes k3 certain.

25G/60: ×.6

[i] Individual letter counts against the three weakest characters on the three messages already used, still fail to make the wheel certain, because the 1st character retains its wrong sign; but a count against the 1st character on a newly set message, MB2009, (decibanned of course from the complete count on that message) is conclusive.

[i] The text 'Individual. . . on the three' appears on p. 180.

p. 182

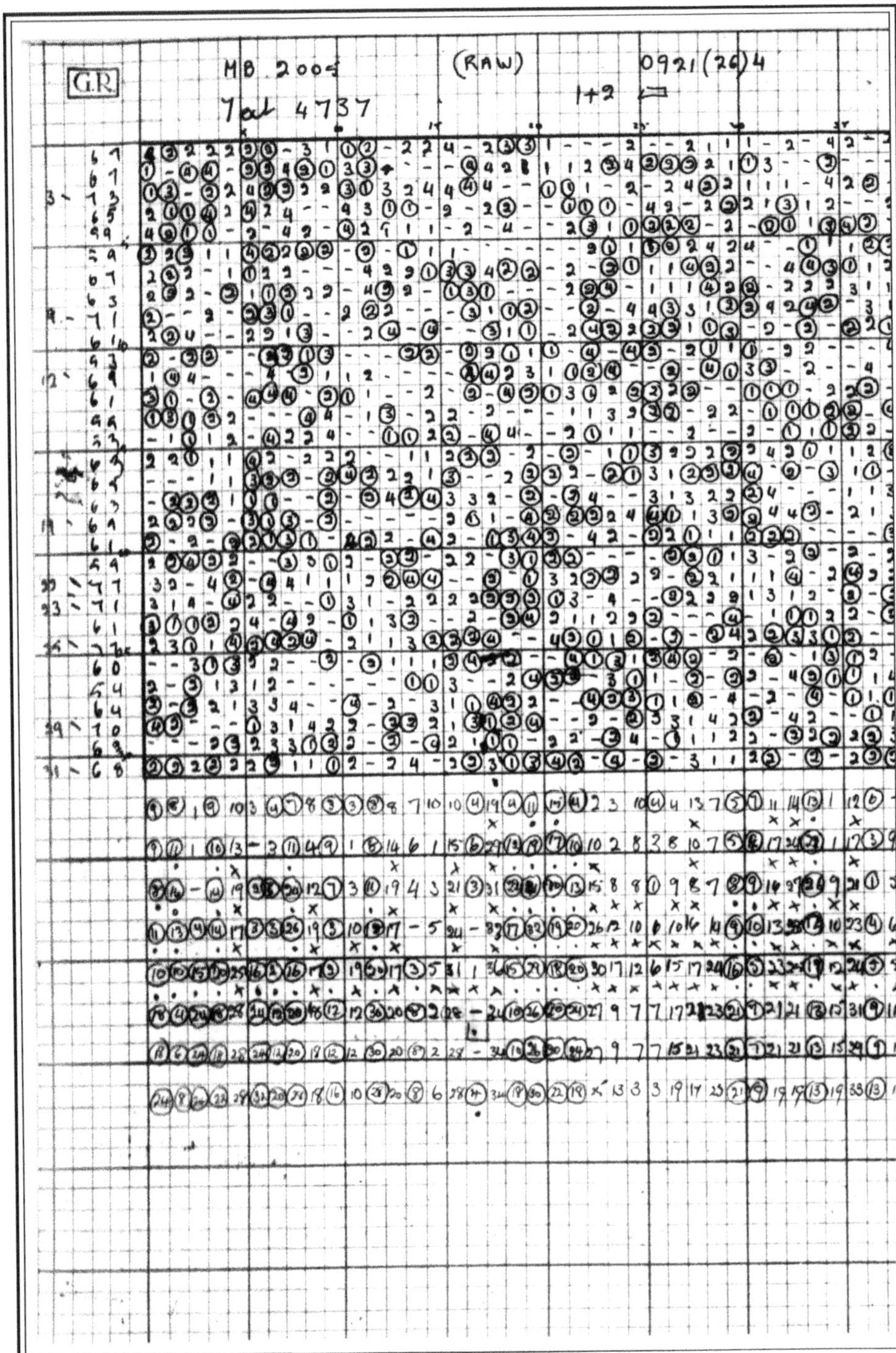

25G/I (left half): ×.55

Fig. 25 (I) (left half)

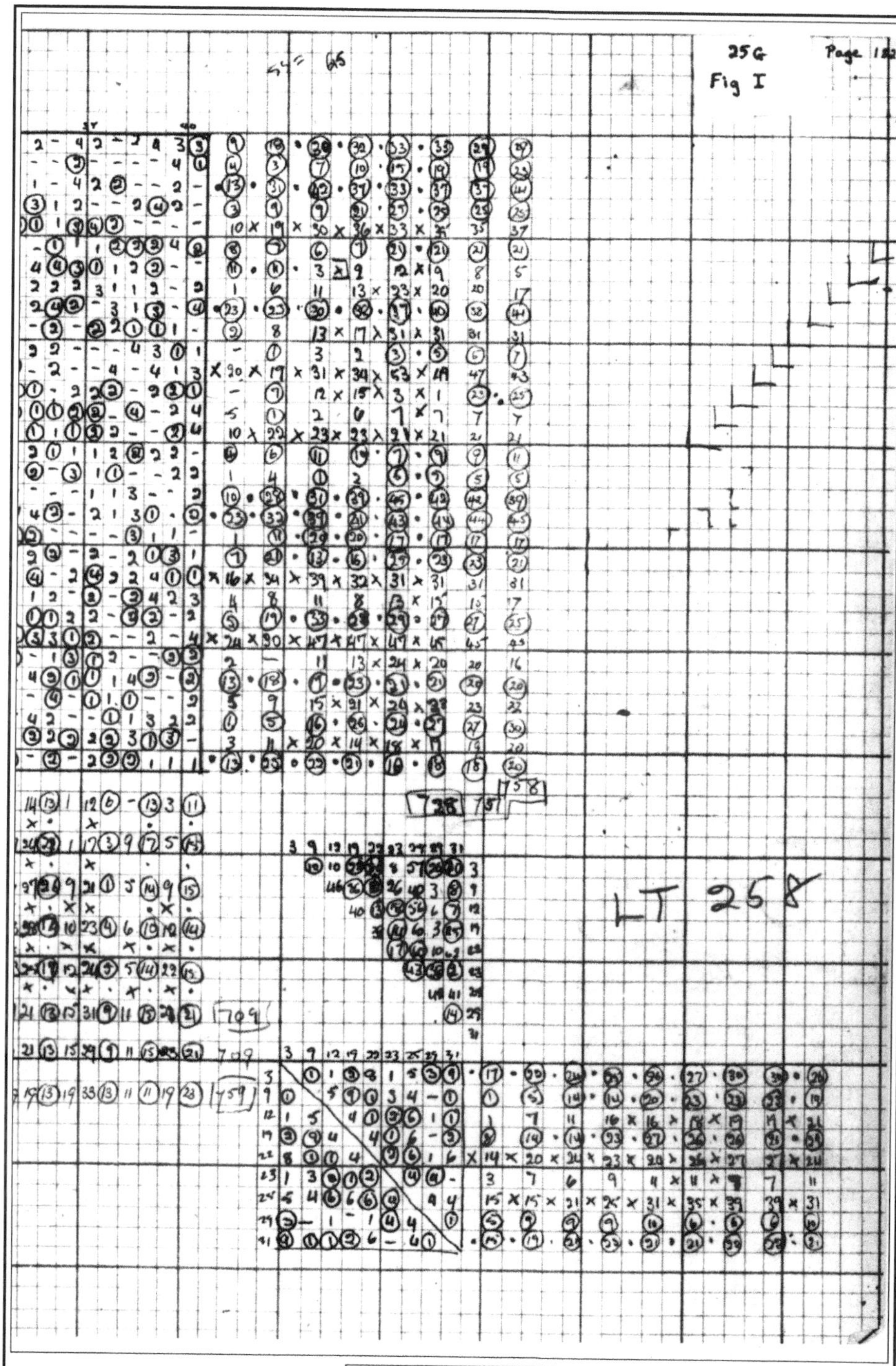

25G/I (right half): ×.55

Fig. 25 (I) (right half)

p. 183

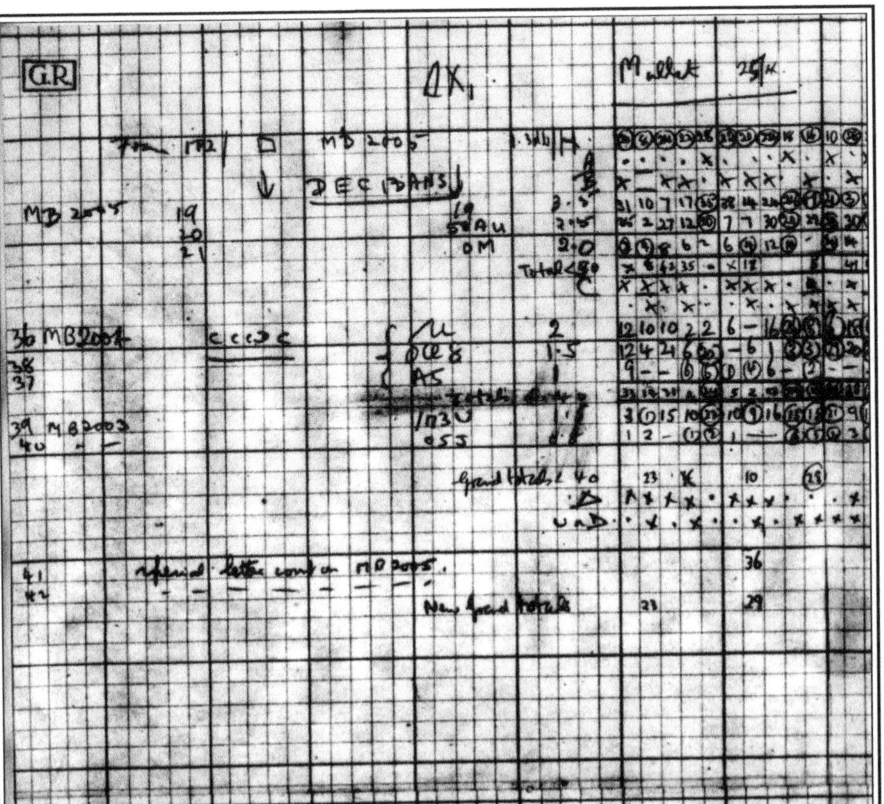

25G/II-III (left half): ×.55

Figs. 25 (II), (III) (left half)

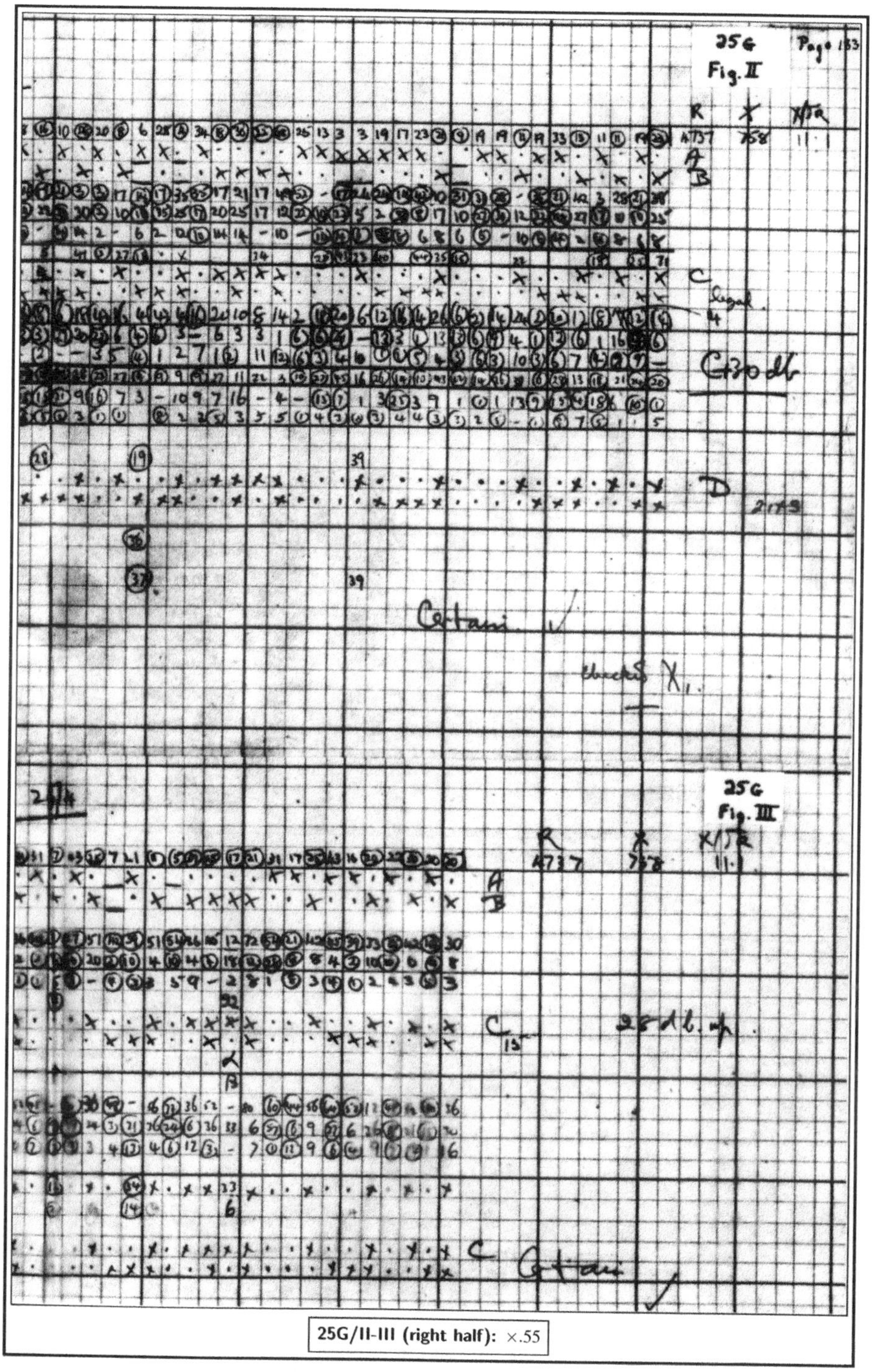

25G/II-III (right half): ×.55

Figs. 25 (II), (III) (right half)

p. 184

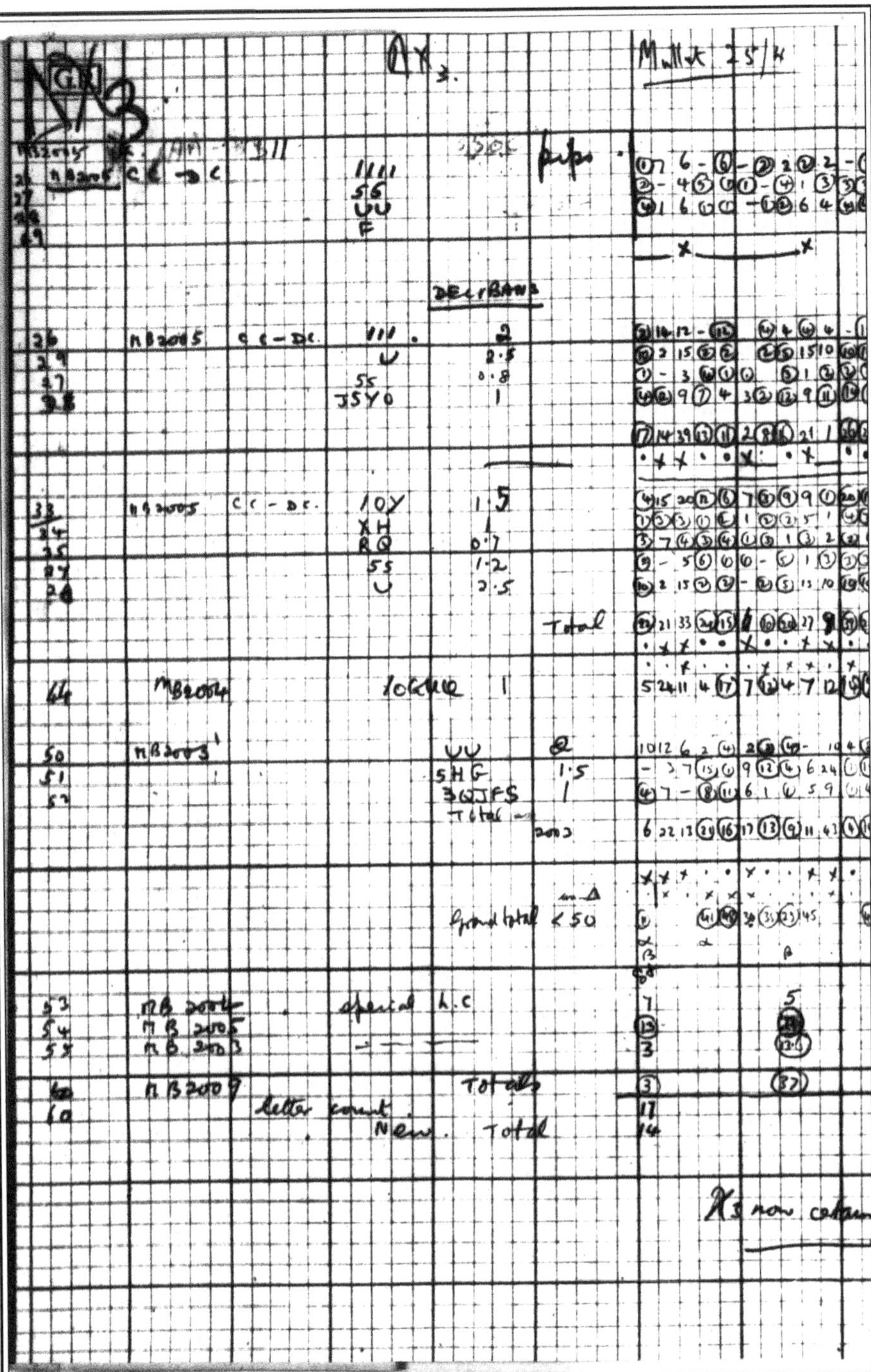

25G/IV (left half): ×.55

Fig. 25 (IV) (left half)

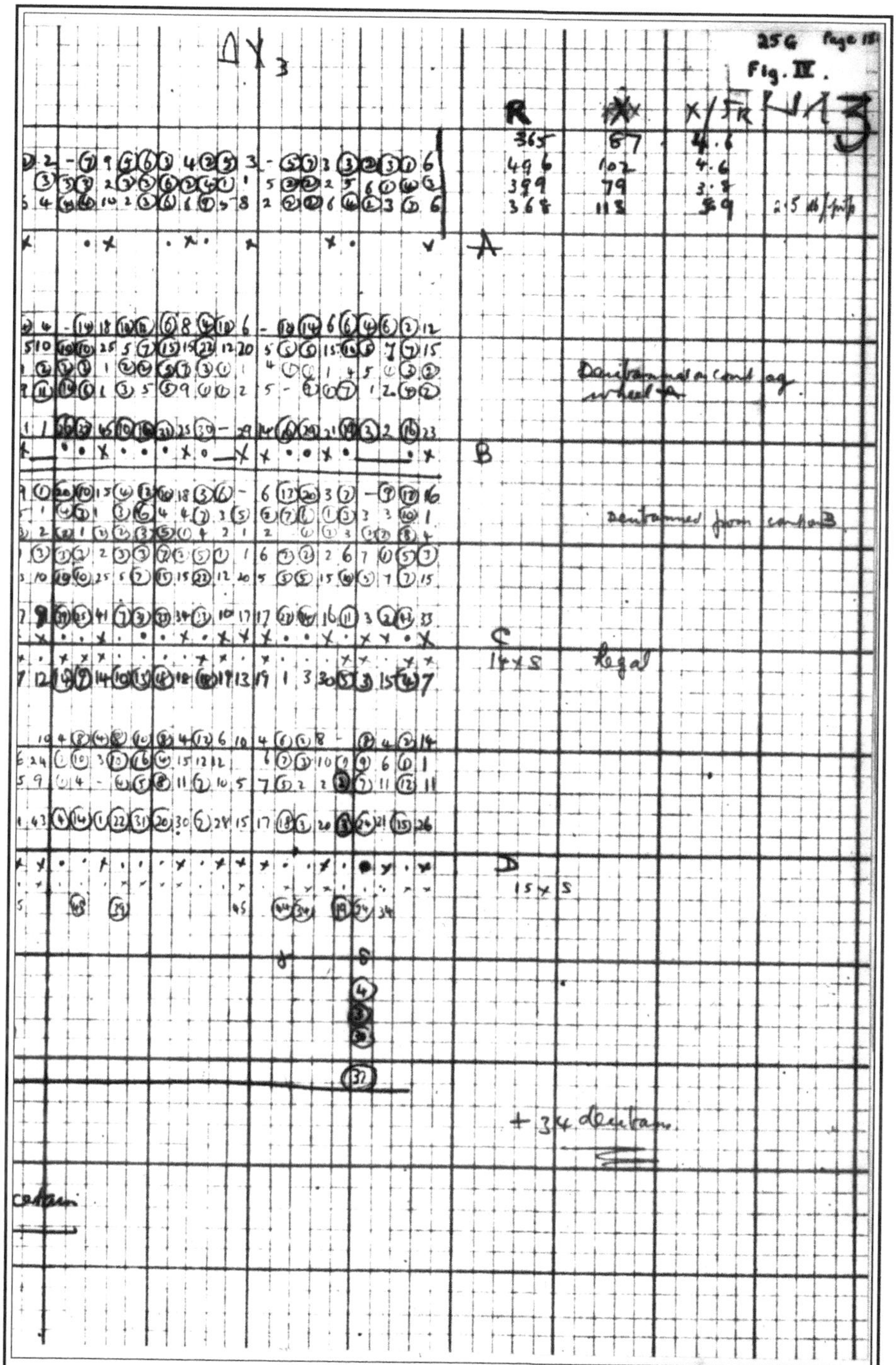

25G/IV (right half): ×.55

Fig. 25 (IV) (right half)

p. 185

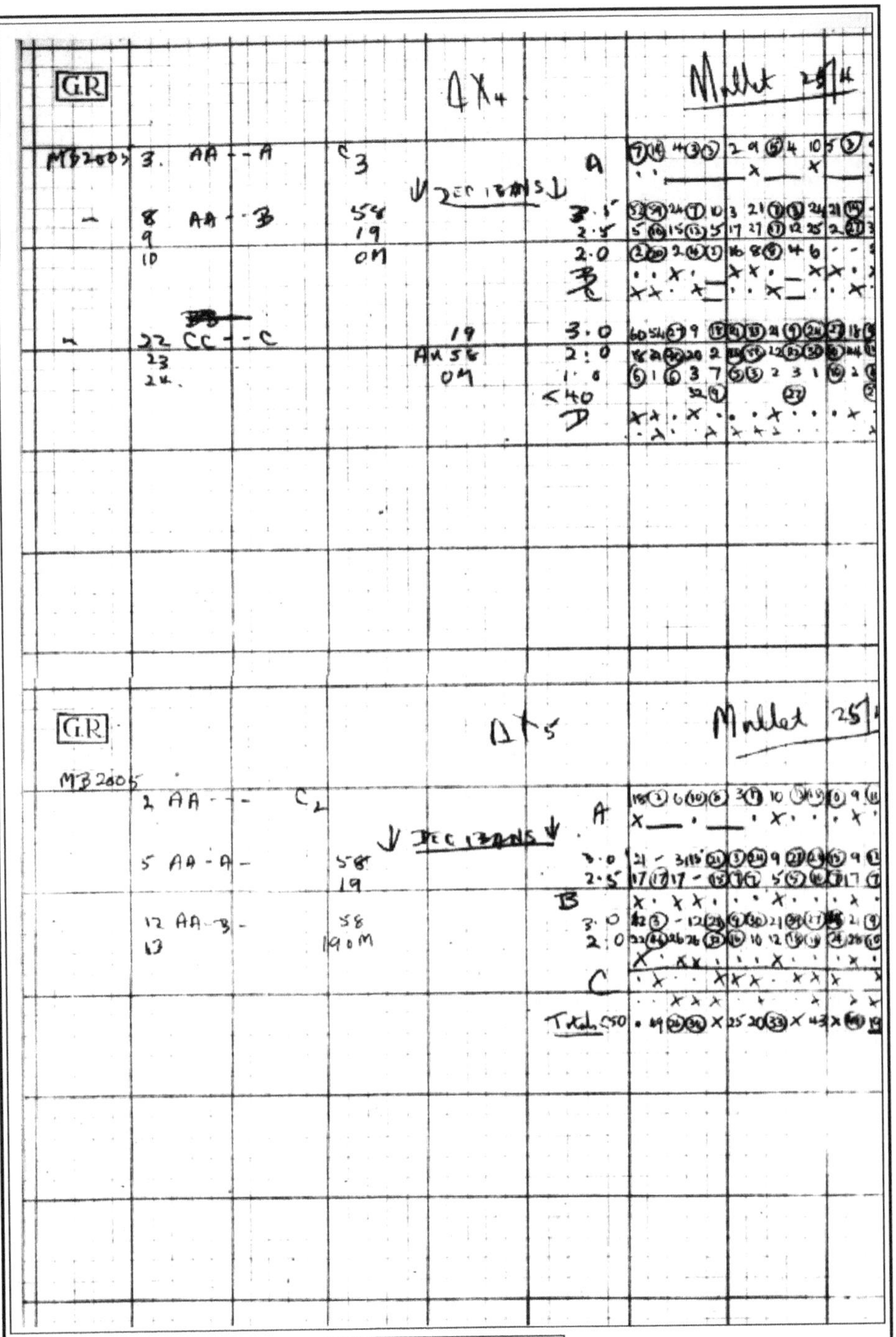

25G/V, VI (left half): ×.55

Figs. 25 (V), (VI) (left half)

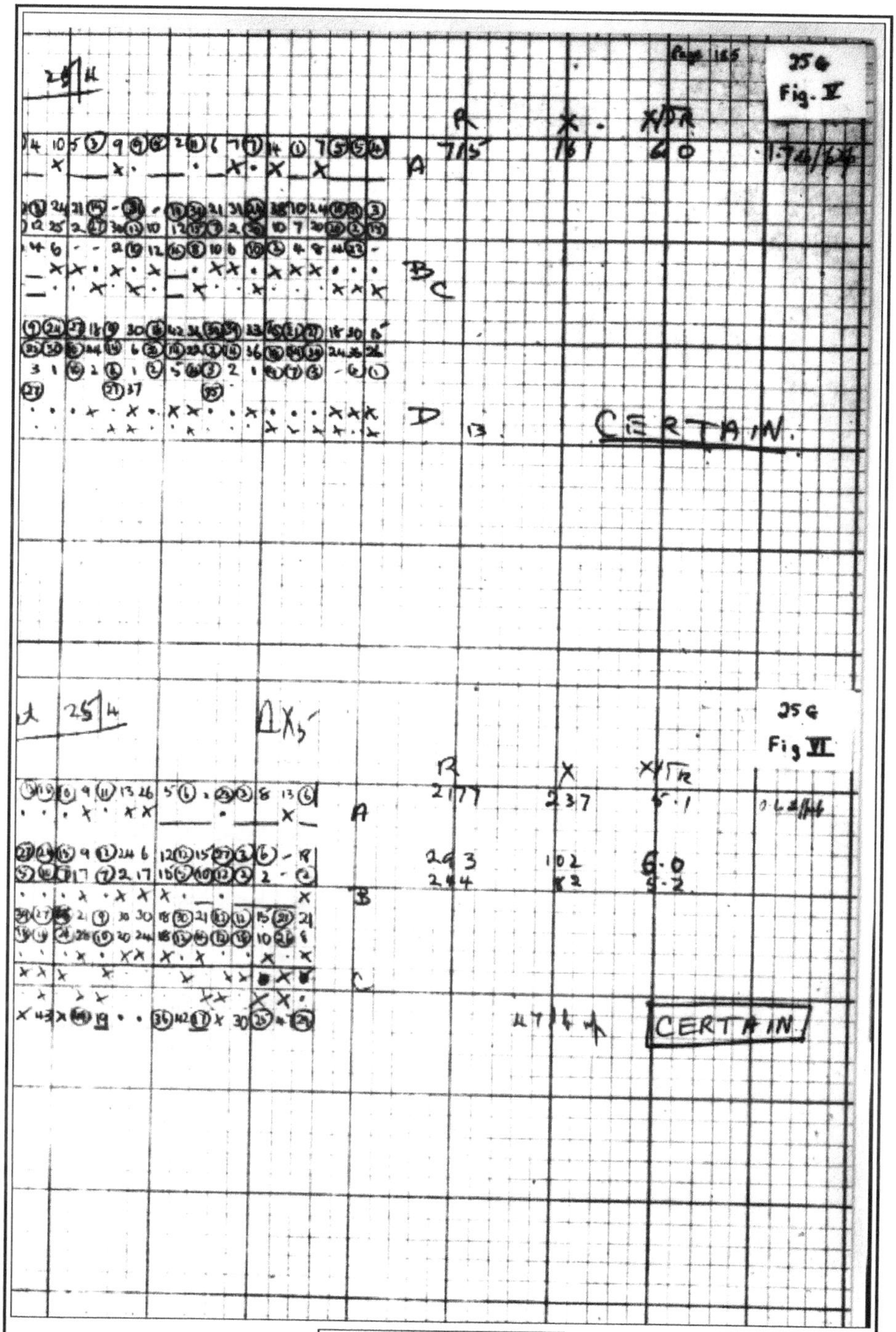

25G/V, VI (right half): ×.55

Figs. 25 (V), (VI) (right half)

p. 186

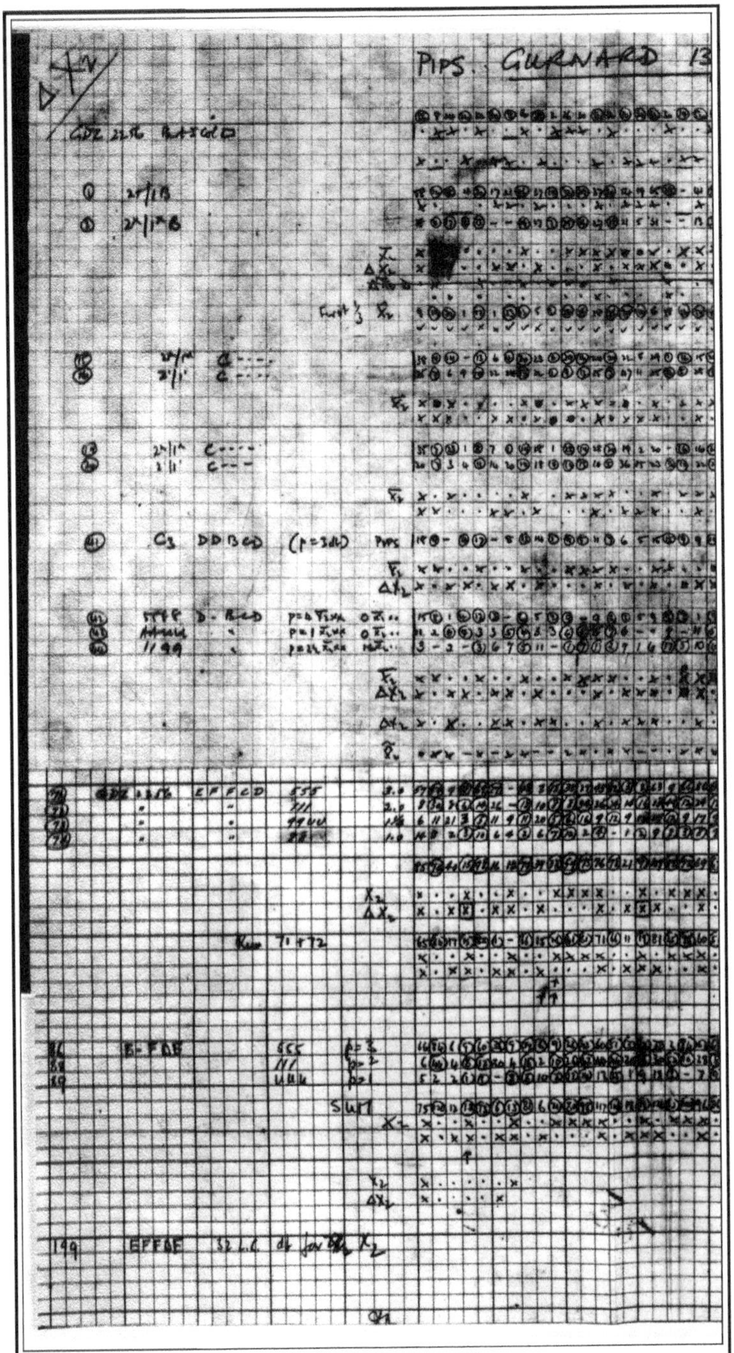

25G/VII (left half): ×.4

Fig. 25 (VII) (left half)

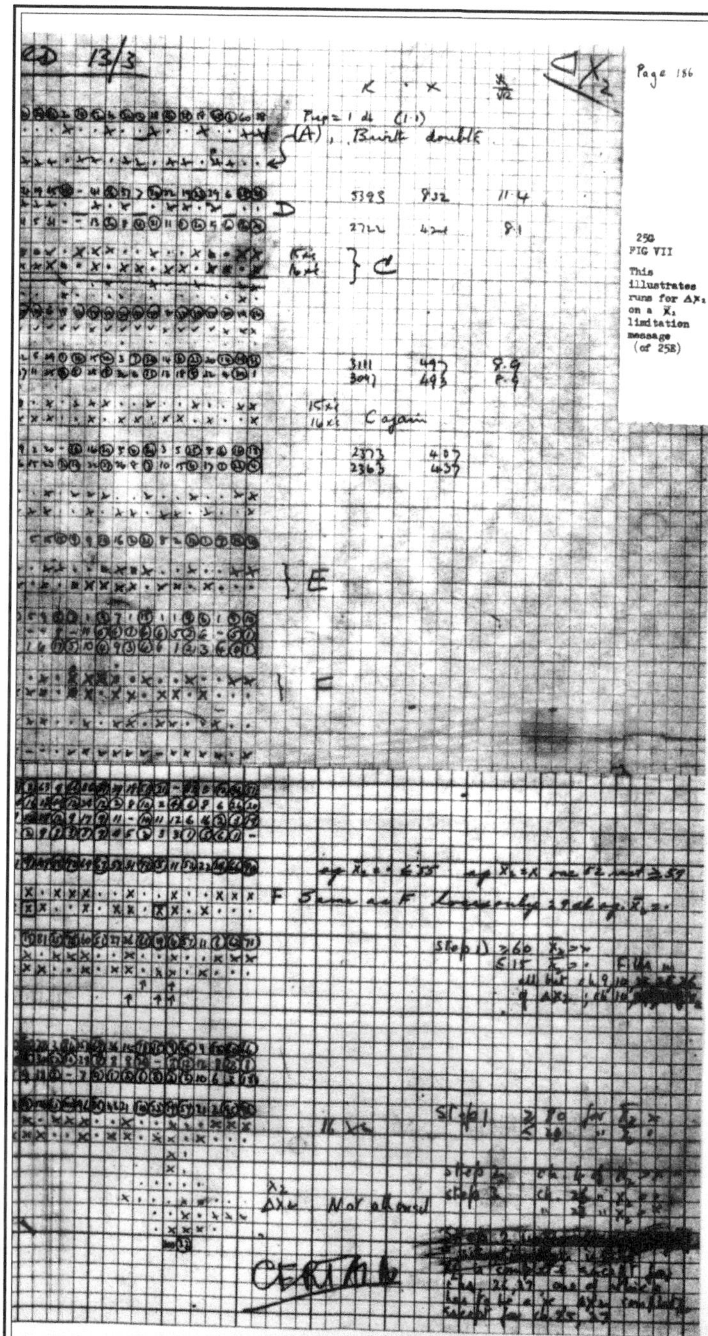

25G/VII (right half): ×.4

Fig. 25 (VII) (right half)

p. 187

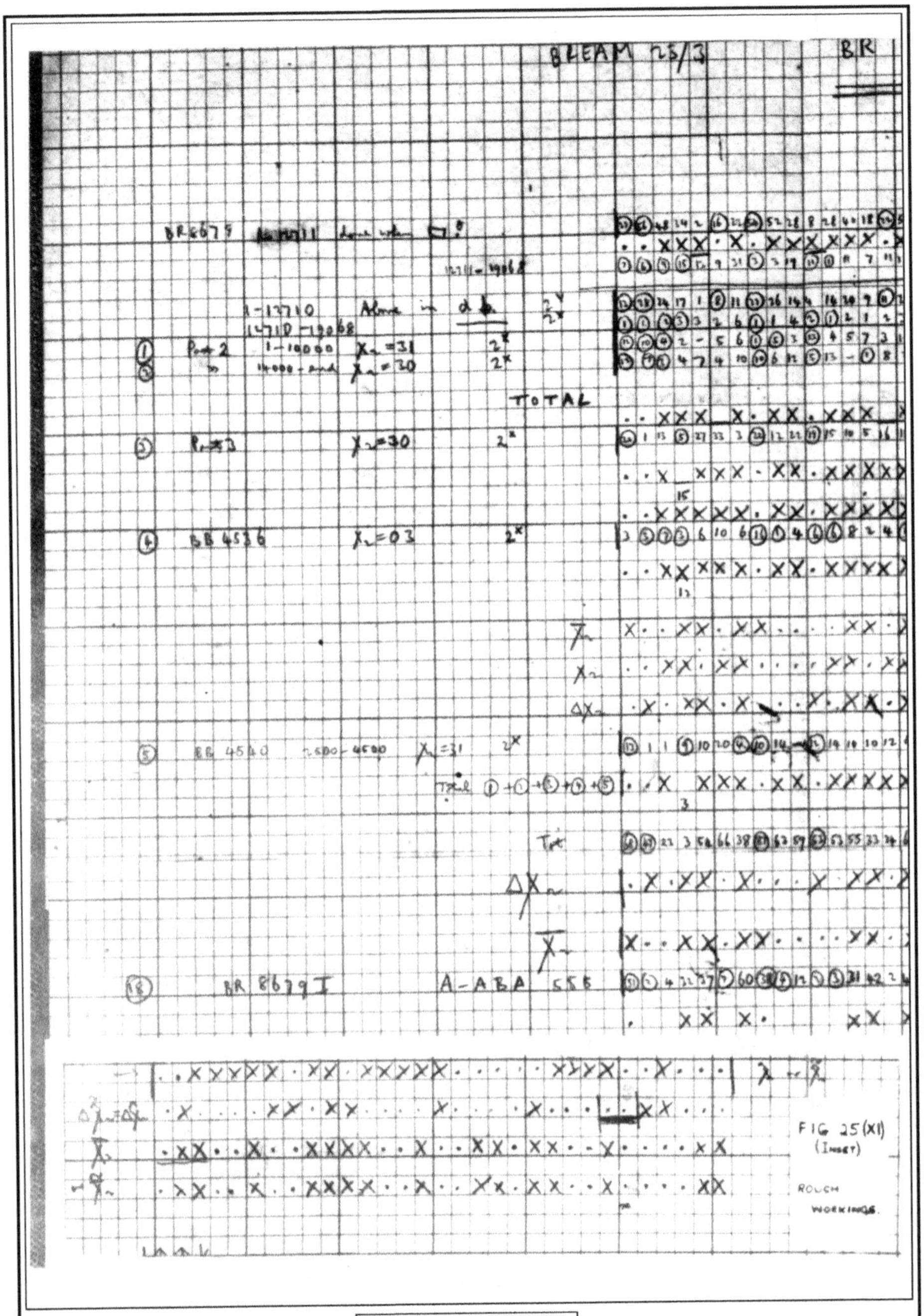

25G/VIII (left half): ×.5

Fig. 25 (VIII) (left half)

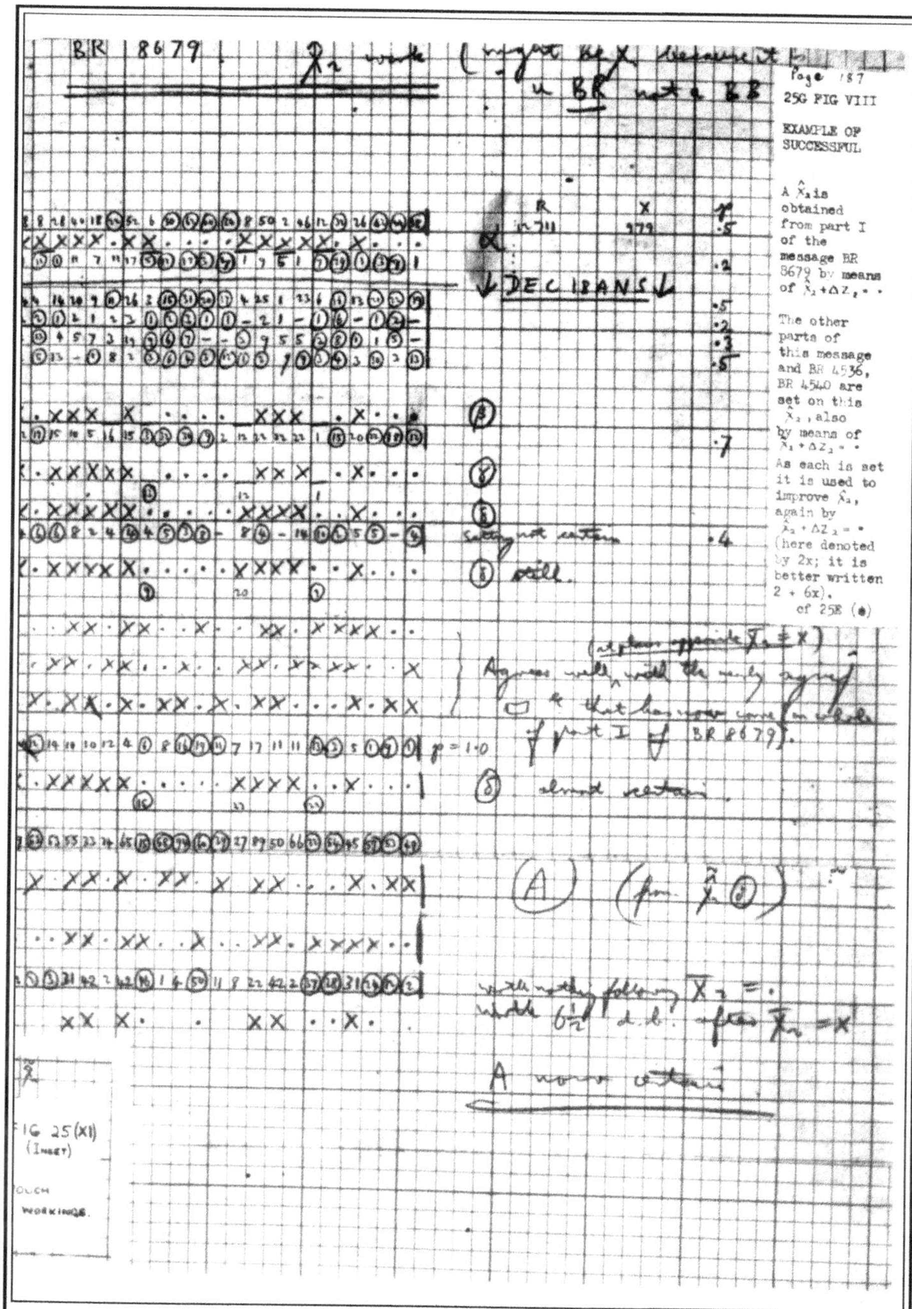

25G/VIII (right half): ×.5

Fig. 25 (VIII) (right half)

p. 188

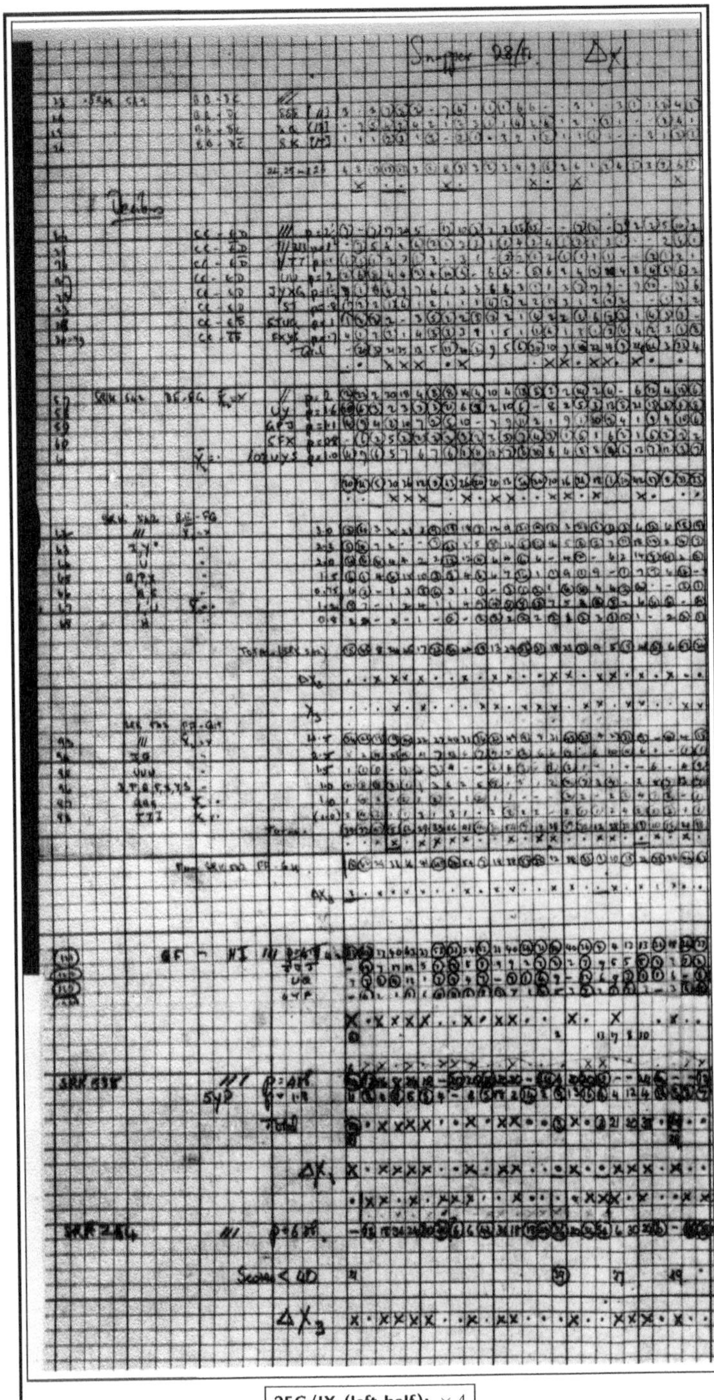

25G/IX (left half): ×.4

Fig. 25 (IX) (left half)

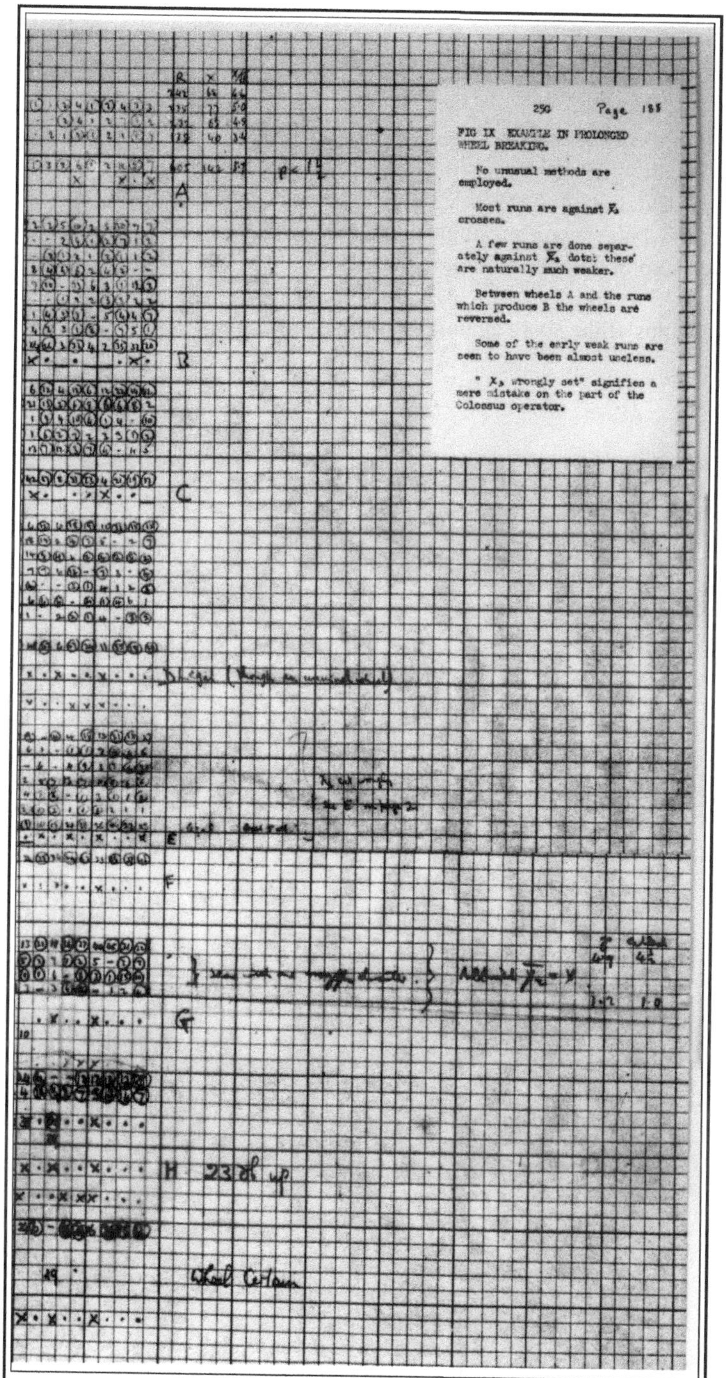

25G/IX (right half): ×.4

Fig. 25 (IX) (right half)

p. 189 25W DERIVATION OF FORMULAE FOR THE WEIGHING OF EVIDENCE

(a) Significance test

Let:

R be the number of places looked at
w be the wheel length
σ be the standard deviation of the double bulge against a single character, viz $\sqrt{R/w}$
z be a typical double bulge against a single character
x be the observed sum of the moduli of double bulges.

i The expected modulus of the score against a single character is

$$\int_{-\infty}^{\infty} \frac{e^{-z^2/2\sigma^2}}{\sqrt{2\pi\sigma}} |z|\, dz$$

$$= 2\int_{0}^{\infty} \frac{e^{-z^2/2\sigma^2}}{\sqrt{2\pi\sigma}} \cdot z\, dz$$

$$= \sqrt{\frac{2}{\pi}}\sigma \qquad \text{(W1)}$$

$$= \sqrt{\frac{2}{\pi}}\sqrt{\frac{R}{w}}. \qquad \text{(W2)}$$

ii Its variance is

$$\int_{-\infty}^{\infty} \frac{e^{-z^2/2\sigma^2}}{\sqrt{2\pi\sigma}} \left(|z| - \sqrt{\frac{2}{\pi}}\sigma\right)^2 \cdot dz$$

$$= 2\int_{0}^{\infty} \frac{e^{\frac{-z^2}{2\sigma^2}}}{\sqrt{2\pi}\,\sigma} \left(z^2 - 2\sqrt{\frac{2}{\pi}}\sigma z + \frac{2}{\pi}\,\sigma^2\right) dz$$

$$= \sigma^2 - \frac{4}{\pi}\,\sigma^2 + \frac{2}{\pi}\,\sigma^2$$

and hence its standard deviation is

$$\sqrt{1 - \frac{2}{\pi}}\,\sigma \qquad \text{(W3)}$$

$$= \sqrt{1 - \frac{2}{\pi}}\sqrt{\frac{R}{w}}. \qquad \text{(W4)}$$

a From (W2), the expected sum of moduli for the whole wheel is

$$w\sqrt{\frac{2}{\pi}}\sqrt{\frac{R}{w}} \quad \text{or} \quad \sqrt{\frac{2}{\pi}}\sqrt{Rw}. \qquad \text{(W5)}$$

---

[a] from

[i] Throughout **25W**, displayed equations are connected to their equation numbers in the margin by leading rows of dots. Throughout **25W**, equation numbers are given without parentheses.

[ii] All the text, starting with 'Its variance…' on up through the end of equation (W6) is one run-on sentence, which we have broken into three.

From (W4), its standard deviation is a

$$\sqrt{w}\cdot\sqrt{1-\frac{2}{\pi}}\sqrt{\frac{R}{w}} \quad \text{or} \quad \sqrt{1-\frac{2}{\pi}}\sqrt{R}. \tag{W6}$$

It is considered that for the significance of a single trial, a sufficient sigma-age is 2, i.e. p. 190

$$x > \sqrt{\frac{2}{\pi}}\sqrt{Rw} + 2\cdot\sqrt{1-\frac{2}{\pi}}\sqrt{R} \tag{W7}$$

or approximately

$$\frac{x}{\sqrt{R}} > 0{\cdot}8\sqrt{w} + 1{\cdot}2. \tag{W8}$$

(For this test **R3**, pp. 5, 6, 7. A slight generalization **R4**, p. 100. Controversy **R4**, pp. 93, 100. Tests based on a letter count χ^2 test **R4**, p. 54; **R5**, pp. 3, 8, 11, 37, 113: $\sum n \log n$ **R4**, pp. 56, 70, b 121; **R5**, pp. 1, 3, 7.)

(b) Fundamental decibanning formula

Let δ be the true proportional bulge of the run.

Suppose that a particular place in the cipher is observed to favour a dot in $\Delta\chi$.

If the corresponding character of $\Delta\chi$ is a dot, the probability of the observation is $\frac{1+\delta}{2}$.

If the corresponding character of $\Delta\chi$ is a cross, the probability of the observation is $\frac{1-\delta}{2}$.

Whence the factor in favour of a dot is $\frac{1+\delta}{1-\delta}$.

Hence if the double bulge in favour of a dot, i.e. the excess of places favouring dot over places favouring cross, is x_i, the total factor is

$$\left(\frac{1+\delta}{1-\delta}\right)^{x_i}$$

whose decibanage is $x_i 10\log_{10}\frac{1+\delta}{1-\delta}$, i.e.

$$10\log_{10}\frac{1+\delta}{1-\delta} \text{ decibans per pip.} \tag{W9}$$

N.B. This is the decibanage for dot rather than cross, not for dot rather than random.

The major problem is to find δ.

(c) Impracticability of exact formulae c

An exact formula is impracticable, for it must use not only the evidence of the run, but also general Fish evidence. Even if it could be evaluated, its precision would be largely illusory. The d formula is

$$\frac{\int_{-1}^{1} p(x|R,\delta)\,p(\delta)\,\delta\cdot d\delta}{\int_{-1}^{1} p(x|R,\delta)\,p(\delta)\cdot d\delta}.$$

(d) Decibanning a run on its own message and correct wheels p. 191

If δ is to be evaluated from the evidence of the message under consideration only, then $\delta = x^*/R$ where x^* is the double bulge on the correct wheels. This is a compact and convenient notion, though until the correct wheels are known, x^* is unknown and must be estimated.

[a] from [b] χ_2 test [c] Impractibility [d] fish evidence

(e) Decibanning a run from its own wheel

To simplify the calculation it is assumed

(i) that a sufficient approximation to the expected δ is *that value of δ whose expected x/R is the observed x/R.*

(ii) that the distribution of x is normal. This is satisfactory if $x \ll R$, a condition satisfied except in key.

It will be convenient, though using the same notation as before, to interpret it more generally
i by taking Z to be the deviation of a typical double bulge from its mean, $R\delta/w$, so that the variance
E.13 of Z will be $\sigma^2 = \frac{R}{w}(1-\delta^2)$. Previously we took $\delta = 0$.

Suppose that the wheel is constructed entirely from the run. Then the score for a single character is

$$\left| Z + \frac{R\delta}{w} \right| \tag{W10}$$

and the expected score, x, for the whole wheel is

$$w\int_{-\infty}^{\infty} \frac{e^{-Z^2/2\sigma^2}}{\sqrt{2\pi}\sigma} \left| Z + \frac{R\delta}{w} \right| \cdot dZ \tag{W11}$$

$$\therefore \quad \frac{1}{q} \equiv \frac{x}{R\delta} = \frac{1}{R\delta}\left\{ -\int_{-\infty}^{-R\delta/w} + \int_{-R\delta/w}^{0} + \int_{0}^{R\delta/w} + \int_{R\delta/w}^{\infty} \frac{e^{-Z^2/2\sigma^2}}{\sqrt{2\pi}\sigma}\left(Z + \frac{R\delta}{w}\right)\cdot dZ \right\}$$

which reduces to

$$\frac{1}{q} = \sqrt{\frac{2}{\pi}}\frac{1}{\xi e^{\xi^2/2}} + 2\int_0^{\xi} \frac{1}{\sqrt{2\pi}} e^{\frac{-t^2}{2}}.dt \tag{W12}$$

where

$$\xi = \frac{R\delta}{w\sigma} \tag{W13}$$

remembering

$$\sigma^2 = \frac{R}{w}\left(1-\delta^2\right) \tag{W14}$$

$$q = \frac{R\delta}{x} \tag{W15}$$

and eliminating σ, δ from (W13), (W14), (W15)

$$\frac{\xi}{q} = \frac{x}{\sqrt{Rw}}\sqrt{1 + \frac{\xi^2 w}{R}} \tag{W16}$$

$$\fallingdotseq \frac{x}{\sqrt{Rw}}. \tag{W17}$$

p. 192 What is required is q as a function of x, R, w and this can theoretically be obtained by eliminating ξ from (W12), (W16).

It is more convenient to replace (W16) by the pessimistic approximation (W17). Then by taking a series of values of ξ, it is easy to construct a table of q as a function of $x/\sqrt{Rw}$. This is given in **25B(c)**.

---

i Throughout **25W(e)**, and especially in handwritten formulae, the symbol Z changes size, often appearing as z, with unchanged meaning.

(f) Decibanning from a letter count

On the correct wheel the expected score is the expected value of $|z+R\delta|$, so that it can be calculated from (W11) by putting $w=1$, and the table of **25B(c)** is applicable (**R5**, p. 109). Inspection of the table shows that when $w=1$, and the total decibanage, roughly $8{\cdot}7(x/\sqrt{R})^2$, is a sufficient to make the run worth while, $q \risingdotseq 1$ i.e. crude decibanning is adequate.

It follows that if the wheel is independent of the run, but not necessarily correct, crude decibanning will tend, in practice inappreciably, to be too pessimistic, except for very feeble runs. This remark applies to decibanning, from a letter count, any run not used in making the letter count wheels, including all runs on a newly set message.

If the run is used, but not alone, in making the wheel, some value of w between 1 and the actual wheel-length is required, but it has not been found necessary to investigate this more precisely. (**R3**, pp. 6, 7. Premonitions **R2**, pp. 57, 72. Non-linearity **R3**, p. 132. Triviality **R5**, p. 70. Further references under methods for $\overline{\chi}_2$ limitation.)

25X THE NUMBER OF LEGAL WHEELS E.14

In order that χ_5 shall generate a $\Delta\chi_5$ with 12 crosses, it must consist of 6 blocks of crosses and 6 blocks of dots. Each block must contain at least one character, and, for legality, not more than four. There must be in all 12 (or 11) crosses and 11 (or 12) dots.

The number of ways in which such blocks can be chosen is

$$\left\{\text{coefft. of } x^{12} \text{ in } \left(x+x^2+x^3+x^4\right)^6\right\}.\left\{\text{coefft. of } x^{11} \text{ in } \left(x+x^2+x^3+x^4\right)^6\right\}$$

$$=\left\{\text{coefft. of } x^6 \text{ in } \frac{1}{(1-x)^6}-\frac{6x^4}{(1-x)^6}\right\}.\left\{\text{coefft. of } x^5 \text{ in } \frac{1}{(1-x)^6}-\frac{6x^4}{(1-x)^6}\right\}.$$

To find the number of legal wheels this must be multiplied by 2, to allow for 11 crosses and b 12 dots; divided by 6 because the first block of crosses may be any one of six; and if different settings of the same wheel are to be distinguished, multiplied by 23. p. 193

In the following table the number of legal wheels is exact: other entries to four figures only.

	Total no. of wheels.	Δ'd wheels with the correct no. of crosses.	Legal wheels.
χ_1	2,193,000,000,000	271,900,000,000	23,314,226,716
χ_2	2,143,000,000	304,000,000	73,241,034
χ_3	535,800,000	78,320,000	14,524,128
χ_4	66,990,000	19,544,000	2,869,568
χ_5	8,434,000	1,364,000	556,416

From this table the factor in favour of a wheel because it is spontaneously legal can be calculated. It should be noticed that any supposed $\Delta\chi$ wheel corresponds to two χ wheels or to none, so that e.g. a $\Delta\chi_5$, constrained to have the correct number of crosses gains a factor $2\times 1{,}364{,}000/556{,}416 \risingdotseq 4{\cdot}4$ if it is spontaneously legal.
(**R5**, p. 4; for factor given by integration **R3**, p. 30.)

25Y PROPORTIONAL BULGES RELATING TO $\widehat{\chi}_2$ i

These will all be derived using $\Delta\chi_6 \equiv \widetilde{\overline{\chi}}_2$. (**22D(g)**.)

The following notation will be used for proportional bulges:

[a] decibannage [b] multipled

[i] Throughout **25Y** equation numbers given without parentheses.

a $(\bullet\bullet\times) \equiv \beta_{\bullet\bullet\times}$	denotes	the	P.B.	of	$1=\bullet$,	$2=\bullet$,	$6=\times$ in	$\Delta\psi'$
$\{\bullet\bullet\times\} \equiv \delta_{\bullet\bullet\times}$	"	"	"	"	$1=\bullet$,	$2=\bullet$,	$6=\times$ in	ΔD
$\pi_{\times}$	"	"	"	"		$2=\times$,		ΔP
$\pi_{\bullet\bullet}$	"	"	"	"	$1=\bullet$,	$2=\bullet$		ΔP
π_{1+2}	"	"	"	"	$1+2=\bullet$			ΔP
θ	"	"	"	"	$\widehat{\chi}_2=\bullet$.			

$$\begin{aligned}\text{P.B.}(\Delta Z_2=\bullet) &= \text{P.B.}(\Delta_2 Z_2+\Delta Z_6=\bullet)\\ &= \text{P.B.}(\Delta\psi'_2+\Delta\psi'_6+\Delta\chi_2+\Delta\chi_6+\Delta P_2+\Delta P_6=\bullet)\\ &= \text{P.B.}(\Delta\psi'_{26}+\widetilde{\widehat{\chi}}_2+\Delta P_{\dot{2}}=\bullet)\\ &= \beta\theta\pi_{\times}. \qquad \text{(Y1)}\end{aligned}$$

i

p. 194

$$\begin{aligned}\text{P.B.}(\Delta D_1=\bullet,\ \Delta D_{26}=\bullet) &= \frac{1}{2}\left[\{\bullet\bullet\bullet\}+\{\bullet\times\times\}\right]\\ &= \frac{1}{8}\left[\pi_{\bullet\bullet}(\bullet\bullet\bullet+\bullet\times\times)+\pi_{\times\times}(\times\times\bullet+\times\bullet\times)\right.\\ &\qquad \left.+\pi_{\times\bullet}(\times\bullet\bullet+\times\times\times)+\pi_{\bullet\times}(\bullet\times\bullet+\bullet\bullet\times)\right]\\ &= \frac{1}{8}\left[\pi_{\bullet\bullet}(4\beta-\beta^2-\beta^2)+\pi_{\times\times}(-2\beta^2)+\right.\\ &\qquad \left.\pi_{\times\bullet}(-2\beta+\beta^2+2\beta+\beta^2)+\pi_{\bullet\times}(-4\beta+2\beta^2)\right]\\ &= \frac{\beta}{4}\left[(2-\beta)(\pi_{\bullet\bullet}-\pi_{\bullet\times})-\beta(\pi_{\times\times}-\pi_{\times\bullet})\right].\end{aligned}$$

By changing the sign of ΔP_1

$$\text{P.B.}(\Delta D_1=\times,\ \Delta D_{26}=\bullet) = \frac{\beta}{4}\left[(2-\beta)(\pi_{\times\bullet}-\pi_{\times\times})-\beta(\pi_{\bullet\times}-\pi_{\bullet\bullet})\right]$$

$$\begin{aligned}\therefore\quad \text{P.B.}(\Delta D_1=\bullet\,|\,\Delta D_{26}=\bullet) &= \frac{\frac{1}{2}\left[\text{P.B.}(\Delta D_1=\bullet,\Delta D_{26}=\bullet)-\text{P.B.}(\Delta D_1=\times,\Delta D_{26}=\bullet)\right]}{\text{P.B.}(\Delta D_{26}=\bullet)}\\ &= \frac{\beta(1-\beta)\pi_{1+2}}{1-\beta\pi_{\times}}. \qquad \text{(Y2)}\end{aligned}$$

Changing the signs of ΔP_1, ΔP_2

$$\text{P.B.}(\Delta D_1=\times\,|\,\Delta D_{26}=\times) = \frac{\beta(1-\beta)\pi_{1+2}}{1+\beta\pi_{\times}} \qquad \text{(Y3)}$$

whence (or otherwise)

$$\text{P.B.}(\Delta D_1+\Delta D_{26}=\bullet) = \beta(1-\beta)\pi_{1+2}. \qquad \text{(Y4)}$$

b Evidently, unless the $\pi_{\times}$ is larger than is probable in cipher, as distinct from key, the P.B.'s of $1\bullet/2+6$, $1\times/2+6\times$ do not differ sufficiently to justify running them separately.

---

[a] denoted the P.B. [b] the P.Bs.

[i] Right hand sides of second and third expressions for $\text{P.B.}(\Delta D_1=\bullet,\ \Delta D_{26}=\bullet)$ given on one line each. We have split them here for clarity.

26 WHEEL-BREAKING FROM KEY p. 195

26A INTRODUCTION

Wheel-breaking from key is normally a hand process performed largely and often entirely by specially trained Testery breakers on key obtained from depth. The length of such key varies from about 100 to 400. Key obtained from a crib is usually at least 1000 in length and is broken entirely E.1
in the Newmanry, largely by mechanical methods. This chapter is concerned only with depth key except where specific reference is made to crib key. This is because

(i) The methods used on crib key are merely extreme simplifications of those used on depth key.

(ii) Depth key is of far more frequent occurrence. a

(iii) Depth key is normally several days more current. It is in fact the quickest way of breaking b
the day's wheels. Frequently it enabled us to decode the traffic of the current day.

The ease with which key is broken depends on three factors: the length, the number of dots in μ_{37} and the type of limitation used. When these factors are particularly favourable the methods here described can often be simplified or short-circuited. For example, in extreme cases depth key can be treated just like crib key and broken rapidly on Colossus.

Five-to-the-inch squared paper of the kind shown in fig. **26 (I)** is used for all hand work. The p. 196
ΔK is written out in ink on a width of 62 with 9 squares intervening between each line, but for convenience we use in this report a width of 31 instead. The 5 rows beneath the ΔK are regarded as corresponding to the 5 TP impulses, and each impulse is marked off with an upright ink line on the period of the chi-length for that impulse. All subsequent work is done with pencil and eraser.

26B STARTS

The first necessity is to obtain a nucleus of $\Delta\chi$ signs of which a substantial majority are right. These are termed 'embryonic wheels' and form the basis of subsequent work.

There are three main types of start, apart from the rarely used Δ^2 method described below.

They are

---

[a] depth key is of [b] depth key is normally

[i] This chapter's analytical contents reproduces what is on the corresponding page of the *Report*, p. 195. The titles given here for sections **26C**, **26X** and **26Y** do not exactly match what is in the body of the chapter.

[ii] Blank line separating **26J** and **26X** not present in *Report*.

(a) the 5 by 5 and 10 by 10 flags (**R3**, p. 93),
(b) the $\widehat{\chi}_2$ count,
(c) the χ_5 composite flag.

i **(a)**

E.2 The 5 by 5 flag is normally used for non $\overline{\chi}_2$ keys which are long enough to give a good
ii expectation of 5 by 5 flag significance provided that the μ_{37} dottage is not very unfavourable. The method is as follows. Fig. **26 (I)** shows the first 44 letters of a ΔK marked off in chi lengths.

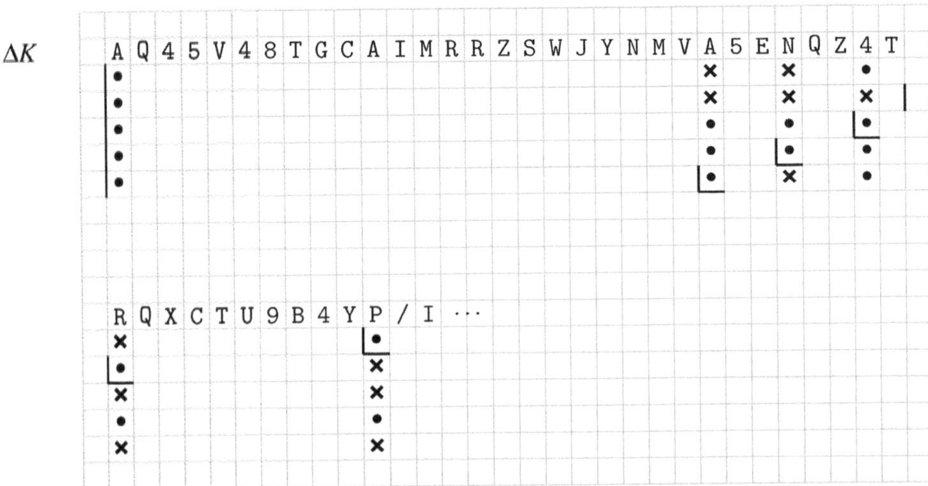

Fig. 26 (I)

p. 197 We assume, arbitrarily, that $\Delta\chi = /$ at the first place of key. We put these 5 $\Delta\chi$ signs in on the period of the χ lengths (underlined in fig. **26 (I)**) throughout the key. Now the property $P(\Delta\psi'_{ij} = \bullet) = b$ implies that if on one impulse $\Delta\chi = \Delta K$ there is a probability b that on any other impulse $\Delta\chi = \Delta K$, and conversely for $\Delta\chi \neq \Delta K$. Thus we make the probability $\Delta\chi$ inferences
a indicated in fig. **26 (I)** by signs not underlined.

These inferences are written into 5 specially prepared "cages", whose widths are the lengths of the 5 χ's. The cages indicate the number of the impulse originally assumed (i.e. underlined) from which each inference is drawn. The $\Delta\chi_5$ cage for the key of fig. **26 (I)** is shown in fig. **26 (II)**.

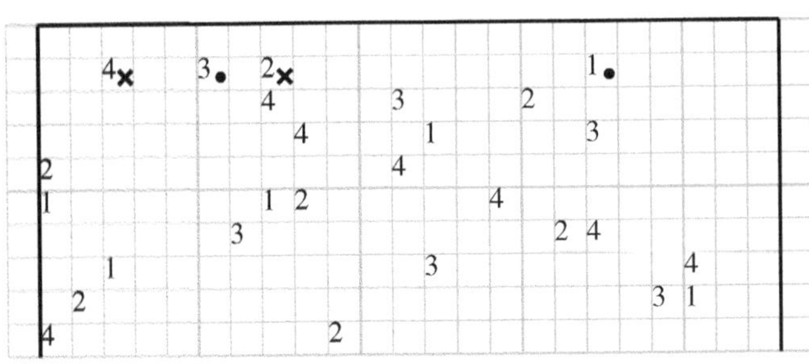

iii **Fig. 26 (II)**

[a] fig I

[i] Subsection (a) untitled; text begins on same line as subhead.
[ii] Word 'unfavourable' handwritten.
[iii] Caption moved from above figure to below.

When the 5 cages have been entered we book all the agreements and disagreements among the signs in each column, using dots for agreements, and crosses for disagreements. For example a column of the $\Delta\chi_5$ cage entered as in fig. **26 (III)** scores a disagreement between 1 and 3, and between 3 and 4, and an agreement between 1 and 4. So when all the comparisons have been booked, we get something like this (fig. **26 (IV)**):

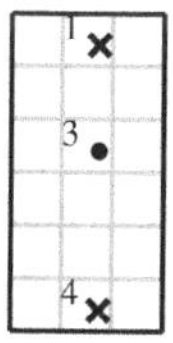

Fig. **26 (III)**

										Dots	Crosses	Excesses
1	2	•	•	×	•	•	•			5	1	(4)
1	3	•	•	•	•	•	×	×		5	2	(3)
1	4	×	•	×	×	×	×			1	5	4
1	5	×	×	•	•	•	×	×	×	3	5	2
2	3	•	×	×	•	•	•	•	•	6	2	(4)
2	4	×	×	×	•	•	×	×		2	5	3
2	5	×	•	×	×	×	•	×		2	5	3
3	4	×	×	×	•	•	•	×	×	3	5	2
3	4	•	×	×	•	×	×	×		2	5	3
4	5	•	•	•	•	×	•	•		6	1	5

ν = total no. of comparisons
$= 35 + 36 = 71$

Fig. **26 (IV)** i

The right-hand column of numbers represents the excess of agreements over disagreements, and these numbers are entered into a double-entry square, which is "converged" thus (see **24C**). p. 198, a

	1	2	3	4	5		
1	\	(4)	(3)	4	2	×	13
2	(4)	\	(4)	3	3	×	14
3	(3)	(4)	\	2	3	×	12
4	4	3	2	\	(5)	•	(14)
5	2	3	3	(5)	\	•	(13)

Sum of moduli = 66 = x

Fig. 26 (V) ii

We infer that the arbitrary assumption of / in the first place of key must be changed to U (or O) to give the maximum number of agreements in the comparisons. So all cage entries numbered 1, 2 and 3 (or 4 & 5) are reversed and the embryonic $\Delta\chi$'s obtained by summing the cage columns. The significance test "$\frac{1}{2}x/\sqrt{\nu} \geq 3$", (where x = the modular sum of the scores and ν = the total number of comparisons) is applied before using the flag as a start. In the example given in figs. **26 (IV)** and **(V)**, $x = 66$, $\nu = 71$, $\frac{1}{2}x/\sqrt{\nu} \fallingdotseq 3{\cdot}9$. b E.3 c

To decide which of the two alternatives for the $\Delta\chi$ letter to accept provisionally, we add them to the first letter of ΔK to give a $\Delta\psi'$ letter. In our example the alternatives are U and O which added to the first letter of ΔK, A, give $\Delta\psi' =$ 9 and 5 respectively. Since 5 is so much more likely

[a] right hand [b] place of must [c] given in figs **IV** and **V**

[i] Caption of fig. **26 (IV)** states $36 + 36 = 71$.
[ii] Fig. **26 (V)** uncaptioned in *Report*.

than 9 in $\Delta\psi'$ we accept $\Delta\chi = 0$. The actual factor in favour of 0 rather than U can be seen to be $\{b/(1-b)\}^3$, which corresponds to 9 db, if $b = 2/3$. This sort of argument can also be used as an additional significance test for the flag. For example, if the $\Delta\psi'$ letter is / or 8 we would be quite satisfied with $\frac{1}{2}x/\sqrt{\nu} = 2{\cdot}5$, since the letter / or 8 is so much more likely a priori than any other pair of $\Delta\psi'$ alternatives.

a The 10 by 10 flag is an amplification of the 5 by 5 flag. It is frequently used when the 5 by 5 flag has just failed to be significant, as the work for the latter flag can easily be included in the 10 by 10 flag. The first *two* letters of $\Delta\chi$, instead of just the first, are assumed to be strokes, the impulses of the second letter being numbered 6, 7, 8, 9, 10. Then we proceed as for the 5 by 5 flag.

The inferences from $\Delta\chi_2$, 2nd place are booked under the heading '7', as distinct from those derived from $\Delta\chi_1$, 1st place, which are headed '1' (**R41**, p. 47). When the comparisons between all 45 possible pairs of the 10 impulses have been booked they are entered in a square 10 by 10,
p. 199 and converged as before. The significance test is $\frac{1}{2}x/\sqrt{\nu} \geq 4$.

(b) The $\widehat{\chi}_2$ count is used

E.4 (i) to establish by means of the standard significance test for short WB runs that the key is on $\overline{\chi}_2$ limitation, if this is in doubt, or if $\overline{\chi}_2$ limitation is certain, possibly to establish the correctness of the key,

(ii) to give a start for key-breaking.

The property used is

$$\Delta K_2 \underset{b}{\rightarrow} \widetilde{\widetilde{\chi}}_2 \,.$$

This can be derived from **22H**(9), by regarding P as / throughout so that $K = Z$.

ΔK_2 is written out on a width of 31 and the excesses per column of dots over crosses are written as ringed and unringed numbers. The deciban value of these pips is $10\log_{10}\{(1+\beta)/(1-\beta)\}$.

Sometimes the length of key and the dottage are sufficient to give a complete $\widehat{\widetilde{\chi}}_2$, from which χ_2 may be derived, as follows:

i $\widehat{\chi}_2$ is deltaed to give $\Delta_3\overline{\chi}_2$, which is integrated and slid one to the left. This pattern is χ_2 or $\widetilde{\chi}_2$, according to the correctness of the original assumption from which the integration was made. The ambiguity is immediately solved by reference back to the $\widehat{\chi}_2$ wheel.

Now we add χ_2 to K_2, and by using the known $\overline{\chi}_2$ limitation we should easily be able to recognise ψ_2 and break the key as described below (**26D**).

Normally, however, the $\widehat{\chi}_2$ count is significant but does not yield a complete wheel. In this case we make our start as follows. The method rests on the concept that $\overline{\chi}_2$ limitation is a *six*-impulse

ii key in which ΔK_6 always $= \bullet$, and $\Delta\chi_6 = \Delta\psi'_6 = \widetilde{\widetilde{\chi}}_2$. (See **22D(g)**.) (**R41**, p. 67)

The first step is to de-chi ΔK_2 with the stronger characters of $\widehat{\widetilde{\chi}}_2$ (say scores ≥ 3). The operation performed can be expressed

$$\Delta K_{26} + \Delta\chi_{26} \quad (\text{since } \widetilde{\widetilde{\chi}}_2 = \Delta\chi_2 + \Delta\chi_6\,)$$

and the resultant signs are $\Delta\psi'_{26}$.

Thus we have a fragmentary $\Delta\psi'_{26}$ pattern from which to make a start. A count for $\Delta\chi_5$ is done first. The properties used are

$$P(\Delta\psi'_i = \bullet \mid \Delta\psi'_{jk} = \bullet) = (1+2\beta-\beta^2)/(2+2\beta)$$

---

[a] frequenly

[i] delta-ed

[ii] Reference '(**R41** p. 67)' handwritten.

and

$$P(\Delta\psi_i' = \times \mid \Delta\psi_{jk}' = \times) = \frac{1}{2}(1+\beta).$$

Therefore a dot in $\Delta\psi_{26}'$ gives a factor of $\frac{1+2\beta-\beta^2}{1+\beta}$ (about 1·5 db if $d = 181/2$) in favour of a $\Delta\psi_5'$ p. 200, a
dot, and therefore in favour of $\Delta\chi_5 = \Delta K_5$. A cross in $\Delta\psi_{26}'$ gives a factor of $\frac{1+\beta}{1-\beta}$ (about 3 db) in favour of a $\Delta\psi_5'$ cross, and therefore in favour of $\Delta\chi_5 \neq \Delta K_5$. For convenience we work in pips worth 1·5 db each, scoring 1 and 2 respectively. From this $\Delta\chi_5$ count strong characters are selected, say $\geqslant 7{\cdot}5$ db with which to de-chi ΔK_5. The count for $\Delta\chi_4$ makes use both of the $\Delta\psi_5'$ characters now in the 5th impulse, and of the $\Delta\psi_{26}'$ characters in the 2nd, while the $\Delta\chi_3$ count also uses the new characters derived from the $\Delta\chi_4$ count. The scoring for these counts is given below. **(26Y(f))**

Having counted for $\Delta\chi$'s 4 and 3 in this way it is usual to scrap the $\Delta\psi_{26}'$ signs in the second impulse and count for $\Delta\chi_2$, (using the signs now in impulses 3, 4 and 5), rather than first counting for $\Delta\chi_1$.

How this count is taken and all subsequent work is described below **(26E)**.

(c) The χ_5 flag (R3, p. 67) is normally used:

(i) on keys not on $\overline{\chi}_2$ limitation which are not long enough for a good chance of 5 by 5 significance,

(ii) on keys known a priori to be on $\overline{\chi}_2$ limitation but which are not long enough for $\widehat{\chi}_2$ significance. The $\widehat{\chi}_2$ start is then considered not to be strong enough, and the χ_5 flag is used. E.5

Method: A type-out is made on Garbo in widths of 23, of ΔK_{15}, ΔK_{25}, ΔK_{35}, ΔK_{45}, and in the case of (ii) ΔK_{65}. These type-outs are entered diagonally into rectangles (for rectangles generally see **24**) of width 23, and length 41, 31, 29, 26, and 31 respectively. The rectangles are flagged (see **24B(d)**(i)) on $\Delta\chi_5$ and the flags combined by straight addition. This is of course equivalent to flagging what is called the long rectangle, shown in the diagram.

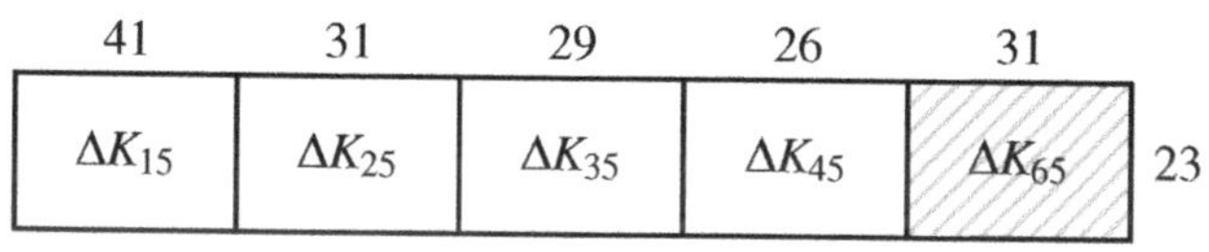

The flag is converged to give $\Delta\chi_5$ in positive and negative scores. The significance test $\frac{1}{2}x/\sqrt{\nu}$ is applied, where x is the modular sum of the scores and ν is the total number of comparisons (**R3**, pp. 46, 97). i

The formula for finding ν is

$$\nu = {\cdot}0648N^2 - 2N + 8$$

and

$$\nu^* = {\cdot}0810N^2 - 2N + 10$$ p. 201

where ν^* is the total number of comparisons when the ΔK_{65} rectangle is included.

A simpler form of the test is ii

---

[a] give a factor

[i] Reference '(**R3** pp. 46, 97.)' handwritten.

[ii] Word 'where' moved from end of first line of following displayed equation to start of second line. Word 'and' handwritten.

$$\frac{x}{\sigma \text{ or } \sigma^*} \geqslant 6$$

$$\text{where } \sigma = 2\sqrt{\nu} = \cdot 51N - 8$$

$$\text{and } \sigma^* = 2\sqrt{\nu^*} = \cdot 57N - 7.$$

Each flag comparison is worth a factor of $\frac{1+\beta^2}{1-\beta^2}$. Since $10\log_{10}\frac{1+\beta^2}{1-\beta^2} \risingdotseq 1$ for $\beta = 1/3$ the scores for $\Delta\chi_5$ from the converged flag will be approximately in decibans.

If significant a partial $\Delta\chi_5$ obtained from these scores is taken through the 4 (or 5) rectangles (as through the long rectangle) to provide embryonic $\Delta\chi$'s for the start. The scores of the embryonics are in units of approximately 3 db as each rectangle entry is worth a factor of

$$\frac{1+\beta}{1-\beta}, \text{ and } 10\log_{10}\frac{1+\beta}{1-\beta} \risingdotseq 3 \text{ for } \beta = \frac{1}{3}.$$

Sometimes a combined χ_4 flag is made, if the χ_5 flag fails to be significant.

The expected x^* for any converged composite flag is $2\beta^2\nu$, and the expected $x^*/\sigma = \beta^2\sqrt{\nu}$
i, a (**R3** p. 97). The meaning of x^* is analogous to that given in **24X(e)**.

Below is a table of the length, N, of ΔK required for expected $x/\sigma > 6$ for different dottages, d (**R3**, p. 98).

d	*N*	*d*	*N*
14	447	22	148
15	377	23	131
16	323	24	118
17	281	25	107
18	244	26	96
19	213	27	88
20	187	28	79
21	167	29	72

For flags which include the ΔK_{65} rectangle these figures will be even smaller.

(d) Δ^2 properties

b In September 1943 (see **R0**, p. 53) it was noticed that $P(\Delta^2\chi_i = \times) > \frac{1}{2}$ and often about 2/3.
ii, E.6 Unlike P. B.$(\Delta\psi_i = \times) = \beta$ the property was found to lack rigidity.

Let P. B.$(\Delta^2\chi_i = \times) = \xi$ and assume P. B.$(\Delta\psi_i = \times) = 0$.

p. 202 Then it can be shown that

$$\begin{cases} \text{P.B.}(\Delta^2 K_i = \times \mid \text{TM} = \bullet\,\bullet) = \xi \\ \text{P.B.}(\Delta^2 K_i = \bullet \mid \text{TM} = \bullet\,\times \text{ or } \times\,\bullet) = \beta\xi \\ \text{P.B.}(\Delta^2 K_i = \bullet \mid \text{TM} = \times\,\times) \risingdotseq 0. \end{cases}$$

So if $\Delta^2 K = 8$ we have a strong factor for TM $= \bullet\,\bullet$, which brings the odds in favour of TM $= \bullet\,\bullet$ up to a little over evens for a μ_{37} dottage of 16, and even higher for higher μ_{37} dottages.

Two points arise in the selection of a possible $\bullet\,\bullet$ in TM.

(i) If we assume TM $= \bullet\,\bullet$ in positions 2 and 3 of K we are automatically (for $\overline{\chi}_2$ limitation) assuming $\times\,\times$ in positions 1 and 2 of χ_2. Therefore we are assuming position 1 of $\Delta\chi_2 = \bullet$ and so it is preferable in our selection of a place in ΔK that we take one in which $\Delta K_2 = \times\,\bullet$ rather than $\bullet\,\times$ so that we have $\Delta^2\chi_2 = \times\,\times$ rather than $\bullet\,\times$.

[a] analagous [b] **R0**, 53

[i] Handwritten reference '(**R3** p. 97)' inserted with caret.

[ii] Symbol 'P. B' used in second and third sentences of **26B(d)** instead of 'P. B.'.

(ii) By a similar argument to that used to infer a possible • • in TM from an 8 in Δ^2K we may infer (with even greater probability) that TM = • × or × • from a / in Δ^2K. This provides a useful check in the case where ΔK reads (say) RYY, where it greatly strengthens the evidence for TM = • • at RY.

Having chosen a double dot in TM we are already provided with 2 $\Delta\chi$ characters on each impulse, 10 characters in all. These we put through the ΔK on the chi-lengths, derive further $\Delta\chi$ assumptions from them in the normal way as in Turingery (see **43B**) and collect them into cages. If the cages look good we proceed as in Turingery.

This method of using Δ^2 properties for key-breaking was never standard practice, but it occasionally yielded spectacular results, especially when the number of 8's in the Δ^2K was significantly high, indicating a strong tendency of $\Delta^2\chi$ to cross and high μ_{37} dottage. The most outstanding success was obtained in the last few weeks of the war, when the shortest key ever to be broken, of length 97 was tackled by assuming *all* 8's in Δ^2K to be double dots in TM, and gradually eliminating those which began to give contradictions.

For the tendency of $\Delta^2\chi$ to cross as a special case of the use of $\Delta\chi$ characteristics see **R3**, pp. 125, 126.

26C HAND COUNTING FOR $\overline{\chi}_2\overline{\Psi}_1'$ LIMITATION p. 203

The embryonic $\Delta\chi$'s already obtained from the 5 by 5, 10 by 10, or χ_5 flags are added to the ΔK to give fragmentary $\Delta\psi'$, and check A is applied (see below fig. **26 (VI)**). Except when a
the embryonics derive from a 5 by 5 flag, a test is immediately applied to determine 'the sign of the key' (**R41**, p. 69), i.e. whether the $\Delta\chi$'s (and therefore the $\Delta\psi'$) are reversed or the right way i
round. In the case of the 5 by 5 flag start, the test is applied after 'counting once round', a phrase E.7
to be explained later.

The total number of $L_{5,0}$'s, $L_{4,0}$'s, $L_{3,0}$'s (a letter $L_{n,m}$ is defined as a letter with n dots and m crosses), and also the total number of dots and the total number of crosses in the 'spoiled columns' are counted. An 'unspoiled column' is a letter where either $n = 0$ or $m = 0$.

For each excess of $L_{5,0}$ over $L_{0,5}$ score +2 db
$L_{4,0}$ over $L_{0,4}$ score +1 db
$L_{3,0}$ over $L_{0,3}$ score +4 cb
and for each excess of cross over dot in a spoiled column score +4 c.bs. for the theory that the ii
$\Delta\chi$'s are the right way round.

Significance level for the test is taken as 20 db. This is generous and allows for the possibility that the embryonics may be considerably less than 80% right, 80% being the standard taken for calculating the above scoring system.

Suppose that the test is not conclusive, or that it has not been applied because the start was a 5 by 5 flag. We then do a count for $\Delta\chi_4$ first (as $\Delta\chi_5$ already has strong evidence) using only iii
unspoiled columns.

For 1 dot or 1 cross in the other impulses score 3 db for $\Delta\psi_4'$ being a dot or cross respectively and therefore in favour of $\Delta\chi_4 =$ or $\neq \Delta K_4$ at the position counted.

For 2 dots or 2 crosses score 5.

For 3 dots or 3 crosses score 6.

For 4 dots or 4 crosses score 7. (These figures are derived from the table in **R41**, p. 56 by iv
putting $q = \cdot 5$.)

---

[a] fig.**26** VI

[i] Reference '(**R41** p. 69)' handwritten.

[ii] The abbreviation 'c.bs' for 'centibans' is used twice in this sentence. We have rendered it as 'cb' by analogy with 'db' for 'decibans'. See endnote 4 to **21**, p. 577 below.

[iii] Handwritten 'first' inserted with a caret.

[iv] Parenthesized remark 'These figures...' handwritten.

From the $\Delta\chi_4$ count we select all characters with scores > 10 db and re-de-chi ΔK_4 with the improved $\Delta\chi_4$.

We now repeat the process for the next shortest $\Delta\chi$, and so on until all 5 $\Delta\chi$'s have been counted once. We have now 'counted once round'. The test for the sign of the key is then applied again. Once significance has been achieved on this test the method of counting is changed.

p. 204 Suppose that the test shows the $\Delta\chi$'s to be the right way round. Then for the next $\Delta\chi_i$ count

For 1 dot in the other impulses and no crosses, score $+1$ for $\Delta\psi_i' =$ dot

For 2 dots and no crosses score $+2$.

For 3 dots and no crosses score $+3$.

For 4 dots and no crosses score $+5$ (**R41**, p. 89).

For 1 or more crosses (and however many dots) in the other impulses score -1. If the $\Delta\chi$'s are found to be inside out, interchange 'dot' and 'cross' throughout the above.

These figures are a crude scaling down for convenience of the decibanages 3, 7, 11, 16 [i] assuming $\alpha = 18\frac{1}{2}$. The pips are each worth approximately 3 db, and the standard normally taken for accepting $\Delta\chi$ characters from the count is 5. The counting is continued until one complete $\Delta\chi$ wheel is obtained.

A useful check for key work on $\overline{\chi}_2 + \overline{\psi}_1'$ key was devised shortly before the end of the war (**R41**, p. 92). Suppose that positions $n+1, n+2, n+3$ of K are consecutive TM dots. Then

(i) $\chi_2 + \psi_1' = \times\times\times$ at $n, n+1, n+2$.

But (ii) $\Delta\psi_1' = \bullet$ at $n+1$ because TM $= \bullet$.

Then (iii) from (i) $\Delta\chi_2 = \bullet$ at $n+1$.

But (iv) $\Delta\psi_2' = \bullet$ at $n+1$ (as in (ii)).

Therefore (v) from (iii) and (iv) $\Delta K_2 = \bullet$ at $n+1$. (The property is of course equally and more obviously true for $\overline{\chi}_2$ key.)

Hence we can only assume 3 consecutive dots in TM where $\Delta K_2 = \bullet$ at the first of the 3 dots. So if in key-breaking we have

ΔK			R	B	D	Q	V
			•	•			
			•	•	•		
			•		•		
				•	•		
			•	•	•		

we know that one of these letters is not a TM dot. If we cannot decide which is the weakest and ignore all motor dot evidence derived from it we should ignore all 3 until the impostor is revealed.

To assist key-breakers on $\overline{\chi}_2\overline{\psi}_1'$ key a chart was made giving a standardised routine for keys started from a χ_5 flag. This chart is given in fig. **26 (VI)**.

[i] Phrase 'assuming $\alpha = 18\frac{1}{2}$' handwritten.

p. 205

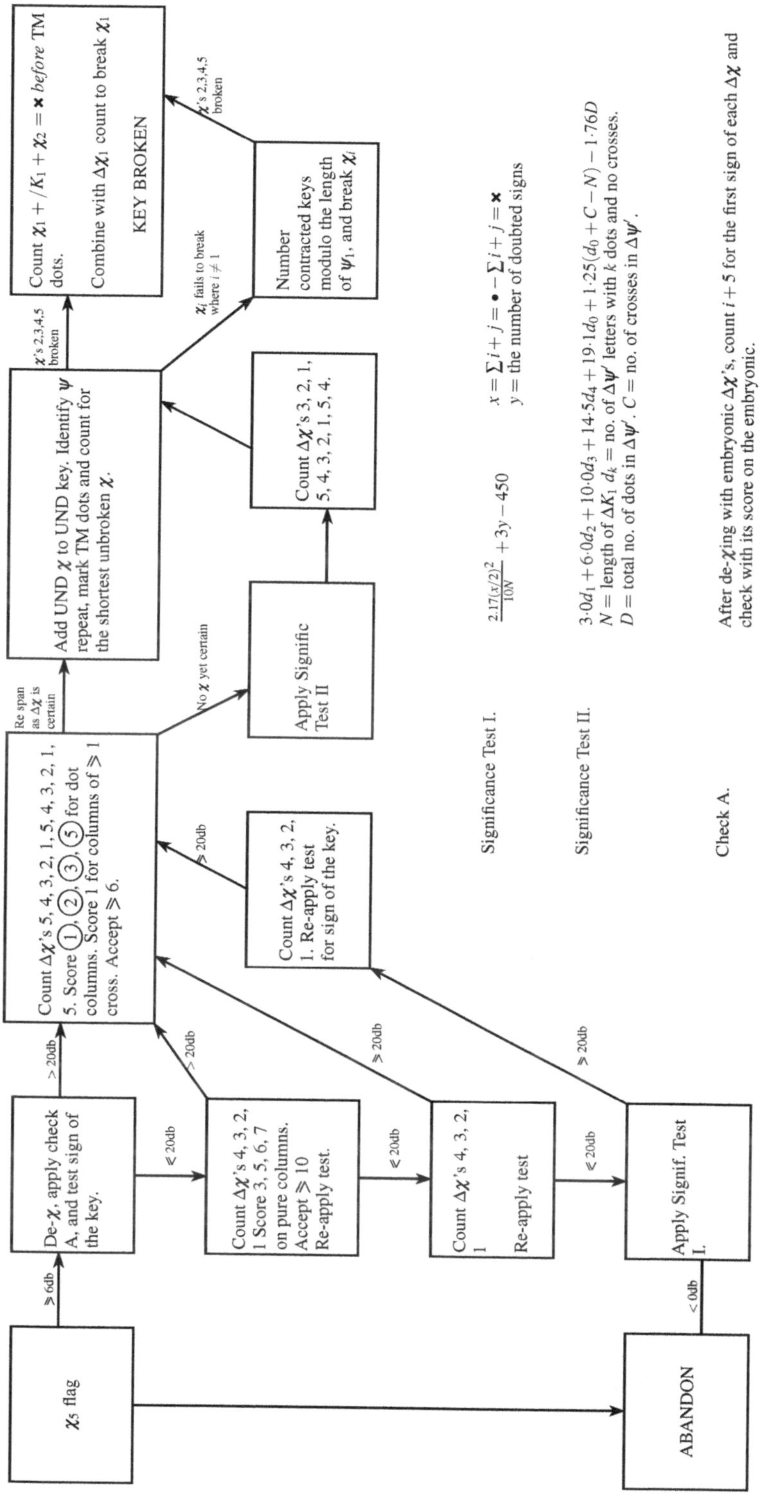

Significance Test I. $\frac{2.17(x/2)^2}{10N} + 3y - 450$ $x = \sum i + j = \bullet - \sum i + j = \times$
$y =$ the number of doubted signs

Significance Test II. $3{\cdot}0d_1 + 6{\cdot}0d_2 + 10{\cdot}0d_3 + 14{\cdot}5d_4 + 19{\cdot}1d_0 + 1{\cdot}25(d_0 + C - N) - 1{\cdot}76D$
N = length of ΔK_1 d_k = no. of $\Delta\Psi'$ letters with k dots and no crosses.
D = total no. of dots in $\Delta\Psi'$. C = no. of crosses in $\Delta\Psi'$.

Check A. After de-χing with embryonic Δχ's, count $i + 5$ for the first sign of each Δχ and check with its score on the embryonic.

Fig. 26 (VI) Standardised key-breaking routine for $\overline{\chi}_2\overline{\Psi}_1$ limitation

p. 206 26D RECOGNISING THE ψ REPEAT AND NUMBERING

As soon as a $\Delta\chi$ is obtained it is integrated, and the undifferenced χ_i is added to undifferenced K_i to give ψ_i'. An attempt is then made to recognise the repeat of ψ_i in its extended form. The number of groups of crosses in ψ_i is known approximately in advance as it is a function of the number of dots in μ_{37}, and some idea of this will have been gained in working on the key. When [a] the repeat has been recognised and the number of groups of crosses established these groups are numbered, returning to 1 each time the repeat comes round. Many TM dots can now be inferred wherever a group or interval between groups is known from one appearance to be a single cross or dot but appears elsewhere extended to two or more. Other TM dots can be inferred but not located exactly (see **41D(e)**). At every TM dot located $\Delta\chi = \Delta K$ and the $\Delta\chi$ values thus deduced for the shortest unknown χ are entered on the width of its wheel length. This will normally bring out the whole $\Delta\chi$, especially if we use the TM $=$ **×** positions, which each give a factor of $\frac{1+\beta}{1-\beta}$ ($\fallingdotseq$ 3 db) for $\Delta\chi_i \neq \Delta K_i$. The new $\Delta\chi$ is integrated to give a χ which is added to its K impulse to give a new ψ'. The new ψ' is numbered in groups as before, thus locating more TM dots. These are used with those already known to break the next shortest unknown χ, and so on.

When the TM dot evidence fails to complete a $\Delta\chi$ the method of 'numbering' is used. First the ψ_i' already produced has to be reduced to ψ_i. This is easy if two or more ψ''s are already known, and nearly always possible for only one. The method is to take the shortest form in which any particular group of crosses or dots in ψ_i' appears as representing its true size in unextended ψ_i. The characters of ψ_i are then numbered from 1 to the length of the ψ wheel, and the numerical co-efficients of the ψ_i characters are transferred to the same characters appearing in ψ_i'.

Thus a ψ':

•	×	×	×	•	•	×	•	•	•	×	•	•	×	×	•	•	•	×	•	×	×	×	×	•

derived from a ψ:

1	2	3	4	5	6	7	8	9	10	11	12	13	14	15	16	17	
•	×	•	•	×	•	•	×	•	×	×	•	×	•	×	×	•	

p. 207 would be numbered

	1	2	2	2	3	4	5	6		7	8	9	9	10	11	12	12	12	13	14	15			16	17
	•	×	×	×	•	•	×	•	•	•	×	•	•	×	×	•	•	•	×	•	×	×	×	×	•
TM	×	•	•	×	×	×	×	(1)		×	×	•	×	×	×	•	•	×	×	×		(2)		×	

The TM deduced is also shown, with bracketed numbers representing dots whose presence but not exact location has been deduced. The process of simultaneously constructing the χ and ψ patterns of a different impulse from that of the numbered ψ' is that described in **42B(d)**, with the difference that instead of taking an arbitrarily assumed sign as the start we can integrate a length of $\Delta\chi$ already made certain in the counting, and with so large a start finish the job easily and quickly.

26E HAND COUNTING ON $\overline{\chi}_2$ KEY

We left the $\widehat{\chi}_2$ start at the stage where the first count for $\Delta\chi_2$ was about to be done, after obtaining signs on $\Delta\chi$'s 5, 4 and 3. This count is taken as in counting on $\overline{\chi}_2 + \overline{\psi}_1'$ key, with the same scoring.

E.8 The scores are in favour of $\Delta\chi_2$ signs, but the aim is to obtain $\Delta\chi_6$ ($\widetilde{\overline{\chi}}_2$) signs as well as $\Delta\chi_2$

[a] group

signs. The process by which this is done is complex and can only be mastered by experience. The methods used depend on mathematical common sense and it is hardly necessary to describe them in detail. If a stage is reached at which a good deal of $\Delta\chi_2$ and $\Delta\chi_6$ are known, considerable use can be made of the connection between these wheels. Otherwise $\Delta\chi_6$ is treated just like a sixth impulse and the scoring system is the same as in non-χ_2 key-breaking, except that the scoring includes another term (**R41**, p. 67). It now reads 1, 2, 3, 5, 7 for a dot in the counted impulse, i
given respectively, 1, 2, 3, 4, or 5 dots and no crosses in the other impulses (**R41**, p. 89). ii

When we start with a χ_5 flag and not a $\widehat{\chi}_2$ count we start at the stage reached in the $\widehat{\chi}_2$ method when partial wheels are known for all six $\Delta\chi$'s. The difference is that unless the compatibility or incompatibility of $\Delta\chi_2$ and $\Delta\chi_6$ is very marked we do not know the sign of the key. This is determined by the test of **26C** except that the score for $L_{6,0}$ over $L_{0,6}$ is $+3$ db (**R41**, p. 69). This p. 208
test allied with the comparison of $\Delta\chi_2$ and $\Delta\chi_6$ should show conclusively the sign of the key. If not we should apply a very careful check of each stage of the work.

Once the sign of the key is determined we proceed with 6-impulse counting as before. The 6th row down on the squared paper is regarded as corresponding to a 6th teleprinter impulse, and contains the known characters of $\Delta\chi_6$ $(= \Delta\psi'_6)$.

26F DEVIL EXORCISM (R41, p. 68)

This is a powerful technique only devised two or three months before the end of the war.

It assumed that we already know the sign of the key. Now we are accustomed to regarding a sign on a $\Delta\chi$ in wheel-breaking as being either cross, dot or undetermined. But a sign can be undetermined for two different reasons — because its scores are feeble or because they are contradictory. It has been found that, especially on low dottage keys, these two cases should be E.9
distinguished. The former is still left as a blank but the latter is entered as a ringed dot. In this way the 'devils' of the key (that is, those letters of the $\Delta\psi'$ which appear, on their known impulses, to a
be motor dots but in reality are not) are rendered impotent and are ultimately exorcised. For once a column of $\Delta\psi'$ gets a ringed character in it we cease to use it as motor dot evidence. Soon the false motor dots thus treated, unable to contribute to their own salvation will take a cross in one of their unknown impulses, thus resolving the contradictions, and restoring the motor dot columns which they contradicted and which have also been ear-marked as devils, to their rightful status. Devilry can also be used to indicate characters of $\Delta\chi_2$ and $\Delta\chi_6$ (on $\overline{\chi}_2$ key) which are mutually incompatible.

26G KEY WORK IN THE NEWMANRY

Apart from the χ_5 flag described above in **26B(c)** there are other key jobs which are done by computers.

(a) The 150 by 150 rectangle (R3, pp. 102, 103) p. 209

If it is specially desired to break a key, and usual methods have failed, the 150 by 150 rectangle can be made, thus:

---

[a] these

[i] Handwritten reference '(**R41**, p. 67)' inserted with a caret.
[ii] Reference '(**R41**, p. 89)' handwritten.

41		ΔK_{12}	ΔK_{13}	ΔK_{14}	ΔK_{15}	ΔK_{16}
31	ΔK_{21}		ΔK_{23}	ΔK_{24}	ΔK_{25}	ΔK_{26}
29	ΔK_{31}	ΔK_{32}		ΔK_{34}	ΔK_{35}	ΔK_{36}
26	ΔK_{41}	ΔK_{42}	ΔK_{43}		ΔK_{45}	ΔK_{46}
23	ΔK_{51}	ΔK_{52}	ΔK_{53}	ΔK_{54}		ΔK_{56}
31	ΔK_{61}	ΔK_{62}	ΔK_{63}	ΔK_{64}	ΔK_{65}	

i Fig. **26 (VII)**

The dotted lines make the rectangle 181 by 181, for χ_2-controlled key.

Care must be taken to ensure that every rectangle is entered in the positive direction of the wheels. (The square labelled ΔK_{26} merely contains the scores of the $\widehat{\chi}_2$ run written down the diagonal.) The rectangle is converged, from a χ_5 flag (or even a $\widehat{\chi}_2$ start for $\overline{\chi}_2$ key). The pattern of length 150 (or 181), which is being taken through, should itself be modified by the new information available after it has been taken through each block.

The 150 by 150 rectangle is merely a quicker way of doing original Turingery counting (see
a **R41**, p.50). Also all rectangle-converging jobs, including this and the 181 by 181 rectangle, can be done on Colossus by a series of runs of the form $i+j$ (see **25**).

An interesting identity in connection with 150 by 150 rectangle is that if we flag the 1st, $41+1$th (= 42nd), $41+31+1$th (= 73rd), $41+31+29+1$th (= 102nd) and $41+31+29+26+1$th (= 128th) rows, we perform *exactly* the same operation as the 5 by 5 flag (see above **26B(a)**).

p. 210 **(b)**

ii With $\overline{\chi}_2$ limitation an extract from the 181 by 181 rectangle was prepared thus: (**R41**, p.65)

	41	29	26	23
31	ΔK_{21}	ΔK_{23}	ΔK_{24}	ΔK_{25}
31	ΔK_{61}	ΔK_{63}	ΔK_{64}	ΔK_{65}

Fig. **26 (VIII)**

[a] rectangle-convering

[i] Caption moved from right-hand side of figure to bottom.
[ii] Text 'With limitation…' on same line as head for **26G(b)**.

The convergence of this rectangle is begun by taking the strongest values of the $\widehat{\chi}_2$ run through the top 4 rectangles, giving fragmentary $\Delta\chi$'s 1, 3, 4, and 5. These are taken right through, giving partial $\Delta\chi_2 + \Delta\chi_6$, which are both taken back again, and so on. After convergence is complete the $\Delta\chi_2$ and $\Delta\chi_6$ patterns are compared for consistency, and if their agreement is striking, as it should be, we can confidently transfer to hand-counting, or to the 181 rectangle, or to Colossus.

Colossus can do many of the operations of hand counting, but since it is unable to 'doubt' on more than one impulse at a time it is not worth trying to use any but the simplest approaches to key when using Colossus. For example to reproduce one normal $\Delta\chi_i$ count on non-$\overline{\chi}_2$ key we would have to do 17 separate Colossus runs.

Colossus is equipped with a switch for the condition "NOT 99" which effectively eliminates all gaps in the key, which are represented as series of 9's on the key tape.

The chief uses of Colossus for key-breaking are

(i) In breaking key from a crib.

(ii) In doing the donkey-work of 150 by 150 or 181 by 181 convergence on sticky keys until significance and the determination of the sign of the key has been attained.

If it is progressing very quickly it may be easier to complete all χ's on Colossus, do a machine de-chi of the key tape on Tunny, and recover the ψ's in a few minutes of hand work. But normally it is best to take it off Colossus and complete the closing and more finicky stages by hand. E.10 p. 211

(c) Key from a crib

This normally exceeds 1000 letters in length. It is therefore so vulnerable that it can be attacked confidently from a random start and may come out in about 10 runs.

The usual random start is from a single $\Delta\chi_5$ character. The runs are of the form $i+/j$ until the sign of the key is known. Then they are of the form $i/j,k,l\ldots$ and $i\boldsymbol{\times}/\overparen{j,k,l}\ldots$

A random start such as this was not in fact generally employed. For $\overline{\chi}_2$ key a $\widehat{\chi}_2$ type-out and for non-$\overline{\chi}_2$ key a converged 4+5 rectangle provided the start as well as giving a preliminary check that the key tape had been made correctly.

(d) Colossus convergence of 150 by 150 and 181 by 181 rectangles (R3, p. 108)

The series of runs below gives the Colossus formulae for converging these rectangles, assuming we start from a $\Delta\chi_5 A$ obtained from the χ_5 flag. Anything bracketed applies only to the 181 by 181 rectangle. Using $\Delta\chi_5 A$;

$$4+/5,\ 3+/5,\ 2+/5,\ (6+/5),\ 1+/5 \text{ giving wheels 4, 3, 2, (6), 1A.}$$

These 4 (or 5) wheels are checked with the embryonics provided by taking $\Delta\chi_5 A$ through the 4 (or 5) ΔK_{ij} rectangles.

Then do the following runs (using the latest versions of the wheels, of course).

$$5+/4,\ 5+/3,\ 5+/2\bullet,\ (5+/6),\ 5+/1.$$

Add the 4 (or 5) runs together to give $\Delta\chi_5 B$.

Then do

$$4+/3,\ 4+/2,\ (4+/6),\ 4+/1,\ 4+/5 \text{ giving } \Delta\chi_4 B.$$

Then do

$$3+/2,\ (3+/6),\ 3+/1,\ 3+/5,\ 3+/4 \text{ giving } \Delta\chi_3 B.$$

Then do (2+/6[*], 2+/1, 2+/5, 2+/4, 2+/3 giving $\Delta\chi_2 B$ *, i

etc. etc.

[*]This is done by adding $\Delta\chi_6 A$ to the scores of the $\widehat{\chi}_2$ run.

[i]Native footnote * uncapitalised: 'this is done...'.

26H GENERAL CONSIDERATIONS

An essential of key-breaking is speed. Only in key-breaking from depth is it likely that one can decode the current day's traffic.

So the best plan is a double attack: a hit-or-miss attempt by a first-class key-breaker to rush it
p. 212 through in record time, and at the same time a slow but powerful second line of defence should be in preparation in case he takes too many chances for the sake of speed and becomes bogged down. In that event he can proceed afresh from the sound start that has meanwhile been prepared by others.

The second line of defence always takes the form of a combined χ_5 flag. The 'spearhead' is normally a 5 by 5 or 10 by 10 flag for non-$\overline{\chi}_2$ key, and a $\widehat{\chi}_2$ start for $\overline{\chi}_2$ key.

p. 213 26J EXHIBITS

Most of the exhibits given in this chapter are taken from actual key-breaking workings. Their purpose is to illustrate some of the processes described in the earlier sections.

The workings on Sailfish of 7th April, 1945 extracts from which are given in figs. **26 (IX)** to **(XVI)** show the breaking of key on $\overline{\chi}_2 + \overline{\Psi}'_1$ limitation from a χ_5 flag start. The correlation of these figs. to the text of Chapter **26** is as follows:

Figs. **26 (IX)** to **(XII)** illustrate **26B(c)**.

Figs. **26 (XIII)** and **(XIV)** illustrate **26C**.

Figs. **26 (XV)** and **(XVI)** illustrate **26D**.

The workings on Grilse of 5th April, 1945, extracts from which are given in figs. **26 (XVIII)** to **(XXII)** show the breaking of key on $\overline{\chi}_2$ limitation from a $\widehat{\chi}_2$ start. The correlation of these figs. to the text of Chapter **26** is as follows:

Figs. **26 (XVII)** to **(XIX)** illustrate **26B(b)**.

Figs. **26 (XX)** to **(XXII)** illustrate **26E**.

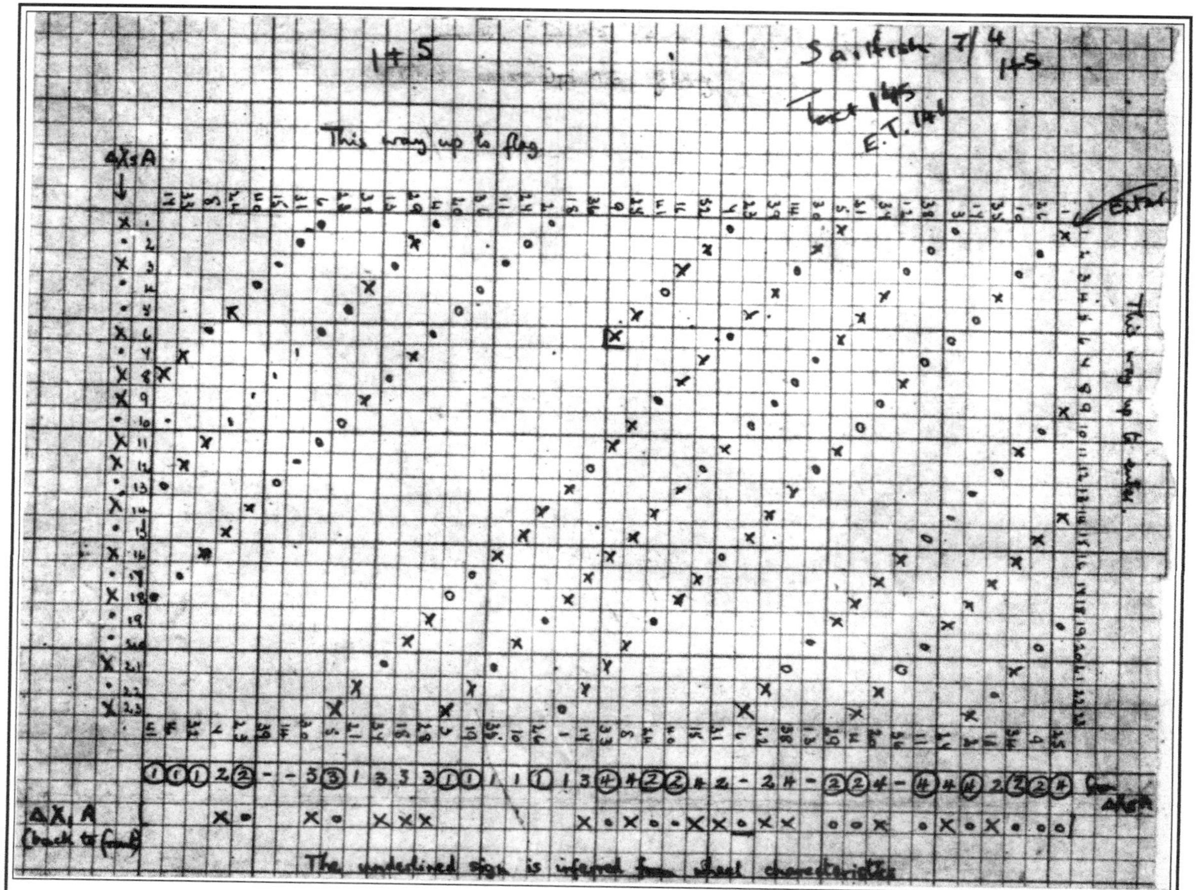

26J/9: ×.6

Fig. 26 (IX) The ΔK_{15} rectangle

The numbers along the top of the rectangle refer to the beginnings of the lines of the Garbage, and those along the bottom to the ends of the lines. These numbers are used as a check when entering.

$\Delta\chi_5 A$, obtained from the converged composite flag (fig. **26 (XII)**) has been taken through the rectangle to give scores for $\Delta\chi_1$, from which an embryonic wheel, $\Delta\chi_1 A$ is constructed.

The embryonic $\Delta\chi$'s all emerge back to front, owing to the method of entering the rectangle, and must be turned the right way round before adding to ΔK at the start of hand counting.

The Garbage and separate flag of the individual rectangles are not shown except in the case of the ΔK_{45} rectangle (figs. **26 (XI)** and **26 (XII)**).

p. 214

p. 215

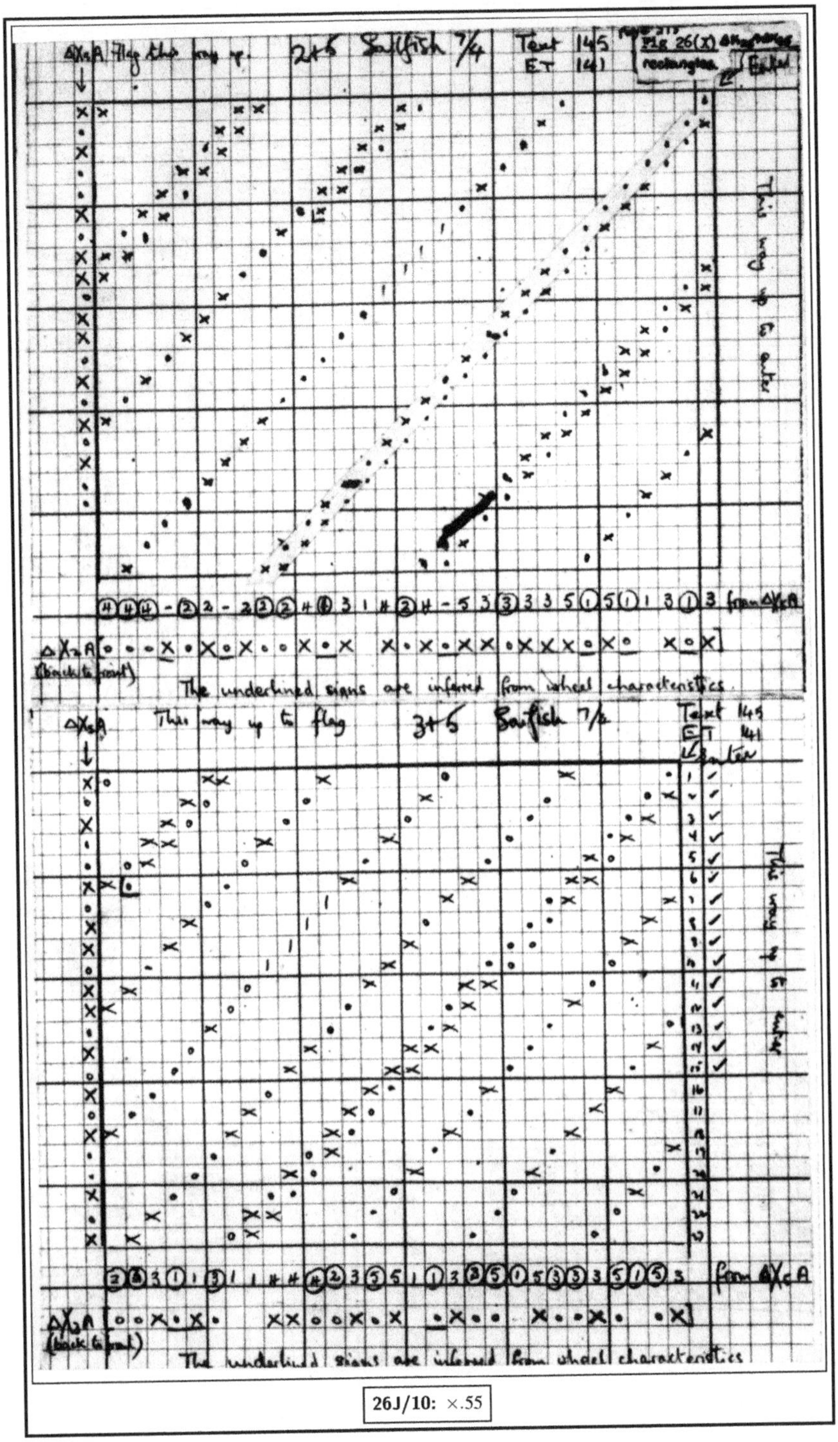

26J/10: ×.55

i **Fig. 26 (X)** ΔK_{25} and ΔK_{35} rectangles

[i] Caption moved from above figure to below.

p. 216

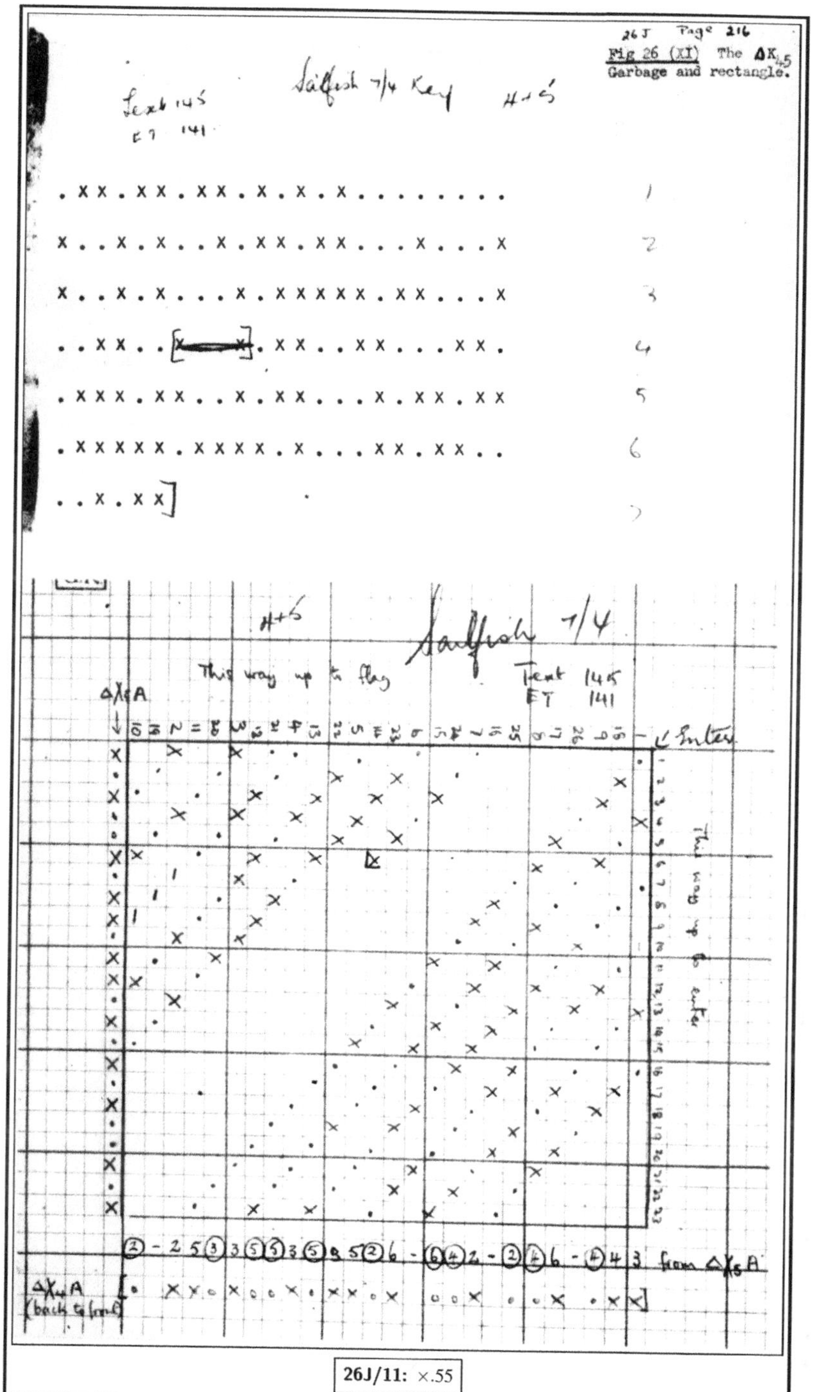

Fig. 26 (XI) The ΔK_{45} Garbage and rectangle[1]

[1] Figure label moved from above figure to below figure.

p. 217, i

Fig. 26 (XII)

The flag of the ΔK_{45} rectangle and the χ_5 composite flag

Note that it is not necessary to enter the individual ΔK_{i5} flags double entry. The double entry is done after they have been added together to form the composite flag.

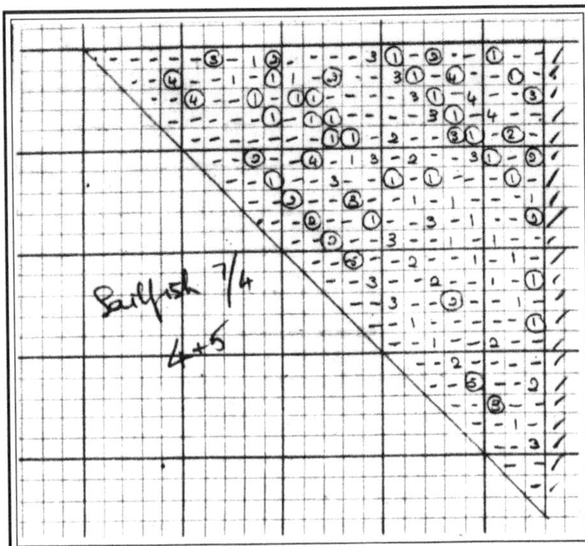

26J/12.1: ×.55

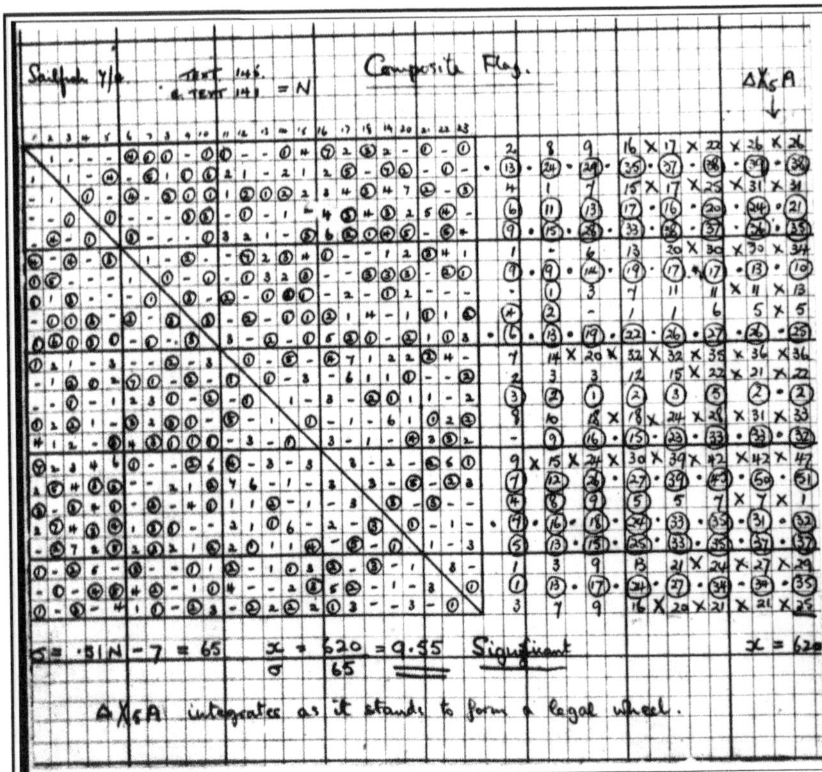

26J/12.2: ×.55

[i] Figure dissected and caption moved.

At this stage there are several possible courses of action. The flag is heavily significant, and gives a complete $\Delta\chi_5$ which integrates to form a legal un$\Delta\chi_5$ assuming that the Δ characters are not inside out. This wheel is very likely to be right, since owing to the high value of β, which can be approximately calculated from the formula $\beta = \sqrt{x/2v}$, the value of the pips is nearer to *3* db than the usually assumed 1 db and further, the weakest scoring character, character 18, is greatly strengthened by wheel characteristics. Thus we might add the un$\Delta\chi_5$ to unΔK_5 to give ψ_5', and identify the ψ-repeat as described in **26D**. But with so short a key and such high dottage ψ_5 would only go about $1\frac{1}{2}$ times round in ψ_5', so that even if the repeat were successfully identified, which would in itself be difficult, it would bring us very little fresh information about TM dots. The best plan is to continue normally until another χ is completed and then to add both the known un$\Delta\chi$'s to the key. The ψ-repeat on both impulses will then be very much easier to recognise (especially with the aid of the embryonic $\Delta\psi'$ now available, which will give considerable evidence about the TM), and when recognised will yield much more information about the presence and position of TM dots. p. 218

It might be argued that the key could be broken more quickly on Colossus. But the shorter the length of key, the greater is the relative advantage of hand over Colossus methods, since the time taken to do hand counts is in direct proportion to the length of key, while on Colossus the length of tape has to be made up to 2000 in any case, so that its speed does not vary with the key length. However we might decide to launch a double attack both by hand and Colossus, with close liaison between the hand breaker and Colossus man. But here this was not done and the following exhibits illustrate hand methods only.

The ΔK is de-χ'ed with the embryonic $\Delta\chi$'s. The $\Delta\chi$ flag suggests, by its integrable $\Delta\chi_5$, that the $\Delta\chi$ signs are the right way out, but not conclusively, so the test for the sign of the keys is now applied (fig. **26 (XIII)**).

p. 219, i

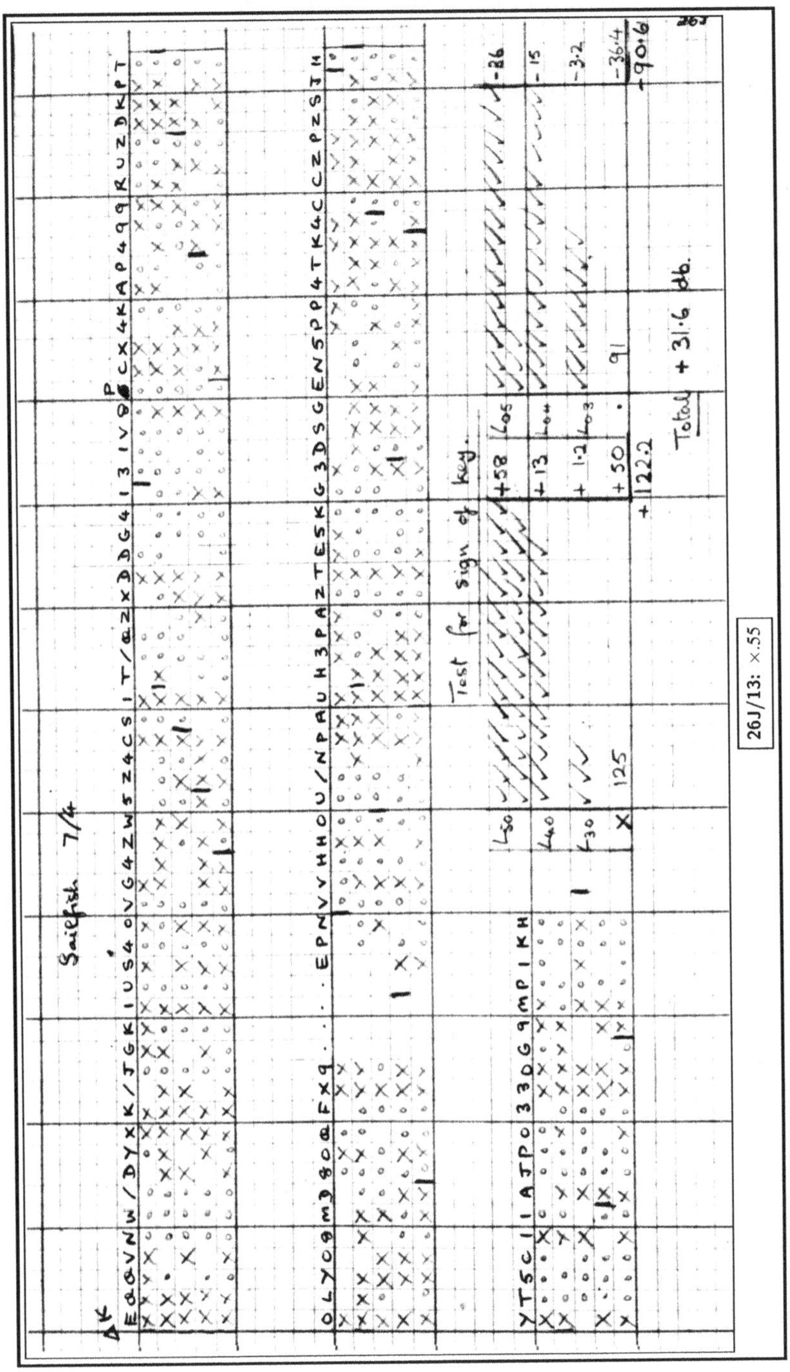

Fig. 26 (XIII) The early stage of hand counting

The ΔK is de-χ'ed with the embryonic $\Delta\chi$'s obtained from the χ_5 flag start. The test for the sign of the key shows conclusively that the $\Delta\chi$'s are right way around. A count for $\Delta\chi_4$ is done on this assumption, and the count is shown in fig. **26 (V)**.

[i] Description 'The ΔK is de-χ'ed…' continues on same line as figure caption.

p. 220

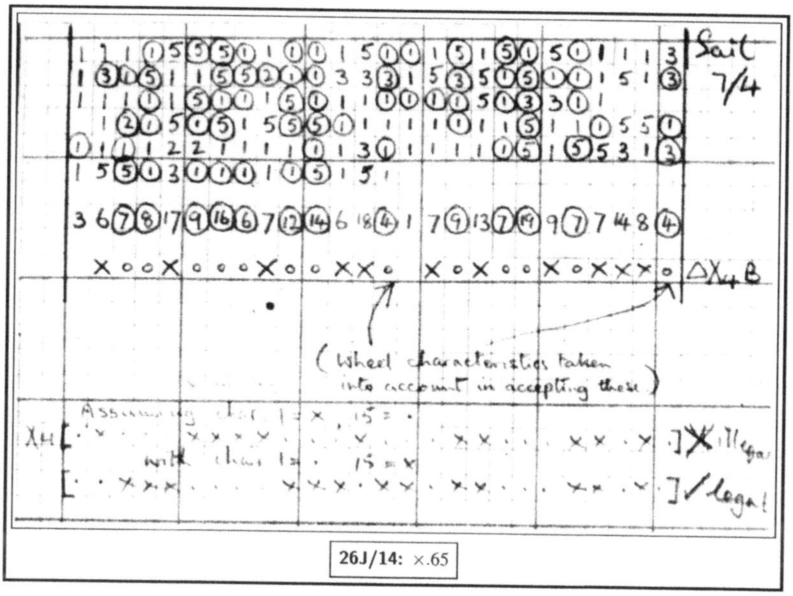

26J/14: ×.65

Fig. 26 (XIV) The count for $\Delta\chi_4$ [i]

By some “fiddling” we have obtained a highly probable un$\Delta\chi_4$ from the count. We now add this χ_4 and un$\Delta\chi_5$ already obtained from the flag to the unΔK and attempt to recognise the ψ repeat (fig. **26 (XV)**).

Fig. **26 (VX)** shows that the attempt was successful, proving that the χ_4 and χ_5 used were correct. With the aid of the embryonic ψ' shown in fig. **26 (XIII)**) all the TM dots have been located except where corruption has made it impossible. The number of groups of crosses in ψ's 4 and 5 fixes the μ_{37} dottage as 28 (see fig. **22 (II)**). It remains to break the remaining χ's by the use of the known TM dots, as described in **26D**. One more exhibit is given to illustrate this final process, as it demonstrates a technique only alluded to above in fig. **26 (VI)**. This is the method of breaking χ_1 if the TM dot evidence does not give all the $\Delta\chi_1$ characters. The property used is

$$\begin{array}{llll} \text{Given} & \text{TM} = & \text{dot,} & \overline{\psi}'_1 + \overline{\chi}_2 = \times\,. \\ \text{''} & \text{''} & \text{''} & \overline{\chi}_1 + \overline{K}_1 + \overline{\chi}_2 = \times\,. \\ \text{''} & \text{''} & \text{''} & \overline{K}_1 + \overline{\chi}_2 = \widetilde{\chi}_1\,. \end{array}$$

K_1 is known and χ_2 has by this time been broken. Hence $\widetilde{\chi}_1$ values at all places preceding TM dots can be filled in on a separate count from the $\Delta\chi_1$ count (fig. **26 (XVI)**). This gives a nearly complete $\widetilde{\chi}_1$ which, combined with the $\Delta\chi_1$ count, yields the whole wheel. Here is the χ_2 used in the $\overline{\chi}_1 + /\overline{K}_1 + \overline{\chi}_2$ count

χ_2 [• × × • × × • × • × × • × × • • × × • • × × × • • × × • • •]

---

[i] Caption moved from right-hand side of figure to bottom.

p. 221

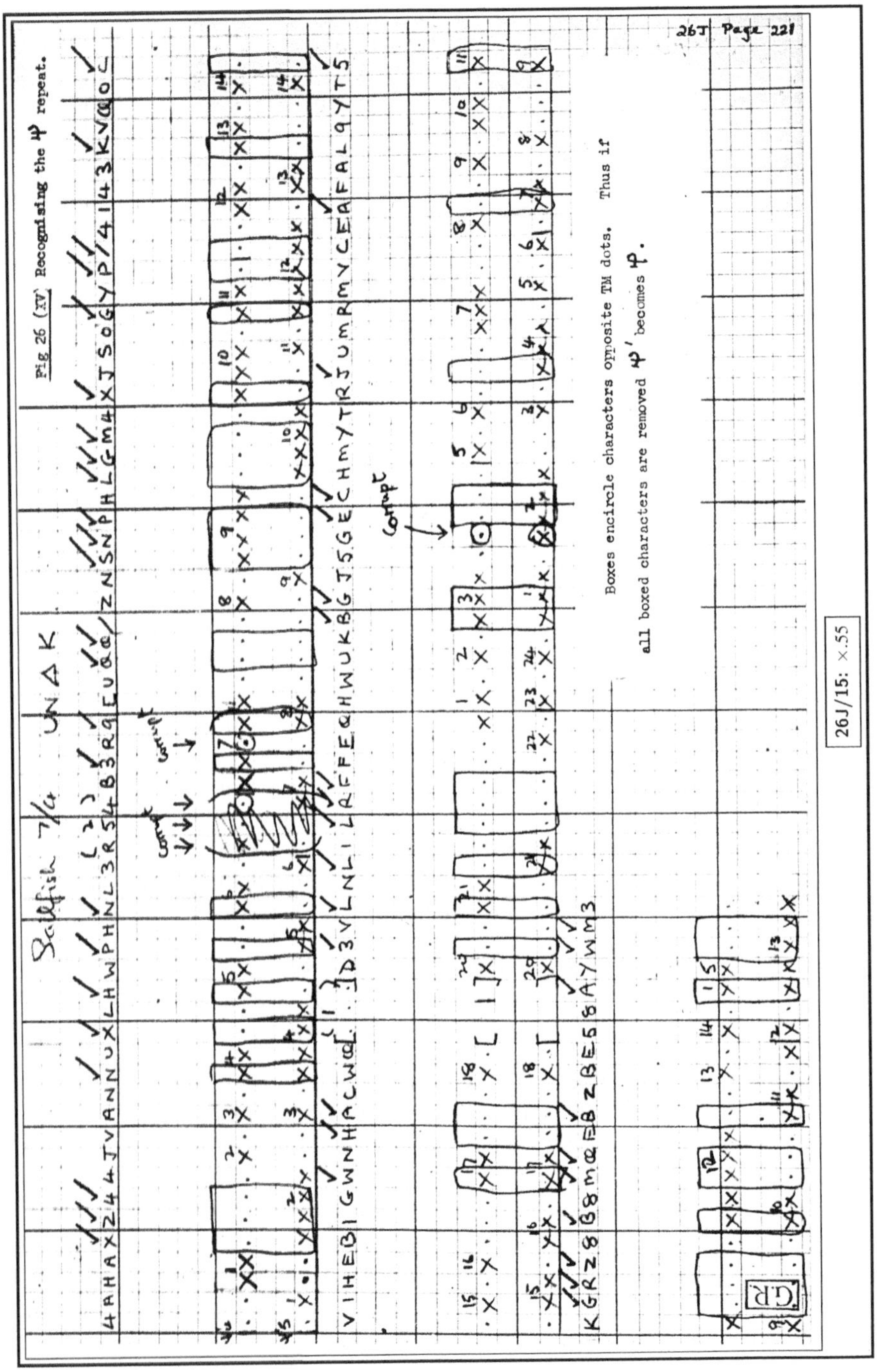

Fig. 26 (XV) Recognising the *ψ* repeat

p. 222, i

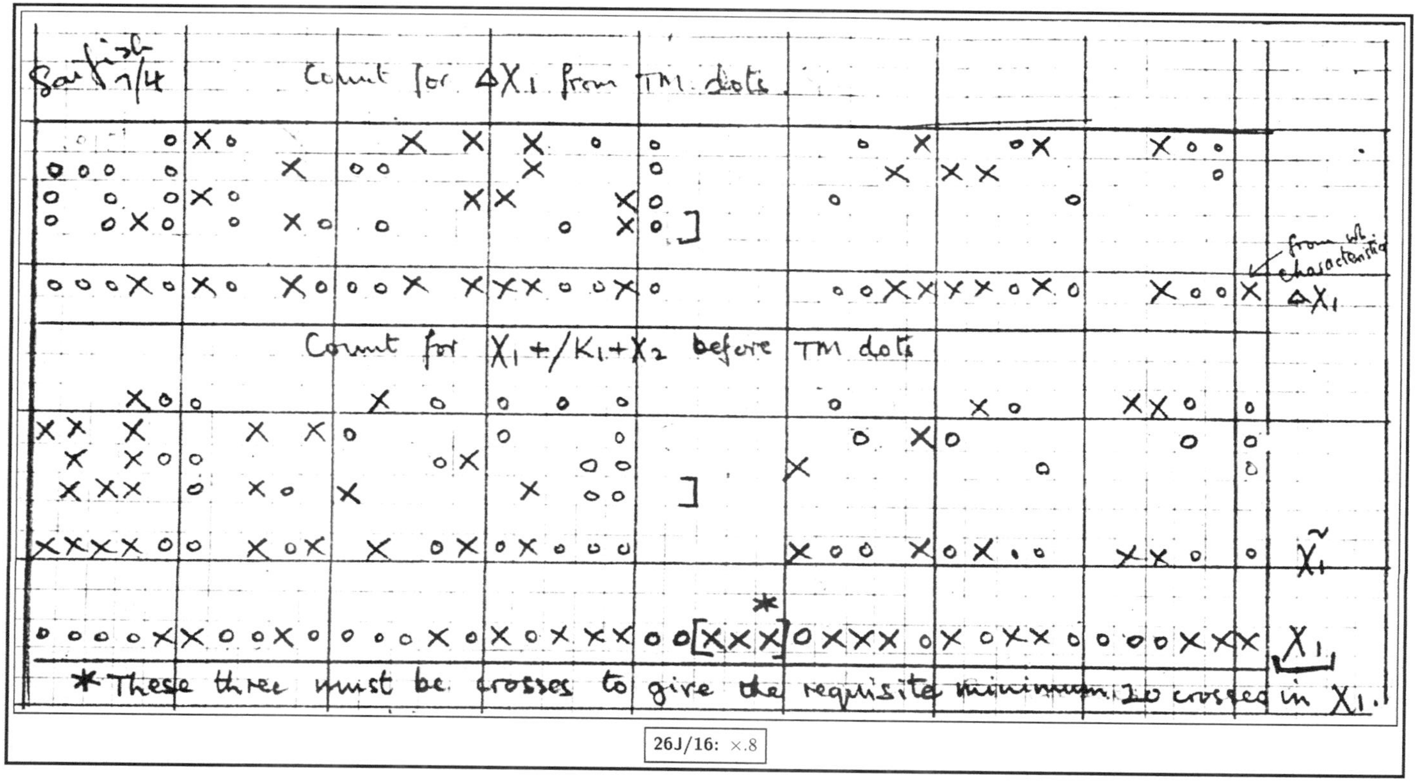

26J/16: ×.8

Fig. 26 (XVI) Final counts for χ_1

By playing off the known $\Delta\chi_1$ and $\widetilde{\chi}_1$ characters against each other, and by using the knowledge that χ_1 cannot have less than 20 crosses, the entire χ_1 is obtained. If this had failed TM cross evidence could be used or the method of 'numbering' described in **26D**. With all χ's complete the remaining ψ' streams can be obtained, and "contracted" by use of the known TM to give 5 ψ wheels. The key will then be broken.

[i]Figure caption moved from right side of figure to bottom.

p. 223 The following series of exhibits show the breaking of a $\overline{\chi}_2$ key from the $\widehat{\chi}_2$ start to the first count for $\Delta\chi_1$.

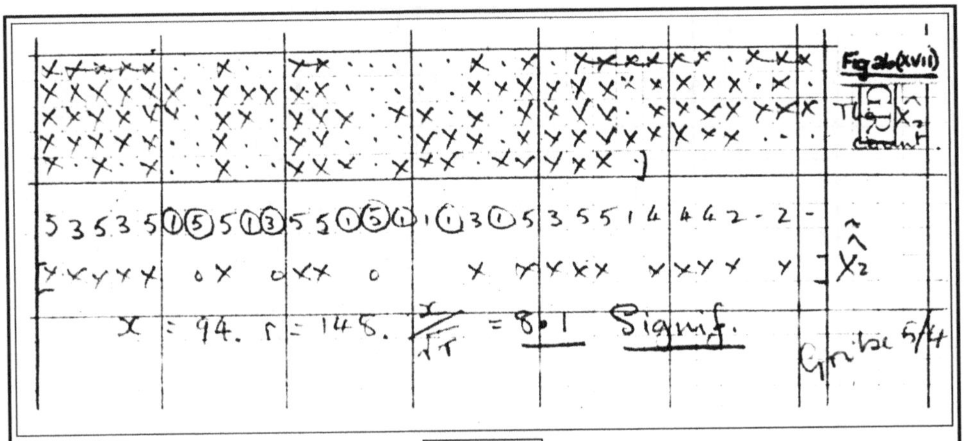

26J/17: ×.7

i **Fig. 26 (XVII)**

Fig. **26 (XVII)** shows the $\widehat{\chi}_2$ count, which is heavily significant, indicating, for so short a key, very high dottage. If we make a conservative estimate of $x^* \doteqdot 80$, β is given by $x^*/r = 80/148 = \cdot 54$ which corresponds to 26 dots in μ_{37} (see fig. **22 (II)**). The value of each pip is $10\log_{10}\frac{1+\beta}{1-\beta} \doteqdot 5$ db. So we can accept $\widetilde{\widetilde{\chi}}_2$ characters with scores of only 2. With the partial $\widetilde{\widetilde{\chi}}_2$ wheel thus formed we de-χ the second impulse of ΔK giving partial $\Delta\psi'_{26}$. We then do counts for $\Delta\chi_5$, $\Delta\chi_4$ and $\Delta\chi_3$ as described in **26B(b)** and **26Y(f)**. Fig. **26 (XVII)** shows work on the key at the stage where the
a $\Delta\chi$'s 5, 4 and 3 obtained from these counts have been added to the ΔK, but the $\Delta\psi'_{26}$ in the second impulse has not yet been erased. The counts are shown in fig. **26 (XIX)**. The reader can therefore check the counts from the workings, remembering that when the $\Delta\chi_5$ count was taken impulses 3, 4 and 5 were blank; when the $\Delta\chi_4$ count was taken, impulses 3 and 4 were blank; and when the $\Delta\chi_3$ count was taken impulse 3 was blank. The $\widehat{\chi}_2$ count can also be checked against the ΔK write-out.

---

[a] ob tained

[i] Figure caption moved from right side of figure to bottom.

p. 224, i

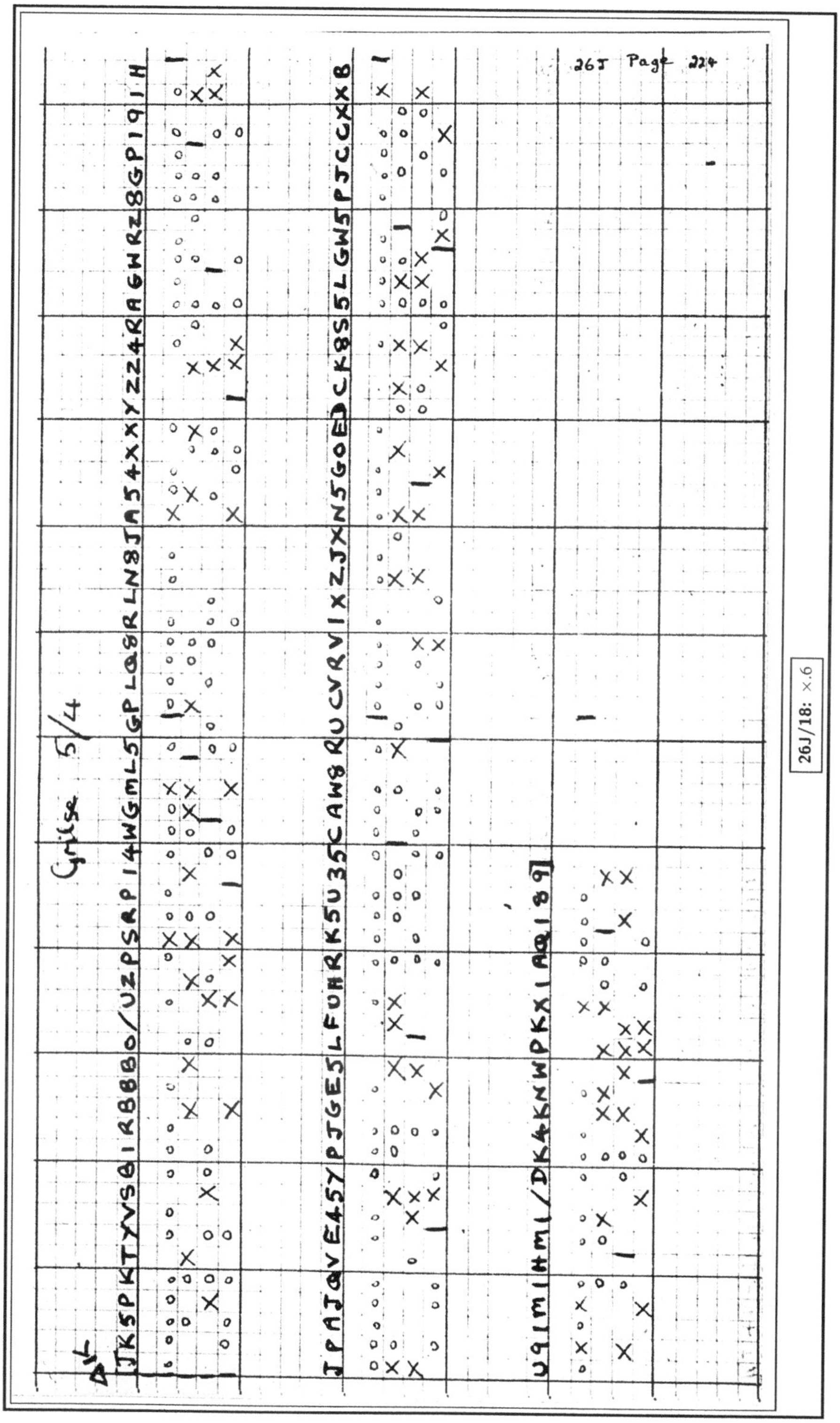

26J/18: ×.6

Fig. 26 (XVIII) Key workings for $\overline{\chi}_2$ key; early stage

[i] Caption moved from top of figure to bottom.

p. 225, i

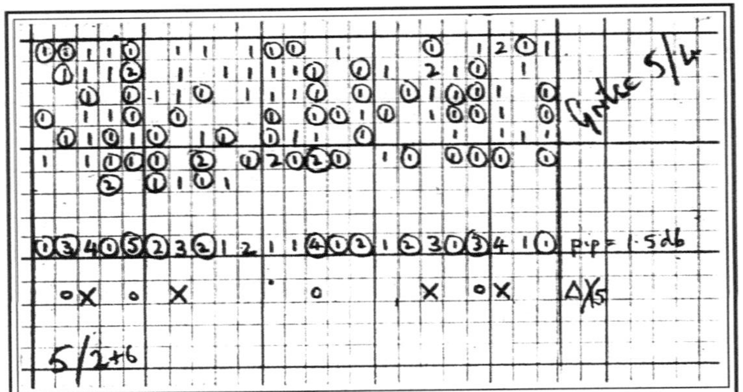

26J/19.1: ×.6

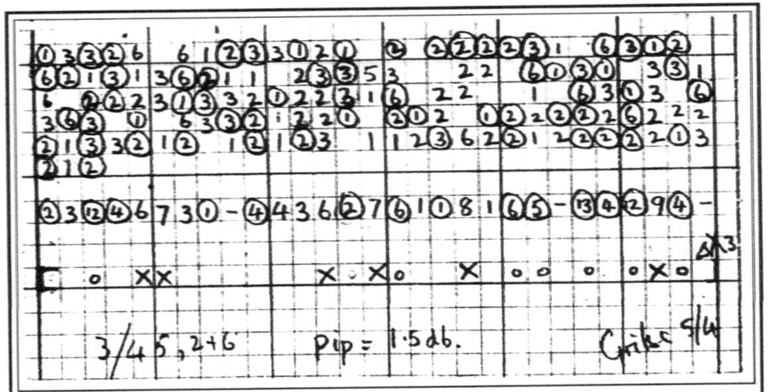

26J/19.3: ×.6

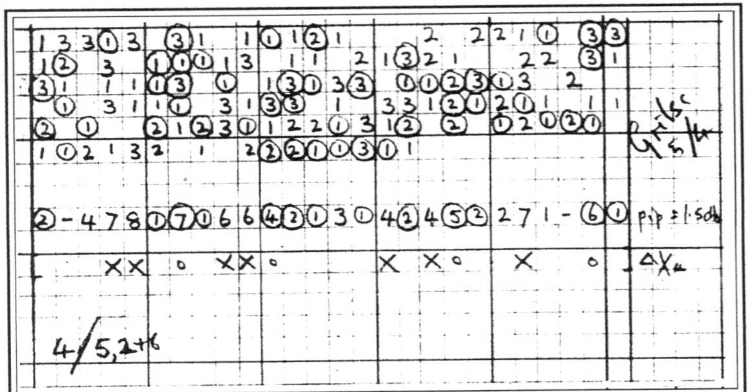

26J/19.2: ×.6

A low standard for accepting characters has been taken — 3 pips for $\Delta\chi_5$, 4 for $\Delta\chi_4$ (except for character 3 where wheel characteristics are unfavourable), and five for $\Delta\chi_3$ (character 28 gains acceptance through wheel characteristics). This is because of the estimated high dottage. The remark on the counts "pip = 1·5" though true for $d = 18\frac{1}{2}$ is clearly in this case a gross underestimate. The practice of holding to a standardised scale of pip values has however the merit of speed and simplicity, and does not mislead much about the *relative* pip values of the different types of count.

Fig. 26 (XIX) The first counts for $\Delta\chi_5$, $\Delta\chi_4$, and $\Delta\chi_3$

[i] Figure caption moved from top of figure to bottom. Figure dissected, and explanatory paragraph formerly below figure moved into lower right area of figure. The dash in dash in 'has been taken — 3' is effectively a colon, not a minus sign.

The next step is to erase the $\Delta\psi'_{26}$ characters from the second impulse and do a count for p. 226
$\Delta\chi_2$ as described in **26E**. The count (shown below, fig. **26 (XX)**) is used to obtain $\Delta\chi_2$ *and* $\Delta\chi_6$ characters. The method, in outline, is to fill in all acceptable $\Delta\chi_2$ scores as $\Delta\chi_2$ characters. Then fill in $\Delta\chi_6$ characters wherever columns of the count strongly suggest the presence or absence of TM dots. For instance the 20th column of the count gives strong evidence of TM dots and a
therefore evidence for $\Delta\chi_6$ = dot, and conversely column 14 suggests $\Delta\chi_6$ = cross. The $\Delta\chi_6$ values are in fact entered at a slide of one to the left, thus becoming $\tilde{\chi}_2$. The relation between $\Delta\chi_2$ and $\tilde{\chi}_2$ is now exploited by a process of "fiddling", the subtleties of which are better acquired by experience than from an involved description. In the example the breaker has produced complete wheels, but they cannot be correct, as $\Delta\chi_2$ has 18 instead of 16 crosses. However since there is no patch which is obviously far weaker than the rest, he has decided to use the entire $\Delta\chi_2$ and $\Delta\chi_6$ wheels as a provisional basis for subsequent counts, rather than 'doubt' a large proportion of the b
wheels.

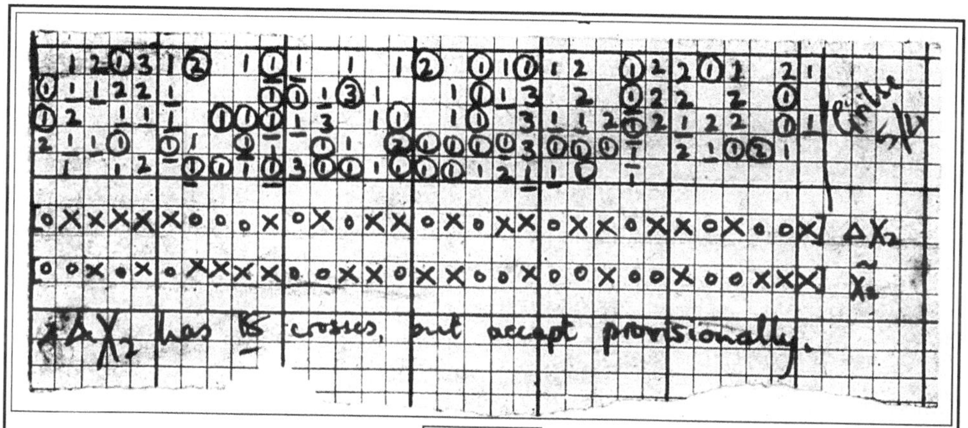

26J/20: ×.7

Fig. 26 (XX) The 1st count for $\Delta\chi_2$ i

$\Delta\chi_2$ is now added to ΔK_2 and the $\tilde{\chi}_2$ pattern is slid one to the right to form $\Delta\chi_6$ and is "added to ΔK_6", i.e. is written along the sixth row down of squared paper. A normal count for $\Delta\chi_1$ is done (see **26E**) and ΔK_1 is de-χ-ed with the $\Delta\chi_1$ thus obtained. Fig. **26 (XXI)** shows the work at this stage, with partial $\Delta\psi'$ on all 6 impulses, and fig. **26 (XXII)** shows the $\Delta\chi_1$ count.

[a] eivdence [b] $\Delta\chi_2$ and $_6$ wheels

[i] Caption moved from top of figure to bottom.

p. 227, i

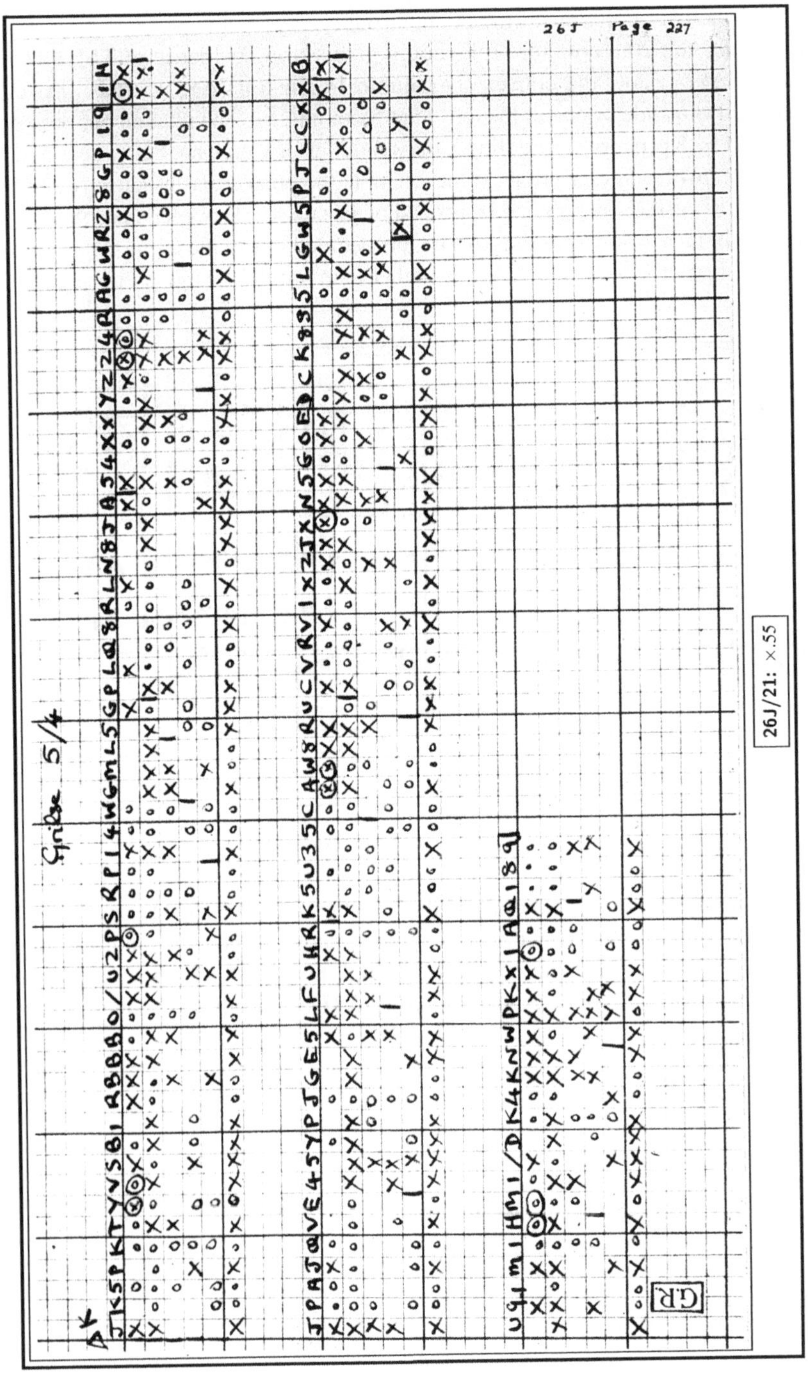

26J/21: ×.55

Fig. 26 (XXI) Work on $\overline{\chi}_2$ key; later stage
The ringed characters come from "devil exorcism" (see **26F**, see also fig. **26 (XXII)**).

[i] Caption and explanatory sentence moved from top of figure to bottom.

p. 228

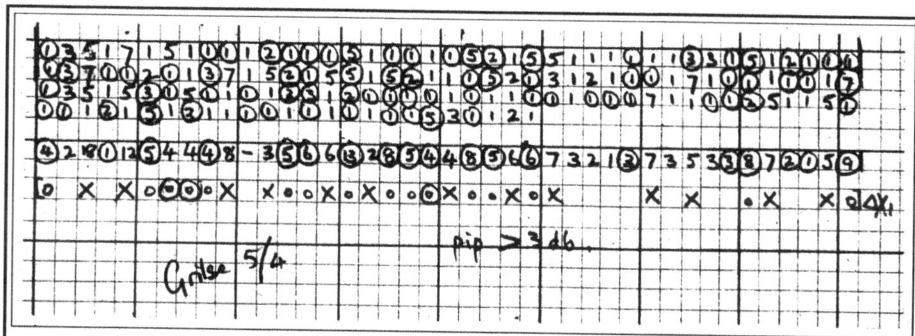

26J/22: ×.55

Fig. 26 (XXII) Count for $\Delta\chi_1$ i

Wherever a character contains a score of 5 or more among its scores, but, owing to contradicting scores, does not qualify for acceptance it is written thus ◎. All $\Delta\psi'$ letters in the key work which would contribute TM dot evidence but have a ringed character derived from de-χing with this wheel are ignored in subsequent counting until the contradictions are resolved. For this technique of "devil exorcism" see **26F**.

From now on, owing to the high dottage and the power of the 6 impulse method, the $\Delta\chi$'s are almost certain to emerge complete at the rate of one for each count done, counting in the order $\Delta\chi_{5,\,4,\,3,\,2,\,1}$. It is therefore not worth de-χing the unΔK with the first one or two χ's to be completed and identifying the ψ repeat as illustrated above (fig. **26 (XV)**), because this would only slow up what should now be a quick and simple job. The ψ's can be broken immediately the five χ's are out by de-χing the unΔK on all impulses and "contracting" the resultant ψ'.

One last point must be mentioned. In making a count for $\Delta\chi_2$ after the sixth impulse has acquired $\Delta\chi_6$ ($=\Delta\psi_6'$) values, these values are ignored, and the count is taken and analysed as in fig. **26 (XX)**. This is because the $\Delta\chi_2$ and $\Delta\chi_6$ values used to de-χ ΔK_2 and ΔK_6 were largely derived from each other, and if we use previous $\Delta\chi_6$ values in counting for a new $\Delta\chi_2$, errors in both wheels will tend to perpetuate themselves. E.11

26X KEY-BREAKING SIGNIFICANCE TESTS p. 229

(a) Significance test for original Turingery (R3, p. 116)(Keybreaking Significance Test I) ii

In original Turingery the method of scoring the characters of a wheel is as follows:

Suppose $\Delta\chi_i$ is the wheel which is being scored. Then for each letter of $\Delta K+\Delta\chi$ score $k-l$ where k is the number of dots in $(\Delta K_{ij}+\Delta\chi_{ij})$ for each $j\neq i$ and l is the number of crosses. Clearly the contribution to the total score of all five wheels due to a letter of $\Delta K+\Delta\chi$ containing r dots and s crosses is

$$\psi(r)-\{5\times 4-\psi(r)\} \qquad \text{(X1)}$$

where $\psi(r)=r(r-1)+(5-r)(4-r)$, and we are assuming for simplicity that all the $\Delta\chi$'s are complete. The reason for this formula is that $\psi(r)$ is the number of dots in $\Delta K_{ij}+\Delta\chi_{ij}$ for all i and j, counting each pair i, j, twice, and $5\times 4-\psi(r)$ is the number of crosses.

The total score of all the wheels is therefore

$$2\sum\psi(r)-20N$$

[i] Caption and explanatory paragraph starting 'Wherever…' moved from right side of figure to bottom.
[ii] Subhead 'Keybreaking Significance Test I' handwritten.

where the summation is over all letters of $\Delta K + \Delta\chi$ and N is the number of letters in ΔK. Incidentally this total score is the same as the double bulge of the converged 150 by 150 rectangle.
E.12 We denote it by x as in Ch. **24**.

Now, for random $\Delta\chi$ wheels, the expected value of $\psi(r)$ is

$$\sum_{r=0}^{5} \psi(r)\frac{1}{2^5}\,{}^5C_r = 10 \qquad \text{(X2)}$$

E.13 and the variance is

$$\sum_{r=0}^{5} \left\{\psi(r) - 10\right\}^2 \frac{1}{2^5}\,{}^5C_r$$

i

$$= 4\sum_{r=0}^{5} \Big\{ r(r-1)(r-2)(r-3) - 4r(r-1)(r-2)$$

$$+ 12r(r-1) - 24r + 25 \Big\} \frac{1}{2^5}\,.\,{}^5C_r$$

$$= 4\left\{ \frac{5.4.3.2}{2^4} - 4.\frac{5.4.3}{2^3} + 12.\frac{5.4}{2^2} - 24.\frac{5}{2} + 25 \right\}$$

$$= 10. \qquad \text{(X3)}$$

Thus the expected value of X, for random wheels, is 0 and its S.D. is $2\sqrt{10N}$. So the sigma-age of the converged rectangle is $X/(2\sqrt{10N})$ and the leading term of the significance test, according to the ideas of significance test IV for rectangles (**24X**), is $2{\cdot}17(X/2)^2/10N$. This is the same as if the ΔK_{ij} streams were independent.

p. 230 Corresponding to the 'ϑ terms' of significance test IV, there will be a bonus for all low scoring characters. However, for simplicity we can replace X by the sum of the moduli of the scores against the high-scoring characters of the differenced wheels, when the partial patterns consisting only of these characters are taken through the 150 by 150 rectangle. Then we get a conservative estimate of the decibanage by allowing 3 db for every doubted character. Thus finally we arrive at
ii the formula (**R3**, p. 116)

$$\left\{ \frac{2{\cdot}17(X/2)^2}{10N} - 454 + 3y \right\} \text{ decibans} \qquad \text{(X4)}$$

where y is the number of doubted characters and $454 = (150-1)\times 3{\cdot}01 + 5$.

a, iii **(b) Significance test for key-breaking** (**R5**, pp. 13, 19.)(Key-breaking Significance Test II)

We now give a more accurate significance test for key than the one just given. The present test does not assume the arbitrary scoring system of original Turingery and is therefore suitable at a later stage of key-breaking, in which a better scoring system has been used.

Suppose that particular $\Delta\chi$ partial wheels are substantially correct, so that we need $3{\cdot}01x$ decibans, where x is the number of characters assumed. If we assume the limitation to be not χ_2 (or neglect the evidence about it if it is χ_2 limitation), then the natural banage in favour of the

---

[a] (**R5**, 13,19)

[i] Second expression for variance of $\psi(r)$ split on two lines for clarity.

[ii] Equations (X4), (X5), and (X6) connected their corresponding equation numbers in the margin with leading rows of dots. Equation numbers given as (X.4), (X.5) and (X6).

[iii] Subhead 'Key-breaking Significance Test II' handwritten.

theory, if β is known, is

$$\sum_{k=1}^{5} d_k \left(1+\frac{2^k\beta}{(1-\beta)^k}\right) + (d_0+C-N)\log(1+\beta)+D\log(1-\beta)$$

where

$N =$ length of ΔK

$d_k =$ number of letters of $\Delta\psi'$ with k dots and no crosses ($k = 0, 1, \ldots, 5$)

$D =$ total number of dots in $\Delta\psi'$

$C =$ total number of crosses in $\Delta\psi'$.

(D should not be confused with the proportion of dots in μ_{37}.)

It is not easy to solve the algebraic equations obtained by maximising the natural banage. However if we assume $\beta = 1/3$, we get, in *decibans*

$$\begin{aligned} &3{\cdot}0\, d_1 + 6{\cdot}0\, d_2 + 10{\cdot}0\, d_3 + 14{\cdot}5\, d_4 + 19{\cdot}1\, d_5 \\ &\qquad + 1{\cdot}25\,(d_0 + C - N) - 1{\cdot}76\, D. \end{aligned} \tag{X5}$$

One could maximise the factor by simply working out the decibanage for different values of β. For complete $\Delta\chi$ wheels the formula becomes

$$19{\cdot}1\, d_5 + 5{\cdot}0\, N - 3{\cdot}01\, D \tag{X6}$$ [i]

and $N = 200$ is required for significance.

26Y FORMULAE USED IN KEY-BREAKING

p. 231

(a) Key Flags

We have already described the χ_5 flag, the 5 by 5 flag and the 10 by 10 flag, used in key-breaking. An entry of $+1$ in any of these flags represents an agreement between two signs each of which has a P.B. β of being a particular sign of $\Delta\chi_{ij}$. Therefore the P.B. of the assertion that the two corresponding signs of $\Delta\chi_{ij}$ are the same is β^2. Therefore every 'pip' in a key flag is worth [a]

$$10\log_{10}\frac{1+\beta^2}{1-\beta^2}\ \text{decibans} \tag{Y1}$$

in favour of agreement of the two signs of $\Delta\chi_{ij}$.

Denote the sum of the moduli of the scores of the pattern obtained by converging a double entry flag by x and denote the number of comparisons in the flag by ν. Then it is easy to see that the sigma-age of the flag is

$$x/\left(2\sqrt{\nu}\right). \tag{Y2}$$

(When proving this it is necessary to remember that all the evidence is counted twice due to the double-entering.) Furthermore, the expected value of x^* (cf. ch. **24**) is given by

$$x^* = 2\beta^2\nu. \tag{Y3}$$

x will often be larger than x^*.

When $\beta = 1/3$, the flag pip value is about 1 db.

For a 5 by 5 flag a sigma-age of 3 is good, of 2·5 usable. If a / or 8 emerges from the flag so much the better.

For a χ_5 flag 6σ is good, 5σ is usable.

---

[a] repesents

[i] Equation number (X6) not at right edge of page.

(b) The χ_5 flag (**R3**, pp. 96, 97)

The number ν of comparisons in a χ_5 flag for ΔK of length N letters can be calculated as
a follows (**R3**, p. 97). Let ν_1, ν_2, ν_3, ν_4 be contributions to ν from the ΔK_{15}, ΔK_{25}, ΔK_{35}, ΔK_{45} flags. Consider ν_i. Let w be the length of the wheel χ_i. Let $N = kw + l$ $(0 \leq l < w)$. Then

$$\nu_i = l\,\frac{k(k+1)}{2} + (w-l)\,\frac{k(k-1)}{2}. \qquad \text{(Y4)}$$

This may be seen by imagining the N letters written out in a row and scoring, for each letter, the number of other letters which are at distances a multiple of w from this letter. We omit the details.
p. 232 (Y4) can be rewritten

$$\frac{N}{2}\left(\frac{N}{w} - 1\right) + \frac{l}{2}\left(1 - \frac{l}{w}\right).$$

Therefore

$$\begin{aligned}\nu &= \nu_1 + \nu_2 + \nu_3 + \nu_4\\ &= \frac{N^2}{2}\left(\frac{1}{41} + \frac{1}{31} + \frac{1}{29} + \frac{1}{26}\right) - 2N + \sum \frac{l_i}{2}\left(1 - \frac{l_i}{w}\right),\end{aligned}$$

with an obvious notation. Now

$$0 \leq \frac{l}{2}\left(1 - \frac{l}{w}\right) \leq \frac{w}{8}.$$

i Therefore

$$0 \leq \sum \frac{l_i}{2}\left(1 - \frac{l_i}{w_i}\right) \leq \frac{1}{8}(41 + 29 + 26 + 23) < 15.$$

So if we replace $\sum \frac{l_i}{2}(1 - l_i/w_i)$ by 8, the error in ν will be less than or equal to 8 (and usually a good deal less). So we can take

$$\begin{aligned}\nu &= \frac{N^2}{2}\left(\frac{1}{41} + \frac{1}{31} + \frac{1}{29} + \frac{1}{26}\right) - 2N + 8\\ &= \cdot 0648N^2 - 2N + 8. \qquad \text{(Y5)}\end{aligned}$$

In order to get 6σ we require

$$x \fallingdotseq 3{\cdot}06N - 50$$

with a small error. (This can be proved with the help of equation (Y2) and the binomial theorem.) If (Y3) is now applied we find as the sort of lengths required for significance of the χ_5 flag:

d	14	17	20	23	26	29
N	447	281	187	131	96	72.

A list of the values of ν for other flags, including those with the '$\Delta\chi_6$' flag added in, see **R4**,
b p. 103.

---

[a] (**R3**,97) [b] **R4**,103

[i] This equation in-line.

(c) Determining the sign of key

Suppose all the characters are correct. Then

$$P(\Delta\psi' = /) = 1 - a + a(1-b)^5$$
$$P(\Delta\psi' = 8) = ab^5.$$

Therefore for each excess of / over 8 the factor for theory "T" that the $\Delta\psi'$ has the right sign is i, a

$$\frac{1-a+a(1-b)^5}{ab^5}.$$

This is $41/16$ if $b = 2/3$.

Similarly the factor for T from ••••? is b

$$\{1-a+a(1-b)^4\}/(ab^4) \qquad \text{etc.}$$

Finally the factor for T from × in a spoilt column (i.e. a column containing at least one dot and at least one cross) is $b/(1-b)$.

In point of fact we do not make the very rash assumption that all our characters are right in applying the test, with the result that the scores are much lower than those resulting from the above formulae. Let p be the probability of each $\Delta\chi$ character assumed. p. 233

$$\text{Let}\begin{cases}\lambda = b(1-p)+p(1-b)\\ \mu = bp+(1-b)(1-p).\end{cases}$$

Then it can be seen that the factor for a / is

$$\frac{(1-a)p^5+a\lambda^5}{(1-a)(1-p)^5+a\mu^5}.$$

If $a = 3/4$, $b = 2/3$, $p = 4/5$ this reduces to a decibanage of 2 db. The decibanage for ••••? is 1 db, for •••?? it is ·4 db and for each cross beyond the first in a spoilt column is ·4db. ii

(d) 'Counting' a $\Delta\chi$ wheel

Similar algebra can be applied to the scores when counting a $\Delta\chi$ wheel. The results depend on whether the sign of the key is assumed to be known or not. The formulae can be simplified a good deal by treating $\widetilde{\chi}_2$ as $\Delta\psi'_6$ in the case of χ_2 limitation. The justification for this is given in **22D(g)**. The scoring is calculated on the assumption of $d = 18\frac{1}{2}$ which makes $a = 3/4$. $b = 2/3$

For a more detailed account, with tables, of **(c)** and **(d)** the reader is referred to Chapter **XI** of the report of Major Tester's Section. E.14

(e) $\widehat{\chi}_2$ run and Δ_{598} significance test

This is dealt with in ch. **27**.

---

[a] over 8 factor [b] Similarly factor

[i] Phrase 'for each excess of / over 8' handwritten.

[ii] Run on sentence 'Then it can be seen... decibanage of 2 db' without punctuation between the displayed formula and the word 'if'. We have split it into two.

(f) Counts involved in the $\widehat{\chi}_2$ start

Given $\Delta K_2 + \widehat{\widetilde{\chi}}_2$ $(\equiv \Delta\psi'_{26}) = \times$, the factor for $\Delta\psi'_i = \times$ is $\frac{b}{1-b}$.
Given $\Delta\psi'_{26} = \bullet$ and n other dots, the factor for $\Delta\psi'_i = \bullet$ is

$$\frac{P(i\bullet\ 2{+}6\bullet\ n \text{ dots})}{P(i\times\ 2{+}6\bullet\ n \text{ dots})}$$

$$= \frac{P(i\bullet\ 2\bullet 6\bullet\ n \text{ dots}) + P(i\bullet\ 2\times 6\times\ n \text{ dots})}{P(i\times\ 2\bullet 6\bullet\ n \text{ dots}) + P(i\times\ 2\times 6\times\ n \text{ dots})}$$

$$= \frac{1-a+a(1-b)^{n+3}+ab^2(1-b)^{n+1}}{ab(1-b)^{n+2}+ab^3(1-b)^n}.$$

Putting $a = 3/4$, $b = 2/3$, this reduces to $\frac{3^{n+2}+5}{10}$, from which the following table can be calculated.

$$\text{Notation:}\quad \begin{aligned} L_{n,m},\bullet &= L_{n,m},\ \Delta\psi'_{26} = \bullet \\ L_{n,m},\times &= L_{n,m},\ \Delta\psi'_{26} = \times \\ L_{n,m},\circ &= L_{n,m},\ \Delta\psi'_{26} = ? \end{aligned}$$

E.15

$\Delta\psi'$ in the other impulses	$L_{0,0},\bullet$	$L_{1,0},\bullet$	$L_{2,0},\bullet$	$L_{3,0},\bullet$	$L_{n,m},\times$	$L_{n,m},\bullet$ $(m\neq 0)$	$L_{1,0},\circ$	$L_{2,0},\circ$	$L_{3,0},\circ$
Score for $\Delta\psi' = \bullet$ (1 pip = 1·5db)	①	③	⑥	⑨	2	2	②	⑤	⑧

27 CRIBS p. 234

27A GENERAL NOTIONS

Given a cipher and the corresponding plain language it is easy to find the (unknown) key, for

$$K = P + Z.$$

From K the unknown wheels on which Z is enciphered can be broken.
The real problem is to find the correct relative positions of P and Z.
In Tunny the problem is necessarily solved in two stages:

(i) log-reading predicts: this Z corresponds to some part of this P;

(ii) Z and P are added in all positions: the correct position can be identified because key has recognisable statistical properties (**27W**, **22F**).

The possibility of a crib depends on the retransmission of the same message (and on the previous decoding of one transmission): the statistical method demands that the retransmission shall be exact: exactitude is in practice possible only if both transmissions are sent automatically from the same plain language tape and if further the one not already decoded is sent without pauses: two hand perforations or two hand sendings of the same message always differ in punctuation and corrections. Thus only retransmissions from the same station can be used as cribs, and for this reason the organisation of the German TP system is more relevant than in other Tunny work.

When K is obtained, ordinary key-breaking methods can be applied. Because of their great length crib keys were easily broken, generally on Colossus from a random start or from a converged 4+5 rectangle. p. 235

For cribs of normal length, not grossly corrupt, it is unnecessary to use very powerful methods unless the dottage is too low for easy χ-setting, and in this case it is not worth while.

Crib setting can begin only after one transmission is decoded, a disadvantage when the value of traffic depends on its currency.

As a matter of history, cribbing was developed when the introduction of $\overline{\chi}_2+\overline{\overline{P}}_5$ limitation prevented the occurrence of depths, which had been the basis of all earlier wheel-breaking.

[i] This chapter's analytical contents reproduces what is on the corresponding page of the *Report*, p. 234. The titles for sections **27F**, **27G** and **27H** given here do not match what is in the body of the chapter.

In this chapter section **G**, which describes the statistical technique, and sections **W**, **X**, **Y**, which explain its mathematical basis, do not assume any knowledge of sections **B**, **C**, **D**, **E**, **F**. Sections **D**, **E**, **F**, **G** deal with the technique of cribbing in roughly chronological order, but **F** will be more intelligible if **G** is read first.

Use of "overlaps" for *setting* messages by crib methods **R2**, pp. 98, 99; **R3**, pp. 1, 22, 64.

For suggested "cribbing" with neither message decoded **22W(c)** (**R3**, pp. 62, 65).

27B GERMAN TP LINKS

E.1 **(a) OKH**

Because, as already stated, statistical crib methods require exact letter by letter correspondence between *P* and *Z* only automatic transmissions from the same tape were cribbable.

In practice this meant messages from OKH to subordinate headquarters, sent from the same TP terminal (of which, unfortunately, OKH always had more than one). The arrangement of these terminals and of the links which they served varied considerably, especially in 1945, and finally became chaotic.

E.2 **(b) Routine messages**

Most cribs were provided by certain of OKH's routine messages, which had several advantages.

(i) they were rather long (3,000–10,000);

(ii) they were sent at about the same time each day thus aiding prediction;

(iii) they followed an elaborate formal procedure;

(iv) they sometimes had double serial numbers.

a Note 1 Most routines were sent by other means than Tunny.

b Note 2 The procedure included the use of Roman numerals or capital letters for designat-
c ing sections, bracketed letters or numerals for subsections.

p. 236 **(c) Routines commonly used for cribbing**

Kriegsmarine Kurzlage

E.3 Daily : Bream, Gurnard, Cod, Whiting.
Regularly : Tarpon, Stickleback, Jellyfish, (irregular after Autumn 1944).
Rarely : Lumpsucker.

Lageberícht West

Daily : Gurnard, Codfish, Grilse,
Bream (not always the same version).
Regularly : Jellyfish (rarely after Autumn 1944).
Occasionally : Mullet, Weever.

OKH Lagebericht

Daily : Gurnard, Codfish.
Regularly : Bleak (erratic after Autumn 1944),
Jellyfish (rarely after Autumn 1944),
Weever.
Occasionally : Grilse (erratic),
Stickleback, Squid, Crooner (after mid-February 1945).

OBSW Tagesmeldung

Daily : Jellyfish, Gurnard (not always the same version).

Daily means not a daily decode, but that log evidence suggested that the routine was sent daily by Tunny unless prevented by circumstances (movement of outstations, reorganisation at OKH). Great activity sometimes caused a routine to reappear, suggesting that it was normally sent by
E.4 other means.

[a] most [b] the procedure [c] of numerals

(d) Suitability of various links

Not all favourably grouped links were equally suitable: long QEP's with few autopauses were helpful. Gurnard and Bream were good in this respect, Grilse fair, Jellyfish and Bleak bad: on Jellyfish an OKH Lagebericht was spread over 16 hours, during which 72 QEP's were sent.

(e) Diagrams of TP links

Comparison with the diagrams of ch. **61**, in which the various TP terminals of OKH are distinguished, will show that the most favourable period was before November, 1944; from then till February, 1945 was particularly bad. The separation of Grilse (high intelligence value) was most unfortunate.

27C GERMAN TP OPERATING PRACTICES

(a) Auto and Hand

In addition to automatic transmission from a punched tape, known as "auto", operators often sent minor corrections, receipts, queries, and personal items directly by operating a typewriter connected to the encoding device, a type of transmission known as "hand". The two kinds of sending were identified on the cipher red forms submitted by Knockholt by marking each p. 237 appropriate stretch as "hand" or "auto".

(b) Use of the same plain text tape on different links

If a message was addressed to two or more different outstations the usual practice was to use a single tape for transmitting to all the addresses concerned. Normally the messages would be sent out on one link and, when transmission was completed, the tape would be taken to another transmitter and sent again and so on. In rare cases, when the message was long and two transmitters were adjacent, the tape was inserted into the second transmitter before sending had been completed on the first link, with the result that we had simultaneous sending of different parts of the same plain language tape.

(c) Change of QEP

A long message was often sent in several QEP's: for 10,000 letters 3 or 4 QEP's was usual, 15 not unknown.

(d) Autopause: go-backs

There were frequently pauses in auto without any change of QEP, i.e. without breaking the continuity of key. When sending was resumed the tape was usually set back 60–300 letters (go-back) so that there was a break in the continuity of plain text.

(e) Go-backs and QEP changes in the decode

The effect of a go-back could generally be remedied, for it was easy to see where 60–300 letters were repeated. This applied to a change of QEP if both QEP's were decoded; but this was often not so.

For editing see **27E(c)**.

(f) Go-backs in cipher

It was impossible to tell how much plain text was repeated, so that only pause-free stretches could be used. Many otherwise favourable cribs failed because there was no sufficiently long pause-free stretch.

(g) Relative length of cipher and decode

Because editing could restore the continuity of P through an autopause, but not that of Z, the available P was almost, though not always, longer than the Z: to simplify descriptions this is sometimes assumed without explanation. E.5

p. 238 27D CRIB PREDICTION

(a) General

Up to this point nothing has been said about how the cipher messages which contained
retransmissions of plain language already at hand, or how cipher messages on two or more
links expected to contain the same plain language could be identified, except to suggest that
they often passed at about the same time on all links. Unfortunately this "about the same time"
covered a period of several hours during which fifteen or twenty messages could be sent. Unless
a conditions were very favourable and we could use judgement based on an intimate knowledge of
b the operating practices of a link, it was not practicable to attempt an identification. Furthermore,
the time required to try all possibilities at random was prohibitive.

(b) Receipts

However, the Germans came to our aid with some most useful practices, the most important
of which was the requirement that each message be receipted by the receiving party when
transmission was completed. The usual method of doing this was to send the last two digits of the
internal serial number together with the time at which the message was cleared at the receiving
c station. The set operator himself was not usually authorized to receipt and sent it only when a
supervisor had examined the message and was satisfied with its reception. Generally this was
done within a few minutes of the end of a transmission although there were exceptions frequent
enough to make such an assumption in a particular case a bit unreliable. At times, too, a whole
block of messages was receipted for at one time, not necessarily in the exact order of transmission.
The most important feature of these receipts was the fact that they were sent, for the most part, in
clear language and were recorded by Knockholt operators on log sheets together with all other
plain language chat between German operators.

(c) Sixta and the identification of receipts

The Sixta Non-Morse section had the task of reading the log sheets of the activity of each
d Fish link and extracting from them any information of cryptographic or intercept value. In the
cribs world we were mainly interested in their ability to predict or identify a retransmission. In
order to give us this information the log readers listed each single serial receipt, together with
p. 239 the time of receipting, numerically according to the last two digits of the serial receipted. It was
possible to record this information for about six links on a single page, making it a simple matter
to see quickly whether or not the same serial was receipted on more than one link. However, when
the same serial was found to be receipted by two or more links, it was not possible to say very
definitely that the same message was involved in all cases. Since most links passed considerably
more than one hundred messages daily, the number of serial coincidences for messages not at
all the same, was quite substantial. Nevertheless if the same serial was receipted by several
links at about the same time of day, the probability that the messages were identical was quite
good. And, indeed, if we had prior knowledge that the links involved received a routine report at
E.6 about this time daily, it was highly probable that the receipt clicks internal serial numbers of the
had identified this routine. In addition to the time element other factors were used to determine
the likelihood of retransmission. For example, the logs could often tell us whether or not the
messages in question had the same priority signal or if they were approximately of the same
length. Sometimes, too, if the operators were quite chatty, they would make queries referring to
E.7, e proforma headings. Thus if one saw references to "8)" or "unter Roem III,A)" on two links and
identical receipts for the traffic in question, the likelihood of a retransmission was very great.

(d) Double serial receipts

Although most receipts were of the single serial type, double serial receipts were fairly
frequent. If, for example, the internal serial number was 7867/7890, the receipt was usually given

---

[a] judgment [b] Further more [c] authorised [d] fish link [e] tow links

as 67/90 and a receipt click kind almost certainly meant a retransmission.

(e) Retransmission Slips

From a consideration of the points just mentioned and any other information revealed by the log sheets, Sixta submitted to the cribs section daily predictions of likely retransmissions.

(f) Use of decodes: Testery Cribs watch

Experience soon proved, however, that not all receipts were intercepted, mainly because of poor intercept conditions. In addition, some receipts were encoded and hence not available to the log readers. For these reasons it was very important that all decoded traffic be examined from a cribs point of view to ensure that no retransmission possibilities were missed. The decodes provided full information about the messages which could be used in conjunction with log p. 240
evidence to spot retransmission. To effect this examination of decodes, a Testery cribs watch was organised. It began making a study of messages with multiple addresses late in June, 1944 and by the middle of July began submitting "crib forms" to Sixta for all messages likely to pass on links other than those on which they were decoded. These crib forms contained all the information about a message likely to be of use to Sixta in attempting to identify it on other links. Most successful retransmission slips were based on these crib forms since it was far easier to identify on another link messages whose serial number and other characteristics were known than to predict a
from log evidence alone. E.8

27E PREPARATION OF DECODE AND CIPHER

(a) Retransmission slips

Work on a crib job usually began with the receipt of a "Sixta Non-Morse Retransmission Slip". These slips were entered, according to the Sixta serial number, in a log headed "List of Slips" and then

(i) worked on immediately if the plain language was already available; or

(ii) if one of the keys of the links involved had been broken, the slip was called active since there was a reasonable prospect that the plain language would soon be available; or

(iii) if none of the keys involved had been broken the slip was called dormant.

Priority in setting and decoding was requested for the messages in question on active slips. If a significant rectangle was obtained on one of the links concerned with a dormant slip, the appropriate messages were ordered from Knockholt for priority treatment when the key was broken.

(b) Ordering of Cipher tapes

Whenever the plain language for a slip became available, or when the cipher message containing it had been set well enough to ensure it becoming available, the first job of the cribs man b
or cribs registrar was to examine the cipher QEP's of the retransmission candidates submitted by Sixta from the point of view of length and order all likely messages from Knockholt under Procedure D. E.9

During the period when $\overline{\chi}_2 + \overline{\overline{P}}_5$ (or $\overline{\chi}_2$) was the most common limitation used and when Knockholt was not overtaxed with slip reading, all D procedure messages were perforated completely and Red Forms submitted for our examination. In February, 1945, a new instruction was issued to Knockholt in the interest of saving time and labour. We informed Knockholt of p. 241
the minimum pause-free auto passage we considered useful and requested a perforation and Red c
Form for all passages as long or longer than this minimum. In all cases the longest possible stretch of cipher was perforated. The usual minimum for a $\overline{\chi}_2 + \overline{\psi}'_1$ link was 1000 letters and for a $\overline{\chi}_2$ link, 600 letters. In some cases the cipher in question was a rectangling message already available.

[a] links message [b] had set [c] pausefree

(c) Editing Decodes

Since several messages were often contained in a single QEP, the one pertaining to the slip in question had to be identified by its serial numbers or other characteristics in case the preamble was missing. Next it was necessary to decide whether or not to use the address as part of the crib. Since October, 1944 this has not been a problem because no example was ever decoded after that date in which the body of the message was identical on two links but with different addresses. A message occasionally passed on a link not included in the address but, in these cases, the new addressee was designated in an explanatory message preceding the transmission or more informally in hand chat between the operators. Before October, however, the Testery Cribs identified several routines having identical plain language for the body of the message but differing in the address.

Go-backs were eliminated by pencilling out the repeated letters, taking great care to ensure exact continuity. Occasionally this was difficult or even impossible due to extreme corruption caused by poor conditions or to a broken tape. In the latter cases the German operator was forced to remove the tape and reset it beyond the point of break. The letters missed were then filled in by hand so that continuity was missed because of invariably different punctuation.

a The problem of correcting corrupt plain language arose only when interception was bad. The occasional wrong letter in a good decode could not affect results much but corruptions of up to twenty-five percent of the text could obscure correct settings. Fortunately bad reception by Knockholt was usually accompanied by bad reception on the part of the Germans, giving rise to numerous repeats. With the help of the Testery Cribs Section we could do a fairly good job of piecing together the original plain language.

(d) Perforation of Plain Language

p. 242 A tape of the edited plain language was perforated by Testery decoders, if available, or in Tunny. These tapes were then printed out in widths of 60 and checked letter for letter, against the decode. Corrections were indicated on tape and printout and the two corrected copies made in
E.10 insert machines.

(e) Checking Decode against Red Form

To ensure letter for letter correspondence between the Testery copy of the decode and the plain language tape used by the Germans for transmitting, Cribs registrars checked each line of the decode against the cipher Red Form. When discrepancies were found, partial decodes of the parts in question were done by the decoders. Failure to check arose from several causes. The decoding machine sometimes printed an extra "8"; carbon copies occasionally had a letter missing at the beginning or end of a line; the decoding operators were known to omit a part of the message when taking up after a breakdown.

(f) Cipher Passages

Two copies of each stretch of cipher to be used were made from a copy of the complete cipher tape and numbered appropriately as ZI, ZII etc. These pause-free passages were selected with regard to length, degree of corruption and position in the message. This last point involved an attempt to fit roughly the position of various cipher stretches with the corresponding plain language. A happy choice of the first cipher passage to try saved a great deal of tape making and running time.

27F TAPE MAKING

(a) General

This section will be more intelligible if the following section, **27G**, is read first.

Tape making was always done on Miles and the processes for different varieties of tape are very similar. Except for $\overline{\chi_2}\overline{\overline{P_5}}$ limitation P^* is made from P exactly as Z^* is made from Z.

---

[a] intercept was

(b) Δ_{598} tapes

Each letter of Z^* involves, (see **27G(b)**), not merely one letter of Z but also the letters 943, 713, 667, 598, forward, so that five Z tapes must be placed in five transmitters of Miles, staggered 943, 713, 667, 598:

In Transmitter	T1	a Z tape	starting	with the	1st	letter	p. 243
	T2	"	"	"	943+1 th	"	
	T3	"	"	"	713+1 th	"	
	T4	"	"	"	667+1 th	"	
	T5	"	"	"	598+1 th	" .	

The output Z^* is to have in its first impulse $\Delta_{943}Z_{15}$ i.e. Z_5 (present) + Z_1 (present) $+Z_5$ (943 forward) $+Z_1$ (943 forward)

Accordingly	$T1_5+T1_1+T2_5+T2_1$	is plugged into the	1st	impulse.
Similarly	$T1_5+T1_2+T3_5+T3_2$	"	2nd	"
	$T1_5+T1_3+T4_5+T4_3$	"	3rd	"
	$T1_5+T1_4+T5_5+T5_4$	"	4th	" .

This can easily be plugged on any existing Miles.

(c) Running on to the end

The tape in T2 (staggered 943) will reach the end $943-598=345$ places before that in T5 (staggered 598). It is preferable to wait till T5 is exhausted, in case it is afterwards decided to run on fewer impulses, or include the extra evidence in the letter count.

(d) Δ_{31}: $\overline{\chi}_2$ limitation

The operation is almost identical, but tapes are staggered (e.g.) 93, 124, 279, 341, and Z^* consists of:

1st impulse	:	$T1_2+T2_2$
2nd impulse	:	$T1_2+T3_2$
3rd impulse	:	$T1_2+T4_2$
4th impulse	:	$T1_2+T5_2$

(e) Δ_{31}: $\overline{\chi}_2+\overline{\overline{P}}_5$ limitation

Z^* as for $\overline{\chi}_2$ limitation.

P^* consists of $\Delta_{31\rho}(\Delta P_2+\overline{\overline{P}}_5)$. For two P^* impulses this can be made on Miles A in one operation. For more impulses an auxiliary tape, $\Delta P_2+\overline{\overline{P}}_5$ in all impulses is made, using three P tapes: present, 1 forward, 2 back.

(f) Tapes for Old Robinson

The only difference was a **×•×•** pattern in the fifth impulse, used as a control (**27G(i)**). On Miles A a **×•×•** tape in the 6th transmitter could provide this. If only 3 impulses of Z^* were wanted, only four transmitters were used for differencing, and on any Miles a 5th transmitter could provide **×•×•**.

If however a Z^* (or P^*) tape was to be made on a Miles other than Miles A, four copies of an auxiliary tape ZQ were made, whose impulses were a, p. 244

$$Z_{15},\quad Z_{25},\quad Z_{35},\quad Z_{45},\quad \textbf{×•×•}\text{ pattern.}$$

These were used in the obvious way to produce Z^*. b

For $\overline{\chi}_2$ limitation ZQ had Z_2 in four impulses, **×•×•** in the 5th.

---

[a] tapes was to be [b] X^*

For $\overline{\chi}_2 + \overline{\overline{P}}_5$ limitation $\begin{cases} \text{ZQ had } Z_2 \text{ in four impulses, } \times\bullet\times\bullet \text{ in the 5th.} \\ \text{PQ had } \Delta P_2 + \overline{\overline{P}}_5 \text{ in four impulses, } \times\bullet\times\bullet \text{ in the 5th.} \end{cases}$

(cf. **27F(e)**.)

i 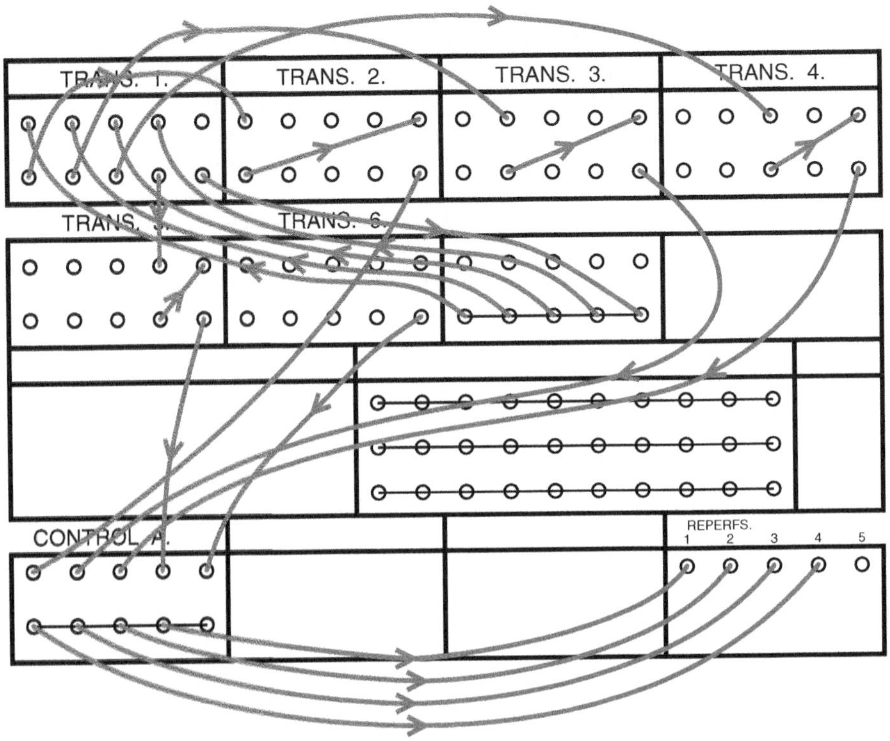

(g) Continued use of auxiliary tapes

The use of PQ, ZQ was continued to avoid disturbing an established routine, and because an undependable Miles was better able to cope with the individually simpler operations.

(h) Number of tapes needed

4 P^* tapes, 2 Z^* running tapes, 2 Z^* checking tapes.

(i) Checking

The first 15 letters of every tape made were checked by hand. Tape sheets were used to record progress.

27G STATISTICAL TECHNIQUE: RUNNING ON ROBINSON

Note: Throughout this chapter it is assumed (cf. **27C(g)**) that Z is shorter than P: if not Z, Z^*
ii should be interchanged with P, P^*. For proofs and references see **22W**.

(a) Basic Formulae

If Z is the encipherment of part of P, then in the correct position

E.11
$$Z + P = K.$$

---

[i] The exact details of the shape of the flex of the cables have not been reproduced in this drawing. The arrowhead missing from the cable connecting 'TRANS. 2' with 'CONTROL A.' is missing in the original.

[ii] Sentence 'For proofs ...' handwritten.

Z and P are added in all positions and their sum examined for resemblance to key. Key is characterized by

$$\Delta_{598}\Delta K_{45} \longrightarrow \bullet$$

where $\Delta_{598}U$ means (present U) + (U_{598} forward) with the analogous results for other pairs of impulses. p. 245

Further, for $\overline{\chi}_2$ limitation, if 31ρ is any multiple of 31,

$$\Delta_{31\rho}\Delta K_2 \longrightarrow \bullet;$$

for $\overline{\chi}_2 + \overline{\overline{P}}_5$ limitation

$$\Delta_{31\rho}(\Delta K_2 + \overline{\overline{P}}_5) \longrightarrow \bullet.$$

For the use of $\Delta_2 K$ characteristics see **22F** (**R2**, p. 80, **R3**, pp. 13, 15, 76).

(b) Δ_{598} method: running for strokes in ΔK^*

The runs used are based on

$$\Delta_{943}(\Delta P_{15} + \Delta Z_{15}) \longrightarrow \bullet,$$
$$\Delta_{713}(\Delta P_{25} + \Delta Z_{25}) \longrightarrow \bullet,$$
$$\Delta_{667}(\Delta P_{35} + \Delta Z_{35}) \longrightarrow \bullet,$$
$$\Delta_{598}(\Delta P_{45} + \Delta Z_{45}) \longrightarrow \bullet.$$

The last of these, for example, could be done on Robinson, by adding a $\Delta_{598}P_{45}$ tape and a $\Delta_{598}Z_{45}$ tape in all possible relative positions, in each of which $\Delta_{598}\Delta P_{45} + \Delta_{598}\Delta Z_{45} = \bullet$ is counted.

For greater power the number of places where all four runs simultaneously give a dot can be counted. This is achieved by a tape Z^* whose first four impulses carry $\Delta_{943}Z_{15}$, $\Delta_{713}Z_{25}$, $\Delta_{667}Z_{35}$, $\Delta_{598}Z_{45}$, respectively, and a tape P^* similarly derived from P. The run is then

$$\Delta Z^* + \Delta P^* = /.$$

(c) Optimum number of impulses

Differencing reduces the length of text, the reductions for Δ_{943}, Δ_{713}, Δ_{667}, Δ_{598} being of course 943, 713, 667, 598. Since the length of Z^* is the length of its shortest impulse, it may be preferable to use fewer than 4 impulses, generally 2 or 3 (see table in para. (**e**)).

(d) Scoring the letter count

The runs for /'s are convenient, but waste the evidence of dots not forming a /.

Accordingly, when the run is completed, at each of the settings which gives a good score for /'s, the total number of dots in all (2, 3 or 4) impulses is counted, actually by means of a letter count, the score for any letter being the number of dots it contains. In one instance this set the crib correctly, though the score for /'s was 3·4σ and only the fourth highest.

It is possible to count dots in impulses not used in the run for /'s and at places thrown away by reducing the length of K^* to that of its shortest impulse. p. 246

(e) Table of formulae

Number of impulses used.	N = text length of Z^* (n being text length of Z)	Running for /'s		Approx. value of σ commonly used	Minimum text for which this number of impulses is preferable.	Scoring the l.c.	
		Random average	σ			Average	σ
1	$n-598$	$N/2$	$\frac{1}{2}\sqrt{N}$			$N/2$	$\frac{1}{2}\sqrt{N}$
2	$n-667$	$N/4$	$\frac{1}{4}\sqrt{3N}$		750	N	$\frac{1}{2}\sqrt{2N}$
3	$n-713$	$N/8$	$\frac{1}{8}\sqrt{7N}$	$\sqrt{N/8}$	860	$3N/2$	$\frac{1}{2}\sqrt{3N}$
4	$n-943$	$N/16$	$\frac{1}{16}\sqrt{15N}$	$\sqrt{N/16}$	6,000	$2N$	$\sqrt{N}$

i Note: The sigma-age needed for "certainty" depends on the number of positions tried. As the number of impulses used increases, the evidence of a given sigma-age decreases (see **27X(e)**).

(f) Running on Robinson

The tape of Z^* is one longer than the tape of P^*, so that at each revolution Z^* steps one forward relative to P^*. Start and stop are taken from Z^*, until Z^* begins to run off the end of P^* (**R2**, p. 99;
ii **R3**, p. 68). A set total of 2σ allows the random scores to act as a crude check that Robinson is not grossly faulty.

When the run is finished (or stopped if a very good score appears) the Z^* tape is replaced by a Z^* checking tape, of the same length as P^*, which is set in all positions giving good scores, and a letter count made. To set the tapes the letter of P^* which corresponds to the first letter of Z is marked with the aid of a hand-counter.

The score for /'s is spanned to detect slides or corruption.

(g) Very long decodes

If P^* is very long, not only must Z^* be tried at many settings, but each revolution takes a long time. P^* may be cut into overlapping sections; if machines are available these may be run simultaneously; log reading may predict which is the best section to try first. Alternatively the
a P^* tape may be made one shorter than a *multiple* of the Z^* tape, so that two or more settings are examined for each revolution of P^*.

(h) Running for dots

p. 247 This means counting the total number of dots in $\Delta_{943}\Delta K_{15}$, $\Delta_{713}\Delta K_{25}$, etc. i.e. obtaining the "score on the letter count" (**27G(d)**) in the actual run. It was not used operationally because

(i) the possible pitfalls in tape-making were so numerous that standardisation was necessary,

(ii) running for /'s, and counting dots at *all* good settings, is equally effective.

It can be done by putting $\Delta_{943}Z_{15}$, $\Delta_{713}Z_{25}$, $\Delta_{667}Z_{35}$, $\Delta_{598}Z_{45}$, end-to-end in the same impulse, and likewise for P; but this demands a roughly four-fold increase of tape length. A two-fold increase will suffice if "either-or" is used on Robinson.

---

[a] mote

[i] This note typed single space.
[ii] '...from Z^* (until Z^* begins to run off the end of P^* **R2** p 99; **R3** p 68)' without a stop at the end.

Length of corresponding tape for P.

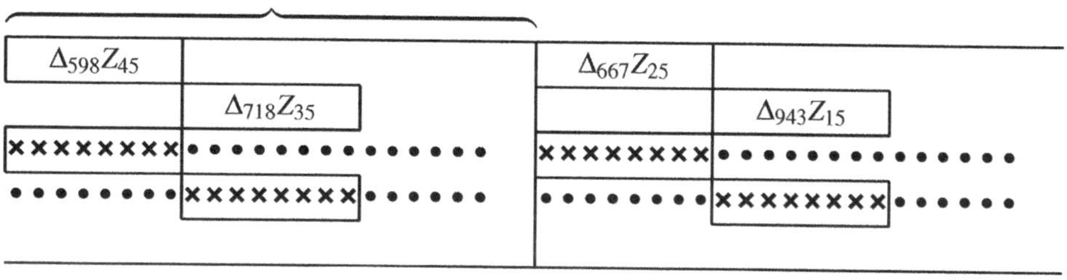

Switch either $\Delta Z_1^* + \Delta P_1^* = \bullet$, $\Delta Z_3^* = \times$
or $\Delta Z_2^* + \Delta P_2^* = \bullet$, $\Delta Z_4^* = \times$.
Tapes could be of normal length if Robinson could count "A or B or C or D".

(i) Running on Old Robinsons

This was complicated because the minimum text length was 2000, there was no spanning and long strings of dots or crosses were technically forbidden (**52(b)**(iv)).

The text of Z^* and P^* was made up to 2000 with RY's except in the 5th impulse, which was used as a control. On each tape the 5th impulse had a ×•×• pattern throughout, but in the shorter text (usually Z^*) there was a phase reversal at the end of the text.

The tapes differed in length by 2, so that the stepping was two at a time: odd and even settings were run separately.

Odd settings P_5^* × • × • × • × • × • × • × For genuine text $P_5 + Z_5 = \bullet$.
Z_5^* × • × • × • × | × • × • × • Setting $= 2 \times$ reading $+ 1$
End of text (reading = number of revolutions).

Even settings P_5^* × • × • × • × • × • × • × • × For genuine text $P_5^* + Z_5^* = \times$.
Z_5^* • × • × • × • × | × • × • × • × Setting $= 2 \times$ reading.
End of text

If only three impulses of K^* were wanted, the 1st and 5th were used for control, no separation into odd and even runs being needed.

P_5^* • × • × • × • × • × • ×
Z_5^* • × • × • × | × • × • × •
End of text i

(j) Checking on Old Robinsons p. 248

Old Robinson had no device to show whether the tapes had in fact been set correctly, and it was necessary to depend on the accuracy of hand counting. It was desirable to make many trials, even a re-run, before abandoning a high score which failed to check.

(k) Δ_{31} ($\overline{\chi}_2$ limitation) Running for strokes

The technique is almost identical with that of the Δ_{598} method, being based on $\Delta_{31\rho}(\Delta P_2 + \Delta Z_2) \longrightarrow \bullet$.

The impulses of P^* are $\Delta_{3\times 31}P_2$, $\Delta_{4\times 31}P_2$, $\Delta_{9\times 31}P_2$, $\Delta_{11\times 31}P_2$.

(There are many references, most of them applicable to $\overline{\chi}_2 + \overline{\overline{P}}_5$ limitation, in the Research Logs: ii

---

i 'End of text' handwritten.

ii 'There are many references. . . ': typed single space.

R2, pp. 70, 71, 73, 75, 102, 105; **R3**, pp. 2, 12, 24, 26. Somewhat different methods **R2**, pp. 65, 66, 68, 73.)

(l) Δ_{31}: Scoring the letter count

This is quite different, e.g. $\begin{smallmatrix}\times\\ \times\\ \bullet\end{smallmatrix}$ scores $2+1+1=4$, because the two crosses imply a dot in

a $\Delta_{124-93}=\Delta_{31}$, and the two dots imply a dot in $\Delta_{341-297}=\Delta_{62}$ (**R2**, p. 70). For one or two impulses this is absolutely equivalent to counting strokes.

(m) Δ_{31}: Table of formulae

i

Number of impulses used	Intervals chosen for differencing 31 times	N, text length of Z^* (n = text of Z)	These are as in **27G(e)** Ave	σ	Least text (n) which makes this number of impulses preferable for counting /'s	Scoring the letter count: Score for a letter having so many dots 0 1 2 3 4	Ave	σ
1	1	$n-31$	$N/2$	$\frac{1}{2}\sqrt{N}$		0 1	$N/2$	$\frac{1}{2}\sqrt{N}$
2	1,3	$n-93$	$N/4$	$\frac{1}{4}\sqrt{3N}$	210	1 1 3	N	$\frac{1}{2}\sqrt{3N}$
3	1,4,6	$n-186$	$N/8$	$\frac{1}{8}\sqrt{7N}$	approx 6000	3 2 3 6	$3N$	$\frac{1}{2}\sqrt{6N}$
4	3,4,9,11	$n-341$	$N/16$	$\frac{1}{16}\sqrt{15N}$		6 4 4 6 10	$5N$	$\frac{1}{2}\sqrt{10N}$

b As the number of impulses increases, the evidence of a given sigma-age diminishes.

It is rarely advisable to use 3 or 4 impulses for counting /'s, but it is useful to have more impulses on the tapes in order to score the letter counts.

(n) Δ_{31}: $\overline{\chi}_2+\overline{\overline{P}}_5$ limitation

$$\Delta_{31\rho}(\Delta P_2+\overline{\overline{P}}_5)+\ \Delta_{31\rho}(\ \Delta Z_2)\longrightarrow\bullet.$$

The P^* tape carries $\Delta_{31\rho}(\Delta P_2+\overline{\overline{P}}_5)$, and P_2^* is not differenced on Robinson.

p. 249 **(o) Δ_{31}: ideal method**

This means to count the dots in $\Delta_{31\rho}\Delta K_2$ for all values of ρ simultaneously (**27Y(b)**). It is considerably more powerful than running for strokes (**27Y(g)**). It might occasionally have been worth while.

Since so powerful a method would be needed only for very short texts, the method of **27G(h)** would be practicable (cf. **R2**, p. 102). Numerous alternatives were suggested. A form of "staircasing" in which all the impulses of "Z^*" are simply ΔZ_2 staggered at multiples of 31 is given in **R3**, p. 2 ($\Delta_{31\rho}$ is effected by adding them: more than one run is needed). Other suggestions **R2**, p. 105, **R3**, p. 24.

ii The 5202 photographic machine (ch. **91**) could be used advantageously, by putting a transparent spot in the $2\rho-1^{\text{th}}$, $2\rho^{\text{th}}$ level, if $\Delta_{31\rho}\Delta Z_2=\bullet,\times$ respectively; and similarly for P. A single place of K^* can contribute several coincidences between transparent spots, an advantage of 5202 not exploited by the method of **91D**.

[a] $\Delta_{347-297}=\Delta_{62}$ [b] impluses

[i] 'Average' in column heads replaced with 'Ave' (twice), to save space.
[ii] Text starting 'by putting...' handwritten.

27H HISTORY OF CRIB ORGANISATION

Work on cribs was shared between

(i) Sixta Non-Morse Section (Log reading).

(ii) Testery Cribs Watch (Decode reading).

(iii) Newmanry Cribs (Statistical machine setting).

Crib prediction was so unlike other work on Tunny and involved so much liaison with Sixta and the Cribs Watch that during most of its existence the Cribs Section was the responsibility of a single cryptographer with special qualifications for such work.

The (Wren) Cribs Registrars (one on each watch) dealt competently with all standardised operations: ordering, editing, checking decode and cipher, making and checking tapes. The amount of checking needed was large even by Newmanry standards. a

Men in charge

Early 1944	Newmanry DO (as one of many duties)	During this period methods were gradually standardised. i, b
Aug. 1944	Cryptographer on each shift (by rota)	
Sep. 1944	Permanent Cribs man and Mr Y.	
Nov. 1944	Permanent Cribs man	
Apr. 1945	Section reorganised as "Robinson Section" (2 men) to facilitate experimental work on Robinsons.	

Some Statistics

Retransmission	slips	produced by Sixta	: 893
"	"	worked on by Newmanry Cribs	: 250
Days broken			: 72

(Early references **R2**, pp. 64, 79.)

27W BASIC CRIB FORMULA

p. 250

The problem is that of recognising key. c

$$\begin{aligned}\Delta_{ij}\ K_{ij} &= \Delta_{ij}(\psi'_{ij} + \chi_{ij})\\ &= \Delta_{ij}\psi'_{ij} \qquad \text{(W1)}\end{aligned}$$

ii

where Δ_{ij} denotes differencing at any common multiple of the lengths of $\chi_i\chi_j$.

Therefore since

$$\begin{aligned}P(\Delta\psi_{ij} = \bullet) &= \frac{1+\beta}{2},\\ P(\Delta_{ij}K_{ij} = \bullet) &= \frac{1+\beta^2}{2}. \qquad \text{(W2)}\end{aligned}$$

Putting $j = 6$ or by elementary methods

$$P\{\Delta_i(\Delta K_i + \text{lim}) = \bullet\} = \frac{1+\beta^2}{2}.$$

[a] standardized [b] reorganized [c] if recognising

[i] Text to right of } sign, 'During this period methods were gradually standardised', handwritten.

[ii] Throughout **27W**, equation numbers are given without parentheses, both in displays and in equation references. We have rearranged the spacing of the displayed equations in the first three paragraphs.

For $\overline{\chi}_2 + \overline{\overline{P}}_5$ limitation

$$P\left\{\Delta_{31\rho}(\Delta K_2 + \overline{\chi}_2 + \overline{\overline{P}}_5) = \bullet\right\} = \frac{1+\beta^2}{2} \qquad (31\rho \text{ is any multiple of } 31)$$

i.e.

$$P\left\{\Delta_{31\rho}(\Delta K_2 + \overline{\overline{P}}_5) = \bullet\right\} = \frac{1+\beta^2}{2}. \tag{W3}$$

Similarly for $\overline{\chi}_2$ limitation

$$P\left\{\Delta_{31\rho}\Delta K_2 = \bullet\right\} = \frac{1+\beta^2}{2}. \tag{W4}$$

U^* is used to denote a stream of letters whose impulses are all of the form $\Delta_{ij}U_{ij}$, so that (W1) may be written

$$K_{ij}^* = \psi_{ij}'^{\,*}. \tag{W5}$$

[a] K, K^* often mean $P+Z, P^*+Z^*$ which should not strictly be called K, K^* except when P and Z are correctly set (Δ_{31} **R2**, p. 70 sqq; Δ_{598} **R2**, p. 90).

$\Delta_{598}, \Delta_{31}$ are treated separately, because each has some simplifying circumstance: in Δ_{598} differencing at *multiples* of 598 etc. is not needed; in Δ_{31} only the second impulse is involved.

27X Δ_{598} THEORY

(a) Ideal method (counting dots)

The theoretically simplest method is to count the total number of dots in the four streams $\Delta_{943}\Delta K_{15}, \Delta_{713}\Delta K_{25}, \Delta_{667}\Delta K_{35}, \Delta_{598}\Delta K_{45}$ (**27G(h)**).

The number, ν, of characters to be considered, is the positive terms of $(n-598)+(n-667)+(n-713)+(n-943)$

i.e.

$$n-598,\ 2(n-633),\ 3(n-659) \text{ or } 4(n-755). \tag{X1}$$

[i]

[ii] As usual,

$$\text{average} = \frac{\nu}{2} \tag{X2}$$

$$\sigma = \frac{1}{2}\sqrt{\nu} \tag{X3}$$

$$\text{expected sigma-age} = \beta^2\sqrt{\nu}. \tag{X4}$$

---

[a] meean

[i] Throughout **27X**, equation numbers are given without parentheses, both in displays and in references.

[ii] Equations (X2), (X3), (X4) and their equation numbers are all given in one line, which we have split to make them more legible.

(b) Practical method (counting strokes)

In practice (cf. **27G(b)**) only those places where *all* these four streams have a dot are counted, i.e. the number of strokes in ΔK^*, the four impulses of K^* being $\Delta_{943}K_{15}$, $\Delta_{713}K_{25}$, $\Delta_{667}K_{35}$, $\Delta_{598}K_{45}$.

The effective text length N is p. 251

$$n-598,\ n-667,\ n-713,\ \text{or}\ n-943 \tag{X5}$$

according to the number, m, of impulses used.

$$\text{Average} = \frac{N}{2^m},\quad \sigma = \sqrt{\frac{1}{2^m}(1-1/2^m)N}. \qquad \text{(X6), (X7)}$$

(c) Effect of non-normal distribution

As m increases the evidence of a given sigma-age decreases because the binomial distribution ceases to approximate to a normal distribution, and approaches, though not very closely, the Poisson distribution for rare occurrences (**22(I)**; **R3**, pp. 24, 26).

In practice this demands no further calculation for good scores are checked by counting the dots in ΔK^*.

(d) Expected frequency of each letter in ΔK^*

The frequency of strokes in $\Delta K^* \equiv \Delta\psi'^*$ is greater than for a distribution, otherwise random, in which each character tends to a dot with probability $\frac{1+\beta^2}{2}$, because all the impulses of a letter in $\Delta\psi'^*$ depend in part on the same letter of $\Delta\psi'$. For this same letter there are three cases viz. [a]

	TM× $\Delta\psi_5$×	TM× $\Delta\psi_5$•	TM •
Probability of each case	ab	$a(1-b)$	$1-a$
” that $\Delta\psi'_{45} = \bullet$	b	$1-b$	1
” ” $\Delta\psi'_{45} = \times$	$1-b$	b	0
” ” $\Delta\psi'_{45}$, 598 forward $= \bullet$	b	b	b
” ” ” ” $= \times$	$1-b$	$1-b$	$1-b$
” ” $\Delta_{598}\Delta\psi'_{45} = \bullet$	$b^2+(1-b)^2$	$2b(1-b)$	b
” ” $\Delta_{598}\Delta\psi'_{45} = \times$	$2b(1-b)$	$b^2+(1-b)^2$	$1-b$

Whence the probability that a letter of ΔK^* has r dots and s crosses is

$$\begin{aligned} p &= ab\{b^2+(1-b)^2\}^r\{2b(1-b)\}^s \\ &\quad + a(1-b)\{ab(1-b)\}^r\{b^2+(1-b)^2\}^s + (1-a)b^r(1-b)^s \\ &= \frac{1}{2^{r+s+1}}\left[(1+\beta^2)^r(1-\beta^2)^s\right. \\ &\quad \left. + \frac{1-\beta}{1+\beta}(1-\beta^2)^r(1+\beta^2)^s + 2\beta(1+\beta)^{r-1}(1-\beta)^2\right]. \end{aligned} \tag{X8}$$ [i]

[a] vix

[i] Equation (X8) and its predecessor are each displayed on a single line. We have split them to make them more legible.

(e) Expected decibanages

E.12 These can be calculated by "$\Sigma n \log n$" (**22Y**3). Since the frequencies are given, this is not optimistic. For counting strokes it reduces to

i
$$N\left[p \log 2^m\, p + (1-p) \log \frac{1-p}{1-1/2^m}\right]. \tag{X9}$$

The corresponding results for counting dots are included in the table, and show that these runs are appreciably stronger. The text for +40 decibans when counting dots assumes the ideal method of para. (**a**).

p. 252, ii

m (number of impulses)	Decibans per letter of Z^* counting strokes or dots, for a motor dottage: 20 /'s	20 •'s	24 /'s	24 •'s	28 /'s	28 •'s	$n-N$ loss of text length due to differencing K^*	Ideal method
1	·041	·041	·116	·116	·31	·31	598	598
2	·073	·088	·214	·23	·59	·61	667	633
3	·087	·132	·28	·35	·80	·92	713	656
4	·091	·176	·31	·46	·93	1·22	943	730
Gross text for 40 decibans, and number of impulses used	1170 (3)	1020 (4)	855 (2 or 3)	770 (3)	730 (1)	700 (2)		

If the whole ΔK^* letter count were scored even more evidence could be obtained than from counting dots.

27Y Δ_{31} THEORY

(a) Preliminary

ΔK_2 is differenced at various intervals which are multiples of 31. In forming these differences a character of ΔK_2 is added only to characters of ΔK_2 against the same character of χ_2, and it is convenient to think of the text as consisting of 31 sets of $n/31 = k$ letters.

(b) Ideal method

The obvious method, which wastes no evidence, is to compare each of the k letters with each
a of the others, thus obtaining $\nu = 31k(k-1)/2$ comparisons for counting $\Delta_{31p}\Delta K_2 = \bullet$, but these are clearly not all independent.

It is easy to prove (as in the analogous problem of **24X(d)**) that the bulge of the score equals the bulge of the square of the half-pippages in the $\widehat{\chi}_2$ run on the same key, i.e. the method is equivalent to using the χ^2 test (**R2**, p. 102: other references in **27G(o)**).

For the standard deviation and expected score see paras (**f**), (**g**) where this method is treated as the limiting case of methods used in practice.

[a] each of the other

[i] Right-hand bracket ']' missing from formula (X9).

[ii] Column heads 'strokes' and 'dots' replaced with "/'s" and "•'s"; multi-line captions rearranged to save space.

(c) Practical method (counting strokes)

In practice **27G(k)** the differencing is done only at m (1, 2, 3 or 4) intervals, each constituting one impulse of ΔK^* (not quite the same as for Δ_{598} etc.). Strokes in ΔK^* are counted.

The evidence of these strokes is not entirely independent, but if the intervals are well chosen (cf. para. **(h)**), the formulae (X6), (X7), above, can be used.

(d) Effects of non-normal distribution

Exactly as in **27X(c)**, the sigma-ages may be misleading, and it is preferable to use the formula for expected decibanages p. 253

$$N\left\{\left(\frac{1+\beta^2}{2}\right)^m \log\left(1+\beta^2\right)^m + \left(1-\left(\frac{1+\beta^2}{2}\right)^m\right)\log 1 - \left(\frac{1+\beta^2}{2}\right)\right\}. \qquad \text{(Y1)}$$ i

(e) Scoring the letter count

To get more evidence from the ΔK^* letter count, consider all the comparisons made at each letter, and count those which give a dot. The number of comparisons is not merely m (as in Δ_{598} method) but (cf. **27G(l)**)

$$m+\frac{m(m-1)}{2}=\frac{m(m+1)}{2}$$

and a letter with r dots and s crosses scores

$$r+\frac{r(r-1)}{2}+\frac{s(s-1)}{2}$$

e.g. when differencing at intervals $1\times 31, 4\times 31, 6\times 31$, denoting each of the k letters against a particular character of χ_2 by its number, the first letter of Z^* involves explicitly the comparisons, 12, 15, 17 and implicitly 57, 72, 25.

Treating the comparisons as independent,

$$\nu = N\frac{m(m+1)}{2}, \qquad \text{(Y3)}$$

$$\text{Average } = N\frac{m(m+1)}{2}, \qquad \text{(Y4)}$$

$$\sigma = \frac{1}{2}\sqrt{N\frac{m(m+1)}{2}}, \qquad \text{(Y5)}$$

$$\text{Expected decibanage} = 2{\cdot}17\beta^4 N\frac{m(m+1)}{2}. \qquad \text{(Y6)}$$ ii

It is shown rigorously in **R3**, p. 70 (and a mathematically identical result is proved in **26X(a)**), that for a single letter the equations (Y3), (Y4), (Y5) are in fact correct, but this particular argument does not apply to the whole text, unless $N\leq 31$ when there is only one letter of K^* against each character of χ_2.

(f) Ideal method as a limiting case

The case $m = k-1$, and therefore $N = 31$, is the ideal method of para. **(b)**. There is only one letter of K^* opposite each character of χ_2 so that (Y3), (Y4), (Y5) are exact.

---

i Throughout **27Y**, equation numbers are given without parentheses.

ii There is no equation labelled (Y2): the numbering series skips from (Y1) to (Y3). The *Report* displays equations (Y3), (Y4), and (Y5) on the same line; we display them on separate lines to make them more legible.

$$\nu = 31\frac{k(k-1)}{2}, \tag{Y7}$$

$$\text{Average} = 31\frac{k(k-1)}{2}, \tag{Y8}$$

$$\sigma = \frac{1}{2}\sqrt{31\frac{k(k-1)}{2}}. \tag{Y9}$$

i

$$\text{Expected decibanage} = 2{\cdot}17\beta^4 31\frac{k(k-1)}{2}. \tag{Y10}$$

(g) Expected decibanages

m (number of impulses)	Expected decibans per letter of K^* for motor dottages: 20, /'s	20, letter count	24, /'s	24, letter count	28, /'s	28, letter count	$n-N$ (loss of text due to differencing)
1	·041	·041	·116	·116	·31	·31	31
2	·058	·123	·174	·348	·49	·93	93
3	·059	·246	·189	·796	·57	1·86	186
4	·054	·41	·176	1·16	·58	3·1	341
Minimum text for 40 decibans and number of impulses used	780 (2)	350 (3)	320 (2)	210 (2)	160 (1)	140 (2)	
Ditto, ideal method	265		165		105		

p. 254 **(h) Choice of intervals for differencing**

Although the comparisons of para. **(e)** cannot be made independent, it is possible to avoid including the same comparison twice viz. by making

(i) the intervals

(ii) twice the intervals

(iii) the sum of any two intervals

all different numbers.

Convenient sets of intervals which satisfy the conditions are (after removal of the common factor 31)

1 ;
1, 3 ;
1, 4, 6 ;
3, 4, 9, 11 .

[i] The *Report* displays equations (Y7), (Y8), and (Y9) on the same line; we display them on separate lines to make them more legible. The equals sign is missing from equation (Y9).

28 LANGUAGE METHODS p. 255, [i]

28A DEPTHS

E.1

(a) Definition

Two messages are said to be in depth if they are enciphered on the same key. A cross depth is a depth in which the legs are sent by different ends of the link. E.2

(b) Importance of depths

In the Tunny era, depths were of enormous importance in obtaining wheel patterns — it was some time before any technique independent of depth was discovered — but, owing to the nature of the indicating system, they were extremely rare.

The introduction of QSN (later QEP) numbers (November 1, 1942) obliged us to concentrate E.3
all our attentions on depths whose number increased enormously as a result of the increase in the [a]
number of links and the indiscriminate use by the enemy of the cipher. (For example, a gadget was installed on the German machine enabling the operator to return the wheels to their original settings — a glorious depth-producing device.)

Statistical analysis enabled the problem of setting the wheels on single messages to be tackled again, but depths were still invaluable for obtaining wheel patterns.

The advent of the P_5 component of the limitation dealt a knockout blow to depths but its subsequent disappearance enabled us once again to employ depth-breaking methods and, in the closing months of the war, depths proved of enormous value in obtaining wheel patterns with a currency which no other technique could achieve.

(c) Evidence

The existence of depths was deduced from the sequence of QEP numbers preceding intercepted messages. There was a possibility of a depth when the same number occurred twice within a short space of time, or when no QEP number was sent and the previous and following numbers were consecutive e.g. as in the sequence (i) 34 (ii) QEP not sent (iii) 35. E.4

Originally depths only occurred between messages from the same end of the same link, but later some links used a QEP system in which both ends jointly used the same consecutive sequence of QEP numbers. After this, depths between messages from different ends of the same link (cross-depths) occurred.

In many cases it was not obvious which pair of messages were in depth, and in many cases alleged depths were in fact follow-ons. However every possible depth was teleprinted from E.5
Knockholt and investigated. There were two categories:

[a] out attentions

[i] All the chapters from **28** to the end of the *Report* are typed single space.

[ii] In the original text of the *Report*, almost all chapters start with an analytical contents list. This one does not. We have accordingly supplied such a list, as a copy editor would have done, for uniformity and the convenience of readers.

a (i) Depths which might give enough key for wheel-breaking purposes. The minimum for this in 1945 was 100 letters.

(ii) Depths which might give enough key to set on known wheels. The minimum for this in 1945 was 15 letters.

(d) Treatment of Depths

From the fundamental equation of the machine

$$P = Z + K$$

E.6 we see that $P_a + P_b = Z_a + Z_b + K_a + K_b = Z_a + Z_b$ if $K_a = K_b$

Since by definition, $K_a = K_b$ for a depth, it follows that the difference of the ciphers is the
p. 256, i difference of the clears. The conditions that $K_a = K_b$ for all places of the key are

identical wheel patterns
identical original settings
identical limitations.

It follows from (iii) that the introduction of autoclave destroys depths and that two messages enciphered on $\overline{\chi}_2$ and $\overline{\chi}_2\overline{\Psi}_1$ lims respectively will also not be in depth.

b Treatment of depths may be divided up into two subsections (1) depth scoring and (2) depth anagramming.

(1) Depth Scoring

Since the frequency distribution of P is non-random, it follows that the $Z_a + Z_b$ of the two messages in depth, differs considerably from a random set of letters, since the frequency p_Θ of a
E.7 letter Θ in $P_a + P_b$ is given by

$$p_\Theta = \sum_\Phi p_\Phi p_{\Theta+\Phi}.$$

It therefore follows that each letter in $Z_a + Z_b$ contributes a factor towards (or against) the theory that the two messages are in depth. [A scoring table was devised to exploit this property (**R41**, pp. 56, 57) (see **22W**.)] It is equally true that trigrams or bigrams in $Z_a + Z_b$ make their contribution to the theory and scoring tables could be devised to make use of their contribution. Two points, however, should be borne in mind. First language properties are very heterogeneous and depths may therefore not appear obvious from a scoring table (in particular, depths on links
E.8 using 'doubles' may usually be recognised purely by a count of /'s in the difference or 'clicks').
c Second the danger of slides is a very real one and their occurrence naturally makes depth scoring more problematical.

(2) Depth Anagramming

Having ascertained that the depth is worth working on, the next stage is reached in which an attempt is made to divide up $Z_a + Z_b$ into its respective P_a and P_b. The original technique of dragging (described in earlier screeds on this subject) has now been completely superseded by 'faffing' or 'fiddling', a process open only to the most experienced and capable breakers. The process consists — insofar as it is susceptible to logical exposition — of recognising common differences (e.g. `F3`, `Y3`, `58`, `KO`, `VLJ`) and assuming the clear equivalents `EN` + `N9`, (`DE` + `9D`), `CH` + `5M`, `89` + `95`, `CH` + `EN`, `SCH` + `5M8`, then trying to extend these rudimentary breaks. It will be readily appreciated that only after considerable experience and practice can sufficient of these 'equivalents' be memorised to enable one to employ the method. In anagramming a depth, the following aids should be borne in mind

[a] wheelbreaking [b] (i) depth scoring and (ii) depth [c] make depth

[i] The following items were originally displayed in a numbered list, whose numbers were then cancelled by pasted-over slips. The next sentence ('It follows…'), however, refers to the third item.

(i) use of autopauses, which would suggest an identical clear repeat or go-back,

(ii) short hand transmissions in the middle of an auto message,

(iii) stereotyped nature of message beginnings

(iv) the common appearance of standardised forms of punctuation and the tendency of stops, when acting as abbreviation marks, to occur in clusters, a

(v) the possibility of a single letter or bigram being repeated several times, particularly before an autopause.

It will be noted that these aids are, as would be expected, fundamentally the same as those employed in de-chi breaking.

(e) Determination of key

Suppose $Z_a + Z_b$ are in depth and suppose that the clears are P_a and P_b (so that $Z_a + Z_b = P_a + P_b$). Without further evidence, it is not possible to say whether $K = Z_a + P_a = Z_b + P_b$ or $K = Z_a + P_b = Z_b + P_a$. I will discuss here what methods are employed to relate the clears to their respective ciphers, omitting only those methods which virtually form part of key-breaking. E.9

They are

(i) The existence of one or more extra messages in depth;

(ii) relating cipher pauses to clear pauses;

(iii) distinguishing between hand and auto language;

(iv) Sixta preferences based on their clear expectations;

(v) distinguishing between language characteristics at either end of a cross depth.

In addition, continuity enables one to keep on the right track, but it is often difficult even for the most experienced depth breakers to associate the clears correctly. p. 257

(g) Proteus i

At the time of writing, Proteus has not yet been completed, but a brief description of its functions may be of interest. Proteus is a machine designed to take a crib through a depth difference and test the resulting letters against a dictionary of common clear-formations. For fuller account see . ii

(h) Setting of depths on known wheels

See Chapter **43C(b)** and **(d)**.

28B ψ SETTING FROM DE-χ

(a) Introduction

When the χ's are set on Colossus, frequently either the motor patterns for the day are not yet known; or else Colossus time is too short to permit the mechanical setting of the motors and ψ's. b So, the χ's are added to the Z at their correct settings to give de-χ (D). Thus $D = Z + \chi = P + \psi'$. The de-χ tape is then printed on a width of 31 and sent over to Major Tester's section, where skilled breakers attempt to set the ψ's by non-statistical methods. This chapter is intended to give an outline of these methods.

The first de-χ was broken by Tutte (**44C**, the second by Tutte and Major Tester's Section combined and the third by Mr Newman's Section (**R0**, p. 95). This last gives the date when it became a routine to send de-χ's to Major Tester's section for ψ-setting by hand, in place of the de-χ's on impulses 1, 2, 4 and 5 *with the motor* which was previously thought necessary for success (see **43C(b)**). c

[a] The common [b] setting the the motors [c] **43(1)(d)**

[i] There is no subsection **28A(f)**: **28A(g)** follows directly after **28A(e)**.
[ii] Reference missing.

(b) The Problem

The breaker is given a single stream of letters which he must resolve into the two components P and ψ'. The partial ψ patterns obtained from stretches of de-χ which he thus resolves, must then be found on the known ψ wheels.

(c) Prior Knowledge

To obtain such 'breaks' in the D four types of prior knowledge are used:

(i) P characteristics

(ii) ψ' characteristics.

(iii) Type of limitation used by the Germans.

E.10 (iv) The 32 L.C.

(i) Knowledge of P characteristics is gained from a wide range of decodes on various links. Stock forms of message beginnings and endings, call signs, priority and secrecy signs, addresses, common syllables, words and phrases of military German — all of these are invaluable, but it is the peculiar nature of Tunny punctuation that the breaker makes most use of. A full stop may be expressed in various forms, e.g. `++M889`, `+M98`, `++M989`, `+M89` etc. Tunny language showed an ever-increasing use of abbreviations, each normally followed by a stop. These abbreviations tended to occur in common sequences, producing clusters of stops. Hand transmission is marked on the de-χ and here use is made of knowledge of the common phraseology of operator's remarks.

p. 258 (ii) The basis of de-χ breaking is the property $\Delta\psi' \longrightarrow /$ with probability $\doteqdot 1-a$. Wherever $\Delta\psi' = /$, $\Delta D = \Delta P$. The breaker therefore reads through the de-χ mentally differencing as he reads, looking for common ΔP combinations which will show through proportion $\doteqdot 1-a$ of the time. He also uses the property $\Delta\psi_i \xrightarrow[b]{} \mathbf{x}$. Thus having recognised a ΔP combination he writes it, in its undifferenced form, beneath the relevant letters of de-χ, adds it to give ψ', and then continues the combination backwards and/or forwards using his knowledge of P. The new ψ' letters thus produced are examined by the two criteria given above, to judge the validity of the break. Clearly the higher the μ_{37} dottage the stronger are these two properties and the easier it is to make and extend breaks. The breaker's knowledge of the reverse Δ of the common P combinations also helps him in making breaks.

(iii) All breaks must satisfy the conditions of the limitation known to have been used. Since the de-χ is printed on a width of 31, the breaker writes in χ_2 (or $\overline{\chi}_2$ if the lim. is $\overline{\chi}_2$ only) which is present in every type of limitation above the top line of the de-χ and it is then correct for every line.

E.11 (iv) The de-χ is accompanied by its 32 L.C., with a comment from the D.O. on its reliability and a note on whether the limitation is $\overline{\chi}_2$ or not. If it is on $\overline{\chi}_2$, a 32 L.C. against $\overline{\chi}_2$ crosses is given. Chapter **22G, H** gives an idea of how useful the 32 L.C. is to the breaker, in revealing the type of language and punctuation used in the de-χ.

(d) Breaking the de-χ

It is impossible fully to describe the subtleties of exploitation used by the expert breaker with his great familiarity with plain language and its Δ forms and his faculty of instantaneous teleprint addition. We can only describe the commonest and most obvious methods of obtaining a break.

In favourable circumstances a single break may be obtained sufficient to set all the ψ's or enough of them to be used as evidence to set the remainder. Here is an example of a line of de-χ on $\overline{\chi}_2$ limitation with $\overline{\chi}_2$ written along the top. In it the breaker sees two likely stops which he writes in, with the ψ' which they produce.

```
χ̄2    • × × × • • • × • • × × × • × • • × × • • × × × • × × ×
D     / W M 5 E E P N / M O R F O R D F 8 T A E 5 O A G I W U
P                                 5 M 8 9       5 M 8 9
ψ'                                A P P D       G U U U
```

The ψ' extensions all work on the limitation and the $\Delta\psi'$ features are good. The ψ letter D cannot be carried forward nor the G backward. But extensions are legitimate at 8TA in the de-χ. The Δ of 8T is K which is the Δ of DI, suggesting the common abbreviation DIV, which would also give 'good ψ changes' ($\Delta\psi$ crosses). Assuming DIV to be correct we look before the first stop for an abbreviation likely to precede DIV, such as 9PZ, 9GREN, 9JAEG, or 9INF. The ORF under $\overline{\chi}_2$ crosses immediately suggests 9PZ, and the likelihood that the number of the division has been given in figure shift suggests an 8 before the 9PZ, which gives an 8 in $\Delta\psi'$. The common word IST is strongly suggested at the end of the break, so we now have

```
χ̄2    • × × × • • • × • • × × × • × • • × × • • × × × • × × ×
D     / W M 5 E E P N / M O R F O R D F 8 T A E 5 O A G I W U
P                       8 9 P Z 5 M 8 9 D I V 5 M 8 9 I S T 9
ψ'                      A M M M A P P D P P X G U U U M A A A
```

The next stage is to write out ψ in impulses

```
× • × • × • × • × • ×
× • × × • × • × × • ×
• × • × • × × • × × •
• × • • × • × × • × •
• × • × • × × × • × •
A M A P D P X G U M A
```

The patterns are then tested against the known ψ wheels. It is found that the patterns obtained for the 1st, 2nd, 3rd, and 5th impulses are unique on their respective wheels, so the patterns can be written out on either side of the break. On ψ_4 the pattern obtained occurs twice only, so it is possible to write in what is common to both positions. i, p. 259

ii

```
      • • × • × • × • × • × • × • × • × × • • ×
      • × • × • • × • × × • × • × × • × • • × •
      × • × • • × • × • × • × × • × × • × • • •
              • × • × • • × • × × • × • × × •
      • × • × • × • × • × • × × × • × • • × • ×
      9 L S G E M A M A P D P X G U M A F O 4 Z
or    N G F L                                 B
```

Using the new material the break can clearly be extended to the left by choosing the ψ alternatives and extensions to give sense, until ψ_4 is also set uniquely and the de-χ broken. In this case the first stretch should read

```
• × × × • • • × • • ×
/ W M 5 E E P N / M O
9 D I V 9 5 Q T M 8 9
9 G G S S G E M M A M   etc.
```

In this example the motor dottage is high and the problem easy. But frequently two short breaks are obtained and nothing can be assumed for the intervening gap, as in the following example (limitation is ignored for simplicity).

---

[i] The lower left corner of p. 258 of the original typescript was dog-eared when photostatted, hiding the first two letters of "that the patterns obtained. . . "

[ii] Third dot from the right of first line of display missing: ••×•×•×•×•×•×•× ××••×.

D	Z Z D Q Q N S W Q T O A J 3 Q N	
P	5 5 M 8 8 9	5 5 M 8 8 9
ψ'	R R Y 3 3 3	A O Q Q 3 3

The ψ is then written out on all reasonable assumptions of the number of ψ's in the gap, and enough impulses of ψ should be identifiable on one of the assumptions, to guess the intervening P (in this case 'GREN'). This will either set the ψ's or reduce the number of positions still possible, to obtain further evidence, or in the worst case merely provide language evidence from which to guess further P.

With difficult de-χ's, the two breaks may be at a considerable difference apart (**R0**, p. 89). Suppose each gives 5 ψ letters. The possible positions for all wheels for each break are listed and the distance apart estimated, thus

7, 12, 15	15, 22, 30	Actual distance = 550
37, 42	15, 19, 32	Approx. unextended ψ distance
5, 19, 27, 31, 50	45	= 550 × known value of a = 400.
4, 38	17, 30, 42	
27, 50	20, 34, 50	

It is calculated that if the distance is taken as 397, both breaks fit all wheels, and the ψ's are set at

12	22
37	15
5	45
4	30
50	34.

To do the somewhat laborious calculation involved, a 'compatibility chart' was calculated and work was begun on an attachment to Dragon, named Salamander which would solve such problems automatically. But the end of the war prevented the machine from being completed and tested operationally.

(e) Autopauses

These signify either that the operator has inserted a new message tape or that he has pulled back the tape and sent the last stretch again. In the first case the autopause is followed by a message head with its vulnerable stock beginning. In the second case the same P occurs both before and after the pause; this is called a 'go-back'.

p. 260 **(f) Go-backs**

The average length of a go-back is between 40 and 100 letters. A go-back can be located in two ways

(i) by making a break on one side of the pause and then looking for the same P on the other side,

(ii) by comparing the two stretches of ΔD.

In the case of (i), once located the two identical breaks can be extended by playing them off against each other. For obstinate de-χ's procedure (ii) is used. A complete and detailed scoring
E.12 system for go-backs for all motor dottages is given in 'Report on Tunny (Major Tester's Section)' **VIII**, Appendix to parts **A** and **B**.

But frequently a go-back can be found by (ii) by inspection.

Let the stretches of de-χ before and after the pause, which contain the same P, be D_a and D_b. Then $\Delta D_a + \Delta D_b = \Delta\psi'_a + \Delta\psi'_b + \Delta P + \Delta P = \Delta\psi'_a + \Delta\psi'_b$. The most striking feature of the sum of two $\Delta\psi'$ streams is the proportion of /'s which is E.13

$$(1-a)^2 + a\left(b^2 + \overline{1-b}^2\right)^5$$

and the next most prominent feature is the proportion of 8's, which is

$$2(1-a)(ab^5) + a\left\{2b(1-b)\right\}^5.$$

These two factors may be sufficient to locate the go-back, by sliding ΔD_a against ΔD_b and looking for 'clicks' and 'anti-clicks'. An additional check is provided by the limitation. /'s are only E.14 strong evidence where $\text{lim}_a = \text{lim}_b$. Even with compound limitation the two lims can be compared. As $P_a = P_b$ the P_5 element of the limitation is identical. Also $\overline{\psi}'_{1a} + \overline{\psi}'_{1b} = \overline{D}_{1a} + \overline{D}_{1b} + \overline{P}_{1a} + \overline{P}_{1b}$, $= \overline{D}_{1a} + \overline{D}_{1b}$ as $\overline{P}_a = \overline{P}_b$. So the first impulse of D can be used supposing $\overline{\psi}'_1$ limitation is present.

A machine, 'Aquarius', was constructed to locate go-backs mechanically, but too late for operational use. i

Go-backs are also used when located by (ii) for resetting a wrongly set impulse of D. Resetting a wrongly set χ by means of a go-back and also by means of a break, is described in 'Report on Tunny (Major Tester's Section)' **VIII 6** and **7**.

(g) Overlaps

It is quite common for the beginning of a transmission to be a repeat of the P at the end of the preceding transmission.

The extent of overlapping varies considerably. The ΔP of the broken de-χ is slid against the ΔD at the start or end of the unbroken de-χ for 'clicks'. The Dragon machine is particularly E.15 suitable for exploiting overlaps.

(h) Rodding

A rod is a stick of cardboard at the head of which is written any of the 32 letters, and below in E.16 a column, the letters resulting from the addition of that letter to each of the 32 letters in order. If it a is desired to rod `QXR40MC` of a de-χ, ten rods headed by these letters are set up adjacent to each other and each level of the rods is inspected for fragments of P. Wherever there are repeats in ψ' the P will appear on a level of the rods (**R0**, p. 99).

(j) Operational Success ii

The following figures (in transmissions) give a picture of the quantity of the work handled and the proportion of success gained. The figures are for April, 1945.

de-χ's	Broken
806	707

p. 261

De-χ's marked 'all certain'	Of these broken	Of those broken incorrectly – marked 'all certain'.
728	680	21

356 transmissions were also set on all wheels mechanically.

[a] in column

[i] 'too late for current operational use', with 'current' struck out.

[ii] There is no subsection **28B(i)**: subsection **28B(h)** is immediately followed by **28B(j)**.

(k) Dragon

Dragon is a machine for the mechanical breaking of de-χ's by means of short cribs. For an account of how it works see **55A** (also see Report on Tunny (Maj. Tester's section) **VIII**).

28C ψ-BREAKING FROM DE-χ

(a) Introduction

When the χ's have been broken from cipher, the breaker must find sufficient *P* in the de-χ to give the entire new ψ patterns. This is clearly a much more difficult task than ψ setting, for a very much longer break of correct *P* must be made. In fact at first it was thought impossible except by using both legs of a depth set on the χ's. This was in fact how the first set of ψ's to be broken from a de-χ were obtained, on Bream of January 1944. But the February Bream ψ's were broken from a single de-χ and it was never necessary again to use a depth. As depths are
a rather infrequent and as from Summer of 1944 wheel patterns changed daily, this regular success in breaking ψ's from single de-χ's was of vital importance. Between August 1944 and May 1945 failures to obtain ψ patterns numbered less than 10 as against about 365 successes, and in some of the failures the χ's were not certain. Moreover, several sets of ψ's were obtained from de-χ's made with incorrect χ's which had to be corrected during the process.

(b) Method

i See figs. (**I**) and (**II**).

The process of ψ-breaking begins with the making of a break in the de-χ. Normally, this break would yield 17 or more letters of ψ key. The ψ-key obtained, with extensions removed is then written out in impulse form, as in fig. **28 (II)**. The fragments of ψ are then "projected" forward, at their respective wheel lengths. Thus ψ_1 is re-written out at a distance of 43, ψ_2 beneath it at a distance of 47, and so on. These patterns found in Break A can now be used.

b (i) For finding another break where the "projected" ψ is expected to occur. The position is calculated as follows. In the unextended ψ, the distance from the last ψ letter of the original break A to the first nearly complete letter of the projected ψ is 36. The original break will have provided an approximate indication of the motor dottage and therefore of the proportion of repeats in ψ'. In this example the first nearly complete letter (`M`) of the projected ψ is found in break B at a distance of 56 from the end of break A, showing a ψ' to ψ ratio of 56/36 or very roughly 3/2.

Or (ii) for identifying a break already found, about two lines ahead in the de-χ. Thus after obtaining break A, the stop giving the ψ'-stream `MMA000` might have been discovered and the ψ identified on the "projected" ψ at places 54, 55, 56.

From the correlation of these two breaks we get much useful information. First our breaks confirm one another. Secondly they give further indication of the dottage of μ_{37} (by defining how many ψ's are used in a given length between break A and break B). Thirdly, if we want to project our ψ-stream forward, once more, or backward, we shall know with fair accuracy where to look for such ψ-letters or partial ψ-letters, as we get by such projections, i.e. where these letters should give clear, and most important, the new break will give us additional signs on our
ii, p. 263 partial jsictextψ-wheelsψ wheels, which can in their turn be played back to break A, to assist in discovering the clear which comes in front of this break. Having obtained this clear, the new signs which it gives are projected forward again to ψ-stream B to assist in getting the clear before break B.

---

[a] succes [b] for finding another

[i] Throughout chapter **28**, figure captions and references use some variant of the style 'Fig **II**' instead of the style 'fig. **28 (II)**' used by the rest of the *Report*. We have silently regularized them to the latter form.

[ii] Figs. **28 (I)** and (**II**) moved from this location in the *Report*.

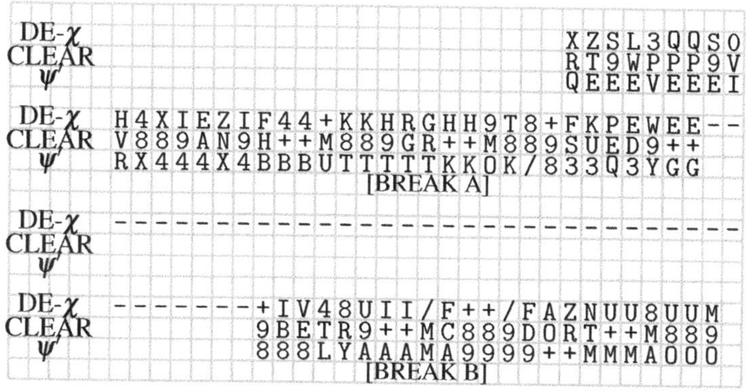

Fig. 28 (I)[i]

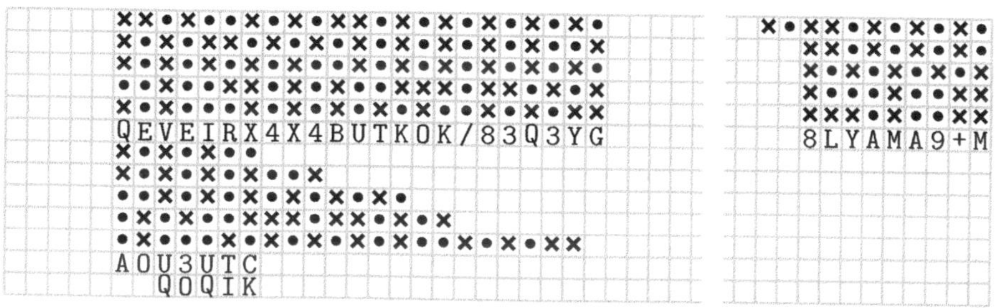

Fig. 28 (II) Unextended ψ Obtained from Breaks[ii]

The reason for the stipulation that the original break should produce 17 or more ψ's may now be clearer. The difference in length between the longest and shortest ψ-wheel is 16, and 17 places thus give a complete new ψ-letter in the projection B (place 60). It is easier, if no break is readily visible in the B area of the de-chi, to look for a complete ψ-letter to give clear when added to the de-chi, than to use only 4-impulse ψ-letters.

There are two ways in which the breaker can have his work simplified.

(i) By the discovery of "pure ψ".

(ii) By discovering a go-back.

In (i) the German operator has sent, instead of clear text, a string of /'s, in which case, when the χ wheels have been stripped off the cipher, ψ′ which is usually easy to recognise, forms the de-chi at that point. (The operator has been sending pure key, in fact.) This pure ψ is the more easily spotted, as the operator usually pauses when he has sent it, and ψ-breaking de-chi's are usually examined at pauses in the text. But he may send a series of 8's instead of /'s, or any other letter. If he sends a string of E's then the last four impulses will fit correctly with the ψ-wheels, but the first impulse will be in reverse (having a cross in the first impulse). As the breaker never

[i] Caption moved from left side of figure to bottom. Figures **28 (I)** and **(II)** have been moved to this position from their location in the middle of the fourth paragraph of this section, where they occupy all of p. 262 as a sideways squared-paper display. To save space we have moved the right-hand side of **28 (II)** closer to the left by 19 grid squares, indicating this with a 'frayed reticulation' effect.

[ii] Figure title in underlined capital letters. Caption moved from top of figure to bottom.

knows which letter has been sent, he has to find a break in the vicinity of the "pure ψ", write down, in impulse form, the ψ's obtained from the break, and look for these patterns, or their reverse patterns, in the write-out of the pure ψ. If he is unable to find a break, then his only alternative is to test the 32 possibilities which the pure ψ (representing the encipherment of one of the 32 signs of the teleprinter alphabet *minus the signs 3 and 4 which do not occur*) offers him. Such a method was used with success on at least one occasion. One breaker tested the ψ write-out with the assumption of / in the clear text, another with the first impulse reversed assuming an E in the clear, and so on.

Case (ii) offers the quickest means of ψ-breaking and the job has been done in 35 minutes with ease with the aid of a go-back. Usually the operator repeats about 60 letters of his tape in a go-back, which is just the right distance for the breaker. Thus the *P* of break A, picked up again after a go-back in position B, can be expanded by the use of the ψ signs derived from write-out of the B ψ-stream. The new clear information is put in at position B, providing new ψ information for position A. Unless the clear is very awkward, this process carries on quite smoothly until the breaks are lined up and the wheels are complete.

A few points:

(i) Naturally the original ψ may be projected forwards, or backwards, and any number of times, though the ψ information gets weaker with each projection, as the impulses get progressively out of phase with each other.

(ii) Use is of course made throughout of the limitation, as in ψ-setting from de-chi.

E.17 (iii) After the completion of the ψ-breaking, the number of dots in the 37 wheel can be discovered as it is in relation to the numbers of crosses in the 5 $\Delta\psi$-wheels ($ab = \frac{1}{2}$). A chart is used, giving the number of crosses in each $\Delta\psi$ wheel corresponding to any given number of dots in the μ_{37}. A copy of the chart is given in **22D(c)**.

p. 264 It is useful as a second check of the ψ patterns obtained (the first check being that each ψ wheel must be an equal number of dots and crosses ± 1), and sometimes as a method of completing

E.18 an incomplete ψ wheel.

Thus dottage can be found before breaking the motor and traffic ordered according to the expected ease of difficulty of χ-setting by machinery.

i (iv) It should be mentioned finally that, about a week after VE-day, a method was successfully used for breaking Motor and ψ patterns by statistical methods.

28D MOTOR BREAKING AND SETTING

(a) Early Motors

Motor breaking and setting were simple operations with the original Tunny type motors. These had

(i) No limitation,

(ii) 11 groups of crosses in μ_{37} separated by singleton dots,

(iii) 11 to 19 singleton dots in μ_{61}.

ii, E.19 Thus the groups of crosses of μ_{37} could be numbered in the BM modulo 11, a μ_{61} dot inferred from every BM double dot, and the rest of the μ_{61} dots inferred by comparison of the several appearances in the BM of the same μ_{37} group. This section however deals with the more complex motors universally used after the first few months of the QEP era, in which none of the above conditions was fulfilled.

---

[i] Handwritten 'that' inserted with a caret.

[ii] Handwritten 'groups of crosses of' inserted with a caret.

(b) Motor Breaking

When the first message of a given motor key date has been broken either from depth or de-χ, the χ and ψ patterns and settings will be known, but those for μ_{61} and μ_{37} have still to be found. If the χ and ψ wheels were obtained from a depth then the anagramming necessary to break the motors is already largely provided. Where the ψ's derive from a de-χ the settings of the χ's may be for the first letter of the cipher and the ψ settings for (say) the 4,000th. Advantage is usually taken of the plain language and ψ' obtained during the breaking of the de-χ, at this letter position, and the calculation of the settings for the start is carried out after the motor has been broken. When the wheels have been broken by means of a crib, anagramming is unnecessary and the key is de-chied to give the required ψ'. This ψ' must be checked against the unextended ψ. Since only ψ movements resulting from the BM are used to reconstruct the motor wheels, the amount of anagramming necessary will depend on (i) the type of limitation and (ii) the μ_{37} dottage. E.20 a

In (i) the case of $\overline{\chi}_2$ lim. the longest group of BM characters that can appear as TM is the length of the longest group of crosses in χ_2. E.21

(ii) The nearer the number of dots in μ_{37} is to $37/2$, the greater is the expected proportion of changes of sign in μ_{37} and therefore the smaller the amount of anagramming required. Where a ψ wheel contains uncertain characters, the correction of the wheel is done during the anagramming by noting the period in which the wrong letter appears. When the anagramming proves difficult the process of "snaking" is used. An example and explanation of "snaking" is given in fig. **28 (V)**. The anagramming is done on a width of 61 to facilitate the writing out of the BM on this width. Motor breaking is begun when a length of from 6 to 12 times 61 has been anagrammed. E.22 b

First of all, changes of sign (**•x** or **x•**) in the BM are marked above the first of the pair of signs as a cross in μ_{61}. It follows that if a block of say 3 consecutive crosses occurs in μ_{61}, all stretches of BM appearing underneath will be stretches of unextended μ_{37} (fig. **28 (III)**). If the number of dots in μ_{61} is say, 25, μ_{37} expands to 62 and the first term of μ_{37} reappears on the next line of the BM one position to the right, as also positions 37, 2, and 3. The "interval" or "Column difference" is therefore -1, and if each term under the block of crosses is numbered accordingly quite a few terms of μ_{37} are revealed and a start can be made on the process of building up μ_{61} and μ_{37} as described later. The formula for the "interval" is $61-37-$ number of μ_{61} dots $= 24-$ number of μ_{61} dots. p. 265

[a] start carried out [b] **28** Fig **V**

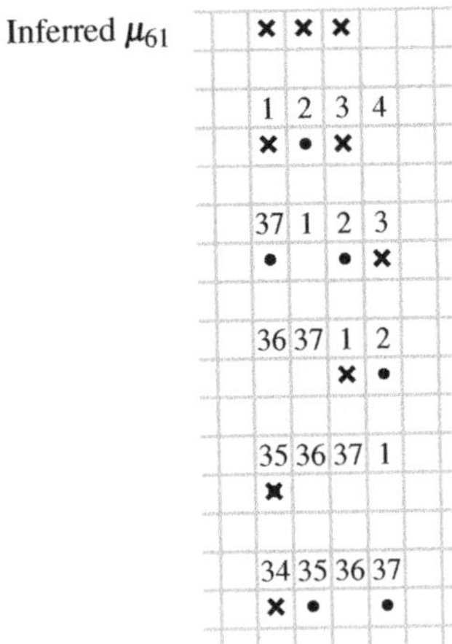

Fig. 28 (III) Section of motor-breaking workings

Where the interval is not a small one the inspection of the terms under a block of inferred μ_{61} crosses is often not helpful, since the terms appearing in the top line may not reappear under the block until many lines down, more than have been anagrammed.[a] The finding of the correct interval and thus the μ_{61} dottage is attempted in 3 ways:—

(i) A simple eye inspection of the columns under a block of inferred μ_{61} crosses as in fig. **28 (III)**.

(ii) Trying out arbitrary intervals and numbering the columns under a block on each assumption.

(iii) Looking for a repetition after a gap of over 37 μ_{61} characters of the columns appearing under a block of crosses (cf. **R0**, p. 69).

As already mentioned (i) only succeeds if the interval is very small. (ii) is very successful when the μ_{61} inferred crosses are frequent and in large clumps, for by using a card stencil assumed intervals which give contradictions are quickly rejected by inspection.[i] The stencil has a series of openings five characters in width, each opening being numbered according to a particular interval assumption. Intervals from +13 to −7 are provided for.

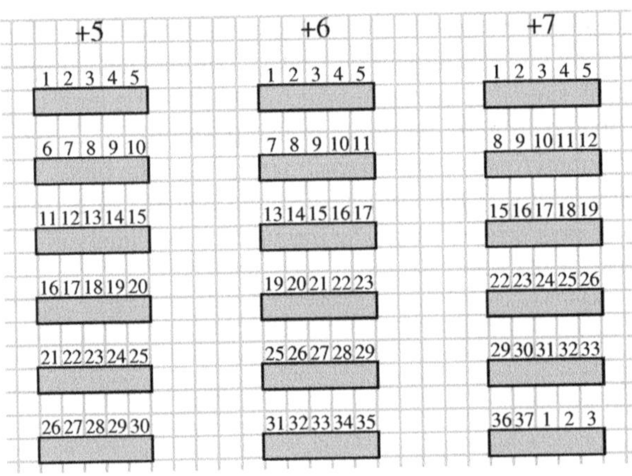

Fig. 28 (IV) Section of Interval Stencil

p. 266 A contradiction is given if a number on the stencil with a sign of BM beneath it, reappears in a different row with the opposite sign. The particular interval assumption being made is then rejected and another one tried. When the stencil fits with no contradictions it is replaced by numbering the columns of the BM according to the stencil (in pencil). Then an attempt is made to extend the numbering of the BM on all rows backwards and forwards assuming whatever μ_{61} characters (in the gaps between inferred crosses) are necessary to avoid contradictions. This will

---

[a] many line down

[i] Figs. **28 (III)**, **(IV)**, and **(V)** all show sections of workings delineated with wavy boundaries, simulating the appearance of the torn edges of a piece of squared paper. We render this with grid lines ending at non-interstitial points, creating a 'frayed reticulation' effect. The captions of all three appear above the figures; we have moved them to their bottoms.

either yield eventually the entire μ_{61} and μ_{37} patterns, with some ambiguities in μ_{61} (an ambiguity is a short stretch of μ_{61} where the number of dots is known, but not their exact position) or lead to inescapable contradictions, in which case the interval assumption must be abandoned and another one tried.

In (iii) the repeating columns are identified as follows. A block of inferred μ_{61} crosses is chosen which has under it a fair number of characters. Column 1 under the block is copied on to a strip of paper which is slid along the columns of B.M. Wherever the characters on the slip give no disagreements with the characters of a column, the figure "7" (for Column 7) is written beneath that column at the bottom of the page. Columns 2, 3 etc. are similarly slid. Examining the results a continuous "staircase" as in fig. **28 (V)** indicates the repeat, and the length of the gap between the repeat and the original columns gives an idea of the μ_{61} dottage and therefore the most likely intervals. [a]

μ_{61}	×	×	×	•	•	×	×	×	•	×	×	×	×	×	×	•	•	×	×	×	×	
	30	31	32	33	33	33	34	35	36	36	37	1	2	3	4	5	5	5	6	7	8	9
			×	×					•	•		•		×		•	•	•			•	
	1	2	3	4	4	4	5	6	7	7	8	9	10	11	12	13	13	13	14	15	16	17
	•			•	•					×	•		×		•		•	•	•			•
	9	10	11	12	12	12	13	14	15	15	16	17	18	19	20	21	21	21	22	23	24	25
	×	×			•	•					•	•		×		•		•	•	×		
	17	18	19	20	20	20	21	22	23	23	24	25	26	27	28	29	29	29	30	31	32	33
	•	×	×			•	•					•	×		×		×		•	•	×	
	25	26	27	28	28	28	29	30	31	31	32	33	34	35	36	37	37	37	1	2	3	4
		×	•	×			×	•					•	×		×		×		×	×	•
	33	34	35	36	36	36	37	1	2	2	3	4	5	6	7	8	8	8	9	10	11	12
	×		×	•	•			•	×					•	×		•		×		×	
	4	5	6	7	7	7	8	9	10	10	11	12	13	14	15	16	16	16	17	18	19	20
	•	•		×	×	×			×	×					×	•		•		×		
	12	13	14	15	15	15	16	17	18	18	19	20	21	22	23	24	24	24	25	26	27	28
		•	•		×	×	•			×	×					•	•		•		•	

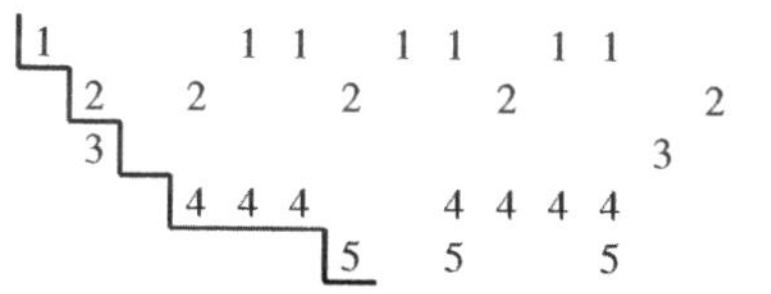

The complete μ_{37}:

1	2	3	4	5	6	7	8	9	10	11	12	13	14	15	16	17	18	19	20	21	22	23	24	25	26	27	28	29	30	31	32	33	34	35	36	37
•	×	×	•	•	•	×	•	×	×	×	•	•	•	×	•	•	×	×	•	•	•	×	•	•	×	•	×	×	•	•	×	×	•	×	•	×

Fig. 28 (V) Section of motor-breaking workings showing the 'repeat column' method of finding the interval [i]

[a] similiarly

[i] Caption moved from top of figure to bottom.

p. 267 According to whether dots or crosses are assumed in positions 9 and 11 of μ_{61}, the possible intervals in the example are +9, +8, and +7. Assuming a dot in position 9 and an interval of +8, column 10 gives 7, 10 and 18 as crosses — which agrees with the numbering already carried out. Position 11 of μ_{61} must be a cross; if a dot is assumed, then in column 13, 33 would be a dot, whereas it has been accepted as a cross in column 1. Similarly, column 17 must be a repeat of column 16, because 9 is a cross, column 18 a repeat of 17 because 1 is a dot and position 18 of μ_{61} must be a cross, otherwise 1 has to be a cross.

Arguing along these lines, μ_{37} takes shape fairly quickly and in turn enables μ_{61} to be completed.

The expected μ_{37} dottage is given beforehand by the number of groups of crosses in the ψ wheels. Where the information given by the BM is scanty, the exact location of a dot or cross in μ_{61} may be uncertain. This "ambiguity" can usually be resolved when the message is being decoded, by simple trial and error methods. The process of setting a message on the motor can also result in an ambiguity being resolved.

An elaboration of the "drag-slip" method of identifying the repeated columns is the use of a squared-celluloid sheet which can be laid over the basic motor; the columns under a chosen block of crosses in μ_{61} are copied on to the celluloid with a "chinagraph" pencil. What amounts to a simultaneous comparison of several columns can then be carried out by sliding the marked celluloid over the BM at various points until the repeating columns are found.

As an assumption regarding a dot or cross in the μ_{61} is made, so can extra columns be copied on to the celluloid, thus playing the repeat against the original and vice-versa, until the columns link up.

When the μ_{61} and μ_{37} patterns have been obtained, the μ_{61} setting is given as 1 and the μ_{37} setting is the μ_{37} character which appears or would appear, under 1 in the μ_{61} in the first line[a] of the BM. The χ and ψ settings are then the settings for the first χ and ψ characters used to anagram line 1 of the BM.

(c) Motor Setting

When a de-χ or depth has been broken on a day for which the motor patterns have already been broken, the setter is given the depth or de-χ with the ψ settings at the break. Usually the break is not at the start, so the ψ settings for the first letter must be found. This is done by calculating approximately the ψ settings for the start, typing a ψ stream from these settings, and attempting to fit the ψ's on the de-χ near the start, either by 'snaking' or by obtaining breaks in the same way as the breaker does and finding the ψ' given by the breaks in the typed ψ stream.

To calculate the approximate ψ settings for the start we multiply the distance from the start to the break by a, and add a small excess for safety. This gives the approximate number of places moved by the ψ's over that distance. It remains to subtract the number thus obtained from the ψ settings at the break.

For this purpose a book of subtractors is used, wherein the remainders after dividing this number by the wheel lengths, are listed; e.g. if the ψ_1 has moved about 2000 places to reach the break[i] the number of revolutions of ψ_1 in 2000 is 46 with a remainder of 22. The position of ψ_1 at start is therefore $40 - 22 = 18$.

When the ψ's giving clear at the start have been found, anagramming can be carried out, in lengths of 61. When a length of 150 letters has been anagrammed (or less, if the motor wheels are distinctive) the BM is written out as for motor breaking and the compulsory crosses on μ_{61} written in.

μ_{37} is next examined for any distinctive feature such as a solitary •×• or ×•× or any other characteristic which would enable a deduction to be made regarding μ_{61}. For example, if μ_{37} has

[a] μ_{61}; in the first

[i] Words 'has moved ... break' handwritten.

no **•xx•** every **xx** in the BM will mean a dot in the 61, or if the largest μ_{37} group is **•xxx•** and **•xxxx** occurs in the BM this will also mean a μ_{61} dot. When all possible use has been made of the μ_{37} characteristics the fragmentary μ_{61} is slid along the actual μ_{61} until a non-contradictory position is found. The BM is then numbered accordingly, enabling a fragmentary μ_{37} wheel to be written out. The actual μ_{37} should fit uniquely on this. The positions on the actual wheels of the first terms of the fragmentary μ_{61} and μ_{37} are then the motor settings.

28E DECODING p. 268

(a) Organisation

This has been described in the Testery report **XII 9**.

(b) Operation

The operator plugs the twelve wheel patterns and settings into the Tunny decoding machine and sees that the limitation switches are correctly thrown. The settings are found written on the red form at the start (fig. **28 (VI)**). She then types the *Z* which is printed as *P* by the machine. If the message has been correctly set and does not have an autoclave limitation, it will decode without difficulty. The operator may find trouble if the cipher text is corrupt owing to poor intercept conditions, bad emendation by the intercept department, or mistakes by the perforating department. Incorrect continuity of the text means that the operator must stop and find the error by means of "sliding" (fig. **28 (VII)**). The correction is written on the red form (fig. **28 (VI)**). New motor keys which have 'ambiguities' (short stretches of μ_{61} where the *number* of dots is known, but not their exact position) are sometimes troublesome, but if the ambiguities are correctly marked the operator can solve them by trial and error methods without difficulty.

Messages with an autoclave limitation are much more difficult to decode. In the case of incorrect continuity key cannot be generated and the cipher has to be corrected by means of a 'snake' (fig. **28 (VIII)**). If the cipher is corrupt on the 5th impulse the operator must decide the exact letter which is corrupt, and type through again correcting it. She can easily determine this letter because there will be two clear letters after the corrupt one before the clear breaks down completely.

The finished decode (fig. **28 (IX)**) has 12 lines of 60 letters to each page with a machine reading of the 12 settings taken at the end of the 12th line and written at the corresponding place of the red form. The first page is headed with message date, the time transmission started and ended, the motor key date, the frequency, the exact amount of the message decoded, the amount (if any) to be decoded, and the serial number. Each subsequent page is headed with the serial number, and all the pages are numbered consecutively. Any clear which has been lost through incorrect continuity or corrupt letters will have been re-constructed by 'slides' and 'snakes' (fig. **28 (VII)** and **28 (VIII)**) is written on the decode. Every letter lost in interception is crossed out on the decode.

This covers normal procedure. There remain messages that are not set at the beginning and those set on the ψ's and motors by machine. Messages with any limitation except pure $\overline{\chi}_2$ which had to be taken back to the start were passed back to the setters. Those with $\overline{\chi}_2$ limitation were taken back on the machines. The procedure was as follows:—

(i) Subtract the χ_1, χ_3, χ_4, χ_5, ψ_1, ψ_2, ψ_3, ψ_4, ψ_5, break-in settings from the lengths of the wheels +1.
Subtract the χ_2 setting from the length of the wheel +4
" " μ_{61} " " " " " " " +3
" " μ_{37} " " " " " " " +1 if the μ_{61} setting-1 = dot
+2 if the μ_{61} setting-1 = cross

(ii) Turn the χ_2, μ_{61} and μ_{37} wheel patterns backwards and plug in the transformed settings.

(iii) Tap the number of letters from the break back to the 1st letter and take a reading.

(iv) Repeat (i) with the reading now obtained.

(v) This should give the settings for the first letter.

If however the continuity of the text is incorrect, key must be taken and the cipher slid against it until it ‘clicks’ into the right place.

p. 269, i

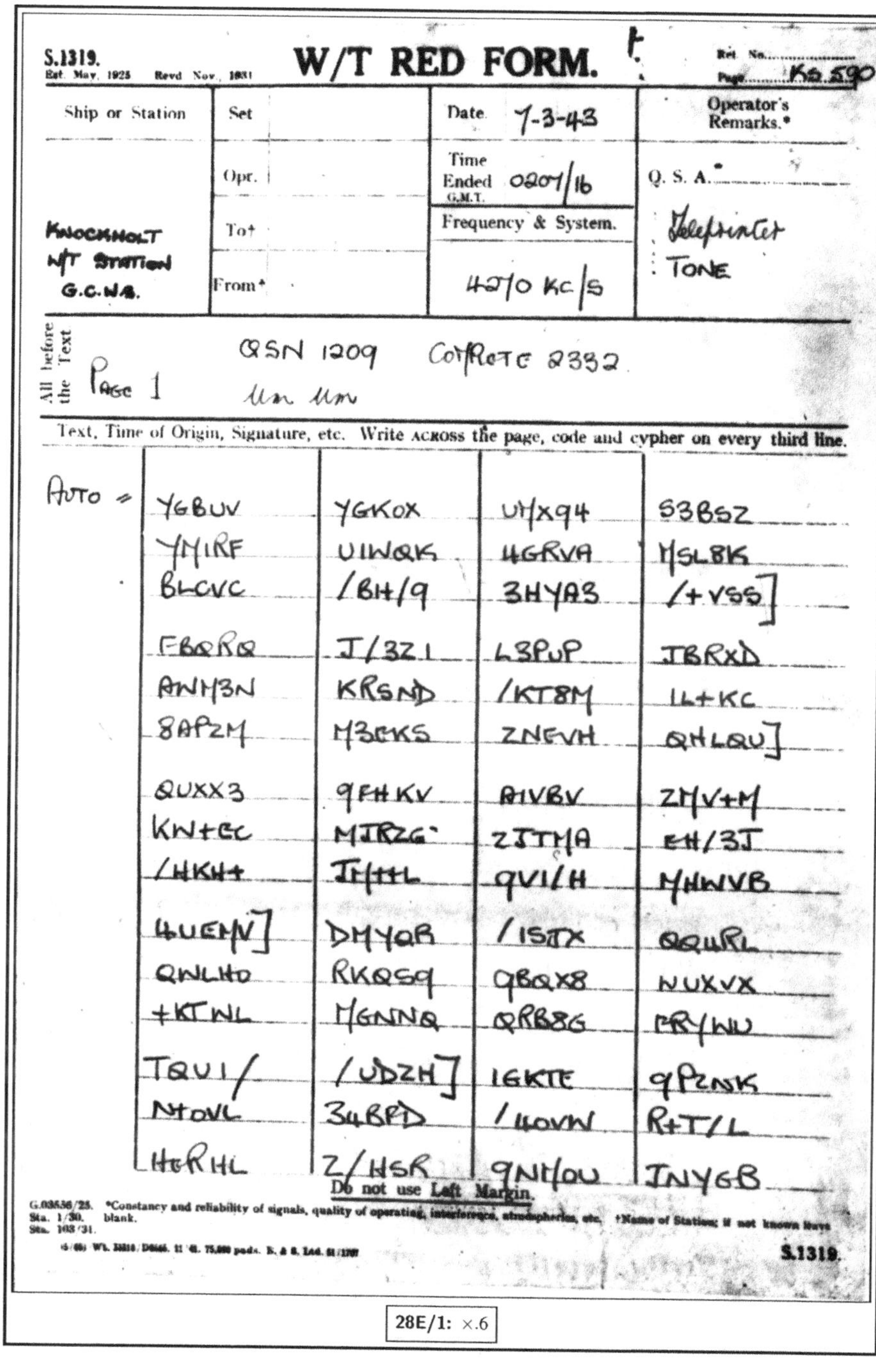

S.1319.
Est. May, 1925 Revd Nov., 1931

W/T RED FORM.

Ref. No.
Page KS 590

Ship or Station			Operator's Remarks.*
	Set	Date 7-3-43	
	Opr.	Time Ended G.M.T. 0201/16	Q. S. A.*
KNOCKHOLT W/T STATION G.C.W.S.	To†	Frequency & System.	Teleprinter
	From*	4210 Kc/s	TONE

All before the Text: QSN 1209 CORRECT 2332
PAGE 1 Um Um

Text, Time of Origin, Signature, etc. Write ACROSS the page, code and cypher on every third line.

AUTO =

YGBUV	YGKOX	UHX94	S3BSZ
YHIRF	UIWQK	4GRVA	HSL8K
BLCVC	/BH/9	3HYA3	/+VSS]
FBQRQ	J/3Z1	L3PUP	JBRXD
ANH3N	KRSND	/KT8M	IL+KC
8APZM	M3CKS	ZNEVH	QHLQU]
QUXX3	9FHKV	AIVBV	ZHV+M
KW+EC	MJRZG	ZJTMA	EH/3J
/HKH+	JH++L	9VI/H	MHWVB
4UEMV]	DMYQB	/ISJX	QQURL
QWLHD	RKQS9	9BQX8	NUXVX
+KTWL	MGNNQ	QRB8G	PRYWU
TQUI/	/UDZH]	IGKTE	9PZNK
NtOVL	34BPD	/4OVW	R+T/L
HERHL	Z/HSR	9NHOU	JNYGB

Do not use Left Margin.

G.03536/25. Sta. 1/30. Sta. 103/31. *Constancy and reliability of signals, quality of operating, interference, atmospherics, etc. blank. †Name of Station; if not known leave

S.1319.

28E/1: ×.6

Fig. 28 (VI) Pages of Red Form, showing settings at start, readings taken every 12th line, cipher corrected by slide

[i] Caption moved from top of figure to bottom.

p. 270, i

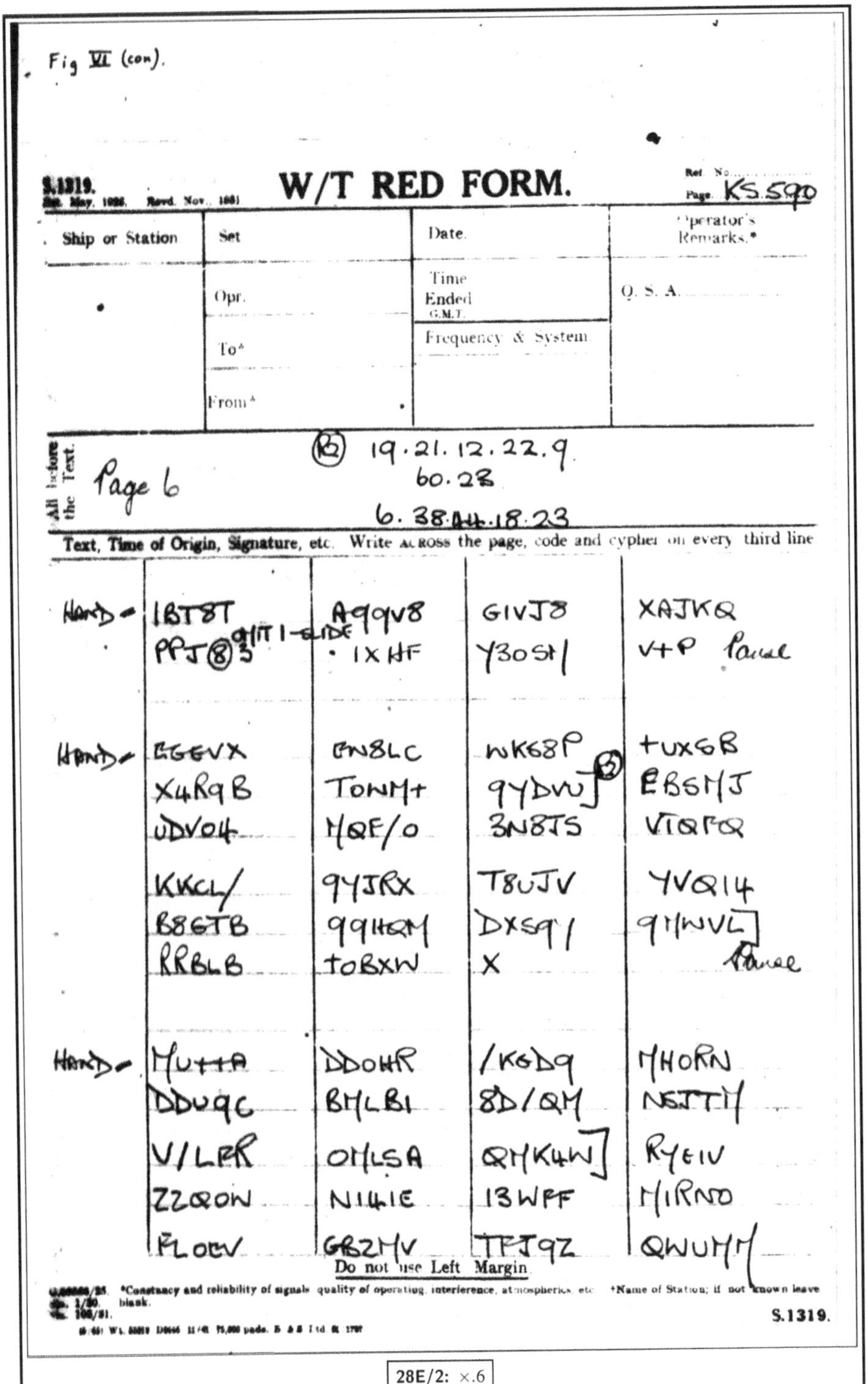
Fig VI (con).

S.1319. Sep. May. 1926. Revd. Nov. 1931

W/T RED FORM.

Ref. No.
Page. KS.590

Ship or Station	Set	Date.	Operator's Remarks.*
	Opr.	Time Ended G.M.T.	Q. S. A.
	To*	Frequency & System.	
	From*		

All before the Text. Page 6 ⓇⒸ 19.21.12.22.9. 60.28 6.38.44.18.23

Text, Time of Origin, Signature, etc. Write ACROSS the page, code and cypher on every third line

HAND-	IBT8T	A99V8	GIVJ8	XAJKQ
	PPJ⑧3	·IXHF	Y30SM	V+P Pause
HAND-	EGEVX	EN8LC	WK68P	+UXGB
	X4R9B	TONM+	9YDVU]	EBSMJ
	UDVO4	MQF/O	3N8TS	VTQFQ
	KKCL/	9YJRX	T8UJV	YVQ14
	B86TB	99HQM	DXS9/	9MWVL]
	RRBLB	tOBXW	X	Pause
HAND-	MUttA	DDOHR	/KGD9	MHORN
	DDU9C	BMLBI	8D/QM	NEJTM
	V/LPR	OMLSA	QMK4W]	RYEIV
	ZZQOW	NI4IE	13WFF	MIRND
	FLOEV	GB2MV	TFJ9Z	QWUMM

Do not use Left Margin

*Constancy and reliability of signals quality of operating, interference, atmospherics, etc. †Name of Station; if not known leave blank.

S.1319.

28E/2: ×.6

Fig. 28 (VI) (cont)

[i] Caption moved from top of figure to bottom.

'Phoney Clear'	WSGO+XMMPZXAEDSHDM4GVFDRV+K+FD4+M
Cipher	83.IXHFY30SMV+PEGEVXEW8LCWKS8P+UX
Key	NFGVIDZDVD088LWYWXMU8VPOT3/VLBBME
Clear	9.MAL99EIN9E99LKLAEINE9PAUSE99VE

By omitting 1 letter from the cipher and adding to the key we can reconstruct the lost clear.

Fig. 28 (VII) A 'slide' i

De-χ

	4	I	M	K	T	T	D	X	X	G	B	R	K	N	F	F	R	C	P	E
3	R																			
U		E																		
T			N																	
J				9	+	+														
Y							M													
4								8	8											
V										9										
W											R									
T												G								
8													T							
3														9						
P															+	+	M			
K																		E		
L																			9	
S																				9

ψ

This example shows the final stage, with the correction made to the cipher, thus giving the correct de-χ, each letter of which is added in turn to each letter of the ψ, and the correct *P*-stream picked out. In the example only the correct *P*, and none of the wrong alternatives, is shown.

Fig. 28 (VIII) A 'snake' ii

---

[i] Caption moved from top of figure to bottom. Explanatory text 'By omitting...' handwritten.
[ii] Caption moved from top of figure to bottom. Explanatory text 'This example...' handwritten.

p. 272

Fig. IX   28E Page 272

MACHINE I   (1)

DATA 7-3-43	TS 0207 TE 0216	FREQ. 4270	MK 6-3-43	DECODED:- 1ST LTR. PAGE 1 TO:- END	TO DECODE NIL	SERIAL NO:- KG 590

HBZCHORNSTEINFEGER..ANNA+X-FF.NR+M.YYQ.UMEMRE.VV.KK-.ANN+X-FF

.NR+M.YYQ.UMEMRE.VVLL-.HAVD.NN.HAVXD.++.QIWYR.TMEM.QREP.VV.K

K-.HAVXD.+UQI.WYR.TMEM.QREP.VVLL-..WN.ART+M-.KDR+M-.+.F.-.BEIM

.PZ+M-.AOK.+.ONK.H+M-.GR+M-.SUED.+VV.KK-.AN.ART.+-.KDR+M-.++.

F.-.FEIM.PZ+M-.AOK.+.QN-..H+M-.GR+M-.SUED.+VVLL-..++.W-.SHNEN

N.++.W.-.SCHW+M-.ART+.-.ABT+M.++.UFT.KK-.++.W.-.SCHW+M-.ART+M-

.ABT+M-.++.UFT.LL-.MUSZTE.DREI.ZWOFLFTONNER.ZUGMASCHINEN.MIT

.GENEHMIGUNG.HOFH+M-.ART+.-.KDR+M.FPI.KK-.HOEH+M-.AE.NN.ARTM-

E.23 .KDR+M-..+EPI.+LL.-.ZUR..++.RM-.PZ+M-.DIV+.M-.+KK+.RM-.PZ+M-

.DIV+MLL-.ASSTEKLEN+M-.ALLE.BEME.NN.BEMUEHUNGEN.DES.BATTR+M-

.CHEFS.+KK-.BATTR+M-.CHEFS+LL-..ZUGMW.NN.ZUGASHCINEN.ZURUECKZU

BEKOMMEN+N-.SIND.B.NN.SIND.GESCHEITERT+M-.BATTR+M-..+KK-.BATT

R1.

28E/3: ×.55

Fig. 28 (IX)[i]

[i] Caption moved from top of figure to bottom.

p. 273, i

Fig IX (con).

28E Page 273 KD. 590 (2)

R+MLL-.BITTET.UEBER.DIE.H+M-.GR+M..+KK-.H+M-.GR+MLL-.DIE.+.R

M-.PZ+M-.DIV+M-.+KK-.++.RM-.PZ+M-.DIV+MLL--.ZUR.HER.USGABE.Z

U.VERANLASSEN+N-.DA.VERLADUNG.IN.ETWA.+.Y.+KK.YLL-.TAGEN.ERF

OLGEN.SOLL+M-.ERBITTET.BATTR+M.+KK-.BATTR+MLL-..MITTEILUNG+N

-.OB.SIE.DIE.RUECKGABE.DER.ZUGMASCHINEN.SO.RECHTZEITIG.EWWARTE

N.KANN+N-.DASZ.SIE..MIT.TRSP+M-..DER.BATTR+M.KK-.TRSP+M-.DER

.BATTR+MLL-..ABROLLEN.KOENNEN+M-.BATTR+M.KK-.BATTR+MLL-.ISTHZ

U.ERREICHEN.UEBER.AOK.+.W..KK-.AOK.+.WLL-.AUFFAGSTAB..+.YQI.N-

.ROMNY.+PV.KBQAN+QFFANGSTAQ++.YQIN.-.ROM.Y.+MVVLL-..DIENSTSTELL

E.FPN+FM.+XXX.WPQ.-MRB-HGFZ+M.-IUSCHR+MZZ-.KK-.DIANSTSTELLE.FPN

R+M.EW.WYQ.-.C..GFZ+M-.RSCHR+MZZ.LL-..-.BERICHTIGUNG.+C-.ZUGM

ASCHINEN..VGL+M-.ZUGMASCHINEN.-.QXA.+.+QPPVV--.QXA.+QPPPVVZZ

-KAFFEH Hand

[SLIDE OMIT !]

MAL..EIN.E..

.......NUN...WIEDER...AWS~~Q+XHHPZXAFB~~ Hand.

LKLAEINE. PAUSE..VE

~~SHBMQVPDRV+K+FD4~~

.+B.-..............

~~+MUK+QRBENK.JA+YOU~~. R2.

28E/4: ×.55

Fig. 27 (IX) (cont) ii

[i] This is the last page of Volume I of the *Report*, that is, of TNA HW 25/4.

[ii] Caption moved from top of figure to bottom.

p. 274, i

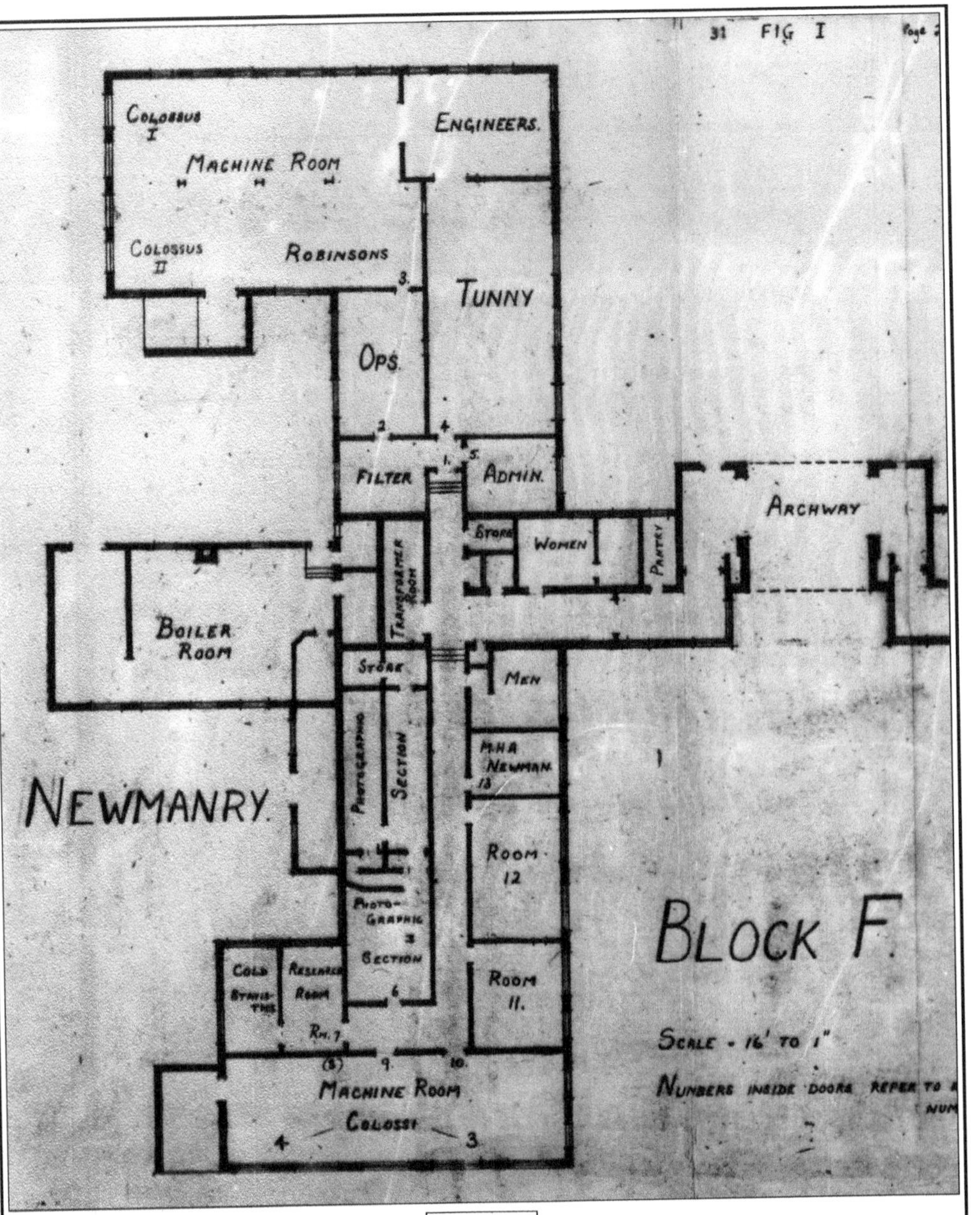

31/I: ×.525

Fig. 31 (I) (left half)

---

[i] This is the first page of Volume II of the *Report*, that is, of TNA HW 25/5.

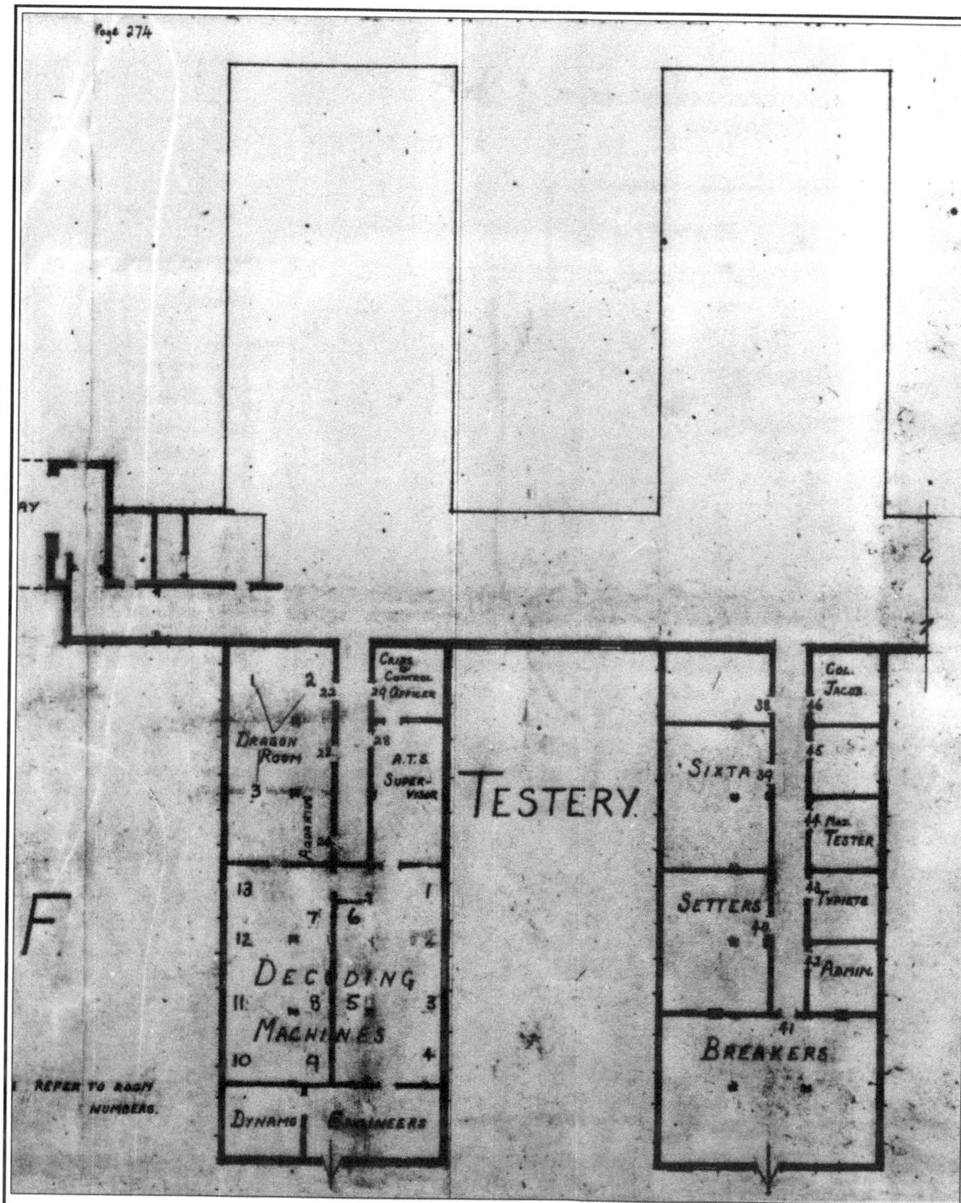

31/I: ×.525

Fig. 31 (I) (right half)

p. 275

E.1

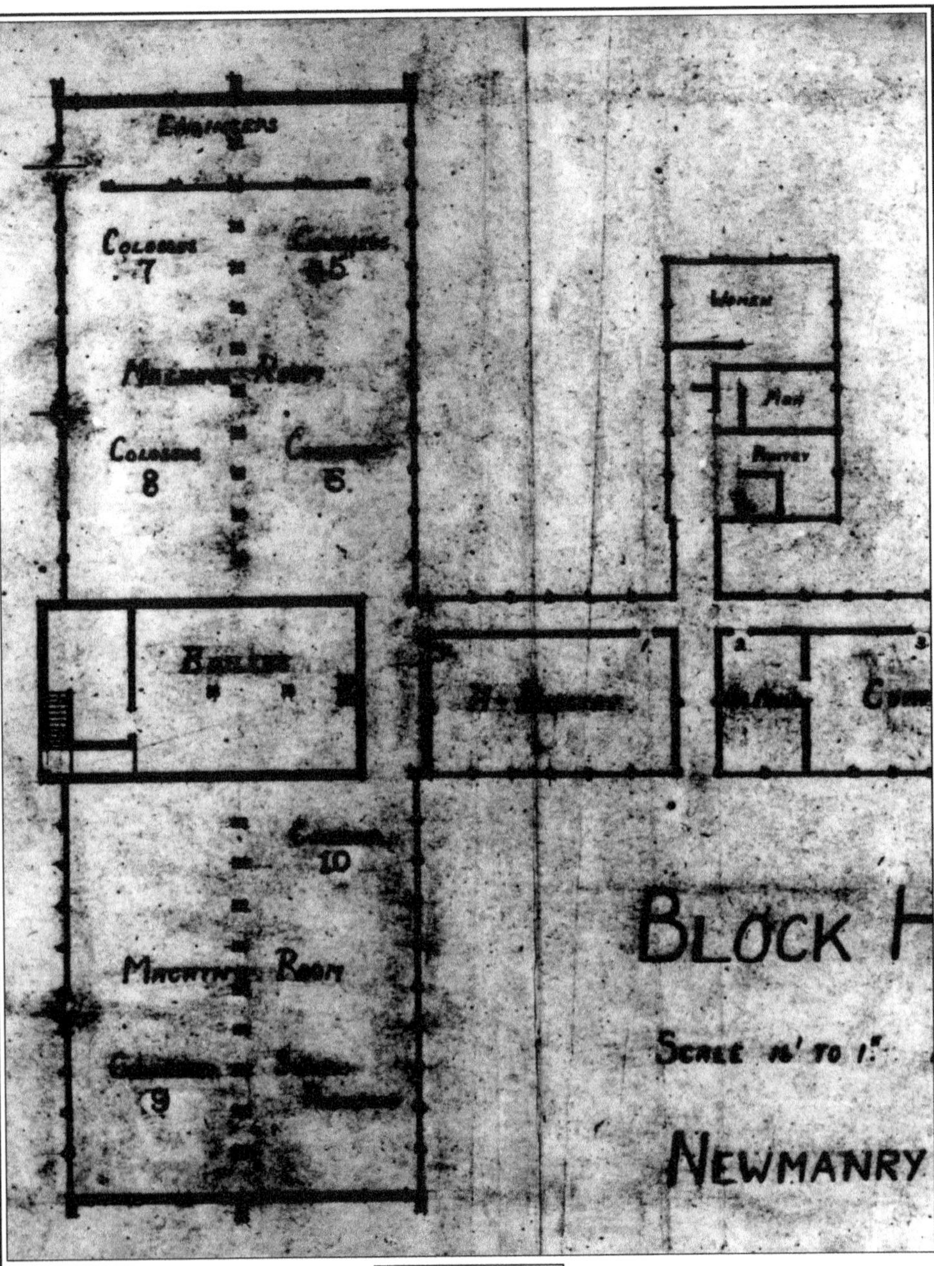

31/II (left half): ×.6

Fig. 31 (II) (left half)

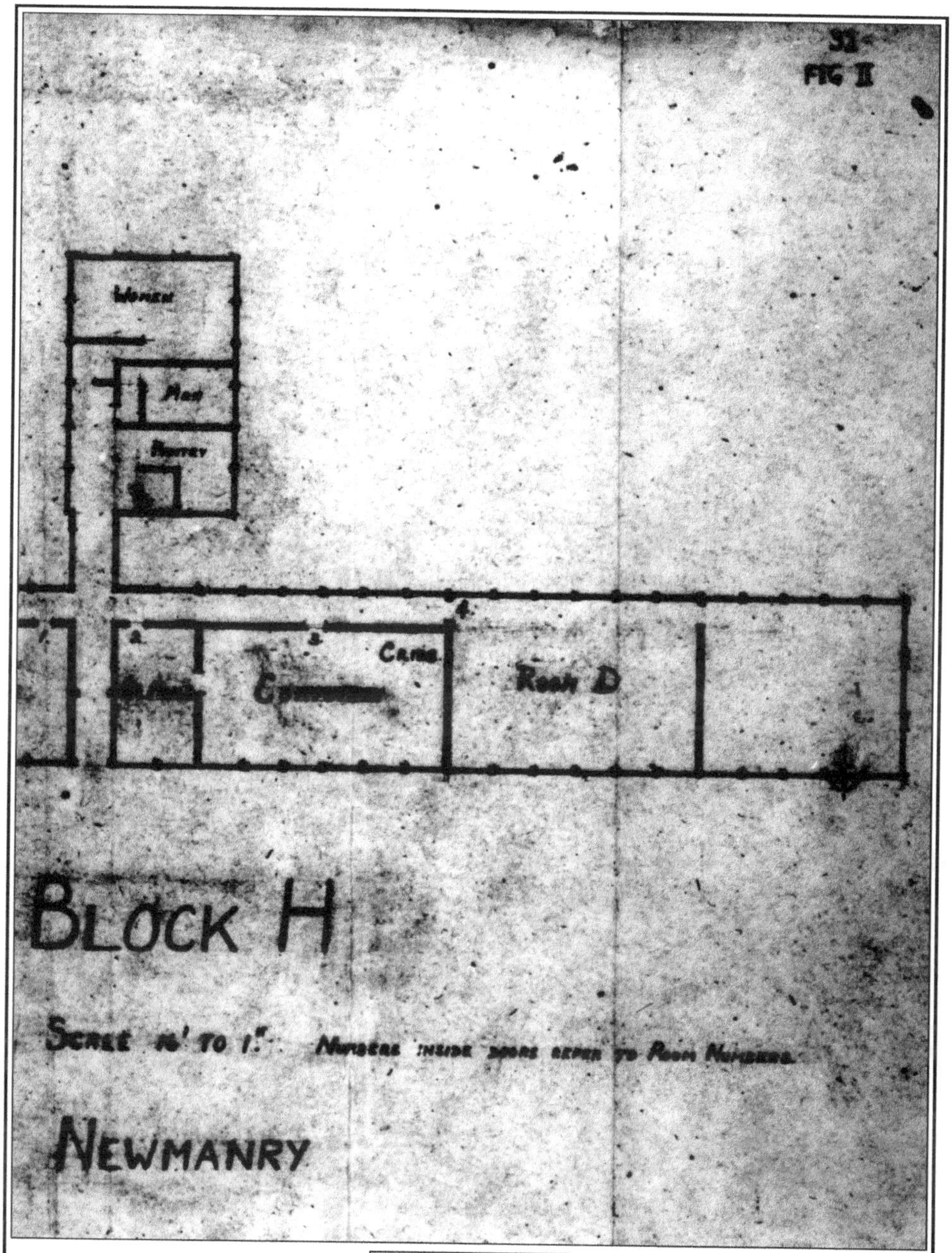

31/II (right half): ×.6

Fig. 31 (II) (right half)

p. 276 31 MR NEWMAN'S SECTION

31A GROWTH

In December, 1942 Mr M.H.A. Newman was given the job of developing machine methods of setting Tunny. In April, 1943 the first machines arrived, a Robinson and a Tunny, pilot models of somewhat uncertain behaviour. Mr Newman formed his section with one cryptographer, two engineers and 16 Wrens. The section was founded and lived (for the most part) in a single room. After three months two or three messages were set each week.

By May, 1945 there were 26 Cryptographers, 28 Engineers, and 273 Wrens with 10 Colossi, 3 Robinsons, 3 Tunnies and 20 smaller electrical machines. The section moved into Block F in November, 1943, and expanded into a new and additional Block (H) in September, 1944, in which all chi-breaking was done. In the week ending March 31st, 358 messages were set on Chis, 151 on Motors and Psis and 23 sets of new wheels were broken.

E.2 The total number of log books used in 2 years was about 500.

31B STAFF REQUIREMENTS

The allocation of staff at 6 monthly intervals is shown in the following table.

		Apr.43	Sep.43	Apr.44	Sep.44	Apr.45
	Administration	—	—	1	2	2
	Cryptographers	2	5	6	20	22
Engineers	Maintenance	—	3	9	12	15
	Construction	—	4	9	11	13
	Wrens	16	16	68	180	273
	TOTAL	18	28	93	225	325

Finally the staff per shift was as follows:

7 Cryptographers :	DO in charge of setting 1 Wheel-man in charge of wheel-breaking 1 in charge of Cribs and Robinson work 2 to supervise Colossus setting 2 to supervise Colossus wheel-breaking
67 Wrens :	7 Registrars 17 Tunny Operators 2 Robinson Operators 20 Colossus Operators 15 Computers 1 "Cribs" assistant 5 "Room 11" maintaining contact with Knockholt.
5 Engineers and a daily requirement of	2 Research Cryptographers 2 Research Wrens 13 Construction Engineers 6 Administrative Staff.

p. 277

31C ADMINISTRATION

As the section expanded, administrative problems became considerable. Co-ordinated policy was established through a "Fish Committee" under Mr Welchman's chairmanship during the period of fastest development (May 1944–January 1945) to determine the policy of machines to be ordered and staff to be recruited. A good deal of attention was given by this committee to the slip-reading and perforation of tape at Knockholt and every effort was made to encourage the production of material at Knockholt on a scale commensurate with the rapidly expanding capacity at this end. E.3

The administration had to keep in touch with operational results. It did this by collecting and analysing facts about success achieved in each part of the section and issuing suitable reports. The log books kept by all operators provided the required information in addition to making operators conscious of their own efficiency.

31D CRYPTOGRAPHIC STAFF

The first thirteen men to join the Section as cryptographers were drawn from other sections of GC & CS. In experience and infectious enthusiasm they preserved their lead to the end, and there were few in the section not affected by their keenness. After July, 1944 they were joined by men from other war jobs and men straight from the universities. The qualifications of men chosen are given in the following table:— E.4

Date of Arrival		June 43– July 44.	Aug. 44– May 45.
Professional Mathematicians etc } Research Students }		8	4
Other University Mathematicians		3	11
Others		2	1
Previous cryptographic experience		12	3
Enigma		8	2
Fish		3	1
Age on joining	over 30	5	2
	25 – 30	3	3
E.5	20 – 25	3	5
	under 20	1	6
British		11	13
American		2	3
TOTAL		13	16

p. 278 Cryptographers were not organised into fixed shifts, but worked with different people each week and took it in turn to do research work and the various operational jobs. This system kept everybody in touch with up to date technique and alive to possible improvements. A weekly change of job led at times to minor administrative inefficiency and the normal term of offices for Duty Officers and wheel-men was eventually extended to three weeks, these two jobs were normally filled by more experienced men.

After the Section was fully staffed there were often two research men each week. Most of the important ideas were developed by men as a result of practical routine work and written up in the Research Logs. In a subsequent research period of a week or more they were at leisure to elaborate their ideas and to tackle any other problems of a pressing operational nature.

Ideas for new methods, and routines for immediate instruction were discussed at the weekly
E.6 "Tea Party" — a democratic assembly of cryptographic staff.

31E W.R.N.S.

Wrens were chosen by interview from those in H.M.S. Pembroke V (Category — Special Duties X). No fixed qualifications were required, though a pass in mathematics in School Certificate
i or (apparently) "good social recommendations" was normally considered essential. Though a few of the earlier Wrens were rather older and more experienced, 96 per cent of those who came
E.7 were between the ages of $17\frac{1}{2}$ and 20. 21 per cent had Higher Certificate, 9 per cent had been to a University, 22 per cent had some other training after school training and 28 per cent had previous paid employment. None had studied mathematics at the university.

On arrival, all Wrens were given up to a fortnight's training in the teleprinter alphabet, the workings of the Tunny machine and (in some cases) in computing. This was followed by a conducted tour of the section and a written test. Wrens (unlike men) were organised in fixed watches and given fixed jobs in which they could become technically proficient. While the section remained small it was possible to try new Wrens at various jobs soon after arrival, but later,

[i] Parenthesized word '(apparently)' handwritten.

allocation was made on the basis of the test held at the end of their initial training period, and on the basis of the jobs available. The cheerful common sense of the Wrens was a great asset. Several of them showed ability in cryptographic work and several others were trained by the engineers to undertake routine testing of machines.

31F ENGINEERS

It was decided at the beginning of the association of the P.O. Research Branch with GC and CS that maintenance of equipment would be an increasingly important part of the undertaking. It was agreed to recruit the best available men from the automatic telephone construction and maintenance staff throughout the country, to employ them at Dollis Hill and the P.O. Factory at Birmingham to build the equipment so that they should be thoroughly familiar with it, and to give them, before taking up their maintenance duties, any supplementary instruction that was necessary. As the work developed, the complexity and novelty of the equipment increased and further maintenance training was needed, but the technical staff were often hard pressed to produce the equipment and instruction was neglected. A number of maintenance men made up for this deficiency by their own initiative and exertions, and passed their knowledge on to others. Full maintenance efficiency can be achieved only after some months of experience, and by May, 1945 p. 279
equipment and maintenance had reached a very high level of performance.

Telephone maintenance work is mainly done by unestablished skilled workmen and skilled workmen Class II. Recruitment for the maintenance force at Station X was made almost entirely from men in these grades aged 20 – 22 years. The first eight men came to Dollis Hill in April, 1942, a number of Chief Regional Engineers having been asked to recommend good men. A [a] selection was made on the basis of paper qualifications, mostly City and Guilds certificates. The selection of the men after the first eight was based solely on their technical qualifications, the type of work on which they had been engaged and (where possible) their performance at the Post Office Training Centre, where men are trained for normal Post Office work. The total number of men engaged in maintenance on "Fish" traffic eventually reached 45.

The allocation of duties to the maintenance men was based on their previous Post Office experience and the aptitude which they had shown for various kinds of work during the time they spent at Dollis Hill. For a long time a rather critical balance of manpower had to be held between maintenance and further construction. The total manpower available at the beginning of 1944 had been so depleted by the demands of the Armed Forces on the Post Office Staff that no further suitable men were available, and the men already engaged — including all the manufacturing force at Dollis Hill and the P.O. Factory — worked over 70 hours a week for many months.

31G EDUCATION

It was the policy of the section that all its members should be encouraged to interest themselves in all its activities and to improve their theoretical knowledge. In practice it became increasingly hard for Wrens to get a complete picture of an organisation in which they might have only done one job. Moreover the mathematical style of the Research Logs made them unreadable for Wrens, and before they (or new men) undertook chi-breaking and Colossus-setting on their own, some other introduction to the theoretical side was needed.

Screeds and lectures on aspects of the work were issued or given from time to time in 1944, but nothing was done systematically till the Education Committee was founded in January, 1945. This committee of four men and 14 Wrens chosen democratically arranged general lectures and "Seminars" for small parties of Colossus operators or other specialized groups. All lectures and [b] Seminars were given outside working hours and were voluntary. The Seminars for Colossus operators were a complete success. The less mathematical general lectures were also appreciated.

---

[a] 1942 a number [b] specialised

The Education Committee co-ordinated the production of screeds and started a General Fish
E.8 Series of papers which were duplicated and available in every room.

31H STATISTICS BUREAU

In August, 1944 a permanent Statistics Section was set up employing one or two Wrens. The Statistics Bureau

(i) Collected routine statistics, in particular 32 letter-counts of various types, significant rectangles and numbers of messages set.

(ii) Helped the administration to prepare statistical reports.

(iii) Looked after the library and the publication of screeds.

(iv) Helped the research man to complete any statistics that he required.

32 ORGANISATION OF THE TESTERY

p. 280

The organisation of Major Tester's Section has been described briefly in **14B(c)**, and more fully in "Report on Tunny (Major Tester's Section)" and also in the separate report entitled "History of the Fish Sub-Section of the German Military Section". We do not go into further details here as they are of no great cryptographic interest and are not necessary for the understanding of the present report. E.1

p. 281 # 33 KNOCKHOLT

i, E.1

33A	Ordering tapes
33B	Treatment of tapes

33A ORDERING TAPES

The work of Knockholt was the preparation of tapes and Red Forms for Station X and consisted of (i) Interception (ii) Slip Reading (iii) Reperforation. A tape with a single letter inserted or omitted in the middle would almost certainly fail to set, hence the need for accuracy at Knockholt. Approximately 600 people were employed there. Nevertheless there were times when the traffic ordered by us was more than they could handle. Once (Aug. 1944) an abortive attempt was made to perforate tapes in Block F.

The priorities of ordering were decided by a morning meeting of various interested parties in Station X. This meeting also decided priorities for machine setting and wheel-breaking. All ordering was done through the 'Control Officer' at Station X by the following procedures:

A procedure	Long tapes on unbroken days (according to a link priority list).
B procedure	Other tapes for wheel-breaking ordered individually.
C procedure	Tapes for setting on broken days.
D procedure	Messages required for Crib purposes.
Depths	The Control Officer was responsible for ensuring that these were teleprinted at once.

33B TREATMENT OF TAPES

There were 30 receiving sets (in the Set Room). 26 covered priority links and the rest were on directed and general search. Intercepted impulses were automatically recorded on undulator
E.2 tape and usually on printed and perforated tape. The undulator tape was the most reliable and was
a used by the "slip-readers" for improving the RF and perforated tape. In March 1945 efforts were made to save time by using the automatic perforation (RAW TAPE) when interception conditions were good. Blurred patches were marked by the operator. Sometimes dubious portions were also slip-read. The method of raw tapes is a good one provided that full slip-reading is continued until and if positive cryptographic results are obtained with the raw tape.

Completely slip-read messages were passed to the reperforating room. The final tape was checked against the RF with the use of a 'hand counter', though it was not until Autumn, 1944 that a hand counter was issued to Knockholt. Increased accuracy was immediately noticeable.

There were 10 transmission lines to our section. At its best the reperforation room achieved an average daily output of 400,000 letters.

For further details, including auxiliary interception stations, the report by Sixta should be
E.3 consulted.

---

[a] effots

[i] In the original text of the *Report*, almost all chapters start with an analytical contents list. This one does not. We have accordingly supplied such a list, as a copy editor would have done, for uniformity and the convenience of readers.

34 REGISTRATION AND CIRCULATION p. 282

(a) Foundation of the Joint Registry

Registration methods were, of course, developed early and in January, 1944 a joint registry was founded for Major Tester's and Mr Newman's sections. This registry kept track of all material entering or circulating in either section, and itself kept all tapes, or documents for tapes, not being worked on. This avoided congestion and delays in the Newmanry. Few messages strayed and those that did were quickly recovered.

(b) Division of work

Work was divided between Room 12 and Block H. Room 12 dealt with tapes required for setting and the T registry in Room A, Block H, with tapes required for wheel-breaking or Cribs.
As soon as a day's wheels were broken all tapes and documents for the wheel-day were sent over a
from Block H to Block F.

(c) Cards and Circulation

The basic system for all procedures was the same: two copies of each tape perforated were teleprinted from Knockholt. Later on the RF and Master Tape were sent by DR. A procedure card E.1
was started for each message and a pigeon-hole allotted for the tapes and RF (See fig. **34 (I)**). b

In addition to the procedure card, a card was made out for each message, which accompanied the tapes on their journeys. These were used in Ops or Block H for the registration of various setting and rectangling processes. The "Ops Card" for instance was used for setting messages and it was returned to Room 12 when the message was abandoned or set.

When a set of wheels was broken the relevant material was transferred from the T-Registry to Room 12 and from the H-Registry to Ops. On the other hand if the wheels for a day were
not broken within a month the pigeon-holes in Block H were emptied, the RF was filed and the c
master and another tape were stored. The pigeon-holes in Block F were not cleared until a setting d
message was abandoned or completely decoded. In the latter case one copy of the decode was sent to the appropriate intelligence section and one copy was filed in Room 41.

(d) Other Records

Other records kept include registers of:

All tapes intercepted.
'A' tapes and their history. E.2
Tapes for setting on broken days.
Tapes transmitted from Knockholt.
Depths.
Settings of decoded messages.

---

[a] days' [b] pigeon hole [c] pigeon holes [d] pigeon holes

p. 283

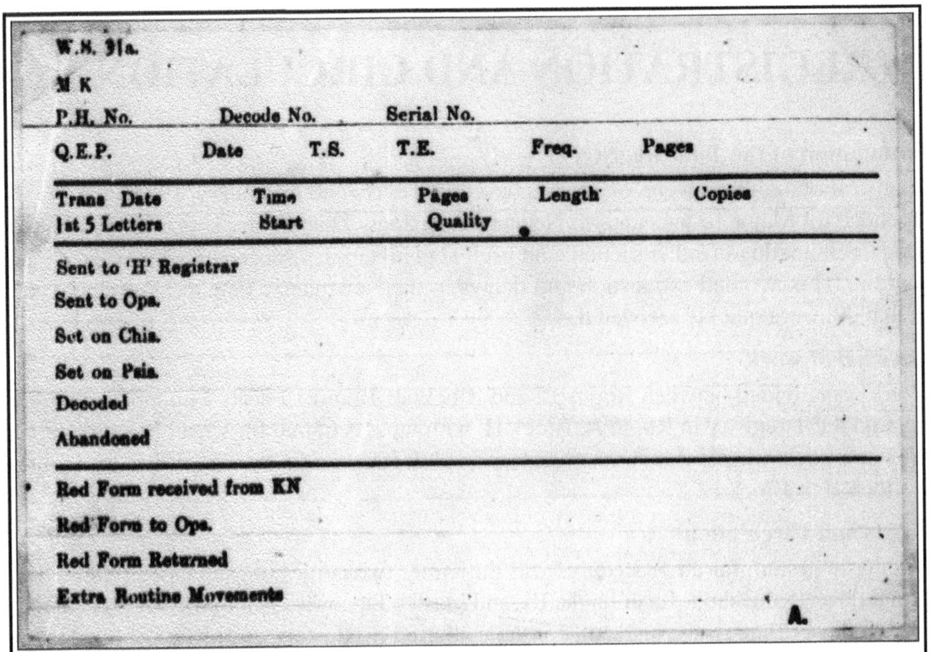

W.S. 31a.

M K

P.H. No. Decode No. Serial No.

Q.E.P. Date T.S. T.E. Freq. Pages

Trans Date Time Pages Length Copies

1st 5 Letters Start Quality

Sent to 'H' Registrar

Sent to Ops.

Set on Chis.

Set on Pais.

Decoded

Abandoned

Red Form received from KN

Red Form to Ops.

Red Form Returned

Extra Routine Movements

A.

34(d)/1: ×.8

Fig. 34 (I) Procedure Card

35 TAPEMAKING AND CHECKING

p. 284

i

35A INTRODUCTION

The successful working of all parts of Mr Newman's section depended on the accuracy and efficiency of the Tunny rooms which were responsible for looking after all copying, reading and tape-making machinery.

An elaborate system of checks for all tapes made was found to be essential to prevent the early introduction of mistakes which might be reproduced unnoticed. The importance of checks was not realised at first and it is generally believed that the comparative lack of success in the earliest days was largely due to the use of incorrect tapes.

35B GENERAL RULES

All tapes were made twice independently and compared to ensure that no letters had been inserted or omitted. Before newly-made tapes were returned to the appropriate registrar their text length was measured on a Hand Counter and marked on the tape. All jobs involving the making of tapes (or prints) other than exact copies, were sent to Tunny with a Hand Check for the beginning which had been worked out by the Registrar. For every tape made two copies (at least) were ordered to save time in case of damage to one of them. All work was very fully labelled.

35C CHECKING AND ALTERATION OF TAPES

(a) Checking tapes against Red Forms

This was not strictly a Tunny Room job, but may logically be described here. For a long time every long rectangling tape and every setting tape which failed to set was checked against the appropriate Red Form.

First Method The number of letters on each page of the RF was calculated and the first few letters at the top of each page recorded. The tape was wound through the hand counter and stopped at the calculated position corresponding to the end of each page. The position of the entries corresponding to the top of the next page were checked on the tape. a

Second Method The tape was measured out on a hand counter, marked at every multiple of 1271, and 10 letters after each mark recorded. When the RF arrived, the letters at similar positions on it were independently noted, and the results compared. This method was suitable for rectangling tapes as it enabled a hand check for the rectangle to be made at once from the tape check.

---

[a] throught

[i] In the original text of the *Report*, almost all chapters start with an analytical contents list. This one does not. We have accordingly supplied such a list, as a copy editor would have done, for uniformity and the convenience of readers.

(b) Comparing two versions of the same tape

It was sometimes necessary to compare two versions of the same tape (say an original version with its rewrite). The tapes were added together on Miles until the output tape showed that there was a slide. The place at which this occurred was marked on both tapes and the tapes were reset (to account for the slide) and the operation continued. A print-out of both versions was made on Garbo wherever discrepancies had been noted so that Knockholt could be asked to reread the undulator tape at these places and decide which version was the most likely. A composite tape could then be made embodying the best of both tapes.

(c) Correction and Doctoring of tapes

E.1 This was normally done on an IBM (preferably) or Angel. The tape to be corrected was marked (with the help of a hand counter) at the places at which a letter was to be inserted or omitted. The IBM or Angel was stopped when the marks were reached and the correction made.

p. 285 The corrected or doctored tape was compared with the first version by hand and the corrected length verified on a hand counter. It was marked CORRECTED TAPE or DOCTORED TAPE in block capitals.

35D PREPARATION OF MESSAGE TAPES

(a) For Colossus

i

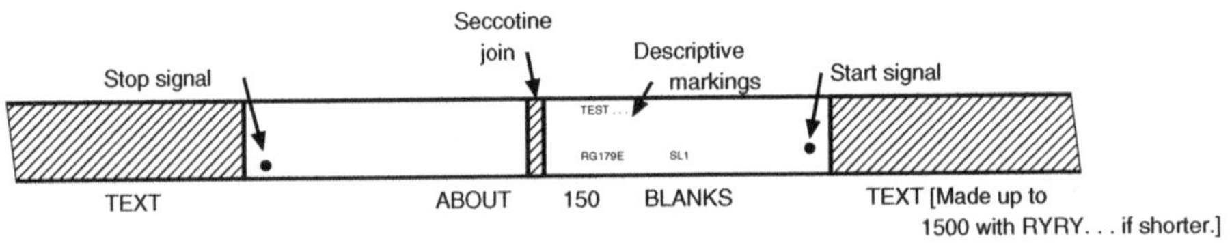

Tapes were copied (on Angel) if sufficient copies were not available, or if available copies had not sufficient blanks at either end. Tapes issued were stuck into closed circuits as shown, and
E.2 stop and start signs punched with a special metal gadget. An overlap of two sprocket holes was allowed at the join; the join had to be made with smooth edges and the end (as opposed to the beginning) of the tape on the outside of the circuit.

The text length was measured before the tapes were returned to the Registrar and if it failed to agree with the Knockholt estimate, Knockholt were informed.

If the text length was below 1500, copied tapes were made on which the text was followed
E.3 by `RYRY...` till the total length of text exceeded 1500. This was done by feeding a tape reading `RYRY...` into the Angel input as soon as the real text had been copied.

For issue to Colossi with short bedsteads very long tapes were stuck in parts of text length 10172 with an overlap of 4 between each part (1–10172, 10169–20340, 20337–end). (See **53B(b)**.)

(b) For Robinson

a Message tapes were prepared for Robinson as for Colossus except that a mixture of Bostik
ii and benzene was used for sticking. The tape to be stuck was inserted between two electrically heated plates (a 'hot sticker') and the benzene was evaporated.

[a] Bostick

[i] Lettering of the descriptive marking is illegible.
[ii] See endnote 28 to **23Z**, p. 589 below.

35E MAKING OF DE-CHIS

(a) Without Colossus check

The settings and wheels for the de-chi were written on the chit by the Tapes Registrar with a hand check of the first 41 letters of the de-chi. The de-chi was made on a Tunny machine [a] twice, and if both makes agreed one make was stuck for Colossus or Robinson and returned to the [i] Registrar. The Tunny was not stopped during either make.

If the ΔD count on the de-chi tape checked with that on the Z tape, the de-chi tape was returned [b] to the Tunny Room for printing (on Garbo) in rows of 31 with double spacing. To check the print the de-chi tape was marked at positions 1, 621, 1241 etc. and the start of every 20th line on the p. 286 print verified.

Lines of the de-chi were numbered and the print marked with the 1st 10 letters of Z.

If the ΔD count on the de-chi tape did not check the wheels set up on the Tunny machine were checked and if no mistake was discovered the Z tape was recounted on a different Colossus.

(b) With Colossus check

The Tunny room was supplied with a chit giving setting and wheels and a Colossus check giving the following letters of de-chi:— 2–9, 621–624, 1241–1244, 1861–1864, 2481–2484, 3101–3104 and the last 5 letters. To this the Tapes Registrar had added the settings for letters 621, 1241 etc.

The de-chi was made on Tunny twice. The first make was stopped automatically every 620 letters and the settings checked. This make was printed while the second make was being made. If the two makes were identical, and the print checked with the Colossus check the de-chi was assumed correct and marked and set over as before.

When the two makes agreed, but the print did not agree with the Colossus check, the Tunny wheels were checked and if correct, the Colossus check was assumed invalid, a hand check made, and the de-chi tape stuck and counted on Colossus.

(c) Contraction of de-chis

In days when psis were set on Robinson (on messages with $\overline{\chi}_2$ lim) the psis were run against a de-chi tape from which all letters occurring against Total Motor dots were omitted. The contracted [c] de-chi was made on a Tunny on which motors and χ_2 were set up. A special switch was used and a hand check supplied.

35F WHEEL TAPES AND TEST TAPES

(a) Chi test tapes

These were made on Tunny. The appropriate wheels were set up at 01 01 01 01 01 and 2002 letters of chi-stream perforated. Before sticking for Colossus every impulse was checked by sliding the tape against itself at a multiple of each wheel in turn.

(b) Psi test tapes

These were made on Tunny with setting 01 01 01 01 01 for Psis and 01 01 for Motors. The limitation appropriate to the wheel-day concerned was used and a hand check of 61 letters supplied by the registrar. Final copies were stuck for Colossus.

(c) Motor tapes

Tunny can be made to perforate Basic Motor tapes from the plugged patterns of μ_{37} and μ_{61} and Total Motor tapes (for $\overline{\chi}_2$ lim) if χ_2 is also set up. Motor tapes were sometimes required for printing the motor over a de-chi or for doing motor runs on Robinsons. A hand check of 15 letters [d] was supplied.

---

[a] dechi [b] dechi [c] occuring [d] dechi

[i] Handwritten 'make' inserted with a caret.

p. 287
35G RECTANGLES

(a) Garbo Rectangles

The method of making 1+2/ Rectangles on Garbo is described in **24B(c)**. The following practical steps were taken to ensure accuracy. The tape was measured on a hand counter and positions of the form $(1271m+2)$ were marked. The second letter of the tape was put in the Garbo (which deltas backwards) and the print-out was started and compared with a hand check prepared for the first few characters. Whenever 1271 characters had been printed and the paper was reset, the tape should have been on the appropriate mark and this was checked. A hand check for the last few characters was prepared, and the position of the last character printed was verified by calculation. Garbo rectangles were only made once.

Different markings of the tape would have been required for a 3+4**x**/ or 4+5/ Rectangle. These were not made on a routine basis.

A further hand check was applied to rectangles when they were returned to the H Registrar. From the check sheet prepared by her from the Z tape (see **35C(b)**) a hand check for the first entries of each cycle of 1271 was made.

(b) Miles and Garbo (Thurlow) Rectangles

This method of rectangling is described in **24B(d)**. The tape was measured and marked at positions of the form $(1271m+1)$. Hand checks for letters 1–10, 1271–1281 etc. of the Thurlow tape were prepared. Marks 1–5 on the Z tape were put in the 5 heads of Miles and the resulting Thurlow tape compared with the hand check. After it had moved 1271 times the Miles was stopped and it was verified that the second mark was in the first head, the third in the second etc. The tape was removed and marks 6–10 put in the 5 heads and so on. The start of each new stretch of 1271 was compared with the hand check.

Thurlow tapes were made twice and measured to ensure that their length was a multiple of 1271 before printing. The positions 2, 1273 etc. were marked and the Thurlow tape printed like a Garbo rectangle. The position of the change of depth was calculated from the Z tape, checked on
a the Thurlow tape and marked on the print-out.
b A further hand check, similar to that for Garbo Rectangles, was done by the H Registrar when a Thurlow Rectangle was returned.

35H OTHER TUNNY JOBS

(a) Hand Perforation

Hand perforations were most easily checked by printing out the perforated text and checking the print-out against the original.

(b) Cribs

The various tapes required for Crib work are described in detail in Ch. **27**.

(c) Other jobs

Tunny Room machinery was very adaptable and numerous non-routine jobs were undertaken. In certain cases it was necessary for hand checks to be prepared by a cryptographer who (at most) supervised the job in person or (at least) provided a sheet of careful instructions.

---

[a] print out [b] Reegistrar

36 CHI-BREAKING FROM CIPHER p. 288

36A HISTORY AND RESOURCES

(a) Early wheel-breaking

Mr Newman's section began as a section for setting messages on wheels broken from depths in Room 41. Wheel-breaking activities came later.

Bream started to use P_5 limitation regularly in the middle of December, 1943, and as there seemed every chance that the use of this gadget would be extended, research activities were devoted to the statistical solution of chis from Z. Tutte's method of rectangles (see Ch. **44**) was elaborated and from January 1944 monthly keys were tackled operationally.

Significance tests were gradually instituted and methods improved. Soon after Colossus 1 arrived in February 1944 it was discovered that it could be used for chi-breaking. It was this discovery that made large-scale wheel-breaking possible even after the introduction of the daily [a] wheel change in July 1944.

(b) The period of expansion

Between July and November 1944 the number of computers increased from 4 to about 16 a watch, and the number of Colossi from three to six, of which three were fitted with a rectangling device. New Garbos, Miles and arrival terminals from Knockholt were installed in Block H which opened in September and housed all wheel-breaking operators from the middle of November onwards.

From August onwards extensive rectangling was rarely applied to any particular day's messages. A few long tapes on each day were rectangled and it was assumed that when the dottage was high and the interception good the rectangle would be significant. Colossus work on significant rectangles largely replaced the more laborious method of the conditional rectangle, and from the end of August a machine and a man to supervise operation could be spared most of the time.

From the middle of November 1944 to May 1945 the number of machines and trained staff continued to increase, and about 15 sets of wheels broken on rectangles each week. In 1945 there were about 15 Computers per shift, whose main job was to converge rectangles on paper. The head of Computers was called the Rectangles Registrar. A man, called the Wheel Man (WM) was in charge of wheel-breaking operators and there were other men called wheel-breakers, each of whom took charge of one wheel-breaking job on a Colossus.

(c) Checking of tapes p. 289

Needless to say the long tapes ordered on A (or B) procedure for rectangling needed to be E.1 particularly carefully checked. Therefore they were checked by us against the Red Form, as described in Ch. **35**. However, after Knockholt had been supplied with a hand counter in Autumn 1944, there were so few mistakes that we stopped checking the tapes in Bletchley. E.2

36B RECTANGLES AND CHI 2 CAP RUNS

There were four methods of rectangling, described in ch. **24**. Priorities were decided by intelligence value, length of tape, supporting tapes and many other considerations. Tapes were often rectangled in parts, in case of a slide in the tape. The $\sum \theta_{ij}^2$ test was done when the Colossus had the required meters. [b], E.3

---

[a] large scale [b] meter

In addition chi 2 cap runs were done on each third and the whole of each message rectangled.

If $x > 7\sqrt{v}$ the WM might start Colossus chi-breaking at once, before the rectangle was converged. If $5{\cdot}6\sqrt{v} < x < 7\sqrt{v}$ the rectangle was given priority. Very rarely the chi 2 cap run revealed a slide in the tape. (See **R5**, p. 98.)

36C TIMES

Here are the average times in hours for various processes and over various periods. The unbracketed figures are for high priority and bracketed for low priority groups.

[i]

	1944 NOV–DEC	1945 JAN–FEB	1945 MAR–APR
Time of interception — Arrival in Block H	39(56)	29(41)	25(30)
Time of arrival — Issue of rectangle	5(6)	3(5)	3(4)
Issue — Abandoning	21(26)	11(12)	12(14)
Issue — Significance	11(13)	9(8)	7(12)
Completion of wheels on Colossus	31(27)	15(14)	13(11)

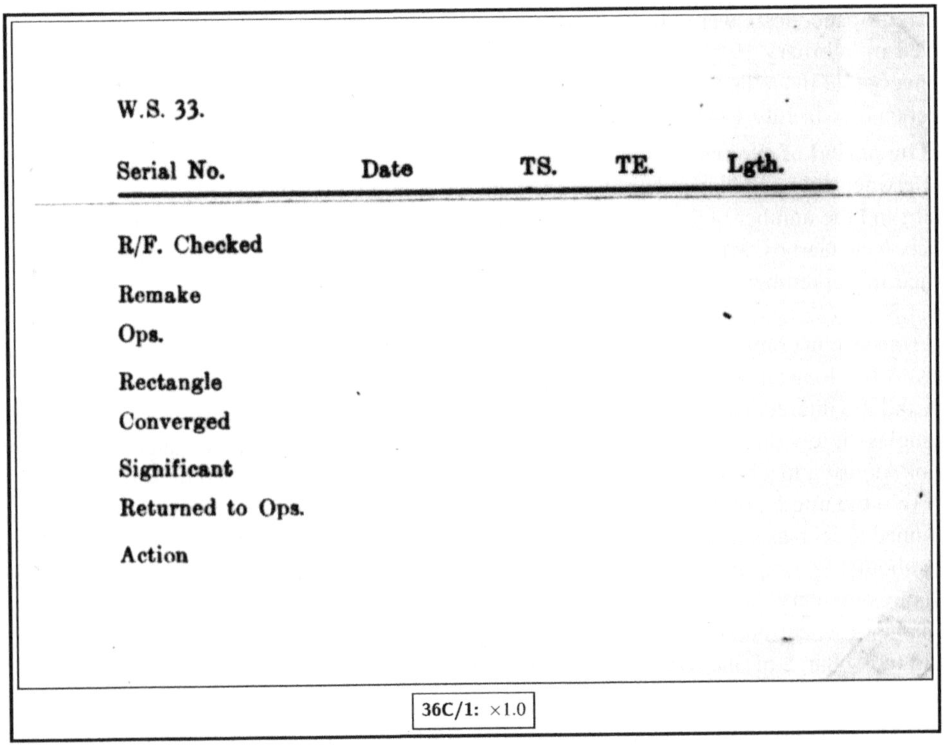

W.S. 33.

Serial No.	Date	TS.	TE.	Lgth.

R/F. Checked

Remake

Ops.

Rectangle

Converged

Significant

Returned to Ops.

Action

36C/1: ×1.0

[ii] **Fig. 36 (I)** Rectangle card used by H Registry

[i] Month heads in tabulation handwritten.

[ii] Figure unnumbered in *Report*.

37 MACHINE SETTING ORGANISATION

p. 290

(a) Ops

The following were housed with the Duty Officer (D.O.)

(i) The Runs Registry, which organised jobs for Robinsons and Colossi. a

(ii) The Tapes Registry, which organised jobs for the Tunny Rooms.

(iii) The Logs Registrar, who maintained liaison with the Joint Registry (Rooms 11 and 12) and the T-Registry (which was the Block H branch of the Joint Registry — see Ch. **34**). See also fig. **37 (I)**.

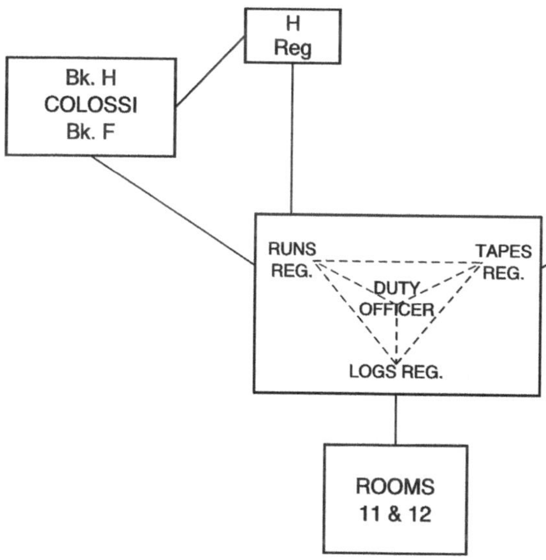

Fig. 37 (I) Function of the Ops. Registry i

In addition there was an H registrar who was effectively the Block H representative of the Runs Registry.

The Runs and Tapes Registrars issued chits with every job ordered. These chits contained accurate descriptions of the job required and were returned with the tapes when the job was completed.

When the Colossus tapes were returned from the Tunny Room the T.R. checked that they were correctly marked, had an adequate join, and stop and start signs in the correct place. To ensure this the first few letters of the tape were checked with those on the Ops. card. The tapes were then passed to the Runs Registrar.

[a] Robinson

[i] Caption moved from lower right corner of figure to bottom.

After a successful setting job the tapes were returned to Ops with a decode check or de-chi check and ΔD letter count. If the job was partially successful a ΔD letter count using as many wheels as possible was provided. When a dossier was given to the D.O. he ordered one of the following: Further runs, Decode, De-chi, or Abandon and returned the dossier to the Runs Registrar.

The Registries had several additional jobs. For example the Tapes Registrar kept an index of $\Delta\chi_5$'s so that any repetition of the same set of wheels could be spotted.

(b) Robinsons and Colossi

In June, 1943, when there was only one Robinson available, each message tried was a research
p. 291 job in itself, and every run was ordered separately by the Runs Registrar the Duty Officer being consulted if necessary. At this time the D.O. was responsible for all work on messages tried in the Newmanry and it was in Ops. that the psis were first set by hand in November, 1943. After this there was an almost immediate change of policy, Room 41 took over the job of psi-setting by hand, and Robinsons were used to set all five chis on as many messages as possible. This policy remained unchanged for almost a year though spasmodic efforts at machine psi and motor-setting were made.

The Newmanry moved to Block F late in November, 1943: the first 'Heath' Robinson was
E.1, a replaced by 2 production models and others came later. Colossus 1 came in February 1944 and runs on the new machine took so short a time that it was necessary to decide policy on the spot and a Colossus man was appointed. Colossi soon replaced Robinsons for setting purposes and the duties of the Runs Registrar were increasingly confined to issuing tapes to machines in the right order and seeing that they did not stay there for too long. By the end of August no Robinsons and up to 4 Colossi were used for setting.

As the number of Colossi increased Wren operators were left more and more on their own. A Colossus man was always available for consultation, and the D.O. kept a check on the accuracy of all Colossus work. From July, 1944 onwards the D.O. saw every Colossus dossier as it returned to Ops. and took over the responsibility for abandoning messages and ordering de-chis. This had previously been done by the Colossus man.

By November, 1944 many new Wrens were working Colossi on their own and considerable time was being wasted. Either too many runs were done, or so few that further runs had to be ordered by the D.O. For this reason the runs normally done were standardised, the 'trees' or runs schedules varying according to the type of language and limitation expected. Departures from schedule were only made in consultation with the Colossus man. The new 'rules' had a remarkably good effect and were interpreted in an increasingly liberal way.

In the Summer and Autumn of 1944 there was so much chi-setting to do that psi runs were not done. But in November, when there were 6 Colossi, Motor and Psi runs were done more often, and after December 25th it became a routine to do them on low dottage days. From March 5th, 1945, a new policy of setting motors and psis on Colossus in every possible case was adopted,
b exceptions only occurring on days of high dottage, or days for which motor patterns were not yet broken. Wrens soon picked up the technique and were able to do motor and psi runs on their own.

The machine resources in 1945 are given in part **5**.

(c) Ordering

The D.O. was responsible for knowing what wheel-breaking was in progress, whether on significant rectangles, key, or crib. As soon as it appeared likely that a day would come out, the D.O. (in consultation with the W.M. or head of Room 41) asked the C.O. to order the traffic
E.2 from Knockholt on C-procedure, and recommended whatever priority and procedure seemed to
c fit the general priority of the link, date, estimated dottage, and estimated time of completion of

[a] Fenruary [b] occuring [c] priotity

the wheels. The priority of the wheel day was assigned by the morning meeting if it was being worked on when this took place: otherwise the priority had to be decided from the general priority list or in consultation with Hut 3 (see **33A**). E.3

(d) Further Runs

We referred in **37(a)** to 'Further Runs'. These were of 5 main types. [a]

(i) Correct Runs, where incorrect runs had been done before. p. 292

(ii) More runs, runs with spanning etc.

(iii) Motor and Psi runs, either immediate or delayed. Messages set on all chis before motors were broken were de-chied, but those set strongly on some chis only, were held for 'delayed motor runs'.

(iv) 4-wheel runs (see **23H(c)**). These were done on long messages for which normal methods gave no result, if and when there was machine time to spare.

(v) Runs on a Doctored tape i.e. a tape altered to counteract a message slide discovered by spanning on Colossus.

In all cases it was best for the D.O. to write out quite precisely what he wanted done. As it was often necessary for the D.O. to calculate the expected score of a motor run in order to decide if it was worth while, many motor runs were issued with E.S. worked out. E.4

Further runs fell naturally into two categories: Runs strongly expected to succeed and runs done because insufficient work had been done to justify abandoning. The first category was marked so that the R.R. could give it suitable priority.

(e) Hut 3 Priority Messages

When Hut 3 believed that messages were of special urgency, the C.O. was sent a chit, E.5
requesting that it should be marked Z, ZZ, or ZZZ. If the tapes had not been set the request was passed to the D.O. and Logs Registrar. All documents were marked with the priority sign and treated specially. If other work was plentiful, Z and ZZ messages were run rather more fully than other tapes. If already abandoned when the request arrived, a rewrite was ordered, and run fully. 4-wheel runs were *not* done. ZZ had priority over Z. ZZZ priority was only ordered in special E.6
cases. All possible runs including 4-wheel runs were done at once on the first tape and a rewrite was ordered. All runs including 4-wheel runs were repeated on the rewrite.

(f) Routine checks for machines

(i) Chi test runs and tapes

Before the first de-chi on a new key day was ordered by the T.R., a chi test tape was ordered from Tunny. This was sent to a Colossus on which the new chis had been set up, and chis and test tape were checked against each other by adding them together. Test Runs were then done on this Colossus and one other, and if they agreed several copies were made and stuck in each Colossus wheel-book. [b]

(ii) Psi Test Runs and Tapes

Psi test tapes were made (with suitable limitation) as soon as psis and motors were known. The routine and uses of psi test runs and tapes were similar to those for chi test runs and tapes.

(iii) Routine Tests

A routine test (using a general test tape) was carried out on two Colossi per shift. The test took about 20 minutes and was done by Wrens specially trained by the Engineers.

---

[a] refered [b] wheel book

p. 293 # 38 WHEEL-BREAKING FROM KEY, ORGANISATION

(a) Development

In the early days of Tunny work when all monthly keys were broken on depths, the recovery of wheels from key was undertaken in Major Tester's section, either by means of special methods available before the QEP system was introduced, or by 'Old Fashioned Turingery'.

After P_5 limitation was introduced on most of the links normally tried (December, 1943) depths were still occasionally anagrammed on any others that still used χ_2 lim. Some monthly keys were broken in this way, but hand methods as practised in Room 41 were rarely strong enough to break wheels from key of under 400 letters. Very long key was sometimes broken on Colossus.

No great advances were made until the autumn of 1944 when $\chi_2\psi_1$ limitation gradually replaced $\chi_2 P_5$ and χ_2 lim was reintroduced on several important links. After the start of the daily key change (July, 1944) it was policy to try as many key days as possible and it became necessary to develop quick and powerful methods on shorter lengths of key. First the $\Delta\chi_5$ flag was invented and introduced, the Modern Turingery (with decibans) and later 6-impulse Turingery for χ_2 limitation.

Therefore, by 1945, the resources and staff employed in the breaking of chis and psis from depth key had expanded outside Room 41 and included some or all of the following:—

A skilled key-breaker in Room 41 (and assistant)
The Wheelsman
The Rectangles Registrar and up to 6 computers.
a 1 Garbo, 1 hand perforator and operators in Room D.
1 Colossus with wheelbreaker and 1 or 2 operators to assist him.

(b) Work in Room 41

Work on Turingery in Room 41 involved very little organisation as each job was undertaken
E.1 by one man with occasional help from an A.T.S.

b Certain members of Room 41 took a particular interest in key-breaking and specialized in the work. Most of the older members could undertake the job in the absence of the specialists, and newer members were gradually trained when it appeared that two key-breakers on each shift might be required.

Unfortunately the specialist key-breakers did not work on a three shift basis and were by no means always available. However they were always willing to work double shifts and odd shifts when there were important key-breaking jobs to be done.

(c) Making of Combined Flag

The flagging of each rectangle was done by one computer, and one computer was employed in adding the flags together, so that 5 or 6 computers worked at once.

It proved profitable for the computer adding the flags to record the entries of each flag on a
p. 294 large sheet and then to add them. Therefore whenever a few lines of a single flag were completed they were torn off and given for entering to the computer in charge of the adding.

The time for making a combined flag was about $3\frac{1}{2}$ hours.

---

[a] handperforator [b] specialised

If the converged combined flag proved significant the $\Delta\chi_5$ pattern was taken through the rectangles and the resulting scores for each character sent to Room 41 with the flag scores for each character of $\Delta\chi_5$.

Results were recorded and further work was normally done in Room 41, unless the key was issued to Colossus.

If the combined flag proved insignificant, all working and entering was rechecked by the wheelsman and if no mistakes were found either:

(a) the key was abandoned

(b) a $\Delta\chi_4$ flag was made,

(c) the key was issued to Colossus for convergence of a 150 × 150 rectangle in the hope that this might prove significant.

In view of the work involved in making a combined flag and the strain on computers, experiments in making the flag mechanically started in 1945. These were never successful enough to produce new operational techniques and are described in an appendix. a, E.2

[a] technique

p. 295 # 39 LANGUAGE METHODS

i

39A CIRCULATION

Circulation of material in the Testery was arranged from Room 12 with the help of a de-chi clerk (in Room 41) who kept track of material in Rooms 40 and 41 and the Supervisor, who kept track of material in the decoding room. Documents for each message worked on in the Testery were circulated in an envelope which included the Red Form (but not the tapes). When the message had been decoded, it was returned to Room 12.

39B CRYPTOGRAPHY

(a) Commitments

Cryptographers in the Testery were divided into two rooms, the so-called 'Breakers' in Room 41 and the so-called 'Setters' in Room 40. Room 41 numbered 5 on a shift plus 4 on permanent days, and Room 40, 8 a shift. Room 41 contained the more experienced men and the Head of Room 41 was responsible for all work in the section, on his watch.

The growth of the Testery and the division of work has been outlined in **14A(b)**. The purpose of this chapter is to describe the organisation in 1945 when there were two major cryptographic commitments.

(i) Recovery and Solution of Key from Depths.

(ii) Psi and motor setting from a de-chi by hand or with the help of Dragon.

(b) Depths

Possible depths noticed at Knockholt were teleprinted at once, not more than 1000 letters being sent. When the interception registers arrived in Room 12 they were carefully examined and a list of other possible depths sent to Knockholt.

(c) De-chis

Before being issued to the Head of Room 41, the annotations "Pause", "Auto" and "Hand" were copied by the de-chi clerk from the Red Form on to the de-chi. The head of shift saw that the de-chis were worked on in a suitable order and that psi breaking jobs were given suitable priority. Various aids to de-chi "breakers" existed in the form of decodes and abstracts of message characteristics.

De-chis were passed to Room 40 when sufficient P and ψ' had been obtained to set or break the psis at some point in the de-chi. Room 40 found the settings for the start of the message and worked out sufficient extended psi to set the motor or break the motor patterns. In the most favourable circumstances jobs took 20 minutes and $1\frac{1}{2}$ hours respectively, but more usually rather longer owing to the unfavourable motor wheels or slides in the text. Messages with χ_2 limitation were sometimes set at the position of the Room 41 break and worked back on a specially adapted machine.

[i] In the original text of the *Report*, almost all chapters start with an analytical contents list. This one does not. We have accordingly supplied such a list, as a copy editor would have done, for uniformity and the convenience of readers.

De-chis worked on in Room 41 without success and any unworked setting de-chis on low dottage days could be sent to Dragon, which was under the control of members of Room 41. When $d < 19$ it was general practice to send all de-chis to Dragon. A few de-chis were returned to the Newmanry for motor runs.

39C DECODING p. 296

Decoding Resources consisted of a Supervisor; 13 machines 10 operators and 3 engineers on each watch. There were occasional interchanges of staff with Room 40.

(a) Supervisor

The Supervisor registered messages to be decoded, and issued them to machines, which had to be set up so that messages could be dealt with, with suitable priority. The supervisor verified from the decodes on their return, that the machines had been set up correctly on all impulses.

(b) Operators

Operators needed to be touch-typists and to be able to recognise P and to be trained sufficiently in Tunny to solve minor breakdown problems. Major breakdowns were passed back to Room 40.

In the later stages, tape decoding was introduced. It was found to be much faster than hand decoding on long messages, but slower on short ones. Corrupt messages were better dealt with by hand methods.

Rewrites of poor or unreliable cipher text could be obtained through the C.O. from Knockholt, [a] and when necessary a slide run on approximate chi-settings could be done in the Newmanry.

(c) Machines

In the early days decoding had to be interrupted for short periods while repairs and adjustments were carried out.

The number of machines steadily increased to the final total of 13 and during the last 12 months or so, it was possible to have the engineers working on the machines which were not actually required for current work.

39D ISSUING

The Cribs Watch was created, to read decoded material "en passant", and contained 5 German linguists covering three shifts. Its duties were:

(i) To pick out possible retransmissions from incomplete decodes still on the machines, to assist operators in correcting breakdowns by suggesting probable clear text, and to expedite the issue of particularly urgent messages.

(ii) To check the general accuracy of completed decodes, and to route the different messages found in each decode, to the appropriate sections. E.1

(iii) Later, to reread the duplicate copy of each decode (returned from Room 12) with the object of marking any information of interest to Sixta and of informing Mr Page's Section of E.2 any possible cribs.

(iv) To sort amended and typed decodes from Hut 3 and extract and file examples of routine messages for the benefit of Room 41.

[a] throught

p. 297 # 41 THE FIRST BREAK

i

41A EARLY TRAFFIC

(a) A first analysis

The first messages on the "Tunny" link (the name "Tunny" was first given to this traffic in the summer of 1942) to be studied cryptographically were sent out shortly after the German invasion
E.1, a of Russia. They passed between Vienna and Athens. The Hellschreiber method of transmission was used. Some earlier traffic, apparently practice transmissions, had been intercepted in May. This had been sent out in the form of a five-unit code, so it was suspected that a teleprinter was being used. This was confirmed by a preliminary examination of the later traffic, which showed that an alphabet of 32 characters was being employed. These characters were the 26 letters of the normal alphabet, and the six extra symbols 3, 4, 8, 9, + and /.

Each message began with a clear preamble in which there appeared first the serial number, repeated several times, and then a set of 12 letters, in the forms of names (Anton, Bertha etc.) which was clearly a 12-letter indicator. The symbol 9 was used as a separator in this preamble, and a group of five 9's separated the clear preamble from the cipher text. Immediately after the cipher text there appeared a sequence of 8's. The serial number was given in letter form by means of a simple keyboard substitution the digits 1, 2, 3, 4, 5, 6, 7, 8, 9, 0, being represented by the
E.2 letters Q, W, E, R, T, Y, U, I, O, P, respectively.

(b) Meanings of teleprinter letters

On the assumption that a teleprinter machine was being used, two problems presented themselves. First, was the correlation of the 26 letters of the normal alphabet with the teleprinter signs the same as that of the international convention, and second, what teleprinter signs corresponded to the symbols 3, 4, 8, 9, + and / ?

b Both these questions were answered by the study of a series of corrupt messages which were sent out on July 22nd. Only sixteen different letters appeared in these messages, and those letters of the normal alphabet which appeared were those whose first impulse was conventionally a dot. Clearly, owing to some fault in the machine, the first impulse of each letter had been transmitted as dot, even when it should have been cross. This effect finally confirmed the hypothesis that a teleprinter machine was being used and answered the first of the above questions in the affirmative.

c The second problem was then solved by a study of the corrupt clear preambles. For example the sequence H / I N R I C H and T H / O 3 O R would be recognised as corruptions of H E I N R I C H and T H E O D O R respectively. Hence it would be deduced that for each of the pairs (E, /) and (D, 3) the teleprinter signs differed only in the first impulse. But by convention E is (x••••) and D is (x••x•). Hence it was deduced that / corresponded to the teleprinter sign (•••••), and 3 to the teleprinter sign (•••x•). By this sort of argument the teleprinter sign corresponding to each of the letters 3 , 4 , 8 , 9 , +, and /, was determined.

[a] Hellschrieber [b] a a series [c] problems

[i] In the original text of the *Report*, almost all chapters start with an analytical contents list. This one does not. We have accordingly supplied such a list, as a copy editor would have done, for uniformity and the convenience of readers.

41B TUNNY SHOWN TO BE A LETTER SUBTRACTOR

The next advance to be made was the demonstration that the cipher was a letter subtractor cipher, and the determination of the law of addition used. E.3

This was made possible by the occurrence of a number of "depths of two", that is, of messages having the same 12 letter indicator. Usually the two messages of such a pair were consecutive, as though an operator had failed to reset his machine between the two messages, but instead had made use of some device for returning all the wheels to their starting points.

The simplest assumptions to make seemed to be that a letter subtractor cipher was being used. The law of addition was fairly easy to guess and was guessed correctly. p. 298

It was argued that if a pair of messages (a, b) with the same indicators were really in depth, the sum of the two cipher messages must be equal to the sum of the two clear messages, it being assumed that the cipher was a letter subtractor.

Now when the sums $Z_a + Z_b$ were formed for a number of depths of two it was noticed that some pairs of them began with the same sequence of five or six letters. This was regarded as a proof of the assumptions that had been made, namely that the cipher was a letter subtractor, and that the law of addition had been inferred correctly. The effect would be expected to arise if stereotyped beginnings were being used.

The proof was completed when about 15 letters of one of the depths were decoded. When a group `++ZZZ88`, which had appeared occasionally in clear preambles was tried as the clear of one message, the clear of the other message, came out as the first letters of the word `S P R U C H N U M M E R` (serial number).

41C A DEPTH READ

(a) Problems of depth reading

The first attempts to reconstruct long key-sequences from depths of two were failures. Depth breakers then had no previous experience of the traffic, and so depth breaking was much slower and much more difficult than it was in later years. Apart from this there was one very serious obstacle in an ambiguity which is inseparable from a depth of two.

For in the process of depth breaking the first step is to construct the sequence $Z_a + Z_b$, and then to express this as a sum of two passages of plain language, which are assumed to be P_a and P_b. But there is usually no way of telling which of the passages is P_a and which is P_b. It can be done when cribs to the messages are known; for example, as in the early days when the serial numbers were given both internally and externally: and it can also be done when the decoding process is carried on to the end of the shorter message, for then the clear message which comes to an end must be associated with the shorter cipher message. But it cannot be done by the depth breaking process alone, without independent evidence.

In the depths which were first attacked, the clear language obtained was not continuous, and the short sequences obtained could not be correlated with one another, so the ambiguity arose fresh in each section.

It is not surprising therefore that for some time little progress was made with the "Tunny" cipher. The construction of long pieces of key was very difficult, and even when it was possible the results were not unique.

(b) The depth "`HQIBPEXEZMUG`"

On 30th August, 1941, the German cipher operators came to the rescue.

On that date two very long messages, with the same indicators `HQIBPEXEZMUG` were sent out from the same end of the link. When a depth was broken into, it was found that the messages were essentially the same, but the spacing, the mis-spellings and the corrections were different. Evidently the same message had been typed out twice, by hand. As a result the two versions, at the same number of letters from the beginning, would be at slightly different places in the true text of the message. This divergence increased slowly, until at the 3,976th letter, where the shorter message came to an end, it had increased to more than one hundred letters.

p. 299 This depth was much easier to read than the earlier depths had been, for at any stage the next letter of clear language in the less advanced message could be predicted from the clear language already derived for the other. The messages were in fact decoded over the entire length of the shorter message, so that the ambiguity in the key was resolved. The practice of giving the serial number externally and internally had ceased some weeks previously.

From this depth a length of subtractor key of 3,976 letters was reconstructed (with a few of the
E.4 letters doubtful, of course). During the remaining months of the year 1941 the Research Section were engaged in attempts to analyse this key, and so discover the nature of the machine which had produced it.

The Germans may have noticed this breach of security, for the traffic almost stopped for a few days, and no more true depths are on record for the remainder of 1941.

(c) Near-depths

Besides the depths in July and August there were a number of "near-depths". These were pairs of messages sent out on the same day whose indicators differed only in one or two letters. One pair whose indicators differed only in the first letter was decoded successfully for 20 or 30 letters on the assumption that the two subtractor keys differed only in the first impulse. Then another pair whose indicators differed only in the first two letters was decoded for a dozen or so on the assumption that its two subtractor keys differed only in the first and second impulses.

It was deduced from this that the first letter of the indicator affected only the first impulse and the second letter only the second impulse of the subtractor key. No further positive information was obtained from near-depths at this stage.

Mention should also be made of some pairs of messages having the same indicator, but not sent on the same day. All attempts to decode the beginnings of these pairs failed.

With luck, we might have had at this early stage a near depth whose indicators differed only in one or two of the last five letters. Such a depth, we now know, should have given very important information. However no such depth seems to have been intercepted until March 1942, except for a hopelessly corrupt one in the January of that year.

41D KEY ANALYSED

(a) Study of Indicators

For a long time no progress was made in the analysis of the subtractor key of the depth H Q I B P E X E Z M U G. This was due to concentration on a hypothesis now known to be wrong —
E.5 that each impulse was the sum of two or more periodic components, the periods being small.

In fact the only positive information obtained during the rest of 1941 was obtained by a study of the indicators used. It was found that, in any particular month, there were two letters (apart from J) which could not appear in the twelfth place of the indicator. This pair varied from month to month. One other fact about the indicators was established: the letters most frequently used were those in the middle of the alphabet, and those at the ends of the alphabet were comparatively rare.

p. 300 The reason for the latter effect remains obscure though there is no doubt that it is only a psychological one, and is not necessitated by the nature of the machine and of the indicator system. The first effect suggested that the last letter of the indicator controlled the setting of a wheel of period 23.

(b) Chis, Psis and extensions

The first success in the analysis of the key was obtained towards the end of January 1942 when it was found almost accidentally that many repeats occurred in the first impulse of the key at intervals which were multiples of 41. This suggested that this first impulse was the sum of a periodic sequence (of period 41) and of an aperiodic but non-random sequence. We here denote the periodic sequence by χ and the non-periodic sequence by ψ.

In order to reconstruct the sequences χ and ψ, the first impulse was written out on a width of 41, and for each set of five consecutive columns a count was made of the five consecutive characters which occupied these columns. When two such counts were made it was found that they were closely related; by adding a constant set of five consecutive characters to each of the five character sequences in one of the sets of columns, the frequency count of this set could be brought into close agreement with that of the other. It was found that these constant five-character sequences could be so chosen as not only to bring all the frequency counts into good agreement, but also to fit together in their proper order to form a periodic sequence of period 41. This sequence was denoted by χ and the result of adding it to the first impulse was denoted by ψ.

When ψ was examined with the object of determining its non-random properties, the following "local" peculiarities were observed:— i

(i) Consecutive signs in the sequence ψ tended to be equal. In fact there was equality in about 3/4 of the cases.

(ii) The sequences **•x•** and **x•x** were significantly rare in ψ, even when the result (i) was taken into account.

It was then seen that the χ pattern could have been reconstructed by considering only pairs of consecutive columns in the rectangle, and that the power of the method was not appreciably increased by taking five columns rather than three. When the method came to be applied to other depths, the counts were therefore made on sets of three consecutive columns.

The most striking property of ψ was that it was roughly periodic; it could be regarded as a periodic sequence of period 43 which had been "extended" by replacing some dots by sequences of two or more consecutive dots, and some crosses by sequences of two or more consecutive crosses. The ψ sequence was evidently generated by a wheel of period 43 which sometimes a moved on one place, and sometimes stayed still when the cipher machine moved from one of its states to the next.

We may here introduce a slight change of notation. The extended key which has been called ψ is now denoted by ψ' and the symbol ψ is used for the periodic sequence from which it is derived by extension.

We have now reached the stage at which the first impulse was shown to be the sum of a periodic sequence χ of period 41, and an "extended" sequence ψ' derived from a periodic sequence ψ b, ii of period 43. An ambiguity arose here, for the patterns of χ and ψ could both be reversed (by replacing dots by crosses, and crosses by dots) without affecting their sum, but this was evidently of very little importance.

The law governing the extension of the sequence ψ was still unknown. p. 301

The four impulses of the key were next attacked, and they were successfully broken down into χ and ψ patterns, just as the first impulse had been. In these cases the periods of the χ wheels were found by booking 7-sign repeats in the first few hundred places of each impulse, factorizing the intervals and selecting the most common, fairly large, prime factor. The periods were found to be 41, 31, 29, 26, and 23 for χ_1, χ_2, χ_3, χ_4, and χ_5 respectively, and 43, 47, 51, 53 and 59 for ψ_1, ψ_2, ψ_3, ψ_4, and ψ_5 respectively.

---

[a] somtimes [b] ψ

[i] Word 'peculiarities' handwritten.
[ii] Word 'derived' handwritten.

(c) The Motor

The next problem was to determine the law governing the extensions of the ψ patterns. This was attacked by means of the concept of the "motor-key".

The motor-key was defined as a sequence of dots and crosses of which each sign was associated with a particular pair of consecutive signs of ψ', and such that the nth sign of the motor key corresponded to the pair formed by the nth and $(n+1)$th signs of the extended ψ key. When two consecutive signs in ψ' correspond to the same positions of the ψ wheel the corresponding motor-key sign was defined to be dot, and when two such signs corresponded to different positions of the ψ wheel the corresponding motor key sign was defined to be a cross.

The motor key corresponding to a particular impulse could only be determined partially from the corresponding ψ' key. When for example a block of 3 consecutive crosses in the ψ wheel was represented by a block of 5 consecutive crosses in ψ', it was possible to say that just two of the pairs of consecutive crosses in this block corresponded to dots in the motor key, but it was not possible to say which two of the four such pairs these were.

A pair of consecutive different signs in ψ' necessarily corresponded to a cross in the motor key, but the position of a dot in the motor key could only be fixed, when it corresponded to the extension of a singleton dot, or cross, in the ψ pattern. As there were very few singleton dots, or crosses in the ψ patterns, very few dots could be fixed in the motor key. Sometimes a group of several consecutive dots, or crosses, in the ψ' key would not be extended at all: each sign in the motor key corresponding to a pair of signs in this block could then necessarily be a cross.

A motor key determined from a ψ' key therefore consisted of a number of isolated groups of one or more crosses, together with a few groups consisting of dots flanked by crosses. These groups would be separated by intervals whose lengths varied from two places up to eight or nine. In each such interval the number of dots, but not their distribution, would be known.

A study of the indicator had suggested the hypothesis that the motor keys of the five impulses were identical. For since the first and second indicators affected only the first and second impulses respectively, it was supposed that each indicator letter gave the setting of a particular wheel in the machine. We have already mentioned the evidence that the twelfth indicator letter gave the setting of a wheel period of 23. This wheel could now be identified with the fifth χ wheel. It seemed probable therefore that the first five indicator letters corresponded to the five ψ wheels, in order, and the last five to the five χ wheels in order.

This left only the middle two indicators to govern the motor key. (This would explain why near depths differing in this pair of indicators have proved unbreakable.)

a, p. 302 But five independent motor keys should need at least five indicators. Hence there was probably only one motor key, controlling all five ψ wheels.

The five partial motor keys, obtained from the five impulses, were therefore compared, and it was found that the assumptions that they were all partial descriptions of the same fundamental
b motor sequence led to no inconsistencies (or at any rate to no more inconsistencies than could be explained by rare corruptions in the text). The five motor keys were accordingly combined to give the true motor key. Even this was not free from ambiguities, but most of its signs were fixed.

The Research Section now tried out a number of hypotheses on the motor key, without success, until it was noticed that the key was nearly periodic. It was then found that it was derived from a truly periodic sequence, of period 37, by a system of extensions just as the ψ' keys were derived from periodic sequences.

The pattern of the 37 wheel was readily determined, as was the law governing its extension. For the "motor-key" governing the movement of the 37 wheel was simply a sequence of dots and crosses of period 61.

---

[a] indpendent [b] inconsistences [twice]

41E TWO MORE DEPTHS

The cryptographic problem presented by the depth H Q I B P E X E Z M U G had now been completely solved. The next problem was to find what changes were made in the machine between the encipherment of different messages. For example, could the wheel patterns be changed, if so how often were they changed? Again, could the actual order of the wheels be changed, so that say, the 41 wheel became the χ wheel of the 3rd. impulse?

The first attack on this problem was made by attempting to set messages of 30th August 1941 and other dates close to this, on the set of wheels found for H Q I B P E X E Z M U G, taken in the same order. In this way it was hoped that the period of time over which these wheel patterns, with this wheel order were valid could be determined. But these attempts at message setting all failed. An attempt was then made to set a depth of July 3rd, the indicator letters of which were D K T N F Q G W A O S H. This depth was usually referred to as "Waosh". Now that a good knowledge of the type of plain language used in the traffic had been obtained from H Q I B P E X E Z M U G, and now that it was known that keys could be broken, depth breaking became a much more rapid and successful process than it had been in July and August, 1941. Two passages of the depth were read, one about 500 letters long, and the other about 300 letters long, and two possible subtractor keys were obtained from each passage.

These possible keys were submitted to the analysis that had succeeded in the case of H Q I B P E X E Z M U G, but the columns were now counted in threes, rather than fives. The [a] alternative which seemed to give the more significant results in the fifth impulse, on a width of 23, was retained in the case of each of the passages that had been read. The information given by both passages was now combined, and the fifth impulse was successfully broken up into a χ-key of period 23, and an extended ψ key of period 59. The ambiguity in the key was now eliminated for all five impulses. The analysis was now applied to the other four impulses on the assumption that the wheel order was the same as in H Q I B P E X E Z M U G, and successful results were obtained in each case. No difficulty was then found in the determination of the motor key.

It was found that the patterns of the ψ wheels in W A O S H were identical with the ψ wheel patterns of H Q I B P E X E Z M U G, but the patterns of all the other wheels were different in the two depths.

Next a depth of July 21st with indicators K O W P A E N G F Q B Z was successfully p. 303 attacked. All the wheel patterns of this depth, with the exception of those of the two "motor" wheels (with periods 37 and 61) were the same as in W A O S H, but these two patterns were different.

From these depths the following conclusions could be drawn:

(i) The order of the wheels was fixed.

(ii) The ψ patterns remained unchanged over periods which could exceed one month.

(iii) The χ patterns remained unchanged over periods of many days.

(iv) The patterns of the motor wheels were changed comparatively frequently.

It could now be assumed that one reason why the attempts to set messages not in depth had failed was that the wrong motor wheel patterns had been assumed. The attempts were now resumed, but no assumptions were made about the motor patterns. Messages intermediate in time between K O W P A E N G F Q B Z and W A O S H were taken, so that there could be no serious doubt about the patterns of the χ and ψ wheels.

---

[a] counted in three

p. 304 # 42 EARLY HAND METHODS

i

42A FIRST EFFORTS AT MESSAGE SETTING

The theory of message setting which was attempted in March, 1942, after the breaking of the first three depths is simple. It had been observed from these, and from depths that had only a been decoded for a few letters, that most messages contained the group S P R U C H 9 + + or S P R U C H N U M M E R 9 + + either right at the beginning or else preceded only by such groups as 89, or + + Z Z Z 8 8 9. In most attempts at message setting therefore, the groups S P R U C H N U M M E R 9 + + or + + Z Z Z 8 8 9 S P R U C H were assumed as the clear language in some position near to the beginning of the message. After the group 9 + + the serial number of the message would be given in letter form. When this was also given in the clear preamble the crib could be extended a little if necessary. (This practice of giving the serial number in clear soon ceased.)

By adding the assumed clear language to the cipher text, a length of about 15 letters of possible keys was obtained. Each impulse of this was treated in the following way. First the corresponding χ wheel was added in all possible settings, and then attempts were made to fit the ψ pattern, suitably extended, to each of the set of sequences of dots and crosses thus obtained. Usually there were two or three sequences which could be interpreted as extended parts of the ψ pattern.

The possibilities were limited by the nature of the ψ patterns, which contained so few singleton dots or crosses. A sequence containing several singletons could be rejected at once.

After this process had been gone through for the five impulses the results were compared to see if the same motor key could be fitted to five of the possibilities, one in each impulse. If so, a possible setting of the 10 χ and ψ wheels had been obtained. It was finally tested by an attempt to decode more of the message. This test depended on the principle that a message can be decoded even when the motor key is unknown, provided that the other ten wheels are correctly set. For suppose we have decoded a message up to the nth letter. Then there are only two possibilities for the nth sign of the motor key, namely cross and dot, and the $(n+1)$th sign of the subtractor key can readily be calculated for each possibility. By applying these two subtractor letters we get two alternatives for the $(n+1)$th clear letter, and considerations of sense are usually sufficient to decide between them. Thus the message can be decoded letter by letter, the motor key being built up sign by sign at the same time.

For a long time the would be setters had no success, but at last came the great day when the first single message was set and decoded.

By the end of April several other July messages had been set, and the Research Section was in a position to attack the July indicator system. But then some messages were broken which were only about a month old. The message setters thereupon forgot all about July 1941 and concentrated on March, 1942.

[a] only be decoded

[i] In the original text of the *Report*, almost all chapters start with an analytical contents list. This one does not. We have accordingly supplied such a list, as a copy editor would have done, for uniformity and the convenience of readers.

42B MACHINE BREAKING FOR MARCH 1942

(a) Depths in February

Interest in current traffic, dormant for six months, revived at the end of February, 1942. The Hellschreiber method of transmission had now been superseded by tone transmission in 5-unit p. 305 code; near depths were once more appearing. Many of these were corrupt, but the beginnings of some were decoded, and were shown to be of the same stereotyped forms as were those of July and August 1941. Two or three hundred letters of one February depth were read and an attempt was made to break the machine. This failed. A near depth of March 3rd was passed over in favour of the February depth.

(b) A depth of three

On March 25th, an unprecedented phenomenon, the interception of a depth of three, occurred. Attention was immediately diverted to it. Reading in depth of three was found to be very easy, and it was soon carried to the end of the shortest of the three messages (973 letters). It was continued for the other two messages without a break up to the 1060th letter. There was no ambiguity about a the subtractor key, as there would have been in a depth of two, and there was hardly any possibility of corruption in it, since all three messages were good, and since two messages would need to be corrupt in the same letter in order to produce an error in the calculated subtractor key. No better length of key could have been desired, and all the energies of the Research Section were thrown into the attempt to break it, but without success. Some evidence was found to confirm the hypothesis that the periods of the χ wheels were the same as of old, but that was all. It was supposed that the Germans had taken steps to eliminate the non-random characteristics of the extended ψ patterns. The Research Section did not manage to anticipate Turing's Method of Key Analysis and work on the depth of three had to be abandoned.

(c) A near depth of March 3rd

However, though depths could no longer be broken, it was thought that a near depth might prove vulnerable. For when a near depth can be read it gives not merely one key, but two closely related, but different keys. Attention was therefore transferred to the rather corrupt near depth of March 3rd. which has already been mentioned.

The two messages of the near depth had indicators which differed only in two of the last five letters, and therefore according to the hypothesis referred to in Section IV the only difference i, E.1 between the two subtractor keys was in the settings of two of the χ wheels.

The near depth was decoded for about 30 letters, and the sum $K_a + K_b$ of the two keys was determined. Crosses (of course) appeared only in the impulses whose χ wheels had different settings in the two messages. Both these impulses of $K_a + K_b$ should have shown the periodicity of the corresponding χ wheels, and were in fact found to do so, though the piece of pattern actually repeated in either impulse was of course very short. Hence, both these impulses were assumed to be χ patterns "differenced" at some unknown interval. By repeating the patterns the sequence $K_a + K_b$ could be extended as far as was desired. So from this sequence and the cipher texts the sum of the two clear texts could be derived. This sum was attacked as in the breaking of ordinary depths, and two or three hundred letters were decoded. So two alternatives for the subtractor key of either of the messages were worked out for this stretch of two or three hundred letters.

This success established the validity of the assumptions which led up to it.

At this stage then, not only were two alternatives for a length of key known but also two χ patterns differenced at unknown interval had been obtained.

---

[a] abiguity

[i] First word of 'to the hypothesis' handwritten.

p. 306 **(d) Chis and Psis completed**

From the χ difference patterns, it was possible to determine the correct χ patterns with some ambiguity. Actually each assumption about the unknown differencing interval led to a different χ pattern, but most of these could be rejected as having too many, or too few, crosses. The justification for this lay in the fact that in July and August 1941 the numbers of dots and crosses in any χ or ψ wheel patterns had been made as nearly equal as possible.

Those few possible χ wheels that remained for one of the impulses were applied in their proper settings to the alternative subtractor keys, and the resulting sums were examined to see if they were nearly periodic. One of them did indeed prove to be an extended ψ key.

So the ambiguity of the subtractor keys was resolved, and one impulse of each key was successfully broken down into χ and ψ keys. By studying the ψ' key in the impulse it was possible to decide, for very many of the subtractor letters just how many ψ movements had intervened between them and the beginning of the message. As the ψ movement was the same for all five impulses, it followed that for very many letters of the key, the settings of all the ψ wheels, relative to their initial settings could be determined. This was done, and then the value dot was assumed for the first character of the χ wheel in another impulse. This assumption was legitimate, since the patterns of both χ and ψ wheels in any impulse can be reversed without affecting their sum. Then from the characters of the key corresponding to the first position in this χ wheel, a number of characters in the ψ pattern were obtained, and put at their proper intervals in the ψ pattern, by the use of the relative settings. From other key characters corresponding to these ψ characters, more χ characters were found, and then by continuing this process the complete χ pattern and ψ patterns were built up.

Hence all the χ and ψ patterns were determined and then the motor key was analysed just as for July and August, 1941.

The message setting method was then applied to the Key from the depth of three and this was successfully set on the χ and ψ wheels which had been derived from the near depth. The motor wheels were however different.

(e) Value of *a* and *b*

When the March wheel patterns were inspected it was seen that there were still 11 dots in Mu 37 (so that $a = \cdot 703$ since there was no lim) and that the value of b was about $\cdot 7$ giving $ab = 1/2$. These values must be compared with those for the patterns for 1941 when $a = \cdot 703$, $b < 1/2$ so that ab was always less than $\cdot 352$.

The change in the value of b explains the failure of the old method of key analysis on the key from the depth of three. It is worth noticing that the Tunny machine would probably never have been broken if there had been no stretch of key susceptible to the single impulse analysis possible when $ab \neq 1/2$.

42C MESSAGE SETTING FOR MARCH 1942

The success obtained with the near depth of March 3rd. confirmed the theory of indicators which has been mentioned above. It was now taken for granted that the setting of each wheel was
p. 307 controlled by a single letter of the indicator, that the first five letters of the indicator corresponded to the five ψ wheels, in order, and the last five letters corresponded to the five χ wheels, in order. The obvious assumption that the same indicator letter in the same place for two messages meant that the corresponding wheel had the same setting in both messages was also made. Justification for it could be found in the fact that the last indicator letter was restricted to the same 23 values over the whole of any one month, which seemed to show that there was no change in the indication of the fifth χ wheel over this period.

The message setters therefore restricted themselves to messages which had for two or more of their χ and ψ indicators values which had appeared in messages which were already set.

The settings of the corresponding wheels could be assumed known, and this greatly simplified the process of message setting described above. In impulses in which the setting of a χ wheel was known, the crib, usually SPRUCHNUMMER9++ could be tried in many different positions, and rejected at once in some of them. When the χ setting was known for two impulses, most of the false crib positions could be rejected.

The process of message setting was very successful, and with each success it became more powerful, since the meanings of more indicator letters were known. In its later stages the settings of the majority of the wheels for the message attacked were known, and the process differed but little from ordinary decoding.

The theory of the indicators was completely confirmed. The results, together with those for April — the two months were soon being attacked simultaneously — also gave new information about the motor wheels. It was found that their patterns changed every day but that the corresponding indicator system, that is the correlation of the indicator letters with wheel *positions*, was fixed over each month. The 6th indicator letter controlled the 37 wheel and the 7th controlled the 61 wheel.

It should be noted that the cyclic order of the wheel settings corresponding to the indicator i
letters was not correlated with the order of those indicator letters in the alphabet.

It was found that the χ and ψ wheel patterns remained constant over each of the months a
March and April, but changed between these two months.

42D APRIL 1942

(a) Breaking the wheels

One or two depths were found in April, but no attempt was made to analyse the keys obtained. The break into April was made on a near depth of April 22nd. The indicators of the two messages concerned were

M H S L P E I S V O I U

and

M H S L P E I . . O I O .

Two of the indicator letters in the second message could not be determined, owing to corruptions. By a curious coincidence both were found, after the near depth was broken, to represent different wheel settings from those used in the first message. The fifth χ indicator differed between the two messages.

It was clear at the beginning therefore that the two message settings differed only in the p. 308
settings of the χ wheels and further that the settings of the 3rd and 4th χ wheels were the same. Moreover the messages were stated in the clear preambles to be 3rd. and 2nd parts of messages (presumably the same message) respectively. From experience with the decodes of July and August 1941, and of March 1942 the clear messages were expected to begin with

DRITTER9TEIL9DES9SPRUCHES9

and

ZWOTER9TEIL9DES9SPRUCHES9 E.2

or equivalent phrases, respectively.

The initial problem was to find two such phrases which when added together gave a result which agreed in the third and fourth impulses with the sum of the two cipher messages. This problem was solved without difficulty and the wheels completed. (The screed of the Research Section contains further details of this job.) E.3

[a] contant

[i] First word of 'the cyclic' handwritten.

(b) Setting

When the wheel patterns had been obtained the April depths were set, and then messages whose clear language was unknown were studied. The process of message setting was carried so far that the indicator system was completely solved.

At this stage, early in May, 1942, it was possible to draw conclusions about the periods over which the wheel patterns remained valid. It was found that the patterns of the motor wheels changed every day, and the χ patterns changed at the beginning of each month. The patterns of the ψ wheels, it was found, had changed at the beginning of April, and they were constant over each of the months March and April. But it was remembered that the same ψ patterns were used in August as in July of 1941 so it was suspected that the ψ patterns were constant over a period of several months. Three months seemed a likely period, since the first set of ψ patterns had presumably come into force at the beginning of July 1941.

A curious difficulty arose out of the first letter of each message, which never seemed to decode according to the rules. This effect was not understood until the studies described in the next section had been made.

42E THE INDICATOR METHOD

(a) General Tunny position in April 1942

The Research Section had achieved great success with the March and April messages. The complete decoding of all this traffic would have been possible if suitable machines had been available at the time. (As a result, while this analysis was proceeding, it was decided to have such
E.4 machines made; the first one came into operation at the beginning of June, 1942).

But the mastery of the problem was not so complete as the March and April success might seem to indicate. No way of breaking a length of key, without independent information was
p. 309 known, and the only independent information that would suffice seemed to be a knowledge of one of the χ patterns, or of a number of alternatives for such a pattern. The only way of getting a length of key with this additional information, seemed to be by the study of a near depth, for which the two indicators concerned differed only in the last five letters. The Germans could not be relied upon to send such near depths at the rate of one a month.

It seemed possible that a pair of messages whose indicators differed only in one of the first five letters, so that only one ψ wheel was differently set in the two messages, might also be breakable. However there was never any occasion for the Research Section to attempt the feat of breaking such a pair.

One possible line of research would have been the search for a new method of breaking into a length of key, so that wheel patterns might again be derived from true depths. It was not until July, 1942 that such a method was discovered, (by Turing).

Even such a method would have been useless in the case of a month in which no depth had been sent, and there had been several such months.

(b) Idea of using indicators for breaking the wheels, May, 1942

The Research Section sought therefore for a method of machine breaking independent of depths. It seemed possible that such a method could be developed from a study of the indicators and first few cipher letters of a sufficiently large number of messages. Even if the process was not
[i] carried on to completion it might give the pattern of a single χ wheel and thus permit the breaking of a machine when a depth was available.

A study of the May messages was therefore begun as soon as about 10 days traffic had accumulated. The workings have not been preserved, but similar workings for June still exist.

---

[i] Word 'the' handwritten.

(c) The first experiment

In the first experiment which was made, the fifth impulse of the second letter of each cipher message was tabulated against the fifth and twelfth indicator letters, corresponding to the fifth ψ and χ wheels respectively. The row, and also the columns, were lettered in order from A to Z, excluding J, which had never been used as an indicator letter. The fifth impulse of the second letter of a cipher message was entered in the row whose letter was the ψ indicator, and the column whose letter was the χ indicator. Several hundreds of messages were used.

Many of the 625 squares contained more than one entry, but it was very rare to find two different signs in the same square. This confirmed the assumption that almost all the messages began in the same way, and also showed that the setting of the ψ wheel for the second letter was [i] fixed uniquely by the ψ indicator. A very similar effect was found when the fifth impulse of the [a] third cipher letter was tabulated in the same way, but when the fifth impulse of the fourth letter was tabulated, very many cases of different signs appearing in the same square were found. It was deduced that the movement of the ψ wheel was the same for all messages up to the third letter, but that between the third and the fourth letters the wheel could either advance one place or else stay still.

Another count was made for the fifth impulse of the first letter. This count differed from all p. 310 the others in that nearly all the entries in any one column were the same. This showed that only the χ wheels were effective in the encipherment of the first letter.

Similar results were obtained for the first and third impulses. The other two were avoided [b] because they are the ones in which + and Z differ, so that these two impulses would, it was thought, present more difficulty than the others.

The difficulty that had been presented by the first cipher letter in March and April was now explained, and it was no longer a matter of complete indifference whether the wheel patterns of a Tunny machine were reversed or not. This property of the first letter was peculiar to SZ 40 (the first model of the German Tunny machine).

(d) Construction of pattern fragments

On the assumption that almost all messages began with a group of +'s, followed by a group of Z's it followed that nearly every message began, in the fifth impulse with a sequence of crosses. (At least 6 crosses, to judge by the March and April traffic). Since the ψ wheel did not operate in the first place, the nature of the χ character in the wheel-setting corresponding to each χ indicator could be determined from the count of the fifth impulse of the 1st letter. Since each setting of the 23-wheel corresponds to some indicator letter, the number of crosses in the pattern of the fifth χ wheel could at once be deduced. It was found to be 11. Of course the count of the first letter did not suffice to determine the pattern of the wheel, since the wheel settings were not in the order of the indicator letters.

The analysis of the count of the 2nd letter was more complicated since the ψ wheels were now operative. Each cipher character was the sum of a clear character assumed to be ×, a χ character fixed by the χ indicator, and a ψ character fixed by the ψ indicator. However, if a particular χ character was assumed to be dot, the values of a number of ψ characters could be deduced from the row of the square corresponding to that χ character. Then more χ characters could be deduced from these ψ characters, and so on. This process was carried on until it terminated, and so sets of χ and ψ characters were obtained. Since these led to very little inconsistency, they were assumed to be the correct ones. Some of the ψ characters were uncertain, since the corresponding rows were almost empty, but all the χ characters were obtained with a fair certainty. The first assumption, that a particular χ character was ×, might have been wrong: it would have then been

[a] similiar [b] Similiar

[i] Phrases 'the setting of' and 'ψ wheel for' handwritten.

necessary to reverse all the χ and ψ characters finally obtained. This point was settled by using the fact that the number of crosses in the fifth χ wheel was 11.

The count of the third letter was analysed in the same way. It was found that the ψ wheel always moved on between the second and third letters.

a We will now summarise the information which had been obtained at this stage. We shall use the term “pattern-fragment for A” to denote a short sequence of dots and crosses in a wheel beginning at the setting which, with the indicator A, corresponds to the first letter of the message in the case of a χ wheel, and to the second letter in the case of a ψ wheel.

The pattern-fragments of the fifth χ wheel were known to three places, and the pattern fragments of the fifth ψ wheel were known to two places. A check on the working was now
p. 311 possible, for by the nature of the ψ wheels the pattern fragments •× and ×• should have been much more common than the pattern fragments •• and ××. The pattern fragments actually obtained were found to fulfil this requirement.

(e) Extension of the fragments

The next step was the analysis of the fifth impulse of the fourth letter. This was expected to be more difficult, as either the second or third characters of the ψ pattern-fragment might be used in any given message. In all the motor keys of March and April the proportion of dots to crosses was 11 to 26, so the effect of the third signs of the ψ pattern-fragments was expected to predominate.

In some rows of the square it very seldom happened that two different characters were entered in the same small square. This evidently meant that the second and third characters of the corresponding ψ pattern-fragments were the same. Conversely rows in which there were many cases of different entries in the same square corresponded to pattern fragments whose second and third characters were different. Thus many third characters of ψ pattern-fragments were deduced merely from the quality of the corresponding rows. The analysis was completed as for the earlier letters, and thus many ψ pattern-fragments were extended to 3 places, and most χ pattern-fragments to four places.

There were more ambiguities this time than there were before, because of the messages in which the second characters of the ψ pattern-fragments were used in the fourth place, so one or two χ characters, and several ψ characters could not be determined by this analysis. But it was known that the results obtained did not need to be reversed, (by the argument from the qualities of the rows).

The missing characters in the χ pattern-fragments were easily filled in by using the fact that the fragments had to fit together to form a wheel. Thus for example the number of fragments four characters long beginning with ×•× had to be equal to the number of such fragments ending with ×•×.

The same kind of analysis was applied to the first and third impulses, but with less satisfactory results, owing to the fact that not every possible pattern-fragment in the corresponding χ wheels corresponded to an indicator letter. Thus although χ and ψ fragments were obtained it could not be decided whether or not these ψ fragments and the parts of the χ fragments from the second letter onwards ought to be reversed, and the argument that the χ fragments must fit together, (with others) to form a wheel was not so readily applicable.

It was now possible to get further characters of some of the χ fragments, and gradually to build up all possible χ_5 patterns. There were rather less than 10. These were applied in turn to key from two rather corrupt depths, and the May wheels were completed before the month was quite
b over. (This was something new). As the settings for most of the χ_5 indicator letters (and some others) were known with certainty, the setting of the other May messages was comparatively easy.

---

[a] summarize [b] som

(f) June and July, 1942

The wheel patterns for June and July were also broken by the Indicator method. In June no depth was found and the problem was correspondingly more difficult. It was necessary to extend the χ_5 fragments until only one wheel could be formed from them. In July a good depth (yielding several hundred letters of key) was intercepted early in the month. The analysis was completed before 18th July and current traffic was read for the first time. p. 312

(g) Later uses of the method

Refinements of the Indicator Method, whereby the second and fourth impulses were given equal status with the others, and whereby a complete and systematic determination of the wheel patterns was made possible, even when the ψ patterns were initially unknown will not be described here.

It may be noted however that analysis by indicators still proved possible and useful, even when the stereotyped beginnings were replaced by arbitrary padding words as was the case from the middle of August onwards. However, after July, Turing's method for analysing key from true [i] depths was available, and wheel patterns for September and October were actually broken on depths and near depths. The indicator analysis was used only for the breaking of the indicator substitution.

At the end of July work on the Tunny cipher by the Research Section came to an end, and was all taken over by a special "Tunny" Section. Later however the Research Section made another contribution in the shape of the Statistical Method.

[i] Word 'true" handwritten.

p. 313 # 43 TESTERY METHODS 1942–44

i

43A BREAKING TUNNY AUGUST–OCTOBER 1942

The first major job of the newly formed Tunny section (see **14A(b)**) was to break the August wheels. The indicator method described in **42E** was applied and for the first 10 days the traffic responded well, except for the bad corruption caused by exceptionally poor intercept conditions. But from the 11th onwards only a very few messages seemed to produce the stereotyped openings. By working only from those messages which were using the regular and predictable openings progress was made until it became clear that the others opened with German words, — the padding sentences or quatsch which continued as the invariable preliminary to the message text throughout Fish history. It was often possible to predict the next letter of partially obtained words and thus progress was made, using much more material than required in previous months, until a χ_5 had been built up by the time the Germans sent a depth on the 27th.

To meet the introduction of quatsch, research into German plain language in its teleprinter impulse form was carried out, and it was thought that the indicator method was still possible though immensely slow and difficult. But the findings were never put to the test for on September 5th a depth was sent which provided easily enough key to break the wheels on the recently evolved Turing method (see below **43B**). At this stage the position of only one indicator on each wheel was known (that of the depth) whereas the indicator method had enabled a number of indicators to be placed on the wheels as soon as the full patterns were obtained. The initial stage of setting individual messages (for method see **42A**) was therefore more difficult. The last month of the indicator era, October, was broken from a near depth.

43B TURINGERY

The original method of key breaking clearly became useless as soon as the Germans introduced the condition $ab = 1/2$. So research was done by A.M. Turing on the key from which the July wheels had been broken by the indicator-cum-depth method, and a method was evolved which produced the correct wheels. The introduction of QSN's (later QEP's) in November 1942 dealt the death blow to the indicator method and left Turingery as the only known way of breaking wheels.

Turingery introduced the principle that key differenced at one, now called ΔK, could yield
E.1 information unobtainable from ordinary key. This Δ principle was to be the fundamental basis of nearly all statistical methods of wheel-breaking and setting. Many improvements and refinements of technique have since been made enabling very much shorter lengths of key to be broken than the 500 or more required by original Turingery. The technique of modern wheel-breaking from key is given in Ch. **26**. The original method is described here. The description gives a certain amount of rationalisation of the process which could certainly not have been given at the time since the principles involved had not been studied and understood to the extent that they were later.

[i] In the original text of the *Report*, almost all chapters start with an analytical contents list. This one does not. We have accordingly supplied such a list, as a copy editor would have done, for uniformity and the convenience of readers.

The property used throughout is simply $P(\Delta\psi'_{ij} = \bullet) = b$, or, in different terms, $\Delta K_{ij} \underset{b}{\longrightarrow} \Delta\chi_{ij}$.

ΔK is written out in ink on squared paper. The 5 rows of squared paper beneath are regarded as corresponding to the 5 TP impulses and each impulse is marked off with an upright ink line according to the chi length of that impulse. All subsequent work is done in pencil. A letter of ΔK is arbitrarily chosen and assumed to have $\Delta\psi' = /$. On the Tunny machine of the time the psis came in at the second letter and moved on automatically from the second to the third place. So the third place of ΔK was the first possible TM dot. At the assumed $\Delta\psi'/$ position we enter the $\Delta\chi$ letter in impulses ($= \Delta K$ since $\Delta\psi' = /$), and the 5 $\Delta\chi$ signs thus derived are entered on their respective chi-periods throughout the ΔK. These signs are underlined to distinguish them from other $\Delta\chi$ signs deduced from them. Now from every $\Delta\chi$ sign thus entered we can use the property $\Delta K_{ij} \longrightarrow \Delta\chi_{ij}$ to deduce one $\Delta\chi$ sign on each of the other four impulses. For if the underlined $\Delta\chi$ character is on impulse i and gives $\Delta\chi_i = \Delta K_i$, then in accordance with the above property we deduce $\Delta\chi_j = \Delta K_j$, for $j =$ each of the other 4 impulses, thus obtaining 4 fresh $\Delta\chi$ characters which each have probability b, provided that the position originally selected is in fact a TM dot. Similarly if we find $\Delta\chi_i \neq \Delta K_i$ we assume $\Delta\chi$ on the other four impulses to be the opposite of ΔK. These deduced $\Delta\chi$ signs are written into 5 'cages' of width 41, 31, 29, 26 and 23 respectively. Thus all signs deduced for $\Delta\chi_3$ from underlined $\Delta\chi$ signs on impulses 1, 2, 4 and 5 are written out on a width of 29. An example of a $\Delta\chi_3$ cage is given below: p. 314

χ_3 Cage

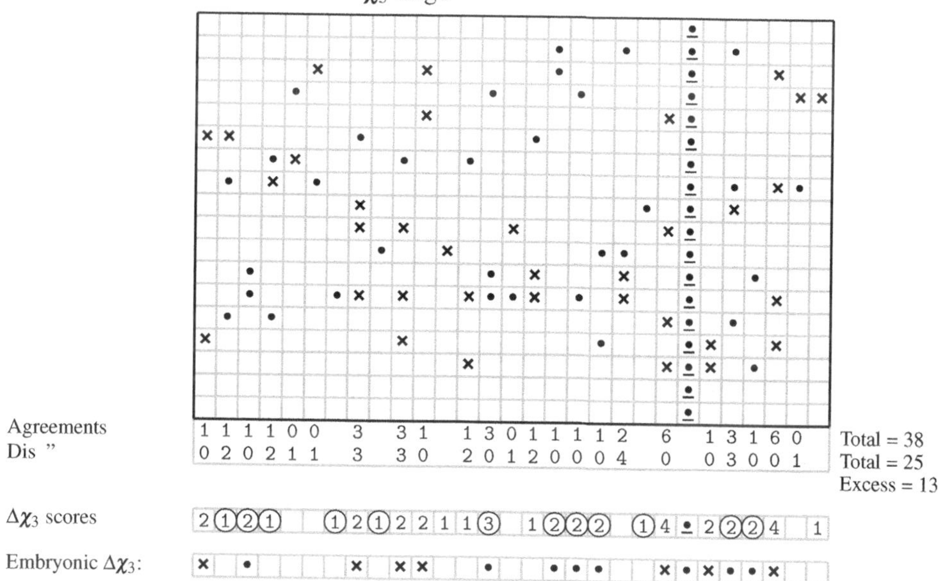

i, E.2

It will be seen that the underlined $\Delta\chi_3$ sign is also written into the cage each time it occurs as a check against inadvertently sliding the cage to the right or left when entering. We now use these 5 cages as a test of the original assumption of a TM dot. For if the original assumption is correct the ratio of agreements to disagreements among the signs in each column of the cage will be $b^2 + \overline{1-b}^2$ to $2b(1-b)$, or $(1+\beta^2)$ to $(1-\beta^2)$. We therefore write the number of agreements and the number of disagreements at the bottom of each column (see fig. (**I**)) and add up the total p. 315 E.3

[i] Illustration redrawn half scale, to fit page width.

excess of agreements over disagreements for all 5 cages. Each excess contributes a factor of $(1+\beta^2)/(1-\beta^2)$ to the theory that the original position has $\Delta\psi' = /$ (or $\Delta\psi' = 8$ which merely makes all our $\Delta\chi$'s inside out). If the result is poor we scrap the cages, erase the workings and take the next ΔK letter as our $\Delta\psi' = /$ assumption. If it is good we accept the original assumption. In that case the cage entries each have a probability b of being correct and can simply be totted up in columns, and written at the bottom as ringed or unringed numbers according to whether they are scores in favour of the particular $\Delta\chi_i$ character being dot or cross (see fig. **(I)**). Accepting scores $\geqslant 2$ we form rudimentary $\Delta\chi$ wheels with which we de-chi the ΔK to give rudimentary $\Delta\psi'$. We examine thus $\Delta\psi'$ to find a character with 3 or more dots, not counting dots generated by an original underlined $\Delta\chi$ sign. This we assume to be another position where $\Delta\psi' = /$, and re-apply the cage test described above. If the proportion of agreements is poor we try another assumed $\Delta\psi'/$. If it is good we derive $\Delta\chi$ scores as before by summing the columns and combine these with the previous scores by straight addition, provided that the agreement between scores is reasonably good. Again taking a standard of $\geqslant 2$ we form 5 embryonic $\Delta\chi$'s from the combined scores, with which we de-chi the ΔK to give embryonic $\Delta\psi'$.

We make a 'count' for $\Delta\chi_5$, which is the shortest wheel and therefore will accumulate the most evidence per character. The system of scoring is as follows. For each $L_{m,n}$ in $\Delta\psi'$ (considering only the other 4 impulses) (where $L_{m,n}$ is a letter with m dots and n crosses) we score $m-n$ for the theory that $\Delta\psi'_5 =$ dot, and that therefore $\Delta\chi_5 = \Delta K_5$ at that place. Thus if the $\Delta\psi'$ letter reads **×?•×** in the first 4 impulses, and the ΔK letter is Q we score ① for $\Delta\chi_5 =$ dot. We write in all these scores throughout the key on a width of 23, and add up the columns to give an improved $\Delta\chi_5$. With this we de-chi ΔK_5 in place of the earlier $\Delta\chi_5$ used, and count for $\Delta\chi_4$. This process continues, going back to $\Delta\chi_5$ after $\Delta\chi_1$, until all the $\Delta\chi$'s are completed. These $\Delta\chi$'s must obviously integrate into legal undifferenced chis, the even or odd number of crosses in the $\Delta\chi$'s will tell us whether the original assumption was a $\Delta\psi'$ / or 8. With the undifferenced chis obtained, from the $\Delta\chi$'s we de-chi the undifferenced K to give ψ', from which we derive the psi wheels by taking out the extensions.

43C THE PRE-NEWMANRY QEP ERA

(a) Introduction of QEP's

i At the end of October, 1942 Tunny was replaced by Codfish (Saloniki–Berlin) and Octopus
p. 316 (see **14A(b)**). Indicators were replaced by the QEP system. This meant a serious reduction in the amount of traffic decoded because we had to rely entirely on depths. Fortunately the Germans sent frequent and sometimes multiple depths — sometimes as many as 10 messages on the same QEP number (or QSN number as it was at first called). Keys were broken from depths as before, but the wheel settings had to be found for each depth broken for a month for which the chi and psi patterns were known. The method for doing this is described below. The motors constructed in the same way as those used in Tunny.

(b) Setting depths with no-limitation motors

The P obtained by anagramming the depth is added to Z to form K. Where it is not possible to determine which P belongs to which Z the second possible K has to be tried if the first fails.

K_5 is written out and de-chied at all 23 possible settings of χ_5 to give 23 possible versions of ψ'_5. This process is called 'making a drag'. The problem is to find the true ψ'_5. The majority can be discarded immediately because it can be seen at once that they cannot fit the known ψ_5's whatever extensions are assumed. This process is greatly helped by the fact that the Tunny type μ_{61} and μ_{37} only have singleton dots and therefore cannot give more than two consecutive dots in
ii TM. The remaining candidates are examined by reference to another impulse in the following

---

[i] Word struck out after 'Saloniki–Berlin'.

[ii] Typed line ends 'The remaining c'; following line begins 'candidates are. . . '.

manner.

For each assumed ψ_5' pattern, all TM dots which have to be assumed for the pattern to fit ψ_5 are marked. At each of these places we know that $\Delta K = \Delta\chi$. So at all χ_4 settings which satisfy this condition we de-chi K_4 and examine the resultant possible ψ_4''s. Unless the key is very short (the length normally used is from 14 to 30) the correct χ_4 setting based on the correct χ_5 setting will yield a ψ_4' pattern which when contracted by using the assumed TM dots will fit on the known ψ_4. We then do the same for ψ_3 and so on until all psis and chis are set. It remains to anagram by using the known psis and chis sufficient to break (or, if the motor patterns are known, to set) the motors.

(c) Advances in Key-breaking

Recognising the psi repeat and numbering, were devised in the winter of 1942 and were never discarded (see **26D**.) a

(d) Setting depths on $\overline{\chi}_2$ limitation

The $\overline{\chi}_2$ limitation first appeared in February, 1943. The number of dots in μ_{37} was doubled to give the same proportion of dots in TM as before. The $\overline{\chi}_2$ limitation necessitated changes in setting and motor working and caused some changes in Key-breaking methods.

The method of setting depths on $\overline{\chi}_2$ limitation is essentially the same as with the "No-limitation" motor. But the drag is made on K_2 instead of K_5 and use is made of the fact that for each setting of χ_2 used, we know where the compulsory crosses in TM fall and therefore we know where we are *not* permitted to assume extensions when trying to fit possible ψ_2' on to ψ_2. On the other hand we no longer have the useful feature of the old type motor, which precludes more than two consecutive TM dots.

(e) The effect of $\overline{\chi}_2$ limitation on key-breaking p. 317

Turing's original method had already been modified in two respects (see above **(c)**). With the introduction of $\overline{\chi}_2$ limitation a certain amount of use was at once made of this new feature in key-breaking, though it was realised at the time that it should be possible to make very much i greater use of it. The powerful methods for using $\overline{\chi}_2$ which were finally perfected in early 1945 are described in **26**. At the time, however, use was only made of the limitation to obtain χ_2 after one other chi had been obtained and the psi repeat recognised. This was done by examining the TM deduced from the ψ' already obtained, when written on a width of 31. All TM dots imply $\overline{\chi}_2 = \times$ and columns where no dots appear are extremely likely to correspond to a $\overline{\chi}_2$ dot. This allows us to infer most of $\overline{\chi}_2$ which is then slid one to the left so that it becomes χ_2 and is then compared with the $\Delta\chi_2$ values obtained from the last Turingery count for $\Delta\chi_2$ to have been made. The combination of the two should give a complete χ_2 which is then added to K_2 to give ψ_2'. This ψ_2' combined with the use of the known $\overline{\chi}_2$ should place most, if not all, of the TM dots whose position is ambiguous.

The disadvantage of the new modification was that recognising the psi repeat was made much more difficult because the old rule disallowing more than 2 consecutive TM dots no longer held.

(f) A new feature

In the early months of the QEP era a new feature appeared. Messages no longer invariably began and ended with the beginning and ending of transmissions, nor did transmissions beginning in the middle of messages start with "Zwoter (etc) Teil… ". No serious difficulties were caused, E.4, b apart from the greater difficulty of breaking depths, and later de-chis, because we could no longer rely on the starts of transmissions containing stereotyped message beginnings, though a fair proportion still did.

---

[a] (See **26D**) [b] teil . . .

[i] Word 'key-' of 'key-breaking' handwritten.

(g) The Herring link and the first appearance of $\overline{\chi}_2\overline{\overline{P}}_5$ limitation

The Rome–Tunis link known as Herring operated between December, 1942 and the final collapse of the German forces in Tunisia in May, 1943. It was on this link that both the $\overline{\chi}_2$ and $\overline{\chi}_2\overline{\overline{P}}_5$ limitations first appeared. The method by which the $\overline{\chi}_2\overline{\overline{P}}_5$ limitation was analysed and its method of working understood is described in Ch. **44**. The $\overline{\chi}_2\overline{\overline{P}}_5$ limitation effectively prevents messages being in depth even when the initial settings are the same owing to the divergence of the two ψ''s under the influence of the different P_5's. Thus work on Herring was made impossible, until the operational difficulties of passing a great quantity of traffic under pressure using the new P_5 attachment proved too great (a single fifth impulse corruption in reception would cause a breakdown, necessitating a complete retransmission) and the attachment was abandoned — (to reappear on nearly all links in December, 1943). From then on the Germans sent an enormous quantity of traffic; the majority was sent in depth (often multiple depth), presumably because they could hardly spare the time to reset their machines. The effort and production of the Testery reached an unprecedented peak, at a time when the messages broken were of great operational importance. In May the section decoded over 1,400,000 letters, a figure which was not equalled until March, 1944, when the Newmanry was in full swing.

p. 318 43D THE FOUNDATION OF THE NEWMANRY AND AFTER

(a) Early days

In July, 1943 Mr Newman formed his section, to set messages not sent in depth, by mechanical and statistical methods. Since the introduction of QEP's these messages had not been touched. For the first few months the Newmanry was struggling to put its work on an operational basis. The Testery occasionally helped them by hand-breaking messages set on χ's $_{124}$ and $_5$ and the motor. A print-out of D_{1245} was provided with TM printed above. A break was obtained opposite a run of dots in the TM and then extending the break both ways with the aid of nearby TM dots until sufficient had been read to set ψ's $_{124}$ and $_5$ uniquely. χ_3 and ψ_3 were set as in setting on a length of K, described above (**43C(b)** and (**d**)). K is produced by adding Z to the P obtained, and since all the TM dots are known it is a simple matter to find the setting of χ_3 which gives $\Delta\chi_3 = \Delta K_3$ at all TM dots, and then to add at the correct setting to K_3 to give ψ_3'.

(b) Further advances in key-breaking

(i) Accurate scoring

In the summer of 1943 the Germans reduced the number of dots in the Bream μ_{37} from 22 to 16. This made key-breaking by Turing's original scoring system extremely slow and difficult, and stimulated the first attempt to make key-breaking scoring more accurate. Accurate scoring in its final form is described in **26C**.

(ii) Δ^2 properties

The next discovery to have an effect on key-breaking techniques was made in September, 1943 (see **R0**, pp. 53, 54). It was that $\Delta^2\chi \longrightarrow \times$ with probability about 2/3. Unlike the property
E.5 $\Delta\psi \longrightarrow \times$ the new property was found to lack rigidity. The way in which it is applied is described in **26B(d)**.

(iii) The discovery of $\widehat{\chi}_2$ (see 26B(b))

a The discovery of $\widehat{\chi}_2$ was made on Squid for November, 1943, for which 880 letters of key had been obtained from depth. It had 22 dots in μ_{37} and $\overline{\chi}_2$ limitation. The discovery had far-reaching repercussions. Its ultimate effect on key-breaking is described in (**26B(b)**), and on chi-breaking from Z in (**25E**). It led directly to the breaking of wheels from cribs. (See **27G**.) And lastly the level of significance of the $\widehat{\chi}_2$ count or run proved an invaluable test as to (i) whether a given key

[a] 880 key

was on $\overline{\chi}_2$ limitation or not and (ii) in the case of certainty of $\overline{\chi}_2$ limitation a priori, but ambiguous key (see **28A(e)**), which of the two alternative keys was the true one.

(iv) Key-breaking rationalised

In the autumn of 1944 the $\overline{\chi}_2\overline{\overline{P}}_5$ limitation began to be dropped on Western links, and, since we were now in the era of daily change, (see above **(f)**) breaking wheels from depth once more came into prominence. The accurate scoring formulae devised in the summer of 1943 on the basis of 16 dots in μ_{37} (see above **(b)**(i)) were dug up and recalculated on the basis of $18\frac{1}{2}$ dots in μ_{37} (see **26CY(d)**) as being nearer to the average expected dottage and also as giving convenient values for a and b ($a = 3/4$, $b = 2/3$). The test for the sign of the key (see **26C**) and the 5 by 5 flag (see **26B(a)**) were devised, and the Newmanry at the same time invented the powerful χ_5 composite flag (see **26B(c)**). The immediate result of this work was that the length of key and the p. 319
length of time thought necessary to break the wheels were divided by about 2 and 4 respectively.

At the same time research on key-breaking for $\overline{\chi}_2$ limitation was begun, and after some months of evolution the method reached its final form as described in **26B(b)**, **26E**.

(c) The first de-chis

When the $\overline{\chi}_2\overline{\overline{P}}_5$ limitation was reintroduced in mid-December, 1943 it was no longer possible with the equipment of that time to set the motors and psis mechanically, and at the same time the main source of decodes and the whole source of employment for the Testery, dried up, since depths could no longer occur. So the Testery had to master the art of setting the psis by hand from the de-chis prepared by the Newmanry, and this became their main job. But, more important, the month's wheel patterns could no longer be broken from depth, and the task of breaking the wheels from Z had to be attempted. The Bream chis for January, 1944 were broken within the first fortnight with the comparatively primitive equipment of the time — Colossus 1 (see **52(e)**) a
was not yet in action. Two messages on the same QEP were set on the chis and de-chied. From these two de-chis, by the method of applying the psis obtained from a break in one to the other de-chi (see **28C(a)**) the psi patterns were obtained within an hour. The μ_{37} proved to have 26 dots which helps to explain this remarkably short time.

The breaking of the February Bream chis was greatly helped by the use of Colossus 1. No b
pairs of messages on the same QEP were available, and attempts by the Testery to break the psis from the de-chis sent over were at first fruitless. Finally however the psis were broken with great difficulty and effort from one de-chi. The μ_{37} dottage proved to be only 19, which explained the difficulty encountered. It was now evident that the problem of the $\overline{\chi}_2\overline{\overline{P}}_5$ limitation had been mastered in both sections. A detailed account of psi-breaking from de-chi is given in **28C**.

(d) The $\overline{\chi}_2\overline{\Psi}'_1\overline{\overline{P}}_5$ limitation

This triple limitation first appeared in June, 1944 on Codfish and Gurnard. Its action is described in **11B(g)**(iv); its stay was brief as in December, 1944 the Germans began taking the $\overline{\overline{P}}_5$ component out of the limitation on the various links; thus it gave rise to the $\overline{\chi}_2\overline{\Psi}'_1$ limitation (see **11B(g)**(ii), **11B(h)**), which became the standard limitation on the majority of links, the remainder reverting to the old $\overline{\chi}_2$ limitation. It did not cause any new difficulties apart from slightly complicating the process of de-chi breaking.

(e) Daily Change

The introduction of daily change of all wheel patterns in the summer of 1944 meant that the time and energy previously expended to release a whole month's traffic for setting now only released one day's traffic. The emphasis in the Testery as well as the Newmanry changed from wheelsetting to the much more difficult job of wheel-breaking. But the concerted efforts of both c
sections met with such success that the production figures for August, 1944, the first month with

[a] Colossus I [b] Colossus I [c] wheelbreaking

daily change on all links, was higher than ever before, and the figures continued to rise steadily month after month.

44 HAND STATISTICAL METHODS p. 320

i

44A INTRODUCTION OF THE QEP (QSN) SYSTEM

(a) Codfish and Octopus

At the end of October, 1942, there was a complete change in the nature of the Tunny traffic. The Tunny link itself closed down, and it was for a time supposed that the Germans had abandoned the "Tunny" cipher machine. Two other teleprinter links (called Codfish and Octopus) came into operation at this time, and it was shown, by the analysis of depths of three that both these links were using the "Tunny" machine. These links did not transmit twelve letter indicators, but only a "QSN" number (QSN was later replaced by QEP). Messages having the same QSN number on the same day and belonging to the same link were, it was found, in depth.

(b) Depths

Messages were soon being sent in greater numbers than ever, but now only those messages which were in depth with others could be read. So during the first half of the year 1943, the Tunny Section confined itself to the reading of depths.

Fortunately the German operators began to send depths in great profusion, and so on many links it was still possible to read a fairly large fraction of the traffic. (From this time on, many new links were coming into operation, or were being discovered.)

Codfish was one of the links which gave a large proportion of depths. Depths of more than a dozen messages were not unknown on this link. Octopus depths were much rarer.

(c) The New Cryptographic Problem

It was found that each link had its own set of wheel patterns, that χ and ψ patterns were changed monthly, and that motor wheel patterns were still changed daily. Here there was one difference from the old Tunny link, for which it had been demonstrated that the ψ patterns were changed only quarterly.

The Germans could not be relied upon to continue to send such a proportion of depths, and in any case the single messages presented an urgent problem. The wheel patterns for a link could be obtained from the depths but there seemed to be no way by which single messages could be set on these patterns.

It was clear that single messages had now to be considered in isolation, for it was no longer possible to relate them to one another by means of their indicators, as in the method of analysis described in **42E**. Had there been reliable cribs, the method of message-setting described in Section VI could have been employed, but the Germans had now taken precautions against the E.1
use of stereotyped beginnings, the chief precaution being the use of padding words. Sometimes a fairly reliable crib for a link would be found, but positions of the crib in the message was then so variable that the method was still not practicable.

The only hope left was that it might be possible to set messages by using the statistical p. 321
properties of the plain language, or extended psi-stream.

[i] In the original text of the *Report*, almost all chapters start with an analytical contents list. This one does not. We have accordingly supplied such a list, as a copy editor would have done, for uniformity and the convenience of readers.

44B SETTING — STATISTICAL METHODS

(a) First ideas — *P* characteristics

An attempt was made early in 1942 to set χ_5 and ψ_5 for a message by using the observed fact that dots predominated markedly over crosses in the fifth impulse of ordinary Tunny plain language. This was not successful but the possibility of using this effect was again investigated. The chief difficulty was the irregular movement of the ψ wheels, but it was hoped that the ψ' key could be approximated to sufficiently closely by using a standard motor key instead of the unknown true motor key. The theoretical investigation showed that success might just be possible with $ab \neq 1/2$ but that no success could be expected with $ab = 1/2$. The reason for this was closely connected with the predominance of changes in the ψ pattern: when the assumed setting of a ψ wheel was one place off the true setting, the resulting sign in the assumed ψ' key was more likely to be wrong than right.

(b) $\Delta\psi'$ characteristics

In another investigation, no attempt was made to use the periodicity of the unextended ψ impulses but an attempt was made to derive a statistical method from a consideration of the other non-random properties of the ψ' key. These are:

(i) All five ψ wheels have the same movement

and (ii) In the unextended ψ impulses, changes are much more frequent than continuation.

These properties, it was thought, could best be expressed in terms not of the actual ψ' key, but of its first difference, which we denote by $\Delta\psi'$. Changes and continuation in ψ' are represented by crosses and dots respectively in $\Delta\psi'$.

At this time, as in March and April, 1942, the Germans always arranged that $ab \fallingdotseq 1/2$, so that dots and crosses were equally frequent in each impulse of $\Delta\psi'$. Hence no statistical method could be founded, it was thought, on the statistical properties of $\Delta\psi'$.

But suppose, it was argued, that two impulses of the $\Delta\psi'$ key, say the first and second, are added together. The resulting sequence $\Delta\psi'_1 + \Delta\psi'_2$ will have a dot in each position corresponding to a dot in the motor key, and in the positions corresponding to crosses in the motor key, the proportion of dots will be $b^2 + (1-b)^2$, and the proportion of crosses $2b(1-b)$, if, as an approximation we take the same value of b for each impulse. But then the proportion of crosses in the entire sequence will be

$$2ab(1-b) = 1-b$$

and therefore the proportion of dots in the sum of any two impulses of $\Delta\psi'$ will be equal to b and about 70%

It was deduced that the first step in any statistical method of wheel setting should be the differencing of the cipher text and the addition of two impulses of the resulting stream of letters.

p. 322 All now depended on the properties of $\Delta P_1 + \Delta P_2$. Counts were made on the clear texts of some Octopus messages, and the value ·63 was derived for the proportion of dots in $\Delta P_1 + \Delta P_2$ averaged over these messages. This effect seemed to be due, largely to the high proportion of
E.2 double letters in Octopus clear, in which long drawn out punctuation signs such as `+++MAA8889` were used.

It followed that, for the sample taken,

$$P(\Delta D_{12} = \bullet) = \cdot 55$$

and that this property of D was sufficiently marked for it to have been possible uniquely to determine the χ_1 and χ_2 settings for one of the Octopus messages whose P had been counted.

(c) Chis set successfully

An attempt was then made to set an unbroken message by this new method of the "1+2 Break In". A systematic method of testing the 1271 possible $\Delta\chi_1 + \Delta\chi_2$ settings had to be devised. The sequence $\Delta\chi_2$ was added to $\Delta Z_1 + \Delta Z_2$ in an arbitrary setting, the numbers of dots and crosses in $\Delta Z_1 + \Delta Z_2 + \Delta\chi_2$ corresponding to each position in the 41 period were tabulated and then this table was compared with each setting of $\Delta\chi_1$. This process was carried out for every setting of $\Delta\chi_2$. It was found convenient for this process to write $\Delta Z_1 + \Delta Z_2$ diagonally into a rectangle, of sides 31 and 41.

A message of length about 4000 letters, which did not belong to a depth, was taken, and a significant result was obtained for the first two impulses. The same process was then applied to some other pairs of impulses and by combining the best results for all these pairs, the other three χ wheels were set. For later messages it was found sufficient, after χ_1 and χ_2 had been set to work only on pairs of impulses for which the setting of one χ wheel was known. The settings of the other χ wheels would then be comparatively simple with good messages.

(d) Motors and Psis set

When all the χ wheels of the first message had been set, the χ key was added to the cipher text, and the sequence $D = Z + \chi$, obtained. This sequence was found to have more than twice the random number of double letters. This was presumably because both P and ψ' contained a high proportion of double letters. But nearly all the double letters in the extended ψ key would correspond to motor dots and therefore most of the double letters in the de-chi would correspond to motor dots.

It was found that, by an analysis of the distribution of the probable motor dots the patterns of both motor wheels could be derived. The method used was analogous to that later used for motor a
breaking on machines with limitation, and described in Ch. **28**.

A controversy broke out in the Research Section over the problem of the best method of continuing the analysis from this point. Some held that the ψ wheels should be set statistically, by striking out from the de-chi all letters corresponding to extensions of the ψ-key and then setting the ψ wheels on the 'contracted de-chi' just as the $\Delta\chi$ wheels had been set on the differenced cipher message. Others held that attempts should be made to guess the clear at some point of the de-chi, and thus to obtain a short stretch of extended ψ key, on which the wheels could easily be set. The best way to do this, they said, was to consider a place where there were two consecutive dots, in the motor key. (There were never more than two consecutive dots in the motor keys p. 323
of those days). For in such a place, three consecutive letters of the extended ψ key would be identical, and there would be only 32 possibilities for corresponding trigram of the plain language.

In the case of the first message, the ψ wheels were set by means of the second method, but the first method was also used successfully later on.

(e) Foundation of Newmanry

When two or three messages had been set by the statistical method, it was seen that new machinery, and a new section to operate it, was needed, for the hand methods took far too long to be of much practical use. Mr Newman was put in charge of developments and his section came b
into operation later in the year. This section set the χ wheels of their messages essentially by the method described above at first, but carried out its processes mechanically. The technique of using only runs of form $i+j$ was soon improved upon (see **23** or Part I). E.3

(f) Statistical Chi-breaking

Statistical methods were carried further by the Research Section early in 1943 when an example of chi-breaking from rectangles was carried out. 'Wheel-breaking' in the sense of chapter

[a] analagous [b] developements

25 was not used — in fact the message was so favourable that all the chis were obtained from three rectangles, namely ΔZ_{12}, ΔZ_{13} and ΔZ_{45}. The motor was obtained statistically.

Further investigation into Rectangling and other statistical chi-breaking methods was carried out by the Newmanry, but it was only after the general introduction of autoclave in Dec. 1943 that these methods were used operationally.

No statistical method for motor-breaking (with limitation) was developed by the Research Section.

44C INTRODUCTION OF P_5 LIMITATION

The autoclave was first used on a single link in March 1943, before the Newmanry came into operation, but it was abandoned and was not used again until December. The analysis of messages showing the autoclave effect was one of the triumphs of the hand methods of statistical analysis.

The first sign that a new device was being used was the sending of a number of pairs of messages on the 'Herring' link the members of each pair having the same QSN number. These pairs should therefore have been depths, but attempts to break them in the usual way all failed. Fortunately this happened in the middle of the month, so the messages were expected to be using the same wheel patterns as the earlier messages of that month, some of which had been broken. One of the messages in the unbreakable 'depths' was about 6,000 letters long, so the statistical method for setting χ wheels was applied to it. The method was completely successful. The de-chi was obtained and investigated. One passage of this de-chi contained so many repeated letters that it looked like an extended ψ key. The passage was

```
Z 3 D D D D V V N A A F G O O E 8 / / / K H R R R
Q Q Q C C C C 3 8 S S W M .
```

p. 324 It was assumed therefore that in the underlying clear language the same clear letter was being repeated over and over again. If this hypothesis were correct, each separate impulse of the passage would either agree with, or else be the complete reverse of, the corresponding impulse of the extended ψ key.

The hypothesis was tested by comparing the actual ψ wheels with the various impulses. It was found that complete agreement could be secured by taking the underlying clear language to consist of a long sequence of Z's followed by a long sequence of 9's. The ψ wheels were thus set and the motor key could now be derived by decoding the message.

This was the first example of hand psi-setting from a de-chi with an unknown motor key, but the de-chi was an exceptionally easy one.

The decoding process was applied to both messages of the 'depth' on the assumption, soon verified, that the initial settings of the wheels were the same for both messages. The two motor keys were different however, and the difference could only be explained on the assumption that the motor key was a function of the clear language, or cipher, as well as of the initial state of the machine.

The nature of the plain language effect was deduced by studying the actual plain language near the places in which the two motor keys differed. It was found that when they differed, there was always a difference in the two clear texts two letters back, in the fifth impulse.

Further investigation revealed that when there was a difference in the motor key, the motor sign in each message was given by the sum of the fifth impulse of the plain language two places back (denoted by $\overline{\overline{P}}_5$) and the second χ sign of one place back (denoted by $\overline{\chi}_2$). This suggested that the total motor key was obtained from the Basic Motor in conjunction with the limitation ($\overline{\overline{P}}_5 + \overline{\chi}_2$). This 'basic motor' could be determined whenever $\overline{\overline{P}}_5 + \overline{\chi}_2$ had the value cross. The fragmentary basic motor was written out on a width of 61 and broken by the methods already devised by the Testery for dealing with motors having the $\overline{\chi}_2$ limitation.

51 INTRODUCTORY p. 325

(a) Character of chapters 51–58

This is a strictly functional and non-technical account of the machines used. A technical account is to be prepared by the post office engineers. E.1

Some attempt is made to avoid statements technically false, but none to avoid statements technically vague.

(b) Terminology

The terminology is that of the layman and cryptographer: for example a switch means a lever to be pushed up and down, or a knob to be rotated. As in other parts of the report, an impulse means one of the five streams of which teleprinter letters are composed, but when the meaning is clear from the context, impulse is also to mean electrical impulse; otherwise called pulse to avoid ambiguity.

(c) Scope of the chapters

Such history as is included is a description of development and lacks chronology.

Colossus and Robinson receive detailed treatment, for in large measure it is the use of these machines which gives Tunny-breaking its distinctive character.

Copying machines are indispensable but less distinctive, and are treated less fully.

The specialized counting machines, Dragon, Aquarius, Proteus are treated rather sketchily because being specialized most of their functions are adequately dealt with in the description of their applications.

(d) Relative importance of machines

The pre-eminence of Colossus and Robinson is manifest.

The need for a "Tunny" machine to decode messages, or, as an intermediate step towards decoding, to de-chi them, is obvious.

The need for efficiency in other copying machines is apt to be overlooked; one of them, Miles, was in fact unduly neglected: in particular the production models of Miles A were vetoed. The supply of spare parts for readers and reperforators generally has been inadequate. The hand counter is very simple and quite indispensable: a long time elapsed before a reliable one was produced. The amount of Colossus time wasted because tapes were delayed or incorrect is difficult to estimate but it is certainly very considerable.

(e) Electronic counters etc

As a matter of general interest it may be mentioned that on the existing counting and stepping [i] machines, counting is in the scale of 10 (strictly, in alternate scales of 2 and 5) and is purely p. 326 electronic: auxiliary circuits which can operate more slowly however, use also mechanical relays and uniselector switches.

The earlier Robinsons counted in four electronic scales of 2, followed by four mechanical relay scales of 5.

Colossus 1 counted electronically, in three scales of 2 followed by four scales of 5.

Copying machines, whose speed per letter is much less, generally employ mechanical relays, but Miles A is largely electronic and Tunny and the decoding machines use a few valves.

---

[i] Handwritten 'existing' inserted with a caret.

(f) Use of standard components

a Many features recognised as desirable in Tunny-breaking machinery were not incorporated because they require equipment which was either non-standard or not readily obtainable, e.g.
b six-impulse tape. Indeed it is a recognised principle that a machine which can be assembled from standard parts, even though more complex, is preferable to a machine requiring special parts. This is due in part to availability, in part to the probability that the special parts will not work properly. This is one advantage of electronic equipment: the amazingly reliable counters of Colossus are of novel design but do not need special parts, being made from standard valves and other standard equipment.

(g) Note on the source of machines

All machines were provided by the Post Office Engineers except the counters of Heath Robinson, and some copying machines due to TRE. The maintenance of the TRE machines by P.O. Engineers was never officially authorized, a most unsatisfactory state of affairs, in consequence of which, despite their relatively simple character, they are less reliable than Colossus.

(h) Readers and Reperforators

There is one example of technical vagueness in this account of which warning must be given. The five impulses which constitute a teleprinter letter are transmitted over distances successively, not simultaneously, for otherwise five separate wires or other carriers would be required. Within a terminal office, however, there is no objection to the use of five wires; in some tape readers and reperforators the five impulses appear simultaneously, in others successively. Both types are used for Tunny cryptography, though for this purpose successive impulse apparatus has no advantage except availability: it is clearly much easier to add and permute simultaneous impulses.

The hand perforator, the Insert machine, Junior, Garbo, and the punch of Colossus 6 use simultaneous impulses.

c Angel, Tunny, and the decoding machine use successive impulses.

Miles (including Miles A) reads the five impulses simultaneously but perforates them successively.

Readers which produce five successive impulses are supposed to be called auto-transmitters.

Reperforators which punch five impulses simultaneously are supposed to be called punches.

p. 327 (i) Typewriters

Similarly "typewriter" and "printer" are used indifferently for various types of electric typewriters, regenerative and non-regenerative.

(j) Impressions of Colossus

It is regretted that it is not possible to give an adequate idea of the fascination of a Colossus at work: its sheer bulk and apparent complexity; the fantastic speed of thin paper tape round the glittering pulleys; the childish pleasure of not-not, span, print main heading and other gadgets; the wizardry of purely mechanical decoding letter by letter (one novice thought she was being hoaxed); the uncanny action of the typewriter in printing the correct scores without and beyond human aid; the stepping of display; periods of eager expectation culminating in the sudden appearance of the longed-for score; and the strange rhythms characterizing every type of run: the stately break-in, the erratic short run, the regularity of wheel-breaking, the stolid rectangle interrupted by the wild leaps of the carriage-return, the frantic chatter of a motor run, even the ludicrous frenzy of hosts of bogus scores.

Perhaps some Tunny-breaking poet could do justice to this theme; but although an ode to Colossus and various fragments appeared, all seemed to have been composed in times of distress and despondency, and consist almost wholly of imprecation or commination.

---

[a] recognized [b] recognized [c] succesive

(k) Number of machines in use E.2

	MAY 1943	MAY 1945				NOTES
		BLOCK F	BLOCK H	TESTERY	TOTAL	
Robinsons	1		2		2	+ 2 nearly complete
Colossi		4	6		10	
Dragons				2	2	+ 1 under construction
Proteus				—	—	+ 1 under construction
Aquarius				1	1	On test
Decoding machines	5			13	13	
Tunnies	1	3			3	
Miles			3		3	
Garbos			3		3	
Juniors		4			4	
Insert Machines		1	1		2	
Angels		2	2		4	
Hand Perforators		1	1		2	
Hand Counters		4	2		6	
Stickers (Hot)	3		3		3	
Stickers (cold)		3	3		6	

p. 328

52 DEVELOPMENT OF ROBINSON AND COLOSSUS

(a) Introductory

Some of the paragraphs in this chapter will not be fully intelligible without reference to the two chapters which follow: **53**, **54**.

A brief description of the two machines has already been given (**15(b)**). The essential difference between them is that on Robinson all streams of letters are on tapes. On Colossus only Z is on a tape, the wheels being set up electrically.

(b) Heath Robinson

In the experimental stages of Tunny-breaking, though other forms of machine were considered, it was inevitable that one using Robinson principles should be chosen because

α it is easy to make.

β it can be adapted to any wheel length by preparing suitable tapes.

The original Heath Robinson was effective, despite what now seem intolerable handicaps:

(i) There was at first no printer: the operators (two in number) had to write down the fleeting figures on display: this was a fruitful source of error.

(ii) The distance between the gate where the tape was scanned and the sprocket-wheel which drove it was six inches, so that the stretching of tapes alone was sufficient to put tapes out of alignment.

(iii) The position counter recorded, not the relative position of the two tapes, but the number of revolutions completed: from this the relative position can be found but with great risk of erroneous calculation.

(iv) Heath Robinson would not tolerate long stretches of dots or of crosses, so that elaborate tapes, with additional opportunities for making mistakes had to be devised to avoid this.

(v) The minimum text length was 2000. If it was less, rubbish had to be inserted in such a way that it was not counted.

(vi) There was no spanning.

a (vii) The forms of imposable conditions were severely limited.

(viii) The counters were only partly electronic.

(ix) At first Heath Robinson was unable to obtain results, even if not itself at fault, because the tapes, not being subject to a proper system of checks, were incorrectly made.

As a direct result of experience with Heath Robinson all the improvements needed to remedy these defects (except spanning, whose value was overlooked till later) were incorporated by stages in Old Robinson and Super Robinson, and incorporated at the outset in Colossus.

---

[a] impos-able

(c) Old Robinson (Figs. **58** I,II)

The old Robinson, which followed Heath Robinson, had a special Gifford printer, which should have been far superior to the ordinary typewriter, for it printed all eight digits at once: in fact it caused endless trouble, and its records were barely legible. The counters were much p. 329 the same as before. The restrictions on strings of dots or crosses and on minimum text length remained.

(d) The basic weakness of Robinson

The disadvantages of Heath Robinson listed above were later overcome, but there is one which is inherent in the Robinson principle, namely, that a pattern cannot be "extended", in particular, in psi-setting, because the psi pattern could not be extended, it was necessary to "contract" the de-chi, i.e. letters opposite a total motor dot were omitted. This wasted evidence, but was quite feasible with no limitation or $\overline{\chi}_2$ limitation.

A related functional disadvantage is that stepping is necessarily uniform, so that to set wheels arbitrarily is extremely laborious: moreover when a wheel which has been stepping, is to remain at a fixed setting, its tape must be replaced by one of different length.

(e) Colossus 1

The flexibility of Heath Robinson for experimental purposes made it easy to discover the essential requirements of a Tunny-breaking machine. As a result, Colossus 1, the original experimental model, really lacked surprisingly little for a first model. The choice of runs, though more extensive than on Robinson, was less extensive than Heath Robinson had shown to be [a] desirable: it was biassed towards runs of the form $i + j = \bullet$: these could be done by switching except in the fifth counter. Most other runs required plugging, though there was a single set of five dot and cross switches for "all counters". There were five counters, two pairs of which could be used independently for double testing on χ_1, but for this it was necessary to set up the same wheel [b] twice with a stagger of one. Operation was not very simple because of the lack of symmetry, accentuated by changes introduced without correcting the "signwriting" on the machine. There was no spanning and only a single bedstead.

(f) Colossus 2 and later

Experience gained from the development of Colossus 1 added to that from Heath Robinson, [i] made possible Colossus 2, the prototype of all later Colossi, in a form which needed very little modification.

Colossus 2 possessed from the first, quintuple testing, a generous switch-panel (including [ii] not-not), a versatile plug-panel, spanning, a double bedstead, and a greatly increased simplicity of operation.

Spanning was introduced originally for P_5 limitation, but was soon found indispensable for all [c] setting.

The chief modifications introduced later were the rectangling gadgets, devices to reduce the effect of doubtful cipher letters, and devices to make wheel-breaking easier.

(g) The rectangling gadgets p. 330

These were added shortly after Colossus 2 came into use, and afterwards fitted, with technical modifications, to several Colossi. Score meters were added later; Colossus 6 has some special gadgets for key rectangles.

Colossus rectangling has been slightly disappointing; although the rectangle is produced in [iii]

[a] had show to [b] this is was [c] P5

[i] Handwritten 'e' inserted with caret in 'development'.
[ii] Word 'switch' in 'switch-panel' handwritten.
[iii] Word 'slightly' handwritten.

the required form, it has been found necessary to copy it onto squared paper for convergence; as a single operation it cannot be used with "not 99".

a **(h) The use of Colossus for wheel-breaking: not 99**

Colossus was designed for chi and psi setting, not for breaking. The first attempts to use it for chi-breaking consisted of setting up some provisional wheels and changing the characters one by one: if the score improved the character remained changed, otherwise it reverted. It was soon
b realised that this was equivalent to the more rapid process of putting only one cross in a trigger, and stepping it, thus in effect using the trigger to select the characters of the wheel one by one. Essentially the same method had already been used on Robinson.

c, i That Colossus (including Colossus 1) should prove suitable for wheel-breaking justified the policy of making it as flexible as possible, but immediately demanded further improvements.

(i) Longer bedsteads, because breaking requires longer texts than setting.

(ii) Uncertain letters replaced by 9's are a nuisance in chi-setting and breaking from cipher, even if there is no slide, but it is in chi-breaking from depth key, where missing letters are a substantial part of the text that the problem becomes acute. It was found necessary to use the Q panel for the condition $Z \neq 9$, there being no "not" facility on the plug-board, and plugging all runs, which was intolerably tedious.
In consequence "not 9" was fitted, a device which imposed $Z \neq 9$, but this lost all genuine 9's also (about $1/17$ of the text after differencing), and was replaced by "not 99".

(iii) Multiple testing on doubted wheels is obviously of great value when setting long messages during wheel-breaking.

(iv) Intolerable delays and mistakes during wheel-breaking were caused by the need for setting up pins at the back of Colossus and complaints finally extorted the wheel-breaking panel on the front of some machines.

(i) Objections to specialized gadgets

The clamour for specialized gadgets continues: the objection to it is the difficulty of maintaining Colossi unless they are all alike: a device worth fitting to all Colossi is much more welcome.

(j) Super-Robinson

Colossus soon replaced Robinson for setting and breaking, but Robinson remained indispens-
p. 331 able for crib runs in which two tapes (derived from Z and P), must be compared in all positions. A successful crib run usually produced key of such length that wheel-breaking was extremely easy. For this reason four Super-Robinsons were ordered to overcome some of the handicaps which persisted on Old Robinson, and to include spanning whose value had been proved on Colossus.

(k) Suggestions for a Super-Colossus

Many suggestions are made in **R4**, pp. 124–125: fundamental, trivial or even frivolous.

Perhaps the most obvious development is the logical completion of devices to deal with corruption, including spanning, on two or more stretches, slide-correction without doctoring tapes, and not 99 for all purposes including rectangling.

The difficulty of not 99 in rectangling is that the most straightforward (though not the only) method demands the subtraction of a variable number. The most satisfactory scheme would be a general facility so that, on the same counter, some letters score positively and others negatively.

---

[a] The use Of Colossus [b] realized [c] wheel breaking

[i] Handwritten 'should prove . . . breaking' inserted with a caret.

A generalization would be that scores from different runs could be added, each multiplied by an arbitrary constant either positive or negative. Given either, wheel-breaking would require no immediate simplification.

A small improvement would be the setting up of wheels by means of punched cards.

(l) Suggestions for Robinson

The most pressing needs are not 99 and a longer bedstead, but the latter is a difficult mechanical problem. Multiple testing and a much larger plugboard and switchboard are desirable.

(m) Synthesis of Robinson and Colossus

There have been various suggestions for a combined Robinson-Colossus in which all patterns are set up electrically, being of adjustable and in many cases, very considerable length. These could be set up from a tape (as on Aquarius). A further suggestion is that of making it possible to examine many positions simultaneously (as on Proteus): this however is more than a mere modification of Colossus, and leads to such flights of fancy as a machine to combine two letters by means of an arbitrary conversion square before counting them.

p. 332 # 53 COLOSSUS

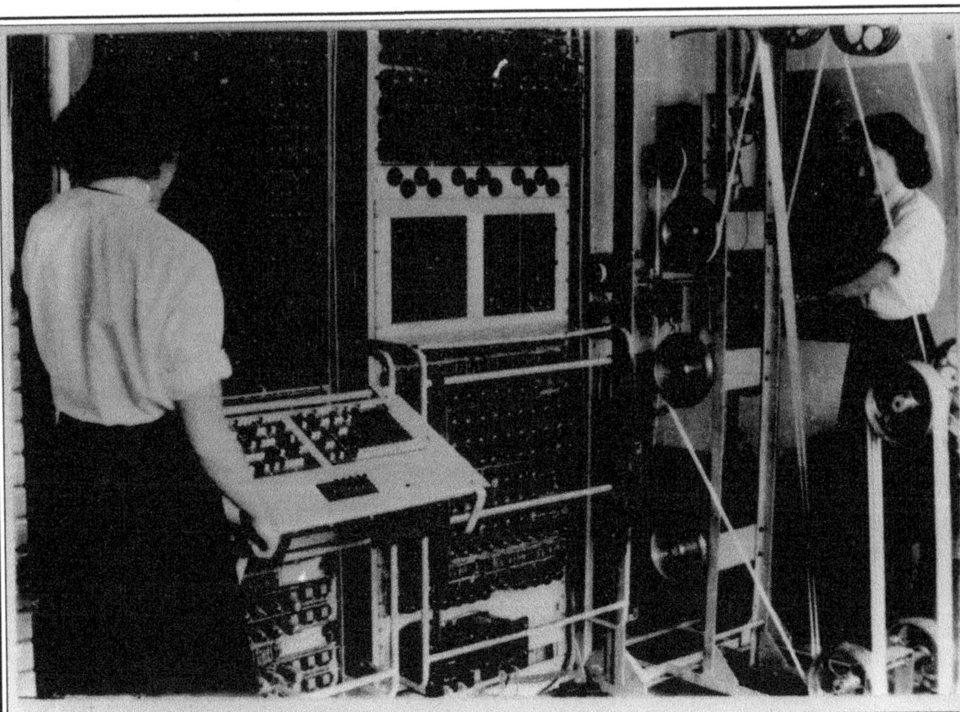

53/1: ×.8

[i] This chapter's analytical contents reproduces what is on the corresponding page of the *Report*, p. 332. The title for section **53N** given here does not match what is in the body of the chapter.

[ii] There is no section **53I**.

53 COLOSSUS i, p. 333

53A INTRODUCTION

The photographs in chapter **58** show the layout both of the whole machine and of individual panels, far more clearly than verbal description, which is therefore omitted. ii

Colossus makes counts concerning certain streams of teleprinter letters. One, denoted by Z and represented on a punched tape, is wholly arbitrary; the others, denoted by χ, μ, ψ and represented electrically, are specialized and composed from certain fixed periods. These patterns χ, μ, ψ, do in fact represent the 12 wheels of the German Tunny machine, and move in the same way. Their 12 components will here be called wheels. For given "settings" there will be, corresponding to each place on the tape Z, definite positions on all the wheels.

Colossus counts the number of places of Z where a condition involving some or all of these streams is satisfied. An essential feature is that the counts can be made in rapid succession with the various wheels in different relative positions ("stepping").

Colossus cannot count a condition involving two different places in the stream except in a limited way by memory circuits, used mostly for delta-ing.

The sum Q of any number of the three 5-impulse streams Z, χ, ψ, each either differenced or undifferenced, can be switched into the Q panel: the switches of this panel suffice to impose the majority of the $2^{32} \doteqdot 5,000,000,000$ combinations of conditions which are theoretically possible. Less specialized conditions can be imposed by the plugboard.

Note 1. Although the streams are named Z, χ, μ, ψ, these are not necessarily used as the real Z, χ, μ, ψ of Tunny. In a short wheel-breaking run (**25**) the pattern set up in χ is really delta χ a
except in the wheel for which the run is made, where it has only one cross and is used merely to select in turn the characters of that wheel.

Note 2. A tape is required in every case, because it controls counting, but Z need not occur in the conditions imposed (e.g. χ test runs).

53B THE Z STREAM

(a) The tape

The tape is a continuous loop of five-impulse tape carrying the Z stream, the usual sprocket holes, a start sign, a stop sign, and 150 blanks.

The sprocket holes are utilized

(i) to cause the machine to count if the conditions imposed are satisfied: the machine counts once, at most, for each sprocket hole.

(ii) to maintain the correct motion of χ, μ, ψ.

The start sign is a hole between the 3rd and 4th impulses, which p. 334

(i) causes the machine to start counting (the start sign has to be punched $2\frac{1}{2}$ sprocket lengths before the first place to be counted),

(ii) sets χ, μ, ψ, in motion.

The stop sign is a hole between the 4th and 5th impulses, $1\frac{1}{2}$ places beyond the end of the text, which

(i) causes the machine to stop counting, and generally prepares for the next start sign.

---

[a] wheelbreaking

[i] Chapter **53** has two opening chapter heads.
[ii] 'in chapter **58**' handwritten.

(ii) transfers to relays the score which has been counted.

150 blanks between start and stop give Colossus time to prepare for the next start sign.

(b) The Bedstead

The bedstead is a system of pulleys round which the tape is driven by friction at about 40 feet or 5000 sprocket holes per second, so as to pass through a gate where it is scanned by eight
i photo-electric cells, one for each impulse and one each for sprocket hole, start and stop.

Each Colossus has two bedsteads; while one is in use a tape can be put on the other. An on-off switch by each bedstead controls both its driving motor and its lamp. There is a switch on the selection panel, whereby either bedstead can be selected (near or far), not both at once.

The maximum length of tape which a bedstead can carry is either 11,000 (short bedstead) or, on Colossi 5, 6, 7, 8, 10 30,000 (long bedstead). On a long bedstead the voltage applied to the motor can be adjusted to maintain the correct speed whatever the length of tape and number of pulleys in use.

Although shorter tapes can be put on the pulleys, Colossus does not work well with a tape less than 2,000 long.

53C THE χ, μ, ψ STREAMS

(a) The triggers

E.1

The twelve wheels constituting χ, μ, ψ, are set up in 'triggers' of length 41, 31 etc. These triggers, except the wheel-breaking panel are inconveniently situated at the back of Colossus.

For each character of a wheel there are two small sockets: a cross is represented by short-circuiting these with a U-shaped pin ("putting in a pin"); a dot by leaving them vacant. (Fig. **58**
ii **(XVII)**.)

There are several alternative triggers for each wheel. The χ, ψ patterns have five triggers (a, b, c, d, e) each selected by a switch on the selection panel. χ a must be used with ψ a.

The μ pattern has seven triggers a, b, c, d, e, f, g, any one of which can be used with any χ, ψ trigger. This discriminatory treatment of μ was arranged when only the μ's changed daily.

p. 335 **(b) Special Patterns**

By using the switch position e′ the χ, ψ trigger e can be used in a different way, as a "special pattern" or "doubting" trigger. Similarly g′ is the special pattern μ trigger.

e′ is *not* added into Q (see Q panel: **53J(a)**).

g′ does *not* motorize the ψ's.

Indeed these patterns appear nowhere except in the seven special pattern jacks on the plug
iii panel, and to have any effect they must be plugged.

These are used in addition to an ordinary trigger.

(c) Wheel-breaking Panel

On wheel-breaking Colossi there is the inestimable boon of a panel on the front of the machine, carrying an ordinary χ trigger and a special pattern χ trigger: in place of U-shaped pins, easily inserted plugs are used: they are so much easier that they are often used for setting. Each of the 5 χ wheels has its ordinary and special patterns adjacent and each is controlled by a 3-way switch whose positions are

{ down: ordinary and special patterns in,
normal: all out,
up: single cross in the last position of the ordinary pattern.

[i] Phrase 'each for' handwritten.

[ii] Figure reference handwritten.

[iii] Handwritten 'they' inserted with a caret.

(d) Motorization and Limitation determiner switches

The motion of μ_{37} and the ψ's is not uniform, but simulates that of the corresponding wheels of the German Tunny machine.

On Colossus the extension of the μ_{37} pattern by μ_{61} is fixed. The extension of the μ pattern is naturally adjustable to suit the limitation. The appropriate switches are near the bottom of the selection panel viz. $\overline{\psi}'$, $\overline{\chi}_2$, $\overline{\overline{P}}_5$: if one or more of these switches are either up or down the corresponding impulses are added and used as the limitation. At the beginning of the text these, since they refer to places one or two back, are indeterminate: the up and down positions of these switches and of $\overline{P}_5$ impose an arbitrary dot or cross, in these places.

BM C/o is the basic motor *cut-out*. When it is used the total motor is simply $\widetilde{\text{lim}}$.

53D STEPPING AND SETTING

(a) Setting

The setting of a wheel is that character of the wheel which corresponds to the first sprocket hole of Z.

All wheels can be given assigned settings, simultaneously, by putting plugs in the appropriate setting jacks and depressing the switch SU. The setting jacks are arranged below the control panel in 12 rows which correspond to the 12 wheels.

(b) Stepping p. 336

Any wheel can be stepped i.e. its setting increased at each revolution of the tape.

This will not of course be confused with the ordinary motion of the wheels at a fixed setting. It should be noticed that increasing settings imply that the patterns move backwards relative to Z. Any number of wheels may be stepped simultaneously.

(c) Stepping Switches

Each wheel has two 3-way switches in the control panel, one in the upper row, one in the lower.

Either of these two switches may be thrown up or down.

	Upper switch up	causes the wheel to step fast
or	Upper switch down	i.e. to step at each tape re-
or	Lower switch down	volution

Lower switch up—causes the wheel to step slowly i.e. to step only when a wheel whose lower switch is thrown down reached the plug in the setting jacks. If in some frenzied fantasy, several wheels have their lower switches down, *each* of them will step a slow stepping wheel.

(d) Repeat Light

When all wheels return to their original settings (strictly to the plug in the setting jack), the repeat light glows. A wheel whose upper switch is thrown *up* is ignored. i

53E DIFFERENCING

Any pattern, except a "special pattern" is available deltaed either on the Q panel (by throwing the Q selection switch to delta) or on the plug panel (by using deltaed output jacks).

The conventional Tunny delta is the sum of present and future i.e. forwards. Colossus deltas by remembering and adding the letter one place back i.e. backwards.

This is immaterial provided that all patterns in use are deltaed by Colossus or all not deltaed ii by Colossus; but if some are and some not, then those which are, are recorded by Colossus as one place back.

[i] Word 'glows' handwritten.

[ii] Second 'deltaed' handwritten and inserted with a caret.

For example suppose that Z is a plain Z tape which is being deltaed by Colossus and added to delta χ set up deltaed on the χ trigger, the two patterns being level so that the recorded setting is 01.

Opposite the second sprocket hole Colossus produces for delta Z: 1st character + 2nd character.

Opposite the second sprocket hole delta χ is plugged as: 2nd character + 3rd character.

It follows that the true setting of χ is 02.

This is in many cases corrected by adjusting the settings, whence the phrase "Settings of deltaed wheels should be one back".

p. 337 A "Special Pattern", however, steps level *with* the corresponding ordinary pattern, and accordingly when the latter is to be deltaed by Colossus, the former must be set up in the trigger one back, in the sense that the 2nd position of the trigger contains the first character of the wheel.

If the same pattern is used both differenced and undifferenced, the correction cannot be made either by setting or by setting up, but must be made internally by Colossus.

The following are all one back so as to be in the present place when used with wheels deltaed on Colossus

(1) The TM switch at the bottom of the Q panel (including $\overset{\sim}{\overline{\chi}}_2$ when BM is cut out and the χ_2 determiner switch is in.)

(2) the jacks $\overline{\mu_{61}}$, $\overline{\mu_{37}}$, $\overline{P}_5$, TM on either side of the special pattern jacks.

It will be noticed that the labelling is inconsistent.

53F COUNTING

(a) The five Counters

Colossus counts up to 9999 and then returns to zero.

To increase the speed of operation, Colossus has five separate counters, which can be used simultaneously either for five (or fewer) distinct runs or for multiple testing on a single run. Spanning and stepping must be the same for all runs. The five counters are labelled 1, 2, 3, 4, 5, but printed on Colossus records a, b, c, d, e.

(b) Switching into counters

To be effective a condition must be switched (on the Q panel) or plugged (on the plug panel), into the proper counter. In particular in multiple testing the condition on *each* of the remembered impulses must be plugged or switched to its proper counter.

53G RECORDING OF SCORES

When a count has been completed, i.e. when the stop sign on the tape is reached, Colossus can transfer it to the "display" and the printer.

(a) Set Total

To avoid displaying and printing useless scores a "set total" can be imposed so that only scores which exceed, or, alternatively, only scores which do not exceed this set total appear, others being cancelled.

The set total controls for the five counters are independent, and for each of the five, consist of decade switches reading 0000–9999, and a three-way switch $<$, Off, $>$. With the off position all

i scores are displayed and printed. (Fig. **58 (XIV)**.)

[i] Figure reference handwritten.

(b) SIP

On Colossus 10 S.I.P. ("Significance Interpretation": switch on control panel) causes all counters to print if one exceeds the set total. p. 338

(c) Storage of scores

Scores which are to be printed, together with the relevant settings, are stored on relays and appear on display. While the next count is being made these relays send impulses to the printer and so clear themselves. If the printing is not completed in time to clear the relays for the next score, stepping is automatically inhibited till the relays are clear: thus no scores are lost.

(d) The display

The display is a glass screen on which the scores are projected by small electric lamps

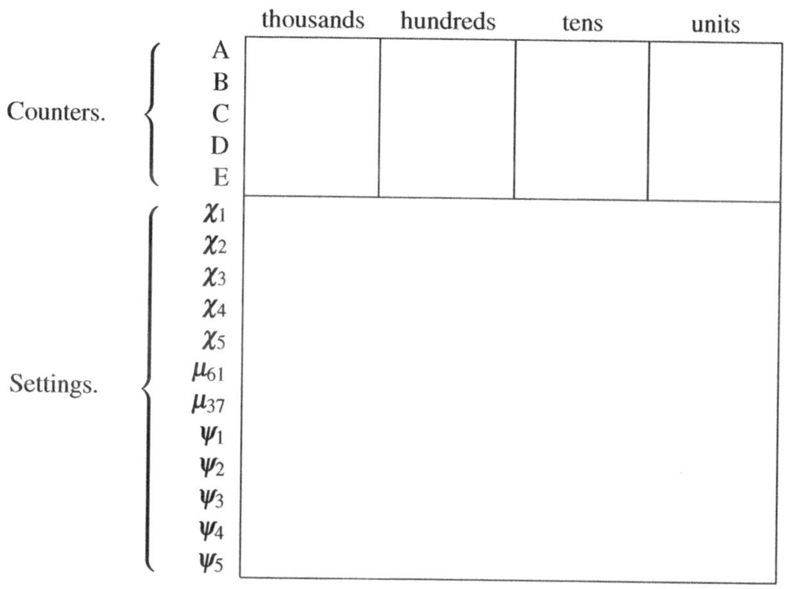

The switch LC/o cuts out the "settings" lamps. The switch KL extinguishes the "settings" lamps when all scores in storage have been printed.

(e) Printing of settings

When the machine is started it prints in a horizontal row the symbols for all wheels which are stepping. In the printed record the settings of these stepping wheels appear before every score, each below its appropriate heading. When runs are done simultaneously, some of these settings may be relevant to certain runs only. To avoid the printing of confusingly meaningless settings there is a 5×12 array of jacks to the right of the χ setting jacks, whose 5 rows correspond to the 5 counters, and 12 columns to the 12 wheels: in order that a score on a particular counter shall cause the setting of a particular wheel to be printed, a shorting plug must be inserted in the corresponding jack.

In all cases the name (a, b, c, d, e) of the appropriate counter is printed before each score.

(f) Printing of Scores

After a score is printed there is an automatic carriage return so that each score is on a separate line.

(g) "Print Main Heading" (PMH switch on control panel).

Prints the settings of all 12 wheels, each below its appropriate symbol. Colossus has to be restarted after printing the symbols.

p. 339 **(h) "Letter Count"** (LEC switch on control panel)

is for making counts at fixed settings. It stops the machine after printing a batch of scores: without it the same count would be repeated. Whilst one batch of scores is being printed, the next batch can be switched.

(i) Printer Cut Out (PCO switch on control panel)

prevents Colossus from sending impulses to the printer, so that stepping ceases (cf. Storage of scores in para. **(c)** above).

(j) Reset (switch on control panel)

clears all scores in storage: in particular if PCO is in use it allows stepping to be resumed.

(k) The Printer

The printer is an electromatic typewriter.

It can be operated manually for the insertion of data (e.g. σ, S.T., span) not printed by Colossus.

Single, double and triple line feed are available.

The inexplicably assorted founts are not intended for cryptography, but this seems to be no handicap: σ has appeared as £, @, ø, $.

53H SPANNING

(a) Spanning

is a device whereby Colossus counts only over a selected stretch of the tape.

i There are three groups of decade switches (fig. **58 (XVI)**) above the plug panel each reading 0000–9999 labelled

START COUNTERS , START PSIS , END OF SPAN.

If "start counters" is set to m when m is not 0000 "end of span" to n, Colossus counts only from the $\overline{m+1}^{\text{th}}$ to n^{th} places on the tape, inclusive.

If "start counter" is set to 0000, spanning is ineffective, the first place on the tape cannot be included in a span.

(b) The Settings

The settings on Colossus refer to the start of the tape, not the start of the span.

Motorizing of the ψ's begins at the place to which "start psis" is set: normally this is 0000, the start of the tape.

(c) On Colossi with long bedsteads

a There is a rudimentary 5th decade in the bottom row of the selection panel. Switches are
p. 340 thrown down for +10,000, up for +20,000.

(d) On Colossi with short bedsteads

b Spanning is unable to distinguish places 10,000 apart so that e.g. 500–1,000 cannot be disentangled from 10,500–11,000.

(e) End of Span cut-out

The ES c/o switch in the bottom row of the selection panel overrides the end of span switches and spans to the end of the tape.

---

[a] there [b] spanning

[i] Handwritten figure reference inserted with caret.

53J *Q* PANEL (Fig. **58 (XIII)**) i

(a) *Q* Selection Switches

At the top right of the selection panel there are three large three-way switches. Each switch has a neutral position and the active positions are Z, delta Z; χ, delta χ; ψ, delta ψ. The streams to which these switches are thrown are added together, and their sum appears in the *Q* panel: the five impulses of this sum are called Q_1, Q_2, Q_3, Q_4, Q_5.
Note: each large switch is really five switches linked together viz. one switch for each impulse: if necessary these can be separated.

(b) The Layout of the *Q* panel

The upper part (10 rows) is used for imposing conditions on individual impulses.
The lower part (5 rows) is used for imposing conditions on the sums of impulses.

(c) Conditions on individual impulses

Every row in the upper part of the panel is arranged as follows. At the left there are five 3-way switches, one for each impulse, each of which can be thrown to dot or cross to make the corresponding impulse of *Q* dot or cross. At the right there are five switches labelled 1, 2, 3, 4, 5, one for each counter, to determine the counters in which the condition is to be imposed.

 ii

Q_1=×, Q_2=×, Q_3=•, Q_4=×
(i.e. *Q*=5 or 3) in counters 1 and 2 iii

Any number of rows may be used: if conditions from two of them are switched into the same counter, *both* will be imposed.

(d) "Not" switches

To impose alternative conditions

"either A or B"

is replaced by the equivalent

"not (not A and not B)".

Just to the left of the counter switches is a "not" switch labelled $\neq$, which negates the conditions. p. 341

[i] Figure reference added by hand.
[ii] These drawings of the *Q* panel differ from those in the *Report* as follows: Switches in the neutral position, seen end-on, are here indicated with hollow circles, to better distinguish them from • labels. The relative spacing of the switches (but not the edges of the switch panel) is less schematic and mimics the actual layout as seen in fig. **58 (XIII)**. The positioning of the plus sign labels in the lower part of the panels is *more* schematic than in the *Report*.
[iii] The annotation Q_1 = ×,... appears to the right of the rectangle, moved here to save space.

means not ($Q_1 = \times$ and $Q_2 = \bullet$): this allows $Q_1 = \bullet$, $Q_2 = \times$, or $Q_1 = \times$, $Q_2 = \times$, or $Q_1 = \bullet$, $Q_2 = \bullet$.

At the foot of each column of ten counter switches is another "not" switch, which negates the whole column.

For example: to impose $Q =$ either / or 5.

This is equivalent to not ($Q \neq /$ and $Q \neq 5$).

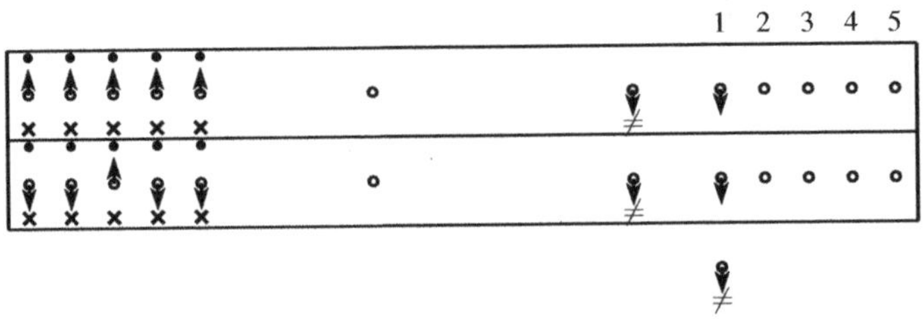

(e) Addition Switches

In a row in the lower part of the Q panel the 5 switches at the left which are separated by +
i signs can be thrown down only, to make the sum of any number of impulses a dot. There are five
a counter switches exactly as in the upper part of the panel. The "not" switch is labelled $\overset{\bullet}{\times}$, but it has the same effect.

Footnote: Clearly not ($i + j = \bullet$) is the same as ($i + j = \times$). These "not" switches actually have a
ii neutral position, but it is not needed and is not alike on all Colossi: on some it causes no condition to be imposed, on others an impossible condition.

The five "not" switches at the bottom of the Q panel labelled $\neq$ negate whole columns, not merely the lower part of the panel; in particular they negate the upper row of "not" switches.

(f) Examples of Switching

It is worthy of emphasis that what is switched is Q, and that Q is whatever is selected by big black switches. In runs to set χ's, Q is $\Delta Z + \Delta\chi$ (though if Δ'd χ patterns are set up it is $\Delta Z + \chi$ so far as Colossus is concerned); in runs to set ψ's it is usually $Z + \chi + \psi$. Use has been made of Q as χ, Z, $Z + \chi$, $\Delta Z + \Delta\chi + \Delta\psi$. The methods of switching on the Q panel are the same in all cases.

(i) 3×/1×2•, 4=/1=2, 5=/1=2 simultaneously on counters 1, 2, 3. The two runs 4=/1=2, 5=/1=2 would ordinarily be done on the same principle: here, for purposes of demonstration, they are done quite differently.

---

[a] the "not" switch

[i] Word 'impulses' handwritten.
[ii] Word 'is' in 'but it is' handwritten.

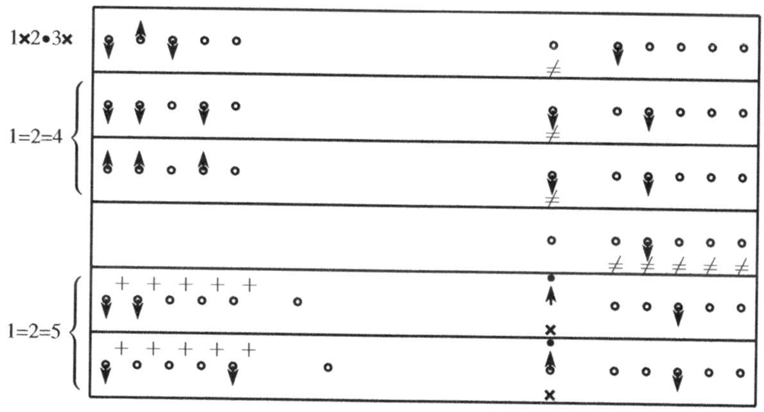

(ii) / H O 3 G P I U Q 5 J F X Y S as a single run p. 342

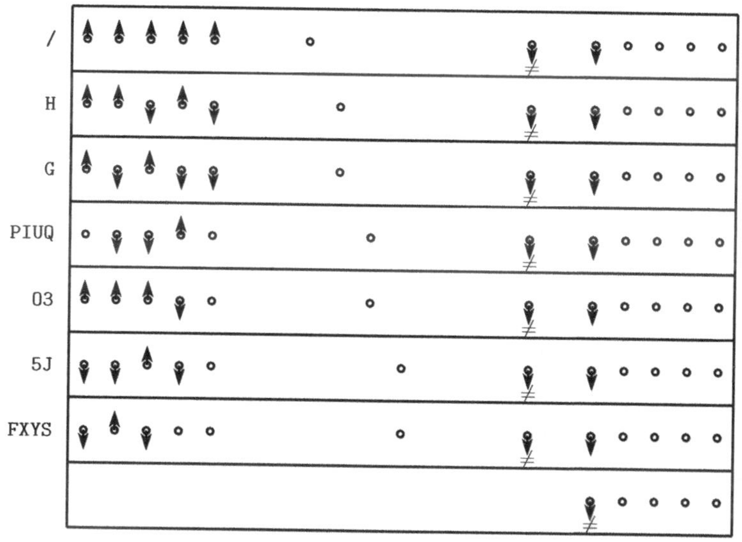

[i]

If this were done in a hurry it would be very easy to overlook that PIUQ can be switched in a single row; if PI, UQ were in separate runs it would not matter, but it *is* necessary to put some of the fifteen letters together, for there are only 10 rows.

(g) Possible Runs

This suggests the problem of whether all possible sets of conditions can be imposed on *Q*, i.e. whether it is possible to run for an entirely arbitrary selection of letters from the 32 letter alphabet.

It is obviously possible to run for any ten letters but, for example, R A S H D O N 8 L I Z, 11 letters, is impossible.

Despite the aid of the addition switches, 15 rows in the upper part of panel are needed to include all runs.

(h) The *R* Switches

These are the multiple test switches carrying the impulses R_1, R_2, R_3, R_4, R_5, (see Multiple Test **53L(c)**): each occurs in two rows in the upper part of the panel and in one row in the lower part.

---

[i] In the *Report* an extraneous end-on view of a non-existent R_5 switch is shown in the bottom row, directly under the two end-on views of the R_5 switches in the two next-to-bottom rows.

Evidently the choice of runs will be much more restricted on multiple test than without it. For examples of multiple test switching see **53L(k)**.

(i) Total Motor Switch

In the bottom row of the Q panel is a three-way switch whose active positions are labelled TM • and TM **×**.

This switch is not used for motorizing, but only for counting against TM = • or TM = **×**. It is rather more general than this, for by use of the limitation determiner switches TM can be made to mean

BM = μ_{37}	:	all switches normal
TM	:	Switches for the appropriate limitation in.
$\tilde{\bar{\chi}}_2$	:	BM c/o , $\bar{\chi}_2$ in.

p. 343 Note: TM is in the present position when used with wheels which are deltaed by Colossus (as it usually will be). Compared to patterns not deltaed by Colossus it is $\overline{\text{TM}}$, i.e. TM one back (cf. Differencing **53E**).

i 53K PLUG PANEL (Fig. 58 (XV))

(a) The Jacks

The jacks in this panel are essentially of four kinds:

ii 1. Jacks carrying streams, (including some combined streams);

2. Addition Field;

3. Common Jacks;

4. Jacks carrying input to counters.

Streams may be plugged into counters, either directly or via the addition field and common jacks. To plug anything into a counter is to equate it to a dot.

(b) Jacks carrying streams are described in paragraphs **(c)** to **(h)**.

(c) Q Jacks

The whole top row of jacks is really a dependency of the Q panel. Q_1, Q_2, Q_3, Q_4, Q_5 are the five impulses switched into Q by the selection switches. R_1, R_2, R_3, R_4, R_5 are the present and remembered items of Q_m when Q_m is on multiple test. All these have two jacks each.

(d) Z, χ, ψ

Each impulse of Z, χ, ψ, has two jacks, one deltaed and one undeltaed.

(e) Special Patterns

χ_1, χ_2, χ_3, χ_4, χ_5, μ_{61}, μ_{37}, have each one jack for the pattern set up, independently of the ordinary pattern in use, in the special trigger.

(f) $\overline{\mu_{61}}$, $\overline{\mu_{37}}$, $\overline{P_5}$, $\overline{\text{TM}}$

These are derived from ordinary patterns. If used with streams deltaed by Colossus they are in the present position. If used with streams not deltaed by Colossus they are one back, as labelled (cf. **53E**).

---

[i] Figure reference handwritten.

[ii] Right-hand bracket missing in *Report*.

(g) Not 99

This is used to inhibit counting at doubtful letters of cipher replaced by $Z = 9$. Such 9's rarely occur singly. Genuine 9's usually do occur singly. It is therefore only imposed at a 9 adjacent to another 9: at such places this jack carries a cross, elsewhere a dot.

Note: Not 99 is intended for use with a Z pattern which is deltaed by Colossus and therefore, since delta Z is rubbish if Z one forward is rubbish, it is in use, for each stretch of 9's, from one place before the first 9 to the last 9. Colossus however, because it deltas backwards, treats this as being from the first 9 to one place after the last 9; and accordingly if not 99 is used with Z not deltaed by Colossus one place will be lost unnecessarily at the end of each stretch of 9's. p. 344

(h) Start Units

These carry a permanent dot or cross as labelled.

(i) Addition Field

These are of course used to add impulses: there are three rows, 28 columns.

All but one of the impulses to be added are plugged into consecutive jacks in the top row.

The odd one is plugged in the middle row below the first of the other plugs.

The output (sum) is taken from the bottom row below the last of the other plugs.

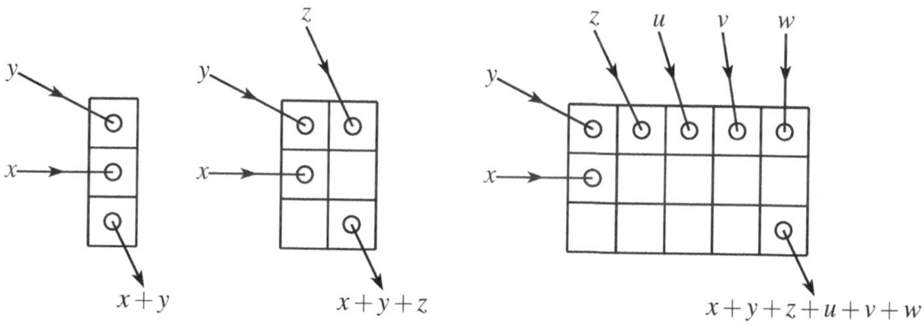

The columns used thus are isolated so that several additions can be carried out simultaneously.

To plug any impulse to equal a *cross*, add a cross and plug normally.

(j) Common Jacks

There are on each Colossus six or more commons of five jacks each. An impulse put in can be taken out four times: if this is insufficient common jacks can be linked together.

(k) Counter Jacks

There are 8 jacks for carrying conditions to each counter.

There are also 6 jacks carrying conditions to all counters. One of these is marked TM because it will not work if the TM switch on the Q panel is thrown.

There is a special counter jack (Multiple Test Doubting) used only for multiple testing on special patterns.

(l) Examples of the use of the Plug Panel

(i) Before not 99 was available it was usual, on corrupt texts, to switch $Q = Z$, $Q \neq 9$, and plug all wheel-breaking runs.

(ii) The wheel-breaking run $\Delta\chi_1 + \Delta Z_1 + \Delta\chi_6 = \bullet$ is normally done by plugging (delta χ_6 is usually set up in the χ_2 trigger). a

If the Q panel were used delta Z_2 would be switched in along with Delta Z_1. This could be avoided, alternatively, by splitting the delta Z selecting switch. p. 345

(iii) the run 1=2=lim (i.e. $\Delta D_1 = \Delta D_2 = \overline{\chi}_2$) can be switched and plugged thus

[a] wheelbreaking

$1 = 2$ on the Q panel, multiple testing on χ_1

$Q_2 + \chi + \text{TM} = \bullet$ on the plug panel

a TM $= \tilde{\overline{\chi}}_2$ on the limitation determiner switches, using BM c/o, $\overline{\chi}_2$.

E.2 53L MULTIPLE TEST

i **(a) To save time**
it is arranged that the same wheel can be examined at five different settings simultaneously, the five scores appearing in the five counters.

(b) Memory Circuits

When the multiple test switch for any wheel is thrown, a memory device is switched in, which stores the characters of that wheel 1, 2, 3, and 4 places back.

Footnote: More explicitly Colossus remembers characters of the wheel opposite places on the tape 1, 2, 3, 4, back; in particular characters of ψ' not of ψ. In the first four places of the text b some of the remembered characters are really those at the end of the text in the preceding tape revolution; and will give random scores, unless the text length is a multiple of the wheel length: it is customary to span from 04 onwards.

Thus when Colossus is examining a particular place on Z, it has available for comparison:—
(i) on the multiply tested wheel, the present character and the characters 1, 2, 3, 4, back. These are associated with the numbers 1, 2, 3, 4, 5 (i back with $i+1$).
(ii) on Z, and on all other wheels, only the present character.

(c) R_1, R_2, R_3, R_4, R_5

Most operators are surprised to find that the remembered characters appear nowhere except as a component of Q, the corresponding five characters of Q are called R_1, R_2, R_3, R_4, R_5.
c e.g. if χ_1 is multiply tested and $Q = \Delta\chi + \Delta Z$ then

R_1	=	ΔZ_1	(present)	+	$\Delta\chi_1$	(present)
R_2	=	ΔZ_1	"	+	$\Delta\chi_1$	(1 back)
R_3	=	ΔZ_1	"	+	$\Delta\chi_1$	(2 ")
R_4	=	ΔZ_1	"	+	$\Delta\chi_1$	(3 ")
R_5	=	ΔZ_1	"	+	$\Delta\chi_1$	(4 ")

Five counts made simultaneously, with R_1, R_2, R_3, R_4, R_5, used instead of the corresponding impulse of Q, are evidently equivalent to a count, for the same conditions, at each of the following ii *settings* for the multiply tested wheel: present, 1 back, 2 back, 3 back, 4 back.

p. 346 **(d) $R_1\ R_2\ R_3\ R_4\ R_5$: Switching and Plugging**

$R_1\ R_2\ R_3\ R_4\ R_5$, must be plugged or switched in the usual way. The provision for them is less generous than for ordinary impulses. On the Q panel they have two switches each in the upper part, one switch each in the lower part. On the plug panel they have one jack each: these jacks are part of Q and are controlled by the main Q selecting switches.

---

[a] BMc/o [b] preceeding [c] χ is

[i] Sentence continues on same line as started by heading.
[ii] Handwritten 'the' inserted with a caret.

(e) R_1 R_2 R_3 R_4 R_5**: Relation to the Five Counters** (regrettably obscure)

R_1 R_2 R_3 R_4 R_5 may of course be switched or plugged into the counters in any order; but Colossus cannot recognise this and therefore always prints the settings for a batch of five scores in the same order, viz. backwards (e.g. 11, 10, 09, 08, 07).

The counters print in the order 1, 2, 3, 4, 5, and therefore if each setting is to be printed opposite the appropriate score, the settings in the five counters must likewise run backwards. (e.g. 11 in 1, 10 in 2, 9 in 3, 8 in 4, 7 in 5).

The settings corresponding to R_1 R_2 R_3 R_4 R_5 also run backwards (R_1 is present, R_2 one back etc.) and, therefore, finally R_1 is switched to counter 1 etc.

It may sometimes be profitable to put R_1 R_2 R_3 R_4 R_5 into the counters in reverse order (e.g. in rectangling).

(f) Manner of stepping

The wheel on multiple test can step either fast or slow (**53D(c)**) but in either case it steps five positions at a time, for obvious reasons. The batches of five settings are not arbitrary but must belong to the sequence 02–06, 07–11, 12–16 ... ending with the batch whose present position is 01 (e.g. ends with 38–01).

(g) Multiple Testable Wheels

Multiple testing is provided for all wheels except μ_{61}. χ_5, ψ_5, were added later and have not been fitted to all Colossi. μ_{37} has its own switch: the others are in pairs, each pair sharing a three-way switch, viz. χ_1, χ_2, χ_3, χ_4 ; ψ_1, ψ_2, ψ_3, ψ_4; χ_5, ψ_5.

(h) Mu37

Multiple testing on Mu 37 has some special features. It can be used only for motor runs in which a count is made against motor = •, or motor = ×. It cannot be used for motorizing the psis.

The Mu37 multiple test switch, not only puts the wheel on multiple test, but also puts Mu 37 i
alone into the switches R_1 R_2 R_3 R_4 R_5 on the Q panel, where it can be switched in the normal manner. (Commonly Mu 37′ = •, but sometimes $M37 + \Delta D_{12}$ = •). The effect of these switches is *not* modified by the limitation determiner switches: they always represent the basic motor. For a total motor run what is required is BM = • and lim = ×. BM = • is imposed by these R switches. Lim = × is imposed by the TM switch on the Q panel, the limitation determiner switches being thrown to BM c/o and the appropriate limitation.

(i) No Multiple Test for Motorizing p. 347

It is impossible, in a run involving the psis, to use multiple test on any wheel which influences the total motor, for this would require that the psis should move in two different ways at once. In practice the wheels thus restricted are Mu 37, psi 1, and, with P_5 limitation, chi 5, psi 5. It is ii
however, possible to use the multiple test switch merely to step one of these wheels five positions at a time, ignoring four settings out of five. This is useful for ψ_1' because of coalescence (**23X**). a

(j) Multiple Test Doubting (Special Patterns)

Multiple test normally applies only to ordinary patterns, not to special patterns. On Colossi 5, 8, 10, however, it can be applied to the corresponding special pattern also. The appropriate switch is in the bottom row of the selection panel. As always with special patterns, it must be plugged, viz. from the appropriate special pattern jack to one of the two jacks labelled: Multiple Test Doubting • or ×: these select places where the special pattern is • or ×, respectively, in all counters.

---

[a] setting

[i] 'test' overstruck with 'tewt'.

[ii] 'practice' overstruck with 'practize'.

(k) Checking of Multiple Test Scores

It is generally undesirable, because of confusion about settings, to check scores with multiple testing in. In place of R_1 R_2 R_3 R_4 R_5 the ordinary impulse is used, and, of course, the wheels must be reset.

For Mu 37 this means that, in the lower part of the Q panel, what is used is not R_1 R_2 R_3 R_4 R_5 but TM. In checking a total motor run the BM c/o must be restored to its normal position.

For special pattern multiple test this means that the special pattern shall be plugged into the ordinary all-counters, not into the multiple test doubting jacks.

(l) Examples of Multiple Test Switching

(i) 1+2=•

i Note: this may be either $\Delta D_{12} = \bullet$ to set χ_1 and χ_2, or $P_{12} = \bullet$ to set ψ_1 and ψ_2. On the Q panel the switching for their two cases is identical.

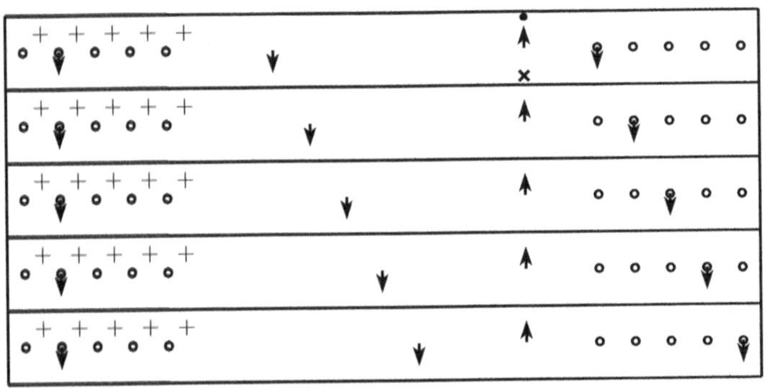

p. 348 (ii) Mu 37 = •/5U/, $\overline{\chi}_2$✖. A total motor run for M61 M37 when $\overline{\chi}_2$ limitation is in use, counting TM = •, where ΔD = /, 5, U.

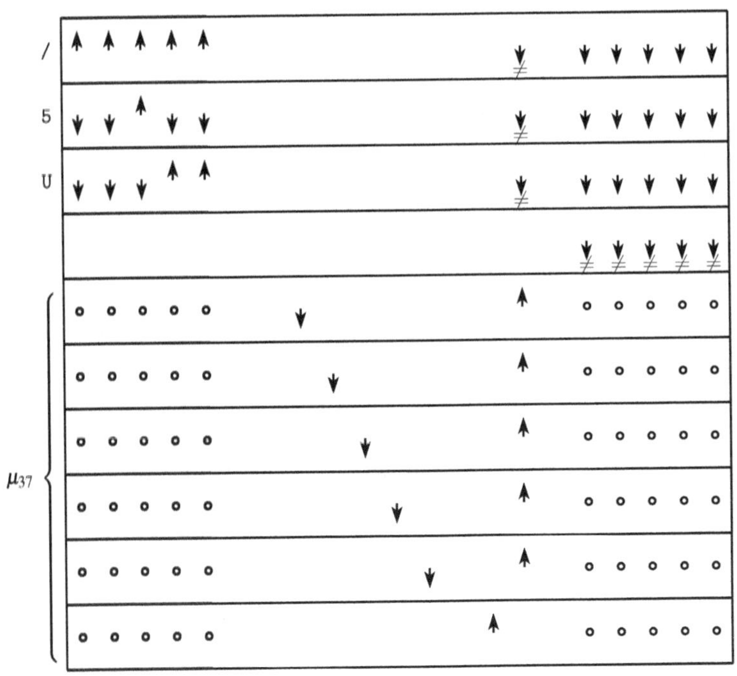

E.3

[i] Both words 'and' handwritten.

Other switching

M37 multiple test, step M37 slow, M61 fast.

Limitation determiner switches: BM c/o, $\overline{\chi}_2$ in.

For checking this run see **53L(k)**.

(iii) *P* /, 3, 4 to set Chi 3, Psi 3, with multiple testing on Chi 3, all other wheels being set.

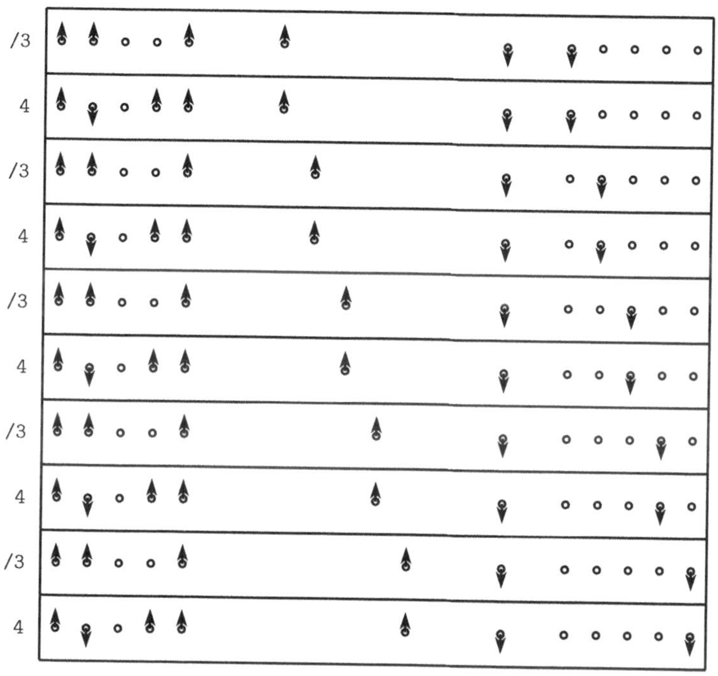

(iv) The short wheel-breaking run 3+/1•2• p. 349

It is not worth while to use multiple test for one-wheel runs, unless the tape is very long, as it may be in chi-breaking.
For the reason why 3+1 is switched to cross see **25**.
R_1 R_2 R_3 R_4 R_5 are switched into counters 5, 4, 3, 2, 1 so that scores shall be printed in the correct order (**53L(d)**).

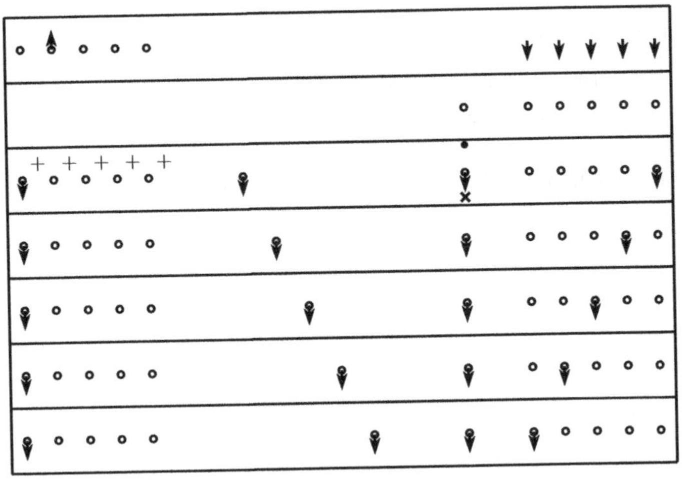

53M COLOSSUS RECTANGLING GADGETS

(a) The principle of Colossus Rectangling

To render the gadget more intelligible the how and why of Colossus rectangling is explained
i (see also **24B(f)**).

Suppose that the Chi 1, and Chi 2 triggers each contain one cross, that $Q = \chi$; and that Q is switched: $Q_1 = \times$, $Q_2 = \times$. This will select a set of places all of which are opposite a particular character of chi 1, and also opposite a particular character of chi 2, i.e. they will belong to the same cell of the rectangle.

Plug $\Delta Z_1 + \Delta Z_2 = \bullet$.

Throw the lower stepping switches, so that chi 1 (down) steps fast and controls chi 2 (up).

Chi 1 will step, producing a row of the rectangle: when Chi 1 reaches the setting plug, chi 2 will step one.

Chi 1 then steps again, producing the next row, and so on.

(b) The Rectangling Gadget

If the rectangle were made exactly as above the entries would be printed on separate lines each preceded by the settings of chi 1, chi 2. It is much better to have the row printed as a row. Accordingly a gadget is fitted such that:

p. 350 (i) Carriage return is operated only after the completion of a row.

(ii) Settings are not printed.

(iii) A score is printed as a single figure.

On Colossus 6 scores exceeding 9 are represented by letters viz. A = 10, B = 11 and so on.

(c) Multiple Test in Rectangling

To increase the speed of rectangling, multiple testing on χ_1 is used. Multiple testing always examines batches of settings whose "present" member belongs to the sequence 1, 6, 11 ... 41. The first batch of settings in each row of the rectangle is chosen to be 02 – 06, 06 being "present", 02, 03, 04, 05 "remembered". In order that χ_2 shall step at the correct position of χ_1, the χ_1 setting *plug* must be at 01. If however χ_1 were actually set at 01, the first row would begin with settings 38, 39, 40, 41, 01. To make the first row begin 02, 03, 04, 05, 06 the wheels are set with the χ_1 plug at 06: the plug is then returned to 01 without resetting.

---

[i] Reference handwritten.

Because the rectangle is made backwards the first five readings should be for the *last* five cells a of the rectangle, which contain places of the cipher whose remainders on division by 41 are 37, 38, 39, 40, 41 so that the required differences (ΔZ_1) are 37 + 38, 38 + 39, 39 + 40, 40 + 41, 41 + 01. Since Colossus differences backwards, the cross in χ_1 must be against cipher places 38, 39, 40, 41, 01. The first batch of settings is 02, 03, 04, 05, 06; and therefore the cross must be in position 02:

Position in cipher (remainder on division by 41)		37	38	39	40	41	1	2
Character of χ_1 opposite each letter of cipher when the setting is <u>06</u> (i.e. 06 of χ_1 opposite 01 of Z.)	R_1	1	2×	3	4	5	<u>6</u>	7
Remembered character of χ_1	R_2	41	1	2×	3	4	5	6
	R_3	40	41	1	2×	3	4	5
	R_4	39	40	41	1	2×	3	4
	R_5	38	38	40	41	1	2×	3

R_1 sees the cross in 02 of χ_1 opposite 38 of Z

R_2 remembers the cross of 02 of χ_1 opposite 39 of Z i

χ_2 has a cross in 02, for symmetry, and it follows that its setting is 02.

The last batch of settings is 38, 39, 40, 41 and 01 of which 38, 39, 40, 41 are also in the last batch but one: the rectangle gadget prevents these from being printed twice.

(d) Print Scores

Done thus, the rectangle would have to be done twice, for $\Delta Z_1 + \Delta Z_2 = \bullet$, and for $\Delta Z_1 + \Delta Z_2 = \times$. Conditional rectangles are done this way; the rectangling switch is thrown to "print scores".

(e) The Subtraction Gadget

If the depth is constant, which will be the case if the text length is a multiple of 1271 and 99's are *not* cancelled, the score for $\Delta Z_1 + \Delta Z_2 = \bullet$ will suffice, for the bulge equals ($\Delta Z_1 + \Delta Z_2 = \bullet$) minus depth. A further rectangling gadget performs this arithmetical operation if the rectangling switch is thrown to "normal", and the appropriate depth switched in on the rectangling panel. p. 351

This is the usual Colossus rectangle method: it is often disadvantageous for short texts because so much is lost by reduction to a multiple of 1271.

Note: Although the subtraction gadget can be used independently of the rectangle gadget proper, it is too limited in scope to be of value.

(f) Switching

The 3-way rectangling switch at the extreme right of the control panel has two active positions: "Print scores" and "normal".

The other switches are on the rectangling panel. Any chi-wheel can be multiply testing for making a rectangle: the corresponding switch of the bottom of the rectangling panel must be thrown. This determines when carriage return is operated and how many surplus scores are cancelled.

The subtraction gadget is controlled by a series of switches labelled 1 to 36, each number indicating the depth to be subtracted.

[a] whould

[i] Lower right block of text in diagram: '39of Z'.

(g) The Cyclometers

The θ_{ij}^2 significance test is based on the number of occurrences of each possible value for the entries in a rectangle.

At the top of the rectangling panel is a row of cyclometers to record these occurrences.

Below these is a row of jacks, one for each cyclometer. A pulse here steps the corresponding cyclometer.

Below these again are two rows of jacks labelled 1, 2, 3... A score of $\pm\theta$ produces a pulse in the jack θ.

These score jacks can be plugged arbitrarily to the cyclometer jacks.

(h) The Punch

Colossus 6 can make a rectangle in the form of punched tape. A negative score is always represented by a cross in the fifth impulse, but otherwise a score can be represented by an arbitrary letter, selected by plugging from a score jack to a punch jack.

There is a score jack labelled CR which carries the pulse of the carriage return at the end of each row of the rectangle. This is normally plugged to the punch jack labelled $\overline{9}$/ which punches / and adds a cross to the third impulse of the preceding letter (cf. Appendix **95**).

(i) Rectangle not 99

In any cell of the rectangle containing a place where Z = 9 adjacent to another 9, this replaces the entry by zero. It is useful only for rectangles of depth one.

p. 352 53N CONTROL PANEL

i See the photograph. (Fig. **58 (XI)**)

MAS is the master switch (upper row, second switch from right; labelling obscured in the photograph). Unless this switch is thrown Colossus can neither count nor step. It is however possible to set wheels and to reset counters.

ii The switches labelled χ, μ, ψ, are the stepping switches **53D(c)**. The switches labelled mult are multiple test switches **53L(g)**. χ_3, ψ_5 are oddly placed.

The other switches are

PMH	Print main heading (**53G(g)**)	PCO	Printer cut-out	(**53G(i)**)
SET $\underline{\cup}$	Set wheels (**53D(a)**)	Lc/o	Lamp cut-out	(**53G(d)**)
RESET	Reset counters (**53G(j)**)	LC	Letter count	(**53G(h)**)
REC	Rectangle (**53M(f)**)	KL	Cancel lights	(**53G(d)**)
		SIP	Significance Interpretation	(**53G(b)**)

53P COLOSSUS TESTING

Any account of the methods used by the engineers to test Colossi would be entirely out of place in this report, but it is appropriate to refer to the methods used by Wrens, chosen to carry out routine tests.

Owing to the complexity of its operations Colossus can produce results so erroneous as to be useless without arousing suspicion till valuable time has been wasted.

Runs have therefore been selected such that a machine faulty in any respect is unlikely to give correct scores, and these have been done on Colossi known to be in good order, using selected standard wheel patterns and a selected standard tape. One set of triggers on each Colossus is now assigned to these standard patterns, and standard tapes are kept in stock: the runs are repeated on all Colossi at frequent intervals.

---

i Figure reference handwritten.

ii Word 'stepping' handwritten.

A single fantastic run could doubtless be devised to check everything, but it is preferable to use a number of runs, which in themselves will aid in locating faults. Z and χ are first tested without ψ. a, i

Of course when there is a fault the ordinary chi and psi tests (**23K(d)**) will fail, thus providing a crude test of Colossus very frequently. ii

---

[a] preferrable

[i] Words 'locating faults' handwritten.

[ii] Reference handwritten.

p. 353 54 ROBINSON

i

p. 354 54A INTRODUCTION

Robinson was made in three versions known as

Heath Robinson,
Old Robinson,
Super Rob(inson).

Super Robinson is described in detail: the others, which do not differ in principle, are mentioned in chapter **52**.

ii For photographs see the end of this volume. (Fig. **58 (III, IV, V, VI, VII)**)

Let four or fewer teleprinter streams punched on tapes, with uniformly spaced sprocket-holes, be imagined laid side by side, so that their letters correspond, sprocket-hole by sprocket-hole.

Robinson can count the number of places in the combined stream where certain conditions are satisfied.

Rather more generally, it can count the number of places such that certain conditions are satisfied, involving that place, and the place *one forward* (this includes differencing) together with two conditions involving the place one back, and one condition involving the place two back.

Apart from this it cannot count a condition involving two different places, except by using two tapes alike, appropriately staggered.

An essential feature is that the counts can be made in rapid succession, with the various tapes in different relative positions (stepping): stepping is necessarily uniform though the step between successive counts may be any number of sprocket-holes.

54B HOW SCORES ARE EXHIBITED

iii The scores so counted are exhibited in two ways

(i) On display,
(ii) By the printer.

Footnote Display can be switched off either entirely or to show position only. There are more printer details later.

---

[i] Chapter **54** starts on p. 353 of the *Report* with a chapter head and a table of contents. The chapter begins again on p. 354, with a fresh chapter head (omitted here) followed immediately by section **54A**.

[ii] Figure references handwritten.

[iii] Footnote reference location (on p. 354) not indicated; context makes section **54B** likely.

The display is a ground glass screen on which numbers can be projected by small electric lamps.

The four upper digits are the *position counter* i.e. they show the relative position of tapes.

The four lower digits are the *score counter.*

The printer simply prints all 8 digits in order, without spacing, so that e.g. 25341798, means [i] position 2534 score 1798.

54C BEDSTEADS AND POSITION COUNTING p. 355

(a) Bedsteads

A bedstead is a system of pulleys round which the tape is driven by a sprocket wheel at about 2000 sprocket-holes per second, so as to be scanned by photo-electric cells.

There are four bedsteads A, B, C, D: to ensure simultaneous scanning of corresponding places on different tapes, their four sprocket wheels are on a common shaft.

(b) Bedstead Drive

To reduce the tearing of sprocket-holes, two of the pulleys are driven at the correct speed. For the same reason the drive is applied gradually when starting, and removed gradually when stopping (by means of relays).

The tapes are draped loosely on the pulleys. Centrifugal action tends to tighten them, and they [a] may need to be slackened. After a long run tapes may stretch.

Between the "Gate" and the sprocket wheel the tape moves past two engraved marks: to ensure that the tape is correctly placed these are aligned with an appropriate pencil mark on the [b] tape (fig. **58 (IV)**).

The tapes, which are of course continuous loops, are jointed flexibly with Bostik. [c]

One spring switch is used both for starting and stopping: it is thrown down (and released) for start, up for stop.

(c) The Gate

Each bedstead has 13 photo-electric cells which scan the tape as it passes (downwards) through [d] the "gate". The gate is placed as near as possible to the driving sprocket to reduce the effect of stretched tapes.

One of the photo-cells scans the sprocket-holes, permitting the counters to add 1 or 0 at each sprocket hole.

In *each* position of the tape 10 of these cells scan the 10 dots and crosses in *two* consecutive places on the tape, the 10 outputs appearing in 10 jacks on the plug panel (the output from each bedstead in the 10 jacks immediately below the corresponding letter), and nowhere else.

(d) Start and Stop Signs

The remaining two photo-cells look for the start and stop signs, which are punched in the $4\frac{1}{2}$th and $3\frac{1}{2}$th impulses of the tape, exactly as on Colossus.

A start sign causes the machine to start counting.

A stop sign causes the machine to stop counting, transfer the count to relays, and prepare for the next start sign.

Only one start sign and one stop sign are used as such at any time; these are not necessarily taken from the same bedstead: they are selected by the switches above the plugboard. Start (on A, B, C, or D) by the first four: stop (on A, B, C, or D) by the second four.

---

[a] pulleys centrifugal [b] mark of the tape [c] Bostick [d] has 12

[i] Word 'means' handwritten.

(e) Position Counter

p. 356 The start signs are used also for finding the relative positions of tapes. If one (say B) of the right-hand switches above the display is thrown, the position counter shows how many sprocket-holes the start sign on B is behind the start sign used as a start sign.

(f) Period Dials

These are above the display reading 0000 – 9999.

If they are set e.g. to 1271, as soon as the position counter reaches 1271 it returns to 0000 i.e. the reading is always the remainder on division by 1271.

(g) Split Position Counter

If one of the left-hand switches above the display is thrown the position counter is split in two, each half working independently reading up to 99. The first two digits show the position of the
a tape selected by the left-hand switch. The second two digits show the position of the tape selected by the right-hand switch.

Splitting splits the period dials also, e.g. if the dials are set to 4131, the first two digits show the remainder on division by 41, the second two digits show the remainder on division by 31. These may refer to the same or different tapes.

(h) Note

By convention the setting of one pattern relative to another is the place on the latter against the 1st and not the 0th place on the former. Thus setting = Rob reading + 1.

(i) Stepping

b Stepping is effected on Robinson by using tapes of different lengths. If A is m sprocket-holes longer than B, and the original setting is 01, then after a revolution, A will return m sprocket-holes later than B, i.e. the 1st place on A is opposite the $\overline{m+1}^{\text{th}}$ place on B, and the setting of A relative to B is $+m$

A is said to have moved forward relative to B.

(j) Repeat light

When the position counter returns to its original reading a *repeat light* appears below the display.

54D THE PLUG PANEL

(a) Layout

The jacks on the plug panel may be grouped thus.

---

[a] shown [b] on

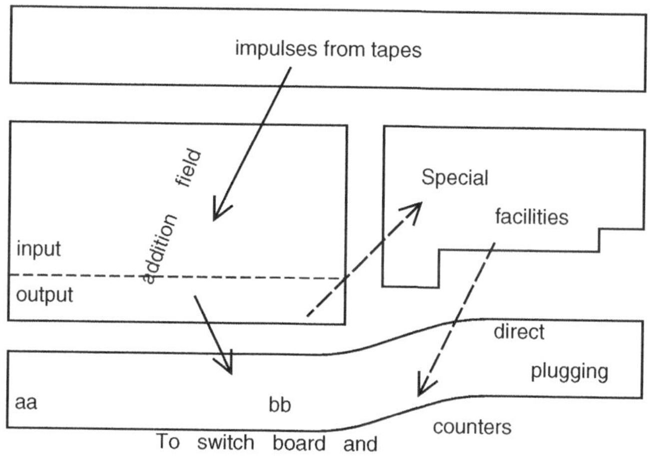

i

Conditions can be imposed only by plugging *both*: p. 357
1. From tapes to Addition Field *input*.
2. From Addition Field *output* to switch panel.
The latter however may be plugged via "Special Facilities". Note that this forbids plugging direct from tapes to switch panel.

Subject to the above rules (and some minor restrictions in the ordinary addition fields) any jack may be plugged to any other. No jacks in the plug panel are permanently linked except the columns of the addition fields (ordinary and special).

(b) Pulses from Tapes

The arrangement is obvious from the picture.
The upper row is one forward on the tape.
The lower row is present position on the tape.

(c) Ordinary addition fields

Pulses (one or more) from tapes, plugged into input jacks in any column, appear added together in both the output jacks of that column. For technical reasons there are certain restrictions on the use of these fields. Each of the left-hand five columns has two *pairs* of input jacks (upper and lower). Each of the right-hand five columns has a single pair of input jacks. Impulses plugged into the two jacks of a pair must come from the same tape. If there is only one impulse in a pair it should be in the upper jack of the pair. Impulses from different tapes can be added only in the five right-hand columns (or in the special addition field). Each column of the addition field has *two* output jacks from which the impulse may be plugged directly to the switchboard or to some special facility.

(d) Special Facilities

These are special addition, Permanent cross, one back and two back.

(e) Special addition field

This is exactly the same as a Colossus addition field e.g.

---

[i] 'To switch. . . ' follows curve of bottom part of drawing.

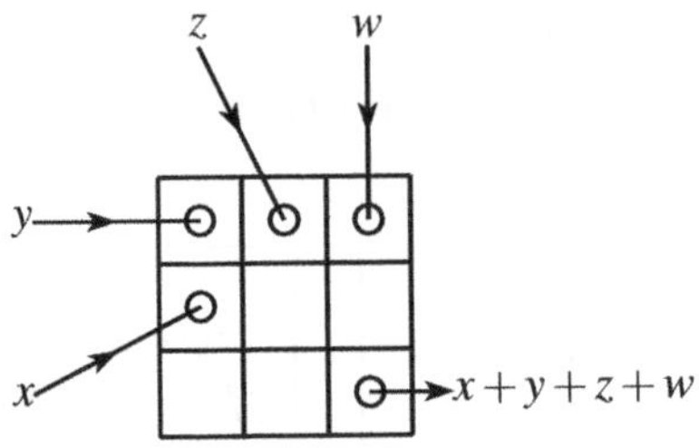

Note: Other columns in the addition field are unaffected by this and can be used separately.

(f) Permanent Cross

There is a column of jacks to the left of the special-addition field: each of them bears a permanent cross, which can be added, in the special addition field, to any impulse. This is useful for making an impulse equal a cross when using "direct plugging".

(g) One back and two back

There are five jacks at the right of the addition field

p. 358

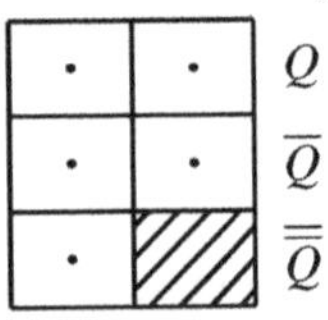

in each column any impulse plugged into Q appears one back in $\overline{Q}$ and, in the left-hand column two back in $\overline{\overline{Q}}$

The notation Q is unfortunate: it is not analogous to Q on Colossus. I would be better.

(h) Plugging into the switch panel

The output of an ordinary addition field, or of any special facility may be plugged into the switch panel where the conditions, a count for which is to be made, can be imposed.

An impulse plugged into one of the 10 jacks in the bottom row of the switch panel appears on two switches, one labelled $\overset{\bullet}{\times}$, and, immediately below this, one labelled $+$. The first five jacks correspond to the five pairs of switches aa, the second five to those of bb. The impulses are called (not written on machine) $Q_1, Q_2, Q_3, Q_4, Q_5, Q_6, Q_7, Q_8, Q_9, Q_{10}$.

Footnote: These are not related to $Q, \overline{Q}, \overline{\overline{Q}}$: they (i.e. Q_1, Q_2 etc.) are broadly analogous to Q on Colossus, but the impulses plugged into them are quite arbitrary.

The five jacks marked "direct plug" in the diagram have essentially the same function, but are permanently switched to dot.

54E THE SWITCH PANEL

(a) Layout

i, E.1 Without the diagram at the end of this volume this description will probably be completely obscure; fig. **58 (VII)**.

(b) Q Switches

The two rows of switches in the left half of the switch panel will be described first: the conditions they impose may be modified (may even be reversed) by the switches in the right half.

---

[i] Handwritten 'at the end of this volume' inserted with a caret.

The switches to the left of aa control impulses Q_1, Q_2, Q_3, Q_4, Q_5.

The switches to the left of bb control impulses $Q_6, Q_7, Q_8, Q_9, Q_{10}$.

A switch labelled $\overset{\bullet}{\times}$ can be thrown either to make its impulse a dot or to make its impulse a cross.

If several are thrown, all their conditions are imposed.

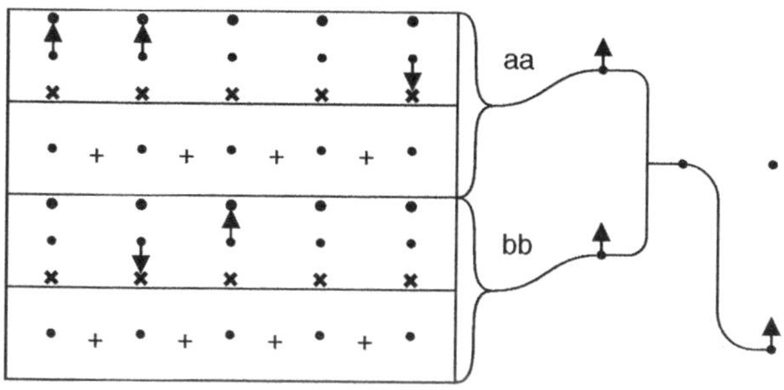

Imposes the conditions
$Q_1 = \bullet$ $Q_2 = \bullet$ $Q_5 = \times$
$Q_7 = \times$ $Q_8 = \bullet$.

Switches labelled + can be thrown (down only) to add one or more impulses and equate their sum to a dot. [i] p. 359

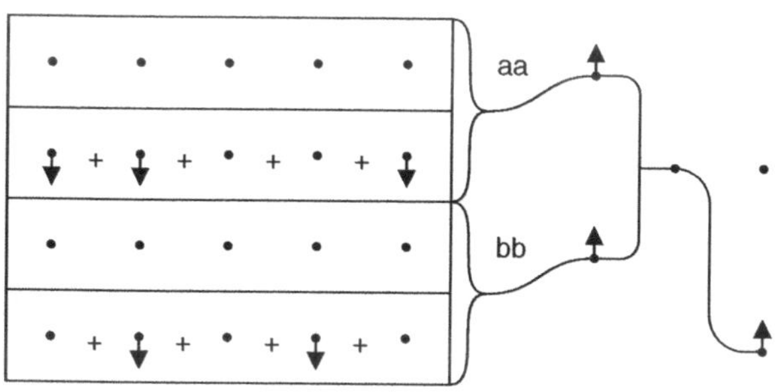

Imposes the conditions
$Q_1 + Q_2 + Q_5 = \bullet$
$Q_7 + Q_8 = \bullet$

(c) Yes Not Switches

On the right half of the switch panel white lines are drawn: conditions imposed must in effect, pass along these lines.

Switches situated on these lines modify the conditions which pass through them: of these aa, bb and the bottom switch are three-way switches labelled

- • which means : condition is unchanged (yes)
- which means : condition is cancelled [a]
- × which means : condition is reversed (not)

The & + and red switches are described later: at present they are supposed to be in their normal positions.

[a] condition in cancelled

[i] Faintly visible in the two diagrams in this section are two dots representing switches not thrown and hence seen end-on. These are the & + switch described **(d)** below, whose dot is to the right of the place where the lines from 'aa' and 'bb' have merged, and the 'red switch' described in **54F(a)**, whose dot is at the far right of the figure, not lying on a curved line. Three of the examples in **54J** show this switch thrown.

Examples.

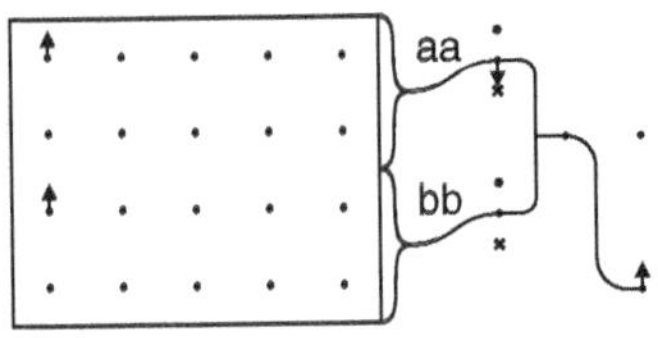

$Q_1 = \times$

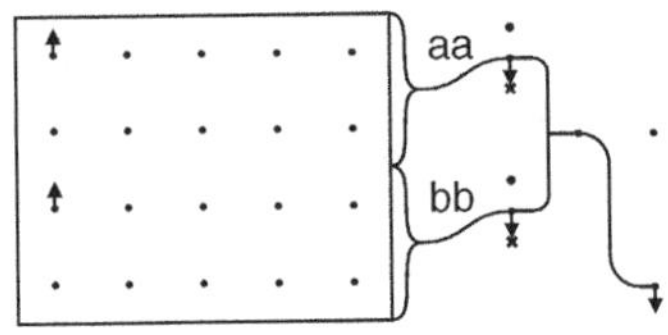

Either $Q_1 = \times$ *or* $Q_6 = \times$.

(d) &+

Two conditions reach this switch, from aa and bb.

& means both;

+ means both or neither.

It is intended for use with $Q+$ switches
e.g. $Q_1 + Q_2 + Q_3 = \bullet$, $Q_8 + Q_9 = \bullet$, +, means

$$\begin{cases} \text{either} \quad Q_1 + Q_2 + Q_3 = \bullet \quad \text{and} \quad Q_8 + Q_9 = \bullet \\ \text{or} \quad Q_1 + Q_2 + Q_3 = \times \quad \text{and} \quad Q_8 + Q_9 = \times \end{cases}$$

i.e. $Q_1 + Q_2 + Q_3 + Q_8 + Q_9 = \bullet$.
Obviously any number of Q's can be added.

54F MISCELLANEOUS COUNTER FACILITIES

(a) Split Score Counter

p. 360 If the red switch to the right of & + is thrown the score counter is split into two, each counting independently up to 99.

The 1st and 2nd digits count for conditions imposed in bb

a The 3rd. and 4th digits count for conditions imposed in aa and direct plugging.

(b) Span Counter

This makes it possible to count on a part only of the text between start and stop.

It controls two sets of decade switches (0000 – 9999) labelled "start", "end", on the panel above the printer.

If "start" is set at m, "end" at n, the places counted on from the $\overline{m+1}$ th to nth, inclusive, on the tape from which the start sign is taken.

Note: The position counter continues to work in terms of start signs not in terms of the beginning of span.

(c) Set Total

A device whereby only scores which exceed, or, alternatively, scores which do not exceed, a fixed score, are displayed or printed. The switches are above the plug panel, viz. a set of decade

i switches (0000 – 9999) and a three way switch $\overset{>}{\underset{<}{\text{off}}}$.

[a] condition

[i] Word 'off' handwritten.

54G THE PRINTER

(a) Lost scores

On Robinson stepping is always uniform, so that when scores appear in rapid succession it is not possible to inhibit stepping till they can be printed and scores may thus be "lost". Various devices are used to prevent this.

1. The printer is made to print as fast as possible, without spacing, in fact too fast to print the same figure twice successively. When two or more digits which are alike occur together, the printer replaces all but the *last* by arbitrary letters (actually a,b,c,d,e,f,g for the first seven digits respectively) for example ab072f39 means 00072339.

2. Two scores can be stored at once (instead of one as on Colossus).

3. The machine is not made to count as fast as it could be.

4. If nevertheless a score is lost, this is shewn in two ways.

   (i) A light appears below the display (labelled "lost counts")

   (ii) A cyclometer records the number of lost scores.

The cyclometer can be reset (but only one at a time) by throwing a switch near the cyclometer up to "meter".

(b) PCO

This switch cuts out the printer: unfortunately if it is thrown to normal during a run it is apt to demoralize the printer and produce rows of dots.

(c) RESET

p. 361

This switch clears the display and all scores which are in storage.

54H CONTROL TAPES

(a) Definition

A control tape is one used to select a set of places on another tape whereon a count is to be made.

These places may be all consecutive, or in isolated groups, either regular or irregular.

(b) Spanning by means of control tapes

In particular if all the places are consecutive, and if still more particularly the tape steps in unison with the tape from which the start is taken, a control tape is equivalent to spanning. Spanning by dials has of course the advantage that it can be adjusted rapidly, and if the spanning required is not known beforehand this advantage is overwhelming.

Spanning by a control tape was used for some early versions of mechanical flags and rectangles, in which several different spans are needed: the spans were represented on the control tape by different letters, and selected by means of a letter count which is easier than respanning. This was [a] discontinued when the split score counter was introduced only because it absorbed too many of the conditions which can be imposed on the bb half-counter.

A compromise, spanning large pieces of text by dial and subdividing these by a control tape is quite feasible.

Old Robinson had no span counter so that spanning had to be effected by control tape, or more commonly by a control impulse replacing an impulse of the tape to be counted. This was often necessary because the minimum text length was 2,000.

---

[a] easier that

(c) Irregularly spaced selection

When the places to be selected are not consecutive a control tape must be used: the method is obvious: it can be employed to eliminate corrupt letters.

(d) Regularly spaced selection

Some simplification is usually possible: the length of the control tape can be any multiple of the cycle which can be put on the bedstead. A proper choice for the length of the other tape will usually suffice for any stepping required. A good example is the 1+2 rectangle (**24B(e)**).

(e) Number of different selections made by one tape

A single control tape `/9/H/T` and so on can, by imposing the conditions $\underline{C} = 9$, $C = 9$, $\underline{C} = \mathtt{H}$, $C = \mathtt{H}$ and so on, be made to select a cycle of 62 or fewer places.

A single impulse of a tape with the pattern **xxxx••••xx•x••x•** , can, by use of $\underline{C}, C, \overline{C}, \overline{\overline{C}}$,
i be made to select a cycle of 16 places (**R3** p. 75).

p. 362 54J SOME ROBINSON PLUGGING USED OPERATIONALLY

E.2 **(a) 1+2 Rectangle (24B(e))**

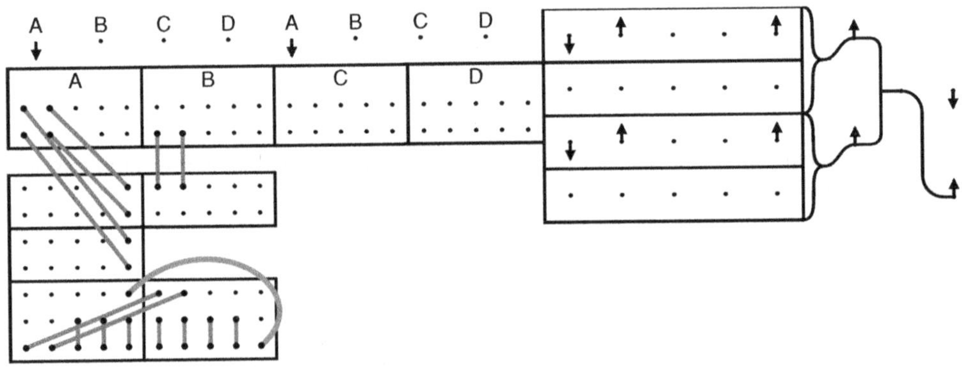

(b) $\widehat{\chi}_2$ (25E(e))

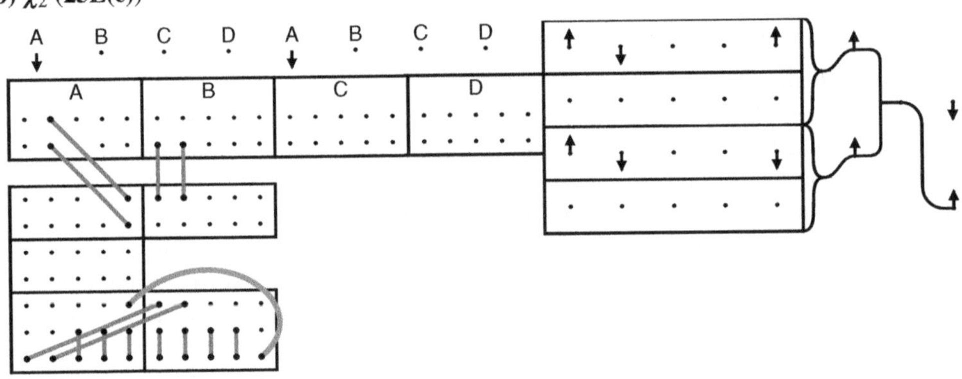

[i] Reference handwritten.

(c) Mechanical Flags (95C(a))

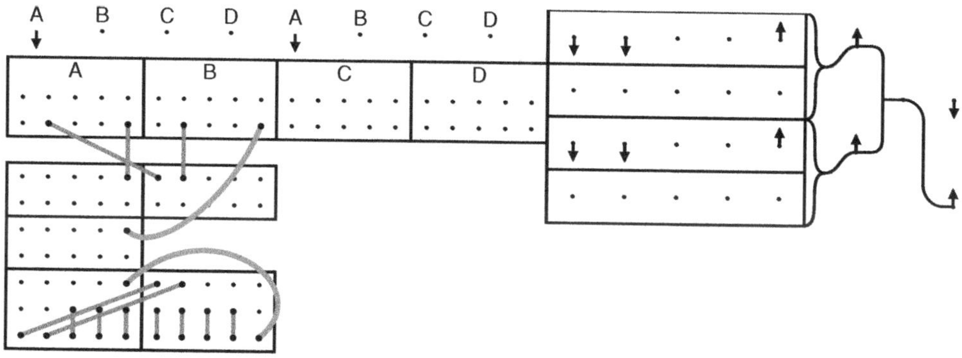

(d) Counting 999 on whole text

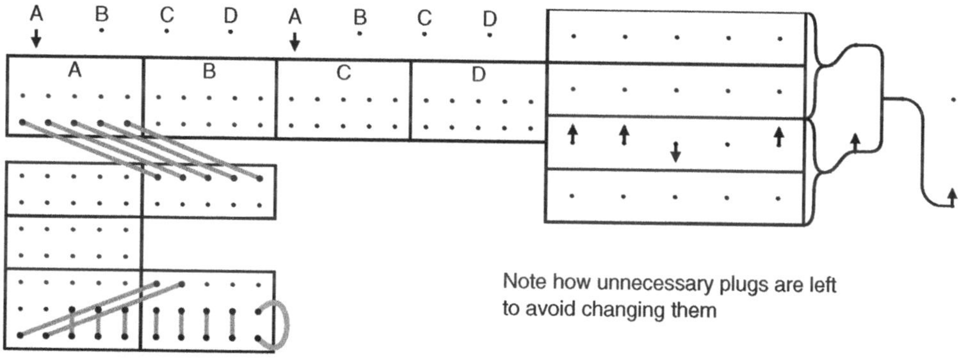

p. 363, a # 55 SPECIALIZED COUNTING MACHINES

i

E.1

ii ## 55A DRAGON (Figs. **58 (XXVI–XXX)**) (Details apply to Dragon 2 only)

(a) Purpose and method

E.2

The purpose is to set a common crib P, of up to 10 letters, in a given de-chi D, i.e. to find a stretch of D (if there is one) where the underlying plain text is P, so that $P + D = \psi'$, which when the extensions are removed, yields ψ.

Dragon adds P to a stretch of D in all positions in turn: in each position it contracts $P + D$, i.e. omits repeated letters, and then compares each impulse of the result, independently, with the corresponding ψ wheel: if all five can be fitted the machine stops and displays the settings of D and all ψ's at the last letter of the crib.

(b) Use of motor or limitation

Although the majority of repeated letters in ψ' are due to extension some are not, and the method will obviously be more powerful if $P + D$ is contracted only at total motor dots.

Dragon 1 cannot do this; Dragons 2, 3 can. In practice if the motor settings are known
b it is unnecessary to use Dragon: the facility can however be used with great benefit to forbid contraction at limitation dots.

(c) Setting up D, ψ, χ_2, μ

E.3 (i) **The de-chi.** D is on a tape fed into a tape-reader. Dragon remembers it ten letters at a time.

(ii) **The crib.** P is plugged on a 10×5 array of jacks. The length of the crib can be reduced by the top row switches: starting at the left, each switch thrown up cuts out one letter. The only letter which can be cut out from the middle of the crib is the fifth, by throwing its switch down.

There are actually two 10×5 arrays, selected by a switch, so that one can be set up while the other is in use.

(iii) ψ. ψ is plugged up as usual: above each jack is a lamp to show the setting at the end of a successful crib.

(iv) μ, χ_2. μ_{61}, μ_{37}, χ_2 have each two rows of jacks, the lower for the pattern, the upper for the setting at the start of the de-chi.

[a] SPECIALISED [b] unneccessary

[i] In the original text of the *Report*, almost all chapters start with an analytical contents list. This one does not. We have accordingly supplied such a list, as a copy editor would have done, for uniformity and the convenience of readers.

[ii] Handwritten figure reference in head not enclosed by parentheses.

(d) The display

When a crib sets, this shews the settings, at the end of the crib, of μ_{61}, μ_{37}, χ_2, D. D is measured in lines of 31.

The display also shows each position (1, 2, ... 9) where $P + D$ has been contracted.

(e) The de-chi display

Above the crib jacks is a display showing, in dots and crosses, the ten letters currently under p. 364 examination.

(f) Miscellaneous facilities

(i) A cut-out switch for each of the five impulses.

(ii) Set total for extensions such that Dragon does not stop unless there is a minimum number of extensions. Switch 5 means 5, switches 5 and i means i.

(iii) Switch for use when setting tapes back, such that the recorded setting of D remains stationary.

(g) Miscellaneous switches

Reset tape, Reset tape and wheels, reset $\chi_2\mu$, limitation, single step, de-chi display cut-out, test, start-stop.

(h) Dragon 1

Always contracts a repeated letter.

(i) Dragon 3

A much larger machine; can deal with a 16 letter crib, or with two or three shorter ones simultaneously. It can cope with a gap of up to 5 letters in the crib, trying every possible number of extensions in the gap.

(j) Salamander

This is a "compatibility" gadget for attachment to Dragon (see **28B(d)**). i, a

55B PROTEUS (Fig. 58 (XXXI))

(a) Purpose and method

E.4

Proteus anagrams depths (**28A(a)**(ii)).

The given depth V is known to be the sum of two plain texts $P_{(a)} + P_{(b)}$. It is expected that at some position one of these will be a very common group of plain text letters, say one of the six ii commonest: this is called the crib, $P^{(1)}$; and that at the same position the other is a fairly common group, one of several hundred, called the dictionary $P^{(2)}$.

Then of course $P^{(1)} + P^{(2)} + V = /$.

What Proteus does is to add $P^{(1)}$, $P^{(2)}$, V in all positions looking for a position where the sum is all /'s.

(b) Setting up $P^{(1)}$, $P^{(2)}$, V

(i) $P^{(1)}$ The crib has a length of seven or fewer letters and is set up by plugging. Each letter has 6 jacks: a cross in the 6th means "ignore this letter". Actually six cribs are set up and examined simultaneously but independently.

(ii) $P^{(2)}$ The dictionary is on a tape running on a Colossus bedstead, with blanks between groups.

(iii) V The depth is on a tape fed into a tape-reader. p. 365

[a] compatability

[i] Handwritten 'a' inserted with a caret.
[ii] Handwritten 'letters' inserted with a caret.

(c) Operation

Proteus is started: it reads and remembers the first seven letters of the depth, adds them to the
i, E.5 crib, and as the dictionary is scanned adds this also in all positions looking for a click consisting entirely of strokes.

If no click is found, the tape reader steps. Proteus acquires the 8th letter and forgets the 1st, so that letters 1–7 are replaced by letters 2–8; and so on.

When a click is found, Proteus stops, and displays

(i) the position in the depth (last letter) measured in lines 31 long.

(ii) the successful crib (1, 2, 3, 4, 5, or 6).

The place in the dictionary must be found by hand, (by addition).

The anagram can be checked throwing a switch to "rerun", so re-examining the same seven letters of the depth.

To resume stepping throw the switch to "reset".

(d) Other Applications

ii Proteus is equally applicable to any mod-2 addition teleprinter cipher which has true depths.

iii 55C AQUARIUS (Fig. **58 (XXXII)**)

(a) Purpose and method

Aquarius sets go-backs (**28B(f)**) using a de-chi.

In the correct position, the two *P*'s are the same, so that $\Delta D_{(a)} + \Delta D_{(b)} = \Delta P_{(a)} + \Delta\psi'_{(a)} + \Delta P_{(b)} + \Delta\psi'_{(b)} = \Delta\psi'_{(a)} + \Delta\psi'_{(b)}$

Aquarius adds a stretch of de-chi immediately after the autopause to a stretch before the autopause, differences the sum, and makes counts for resemblance to the sum of two $\Delta\psi'$s. The proportional frequency of each letter depends only on the number of crosses in it, and the six switches are for counting letters with 0, 1, 2, 3, 4, 5 crosses: throwing more than one switch provides "either - or",

Two counters are provided (generally used for all dots, all crosses).

(b) Stepping

At first the comparison is made on a steadily increasing text, thus: first 11 letters after the auto-pause with last 11 before; then first 12 after with last 12 before, and so on.

After the text length has reached 97 there is no further increase, but the 97 letters following the autopause are stepped back relative to the part before the autopause. 97 letters are sufficient: in a long go-back the letters immediately before the autopause may be rubbish.

p. 366 **(c) Setting up the de-chi**

The most entertaining feature of Aquarius is that the tape is used only at the outset, to set up the de-chi electrically, viz. on condensers: a charge represents a cross: these are automatically recharged at least once every two minutes, according to the rule "to him that hath shall be given".

The tape is marked at the 97th letter beyond the autopause and (switch: reading position, home, charge operating length, start reader) run backwards through a tape-reader and so transferred to the condensers. It stops automatically at the autopause, where its position is checked. Then (switch: charge comparison length, start reader) 218 letters before the autopause are similarly transferred. Switch: comparison length off, reader off, comparison position, home.

---

[i] Word 'consisting' handwritten.

[ii] 'mod-2-addition', with 'mod' handwritten.

[iii] Handwritten figure reference in head not enclosed by parentheses.

(d) Running

A set total is imposed on each counter (for /'s and 8's) and the machine is started.

In a position where the score on either counter exceeds the set total, the machine stops. The set total is taken off and the switch thrown to "rerun" (i.e. count again without stepping). This checks the score and finds the score on the other counter.

To resume stepping the switch is thrown to "go on".

Because the text length increases the set total requires occasional adjustment. [a]

(e) Impulse cut-out

Switches labelled 1, 2, 3, 4, 5 cut out these impulses, causing them to be treated as all dots.

(f) The Buzzer

This is provided to call attention to imminent catastrophe.

[a] occassional

p. 367 # 56 COPYING MACHINES

iii, E.1 For general description and classification see chapter **13**.

56A HAND PERFORATOR

Operation of the keyboard produces punched tape.

56B ANGEL

This simply copies tapes. It consists of a tape-reader linked to a reperforator. To make corrections by hand, it is necessary to stop the machine, and replace the input tape by one bearing the letter to be inserted.

56C INSERT MACHINE

(Vulgarly known as the IBM machine)

Functionally this is an Angel with a device for making corrections by hand easily. In addition to the reader and reperforator it has a punch insertion typewriter to which nine

E.2 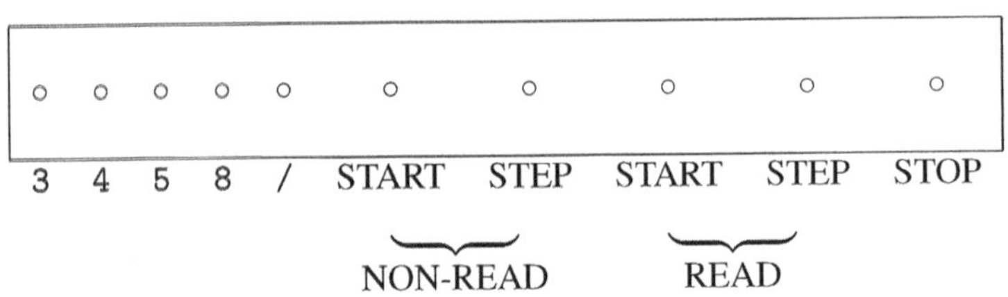

special keys have been added, thus

For normal running use "read": "start" means start and continue to run; "step" means step one letter.

To *insert* letters, "stop" and

for A to Z use the ordinary keyboard;

for 9 use the space bar;

[i] There is no item 56I. Items 56J, 56K, and 56L handwritten.

[ii] This chapters analytical contents reproduces what is on the corresponding page of the *Report*, p. 367. The title given here for sections **56K** does not exactly match what is in the body of the chapter.

[iii] Sentence 'For general...' handwritten in a typewriter-like script, possibly a hand reenforcement of too-faint typescript.

for 3458/ use the special keys.

To step the reader but not the reperforator use "non-read".
To step the reperforator but not the reader use special key "/".
To *correct* a letter, use "non-read", and insert.
The tapes produced are unsuitable for Colossus and need to be copied. p. 368

56D JUNIOR

(a) Function

Junior prints from a tape. It consists of a tape-reader, a steckerboard, and an electric typewriter.

By steckering any character can be made to print any other character. Any number of characters can be steckered to print the same character.

(b) Details of steckering

The three upper rows of jacks carry the output from the reader.

The three lower rows carry the input to the typewriter.

Steckering is effected by plug cords.

Letters not steckered are printed normally (as Tunny letters, e.g. 5 as 5 not by actual figure shift).

Different letters to be printed alike are plugged into a common jack and thence to the desired letter.

To common a large group of letters a *Ring Common* can be used.

The reader output has two jacks for each letter, a mere shorting plug in the upper jack connects the letter to Ring Common RC 1; a plug in the lower jack connects it to RC 2. RC 1, RC 2 can be plugged to any desired letters: if they are left blank the letters commoned into them are printed as •, × respectively.

In a jack carrying input to the typewriter FS means literally figure shift; 5 means 5; similarly for CR etc.

Note: some Juniors have a different and much smaller steckerboard, unsuitable for rapid steckering.

(c) The Typewriter

This has three switches: "start"; "stop" and "insert". "Insert" causes the whole machine to stop at the end of each line. The arrangement of these switches varies considerably.

The typewriter can be set to print in any width up to 60.

Letters can be inserted by using the keyboard.

56E GARBO Fig. 58 (XXI).

p. 369

Everything said about Junior applies to Garbo: the only difference is that, in addition, Garbo has a row of switches for Δ'ing. Garbo always Δ's backwards.

Clear	Δd								
↑	↑								
○	○	○	○	○	○	○	○	○	
	↓	↓	↓	↓	↓	↓	↓	↓	
	$\Sigma\Delta$	ΔZ_1	ΔZ_2	ΔZ_3	ΔZ_4	ΔZ_5	PUNCH	DC	(supply)

1. If the switch labelled $\frac{\Delta d}{\Sigma\Delta}$ is thrown to Δd , each letter is differenced; it may thereafter be steckered.

2. If the same switch is thrown to $\Sigma\Delta$, and some ΔZ switches are thrown the corresponding impulses are differenced and added, being printed as • or ×: no steckering is needed.

"Clear" merely clears any letter left from the preceding run.

"Punch" is thrown if the output is connected to a punch instead of a typewriter.

56F MILES

(a) Function

E.3 A Miles is a machine which when fed with one or more tapes produces a tape combining them in some way.

(b) The early Miles

The early Miles could combine tapes by adding them (in the Tunny sense). Impulses could not be permuted, though an impulse could be cut out. No further description is given.

(c) Miles B, C, D

These are a development of the early Miles. With no plugging and switches all normal the tapes are merely added. By plugging impulses can be permuted. Differencing is not possible except by using two tapes at a stagger of one. (Details: **56G**.)

(d) The Mechanical flag Gadget (Miles D)

This introduced an extension of the notion of combining tapes, viz. that one tape can be used to control the stepping of another, or of itself. (Details **56G(m)**.)

(e) Miles A

This was designed to be as flexible as possible: nothing is transferred from input to output without being plugged. Plugging is therefore usually more extensive than on Miles B, C, D; but because it is based on a simple uniform principle (**56H(c)**), it is very easy and can be made quickly.

Differencing, up to eight times, is provided by means of memory circuits. (Details **56H**.)

p. 370 (f) Performance of Miles

This has not been entirely satisfactory. These machines could not of course claim the attention devoted to Colossi, but even relatively they have been rather neglected. The design is believed to be sound, but there has been no adequate supply of spare parts. In particular Miles A has been rarely in proper working order, the existing model being the experimental one, not really intended for regular use: this rather than the extra plugging, explains the operators' preference for B, C, D.

(g) Possible Improvements

The ideal Miles would probably be on the lines of Miles A. It would be desirable to include a generalization of the Flagging Gadget (**56G(m)**), viz. an automatic stepping control such that any reader or reperforator control could be started or stopped either by pulses from any tape or after a fixed number of letters: one suggestion is two automatic control jacks (stop and start) on each reader and reperforator control, into which any pulse could be plugged.

If Miles were required to combine letters in accordance with a general combination square, extensive changes would be needed.

The counters would probably be of real use only if they could be reset to zero.

56G MILES B, C, D

(a) Layout

Each of these consist of 5 tape-readers, a plugboard, and 2 reperforators.

B is now incomplete.

The control panel is arranged as in the following diagram.

This may be compared with the photograph (fig. **58 (XXII)**). i

In the description of Miles, tape-readers will be called transmitters, as is customary: these are *not* auto-transmitters.

p. 371

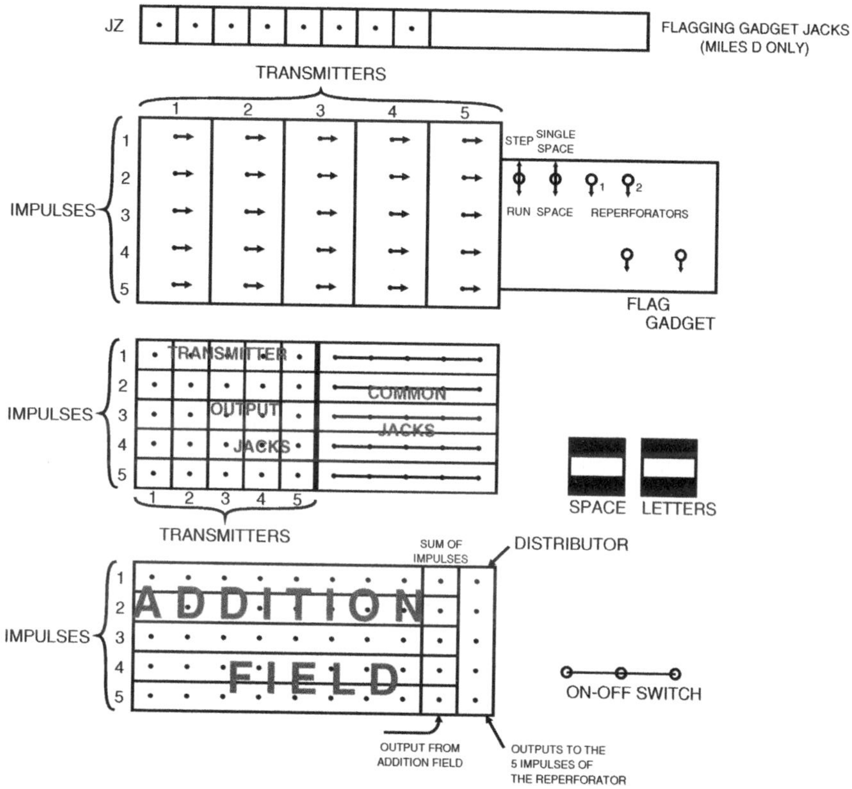

(b) The items of the plugboard

1. Transmitter impulse cut-out switches.
2. Transmitter output jacks, each carrying one of the 5×5 impulses for the 5 transmitters.
3. Addition field: this has 5 rows of jacks, one for each impulse.
4. Sum of impulses: these 5 jacks are the output jacks for the 5 sums of the addition field.
5. Distributor: these 5 jacks carry the input to the 5 impulses of the reperforators.
6. Commons: each row constitutes one common jack.

(c) Normal Connection, i.e. without plugging

The first impulses (for example) from all five transmitters are added in the first row of the addition field and taken to the first impulse of "Distributor".

(d) Plugging and Switching

The more important items are described in paras **(e) (f) (g) (h) (i)**.

---

[i] Figure reference handwritten.

p. 372 **(e) Impulse cut-out switches**

Any impulse can be cut out completely by its impulse cut-out switch: if all the impulses of a transmitter are cut out it does not step.

(f) Transmitter output jacks

Any one of the 25 impulses in the transmitter output jacks can, by the obvious plugging, be transferred to a different row of the addition field. This means that it is

(i) cut out from its own row

(ii) added to the impulses already in its new row.

For example, if T4 T5 are cut out, and a plug cord is taken from $T3_1$, the first impulse of T3, to the second row of the addition field the first row now carries $T1_1 + T2_1$ and the second row $T1_2+T2_2+T3_2+T3_1$.

(g) Adding a cross

A shorting plug in a jack of addition field adds a cross thereto.

(h) Permuting sums of impulses

The outputs from the addition field can be transferred to other impulses, cancelling what is already there e.g. if the 2nd impulse in 'Sum of Impulses' is plugged to the 5th impulse of 'Distributor', the reperforators will have nothing in the 2nd impulse, and whatever is in the 2nd row of the addition field in the 5th impulse.

(i) Common jacks

These, unlike the other jacks, are not permanently connected to anything else.

Impulses plugged into a common jack are added, not in the ordinary way, but by the rule that the output is a cross unless *all* inputs are dots (Boolean addition).

Two or more outputs can be taken.

(j) Reperforators

Either one or both can be used.

(k) Counters

(Cyclometers) are supposed to record the number of blanks and letters punched: they were used very little and all but one are out of order.

p. 373 **(l) Miscellaneous switches**

Step ("run" on Miles D) causes both the transmitters and reperforators to start and continue to step.

a **Space** causes the reperforators to step, and punch blanks, the transmitters remaining stationary.

Single step, single space can be flicked on and off for a single step or space.

The unlabelled switch to the right of the reperforator switches on Miles C controls an improvised gadget used for making motor tapes when Tunny was disabled by the Fire (See Glossary).

The pair of switches below these on Miles D are for flagging. (Next para. **56G.**)

i The Triple switch is the on-off switch.

---

[a] stationery

[i] Sentence 'The Triple switch...' handwritten.

(m) Mechanized Flag Gadget (Miles D only)

The basic idea is to control the stepping of transmitters automatically by means of impulses from the tapes themselves. a

This may be needed if tapes are to be combined not concurrently, but consecutively, in a large number of stretches.

The gadget was made specially for Mechanical Flagging (ch **95**) without much regard to flexibility. Nevertheless, though designed for ordinary flags it proved suitable for combined key flags, when it is used quite differently.

This explains the rather odd facilities available.

The gadget manifests itself as a series of jacks JZ1 – JZ8. A cross in:

JZ1, 2, 3, 4 starts transmitters 1, 2, 3, 4, respectively.

JZ5 produces a cross in JZ7 and, if JZ1, 2, 3, 4 are all dots, produces a cross in JZ8 & steps transmitter 4 i

JZ6 stops transmitters 1,2,3,4 and steps transmitter 5 one sprocket hole.

The gadget has two switches: the right-hand one switches in the gadgets, the left-hand one then acts as an off switch. b, c

56H MILES A

(a) Layout (see photograph fig. **58 (XXIII)**) ii

There are

6 Transmitters.
3 Reperforators.
3 Controls (which control the stepping of both transmitters and reperforators).
6 Common jacks.
8 Sets of jacks for differencing an impulse (backwards) or taking an impulse one back.
2 Sets of extra jacks for addition.

(b) All 28 items are completely independent p. 374

Three different tape-making jobs may be done simultaneously, each being started and stopped by its own control without interfering with the running of the others. The allocation of items to each job is quite arbitrary.

At the other extreme one control may control everything, producing identical tapes from all three reperforators.

The linking of items is by plug cords.

(c) Principle of plugging

Plugging depends on a very simple principle

Each item has a series of corresponding $\begin{cases}\text{IN jacks}\\ \text{OUT jacks}\end{cases}$

Any impulse plugged into an IN jack appears suitably modified in the corresponding OUT jack.

---

[a] be [b] right hand [c] left hand

[i] Word 'if' and phrase '& steps transmitter 4' handwritten.
[ii] Typed 'see phograph', handwritten figure reference.

NOTES. Reperforators have, naturally, no OUT jacks.
Even transmitters have IN jacks.
In a common jack, IN and OUT jacks are the same.
In a control, OUT jacks are common to all 5 impulses.
Corresponding IN and OUT jacks are in the same column.

(d) The effects of the various items on an impulse taken through them.

(i) **Any one of the 5 impulses of a transmitter**: adds that impulse.

(ii) **Common jack**: the impulse can be taken *out* on several cords.

(iii) **Delta***: from $\overline{I}$: the same impulse one back. a
from $\overline{\Delta}$: the same impulse Δ'd backwards
(Δ'd). i

(iv) "**Add**": two inputs can be added (may be useful for adding two impulses already complex).

(v) **Controls**: the impulses plugged into a control can be taken out into reperforators (only *one* cord for each reperforator); each impulse is punched in the corresponding impulse of the tape.

"IN and OUT" can be continued without restriction as long as there are jacks to spare

(e) Examples:

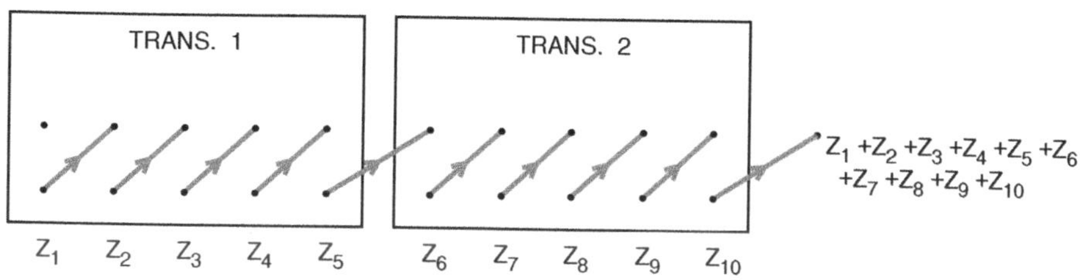

p. 375

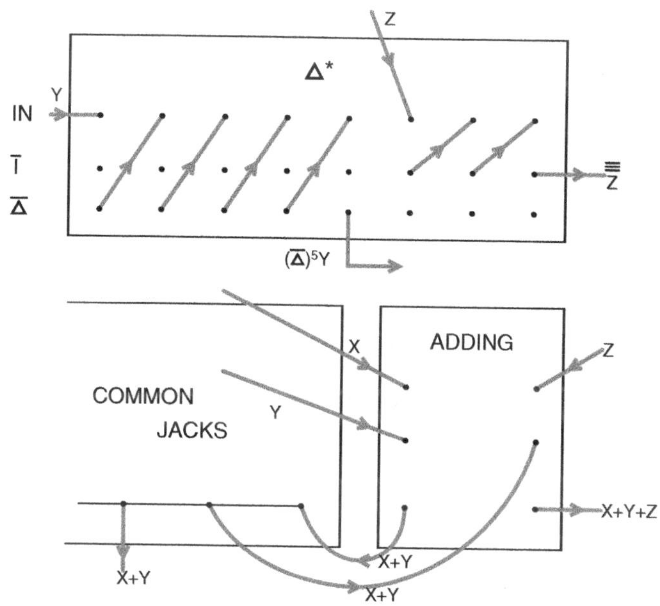

ii

A good practical example is given in **27**.
An amusing example is to take an impulse to a common jack thence

[a] **Delta***;

[i] 'Δ'd' handwritten between typewritten parentheses.

[ii] The labelling in this drawing has been altered: The 'elbow' output from the upper, Δ*, box is labelled $(\Delta^*)^5 Y$ in the *Report*. The three labels IN, $\overline{I}$ and $\overline{\Delta}$ name the three rows of sockets in the Δ* box, and they have been moved to make this more clear. The *Y* to the left of the box names the input to the first socket in the top row. Finally, the lines representing jacks have been rendered as in the other diagrams; in the *Report* they are the same thickness as the lines representing boxes.

(i) to control

(ii) one back ($\overline{1}$) to the IN jack of the same impulse.

i This integrates (un-Δ's) the impulse: it can be applied to five impulses simultaneously.

p. 376 56J TUNNY AND DECODING MACHINES

The original Tunny machine was simply a functional reproduction of the German Tunny machine, operated electrically instead of largely mechanically. It was intended primarily for
a straightforward decoding. It was developed in two directions:

(i) as a decoding machine improvements were effected and gadgets added for ease of operation, not for versatility.

(ii) as an aid to Newmanry setting and breaking, much more versatile models were produced.

There were several versions of each, some of the early ones being very awkward in operation e.g. patterns were set up by means of U-shaped pins, and wheels were reset by stepping each uniselector switch by hand, one position at a time, and forwards only. Only the later models will be described.

A weakness common to all Tunnies is that the five impulses of each letter of Z are sent through the machine successively, though by different routes, and can be added or permuted only with the aid of remembering circuits. This restriction does not apply to the wheels.

ii 56K THE (NEWMANRY) TUNNY MACHINE (Fig. **58 (XXV)**)

(a) General description of operation

The tape is fed into an auto-transmitter: Chi, psi, unless cut out, are added automatically, and the sum appears on another tape, letter by letter. At each letter the current settings of all wheels are exhibited.

b **(b) Wheel patterns**

Each wheel has two rows of jacks, in which shorting plugs can be inserted. The upper row represents the pattern; the lower row determines the initial setting. Each wheel has also one row of indicator lamps to show its current setting.

The "display" shows not the wheel settings but the number of positions through which the wheels have moved: the three rows of figures correspond to Chi, (with Z and μ_{61}) μ_{37}, Psi. Each row has a cut-out switch.

(c) Limitation

Switches K P S (for $\overline{\chi}_2, \overline{\overline{P}}_5, \overline{\psi}'_1$) one or more being thrown determine the limitation.

The characters of $\overline{\psi}'_1, \overline{\overline{P}}_5, \overline{P}_5$, which are just before the start of Z can be preset by spring switches: $\overline{\overline{P}}_5$ $\overline{P}_5$ are set simultaneously by switch positions: ••, •×, ×•, ××.

p. 377 **(d) Wheel switches**

Each wheel has a separate switch. Unless a wheel is switched in, it has no effect whatever, e.g. if χ_2 is not in, the limitation will be incorrect and the psis will move incorrectly (cf. Para. **(e)**).

The chi, psi master switches merely determine whether the wheels move or remain stationary.

---

[a] straight forward [b] Wheel-patterns

[i] Word 'un-Δ's' handwritten.

[ii] Figure reference handwritten.

(e) Plug panel

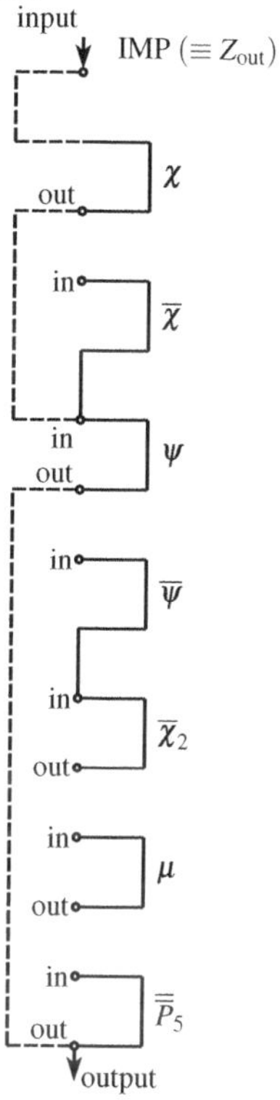

In normal operation the motion of the psis depends on some or all of Z, Chi, Psi, Motor, but only Z, Chi, Psi are added in the resultant tape. It is sometimes desirable to modify this in various ways, e.g. in a total motor tape μ_{37} and the limitation are involved in the resultant tape; Z, Chi, Psi are not to be added to it, but Z, Chi, Psi (or χ_2 at least) cannot be switched out (compare para. **(d)**) because they determine the limitation.

To each of the five impulses corresponds a column of jacks (see diagram: where no suffix is shown, that corresponding to the column is to be assumed). It will be seen that Psi, $\overline{\chi}_2$, μ, $\overline{\overline{P}}_5$ have each an "in" jack and an "out" jack. Anything put into "in" appears at "out" with the appropriate impulse added to it. Chi has no in jack being normally connected to "IMP", which is in effect, "Z out". $\overline{\chi}$ ψ have no out jacks being permanently connected to ψ, $\overline{\chi}_2$ respectively. Chi and psi are normally connected both up and down (dotted lines), but a plug inserted in one of their jacks automatically breaks the normal connection to that jack.

Wheels may be transferred from one column to another, but Z cannot.

There are a few common jacks.

(f) Stop setting

Decode switches reading 0–9999 can be set so that the machine stops after so many letters of Z.

(g) Contraction

Because Robinson psi-setting required a de-chi tape contracted by the omission of letters against total motor dots (**52(d)**), several Tunnies included a facility for making such tapes.

(h) Miscellaneous facilities p. 378

(i) Reversing one or more of the five impulses. [i]

(ii) Making blank one or more of the five impulses.

(iii) Running backwards.

(iv) Encoding with P_5 limitation.

(v) Innumerable switches for cutting out lamps.

(i) Differencing

Tunnies "1" and "3" can produce differenced tapes.

---

[i] Handwritten 'or more' inserted with a caret, both in items (i) and (ii).

i 56L DECODING MACHINE (Fig. 58 (XXIV))

(a) General description of operation

Given a cipher text all of whose settings are known, the appropriate patterns, settings and limitation are imposed, and the machine is started.

As each letter of cipher is typed out on the keyboard, Chi, Psi, are automatically added so that a letter of clear text is printed.

In place of the keyboard an auto-transmitter reading a cipher tape can be plugged in, but its speed is apt to be too great for the machine.

The settings of all wheels at each letter are shown by indicating lamps.

For swift operation some switches are on a control box adjacent to the keyboard.

(b) Wheel patterns

See **56K(b)**, but there is no display of positions moved through, only of current settings.

(c) Limitation

See **56K(c)**.

(d) Chaser settings

In early models if it were necessary for any reason, such as typists' error or corruption, to start again a few places back, the position of each wheel had to be calculated and set separately. This is now avoided by "chaser settings" which are stationary during ordinary running, but

(i) the "set reading" switch causes the chaser settings to move forward to current settings (used once per line or so)

(ii) the "reset" switch causes the current settings to move back to the chaser settings.

These switches are duplicated on the control box.

The same lamps are used to indicate both current and chaser settings, but confusion is avoided by "DCL" which extinguishes the chaser settings.

p. 379 ### (e) Snaking

On corrupt texts using P_5 limitation the psis may be incorrectly motorized. If the SN and the
a psi cut-out switches are in the active position, then each time SS is thrown the psi settings are increased by one. Several versions for different psi settings can be printed: by "snaking" through these the clear text can be found. In practice it was done better by hand.

(f) Chi, mu, Psi cut-out switches

These switches (on the control box) cut out a set of wheels completely, including their effect in the total motor.

Cutting out Psi produces de-chi, which may be checked against that provided by the Newmanry.

(g) χ_2 inside out

This switch interchanges dot and cross in χ_2.

---

[a] posision

[i] Handwritten figure reference in head not enclosed in partentheses.

57 SIMPLE MACHINES p. 380

(a) Slide-rules

The operations required are multiplication, division, squaring, extracting square roots, and taking logarithms to base 10. Many of the slide-rules used lack logarithms, and have elaborate useless scales. a

(b) Adding Machines

"Plus" comptometers are used, reading up to 10^9. For each digit there is a column of five keys 1, 2, 3, 4, 5. These are quite suitable, though a few specimens wasted three columns by provision for adding £.s.d. E.1 E.2

(c) Hand Counter (For counting sprocket holes in tapes)

The tape is carried forwards by a sprocket wheel, against which it is held by a hinged wedge made of perspex. The wedge is made transparent so that characters can easily be identified; its edge is used as a ruler for marking the tape.

A single handle drives both

(1) the sprocket-wheel,

(2) a cyclometer. i

The cyclometer is geared so that each movement of one sprocket increases the reading by 1. The cyclometer can be reset to zero.

Hand counters were at first very troublesome.

(d) Sticker

This is a long tape guide with four dummy sprocket teeth to hold two tape ends in the correct relative position for jointing ("sticking") them.

For Colossus tapes Seccotine was used as the adhesive. For Robinson tapes Bostik, which yields a weaker but flatter and more flexible joint, was used, the central part of the sticker being heated electrically. b, c E.3

(e) Stop and Start

A simple hand punch for punching the holes, in the $4\frac{1}{2}$th and $3\frac{1}{2}$th impulses, used as start and stop signals. To make it easy to place the tape correctly the slide which holds it has an engraved mark (for the first or last letter) and a dummy sprocket tooth.

---

[a] slide rules [b] Secotine [c] Bostick

[i] Items (1) and (2) are indented to the middle of the page.

p. 381, i

58 PHOTOGRAPHS

ii

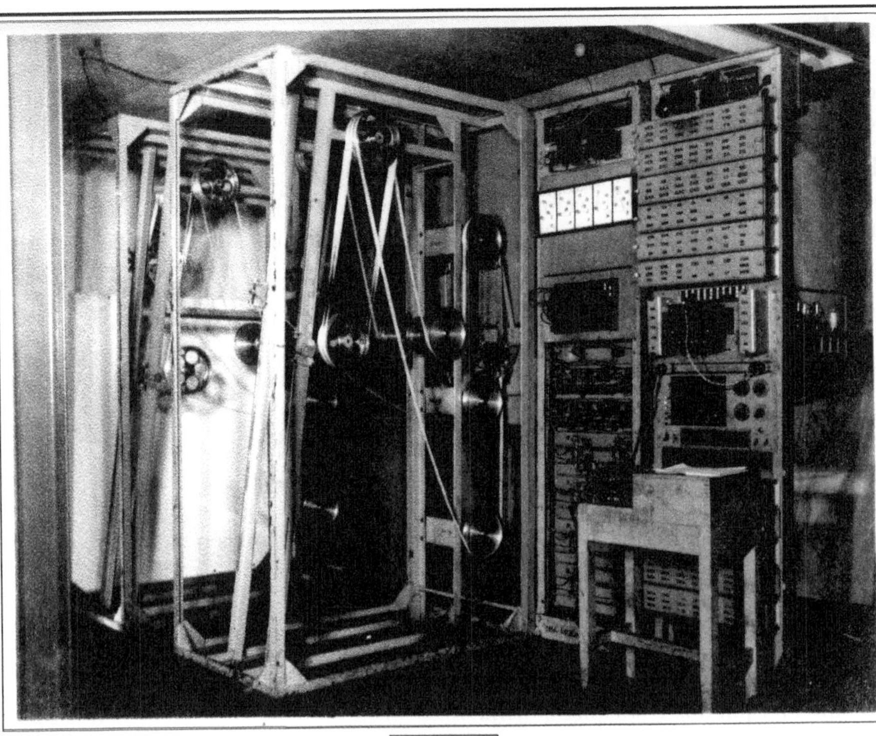

58/1: ×1.0

Fig. 58 (I) Old Robinson **(52(c))**

[i] Chapter **58** has no head; title supplied here from Table of Contents on p. i. In this chapter the figure captions have been rearranged. In the original they all stand to the right of the corresponding images, except for Fig. **58 (IX)**'s, which stands to the left. We have moved them all below the image. The figure numbers have been standardised to fit the pattern of the rest of the *Report*: 'Fig. **58 (I)**' instead of 'Fig. **I**', and so on.

[ii] This image copied from TNA HW 25/26.

[i]

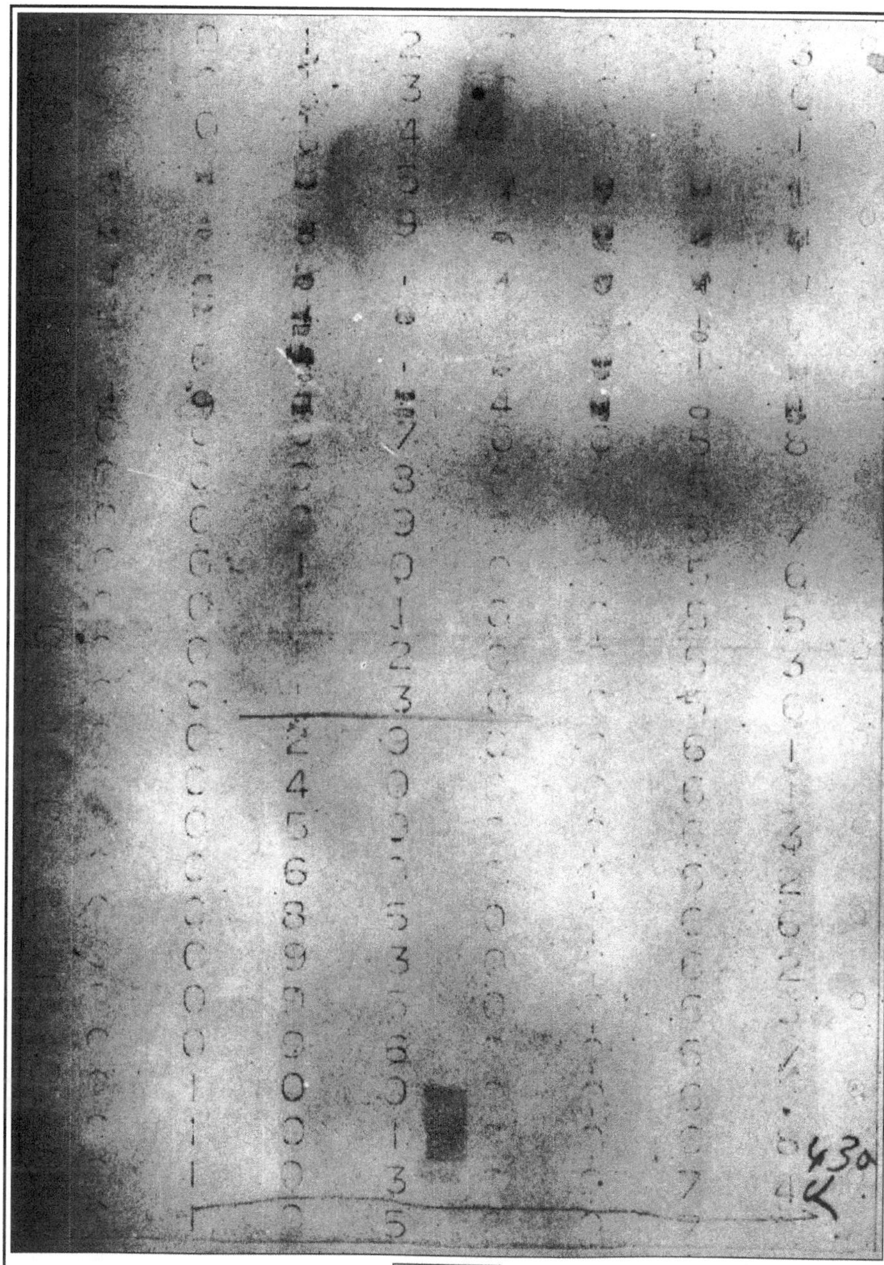

58/2: ×1.0

Fig. 58 (II) Specimen of Old Robinson printing (**52(c)**)

[i] Fig. **58 (II)** illegible in TNA HW 25/5; this image scanned from the GCHQ copy of the *Report* by a 'discretionary release of retained material by GCHQ historian'. This image ©Crown Copyright. Used with permission of Director GCHQ. Image contrast digitally enhanced.

p. 382

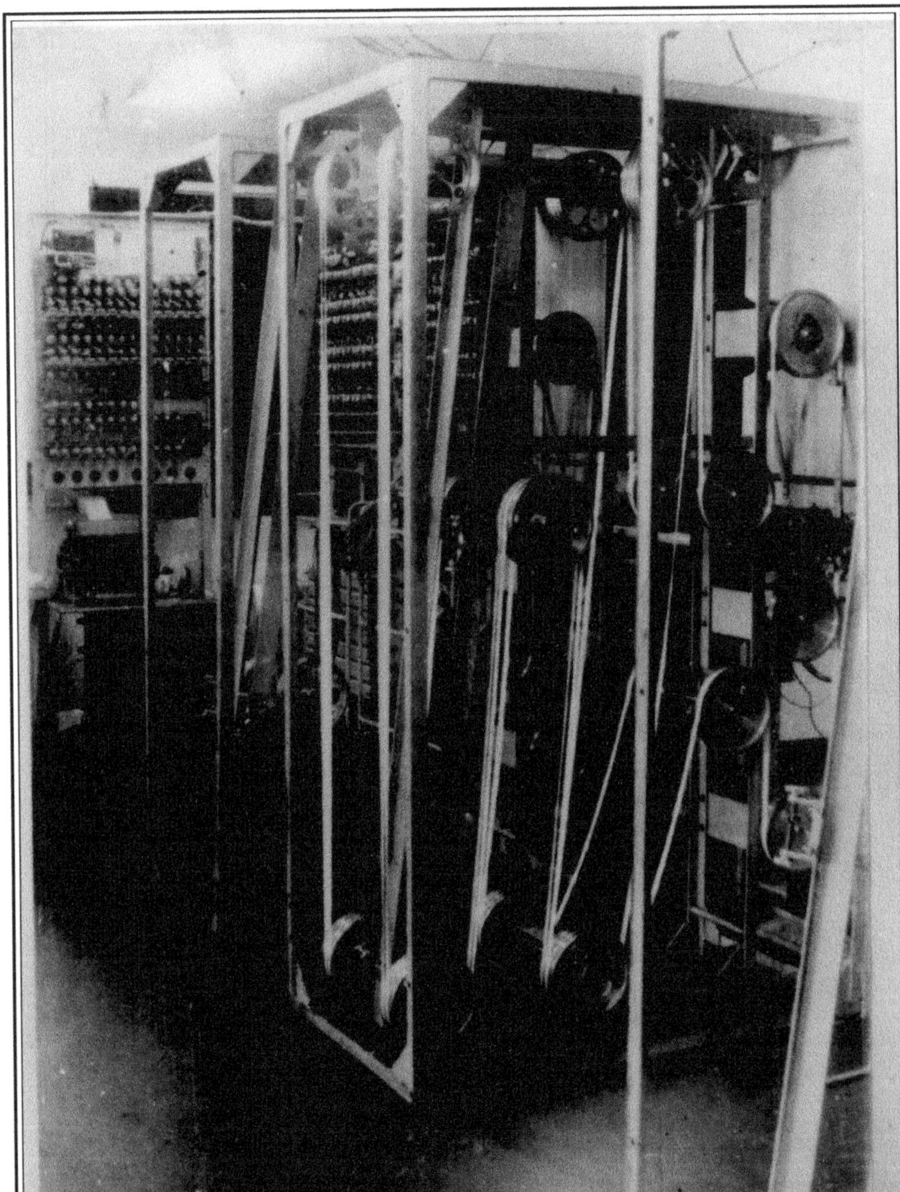

58/3: ×1.0

Fig. 58 (III) Super-Robinson (**54**)

58/4: ×.65

Fig. 58 (IV) Super-Robinson: details of gate
Note sprocket teeth and 13 holes through which light passes to photo-cells (**54C(c)**).

p. 383

58/5: ×.65

Fig. 58 (V) Super-Robinson position counter switches (**54(C)(e,f,g)**), display (**54B**), miscellaneous switches

58/6: ×.65

Fig. 58 (VI) Super-Robinson: panels

58/7: ×.65

Fig. 58 (VII) Super-Robinson: plug Δ switch panels (**54D, 54E**) "start" & "stop" switches (**54C(d)**)

p. 384

58/8: ×.65

Fig. 58 (VIII) Colossus 5: back view **(53)**

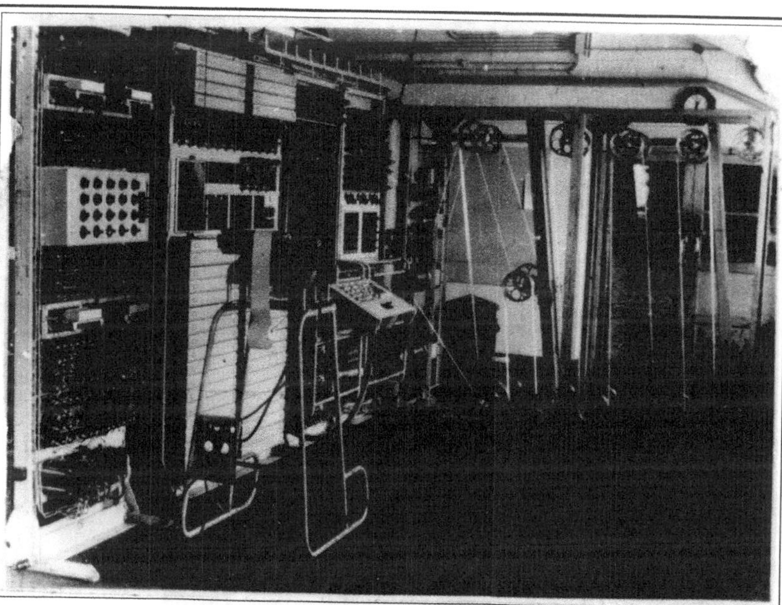

58/9: ×.65

Fig. 58 (IX) Colossus 10 **(53)** [i]

[i] Caption placed to left of image in original.

58/10: ×.65

Fig. 58 (X) Colossus 7 **(53)**

p. 385

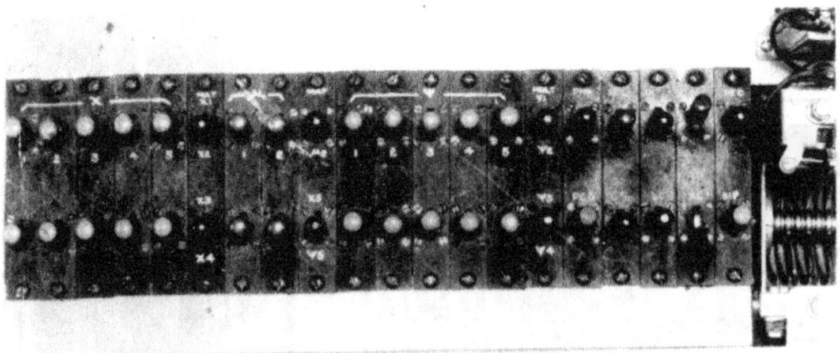

58/11: ×.65

Fig. 58 (XI) Colossus 10: control panel **(53N)**

58/12: ×.65

Fig. 58 (XII) Colossus 10: display (**53G(d)** control panel setting jacks (**53D**)

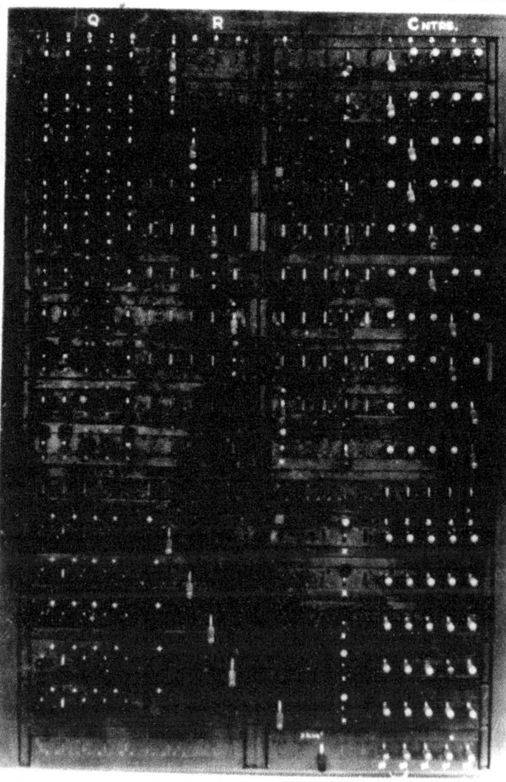

58/13: ×.65

Fig. 58 (XIII) Colossus 6: Q panel **(53J)**

p. 386

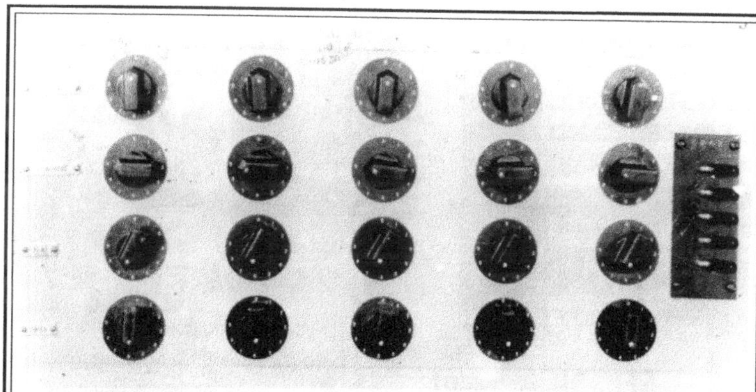

58/14: ×.65

Fig. 58 (XIV) Colossus 10: set total switches **(53G(a))**

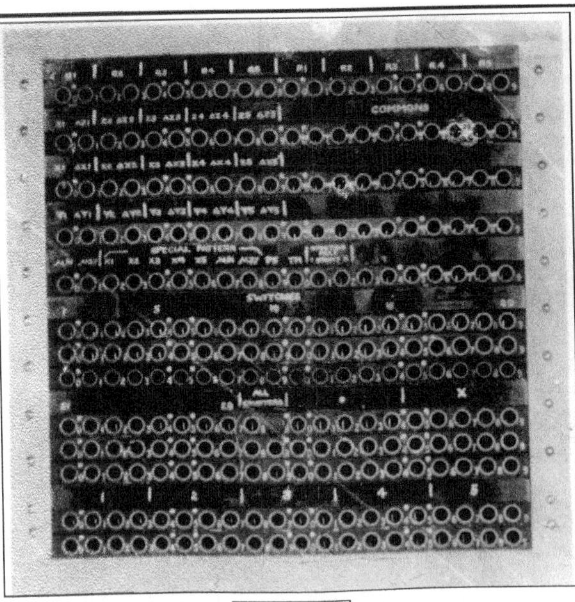

58/15: ×.65

Fig. 58 (XV) Colossus 10: plug panel **(53K)**

58/16: ×.65

Fig. 58 (XVI) Colossus 6: span counters (**53H**), plug panel (**53K**), selection panel **(53C)**

p. 387

58/17: ×.65

Fig. 58 (XVII) Colossus 10: χ_2 wheel triggers and part of μ_{61} (**53C**)

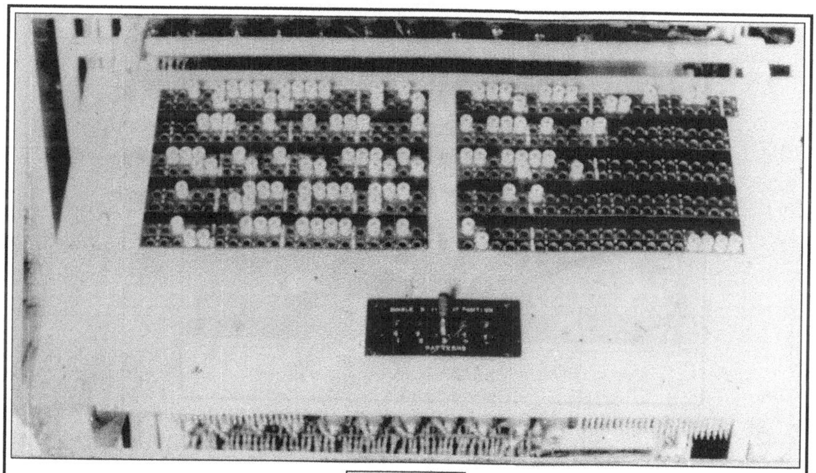

58/18: ×.65

Fig. 58 (XVIII) Colossus 10: wheel-breaking panel (**53C(i)**)

58/19: ×.65

Fig. 58 (XIX) Colossus 6: rectangling panel **(53M)**

p. 388

[i]

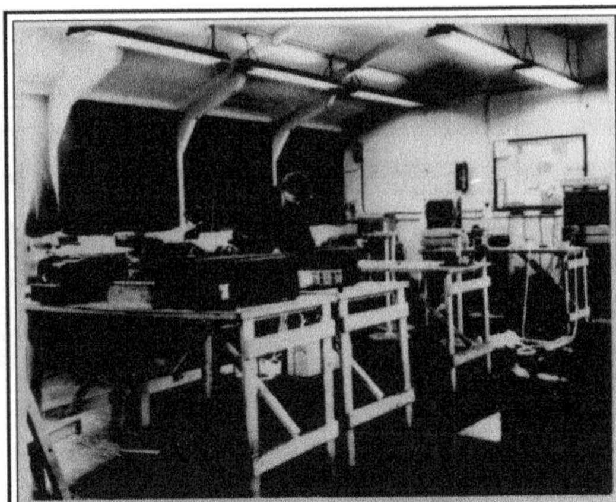

58/20: ×.65

Fig. 58 (XX) In foreground Insert Machine **(56C)**; in background Miles C, D. **(56G)**; stickers and hand-counters **(57)**

[i] This image copied from TNA HW 25/26.

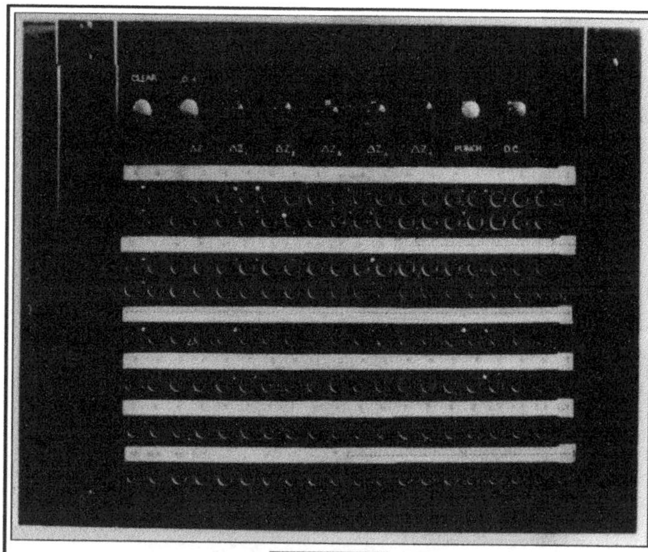

58/21: ×.65

Fig. 58 (XXI) Garbo Panel (**56E**)

p. 389

58/22: ×.65

Fig. 58 (XXII) Miles D panel (**56G**)

58/23: ×.65

Fig. 58 (XXIII) Miles A panel **(56H)**

p. 390

i

58/24: ×.65

Fig. 58 (XXIV) Decoding machines **(56L)**

---

i This image copied from TNA HW 25/26. This figure reversed in *Report*; here printed unreversed.

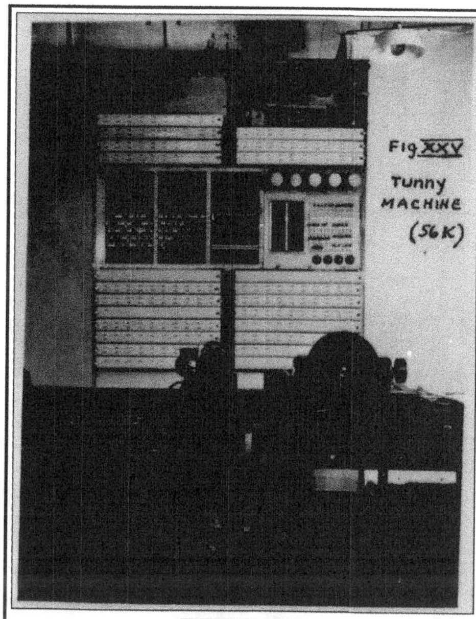

58/25: ×.65 [i]

Fig. 58 (XXV) Tunny machine **(56K)**

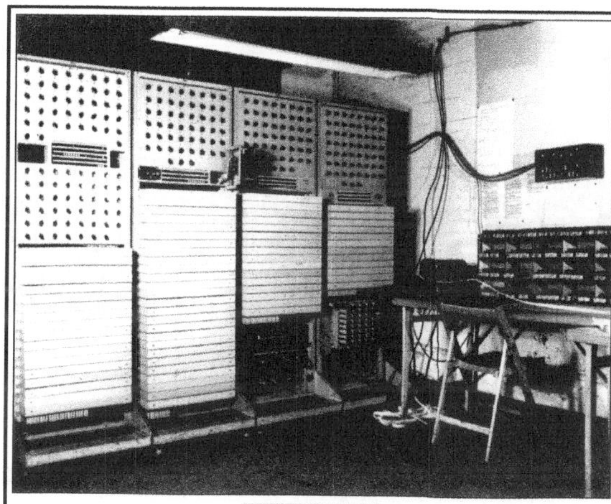

58/26: ×.65 [ii]

Fig. 58 (XXVI) Dragon 1 **(55A)**

[i] This image copied from TNA HW 25/26.

[ii] This image copied from TNA HW 25/26. The right edge of the version in the *Report* is slightly cropped, at roughly the right-hand edge of the wall-mounted indicator lamp box, continuing down just to the right of the right most table leg.

p. 391

58/27: ×.65

Fig. 58 (XXVII) Dragon 2

58/28: ×.65

Fig. 58 (XXVIII) Dragon 2: switch panel

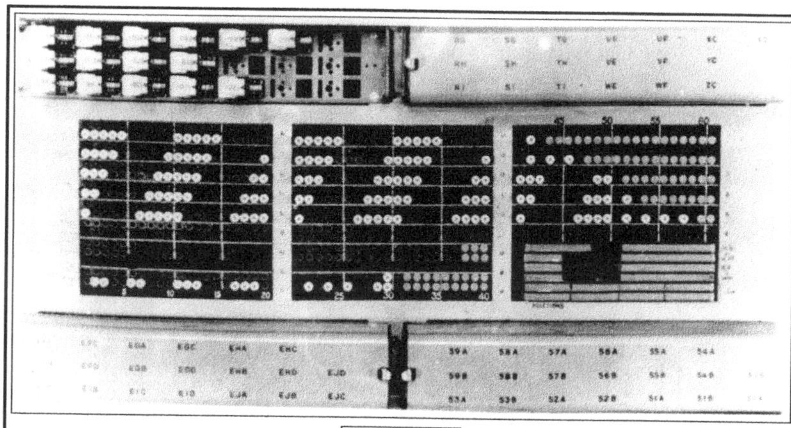

58/29: ×.65

Fig. 58 (XXIX) Dragon 2: wheel patterns etc

p. 392

58/30: ×.65

Fig. 58 (XXX) Dragon 2

58/31: ×1.0

Fig. 58 (XXXI) Proteus (panel on right belongs to a decoding machine)

58/32: ×1.0

Fig. 58 (XXXII) Aquarius

58/33: ×1.0

Fig. 58 (XXXIII) Aquarius panel

61 RAW MATERIALS – PRODUCTION, WITH PLANS OF TUNNY LINKS

p. 394

The development of German Army links is shown in figs. **61 (I)** to **(V)**. [i]

The table below shows the amount of material used and the results obtained. This table does not show the strong correlation between success and high μ_{37} dottage. E.1

Period	Transmissions received at Knockholt	Tapes received	Tapes set on χ's	Decodes	Decode in thousands of letters	Keys broken.
1942						
Nov.–Dec.	12,180	–	–	872	4,467	† 4
1943						
Jan-Mar	16,615	–	–	991	3,386	† 10
Apr-June	23,970	73	2	965	3,063	† 15
July-Sep	21,550	272	17	745	3,047	† 19
Oct-Dec	34,740	955	199	733	3,145	† 18
1944						
Jan-Mar	28,000	1,670	1,205	680	3,189	13
Apr-June	6,215	4,160	1,446	1,044	4,695	19
July-Sep	5,210	4,450	1,638	1,139	6,860	‡ 80
Oct-Dec	6,922	5,496	2,182	1,861	9,607	‡ 166
1945						
Jan-May 8th	12,325	10,555	*4,332	4,478	21,972	‡ 374
TOTAL	167,727	27,631	11,021	13,508	63,431	‡ 718

* Of these, 1040 were set mechanically on all 12 wheels.
† These were all broken by means of depths.
‡ Over half of these were broken by rectangles.

[i] See endnote 2 to this chapter, p. 615 below, for a description of our redrawing of these figures.

p. 395

E.2

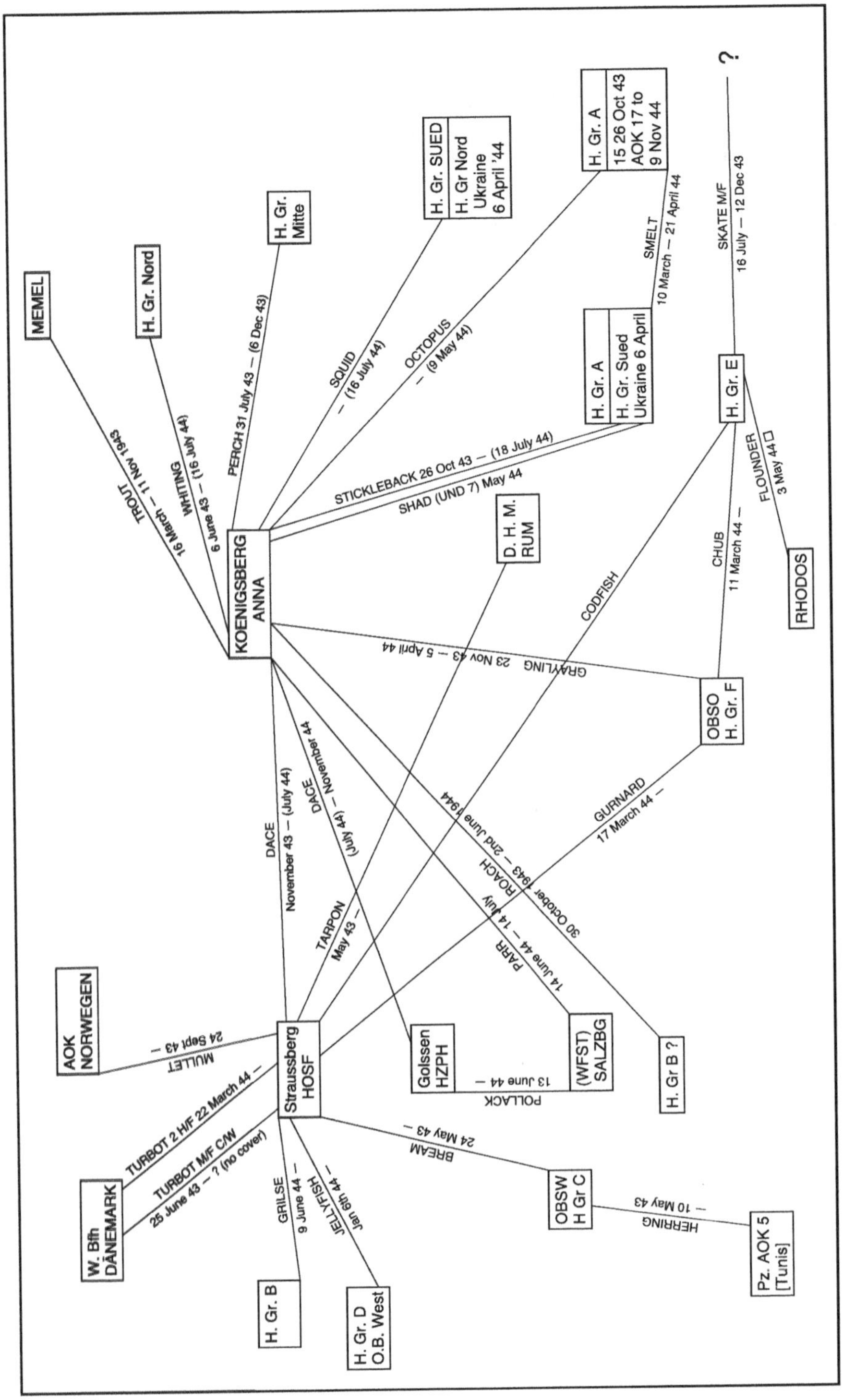

Fig. 61 (I) German Army: March 1943 – July 1944

p. 396

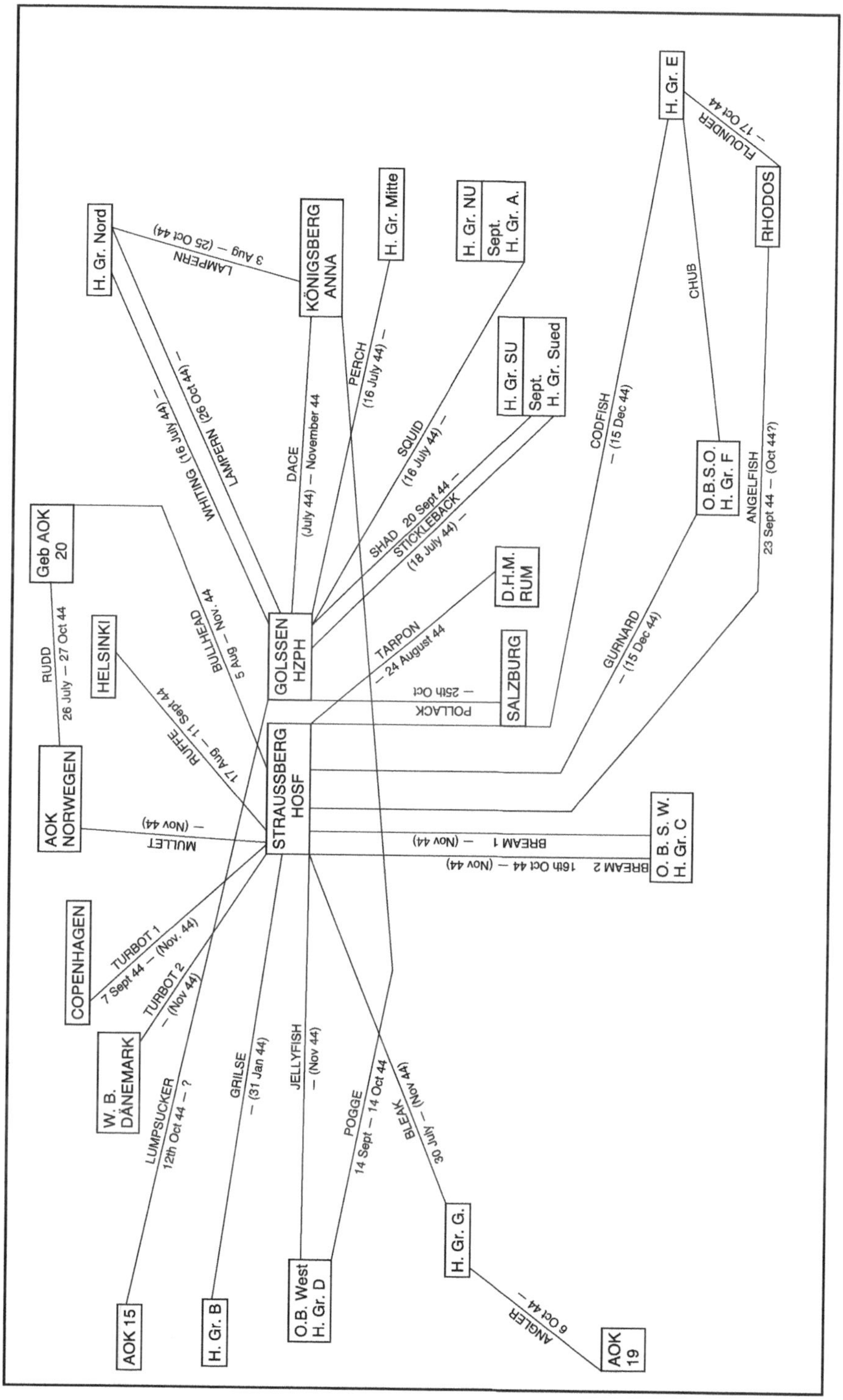

Fig. 61 (II) German Army: July 1944 – October 1944

p. 397

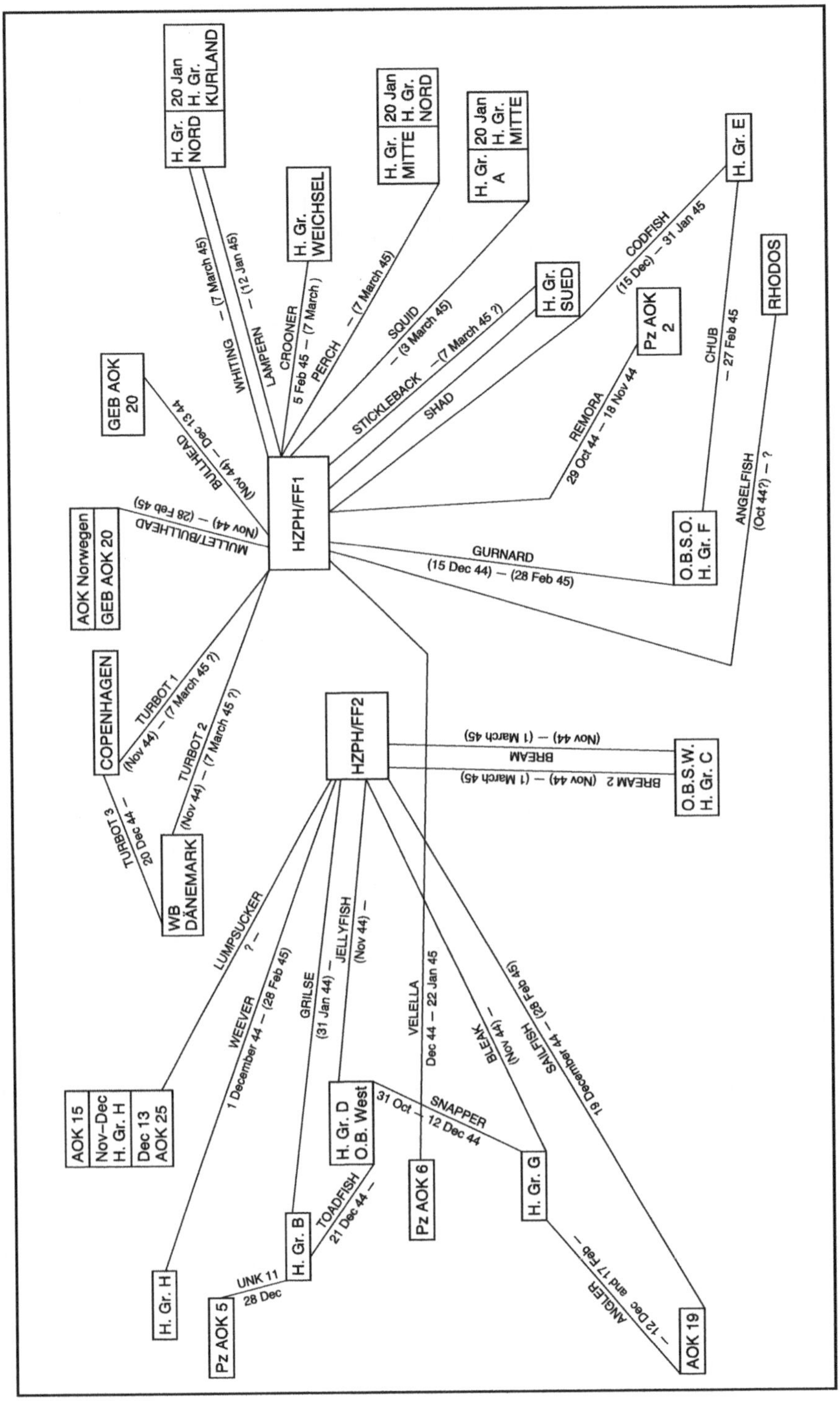

Fig. 61 (III) German Army: October 1944 – February 1945

p. 398

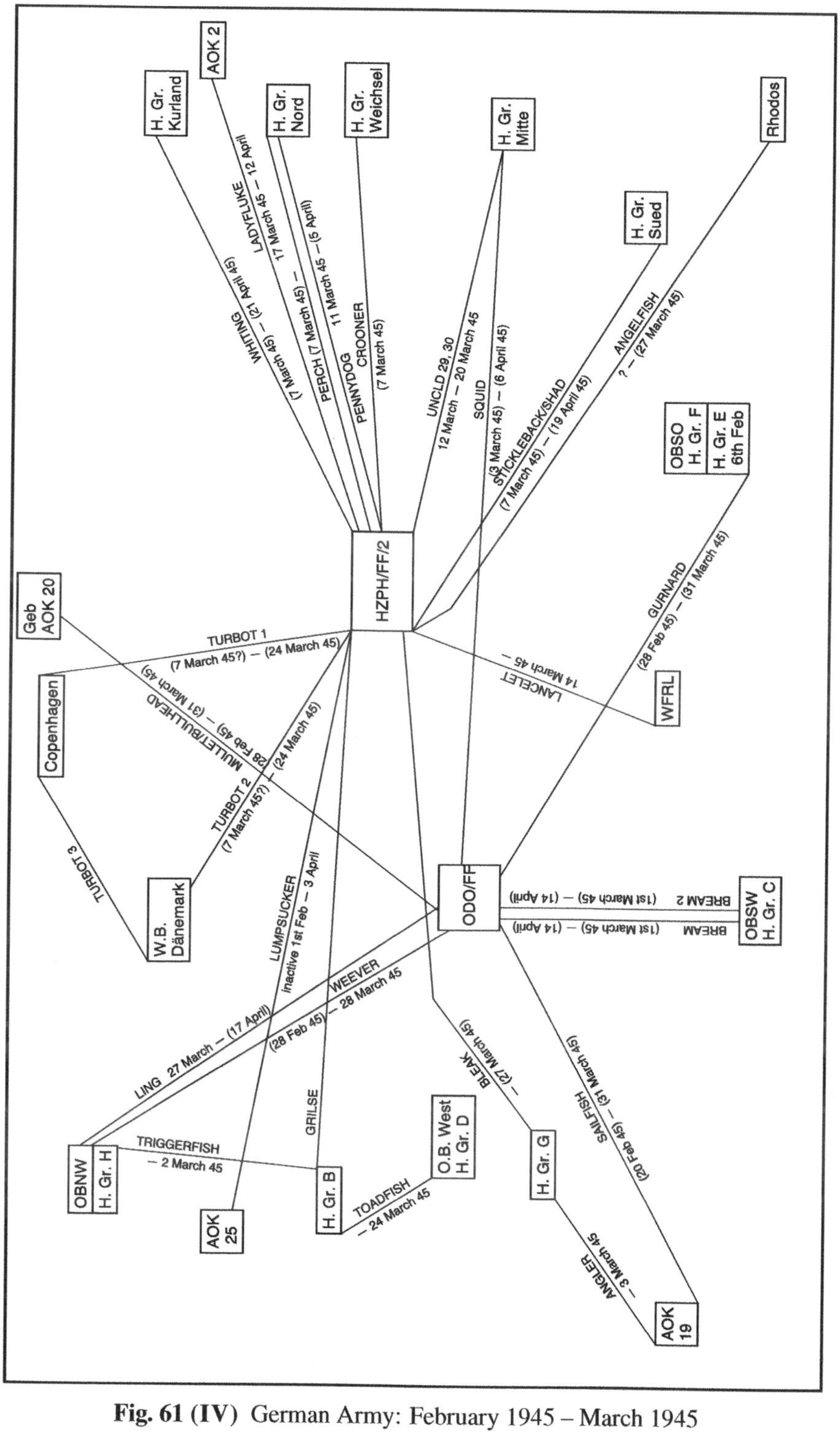

Fig. 61 (IV) German Army: February 1945 – March 1945

p. 399

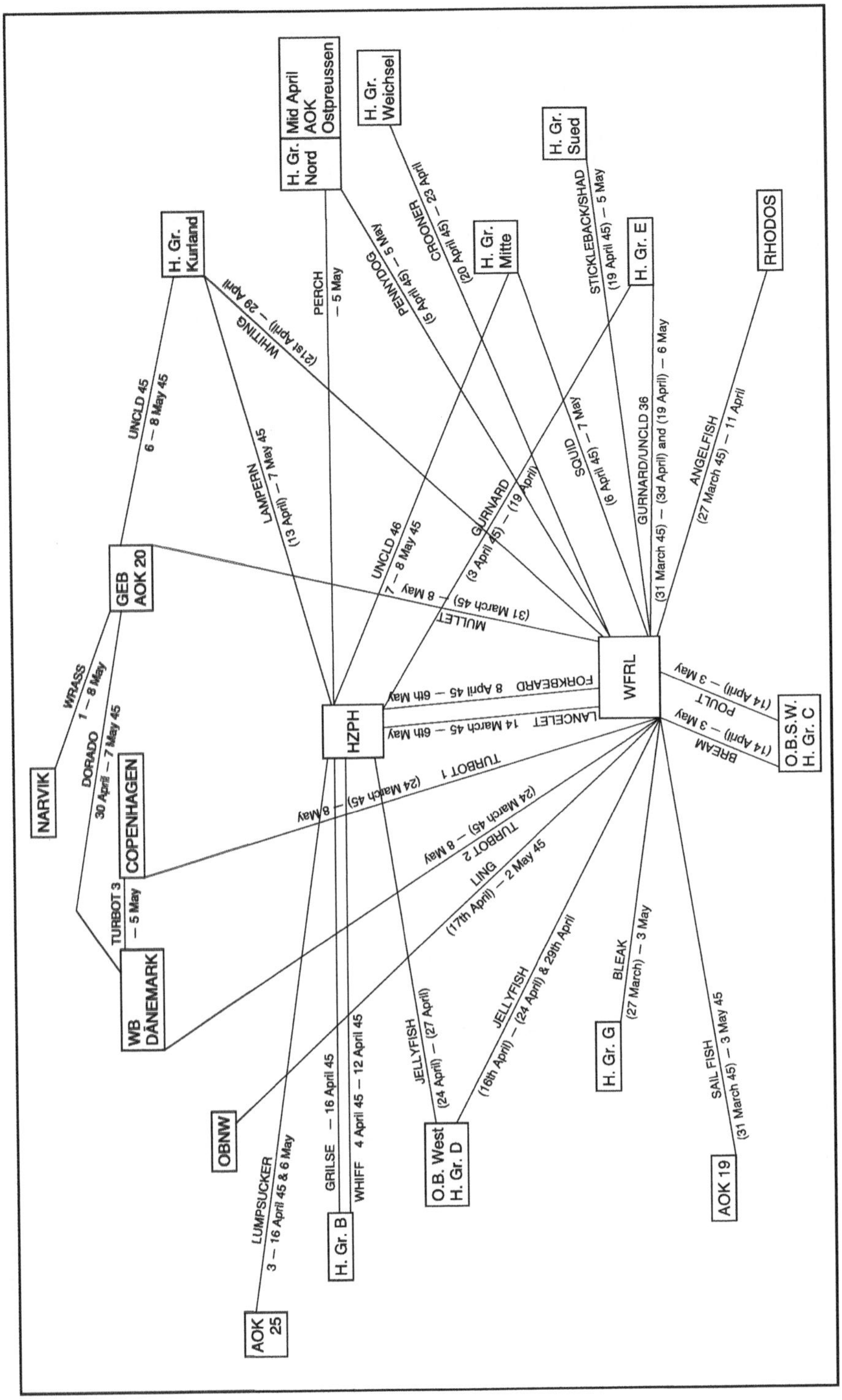

Fig. 61 (V) German Army: March 1945–VE Day

71 GLOSSARY AND INDEX

p. 400

a	Proportion of crosses in Total Motor **11C(d)**
aa	**54E**; **54D(h)**, **54F(a)**
A	Average **23D**; **23E(c)**
'A' PROCEDURE	A procedure for ordering long tapes for rectangling
'A' TYPE	Traffic with a high proportion of double punctuation **22G(c)**(3)
ab	Proportion of crosses in $\Delta\psi'$ **11C(d)**,**(e)**; **12A(d)**, **42B(e)**, **74** Mar'42 a, E.1
ACCURATE CONVERGENCE	Method of converging a rectangle by means of accurate scoring **24W**; **R2**, p. 21
ACCURATE SCORING	Method of decibanning the odds that the sum of two characters is a dot, given the decibanages that each is a dot **24W**
ACCURATE SCORING, KEYBREAKING	See Key-breaking
ACCURATE SCORING, PROOF OF FORMULA	**24W(b)**
ACTIVE	See Crib Retransmission Slips
ADDER	Adding machine (for ordinary addition) **57(b)**
ADDITION	Usually means teleprinter addition, that is modulo 2 addition with • = 0, × = 1 (i.e. • + • = × + × = •, • + × = × + • = ×) **11B(a)**
ADDITION ON MILES	**56G(c)**, **56G(f)**, **56H(d)**
ADDITION FIELD (COLOSSUS)	**53K(i)**
ADDITION FIELD (ORDINARY ON ROBINSON)	**54D(c)**; **54D(a)**
ADDITION FIELD (ROBINSON SPECIAL)	**54D(e)**
ADDITION OF STREAMS	See Sum of Streams
ADDITION SQUARE	A square table of 1024 entries giving the sum of any two TP letters **11**(I)
ADDITION SWITCHES (COLOSSUS)	**53J(e)** sqq
ADDITION SWITCHES (ROBINSON)	**54E(b)**; **54E(d)**
ADDITION TABLE	The 155 independent trios of different letters which add up to /

[a] **42C(e)**

	ADDRESSES (IN TUNNY MESSAGES)	**22G(b),(c)**
	AGREEMENTS	**43B**
	ALPHABET	Teleprinter alphabet
p. 401	ALPHABETICAL COUNT	Letter count q.v.
	AMBIGUITY	A short stretch of μ_{61} where the number but not the exact position of dots is known **28D(b)**; **28E(b)**
E.2	ANAGRAM	To anagram a depth is to express it as the sum of two *P*'s by language methods. To anagram a de-chi is to obtain *P* by hand, given the chi and psi settings but not the motor **28A(d)**, **(f)**; **55B**
	ANALYSIS OF SETTINGS	See Settings, Analysis of
	AND/OR MACHINE	A machine which will score one unit when some logical proposition involving the symbols 'and' and 'or' is satisfied **R0**, p. 43; **74** Sept'43
	AND PLUS (&+)	**54E(d)**
	ANGEL	A tape-copying machine **56B**; **13C**
	ANTI-REPEAT	A letter in a differenced stream with any number of impulses from 2 to 5 all of which are crosses **23Z**
	ANTI-SLIDE	If a wheel (or differenced wheel) when differenced at distance *n* has a high proportion of crosses, the wheel (or differenced wheel) is said to have an anti-slide at distance *n* **R5**, p. 6; **23G(d)**
	APPROXIMATE μ_{37} AND μ_{61}	**92F**
	AQUARIUS	A machine for locating go-backs **55C**; **13B(c)**, **28B(f)**, **58**(XXXII),(XXXIII)
a	ARROW (→)	A symbol meaning "tends to" **22A(b)**
	ASTERISK	See Star
E.3	ATKIN COUNT	A combination count on *P*. The point was that the corresponding ψ-setting combination runs all had the same *R* and σ.
	AUTO	The part of a message which is sent (by the enemy) by running a tape through an auto-transmitter. **11A(b)**; **27C(a)**
	AUTOCLAVE	In our work, limitation involving $\overline{\overline{P}}_5$. **44C**; **11B(g)**(iii),(iv)
	AUTOMATIC RECORDING	**15A(e)**
	AUTO-PAUSE	A pause in auto-transmission while tape is reset or replaced by another tape. **28B(e)**, **11D(c)**; **27C(a)**,**(d)**, **55C**
	AUTO-TRANSMITTER	A tape-reader from which the five impulses of each letter are sent successively along a single wire. Sometimes incorrectly used for transmitters (tape readers) in general. **51(h)**

[a] **22B(b)**

AUXILIARY TAPES	**27F(f),(g)**
AVERAGING GADGET	A gadget that was fitted on Heath Robinson, which would give the total for 50 consecutive readings.
b	Proportion of crosses in a $\Delta\psi$. **11C(d)**; **22D** p. 402
B	Bulge. Excess of score over random. See also Proportional Bulge
bb	See aa
BM	Basic Motor. **11B(f)**; **44C**
BM C/O	Basic motor cut-out. **53C(d)**; **53L(k)**
BM+/1+2	**23L(i)**
BI	Break-in. A setting run for a message which does not involve knowledge of the setting of any other wheel. **23B(c)**; **74** Nov'42, Aug'43
BI WITH SPANNING	**23F(f)**
BI FLOGGING	**23H(b) 91C(c)**
B PROCEDURE	A procedure for ordering individual priority tapes.
B TYPE	Strictly traffic with a high proportion of single punctuation. Commonly used to include C (language) type. **22G(c)**(2)
BAN (10 db)	Logarithm of a factor to base 10.
BAN (NATURAL)	Logarithm of a factor to base *e*.
BAR ($\overline{U}$ or $\underline{U}$)	**22A(b)**
BAYES' THEOREM	**21(f)**; **21(o)**, **24W(a)**, **24X(d)**, **(e)** [a]
BEDSTEAD	The part of Colossus or Robinson on which the tape runs, together with the photo-electric cells, etc (also used erroneously in **R0** for Heath Robinson). **13B(a)**; **52(f)**
BEDSTEAD, COLOSSUS	**53B(b)**; **52(h)**
BEDSTEAD, ROBINSON	**54C**
BIBLE	A book in which wheel patterns are kept.
BIG RECTANGLE	See Rectangle, 150 × 150.
BIG BLACK SWITCHES	See *Q* selection switch.
BIGRAMS, ΔD	**22H(h)**; **23H(g)**
BIGRAMS, UN ΔP	**22**(IV); **22G(a)**,**(g)**
BITING TAPE	A tape with the end of the text running straight on to the beginning.
BLANKS (REQUIRED BY COLOSSUS)	**53B(a)**

[a] BAYE'S

	BLATT	Sheet. **94(d)**
	BLOCK F	**14B(b)**
	BLOCK H	**14B(b)**; **15C(b)**
	BOOK OF SETTINGS	See Settings, Book of
a	BOOLEAN ADDITION	$1+1=0, 0+1=1+0=1, 0+0=0$ **R1**, p. 14; **56G(i)**
b, i, c	BOSTIK	A substance for sticking tapes for Robinson. Benzine is used as a solvent. **57(d)**; **54C(b)**
p. 403	BREAK	A stretch of *P* obtained by hand methods in depth or de-chi. **28A, B**
	BREAKING	Obtaining patterns of wheels (see wheel-breaking). Breaking a de-chi: setting or obtaining patterns of psis by hand from de-chi. **28B, C**
	BREAKERS	Testery language and key-breaking experts. **39B(a)**; fig. **31 (I)**
	BRUSSELS	An intercept station set up rather late in the war.
	BULGY	Showing bulges not easily ascribed to random variation.
	BUZZER	**55C(f)**
	C	Number of crosses in μ_{61}. **92B(a)**
	C PROCEDURE	The normal procedure for ordering tapes for setting.
	C TYPE	Type of message likely to set on 3+4**x**/ (high proportion of German language). **22G(c)**(1)
	C1, C2, C3, C4	(i) Runs: C1 is 1=2=4, C2 is 1=2=5, C3 is 1=2=4=5, C4 is 1=2=3. **R0**, p. 80; **R5**, p. 60 (ii) Procedures for ordering tapes. C_n means over 500 $(n+1)$ in length. $(n=1,2,3,4,5)$
	CAGE	**26B(a)**; **43B**
	CAMERA	**91B(c)**
	CAP	Cap as in chi 2 cap, or $\widehat{\chi}_2$, means sum of the past, present and future characters. Thus $\widehat{\chi}_2 = \overline{\chi}_2 + \chi_2 + \underline{\chi}_2 = \overline{\chi}_2 + \Delta\chi_2$ See also $\widehat{\chi}_2$.
	CARRIAGE RETURN	**53M(b),(h)**
	CELL (OF A RECTANGLE)	A compartment, fixed by a definite row and column of a rectangle. **24B**
	CERTAIN	Used with different shades of meaning, (i) in a single setting run 50:1 on (ii) in setting a message 10:1 that all wheels are set correctly (iii) in chi-breaking, for one wheel, ostensibly 10,000:1 on. **23C**; **R3**, p. 134, **R5**, p. 58, **25D(g)**

[a] $1+1=0+1=1+0=1, 0+0=0$ [b] BOSTICK [c] **54C(D)**

[i] See endnote 28 to chapter **23Z**, p. 589 below.

CH	Checked (occasionally character).	
CHAIN OF WITNESSES	See Witnesses, Chain of	
CHARACTER	Dot or cross.	
CHARACTERISTIC FUNCTION	**21(n)**	
CHARACTERISTICS, WHEEL	See Wheel Characteristics.	
CHARACTERISTICS, *P*	See Plain Language, Counts and Characteristics.	
CHASER SETTINGS	**56L(d)**	p. 404
CHECKS	**15B(b)**; **81A(a)**, **74** Jan'45, **25A(b)**	
CHECKS ON DE-CHIS	**23K(f)**	
CHECKS ON KEY-WORK	**26C**	
CHECKS, NATURAL, FOR MECHANICAL FLAGS	**95C(b)**	
CHECKS ON SETTING	**23K**	
CHECKS ON *Z*	**23K(e)**	
CHECKS ON χ's	**23K(b),(c),(d),(g)**; **53P**	
CHECKS, USE OF	**52(b)**(ix)	
CHESS OPENINGS	A method for setting out routines for break-ins. **R2**, p. 42	
CHI	See χ	
CHITS	Forms issued by Run and Tapes Registrars for each job. **R0**, p. 91	
CIPHER OR CYPHER	The sequence of letters making up a message as received. Written as *Z*, where $Z = P + K$ in Tunny. **11A(c)**	
CIPHER-BREAKING	**12**(I), **12B**	
CIPHER-MACHINES	**11A(c)**	
CIPHER-STREAM	**22J**	
CIPHERING BY THE GERMAN MACHINE	**11B(i)**	
CIRCULATION	**14C**; **39A**	
CLEAR	See Plain Language.	
CLICK	A coincidence in the matching of two streams, also a confirmation of a theory, e.g. a pick-up.	E.4
COALESCENCE	The effect of the setting of a motorizing psi 1 wheel becoming independent of the initial setting after a sufficient length of text. **23N**; **74** Dec'44, **53L(i)**	[a]
COALESCENCE THEORY	**23X**	
CODFISH	A Tunny link. **43C(a)**, **44A(a)**; **74** Oct'42, Feb'43	
COL F, COL H	Men in charge of setting in Block F and H respectively.	
COLOPERATOR	Colossus Operator.	

[a] motorising

	COLOSSUS	The chief setting and breaking machine. **53**; **52**, **12C(d)**, **13B(a)**, **15C(b)**, **51(j)**, **37(b)**, **58**(VIII–XIX), figs. **31** **(I)(II)**, **91C(a)**.
	COLOSSUS 1	**52(e)**; **74** Feb'44
	COLOSSUS 2	**52(f)**; **74** June'44
	COLOSSUS DECODING	**23M(b)**; **23D**, **74** Dec'44, fig. **23 (I)**
	COLOSSUS, FURTHER PLANS FOR	**74** Sept'43
	COLOSSUS KEY WORK	**26G**
p. 405, a	COLOSSUS MOTOR-BREAKING	**92K**, **92E(d)**; **74** Apr'44
b	COLOSSUS RECTANGLING	**24B(f)**
	COLOSSUS RECTANGLING SIGNIFICANCE TEST	**24E(b)**
	COLOSSUS TESTING	**53P**
	COLOSSUS χ-BREAKING	**12C(e)**, **25**
	COLUMN	Often means a letter of $\Delta\psi'$ in hand key-breaking.
	COLUMN DIFFERENCE	See Interval
c, E.5	COMBINATION COUNT	Count of the form $i+j+\cdots+k=\bullet$ **22X(d)**
	COMBINATION SWITCHES	See Addition Switches
	COMBINED FLAG	See Flag, χ_5
	COMMON JACKS (or COMMONS)	Holes in a plug-board having direct electrical connection. **56D(b)**, **56G(i)**
	COMMON JACKS, COLOSSUS	**53K(j)**
	COMPARATOR	**91B(b)**, **91C(b)**(iii)
	COMPARISON	A comparison of two characters of ΔK_{ij} in a key rectangle. The aggregate of all the comparisons in all the rectangles constitutes the combined flag. The total number of comparisons made is denoted by ν or $\nu^{\star}$ **26B(c)**
	COMPATIBILITY CHART	A chart for finding the common difference between two sets of ψ settings. **28B(d)**
	COMPETITION	The rivals of the most probable setting. See also Rival Settings. **23L(g)**
	COMPUTERS	Wrens who enter, flag and converge rectangles. **14B(b)**; **36A(b)**, **31**(II)
	COMPUTERS' KEY JOBS	**26G(a)**,**(b)**
	CONCLUSIONS	**81**
	CONCLUSIONS ON 5202	See Photographic Machine. **91E**
	CONDENSERS, STORAGE OF DE-CHIS ON	**55C(c)**
	CONDITIONAL RECTANGLE	A rectangle such as 3+4**x**/1**x**2**x** with only part of the text "looked at". **24F**; **53M(d)**

[a] **92F(d)** [b] **23B(f)** [c] Count of the for

CONSTRUCTION OF RUNS	**23H(e)**
CONTRACTED DE-CHI	A de-chi with the letters at total motor dots omitted (for setting psis on Robinson). **R0**, pp. 5, 116; **23Z**, **52(d)**, **56K(g)**
CONTRACTION OF ψ	**55A(a),(b)**; **43C(b)**
CONTROL IMPULSE	Analogous to a control tape, q.v. but in a single impulse.
CONTROL OFFICER (CO)	Man in charge of liaison with Knockholt. **14B(a)**, **31**(I)
CONTROL PANEL	**53N**
CONTROL TAPE	(or Special Counter Tape) A tape used on Robinson for picking out letters on another tape. **54H**
CONTROLLED STEPPING	**53D(c)** p. 406
CONTROLS (MILES A)	**56H(d)**
CONVERGENCE (OF RECTANGLES)	Method of analysing a rectangle by successive approximation. **12C(e)**
CONVERGENCE, ACCURATE	**24W(a)**; **24W(c),(d)**
CONVERGENCE, CRUDE	**24C**; **24W**, **R2**, p. 11
CONVERGENCE PANEL	See χ-breaking Panel.
CONVERGENCE, SCALAR PRODUCT	**24W(c),(d)**
CONVERGENCE, STARTS FOR	**24D**; **24W(c)**, **R2**, p. 6
CONVERGENCE, TWO-WHEEL	**25C(e)**
CONVERGENCE, WRONG	**24W(c)**, **24C(b)**
COOKED TAPE	A tape carefully slip-read at Knockholt.
CORRECTED EXCESS	If an experiment has only a probability p of being relevant and when it is relevant, give a factor f to a theory, then this factor has to be corrected to $pf+1-p$. **21(i)**; **25D(b)**
CORRECTED TAPE	A tape altered to agree with the red form.
CORRUPT PLAIN LANGUAGE IN CRIBBING	**27E(c)**
CORRUPTION	See 'Nines'. **41A(b)**, **54H(c)**, **56L(e)**, **28E(b)**
CORRUPTION AND CONVERGENCE	**24W(a)**
COUNT, HAND	A hand process in key-breaking for collecting the evidence for one wheel. **26C**, **D**; **26Y(d)**
COUNTER	A system of circuits for counting electrical impulses at great speed. **51(e)**
COUNTER, HAND	See Hand Counter.
COUNTER, POSITION (ROBINSON)	See Position Counter
COUNTER JACKS	See also cyclometers. **53K(k)**
COUNTER SCORE (ROBINSON)	See Score Counter.
COUNTER SPAN	See Spanning.

COUNTER WHEELS	**91B(c)**
COUNTING	**53F**
COUNTING, HAND	Taking hand counts. **26C**, **26E**
COUNTING MACHINES	Colossus, Robinson and the Hand Counter are all counting machines.
COPYING MACHINES	**13C**; **56D**
CP	Letters written on crib jobs at first, to give them priority. The practice continued long after cribs were generally of top priority.
CRIB	A stretch of clear believed a priori to occur in a length of de-χ or cipher. Usually means a long retransmission of a routine message on another key. **12E(b)**, **27**: **41C(a)**, **12B(c)**, **14B(b)**, **15C(f)**, **74** May'44, **25D(g)**8, **31**(I)
p. 407 CRIB FORM	**27D(f)**
CRIB (GENERAL NOTION OF)	**27A**
CRIB KEY	**26G(c)**
CRIB, MINIMUM LENGTH	**27G(e)**, **(m)**
CRIB, 5202	**91D**
CRIB, ORDERING OF, TAPES	**27E(a)**,**(b)**
CRIB, ORGANISATION, HISTORY OF	**27H**
CRIB PREDICTION	**27D**
CRIB REGISTRAR	**27H**
CRIB RETRANSMISSION SLIPS	**27D(e)**, **27E(a)**
CRIB SCORING OF LETTER COUNTS	**27G(d)**,**(l)**; **27X(a)**,**(d)**,**(e)**, **27Y(e)**,**(g)**
CRIB STATISTICS	**27H**
CRIB, SHORT SETTING IN DE-χ	**55A(a)**
CRIB, DISADVANTAGES OF, FOR CURRENT TRAFFIC	**27A**
CRIB TAPE-MAKING	**27F**
CRIBS WATCH (TESTERY)	**27H**(ii); **39D**, **27D(f)**, **14B(c)**
CROSS	See under "dot". **11A(a)**,**(b)**; **11B(f)**
CROSS, PERMANENT (ON COLOSSUS)	**53K(h)**
CROSS, PERMANENT (ON ROBINSON)	**54D(f)**
CROSS, PERMANENT, ADDING ON MILES	**56G(g)**
CROSS DEPTH	See Depth, Cross
CROSS PRODUCT / CROSS MULTIPLICATION	Scalar product (not what is called cross-product in vector theory).
CRUDE (AS IN "CRUDE CONVERGENCE")	Method of assuming that all characters used in a wheel are certain. See Convergence.

CRYPTOGRAPHY	The science of breaking codes and ciphers. Usually applied specifically to hand processes. **39B**	
CUMULATIVE TOTALS FOR RED FORMS	The number of letters on each page of the red form was counted and cumulative totals of these were used for checking the tape against the red form.	
CYCLOMETER RECTANGLE	**53M(g)**	
CYCLOMETER LOST SCORES	**54G(a)**	
CYCLOMETER, MILES	**56G(k)**	
CYCLOMETER HAND COUNTER	**57(c)**	
d	No. of dots in μ_{37} **22D(c)**	p. 408
d INFERRED FROM $\Delta\psi$ PATTERNS	**28C(b)**	
D	Proportion of dots in μ_{37} **23L(b),(c) 92B**	i
D PROCEDURE	Used for ordering crib priority tapes.	
db	See deciban	E.6
DB	Occasionally used for double bulge.	
DCL	**56L(d)**	
DO	Duty Officer. Man in charge of all work on a given shift. **14B(b); 37(b)**	
DR	David Rees, Decoding Room, Dispatch Rider, Double Robinson.	
DAILY CHANGE	The daily change of all 12 wheel patterns on a link. **43D(e)**	
DAILY FILM	A quaint term for "message film", used by the photographic section, but not in this report.	ii
DECENTRALISATION	**81A(e)**	
DE-CHI	See De-χ	
DECIBAN(db)	The unit of decibanage. **21(g); 25B(b), (c),(d),(e)**	
DECIBANAGE	10 × logarithm to base 10 of a factor.	
DECIBANAGE EXPECTED IN CRIB RUNS	**27X(e); 27Y(f),(g)**	
DECIBANAGE, NON LINEAR	**24W(a)**	
DECIBANAGE OF ΔD LETTERS	**92B**	
DECIBANNING	Calculating decibanages.	
DECIBANNING "FROM A LETTER COUNT"	**25W(e), 22Y**	a

[a] **25W(f)**

[i] Reference **92B** handwritten.
[ii] Entry 'A quaint…' handwritten.

DECIBANNING, FUNDAMENTAL FORMULA	**25W(b)**
DECIBANNING A LETTER COUNT USING THE MESSAGE AS ITS OWN SAMPLE	**22Y**; **23J**, **25B(c)**
DECIBANNING MACHINE	A machine which would score different numbers for different conditions (Colossus only scores one or zero). **23Z**; **R0**, p. 43
DECIBANNING RUNS	**25W(d)**; **25W(e)**
DECIPHER	Make intelligible (applied more often to bad handwriting than to cipher). **11B(i)**
DECODE	$Z+K$ even if K is wrong, e.g. the Colossus decode from the second letter with psis set only at a slide. Since Tunny is a cipher the word decipher would be logically better. **39D**
DECODE, EDITING OF	**27E(c)**
DECODE, READING OF	**27D**
DECODE, VERY LONG	**27G(g)**
p. 409 DECODING	**28E**; **39C**
DECODING, COLOSSUS	**23M(b)**; **74** Dec'44
DECODING MACHINE	**13C**, **56L**; **74** Apr, June'42, **58**(XXIV), **31**(I)
DECODING OPERATORS	**39C(b)**
i DELTA	See Δ
DEPTH [a]	A set of messages enciphered on the same key. **28A**; **11D(d)**, **12B(c)**, **22G(h)**, **33A**, **39B(b)**, **74** Oct'42, **55B**, **44A(b)**
DEPTH, ANAGRAMMING	See also Anagram. **28A(d)**; **41C(a)**, **41E**
DEPTH, CROSS	A depth, the two legs of which are sent from opposite ends of a link. **28A(a)**
DEPTH, EVIDENCE FOR	**28A(c)**
DEPTH, MYSTERY OF ALLEGED	**93(d)**
DEPTH, OBSOLETE PHRASE "setting in depth"	Getting wheels at the same settings by staggering messages.
DEPTH OF RECTANGLES	The number of elements of ΔZ_{ij} contributing to each cell of the rectangle.
DEPTH SCORING	**28A(d)**,**(i)**
DEPTH TREATMENT	**28A(d)**
DEPTH OF TWO	**41B**
DEPTH OF THREE	**42B(b)**
DETERMINATION OF KEY	See Key, Determination of

[a] **22H(h)**

[i] Word 'See' handwritten.

DEVIATION, STANDARD	See Standard Deviation.
DEVELOPING	**91C(b)**
DEVIL	A TM dot hypothesis in key-breaking which leads to a contradiction. **26F**
DEVIL EXORCISM	The technique for resolving such contradictions. **26F**; **26**(XXI),(XXII)
DE-χ (Also written de-chi, *D*)	$Z+\chi$ usually on tape or printed out. **12A(a)**; **14B(c)**, **35E**, **39B(c)**, **74** May'43, Sept'43, Jan'44, **43D(c)**, **44C**, **91B(i)**
DE-χ BREAKING	**28B, C**
DICTIONARY	**55B(a),(c),(b)**
DIFFERENCING	See Δ
DIFFERENCING OF SETTINGS	See Settings, Analysis of
DIFFICULTIES, EARLY	**23Z**
DIRECT PLUGGING (ROBINSON)	**54D(a),(h)**
DISAGREEMENT	Dot against cross. **43B**
DISCRIMINANT	Control Tape
DISPLAY	Details of settings and scores are displayed by being lit up on a 'display panel'. The term is used in contrast to the printer.
DISPLAY, COLOSSUS	**53G(d)** p. 410
DISPLAY, DRAGON	**55A(d),(e)**
DISPLAY, ROBINSON	**54B**
DISPLAY, TUNNY	**56K(b)**
DISTRIBUTION, BINOMIAL	**21(l)**; **27X(c)**
DISTRIBUTION, GAUSSIAN	See Distribution, Normal
DISTRIBUTION, MATCHING OF PENNIES	The distribution that actually occurs in Tunny work. **21(n)**
DISTRIBUTION, NORMAL	**21(l)**; **21(o)**
DISTRIBUTION, POISSON	In this report this always means Poisson distribution of rare statistical frequency. **21(l)**, **27X(e)**
DISTRIBUTION, χ^2	**21(l)**; **24X**. See also "χ^2 Test"
DISTRIBUTOR	The part of a Mrs. Miles which distributes the electrical impulses in the correct order. **56G(b)**(v)
DIVISION OF WORK	**14A(b),(c)**; **15C(d)**
DOCTORING	Inserting or removing letters in a tape to eliminate slides found by spanning. It thus differs from 'correcting' a tape, which means altering the Tape to agree with the Red Form. **23F(e)**; **25D(c)**
DONALD'S THEOREM	$\Delta^m = \Delta_m$ if and only if m is a power of 2. **22A(c)** E.7

	DORMANT	See Crib Retransmission Slips
	DOSSIER	Collection of Colossus records of a job.
	DOT	Dot, and cross are the conventional signs used in the TP alphabet, e.g. E is × • • • • **11A(b)**; **11B(f)**
	DOTS, DOUBLE	See Double Dots
	DOTS, RUNNING FOR (CRIB)	**27G, X, Y**
	DOTTAGE	The number of dots in μ_{37}. See *d*. **11C(e),(f)**; **22C(a)**, **22D(c)**
	DOTTAGE, IMPORTANCE OF	**22H(a),(c)**; **27A**
	DOTTERY	Method of forecasting best settings of a long ψ run. Corresponding to a setting (a,b) dots are put on two sheets of paper opposite numbers *a* and *b* respectively. Several dots opposite a number suggest it is the correct setting. **23Z**(vii)
	DOUBLE BEDSTEAD	**74** Jan'44
	DOUBLE DOTS IN μ_{37}	**22C(e)**
	DOUBLE DOTS IN TM	**26B(d)**
	DOUBLE PUNCTUATION	See Punctuation, Double and Single
	DOUBLE TESTING	**52(e)**
a	DOUBTING	A device used in χ-breaking for ignoring all letters of ΔZ against $\Delta\chi$ characters which are still indeterminate. **25D(a)**
p. 411	DOUBTING TRIGGER	See Special Pattern
	DOUBTING ON ψ's, IMPOSSIBILITY OF	**92H**
	DOUBTS	Places in a $\Delta\chi$ at which neither a dot nor a cross is assumed.
	DRAG	Trial of a short crib in all places of de-χ or depth, or trial of a χ wheel at all settings against a short length of key. **43C(b),(d)**
	DRAGON	Machine for dragging short cribs through de-χ's. **55A**; **13B(c)**, **14B(c)**, fig. **31 (I)**
	DRAGON, PHOTOGRAPHS OF	**58**(XXVI) to (XXX)
	DRAGON III	**55A(i)**
b	DRIVING	Motorizing
E.8	"DRUNKEN MAN"	A mathematical problem with some applications to Tunny in which the total length of several attempts to travel along a straight road is known but the direction of each is random.
	DUPLEX	**11D(b)**

[a] A device using [b] Motorising

E as in $P(ET)$	Event. **21(b)**
E_1, E_2	Starts for convergence. **24D(g)**, **24D(e)**
e′	The only doubting trigger on the Colossi which are not fitted with a χ-breaking panel. **53C(b)**
EB	Expected Bulge
ES	Expected score.
ES c/o	End of span cut-out. **53H(e)**
ET	Effective text.
EARLY MOTORS	See Motors, Early
EDITING DECODES	See Decodes.
EDUCATION COMMITTEE	Committee formed for the education of Wrens in Tunny theory and practice. **31G**; **74** Jan'45
EITHER-OR	**53J(d)**, **54E(c)**; **27G(h)**, **91A(d)**
ELECTRONIC COUNTERS	**51(e)**; **74** Nov'42, **91B(b)**
EMBRYONIC WHEELS	Partial wheels used as a basis for hand-counting on key. **26B(a)**,**(c)**
ENCODING	**56K(h)**
END	(e.g. Rome, Paris) End of a 'link'.
ENGINEERS	**31F**; **31**(I,II)
"ENGLISH SETTINGS"	**94(d)** p. 412
ENIGMA	Another German high-grade machine cipher. **93(d)**
EQUIPMENT, STANDARD	**81C(e)**
EVENING MEETING	Meeting of DO, WM, CO and representative of Hut 3 at 2300 hours, to decide policy.
EVIDENCE, AMOUNT DERIVED FROM A LC	See letter count.
EVIDENCE, AMOUNT DERIVED FROM ΔD	See letter count.
EVIDENCE, FLOGGING THE	**23J**
EVIDENCE FOR DEPTHS	See Depth
EVIDENCE FOR SETTING	**23A(a)**
EVIDENCE FOR SETTING, OTHER THAN FROM ΔD	**23H(h)**
EVIDENCE, WEIGHING OF	**25B**. See also decibanning.
EVIDENCE, WEIGHING OF, DERIVATION OF FORMULAE	**25W**
EVIDENCE, WEIGHING OF, IMPRACTICABILITY OF EXACT FORMULAE	**25W(c)** a

[a] IMPRACTIBILITY

	EVIDENCE, WEIGHING OF, USING A MESSAGE AS ITS OWN SAMPLE	**22Y**, **23J**, **25B(c)**. This is usually too optimistic: see **21(i)**, **22Y**, **24X**, **23J**, **25B**, **25W**
	EXHIBITS, KEY BREAKING	**26J**
	EXHIBITS, MACHINE SETTING	**23D**
	EXHIBITS, μ and ψ SETTING:	**23**(I)
	EXHIBITS, χ-BREAKING	**25G**
	EXPANSION	**36A(b)**
	EXPECTED SUM OF MODULI	**25W(a)**
	EXPECTED VALUE	**21(k)**; **21(p)**
	EXPOSURE RATE	**91B(d)**
	EXTENSION	Repetition of the same ψ letter due to the action of a TM dot. **11B(e),(f)**; **22D**, **55A(b),(f)**, **41D(b)**
	EYE	See Peckers.
	EYE-START	A start for convergence of a rectangle by eye. See also E_1 and E_2.
p. 413	f_i	**92D**
	FACTOR, f	**21(f)**
	FACTORS, WEIGHTED AVERAGE OF	**21(i)**; **22Y**
	FAFFING	An unsystematic and intuitive hand method of obtaining breaks in depth or de-χ. **28A(d)**(2)
	FALLACY, STATISTICIANS	See Statistician's Fallacy.
	FALTUNG	**22E(b)**, **22X(d)**; **21(m)**
	FAST (STEPPING)	Stepping at every revolution of the tape.
	FERTILISER	**21(o)**
	FIDDLING	Process of finishing off key-breaking unsystematically. Not advisable for inexperienced people. Also equals faffing.
	FILM	**91B(a)**, **91A(b)**
	FILM, SPECIAL COUNTER	**91B(b)**
	FILTER	fig. **31 (I)**
	FINISHING OFF THE μ's	**92G**
i	FIRE, THE	A fire in Block F caused by a broken bottle of benzine. The damage was serious but not crippling. **74** Nov'44.
a	FISH	Any TP machine cipher, notably Tunny and Sturgeon. **11A(c)**

[a] notable

[i] See see endnote 28 to chapter **23Z**, p. 589 below.

FISH COMMITTEE	**31C**	
FISH LINKS	**11D(a)**; **61**(I) – (V)	
FIVE DIMENSIONAL CONVERGENCE	See Convergence, Five Dimensional	E.9
FIVE-IMPULSE TAPE	**11A(b)**	
FIVE-UNIT CODE	**41A(a)**	
FLAG	Method of comparing rows of a rectangle to obtain a start for convergence. Even the 5 by 5 flag can be so described. **26G(a)**; **24D(b)**	
FLAG, COMBINED	See Flag, χ_5	
FLAG, JACOB'S	**74** Nov'44	
FLAG, MECHANICAL	**95**	
FLAG, MILES, GADGET	**56G(m)**	
FLAG, ROBINSON	See Flag, Mechanical	
FLAG, SIGNIFICANCE TEST FOR	**24X(f)**; **26B(c)**	
FLAG, THEORY OF	**24W(d)**; **24W(b)**	
FLAG, χ_5	**26**(XII), **26B(c)**; **26Y(a)**,**(b)**, **26G(a)**, **38(c)**	
FLAG, 5 by 5	**26B(a)**; **26Y(a)**	
FLAT	Used variously to mean too nearly random, random, or even having a zero bulge.	
FLOGGING	Working exhaustively on a particular method or hypothesis. **23H**; **25D(g)**, **91C(c)**	p. 414
FLOGGING THE EVIDENCE	**23J**	
FOLLOW-ON	Messages sent consecutively without resetting the wheels. **11D(d)**; **23F(h)**	
FORMULAE, FOR KEY-BREAKING	See key-breaking, Formulae	
FOUR-LETTER COUNT	See Letter Count, Four-	
FOUR-WHEEL RUN	Commonly used in the sense as doing a two-wheel run and using all scores above the set total for a further run on two other wheels. **23H(c)**	
FOURIER TRANSFORMS	**22X(d)**; **22X(c)**	
FREAK ΔP COUNTS	See Plain Language Freak Counts.	
FREEBORNERY	Any catalogue produced by Freeborn's section. See also Hollerith Section.	
G CIRCUIT	**91B(i)**	
g′	Special pattern (doubting) trigger for μ_{37}. **53C(b)**	
GPO	General Post Office. **51(g)**	
GADGET FOR RESETTING	See Resetting Gadget.	

	GAMMA TAPE (γ)	A tape punched /L/L/L, etc.
	GARBAGE	Type-out done on Garbo (or Junior). **24**(I); **26**(XI)
	GARBO	A machine for printing from a tape with (i) steckering (ii) differencing (iii) addition of differenced impulses. At one time it possessed a reperforator. **56E**; **13C**
	GARBO RECTANGLE	See Rectangle, Garbo
	GATE	The part of Colossus or Robinson through which a tape passes when being examined by the photo-electric cells.
	GATE, ROBINSON	**54C(c)**; **58**(IV)
	GAUSS (IAN DISTRIBUTION)	See Distribution, Gaussian.
	GENERATING FUNCTION	See Characteristic Function.
	GENERATING UNIT	**91B(b)**
	GERMAN TUNNY	**74** June'45
	GERMAN WHEELS AND SETTINGS	**94(b)**, **(d)**
	GIFFORD	Inventor of the original Robinson printer.
	GIFFORD PRINTER	**52(c)**
	GOAT	Type of Colossus pin, as opposed to a "sheep". Used variously for good ones, bad ones, thin ones, thick ones.
p. 415	GO-BACK	A repeat of plain language in auto, due to resetting of tape. **11D(c)**, **28B(f)**; **55C(a)**, **27C(d)**,**(e)**,**(f)**
	GO-BACK SCORING	**22W(b)**
	GOOD I.J.	A cryptographer. **21(f)**, **R3**, p. 55
	GOOD AND BAD LETTERS	**22Y**
	GOOD SETTINGS	6:1 on. **23C(a)**,**(b)**
	GREEK ORTHODOXY	A system of calling various editions of wheel-patterns by names $\alpha, \beta, \gamma \ldots$
	H	Hypothesis. **21(b)**
E.10	HC	Hand check. See Checks, Hand.
	H REGISTRAR	**37(a)**
	H REGISTRY	**14B(b)**; **31**(II)
	HAND	Non-auto transmission (i.e. not from a tape). **11A(b)**; **27C**, **22G(b)**,**(c)**
	HAND COUNT ON KEY, $\overline{\chi}_2 + \overline{\psi}_1{}'$ LIM	**26**(XIV)
	$\overline{\chi}_2$ LIM	**26**(XXII)
	for $\Delta\chi$'s 2 & 6	**26**(XX)

HAND COUNTER	Small and extremely important machines for counting tape-lengths. **13D**, **57(c)**; **51(d)**	
HAND METHODS	See Language Methods.	
HAND METHODS (EARLY)	**42**	
HAND PERFORATOR	Machine for perforating a tape by typing. **13C**, **56A**; **35H(a)**	
HAND STATISTICAL METHODS	**44**	
HEAD, OF MILES	A tape reader on Mrs. Miles (see also Peckers).	
HEAD OF ROOM 41	Man in charge of Room 41 for each shift.	
HEATH ROBINSON	The original form of Robinson, housed in Hut 11. **52(b)**; **15A(c)**, **74** June'43	
HELLSCHREIBER	Method of facsimile wireless transmission of letters. **41A(a)**	
HERRING LINK	**43C(g)**; **74** Mar'43	
HETEROGENEITY OF P and ΔP	See Plain Language, Heterogeneity of.	
HISTORY SECTION	**74** May'45	
HOLLERITH SECTION	Mr Freeborn's Section for the application of commercial tabulatory machinery to cryptography. **94(b)**	
HUT 3	The main hut for 'intelligencing' decodes. **14A(a)**; **39D**	p. 416
IBM	See Insert Machine	
IST	Intelligence Section Tester. An unofficial name for the Testery.	
IMPORTANT (HUT 3 TERM)	Having high intelligence value.	
IMPULSE	A character of a TP letter. **11A(a)**.	
IMPULSE, GENERALIZED	**91A(d,c)**; **91B(a)**.	[a]
IMPULSE, SIXTH	See Sixth Impulse.	
IMPURE COLUMN	Same as spoilt column, q.v.	
IN and OUT JACKS, MILES A	**56H(c)**	
IN and OUT JACKS, TUNNY	**56K(e)**	
INDEPENDENCE	Two counts or runs are said to be independent if a knowledge of the score for one does not affect the probability of any score for the other, if both are supposed to be random it follows that the evidence of the counts is independent.	[b]
INDICATOR	**12A(d)**	
INDICATOR METHOD	**42E**	
INDICATOR, 12-LETTER	**41A(a)**	
"INSERT"	**56C**; **56D(c)**	

[a] GENERALISED [b] does not not affect

INSERT MACHINE (IBM)	**13C**, **56C**
INSIDE OUT	Dots instead of crosses and vice versa. See also Sign of Key. **25D(f)**; **25G(c),(d),(e)**
INSTRUCTION BOOKS	**81A(f)**(ii)
INTEGRATION	Recovery of the unΔ patterns from a Δ pattern, i.e. Δ^{-1}
INTEGRATION, MILES A	**56H(e)**
INTEGRATION OF $\widehat{\chi}_2$	**26B(b)**
INTERVAL OR COLUMN DIFFERENCE	**28D(b)**
ISSUING	Routing decodes to appropriate intelligence authorities. **39D**
JACK, JACKFIELD	See Plug Panel.
JACK, COMMON	See Common Jack
JACOB'S FLAG	Operative **24D**; Theory **24W(d)**
JIGGERS	Corruption of peckers q.v.
JUDGEMENT, PROBABILITY	**21(h)**
p. 417 JUICY	Having large proportional bulges in ΔD.
JUNIOR [a]	Machine for printing from a tape with steckers. **56D**; **13C**, **R1**, p. 11
JZ	Mechanical flag jacks on Miles D. **56G(m)**; **95B(d)**, **95C(e)**
K	Symbol for Key
K	Symbol in Significance Test IV (much disputed). **24X(e)**
KL	"Cancel Lamps". **53G(d)**; **53N**
KEDLESTON HALL	A subsidiary interception station, (details in Sixta report).
KEINE	See "Nocke".
KEY	The stream of teleprinter letters added to *P* to give Z. **26**
KEY (INTRODUCTORY)	**11B**, **12E**; **12B(c)**
KEY CAUSED BY STUCK TAPE	**22G(b)**
KEY, CRIB	**26G(c)**; **27A**
KEY, "DETERMINATION" OF	**28A(e)**
KEY, RECOGNITION OF	**22F**, **27W**; **27G**, **X**, **Y**
KEY, SIGN OF	See Sign of Key
KEY, SUM OF TWO STREAMS	**22W(c)**

[a] **13(c)**

KEY THEORY, STATISTICAL	**22F**	
KEY-BREAKING, ACCURATE SCORING	**43D(b)**(i),(iv)	
KEY-BREAKING, COMPUTERY and COLOSSUS	**26G**	
KEY-BREAKING EXHIBITS	**26J**	
KEY-BREAKING FORMULAE	**26Y**	
KEY-BREAKING, GENERAL CONSIDERATION	**26H**	
KEY-BREAKING, HISTORICAL	**43C(c),(e)**; **43D(b)**, **74** July, Aug'44	
KEY-BREAKING, INTRODUCTORY	**12E(c)**	
KEY-BREAKING, MECHANICAL FLAG FOR	**95C**	
KEY-BREAKING WORKINGS		
$\bar{\chi}_2 + \bar{\psi}'_1$ LIM	**26**(XIII)	
$\bar{\chi}_2$ LIM, EARLY STAGE	**26**(XVIII)	
$\bar{\chi}_2$ LIM, LATER STAGE	**26**(XXI)	
KEYBOARD OF GERMAN TUNNY MACHINE	**11A(a)**; **41A(a)**	p. 418
KNOCKHOLT	Principal interception station. **33**; **14A(a)**	a
"KNOCKING OFF SOMETHING"	The sum of moduli in a wheel-breaking run (score on its own wheel) is called x and it is necessary to "knock off something" to get x^* the score on the correct wheel. **25B(b),(e)**	
$L_{n,m}$	Letter with n dots and m crosses. **26C**	
$\textcircled{L}$, $\textcircled{L_r}$	Generalized Teleprinter letter. **91A(d)**	i
LABOUR, DIVISION OF	**81A(c)**	
LAGRANGE	**23X**	
LAMPS	**91B(c,f,g)**	
LANGUAGE METHODS	**28**; **39**	
LC	Letter count (q.v.); Leslie Chown.	
LC/O	Lamp cut-out on Colossus. **53G(d)**; **53N**	
LEC	Colossus sign-writing for letter count. **53G(h)**; **53N**	E.11
LEG	One message of a depth. Also used in an electrical sense.	
LEGAL	Satisfying the conditions imposed by the Germans on wheel patterns. **22B**; **25D(e)**	b
LEGAL WHEELS, NUMBER OF	**25X**	
LENGTH REQUIRED TO BREAK WHEELS	**24Y(a)**	

[a] Principle [b] wheel-patterns

[i] Entry 'Generalized...' handwritten.

	LENGTH OF KEY	**26A**, **26B(c)**
	LENGTH OF SLIDES	**23G(c)**
	LENGTH OF WHEELS	See Wheels
	LEOPARDRY	Filling up a tape with RYRY... Early Robinsons (and in a less degree all Colossi) disliked long runs of dots or crosses. Preferred to Tigering (q.v.) for increased tape strength.
	LETTER	Always means Teleprinter letter. **11A(a)**
	LETTERS, TELEPRINTER, ALGEBRA OF	**21(m)**; **22E**
	LETTER COUNTS	**12C** (especially **(a)**, **(b)**, **(c)** and (II)), **22** (all figs), **23B(a)**, **23D**, **53G(h)**, **25G(c)**, **(e)**, **(g)**, **(h)**, **(j)**, **(l)**, **(n)**
	LETTER COUNTS, AMOUNT OF EVIDENCE DERIVED FROM	**22Y**
	LETTER COUNTS, DECIBANNING FROM	**25B(e)**, **25W(f)**; **25G**
	LETTER COUNTS, AGAINST INDIVIDUAL CHARACTERS	**25D(g)**(3); **25G(l)**,**(n)**
	LETTER COUNTS, CRIB, SCORING OF	See Cribs
	LETTER COUNTS, FOUR-	**25E(d)**; **23E(h)**
p. 419	LETTER COUNTS, SAMPLING ERRORS IN	**22K**
	LETTER SUBTRACTOR CIPHER, TUNNY SHOWN TO BE	**41B**
	LIKELIHOOD, MAXIMUM	See maximum likelihood.
a	LIMITATION	The modifier of the motor such that if it is a dot it forbids a motor dot. (i.e. $\overline{\chi}_2$ not $\widetilde{\overline{\chi}}_2$) **11B(g)**,**(h)**; **22D(g)**, **22H(d)**,
i		**22W(b)**, **22C(d)**. See also under.
	LIMITATION, HISTORICAL	**43C(d)**,**(g)**; **43D(d)**
	LIMITATION, CHRONOLOGY $\overline{\chi}_2$	**74** Feb'43
	$\overline{\chi}_2\overline{\overline{P}}_5$	**74** Mar'43
	$\overline{\chi}_2\overline{\Psi}'_1\overline{\overline{P}}_5$	**74** June'44
	LIMITATION, REVERSED EQUIVALENT TO $\Delta\psi'_6$	See sixth impulse.
	LIMITATION ON COLOSSUS (WITH DETERMINER SWITCHES)	**53C(d)**; **53J(i)**
	LIMITATION CROSSES, COUNTS AGAINST	**22H(b)**, **22**(VI),(VII),(VIII)
	LIMITATION, DRAGON	**55A(b)**
	LIMITATION, TUNNY AND DECODING MACHINE	**56K(c)**
	LIMITATION, WORKING OUT THE	**25E(c)**; **25G**(VII), (VIII)

[a] is forbids

[i] 'See also under' presumably meaning, 'see following few entries'.

LINK	The traffic between two particular German stations. **61**; **27B**	
LOG-BOOKS	**31A**; **81A(f)**(iii)	
LOGIC, SYMBOLIC	**21(a)**	
LOG-READING	**27D**	
LOGS REGISTRAR	**14B(b)**; **37(a)**	
LONG BEDSTEAD	A Colossus bedstead (q.v.) which can carry a tape 30,000 long.	
LONG RUN	A two-wheel run.	
LOOPS	Tapes stuck in short lengths for periodic effects in special jobs on Miles.	
LOST COUNTS	A score missed on Robinson (or Colossus). **54G(a)**	
LYLE	A special tape used in mechanical flagging. See Tate.	E.12
MACHINES	Part **5**, **13**, **15(c)**; **74**, **81C**	
MACHINES, ACCURACY OF	**81C(a)**	
MACHINES, ADAPTABILITY OF	**81C(b)**; **52(e)**,**(h)**	
MACHINES, DEVELOPMENT OF	**15A**; **51**, **52**, **81C**, **74** Dec'42, **14A**	
MACHINES, MAINTENANCE	**14B(b)**	p. 420
MACHINES, SMALL	**57**; **81C(d)**, **51(d)**	
MACHINES, GERMAN, BREAKING	**42B**; **74** Jan'42, April'42	
MAKES, TWO	All tapes were made twice independently before copying was permitted. The two originals were called "makes".	
MAS(TER SWITCH)	**53N**	
MASTER-DAILY	Variously interpreted; a "master" film is a $\Delta\chi$ film. Cf. "daily film".	i
MASTER TAPE	**34(c)**	
MAXIMUM LIKELIHOOD	**21(p)**; **22Y**	
MEAN	**21(k)**	
MECHANICAL FLAGS	Flags made mechanically (see also Flags). **95**	
MECHANICAL FLAGS, MILES D GADGET	**56G(m)**, **56F(d)**	
MEMORY SWITCHES	(i) The switches R_1, R_2, R_3, R_4, R_5. **53L(c)** (ii) The limitation determiner switches. **53C(d)** The term was rarely used in either sense.	
MEMORY CIRCUITS	**53L(b)**; **53A**, **56F(e)**	a

[a] **53:(b)**

[i] Entry 'Variously...' handwritten.

	MESSAGE, LAST, USING TUNNY CIPHER	**74** May'45
	METERS	Cyclometers.
	MHAN	Maxwell H.A. Newman. **31**(I)
E.13	MILES	Machine for combining two or more tapes. Originally called Mrs. Miles. **56F**, **13(c)**; **27F**
	MILES A	**56H**; **58**(XXIII)
	MILES B, C, D	**56G**; **58**(XXII)
	MILES D, MECHANICAL FLAG GADGET	**56G(m)**; **95C(e)**, **95B(d)**
	MODULI, EXPECTED SUM OF	**25W(a)**
	MODULUS	Used in its ordinary mathematical senses: (i) the positive value of number, e.g. the modulus of $+3$, -3, written $\|+3\|$, $\|-3\|$ respectively is 3. (ii) in respect of certain types of addition, a number equivalent to zero (e.g. Teleprinter addition has modulus 2) cf.: Addition.
E.14	MODULUS OF A DOT	A notorious example of bad writing in which 1·1 was interpreted independently by several people as "modulus of a dot"! **R3**, p. 50
	MORNING MEETING	A meeting held at 1100 hours (of the administration, DO, CO, WM, representative of Hut 3 and Room 11) to discuss policy.
	MOTOR	Usually means total motor, i.e. basic motor (μ_{37}) modified by the limitation. **11B(f)**; **22C**
p. 421	MOTOR, HISTORICAL	**41D(c)**; **44B(d)**
	MOTOR, BASIC, PERIOD OF	**22C(c)**
	MOTOR, BASIC, ΔD COUNTS AGAINST	**22H(e)**; and **22** figs.
	MOTOR-BREAKING, HAND	**28D(b)**; **12D(b)**
	MOTOR-BREAKING, MACHINE	**92**
	MOTOR-BREAKING, MACHINE, PROBABILITY OF SUCCESS	**92A**.
	MOTOR-BREAKING, MACHINE, (SMOOTH MOTOR)	**92K**
	MOTOR-BREAKING, MACHINE, STATISTICAL, REFERENCES	**92K**
	MOTOR-BREAKING ON COLOSSUS	**53C(d)**, **53L(h)**; **53H(b)**, **53J(i)**, **53L(i)**
	MOTOR CROSS LETTERS	**22H(a),(c)**
	MOTOR ON DRAGON	**55A(b)**
a	MOTOR, EARLY	**28D(a)**

[a] **29D(a)**

MOTOR KEY DATE	An obsolete term for wheel date, introduced when only the motor patterns were changed daily. Still used in dialect.	
MOTOR RECTANGLE	See Rectangle, Motor	
MOTOR, SMOOTH	**92K**	
MOTOR-SETTING, HAND	**12D(b)**, **28D(c)**	
MOTOR-SETTING, MACHINE	**12D(c)**, **23L**; 23(I), **53L(l)**(ii), **23N**	
MOTOR-SETTING, APPLICATION OF PROPORTIONAL BULGE ALGEBRA	**22X(b)**	
MOTOR, TOTAL, PROPORTION OF CROSSES IN	**22C(d)**; **11C(d),(e)**	
MR MINUS X	Man lent by Newmanry to Testery for a week on key-breaking. Introduced too late in war to be of much value.	
MR X	Man lent by Testery to Newmanry for a week on chi-breaking.	
MR Y	Man lent by Testery to Newmanry for a week on Cribs. (scheme in operation only a few weeks) **27H**	
MRS MILES	See Miles.	E.15
MULTIPLE TEST	Examining more than one wheel-setting simultaneously on Colossus. (Double on Colossus 1; quintuple on the others). See quintuple test, double test.	
MUTUALLY EXCLUSIVE	**21(d)**	
MYSTERIES	**23Z**(11), (14)	

n_α	**92B(b)**	p. 422
$N^{\bullet}_{\alpha}\, N^{\times}_{\alpha}$	**92B(a)**	
$n \log n$	**22Y**(3) **27X(e)**, **27Y(d)**	
NATURAL BAN	See Ban, Natural	
NEAR DEPTH	Two messages are said to be in near depth if the settings of all wheels except one are the same. **41C(c)**; **42B(a),(c)**	
NEEDLES IN HAYSTACKS	**21(h)**	
NEGATION SWITCH	See 'Not' Switch.	
NEGATIVE	(meaning cross) **11A(a)**	
NEWMANRY	Mr Newman's Section: the Tunny breaking section which used machine and statistical methods.	
NEWMANRY, EARLY DAYS OF	**74** June'43, **43D**, **44B(e)**	
NEWMANRY, EXPANSION OF	**14A**, **14B(b)**, **15C**; **15A**	
NEWMANRY, KEY-WORK IN	**26G**; **15C(e)**	
NINE	The letter 9 is used for letters not recognisably intercepted (as well as the genuine 9's of the cipher). Originally eight was used, but strings of these unduly weakened the tape. These 9's are often referred to as "corruption" (q.v.)	

	NINE BAR STROKE ($\bar{9}$/)	**95C(d)**; **53M(h)**
	NM	Typewriterese for norm.
i, E.16	NOCKE	One of the pegs (or cams) on a wheel of the German Tunny machine. It can be put in two positions, active and inactive. The active position is referred to simply as "Nocke", the inactive as "keine". On all wheels except μ_{37} Nocke is cross, keine is dot. **11B(j)**, **22G(c)**(7)
	NON-FLOGGING	Setting by quick but not very powerful methods, for dealing with a large bulk of traffic. (**R0**, p. 22)
	NON-READ	**56C**
	NORM	The score in a wheel-breaking run if the wheel is assumed to be all dots. **25A(b)**; **25G(c)**
	NORMAL RECTANGLE	Colossus rectangling for constant depth, using the subtraction gadget. Rectangling without the subtraction gadget is called "print scores". **53M(e)**
a	NORMALISE	To scale a letter count to make the total 3200.
	NOT (SYMBOL FOR)	**21(a)**. A somewhat different use of this symbol is in **22A(b)**.
	NOT SWITCH	A switch which insists that the condition to which it is applied shall *not* be satisfied. **13B(a)**
	NOT SWITCH, COLOSSUS	**53J(d)**
	NOT SWITCH, ROBINSON	**54E(c)**
	NOT NOT	The importance of this is that NOT (NOT A, NOT B) is equivalent to EITHER A OR B. **53J(d)**; **54E(c)**
p. 423	NOT 9, NOT 99 ($\widetilde{9}$, $\widetilde{99}$)	A device on several Colossi to prevent counting parts of the tape not properly intercepted. $\widetilde{99}$ is an improvement on $\widetilde{9}$. **53K(g)**, **52(h)**(ii); **13B(a)**
	NOT 99, FOR KEY RECTANGLES	**53M(i)**; **95C(d)**
	NOTATION	**22A(a)**,**(b)**,**(c)**; **81B(b)**, **11B**. See also Probability Notation.
	NUMBERING	**26D**
	NUMERALS IN TEXT OF MESSAGE EFFECT ON *P* AND ΔP COUNTS	**22G(c)**6
	O	Odds. **21(b)**; **24Y(c)**
	OCTOPUS	**44A(a)**; **43C(a)**, **74** Oct'42
	OKH	Oberkommando des Heeres: the chief German Army Headquarters. **27B**
	OLD FASHIONED TURINGERY	Original form of key-breaking: equivalent to the "big rectangle".

[a] NORMALIZE

[i] 'nocke' in definition: uncapitalised both times.

OLD ROBINSON	**52(c)**; **58**(I),(II)
ONE BACK, ON ROBINSON	**54D(g)**
ONE BACK, ON MILES	**56H(d)**
ONE PLUS TWO (1+2)	**12C(d)**, **15A(a)**, **44B(c)**; **23B(c)**, **22H(f)**
OPENINGS	Routine in tree (q.v.) form for Colossus setting, not including difficult fifth wheels and the like.
OPERATING PRACTICE, GERMAN	See procedure and operating practices, German.
OPS REGISTRY	**14B(b)**; fig. **31 (I)**
OPS CARD	**34(c)**
OPERATIONAL SUCCESS	Part **6**
ORDER BOOK	Book (with carbon paper) for ordering messages, used by DO and WM.
ORDERING	**33A**; **37(c)**
ORDERING OF CRIB MESSAGES AND TAPES	See Cribs.
ORGANISATION	**14**, **15B**; **74**, **81A**
ORDINARY ADDITION FIELD	See Addition Field, Ordinary.
OSCILLATING CONVERGENCE	**24X(f)**
OUT (MACHINES)	Not working properly.
OUT (WHEELS)	Broken and issued as certain.
OVER DECIBANNING	Decibanning for wheel-breaking assuming the letter-count on partial wheels to be a fair sample. **25B**, **25W**
OVERLAP	The end of one message (QEP) and the beginning of the next when they have the same plain language. **28B(g)**, **11D(c)**; **27A** p. 424
p	Probability
P	Priority sign.
P	Symbol for Plain Language (Plain Text, Clear). Sometimes denoted by PL. See also Plain Language.
P^*	(i) A modification of P used in crib runs. **27G**, **27W** (ii) (a nonce-use) $P_5^* = \overline{\overline{P}}_5 + \Delta P_5$.
PQ	A tape used in making P^*. **27F**
P_5 LIMITATION ($\overline{\chi}_2 + \overline{\overline{P}}_5$)	**11B(g)**(iii), **14A(b)**, **43C(g)**, **44C**; **27A**, **11E(c)**, **74** Sept,Dec'44. See also Limitation.
P_5 LIMITATION, CRIBS	**27G(n)**
P_5 LIMITATION, CRIBS RUN	**27G(n)**
P_5 LIMITATION, ΔD COUNTS	**22H(d)**

P_5 LIMITATION, χ-BREAKING	**25E(h)**
$P_5\psi_1$ LIMITATION	See Triple Limitation.
PARALLELEPIPEDS	See Rectangles.
PARTIAL DE-CHI	De-chi on fewer than 5 chis. **23H(h)**
PARTIAL WHEELS	Wheels with some characters doubted. **25D(a)**
PATTERN	The dots and crosses constituting a wheel: also the corresponding part of Colossus (see trigger, ptrigger, also wheels).
PATTERN FRAGMENTS	**42E(d)**
PAUSE	See Autopause.
PBA	Proportional Bulge Algebra (q.v.)
PB FUNCTION	Proportional Bulge Function (q.v.)
PBI	Partial break-in, i.e. setting on partial wheels (q.v.)
PCO	Printer cut-out. **53G(i), 54G(b); 53N**
PECKERS	The pins in a tape-reader, which when a hole in the tape permits them to rise, produce the electrical impulse which represents a cross. A vulgar corruption is 'jigger'. In the absence of a tape the peckers can be seen through a rectangular aperture, known as the window, eye, or (a loose usage) the head. Thus all the phrases: on the peckers, on the jiggers, in the window, in the eye, in the head, have the same meaning, viz. that the letter referred to is the next to be copied.
p. 425 PENNY, DOUBLE HEADED	**21(h)**
PENNY, TOSSING OF	**21(g)**
PERFECT WHEEL	A χ wheel with as large a patch of • • × × • • × × (producing • × • × • × • × • × in the deltaed wheel) as is legal. **22B; 23G(a), 25D(e)**
PERFECT WHEEL, RANDOM SETTING OF	**23G(f)**
PERFORATION (IN TUNNY TRANSMISSION)	**11A(b)**
PERFORATION, HAND	**35H(a)**
PERFORATOR, HAND	**56A**
PERIOD OF BASIC MOTOR	See Motor
PERIOD DIALS	**54C(f),(g)**
PERMANENT CROSS	See Cross, Permanent.
PERMUTING OF IMPULSES	**56G(f),(h); 56F(b)**
PHOTO-ELECTRIC CELLS	**53B(b), 54C(c), 91B(b)**
PHOTOGRAPHIC MACHINE AND SECTION	**91; 13B, 74** May'45, fig. **31 (I)**

PICKUP	A confirmation of the setting of a wheel involved in two different runs. **23C(b)**; **23L(e)**
PICKERING PAPER	A special tape used for cutting out an operation in an early type of Robinson de-chi tape.
PIGEON-HOLES	Wooden pigeon-holes for tapes. [i]
PIN-JUGGLING	In the final stages of chi-breaking doubtful characters may be resolved by counts on two or more versions of the wheel. This is equivalent to letter counts against the doubtful characters. **25D(g)**(3), **25G(l)**
PINK AND WHITE BUTTONS	Shorting plugs, with pink and white heads, used for several purposes, including wheel-setting on Colossus, wheel patterns on Colossus wheel-breaking panel, Tunny, Dragon, etc. [a]
PIP, PIPPAGE	(i) The excess of dots over crosses is called the pippage. The unit is called a pip. **24A(b)**; **25A(a)**, **24W(a)** (ii) A protuberance on a relay contact, caused by over-heating.
PIPPETTE	A pip in a (scalar-product) flag. **24W(d)** [b]
PLAIN LANGUAGE (*P*)	Plain text or clear. **22G**
PLAIN LANGUAGE BIGRAMS	See Bigrams.
PLAIN LANGUAGE COUNTS AND CHARACTERISTICS	**22G(a)**,**(c)**; **44B(a)**, **22** IV,V,VI,VII,VIII,IX
PLAIN LANGUAGE COUNTS ON ONE OR TWO IMPULSES	**22G(d)**,**(e)**
PLAIN LANGUAGE FREAK COUNTS	**22G(c)**
PLAIN LANGUAGE COUNTS, $\Delta^2 P$	**22G(f)** p. 426
PLAIN LANGUAGE, RECOVERY OF ΔP FROM ΔD	**22X(a)**
PLAIN LANGUAGE, OBTAINING OF ΔD FROM ΔP	**22H(a)**
PLAIN LANGUAGE, HETEROGENEITY	**22G(b)**
PLAIN LANGUAGE, SUM OF TWO *P* STREAMS	**22W(a)**
PLUG	Commonly used to mean two plugs and lead, or "plug cord".
PLUG, SHORTING	Commonly called pink and white buttons.
PLUGBOARD (PHOTOGRAPHIC MACHINE)	**91B(d,e,f,g,i)**, **91**(I,II)
PLUG PANEL	A panel with jacks (often called 'holes') for the insertion of jacks to link various circuits.
PLUG PANEL, COLOSSUS	**53K**
PLUG PANEL, ROBINSON	**54D**

[a] wheel-patterns [b] PIPETTE

[i] 'Pigeon holes' (twice).

	PLUG PANEL, TUNNY	**56K(e)**
	PLUS (& +)	See "and plus"
	PLUS SWITCHES	See Addition Switches.
	PMH	Print Main Heading. **53G(g)**, **53N**
	POISSON DISTRIBUTION	See Distribution, Poisson.
	POSITION COUNTER	The counter which shows the relative position of two tapes on Super Robinson; also the more primitive devices to the same end on earlier Robinsons. **54C(d)**,**(e)**,**(f)**,**(g)**,**(h)**; **52(b)**(iii), **54B**, **54F(b)**
	POSITIVE (DOT)	**11A(a)**
	POWER OF A RUN	*Roughly* sigma-age. **R1**, pp. 64, 67
	POSTERIOR ODDS	**21(f)**,**(g)**
	PREAMBLES	**41A(b)**
	PREDICTION	See Crib Prediction.
	PRESETTING SWITCHES (FOR LIMITATION)	**53C(d)**, **56K(c)**
	PRIGGISH PRINCIPLES	**R3**, p. 55
	PRINTER	The electrical printer (Electromatic or Gifford) of a Robinson or Colossus. **51(i)**
	PRINTER, COLOSSUS	**53G(k)**; **53G(e)**,**(f)**,**(g)**,**(i)**, **53L(e)**
	PRINTER, ROBINSON	**54G**; **52(b)**, **54B**
	"PRINT SCORES"	The sign-writing on Colossus to denote the use of the rectangling gadget without the subtraction gadget. **53M(d)**
	PRIOR ODDS	**21(f)**,**(g)**
	PRIORITY MESSAGES	**37(e)**
p. 427	PROBABILITY	**21**; **81B(a)**
	PROBABILITY, LAWS OF	**21(e)**
	PROBABILITY NOTATIONS	**21(b)**
	PROCEDURES, CURRENT, REFERENCE, OBSOLETE	DO's list of various routines.
	PROCEDURES, A, B, C, D	Message ordering procedures. **33A**
a	PROCEDURE CARD	**34(c)**; **34(I)**
	PROCEDURE AND OPERATING PRACTICES, GERMAN	**27C**; **27B**, **27D** (receipts).
	PRODUCTION CHART	Chart showing number of messages set and abandoned, classified by day and link.
	PROJECTING ψ	**28C(b)**

[a] **34C**

PROPORTIONAL BULGE (PB)	If the probability in a random case is p, and in the "right" case is $p(1+\xi)$, ξ is called the proportional bulge. **21(j),(m), 22E**
PROPORTIONAL BULGE	Algebra **22X**; Function **22X(d)**
PROTEUS	A machine which uses short cribs and a "dictionary" to anagram depths (q.v.). **55B, 28A(g); 13B(c), 58**(XXXI)
PROVING (WHEELS)	Make wheels complete and certain by decoding. Occasionally used for making wheels + 40 db in χ-breaking.
PROVING MOTOR SETTINGS	**23L(k)**
PTRIGGER	See Trigger.
PSI	See ψ
PSI 1 LIMITATION	$\overline{\chi}_2+\overline{\psi}'_1$ Limitation. See ψ
PSI 1 P_5 LIMITATION	$\overline{\chi}_2+\overline{\psi}'_1+\overline{\overline{P}}_5$ Limitation. See ψ
PUNCH	A 5-wire perforator, attached to various machines, including Colossi 2 and 6. **51(h)**
PUNCH, COLOSSUS	**53M(h); 95B(c), 95C(d)**
PUNCTUATION, DOUBLE and SINGLE	**22G(c)**
"PURE ψ" (IN DE-CHIS)	**28C(b)**
PURGING	Method of starting a rectangle convergence by removing, from an eye start, characters which do not score well. **24D(g)**
Q	Whatever is switched into the Q panel of Colossus by means of the Q selection switches (big black switches). Q is necessarily of the form $\varepsilon_1 Z+\varepsilon_2\chi+\varepsilon_3\psi'$ where ε_1 ε_2 ε_3 independently are 0, 1, or Δ
Q PANEL	The switch panel on Colossus where conditions are imposed on Q. **53J, 13B(a); 53K(c)** p. 428
Q SELECTION SWITCHES	**53J(a)**
Q SWITCHES (ROBINSON)	**54E(b)**
$Q_1, Q_2, Q_3, Q_4, Q_5, Q_6, Q_7, Q_8, Q_9, Q_{10}$	**54D(h); 54E(b)**
$Q, \overline{Q}, \overline{\overline{Q}}$	**54D(g)**
q	Symbol for $R\delta/x$. **25W(e)**
QEP	A number giving message settings (taken from a numbered list). Used also for the whole of a transmission on the same settings. (It is of course a German Army Q signal) **43C(a); 44A(a)**
QEP SYSTEM, INTRODUCTION OF	**74** Oct'42
QEP SYSTEM, RESEARCH INTO	**94**
QEP BOOK	**11D(b); 14A(b)**

	QEP BOOK, CAPTURED	**94(c)**
	QEP CHANGE (Ref. Cribs)	**27C(c),(e)**
	QEP NUMBERS, RECOVERY OF	**74** Nov'44
	QEP SHEET, WHITING	**94(d)**
	QEP THRASHER, ABNORMAL USE IN	**93(a)**
	QSN	Old signal for QEP
	QTQ	Signal for limitation
a, E.17	QUATSCH (WAHL-WÖRTER)	Arbitrary trivialities which German operators were required to insert at the beginning of a QEP to prevent the use of stereotyped beginnings as Cribs.
	QUINTUPLE TESTING	**53L, 13B(a); 52(f), 53J(h)**.
	QUINTUPLE TESTING, RECTANGLING	**53M(c)**
	QUINTUPLE TESTING, IN WHEEL-BREAKING	**53L(l)**(iv)
	QZZ	Signal for changing wheel patterns.
	R	Number of places looked at. (Occurs very frequently).
	R (5202)	
	$R - 2\times$ NORM.	**25A(b), 25G(c)**
	R (Ri)	Research log.
	R (Ri)	Room
	R (R_i)	Remembered impulses of *Q* (in multiple test). **53L(c)**
	R (R_i) (SWITCHES FOR)	**53J(h)**
p. 429	RANDOM KEY	**93**
	RAW TAPE	Tape not slip read. **33B**; **74** Mar'45
	READ (INSERT MACHINE)	**56C**
	READERS AND REPERFORATORS	**51(h)**
	READER	A machine which reads a tape, that is converts the punched letters into electrical impulses. **56B**, **56C**, **56D**, **56F(g)**, **56G(a)**, **81C(g)**. See also auto-transmitter.
	RE	Re-encodement (otherwise called retransmission) of the same message on different keys. **27A**
	RECEIPTS (GERMAN ARMY)	**27D(b)**
	RECTANGLE	See also convergence. **24**, **44B(c)**; **12C(e)**, **35G**, **36B**, **74** Nov'42, Feb'43, Nov'44.
	RECTANGLE, COLOSSUS	**24B(f)**, **53M**; **52(k)**, **(g)**, **53N**
	RECTANGLE, CONDITIONAL	**24F**; **25C(e)**, **53M(d)**

[a] WORTER

---

[a] GENERALISED [b] IMPRACTIBILITY

REGISTRAR RUN TAPES LOGS H RECTANGLES T ROOM 12 CRIBS	Person whose duty is registration, and control of a special job.
RELAY	**51(e)**
RELIABILITY OF WITNESSES	**21(j)**
REPEAT	Usually repeated letter in *D*, i.e. / in ΔD.
REPEAT (ψ REPEAT)	When taking off a complete χ wheel in the last stages of key-breaking, a repeat in the pattern of the unextended ψ wheel must be obtained. This is called a ψ repeat. **26D**, **26**(XV)
REPEATS AND ANTIREPEATS	Letters in ΔD which are all dots or all crosses (e.g. C_2 is repeats and antirepeats on 1, 2, 5.)
REPEAT AND REPEAT LIGHT	In a setting run the reappearance of settings already tried. When this first happens a lamp called the repeat light glows.
REPEAT LIGHT, COLOSSUS	**53D(d)**
REPEAT LIGHT, ROBINSON	**54C(j)**
REPEAT COLUMNS	**28D(b)**(iii); **92A**, **92E(b)**
REPEAT OF SETTINGS	See settings, analysis of
REPERFORATOR	A perforator in a copying machine, strictly one operated by a train of impulses on one wire. See also Reader. **56B**, **56C**, **56E**, **56F(g)**; **56G(a),(b),(j)**, **56H(a),(b),(c),(d)**.
REPERFORATING ROOM	**33B**
RERUN	Run again (also used as a noun).
a RESEARCH	**81A(i)**, **31D**
RESEARCH PERIOD	**14A(b)**, **74** June'41
RESEARCH SECTION	**41**, **42**
RESET, COLOSSUS	**53G(j)**; **53N**
p. 431 RESET, ROBINSON	**54G(c)**
RESET, DECODING MACHINE	**56L(d)**
RESETTING GADGET, GERMAN MACHINE	**28A(b)**
RESETTING GADGET, DECODING MACHINE	**56L(d)**
RESPONSIBILITY, ALLOCATION OF	**81A(d)**

[a] **31**(I)

RESTART	Method of taking a new start during the convergence of a rectangle, generally in a manner depending on the result of the first convergence. **24D(f)**; **24W(c)**
RETRANSMISSION	**27A**
RETRANSMISSION SLIPS	**27D(e)**, **27E(a)**
REWRITE	The result of reperforating a message after additional slip-reading.
RING, QEP NUMBERS	**94D**
RING	A term used in early PB Algebra
RING COMMONS	A device on Garbo or Junior for the easy common steckering of two sets of letters by means of shorting plugs. **56D(b)**
RINGED	**43B**
RIVAL SETTINGS	**23F(b)**, **23G(b)**, **23C(a)** [a]
ROBINSON	A counting and stepping machine which examines two synchronised tapes simultaneously. **54**, **12C(d)**, **13B(b)**; **27G(f),(g),(h),(i)**, **52(l)**, **14B(b)**, **15C(a)**, **74** Jan'43, **31**(I),(II)
ROBINSON-COLOSSUS (SYNTHESIS)	**52(m)**
ROBINSON FLAGGING	**95** especially **95A(d)**, **95B(a)**, **95C(a)**
ROBINSON, HEATH	**52(b)**; **23Z**, **15A(c)**
ROBINSON MECHANICAL FLAGS	See Robinson Flagging and Mechanical Flags.
ROBINSON, OLD	**52(c)**, **58**(I)
ROBINSON, OLD, CONTROL IMPULSE	**54H(b)**
ROBINSON RECTANGLE	See Rectangle, Robinson.
ROBINSON SECTION	**27H**
ROBINSON WEAKNESS, BASIC OF	**52(d)**; **54G(a)**
ROD	A strip of cardboard consisting of a column of the addition square arranged in a certain order. **28B(h)** E.18
ROLLE	**93(a)**
ROOM D	**14B(b)**; **58**(XX), **31**(II)
ROOM 11	**14B(a)**
ROOM 12	**14B(a)**; **34(b)**, **31**(I)
ROOM 40	**14B(c)**; **31**(I) p. 432
ROOM 41	**14B(c)**; **31**(I)
ROUTINE	(i) Technique formulated in detail and used frequently. (ii) Routine message. **27B**, **27D**
ROUTINE, KEY-WORK	**26**(VI)
ROUTINE FOR 5202	**91C(c)**

[a] **23G(c)**

	RUN	A setting or breaking operation on Robinson or Colossus which, when started, the machine can complete without human intervention.
	RUN FOR LAST WHEEL	**23H(f)**
	RUNS, REGISTRAR	**14B(b)**; **37(a)**
	RUNS, SUBSEQUENT (FLOGGING)	**23H(d)**
	RUNS, TEST	See Test Runs.
	RUNS, 3 and 4 WHEEL	**23H(c)**, **91C(c)**, **91E**
	RUNNING BACKWARDS	**56K(h)**
	S	Typewriterese for ψ
	$S_2\ S_4\ S_6$	$S_r = \Sigma\ \theta^r_{ij}$ **24X(d)**
	S and S TESTS	Slide and Significance Tests. See Significance Test, Slide and.
	SALAMANDER	A compatibility gadget (see compatibility chart) **55A(j)**; **28B(d)**
	SAMPLING ERRORS	Alphabetical counts. **22K**
	SC	Score on Colossus dossier.
	SCALAR PRODUCT	**24D(b)**, **24W(a)**, **24Y(d)**
	SCALE OF 2 COUNTER	See Wynn-Williams' counter.
	SCORE, COUNTER (ROB)	**54B**; **54G(a)**
	SCORE OF A RECTANGLE	Double-bulge, or sum of moduli of scores of either wheel, after the rectangle has been crudely converged.
	SCORES (EXHIBIT OF A ROB)	**54B**
a	SCORING CHART	A deciban chart for setting. **R2**, p. 7, **R5**, pp. 73–77, 89
	SCORING OF COLUMNS IN SOLUTION OF MOTOR PATTERNS	**92D**
b	SCREEDS	**81A(f)**(v)
	SD	See Standard Deviation.
c	SECCOTINE	**57(d)**
p. 433	SECONDARY RECTANGLE	See conditional rectangle.
	SELECTION SWITCHES	See *Q* Selection Switches.
	SEMINAR	A meeting of Wrens and one or two cryptographers for instructional purposes.
	SERIAL	See Receipts.
	SERIAL NUMBER	**41A(a)**. See also Receipts.
	SET READING	**56L(d)**

[a] **R2** 7, **R5** 73–77, 89 [b] **81A(f)**(iv) [c] **57D**

SET TOTAL	A number set up on Robinson or Colossus such that lower (or if you wish higher) scores are neither printed nor displayed. **53G(a)**; **54F(c)**, **55C(d)**, **13B(a)**
SET WHEELS (SU SET U)	**53D(a)**; **53N**
SETTERS	**39B(a)**; **31**(I)
SETTING	A position of a wheel at the start of a message is called a setting. Setting wheels means finding the settings. A wheel is set if its setting is found. A message is set if all the wheels are set. To set up the wheels means to put patterns in the triggers. When copying, or in setting short cribs, setting often means a position at the letter currently under examination. **23**; **12B**, **12A(b)**, **14C(a)**,**(b)**
SETTING, EARLY	**42A**; **41E**
SETTING, HISTORY OF MACHINE	**23Z**, **74** Mar'43
SETTING MESSAGES IN DEPTH ON $\chi_1\ \chi_2$	**24Y(d)**
SETTING, MOTOR	**23L**
SETTING OTHER MESSAGES IN χ-BREAKING	**25D(b)**
SETTING SLIDY WHEELS	**23G(d)** [a]
SETTINGS, ANALYSIS OF	**94(b)**
SETTINGS, BOOK OF	**94(a)**
SETTINGS, MEANING RELATIVE POSITION	**53D(a)**; **53H(b)**, **54C(e)**,**(h)**, **55A(d)**, **91B(c,b)**
SETTINGS ON TUNNY	**56K(b)**
SETTINGS ON DECODING MACHINE	**56L(a)**
SHAUN COUNT	A count of the 32 numbers of occurrences of $\Delta D_{ij\cdots k} = \bullet$ Sometimes loosely used for the corresponding thing for $P_{ij\cdots k} = \bullet$ (Atkin Count) E.19, [b]
SHEEP	Pins which are not 'goats' q.v.
SHIFT, LETTER AND FIGURE	**22G(b)**, **11A(a)**
SHORT BEDSTEAD	A bedstead which can carry a tape not more than 11,000 long. [c]
SHORT RUN	A setting run for one wheel.
SHORT WB RUNS	**25A** p. 434
SICKNESS	**23Z**(26)
SIGMA	See $\boldsymbol{\sigma}$
SIGMA-AGE	See $\boldsymbol{\sigma}$-age
SIGMA-AGE EXPECTED IN MOTOR RUNS	See $\boldsymbol{\sigma}$-age expected in motor runs.

[a] **23G(e)** [b] occurences [c] SHORT, BEDSTEAD

SIGN (MATHEMATICAL SYMBOL FOR $x/\lvert x\rvert$)	**24Y(c)**; **24W(a)**, **24W(d)**
SIGN OF KEY	If in keybreaking the $\Delta\chi$'s are not reversed the key is said to have the right sign and if they are reversed the wrong sign. **26C**; **26Y(c)**, **26**(XIII)
SIGNIFICANCE OF μ_{37} RUNS	**92K**
SIGNIFICANCE TEST	A mathematical test to determine whether a result is sufficiently bulgy to be unlikely to have occurred at random. **36A(a)**
SIGNIFICANCE TEST FLAG	**24X(f)**,**(b)**
SIGNIFICANCE TEST FOR KEY-BREAKING	**26X(b)**
SIGNIFICANCE TEST FOR RECTANGLES	**24X**, **24E**, **74** Apr'44
SIGNIFICANCE TEST FOR SHORT WB RUNS	**25B(a)**; **25W(a)**, **74** July'44
SIGNIFICANCE TEST ON ORIGINAL TURINGERY	**26X(a)**, **25W(a)**
SIGNIFICANCE TEST, SLIDE AND	**24X**, **24E(c)**, **93**
SIGNIFICANCE TEST, 5×5, 10×10 FLAG	**26B(a)**
SIGNIFICANCE TEST 0	**24X(d)**
SIGNIFICANCE TEST, χ_5 FLAG	**26B(c)**
SIGNWRITING	The labelling of switches, jacks, etc.
SIMPLEX	**11D(b)**
SIMPLICITY	**81A(b)**
SINGLE PUNCTUATION	See Punctuation, Single
SIP	'Significance inter penetration'. A device on Colossus 10 for bringing up scores on all counters if the set total is exceeded on one counter. **53G(b)**; **53N**
SIX DIMENSIONAL CONVERGENCE	cf. 5 dimensional convergence. $\Delta\chi_6$ is the limitation reversed and is treated in the same way as the other $\Delta\chi$'s, when six dimensional convergence is carried out. **26G(d)**
SIXTA	Six Traffic Analysis. Log reading section. **27D(c)**; **39D**, **27H**, **31**(I)
p. 435 SIXTH IMPULSE	Limitation reversed. **22D(g)**, **26B(b)**, **R41**, p. 67, **26**(XXI), **26E**
SKELETON FLAG	A rectangle in which the unit is replaced by a large unit and is entered in dots and crosses instead of numbers is called a skeleton (rectangle). It can be flagged and the result is called a skeleton flag. **24D(d)**; **24W(c)**
SLAVE	See 'Chaser Settings'.

SLIDE, MESSAGE	If *n* cipher letters are omitted in a tape the tape is said to have a slide of *n* forwards since the key is *n* places further forward after the omission than it would have been without the omission (similarly for letters inserted). **23F**; **23Z**(21); **25D(c)**	
SLIDE OF COLUMNS	**92D**, **92E(a)**	
SLIDE OF THE MOTOR	**23L(g)**	
SLIDE RUNS	Setting runs with all five chis, for determining a slide in a message with at least some of the chis already set on part of the message. **23F(d)**; **74** July'44	
SLIDE AND SIGNIFICANCE TEST	See 'Significance Test, Slide and'.	
SLIDE (WHEEL SLIDE)	**23G**	
SLIDE-RULES	**57(a)**	a, b
SLIDE-RULES FOR ACCURATE CONVERGENCE	Device for making the accurate scoring table, consisting of a slide-rule made of cardboard. **24W(a)**	c
SLIDES, LOOKING FOR GOOD	**92E(c)**	
SLIDING	**28**(VII)	
SLIDING MACHINE	Hypothetical machine for sliding columns of a motor rectangle for motor breaking. **R0**, p. 68	
SLIP READING	Examination of undulator tape (or 'slip') for production of cipher tape and red form.	
SLIPS, RE and CRIBS	See 'Crib Re Slip' and 'Crib Slips'.	E.20
SMOOTH MOTOR	An artificial motor which gives (or is hoped to give) the correct number of motor dots up to the *n*th letter of a message for a large proportion of values of *n*. **92K**; **92E(d)**	
SNAKE	**28**(VIII): **92F**	
SNAKING	**56L(e)**	
SORTING OF SETTINGS	See 'Settings, analysis of'	
SOURCE OF MACHINES	**51(g)**	
SPANNING	To span a message from the *m*th to the *n*th letter means that only this part of the message is looked at. This can be done on Colossus and Super Robinson by setting up the 'span counters'. **53H**; **52(f)**, **23F(c)**; **23F(f)**, **23L(j)**, **25D(c),(d)**, **13B(a)**	
SPANNING, COLOSSUS	**53H**	
SPANNING OF RECTANGLES	**25D(c)**; **25G(b)**	
SPANNING, ROBINSON	**54F(b)**; **54H(b)**	
SPECIAL COUNTER TAPE	See 'Control Tape'.	p. 436
SPECIAL FACILITIES (ROB PLUG PANEL)	**54D(d)**	d

[a] SLIDE RULES [b] **57A** [c] SLIDE RULES [d] **54D(c)**

SPECIAL METHODS FOR $\overline{\chi}_2$ LIMITATION	**23E; 25E**
SPECIAL PATTERN	The trigger (e′) used for doubting — independent of Q, or the corresponding trigger on the χ-breaking panel. **53C(b); 53E, 53L(j), 53K(e), 25D(a), 25D(g)**(3)
SPEED	**81A(g)**
SPLIT POSITION COUNTER	**54C(g)**
SPLIT SCORE COUNTER	A counter on Super Robinson which can be split into two counters, each of which, however, will then not count beyond 99. **54F(a)**
SPOILT COLUMN	A letter of $\Delta\psi'$ in key-breaking containing at least one dot and at least one cross. **26C**
SPROCKET HOLES	The small guiding holes at every letter of a tape. **53B(a)**; **54C(a),(b),(c), 54C(i), 11A(b), 23Z(iv)**(1), **58**(IV)
SPWM	Semi-permanent wheels man. Man in charge of all wheel men usually for period of three weeks.
SQUARE-SUMMING	Method used in significance test 0, in all χ^2 tests and in particular for the hypothetical machine for testing heterogeneity as a help in setting chis. **24X(b)**; **23Z(iii), 53M(g), 21(l)**
SQUARE-SUMMING OF COLUMNS	**24X(e)**
ST	See Set Total
STAFF	**15B(a)**; **15C(c), 31B, 31D, 31E, 31F, 74** Apr'43, **74** Aug'44
STAGGERING OF TAPES	**54A, 56F(c)**
STAIRCASING	Method of staggering a stream S of dots and crosses in the 5 impulses of a tape, at various multiples of a length l so as to be able to plug $\Delta_{il}S$ for many values of i. Note: this is very similar to the methods of crib setting especially that of **27Y(b)**. **27Y(b)**; **74** July'44
STAIRCASING and χ^2 TEST EQUIVALENCE OF	**27Y(b)**
STAND OFF	Scheme of 3 or 4 days leave for Wrens.
STANDARD DEVIATION[a]	**21(k), 21(l), 21(n), 22K, 23E(c)**
STANDING ORDERS	Instruction books for Colossus operators.
STAR[*] (FOURIER TRANSFORM)	**22X(d)**
STAR (CRIBS)	**27G(b)**
STAR (χ_5 FLAG)	**26B(c)**
START	A pattern used for the starting of convergence of a rectangle. **24D**
START (INSERT MACHINE)	**56C**

[a] **21K**

START (START SIGN)	A signal in front of the text of a message produced by a special hole in the tape causing counters to come in and (on Colossus) the 'wheels' to go round. **53B(a)** p. 437
START SIGN (ROB)	**54C(d)**
START UNIT	A jack which provides a constant dot or cross. **53K(h)**; (Rob) **54D(f)**
STARTING SWITCH (ROB)	**54C(b)**
STARTS FOR KEY-BREAKING	**26B**
STATISTICAL METHODS	**22**; **15A(a)**, **44B**, **74** Oct'42
STATISTICIANS' FALLACY	**21(o)**; **24X(e)**
STATISTICS BUREAU	Department of one or two Wrens which collects letter counts and other statistics. **31H**; **31**(I)
STECKERING	Plugging in order to produce a permutation of the alphabet. **56D(b)**,**(a)**, **56E**
STEPPING	A 'wheel' on Colossus (etc.) which moves on to a setting when the tape goes round once, is said to be stepping. **53A**; **53D(b)**, **53D(c)**, **53L(f)**, multiple test.
STEPPING, AQUARIUS	**55C(b)**
STEPPING, ROBINSON	**54C(i)**; **54A**
STEPPING, COPYING MACHINES	On a copying machine stepping merely means to move on, and is sometimes used to mean move one position for each throw of the switch. **56C**; **56G(l)**
STICKER	Electrically heated device for helping to stick tape for Robinson. Used cold for Colossus. **57(d)**; **13D**
STOP (INSERT MACHINE)	**56C**
STOP (STOP SIGN)	On Colossus or Robinson: causes counting to cease, cf. start sign.
STOP (ON DRAGON)	A place where crib plus de-χ gives possible ψ'
STOP SETTING	**56K(f)**
STOP and START (PUNCH)	**57(e)**; **13D**
STORAGE OF SCORES	**53G(c)**; **53G(j)**, **54C(d)**, **54G(a)**(ii)
STORING OF DE-CHI IN CONDENSERS	**55C(c)**
STREAM	A sequence of TP letters with fixed number of impulses (not necessarily five, and, in fact, commonly used for 1)
STRETCHING OF TAPES	**52(b)**, **54C(b)**, **54C(c)**, **23Z**(1)
STRIPED SHEET	Chit used in wheel-breaking to record numbers and length of tapes for the specific day.
STURGEON	A TP cipher involving permutation of impulses. **11A(c)**
SUBSETS	On plugboard of Robinson and Colossus. **R0**, p. 43
SUBSTANTIALLY RIGHT	**24X(e)**

p. 438	SUBTRACTION GADGET	**53M(e)**
	SUBTRACTORS, BOOK OF	**28D(c)**
	SUCCESS ON DE-χ BREAKING	**28B(j)**
	SUCCESS ON ψ BREAKING FROM DE-χ	**28C(a)**
	SUCCESSIVE APPROXIMATION	**81B(c)**
	SUM OF STREAMS	**22E**
	SUPER COLOSSUS, SUGGESTIONS FOR	**52(k)**; **R4**, pp. 124–128
	SUPER ROBINSON	The latest and best type of Robinson. **52(j)**; **13B(b)**, **15C(f)**
	SUPPLIES	**81C(f)**
	SWITCH	A place where the relative positions of the two plain languages of a depth are interchanged, on the workings. The word "switch" is written to prevent incorrect determination of key.
a	SWITCHBOARD	The *Q* panel of Colossus: it has a great many switches, all but one, for putting conditions involving *Q* into the counters. **53J**, **53E**;
	SWITCH PANEL (ROB)	**54E**; **54D(h)**
	SWITCHING, MOTOR RUNS	**23L(f)**; **53L(h),(l)**
	SWITCHING, RECTANGLING	**24B(f)**, **24F**
	SYMBOLIC LOGIC	**21(a)**
	T REGISTRY	**14B(a)**; **34(b)**
b	TAPE	A paper tape containing one TP letter every $1/10''$ and a sprocket hole at each letter. **11A(b)**; **14B(a)**, **33A**, **33B**
	TAPE, COLOSSUS	**53B(a)**
	TAPE, MINIMUM and MAXIMUM LENGTHS OF	**53B(b)**
	TAPE, OILED	**23Z**(3)
	TAPE, RAW	See Raw Tape
c	TAPE, ROBINSON	**54A**; **54D(b)**
	TAPE, PLAIN LANGUAGE SETTING BOOK	See Go-backs.
	TAPE, PLAIN TEXT, USE OF SAME ON DIFFERENT LINKS	**27C(b)**
p. 439	TAPE-MAKING and CHECKING	**35**
	TAPE-READER	See Reader.

[a] SWITCH BOARD [b] **33(a)**, **33(b)** [c] **53A**

TAPES REGISTRAR	**14B(b)**; **37(a)**
TARGET	**91B(c)**
TARGET CONTROL, ARRANGEMENT OF	**91**(III)
TATE	A special tape used in crib runs. **95B(a),(d),(g)**
TEA PARTY	Meeting of cryptographers held frequently at 1600 hours to discuss changes of routines and subjects for research. It was a democratic assembly with legislative powers. **81A(f)**(iii) E.21 [a]
TEACHING	**81A(h)**
TELEPRINTER (TP)	A machine which sends or receives letters in 5-impulse code. **11A(a)**
TELEPRINTER ALPHABET	**11A(a)**
TELEPRINTER LETTERS	**11A(a)**
TELETAPE	Five-impulse tape.
TEST FOR SIGN OF KEY	**26C**, **E**; **26**(XIII)
TEST RUNS	**23K**; **53P**, **37(f)**
TEST WHEELS	Wheels of a standard type for testing machines. **53P**
TEST $\overline{\chi}_2$ LIM	**23E(g)**,**(h)**; **25E(d)**
TESTERY	Major Tester's Section — the original Tunny section, which deals with Tunny by hand and particularly language methods. **14A(b)**; **14B(c)**, **15C(d)**, **32**, **74** July'42, **31**(I)
TESTERY CRIBS	**27H**, **27D(f)**
TESTERY METHODS	**28**; **26**, **43**
TESTING OF COLOSSUS	**53P**
THRASHER	A TP cipher with one-time key tapes. **93**; **22J**
THEORY	**81B**
THREE-HEADED PLUG	A plug which was promised for use on Robinson, for the purpose of making double use of an electrical impulse
THREE-WAY SWITCHES	The original scheme for the convergence panel was conceived as a set of three-way switches having values dot, cross and doubt.
THREE-WHEEL RUNS	**23H(c)**
THURLOW TAPE	Tapes of a special type for convenient making of rectangles on Garbo. **24B(d)**
THYRATRONS	
TIGERING	A sequence of `/8/8/8...` on a tape (see Leopardry).
TIMES OF RETRANSMISSIONS	**27B**; **27D**
TIMES	**36C**

[a] **81F(iii)**

	TIMES FOR 5202	
p. 440 E.22	TM	Total Motor. TM = dot, if and only if $\mu'_{37} = \bullet$ and limitation $= \times$. **11B(f)**; **11C(d)**. Tim Moilien.
	TM SWITCH	**53J(i)**
	TOILET ROLLS	Rolls of paper for printers on Robinson and Colossus
E.23	TONE TRANSMISSION	**74** Mar'42
	TOTAL MOTOR	See TM
	TP	See Teleprinter and Tea-party.
	TRAFFIC, CURRENT	**74** July'42
i	TRANSLATING CIRCUIT	**91B(e)**
	TRANSMISSION	**11D(b)**
	TRANSMISSIONS RECEIVED	**61**
	TRANSMITTER	A tape-reader.
	TRE	Telecommunications Research Establishment. A source of some machines. **51(g)**
a	TREE	A scheme of routine for setting messages in the form of a tree, i.e. giving instructions depending on what happens at each stage. Usually applies to fairly simple cases only. **23B(c)**; **26**(VI)
b	TRIGGERS	Method of starting action in a circuit which then functions for a time under its own control. Hence used for the wheel patterns panel on Colossus 1. The term was naturally extended to the wheel pattern panels on later Colossi, but as this was technically incorrect the word was modified to Ptrigger to appease the engineers. Later the p was dropped by everybody. **53C(a)**; **13B(a)**
	TRIPLE DOTS IN TM	**26C**; **R41**, p. 92
	TRIPLE LIMITATION	$\overline{\chi}_2, \overline{\psi}_1, \overline{\overline{P}}_5$ lim. **11B(g)**(iv), **74** June'44
	TUNNY	Statistical determination whether cipher is Tunny cipher. **93**.
	TUNNY	The cipher dealt with in this work. **11**, **11B(i)**, **14A**, **12A(a)**,**(b)**,**(c)**, **41A**
	TUNNY (AND DECODING MACHINE)	**31A**, **74** June'43, **56K**, **56J**, **13C**, **51(k)**, **15A(d)**
	TUNNY LINK (EXPERIMENTAL)	**74** Oct'42
	TUNNY MACHINE (GERMAN)	**11**(II), **11B(j)**
	TUNNY ROOM	**14B(b)**, **31**(I)
	TUNNY, SZ40, ON FIRST LINK	**74** June'41
	TURING	**21(f)**,**(g)**

[a] **51G** [b] wheel-pattern

[i] Entire entry 'Translating circuit...' handwritten.

TURINGERY	Method of key-breaking. The essential idea was differencing. **43B**; **74** July'42. See Old-fashioned Turingery.
TURINGERY COUNT	**43B**
'TWO BACK' (ROBINSON)	**54D(g)**
TYPE A, B, C	**23B(a)**, **22G(c)**
TYPEWRITERS	See Printer. p. 441
U-SHAPED PIN	**53C(a)**
UN-Δ	See Integration.
UND	Undifferenced, i.e. not Δ'd.
UNDULATOR TAPE	A tape on which the electrical impulses of Tunny transmissions are graphically recorded (at Knockholt). **33B**
UNEXTENDED	See Contraction.
UNISELECTOR SWITCHES	**51(e)**; **56J**
UNRINGED	**43B**
UNSTEADY	A count which is not exactly constant when checked (on Robinson or Colossus).
URGENCY (HUT 3)	A link is 'urgent' if its value decreases rapidly with time. **R4**, p. 101
USABLE	Settings that are evens. **R3**, p. 135
VARIANCE	Square of standard deviation. (q.v.)
VETTING	Rewriting. (q.v.)
VICTORY	**74** May'45
WB	Wheel-breaking (usually χ-breaking).
WEIGHTED AVERAGE OF FACTORS	See Factors, weighted average of.
WHEEL-BOOK and WHEEL-BIBLE	Book containing record of wheel patterns. A bible was an [a] authoritative version.
WHEEL-BREAKER	Cryptographer whose job, for a week, is wheel-breaking.
WHEEL-BREAKING	See also χ-breaking, key-breaking and motor-breaking. **12B**, **12A(b)**; **14C(c),(d)**, **15C(e)**, **74** Feb'44, **25**, **26**
WHEEL-BREAKING (EARLY)	**36A(a)**; **74** May'42, **42D**, **43B** p. 442
WHEEL-BREAKING (χ-BREAKING) GENERAL PLAN OF	**25C**

[a] wheel-patterns

	WHEEL-BREAKING, LENGTH REQUIRED FOR	**24Y(a)**
	WHEEL-BREAKING PANEL	See χ-breaking panel.
	WHEEL-BREAKING RUN FOR μ_{37}	See μ_{37}
	WHEEL-BREAKING RUN, SHORT	See χ-breaking Run, Short.
	WHEEL CHARACTERISTICS	**22B**; **25D(e)**
	WHEEL CHARACTERISTICS OF MOTOR	**22C**
	WHEEL CHARACTERISTICS OF ψ	**22D(a)**,**(i)**
	WHEEL DATE	The period between the QZZ time on a given calendar date, and the QZZ on the following day.
	WHEEL-MAN	The man in charge of wheel-breaking and rectangle organisation and Block H as a whole. **14B(b)**
a	WHEEL PATTERNS	**11C**, **11**(III); **44A(c)**. See also Wheel Characteristics.
b	WHEEL PATTERNS (TUNNY MACHINE)	**56K(b)**
	WHEEL PATTERNS (DECODING MACHINE)	See also Triggers **56L(b)**
	WHEEL PATTERNS (DRAGON)	**55A(c)**
	WHEEL-SHEETS	Sheets with information about one wheel in wheel-breaking. **25C(b)**; **25G**(II–VIII)
	WHEEL-SLIDING	**24Y(c)**
c	WHEEL SLIDES	See Slides (Wheel Slides).
	WHEELS	The chis, psis and motors. For Colossus the word 'wheel' is applied to the corresponding electrical circuits. **11B(c)**; **41D(a)**
	WHEELS, PARTIAL	**25D(a)**,**(b)**; **24W**
E.24	WHITEHEAD'S CHECK	$\Sigma x_i = r - 2 \times$ norm, in a short wheel-breaking run. Usually called Henry's check.
	WIDTH	Number of letters in a row of a print-out. **56D(c)**
	WINDOW	See Peckers.
	WITNESSES, CHAIN OF	**21(j)**; **24W(b)**
	WITNESSES, RELIABILITY OF	**21(j)**, **21(i)**
	WITNESS, UNRELIABLE	**21(i)**
	WM	See Wheel-Man.
	WORKED-ON (NOT)	A rectangle which is considered merely as 1271 different numbers (the entries in each cell) is said to be 'not worked on'.
	WRONG CASE	**21(j)**
	WYNN-WILLIAMS' COUNTER	A thyratron counter of electrical impulses usually based on a scale of two.

[a] WHEEL-PATTERNS [b] WHEEL-PATTERNS [three times] [c] WHEEL-SLIDES

X	Cross, also typewriterese for χ	p. 443
X (MR)	See Mr X	
Y (MR)	See Mr Y	
YES, NOT SWITCH, (ROBINSON)	**54E(c)**	
Z	Cipher. **11B(b)**	
Z^*	**27F, G, W, X, Y**	
Z ZZ ZZZ	Degrees of urgency.	
z	Symbol used in **25W(a),(e)** (q.v.).	
ZIG-ZAG (ON GARBO)	Succession of • × • × • etc. in each of two impulses of a tape, at a stagger of one, so that the sum of the two impulses is a cross.	
$\alpha, \beta, \gamma, \delta$	See Greek Orthodoxy.	[a]
β	**22D(h)** See **72**	[b]
γ TAPE	/L/L/L used in cribs. **R2**, p. 107	
δ	See Ch. **72**	
δ (RECT) MAXIMUM LIKELIHOOD VALUE OF	**24X(d)**	
δ_0	**24X(d); 24Y(a)**	E.25
δ'	**24X(d)**	
Δ (DELTA)	Difference in the sense of adding future to present (modulo 2). Used for whole or partial letters or for a single impulse. **11C(b)**, **22A(b)** definitions. **43B**, **22A(c)** manipulation of Δ	
Δ^2	The effect of applying the operation of Δ twice. Similarly for Δ^n. **22A(b)**; **43D(b)**(ii)	
Δ_n	Differenced at interval n, i.e. 1st $+(n+1)$th, 2nd $+(n+2)$th … etc.	
Δ_{31}	**27F, G, W, Y**	p. 444
Δ_{598}	**27F, G, W, X**	
Δ_{1271} TEST	See Significance Test, Slide and	
Δ^*	Notation on Miles A. Differencing backward, i.e. by adding the past character to the present one. **56H(d)**	

[a] Orthodox. [b] **22(d)**

[a] AN EMPIRICAL [b] χ^x DISTRIBUTION [c] **23G**,(II–VIII) [d] **25(f)**

72 NOTATION

p. 447

Obsolete and rare notations are enclosed in brackets. The letters are arranged in the order large Latin, small Latin, large Greek, small Greek.

A	Average (expected random score)
A, B, C, D,	Ordering procedures; bedsteads of Super Robinson; Wren shifts
A, B, C, D, ...	Versions of wheels in χ-breaking.
B	Bulge.
[B_1, B_2	Bulge of best and second best scores]
BM	Basic Motor.
C	Number of crosses in μ_{61}
[C	Total number of crosses in $\Delta\psi'$ in key-breaking significance test II]
[$\mathscr{C}$	A class of teleprinter letters.]
D	De-chi.
D	$d/37$
[D	Total number of dots in $\Delta\psi'$ in key-breaking significance test II.]
[DB	Occasionally double bulge.]
E	Expected value of, as in EB, ES.
ET	Effective text (similarly ER)
E_1, E_2	Eye-starts for convergence.
H	Hypothesis.
K	Key.
K	Typewriterese for χ
[K	Symbol in significance test IV.]
L	Limitation.
$L_{n,m}$	Letter with n dots and m crosses.
[$L_{n,m,\bullet}$, $L_{n,m,\times}$, $L_{n,m,\circ}$	See **26Y(f)**]
[Ⓛ	Generalized teleprinter letter.]
M	Typewriterese for μ: M1, μ_{61}; M2, μ_{37}
[M	Message tape (Old Robinson).]
N	Text length (especially for rectangles).

$N_{\times}\ N_{\bullet}$	Text length against $\overline{\chi}_2\times$, $\overline{\chi}_2\bullet$
[$N_{\alpha}^{\times}\ N_{\alpha}^{\bullet}$	Number of occurrences in ΔD of α against $\overline{\chi}_2\times$, $\overline{\chi}_2\bullet$]
NM	Norm.
P	Probability, especially in $P(E\|H)$
p. 448 P	Plain language.
P^*	Modified plain language (see **27G**)
PB	Proportional bulge.
Q	Whatever is switched into the Q panel of Colossus.
[Q	Used, unhappily, in Robinson sign-writing.]
R	Number of places looked at.
R_i	Remembered impulse of Q.
S	Typewriterese for ψ
S	Score.
S	Amount of column slide in a motor rectangle.
[S_r	$\Sigma\theta_{ij}^{r}$]
SD	Standard deviation.
ST	Set Total
T	Text length.
T	Theory.
TM	Total motor.
U, V	Typical teleprinter letter or stream.
[V	Depth.]
[W	Wheel tape on old Robinson.]
X	$\Sigma\|x_i\|$, more generally double bulge.
X	Typewriterese for χ
[X_n^m, Y_n^m, Z_n^m	Nonce-use in scoring go-backs.]
Z	Cipher.
Z^*	Modified cipher (see **27G**).
a	$P(\text{TM}=\times)$
[a] a'	$P(\text{BM}=\times)$ $(=1-D)$

[a] $P(\text{BM}=\times$ $(=1-D)$

[a	average.]	
b	Ideal value for b_i, so that $ab = \frac{1}{2}$.	
b_i	$P(\Delta\psi_i = \times)$	
b	Bulge.	
[c	Number of crosses in χ_2]	[i]
d	Number of dots in μ_{37}	p. 449
[d	Decibanage.]	
d_k	Number of $\Delta\psi'$ letters with k dots and no crosses in key-breaking significance test II.	
db	Deciban.	
f	Factor.	
i, j }	Suffixes most commonly denoting impulses, but also columns and rows of a rectangle.	
[k, l	Number of dots, crosses, in the other impulses in Turingery.]	
[k, l	Constants in **26Y**(4)]	
k	Depth (of rectangle $\widehat{\chi}_2$ etc.)	
[k	Number of crosses in μ_{61}]	
[l	Tape length.]	
m	Number of crosses in a letter.	
[m	Number of impulses in a crib run.]	
n	Text length.	
$n_\times$, $n_\bullet$	Text length against $\overline{\chi}_i\times$, $\overline{\chi}_2\bullet$	
n'	Obsolete form of $n_\times$	[ii]
n	Number of dots in a letter.	
[$n(\Theta)$	Number of occurrences in a score Θ]	
n_Θ, n_α	Number of occurrences of a letter Θ, α	
o	Odds.	
p	Probability.	
[p	(Specialized uses) Probability that each $\Delta\chi$ character is correct.]	[a]
P_Θ	Probability of a letter Θ	
P_x	Probability of a score x if the character is a cross. **24Y(c)**	
p	(originally $\wp$) Pip.	

[a] Specialised

[i] Line ends with) instead of].
[ii] Entire entry handwritten.

q	$= x^*/x$
[q	Probability that the right score has bulge $< B_2$.]
r	Number of places looked at.
$r_{\times}, r_{\bullet}$	(in motor run) Number of places looked against $\overline{\chi}_2\times$, $\overline{\chi}_2\bullet$
[r	Number of dots in a letter.]
[r	Number of dots in a cell of a rectangle.]
s	Sigma-age.
[s	Number of crosses in a letter.]
[s	Number of crosses in a cell of a rectangle.]
[s	Distance between settings (coalescence).]
p. 450 t	$s/43$ (coalescence)
w	Wheel length.
x	$\Sigma\lvert x_i\rvert$, more generally double bulge.
x_i	Pippage of character (sometimes specifically $\Delta\chi_1$ character)
x^*	Double bulge on correct wheels.
[y	Number of doubled signs in key-breaking significance test I.]
[y_i	$\lvert x_i\rvert$. Inconsistent with the following use.
y_i	Pippage of character of $\Delta\chi_2$ in converged rectangle.]
[z	Double bulge against a typical character. **25W(a)**, **(e)**.]
Δ	$\Delta U = U +$ (U one forward)
Δ^n	Δ applied n times.
Δ_n	$\Delta_n U = U +$ (U n places forward)
Δ^*	$\Delta^* U = U +$ (U one back)
Θ, Φ	Typical letter of the teleprinter alphabet (often written Ⓗ)
Σ	Sum of
$\alpha, \beta, \gamma, \delta$	Editions of wheels, or special tapes.
β	Proportional bulge of $\Delta\psi = \times$
[β'	Proportional bulge of $\Delta\psi' = \times$, commonly written β]
For β_Θ β_{ij} &c.	see ξ
[γ	$\delta/2$, obsolete]

δ	Proportional bulge of $\Delta D_{ij} = \bullet$ (most commonly $\Delta D_{12} = \bullet$)	i
δ_0	Observed bulge of $\Delta D_{ij} = \bullet$ (most commonly $\Delta D_{12} = \bullet$)	
$\overline{\delta}$, $\underline{\delta}$	δ against $\overline{\chi}_2$×, $\overline{\chi}_2$•	
δ_Θ &c.	See ξ	
ε_i	± 1, or 0. (reprints •, × or ?)	
ζ	$\dfrac{1+\delta}{1-\delta}$	
ϑ	ϑ term in significance test IV.	
[θ	Proportional bulge of $\widehat{\chi}_2 = \bullet$]	
[θ_i, θ'_j	Pippages in accurate scoring.]	p. 451
θ_{ij}	Excess of dot over cross in a cell of a rectangle.	
[$\theta(x)$	See **92D**.]	
[λ	$\pi/2$ (obsolete).]	
[λ, μ	Co-efficients in series for banage that $\delta > \delta_0$]	ii
[λ	$b(1-p)+p(1-b)$]	
[μ	$bp+(1-b)(1-p)$]	
μ	Motor.	
ν	Number of comparisons, generally in a composite flag, but also in crib scoring.	
ν^*	ν when $\Delta\chi_6$ is included.	
[ν	Number of different letters looked at in motor run.	
ν'	Number of different letters looked for in motor run (obsolete).]	
ν_i	Number of clicks between A_i, B_i in general formula for standard deviation.	
ξ	Typical proportional bulge: in full ξ_Θ^U is the proportional bulge of Θ in the stream U.	
ξ_Θ	Proportional bulge of Θ.	
$\xi_\times$, $\xi_{\bullet\bullet\times}$ &c	Proportional bulges of $i=$×; $i=\bullet$, $j=\bullet$, $k=$×, etc.	
ξ_i, $\xi_{ij} = \xi_{i+j}$ &c.	Proportional bulges of $i=\bullet$; $i+j=\bullet$, etc.	
[ξ	Proportional bulge of $\Delta^2\chi =$ ×]	
[ξ	$\dfrac{R\delta}{\omega\sigma}$]	
π	Proportional bulge in ΔP.	

[i] Words 'most commonly' handwritten in entries for δ and δ_0.

[ii] Word 'that' handwritten.

	For π_Θ &c.	see ξ
	$[\pi$	$\log_\zeta$ odds.]
	$[\rho$	31ρ is an interval used for differencing in $\overline{\chi}_2$ limitation crib tapes.]
	$[\rho$	$\frac{1}{32}$P.B.$(\Delta D = /)$, obsolete.]
	σ	Standard deviation.
	ϕ	A distribution function (χ^2 distribution)
	$[\phi$	A distribution function for δ]
a	$[\phi$	P.B.$(\Delta Z_2 = \bullet)$]
	$[\phi$	in statistical motor-breaking: see ch. **92**.]
	χ	χ-stream.
	$\Delta\chi_6$	$= \Delta\psi'_6 = \widetilde{\text{lim}}$. **22D(g)**, **26B(b)**, **26E**
	χ^2	In χ^2-distribution **21(l)**.
p. 452	ψ	ψ-stream.
	$[\psi(r)$	$r(r-1)+s(s-1)$ in key-breaking significance test II]
	ø, £, @	Typewriterese for σ
	$\widetilde{U}$	$U + \times$
	$\overline{U}$	U one place back.
	$\underline{U}$	U one place forward.
	$\widehat{U}$	$\overline{U} + U + \underline{U}$
	U'	Extended U
	U^*	U modified in various ways.
	$\longrightarrow$	$U \longrightarrow \bullet$ means $P(U = \bullet) > \frac{1}{2}$
	$\underset{p}{\rightarrow}$	$U \underset{p}{\rightarrow} \bullet$ means $P(U = \bullet) = p$
	$\textcircled{z}$, z	To reduce errors, scores are usually entered thus $\begin{cases} +z \text{ as } \textcircled{z} \\ -z \text{ as } z \end{cases}$
	$\textcircled{o}$, $\textcircled{x}$	Symbols used in devil exorcism.
	$\square$	Rectangle.

[a] PB$(\Delta Z_2 = \bullet)$

73 BIBLIOGRAPHY p. 453

This bibliography is by no means exhaustive, especially in the case of **73C** and **73E**, where the specimens included owe their preservation as much to chance as to deliberate selection. E.1

73A RESEARCH LOGS

R0, **R1**, **R2**, **R3**, **R4**, **R5**, **R41**.

Index to Research Logs, **R0** to **R5**.

Black File. E.2

73B SCREEDS

(a) General

An Introduction to Fish.

Elementary Screed on ΔD Counts and Colossus Runs.

Sigmas and Decibans.

From De-χ to Decode.

Elementary Theory of Wheel-breaking.

Motor and ψ Runs.

Treatment of Key.

Checks and Tests.

Super-Robinson.

(b) For Coloperators

Setting on Colossus, Elementary Openings.

ψ and Motor Runs.

Wheel Slides and Message Slides.

Colossus Testing for Wrens.

(c) Rectangles (largely obsolete)

I Theory of Rectangles. E.3

II The Practice of Rectangle-making.

III What to do when a Significant Rectangle is Obtained.

---

[i] In the original text of the *Report*, almost all chapters start with an analytical contents list. This one does not. We have accordingly supplied such a list, as a copy editor would have done, for uniformity and the convenience of readers.

p. 454

73C STATISTICS

Rectangle Statistics.

Significant Rectangles, Letter Counts.

Alphabetical Counts and Runs Statistics.

ΔD Counts on Set Messages, Volumes A, C and D.

Plain Language Alphabetical Counts.

Un ΔP Combination Counts.

$\Delta\chi_5$ Wheel Research.

73D ADMINISTRATION, STANDING ORDERS, ETC

Grey File of Standing Orders.

Robinson Standing Orders.

Wheel Man's Compendium.

Specimen Ops Log, **O5**.

Tea Party Minutes.

73E CHARTS AND TABLES

(a) For Coloperators

i A Colossus Bible, containing

Table for Estimating Odds of Runs,

Fifth Wheel Runs (χ_3 and χ_5) and (on back)

χ Runs for Colossus,

Decibanning of Single Wheel WB Runs,

Rectangling on Colossus (χ-length multiples),

Average 32 Letter Counts (Whiting and Lumpsucker),

Normalised Un ΔP Counts for ψ-setting,

Runs Statistics.

Sigma Chart.

"Good Certain" Chart.

Elementary Setting.

Dottages for Colossus.

p. 455

(b) For Wheel Man and Computers

Significance Test IV, χ_5 Flag Formulae, Wheel Characteristics, and General Formula for calculating ϑ Terms.

Value of X for Significance, for different Text Lengths.

Number of db up for given X, for Text Length 10168.

Table for Calculating ϑ Terms for $N = 10168$, and (on back)

Significance Test IV and General Formula for ϑ Terms.

$10 n \log_{10} n$ Table.

Accurate Convergence Scoring Table.

Accurate Convergence Slide Wheel.

---

[i] Contents list for 'Colossus Bible' bracketed on left margin by large { sign.

(c) Miscellaneous

Decibanage of Error Function.[a]

Centiban Table.

Ratio of EB/σ on /1+2 BM Run to the β/σ of 1+2/.

Wheel-sliding Table.

Psi Test Tapes (for Tapes Registrar).

Tape Sub-section General Instructions (for Tunny and Angel Rooms).

[a] Erro

p. 456

74 CHRONOLOGY

E.1

1941	Changes in Tunny	Organisation Changes	Machines	Theoretical Discoveries and Achievements
June	SZ40 first Tunny link	Work in Research Section Starts		
July				
August	The depth HQIBPEXEZMUG sent . . . and read			
September				
October				
November				
December				

p. 457

a

1942	Changes in Tunny	Organisation Changes	Machines	Theoretical Discoveries and Achievements
January				Machine broken for Aug. 1941
February				
March	Broken traffic shows $ab = 1/2$ Tone transmission			
April			Decoding machine ordered	Machine broken for March 1942. First attempts at setting
May				Wheels broken before the end of the month by indicator method
June			First decoding machine arrives.	

[a] March 1943

p. 458

1942	Changes in Tunny	Organisation Changes	Machines	Theoretical Discoveries and Achievements
July		Testery founded to take over work on Tunny from Research Section.		Current traffic read for first time Turingery.
August	Introduction of Quatsch			
September				
October	Experimental Tunny link closed. Codfish and Octopus start with QEP system and monthly change of Psi patterns	Testery confined to depths. Research Section begin investigating Statistical Methods.		
November			Newman suggests electronic counters	1+2 break in invented by Tutte. Message set statistically using $\Delta Z_1 + \Delta Z_2$ rectangle
December		Newman given task of developing machines for setting Tunny		

p. 459

1943	**Changes in Tunny**	**Organisation Changes**	**Machines**	**Theoretical Discoveries and Achievements**
January			Early Robinson designed and ordered	
February	SZ42A (with $\overline{\chi}_2$ lim.) makes first appearance on Codfish			Research section breaks chis statistically from Z by rectangles
March	$\overline{\chi}_2\overline{\overline{P}}_5$ lim. tried experimentally on Herring		Plans for mechanical setting of Tunny and Sturgeon well under way	$\overline{\chi}_2$ lim broken
April		First 16 Wrens arrived.		$\overline{\chi}_2\overline{\overline{P}}_5$ broken by Testery and Research Section.
May			Method of contracted de-χ successful.	
June		Newmanry work starts	Arrival of Heath Robinson & first Newmanry Tunny	

a

[a] (with χ_2 lim.)

p. 460

1943	**Changes in Tunny**	**Organisation Changes**	**Machines**	**Theoretical Discoveries and Achievements**
July				
August		**R0** started		Recognition that 4σ in a break-in is not by any means certain. Discovery that Knockholt (at the time) were producing a lot of slides in tapes.
September			Suggestion of 'and/or' machine and repeated use of character on Colossus or Robinson	Discovery that best ΔP letter is not necessarily / Expected score of motor run in terms of ΔD.
October		Change over from two to three shifts.		
November		Newmanry moved from Hut 11 to Block F.	First (production) Robinson arrived	Recognition that de-χ's can be broken by hand. Discovery of $\widehat{\chi}_2$
December	Reappearance of $\overline{\chi}_2 + \overline{\overline{P}}_5$ limitation in Bream and Codfish traffic	Testery take on psi and motor setting and Newmanry concentrate on chi setting and breaking.	Second (production) Robinson arrived	Recognition that ΔD statistics (rather than ΔP) are the quickest way of finding new runs.

p. 461

1944	Changes in Tunny	Organisation Changes	Machines	Theoretical Discoveries and Achievements
January		General Registries of Newmanry and Testery amalgamated.	Direct TP line from Knockholt to Block F installed. Robinson 3 (first double bedstead Rob.) installed.	χ_3 now set in Newmanry, rather than sending de-χ's on only 4 impulses to Testery.
February			Colossus I installed. Spanning suggested	Colossus first used for wheel-breaking
March			Robinson IV installed	
April		First motor runs successfully done on Colossus	New Tunny machine, new Garbos and one Mrs. Miles installed	Significance tests for rectangles.
May				Cribs, predicted by Sixta successfully used for wheel-breaking for first time.
June	SZ42B first used on Codfish (with $\overline{\chi}_2\overline{\Psi}'_1\overline{\overline{P}}_5$ lim)	Daily meetings started	Colossus II installed.	

p. 462

1944	Changes in Tunny	Organisation Changes	Machines	Theoretical Discoveries and Achievements
July	Invasion of Europe Daily wheel changes on Jelly Koenigsberg Exchange closes and moves to Golssen.	Slide-runs started using test-tapes, to check machines	Colossus III installed More reliable Robinsons designed suitable for work on cribs	New 'staircasing' method evolved for Cribs. Significance tests for wheel-breaking runs introduced.
August	Daily wheel changes on almost all Tunny links.	No. of computers increased very considerably	First rectangles made on Colossus. Colossus IV finished.	
September	Several links ceased using P_5 limitation	Work started in Block H	Colossus V installed	Thurlow rectangles first done. Combined χ_5 flag for key introduced, with significance test
October	Further reorganisation of Tunny		Colossus VI and first super Robinson installed Colossus VI takes tapes up 25,000 long.	Copy correction units (for correction of tapes) introduced.
November		15th November. The Fire. New type of test runs for checking Colossus — test runs. Kedleston Hall started operating. Reorganisation at Knockholt.	Colossus VII installed	New adaptation of rectangling methods used to break short stretches of key. Complete page of QEP nos. with corresponding wheel-settings recovered from Whiting decode. Jacobs Flag started.[a]
December	P_5 limitation largely abandoned by Germans.	Extensive motor and psi setting by machine.		Colossus decoding invented Theory of coalescence

E.3, E.4

[a] Jacob's Flag

p. 463

1945	Changes in Tunny	Organisation Changes	Machines	Theoretical Discoveries and Achievements
January		Psi test-runs first made De-χ checks first done Education committee formed	Colossus VIII installed. Second Super-Rob. finished	
February		$\widehat{\chi}_2$ runs started	Device installed on Colossus VI enabling sum of squares of rectangle entries to be computed quickly. Rectangles now produced on tape to mechanize computing on keys. Colossus IX installed.	Tests carried out on Thrasher (on new Robs) gave negative results, with regard to Tunny-type machines.
March	Exchange set up at Salzburg	Raw tapes sent from Knockholt 4 wheel-runs instituted Setting of Psis now considered as responsibility of Newmanry rather than Testery Wrens taught wheel-breaking	Mechanical flags instituted Machines tested regularly by Wrens	
April		Rectangle making started on Super-Robs.	Colossus X installed "5202" arrived to start work experimentally	
May	Victory in Europe Last Tunny message sent	Change from 3 to 2 shifts Work on back traffic (1943–4) History and 5202 section formed		
June			Two sets of German Tunny equipment arrive	Experimental operations using 5202.

a

[a] mechanise

p. 464 81 CONCLUSIONS

i

ii 81A ORGANISATION

(a) Checking

The number of operations performed on a message from the time it is received at Knockholt to the time it is decoded is very large and therefore it is essential to have systematic checks at every stage. These checks are equally important for processes which are done by hand and by machine. Checking has become a mental habit with all the cryptographers who have been in the section for any length of time.

(b) Simplicity

Another method of avoiding mistakes is to choose simple processes if possible, even if some power is sacrificed. Mistakes are always made when a new routine is introduced. On the other hand the Wrens are quite capable of assimilating a complicated routine with practice, provided that they are specialists at a particular job (e.g. cribs). Sometimes there are alternative methods with not much to choose between them and then the choice can profitably be left to individual preference (e.g. methods of starting the convergence of a rectangle).

---

[i] Chapter number lacking in chapter head, sections heads, and in sections listed in chapter table of contents. Chapter numbers are present in running heads, as usual. That is, the digit string '81' *only* appears in the running heads of the typescript original.

[ii] Head (but not running head) labelled as 'A', not '81A'.

(c) Division of Labour

We have just referred to one advantage of specializing. The method of division of labour is a principle which applies to all grades. Cryptographers are given a definite job for at least a week at a time. Wrens have a definite job more or less permanently. An experiment was tried once of changing the jobs of the Wrens round, but it was unsuccessful. The cryptographers, on the other hand, need to have a complete and detailed knowledge of the entire section if they are ever to act as duty officer. The principle of moving from one job to another after a week or two is particularly important as regards research. No important theoretical advance was made by anyone who did not have a good knowledge of the practical side. a p. 465

(d) Allocation of responsibility

The method of division of labour is much the same as that of allocation of responsibility for particular jobs. The possibility of cribbing by long retransmissions would probably have been discovered much earlier if a definite individual had been made responsible for looking into the question (as a part time job).

(e) Decentralisation

decentralisation

Division of labour should not be confused with geographical decentralisation. This has nothing to be said for it except security from aerial attack. The spreading into three blocks of the people who broke Tunny was due to historical causes and could not be remedied once it had happened. The Colossi were housed in four rooms. This necessitated a larger staff of cryptographers. A larger supply of PAX telephones would have helped in this connection. E.1

(f) The Written Word

(i) Without a printer, runs on a Colossus would take about 50% more time to do and the results, written down from the display panel would be much less reliable.

(ii) Notices and Instruction books. When routines were first spread round the section in the form of notices there was an immediate decline in the number of mistakes. Previously the Wrens had been taught mainly by word of mouth. Later instruction books were introduced and each entry was signed by all who read it. This is the best method. Technical instructions prepared by the administration should be checked by someone with particular knowledge of the technique involved.

(iii) Log books. These have the following advantages:

(a) to show what work is done in each department and to help the administration.

(b) to help with the efficient handing over from shift to shift (though a short overlap of shifts is useful in addition). When a mistake is made that is so incredible that no single individual could have perpetrated it, the reason is always that there has been an inefficient handover from one shift to another.

(c) to encourage people to take a pride in their work. b

(d) to provide a permanent record for research purposes.

(e) the research logs help new men to learn the work.

The only alternative to log books is a very great deal of talk. Verbal discussion should in any case be encouraged, as in the 'Tea Parties'. (The Tea Parties are meetings of the cryptographers held about once a week).

(iv) A form of log book appropriate for some purposes, e.g. Tea Party Agenda is a blackboard.

---

[a] specialising [b] peaple

(v) Screeds. These are valuable if well written for teaching Wrens and new cryptographers. Men employed in operational work are usually too busy to teach new men by word of mouth though
p. 466 lectures for Wrens were fairly frequent.

(vi) Signing work, Labelling, Neatness. The importance of these three things is often overlooked and thereby much time is wasted.

(vii) Reading. A failure to read the log books, instruction books, blackboard suggestions, etc. should be regarded as a 'howler'.

(g) Speed of work

In estimating in advance how long a particular job will take, it is useful to hold in mind that some time must be allowed for every transference of the job from one person to another. A rough estimate is about half an hour. This is a necessary evil of the shift system, and is most noticeable when cryptographers are being transferred from one job to another. It is accentuated by being housed in significantly separated buildings.

(h) Teaching

In addition to the value of screeds there is a general principle of learning that is only too easily overlooked. The principle is that of alternating theory and practice. The level of theory that can be assimilated without some experience is not very high with most people. Hence the best plan is to give theoretical lectures to all Wrens whether they are new arrivals or old hands.

(i) Research

An aspect of research not yet mentioned is the fact that it is useful to think from time to time about the theory even if no tangible result emerges. The effect is to make the practice easier, and in particular to make it easier to cope with unexpected practical situations. Incidentally the best ideas are often had outside working hours.

[i] 81B THEORY

(a) Probability

The most obvious conclusion, from the point of view of theory, is the value which the subject of probability has in certain types of cryptography. In particular the use of significance tests is noticeable and is a way of replacing the cryptographer's intuition by something more accurate, in certain cases. The 'deciban' has again proved its worth. On the whole the point of view of the theory of probability (including the so-called principle of inverse probability) is more powerful
E.2 than that of the subject of statistics.

(b) Notation

If a mistaken notation is introduced it is sometimes difficult to change because everybody becomes accustomed to it. Improvements were made in the notation in 1943 in spite of a certain amount of ossification. The only outstanding flaw in notation now is the habit of using $\overline{\chi}_2$ crosses to permit motor dots. Though known to correspond to the German practice it would nevertheless have been better to reverse the convention.

(c) Successive approximation

Several of our processes are examples of the method of successive approximation. This is a well known part of ordinary scientific method.

p. 467 **(d) Key and Cipher**

Key can be regarded as a special case of cipher with plain language all strokes. The statistical methods which apply to one, will also apply to the other. This idea should have application to other subtractor ciphers.

---

[i] Head (but not running head) labelled as 'B' instead of '81B'.

(e) Cipher makers and cipher breakers

With our experience of Tunny it would be easy to make suggestions for making Tunny unbreakable. Independent motorizing of the ψ's would achieve this, except that depths could be read if an autoclave were not introduced also (see **R4**, 116). a b

Anyone who designs a cryptographic machine should avoid the use of a gadget for returning the settings to the start of the message. Such gadgets are liable to encourage the production of depths.

81C MACHINES (Cf. ch. **51, 52**) i

(a) Accuracy

The most remarkable feature of our machines is the accuracy of Colossus, especially when doing ψ runs.

(b) Adaptability

For Tunny wheel setting and breaking Colossus is a much more powerful machine than Robinson, but Robinson is more adaptable to other problems. The design of the Colossus switchboard and plugboard were also based on the principle of adaptability and this paid good dividends. The method of making a machine adaptable is first to think of a number of things required of it and then design the machine to cope with a general class of problem which includes all the special ones as particular cases.

(c) Strength of paper

We had several tape breakages, especially on the Robinsons, but on the whole the strength of the tapes, when run at speed, is very surprising to the layman.

(d) Small Machines

There is a danger of underestimating the importance of small machines and devices like hand counters, printers, adding machines, slide-rules, charts and rubbers. Shortage of these things can cause bottle-necks. Our production increased considerably when we were able, in 1944, to present Knockholt with a few hand counters. c, E.3

(e) Use of standard equipment

It is helpful in avoiding bottle-necks to use standard equipment as far as possible, even if not as efficient as some other device. For example the use of perforated tape rather than photographic apparatus was justified in this way. ii, E.4

(f) Adequate Supplies

As already implied, the supply of certain small machines was inadequate, while the supply of standard equipment was fairly plentiful. At times it looked as if the supply of electrical power would be definitely insufficient, but fortunately no very great trouble was caused on this account, partly owing to the economies effected in the Park as a whole.

(g) Tape-readers and electromatic typewriters p. 468

These are of great value for quickly typing out a length of cipher in given widths. They should be useful in other cryptographic work. The original discovery of the χ_1 wheel length, which led to the breaking of Tunny, was almost an accident. It would have been a routine if systematic use of a tape-reader and electromatic typewriter had been applied.

---

[a] motorising [b] See [c] slide rules

[i] Head (but not running head) labelled as 'C', not '81C'.
[ii] Word 'than' handwritten.

p. 469 # 91 THE 5202 MACHINE

i

91A PRINCIPLE OF THE 5202

(a) Introduction

The 5202 is a photographic machine designed for setting messages enciphered on the Tunny machine. It is based on counting the number of coincidences between two sequences of (teleprinter) letters, one derived from the cipher and one from the chi wheels.

The machine was produced just too late for the European war, but it was decided to experiment with it for two months.

The theory of the method is simple. It depends on the equation

$$\Delta\chi = \Delta Z + \Delta D.$$

(b) Example: 1×2•3×

Suppose that we are dealing only with the first three impulses of ΔD and that the letter (from an eight letter alphabet), $\Delta D_1 =$ ×, $\Delta D_2 =$ •, $\Delta D_3 =$ ×, has a frequency above random. In order to count the number of times the above three-impulse letter occurs in ΔD, using the 5202, we record the data on 35mm film as a series of transparent spots on an opaque background.

		$\Delta\chi$ Film			ΔZ Film	
ii A transparent spot in level	$\Delta\chi_1$	$\Delta\chi_2$	$\Delta\chi_3$	ΔZ_1	ΔZ_2	ΔZ_3
1	•	•	•	×	•	×
2	×	•	•	•	•	×
3	•	×	•	×	×	×
4	×	×	•	•	×	×
5	•	•	×	×	•	•
iii 6	×	•	×	•	•	•
7	•	×	×	×	×	•
8	×	×	×	•	×	•

It will be seen on inspection that the spots will appear on the same level in both films, and thus give a coincidence when superimposed, only if $\Delta D_1 =$ ×, $\Delta D_2 =$ •, $\Delta D_3 =$ ×.

(c) Example 1=2=4

Although we are dealing with an eight-letter alphabet, we can put the data into four levels of the film as follows:

[i] In the original text of the *Report*, almost all chapters start with an analytical contents list. This one does not. We have accordingly supplied such a list, as a copy editor would have done, for uniformity and the convenience of readers.

[ii] A little arrow leads from the caption 'A transparent spot in level' to the first entry in its column, the number '1'.

[iii] Row 6 reads '×•× •×•'.

Level		$\Delta\chi_1$	$\Delta\chi_2$	$\Delta\chi_3$	ΔZ_1	ΔZ_2	ΔZ_3
		•	•	•	•	•	•
1	or	×	×	×	×	×	×
2		×	•	•	×	•	•
	or	•	×	×	•	×	×
3		•	×	•	•	×	•
	or	×	•	×	×	•	×
4		×	×	•	×	×	•
	or	•	•	×	•	•	×

i

In this case a spot will appear at a given level in the $\Delta\chi$ and ΔZ films if one or the other of the two three-impulse letters shown for that level is generated. This will be seen to be equivalent to working with two generalized impulses, $1+2$, and $1+4$.

(d) Generalized statement of principles p. 470, a

The fundamental equation

$$\Delta\chi = \Delta Z + \Delta D \tag{A1}$$

can be generalized by generalizing the idea of an impulse. b, c

Definition. A generalized impulse is any (non-null) sum of ordinary impulses. For example Z_{34}, i.e. $Z_3 + Z_4$, is a generalized impulse of Z. We refer to an impulse in this sense as an 'impulse' (in d inverted commas).

If $\Delta\chi$ is considered as a letter in an n-'impulse' alphabet we write it as $\textcircled{\Delta\chi}$. Similarly for $\textcircled{\Delta Z}$ and $\textcircled{\Delta D}$. Then (A1) can be written in the generalized form e

$$\textcircled{\Delta\chi} = \textcircled{\Delta Z} + \textcircled{\Delta D} \tag{A2}$$

Let $L_1, L_2, \ldots L_r$ be letters in ΔD which have a frequency above random. Then

$$\textcircled{\Delta\chi} \longrightarrow \textcircled{\Delta Z} + \textcircled{L_i} \tag{A3}$$

These can be represented on 2^r levels of film. On one film we can record $\textcircled{\Delta\chi}$ (a single spot) and on the other $\boxed{\Delta Z + L_i}$ (r spots for the r alternative letters L_i). (Or we can interchange $\Delta\chi$ ii and ΔZ and obtain an equivalent result.) Then if the two films are superimposed the number of coincidences of transparent spots gives us the number of occurrences of one or other of $L_1 \ldots L_r$ in ΔD.

The spots are made visible by shining a light through the film thus activating a photo-electric cell. A fundamental difference between the 5202 and Colossus or Robinson is that the 5202 measures the amount of light rather than the number of spots of light. If the amount of light exceeds a certain amount (cf. set total on Colossus) the position is indicated by a lamp. Later on, an exact count can be made of the number of spots of light in these positions by means of a special counter film (see below **91B(b)**).

---

[a] Generalised [b] generalised [c] generalising [d] generalised [e] generalised

[i] Right-most column label given as Δ_3

[ii] $\Delta Z + L_i$ circled.

(e) Example of conditional run

Assume that χ_1 and χ_2 have been set and that we wish to make use of the evidence of ΔD_1 and ΔD_2 in doing a run to set the other three chis. The example considered is the run for the letters `5U/F` in ΔD.

5	×	×	•	×	×
U	×	×	×	•	•
/	•	•	•	•	•
F	×	•	×	×	•

It is seen that a `5` or `U` can occur only if $\Delta D_1, \Delta D_2$, is **××**, a stroke if $\Delta D_1, \Delta D_2$ is •• and an `F` only if $\Delta D_1, \Delta D_2$ is ×•. The machine, which makes the film (the generator), has circuits available for each of the letters `5U/F` which can be plugged to prevent any data appearing on film unless the required conditions of $\Delta D_1, \Delta D_2$ are satisfied

[i]

LEVEL	$\Delta\chi$ Film One spot in each group of 8 levels			ΔZ FILM. When $\Delta D_1, \Delta D_2$=××, two spots in each group of 8 levels.						When $\Delta D_1, \Delta D_1$=•• one spot			When $\Delta D_1, \Delta D_2$=×• one spot			When $\Delta D_1, \Delta D_2$=•× No spot
				5			U			/			F			
	$\Delta\chi_3$	$\Delta\chi_4$	$\Delta\chi_5$	ΔZ_3	ΔZ_4	ΔZ_5	ΔZ_3	ΔZ_4	ΔZ_5	ΔZ_3	ΔZ_4	ΔZ_5	ΔZ_3	ΔZ_4	ΔZ_5	
1	•	•	•	•	×	×	×	•	•	•	•	•	×	×	•	
2	×	•	•	×	×	×	•	•	•	×	•	•	•	×	•	
3	•	×	•	•	•	×	×	×	•	•	×	•	×	•	•	
4	×	×	•	×	•	×	•	×	•	×	×	•	•	•	•	
5	•	•	×	•	×	•	×	•	×	•	•	×	×	×	×	
6	×	•	×	×	×	•	•	•	×	×	•	×	•	×	×	
7	•	×	×	•	•	•	×	×	×	•	×	×	×	•	×	
8	×	×	×	×	•	•	•	×	×	×	×	×	•	•	×	

p. 471

91B TECHNICAL ASPECTS

(a) The Film

The actual width of the transparent spots is ·006 inch. Hence if we only had sufficient levels on the film for one letter per column, a message of 5000 letters would require 2ft 6 ins of film whereas, as will be seen later, only three inches of film can be scanned at one time. Hence the film has 80 levels, divided by an opaque strip into two groups of 40, which if desired, can be used to record two different alphabets derived from the same stream. Thus with a 3-'impulse' (8 letter) alphabet, using the whole film we could record 10 consecutive letters of ($\Delta\chi$) or (ΔZ) on one column of film, or using the top half of the film for one alphabet and the bottom half for another, we could record 5 consecutive letters. For a 4-'impulse' (16 letter) alphabet, the whole film would be necessary to record five letters. It would seem that with a 2-'impulse' alphabet, using only 4 levels, 20 letters could be recorded. In practice this is not so. The reason is that it is necessary to expose the film a column at a time. Hence a method of storing data is necessary, in order that all the data for one column should be transferred to film simultaneously. This storage circuit is only capable of storing data from 5 or 10 consecutive letters.

To summarise we are concerned with 3 cases.

Case (i) Two impulse run. Uses 4 levels. Two alphabets can be run, one on each half of the film. 10 positions recorded in each column.

---

[i] Column captions written here in 6 lines instead of 5 to save width.

Case (ii) Three impulse run. Uses 8 levels. Either 10 positions recorded using whole film or if we have two alphabets, one on each half of the film, then 5 positions recorded.

Case (iii) Four impulse run. 16 levels required for each position. 5 letters recorded in each column.

There is one further point to consider about the film. In preparing the ΔZ film, the initial letters will always be placed in the top set of levels. As it would be very inconvenient to have to give the films two dimensional, relative motion in comparing them, it is necessary for all possible combination of chi settings to occur in the top level in order to try all possible initial chi settings. Hence it is necessary to repeat the complete $\Delta\chi$ stream, 10 times over (or if only 5 letters are recorded in each column 5 times over). If we record 10 letters in a column we strike a snag if $\Delta\chi_4$ is involved, since 26, the length of the wheel is not prime to 10. In this case it is necessary, half way through making the film, to move all the χ wheels one place in order that both odd and even positions of $\Delta\chi_4$ should occur in the top levels.

We will now consider the equipment of the 5202 in more detail. This is not meant to be a technical description, as one already exists in the American "reference Manual for 5202 Equipment". This account, which is only meant as a basis for explaining the cryptographic use E.1
of 5202, is based on the reference manual.

The equipment falls into three parts.

(1) The camera and target for preparing the film.

(2) The generating unit for controlling the target.

(3) The comparator for examining the two superimposed films in all possible relative positions.

(b) The Comparator p. 472

This is the machine which examines the film in all possible relative positions and measures the number of coincidences between the film.

This is done as follows. The message film, of which 3 inches or 500 columns can be examined at one time, is kept stationary. The $\Delta\chi$ film is moved over it. Light is directed down on the two films in such a way that the light intensity is uniform over the whole message film. Then the light shining through the two films is proportional to the number of coincidences of transparent spots. This light is focussed on to a photocell. The photo-cell controls a light, which flashes on when the amount of light focussed on the photo cell exceeds a certain amount. The actual amount of light necessary to flash the lamp can be varied by means of two dials on the machine. It is not possible to correlate the number of coincidences on the film with the readings on these dials, as the photo-cells tend to vary. Hence it is only possible to cut down the stops to a pre-determined number and then record these. When we have cut the number of stops down to say three or four we can set the films to these settings as follows. We throw the automatic stop switch. When the $\Delta\chi$ film reaches a place where the lamp is flashed, the $\Delta\chi$ film is automatically stopped and reversed. [a]
It then runs back slowly until it reaches the hit when it stops again. Due to the momentum of the film it will not set exactly on the correct place. It is necessary to do the final setting by hand, using the flashing of the lamp as a guide. When the film is correctly set the lamp should remain on.

We can then throw onto a screen a magnified image of the identification strip (described in more detail in para. (**c**)). This enables us to read the settings by seeing which letters on the $\Delta\chi$ film come against the arrow at the beginning of the message film. Because there is an identification letter only for every other column, it is important to see whether the arrow points to an identification or between two of them.

We can count the score by means of a special counter film: this has transparent spots 4 levels high, one and only one in each set of 4 levels i.e. one in levels 1–4, one in levels 4–8 and so on.

---

[a] reaches a places

These spots are spaced at a distance of 3 inches, so that only one of them is viewed at a time. The rest of the film is opaque but at one end a section is cut away except for a thin strip in the middle. This strip is in the same position on the film as the opaque sections (between lamps 40 and 41) of other films, making it possible to keep the counter film in the machine without interfering with setting operations. When we wish to count, this film is moved along under the other two films and light shines through all three only when the counter film spot is beneath a coincidence on the other two. The number of these coincidences can be counted on an electronic counter and this total gives us the score for the run.

(c) The camera and target

The camera affords a means of exposing the film and synchronising the exposures with the generating unit. The film is moved on ·006 inches after each exposure so as to be in a position to expose the next column in the next exposure. The camera has two rates of exposure: 1 per sec. or 10 per sec.

The "target" consists of a row of 80 lamps, divided into two groups of 40, one corresponding to each level of the film. These lamps are controlled by the generating unit, which selects which of the 80 lamps should light up. After exposure and development, the levels corresponding to lamps which have lit, have transparent spots produced on them.

In addition it is necessary to have some sort of identification on the films in order that it should be possible to read off the settings when running the film in the comparator. This is done on the chi film by photographing the chi settings onto the film, at the top of the column in five levels used for this purpose. In order to make the settings readable this is done for every other column. The settings are recorded on five counter wheels which are illuminated internally by a lamp flashing in phase with the chi wheels. The counter wheels move in step with the chi wheels themselves. In
p. 473 order that it should be possible to read this identification through the message film another lamp photographs a transparent channel onto the message film in the same position as the identification on the chi film.

In addition another level on the message film is also transparent, but has a small arrow photographed on it at the beginning of the message and if required, at preassigned intervals throughout the message. The chi film has a clear channel in order that the arrow may be seen.

(d) Generating unit: χ wheels

The chi films are made with the camera working at an exposure rate of about 10 per second. Since in most types of run used each exposure records 10 positions of the chi wheels, the chi wheels must operate at the rate of 100 characters per second. The generator consists of 5 wheels geared to a shaft with ratios 41:10, 31:10, 29:10, 26:10, 23:10 i.e. in ratios proportional to the wheels lengths. In addition there is another wheel termed the master storage strip cam which is geared 1:1 to the shaft. Each χ wheel carries two wire brushes, one making contact with a metal disc connected to −310 volts, the other contacting one of a set of equally placed metal segments equal in number to the wheel length and corresponding to a position on the χ wheel. These segments are wired to the corresponding position on the χ pattern board I. This board is so plugged that a connection is made when there is a × in the $\Delta\chi$ wheel. Thus we get a signal of −310 volts if there is a cross in the $\Delta\chi$ wheel, and if there is a dot there is no connection through the plugboard, in which case the voltage of the line is −330 volts. Whatever wheels we require are connected through plugboard V to a set of five double triodes which have the effect of putting potentials of −175 volts on one line of a pair, and −300 on the other, if a dot signal is received. We will term a line active if it is at −175 and inactive if it is at −300. We will term the line of a pair which is active when a dot signal is received the dot-line and the other the cross-line. Then we have 5 pairs of lines, each consisting of a dot-line and a cross-line, which can be made to correspond to the five impulses of the $\Delta\chi$ stream. These 5 pairs of lines come out on plugboard

III at the plug holes $P_1^-, P_1^+, P_2^-, P_2^+ \ldots P_5^-, P_5^+$. The $-$ corresponds to a dot-line and the $+$ to a cross line. There are 7 plug-holes for each line. [i]

(e) Translating Circuit

This translates a letter in teleprinter form (a pattern of r dots and crosses) into a "single spot in one of 2^r levels."

The 5 pairs of χ lines can be joined across to 4 pairs of lines which form part of the translating circuit. These 4 lines come out at the plug-holes $T_1^-, T_1^+, T_2^-, T_2^+ \ldots T_4^-, T_4^+$. We can therefore join whatever impulses we are interested in across to these lines. These lines constitute a resistor matrix which controls a set of 16 valves $T_1 \ldots T_{16}$ termed the translator tubes. These valves are each connected to one and only one line of each pair, this being possible in 16 ways. A translator tube operates if all the lines to which it is joined are active. Hence each possible 4 impulse character (here we mean teleprinter impulse) will operate one valve. The actual scheme is as follows.

T_1	•	•	•	•	T_9	•	•	•	×
T_2	×	•	•	•	T_{10}	×	•	•	×
T_3	•	×	•	•	T_{11}	•	×	•	×
T_4	×	×	•	•	T_{12}	×	×	•	×
T_5	•	•	×	•	T_{13}	•	•	×	×
T_6	×	•	×	•	T_{14}	×	•	×	×
T_7	•	×	×	•	T_{15}	•	×	×	×
T_8	×	×	×	•	T_{16}	×	×	×	×

If on the other hand we are only interested in 3 impulses then we can make both T_4^- and T_4^+ active by connecting both valves to -175v on Plugboard III. In this case each possible three impulse character operates two valves.

(f) Combining tubes

The 16 translating tubes control the inputs to 16 further tubes termed the combining tubes. The p. 474
connection between the translator tubes and combining tubes is not fixed but is done on Plugboard II. Each of the inputs controlled by $T_1 \ldots T_{16}$ has plug-holes. The 16 combining tubes $G_1 \ldots G_{16}$ have 4 plug-holes. Those for $G_1 \ldots G_8$ are numbered G_{1-i}, G_{2-i} G_{3-i}, G_{4-i} (i=1–8) and those for $G_9 \ldots G_{16}$ are numbered G_{5-i}, G_{6-i}, G_{7-i}, G_{8-i} (i=9–16). A combining tube operates unless one of the translator tubes to which it is connected is operated. The combining tubes act as part of the control of a bank of 80 pairs of thyratrons. These are arranged in 16 columns of 5 each, each column being associated with one combining tube. These thyratron pairs are associated in [ii] groups of 4, which receive a pulse from the master storage trip cam through a connection made on plug-board VIII. This pulse goes through a phasing switch which has 10 positions and comes out at the 10 plug-holes $P_1 \ldots P_{10}$. The groups of 4 mentioned above come out to the plug-holes $L_1 \ldots L_{20}$, on the same plugboard. The actual arrangement of these groups of 4 is shown on diagram III. These thyratron pairs correspond to the 80 lamps. The groups $L_1 \ldots L_{10}$ correspond [iii] to lamps 1–40 in that order and $L_{11} \ldots L_{20}$ to the lamps 41–80.

(g) Illustrative example

The actual control of the lamps is best shown by a simple example. We will consider the case of a $\Delta\chi$ film which $\Delta\chi_1$, $\Delta\chi_2$, $\Delta\chi_4$ are involved and the alphabet used is the ordinary 3-impulse alphabet, the impulses being ordinary teleprinter impulses. [iv]

---

[i] Sentence 'There are...' handwritten.
[ii] Words 'tube' and 'Thyratron' handwritten.
[iii] Word 'thyratron' handwritten.
[iv] Word 'impulses' handwritten.

In this case we put $\Delta\chi_1$ signals on the pair of lines $T_1^- T_1^+$, the $\Delta\chi_2$ signals on to the second pair of lines and $\Delta\chi_4$ on to the third pair. The fourth pair of lines are both made active. In this case two of the translating tubes will be operated by each impulse, one being in the set $T_1 \ldots T_8$, the other in the set $T_9 \ldots T_{16}$, the tubes operated being similarly placed in each set.

This run clearly uses 8 levels. Hence we need 8 lamps for each character and consequently 8 thyratron pairs to control them. Accordingly we connect the sets L_1 to L_2 to P_1, L_3 to L_4 to $P_2 \ldots, L_{11}$ to L_{12} to P_6 L_{19} to L_{20} to P_{10}. The connection between translating tube and combining tube is simply straight across i.e. T_1 to $G_1, \ldots, T_{16}$ to G_{16}.

Now suppose we start the run. In the first position the master storage trip cam sends a pulse to the 8 thyratron pairs in $L_1 L_2$. This puts the first thyratron in each pair in a condition to fire. The actual one that fires is determined by which combining tube is not operated and hence in this case, by which translating tube is operated. In the next position the first thyratron in one of the pairs in $L_3 L_4$ is fired and so forth up to the tenth position. When the 10th impulse is received the
a information on the first thyratron of the 80 pairs is transferred to the second of each pair, the first thyratrons now being ready to receive the data from the next 10 positions. When the camera is
b operated, it clears the second thyratrons and lights the lamps corresponding to the thyratrons that have struck. In this way the data is transferred to the film.

There is one further case to consider, and that is the case when 16 levels are required. In this case it is necessary to transfer the information every 5 instead of every 10 positions. This is done by commoning P_1 to $P_6 \ldots, P_5$ to P_{10} so that the special 10th pulse is received every 5th position instead of every 10th. In this case of course, 4 groups of 4 thyratron pairs have to be plugged to each P plug-hole.

(h) Message film

i The message is recorded on six impulse tape. This is read on an ordinary tape reader and is then transmitted via a special deltaing circuit; from then on the process is essentially the same as the recording of patterns. The only important difference is that the exposure rate of the camera is only 1 per second.

p. 475 **(i) Conditional de-chis and *G*-circuits**

The case sometimes arises that we have set two of the chis and we wish to use this information to set the other three wheels. In this case we can actually add the $\Delta\chi$'s to the impulses which are set and thus obtain ΔD on these two pairs of lines. To do this we have to reset the chi wheels to their known settings. Since the wheels cannot be moved independently, the time taken becomes prohibitive if we deal with more than two wheels.

To consider the actual operation of the *G*-circuits it is easier to consider a definite example. The example considered is one that we actually used, that is, running for 5U/F when $\Delta\chi_1, \Delta\chi_2$ are set and we are trying to set $\Delta\chi_3, \Delta\chi_4, \Delta\chi_5$ (see **91A(e)**). In order to do this we require a straight 345 chi film i.e. one where the impulses are the ordinary 3rd, 4th and 5th, teleprinter alphabets. The message film however is modified by the information we obtain from the de-chi on impulses 1 and 2.

It will be remembered that each of the combining tubes had 4 plug-holes for its input which were numbered, in the case of the tube G_i, $(i \leq 8)$ G_{1-i}, G_{2-i}, G_{3-i}, G_{4-i}. So far it has not been necessary to distinguish between these 4 plug-holes. However in the type of run now being considered, these 4 plug-holes serve slightly different functions. Between the plug-hole and the cathode of the combining tube to which it is connected, is a relay. Normally, that is, when the *G*-circuits are not in use, this relay is closed. If however, the relay operates and thus opens the circuit, no signal is received from the translating tube, and the combining tube, unless prevented

[a] thratron [b] crresponding

[i] Handwritten 'is' inserted with caret.

from operating by another translating tube connected via another plug-hole, will be in its normal, i.e. operating, state. The relays in all the lines terminating in plug-holes with the same lower suffix are all operated when a thyratron connected to all of them strikes. This thyratron, in turn, strikes unless a controlling triode conducts. The grid of this triode is connected on plugboard III to one line of either one or both pairs of lines, carrying the $\Delta D_1, \Delta D_2$ signal, and if either line to which it is connected is inactive, prevents the triode from conducting.

We can now consider in detail the plugging which effected the result shown in the example given. The letters 5U/F are controlled by G_1G_5, G_2G_6, G_3G_7 and G_4G_8 respectively by means of the $\Delta D_1, \Delta D_2$ signals through plugboard III. To obtain the $\Delta D_1, \Delta D_2$ signals we synchronise the chi wheels with the tape reader, preset $\Delta\chi_1$ and $\Delta\chi_2$ to the known settings and bring out the known ΔD_1 and ΔD_2 impulses to the pairs of lines terminating in P_4^+, P_4^- and $P_5^+P_5^-$ in plugboard III. The reason for bringing them out on these pairs of lines is that we can then put the 3rd, 4th and 5th impulses on to lines $P_1^+, P_1^-, P_2^+, P_2^-, P_3^+, P_3^-$ and plug them straight across the top three lines of the resistor matrix, which simplifies the plugging on plugboard II from translating tubes to combining tubes. a

On plugboard III all the plug-holes not marked correspond to the G symbol at the end of the row. Since 5 and U are controlled by G_1G_5 and G_2G_6 respectively, we join G_1G_5 and G_2G_6 to the lines P_4^+ and P_5^+ by means of bottle plugs. This ensures that the relay will open unless the de-chi signal is **××** and so spots will be put on the film only if $\Delta D_1 \Delta D_2$ is **××**. Similarly G_3 and G_7 are joined to $P_4^-P_5^-$ and G_4G_8 to $P_4^+P_5^-$. If now the signal received on lines $P_4^+P_4^-, P_5^+P_5^-$ is •**×**, all relays operate and no spot appears.

Remembering that G_1 and G_5 control the letter 5, we plug from the T plug-hole to the G plug-holes in the following manner to get the arrangement shown in the example given previously. b

$T_1 \to G_{1,7}$	$T_9 \to G_{5,15}$
$T_2 \to G_{1,8}$	$T_{10} \to G_{5,16}$
$T_3 \to G_{1,5}$	$T_{11} \to G_{5,13}$
$T_4 \to G_{1,6}$	$T_{12} \to G_{5,14}$
$T_5 \to G_{1,3}$	$T_{13} \to G_{5,11}$
$T_6 \to G_{1,4}$	$T_{14} \to G_{5,12}$
$T_7 \to G_{1,1}$	$T_{15} \to G_{5,9}$
$T_8 \to G_{1,2}$	$T_{16} \to G_{5,10}$

In the resistor matrix the wiring of the first three pairs of lines of $T_9 - T_{16}$ is the same as for $T_1 - T_8$ so the plugging of $T_9 - T_{16}$ to $G_{5,9-16}$ simply puts data on the lower half of the film in the same way that the plugging $T_{1-8} \to G_{1,1-8}$ does in the upper half. We are thus able to record data for ten letters in each column, five groups of eight levels in the top half and five more groups in the lower half. The plugging for U, / and F is simply a variation of the above. p. 476

(j) $\overline{\chi}_2$ limitation

It is convenient to be able to consider only characters occurring against $\overline{\chi}_2$ **×**'s. This is done by modifying the $\Delta\chi$ film when it involves $\Delta\chi_2$. The χ_2 pattern is set up reversed (i.e. interchanging dot and cross on plugboard I). This is read one back and a special suppressor circuit causes no light to light up if a cross signal appears i.e. $\overline{\chi}_2 = \bullet$. i, c

[a] synchronize [b] plugholes [c] occuring

[i] Word 'able' handwritten.

i 91C TIMES AND ROUTINES

(a) Colossus time

In order to understand the reasons for the uses we made of the 5202 machine it is necessary to consider how the machine compares with the other method of breaking Fish messages, i.e. by means of Colossus.

When a message is run on Colossus the following processes have to be gone through. The message is obtained in the form of 5-impulse tape and this has to be copied and stuck into a loop. This process, including checking takes an average time of 40 minutes for a message 5000 letters.
ii The actual time for setting 5 chis on Colossus on a reasonably easy message is about 30 minutes, 4 minutes for a 1+2 break-in, 12 minutes for runs for the next two wheels, and 15 minutes or so, for the last wheel, letter counts, and checks.

(b) Time for 5202 processes

For comparison, the times for the 5202 set-up are considered below. We usually run message
a films in groups of three in order to save time in the developing process as it takes no longer to develop 3 films on the same strip than to develop 1 film. The first process in England was to transfer the data from the 5-hole tape to the 6-hole tapes used on the Generator. This, presumably, would not be necessary in America. This was done before we started operations on the machine
iii and so need not be counted in the time taken to run a message.

We will now give an estimate of the times taken to run a single film through the three parts of the process.

(i) The Generator

The time taken for the generator to run through three message films of 5000 letters each seemed to average 40 minutes. As the actual speed obtained on the generator was 550 letters per minute, this gave a total running time of 27 minutes leaving 13 minutes for changing tapes, loading the camera, and resetting the dials after each message. This time seems reasonable.

p. 477 In the case of a conditional de-chi extra time is needed to set the chi wheels to the predetermined settings. This on an average seems to take about 5 minutes putting the time for three films up to 55 minutes. This, of course, assumes no mistakes by the operator or machine faults such as lamps burning out.

(ii) Developing

The times obtained here were not a fair sample due to the fact that the temperature control on our air conditioning system was not adequate. This meant that a considerable time had to be spent in bringing the various baths to the required temperature of $70^\circ \pm 1^\circ$ F. This usually took as long as 10 minutes. The actual developing time was 15 minutes. The other stage which seemed to take a long time was drying the film. It seemed to be necessary to keep the film in the drier for 30 minutes in order to dry it adequately.

(iii) Comparator

The time taken to run a 3-wheel film through the comparator, to set it and to count the score, seems to be about 10 minutes. This assumes good films and clear identification on the master film. One of our chief troubles with the comparator was the fact that the identification was often very nearly unreadable, with the result that settings could often only be determined by finding the nearest clear reading and calculating the settings, a rather tedious process. To sum up, the times that it seems reasonable to expect are:—

---

[a] to same time

[i] Words 'AND ROUTINES' in section head handwritten.
[ii] Word 'minutes' handwritten.
[iii] Word 'need' handwritten.

Generator	(i)	Break-in run 13–15 minutes per message
	(ii)	Conditional de-chi 18–20 minutes per message.
Developing	(i)	Actual developing 15 minutes
	(ii)	Drying 30 minutes. This should be reducible.
Comparator		Ten minutes per run.

Since each message will require at least one conditional de-chi in addition to the break-in run, it follows that at least 30 minutes of generator time, 30 minutes of developing time, 1 hour of drying time and 20 minutes of comparator time are required to completely set a message. Hence the number of messages that could be dealt with completely by the unit cannot exceed 2 an hour, and this will cause an accumulation in the drier. The time taken to set a message is 2 hours and 20 minutes as a minimum. This, as a whole, does not compare particularly favourably with Colossus as an operational method. But considered from another angle, the 5202 compares very favourably. This is the very large number of positions which can be examined by the comparator in a short time. The comparator can examine 2000 $\Delta\chi$ settings in one second. Colossus can only examine, with multiple testing, 5 $\Delta\chi$ settings in one second.

(c) Routines employed in practice

Hence it seemed to us that the best use of the comparator was on 3-wheel or 4-wheel runs and we decided to start doing 3-wheel runs. The materials used were 2 months Squid traffic namely Squid of January and February, 1944. Both months were on $\overline{\chi}_2$ limitation. The January Squid had a motor with 26 dots and the February, 22 dots. Due to considerable trouble with the machinery we were not able to try as many messages of these months as we had hoped and in fact only 34 messages of January and 10 of February were attempted.

We decided on the following routine for these messages. The following films were made.

(a)	"Standard"	1=2=4
(b)	"Standard"	1=2=5
(c)	Straight	345 film

The Standard films mentioned above have not yet been described, and it seems convenient to do so now. The standard message film was designed to do runs on 4 impulses for any set of letters which contained with any letter, the complete opposite of that letter. p. 478

Hence the message film plugging was of the form

T_1	T_{16}	$\rightarrow$	G_1	G_9	T_5	T_{12}	$\rightarrow$	G_5	G_{13}
T_2	T_{15}	$\rightarrow$	G_2	G_{10}	T_6	T_{11}	$\rightarrow$	G_6	G_{14}
T_3	T_{14}	$\rightarrow$	G_3	G_{11}	T_7	T_{10}	$\rightarrow$	G_7	G_{15}
T_4	T_{13}	$\rightarrow$	G_4	G_{12}	T_8	T_9	$\rightarrow$	G_8	G_{16}

The plugging for the 1=2=4, and 1=2=5 chi films was exactly the same but in the first case the fourth pair of lines are both made active and in the second case the third pair of lines are both made active. In these cases the first pair of lines carried $\Delta\chi_1$, the second $\Delta\chi_2$, the third $\Delta\chi_4$ and the fourth $\Delta\chi_5$.

The other standard film of the ordinary type which was made, was made to run 1+2=• 3+4=**×**. This was run with a standard message film using impulses 1,2,3,4 instead of 1,2,4,5 as above. The plugging for the master was

T_1	T_{16}	$\rightarrow$	G_5	G_8	G_{13}	G_{16}	T_5	T_{12}	$\rightarrow$	G_1	G_4	G_9	G_{12}
T_2	T_{15}	$\rightarrow$	G_6	G_7	G_{14}	G_{15}	T_6	T_{11}	$\rightarrow$	G_2	G_3	G_{10}	G_{11}
T_3	T_{14}	$\rightarrow$	G_6	G_7	G_{14}	G_{15}	T_7	T_{10}	$\rightarrow$	G_2	G_3	G_{10}	G_{11}
T_4	T_{13}	$\rightarrow$	G_5	G_8	G_{13}	G_{16}	T_8	T_9	$\rightarrow$	G_1	G_4	G_9	G_{12}

It was hoped that by making a single message film and running 1=2=4, 1=2=5 we could set with certainty $\Delta\chi_1$ $\Delta\chi_2$ and either or both of $\Delta\chi_4$ $\Delta\chi_5$. To do this it was essential that the counting of the scores obtained should be reliable, since it was necessary that we should have a numerical check of the significance of the score obtained. Unfortunately the counter was never completely
E.2 reliable, chiefly due, I suspect, to faults in the film, such as stretching, imperfectly exposed spots on the film, and fortuitous spots on the film. Hence the only check on the runs which we would have had would have been agreement between the $\Delta\chi_1$ $\Delta\chi_2$ settings. In fact, we could always, if necessary, check the settings obtained as these messages were already set on Colossus and the
a Colossus dossiers were available. In practice we found that the $\Delta\chi_1$ $\Delta\chi_2$ settings obtained were usually correct but that the $\Delta\chi_4$ $\Delta\chi_5$ settings were not always reliable. The next step was to run a conditional de-chi using the $\Delta\chi_1$ $\Delta\chi_2$ settings obtained. The letters chosen for these de-chis were `/5UF`, one of the first two being usually the best letter in a 32-letter count on Squid and the other two being reliable letters. (It should be mentioned that Squid messages seem to be of two main types, one with high `/`'s and the other with high `5`'s. On both types of message `U` and `F` score fairly high.) This run was usually successful, when the film was made correctly. However difficulty in reading the identification film occasionally led to wrong settings being used for $\Delta\chi_1\Delta\chi_2$ if the
b settings had not been checked against Colossus first. Of the 34 January Squid messages tried, 24 came out without much trouble on the runs mentioned, 2 failed to set on χ_3 although the other chis set correctly, 6 were abandoned after unsuccessful initial runs and two were retried successfully on 4-wheel runs.

It had been thought that 4-wheel runs would be impossible since the length of the film for
i a 1245 run with the usual tenfold chi film would be 380 feet. Fortunately, a way was found round this difficulty as follows. A 1245 chi film (with standard plugging) was made with every
c setting occurring somewhere on the film. The standard message film was then made ten times over starting at the first, second, third etc. letter in the message. Then the setting for the beginning of one of the films will occur at the head of a column of the $\Delta\chi$ film. As a result of this method of making films it took ten times as long to set a message on the comparator since we had to record at least one reading on each of the ten message films. The length of the $\Delta\chi$ film, however, was reduced to 38 feet, and the time taken to make the $\Delta\chi$ film worked out, in practice, at $2\frac{1}{2}$ hours instead of (theoretically) 21 hours.

The February Squid messages were not particularly notable and gave a certain amount of
p. 479 trouble from the machine point of view. However 5 of them were set by the original method of running 1=2=4, 1=2=5 and 345/12.

One other class of message in which we were particularly interested was messages which set with certainty on two impulses, usually 1 and 2, but failed to set on any other impulses by the normal Colossus technique of one or two impulse runs, using the two known impulses. We obtained 4 of these messages on July, 1943 Squid, using the 1 and 2 settings given (which were certain according to our accepted conventions) and tried 3-wheel runs. Two such runs were tried, namely the run mentioned before, for `/5UF` and a run for letters which are strong on German language counts, namely `3JGF`. These were not very successful. The second best score on one turned out to be correct but had been missed by Colossus. It seems that not much is gained by running for the last 3 wheels together but the size of the sample is very small and it seems hardly fair to damn the method on such faint hearing.

As the rest of the Fish section broke up 10 days before the end of the experiment, we decided to run a few unset messages of Squid of May, 1943, using Colossus to do letter counts to check the settings afterwards. We had 4 of these messages, all 4 being set on a 4-wheel run followed by a 3-wheel run using the 1 and 2 settings. The 4-wheel run used for these messages was 1=2=4=5.

---

[a] dossiers available [b] message [c] occuring

[i] Handwritten 'a' in phrase 'film a 1245 run' inserted with caret.

Lastly a few Dace messages of December, 1943 were tried on 4-wheel runs using the run which seemed best on the Dace type of message namely 3+4=**×**, 1+2=•. Only one was successful, this being a message which set with difficulty on Colossus, but set with ease on the 4-wheel run. In addition a run was done to set a crib. This is the subject of **91D**.

To finish, here is a complete summary of the time taken to make various films.

Standard Message Film	13 minutes
Conditional de-chi	18 minutes
Standard 1=2=4 chi film	1 hour and 5 minutes
1=2=5 chi film	55 minutes
Standard 1=2=4=5 chi film	$2\frac{1}{2}$ hours
Standard 1+2, 3+4**×** chi film	3 hours

91D CRIB RUN

The crib chosen was a Jellyfish-Gurnard combination of May, 1944 which had previously been set on Robinson. Standard three impulse running tapes were made on Mrs. Miles by the method independent of limitation giving

$\Delta_{713}(Z_2+Z_5)$ in the second impulse
$\Delta_{667}(Z_3+Z_5)$ in the third impulse
$\Delta_{598}(Z_4+Z_5)$ in the fourth impulse

for the cipher tape (Z^*) and an identical set up for the plain language (P^*). As boards were plugged to put five letters of text on the films per exposure, we got all possible starting positions by copying the plain language (3259 letters of text) five times and filming the resulting tape. Identification was put on this film by engaging the "master-daily" clutch.

Boards were plugged in such a way that a coincidence in the upper half of the film, when films were superimposed, meant • • • in $\Delta P^*+\Delta Z^*$ and, in the lower half, a coincidence meant one of the letters • • **×**, • **×** • and **×** • •. We were thus able to make a simultaneous run for all the letters of $\Delta P^*+\Delta Z^*$ which are expected to score well in a crib run of this type.

There was a single big hit on the comparator and a count that compared very well with the Robinson run. The score for • • • on the high side was indeed only four away from the original. The identification of the position at which the plain and cipher set relative to each other was not entirely satisfactory since we arrived at a calculated setting of 973 compared with 993, the correct p. 480
position. The films, however, were faulty inasmuch as the identifying arrow could not be seen, so the reading of the identification was guess work to some extent.

91E CONCLUSIONS

The machine is clearly a very good method for dealing with cryptographic problems at very high speeds. Its chief trouble,[a] as far as Tunny traffic was concerned, was lack of flexibility. This was not important in the case of the normal settable message but unfortunately a large proportion of messages are not normal. Thus the standard procedure which we adopted could set messages which conformed to the usual long supply reports with a considerable amount of punctuation, but would fail on a message which was say, an appreciation of the chances of an expected operation, in which case strong language differences would predominate and different types of run would be successful. On Colossus it is very easy to try both hypotheses, but at the moment to try both hypotheses on the 5202 requires the making of two films. It would be possible to use one film if all the data from the message tape could be recorded on one film, but this would require 32 levels. This could be reduced to 16 if we only considered runs for groups of letters defined by relations of the type $i+j=$ dot or cross, but this is not always a good method of setting the last wheel or wheels (e.g. a run for /8 is not usually as good as a run for /).

[a] It chief trouble

The other place where lack of flexibility was apparent was in the *G*-circuits. When the whole film was being used, only 4 of these circuits were available, unless we were prepared to cut the effective text down to 2500.

It seems that if the 5202 had been available whilst Tunny traffic was still active, it would have been of immense value for setting, by 3- or 4-wheel runs, messages which failed on Colossus, but the setting of the remaining wheels would have been completed on Colossus.

In χ-setting the advantages of Colossus over 5202 include:—

1. Flexibility
2. Shorter time of preparation
3. Maximum message length 30,000 instead of 5000
4. Letter counts
5. Spanning
6. Not 99

χ-setting is only one of the Tunny-breaking operations performed on Colossus: The following
[a] are impossible or impracticable on 5202:

7. χ-breaking
8. Rectangling
9. ψ-setting

The lack of these facilities is due in some cases to inherent characteristics of the 5202 principle; in others their provision would require a very precise technique. At the other extreme spanning could easily be improvised.

---

[a] impractible

p. 481

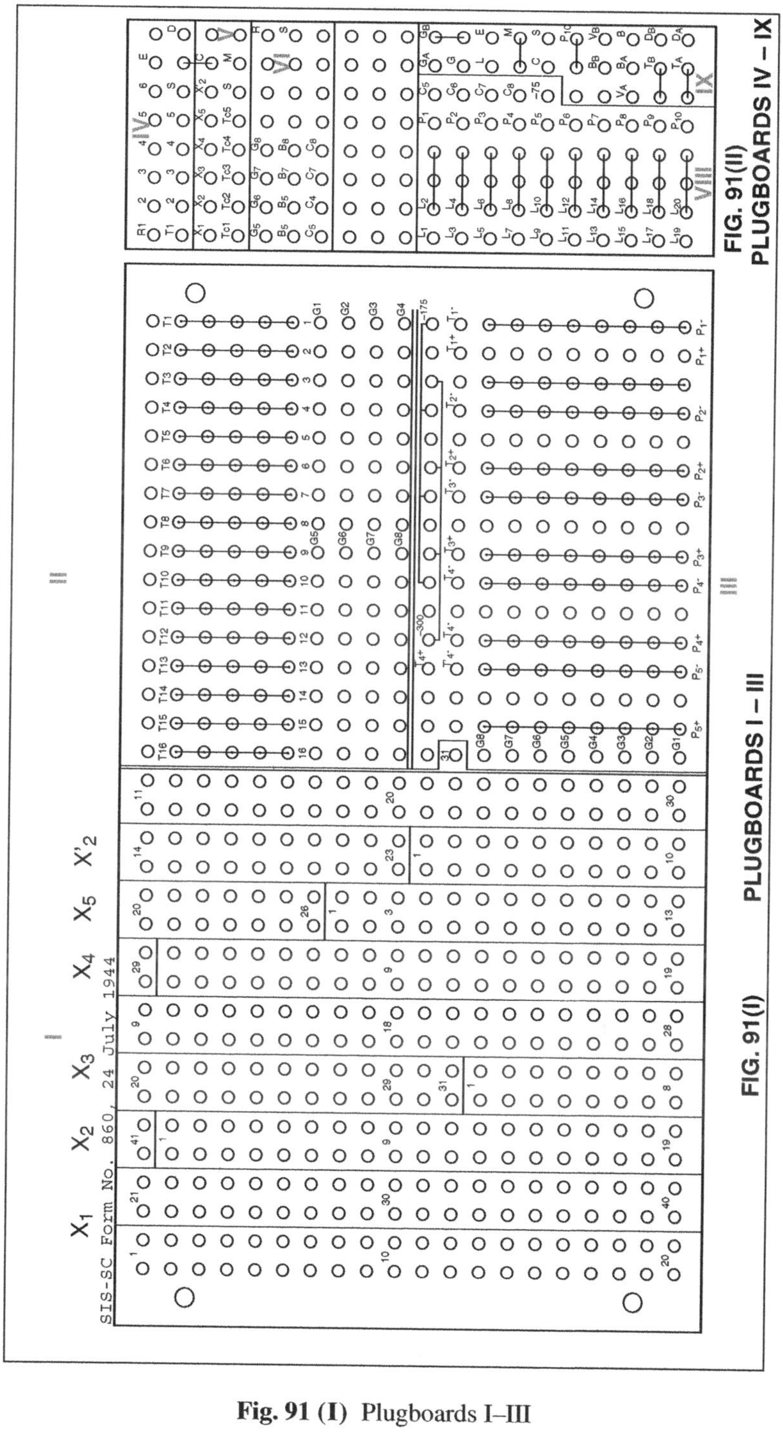

Fig. 91 (I) Plugboards I–III

Fig. 91 (II) Plugboards IV–IX

p. 482

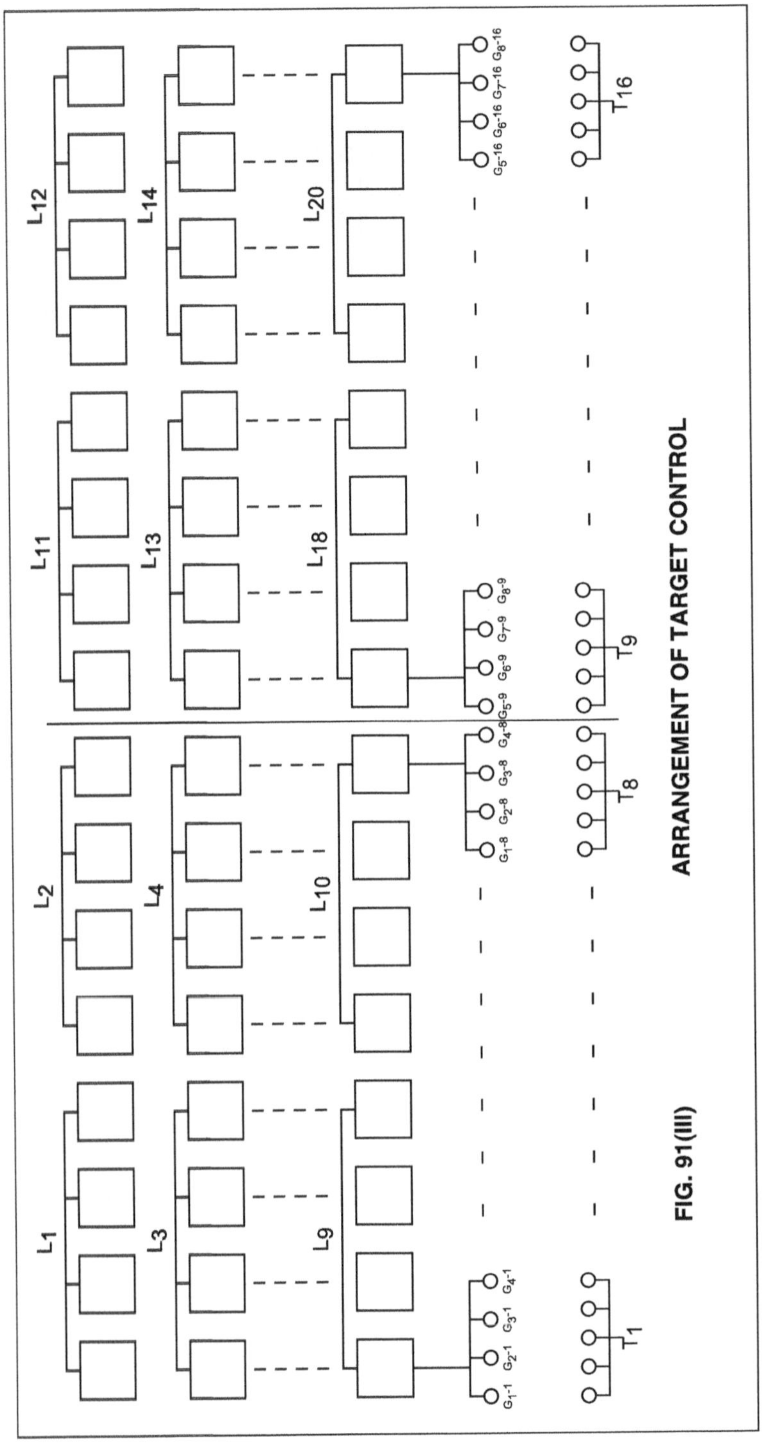

Fig. 91 (III) Arrangement of target control

92 RECOVERY OF MOTOR PATTERNS FROM DE-CHI p. 483, i

ii

92A Introduction and outline iii

An account has already been given (**28D**) of the methods of recovering the patterns of μ_{37} and μ_{61} from a stretch of ψ'. In that case a length of about 500 is needed, and eight lines of the motor rectangle are filled in; each square contains one of three entries — dot, cross or blank. The methods of recovering depend mainly on two ideas: first that consecutive columns of the complete motor rectangle match perfectly when compared level, if the earlier comes under a μ_{61} dot, and; when compared at a constant slide (dependent only on the dottage of μ_{61}), if it comes under a μ_{61} cross; secondly that any column matches perfectly, if slid one down, with some column between 20 to the left and 10 to the right, and that the distance away of this repeat column is determined to within a range of about 4 by the dottage of μ_{61}. iv, E.1

The following account shows how motors can be recovered from ΔD. Probability methods must be used, and the dots, crosses and blanks in the $\Delta\psi'$ motor rectangle replaced by deciban scores in favour of dot or cross, (with the prior decibanage not added in). The sort of length required appears to be about 8,000; additional lengths will nearly always be worth including. The count of ΔD is examined and an estimate made of the ΔP count underlying it: from this estimate it is possible to work out, for any given letter of ΔD, the probability that it comes against a basic motor dot, or rather the factor that the occurrence contributes to the odds on that character being a dot. These 32 factors are expressed as decibanages.

If we have a length of 10,000, any given character of the motor rectangle (which has 2257 squares) will occur 4 or 5 times in the de-chi and so there will be 4 or 5 letters of ΔD contributing factors to the prior odds on that character being a dot. All this evidence, in deciban form, is put together and entered into a 61×37 rectangle.

The basic operation, from now on, is to see whether two columns match well at a given slide: in the $\Delta\psi'$ motor rectangle the match is either admissible or inadmissible; in the present case the answer is a decibanage in favour of the match (except, again, that the prior decibanage is not

[i] This chapter consistently uses the spelling 'wheelbreaking', instead of the *Report*'s usual 'wheel-breaking'.

[ii] In the original text of the *Report*, almost all chapters start with an analytical contents list. This one does not. We have accordingly supplied such a list, as a copy editor would have done, for uniformity and the convenience of readers.

[iii] Head (but not running head) labelled as **A**, not **92A**, and similarly for subsequent sections; sections **92H** on labelled **(H)**, and so on. This chapter is the only one in the *Report* whose section heads are not typed with all capital letters.

[iv] Words 'a constant' handwritten, with 'a' inserted with caret.

usually included). The scoring is done from a table and will be described in detail later. Such small experience as there is available, indicates the method of finding repeat columns to be less powerful than that of finding the slide at which adjacent columns are to be matched. The reason seems to be that this slide is uniquely determined by the μ_{61} dottage, but the distance between repeat columns is only determined to lie in a range of about four; since the decibanages in favour of slides are small compared with the prior decibanage, it is important to be able to collect a large number of scores for a given hypothesis.

Once the dottage of μ_{61} is established, it is a simple hand process to construct an approximate μ_{61} and an approximate μ_{37}. The hand work should be checked on Colossus: indeed Colossus gives the final scores for μ_{37} in a manner not very liable to error, and the possible variation of μ_{61}, can be fairly conveniently assessed. If certainty is reached for both patterns, well and good; if not, there should be little trouble in setting the probable patterns on another de-chi and using this message to settle the doubts.

p. 484 When there is χ_2 limitation or no limitation at all the total motor is now known and the ψ's can easily be recovered on Colossus by normal wheel-breaking methods. If the limitation is more complex, the natural way to recover the ψ's would be to have recourse to the usual method of ψ
a breaking from de-chi (**28C**). This is made considerably easier by the recovery of the basic motor.

Before work is started, some assessment can be made of the probability of success. Setting aside limitations on the number of dots in μ_{37} and μ_{61} there are 2^{98} different pairs of patterns; so the prior decibanage of a given pair is 295. The decibanages in favour of a hypothesis in virtue of a score of 3σ above the average is approximately $2{\cdot}17s^2$; consequently a pair of patterns scoring 12σ is rather better than evens. Now it is a routine operation to estimate the expected σ-age of a motor run. Let this be done for all letters. The sums of the squares of the σ-ages on the separate letters gives the square of the σ-age for the correct patterns.

Sometimes a single letter in ΔD can be sufficient, as in the motor broken in August, 1943 (**R0**,
b pp. 11, 14 etc). This simplifies the work a lot.

i 92B Decibanage of ΔD letters

The first job is to determine the decibanage contributed by each of the 32 letters of ΔD to the hypothesis that the basic motor underlying it is a dot. The problem is slightly different with $\overline{\chi}_2$ limitation and not χ_2 limitation.

(a) With $\overline{\chi}_2$ limitation

Places where $\overline{\chi}_2 = \bullet$ provide no evidence about the BM and we need only consider places where $\overline{\chi}_2 = \times$. Let

$$37D = \text{Number of dots in } \mu_{37}$$
$$C = \text{Number of crosses in } \chi_2$$
$$N_\alpha^\times, N_\alpha^\bullet = \text{Number of occurrences of } \alpha \text{ at } \overline{\chi}_2 = \text{cross, dot.}$$

Then, by regarding the $\overline{\chi}_2$ dot positions as a sample of what happens at motor crosses (e.g. 23), the factor in favour of a BM dot can be seen to be

$$\frac{1}{D}\frac{N_\alpha^\times}{N_\alpha^\bullet}\frac{31-C}{C} - \frac{1-D}{D}.$$

[a] this [b] (**R0** 11,14 etc)

[i] Head (but not running head) labelled as **B**, not **92B**.

We can estimate D from the relations

$$\frac{\text{P.B.}(\Delta D_{ij} = \bullet \mid \overline{\chi}_2 = \times)}{\text{P.B.}(\Delta D_{ij} = \bullet \mid \overline{\chi}_2 = \bullet)} = \frac{2-\beta}{\beta}.$$

Both formulae are liable to error due to random variation and prior knowledge must be taken into account.

(b) With other limitation, or no limitation

Let

$$\begin{aligned} n_\alpha &= \text{number of occurrences of } \alpha \text{ in } \Delta D \\ T &= \text{Text length} \\ \phi_\alpha &= P(\Delta D = \alpha \mid \text{TM} = \times). \end{aligned}$$

Then factor in favour of BM dot is

$$\frac{n_\alpha}{TD\phi_\alpha} - \frac{1-D}{D}.$$

$\phi_\alpha = 1/32$, with an adjustment that depends on how good are the complements and near complements of α (with respect to 8). The adjustment is made by judgement — there is in any case no theoretical solution without using prior knowledge (see e.g. **R3**, 48). p. 485

92C Construction of Motor Rectangle i

The most thorough method of transferring the available information into the rectangle would be something of this kind:— Print out the delta D in widths of 2257: if there is χ_2 limitation, strike out those characters occurring against a $\overline{\chi}_2$ dot; using the decibanages already worked out for each letter, total up the decibanages for each of the 2257 columns; enter these in a 61×37 rectangle writing them in horizontally from the top left-hand corner in 37 rows of 61. When this has been done what appears in a given square is the decibanage in favour of that character being a dot (except that the prior decibanage has not been added in.) a

There is a short cut to this thorough method, making use of the plugging facilities on Garbo. The decibanages for ΔD can be taken to the nearest deciban or half-deciban; and instead of printing the letter itself, the plugging can cause the machine to print the score in the unit chosen; the ordinary numbers can be used for negative scores and A, B, C... for ①, ②, ③... This makes the totalling in the 2257 columns a great deal easier and sacrifices little in accuracy. If there is χ_2 limitation, it will still be necessary first to strike out the scores opposite $\overline{\chi}_2$ dots. Of course the machine does not print in widths of 2257 but in widths of 61 so that there are 37 rows. The technique of operating Garbo for this job has been described in the section describing the making of Garbo rectangles (**24**).

92D The Scoring of Columns against each other ii

It has already been stated that the elementary operation that underlies all attempts to recover μ_{37} and μ_{61} is that of comparing two columns against each other at some slide, and of determining how likely it is that the true columns have a perfect match at that slide. Any such comparison consists of making 37 separate comparisons of the factors in the first column against the corresponding factors in the second. f_1 and f_2 may be regarded as a typical pair of corresponding iii, b

[a] left hand [b] typical plan

[i] Head (but not running head) labelled as **C**, not **92C**.
[ii] Head (but not running head) labelled as **D**, not **92D**.
[iii] Word ‘as’ handwritten.

factors. Consequently the first thing to do is to find what factor is contributed to the odds on the slide being correct by the pair f_1 and f_2.

Let the probability of observing a factor f_i in a square that is really a cross be ϕ_i; then the probability of seeing it in a square that is a dot is $f_i\phi_i$. Then

i $$P(f_1, f_2 \mid \text{slide correct}) = Df_1\phi_1 f_2\phi_2 + (1-D)\phi_1\phi_2$$

and

$$P(f_1, f_2 \mid \text{slide incorrect})$$
$$= D^2 f_1\phi_1 f_2\phi_2 + D(1-D)f_1\phi_1\phi_2 + D(1-D)\phi_1 f_2\phi_2 + (1-D)^2\phi_1\phi_2$$

∴ factor in favour of slide being correct given f_1, f_2

$$= \frac{Df_1 f_2 + (1-D)}{[Df_1 + (1-D)][Df_2 + (1-D)]}.$$

p. 486 Let $d = 10\log_{10}(f)$ or $f = 10^{d/10}$.

Let

$$10\log_{10}[D10^{x/10} + (1-D)] \equiv \theta(x).$$

$$\text{Decibanage in favour} \equiv \phi(d_1, d_2)$$
$$\equiv \theta(d_1 + d_2) - \theta(d_1) - \theta(d_2).$$

a (See **R0**, p. 63) $\phi(d_1, d_2)$ can now be tabulated.

ii 92E The Recovery of patterns (A). Finding the dottage of μ_{61}

In our present state of inexperience, it would be absurd to dogmatise on the subject of
iii techniques. One point that seems clear is that the first thing is to determine the dottage of μ_{61}, and then the finding of the approximate patterns is easy. In this section some account will be given of four methods of finding this dottage.

(a) The method of determining the slide between adjacent columns

This is the simplest of the four methods and probably the most reliable. The general idea is that every pair of columns has a correct match; for a pair under a μ_{61} dot this match is level; for a pair under a μ_{61} cross it is at a slide determined uniquely by the dottage of μ_{61}.

Let us adopt a convention about slides; a slide between a column n and a column $(n+a)$ in which the $(S+1)$st character of n is opposite the first of $(n+a)$ is called a slide of S. In this paragraph 'a' is always 1 because we are comparing consecutive columns; but later we shall want to compare a column with another several places to the right.

It can be proved without difficulty that if C = number of crosses in μ_{61},

$$SC \equiv 1 \pmod{37}.$$

This method consists of comparing a large block of pairs of consecutive columns at all possible slides and entering the scores in a 61×37 rectangle. The slide of S between columns n and $(n+1)$ is scored and the score entered in the Sth row of the nth column. It will be most worth while

[a] (See **R0**, 63)

[i] Equation split on two lines.

[ii] Head (but not running head) labelled as **E**, not **92E**.

[iii] Handwritten 'that' inserted with caret.

comparing columns which score badly as a level match, because for these the chance of a μ_{61} cross is high.

In this scheme of entering, the last row of the rectangle contains all the scores for level comparisons. To estimate the relative probabilities of two slides, we could add up the scores for each slide and see by how much one exceeded the other. This would be accurate only if μ_{61} had no dots in the places considered, and better methods can be devised.

After about 15 of the columns of this slide rectangle have been completed (particularly if the columns with large negative scores for the level comparison are selected), it should be possible to narrow down the preference to three or four slides. Not all of these need correspond to admissible dottages. (It would be possible, of course, not to make the comparisons for inadmissible dottages, but the job is a mass-produced affair and probably the time saved by omitting some of the rows [a] would be lost in the mistakes arising). The best admissible slides can now be scored in some more of the columns — if necessary in all, — and in this way there seems to be an excellent chance of p. 487 finding with great confidence the correct slide (and hence the correct dottage of μ_{61}).

(b) The Method of Repeat Columns

The general idea will be familiar from the account of ordinary motor-breaking: it is that of a search for the approximate distance away of the column which is a match at a slide of -1. This distance is only roughly determined by the dottage of μ_{61}: the formula is:—

Dottage of μ_{61} given a repeat column at a distance x to the right, is approximately

$$\frac{61(x+24)}{x+61}.$$

This will not be wrong by more than 2, (cf. **R0**, p. 9). [b]

The scheme of work recommended is to compare every column at a slide of -1 with every admissible column, i.e. from 20 to the left to 10 to the right. These scores should be entered in a square 61 by 61: the score between column n and column $n+x$ at a slide of -1 is entered in the nth column and the $(n+x)$th row. In this way there will be at least one 'correct' score in each column and in each row: the presence of μ_{61} dots can increase the number from one up to three or four. The 'correct' scores will form a connected pattern (allowing diagonal connection) and will lie in a band going down diagonally to the right: the width of the band including them will be 4 or 5 squares.

The plan would be to guess what that band approximately is, by noticing the occurrence of very high scores: when the band has been settled, the dottage of μ_{61} should be clear with a possible error of ± 1. The candidates can then be tried out by the basic method of **(a)**, and (it is hoped) the correct one established.

To put this method in perspective, — it is hoped by doing rather less work than that entailed in **(a)**, to get an approximate μ_{61} dottage; and, with that information, to use the method of **(a)**, to distinguish between these candidates.

It should here be mentioned that in extremely favourable cases something more could be done. When the 61×61 rectangle has been filled with all the relevant scores, the attempt can be made to trace the pattern of 'correct' scores. This pattern is determined uniquely by the μ_{61} pattern (and is quite uninfluenced by the μ_{37} pattern); each character of μ_{61} influences the pattern of 'correct' scores in two places, and judicious use of this fact might enable one to construct a nearly complete μ_{61}. However, even at that stage the dottage of μ_{61} may conceivably not be uniquely settled.

(c) The method of looking for good slides

Select a column that has a lot of large decibanages, or a pair of consecutive columns which score so well level that a μ_{61} dot can be assumed. Try this column (or the composite column

[a] ommitting [b] **R0**,69

got by adding the scores of the pair together) against all other columns at all slides. The idea of this method is that it should be done unsystematically; the good portions are selected by eye and scored and recorded. For any given slide at a given distance, it is possible to narrow down the dottages of μ_{61} that could reasonably have given rise to it. This is done for all the good positions recorded, and a dottage of μ_{61} is credited with any of the good scores that it could reasonably p. 488 have picked up. In this way a total score is given for each possible μ_{61} dottage and preferences between the dottages now exist. The final choice can be made by the method **(a)**.

a This method has had a success (**R0**, pp. 1, 14).

(d) The smooth μ_{61} method

For all conceivable μ_{61} dottages make up a μ_{61} pattern or a partial μ_{61} pattern, with the correct numbers of dots evenly spaced. Assuming that pattern correct, add together all the columns and observe the sum of the moduli of the scores. The hope is that the smooth μ_{61} constructed for the correct μ_{61} dottage will sufficiently resemble the true μ_{61} for the μ_{37} scores to be significantly high. If this hope is fulfilled the μ_{61} dottage immediately emerges.

This method has the advantage that it can be conveniently done on Colossus. For every assumed μ_{61} dottage a smooth μ_{61} is plugged up and wheel-breaking run(s) are done for μ_{37}. The correct assumption is picked out by the significance of the wheel-breaking runs. This is identically the same as the hand process of adding together all the columns, described above. When the dottage of μ_{61} is selected, a μ_{37} can be put up and with the use of that, μ_{61} can be improved; and so on backwards and forwards between the two wheels.

Several smooth μ_{61}'s can be tried in the time taken for any hand process.

i 92F The Recovery of Patterns (B). The approximate μ_{37} and μ_{61}

It is now assumed that the dottage of μ_{61} has been established. The μ_{37} and μ_{61} can now be worked out approximately by a 'snaking' process, similar to that sometimes used in anagramming a de-chi after the ψ's have been set. Select a few columns where the μ_{61} pattern can be written in with confidence: such a patch will almost certainly exist if method **(a)** or **(b)** has been used. The b slide S between consecutive columns is now known; so that the left-hand column of the patch can be used as a start and the scores of the other columns of the patch can be added to it at the slides determined by S and the partial μ_{61} pattern.

Now make a rectangle 61 × 37; label across the top with the column numbers starting with the selected column, and down with the numbers 0, S, $2S \ldots 36S$, (all reduced modulo 37) which ii stand for the slides of the selected first column against the other different columns). Suppose there are 12 dots in μ_{61}, this means that $S = 34$; and that it can be assumed that the 19th character of μ_{61} is a cross, the 20th a dot and the 21st a cross; let the evidence for these three characters be scores of (50), (40), (63) as opposed to 60, 89, 35, for the contrary hypotheses. These facts can be entered in the rectangle as shown:—

	×	•	×			
	19	20	21	22	23	
0	✓	60				
34		(50)	(40)	35		
31			89	(63)		
28						
25						

[a] (**R0**, 11, 14) [b] left hand

[i] Head (but not running head) labelled as **F**, not **92F**.
[ii] Sentence ends with stray parenthesis: '... different columns).'

We now have a composite column made from the scores of columns 19, 20, 21 and 22 at their correct slides (of 0, 34, 34 and 31); this is our best approximation so far to the true pattern in a column. There are only two possible slides at which this should be compared with column 23; if the 22nd character of μ_{61} is a dot, the slide is 31, if it is a cross the slide is 28. Make these two comparisons and enter the scores in the rectangle. p. 489

Suppose we now have:—

	× 19	• 20	× 21	22	23	24
0	✓	60				
34		(50)	(40)	35		
31			89	(63)	33	
28					(9)	
25						

This gives an advantage of 42 centibans to the hypothesis of this μ_{61} character being a cross.[i] It already had the advantage of 60 centibans (because μ_{61} has 12 dots and 49 crosses) so that it would be reasonable to accept it. But if that is felt to be a risk, then the column already used can be compared at slides 31, 28 and 25 against column 24.

This might give:—

	× 19	• 20	× 21	22	23	24	25
0	✓	60					
34		(50)	(40)	35			
31			89	(63)	33	(6)	
28					(9)	83	
25						(42)	
22							

Now there are two characters of μ_{61} in question, the 22nd and 23rd. The most probable are clearly **××** which gain (51) centibans from these scores; the next best is •• which loses 27. This advantage of (78) centibans combined with the prior advantage of (120) centibans is overwhelming. When this has been decided the μ_{61} characters can be filled in and the accepted scores underlined in red; and, the most important, the two new columns can be added into the composite column at the slides now determined. There is one point of apparent discontinuity in the path of 'correct' scores; this occurs between column 61 and column 1. It is advisable to draw a heavy line down between these columns to avoid having this fact forgotten. If the correct slide for the 61st column is K, then the slide against the first column is $(K-1)$ if the 61st character of μ_{61} is a dot, and is $(K-1+S)$ if that character is a cross.

Doubts as to the exact cause of 'correct squares' can be left until the snake is completed and μ_{37} is nearly certain; indeed it may not be possible to settle such a doubt on the message itself. It

[i] Word 'the' handwritten.

is a check that the right number of dots in μ_{61} have been taken that the snake leaves the rectangle
a, b either through its bottom right-hand or its top right-hand corner. The μ_{61} pattern will have been
constructed during the operation and the μ_{37} can be written in from the decibanages collected
from the cumulative total of all the columns. It is reasonable to hope that there will be only two or
p. 490 three doubts in either wheel. The pattern deduced from the composite column will not be the μ_{37}
itself but will have to be disentangled. The details of the disentangling depend on the value of S,
or on the dottage of μ_{61}. If there are C crosses in μ_{61} then the first character in the column labelled
1 is the first character of μ_{37}; the second character in this column is the $(C+1)$st character (of
course reduced modulo 37); the third is the $(2C+1)$st and so on.

i 92G Finishing off the μ's

Once the μ_{61} pattern has been approximately established the rest of the work can be done
on Colossus. Set up the μ_{61} pattern as near as may be: it will have to be remembered that the
hand work did not start from the first column of the motor rectangle; also set up the μ_{37} pattern,
about which a necessary warning has been given at the end of the last paragraph. Do a count
against basic motor dots (also against $\overline{\chi}_2 = \times$ if there is the χ_2 limitation) and against basic
motor crosses (or against $\overline{\chi}_2 =$ dot if there is χ_2 limitation). From these counts the letters can be
re-decibanned with a considerable improvement in accuracy over the original estimates. From
c this new decibanning the letters can be grouped for further wheel-breaking runs for μ_{37}, — in just
d the usual manner of grouping letters in wheel-breaking. Do wheel-breaking runs for μ_{37} in the
way to be described, decibanning the runs and totalling the scores, and so get a more accurate
approximation to the wheel than the hand methods gave.

e In doing a wheel-breaking run for μ_{37} first count the score with a trigger consisting only of
dots — giving R. As usual put a cross in the last position and do a run. The 37 scores must all be
subtracted from R to give the scores for the various positions; and, as a check, the total of the 37
answers must be R.

In selecting the groups of letters it is important to include all letters except those scoring almost nothing: unless a correct balance is preserved between positive and negative letters there may be confusion about the number of dots in μ_{37}. For instance, if no negative letters are run for, all scores will be positive and the distinction between dots and crosses will only be that the scores against the dots are much larger than the cross scores.

ii μ_{61} can also be confirmed in a slightly less convenient way. Use the new μ_{37} and select the
five groups of letters that give the best decibanages; count them on the five different counters.
Now vary the position of the dots in μ_{61}. The correct μ_{61} must be reachable from the one set up
by a comparatively small number of moves, each of which consist of moving a dot one place to
iii the right or to the left. If this series of moves is made in a sensible manner, after each operation
the basic motor pattern resembles more closely the true pattern. Consequently a test of the μ_{61} is
afforded by moving all dots in either direction and seeing whether the score improves. So, first
count the five groups with the supposed μ_{61} pattern; list all possible dot moves (there will be twice
as many as there are groups of dots in the original μ_{61}); perform these moves in order, counting
iv the five scores, with each move and remembering, between moves, to return the dot to its original
v position. Comparison of the sets of five scores, with the use of decibanning of the groups, leads to
a decibanage in favour of each of the possible moves. If some dot move seems clearly to be an

[a] right hand [b] right hand [c] wheelbreaking [d] wheelbreaking [twice] [e] wheelbreaking

[i] Head (but not running head) labelled as G, not **92G**.
[ii] Word 'new' handwritten.
[iii] Word 'operation' handwritten replacing struck out 'move'.
[iv] Words 'each move' handwritten.
[v] Phrase 'the dot... position' handwritten.

improvement, then it is necessary to continue that move, or (more generally) to try all dot moves newly made available. This does no more to μ_{61} than can be done by hand, but it is easier to do it a accurately.

It is quite likely that the patterns will remain in doubt at the end of these operations; it would p. 491 be a mistake to spend too long on refinements on one message before trying to set the other messages on the presumed patterns. Once a new message had been set, the additional decibanages can be added in.

92H Recovery of the ψ patterns i

This is a mere appendix but it gives completeness. It is well, before attacking the ψ's to think whether any χ was at all doubtful; in particular a wrong χ_2 makes the ψ's unobtainable by statistical methods. Any χ thought to be worth confirming can be run for against basic motor dots.

If there is some limitation other than χ_2, no workable proposals have yet been made for statistical attack on the ψ's. For instance, if there is $\chi_2 + \psi_1'$ limitation, it is necessary to know the complete ψ_1 before the motorization is known. In cases of this kind the best plan is to print out b the de-chi with basic motor above it and hope that the ψ's can be broken by the usual method of guessing the plain language. The basic motor will certainly be of great assistance.

If there is no limitation at all, or χ_2 limitation, then the total motor is known, and the ψ's can be broken on Colossus without difficulty. The ordinary short runs for ψ's ($P_1 = \bullet$, $P_2 = \bullet$, $P_3 = \times$, $P_4 = \bullet$, $P_5 = \bullet$) can be tried as wheel-breaking runs; it will be very surprising if none of these is c significant. If that should happen, and if careful checking disclosed no new doubts or mistakes it would still be possible to converge the P 1 +2 rectangle for ψ_1 and ψ_2 from a random start. The only difficulty is the technical one, that there is no facility on Colossus for doubting a ψ wheel. However P 1 + 2 is so powerful that the convergence should not be much held up by the necessity to take a complete wheel each time.

92I Example of method (b) ii

For the interest of comparison the work of method **(b)** was done (later). The method was not found strong enough, on its own, to determine a substantially right μ_{61}. The best use of the method would have been to stop after about the 20th column, by which time the μ_{61} dottage had been narrowed down to 13, 14, or 15. These could have been tested out by method **(a)**.

92K Experiment in recovery by method of the smooth μ_{61} iii

There are here, as with other methods, two distinct phases of the work. The first phase is devoted to determining the dottage of μ_{61} and the second to the recovery of the patterns. The distinctive feature of this method is that it is done entirely on Colossus although it would be possible after the successful completion of phase one, to return to hand methods for the patterns themselves. The results and times seem to encourage the belief that machine methods are the most promising.

An experiment was done on a message KOA 4400 of length 7005. It was known to have no limitation and 11 dots in μ_{37}. It was reasonably certain that the μ_{61} dottage lay between 11 and 19. These facts were known because the message was of a date when the monthly keys were used, and before the introduction of limitation. An earlier experiment had been done with 31 dots in μ_{61}. This made the earlier experiment more difficult, since the smooth μ_{61} is a more powerful method when the μ_{61} dottage is not close to $\frac{1}{2} \times 61$.

---

[a] but it easier [b] motorisation [c] wheelbreaking

[i] Head (but not running head) labelled as **(H)**, not **92H**.
[ii] Head (but not running head) labelled as **(I)**, not **92I**.
[iii] Head (but not running head) labelled as **(K)**, not **92K**.

p. 492 The message KOA 4400 had an expected 17 sigma for the motor run on ///, so only /// was used at first.

To estimate the significance of μ_{37} runs, a crude approximation was used. If the number of occurrences of the letters used for a run is R, these R occurrences will be spread over the 37 places; so $R/37$ is used as a norm and subtracted from each of the 37 scores. The resulting numbers are treated just as the numbers in a wheel-breaking run, i.e. their absolute values are summed. This sum is considered as having an expected score of $\cdot 8\sqrt{37R} = 4{\cdot}9R$, and a standard deviation of $\cdot 6\sqrt{R}$. If it exceeds $6{\cdot}1\sqrt{R}$ it is considered to be significant. This ignores the fact that the
i distribution is Poissonian rather than normal, and that the sum of the scores is restricted, — (in fact they must add up to R.) It is thought to be a reasonable approximation becoming unreliable as $R/37$ decreases. The accurate test would be to sum squares of the scores and apply the χ^2 test,
a but that is in practice laborious. (**R0**, p. 65).

For each μ_{61} dottage from 11 to 19 a smooth μ_{61} was chosen. With this pattern a wheel-breaking run was done on /// for μ_{37}. In order to try shorter patches of smooth motor, the doubting trigger was set up with crosses in the last 40 places; runs were done on the remaining 1/3 of the wheel set at 01, 21 and 41 by plugging the special μ_{61} pattern to a dot. So 4 runs were done for each dottage; for each run the scores (with $R/37$ subtracted) were entered and the sums taken to test for significance; $x/\sqrt{R}$ should reach 6·1 before any attention need be paid. The
ii values of $x/\sqrt{R}$ for the four runs and the different dottages given:—

μ_{61} Dottage	11	12	13	14	15	16	17	18	19
$x/\sqrt{R}$ on Full Wheel	5·9	5·1	5·2	4·4	4·3	6·8	6·0	5·4	5·2
" " " " at 01	5·1	3·8	4·9	5·0	4·6	7·0	6·4	4·1	5·3
" " " " at 21	5·3	5·7	4·6	4·9	4·4	5·4	6·7	5·0	5·2
" " " " at 41	6·0	4·9	5·0	4·7	4·9	6·6	6·1	5·0	4·2

This gave a clear preference for 16 dots, with 17 dots as a rival to consider and 11 dots as a poor third. The smooth μ_{61}, with 16 dots was then used for further runs and from now on four groups of letters were used:—

///	at	(7)
P,U,O,3	at	(2)
N,D,X	at	6
V,8,W,B,E,	at	$3\frac{1}{2}$

Runs for the other three groups were done, both on the full wheel and on the partial wheel set at 01 and 41; the 4 runs were added together at their own decibanages and the totals were tested for significance. If runs with R's of R_i and decibanages of k_i are added in this way the usual test can be used on the totals if $\sum_i k_2^i R_i$ is used as the R for the composite run.

The additional evidence was decisive. It gave $x/\sqrt{R}$ for the full wheel as 8·3 and for the parts as 7·3 and 6·5. At this stage phase one is over; the μ_{61} dottage is certain. The time for this work was of the order of one shift not counting the time for preliminary calculations. As already mentioned, phase two can be carried out by hand methods without much difficulty. But it can be done much more quickly on Colossus, provided that it is always held in mind that the first
iii approximation to μ_{37} is liable to be the result of adding together better approximations at a slide.

[a] (**R0**,65)

[i] Word 'Poissonian' handwritten, possibly with spelling 'Poissonion'.
[ii] '. . . dottage are given' with 'are' struck out.
[iii] Word 'be' handwritten.

Therefore it is best to see what are the contributions to μ_{37} due to a number of different patches of p. 493
μ_{61} and to see if the most significant contributions to μ_{37} can be set well at a short slide. Only after this is the next approximation to μ_{61} attempted. This can be done by moving a 'doubting cross' by hand. If instead this is done as an ordinary wheel-breaking run it is necessary to allow [a] for the fact that the smooth μ_{61} is also going round. By this method phase two was completed in one shift, but not until after another method had been used which took 3 or 4 shifts. The patterns were proved correct by the setting of the ψ's (which were already known). [i]

References to the subject of breaking the motor by statistical means may be found in the following places:—

R0, pp. 1, 7, 8, 11, 12, 13, 14, 16, 45, 47, 56, 63, 68, 69, 70. **R3**, pp. 50, 58. [b, c]

The account given here of motor breaking from a de-chi is a paraphrase of work that has been filed away.

[a] wheelbreaking [b] **R0**,1,7,8,11,12,13,14,16,45,47,56,63,68,69,70 [c] **R3**, 50.58

[i] Word 'correct' handwritten.

p. 494 # 93 THRASHER

(a) General Description

a Thrasher was a Fish link whose only manifest abnormality was its QEP system. Between consecutive transmissions the QEP number increased not by one, but by an amount roughly proportional to the length of the earlier transmission, approx. 1 per 120 letters. After some 30,000
E.1 – 40,000 letters there was a change of 'Rolle'. The obvious interpretation was that the Rolle was an expendable key tape of which each terminal had a copy, containing 30,000 – 40,000 letters, marked with intervals of about 120 letters. At the start of a new transmission the tape was presumably moved forward to the next mark.

Whether or not this interpretation was correct, it remained possible that the key was Tunny
b key: this is plausible only because a Tunny machine would be an easy source of key tape, and the Germans were confident that it was unbreakable. Rectangles had already failed but it was thought not unlikely that the Tunny settings would be changed every 2,000 letters or so, which would defeat rectangling.

(b) The statistical method

This appendix describes an attempt to discover statistically whether Thrasher was Tunny. The interpretation of log evidence is dealt with in a Sixta report.

The basic method was the Δ_{1271} test (**24E(c)**) i.e. for Tunny cipher the proportional bulge,

c
$$\text{P.B.}(\Delta_{1271}\Delta Z_{12} = \bullet) = \delta^2.$$

Since $\delta \doteqdot 1/10$ the expected sigma-age was about $\frac{1}{100}\sqrt{N}$.

Corruption would reduce this. If the settings were changed every 2,000 letters the score would be reduced in the ratio $\frac{2000-1271}{2000}$

The value of N required to reach definite conclusions implies the use of many messages.

Further evidence was obtained by differencing at intervals which are multiples of 1271, but this was kept separate lest the settings were changed frequently.

The test for each message was carried out by putting two identical cipher tapes on Robinson with the first character of A opposite the $1271+1$th character of B.

Then the count $\Delta A_{12} + \Delta B_{12} = \bullet$ is clearly equivalent to $\Delta_{1271}\Delta Z_{12} = \bullet$

The count should of course be made only on the overlap of the texts A and B: this was arranged by using A for start, B for stop.

A similar count was made with the tapes staggered by 2×1271, 3×1271 and so on, till the message was exhausted.

The aggregate score for many messages were

Δ_{1271}: effective text 381,701, bulge + 366 sigma-age 1·18
Δ_{2542}: effective text 268,573, bulge + 428 sigma-age 1·65 .

This was unconvincing, but the poor score might have been due to corrupt texts, there-
d fore only messages which had scored well were used in similar tests on other impulses; firstly $\Delta_{598}\,\Delta Z_{45}, \Delta_{1196}\,\Delta Z_{45}$.

p. 495 Messages that still scored well were then tested by

---

[a] fish link [b] because Tunny [c] $\text{PB}(\Delta_{1271}\Delta Z_{12} = \bullet) = \delta^2$ [d] similiar

$\Delta_{754}\Delta Z_{34}$, $\Delta_{1509}\Delta Z_{34}$; $\Delta_{713}\Delta Z_{25}$, $\Delta_{1426}\Delta Z_{25}$; $\Delta_{806}\Delta Z_{24}$, $\Delta_{1612}\Delta Z_{24}$. [i]

For each of the first three of these the aggregate score was negative.
It was concluded that Thrasher was almost certainly not Tunny.

(c) Note on precautions adopted

To provide checks and eliminate spurious effects in the tests just described, all the following were counted for each message and entered in appropriate columns:

Message number,
Text length,
Stagger,
Calculated effective text,
Measured effective text,
Average (half effective text),
9's in whole text (an excess indicates corruption),
$\Delta Z_{12} = \bullet$ (A Tape) and its bulge.
$\Delta Z_{12} = \bullet$ (B Tape) and its bulge.
Δ stagger $\Delta Z_{12} = \bullet$ and its bulge.

It was found that the correction for 9's and consequent bulges on $\Delta Z_{12} = \bullet$ was negligible.

(d) Mystery of alleged depths

Log evidence, which appeared to be unambiguous, suggested that Rolle 40,034 was used twice, once by each terminal. It seemed that in several instances two messages must be in depth though the exact settings were uncertain: an attempt was made to set them by running for ///'s in

$$Z^{(1)} + Z^{(2)} = P^{(1)} + K + P^{(2)} + K = P^{(1)} + P^{(2)} .$$

The attempt was unsuccessful, which was equally unexpected whatever the nature of the key tape; it is inconceivable that the designer of a random tape machine would provide an autoclave.

It is however possible that the originator of a message, not understanding the principle of random key, or merely mistrusting the new-fangled machine, might demand double encipherment, which would destroy the expected properties of $P^{(1)} + P^{(2)}$.

In fact at various times a machine fault caused clear text to be transmitted, and in one case what appeared to be Enigma, though it was not broken.

[i] Last test given as $\Delta_{1612}\Delta Z_{25}$.

p. 496 # 94 RESEARCH INTO THE QEP SYSTEM

i **(a)**

The output of TUNNY decodes would obviously have been enormously greater if the indicating system in use in 1943 to 1945 had been broken. It was suspected, correctly, to be of the 'Book of Settings' type from the following known facts:—

(i) The only part of the preamble of messages which could possibly indicate the settings was the QEP number which was usually between 1 and 100, though very occasionally of three of four figures.

(ii) Messages on the same link and with the same QEP number were in depth only if the sequence of QEP numbers had not passed through a 100 between their transmission.

(iii) A book of settings was captured in the early days, which was thought to apply to similar traffic. The settings had four figure numbers. Settings were given for all twelve wheels.

Work on the QEP system before FISH traffic ceased in 1945 consisted of three pieces of analysis.

(i) Analysis of settings of messages set in the Sections.

(ii) Analysis of the captured QEP book.

(iii) Analysis of a partial QEP sheet transmitted in a Whiting message in November, 1944.

(iv) Analysis of allocation of QEP Books (not discussed below).

(b) Analysis of message settings

When the number of messages set per month began to reach three figures the possibility of breaking the QEP book had to be considered. Obviously everything depended on the size of the book. It might be infinite in the sense that fresh books of settings might be issued as the old ones were used. On the other hand it might consist of a limited number of settings, say 10,000, used over and over again.

The first step was to record the settings of all messages. This was done in Room 12 when they received the Red Forms back from the decoding section. The settings were recorded on cards, one for each message. The obvious method of attack was to sort the settings for repeats. Unfortunately the settings we obtained were only slides of the German settings, since the starting points of wheels are chosen arbitrarily by the wheel-breakers. The slide was of course constant
a for a day's traffic on a given link. The method adopted was to difference the settings for pairs of messages on the same day and link and sort these different settings for repeats over several months. There was a further complication. The initial break of a message was often a hundred or more letters from the beginning. It was necessary to work back the settings to the beginning. The working back and differencing which had to be done modulo the lengths of the various wheels, was done by Mr Freeborn's Hollerith Section (Block C) mechanically. Only the chi settings were used for this purpose. This was sufficiently powerful to eliminate almost all random repeats.

The information was sent to Block C in the following form:—

Msge. No.	Date.	QEP	No. of ltrs. before initial break	Chi settings	Motor Settings	Psi Settings
JP 2374	5.7.44.	40	46	23.14.21.16.03.	36.21.	16.43.21.50.26.

All messages decoded between July and November 1944 were sent.

p. 497 The following processes were carried out mechanically

[a] or pairs

[i] Section **(a)** lacks a section head, and the text 'The output. . .' starts on same line as the **(a)** mark.

(i) The settings were punched on Hollerith cards and printed out in book form for reference, sorted by Link and serial number.

(ii) These books were gone through by hand and a reference bigram given to each message corresponding to the day's keys on which it was decoded.

(iii) New settings cards including the bigram were punched from the book.

(iv) The number of letters before the initial break were subtracted modulo 41, 31 etc. from the chi settings.

(v) The correct settings of messages on the same day's keys were differenced, again modulo 41, 31 etc.

(ii) The differences were sorted by Chi 1 difference, then Chi 2 difference etc. and the results were printed.

The results were examined for repeats, which could be further tested by looking up the μ_{61} settings to find if they also gave identical differences. The psi differences though not the same should be simple slides of each other.

Only one case of a genuine repeat was found. The differences of the settings of two Stickleback messages in September, 1944 were the same as those of two others retransmitted a week later.

The conclusion to be drawn, was that no large scale reuse of QEP sheets was taking place over the period worked on. The isolated instance was probably due to a temporary use of an old sheet. Evidence from the Whiting QEP sheets of November, 1944 shows that the Germans number their wheel positions in the reverse order to us (e.g. the German Chi 1 set at 2 was in our sense 1 back compared with the wheel set at 1), but this unexpected fact makes no difference to the validity of the method used to test for repeated settings.

(c) The Captured QEP book

A QEP book was captured during the Sicilian campaign. The settings were evidently Tunny machine settings since there were twelve wheels and the limitations on the numbers involved corresponded to the lengths of the Tunny wheels arranged in the order:

$$\psi_1\ \psi_2\ \psi_3\ \psi_4\ \psi_5 \qquad \mu_{37}\ \mu_{61} \qquad \chi_1\ \chi_2\ \chi_3\ \chi_4\ \chi_5$$

The following further discoveries were made:—

For each value of k all QEP's of the form $21n+k$ were associated with a group of letters.

p. 498 Thus:

k	ψ_1	ψ_2	ψ_3	ψ_4	ψ_5	μ_{37}	μ_{61}	χ_1	χ_2	χ_3	χ_4	χ_5
1	E	P	C	N	D	B	U	M	F	I	G	A
2	C	G	M	I	L	K	P	D	J	F	A	H
3	J	N	H	A	N	E	T	M	B	D	F	G
4	D	A	Q	K	R	I	F	N	C	J	B	E
5	H	N	D	E	A	K	C	L	I	G	F	B
6	N	L	J	C	Q	D	B	F	K	E	H	G
7	I	O	K	F	J	H	A	C	E	G	B	D
8	G	C	M	B	F	I	O	L	J	H	E	A
9	F	B	A	P	I	G	R	J	E	D	H	C
10	A	L	E	J	H	M	O	B	K	I	C	D
11	K	E	I	O	S	C	H	N	G	J	D	F
12	N	F	G	L	E	A	K	H	D	C	I	B
13	H	M	K	D	T	G	J	F	B	I	A	C
14	L	J	Q	G	C	F	I	A	H	B	D	E
15	F	D	P	H	B	L	Q	E	C	A	I	G
16	A	K	O	G	S	C	E	I	D	B	F	H
17	B	I	F	D	M	L	S	K	H	A	G	E
18	O	H	L	N	K	M	G	J	A	C	E	B
19	M	P	I	R	O	E	L	D	G	F	A	C
20	C	E	N	Q	G	I	M	K	F	H	D	A
21	J	H	B	M	P	A	D	G	I	E	C	F

Where A means one of the settings 1,2 or 3; B one of 4,5,6; C 7,8,9; D 10,11,12; E 13,14,15; F 16,17,18; G 19,20,21; H 22,23; I 24,25,26; J 27,28,29; K 30,31; L 32,33,34; M 35,36,37; N 38,39,40,41; O 42,43; P 44,45,46,47; Q 48,49,50,51; R 52,53; S 54,55,56; T 57,58,59; U 60,61.

It will be seen that if a letter has been used for a setting of one wheel for a given value of k, it has been used for no other wheel for the same k. In other words a letter occurs not more than once in a given row.

Further investigation suggested that within these limits the book was compiled by hand. Depths on different QEP's are almost completely ruled out by the design of the book.

Probably this system is not a regular feature of QEP books on Tunny links.

(d) The Whiting QEP Sheet

At 1105 on 13th November 1944 Berlin sent QEP 45 which was intercepted as W.B.3756, and decoded by us soon after the wheels had been broken on another message. QEP 45 consisted in part of a message which said: "To Heeresgruppe Nord. You will shortly receive the following

E.1 QEP Blatt 1, from 001 to 035. Wheels 1, 2, 3 … 12.

001,	20	47	26	50	17	35	13	02	12	10	24	09
002,	… etc.											

Though several messages on Whiting 12th November were read there was no information that Riga was without any cypher equipment.

At 1149 the first message on Blatt 1 (QEP 01) was sent. In QEP's 08–9 there was another transmission of wheel settings, this time Blatt 3 from 071 to 105 (WB 3761–2). It seems certain that Blatt 2 was never sent or used. QEP 30 was followed, at an interval, by QEP 77 and it certainly looked as if the transmitted Blatt 3 was used from QEP 77 to QEP 96. All these QEP's were on the same day's keys. It is improbable that any further QEP Blatt was transmitted.

All traffic intercepted in QEP Blatt 1 was decoded except for 6 short or corrupt messages. To p. 499
get 'English Settings', the German settings were taken in the order Psi 1, Psi 2, Psi 3, Psi 4, Psi 5, M_{37}, M_{61}, Chi 1, Chi 2, Chi 3, Chi 4, Chi 5 and *subtracted* from

26 33 48 28 50 19 50 30 07 54 21 05. (Defined as rings).

On messages connected with QEP Blatt 3 such messages as had been set on Colossus had settings which bore no obvious relation to the expected settings deduced from the QEP number and the rings deduced from Blatt 1. Settings on Blatt 3 messages were not even consistent among themselves in giving a different set of rings.

It is possible that a slide may have been put on the QEP sheet or that some other transposition or substitution was applied to the printed settings. But it seems more probable, that in spite of the logs evidence, a courier with the missing QEP sheets had arrived at Riga before QEP 78 was sent. This would imply that Berlin transmitted for temporary use a set of QEP's different from those whose transit was delayed and which would otherwise have been used.

A fuller account (of the Whiting QEP sheet) is given in **R4** pages 17, 18, 36 to 38.

p. 500 # 95 MECHANICAL FLAGS

i

95A GENERAL DESCRIPTION

(a) Experiments to be described

This appendix deals with experiments in obtaining mechanically

(1) The complete ($\Delta\chi_2$) flag of an ordinary rectangle.

(2) The flag of a combined key rectangle.

The corresponding hand processes are described in **24D(b,c,d)** and **26B(c)**.

(b) Results obtained

In neither case was mechanization operationally successful. This is probably due to a combination of circumstances, among them:

Both needed complicated processes on Miles D, which was unreliable.

Both used Super-Robinson before it was reliable.

The key-flag, in its final form, requires gadgets on Colossus and Robinsons which were not available till the end of the war in Europe was imminent.

The ordinary flag involved very long tapes.

Neither was even theoretically much faster than computation by hand.

(c) Simplification of this account

The account describes the processes in their final form, and indeed, for the ordinary flag, exceeds this by ignoring certain complications introduced to deal with a mistakenly alleged weakness of Super Robinson. Some ingenious improvisations are thus omitted, but so are many tedious instances of failure to see the obvious solution.

(d) The common basis of mechanical flagging

The basis of the run on Robinson is the same for both types of flag.

Two tapes, *A*, *B*, are used, each bearing the entries, in the cells of the rectangle arranged by rows, thus

A		Row 1	Row 2	Row 3	Row 4	
B	Row 1	Row 2	Row 3	Row 4	Row 5	

To find the flag entry corresponding to rows 1 and 2 of the rectangle, it is arranged that row 2
p. 501 of *B* is opposite row 1 of *A*, and row 1 of *A* is spanned. What is required is the sum of products of corresponding scores on *A* and *B*.

When each score is ± 1 (as in the key flag) this is easy, for if $\pm$ 1 are represented by dot and cross, the correct result is obtained by counting $+1$ when $A+B=\bullet$; -1 where $A+B=\times$.

The complexity of the Mechanical Ordinary Flag is that of summing the products when the rectangle scores are not all ± 1.

[i] In the original text of the *Report*, almost all chapters start with an analytical contents list. This one does not. We have accordingly supplied such a list, as a copy editor would have done, for uniformity and the convenience of readers.

The complexity of the Mechanical Combined Key Flag is that of combining the four rectangles on one tape.

NOTE. The flag of a single rectangle of depth 1 can be obtained on Super-Robinson directly from two message tapes, the selection of a row being made, not by spanning, but by a control tape (cf. **54H**).

95B MECHANICAL ORDINARY FLAG

(a) The Robinson run

Suppose that the depth is 8 so that the score in a cell of the rectangle may be −8, −6, −4, −2, 0, 2, 4, 6, 8. Because the common factor 2 is irrelevant these may be treated as −4, −3, −2, −1, 0, 1, 2, 3, 4.

The contribution to the score of two rectangle entries opposite one another on tapes *A*, *B* is the product of these entries, which may be as great as 16. Super-Robinson can count only 1 at most for each sprocket hole, and thus each score of the rectangle must be represented on the tape by a symbol extending over 16 sprocket holes at least.

Further, Robinson cannot record negative scores, and accordingly positive and negative scores are counted separately, actually in the two halves of a split counter. The score is positive where *A* and *B* entries have like signs, negative when they have unlike signs: minus is represented by a cross in the fifth impulse, and the switching is $A_5 + B_5 = \bullet$ for positive scores, $A_5 + B_5 = \times$ for negative scores.

The magnitude of each score, apart from sign, is represented in the first impulse:

		A Tape (Tate)			B Tape (Lyle)
0	by	••••••••••••••••	0	by	••••••••••••••••
1	by	×•••×•••×•••×•••	1	”	××××••••••••••••
2	”	××••××••××••××••	2	”	××××××××••••••••
3	”	×××•×××•×××•×××•	3	”	××××××××××××••••
4	”	××××××××××××××××	4	”	××××××××××××××××

The switching $A_1 = \times$, $B_1 = \times$ gives the correct products, as will be seen on inspection.

For a $\Delta\chi_2$ flag, tape *A* comprises the 31 rows of the rectangle, each represented Tatewise by 41 × 16 characters, and further 41 × 16 blanks, with start and stop. Tape *B* comprises the 31 rows of the rectangle, each represented Lylewise by 41 × 16 characters, with a start (for checking p. 502 relative positions).

Start tapes level. Span *A* 1–657. *A* will step relative to *B*, and the scores obtained will be those of the first row of the flag.

Then span *A* 657–1313, to obtain the second row, and so on.

(b) Tape-making

This needs two processes, on Colossus and Miles D respectively.[a]

(c) Colossus rectangle tapes

On Colossus with a punch (**53M(h)**) make an ordinary 1+2 rectangle, and in addition plug scores to punch thus 0 to /, 2 to E, 4 to 4, 6 to 9, 8 to 3.

The machine adds a cross in the fifth impulse for negative scores so that on the resulting tape, the representation of scores is

	8	6	4	2	0
+	•••×•	••×••	•×•••	×••••	••••×
−	•••××	••×•×	•×••×	×•••×	

[a] need two processes

(d) Making Tate tapes on Miles D

In	the	first	transmitter	a	loop	E///E///E///E//9	with the 1st E in the window.
”	”	2nd	”	”	”	EE//EE//EE//EE/9	”
”	”	3rd	”	”	”	EEE/EEE/EEE/EEE9	”
”	”	4th	”	”	”	EEEEEEEEEEEEEEES	”
”	”	5th	”	”	”	the rectangle tape just made,	

[i] and plug as in the diagram: (not to scale).

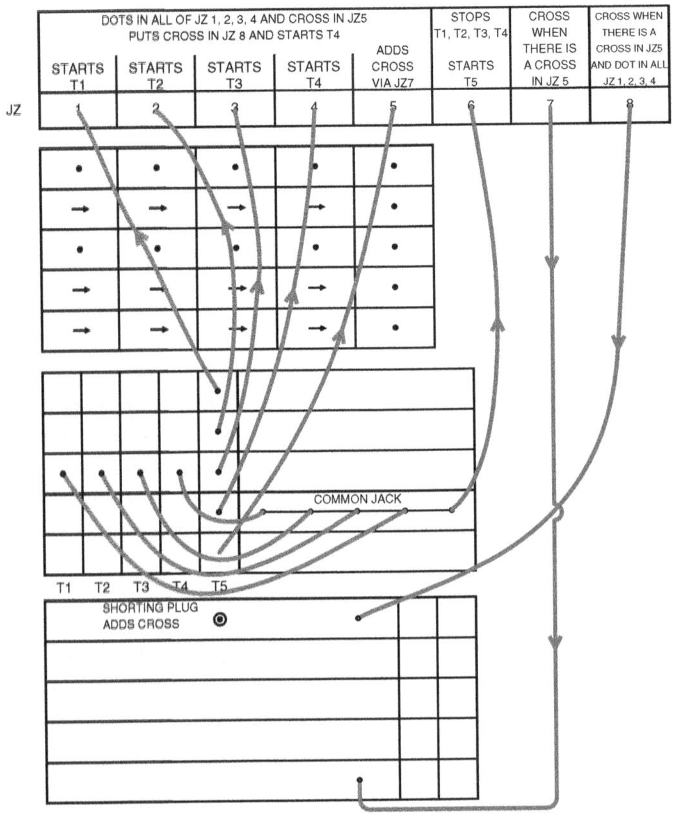

p. 503 Suppose there is a score of +4 on the rectangle tape i.e. •×••• in the eye of T_5: this starts T_2 and produces EE//EE//EE//EE/9, which is the sum of the tape in T_2, the three E's in T_1, T_3, T_4 and the cross in impulse 1 of output. When the 9 is reached, the × in the third impulse stops T_2 (via JZ6), and steps T_5 one place.

If the score is −4, i.e., •×••×, the × in the fifth impulse will add a cross to the output via JZ7, giving ZZTTZZTTZZTTZZTH.

If the score is 0 i.e. ••••×, this will start T_4 (via JZ5) and add a cross to impulse 5 (via JZ7) and a cross to impulse 1 (via JZ8), giving TTTT TTTT TTTT TTTH.

(e) Lyle tape

A "Lyle" tape is made in an essentially similar manner.

[i] Phrase 'and plug . . . (not to scale)' handwritten.

(f) Checks

Tate and Lyle tapes are elaborately checked, being marked at intervals of 656; the letters following each mark are checked against the printed rectangle.

(g) Practical modifications

In fact the Robinson bedstead can hold only 16 rows, and the runs would have to be done piecemeal: nearly all the rectangles used experimentally were of depth 6. Most of the experiments were made on the old Robinsons, so that strings of dots and crosses had to be avoided. What is here called the first impulse was really the sum of the first two. The original Tate tape bore the word "Tate" thrice for each score +1. In the fifth impulse + was represented by •×•×•× and – by ×•×•×• etc.

The Colossus punch is now wired to punch / instead of T for zero.

95C MECHANICAL COMBINED KEY FLAG

The flag is specifically that of the combined 1+5, 2+5, 3+5, 4+5 rectangle.

(a) The Robinson run

The method is applicable only when the overall text length is less than 598

On the two Robinson tapes *A*, *B*, (tape-making is described in **95C(c,d,e)**). [i]

+1	is represented by	R
0	"	E
−1	"	G

Robinson is plugged: p. 504

$$\begin{cases} A_2 = B_2 = \times & \text{(excluding a zero on either tape)} \\ A_5 + B_5 = \bullet & \text{in one half counter for positive products.} \\ A_5 + B_5 = \times & \text{in the other for negative products.} \end{cases}$$

which will obviously give the correct result.

A consists of the 23 rows of the combined rectangle, 2 row-lengths of blanks, start and stop.

B consists of 23 rows of the combined rectangle. 1 row length of blanks, start and stop.

Span the first row of *A*: owing to the difference in tape lengths it will step so as to be opposite each row of *B* in turn: the scores obtained will be those of the first row of the flag. They can be identified by the position counter. Span the other rows in turn.

(b) Some natural checks

When the 1st row of *A* is opposite the (identical) first row of *B*, thus

$$\begin{array}{ccccccccccc} +1 & +1 & 0 & 0 & -1 & 0 & 0 & -1 & +1 & \dots \\ +1 & +1 & 0 & 0 & -1 & 0 & 0 & -1 & +1 & \dots \end{array}$$

the score for positive products is the number of non-zero scores in the first row of the combined rectangle, i.e. the total number in the first rows of all constituent rectangles, and the score for negative products is zero.

Likewise when the nth row is opposite the nth row.

Further, when the spanned row of *A* is opposite the blanks in *B* both scores are zero.

(c) Tape-making

The tapes R_1 R_2 R_3 R_4 of the four rectangles are made separately on Colossus and combined into a single rectangle on Miles D.

---

[i] Sentence ends without a closing parenthesis.

(d) Making the four rectangle tapes

In a key rectangle there are many doubtful characters (**26B(c)**) for which no provision is made in an ordinary Colossus rectangle.

The ordinary not 99 circuit is useless. Colossus rectangling works by counting places where $\Delta Z_{ij} = \bullet$ and then doubling and subtracting the depth. With not 99 in use, a doubt is not counted, p. 505 i.e. it is treated exactly as though $\Delta Z_{ij} = \times$, and will score -1 not 0.

To overcome the difficulty Colossus 6 has been fitted with 'rectangle not 99' directly controlling the score, making it zero: it overrides the score produced normally. It works only for a depth of 1.

The punch is plugged	0	to punch	E
	+1	"	R
	−1	"	G

Carriage Return to punch $\overline{9}$/ i.e. to punch / and add a cross in the 3rd impulse of the preceding character.

The four rectangle tapes R_1, R_2, R_3, R_4 are, otherwise, made normally from the cipher tape as rectangles of depth 1. Owing to the spanning from 04, the first four scores are lost: it may be worth while to preface a short text with four 9's.

The first few scores in each rectangle are checked by hand. Machine faults generally produce an obvious irregularity in the pattern of 0's and 1's.

(e) Combining rectangles on Miles D

R_1, R_2, R_3, R_4 are placed in T_1, T_2, T_3, T_4 with the stroke before the text on the peckers.

In T_5 is a control tape consisting of E43T... repeated 23 times. Plug as in the diagram below (not to scale).

The 'E' in T_5 starts R_1 (in T_1) which is reproduced till the cross in the 3rd impulse at the end of the first row stops it, leaving / on the peckers and steps T_5 to '4'. The '4' starts R_2 (in T_2) and so on.

The tape produced is

1st row of R_1,/, 1st row of R_2,/, 1st row of R_3,/, 1st row of R_4,/, 2nd row of R_1,/ and so on.

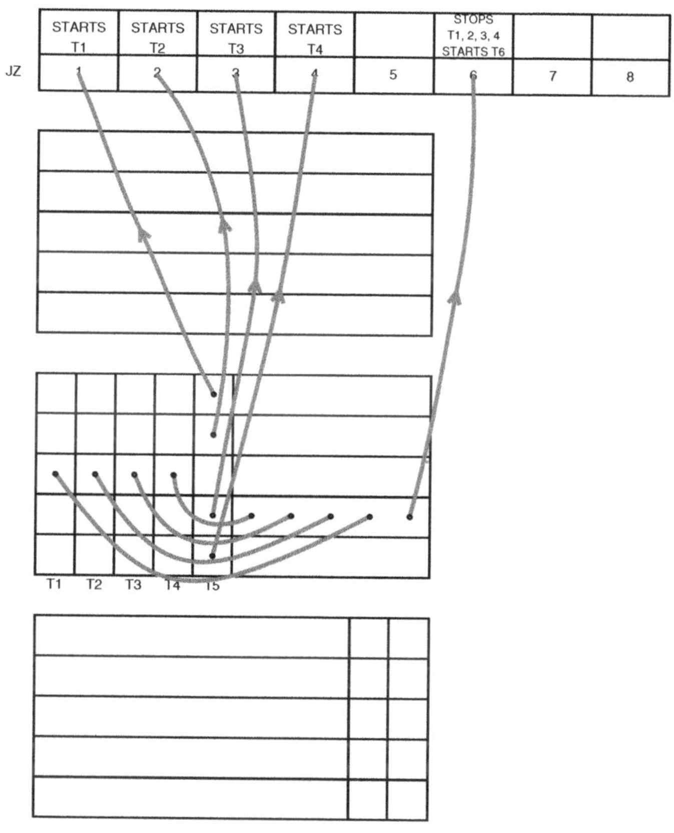

[i]

[i] The *Report* ends here, on p. 505.

Appendix A: Transmission of Teleprinter Signals*

J. A. Reeds

Tunny was used to encipher traffic over a portion of the German military teleprinter network, a network which for the most part used the same technology as its civilian counterparts, operated in Britain and Germany by the national postal services and in the U.S. by commercial enterprises. This same technology was widely applied throughout the world in the half century 1930–1980, especially in the international Telex and American TWX services. Many aspects of this technology were well established by the beginning of the war, but those connected with transmission of teleprinter signals over radio were comparatively new, or in a state of flux. This Appendix attempts to sketch the relevant parts of this technology and its history and to explain the terminology found in the *Report* and other wartime sources.[1]

The idea of a printing telegraph is as old as that of the electric telegraph itself, and several systems for printing telegraphy were developed in the 19th century. These were of varying degrees of practicality, and the widespread use of teleprinters began only in about 1920, with the perfection of the so-called 'start–stop' principle described below.

Everything worked according to a conventional alphabet of $2^5 = 32$ codes for letters, digits, and a few punctuation marks, each code consisting of a pattern of five elements, each element either a 'mark' or a 'space'. The details of this code are irrelevant to the matters under discussion in this Appendix, except to note that the two communicating ends of a teleprinter link used the same code. But in fact by 1939 essentially all start–stop teleprinters in the parts of the world that used the Latin alphabet employed some version of a particular standard code, the International Telegraph Alphabet Number 2 (ITA 2), which we discuss in endnote 4 to **11A(a)**, p. 564 below. The codes could be punched on paper tape, with a punched hole representing mark, or they could be represented electrically on the telegraph wire. In the simplest scheme ('single current working' or 'neutral keying', German *Einfachstrombetrieb*) a mark was represented by a direct current (d.c.) flow of electricity, space by no flow. In another ('double current working' or 'polar keying', German *Doppelstrombetrieb*) a mark was represented by a d.c. flow in one direction, and space by flow in the opposite direction. In either scheme, 'marking current' and 'spacing current' named the corresponding electrical conditions. The German terms, by a quirk of language, in the case of start–stop telegraphy, were *Trennstrom* and *Zeichenstrom*, respectively, even though these terms reverse the usual literal dictionary meanings (spacing current and marking current, respectively).[2]

In teleprinter use, the wire, when idle, carried marking current. To send a letter, first a 'start pulse' of spacing current was sent, then in succession the pulses for the five code elements, and finally a 'stop pulse' of marking current. All these pulses were of equal fixed duration, except for the stop pulse, which was longer, usually about 1.5 times as long as the others. If a letter was sent followed by a pause before the next letter, the first letter's stop pulse was prolonged until the next letter's start pulse was sent.

The purpose of the start and stop pulses was to help the receiving teleprinter know when one letter ended and the next began. The transition from the old letter's stop pulse's marking current to the new letter's start pulse's spacing current triggered the receiver's handling of the new letter. Without the start and stop pulses the sender and receiver would have to maintain a strict synchronisation. In effect, the start and stop pulses impose a 50% tax on the duration of

*The notes to this Appendix are at its end. They use the citation system used in the notes to the *Report*, explained on p. 561.

a transmitted letter, in return for sidestepping the synchronisation problem. In German Tunny traffic the first six elements lasted .02 seconds apiece and the stop pulse lasted .03 seconds, so the whole letter lasted .15 seconds, making for 400 letters per minute, or (figuring a word as having 6 letters) about 66 words per minute. (This speed is called '50 baud', as the shortest element lasts 1/50-th of a second.)

The main pieces of equipment the end user saw were the teleprinter (in German, *Fernschreibmaschine*, colloquially *Fernschreiber*; in American English, 'teletypewriter'), the tape perforator, the tape transmitter, and the tape receiver.[3] Typing at the typewriter-like keyboard of the teleprinter sent its electrical representation of the letters out on the wire. Typing at the keyboard of the perforator caused the letters' codes to be punched on the paper tape. The tape transmitter could send a previously punched message out on the wire or could send it to the local teleprinter to make a printed copy.[4] Incoming messages could be handled by the tape receiver (which punched a paper tape copy), or by the teleprinter (which printed it), or by both.

Many of the components of the scheme described so far had been introduced in the 19th century, including the use of a 5-element code and of punched tape, and all had reached their mature form by (say) 1935.

One innovation in the 1920's was the use of a new electrical representation of mark and space, variously known as 'carrier telegraphy', 'carrier current telegraphy', or 'voice frequency telegraphy' (VFT), and in German *Wechselstromtelegraphie* (WT, literally, alternating, or oscillating, current telegraphy). The *Report* calls it 'tone transmission'. In its simplest form, 'single tone VFT' (*Einton* WT) or amplitude modulated (AM) VFT, a mark (say) is represented by a tone of some audible pitch, and a space by the absence of tone. This makes it easy to carry several independent teleprinter connections on a single telephone line: each channel in a multi-channel voice frequency telegraph system uses a different pitch. This became the preferred way to transmit teleprinter signals over long distances during the 1930's, because of the way it economized on the use of trunk lines.[5] A similar system, of limited use on wired connections, is two-tone VFT, or *Zweiton* WT (WTZ), also described as frequency modulated (FM) VFT, most commonly referred to in the late 20th century as frequency shift keying (FSK) or, more properly, as audio FSK (AFSK). In this system, one tone is assigned to mark and another assigned to space. A modem converts between polar keyed and VFT signals.

The German military used a form of VFT for its land line teleprinter traffic, using a modem designated WT 40. In one mode, at least, it could use AFSK to carry three teleprinter channels over one voice channel, with these pitches[6]:

Channel 1	Channel 2	Channel 2	
540 Hz	1260 Hz	1980 Hz	Mark
900 Hz	1620 Hz	2340 Hz	Space.

In principle, one could transmit three separate teleprinter channels over high frequency (HF) radio by multiplexing them into one telephone channel as above and using it to amplitude modulate an HF radio signal. To protect themselves from the vagaries of HF reception, when sending Tunny enciphered signals by radio, the Germans did something a little more conservative with their system of VFT over short wave, *Wechselstromtelegraphie auf Kurzwelle* (WTK). In effect, they multiplexed three identical copies of the same teleprinter signal into a telephone channel and sent it as above. Thus, mark was represented by a mixture of the three tones 540, 1260, 1980 Hz, and space by a mixture of the three tones 900, 1620, 2340 Hz. The resulting audio signal was then sent by HF AM. The conversion was done by a WTK set, a close cousin of the WT 40 modem used with long-distance telephone wires.[7]

High frequency radio reception is notoriously fickle, as the signal bounces off the ionosphere, whose location and electrical characteristics change with time of day, season of year, and sunspot activity. In addition to interference, HF signals are subject to fading, that is, the intermittent loss of the signal, or loss of frequency components of the signal. A simple result is that AM VFT is unsuitable for HF applications: the receiver cannot tell the difference between not hearing a tone because a space is being sent or because a mark is being sent during fading. With AFSK, since at every time one of the two tones is being sent, the receiver can tell when it is suffering fading. Standard methods for overcoming fading are to use so-called diversity transmitting and receiving, the radio equivalents of saying the same thing more than one way and listening with more than one ear. The use of combinations of three tones instead of single tones to represent mark and space is a form of transmitting (or frequency) diversity: it gives protection against loss by partial fading of one or two of the three tones.[8]

Both the Germans and the British used well-spaced multiple receiving antennas for space diversity, each with its own receiver. A controlling circuit combined the outputs of the receivers, adjusting their output levels so the better signal counted for more.

The resulting audio output was fed into six filters matched to the six information-bearing tones. The filters' outputs were rectified and combined to determine an opinion about whether a mark or a space was being sent. Unfortunately we have been unable to find out precise details of how these combinations and decisions were carried out, in either the German or the British equipment.

The equipment used by the Germans is described, with the help of a diagram showing the main components discussed above, in a 1942 handbook of telephony and printer telegraphy for signals officers, *Merkblatt Fernsprech- und Fernschreibtechnik für den Nachrichtenoffizier*, a copy of which is in NARA HCC 15:139. As discussed in **11A(c)**, Tunny equipment was operated by special signals units (*Funkfernschreibtrupps*), established with a strength of 3 officers, 6 non-commissioned officers, and 31 enlisted men, 15 of whom were radioteleprinter operators.

The unit's teleprinter equipment was two teleprinters, two Tunny machines, two teleprinter line terminating sets (for converting between neutral and polar keying), one punched tape transmitter, one tape receiver, and one perforator. To convert between polar and FSK forms of signals, it had a WTK set used with transmitting and receiving, and one or two more WTK sets for receiving only. It also had a mixer (*Sammel- (misch) Gerät*) for combining the outputs of the several receiving WTK sets into the polar signal sent on to the receiving teleprinter. The transmitter was an 800-Watt 'Ehrenmal' 3- to 23-MHz transmitter (with corresponding wavelengths between 100 and 13 metres). This was evidently a Lorenz transmitter, model number Lo800FK36, originally designed in 1936 for shipboard use.[9] The transmitter was connected to a long wire antenna. There were two or three receivers, with the designation '*Funkhorchempfänger* c' or 'Fu. H. E. c', a radio intercept model,[10] each connected to a rhombic antenna of unspecified dimensions, spaced about 3 or 4 wavelengths apart. The *Merkblatt* also lists one receiver controller and a '*Mehrfach-Funk-Anlage Ausführung*', a multiplex radio implementation. These together must be the added apparatus needed for diversity reception, but the *Merkblatt* does not give details.

Additional equipment for the unit included: a transmitter truck (*Sendewagen*), operations truck (*Betriebswagen*), both mentioned in **11A(c)**, two more trucks (of 5 and 3.5 tonnes), a passenger car, a motorcycle, generator sets, and a radio direction finder trailer (*Peilanhänger*).

We redraw the diagram in the *Merkblatt* showing how the main components connect together. We have retained the abbreviations as found in the boxes and have enlarged its legend by giving the English meanings of the abbreviations. The other lettering in the diagram has been translated; the originals are listed below the legend.

Teleprinter over Shortwave (WTK)

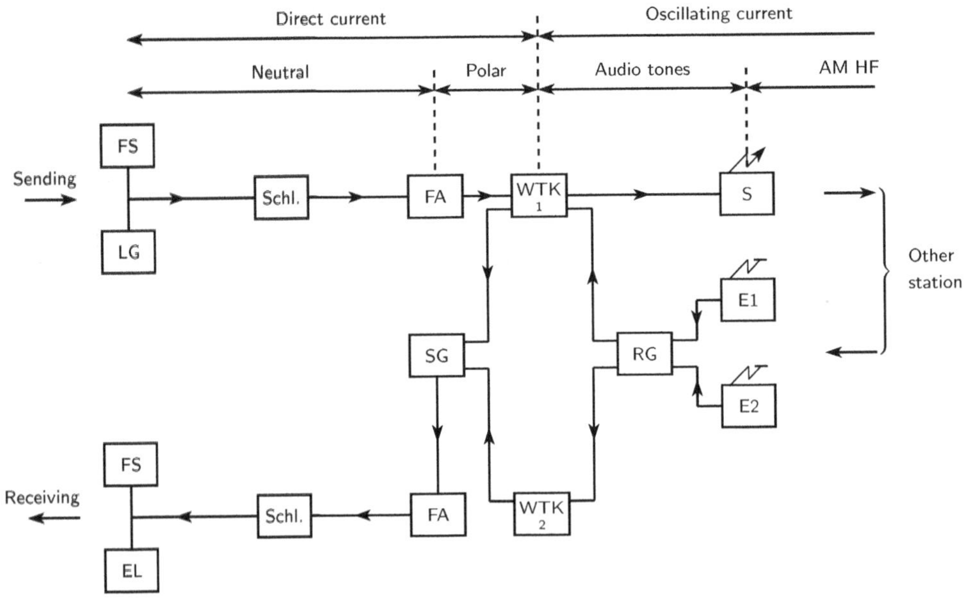

LEGEND

FS	Teleprinter	Fernschreiber
LG	Punched tape transmitter	Lochstreifengeber
Schl.	Cipher attachment	Schlüsseleinrichtung
FA	Teleprinter line termination set	Fernschreibanschlussgerät
WTK	FSK modem	Doppelton-Wechselstromtelegraphie
S	Transmitter	Sender
E	Receiver	Empfänger
RG	Diversity controller	Regelgerät
SG	Mixer	Sammelgerät
EL	Tape punch	Empfangslocher

CAPTION TRANSLATIONS

Teleprinter over Shortwave (WTK)	Fernschreiber auf Kurzwelle (WTK)
Direct current	Gleichstrom
Oscillating current	Wechselstrom
Neutral	Einfachstrom
Polar	Doppelstrom
Audio tones	Niederfrequenz (Tonfrequenz)
AM HF	mod Hochfrequenz
Sending	Geben
Receiving	Empfangen
Other station	Gegenstelle

Redrawn from *Merkblatt*

It should be no surprise that by the end of the war German practice deviated slightly from what was described by the 1942 *Merkblatt*. Thus, when a Tunny unit (Kesselring's 'fish' train) was captured by a TICOM team in May 1945, it was found that its receivers were of type 'Kurzwellenempfänger a' and its transmitter was a '1 kW Sender b'.[11] An unpublished report summarizing the state of German radio teleprinter technology up to 1944 written soon after the war, F. J. Maas, 'Der Stand der Funkfernschreibtechnik in Deutschland bis 1944', 15 Feb. 1946, supplied by Frode Weierud, describes a number of radio teleprinter equipments, with designations *Sägefisch* types I, II, III, IV, and V, WTK types I and II, and EFFK types I and II, not all of which entered service. None of them exactly matches either the description in the *Merkblatt* or what was found in the Kesselring 'train', although *Sägefisch* I comes closest to the *Merkblatt* (differing only in the power of the transmitter).[12] One suspects, however, that the German Air Force was the main consumer of most of the wartime advances in telecommunications technology, which the Army was slower to adopt, and that at the end of the war Tunny transmissions were sent much as the *Merkblatt* had described.[13]

Notes

1. (p. 495) Our general description of teleprinter telegraphy is a synthesis of information found in J. W. Freebody, *Telegraphy* (London: Pitman, 1958), E. A. Rossberg and H. E. Korta, *Teleprinter Switching* (Princeton: Van Nostrand, 1960), N. Biswas, *Principles of Telegraphy* (London: Asia Publishing, 1964), and Lothar Wiesner, *Telegraph and Data Transmission over Shortwave Radio Links* (London: Heyden & Son, 1977). Of these works, only Freebody attempts to attach dates to particular technical developments, and then only sporadically. One can reconstruct an approximate chronology for their appearance by seeing which are described in the various editions of the *Encyclopedia Britannica*; we have consulted the article on 'Telegraph' in the 1911 and 1929 editions: H. R. Kempe, 'Telegraph' in *Encyclopedia Britannica*, 11th ed. (Cambridge: Cambridge University Press, 1911) and Newcomb Carlton, 'Telegraph' in *Encyclopedia Britannica* (London, 1929). The works *A History of Engineering and Science in the Bell System, [vol. 1:] The Early Years (1875–1925)*, ed. by M. D. Fagen (New York: Bell Telephone Laboratories, 1975) and *A History of Engineering and Science in the Bell System, [vol. 7:] Transmission Technology (1925–1975)*, ed. by E. F. O'Neill (New York: AT&T Bell Telephone Laboratories, 1985) are also helpful in assigning dates to technological developments. Volume 1's chapter 7, 'Non Voice-Communications', by F. J. Singer contains a less sketchy summary of early 20th century teleprinter technology than we give in this Appendix.

Our description of German military radio teleprinter telegraphy during World War II is based primarily on a 1942 handbook of telephony and printer telegraphy for signals officers, *Merkblatt Fernsprech- und Fernschreibtechnik für den Nachrichtenoffizier*, a copy of which is in NARA HCC 15:139, supplemented by two technical appendices appearing in Karl Otto Hoffmann, *Ln–. Die Geschichte der Luftnachrichtentruppe* (Neckargemünd: Kurt Vowinckel, 1973), vol. 2, part 2, namely Appendix 2, *Erklärungen zu einigen in diesem Bande benutzten Fachausdurücken* (Explanation of some of the technical terms used in this volume) and Appendix 4, *Die gebräuchlichsten Geräte und Gerätsätze im Drahtnachrichtenwesen* (the most common wired communications devices and sets). Hoffman's Appendix 6, *Fernschreibverschlüsselung* (Teleprinter encryption) is disappointing: it gives scanty information, and only about the Siemens T52 devices, known to GCCS as 'Sturgeon'.

2. (p. 495) The literal dictionary meaning of the noun *Zeichen* is mark, and of the verb *trennen* is to separate, divide, or disconnect, so plausible meanings (plausible, that is, to a bilingual non-telegrapher) for *Zeichenstrom* and *Trennstrom* are marking current and spacing current, respectively. With regards to Morse code use, these plausible translations are in fact exactly correct, but in the case of start–stop telegraphy, are reversed. Hence, an English-speaking reader of German descriptions of teleprinter apparatus might well, unless also expert in the German technical vocabulary, confuse mark and space.

That *Zeichenstrom* in this context means spacing current, and so on, is stated in telegraphy textbooks and is implied by German language ITA-2 code charts and circuit diagrams. According, for instance, to Rossberg and Korta, *Teleprinter Switching* (see note 1 to this Appendix, above), p. 321, for start–stop telegraphy, 'The German and English terms "space" and "mark" are contradictory in their technical significance when translated literally'; similar statements are found in Fritz Schiweck, *Fernschreibtechnik* (Prien (Bavaria): C.F. Winter, 1962), pp. 13, 17. That this German terminology was also used before the war is confirmed, for instance, by a 1936 description of a Lorenz punched tape transmitter, *Beschreibung und Einstellvorschrift des Lochenstreifensenders LS 36*: 'Vor diesen fünf Segmenten liegt das Segment für den Anlaufschritt, hinter ihnen das Segment für den Sperrschritt. Wenn die Bürste über das Anlaufsegment streicht, wird ein Zeichenstomschritt [...] in die Leitung gesandt. Beim Sperrsegment dagegen wird ein Trennstromschritt angeschickt.' (Preceding these five segments is the segment for the start pulse, and following them the segment for the stop pulse. When the brush passes over the start segment a *Zeichenstrom* pulse is sent to the wire. But when passing the stop segment a *Trennstrom* pulse is sent.) An accompanying diagram shows the start pulse represented by *Zeichenstrom* and the stop pulse by *Trennstrom* (NARA HCC 15:140, p. 2 and illustration 1).

3. (p. 496) In American usage, a 'teleprinter', strictly speaking, can only be used to receive messages, but not send them. That is, it has no keyboard. A unit which can both receive and send messages is a 'teletypewriter'. In British usage, the term 'teleprinter' is used for both kinds of device. An informal American equivalent of this is 'teletype'.

4. (p. 496) Some teleprinters were 'page printers', in effect electrically operated typewriters. Others, less complex and hence cheaper and more reliable, were 'strip printers' which printed onto a strip of paper which would subsequently be pasted by hand in lines on a message form. The teleprinters involved with Tunny were of this latter sort. This gives rise to a possible terminological ambiguity, between the hole punched paper tape bearing the codes of the letters of a message, and the gummed paper tape the message might be printed on. In the *Report* the term 'tape' almost always refers to punched paper tape.

5. (p. 496) The first American voice carrier telegraphy circuits were installed between Philadelphia and New York in 1923, with twelve teleprinter channels using twelve tones with pitches 425, 595, ..., and 2295 Hz (spaced 170 Hz apart) packed into one telephone channel (Fagen, *A History of Engineering and Science in the Bell System, [vol. 1:] The Early Years (1875–1925)* (see note 1 to this Appendix, above), pp. 772–776). (At that time, a telephone channel was considered to cover the frequency range 300–3200 Hz; at the end of the 20th century, when carried over digital media, 0–4000 Hz.)

6. (p. 496) These pitch assignments are listed in the *Merkblatt* mentioned above. They agree with those given in the liaison report of M. Gaschk transcribed in our Appendix B, 'Activities at Knockholt', this volume, pp. 503–524 below, esp. p. 505, and differ from those listed in H. C. Kenworthy's *Knockholt Report* ('The Interception of German Teleprinter Communications by Foreign Office Station Knockholt', TNA HW 3/63 and TNA HW 50/79, reprinted this volume, pp. 513–524), paragraph 3.8, and in the U.S. Navy *Report on British Attack on Fish* (NARA HCC 579:1407, p. 12), to the extent that mark and space are interchanged. It is tempting to believe that the authors of both these reports (the U.S. Navy one being almost certainly by Cdr. H. Campaigne) relied on a German-language source such as the *Merkblatt* but were unaware of the correct but counter-intuitive translations for *Trennstrom* and *Zeichenstrom* as marking current and spacing current, respectively, as discussed in our endnote 2 to this Appendix, p. 499 above.

In any case, the spacing between the listed pitches is greater than commonly found in land line VFT, and especially land line AM VFT. Late 20th century practice with VFT was to space the separate pitches 60 or 120 Hz apart, instead of the 360 Hz seen here. According to O'Neill, *A History of Engineering and Science in the Bell System, [vol. 7:] Transmission Technology (1925–1975)* (see note 1 to this Appendix, above), p. 10, American practice in the 1930's was to space VFT channels 160 Hz apart. A 1942 German paper surveying telegraph technology describes systems carrying 12 or 18 telegraph channels, spaced 120 Hz apart: H. Simon, 'Bedeutung und Grundlagen der modernen Telegraphieverbindungen', *Funktechnische Monatshefte für Rundfunk / Hochfrequenztechnik und Grenzgebiete*, 5 (May 1942), pp. 61–76, URL: `http://www.cdvandt.org/FTM%201942%20H5%20telex.pdf` (visited on 07/06/2014). Hoffmann, *Ln–. Die Geschichte der Luftnachrichtentruppe* (see note 1 to this Appendix, above), vol. 2, part 2, p. 482, lists the WT 40 as usually configured to carry 5 or 12 teleprinter channels over two- or four-wire connections, instead of the three channels shown here. The relatively wide pitch spacing used by the Germans when sending VFT via high frequency radio gave a measure of protection against simultaneous loss of all pitches by frequency-dependent fading.

7. (p. 496) Paragraph 3.13 of the *Knockholt Report* cited in endnote 6 to this Appendix, p. 500 above, states that late in 1944 the Germans began using carrier shift frequency keying, with a 360 Hz shift. That is, the teleprinter signal causes the radio transmitter to switch between two unmodulated HF carrier frequencies, spaced 360 Hz apart. This is the system of radio teleprinter transmission that was common in the second half of the 20th century, under the name 'RTTY'. It is not clear if it was ever used for Tunny transmissions.

8. (p. 497) All these considerations are described in a pre-war textbook, F. E. Terman, *Radio Engineering* (New York: McGraw-Hill, 1937).

9. (p. 497) For photographs and description of the Lorenz 'Ehrenmal' transmitter, see Rolf Marschner, 'Lorenz Lo 200 L36 bis Lo 500 FK41: "Ehrenmal"-Sender', URL: `http://www.seefunknetz.de/laboe.htm` (visited on 07/06/2014). See also K. G. Beauchamp, *History of Telegraphy* (London: Institution of Electrical Engineers, 2001), p. 337. The name 'Ehrenmal', meaning war memorial, derives from the supposed likeness of the transmitter's cabinets to the Naval Memorial at Laboe in Schleswig-Holstein.

10. (p. 497) The Fu. H. E. c is apparently described in the German service regulations D 1054/1, 'Funk-Horch-Empfänger c (Fu. H. E. c) Gerätbeschreibung' of 1942 and D 1054/5, 'Merkblatt zur Bedienung des Funk-Horch-Empfängers c' of 1940, neither of which we have seen. These documents are listed on the web page 'Archiv für technische Dokumente 1900–1945', URL: `http://www.superborg.de/d1050.htm` (visited on 07/06/2014); images and circuit diagrams can be found at Helge Fyske, 'Fu.H.E.c FunkHorcEmpfänger - c / Monitoring Receiver', URL: `http://www.laud.no/ww2/fuhec/index.htm` (visited on 07/06/2014).

11. (p. 498) This 'train' was not a railway train but a convoy of six Diesel trucks, comprising the equipment of Funk-Fernschreib Trupp 19 which operated the O.B. West end of the Jellyfish link, that is, served the headquarters of Albert Kesselring (1885–1960). Its capture and subsequent transfer to the UK by A. Levenson and R. Tester, is described in TICOM IF-15, 'Final Report of TICOM Team 1', NARA RG 457, Entry P 11, Box 114, Item 10248, pp. 25, 31 and in R. D. Farley, 'Oral History Interview OH-40-80 with Arthur J. Levenson', interview transcript, 25 Nov. 1980, URL: `http://www.nsa.gov/public_info/_files/oral_history_interviews/nsa_oh_40_08_levenson.pdf` (visited on 07/06/2014), pp. 42–49; the demonstration of its equipment in the UK is described in TICOM M-5, 'Demonstration of Kesselring Fish Train', NARA RG 457, Entry P 11, Box 45, Item 6858. (In his oral history interview, held 35 years after the event, Levenson remembered the train as being von Rundstedt's communications centre, not Kesselring's.) The receiver is named on the first page of in the German inventory of the equipment

of one of the trucks: PAAA T-688, described in an affixed TICOM record entry of 26 July 1945 as '2 booklets describing equipment of mobile teleprinter van, dated 1940. Receipts for teleprinter parts, 1945. Received from Kesselring's "fish'-train" '. The transmitter is described in PAAA T-687, whose affixed TICOM description is 'Der 1 kW Sender b (1 kW S.b) [Description with diagrams of transmitter. Dated 1942. Received from Kesselring's 'fish'-train]' dated 16 July 1945. Somewhat puzzling is the fact that the receipts in PAAA T-687 are for Funk-Fernschreib Trupp 20, which at the end of the war served a different headquarters.

12. (p. 499) It is not clear if Maas is surveying all of German radio teleprinter developments, or only those associated with the Telefunken and the Siemens & Halske firms, or only those associated with the German Air Force.

13. (p. 499) This is the impression conveyed by Hoffmann, *Ln–. Die Geschichte der Luftnachrichtentruppe* (see note 1 to this Appendix, above).

Appendix B: Activities at Knockholt*

J. A. Reeds

The *General Report on Tunny* contains many references to the interception station at Knockholt and a few to its subsidiary outstations, but gives little detail of how the work at these stations was carried out.[1] Some of this missing detail is found in a series of reports, ultimately deriving from Harold Charles Kenworthy (1892–1987), the head of Government Communications Wireless Station (GCWS) Knockholt and of its attached laboratory and workshop, the Foreign Office Research and Development Establishment (FORDE). We reproduce four of these reports, with minor editing,[2] with comments in endnotes. These reports, and to some extent our commentary, use a technical language. We refer the reader to our Appendix A, 'Teleprinter signals', pp. 495–502, for a sketch of radio teleprinter technology and its vocabulary.

Three of these reports are by American liaison officers, writing in May, October, and December of 1944 to their masters in Washington after spending what must have been day-long visits to Knockholt during which they were given briefings by Kenworthy or by his staff members. The level of detail in these reports is consistent with the liaison officers having kept notebook records of what they were told. These reports must be, on the whole, accurate records of what the liaison officers were told, at least for matters they understood. For matters they were not expert in, the possibilities of mishearing or of mistranscribing what they were told cannot be ruled out.

The fourth, and much longer, report was written in March 1946 by Kenworthy himself; this is what we refer to as the *Knockholt Report*. This report seems on the whole to have been written without reference to contemporary files, although portions might have been written while referring to a personal diary. In general, the more interested Kenworthy was in a particular topic, the more detail. This report presents a different set of evidentiary problems from the three earlier reports. The author had a complete understanding of all the technicalities, but was writing ten months after the war in Europe had ended, and so might have misremembered minor details.

All four reports are mostly concerned with details of the radio equipment and radio interception operations, with the flow of slip reading and slip checking work, and to a lesser extent with problems of staffing and training. In addition, Kenworthy addresses the linked stories of the organisational history of GCWS Knockholt and of FORDE, and of the progress of technical development of non-Morse intercept capabilities before the war.

Taken together, these reports give more detail than found in chapter **33** of the *General Report on Tunny* about the activities at Knockholt.[3]

The main problems facing Knockholt were as follows.

It was harder for the British to intercept German Tunny radio signals than it was for the Germans to receive them, for several reasons. First, the British interception sites were typically at different distances from the German radio transmitter than the German radio receivers were.[4] Second, the Germans used directional antennas. They would of course direct their antennas at their intended recipient, and that direction might not point towards Knockholt. For instance, an antenna in Stalingrad or Kharkov aimed at Berlin would be also aimed at Knockholt, but one in Tunis aimed at Rome would not be.[5] Such effects tend to exacerbate the effect of distance. And finally, the German receiving end could tell the sending end when it was having trouble hearing

*The notes to this Appendix are at its end. They use the citation system used in the notes to the *Report*, explained on p. 561.

the signal and request use of a different radio frequency, which of course the British interceptor could not do.

The British interceptors, like the German recipients, used diversity-fed receivers to overcome the intermittent fading which plagues high frequency radio reception. Typically each of two radio receivers, connected to widely separated rhombic antennas, produced its own version of the signal. An automatic volume control circuit allowed the two versions to be mixed, weighting the louder (better) version more. Finally, the German system (WTK) of representing Tunny teleprinter signals by radio waves, described in Appendix A, p. 496, involved sending each transmitted symbol (mark or space, that is, cross or dot) redundantly, as a mixture of three different audio tones. This meant that loss of part of the audio band by fading was not always fatal: as long as one of its three tones was received, the sent symbol got through. These factors, to a degree, eased the interceptor's problems.

The net result was that the intercepted signal was rarely as clean as the intended recipient's version. As these reports make clear, it was typically not good enough to feed into a tape perforator, even though it was often good enough for the labour-intensive process of sight-reading the slips produced by the undulators, that is, from the inked traces of the changes in current flow corresponding to mark and space. The slip reader (typically female) wrote what she read off the slip onto the Red Form, and the Red Form was then punched onto perforated tape.

Essentially all the Tunny-breaking processes described in the *Report* are vitiated by dropped or inserted letters in the cipher text, to a much greater degree than merely mistaking the occasional letter in the cipher text. Since the processes of slip reading and tape perforating seem to have been especially prone to dropping and inserting letters, the staff at Knockholt were forced to use an elaborate quality control system of checks and rechecks, with duplication of each sensitive processing step, to deliver usable (that is, perfect) versions of the intercepted signals to the Newmanry and Testery. Training the staff to carry out these specialized processes was part of this quality control system.

Anonymous, May 1944

In his liaison report F 43 to the SSA in Arlington, Virginia, 27 May 1944, Walter J. Fried wrote: 'One of the U.S. Navy liaison officers here has recently paid a visit to Knockholt, the intercept station which covers all Fish traffic. He is a radio expert and a copy of his report, which is enclosed, may be of interest to E branch[6] although it means very little to me.' (NARA HCC 1009:3179.) We do not know who this officer was. It may have been Ens. Milton Gaschk, the author of the October 1944 report we reproduce below, or Lt. M. A. Anderson, USNR, mentioned in Gaschk's report (on p. 507), or someone else.[7]

Non-Morse Activity. Thirty type-printer radio circuits are actively covered by the British at the present time.[8] The enemy has been placing at least one new circuit of this kind in operation each month for the past year and a half. Most of the frequencies in use are in the medium high frequency range between 5 and 12 megacycles, although they are also known to operate this equipment in the ultrahigh frequency range. Most of the transmitters are said to have a carrier power of 1 kilowatt and high gain directional antennas are apparently used. The circuits are used to establish communications between Germany and the Fronts, the Balkans, Norway and France.

The transmissions are of the amplitude modulated carrier type. The carrier is modulated with three separate audio frequencies for the mark signal and three additional frequencies for the space, as follows, 540 cycles mark, 900 cycles space, 1260 cycles mark, 1620 cycles space, 1980 cycles mark, 2340 cycles space.[9] The signal produced by the above modulation is quite easy to recognize.

It is similar to the A.T.&T.[10] single side band transmission but can be distinguished from it very easily by its higher audio pitch and the fact that a strong carrier is present.

The receivers used for this intercept are National type HRO and RCA type AR 89.[11] The audio output of the receiver is fed to suitable band pass filters, amplifiers, neon bulb type limiters, a mixer, a keyer and a thirty watt direct current amplifier. The direct current amplifier supplies the necessary power to operate simultaneously an undulator tape recorder, a tape teleprinter (Creed) and a Teletype tape perforator.[12]

On very excellent signals the tape perforator can be used but the copy is always compared and corrected by the reading of the undulator tape. The teleprinter machines are used to a greater extent on good signals but this copy is also always checked by comparing with a reading of the five unit code from the ink recorder tape. The undulator tape which is recorded at a constant speed is the most used type of recording because it is considered more reliable as it shows the errors that occur. The determination of skips or misses is very important.

Some of the very skilled operators are able to read the five unit code on undulator tape at a rate of 30 w.p.m. by visual inspection. Because accuracy is so essential the tape is usually divided into the five unit groups with a pencilled mark and then read accurately at a considerable speed. Civilian girls do this work.

Five unit code with start stop is used and the speed of transmission is 66 words per minute. Creed teleprinters are modified to operate at this speed. The teleprinters are supplied with direct current motors so the speed modification is possible by adjustment of the governor. Because of the nature of the transmissions the teleprinters were modified to type-print on tape instead of the usual page printing method. This is also a convenience for a skilled operator in comparing the tape as it is received. The available undulator tape recorders are modified to operate at a fairly constant speed.

The band pass filter used for each existing audio frequency is a three section tuned circuit network, with general characteristics as follows:

1. The pass band with a flat peak 2 db for a 120 cycle band width or 60 cycles from mid frequency.[13]
2. Down at least 20 db at the adjacent channel frequency.
3. A filter loss of 2 or 3 db.

The station that is engaged in this intercept work is provided with a machine shop and a laboratory. They design, modify, and build all the necessary auxiliary equipment for this work at the station. Such work includes the complete construction of audio filter inductors (coil winding and cores) modification of teleprinter machines and the construction of amplifier and keyer units.

Gaschk, October 1944

Fried report F-105 of 25 Oct. 1944 contains another account of a visit to Knockholt by a U.S. naval officer, Ens. Milton Gaschk, dated 16 Oct. 1944 (NARA HCC 950:2821). Gaschk's cover letter to his account names Mr Mason and Mr Janes and other supervisors at Knockholt as the sources of his information.

Non-Morse operating procedure

Receiving Room The main type of intercept work confronting this activity is that of covering non-Morse point-to-point transmissions. Two stations compose a 'link' or 'network' which are independent of all other circuits. The two stations concerned on any one 'link' operate on independent frequencies — thus, one frequency carries *only one* station. To cover each station, two receivers, diversity fed, are employed.

For operating convenience, the two receiving positions, covering each end of a 'link' are adjacent. In addition to the receiving equipment, each position consists of one teleprinter and one perforator. An extra operator is required for the latter two instruments. Therefore, four persons are necessary for each 'link'.

Recording Traffic The manner in which traffic is recorded depends on existing conditions. These can be classified as follows:

1. If reception is good, with no interference, atmospherics, or fading, the teleprinter and perforator are cut in, giving three versions of the transmission:

(a) Undulator tape.
(b) Teleprinter tape.
(c) Perforated tape.

The teleprinter tape, recorded in groups of five (five letters to a group) is affixed to a W/T form.[14] All three (a, b, and c) when complete are given an identical station serial number and passed to the Slip Reading Room.

2. When slight QRM[15] or fading is present, no perforated copy is made, only the teleprint and undulator tapes are produced.

3. When conditions are such that too many corrections would be required on the teleprint tape, then only the undulator tape is recorded. These corrections will be covered later in this report.

Operating Procedure Each link has its own peculiarities. Normally, the practice is somewhat similar to C.W. interception.[16] Accurate logs must be maintained. It is in this phase where close cooperation and physical proximity between the two operators of the same 'link' is important. Messages are infrequently sent singly. The German operator when in the process of constructing the perforated tape for automatic transmission, punches three or four messages in series, and as these are sent enciphered, no breaks, separations, or space signs are apparent to the intercept man. Each message of the series carries its own internal serial number. This tape is then introduced to the transmitting head and sent complete as one transmission. In addition, each tape contains an external serial number preceded by the 'Q' signal 'QEP', which is sent '*en clair*' prior to the switching of the machine to 'cipher' position.[17]

Once the tape has started on its way through the transmitting head, with the machine set at 'cipher', there is no indication to the intercept operator on his undulator tape, of where one message ends and the next begins. Now, however, intercept man number two, straddling the German receiving station on the other frequency comes into the picture. Let us assume Berlin is transmitting two tapes, each containing three messages, to Sofia. Internal serial numbers 60, 61, 62, 63, 64, 65. External numbers, QEP 40 for the first tape, QEP 66 for the second. The Sofia operator having his machine set at the proper 'decipher' position, receives the traffic in plain language, and thus can tell where one message ends and the second begins.

At the point where number 60 is complete, Sofia transmits to Berlin (machine set at '*klar*') 'R R 60' followed by the time of receipt. Transmission from Berlin continues uninterrupted. 'R R 61' and T.O.R is given again when the tape has progressed this far. This information is logged and also passed verbally to the intercept operator on the Berlin side. All subsequent receipts on this tape are logged and these logs eventually reach the cryptanalytic section.

During the process of recording a transmission, a constant stream of chit-chat goes on between the two intercept men, and is simultaneously logged as it is read from the undulator tapes.

Before continuing, it might be explained here that the QEP number is the indicator group, and gives the set-up for the machine. Thus the multiple-message single tape (sometimes containing as many as 35000 letters) will be enciphered as if it were a single message.

As QEP 40 reaches the end of its run, two things can take place. Either QEP 40 continues until completed and QEP 66 is transmitted immediately following number 40, or else, on the completion of 40, transmission ceases, the German operator pulls back the same tape as much as 200 or 1000 letters, then transmits QEP 66 in the '*klar*' position, switches the machine to 'cipher' and proceeds through the remainder of tape 40, followed immediately by tape 66, without any further introduction to the new QEP 66 tape. This superficially sound attempt to confuse gives us part of the text of tape 40 enciphered in two positions. The real reason for this helpful cooperation on the part of the German operator is not altogether understood. It sometimes occurs when a repetition, necessitated by QRM or the dropping of a character or two, is requested. Since there is no way in which the machine can be returned to that particular position, it is easier to re-run on a new position (setting), and the setting of the succeeding tape is chosen. If the entire tape has not been recorded satisfactorily, then the re-run is made at the original setting.

The fact that the intercept operator covering Sofia can establish the approximate position on the tape where one message terminates, or the number of messages in each transmission is not of prime importance. But, the identification of the internal serial number is a major factor.

A message requiring transmission on more than one link is not 'reperfed' with a new internal serial number, but the same tape is used for the re-transmission. When introduced on another circuit, a new QEP number is given which has no relation to the previous setting. Identification however is made when the receiving operator receipts, using the procedure outlined previously.

The result is, *two encipherments of the same text on independent settings!*[18]

Note: as it takes a few minutes to re-set the deciphering position of the machine, the QEP number is followed by a 3 minute pause before the transmission resumes.

Search Group Two operators are on continuous search. No teleprinter or perforator is employed. The procedure is much the same as in C.W. search. D/F stations are available for determining locations of new stations.[19]

Antenna distribution panel This equipment is located near the supervisor's desk. Twelve receivers can be plugged to each rhombic.[20]

Slip Reading Room All material, teleprinter, perforated, and undulator tape is canalized to this section.

If receiving conditions are ideal, the chances are favourable that all three tapes, recorded simultaneously, will agree. The purpose of this section is to compare the teletype copy against the undulator tape and make corrections on the former where necessary. The undulator copy will always be the most reliable. When conditions are adverse, the undulator tape will show up bad copy in a more recognizable form than teleprinter. The experienced slip reader has a better chance of reconstructing bad characters and determining the number of missing letters from the undulator copy than would be possible through the teleprint medium.

No amount of writing can demonstrate how to correct a bad group of letters, this technique comes only through constant practice.

For accurate reading, the slip reader manufactures a pencilled gauge to conform to the particular copy at hand.

The question was brought up by Lt. M. A. Anderson, USNR, in a previous report, why a metal gauge with prearranged distances could not be constructed and permanently mounted on the 'slip table' to be used for all measuring work. This idea was mentioned to the slip supervisor, who explained that few undulator tapes are truly identical with respect to distances, but depend on character of signal being recorded plus motor speed.

When the correct gauge has been constructed, the slip is marked off in groups of ten letters. These ten letters are then checked against the W/T form — corrections or missing letters indicated (on the W/T form) where appropriate.

When no teleprint copy is available, the undulator material is transcribed by pencil on the W/T form.

To facilitate checking, if the transmission is a long one, the undulator tape is split and divided among three or four readers. Usually four W/T sheets and the equivalent amount of tape is distributed to each person.

About fifty readers constitute a watch in this room. A floor supervisor distributes work and directs operations on each watch.

The following records are kept on each tape:

Station serial number of roll.
Time of receipt from receiving room.
Name of floor supervisor
Time the roll (tape) is given to floor supervisor.
Time completed
Number of letters
Time sent to perforation room
Remarks (good, fair, poor)
Procedure

'Procedure' as used here is a criterion of acceptability in regard to length of tape to the cryptanalytical section. Each circuit (link) has a name, z.b. SQUID, TUNA[21], etc. Each name then has a procedure sign, such as A1 = 9000 letters, etc. Thus, only traffic fulfilling these requirements is acceptable to Station X.

Three samples of this check were taken at random. This shows time delay only in Slip Reading Room:

T.O.R. from Receiving Room	Time given to Floor Supervisor	Time Completed	Number of Letters
0005	0125	0950	9000
0600	0655	1733	12500
1910	0755 (next day).	1940	15400

How smoothly a message will flow through all stages of processing without interruption depends on its degree of priority. Station X decides from day to day which circuit has the highest urgency. A tape of lesser importance can easily be sidetracked for many hours if one is received later with a higher classification.

Upon completion of all checking and corrections, the undulator tape is transferred to a storeroom for filing.

The W/T form is sent to the perforating room for the final stage of processing.

Perforation Room All W/T forms and perforated tapes eventually terminate in this room.

The equipment in this section consists of:

1. Teletype perforating machines.

2. Perforator duplicators.
3. Perforator tape counting machine.
4. 2 Perf. transmitting channels to Station X.
5. Tape vulcanizing equipment.[22]

Two conditions are dealt with:

1. Quality of signal was such that perforated tape was made.
2. Signal too poor for perforation of tape.

Dealing with the first condition, a new perf. tape is made from the W/T form, this is then checked against the original tape. If disagreement arises, both tapes are checked against the W/T form, this continues until one tape agrees, which by this time will contain a few patches. From this master, or patched copy, two clean duplicates are produced. One tape becomes the station file copy and is stored in the perforating storeroom. The other, after having been count checked and transmitted, is forwarded to Station X together with its W/T counterpart via courier.

If no perforated tape accompanies the W/T form, then two tapes are punched by different typists — then compared. If no discrepancies appear it is ready for counting and transmitting.

Two multiplex channels connect this section with Station X. Each tape is sent once over each channel. Station X compares the two copies, if they agree it is assumed they have been correctly transmitted. Considerable trouble has been experienced in the transmission stage, this is thought to be due to lack of sufficient maintenance personnel. It is here that much of the time delay is caused, a common source of annoyance is the tendency to drop characters.

Letter Count Check One important factor must be brought forward at this point. The enemy uses no group or letter count in this traffic, which necessitates an above normal practice of accuracy throughout the entire processing procedure. It has happened that two typists punching tape off the same W/T form *have dropped the same line*, and on rarer instances, *the same letter*. (Typists *do not* copy simultaneously from the same W/T form.) When this happens, the two tapes will agree on checking, but of course still be wrong. To prevent this, a perf. counter is used. The W/T form has 25 letters on each line.[23] On starting the counter, the first letter on the perf. tape is checked against the first letter on the form, which must be the same. The tape is then run through the counter until the indicator shows '25', at this point the 25th position of the tape is compared with the same position on the form — this continues through each stage of 25 letters until complete.

Message Progress Sheets A progress sheet is maintained on each tape, showing the time delays through each section, from the time the tape is received until it reaches Station X. Sample form is enclosed.

Four random samples were taken to show time elapsed from T.O.R. to T.O.T. to Station X.[24]

T.O.R. in Receiving Room	T.O.T. to Station X	Number of Letters
0048/4	0925/10	3400
1617/6	0859/10	24568
1619/9	1135/10	3860
0034/10	1247/10	7200

Training An independent group carries on all training, which can be subdivided into three stages:

1. Teletype keyboard instruction for girls being trained for perforation work.
2. Undulator tape reading for both radio operators and slip readers.
3. Radio operating instruction.

The source of civilian trained typists has long been exhausted. Consequently, many of those hired now require typing instructions. Little need be said about this phase of training. The problems are much the same as teaching punch tape operators in 20-G.[25]

Teaching undulator tape reading is one of the major problems in this work. Both slip readers and radio operators must become highly proficient at this. Examples of gauges, exercises and instruction sheets are forwarded with this report.

The undulator alphabet is usually learned in three days, then three more days are allowed for practice. The instruction from here on is as follows:

1. Introduction to automatic and hand sent signals.
2. Teaching the perforator code, which is the same but read in terms of 'holes' instead of the undulator tape.
3. Familiarization with operators' remarks.
4. Attack on actual tapes, practice in correct gauging.

After one month's training, a slip reader should be able to transcribe undulator tape to a W/T form at a speed of about 30 *letters* per minute. Another month is allowed for building up speed. This takes care of the slip reader, now qualified for actual work. Girls are used exclusively for slip reading. Extended observations have proved the advisability of using the superior patience of women in this monotonous work.

The operator must now be considered. His course of instruction parallels that of the slip reader for the first month. During the second month of training, the mornings are devoted to continued slip reading. Afternoons are spent in the operating training room. Here the following subjects are covered:

1. Log keeping.
2. Recognition of tones.
3. Efficient receiver control.
4. Proficiency in translating operators remarks.
5. Q signals.
6. Learning upper and lower keyboard characters as 5-unit symbols.

After a month of half days, the operator spends another two or three full weeks in this practice. He is then used as a relief operator or on slack circuits until considered capable of holding down a regular circuit without supervision.

The speed of transmission is 66 wpm. The operator must be able to keep up with all remarks and Q signals, recording them in his log, keeping the other operator informed of conditions on his side of the 'link'. Keep his tape rolled, marking it with the correct station serial number and cutting it at the appropriate position when the transmission culminates.

Frequency shifts occur even during periods of good signals, apparently in an attempt to throw off the intercept operator. Generally when conditions deteriorate, the appropriate Q signal, requesting or directing to shift to ______ kcs., or to shift up or down followed by a number denoting the number of kcs., is given. Thus the operator must be able to scan the tape at transmission speed. Fortunately most requests for frequency shifts are sent in the *'klar'* position. Sometimes this helpful bit of information is hidden when the German operator keeps his machine in 'cipher' and the transmission ends abruptly. The operator must then decide whether this is the end of a message, or a frequency shift. Experience now helps in making the correct decision.

About 25 frequencies are available to the German operator. The intercept man must decide on which of these he is most likely to pick up the new 'link'.

The majority of the operators are former radiomen. At first it was thought that experience gained in C.W. transmissions was of little aid, until one day they [the German operators] shifted to C.W. and used international Morse. Another trick is keying the tone. The few men having no knowledge of Morse, are given an hour's introduction daily.

A few women are used on circuits, but the preference is for men. Although many reasons were given for this preference, it is not deemed necessary to go into detail on this subject.

Some HRO receivers are used, but they have been mostly replaced with the RCA-AR89. The HRO was found to be a bit too selective for this work.

On links where the quality of signal is consistently poor, the reception is augmented by the use of distant antennas. One antenna is located 500 miles to the north, the other less than 100 to the south.[26] The transmission lines have boosters every 50 miles. The three signals cannot be mixed as in diversity, but are recorded independently.

Small, December 1944

The third report, of two typewritten pages, is liaison report 'G 12', sent on 23 December 1944 by the American cryptanalyst Albert Small to Maj. Seaman of the SSA in Arlington, Virginia. (Seaman was the head of the American Tunny-breaking effort.) It, along with one copy of the instructional material referred to in paragraph 4, is contained in NARA HCC 1424:4682. The instructional material, titled 'Brief notes for instructors who are required to teach the reading of teleprinter signals from undulator tape', consists of three pages of notes covering the basics of slip reading; the last of these bears a rubber stamped date '20 March 1944'.

---

1. Knockholt is an intercept station south of London which has the specific job of intercepting Fish traffic only. The report on Knockholt made by Col. Rowlett last summer described the personnel, administration, and manner of handling traffic. This is a brief summary of the radio side.

2. Antennae are 105 feet high, mounted on masts which are formed from pairs of 50-foot masts fastened together at the bases and stood on end, then guyed from the joints to buried concrete blocks. There are in all 12 rhombic antennae, horizontal, 900 feet across the main diagonal, 600 feet across the minor.[27] The earth below is by nature clay and chalk, usually quite damp. Each rhombic has one pair of ends shorted with 750 ohms; the opposite pair of ends is connected to an 800 ohm 2-wire lead-in, which goes straight down 100 feet to ground level and feeds into the primary of a toroidal transformer. Secondary of the toroid looks into[28] either a 500 ohm 2-wire line, or a 250 ohm 4-wire line (with opposite wires connected in parallel.) Spacing of the lines is about 3 inches, and diameter of wires is of course whatever gives the required 500-ohm or 250-ohm surge impedance at the 3-inch spacing.[29] Wires of these lines do not cross over at intervals, but the line as a whole has a slow twist that accomplishes the same result. Centre taps on the windings of each toroid are connected together, and to earth, for lightning protection. Formerly lightning protection was obtained by a pair of 10,000 ohm resistors from each side of the toroid primary to ground, but resistors kept burning out from static

charges. Each 500 or 250 ohm line feeds into a transformer, the secondary of which looks into a 100-ohm concentric cable. This shielded cable leads to a set of 3 2-stage pre-amplifiers, the set putting out 1.5 – 3 mcys., 3 – 7 mcys., and 7 – 16 mcys. There is a cable for each antenna. Each amplifier has 12 outputs, so that 36 sets could actually be fed from one antenna if desired. Twenty db's[30] are gained by the amplifier, just offsetting all line losses, so the net result is as though the final receiver were connected up on the pole to the antenna. Rhombics are directed in pairs from 40° E of N through 197°. Pairs of rhombics in the same direction are placed as far apart as possible for diversity reception. The antennae are good as rhombics for equal to or greater than 4 megacycles; below 4 megs they are just antennae. Signals coming from paired rhombics to paired receivers are amplified, detected, flat topped, added together, then combined [to] operate Marconi undulators. Another method is to amplify, rectify, combine, then flat top, then operate undulators. No recording of tones as such is done. Tone frequencies used by the German teletype are 540, 900, 1260, 1620, and 1980 cycles.[31] Sound recording apparatus is used at Knockholt on occasion to record speech transmissions. Recording is done by stylus-cutting-into-film standard equipment.

3. Knockholt always has at least two receivers searching the spectrum for non-Morse transmissions. Other receivers are assigned to 'directed search' when needed to pick up known wanted transmissions; these transmissions are then turned over to 'task' receivers. All receivers are carefully calibrated and may be pre-set on frequencies desired. RCA AR-88's are used exclusively. About 25% of the receiver operators are girls.

4. About 200 persons are employed to read, check, and record undulator tapes. I am enclosing material used in a course at Knockholt to teach tape reading. This was requested by Major Seaman. The gauges he requested are just pencil marks on scrap paper, made new for each tape, or even for different positions of the same tape, since they depend upon the speed of the tape puller. Two copies of the course material are enclosed, marked Copy No. 7 and Copy No. 11, and there are two rolls of tape enclosed.

5. If our intercept people are interested in antennae layouts I can obtain a map, or will be glad to get further technical details along any lines requested. Was I correct in stating that some of our pen recorders at Vint Hill[32] operate by sound coupling rather than magnetically? Knockholt would be interested in details if so.

Kenworthy, March 1946

The March 1946 report, *The Interception of German Teleprinter Communications by Foreign Office Station, Knockholt*, is by the former head of Knockholt, H. C. Kenworthy (TNA HW 50/79 and HW 3/163). This report addresses all the issues mentioned by the American liaison officers' reports and includes accounts of the history of non-Morse interception technique, of the history of the Foreign Office non-Morse intercept organisation, of the outstations connected with Knockholt, and of the problems of staffing.

Two features stand out: First, Kenworthy is not interested in cryptography, and so rarely names the kinds of signal being transmitted by the wide variety of modulation techniques he loves to describe. In particular, he typically does not distinguish between unencrypted, Sturgeon encrypted, and Tunny encrypted teleprinter transmissions. Hence, it takes a close reading to realise that his paragraphs 1.7, 1.8, and 3.16 cannot be about Tunny signals, and it is unclear whether 3.13 is. And second, for him, history means history of the immediate organisation he is associated with. This part of his account seems to have been written entirely from memory, and such details as he gives seem to be present because they had been important in interdepartmental fights. His formal transfer from the Metroplitan Police to the Foreign Office is hardly mentioned in paragraph 2.6, possibly because his circle of co-workers did not change, but the establishment of an in-house equipment workshop in 2.10 is treated as a triumph.

THE INTERCEPTION OF GERMAN TELEPRINTER[33] COMMUNICATIONS BY FOREIGN OFFICE STATION KNOCKHOLT.

G.C. & C.S. (F.O.R.D.E.) [signed H.C. Kenworthy]
428/2378
March, 1946.

FOREWORD

The story of the Fish Campaign is complicated and covers so wide a range as to make it impossible to deal with in any other way than as follows. It has been necessary to add items which had a bearing on the policy eventually decided upon. The matter has been treated in a series of general statements and it is hoped that the whole will show the tremendous amount of detail that had to be covered in the successful completion of this complicated task.

THE INTERCEPTION OF GERMAN TELEPRINTER COMMUNICATIONS BY FOREIGN OFFICE STATION, KNOCKHOLT.

I General

1.1 The first indication that teleprinter transmissions were being used was in the latter half of 1940 when two stations using C.W. transmissions were intercepted.[34] It did not make sense and owing to a shortage of cryptographers, was put aside.
1.2 Observation was kept on these two stations but after a time they ceased operation. They had apparently been testing.
1.3 The next evidence of non-Morse was in the early part of 1941 when teleprinter and Hellschreiber[35] transmissions were intercepted.
1.4 It should be mentioned at this point that no special apparatus existed to print any of these transmissions direct. In the case of the teleprinter the signals were not good enough to operate a printer. At that time it was not realised that some of the apparent faults in printing were due to the special coding of the signals themselves. Then, when the Hellschreiber first came along, only two machines were available and these were only suitable for the normal pre-war seven and twelve line commercial transmissions. These machines would not take the new transmissions as the speed was entirely out of the speed range.
1.5 Recourse[36] was therefore made to undulator recording. This necessitated learning the 'pictures' made of the various characters and translating them into longhand.
1.6 An analysis of the Hellschreiber signals showed that special signs were being used and these were at first thought to be equivalent to 'barred' letters, similar to the practice used in Morse transmissions.[37] Six were used and consisted of a triangle, square, inverted '7', inverted '4' and two other signs. Another edition of these six extra characters appeared when the odd signs were replaced by three, four, eight, nine, oblique and plus. By comparison with some teleprinter retransmissions it was found that these six extra signs were used to represent the special functions of teleprinter transmissions, viz. carriage return, line feed, letters, space, blank and figure combinations. This valuable intercept pointed to the fact that these signs were not being used to indicate their normal functions and it was submitted that by combining the units of the

characters together a coded version of a message was obtained. The transmissions in Hellschreiber went on for several months interspersed with teleprinter transmissions.

1.7 About the middle of 1941, the Royal Air Force V.H.F. station at Capel, attached to Hawkings, Kent, began to report an unknown type of communication, apparently coming from German stations on the other side of the English Channel. These were investigated and the results showed that speech, Hellschreiber and teleprinter were at times being intercepted on decimetre wavelengths.

1.8 The transmissions were erratic. Personnel and gear were the difficulty. The operators employed on V.H.F. search were not trained in teleprinter and Hellschreiber. Temporary arrangements were made. On one occasion, a secret teleprinter message in clear was intercepted reporting the removal of a flak battery to the Eastern front. The type of transmission was in this case supersonic and it was discovered by the fact that although the undulator was recording signals, only an apparently steady tone was being transmitted.[38] Investigation proved that the transmitter was actually capable of being keyed simultaneously with tone and supersonic frequencies. It was probably a version of the DM5K apparatus.[39]

1.9 After this, it was decided that special investigations should be made into this form of communication. It was not convenient to do this at Capel but the Admiralty offered accommodation at Abbotscliffe House, a few hundred yards nearer to Dover. This was accepted and a small station was set up with special aerials. Two first class operators were loaned by Admiralty and after training at Denmark Hill took over the investigations. The Army and Air Force followed suit and loaned two operators each. No further decimetre transmissions of teleprinter were heard but some were picked up spasmodically on 40 megacycles.

1.10 This station was used to supplement Denmark Hill in the investigating of H/F non-Morse signals.[40]

1.11 The early days of non-Morse investigations were beset with many difficulties. The specialised type of transmissions meant different training; the reading of undulator slip was far more difficult and tedious than Morse, coupled with the fact that no sets could be spared without a sacrifice of other — at the time — more wanted traffic. Early in 1942 it became obvious that the Germans were carrying out numerous tests with teleprinters using different methods of keying their transmitters. These were originally classified as under:

Nomo 1. Ordinary on/off C.W.

Nomo 2. Two tone keying with steady tone superimposed.

Nomo 3. Multichannel using two, three or four channels with mark space tones. (The forerunner of the multitone keying adopted later on with WTZ units.)[41]

Nomo 4. Single channel two tone without the steady superimposed tone of nomo 2.

1.12 What little interception could be done was being carried out at Denmark Hill and development in gear, privately by Mr. Mason — a technical officer in the Receiver's Staff (Metropolitan Police).[42]

1.13 It became urgent, in February 1942, to open up a special station for this work, gather together operators and train them, also get more slip reading personnel trained to read teleprinter signals from undulator tape.

1.14 First of all arrangements were made to transmit two signals to Station X where they were printed on a slip teleprinter modified to print a character for every function. This became known as a shiftless printer and the German signs three, four, eight, nine, oblique and plus were adopted for the carriage return, line feed, letters, space, blank and figure shift combinations.

1.15 An undulator tape was taken at Denmark Hill at the same time and all slip was sent away to another centre to be read up.

1.16 It was obvious that this method was not good. Peculiarities in the transmission due to bad signals, fading, interference, etc., showed the necessity for checking with a closer liaison with the receiving station.

1.17 Authority was obtained and a search made for a suitable location. Eventually, late in May 1942, a converted farm house at Knockholt was found and requisitioned together with upwards of 30 acres of land — subsequently extended to about 160 acres in July 1942.

1.18 From this time onwards the station gradually expanded with almost continuous building programmes.

II Technical

2.1 It is necessary at this point to throw light on the set-up whereby Metropolitan Police operators and Receiver's Office technical staff and facilities were used for the Foreign Office Y organisation. The liaison started in 1926 when the Metropolitan Police commenced interception. They soon took the lead in development of high speed interception by the introduction of commercial practice.

2.2 As the Metropolitan Police wireless service gradually expanded better facilities became available for the making of experimental apparatus for Y work. Early in 1930 the Foreign Office commenced to finance the Y section. In 1932 the first non-Morse wireless circuits were discovered (Berlin–Moscow) and these were taken in conjunction with officers of the lines branch of the Central Telegraph Office. These experiments went on for ten months. Useful design work was also undertaken in relation to special Japanese cryptographic machinery. The seeds were sown and they were given the task of investigating any curious type of transmission. At one time a new form of picture transmission was introduced by the Germans — known as the Fulltograph and this required expensive machines if the pictures were to be taken. The French developed a modified version using different drum speeds. Experiments were undertaken and the undulator was used to receive the picture signals. By cutting these up into strips a passable reproduction was secured. This is only mentioned as it points to specialized work for Y service interests.

2.3 It became generally accepted by the other services that the Foreign Office Y party were best provided for investigations of strange noises.

2.4 In 1934 the Police Wireless Telegraphy Service expanded and workshops were built at West Wickham.[43] It was always difficult to get money to buy special gear for Y work and even if this was forthcoming no very suitable apparatus was available for the difficult type of search work involved. Therefore experiments in various types of gear were made in these new workshops and a few longwave sets and special recording bridges were built.[44]

2.5 The idea was to produce good square shaped signals on undulator tape making for easier reading of Morse signals and where non-Morse signals were concerned the square shaped signals helped in the accurate measurement of the lengths of the units.

2.6 This service gradually expanded and at the outbreak of war in September 1939 was well established at Denmark Hill, Camberwell, for interception, with workshop facilities at West Wickham. The Receiver's Wireless Engineer was seconded to the Foreign Office shortly after war started and the services of a very competent technical assistant were obtained to work on special Y problems.

2.7 Experimental work went on. A new type of recording bridge, a special Hellschreiber machine and amplifier, were designed and produced in small numbers. Difficulty was experienced in getting the small motors but these were eventually squeezed out of the War Services Boards

— rather reluctantly as no special provision was foreseen for Y work for components in small quantities and contracts were placed for huge numbers of mass produced lines which does not help a very specialized section.

2.8 Then the German teleprinter traffic came along and in the early part of 1942 it became evident that rapid expansion would be essential. As previously stated Knockholt was opened up. Sets were installed in the house — HRO receivers being made available by the services.[45] Eight single sets were installed. Special filters were made up at West Wickham. At various meetings plans were laid to manufacture twenty-five sets of filters, together with the new improved recording bridge. As this work progressed, much experimental work was being carried out and the detail design of the circuits of this apparatus had to be modified several times.

2.9 Unfortunately these facts began to cause friction with the Police Engineer who wanted to set up the workshop on mass production. One or two jobs had been done by the workshop for the R.A.F. and the engineer secured a contract to make automatic beacon-transmitters. From that time onwards continual trouble was experienced as to which job had the higher priority. Although our Y work was very important, no special priorities had been allocated by the production boards and that meant that materials were very difficult to get. At one time it was almost impossible to get small transformers made.

2.10 The matter was brought to a head in early 1943 when the Police engineer accepted an extension of the beacon contract and practically squeezed the Foreign Office work out. The Director of G.C. & C.S. decided that it was best to cut our losses in this direction and authority was obtained at a high level to build and equip a suitable Laboratory and Workshop at Knockholt entirely under Foreign Office control. This was completed and equipped including the provision of stores in just about three months. The value of this Establishment cannot be over estimated as added security to our investigations was possible.

III Equipment

3.1 As soon as the particular type of work at Knockholt was authorized, the allocation of the supply of receivers and undulators was handed over to the Y Committee. A certain proportion of HRO and S-27 receivers were divided among the Y stations.[46] This system did not allow of enough apparatus for the vastly expanding non-Morse commitment. Therefore our requirements were supplemented by special supplies of AR 88 receivers and USA type undulators.[47]

3.2 Diversity reception was developed. The practice in this respect was as follows: we wanted to erect the best and latest aerials, therefore all possible data was gathered together from all sources regarding aerials, aerial amplifiers, feeder lines and so on. Where improvements were possible they were made. By this method the station was very soon equipped with a number of rhombic aerials and special wide band amplifiers to cover the very wide band of frequencies used by the Germans. Aerial transformers were based on a B.B.C. design. Whilst the 200 ohm four wire transmission line was developed from U.S.A. practice. One feature of the latter introduced at Knockholt was the continual rotation of 360 degrees every 60 feet, instead of the usual transposition on widely spaced poles. Our lines were erected under tension and polystyrene spreaders were used every 10 feet. Those on the poles were approximately 2 1/2' x 2 1/2' and screwed up in place — slots 1 7/8" apart allowed the wires to be held in place. Although it was originally intended to fill the gaps by melting polystyrene it was not found to be necessary in practice. The tensioning was more than is usual with overhead wires but no trouble has been experienced in this direction. No proper tools were available for tensioning so double purchase mast tackle and bulldog clips were used for straining the wires. The feeders were made up with tensioning screws in each wire, that is, four screws to a large metal plate which in turn was tensioned by a large turnbuckle and secured to a specially built gantry to which all the feeders were brought. The rhombic aerials were fed by 600 ohm twin wire feeders and aerial transformer to the 200 ohm four wire line and at the gantry end another step down transformer was inserted to match the AS48 (100 ohm) transmission concentric cable. Rhombics between 700 and 1000 feet across the major axis were erected on semi-self supporting 105 ft. towers (wooden lattice structures) supplied by the Air Ministry.

3.3 A number of smaller rhombics were erected on 70 ft. steel sectional masts. To prevent damage by cattle, iron pickets were used instead of wood and once the main masts were set up the stay adjusters were removed and replaced by the insertion of thimbles held in a wire by bulldog clips and then shackled to the steel pegs. It was not a difficult operation to undo these when a new direction of aerial was required. The feeders for these aerials were 400 ohm two-wire lines and rotated continuously in a similar fashion to the four wire lines. Aerial matching transformers were used.

3.4 The concentric cable was taken into the building to the aerial amplifiers. The inputs of these were arranged in pairs so that although each amplifier only covered a two to one frequency range, viz: 3 – 7 megacycles and 7 – 16 megacycles, only one input was necessary. The outputs of these amplifiers were taken to distribution panels of correct impedance to match the HRO input.

3.5 Everything possible was done to screen the receivers from pick up from undulator and teleprinter motors and any other local disturbance. Each receiver was fitted with a coaxial socket and a direct concentric cable was taken to each receiver. Any aerial switching was done on the aerial switching panels. This practice was quite different from other Y stations where concentric feeders were taken to switches and the operator allowed to make his own choice. No amount of screening can make up for the single coaxial cable direct to the set. The results justified the decision to do this as no trouble has been experienced as the station gradually grew and not only teleprinters but reperforators and relays were added to each receiving position.

3.6 Before the acquisition of AR 88 receivers, two HRO's were installed in each bay. No attempt was made to couple these receivers for diversity on the HF side and it was found advantageous to keep the receivers independent to allow quick search for a change of frequency whilst retaining the previous one. It allowed cutting out a receiver temporarily if jamming appeared to be affecting one rhombic more than another.

3.7 After some months of variations in the use of tones the Germans settled down to the use of six tones for transmission — three for mark and three for space — although only five were used by us for some time.[48] We were handicapped by the lack of suitable measuring apparatus and it appeared that very little was to be gained by the use of the highest frequency due to its attenuation by the normal receiving selectivity.

3.8 The use of multi tone for mark and space gave the Germans a safety factor against selective fading — thus they used:—[49]

540	cycles	
1260	"	space
1980	"	
900	"	
1620	"	mark
2340	"	

3.9 Each receiver had its own set of filters. The outputs were rectified and the resultant DC keyed a tone-oscillator by a relay.[50] The oscillator in its turn keyed the bridge and so on to the undulator and teleprinter etc.

3.10 Each of these filters were made as three stages with AVC control — four valves in all.

3.11 Later, experiments were made on different types of filter arrangements and a unit designed for tone teleprinter only was made. In this apparatus land line practice was followed although very special design work was put into the filters so that components of wider range tolerances could be used instead of the close tolerances normally called for in V/F filters.[51]

3.12 The introduction of this filter unit combined with a special bridge was made possible when AR 88 receivers became available. These had provision for linking the sets for diversity operations although it was still possible to operate one set independently of the other for search, etc. The units were very successful and a large saving in space (one 7 ft. rack) and valves etc. was made.
3.13 A further development in teleprinter communication appeared in the latter part of 1944 when the Germans introduced carrier frequency shift keying using a 360 cycle shift on their standard transmitters.[52] The early experimental transmission had been intercepted. Work which had been done on picture reception and the technique developed in that line was adapted to the special filter design and fortunately the necessary prototype receiving equipment had been developed. Several carrier shift units were made up quickly to cover this alteration in German technique.
3.14 Whilst on the subject of variations. Any German experimental work was watched. At one time a multiplex system was tried out involving four channels and using harmonically related V/F tones but nothing came of it after several months.
3.15 On several occasions control circuits were intercepted which were known to be associated with teleprinter transmissions. It was not discovered until after the war that low power single side band transmissions (*Taube*) were being tested in parallel with a normal high power tone and frequency shift teleprinter circuit.[53] The tests were extremely successful and practically defied interception due to their rapid change of spot frequency operation.
3.16 Another type of teleprinter transmission which was used with a parallel control circuit was after the war discovered to be the 'Gleichlauf'.[54] This used synchronous transmitter and receiving apparatus and sent out a continuous stream of cypher. The messages were interspersed at intervals. Although these transmissions were intercepted no definite conclusion had arrived at although synchronism of some sort was suspected. Thus it is seen that many problems were still to be solved had the war gone on much longer.

IV Auxiliary Apparatus. Teleprinters etc

4.1 The natural aim of such a system of communication is to save time by printing messages direct instead of writing them up from Morse. Further, as the method of transmission included the cyphering of the signals, two systems were possible.
4.2 (a) The preparation of coded signal in such a form that it could be passed to a transmitting device and be received by a receiving office and thence to a decoding office.
4.3 Early German transmissions pointed to this practice. It was thought that five unit tapes were prepared by coding sections and passed to W/T offices for transmission. As evidence of this, the original types of teleprinter transmissions were often stopped and sections repeated from any requested point, showing that a prepared tape was being used. This applied to Hellschreiber transmission also as this machine was controlled by a standard five unit teleprinter tape. The teleprinter transmissions were most likely received on a reperforator whilst perforated slip was punched up from the Hellschreiber signals. These were then passed to decoding offices for them to put through their cypher machines.
4.4 (b) As the communications network grew, these methods became cumbersome, and provided special precautions were taken, it would obviously be quicker for the trained telegraphic staff to handle the original traffic. This was done and the cypher machines inserted before the W/T transmitter. Hours of time were saved as corrections could be obtained immediately and a saving of more than fifty percent of time was effected.
4.5 That is all very well when the original plain language copy is being handled but it is a different story from the interceptors angle.
4.6 Originally it was considered impracticable to run teleprinter machines or relays anywhere near receivers — in fact the Post Office made elaborate arrangements of screened rooms for

teleprinters in the Y stations. This led to the belief that all our signals would have to be transmitted by line to a distant centre for printing. The first two circuits were arranged that way and worked with moderate success whilst the Germans were using system (a) and also whilst the coding was in its elementary stages.

4.7 Additional circuits complicated matters as lines were wanted and special terminal equipment was required. Also, where one or two experienced telegraph men could watch over one circuit they were not available for more numerous circuits. Again corrections were difficult. If obvious errors occurred, undulator slip had to be referred to. Work was therefore undertaken to make it possible to install the printer alongside the receiver. The lines of communication were rapidly increasing, far quicker than the supply of machines. The bottleneck was again the services who had their war allocation and the latecomer — ourselves — could or would not be fitted into the picture. It points to the inflexibility of the war machine which could not tolerate something new and unforeseen. Fortunately the U.S.A. were approached and at a later date a supply of American teletype equipment was forthcoming.

4.8 Another problem was maintenance of teleprinters. On the outset, the few machines that were available had to be sent away for maintenance. As the number of machines were increased to include transmitters, reperforators, keyboard perforators, it was found desirable to set up a special teleprinter maintenance staff on the spot. A careful check on such things as speed variations from one German circuit to another enabled a greater output of good traffic to be produced. This came to notice when 'serviced' machines were put onto circuit and apparently found to be out of adjustment. The teleprinter maintenance section was increased and finally a full twenty-four hours service established along with the normal station maintenance.

4.9 During the long interim period of waiting for teleprinters the technique of slip reading was developed. Here again we were faced with an established practice of sending practically all Y station Morse slip to a central pool. A few of the Morse slip personnel were taught to read the teleprinter signals. The results were not entirely satisfactory as proper contact with the receiving station was difficult with the result that very often the cryptographic section were given poor copy to work on. The matter was eventually brought to a head through continual increase in traffic. Steps were undertaken to bring in directed girls to Knockholt. A local hut was rented for several months and a school set up where they were trained from scratch to read teleprinter tape by gauge. It was then possible to take further steps to secure more accurate copies and to correct what printed slip was taken.

4.10 As time went on it became evident that errors were getting by, due to failure to appreciate the extreme accuracy required if any progress was to be made by the cryptographers. The errors likely to be made in checking were due to the difficulty of correctly assessing the number of characters sent when interference spoilt the signal. Jamming caused the teleprinters to race and print extra characters whilst failure produced drop outs which were difficult to detect.

4.11 Every care had been taken to make the undulators give a close approximation to a steady speed and thus it was possible to gauge the tape. The human element came into the picture as even the best were not infallible. Moreover, new methods were being developed at Station X which called for a hitherto unknown degree of accuracy in interception, primarily for the number of characters. An error of one character in several thousand was enough to cause trouble in the methods being adopted.

4.12 A system was introduced to overcome this on the principle that two separate people would hardly be likely to make the same mistake. All tape was therefore measured by two girls before being read up and this made a definite step towards accuracy. The system was not liked but it was persisted in. Very little encouragement could be given to the staff as strict secrecy was kept as to any reason for wanting double checking. The process slowed down the work considerably. It did bring out the fact that printer copies were not always an advantage, particularly if circuits were suffering from interference or poor conditions.

4.13 The next stage came when a new technique, using perforated slip, was developed at Station X. At first they were faced with the problem of preparing tapes from the corrected W/T Red forms. Reperforators were added to the receiving positions so that a perforated slip was obtained as well as the undulator and teleprinter copies. Another system of checking developed from this, as it was necessary to correct the perforated slips from the corrected slip copy. It was undertaken to prepare perforated slips on keyboard perforators from the written up copies. To guard against errors, two girls perforated a message independently. The two tapes were laid against one another and it was easy to see if they differed. From these two tapes a patched master copy was obtained and this was put through a transmitter coupled to a local reperforator thus making a copy without any patches. This copy was checked against the patched master and was finally dispatched to Station X with the written up forms.
4.14 The next step developed from this was the transmission by land line to Station X. Here again precautions were taken to prevent errors occurring by using two transmitters. The perforated slip was fed into the first transmitter and then into the next one giving an interval of twelve to eighteen inches of tape — Any fault in the V/F gear or on the line or in the apparatus at either end was capable of being detected within a few seconds.[55] At Station X the perforated slips were laid up against one another for checking.
4.15 At a later stage a further guard against missing characters was introduced by using automatic counting machines. Each sheet of written or printed form contained approximately 500 characters. These were counted and the number set up on the machine counter. The perforated tape was then run through until that number showed up when the character at that point was checked with the form. A block diagram of these operations is shown at sketch 'A'.

V Outstations

5.1 In July 1943, it became necessary to consider the expansion of the Foreign Office Y Service, for Japanese and German cover. An ex R.A.F. site was made available and tests were carried out towards the end of the month. Negotiations were then commenced which ended in the Foreign Office being made responsible for equipping and maintenance of the new station at Wincombe (Shaftsbury) Dorset. Before final approval was given, similar tests were carried out at Brora[56] but our observations were in favour of Wincombe.
5.2 Observations were also noted relating to German non-Morse traffic and these stood us in good stead a month or so later when it became evident that all German traffic could not be entirely received at Knockholt throughout the twenty-four hours. Gear was specially made up and taken to Wincombe where control and not circuit lines were connected through to Knockholt.
5.3 We occupied ex R.A.F. huts and continued to do so until the main building was completed in the early part of 1944 when a special section was taken over and better gear installed together with a four channel V/F to Knockholt.
5.4 That was the first outstation. Undulators were used at Knockholt and the circuit was usually run there as well. Both tapes were read up together with very good results.
5.5 In April 1944, more reception difficulties were being experienced — this time with the German station in Paris. It was necessary to get as far north as possible to open up temporarily at either Kedleston[57] or Forest Moor[58] (both Army stations) or failing them, Hawklaw[59] or Brora. Some gear was got together and tests were carried out at Kedleston on Wednesday, 26th April. Results were poor. Forest Moor was next visited and tests carried out until Saturday, 29th. Again results did not warrant choosing that site. Hawklaw was next tried — special facilities were arranged here and tests were conducted from the 30th April until the 2nd May. It was very nearly certain that Hawklaw would be the place but to make sure we proceeded to Brora on the 3rd. Two days at Brora convinced the party that the gear and conditions there were not as good as at Hawklaw. Difficulties would have been severe with land lines. Therefore they returned

to Hawklaw on May 6th. Arrangements were made to suspend some of the normal teleprinter communications and some V/F channels were rerouted to Knockholt. Apparatus was set up on the 7th May and Knockholt sent up operators to man the gear. After a lot of work both at Hawklaw and at Knockholt the circuits were working smoothly and well by Tuesday 9th. Full twenty-four hour cover commenced on the 10th.

5.6 This was a temporary arrangement and in a week it was approved that an obsolescent D/F hut in the vicinity at Kingask[60] should be taken over, additional land requisitioned for the erection of rhombic aerials for diversity reception. It was agreed to make this an outstation of four bays of receivers. Apparatus was gathered together and a party again went to Scotland on May 26th. The station was equipped and masts and aerials erected — 2 rhombics on Paris. A new type of aerial was used as well viz., the sloping 'V'. In order to facilitate the full opening of the station it was necessary for a six line V/F system to be made at Knockholt. This was installed by June 18th. The temporary service at Hawklaw was closed down on Wednesday, 21st June, when full service commenced at Kingask. The party returned to Knockholt on June 23rd.

5.7 Later in the year — October — it became necessary to swing the aerials directed on Paris round towards Germany. A long Beverage[61] was erected. Very good results were obtained from this station right up to the end of the war.

5.8 The third outstation was at Kedleston (Army). After prolonged tests with Army personnel, with Kedleston as a self contained unit, it was finally decided that the A.T.S. personnel who had been trained at Knockholt should be drafted to Knockholt, leaving a nucleus to man sets at Kedleston. V/F apparatus was installed and the signals received at Kedleston were read at Knockholt with the other two outstations.

5.9 The next occasion when an outstation was considered necessary was in December 1944. By this time the Germans were being pushed back towards Germany and their communication lines were getting shorter. Arrangements were made with 21st Army Group and a party went out to Brussels in January to test for a site. Tests were made at a Signal Centre in Genval near Brussels from the 14th to the 23rd. Then the party went further south to Verdun (12th Army Group). A few days there proved that Brussels was the better site.

5.10 Room was made available at Genval and special aerials were erected. Four sets of gear were installed and V/F channels connected through to Knockholt.[62] Incidentally this was the only station connected with Knockholt which received any damage from enemy action. A V-1 dropped very close to the building rendering it unserviceable. Very little damage was done to the gear and it was then installed in the W/T vans which were part of the special 'G' type W/T section operating the equipment.[63]

5.11 The Brussels station moved up later in the year in accordance with 21st Army Group advancement.

VI Direction Finding

6.1 Direction finding was a very important factor as each enemy station had identical transmitters and used many frequencies. They were allowed very elastic use of allotted frequencies and changed the frequency up and down to clear jamming. Although call signs were made, these were not self evident unless taken on the undulator or printer. Recourse had to be made to the D/F net work for information.[64] The D/F operators did not find it an easy job, particularly when numerous stations were changing frequency at the same time. Signals were sent to line, via a signal level indicator, over a direct telephone line to the D/F centre. In the latter half of 1944 a DFG 24[65] was erected at Knockholt and this, being manned by operators familiar with the signals, relieved the pressure on the main D/F network. A single line bearing was very often sufficient to locate a wanted station. The importance of D/F in regard to non-Morse interception cannot be too strongly emphasised.

VII Staff at Knockholt

7.1 Continual difficulties were experienced throughout the war to get enough personnel for all the varied branches. There were never enough operators to take every circuit on the air and it was fortunate that at later periods Station X were able to discriminate and know that certain lines were not required. Even then the entire slip was never read up but this again was covered to a point by the fact that insufficient staff were available to cope with the 'workable' material at Station X. It was therefore possible to concentrate on certain particular lines and special requests from time to time as research advanced. The staff figures for each year were as follows:—

June 1942	6.
June 1943	120.
June 1944	600.
May 1945	685 + 84 A.T.S. + 46 F.O.R.D.E.
	815 in all.

7.2 Billeting has always been difficult. Transport another big problem. It was only after very long negotiations that the Ministry of Health allocated certain areas in and around Knockholt up to a radius of ten miles. Neither the Railway or the Town and Country bus services fitted in for watch keeping. Finally, after the Public Transport had met us as much as possible it became necessary to supplement by our own coach and utility van services. Billeting was latterly helped by two hostels, one at Halstead and one at Sevenoaks. Feeding was difficult and in February 1944 a canteen was erected by the Ministry of Works to serve both Ministry of Supply people and ourselves.

VIII Special Training

8.1 From time to time serving personnel were drafted to Knockholt for special training in non-Morse. One of the most successful parties was No. 1 G. Type Section which went out to North Africa, Sicily and Italy. They successfully located some decimetre links, V.H.F., and for a very short period, a German Baudot link between Corsica and the South of France.[66] This on forty megacycles was interesting. No 1 G. Type Section intercepted the French end — beamed to Corsica — in North Africa, while Knockholt intercepted the Corsican end. This link did not last very long. Later, this same unit was set up near Ancona and intercepted decimetre traffic passing over the W/T section of landline carrier frequency circuit between Berlin, Pola and Greece.[67] At the outset this party was handicapped by the refusal of the Italian Headquarters to allow them anywhere near the fighting line but these troubles were overcome when the situation and technical aspects of decimetre work were explained. In this connection it might be interesting to note that decimetre aerial gear captured in Tunisia and sent to Knockholt was repaired and sent out to the No. 1 G. Type Section for use and proved to be a very valuable asset.

8.2 Another G. Type Section was trained and sent out to India. They had greater difficulties to overcome and the results were not too good. The party went to Australia for a time but distance made the proper analysis and co-ordination of results practically impossible.

8.3 Other War Office personnel were trained. Instrument mechanics for servicing gear and A.T.S. for operating and slip reading. It was always felt that there should be a second place fitted up with gear to cover any possible damage to Knockholt. The site chosen was Kedleston and later Forest Moor but as mentioned earlier in this history it was eventually found better to absorb the personnel at Knockholt, leaving Kedleston to operate as an outstation.

SKETCH 'A'
Diagram of Operations

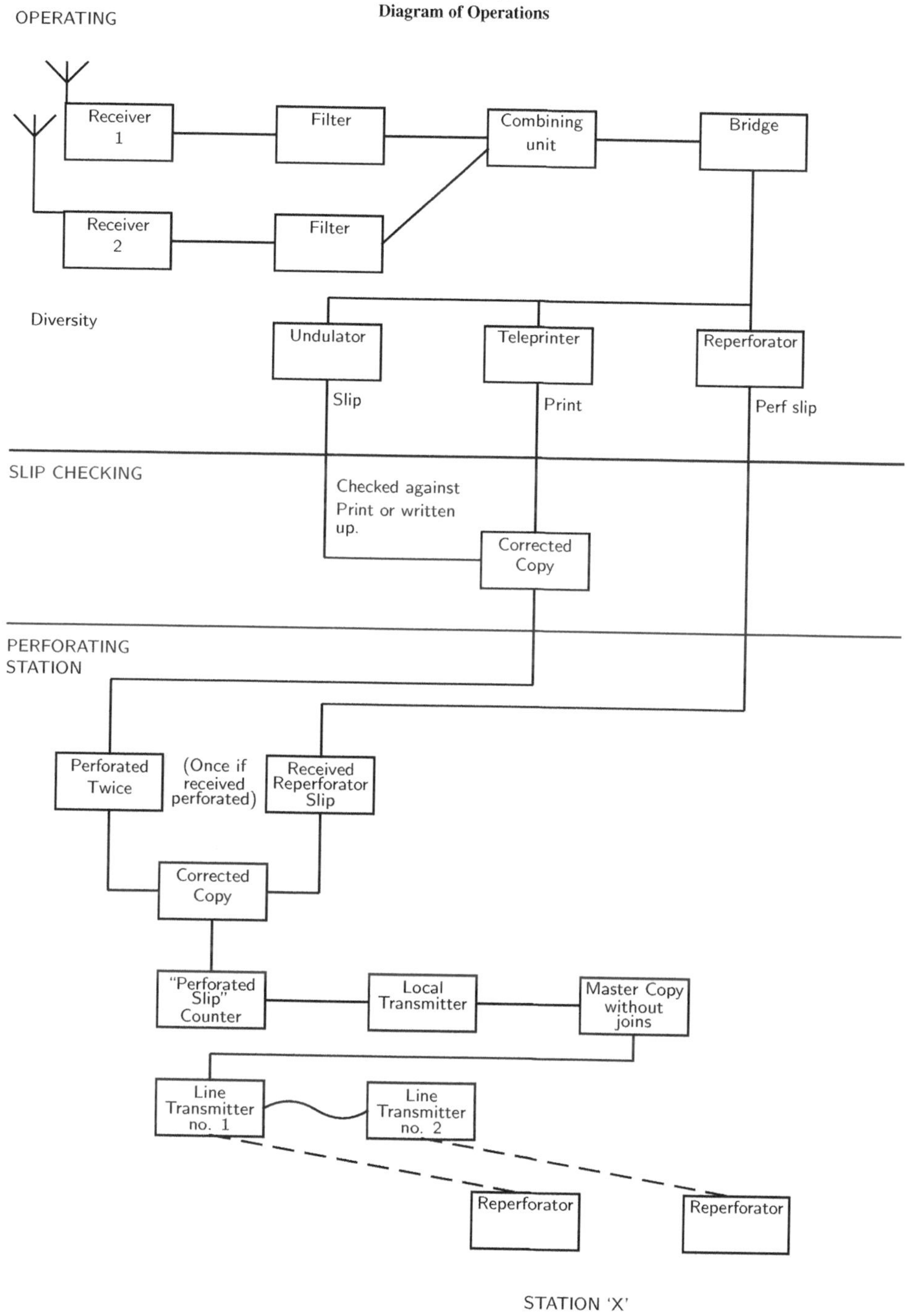

Sketch A redrawn from *Knockholt Report*

IX Additional Commitments

9.1 On several occasions it was possible to undertake special research work and supply of special equipment for other branches directly connected with Headquarters.
9.2 Examples of help given to the Royal Navy and Air Force in the examination of curious types of transmissions may be mentioned. Some analysis of 'Squash' (*Kurier*) helped considerably in this type of pulse transmission.[68]
9.3 Later, assistance was given to 192 Squadron of the Royal Air Force in regard to '*Bernhardine*' where knowledge of Hellschreiber signals pointed the way to the solution.[69] Some special filter gear was made up quickly to help the squadron in their work.

Summary

From the foregoing it can be said that the difficulties encountered were due to the unforeseen and entirely unpredictable rapid increase of teleprinter transmissions. The supply of personnel and apparatus was extremely difficult and although in some respects barriers were broken down quickly, in others there were continual hold ups in manpower — on the operating side particularly.

The outstanding achievement was the set up of the Laboratory and Workshop under direct G.C. & C.S. control which enabled work to be carried out quickly and with utmost security.

Notes

1. (p. 503) Knockholt was the main Tunny interception site, but not the only one. As far as we know the following sites were engaged in Tunny intercept operations, with approximate dates of Tunny work:

- St. Albans, a long-established Post Office site, from mid 1941 into 1942
- Denmark Hill, Camberwell, a long-established Metropolitan Police intercept site, from mid 1941 into 1942
- Knockholt, Kent, from mid-1942
- Wincombe, near Shaftsbury, Dorset, from late summer 1943
- Hawklaw, near Cupar, Fife, May–June 1944
- Kingask, near Cupar, Fife, from June 1944
- Kedleston Hall, Derbyshire, an Army site, from late 1944
- Genval, near Brussels, from January 1945

2. (p. 503) We silently regularize spelling, capitalisation, and punctuation, and note changes of diction.

3. (p. 503) We do not attempt to give a complete account of teleprinter intercept operations during the war, nor of the first discovery of transmitted Tunny signals, nor of the tense relations between Bletchley Park, Knockholt, and the rival intercept site at St. Albans run by the Post Office. Such an account would fill a book. Chapter 8, 'Knockholt', in Paul Gannon, *Colossus:*

Bletchley Park's Greatest Secret (London: Atlantic Books, 2006), pp. 124–133, gives a sketch of the intertwined main issues, concerning changes in technical requirements, organisational rivalries, equipment and staffing shortages, and the clash of personalities. Essentially every mention of Knockholt in the *Report* is a complaint that either it did not send enough intercept or that it did not send good enough intercept, the exceptions being statements to the effect that Knockholt did better once they had been supplied with hand counters. This opinion was not confined to the Newmanry. In its entry for January 1944 the 'History of the Fish Section' (that is, of the Testery, TNA HW 50/63, p. 4) complains: 'Mistakes in slip-reading or imperfect interception at Knockholt on autoclave links had two important results: first, mistakes in continuity prevented the recovery of wheel patterns and made decoding difficult, second, mistakes in individual letters could slow up the decoding process considerably.' According to the entry for July 1944 (p. 10), 'The staff at Knockholt proved quite inadequate for dealing with the changing requirements, traffic ready for perforation could not all be handled and some traffic could not even be checked. Hence a system of priority had to be enforced rigidly to ensure that we at least had material for links of high intelligence value.'

4. (p. 503) Since high frequency radio signals bounce off of the ionosphere the effect of distance on reception quality is not straightforward. It is commonplace to hear of examples of a more distant HF transmission being heard much more clearly than a nearer one, even when the transmitters have equal power.

5. (p. 503) For this reason a number of outstations were established, better situated for intercepting certain Tunny links.

6. (p. 504) E Branch was the communications branch of SSA.

7. (p. 504) According to personal communications from Frode Weierud and Ralph Erskine to JAR, April 2014, based on a list contained in NARA HCC 808:2336, the following U.S. Navy liaison officers were present at GCCS in April or May 1944: Anderson, Eachus, Gaschk, Hall, and Ladouceur. Anderson and Gaschk are as above, Eachus is Joseph Eachus (1911–2003) and Hall is Marshall Hall Jr. (1910–1990), later an eminent mathematician. We do not know who Ladouceur was. According to one of his students, Hall was unlikely to have known much about radios. (Personal communication from A. R. Calderbank, 1 May 2014.)

8. (p. 504) 'Type-printer radio circuits' is presumaby means 'teleprinter radio circuits' or 'Teletype radio circuits', which (in American English) are synonymous.

9. (p. 504) See our Appendix A, 'Transmission of Teleprinter Signals', this volume, pp. 495–502, above, esp. p. 496.

10. (p. 505) This probably refers to the high frequency single side band transmitter described in *A History of Engineering and Science in the Bell System, [vol. 7:] Transmission Technology (1925–1975)*, ed. by E. F. O'Neill (New York: AT&T Bell Telephone Laboratories, 1985), p. 35: 'In 1935, designs went forward for commercial single-sideband operation... Later, in the 1940's, large numbers were manufactured by Western Electric [the manufacturing arm of A.T.&T.] and sold to foreign customers of AT&T, government departments, and others. This set a standard for excellence, with performance far better than any previous HF radio equipment. This promoted the world-wide shift from double-sideband to single-sideband operation.'

11. (p. 505) The HRO, manufactured in vast quantities and widely used as an intercept receiver, was built by the National Radio Company, in Massachusetts. AR 89 is evidently a mistake for AR 88 or for DR 89. According to Kenworthy's report, reprinted here, pp. 513–524, paragraphs 3.1

and 3.6, AR 88 is correct. The AR 88, built by the Radio Corporation of America, was widely used for intercept operations during the latter half of the war. According to *War Department Technical Manual TM 11-889, Diversity Receiving Equipment (RCA Model DR-89)* (Washington, D.C.: USGPO, 1945), the DR 89 consisted of three AR 88F receivers, a tone keyer, and a monitoring unit, mounted on a 7 foot rack. Each of the AR 88F's was a 12-tube (or 14-tube, depending on how you count) superheterodyne receiver, covering the frequency range 540 kHz to 32 MHz. The DR 89 automatically selects the strongest of the three AR 88F signals and suppresses the others; this selection can change in a fraction of a second.

This fits Kenworthy's description of Knockholt's use of the AR 88s: '... these had provision for linking the sets for diversity operation although it was still possible to operate one set independently of the other for search, etc. The units were very successful and a large saving in space (one 7 ft. rack) and valves etc. was made' (TNA HW 50/79 and HW 3/163, reprinted in this volume, pp. 513–524, paragraph 3.12).

So AR 89 might be a simple mistake for either AR 88 or DR 89, although it might be possible that RCA AR 89 was the proper designation for an earlier development of what became the DR 89. (If 'AR 89' is a mistake for either AR 88 or DR 89, it might have been one committed by the staff at Knockholt, as 'AR 89' also occurs in the Gaschk report of October 1944 below.)

12. (p. 505) Creed was the main British manufacturer of teleprinter equipment, Teletype the main American one. Elsewhere in these reports the term 'Teletype' is — as is common in American English — used ambiguously, both as a particular brand of teleprinter and as a generic term for teleprinter.

13. (p. 505) Here 'db' stands for the electrical engineer's 'decibel', not the *Report*'s 'deciban'.

14. (p. 506) 'W/T form' = Red Form.

15. (p. 506) QRM = radio interference. QRM is the international Q-code for 'I am being interfered with'.

16. (p. 506) C.W. = 'continuous wave'; in this context, ordinary Morse.

17. (p. 506) *en clair* = in the clear, unencrypted.

18. (p. 507) This is the process described in **12E(b)**, of identifying retransmissions.

19. (p. 507) D/F = direction finding.

20. (p. 507) 'Rhombic' = rhombic antenna.

21. (p. 508) 'z.b.' = '*zum Beispiel*' = e.g.; 'TUNA' = TUNNY.

22. (p. 509) We do not know what this vulcanizing equipment was for, but we are grateful to Jim Haynes for a very plausible suggestion: Teleprinter tape was often made of oiled paper, to help keep the punch machinery lubricated. If a tape broke it would be need to be mended with an adhesive that would stick to oiled paper, which in practice meant a heat treatment. (Personal communication, 1 Nov. 2008.)

23. (p. 509) The W/T form illustrated in fig. **28 (VI)** show 20 letters per line: four groups of five letters each.

24. (p. 509) The times of receipt and of transmission in this table are given in 'time/date' format. Thus, the message of 3400 letters took about six days to reach Bletchley Park after interception at Knockholt.

25. (p. 510) '20-G' = OP-20-G, the U.S. Navy SIGINT organisation.

26. (p. 511) According to the 1945 U.S. Navy *Report on British Attack on 'FISH'*, NARA HCC 579:1407, p. 17, the subsidiary Fish interception stations were near Cupar (but it spells it Coupar) in Fife, Scotland and at Shaftesbury in Dorset, England. The former is about 400 miles (about 600 km) north of Knockholt, the latter about 90 miles (about 140 km) west of Knockholt. Knockholt itself is in Kent, just south of London.

27. (p. 511) The antennas were about 32 metres high, the mast sections about 15 metres apiece. The rhombic antennas were about 275 metres across the main diagonal, 180 metres across the minor.

28. (p. 511) 'Looks into': electrical engineer's jargon for 'is connected to, possibly with an impedance mismatch'.

29. (p. 511) The spacing was about 75 millimetres.

30. (p. 512) See endnote 13 to this Appendix, p. 526 above.

31. (p. 512) Small here omits the 2340-Hz tone mentioned by the May visitor to Knockholt, whose report appears on p. 504. See our Appendix A, 'Transmission of Teleprinter Signals', this volume, pp. 495–502 above, esp. p. 496. The explanation is in paragraph 3.7 of the *Knockholt Report*, and repeated in Albert W. Small, 'Small Report G-34', 10 Feb. 1945, FOIA release of liaison report, NSA DOCID: 3524356, p. 2: '. . . in the early days of interception, only five tones were selected for recording; all six are now used [at Knockholt] however and I am glad to be able to correct my earlier report'.

32. (p. 512) Vint Hill, Virginia, was an SSA intercept station.

33. (p. 513) Spelling, capitalisation, and punctuation are silently regularized. Major diction errors are corrected and noted. Kenworthy frequently capitalises 'teleprinter' and consistently writes 'morse' for 'Morse'. Kenworthy consistently uses single quotes around the X in Station 'X' and double quotes around the Y in "Y" work; we have eliminated both.

34. (p. 513) C.W. = continuous wave. The transmitter emits a continuous signal at its carrier frequency; information is conveyed by switching this signal on and off. This was the usual means of transmitting Morse code, but in this instance was being used to transmit something else.

35. (p. 513) See endnote 32 to **11E**, p. 571.

36. (p. 513) 'Resource was. . . '.

37. (p. 513) Morse code operators use, in addition to the codes for the 26 letters and 10 digits, a number of dot and dash sequences representing punctuation marks, accented letters, and 'prosigns' or procedural signals. The latter do not code for text but are rather used to control the flow of a message while sending, by indicating, for example, that the preceding character should be discarded. These extra-alphabetic codes are written down by putting a bar over alphabetic sequences, the concatenation of whose dot-dash patterns equals the received sequence. The German Navy used a number of such for some Greek letters: alpha, beta, and so on.

38. (p. 514) That is, the carrier was modulated by a tone outside the audible frequency range.

39. (p. 514) Probably DMG 5K, *Dezimeter-Gerät 5K*, a German military transmitter/receiver set used for line-of-sight communications in the 500–550 MHz. band, capable of carrying voice or multiplexed ASFK teleprinter traffic.

40. (p. 514) '... investigating of H/F non-Morse investigations.'

41. (p. 514) WTZ = *Wechselstrom-Telegrafie-Zweitongerät*, two-tone AFSK set.

42. (p. 514) Here, and below, 'Receiver's' refers not to wireless receivers but to the office of the 'Receiver of the Metropolitan Police District', its chief financial officer.

43. (p. 515) In South East London.

44. (p. 515) 'Bridge' is a somewhat vague term, similar to early 21st-century 'adaptor' or 'interface'. Its input would have been a voltage output by (presumably) the rectified filtered output of the receiver, and its output would have been whatever it took to drive the undulator pen.

45. (p. 516) HRO receivers made by the National Radio Company.

46. (p. 516) Hallicrafters S-27 VHF receivers, tuning from 27–145 MHz.

47. (p. 516) It is not clear from this if Knockolt used the three receiver types HRO, S-27, and AR 88 in Tunny operations, or only just the two types HRO and AR 88, as implied by 3.6 below and by Small's December 1944 report.

48. (p. 517) This explains why Small's December 1944 report lists only five tones at the end of his paragraph 4, discussed in our endnote 31 to Small Report, §4, p. 527 above.

49. (p. 517) We believe Kenworthy has space and mark interchanged here. See endnote 6 to Appendix A, p. 500 above.

50. (p. 517) 'a note-oscillator...'.

51. (p. 517) V/F = 'voice frequency', meaning AFSK, the means used by the Germans to send teleprinter signals by radio, as described in our Appendix A, 'Transmission of Teleprinter Signals', this volume, pp. 495–502.

52. (p. 518) Carrier FSK is an alternative to WTK or VFT as described in endnote 7 to Appendix A, p. 501. It is not clear if it was ever used for Tunny transmissions.

53. (p. 518) *Taube* was a high-speed burst transmitter, meant for use by clandestine agents. See United States Army Security Agency, *European Axis Signal Intelligence in World War II as Revealed by 'TICOM' Investigations and by other Prisoner of War Interrogations and Captured Material, Principally German*, FOIA release of 9-volume typescript report (Washington, D.C., 1946), URL: `http://www.nsa.gov/public_info/declass/european_axis_sigint.shtml` (visited on 07/06/2014), vol. 8, p. 41.

54. (p. 518) This is the system of synchronous teleprinter transmission mentioned in our endnote 19 to chap. **11**, p. 567, in connection with the SZ 42 C; see also NARA RG 457, Entry P 11, Box 46, Item 6897, and United States Army Security Agency, *European Axis SIGINT* (see note 53 to this Appendix, above), vol. 8, p. 42.

55. (p. 520) Here V/F means the AFSK used for sending the teleprinter signal from the Knockholt to Bletchley Park, over a land line. Subsequently it means this, or the means for transmitting an undulator trace from outstations to Knockholt, again over land lines.

56. (p. 520) Brora, in the east of Sutherland.

57. (p. 520) Kedleston Hall in Derbyshire.

58. (p. 520) Forest Moor in Harrogate in North Yorkshire; now a Navy intercept site: HMS Forest Moor.

59. (p. 520) Hawklaw, north of Cupar in Fife.

60. (p. 521) Kingask, north of Cupar in Fife.

61. (p. 521) 'Beveridge' in text is a mistake. This kind of antenna (a doubled long wire one or two wavelengths long, fed at the fold) was invented in 1919 by Harold H. Beverage (1893–1993).

62. (p. 521) 'Four sets of double-diversity AR 88 RCA receivers will drive Marconi UG6A undulators. Inverted V antennae are to be used initially... The undulator signal will be re-transmitted to Knockholt over voice frequncy channels, by means of automatic keying units. Thus Knockholt will have a replica of the tape recorded at Brussels. Slip reading of the tape and its conversion to perforated form will be done at Knockholt.' (Small, 'Small Report G-34' (see note 31 to this Appendix, above), p. 1.)

63. (p. 521) This happened on 24 March 1945. The flying bomb landed about 50 yards (or 45 metres) from the operations building, ruining two of the four sets and hospitalizing four operators. (TNA HW 3/92, p. 261.)

64. (p. 521) 'Resource had to... '.

65. (p. 521) A Marconi HF DF set.

66. (p. 522) This was apparently not a Tunny link.

67. (p. 522) Pola, on the eastern Adriatic coast, now Pula in Croatia, was part of Italy in 1943. It was the site of a German U-boat base.

68. (p. 524) *Kurier* was a burst transmission system for U-boats. See Arthur O. Bauer, Ralph Erskine and Klaus Herold, *Funkpeilung als alliierte Waffe gegen deutsche U-Boote 1939–1945: Wie Schwächen und Versäumnisse bei der Funkführung der U-Boote zum Ausgang der 'Schlacht im Atlantik' beigetragen haben* (Rheinberg: Liebig Funk, 1997), pp. 206–227, and Ralph Erskine, 'Kriegsmarine Short Signals Systems — and How Bletchley Park Exploited Them', *Cryptologia*, 23.1 (1999), pp. 65–92, esp. pp. 89–92.

69. (p. 524) This refers to a German fighter ground control system developed late in the war; see Alfred Price, *Instruments of Darkness* (London: William Kimber, 1967), pp. 236–237.

Appendix C: The 5202 Machine*

J. A. Reeds

The 5202 machine,[1] built by the Eastman photographic company of Rochester, New York, was in its time the most advanced example of the series of photographic film-based cryptanalytic machines built for the U.S. Army's SSA and its Navy counterpart, OP-20-G. The use of such film and photocell-based machinery for cryptanalysis had been suggested in 1935 to OP-20-G by Vannevar Bush.[2] But Bush's suggestion underwent a tortuous course of development before becoming useful in practice, as is well described in Colin Burke, *Information and Secrecy: Vannevar Bush, Ultra, and the Other Memex* (Metutchen, New Jersey: Scarecrow, 1994) and in a redacted version of a classified study, Colin Burke, *It Wasn't All Magic: The Early Struggle to Automate Cryptanalysis, 1930s – 1960s* (Ft. Meade, Maryland: National Security Agency, 2002), URL: `http://www.nsa.gov/public_info/_files/cryptologic_histories/magic.pdf` (visited on 07/06/2014), FOIA release of Center for Cryptologic History study CCH-E05-02-01, NSA DOCID: 4057009.

Bush's original interest was to film digital tracks of data (with opaque and transparent dots) on the same film as conventional microfilmed images of documents. The film would be scanned by a 'Selector' which, when the data in the digital tracks (read by photocells) matched a pre-programmed pattern, stopped the film, and printed a copy of the image.

This plan was replaced by one for a 'Comparator', in which the photocells saw light passing through two superimposed films and where digital logic counted, for each relative offset of the two films against each other, the number of matching places on the films. (These films had no images, just tracks of digital data.) Such a machine would be, in effect, a kind of Robinson using photographic film instead of paper tape. Since the photocells only saw light which passed through both films, a special coding had to be used. If the goal was to count the number of agreements between two bit streams at various offsets, each bit could be coded by two dots: the bit value 0 represented, say, by the pair (transparent, opaque) and the bit value 1 represented by (opaque, transparent). Superposition of 0 with 0 gives (transparent, opaque), of 1 with 1 gives (opaque, transparent), but of 0 with 1 or of 1 with 0 gives (opaque, opaque). Thus, the photocell sees light precisely if the two bits agree. An elaboration of this scheme was used in the 5202.

In a further modification the digital counter was abandoned. Instead of looking at each place on the superimposed films in turn, a photomultiplier saw the total amount of light passing though a stretch of several centimetres of superimposed film, simultaneously. By measuring the intensity of light the photocell could — in effect, although with some measurement error — count the number of spots passing light. One film moved to produce a new alignment relative to the other, stationary film. This arrangement is inherently faster than the previous one. A Robinson comparing two tapes of length 999 and 1000 characters, say, had to make 1000 revolutions of the shorter tape, requiring 999,000 outputs from the photocells. At full speed this would take 500 seconds (eight minutes) to run. A photomultiplier Comparator would only have to consult its photomultiplier 1000 times, stepping the moveable tape that many times; this might take a few seconds.

In its simplest form, then, a comparator computed the cross correlation function corresponding to the data streams on the films, or in American cryptanalysts' jargon, calculating the 'Index of Coincidence' (I.C.) between the two data streams at all possible offsets. This calculation is

*The notes to this Appendix are at its end. They use the citation system used in the notes to the *Report*, explained on p. 561.

generally useful in cryptanalysis, and a number of photographic I.C. machines were built for the U.S. Navy and Army, for use against various ciphers. Several of these are described (with illustrations) in Burke's books and in Budiansky's *Battle of Wits*.[3] An oral history interview with Arnold I. Dumey (1906–1995), one of the designers of the 5202, gives an indication of the degree of Army enthusiasm for this technology, although Dumey was still constrained by considerations of security. Dumey guardedly refers to the 5202: 'They [Eastman Kodak] supplied these things to us, as I said, in several versions. They supplied it to the Navy but not the same as ours. We had a slightly different idea about it. And they also supplied it to the other side of the water. It was used in a rather special way which again I am prevented from talking about.'[4]

This whole genre of photographic cryptanalytic machinery is summed up by Budiansky. Although useful during the war, these machines were '... expensive ... and temperamental; they pushed to the very limits electro-optical technologies that within a few years were to be rendered completely obsolete by the digital computer, and it is unlikely that until the emergency of war these technological avenues — or perhaps they are more accurately described as dead ends — would ever have been explored'.[5]

But in early 1944 the idea of a photographic I.C. machine was very attractive to M. H. A. Newman. Cable TRA 9 of 17 Mar. 1944, from Welchman to Newman, while Welchman was visiting SSA shows that a long-distance technical dialogue had been going on between Newman and SSA.[6] Welchman reports that thinking at SSA favours a film (as opposed to rigid plate) I.C. machine, and he discusses how a plate machine could not support the 3-wheel runs that Newman sees as the likely application for the machine. In another cable, 21 Mar. 1944, Welchman conveys SSA's case: 'Arlington film comparator more flexible than I.C. plate modification. Development time probably no longer. Will press for priority. Main gain is method of photography. Pattern to be recorded on each position of film is displayed by lamps on target at some distance from camera. Size of light spots on film, number of places in each position, and grouping can be varied by change of target and of wiring between target and reader. System works well on HYPO [a photographic machine used in Enigma solution].'

About a year later the machine is nearly ready, but GCCS needs to make a case for using it. Cable SSA 8875 to GCCS, of 10 Feb. 1945, announces 'MARSTON has gone to EASTMAN to test 5202.[7] If satisfactory [it] will be here in about ten days. Please give us your careful estimates based on feelings of Welchman and Newman of current need this machine in England for Fish purposes taking into consideration use for crib runs described annex cast letter 9, part 3. At time it was ordered there was only one COLOSSUS. If present supply of COLOSSI is adequate we could use 5202 for many other problems. See SSA 1559 of 29 June for machine details. Will include scanner.'

The case is made in cable GCCS 0934 of 24 Feb. 1945, from A. W. Small (the SSA liaison officer at GCCS) to F. Rowlett (the head of the cryptanalysis branch at SSA): 'Reference 8875. NEWMAN sees 5202 as very useful here. Last week COLOSSI ran 501 tapes solved 293 then went operationally idle because KNOCKHOLT reached tape checking limit on COLOSSI material. Machine 5202 would have filled gap by tackling unbroken 208 transmissions. Also more than 20 special messages per week requested by Hut 3 all vital many unsuited to COLOSSI could be attempted by 5202. Also 5202 might provide breaks on low dottage days. Unforseen possibilities also great for 5202. Group here figuring math for 4 wheel runs. Darkrooms ready floorspace available operators available. NEWMAN can promise no success but anxious to obtain 5202 would start using on arrival. Does not believe it could be worked by group at SSA with as much chance of success... '

Small's pleading seems to have done the trick: a month later, practicalities of installing the machine are being discussed. Cable GCCS 5006 of 20 Mar. 1945 to Col. William P. Corderman (1904–1998), the head of the SSA, asks 'What is permissible range of temperature in developing and projecting rooms?' The reply, in SSA 679 of 23 Mar. 1945: 'Temperature not too important except that if reasonably constant it is easier control humidity reference GCCS 5006 best range probable 65 to 70'. The following day, Nigel de Grey (1886–1951), Travis's chief deputy (and thus in effect second in command at GCCS), sent Corderman a thank-you note in GCCS 5647:

> A. Am advised that air conditioning and temperature control can be installed in about 6 weeks. Ministry of Works are ready to start immediately.
>
> B. Thought here that 5202 would increase FISH output by making new techniques possible. FISH results now have the highest priority.
>
> If anything 5202 even more important than electronic autoscritcher[8] that we have recently undertaken. Also 5202 is built where our scritcher cannot be built before August.
>
> C. If you are willing to send 5202 here, we shall proceed installations immediately.
>
> D. Fully appreciate your wish to use 5202 for general purposes and generosity in offering to send it here. Suggest return of machine to you as soon as FISH problem dies. We all hope this will be soon, though we consider it may be the last to go. In view of extreme operational importance of FISH feel we cannot relax effort yet.
>
> E. Should be most grateful for your concurrence and for estimate date of arrival. Will not contact BICHER until I hear. Shall of course welcome your personnel here.

In SSA 995 of 30 Mar. 1945, Corderman replies to De Grey: 'Concur in shipment of 5202 equipment to GCCS at earliest practicable date to save time you should initiate request for shipment of equipment, 1 officer, and 1 enlisted man through Bicher. Total estimated weight of equipment is 2900 lbs in six separate boxes of which largest will weigh about 1430 lbs. We are prepared to make shipment as soon as official request is received from ETO'. (Col. George A. Bicher was the Director of SIGINT in the U.S. Army's European Theatre of Operations — in effect, Corderman's representative in England.)

Cable GCCS 9591 of 18 Apr. 1945 to SSA announces 'Lieutenant Dixon Sergeant O'Donnell and 5202 equipment arrived GCCS late today. Equipment has been unloaded will be unboxed in morning. GCCS expresses appreciation for speed of shipment'. On 24 Apr., in cable GCCS 00501, De Grey writes to Corderman: '5202 arrived safely with Lt. Dixon and Sgt. O'Donnelly [*sic*]. Preliminary tests now ending show machine in good condition. Most grateful to you for speedy shipment.'

In his 29 April 1945 liaison report, Small noted 'Lt. Dixon is having trouble with his projector's trigger circuit, in machine 5202. The oscillograph shows it to be breaking into and out of oscillation. Also, film developing troubles are arising, with the first developer seeming to fog the films." (NSA Small G-66, Albert W. Small, 'Small Report G-66', 29 Apr. 1945, FOIA release of liaison report, NSA DOCID: 3524493, para. 7.)

On 7 May 1945, Newman writes to de Grey (in TNA HW 62/6) at the request of Capt. Alan Bradshaw, the Deputy Director (Administration), for permission to go ahead with the air conditioning work, citing the desirability of testing the 5202 at GCCS, where there is more practical experience with Tunny than at SSA, and where it is easy to produce test material in the bulk needed to discover those faults which show up only in work of production scale. 'The apparatus is about to work electrically after some preliminary troubles. It is clear that no results can be obtained without the air conditioning.'

When the machine had arrived, it turned out that not all the necessary supplies and spare parts were at hand. On 2 May 1945, Small wrote to Rowlett, in GCCS 1093: 'Will soon need an IBM six-hole punch for machine 5202. Ref GCCS 8901. GCCS would be most grateful if you could sent one over on loan to be returned with machine 5202.' And on 5 May, in GCCS 2150, 'Punch is all that is required. Re SSA 3618. GCCS is going to swipe typewriter from other machinery in use unless you can easily spare one, in which case of course it would be gratefully received. Reader available.' On 26 May, SSA 4853, addressed to Lt. Dixon, 'Shipping 20 units 404 developer by boat to Colonel BICHER 59 Weymouth Street. Be on lookout 5th June for box number (S-241112). Replaces 600 you have. Process is 2 1/2 minutes for first developer and 2 minutes for all rest. How many 30 × 34 plugboards do you have. Have you received PUNCH?' And on 28 May 1945, in GCCS 04130, 'Punch not yet received ref SSA 4853. Will start tracing back for it. We have 24 plugboards 20 × 34 here. DIXON will send complete report of progress, new developments, etc., in few days.' GCCS 06355 of 26 June 1945, to SSA: 'DIXON has rush need for two high speed IBM Jack type relays. These are used as storage shift relay for 5202. Can find no suitable substitute here. Advise shipment channel.'

The fighting in Europe had in the meantime ended 7 May, just six weeks and two days after de Grey's cable to Corderman predicting that the installation of air conditioning would take about six weeks.

GCCS's post-hostility experimentation with the 5202, reported in chapter **91**, must have ended in late July, as the cable traffic discusses its return to America. Cable GCCS 08313 of 20 July 1945, from GCCS to Rowlett at SSA: 'Johnson feels 5202 should not go by air unless urgently necessary because situation is tight and it would use up entire U.K. base weekly allotment of space. What is your view of shipping by sea? It will be ready to go by 26th July.' GCCS 10113 of 12 August 1945, to SSA: 'DIXON, O'DONNELL and 5202 left today by air'.

Notes

1. (p. 530) As far as we know, the best descriptions of the 5202 are chapter **91** of the *Report* and a 73-page document, *The 5202*, dated 20 Aug. 1945, in NARA HCC 942:2748. Both of these descriptions refer to a 'Reference Manual', written by the 5202's builder, the Eastman Kodak company of Rochester, NY. We have been unable to locate this manual.

2. (p. 530) Vannevar Bush (1880–1974), then Vice President and Dean of Engineering at the Massachusetts Institute of Technology and famous as the inventor of the Differential Analyzer, and hence in 1941 the country's foremost expert in computing machinery.

3. (p. 531) Stephen Budiansky, *Battle of Wits: The Complete Story of Codebreaking in World War II* (New York: Free Press, 2000).

4. (p. 531) William Aspray, 'An Interview with Arnold Dumey', 9 Oct. 1989, URL: `http://conservancy.umn.edu/bitstream/11299/107760/1/oh088ad.pdf` (visited on 07/06/2014).

5. (p. 531) Budiansky, *Battle of Wits* (see note 3 to this Appendix, above), pp. 246–7.

6. (p. 531) This and all cables cited below in this Appendix are in TNA HW 57/1.

7. (p. 531) Marston is Maj. E. Dale Marston, an expert in cryptanalytic computing. An organizational memo for SSA's general cryptanalysis section, B-III, dated 9 July 1943, shows Marston, then a Captain, as both executive officer (under Rowlett) of B-III and as head of the sub-section of B-III that contained the Rapid Analytical Machinery (RAM, that is, cryptanalytic machinery) group. An organizational chart of 1 October 1943 shows Marston as both head of sub-section C of B-III and of B-III-C's RAM group. (Both in NARA HCC 1114:3568.)

8. (p. 532) The autoscritcher was an American special-purpose device for attacking Enigmas with pluggable reflectors. See David J. Crawford and Phillip E. Fox, 'The Autoscritcher and the

Superscritcher: Aids to Cryptanalysis of the German Enigma Cipher Machine, 1944–1946', *IEEE Annals of the History of Computing*, 14.3 (1992), pp. 9–22, and Budiansky, *Battle of Wits* (see note 3 to this Appendix, above), pp. 335, 360. This passage, in a message from GCCS to SSA, suggests that GCCS was at least contemplating building one in Britain; we have seen no other suggestion of this in the secondary literature.

Appendix D: Initial Conception of Colossus*

J. A. Reeds

We reproduce two official minutes from M. H. A. Newman to E. W. H. Travis, the head of GCCS, dated 1 March and 12 March 1943, describing T. H. Flowers's earliest ideas for what eventually became Colossus. Design of Robinson had begun in January of that year, and by March some construction had taken place; the machine was completed in June 1943. While working on Robinson at the Post Office Research Station at Dollis Hill, Flowers knew that there was a better way to do what Robinson was meant to do. As Flowers explained in his retrospective essay 'The Design of Colossus', *Annals of the History of Computing*, 5 (1983), pp. 239–252, esp. p. 244, he realised that digital electronics could bypass many of the problems connected with Robinson's temperamental paper tape reading apparatus.

The two minutes reproduced here show different forms of Flowers's idea. Originally Flowers proposed replacing both of Robinson's punched paper tape loops (one for the cipher message, the other the 'key tape' with the regularly stepping, recovered, χ wheels) with electronically stored or generated bit patterns. The second version of Flowers's proposal, which is what was built as Colossus, replaced only the key tape with its electronic equivalent, in the form of the output of an electronic simulation of a Tunny machine.

An apparent disadvantage of Flowers's earlier proposal was the large number of valves required to store the cipher message, and the second proposal can be understood as a cost-saving compromise. But Newman's second minute presents a different objection to the proposal as being the most serious: such a machine would be insufficiently 'flexible'. We take this matter up at the end of this Appendix.

It seems possible that when Flowers had his first idea he had only partial information about the contemplated application of Robinson and about the lengths of the tapes involved. If this is the case, Newman must eventually have given him a more realistic view of what was needed, and this view is reflected in the second form of Flowers's proposal.

In both minutes Newman uses a terse vocabulary, which makes some passages obscure. We give explanations of most of these passages following each of the minutes.

Newman's Minute of 1 March 1943

The earlier minute, of 1 March 1943, is in the possession of GCHQ, Cheltenham, Glos.† We reproduce its text here,

---

For Commander Travis	From M.H.A.Newman 1 March 1943

Report on progress

*The notes to this Appendix are at its end. They use the citation system used in the notes to the *Report*, explained on p. 561.

†Original held by GCHQ, Cheltenham, and quoted by permission of the Director, GCHQ. UK Crown Copyright Reserved.

1. The plans for the mechanical setting of Tunny and Sturgeon are going ahead. The tests at Dollis Hill on speed of moving Teleprinter tape came out favourably. They have been able to get the tape past a given point at the rate of 2000 letters a second without any signs of excessive strain. This would be enough to carry out the difference-method of setting in a moderate time, if several machines and counters were available, though something faster would be required to keep current if the traffic were considerable.

This machine will in any case be most valuable as a means of carrying out in a reasonable time experiments which cannot be tried at all at present, owing to the excessive labour involved.

2. Flowers, of the P.O., has produced a suggestion for an entirely different machine, in which the message, and the wheels to be compared with it, would be set up on valves, by means of relays. This would involve 5000 or so valves, and about 2500 relays. (The heat the valves would generate would be equal to that of 8 two-bar electric fires!) Mechanical movement would be avoided altogether, and speeds of 5000 to 10,000 a second would be possible.

This is, of course, a much more ambitious scheme. I feel that this is basically the right sort of approach, and that it is very much to our advantage to try out these techniques, and if possible get a step ahead with them. At the same time, since there is risk of hold-ups along these new paths, I emphasized that the simpler tape-machine (which has also the advantage of easy adaptability to all sorts of purposes) should be gone on with also, at full speed. They are quite willing to follow up both lines at once, and that is what I recommend should be done.

A pretty strong priority will be wanted to get that number of valves and relays in a finite time.

3. The rather alarming German instructions on the future use of 52 A B and C, (Tunny and Sturgeon), intercepted during the past two weeks, suggest that it may soon be necessary to read

(i) Tunny over E,

(ii) Sturgeon without depths or indicators.

Of these (i) should be possible, by making use of the fact that the TP characters 3, 4, 8, /, + do not occur in E, and using a method of "conventionally motorising" Tunny which I have recently worked out as an alternative to Tutte's difference methods. The problem (ii) of setting Sturgeon also seems tractable; but both (i) and (ii) involve looking at much larger numbers of characters (running up to nearly 10^9) than in the difference-methods for which the tape-machines are intended.

The only machines capable of anything like such speeds are the I.C. machines. It is therefore urgent to discover as soon as possible whether theese [*sic*] machines have the necessary degree of accuracy, — a point now in doubt —, and if so to set them to work

4. I am continuing to work my way round those departments which might offer opportunities for mechanical aids; and also getting a closer acquaintance ['acquaintance' handwritten] than before with the activities of Huts 8 and 6, and of Freeborn.

/MHAN/ [signed]

Parts 1 and 3 mention 'Sturgeon'. This was the GCCS cover name for a different German teleprinter cipher machine, mentioned briefly in a few places in the *Report* and never at length. There was in fact a series of such machines, the Siemens T 52 A, T 52 B, up through T 52 E, of varying degrees of security. According to F. H. Hinsley, E. E. Thomas, C. F. G. Ransom and R. C. Knight, *British Intelligence in the Second World War: Its Influence on Strategy and Operations*, 5 vols. (New York: Cambridge University Press, 1979), vol. 3 part I, p. 477, GCCS decided late in 1941 to concentrate on Tunny instead of Sturgeon. See Frode Weierud, 'Bletchley Park's Sturgeon — the Fish that Laid No Eggs' in B. Jack Copeland, ed., *Colossus: The Secrets of Bletchley Park's Codebreaking Computers* (Oxford: Oxford University Press, 2006), pp. 307–327 and Frode Weierud, 'Bletchley Park's Sturgeon — The Fish that Laid No Eggs', *The Rutherford Journal: The New Zealand Journal for the History and Philosophy of Science and Technology*, 1 (Dec. 2005), URL: `http://www.rutherfordjournal.org/article010106.html` (visited on 07/06/2014). We do not know if Robinson was intended to be of direct use in attacking Sturgeon, or if it was meant to be an exemplar of the type of machine which might be used to attack Sturgeon.

The matters in the first three numbered parts had almost certainly been discussed earlier with Travis. In each case the purpose is to lay the groundwork for the possible acquisition of new equipment. The second paragraph under part 2 reports the acceptance by the Post Office of a bet-hedging strategy: to pursue the by-now standard approach represented by Robinson and also, simultaneously, pursue the riskier but potentially more valuable proposal of Flowers. Modern two-bar electric fires (electric radiators) draw about 1.8 or 2 kilowatts of power, so the contemplated machine might have drawn 15 kW. Part 3 is confusing, as it seems to be about German Sturgeon traffic (enciphered by variants of the Siemens T52 machine) but Newman mentions it in connection with Tunny. New usages (avoiding depths, and superenciphering Enigma messages by Tunny) by the Germans might make this traffic much more difficult to read, and the use of 'I.C.' machines might be required. (These 'Index of Coincidence' machines were much used by American SIGINT organisations during the war, but apparently not by GCCS. They used photocells and photographic plates or films, slid against each other, to do what Robinson did, but at potentially higher speeds. See chapter **91** of the *Report* and our Appendix C, 'The 5202 Machine', this volume, pp. 530–533 above, for a discussion of a related machine, intended for Tunny breaking.) We do not know what the 'conventionally motorising' method is, mentioned in the end of part 3.

Part 4 refers to Huts 8 and 6, where German Naval (Hut 8) and Army and Air Force (Hut 6) Enigma breaking took place, with the aid of the special-purpose Bombe machines. Frederic Freeborn was the head of the Hollerith Section, which used commercial punch-card tabulating equipment for a wide range of cryptanalysis tasks. This part of the minute is probably related to a recent addition to Newman's duties, ordered by Travis on 1 February 1943: 'In many cases cyphers are becoming so difficult that solution depends on the provision of specially designed machinery to bring to notice clues upon which a cryptographer can work. It is desirable therefore to centralise research on special machinery, and I have appointed Mr. Newman of the Research Section for this work and all enquiries in regard to such matters should be made to him.' (1 February 1943, TNA HW 14/66.) Eight months later these duties were taken over by W. G. Welchman, who was appointed head of a new Machine Co-ordination and Development Section: 'Mr. Welchman should be consulted on all questions of machine aids (other than the BTM machines in Mr. Freeborn's Section.)' (10 September 1943, TNA HW 14/87.)

Newman to Travis, 12 March 1943

Less than two weeks later Newman reports a change in plan in a handwritten note to Travis, TNA HW 14/70, dated 12 March 1943.

Commander Travis 12 March 43
From Newman

Morell [*sic.* F. O. Morrell was the chief engineer for Robinson] & Flowers were here this morning. There seems to be no doubt that they are putting the simple machine, with tapes, first, as we want, and they hope to have their part ready in 2 months. Wynn-Williams also hopes to have his part (the counting apparatus) done by then, & both parties seemed to have a healthy desire not to be finished last.

When the operators have got the hang of it this machine should set six or eight messages a day. More machines will do more messages, but this means another 2 or 3 months wait I suppose.

For the more ambitious machine they now propose to use tape for the message and valves only for the fixed wheels. This does away with the main objection to their first scheme (lack of flexibility of use). About 1?00 [second digit illegible] valves are still needed & they recognise that there will be teething troubles. No date is given for this.

One such machine would do about 50 messages a day, which is just about the average traffic at present.

MHAN

12 March

The third paragraph mentions lack of flexibility of use as an objection to the earlier proposal. Throughout the *Report*, and in GCCS usage in general, the word 'flexibility' means 'versatility', the capability of being useful for more than one particular task, including unanticipated ones.

We give a tentative explanation of the nature of this lack of flexibility, based on the discussion of χ wheel setting in sections **23B(b)** and **23B(c)** of the *Report*, which are applicable equally to Robinson and Colossus. We maintain that although the proposed tapeless Colossus would be able to do what may be called simple wheel-setting runs, it would not be able to do compound ones. (We explain these terms below.)

Since we have no clear statement of Newman's understanding in March 1943 of the details of how Robinson would be used, and no more detailed description of Flower's original proposal than that in the 1 March 1943 minute reproduced above, our explanation is conjectural. Indeed, many of the details in sections **23B(b)** and **23B(c)** were worked out experimentally in the first few weeks *after* Robinson was completed, and hence not known to Newman in March 1943. (See, for example, the accounts by Good and by Michie, who did the experimental work: Good, 'From Hut 8 to the Newmanry' (see p. 215) and Michie, 'Codebreaking and Colossus' (see pp. 240–241), both in B. Jack Copeland, ed., *Colossus: The Secrets of Bletchley Park's Codebreaking Computers* (Oxford: Oxford University Press, 2006).) So our explanation requires that although Newman's understanding in March 1943 of wheel-setting was not as complete as that found in **23B(b)** and **23B(c)**, he still *did* understand the following main point: once the first χ wheels had been set, compound runs are better than simple runs.

In a given run, all combinations of starting positions for one or more of the χ wheels are tried out, and applied to the cipher stream to obtain a tentative 'de-chi' stream, denoted D in the algebraic formalism explained in chapters **11** and **12** of the *Report*. What was counted was occurrences of particular combinations of characters in ΔD, the stream of mod two differences between successive D values. For the initial step, setting χ_1 and χ_2, it sufficed to count the number of instances that $\Delta D_1 = \Delta D_2$. The occurrences and non-occurrences can be computed by referring to a single bit stream derived from the cipher stream, namely the stream of $\Delta Z_1 + \Delta Z_2$ bits.

The next step might be to set χ_4 and χ_5, taking advantage of the newly-set χ_1 and χ_2, following the procedure of the first branch of the recipe laid out in a diagram in section **23B(c)**. To do this, Robinson or Colossus must (for each tentative setting for χ_4 and χ_5, and hence for each tentative ΔD stream) count the number of occurrences of what the *Report* symbolizes as 4=5=/1=2, that is, of cases where $\Delta D_4 = \Delta D_5 = \Delta D_1 = \Delta D_2$. The occurrences and non occurrences of this cannot be computed from a single bit stream derived from the cipher stream, but rather requires examination of three bit streams derived from the cipher stream, in effect, one per equals sign in the formula for the run. Call such a run a 'compound run', in distinction to the 'simple' 1=2 run.

Newman might not have known in March 1943 that the particular compound run 4=5=/1=2 would be a good successor to a successful 1=2/ run. But he would have known that if the results of setting some χ wheels were to help set the others, some form of compound runs would be needed. Otherwise, each wheel or set of wheels would have to be set independently. Oversimplifying only slightly, with compound runs, the complex of all the χ wheels is as easy to set as the easiest of them, but without compound runs it is as hard as the hardest of them.

The practical implication is that a compound run requires more data to be stored in the putative tapeless machine's electronic memory. If a cipher message was 1,500 or 2,500 letters long a compound run would require two or three times as much electronic memory as a simple run, that is, between 3,000 and 7,500 characters (bits) of information instead of 1,500 to 2,500 characters. According to section **12C(d)** of the *Report*, depending on the difficulty of the day's key, messages might need to be as long as 4,000 or even 6,200 letters long if their χ wheels were to be set, even if 1,200 or 1,700 sufficed on easier days.

We do not know exactly how Flowers proposed to represent cipher data in his first proposed machine, but he would have required at least one valve per character of data. With an estimated valve count of 5,000, compound runs would not be possible on long messages.

So we believe Newman's objection was that, in effect, the proposed machine could not perform compound runs on any but the shortest messages.

Appendix E: List of Scanned Exhibits

We have supplied an 'exhibit name' for each digitally scanned image in this edition, for ease of reference. These scans come from three kinds of pages in the *Report*. Some pages are themselves full-page images, typically of work sheets or machine-generated printout. Others contain one or more clearly demarcated illustrations, as usually seen in books. A third kind (mostly in chapter **25**) consists of pasted-up montages of several different Colossus output slips, often combined with text paragraphs. We consider each output slip a separate exhibit. We have dissected these montages into their constituent exhibits and, because the sizes and shapes of the pages in this edition do not match those of the original *Report*, sometimes arranged them differently on the printed page. In some cases we were forced to chop exhibits further, to create sub-exhibits. (We note that the authors of the *Report* followed the same procedure. The first exhibit in section **25G**, for instance, giving the result of a spanning run, has the first 36 results presented in one column and the remaining 12 in another column, even though the Colossus output was originally on one long strip of paper, about 12 inches (30 cm) long, which was too long to fit on the original *Report*'s 10 inch (25 cm) typing area. Since our available vertical space on the page is even less, we are forced to dissect more.)

Our exhibit names, listed in the chart below and in the distinctive border surrounding each scanned image, contain two or three components: the number of the containing section, an exhibit name proper, and, if we were forced to dissect the exhibit, a fragment number. Thus, '23D/1.2' names the second piece of the first exhibit in section **25D**. In numbering the exhibits within any given chapter section, we tried to follow whatever system of reference the *Report* used. In section **25G**, for example, the *Report* numbers the exhibits 1, 2, and so on, referring to them with circled numbers, as in ①, and so on. But the numerical series is imperfect. Exhibit 49, which should appear on p. 180 of the *Report*, is missing. On that page there are exhibits 52 and 52 (bis), and there are different exhibits numbered 53 on pages 180 and 181. So we have exhibits 25G/52 and 25G/52bis, and 25G/53 and 25G/53a, and no exhibit 25G/49.

In this chart, the first column gives a range of exhibit names, in condensed form. The third line, for instance, reads '23D/1.1, 1.2', meaning exhibits 23D/1.1 and 23D/1.2. The second column gives the scale factor used in this edition, relative to the original *Report*. Not all images in the original were presented at full scale. The image we exhibit as 26J/12.2, the lower half of figure **26**(XII), showing a squared paper work sheet, is approximately 7 inches wide in the *Report*, but the actual original work sheet itself was 7.8 inches wide (39 squares, of 1/5 inch apiece), so the *Report* itself uses a scale factor of .975 for this exhibit. Our chart shows a scale factor of .55 for this image, relative to the *Report*'s version; relative to the original work sheet, our overall combined scale factor is $.55 \times .975 \approx .536$. The third column gives the page location, in the original *Report*, of the images in question, together with a code letter D if we had to dissect the images, a code letter F if the page in the original *Report* is a fold-out page, and a code letter ϕ if the original image was a photograph. The final column gives the caption (if any) accompanying the image(s).

These images were taken from TNA HW 25/4 and TNA HW 25/5, with the following exceptions. Figs. **11 (II)**, **58 (I)**, **58 (XX)**, **58 (XXIV)**, **58 (XXV)**, and **58 (XXVI)** were taken from TNA HW 25/26; and figs. **11 (III)** and **58 (II)** were obtained from GCHQ by a discretionary release of retained material by the GCHQ historian. We used these replacement images because they seemed to have been made from the same negatives but were of better photographic quality; in the case of **11 (III)**, because the image had been excised from TNA HW 25/4.

11B/1	.95	9	ϕ	Fig. **11 (II)**
11E/1	.65	15		Fig. **11 (III)**
23D/1.1, 1.2	.5	82	D	
23D/2.1, 2.2, 2.3	.5	83	D	
23D/3, 4, 5	.5	84	D	
23D/6, 7	.5	85	D	
23Z/1.1	.7	111	D	Fig. **23 (I)**
23Z/1.2	.7	112	D	Fig. **23 (I)** continued
24B/1	.55	116bis	F	Fig. **24 (I)**
25G/1, 2, 3	.55	172	D	
25G/4, 5, 6	.6	173	D	
25G/7, 8, 9, 10	.5	173	D	
25G/11, 12, 13, 14, 15, 16, 17	.5	174	D	
25G/18, 19, 20, 21, 22, 23	.5	175	D	
25G/24, 25, 26, 27, 28, 29	.5	176	D	
25G/30, 31, 32, 33, 34, 35	.5	177	D	
25G/36, 37, 38, 39, 40	.4	178	D	
25G/40a, 41, 42, 43, 44, 45	.5	179	D	
25G/46, 47, 48, 50, 51, 52, 52bis, 53	.5	180	D	
25G/53a, 54, 55, 60	.6	181	D	
25G/I	.55	182	F	Fig. **25 (I)**
25G/II, III	.55	183	F	Figs. **25 (II)** and **(III)**
25G/IV	.55	184	F	Fig. **25 (IV)**
25G/V, VI	.55	185	F	Figs. **25 (V)** and **(VI)**
25G/VII	.4	186	F	Fig. **25 (VII)**
25G/VIII	.5	187	F	Fig. **25 (VIII)**
25G/IX	.4	188	F	Fig. **25 (IX)**
26J/9	.6	214		Fig. **26 (IX)**
26J/10	.55	215		Fig. **26 (X)**
26J/11	.55	216		Fig. **26 (XI)**
26J/12.1, 12.2	.55	217	D	Fig. **26 (XII)**
26J/13	.55	219		Fig. **26 (XIII)**
26J/14	.65	220		Fig. **26 (XIV)**
26J/15	.55	221	D	Fig. **26 (XV)**
26J/16	.8	222		Fig. **26 (XVI)**
26J/17	.7	223		Fig. **26 (XVII)**
26J/18	.6	224		Fig. **26 (XVIII)**
26J/19.1, 19.2, 19.3	.6	225	D	Fig. **26 (XIX)**
26J/20	.7	226		Fig. **26 (XX)**
26J/21	.55	227		Fig. **26 (XXI)**
26J/22	.55	228		Fig. **26 (XXII)**
28E/1	.6	269		Fig. **28 (VI)**
28E/2	.6	270		Fig. **28 (VI)** continued
28E/3	.55	272		Fig. **28 (IX)**
28E/4	.55	273		Fig. **28 (IX)** continued
31/I	.525	274	F	Floor plan
31/II	.6	275	F	Floor plan
34(d)/1	.8	283		Fig. **34 (I)**
36C/1	1.0	289		Untitled. (Rectangle card)
53/1	.8	332	ϕ	Untitled. (Wrens attending Colossus)
58/1, 2	1.0	381	ϕ	Figs. **58 (I), (II)**
58/3	1.0	382	ϕ	Fig. **58 (III)**
58/4	.65	382	ϕ	Fig. **58 (IV)**
58/5, 6, 7	.65	383	ϕ	Figs. **58 (V) – (VII)**
58/8, 9, 10	.65	384	ϕ	Figs. **58 (VIII) – (X)**
58/11, 12, 13	.65	385	ϕ	Figs. **58 (XI) – (XIII)**
58/14, 15, 16	.65	386	ϕ	Figs. **58 (XIV) – (XVI)**
58/17, 18, 19	.65	387	ϕ	Figs. **58 (XVII) – (XIX)**
58/20, 21	.65	388	ϕ	Figs. **58 (XX), (XXI)**
58/22, 23	.65	389	ϕ	Figs. **58 (XXII), (XXIII)**
58/24, 25, 26	.65	390	ϕ	Figs. **58 (XXIV) – (XXVI)**
58/27, 28, 29	.65	391	ϕ	Figs. **58 (XXVII) – (XXIX)**
58/30	.65	392	ϕ	Fig. **58 (XXX)**
58/31	1.0	392	ϕ	Fig. **58 (XXXI)**
58/32, 33	1.0	393	ϕ	Figs. **58 (XXXII), (XXXIII)**

Supplementary Glossary

The following glossary is intended to supplement the glossary provided in chapter **71** of the Report. We have included terms that seem to have been overlooked (or perhaps were too well known to to the intended readership to require comment in 1945) together with special terms and abbreviations that appear in the introductory essays, the endnotes or other editorial contributions to the present volume.

Arlington Hall (Used in our endnotes.) The location, in Arlington, Virginia, from 1942 on, of the U.S. Army's SIGINT service, the Signal Security Agency (SSA), and later, the Army Security Agency (ASA).

ASA (Used in our endnotes.) Abbreviation for Army Security Agency, the SIGINT organisation of the U.S. Army after 15 September 1945.

autoclave, autokey A cipher system is said to employ autokey if parts of the earlier plain text or cipher text are used in the construction of the key stream. At GCCS autokey was known as 'autclave'.

bulge (Bletchley Park jargon.) Loosely, a statistical bias. The *Report* defines three slightly different concepts named 'bulge', all referring to the deviation between data and a null hypothesis model, or between the true model and a null model. First, the ordinary bulge (defined in **23C**) is the amount by which a random quantity exceeds its expectation figured according to the null model. Thus, when tossing pennies, if the outcome of 100 tosses is 81 heads and 19 tails, the bulge of the number of heads (with respect to the fair-coin model) is $31 = 81 - 50$. Second, the 'double bulge' (used in chapters **22**, **24**, **25**, and **26**) is twice that; in such coin-tossing examples this works out to be the same as the number of heads minus the number of tails. Third, the 'proportional bulge' (defined in **21(j)**) of an event is the ratio $(p - p_0)/p_0$, where p is the event's actual probability and p_0 is the probability it is assigned by the null model. If the event is to come up heads in a single coin toss, with the fair-coin null model ($p_0 = 1/2$), with true probabilities for heads and tails being p and q, the proportional bulge works out to $2p - 1 = p - q$. The numerical value of the bulge and double bulge depend on the particular outcome; the proportional bulge gives a probability statement about all possible outcomes. (That is, in statisticians' jargon, the first two are sample statistics and the third is a population parameter.) When tossing a single coin, with probabilities as above, the double bulge will be either $1 = 2(1 - 1/2)$ or $-1 = 2(0 - 1/2)$ if heads or tails come up, respectively; its expectation under the true model is $2p - 1 = p - q$, the proportional bulge.

c.b. An abbreviation for 'centiban'.

centiban One hundred times the common logarithm of a probability or ratio of probabilities. So if outcome A is 1,000 times more likely than B, then $\log_{10}(P(A)/P(B)) = 3$, and the *Report* would say 'A is 300 c.b.'s up, relative to B'.

character As used in the *Report*, a bit: either • (a zero) or × (a one). Five characters make up a teleprinter letter. (The term 'bit' for 'binary digit' was invented shortly after the war.)

cipher The *Report* uses this term ambiguously, to mean either a cipher method (such as the Tunny cipher) or a quantity of cipher text.

corruption Errors in the copies of Tunny cipher messages worked on by GCCS. These resulted from poor wireless intercept conditions and from carelessness in transcribing the intercepted data.

cryptographer; cryptography As used in the *Report*, a cryptanalyst or code-breaker; cryptanalysis or code-breaking.

db, d.b., deciban Analogous to a centiban, a deciban is ten times the common logarithm of a probability or ratio of probabilities. See entry for 'centiban' and editorial endnote 4 to the *General Report on Tunny*, chapter **21**, p. 577 below.

decode As a verb: to decipher a Tunny message by running it through a Tunny machine with the proper wheel patterns and settings. As a noun: the result of such a process. For the Germans to be able to decode they had to consult their QEP book and key sheets for the day. For GCCS to decode, they had to first have worked out wheel patterns and settings.

diagnosis A cipher machine is said to have been diagnosed when its mathematical operations are known, for instance by finding the number of wheels and the number of elements on each. The diagnosis of the Tunny machine was carried out by Tiltman and Tutte (*GRT*, chapter **41**).

Dollis Hill The north-west London location of the Research Station of the General Post Office (GPO; until 1981, the state-owned domestic telecommunications monopoly); by synecdoche, the Research Station itself. The Station worked on technical problems connected with operating the British telephone and telegraph system; its main task during the 1930's seems to have been the automation of the dialling system.

D.O. Duty Officer, that is, the man in charge of all work in the Newmanry during a shift.

GCCS Government Code and Cypher School; formally a branch of the Foreign Office. The main British SIGINT organisation during the Second World War, with headquarters at Bletchley Park, Buckinghamshire, and outstations at all theatres of the war. (Variously abbreviated GCCS, G.C.&C.S., GC and CS, and GC&CS.)

GCHQ Government Communications Headquarters, the successor of GCCS.

GPO General Post Office. See 'Dollis Hill', above.

ISOS An abbreviation for 'Intelligence Services Oliver Strachey'. See our endnote 3 to *GRT*, section **14A**, p. 574 below.

key Ordinarily in cryptography, a key is the complete specification of the secret data needed by the senders or recipients of messages to encrypt or decrypt them. But in the *Report*, however, this term is used in several different senses: (1) In Tunny, that which is added modulo 2 to plain text to produce cipher text. (2) Especially in **26**, a stretch of consecutive key letters, obtained from depths or from cribs. (3) The wheel patterns in effect for a particular Tunny link for a particular period of time. 'Key breaking' is determining a key in sense (3) from study of a (stretch of) key in sense (2). To the extent that sense (3) does not specify wheel settings for particular messages, it is not a key in the ordinary cryptographic sense.

Newmanry The Tunny-breaking section of GCCS headed by Mr M. H. A. Newman (1897–1984).

one back The previous letter or character in a stream of letters or characters.

OP-20-G The U.S. Navy's SIGINT organisation during World War II.

Q-code A conventional system of three letter codes used by radio and radio-teleprinter operators to *manage* the traffic they are sending, with code groups specifying such things as signal strength, message priority, and the like. It was originally specified by an appendix to Article XXII of the 'Service Regulations' affixed to the International Radiotelegraph Convention, London 1912, which contained 45 items like QRJ = 'how many words have you to send?', QRS = 'shall I send slower?', and so on. (Other items have been added by subsequent international agreements; the 1990 list of standard Q codes contains more than 200 items.) To these the Germans added code groups for general use in military communications, and yet others for Tunny-specific functions. Most notable among these were QSN and QEP to indicate choice of wheel settings, and QZZ to signal changeover to the next day's wheel patterns.

SD, S.D. Abbreviations for the standard statistical term 'standard deviation'. See **22(f)**.

SIGINT (Used in our endnotes.) An abbreviation for 'signal intelligence', that is, intelligence derived from intercepted signals. Even though neither form appears in the *Report*, both were in common use at GCCS during the latter half of the war. (The form 'signals intelligence', found in the 1993 edition of the *Shorter Oxford English Dictionary*, seems to have been uncommon until about 1960.)

SIS In a British context, the U.K. Secret Intelligence Service. In the context of the history of World War II cryptography, as used in our endnotes, it is an abbreviation for Signal Intelligence Service, the SIGINT organisation of the U.S. Army from 1929 to 1942; located in Washington DC. Relocated to Arlington Hall, Virginia, in 1942, with many successive name changes, including the Signal Security Agency (SSA) in 1943, and the Army Security Agency (ASA) on 15 September 1945.

slide The *Report* uses this term for several different concepts. (1) A message slide (or tape slide) is a mistake in the transcription of a cipher message, in which one or more consecutive letters were missing. It is a form of 'corruption'. (2) A wheel slide is when the pattern on a wheel closely matches some rotation of itself. When this happens, it becomes difficult to set that wheel in messages. (3) More generally, any rotation or translation of a wheel pattern or of a sequence of symbols.

SSA (Used in our endnotes.) Abbreviation for Signal Security Agency, the SIGINT organisation of the U.S. Army; located in Arlington, Virginia. Replaced by Army Security Agency (ASA) on 15 September 1945.

ST, S.T. Abbreviations for 'set total', the thresholds used by Robinson and Colossus to determine which scores to print. See entry 'Set total' in chapter **71**.

Station X A cover name for Bletchley Park, the location of GCCS's headquarters.

stroke The Newmanry name of the teleprinter letter denoted / in Tunny work, whose code is five dots (that is, zeros). It is the letter transmitted when an unpunched tape is fed into a teleprinter, and is assigned no meaning. Since it consists of all dots (that is, zeros), it also plays the role of zero when teleprinter letters are added modulo 2: $/ + \texttt{B} = \texttt{B}$, and so on.

tape Paper tape. Usually (1), 'perforator tape', standard 5-hole teleprinter tape carrying a representation of the teleprinter code symbols, occasionally (2), gummed printed tape produced by a teleprinter, meant to be pasted on telegram forms, or (3), 'undulator' or chart-recorder tape used in radio interception operations.

Testery The Tunny-breaking section of GCCS headed by Maj. Ralph Tester (1901–1998).

tone transmission The *Report*'s term for carrier telegraphy, the method used by the Germans for sending teleprinter signals by radio. The binary elements of the teleprinter letters (the dots and crosses) are represented by two distinct audio tones, or combinations of tones; this audio signal was then sent by shortwave. See our Appendix A, 'Transmission of Teleprinter Signals', this volume, pp. 495–499, for further details.

TP, T.P. Teleprinter, teletypewriter.

TRE, Telecommunications Research Establishment The radar laboratory of the Air Ministry, established in May 1940 at Swanage, Dorset, relocated to Malvern, Worcestershire, in August 1942.

Tunny As used in the *Report*, this term is ambiguous. It can mean any of: (1), a particular Tunny link active in 1942, between Berlin and Athens, (2), any of the cipher algorithms implemented by the SZ 40, SZ 42 A, or SZ 42 B machines, (3), German equipment implementing the cipher, and (4), British equipment implementing the cipher. Context usually makes it clear which sense is meant; in the *Report* it is usually sense (4). The circumlocutions 'the German machine' and 'German Tunny' mean sense (3).

valve Thermionic valve; used as an electronic switching device. The equivalent American English term, vacuum tube, is somewhat misleading, as some valves (including the thyratron used in Colossus) were gas-filled.

Vigenère ciphers Since the nineteenth century, the name of Blaise de Vigenère (1523–1596) has been given to cipher systems that employ repeated application of some particular key word (as this does not change, the key stream is periodic). The nineteenth-century cryptographers had, however, underestimated Vigenère's ingenuity. What he actually describes, in his influential book,*Traicté des chiffres, ou secretes manieres d'escrire* (Paris: Abel L'Angelier, 1586), is a different and much more complicated form of cipher that used autokey.

Wren A member of the WRNS, the Women's Royal Naval Service. Most of the Newmanry staff were Wrens.

W/T Abbreviation for wireless telegraphy, that is, non-voice radio. This includes conventional Morse code signals as well as radio-teleprinter signals, facsimile signals, and so on.

Biographical Notes

We list persons mentioned in the *Report* or in our notes, for ease of reference. Unless otherwise noted, they are British. We use the abbreviation ODNB for *Oxford Dictionary of National Biography* (*Oxford Dictionary of National Biography: In Association with the British Academy: From the Earliest Times to the Year 2000*, ed. by H.C.G. Matthew and Brian Harrison (London: Oxford University Press, 2004), URL: `http://www.oxforddnb.com/subscribed/` (visited on 07/06/2014)). Archival references follow the system used in our notes to the *Report*, explained on p. 561.

(Conel) Hugh O'Donel Alexander (1909–1974) was born in Cork, Ireland. Studied at King's College, Cambridge (1928–1931), obtaining a first class degree in mathematics in 1931. From 1932, he taught mathematics, but in 1938 became head of research at the John Lewis Partnership (a department store with headquarters in London).

In February 1940 Alexander moved to Bletchley Park, where he joined Hut 6. In 1941, he moved to Hut 8, where he took charge around November 1942. After the war, Alexander joined GCHQ where, by 1949, he had become head of Section H (cryptanalysis), a post he retained until his retirement in 1971.

Alexander had a distinguished career as a chess player. He wrote many books on chess and repeatedly represented Cambridge University and England in competitions.

For further indormation see ODNB.

Michael Arbuthnot Ashcroft (1920–1949) was educated at Eton and Magdalen College, Oxford, where he read Philosophy, Politics and Economics and became friendly with Roy Jenkins. He worked at Bletchley Park from June 1941 to January 1946, first in Hut 8 (June 1941 to mid 1944) and then, from mid 1944, in the Newmanry. Later he moved to the Secretariat as Assistant to Nigel de Grey. From 1946 he worked as an administrator in the Treasury, where he was regarded as a high-flier.

Arthur Oliver Lonsdale Atkin (1925–2008) was educated at Winchester College and Magdalene College, Cambridge, where he read mathematics (BA 1944). He was called up in 1944 and spent the next year at Bletchley Park, where he was a member of the Newmanry. When the war was over, he was transferred to the National Physical Laboratory (Teddington). He returned to Cambridge in 1947, obtaining a PhD in 1952. He later taught at various universities in the USA. His main research interest was computational number theory.

Henry Frederick Baker (1866–1956). A leading expert on pure geometry, Lowndean Professor of Astronomy and Geometry at Cambridge, 1914–36, and a Fellow of St John's College.

Thomas Bayes (1702–1761). English Presbyterian minister and mathematician. Elected Fellow of the Royal Society 1742. Posthumous author of 'An Essay Towards Solving a Problem in the Doctrine of Chances', *Philosophical Transactions of the Royal Society of London*, 53 (1763), pp. 370–418, 'An essay towards solving a problem in the doctrine of chances', now regarded as the first enunciation of 'Bayes' Rule', the cornerstone of the method of 'inverse probability', now known as Bayesian statistics.

Peter James Henry Solomon Benenson (1921–2005), who was educated at Eton and Balliol College, Oxford (1939–40, BA 1944), was in the Army from 1941 to 1946. He worked in the Testery and was a temporary member of the Newmanry (or possibly a part-time member, see endnote 4 to *GRT*, chapter **31**, p. 599 below). After the war, he practised as a barrister and became a leading member of the Society of Labour Lawyers. In 1961 he founded Amnesty, a human rights organisation concerned with freedom of speech and fair trials. For further information see ODNB.

Francis Lyall (Frank) Birch (1889–1956), the son of a banker, was born in London and educated at Eton and King's College, Cambridge, where he read Modern Languages and History. In WWI he served in the naval cryptanalysis organisation, 'Room 40', from 1916 to 1919. He then returned to Cambridge as a Fellow of King's College and a lecturer in History (1921–28). He joined GCCS in September 1939 as Head of the (German) Naval Section. After the war he wrote an internal *History of British Sigint* (TNA HW 43/1 and 43/2). For further details see ODNB.

S. W. Broadhurst was an employee of the Post Office, working directly under Flowers on Colossus. Horwood states that Broadhurst 'was almost entirely responsible for the design of the electromechanical elements of the machine, mainly comprising several hundred relays which were used in the control and printing areas where the speed of electronic valve techniques was not required' (D. C. Horwood, *A technical description of COLOSSUS I* [August 1973], TNA HW 25/24). After the war, Broadhurst worked on the development of computers.

Howard H. Campaigne (1910–1988) earned a PhD in mathematics from Northwestern University in 1938 and entered the U.S. Navy two days before Pearl Harbor, joining its cryptanalytic organisation, OP-20-G. In August 1944 he went to England to work in the Newmanry; at the end of the war he took part in two TICOM trips. After the war, as a civilian, he became the chief of mathematical research for OP-20-G, and later, of research for NSA, spending much of his efforts on the development of computer technology. After retirement from NSA in 1973 he became professor of computer science at the University of New Mexico.

John Chadwick (1920–1998) was educated at St Paul's School (London) and Corpus Christi College, Cambridge (1939–40), where he read classics. During wartime service in naval intelligence he worked on breaking Italian messages. He then studied Japanese, taking the course organised at Bedford, and came to GCCS as a Japanese translator (see John Chadwick, 'A Biographical Fragment: 1942–3' in Ralph Erskine and Michael Smith, eds., *Action This Day* (London: Bantam Press, 2001), pp. 110–26). After the war he taught in the Classics department at the University of Cambridge and became the leading expert on Mycenaean Greek. His publications include John Chadwick and Michael Ventris, *Documents in Mycenaean Greek* (Cambridge: Cambridge University Press, 1956) and John Chadwick, *The Decipherment of Linear B* (Cambridge: Cambridge University Press, 1958). For further details see ODNB.

Arthur Cyril Chamberlain (1920–1996) was educated at Liverpool College and Magdalene College, Cambridge, where he read mathematics (matriculation 1937, BA 1940). He served in the Army Intelligence Corps and worked at Bletchley Park from 1941 until 1945, first in Hut 8 (March 1941 – end 1943) and then in the Newmanry until 1945. After the war, he took up an appointment the scientific civil service.

W. W. Chandler was employed by the Post Office to work on Colossus. He joined the team in 1945 and, under Flowers, worked on all the Colossi. Earlier, he had worked under Wynn-Williams at TRE. After the war, Chandler worked on the development of computers.

Leslie Newton Chown, born 1926, Wolverhampton, England. Studied at Balliol College, Oxford, 1943–4, obtaining a first class in mathematics (Mods) in 1944. Worked at Bletchley Park, in Newman's group, 1944-5. Returned to Balliol 1947–51; first class degree in mathematics finals and BA 1949, MA 1950. Taught mathematics in schools, eventually becoming head of department at Tettenhall College.

Thomas Amner Colvill (1911–1998), whose father worked at the Patent Office, was born in Gravesend (Kent) and educated at the local state school, where he excelled at mathematics. He studied to become an actuary and, apart from his wartime service at Bletchley Park, spent all his working life in the insurance industry. It may have been through his friend Arthur Chamberlain that he came to join GCCS (via Tiltman's cryptography course at Bedford).[1] At GCCS Colvill worked in the Research Section and the Testery. In 1958 I. J. Good recollected that Colvill was also a temporary member of the Newmanry (or possibly a part-time member, see endnote 4 to *GRT*, chapter **31**, p. 599 below).

Allen William Mark Coombs (1911–1995) was employed by the Post Office from 1936. He worked on the Colossus project first as Flowers' second in command and then, when Flowers moved to other work after the completion of Colossus II, as the leader of the team. After the war Coombs worked on computer development, with Turing on the pilot ACE machine and then with the Ministry of Supply.

Michael Maurice Crum (1916–1992) was the son of a clergyman (who became a Canon of Canterbury cathedral). Because of ill health, he was educated at home by private tutors. He went on to New College, Oxford, where he read mathematics, obtaining first class honours in both university examinations (matriculation 1934, Mods 1936, Finals 1938). He then became a Harmsworth Senior Scholar at Merton College, before being elected to a fellowship in Mathematics at New College with effect from April 1945. He remained a fellow there until the end of September 1954. Throughout his life Crum was very good at crossword puzzles and at solving chess problems.

He worked at Bletchley Park from April 1940 to June 1945, but details remain unclear. He is known to have worked in Hut 8 and in the Newmanry but he is not mentioned by name in the *General Report on Tunny*. His most important work was to diagnose the Sturgeon machine (Siemens T52), traffic from which was first received in the summer and autumn of 1942.[2] The Newmanry was created in December 1942 with the remit of mechanizing the breaking of Tunny (the machine had already been diagnosed and a breaking technique had already been devised, see *GRT*, **41**) so Crum's more basic work on Sturgeon (a different machine) is likely to have been carried out in the Testery or in the Research Section. Crum is also known for having invented 'Crum's Square', an alphabetical table for obtaining Sturgeon keys. After working in the Newmanry (where he was for some time after mid 1944),[3] Crum moved to ISOS. After the war he worked for GCHQ but for health reasons retired in 1968. After that he worked for Oxfam.[4]

Nigel Arthur de Grey (1886–1951). British cryptanalyst, veteran of the World War I naval cryptanalysis organisation, 'Room 40'. De Grey was 'Assistant Director (Services)' of GCCS

[1] M. A. T. A. Colvill and R. H. Colvill (sons of T. A. Colvill) in private conversations with JVF, December 2013.

[2] See Frode Weierud, 'Bletchley Park's Sturgeon — The Fish that Laid No Eggs', *The Rutherford Journal: The New Zealand Journal for the History and Philosophy of Science and Technology*, 1 (Dec. 2005), URL: `http://www.rutherfordjournal.org/article010106.html` (visited on 07/06/2014).

[3] G. B. Preston, 'Oxford in the forties', *Magdalen College Record* (2008), pp. 105–111, esp. p. 111.

[4] Personal information was supplied by Crum's niece, Professor C. J. Fowler, CBE, FRCS, University College, London, in private correspondence with JVF, February/March 2014.

from February 1942 and 'Deputy Director 1' (chief deputy to GCCS's director, Travis) from 1 March 1944. (See entry for E. W. H. Travis, p. 557.) For further details see ODNB.

Arnold I. Dumey (1906–1995) was born in the Bronx and obtained degrees in mathematics and Latin (1926) and law (1929), both from Columbia University. After practising law for about a decade, his interest in cryptography became known to the U.S. Army's SIS, which he joined in 1942, working as a cryptanalyst. He retired from the Army as lieutenant colonel in 1946 and from SIS's successor, NSA, in 1952. For several decades after that, he was an advisor to NSA. During the 1950s he was a consultant, developing data processing techniques using electronic computers for various businesses. He was a co-inventor of the important programming technique known as 'hashing' or 'open addressing'. Everyone who met him was struck by his gracious affability, high intelligence, and scintillating wit.

Thomas Joseph Eddleston (1924–2005) was born in Blackburn (Lancashire) and educated at Darwen Grammar School and Queen Elizabeth Grammar School, Blackburn, before going to Manchester University (1942), where he obtained a degree in mathematics (1944). He worked at GCCS from 1944 until 1945, first in the Newmanry, then in the Japanese section. After the war he went into teaching. He planned to do a doctorate at Manchester University, but family commitments prevented this — he was by then married with two sons. His teaching career took him to Burnley, Bedford and Liverpool and he eventually retired as Head of the Mathematics Department at Redland College (now part of Bristol University). One of his great passions and hobbies was dealing in stocks and shares, which seemed to make use of his mathematical abilities.[5]

Harry Fensom (1921–2010) was born in the East End of London and educated at a grammar school. At 16 he went to work for the Post Office while studying for City & Guilds certificates in electrical engineering. On the outbreak of war, he was transferred to the PO Research Station, where he worked with Tommy Flowers on building Colossus, and (after the war) ERNIE. He remained with the Post Office until his retirement in 1974.

Thomas ('Tommy') Harold Flowers, (1905–1998) was born in Poplar (in the East End of London). With the help of a scholarship, he attended technical college. From 1921 to 1925 he served a mechanical apprenticeship at the Royal Arsenal in Woolwich, while attending evening classes to obtain a London University degree in engineering. He joined the Post Office in 1926 as an electrical engineer, moving to the PO Research Station in 1930. He led the Post Office team working on the Colossus project until after the completion of Colossus II, when he was succeeded by Coombs. He continued at the Post Office after war and as its chief engineer designed the only computer the British public ever took to its heart: an electronic random-number generator called ERNIE that from 1957 picked winners among holders of premium bonds. For further details see ODNB.

Frederic Victor Freeborn, Chief of Research Department, British Tabulating Machine Company. Boss of Hollerith card operations at GCCS for most of the war.

Walter J. Fried (1904–2003) was born on Long Island, New York. He graduated from Harvard (1924) and Columbia Law School (1928) and began a life-long career as a lawyer, interrupted only by service in the U.S. Army, spending April to October 1944 as the SSA's liaison officer at

[5]Information from Richard Eddleston, Thomas Joseph Eddleston's son, in private correspondence with JVF, Jan/Feb 2014.

GCCS. After the war he returned to his law firm, and retired in 1979.

Milton Werner Gaschk (1909–2008) was born in North Dakota and grew up in Washington state. He enlisted in the U.S. Navy in 1927 and served as a ship-board radioman and radio intercept operator until being commissioned in 1943 and sent to Bletchley Park as assistant liaison officer for OP-20-G at GCCS, serving there from December 1943 through September 1945. After the war he continued working in SIGINT, retiring from the Navy in 1958.

Joseph Gillis (1911–1993) was educated at St Bede's Collegiate Boys' School (Sunderland) and Trinity College, Cambridge, where he read mathematics (admitted 1929, Part I 1930, Part II 1932). He went on to obtain a PhD (his supervisor was A. S. Besicovitch). From 1940 to 1945 Gillis worked at Bletchley Park, first in Hut 8, then in Hut 10, Air Section, including meteorological work. He then worked in the Newmanry. After the war he emigrated to Israel, where he taught at the Weizmann Institute of Science (Rehovot).

I. J. Good (1916–2009). See 'Biographies of Authors', this volume, p. ciii.

James Alexander (Sandy) Green (1926–2014), born in Rochester, New York, was the son of a Scottish professor of French literature who had taught in a number of Canadian and American universities between 1921 and 1935 before taking a professorship at Cambridge. Green entered the University of St Andrews in 1942, but, on reaching the age of 18, joined the Newmanry in August 1944. After the war he returned to St Andrews, obtaining a BSc with first class honours in mathematics (1947), and a PhD from Cambrige University in 1951. After that he had a distinguished career as a research mathematician, at the universities of Manchester and, as professor, of Sussex and Warwick. He was elected FRS in 1987 and awarded the De Morgan medal in 2001. He specialized in group theory, semigroup theory, and group representations; some of his early work was done in collaboration with Newmanry veteran David Rees.

John Herivel (1918–2011) was educated at Sidney Sussex College, Cambridge, where he read mathematics. He arrived at Bletchley Park in January 1940, served in Hut 6 and in October/November 1943 was transferred to the Newmanry (see memo by J. N. Seaman, dated 3 November 1943, NARA HCC 1033:3315). Later a historian of science. He wrote on the work of Joseph Fourier and Isaac Newton; and on his own work at GCCS in John Herivel, *Herivelismus and the German Military Enigma* (Kidderminster: M.&M. Baldwin, 2008).

Peter Hilton (1923–2010) was a temporary member of the Newmanry (or possibly a part-time member, see endnote 4 to *GRT*, chapter **31**, p. 599 below). He was educated at St Paul's School (London) and The Queen's College, Oxford, where he read mathematics. In Oxford, a team looking for mathematicians who knew some German interviewed him and arranged for him to work at Bletchley Park, where he arrived in January 1941 to work in Hut 8. From 1942 he worked in the Testery and then in the Newmanry. Hilton returned to Oxford after the war, obtaining a DPhil in mathematics in 1949. He later taught mathematics in several universities in the USA and carried out important original work in the subject.

Parker Hitt (1878–1971). American signal officer interested in cryptanalysis; inventor of an early teleprinter cipher machine. See Betsy Rohaly Smoot, 'Pioneers of U.S. Military Cryptology: Colonel Parker Hitt and His Wife, Genevieve Young Hitt', *Federal History Journal* (Issue 4, 2012), pp. 87–100, URL: `http://shfg.org/shfg/wp-content/uploads/2012/12/6-Smoot-Web-final.pdf` (visited on 07/06/2014).

Walter W. Jacobs (1914–1982), born in Newark, New Jersey, obtained a BS in mathematics from City College of New York in 1934 and an MA in mathematical statistics from George Washington University in 1940. He joined the U.S. Army and the SIS in 1941 and spent about six months in 1944–1945 in the Newmanry. After the war he stayed in government service, helping the Department of Commerce and the Air Force with their first efforts at using electronic computers. In 1961 he joined NSA, serving at times as its deputy chief of mathematical research, its deputy chief of research, its chief of machine processing, and as commandant of its National Cryptologic School. After retiring from NSA in 1969 he became mathematics professor at American University (Washington DC), retiring from there in 1981.

Roy Harris Jenkins (1920–2003) obtained a first class degree in Philosophy, Politics and Economics at Balliol College, Oxford, in 1941. His wartime service in the army included working at Bletchley Park, to which he was recruited after taking the course on cryptography at Bedford. He mainly worked in the Testery but was a temporary member of the Newmanry (or possibly a part-time member, see endnote 4 to *GRT*, chapter **31**, p. 599 below). He later became a successful politician: a notably reforming Home Secretary (1965–1967) and the first British President of the European Commission (1977–1981). For further information see ODNB and John Campbell, *Roy Jenkins: A Well-Rounded Life* (London: Jonathan Cape, 2014).

Harold Charles Kenworthy (1892–1987) was born in Tottenham (Middlesex, now in Greater London). His father is described in the 1901 census as a 'spirits and wines cellarman'. The 1911 census records Harold Kenworthy as already in employment, as a clerk. From 1917 to 1919 he served in the Royal Navy, working on Wireless Telegraphy in Gibraltar. In 1919 he transferred to the Marconi Wireless Telegraphy Company, on whose behalf he visited India in 1922 to give demonstrations of wireless equipment, following the government's lifting its embargo on the use of wireless telegraphy by private organisations. Later in the same year, Kenworthy married Ivy L. Ford, in Tottenham, and in 1932 it was Ivy Kenwothy, using an undulator installed in their home in Croydon, who was the first to detect teleprinter radio transmissions.

At the time of the General Strike, in 1926, the Metropolitan Police had become interested in detecting unauthorized radio transmissions. Kenworthy, while (it seems) still technically employed by Marconi, assisted the Metropolitan Police in this work and oversaw the installation of a new radio station, for interception and communication, at Denmark Hill (South London) in the early 1930s. From 1938 this station received financial support from the Foreign Office. Under Kenworthy's guidance, other interception stations were set up in the early years of the war, and in May 1942 the centre of interception for non-Morse transmissions was moved to a purpose-built station at Knockholt (near Sevenoaks, Kent), of which Kenworthy was the Director. At the same time, he became Chief of the Foreign Office Reseach and Development Establishemnt, whose remit included the design of new equipment.

After the war, Kenworthy worked for GCHQ until his retirement at the end of June 1957. Much of the above information on Kenworthy's career is taken from *A Brief History of Events Relating to the Growth of the 'Y' Service* (TNA HW 3/81), which he wrote just before his retirement in June 1957 (he retired at the end of the month and the *Brief History* is dated 11 June); it was declassified in 2004.

Pierre Simon Laplace (1749–1827) was a French astronomer and mathematician whose most important contribution to science was in celestial mechanics, where he explored the effects of universal gravitation. His work is notable for its clarity and rigour.

Kenneth James Le Couteur (1920–2011), born in St Helier (Jersey, Channel Islands), was educated at Victoria College, Jersey. In 1937 he won a scholarship to St John's College, Cambridge, where he read mathematics (matriculation 1938, Part II 1940, BA 1941). He spent the remaining years of the war at Bletchley Park, where he worked in the Newmanry and the Research Section. After the war, Le Couteur completed his PhD at Cambridge (1949), and worked in the University of Manchester and then, in 1951, moved to Liverpool, where he began to establish an international reputation as a theoretical physicist with wide-ranging interests. He emigrated to Australia in 1955 and in 1960 was elected to the Australian Academy of Science (then only six years old and with about 90 fellows).

Arthur J. Levenson (1914–2007) obtained a BS in mathematics from City College of New York before enlisting in the U.S. Army Signal Corps in January 1942. He worked for the SIS at Arlington Hall, and (after being made an officer) was sent to GCCS in August 1943, first to Hut 6 and, in the spring of 1944, to the Newmanry and the Testery. At the end of the war he went to Germany on a TICOM trip with Maj. Tester, bringing back a Tunny mobile communications unit and equipment. After the war he continued to work for the Army and then, as a civilian, for NSA, where he held a number of important positions before retiring in 1973.

Frank Laurence Lucas (1894–1967), who worked in Hut 3 at Bletchley Park, was a friend and correspondent of Max Newman. Before and after the war, Lucas taught in the English Department at the University of Cambridge and was a Fellow of King's College. He was well known both as a scholar and as the author of highly readable books for the general public, including *Style* (London: Cassell, 1955). For further details see ODNB.

Arnold Lynch (1914–2004) was born in London, where his father was headmaster of a school. He was educated at Dame Alice Owens School (Islington) and Emmanuel College, Cambridge. After a competitive examination, he was employed by the Post Office at its Research Station from 1936 to 1974. Lynch was a senior member of the team that, under Flowers, worked on the design and construction of the Colossus machines, in which Lynch's specific concern was with optical tape readers. Over the years, Lynch's work on the electrical and magnetic properties of various materials greatly assisted the miniaturisation of radio and radar apparatus.

Angus McIntosh (1914–2005) was educated at grammar school and Oriel College, Oxford, where, in 1934, he took first class honours in English. He went on to study comparative philology. During the war he served in the Tank Corps and then in military intelligence, which brought him to Bletchley Park, where he worked in the Testery. This exposure to numerical methods was to influence his subsequent extensive and pioneering research in linguistics.

John Brook Marriott (1922–2001) was educated at Merchant Taylors' School, Northwood, and St John's College, Cambridge, where he read mathematics. During the war he was in the Army Operational Research Group and in 1944 was posted to Bletchley Park to work in the Newmanry, After the war, Marriott became a mathematics master at Charterhouse.

Tilmar A. Moilien (1912–2001) was born in Coon Valley, Wisconsin, educated at Luther College, Iowa (BA 1934) and at the University of Iowa (MS statistics 1935). He practised as an actuary. During the war he was a cryptanalyst in the U.S. Army, and was assigned to the Newmanry in July 1944. After the war he returned to working in the insurance business in Iowa, from which he retired in 1976.[6]

[6]See *Technical History of the 6813th Signal Security Detachment* (NARA HCC 970:2941), p. 17, and '[Obituary of Tilmar Moilien]', 2003.

Donald Michie (1923–2007). See 'Biographies of Authors', this volume, p. ciii.

James Crain Michie (1927–2007) was educated at Marlborough College and Trinity College, Oxford. He became a poet. His verse translation James Crain Michie, *The Odes of Horace* (London: Rupert Hart-Davis, 1964; reprinted London: Penguin, 1967) was dedicated to his brother Donald. For further information see ODNB.

Gilbert Walter ('Gerry') Morgan (1911–1989) was born in New Cross (London). He was educated at St Olave's Grammar School (London) and Trinity College, Cambridge (entrance scholarship 1929), where he read mathematics (BA 1932, PhD 1935, MA 1936) and received a Smith's Prize for an essay on a topic in pure mathematics in 1934. He was the author of important papers on Fourier transforms and Fourier series published in the *Journal of the London Mathematical Society* in 1934 and 1936. Morgan worked at Bletchley Park from 1940 to 1945, first in Hut 5 (Military Section) and, from 1 May 1941, as head of the new Research Section set up in April (see TNA HW 14/14, minutes dated 11 April 1941 referring to a meeting held on 8 April). After the war he worked for GCHQ until his retirement in 1971.

Maxwell ('Max') Herman Alexander Newman (1897–1984), born in London of a German father (whose original surname was Neumann) and an English mother, was educated at the City of London School and, with the help of a scholarship, St John's College, Cambridge, where he arrived in 1915 to read mathematics. Because his academic work was disrupted by army service in the First World War, he did not obtain his degree until 1921. He was appointed a university lecturer in 1927. In the late 1920s he carried out pioneering work in geometric topology. He was elected FRS in 1939. His publications of the early 1940s relate to logic and Boolean algebras.

Newman worked at GCCS from August 1942 to June 1945, first (briefly) in the Research Section and then running a separate section devoted to mechanizing the breaking of teleprinter traffic. The section started as consisting merely of himself, Donald Michie and some auxiliary Wrens, but later expanded and was known as 'the Newmanry'. The official (internal) report of this section was the *General Report on Tunny with emphasis on statistical methods*, edited by three members of Newman's group between June and September 1945. On leaving Bletchley Park, Newman resumed his already well established career as an academic.

Many of Newman's papers are now held in the library of St John's College, Cambridge. For further details see ODNB.

Noël Kevin O'Neill (1917–1986), born on 25 December, was educated at Beaumont College (Old Windsor, Berkshire) and Wadham College, Oxford, where he read Classics (matriculation 1935, Mods 1937, Greats 1939). He played an active part in College life in Rugby, debating and dramatics, and was President of the Junior Common Room in his final year. He entered the Army as a private in 1939, becoming a Second Lieutenant in the Royal Fusiliers in March 1941. At GCCS he served in the Military Section (Block D) and then in the Testery. In 1958 I. J. Good said O'Neill had been a temporary member of the Newmanry (or possibly a part-time member, see endnote 4 to *GRT*, chapter **31**, p. 599 below). In 1946 O'Neill was recruited into the Canadian signals intelligence service, of which he eventually became Chief. He retired in 1980.

Denys Lionel Page (1908–1978). From early 1942, head of ISOS, a section handling decoded German intelligence service messages, and from early 1944, Assistant Director (ISOS and ISK) of GCCS, of all the sections decoding and handling such messages. Before the war he was at Christ Church, Oxford; in 1950 he was appointed Regius Professor of Greek at Cambridge. For further details see ODNB.

Henry John (Harry) Peake (1923–1998) was educated at High Pavement Grammar School (Nottingham) and The Queen's College, Oxford (Open Scholarship 1942), where he read first Mathematics (Mods 1943) and then Physics (Hons 1944, BA awarded 1946). Peake worked at Bletchley Park from 1944 until November 1945, in the Newmanry and in the Japanese section. On leaving, he returned to teach at his old school. In 1947 he went back to Queen's, completing an Honours course in Mathematics in 1949. He then became a mathematics lecturer at Marlborough College. In 1962 he was Headmaster of Bilborough Grammar School (Nottingham). He later became Principal of Sheffield College of Education.[7]

Gordon Bamford Preston (b. 28 April 1925) was born in Workington (a colliery and steel-making town in Cumbria) and educated at Carlisle Grammar School. In 1943 he won a scholarship to Magdalen College, Oxford, where he read mathematics (Mods 1944). In July 1944 he went to Bletchley Park, where he worked in the Newmanry. He returned to Magdalen in 1945 (Finals 1948). He kept up contacts he had made at GCCS, visiting the National Physical Laboratory (Teddington) to see progress on the pilot ACE. He earned his living by teaching while carrying out research on semigroups (DPhil 1954) and went on to have a distinguished career as a mathematician. He became Professor of Pure Mathematics at Monash University (Australia), where there is a prize named in his honour. For further details see G. B. Preston, 'Personal reminiscences of the early history of semigroups' in Thomas Eric Hall, P. R. Jones and J. C. Meakin, eds., *Monash Conference on Semigroup Theory, in Honour of G. B. Preston; Clayton, Australia, 11-13 July 1990* (Singapore: World Scientific, 1991), pp. 16–30; see also G. B. Preston, 'Oxford in the forties', *Magdalen College Record* (2008), pp. 105–111.

Marian Adam Rejewski (1905–1980). Polish mathematician. In 1932 a group led by Rejewski succeeded in breaking German Enigma traffic. Their work was passed on to the French and British before war broke out in 1939. Rejewski never visited or worked at Bletchley Park.

David Rees (1918–2013) was educated at King Henry VIII Grammar School, Abergavenny, and Sidney Sussex College, Cambridge, where he read mathematics (admitted 1936, Part III, with distinction, 1939). He worked at Bletchley Park, in Hut 6 (German Army and Air Force Enigma). In October/November 1943 he was transferred to the Newmanry (see memo by J. N. Seaman, dated 3 November 1943, NARA HCC 1033:3315). After the war he taught at Manchester University (1945–49). He then returned to Cambridge as a University Lecturer (1949–58), before being appointed Professor of Pure Mathematics at Exeter University (1958–83). Rees was elected a Fellow of the Royal Society in 1968 and was awarded the Polya Prize of the London Mathematical Society in 1993.

Frank Byron Rowlett (1908–1998). American cryptanalyst. Head of general cryptanalytic branch at SSA during World War II. (See Frank B. Rowlett, *The Story of Magic: Memoirs of an American Cryptologic Pioneer* (Laguna Hills, Calif.: Aegean Park Press, 1998) and Theodore M. Hannah, 'Frank B. Rowlett — A Personal Profile', *Cryptologic Spectrum* (Spring 1981), pp. 6–21, URL: `http://www.nsa.gov/public_info/_files/cryptologic_spectrum/frank_rowlett.pdf` (visited on 07/06/2014).)

Michael Robert Sampford (1925–1983) was educated at Dartford Grammar School and Imperial College (University of London), where he read mathematics (matriculation 1942, BSc 1944, having joined the second year of the course). He worked at Bletchley Park from 1944 to November

[7]Much of this information was supplied by Colin Salsbury, editor of *The Pavior*, the newsletter of The High Pavement Society, in private correspondence with JVF, Jan/Feb 2014.

1945, in the Newmanry and then in the Japanese section. In 1945 he was a Demonstrator in Mathematics at Imperial College and applied to study for a Higher Degree in Statistics; he transferred to a PhD in 1946. His academic career as a statistician took him to a number of universities in Britain, including Oxford, Liverpool, Edinburgh and Aberdeen. Lectures he gave in the Ivory Coast for the United Nations Food and Agriculture Organisation were expanded into a book, *An Introduction to Sampling Theory, with Applications to Agriculture* (Edinburgh and London: Oliver & Boyd, 1962). His inaugural address when taking up the Chair of Mathematical Statistics in the University of Liverpool, in 1967, was published as *Conscience of a Statistician* (Liverpool: Liverpool University Press, 1967). Details of Sampford's academic career are given in his obituary by R. M. Cormack, in *Biometrics*, 39.4 (1983), pp. 1109–1110.

John Norman Seaman (1914–2002) was born and educated in Michigan, obtaining a bachelor's degree from Michigan State College (now University) in 1935 and (after an intervening year of study at Princeton University) a law degree from the University of Michigan in 1939. He joined the U.S. Army's SIS as a lieutenant in 1942, working first as a cryptanalyst in Washington and Arlington Hall, and then, between August 1943 and March 1944, as SSA's liaison officer at GCCS. Back at Arlington Hall he headed the SSA's Fish-breaking team. He returned to GCCS just as the fighting ended in Europe, to again be SSA's liaison officer, during which time he took part in the TICOM project in England and Germany. He retired from the Army as Lieutenant Colonel in 1946 and resumed his legal career in Lansing, Michigan.[8]

Walter Penrose Sharp, Jr. (1918–2013) was born in Newark, New Jersey. He studied mathematics at Drew University in New Jersey (BA 1939), Syracuse University in New York (MA 1940), and at Ohio State University before enlisting in the U.S. Army Signal Corps in 1942. After receiving training in cryptanalysis at Vint Hill, Virginia, he was assigned in 1944 to GCCS with the 6813th Signal Security Detachment. He worked in the machine room in Hut 6 and, for a short while, in the Newmanry. After leaving the Army in 1946 he taught mathematics at Newark College of Engineering before joining the ASA in 1947, retiring from NSA in 1973. While working for NSA he earned an MBA degree (Harvard, 1957), and after he retired he worked as a tax preparer.[9]

Albert W. Small (1910–1966) was an American cryptanalyst. He was a member of the team that broke the Japanese PURPLE cipher in 1940. He served as SSA liaison officer to GCCS, October 1944 to May 1945, and continued working in SIGINT until the end of his life.

Oliver Strachey (1874–1960), brother of the author Lytton Strachey (1880–1932), was educated at Eton College and attended Balliol College, Oxford for one term (Hilary 1893). In the First World War Strachey worked in the War Office's code-breaking unit, joining GCCS when it was formed after the war. In the Second he worked at Bletchley Park, where he was head of the ISOS section solving German agent ciphers until the end of 1941, when he was seconded to the nascent Canadian SIGINT organisation for about half a year. For further details see ODNB.

Brian Stapleton Stratford (1926–2010) was educated at Sutton High School for Boys, Plymouth, and Balliol College, Oxford, where he read mathematics (matriculation 1943, Mods 1944). From February 1945 he worked in the Newmanry and was later transferred to the Japanese section, leaving in September 1945. From October 1945 to September 1947 he worked for the Bristol Aeroplane Company (Filton, Bristol). After that he returned to Balliol to read Engineering (BA

[8]From information supplied to JAR by his sons, W. E. Seaman and J. N. Seaman, Jr., January 2014.

[9]In part from information supplied to JAR by Sharp's daughter Pam Camp, and by his friend Selmer Norlund, February and March 2014.

1949). He then joined the Aeronautics Department at Imperial College (University of London), where he obtained a Diploma of Imperial College in Aeronautics in 1952 and a PhD in Engineering in 1954 (Dissertation title: 'Flow in the Laminar Boundary Layer Near Separation'). He became a Fellow of the Royal Aeronautical Society in 1956. From 1952 to 1964 he worked for the National Gas Turbine Establishment (NGTE Pyestock, Fleet, Hampshire). From 1964 onwards he worked for Rolls-Royce Ltd, Derby. Stratford published scientific papers on aerodynamics and held a number of patents relating to aeronautical engieeering. For further details see *'Flight' Directory of British Aviation* (Kingston upon Thames: Kelly's Directories, 1981), p. 422.

Ralph Tester (1901–1998) was a senior accountant at Unilever before and after the war. He had a good command of the German language and had in 1942 headed a small section working on a German hand cipher. See 'Ralph Tester', Wikipedia article, URL: `http://en.wikipedia.org/wiki/Ralph_Tester` (visited on 07/06/2014).

John Hessell Tiltman (1894–1982), the son of an architect, was educated at Charterhouse School. At thirteen he was offered a place at Oxford University, but the family was unable to take it up. On the outbreak of war in 1914 he enlisted in the army, and between 1915 and 1917 served in France, where he won the Military Cross. In 1920 he was attached to the signal intelligence organisation in London. In the following year he was transferred to Simla (India), where he spent eight years breaking ciphers. He moved to the War Office, as a civilian, in 1925, some of his work being concerned with cryptanalysis. He was recalled to the military in September 1939 and appointed head of the Military Section of GCCS, then chief cryptographer of GCCS, and, from March 1944, Deputy Director. Tiltman made a crucial contribution to the breaking of teleprinter ciphers (see *General Report on Tunny*, chapter **41**). For further details see ODNB.

Geoffrey Timms (1903–1982). See 'Biographies of Authors', this volume, p. civ.

William (Bill) Tipler (b. 27 November 1921) was the son of two schoolteachers. He was educated at Watford Grammar School and Queens' College, Cambridge, where he read mathematics (matriculation 1940, Part II 1942). He served in the RAF from 1942 to 1944, and then worked at GCCS, in the Newmanry, from July 1944 to September 1945. He described the work as hard slog, requiring fanatical attention to detail. After the war he went into industry, working for Shell and then Perkins Engines.[10]

Edward Wilfrid Harry Travis (1888–1956), the head of GCCS at Bletchley Park from 1942, and of GCCS from 1944. (The confusing organisational history of GCCS, and Travis's place in it, is described in Christopher Grey, *Decoding Organization: Bletchley Park, Codebreaking and Organization Studies* (Cambridge: Cambridge University Press, 2012).) For further details see ODNB.

Alan Mathison Turing (1912–1954) was born in London, the second son of a father who worked in the Indian Civil Service and a mother who was the daughter of a chief engineer of the Madras Railways. Turing was educated at Sherborne School and from 1931 at King's College, Cambridge, where he obtained a first class degree in mathematics (1934) and a Fellowship (1935); in 1936 he won the Smith's Prize for an essay on probability theory (then not a fashionable subject). He became interested in the logical foundations of mathematics and turned his attention to the famous 'decision problem' (*Entscheidungsproblem*). His paper on the subject was sent to Max Newman for refereeing. Newman was at first baffled, and inclined to reject it, but a few weeks later wrote

[10]This information was provided by Tipler himself in a telephone conversation with JVF, 2 February 2014.

again to the London Mathematical Society saying he now understood and strongly recommended publication, so the paper duly appeared in 1936 (A. M. Turing, 'On Computable Numbers, with an Application to the *Entscheidungsproblem*', *Proc. London Math. Soc.*, 42 (1936), pp. 230–265). This is one of the most important mathematical works of the twentieth century. Its immediate relevance to the *General Report on Tunny* is that it describes what came to be known as the 'Universal Turing machine' which, conceptually, is a modern stored program computer. This was to become a physical reality in the Manchester 'Baby' of 1948.

In 1938, after two years studying in Princeton (NJ), Turing returned to Cambridge and began to do some work for the government cryptanalytic service. In 1939 he moved to GCCS, where he at first worked on Enigma. In the 1930s, a group of Polish mathematicians had devised a mechanical means of breaking Enigma messages (the 'bombe') but during the war the Germans modified the Enigma machine. Together with Gordon Welchman (1906–1985), Turing developed a modified electromechanical bombe that effectively represented a successful mechanization of the breaking of Enigma messages.

As is clear from the *General Report on Tunny*, Turing also worked on breaking teleprinter ciphers, but the exact nature of his contribution is hard to assess since relevant documents remain classified (see the Editors' Introduction, pp. xxv–lxxiv above).

After the war, Turing worked on the Advanced Calculating Engine (ACE) at the National Physical Laboratory (Teddington, near London). In 1948 he went to work at the University of Manchester. The extent of his contribution to the design of the Manchester computers is still a matter of dispute among historians, but it is certain that he wrote programs for the machines. He also worked on the philosophical side of what was to become known as 'machine intelligence' or 'artificial intelligence' (A. M. Turing, 'Computing Machinery and Intelligence', *Mind*, 59 (1950), pp. 433–460).

Following on from his activities at Bletchley Park, Turing also worked for GCHQ, but his known homosexuality (which put him on the wrong side of the law of the time) meant that he was considered a security risk. Thus his skill as a cryptanalyst bore less fruit than the other logico-mathematical talents to which his writings bear witness.

Turing died of cyanide poisoning in 1954, at the age of 41. The inquest verdict was suicide.

See Andrew Hodges, *Alan Turing: The Enigma* (New York: Simon and Schuster, 1983; reprinted London: Vintage, 1992) and David P. Anderson, 'Was the Manchester Baby Conceived at Bletchley Park?', British Computer Society: Electronic Workshops in Computing, Nov. 2007, URL: `http://www.bcs.org/upload/pdf/ewic_tur04_paper3.pdf` (visited on 07/06/2014). For further details see ODNB.

William Thomas Tutte (1917–2002), the son of a gardener, went up to Trinity College, Cambridge in 1935, to read Chemistry. He was, however, also interested in mathematics, and some work he published together with undergraduate colleagues seems to have attracted the attention of the intelligence community's talent scouts. Tutte arrived at Bletchley Park in 1941. He was assigned to the Research Section, which in late 1941 attacked Tunny. A pair of almost identical long messages had been read by Tiltman, giving the cryptanalysts a long stretch of key. Tutte succeeded in deducing from this how the Tunny machine worked. He thus made a crucial contribution to the breaking of teleprinter ciphers (see *General Report on Tunny*, chapter **41**).

After the end of the war, Tutte returned to Cambridge, where he obtained a PhD in 1948 (his supervisor being Shaun Wylie). Later, Tutte emigrated to Canada.

In 1998 Tutte gave a lecture on his work at Bletchley Park, published as 'Fish and I' in W. D. Joyner, ed., *Coding Theory and Cryptography: From Enigma and Geheimschreiber to Quantum Theory* (Berlin: Springer, 2000), pp. 9–17, URL: `http://math.uwaterloo.ca/combinatorics-and-optimization/sites/ca.combinatorics-and-optimization/files/uploads/files/corr98-39.pdf` (visited on 07/06/2014). For further information see

ODNB.

George Herman Vergine (1914–2001) was born in Lafayette, Indiana, educated at American University (Washington DC) and, as an architect, at the University of Maryland. He enlisted in the U.S Army Signal Corps the day after the Japanese attack on Pearl Harbor (7 December 1941), trained as a cryptanalyst, and served with the SIS. He was sent to Bletchley Park in the spring of 1944, where he worked in the Newmanry until the end of the war. He was made lieutenant while in England. He remained in government service as a cryptanalyst after the war, and retired from a high position in NSA in 1970.

Philip Dixon Watson (1925–2009) was educated at Mount St Mary's College (Spinkhill, Derbyshire) and in 1943, with the help of a State Scholarship, went up to New College, Oxford, where he read mathematics, obtaining first class honours in Mods in 1944. He was then recruited to Bletchley Park, where he worked in the Newmanry and the Research Section. He returned to Oxford after the war, obtaining a BA in 1947, after which he began to work for a doctorate. In the year 1949–50 he was a Fellow of Magdalen College, where he completed his DPhil (on topology) in 1950. From 1950 to 1993 he was Tutor in Mathematics and a Fellow of Merton College, Oxford.

John Henry Constantine Whitehead (1904–1960), educated at Eton and Balliol College, Oxford, was an eminent topologist who had been a mathematical collaborator and friend of M. H. A. Newman before the war. During the war he at first worked at the Admiralty with P. M. S. Blackett, but in September 1943 transferred to GCCS, where he worked in the Naval Section (Hut 8) and then in the Newmanry. He was elected an FRS in 1944. For further details see ODNB.

(William) Gordon Welchman (1906–1985) was educated at Marlborough College and Trinity College, Cambridge, where he read mathematics (matriculation 1925, Part II 1928). He became a Fellow of Sidney Sussex College in 1929. He served at GCCS throughout the war and was assistant deputy director for mechanization at GCCS from September 1943. Before that, he had been the head of Hut 6, in charge of cryptanalysis of German Army and Air Force Enigma traffic. See Gordon Welchman, *The Hut Six Story* (New York: McGraw-Hill, 1982). For further details see ODNB.

Shaun Wylie (1913–2009) was educated at the Dragon School (Oxford), Winchester and New College, Oxford, where he took a degree in mathematics in 1934. He obtained a PhD at Princeton University in 1937. From 1937 to 1938 he was a Robbe Scholar at the University of Aberdeen; and was a Research Lecturer at Christ Church, Oxford, in 1938-9. From 1939 to 1958 he was a Fellow of Trinity Hall, Cambridge, and he was an Honorary Fellow of the college from 1980 until his death.

Wylie worked at Bletchley Park from January 1941 to September 1945, first in Hut 8 and then, from 1943, in the Newmanry. In 1945 Wylie returned to Cambridge, where he became a Fellow of Trinity Hall and a University lecturer in mathematics. His research students included W. T. Tutte (PhD 1948). In 1958 Good left GCHQ, where Wylie then succeeded him as Chief Mathematician, thus resuming a wartime partnership with Hugh Alexander. Wylie retired from GCHQ in 1973. After this, he taught for seven years at the Hills Road Sixth Form College in Cambridge.

Charles Eryl Wynn-Williams (1903–1979), the son of a physics teacher, was educated at Bangor University where, having obtained a degree in 1923, he carried out research in electrical instrumentation. In 1925 he moved to Cambridge. He worked at the Cavendish Laboratory where, under Rutherford, he invented and developed the use of thyratron rings in high-speed counters attached to α-particle detectors: C. E. Wynn-Williams, 'The Use of Thyratrons for High Speed Automatic Counting of Physical Phenomena', *Proc. Roy. Soc. A*, 132 (1931), pp. 295–310. About a dozen years later, thyratrons were used in Colossus.

In 1935 Wynn-Williams became an assistant lecturer at Imperial College (University of London). During the Second World War he worked on radar at TRE and collaborated with the Post Office Research Station on a faster bombe (for use against Naval Enigma).

After the war, Wynn-Williams returned to Imperial College, where he remained until his retirement in 1970. For further details see ODNB.

Notes

The page numbers given next to the note numbers refer to this edition, not to the original. References such as **22X(c)** are to places in the text of the *Report*, using the *Report*'s own system of naming (in this instance, to chapter **22**, section **X**, subsection **(c)**). References of the form TNA HW 14/16 or of the form NARA HCC 970:2941 are to items in the National Archives of the United Kingdom or the United States, respectively; the latter example is our shorthand for NARA, Record Group 457 ('Records of the National Security Agency'), Entry 9032 ('Historic Cryptologic Collection'), Box 970, Item 2941. References of the form NSA TICOM I-45 are to partly redacted electronic versions of documents held by the National Security Agency (NSA), Ft. Meade, Maryland, obtained by Freedom of Information Act (FOIA) requests. (Such documents need not have been NSA-created. All the TICOM documents were, for example, British issued documents.) References of the form PAAA T-1437 are to items in the *Bestand Rückgabe TICOM, Politisches Archiv des Auswärtigen Amts*, Berlin. See our 'Bibliography', pp. 624–644, for further details.

Chapter 01: Preface

1. (p. 3) TNA HW 25/28. This report is listed in the TNA catalogue as TNA HW 25/28, *Solution of German Teleprinter Cyphers (Testery) Linguistic Methods*. At the time of writing (February, 2015) it is marked as 'retained by Department', that is, still secret and not available for public inspection.

2. (p. 3) This report seems never to have existed.

3. (p. 3) An approximate American equivalent of 'sixth form standard' is 'AP level'.

4. (p. 3) 'Foreign Office': euphemistic synecdoche for GCCS.

5. (p. 3) These Research Logs are cited more than 300 times in the *Report*, mainly from Chapters **21** through **28** and Chapter **71**. There is no evidence they have been destroyed but at the time of writing (February 2015) they have not been found. They were evidently notebooks in which ideas were jotted down, dated and presumably signed, with entries which might have been as short as a paragraph or as long as a few pages, developing ideas with greater terseness (if such can be imagined) than found in the *Report*. In effect they played the role of a scientific journal for the small, closed community of Tunny researchers, but the entries probably lacked the formality and polish usually found in published journal articles. One gets the impression that a form of technical dialogue took place in these Logs, as evidenced by, say, the list of citations in **22X(c)** or at the end of **25W(a)**. It seems likely that portions of the *Report* (especially the **WXYZ** sections of Chapters **22** to **27**) were taken directly from the Logs, summarising and synthesizing the discussions found in them. This is especially clear in sections **26B(d)** and **43(b)(ii)**, both citing p. 53 of **R0**, both using the unexplained phrase '...property was found to lack rigidity'.

There are references to 'Operational Logs' **O1** and **O5**, in chapters **23** and **73**, and to a 'Wheel Man's log book **II**' in chapter **24**. These must have been more like a ship's log, recording what was done rather than recording ideas.

In 1945, soon after the war, the American Newmanry veteran Lt. George H. Vergine (1914–2001) wrote (in an otherwise laudatory account)

> I shall never forget the maze of abstractions that confronted me the day I started in the section. That was on 9 March 1944. I was ushered into what was called the research room and given the log books to read. Log book number one could not be found; I had difficulty in reading the scribbling; and many of the common terms used such as *deciban* and *bulge* were never seen in a book on probability. Any hope of finding out what the underlying theory of solution might be depended entirely on jumping into the middle of endless daily notes and a mess of unidentified symbols.
>
> There was the Black Book, as it was called. It was supposed to give a coherent summary, but truthfully half of it was obsolete. Dr Newman claimed that perhaps the best summary of Fish theory could be found in Major Seaman's special Fish notebook. He had been our American Mission officer who unfortunately had just returned the week before to Washington — with his notebook.

(*Technical History of the 6813th Signal Security Detachment*, NARA HCC 970:2941, p. 16.) We have been unable to locate Major Seaman's notebook.

6. (p. 3) In fact, only a very few formulae are ever referred to this way: **22H**9, **22Y**3, **25Y**1, and **25Y**4, once each. The preface might have added that a reference of the form **22G(c)**(1) is to numbered subsection (1) of **22G(c)**, and, in chapter **71**, references such as **74** Jan'45 are to dates in the chronology charts of chapter **74**.

7. (p. 3) The main authors were Good, Michie, and Timms; some of the appendices were by D. Rees and S. Wylie.

8. (p. 4) At the time of writing this document has not been declassified. See our endnote 1 to this chapter, p. 561 above.

9. (p. 4) Sixta = [Hut] Six T[raffic] A[nalysis] = a branch of GCCS concerned with traffic analysis and reading of plain texts with a view to assist cryptanalysis of German Army and Air Force traffic, the main work of Hut Six. In the *Report*, 'Sixta' almost always means the non-Morse section of Sixta. TNA Catalogue entries for the 'Sixta History' exist, presumably describing two copies, one of which is subdivided: TNA HW 43/63 and the series TNA HW 43/82–43/93 but the documents themselves have not been released to the public.

Chapter 11: German Tunny

1. (p. 6) 'Electromatic', a trade name for an early electric typewriter (the IBM Electromatic Typewriter) marketed between 1935 and 1947. It was typically *not* used in teleprinter communications; specialized equipment being used instead. The Germans used equipment built by the Siemens or Lorenz firms under licence from the Teletype Corporation (in America, 'teletype' is the colloquial synonym for 'teleprinter'); the British used equipment built by Creed and Co.

2. (p. 6) This is the ordinary civilian system of 5-level start–stop telegraphy, as described in our Appendix A, 'Transmission of Teleprinter Signals', this volume, pp. 495–499, using the ITA 2 code described in endnote 4 to this section, p. 564 below. The standard terms in the modern

English-language telegraphy literature for dot and cross are 'space' and 'mark', respectively; 'dot' and 'cross' are Bletchley Park jargon.

The use of the terms 'dot' and 'cross' by GCCS predates its interest in Tunny: they appear (starting on p. 9) in an undated GCCS paper 'Theory and analysis of a letter-subtractor machine' by Capt. G. W. Morgan, about the C-38 cipher machine, which must have been written in the summer of 1941 when Morgan and his Research Section broke into that cipher machine. A copy of this paper is in NARA HCC 185:862. It was written no earlier than June 1941, when Morgan was 'Mr Morgan' (as he is styled in the minutes of the 23 June 1941 meeting of the Research Section Directing Sub-Committee, TNA HW 14/16, and hence still a lieutenant), and no later than Nov. 1941 as the NARA copy is filed with 4 pages of errata bearing that date. (Morgan was commissioned as second lieutenant in the Intelligence Corps on 4 December 1940. We are indebted to Stephen Freer for explaining the military meaning of 'Mr'.) There dot and cross mean inactive and active 'pegs' on the periphery of a wheel in the cipher device, as they do in the *Report*, but (as it is irrelevant to the C-38 machine) they do not carry the *Report*'s connotation of modulo 2 arithmetic as described in **11B(a)**. The C-38 machine was used by the Italian Navy. See Patrick Wilkinson, 'Italian Naval Decrypts' in F. H. Hinsley and Alan Stripp, eds., *Codebreakers: The Inside Story of Bletchley Park* (Oxford: Oxford University Press, 1993; paperback repr. with corrections, 1994), pp. 61–67, esp. p. 64, Paul Gannon, *Colossus: Bletchley Park's Greatest Secret* (London: Atlantic Books, 2006), p. 86, and F. H. Hinsley, E. E. Thomas, C. F. G. Ransom and R. C. Knight, *British Intelligence in the Second World War: Its Influence on Strategy and Operations*, 5 vols. (New York: Cambridge University Press, 1979), vol. 2, p. 22.

3. (p. 6) Even though it meshes well with the algebraic rules for combining impulses presented in **11B(a)**, the *Report*'s ascription of positive and negative electrical current to space and mark is non-standard, at best descriptive of British but not German practice. Older statements of the ITA 2 code describe marking current as being positive and spacing current as being negative; this contradicts the third sentence of **11A(a)**. These older ITA 2 statements include the code charts in the references cited in endnote 4 to this chapter, p. 564 below, in a 1942 German Air Force teleprinter instructional pamphlet (*Der Blattfernschreiber Lo15*, fig. 17, NARA HCC 17:154), and in J. W. Freebody, *Telegraphy* (London: Pitman, 1958), p. 9; the equations mark = positive and space = negative are also implied by the language in Gilbert S. Vernam, 'Secret Signaling System', US Patent 1,310,719, issued 22 July 1919, p. 3, lines 5–9. More recent statements (such as E. A. Rossberg and H. E. Korta, *Teleprinter Switching* (Princeton: Van Nostrand, 1960), p. 311 and Lothar Wiesner, *Telegraph and Data Transmission over Shortwave Radio Links* (London: Heyden & Son, 1977), p. 33) avoid this identification; it is not present in the version of the ITA 2 code published in the International Telecommunications Union's *ITU-T Recommendation S-1* of March 1993. We have not been able to discover when specification of the polarity of spacing and marking currents was dropped from the international standard.

Curiously, however, the symbols + and − were used in their mathematical and not electrical senses for • and **×** in studies of the security of the SZ 40 and 42 prepared by the German Army's signal security agency, OKH/Ins 7/IV, so where GCCS said $\bullet + \times = \times$, OKH/Ins 7/IV said + times $- = -$. This notation is found throughout the documents in NARA HCC 1405:4541, box 1408, folder 13, as described in endnote 19 to **11B(i)**, p. 567 below, and in Dr. Erich Hüttenhain and Sonderführer Dr. Walther Fricke, 'OKW/Chi Cryptanalytic Research on Enigma, Hagelin and Cypher Teleprinter Machines', 1 Aug. 1945, URL: `https://sites.google.com/site/ticomarchive/the-targets/okw-chi/related-reports` (visited on 07/06/2014), FOIA release of TICOM document I-45, NSA DOCID: 3422500 (a copy of which is in the National Cryptologic Museum (NCM), Ft. Meade, Maryland).

4. (p. 6) This is a British variant of the standard 'International Telegraph Code No. 2' (ITA 2) for start–stop telegraphy, designed in 1931 by the *Comité Consultatif International Télégraphique* (CCIT), the standards body then governing telegraphy, and written into the International Telegraph Regulations at the International Telecommunications Conferences of Madrid in 1932 and (with slight revisions) of Cairo in 1938. (The somewhat turbulent process by which this code was chosen is described in Eric Fischer, 'The Evolution of Character Codes, 1874–1968', unpublished paper, 2001, URL: `http://www2.units.it/hirema/didattica/materiali/charset/ASCII/ascii.pdf` (visited on 07/06/2014).) The final version of ITA 2 was published in International Telegraph Union, *Règlement Télégraphique (Revision du Caire, 1938) Annexé à la Convention Internationale des Télécommunications (Madrid, 1932): Protocole Final audit Règlement* (Berne: Bureau de l'Union Internationale des Télécommunications, 1938) and reprinted in such places as United States Delegation to the International Telecommunications Conferences, Cairo, 1938, *Report to the Secretary of State by the Chairman of the American Delegation, with appended documents* (Washington, D.C.: USGPO, 1939). We have not seen a printed version of the original 1932 'Madrid' statement of ITA 2, but its text is included in the law of 14 April 1934 of the Grand Duchy of Luxembourg ratifying the International Telecommunications Convention of Madrid, 9 December 1932, and the attached International Telecommunications Regulations. This law is printed in Grand Duchy of Luxembourg, 'Loi du 14 avril 1934 portant approbation de la Convention Internationale des Télécommications de Madrid du 9 décembre 1932 et des Règlements télégraphique et téléphonique y annexés', *Mémorial du Grand-Duché de Luxembourg*, 24 (23 Apr. 1934), pp. 415–533, URL: `http://www.legilux.public.lu/leg/a/archives/1934/0024/a024.pdf` (visited on 28/02/2015).

The CCIT merged with a telephonic standards body in 1956 to form the *Comité Consultatif International Télégraphique et Téléphonique* (CCITT); in the late 20th century the code was commonly also called CCITT-2. It is also commonly called the Baudot or Murray code; the above-cited paper by Fischer explains in detail the extent to which these names are imprecise.

The standard allows a national version of the ITA 2 code to assign meanings to the figure-shift versions of F, G, and H; in Britain but presumably not in Germany they were taken to mean %, @, and £, respectively. We do not know what figure-shift meanings (if any) the German Army generally assigned to them; the teleprinter code charts for the Lo 15 machine cited in endnote 2 to this chapter, p. 562 above, does not assign any meanings for them. Inspection of the typewheel of another wartime German teleprinter encryption device, a Siemens T52d belonging to Jon D. Paul, Crypto-Museum, shows that the figure-shift of F is two vertical lines, ||, and of G and H is blank.

5. (p. 6) As pointed out in I. J. Good, 'Enigma and Fish' in Hinsley and Stripp, *Codebreakers* (see endnote 2 to this chapter, above), pp. 149–166, esp. p. 164, this is 'reflection order', intended to make the grossest statistical biases in German plain text letter counts especially easy to notice. According to fig. **12 (II)**, the letters of ΔP whose first impulse is a × are more likely than those whose first impulse is a •, and similarly for the second impulse. In reflection order, the letters whose first impulse is a × are the 16 consecutive letters A through E, and those whose second impulse is a × are the 16 consecutive letters R through J. Thus, in a 32-letter count, the sums of the corresponding blocks of 16 consecutive numbers should be large; this is easy to spot by eye. (If the letters were arranged in numerical order, this would hold for the first impulse but not the second; if they were arranged alphabetically, nothing like this would hold at all for any impulse.) Reflection order is an example of a Gray code, that is, each pair of consecutive letters differs in a single bit position. See D. E. Knuth, *The Art of Computer Programming, Volume 4A: Combinatorial Algorithms, Part 1* (Upper Saddle River, New Jersey: Addison-Wesley, 2011),

pp. 282–301 for a general account of Gray codes and, in particular, p. 284 for an account of early independent re- or pre-discoveries of this idea: É. Baudot in 1878, G. Stibitz in 1943, F. Gray (1887–1969) in 1953.

6. (p. 7) That is, the top row reading `QWERTYUIOP`, the order used on English-language and not `QWERTZUIOP` as on German-language keyboards. This is what the ITA 2 code specifies. (See endnote 4 to this chapter, p. 564 above.)

7. (p. 7) As is clear from **11E** below, p. 20, these six conventional names were the graphical forms used by the Hellschreiber to represent the six non-alphabetic impulse patterns in question.

8. (p. 7) More precisely, these are the signals for a full stop followed by a space and for a comma followed by a space.

9. (p. 8) This standard paper perforator tape was 11/16 inches (about 17.5 mm) wide. The centres of the holes were 1/10-th of an inch (about 2.5 mm) apart; the sprocket holes spaced the same way, but of smaller diameter. Thus, a message of 1,000 letters would require a tape about 100 inches long (about 8 feet or 2.5 metres), and one of 10,000 letters would require ten times the length.

10. (p. 8) 'WT' (also 'W/T') = wireless telegraphy = non-voice radio.

11. (p. 8) *Schüsselzusatzgerät* = cipher attachment. Many English-language accounts of Tunny, both contemporary and modern, but not the *Report*, frequently use the word *Geheimschreiber*, meaning 'secure [tele]printer', or 'cipher [tele]printer'. This seems to have been a widely used but unofficial German term, subsequently adopted by the Allies, to refer to German teleprinter cipher equipment. The official German generic term was *Schlüsselfernschreibmaschine*, also meaning 'cipher teleprinter'.

12. (p. 9) *Betriebswagen* = operations truck; *Sendungswagen* = transmissions truck. According to reference sheet 64 of a German Army handbook of telephony and telegraphy for signal officers, *Dienstvorschrift 794/1: Merkblatt Fernsprech- und Ferschreibtechnik für den Nachrichtenoffizier* dated 1 April 1942 on the title page and 17 July 1943 on the sheet in question, the correct term is *Sendewagen*. (A copy of this handbook is in NARA HCC 15:139.) For further details about the equipment of a mobile Fish signal unit (a *Funk-Fernschreibtrupp*), see our Appendix A, 'Transmission of Teleprinter Signals', this volume, pp. 495–499.

13. (p. 11) Here the *Report* strays from its usual course of explaining new technical vocabulary, at least for the most important terms. As used in the *Report*, a 'character' is a binary digit, a modern 'bit', capable of taking on either of the two values • or ×, that is, 0 or 1. With the introduction of the term 'character', its approximate synonym 'impulse' drops out of use.

Addition of characters and of teleprinter letters is addition done modulo 2; equivalently by 'exclusive or' (XOR). More precisely, the alphabet of teleprinter letters is a five-dimensional vector space over the integers modulo 2. Modulo 2, addition is the same as subtraction, and the *Report* makes free use of this without comment in formulae involving the quantities P, Z, K, χ, ψ, ψ', and D, introduced in **11B(i)** and **12A(a)** below.

14. (p. 11) Starting in **11B(g)**, notations like P_5, Z_1, and so on are used freely, without comment, to denote particular impulses (or bit levels) in P and Z. The letter Z might have been chosen as the symbol for cipher because of cipher's German cognate, *Ziffer*.

15. (p. 11) The notation ψ' is explained in **11B(e)** below.

16. (p. 12) ψ' was pronounced 'sigh dash'.

17. (p. 12) This is the GCCS model of how Tunny worked but not a correct description of the actual German Tunny device. According to D. W. Davies, 'The Lorenz Cipher Machine SZ42', *Cryptologia*, 19.1 (1995), pp. 39–61, esp. p. 56, who examined several SZ 42 machines in great detail, 'The logic of M1 [that is, of μ_{61}] and M2 [μ_{37}] can be summarised thus; The moter wheel, M1 moves at every cycle. When there is a "0" [that is, • or *keine Nocke* (see **11B(j)**)] on its camlets it causes M2 to be locked. When there is a "1" on M2, wheels A [that is, the ψ wheels] are locked for the next cycle, unless pin P [the "limitation", see below] is raised by either of the magnets.' That is, a dot on μ_{61} means STOP and a cross on μ_{37} means STOP. That an active character on μ_{37} means STOP is consistent with the German name for μ_{61}, *Hemmrad*, or 'blocking wheel'; see endnote 20 to **11B(j)**, p. 569 below.

This 'mistake', which amounts to one of notation, means that GCCS recoveries of μ_{37} patterns were consistently the complements of the actual μ_{37} patterns used by the Germans. This was of no operational importance until the Germans occasionally, very late in the war, passed Tunny wheel patterns over Tunny, as described in **22G(c)(7)**. Only then, or only when GCCS had a chance to inspect captured German Tunny machines and wheel pattern specifications such as the one illustrated in fig. **11 (III)**, after the war, would the discrepancy become apparent. See the entry for 'Nocke' in **71**, and our endnote 36 to fig. **11 (III)**, p. 571 below.

18. (p. 13) 'Autoclave', an older form of the standard cryptographic technical term 'autokey'. According to the 1944 GCCS *Cryptographic Dictionary* (NARA HCC 1413:4559 and TNA HW 25/33), an autoclave is 'a cipher system in which successive groups of one or more letters or figures are enciphered in a manner determined or partly determined by the key and/or plain language of the preceding group or a fixed combination of preceding groups; a cipher having a self-generating key'. The term was possibly borrowed from M. Givierge, *Cours de Cryptographie* (Paris: Berger-Levrault, 1925), Chapter VI (*Autoclaves et procédés divers pour compliquer le système de Vigenère*, 'Autoclave and various procedures for increasing the complexity of Vigenére's system'), p. 83; and appears in such English-language works as Helen Fouché Gaines, *Elementary Cryptanalysis — A Study of Ciphers and Their Solution* (Boston: American Photographic Publishing Company, 1939); reprinted as *Cryptanalysis* (New York: Dover, n.d. [*c.*1950]) and Fletcher Pratt, *Secret and Urgent — The Story of Codes and Ciphers* (Indianapolis: Bobbs-Merrill, 1939). It was not, as implied by B. Jack Copeland, 'The German Tunny Machine' in B. Jack Copeland, ed., *Colossus: The Secrets of Bletchley Park's Codebreaking Computers* (Oxford: Oxford University Press, 2006), pp. 36–51, esp. p. 49, a Bletchley Park coinage.

William Tutte, writing in 2000, commented '...Sometimes even a delayed impulse of plain text would be added. The latter device was called an autoclave. From the German point of view, it had the advantage of making depth-reading impossible. On the other hand, a single wrong letter could wreck the remainder of the message. It seemed that the autoclave, when used, gave more trouble to the Germans than to the Bletchleyites.' (William T. Tutte, 'My Work at Bletchley Park', Appendix 4 in Copeland, *Colossus*, pp. 352–369, esp. p. 368.) Here a 'depth' means a pair of messages enciphered by precisely the same key stream, the occurrence of which allows their mutual solution by 'depth reading', as described in **28B** and **41C**. By preventing depths, the autoclave inhibited the use of what the writers of the *Report* call 'the third method'; see **12B(c)** below.

The Germans experimented with autoclave in March 1943 and put it into regular use in

December 1944. (See **24X(b)** (which gives a January 1945 date), the end of **44B**, the beginning of **44C**, and the chronology in **74**.)

19. (p. 14) At the time of its writing, the *Report*'s authors did not know that there were other models of the Tunny machine: a predecessor to the machines GCCS knew about, and a planned successor. Information about them was uncovered by the postwar U.K./U.S. TICOM ('Target Intelligence Committee') effort, which had several teams scouring Europe for information about German cryptographic and cryptanalytic techniques and successes. This project generated masses of document translations, interrogation reports, and summaries, three of which we use. One, Hüttenhain and Fricke, 'NSA TICOM I-45' (see endnote 3 to this chapter, above), is a translation of several short papers written by Oberregierungsrat Dr. Erich Hüttenhain (1905–1990) (the former chief cryptanalyst of the German Armed Forces cryptographic organisation, OKW/Chi) and Sonderführer Dr. Walther Fricke (the former head of the branch of OKW/Chi in charge of developing German cipher systems). Another, 'Enciphering Devices worked on by Dr. LIEBKNECHT at Wa Pruef 7', 2 Aug. 1945, URL: `https://sites.google.com/site/ticomarchive/the-targets/okw-chi/related-reports` (visited on 07/06/2014), FOIA release of TICOM document I-57, NSA DOCID: 3541302, is an interrogation report of a member of the section of the *Heereswaffenamt* (Army Ordnance Office) in charge of building cryptographic machinery. Much of the information in these and similar reports is synthesised in a nine-volume United States Army Security Agency, *European Axis Signal Intelligence in World War II as Revealed by 'TICOM' Investigations and by other Prisoner of War Interrogations and Captured Material, Principally German*, FOIA release of 9-volume typescript report (Washington, D.C., 1946), URL: `http://www.nsa.gov/public_info/declass/european_axis_sigint.shtml` (visited on 07/06/2014). Photocopies of these documents are in the National Cryptologic Museum (NCM) at Ft. Meade, Maryland.

Additional information is also contained in a mass of documents captured from the German Army signal security agency, OKH/Ins 7/IV, faded prints of microfilms of which are preserved as NARA HCC 1405:4541, spanning boxes 1405 through 1409. Box 1408, folder 13 contains twenty-six studies of German teleprinter cipher security. A related item is NARA HCC 1430:4737, *Documents of the Oberkommando des Heeres*, apparently an undated appendix to TICOM report IF-272. It is an inventory of the documents in NARA HCC 1405:4541, probably compiled when the documents were microfilmed.

According to the first three TICOM sources named above, the German Army and the firm C. Lorenz began development of the Tunny machine in 1937, and a predecessor of the SZ 40, called 'SZ 40 (old type)' in Hüttenhain and Fricke, 'NSA TICOM I-45' (see endnote 3 to this chapter, above), p. 16, was put into limited service. (The form 'SZ 40 (old model)' also occurs in TICOM documents. Lorenz cipher machines SZ 38 and SZ 42 are referred to in *Miscellaneous*, p. 42, vol. 8 in United States Army Security Agency, *European Axis SIGINT*, citing TICOM report E-14, *Detailed Feuerstein Technical Project Report, Ref. No. 7: Investigation of SZ Cipher Machines at Feuerstein Laboratory*, which we have not seen. It is tempting to believe that SZ 38 was the correct designation for the SZ 40 (old type). According to I-45, roughly 40 units were built. According to *The Signal Intelligence Agency of the Supreme Command, Armed Forces*, p. 80, vol. 3 in United States Army Security Agency, *European Axis SIGINT*, citing another TICOM report, I-31, *Detailed Interrogations of Dr. Huettenhain, formerly head of research section of OKW/Chi, 18th-21st June 1945*, which we have not seen, about 100 units were built.) This machine had 10 wheels, all regularly stepping, with fixed wheel patterns of about 90 cams per wheel. In effect, this machine used the equation $K = \chi + \psi$, where — unlike subsequent Tunny models — the ψ wheels stepped regularly.

This machine is almost identical to a cipher machine invented by Parker Hitt (1878–1971), the 'Ciphering and Deciphering Apparatus', U.S. Patent 1,848,291 awarded 8 March 1932, assigned to the 'International Communications Laboratories', a subsidiary of the International Telephone and Telegraph Company (ITT). Since the Lorenz firm was also a subsidiary of ITT, it seems very likely that the design of the SZ 40 (old model) was directly based on that of the Hitt machine. (We are indebted to Betsy Rohaly Smoot, an expert on the life and career of Parker Hitt, for pointing out to us the Lorenz/ITT connection.) The near identity of the Hitt machine and the SZ 40 (old model) had been pointed out in *Notes on German High Level Cryptography and Cryptanalysis*, p. 21, vol. 2 in United States Army Security Agency, *European Axis SIGINT*: 'In this respect this [SZ 40 (old model)] was identical with that developed by the International Telephone and Telegraph Company in the United States in 1931, employing 10 mechanical wheels and the property of pairing'. Similarly, the fact that the subsequent Tunny models SZ 40, SZ 42 A, and SZ 42 B could be regarded as improved versions of the Hitt machine had been commented by various authors: Harvey C. Cragon, *From Fish to Colossus: How the German Lorenz Cipher Was Broken at Bletchley Park* (Dallas: Cragon, 2003), pp. 12, 123–128; by Gannon, *Colossus* (see endnote 2 to this chapter, above), p. 38; and by I. J. Good and Donald Michie, 'Motorless Tunny', Appendix 11 in Copeland, *Colossus* (see endnote 18 to this chapter, above), pp. 409–410. The SZ 40 (old model) as discussed in the TICOM reports is thus, in effect, the missing link between the Hitt machine and the SZ 40 and SZ 42 machines.

The insecurity of the SZ 40 (old model) was recognised by the German Armed Forces cryptanalysis organisation, OKW/Chi, and the few copies actually constructed were used only on land lines. OKW/Chi suggested the introduction of the μ wheels to step the ψ wheels irregularly and seems to have regarded the period and complexity of the total motor stream TM as Tunny's main source of security; the successive improvements to the machine simply elaborated the TM stream. In the SZ 40 the TM stream had period $37 \times 61 = 2257$, in the SZ 42 A with $\overline{\chi}_2$ limitation it had period $37 \times 61 \times 31 = 69{,}967$, and with the SZ 42 B with $\overline{\chi}_2 + \overline{\psi}'_1$ limitation it had an even larger period. And with the introduction of the autoclave, the TM stream became non-periodic.

The TICOM reports also make it clear than another Tunny model, the SZ 42 C, was under development at the end of the war. This machine was to have 10 wheels, all irregularly stepping. In the judgement of *Notes on German High Level Cryptography and Cryptanalysis*, pp. 2–3, vol. 2 in United States Army Security Agency, *European Axis SIGINT*, this would have been a secure device.

The intended application of the SZ 42 C was somewhat different from that of the earlier Tunnies. They were used to encrypt ordinary start–stop teleprinter circuits, as described in our Appendix A, Transmission of Teleprinter Signals, this volume, pp. 495–499, but the SZ 42 C was meant for synchronous teleprinter circuits, that is, ones where the five impulses of a letter were sent out on a strict predictable rhythm maintained by crystal oscillators, but without start and stop bits. (See our endnote 54 to Appendix B, p. 528 above.) In start–stop telegraphy if a start bit was damaged by a transmission error, the framing of subsequent letters could be thrown off, spoiling more than just the single letter containing the original start bit. In synchronous telegraphy, data transmission errors did not have such an effect. In synchronous links teleprinter letters are always being sent, padding out spaces between the letters of meaningful messages with the all-dots letter /. This stream would be enciphered by the SZ 42 C, resulting in what would appear to be a seamless stream of random letters in which genuine message boundaries would not be visible. (In early 21st-century terminology, it was to be a 'link encryptor'.) A corollary is that the SZ 42 C would inevitably send pure key when messages were not being transmitted, but the German experts and the TICOM experts agreed that the cipher would be secure even when this happened.

The descriptions in the TICOM documents differ in some details. In the language of the *Report* (but not of the TICOM documents) there were to be five χ wheels and five ψ wheels, key was to be $\chi + \psi'$, and the ψ wheels all stepped together or stood still together, as before. Unlike the earlier Tunny models, the motion of the ψ wheels was controlled by two of the χ wheels, and each χ individually stepped or stood still, each one under the control of two others. According to 'NSA TICOM I-57', p. 6, χ_1 was controlled by ψ_1 and χ_4, but according to *Notes on German High Level Cryptography and Cryptanalysis*, (the second volume of United States Army Security Agency, *European Axis SIGINT*), p. 23, the motion of χ_1 was controlled by ψ_2 and χ_3. Both describe an additional mechanism to prevent the machine from getting stuck in a motionless state. Yet another description of the SZ 42 C is in a document of the German Army Signal Security Agency, OKH/Ins 7/IV, *Schlüsselzusatz 42 C* (cipher attachment 42 C) with letter of transmittal to OKW/Chi, *Gleichlaufgerät und SZ 42 C*, (synchronous device and SZ 42 C) dated 9 August 1944. (Both are in NARA HCC 1405:4541, box 1408, folder 13. Unlike most of the photocopies in this folder, these documents are fairly legible.) It agrees with *Notes on German High Level Cryptography*... as to which wheels control the motion of which other wheels, but adds the detail that each wheel was to have two reading stations (cam-followers), one for generating the key and one for generating the motion. Also, there were to be various plug boards and Enigma-like rotors for an additional layer of encipherment, and there was to be an autoclave feature.

20. (p. 14) Approximately $48 \times 39 \times 43$ centimetres.

21. (p. 14) The German terminology for the wheels was as follows. The ψ wheels were called the *Springcäsarräder* (irregular additive key wheels, literally the 'jumping Caesar wheels', the OKH/Chi term for additive key being 'Caesar'), the χ wheels were the *Spaltencäsarräder* (regular additive key wheels, literally the 'column Caesar wheels'), the motor wheels were the *Sperräder* (inhibiting wheels), the motor wheel μ_{61} was the *Steuerrad* (controlling wheel) and μ_{37} was the *Hemmrad* (blocking wheel). This terminology is illustrated in the 27 Sept. 1944 paper *Wirkungsweise des Schlüsselzusatzes 42 (neue Type) mit und ohne Klartextfunktion* ('Functional principle of the cipher attachment 42 (new type) with and without autoclave', i.e., of the SZ 42 B), one of the subitems in NARA HCC 1405:4541, box 1408, folder 13 described in endnote 19 to **11B(i)**, p. 567 above.

These names explain the markings *spri* and *spa* which puzzled Davies (Davies, 'The Lorenz Cipher Machine SZ42' (see endnote 17 to this chapter, above), p. 51): *spri* means *Springcäsarräder* and *spa* means *Spaltencäsarräder*.

22. (p. 14) The text does not explicitly state that an operative, vertical cam (*Nocke*) meant **×** and an inoperative, oblique cam (*keine*) meant •, on all wheels except μ_{37}, where the meanings are reversed, but this is the case. See the entry for 'Nocke' in **71**, endnote 17 to **11B(f)**, p. 566, and endnote 36 to fig. **11 (III)**, p. 571.

23. (p. 14) *Nocke* = cam; *keine* = none.

This drawing is misleading. Each cam is hinged. In the active (*Nocke*) position, it lies in the plane of the wheel, acting as a cog in a cogwheel, where it can be detected by a pawl feeling protrusions from the periphery of the wheel within the plane of the wheel. In the inactive (*keine*) position, the cam is swung out of the plane of the wheel, to the side. When the cam is in its inactive position the pawl misses it. As explained by D. W. Davies: '...each wheel has cam segments...which can be pushed sideways, having two positions. In their upright position these segments, which I shall call *camlets*, can engage a cam follower ...and when pushed sideways they are inoperative.' (Davies, 'The Lorenz Cipher Machine SZ42' (see endnote 17 to this chapter, above), pp. 44–45.) The sideways swing of the hinged cams is clearly visible in an illustration for the Wikipedia article about Tunny, 'Lorenz cipher', Wikipedia article, URL: `http://en.wikipedia.org/wiki/Lorenz_cipher` (visited on 07/06/2014).

All the wheels have equal circumferences, so the cams on the wheels with longer patterns, such as μ_{61}, are more crowded and hence narrower. The drawing evidently shows a side view of a cam from a shorter wheel (χ_5, say), having roughly the shape of the letter T, whose cross bar is the cam and whose vertical stalk is the arm of the hinge. The profiles of the cams on the longer wheels more nearly resemble the letter I. When drawn in profile, the direction of swing is out of the plane of the paper, and the tilt in the drawing of the cam in the inactive position is presumably an attempt to render this in oblique perspective.

24. (p. 16) *Ein, aus* = on, off, meaning not to switch electrical power on or off but rather to switch the machine between cipher and non-cipher operation, that is, to put the cipher device on-line or off-line.

25. (p. 16) The definition of difference in terms of addition seems somewhat perverse, but in arithmetic modulo 2 the two are, of course, equivalent. The use of Δ to denote the forward difference operator dates back at least to the 19th century, as by George Boole, *A Treatise on the Calculus of Finite Differences*, 2nd ed. (London: MacMillan, 1872; reprinted New York: Chelsea, 1957), p. 3, and was used early in the 20th century in such works as Edmund Whittaker and G. Robinson, *The Calculus of Observations, a Treatise on Numerical Mathematics* (London, Glasgow: Blackie, 1927). These works of course took Δ to act on sequences of real or complex numbers, not modulo 2 quantities as in the *Report*. Elsewhere in the *Report* 'delta' is used as a verb, with past tense 'deltaed'.

26. (p. 16) Here 'groups' are figured with respect to the circular structure of the wheel, in the wraparound sense. Since there are as many groups of crosses as of dots, the number of crosses in the differenced wheel pattern is also equal to the number of groups of characters in the original wheel.

27. (p. 18) The authors consistently write Straussberg instead of the correct Strausberg, possibly confusing the latter, near Berlin, with Strassburg, the German form of the name of Strasbourg in Alsace, or with Straussberg in Thuringia, near Erfurt. There is also a Straussberg in Styria, near Graz. (See our discussion of the 'HOSF' teleprinter exchange in endnote 2 to **61**, p. 615 below.)

A 'Fish Traffic' report of 24 Nov. 1943 by Lt. Col. Pritchard (TNA HW 14/92) gives Berlin as the end of the Bream, Codfish, Mullet, Pilchard, Swordfish, Tarpon, Trout and Turbot links; all are shown on **61(I)** as ending at HOSF, except for Trout which is shown ending at ANNA, and Pilchard and Swordfish are not shown. (In May 1942 Maj. R. C. Pritchard was deputy head of the Military Section of GCCS, according to a telephone directory in TNA HW 14/38; he appears in John A. N. Lee and Golde Holtzman, '50 Years after Breaking the Codes: Interviews with two of the Bletchley Park Scientists', *IEEE Annals of the History of Computing*, 17 (1995), pp. 32–43, esp. p. 40 and Donald Michie, 'Codebreaking and Colossus' in Copeland, *Colossus* (see endnote 18 to this chapter, above), pp. 223–246, esp. p. 233, presumably in this capacity.)

The *Report*, we conclude, is right in placing the link ends near Berlin, and wrong in its spelling of the exact place name.

The names 'Strausberg' and 'Straussberg' are (or can be) pronounced differently in German, so the spelling mistake was probably made by a non-German speaker. This mistake seems to have crept into Hinsley, Thomas, Ransom and Knight, *British Intelligence* (see endnote 2 to this chapter, above), vol. 3 part I, p. 478 et seq.

28. (p. 18) *Heeresgruppe D* = Army Group D; *Oberbefehlshaber West* = Commander-in-chief, West[ern Theatre]; *Heeresgruppe Nord* = Army Group North. Königsberg in East Prussia = modern Kaliningrad, now in Russia. See also endnote 2 to chapter **61**, p. 615 below.

29. (p. 18) Invasion: Allied invasion of Normandy, 6 June 1944.

30. (p. 19) In 1942 the German armed forces regulation governing cipher teleprinter operations specify that with the SZ 40, at most 20,000 letters may be sent with the same message key. (Clause 132, in a 45-page typewritten translation prepared by the U.S. Army in 1944 of *Schlüsselfernschreibvorschrift (SFV), Gültig fur die Wehrmacht v. 1. 12. 42*, NARA HCC 950:2816.) It would have taken about 50 minutes to transmit 20,000 letters at full speed. The 1 May 1945 edition of this regulation was sticter, with a 10,000-letter limit. (*Schlüsselfernschreibvorschrift (SFV), Gültig fur die Wehrmacht v. 1. 5. 45*, PAAA T-1437, clause 111, p. 26.)

31. (p. 19) 'Saloniki', the German form (as seen in Tunny traffic) of Salonica, now usually known as Thessalonica, in Greece. See the use of 'Rhodos' in the network diagrams in chapter **61**, the German form of Rhodes.

32. (p. 20) The Hellschreiber, invented in 1929 by Rudolf Hell (1901–2002), was widely used in Germany for several decades from about 1935. The transmitting apparatus converted an operator's key strokes (or 5-impulse teleprinter letters from a pre-punched tape) into 49-bit code words which were really 7 by 7 bit raster images of the letters typed, transmitted column by column. The receiving apparatus interpreted the signal as a fax signal, printing a picture of the writing on a paper tape. In effect it was a dot matrix printer (of the sort in use in the second half of the 20th century) with the print head at the remote end of a radio link. (See Rudolf Hell, 'Die Entwicklung des Hell-Schreibers', *Hell Technische Mitteilungen: Gerätentwicklungen aus den Jahren 1929–1939* (Heft 1, 1940), pp. 2–11, URL: `http://www.cdvandt.org/Hell%20Mitteilungen.pdf` (visited on 07/06/2014), esp. pp. 2–11, an article in an advertising brochure.) The disadvantage of using a Hellschreiber for Tunny traffic must have been the need for the receiving operator to enter the cipher text into the keyboard of the deciphering SZ 40 machine. That is, although the transmitting Tunny could be used on-line, the receiving Tunny had to work off-line.

33. (p. 20) That is, through the end of October, 1942. See **43A**, **44A(a)**, and *History of the Fish Section*, p. 2 (TNA HW 50/62).

34. (p. 20) 'Tone transmission' = carrier telegraphy, representing dot and cross by combinations of voice-frequency tones. See our Appendix A, this volume, pp. 495–499.

35. (p. 20) See endnote 2 to **61**, p. 615 for further details.

36. (p. 21) Fig. **11 (III)** and its caption excised from TNA HW 25/4; this image scanned from the GCHQ copy of the *Report* by a discretionary release of retained material by GCHQ historian. This image ©Crown Copyright. Used with permission of Director GCHQ.

Geheime Kommandosache = Top Secret. *Wehrmacht-Fernschreib-Grundschlüssel Nr. 863* = Armed forces teleprinter basic key number 863. *Monatstag* = day of month. *Rad* = wheel. *Pr.-Nr. 1* = copy number 1. (*Pr.-Nr.* = *Prüfnummer*, literally, control number or check number.)

This wheel pattern sheet is similar to those preserved in a month's collection of daily wheel patterns, *Fernschreib-Grundschlüssel SZ 42 Nr. 1012*, PAAA T-3376, except, of course, that the patterns are not identical.

The wheel patterns are expressed in terms of the two symbols 0 and +, which apparently mean • and ×, on all wheels except the sixth, μ_{37}, where they mean × and • respectively. (This is what is asserted in the entry for 'Nocke' in **71**.) That this is the case, instead of the seemingly more natural correspondence • = 0 which holds on the other wheels, can be seen by noting that the one assignment verifies the consequences of the restriction $ab = 1/2$ spelled out in **11C(e)** and the other does not.

In greater detail: The line in the sheet corresponding to μ_{37} is line 6, in which there are 17 zeros and 20 plusses. Following endnote 26 to **11C(b)**, p. 570 above, the number of crosses in the five $\Delta\psi$ wheels is equal to the number of groups of consecutively equal symbols in the first five rows of the key sheet, in this case 30, 32, 34, 36, and 40, respectively. Under the correspondence • = 0 for μ_{37} the dottage would be $d = 17$, and then the formulae of **11C(e)** (or the chart in **22D(c)**) predicts the numbers of crosses on the $\Delta\psi$ wheels as 28, 30, 34, 34, and 38. Under the correspondence • = + the dottage would be $d = 20$, resulting in the predicted numbers of crosses on the $\Delta\psi$ wheels being 30, 32, 34, 36, and 40. Thus, for μ_{37}, 0 means × and + means •.

Chapter 12: Cryptographic aspects

1. (p. 22) 'Other contemporary Tunny documents' presumably refers to such items as those mentioned in **73**, or the manuscript essays, '$\Delta\chi$-method' (10 pages, item 3/2/4) and 'Exp. values, Set totals, & necessary lengths' (12 pages, item 3/2/3), in the M. H. A. Newman papers in the Library of St. John's College, Cambridge.

2. (p. 23) If both of χ_1 and ψ_1 (say) were complemented, their sum will be unaffected, and similarly for all wheel pairs not involved in the limitation.

3. (p. 25) Literally, 55M889 = FIG-shift FIG-shift full stop LET-shift LET-shift space, and 5M89 = FIG-shift full stop LET-shift space. By double-striking the shift keys the operators made sure the shift 'took'.

4. (p. 27) More general in these two senses: Robinson could compare two arbitrary sequences of letters, punched on two tapes, but in Colossus one of the two sequences had to be derived from Tunny key stream ingredients. And, Robinson's repertoire of logical comparison functions was richer than Colossus's. (See endnote 13 to chapter **23**, p. 587 below.) But, as pointed out in **52(d)**, Robinson could only step uniformly, and thus unlike Colossus, could not automatically track the action of the motor wheels. This in turn meant Robinson could not automatically track the ψ wheels.

5. (p. 27) According to an anonymous author, evidently from the group in Hut 3 which set intercept and cryptanalysis priorities, writing some time after the war, 'As a rule about 50% of the messages of 2,500 letters or over could be sucessfully set. The proportion of successes was less on shorter messages and also varied according to the nature of the key in a manner that could be fairly accurately forecast.' ('3L Liaison with Fish (non-Morse)', TNA HW 3/92, p. 279.) This refers to the task of setting both χ and ψ wheels, of which the harder part was χ setting. According to **28B(j)**, once the χ's were set, setting the ψ wheels was more likely to succeed. One contributory reason for this must have been that any message slides present had been resolved in the process of setting the χ wheels. See also the table appearing at the beginning of **61**, showing for the latter

part of the war, roughly half of the tapes received from Knockholt as being set on χ's.

6. (p. 27) As explained in chapter **24**, a rectangle is a large numerical array of counts or of scores, the rows corresponding to positions on one wheel, the columns corresponding to positions on another, and the cells corresponding to all places in the cipher sharing positions of the two wheels in question. The two principal operations carried out on a rectangle were *flagging* and *convergence*. Flagging in its simplest form can be viewed as matrix multiplication of the rectangle by its transpose. To converge a rectangle is, in effect, to apply a variant of the 'power method' in matrix algebra to obtain an approximation to the dominant left and right singular vectors of the rectangle, or to the dominant eigenvector of the flag of the rectangle.

7. (p. 27) Garbo: a tape printing machine. See **56E**.

8. (p. 27) That is, the more this frequency exceeds $1/2$, the more likely the optimum patterns (that is, the highest scoring patterns) are correct, and the more suitable they will be for setting other messages and for starting wheel-breaking on Colossus.

9. (p. 28) Grilse: a particular Tunny link. See **61**(III).

10. (p. 28) 'Bulge': see entry in our Supplementary Glossary, p. 542 above.

Chapter 13: Machines

1. (p. 32) This chapter, in effect, serves as a brief introduction to chapters **51–57** and **91**. In particular: Colossus (mentioned in **13B(a)**) receives a fuller treatment in chapters **52** and **53**; the photographic 5202 machine (also mentioned in **13B(a)**) is discussed at length in **91**; Robinson (mentioned in **13B(b)**) is described in chapters **52** and **54**. The specialized counting machines (Dragon, Aquarius, and Proteus) mentioned in **13B(c)** are further described in chapter **55**. The copying machines mentioned in **13C** are described in chapter **56** and the miscellaneous machines mentioned in **13D** are described in chapter **57**.

2. (p. 33) The *Report* uses the term 'trigger' to name the Colossus circuitry holding a set-up wheel pattern, essentially an array of switches, one per character on the wheel. See the discussion in our endnote 1 to chapter **53**, p. 606 below.

3. (p. 34) The Miles machines listed below were sometimes called 'Mrs Miles', especially in **71**, and occasionally in **74** and **91**. See our endnote 3 to **56F**, p. 610 below.

4. (p. 34) Here (and everywhere else in the *Report*) 'start sign' and 'stop sign' refer to special punches marking the beginning and ends of the actual message contents a message tape, as illustrated in **35D** and described in **53B(a)** and **54C(d)**. They do not refer to the start and stop pulses at the beginning and end of every teleprinter letter in the system of start–stop telegraphy, as explained in our endnote 4 to **11**, p. 564 above, and our Appendix A, 'Transmission of Teleprinter Signals', this volume, pp. 495–499.

Chapter 14: Organisation

1. (p. 35) 'Station X' = Bletchley Park, the main centre of GCCS.

2. (p. 35) GCWS = Government Communications Wireless Station, 'Government Communications' being a bland cover term for SIGINT activities, used sporadically during the war. In a memorandum to the head of the Secret Intelligence Service dated 15 June 1942 (TNA HW 14/40), the operational head of GCCS, E. H. W. Travis (1888–1956), discusses the problem of maintaining security, when the scale of activity at Bletchley Park is widely evident. 'I feel that "Government Communications Headquarters" is really a very good title. It explains T/Ps [teleprinters], uniforms, D.Rs [motorcycle dispatch riders], constant Post Office maintenance vans, and if anyone talks out of turn it is consistent with coding and decoding. It should account for the presence of service personnel as well as that of the F.O. [Foreign Office].' Indeed, for the rest of the war the cover name 'Government Communications Headquarters' was used instead of 'Government Code and Cypher School' in correspondence with firms and with government offices not privy to SIGINT secrets.

3. (p. 35) Evidently some German Naval traffic was passed over Tunny links. See Ralph Erskine, 'Tunny Reveals *B-Dienst* Successes Against the "Convoy Code"', *Intelligence and National Security*, 28.6 (2013), pp. 868–889, URL: `http:dx.doi.org/10.1080/02684527.2012.746414` (visited on 07/06/2014), esp. pp. 870–872, which is based on surviving translations of German Naval messages sent via Tunny on the Berlin/Athens link in the second half of 1942, before Newman's group was set up.

ISOS = 'Intelligence Services Oliver Strachey', a section of GCCS handling intercepted German intelligence services traffic, formerly headed by Oliver Strachey (1874–1960), but during the Tunny period headed by Denys Page (1908–1978), later Regius Professor of Greek at Cambridge. (See entry in Biographical Notes, p. 554.)

ISOS did cryptanalysis of hand systems used by the German intelligence services, and it processed those decrypts, together with ones supplied by other cryptanalytic groups, to produce intelligence reports about German intelligence activities. Some of its decrypted messages (the Tunny ones) were supplied by the Testery, some by ISK ('Illicit Series Knox' or 'Intelligence Services Knox', named after Dillwyn Knox), which solved Abwehr Enigma traffic, and some by the Research Section, which solved Italian Intelligence Service messages. Most of ISOS's reports were published in series with names like ISOS, ISK, ISTUN, ISMEW, ISBA, and ISOSICLE. The names of the first three (which apparently formed the bulk of the output) give a hint about the sources of the messages (viz˙ hand systems, Enigma, or Tunny) and those of the other three give a hint about the recipients of the reports or their subjects: those for the Ministry of Economic Warfare, those concering British secret agents, and those meant for the London Office of the Chief of the Secret Service. (See David P. Mowry, *The Cryptology of the German Intelligence Services* (Ft. Meade, Maryland: National Security Agency, 1989), URL: `http://www.nsa.gov/public_info/_files/cryptologic_histories/cryptology_of_gis.pdf` (visited on 07/06/2014), Release of NSA Office of Archives and History, United States Cryptologic History, Series IV, Volume 4, NSA DOCID: 3525898, pp. 26–30.)

4. (p. 35) Maxwell H.A. Newman, FRS (Max), (1897–1984). See entry in Biographical Notes, p. 554, and J. F. Adams, 'Maxwell Herman Alexander Newman, 7 Febuary 1897 – 22 February 1984', *Biographical Memoirs of Fellows of the Royal Society*, 31 (Nov. 1985), pp. 436–452.

5. (p. 36) Dragon: see **55A** and endnote 2 to **55A**, p. 608 below.

6. (p. 37) Until 1950 or so, the term 'computer' meant a clerk performing calculations. In the *Report*, as explained in **71**, the term refers to the Wrens working on rectangles.

7. (p. 37) QZZ: Q-code to signal change to new day's wheel patterns. See **11D(e)**.

8. (p. 38) 'RF' = Red Form.

Chapter 15: Some historical notes

1. (p. 39) This, and a similar passage in **81C(e)**, gives the *Report*'s only hint about how the original idea for Robinson came about. The secondary literature simply suggests that the idea for implementing Tutte's 1+2 break-in with paper-tape loops and electronic counters popped, fully-formed, out of Newman's head, a few months after he arrived at Bletchley. (See, for instance, Brian Randell, 'The COLOSSUS' in N. Metropolis, J. Howlett and Gian-Carlo Rota, eds., *A History of Computing in the Twentieth Century: A Collection of Essays* (New York: Academic, 1980), pp. 47–92, esp. p. 60.) Randell, citing a 1975 interview with Newman, reports that Newman's clumsiness in carrying out the Testery procedures predisposed him to thinking about means of mechanizing the attack; this is consistent with reminiscences by Good and Michie (Lee and Holtzman, '50 Years after Breaking the Codes: Interviews with two of the Bletchley Park Scientists' (see endnote 27 to Chapter **11**, above), p. 36) stating that Newman was no good at, and hated, the hand techniques of the Testery, and thought that they ought to be mechanized. Good, in a personal communication to JAR, pointed out that Newman probably would have been informed about the existence of the special-purpose machines used to help read Enigma traffic, the Bombes. But Good and Michie were not witnesses to the intellectual birth of Robinson in November 1942, and Newman was evidently not forthcoming with details in his 1975 interview with Randell, so the evidence we have does not address the particular form that Robinson took. Nor do they suggest why Newman, rather than someone else, made the crucial suggestion.

A speculation of our own, for which we have found no concrete evidence, is that Newman knew something about the photoelectric sieving machines built by the American number theorist D. H. Lehmer (1905–1991) in the 1930's. (One such machine is described in D. H. Lehmer, 'A Photo-electric Number Sieve', *American Mathematical Monthly*, 40 (1933), pp. 401–406 and, retrospectively, in D. H. Lehmer, 'A History of the Sieve Process' in Metropolis, Howlett and Rota, *History of Computing*, pp. 445–456.)

We do not know, for instance, if they ever met. Newman was in Princeton in 1928–29 and again in 1937–38, and must have had many friends (including Oswald Veblen (1880–1960), the then head of the Princeton mathematics department) in common with Lehmer, who spent the years 1933–34 in Princeton and 1938–39 in Cambridge. I. J. Good (personal communication to JAR, 14 December 2006) remembered hearing Lehmer speak in G. H. Hardy's seminar in Cambridge, but did not remember if Newman was present. (As a topologist, Newman would not have been a regular attendee of Hardy's number theory seminar.) A further speculation is that Newman knew about the work of Charles E. Wynn-Williams (1903–1979) in the 1930's at the Cavendish Laboratory, Cambridge, on electronic counters connected to α-particle detectors. (See C. E. Wynn-Williams, 'The Use of Thyratrons for High Speed Automatic Counting of Physical Phenomena', *Proc. Roy. Soc. A*, 132 (1931), pp. 295–310.) Knowledge, however superficial, of Lehmer's and Wynn-Williams's work might have given Newman a hint about how a Robinson-like machine might work. (Interestingly, Lehmer himself had known about Wynn-Williams's work: 'The other interesting feature of this machine [i.e., his 1932 sieving machine] is that is was photoelectric and a beam of light entered on one side and tried to run the gauntlet of the holes to reach a photocell and find the first answer. We had to have an amplifier for this and at the output of the amplifier we had to have a flip-flop. As far as I know this was the first place in which a flip-flop was used in computing. It had just been used in counting cosmic rays and that's where I got the idea.' (Lehmer, 'A History of the Sieve Process', pp. 448–449.))

The last sentence in **81C(e)** suggests that a photographic apparatus ('comparator' or 'IC machine', presumably to work on similar principles to the later, American, 5202 machine described in chapter **91** and our Appendix C, 'The 5202 Machine', pp. 530–533 above) was also considered, but was deemed to be, on balance, not as suitable as a machine using standard perforated tape. This consideration might be reflected in message dated 26 Dec. 1942, preserved in TNA HW 14/62. In it, Travis asks Tiltman, while the latter was on a liaison visit to Washington, to 'please take a look at the [U.S.] Navy department's "comparators" and associated machining [*sic*] operating with teleprinter tape, with modified Hollerith, or with cine film and photo electric cells'. The intended use is to discover depths in systems using long subtractor 'tables', such as Italian Naval and Japanese Army codes, and the question is whether a new kind of machine 'can be used to make rapid tests of any overlap that we present to it. That is to say a machine on which the whole texts of two or more messages believed to overlap could be set up at any required relative postion [*sic*] and all differences quickly taken and recorded.' The next paragraph names Tunny as a possible application for such a machine: 'Also the Tunny section is concerned in setting messages, now that there are no indicators. The plan is to present and compare and count long series of impulses many times at great speed.' Thus, by late December 1942 the highest management at GCCS was considering technical alternatives to what became Robinson.

The possibility of using a photographic machine is also discussed in a minute of 1 March 1943, from M. H. A. Newman to E. W. Travis, which we reproduce in full in Appendix D, 'Initial Conception of Colossus' this volume, pp. 535–539. This letter, written during the early stages of the construction of Heath Robinson, reports Flowers's initial conception of a completely electronic counting machine. It goes on to discuss the possibility of improvements in German cipher teleprinter usage, which might make both the tape counter (the Heath Robinson under construction) and the contemplated electronic counter (which in scaled back form became Colossus) insufficiently fast. 'The only machines capable of anything like such speeds are the I.C. machines. It is therefore urgent to discover as soon as possible whether these machines have the necessary degree of accuracy, — a point now in doubt —, and if so to set them to work.' (Original held by GCHQ, Cheltenham, and quoted by permission of the Director, GCHQ. UK Crown Copyright reserved.) The American I.C. (Index of Coincidence) machines operated by sliding superimposed photographic plates or films, using photocells to measure how much light came through at each possible offset; they were used both by the U.S. Navy and, to a lesser extent, Army. Newman's lack of precise knowledge about these machines *after* the decision to build Heath Robinson had been taken shows that the possibility of building an I.C. machine instead of Heath Robinson had not been considered seriously.

2. (p. 39) 'Robinson', an oft repeated joke: in the 1930's, the cartoonist Heath Robinson (1872–1944) was famous for his drawings of absurd machines, like those of his American contemporary, Rube Goldberg (1883–1970).

3. (p. 39) Charles E. Wynn-Williams (1903–1979), physicist. Inventor and developer (at the Cavendish Laboratory, Cambridge, under Lord Rutherford) of the use of thyratron rings in high speed counters attached to α-particle detectors: Wynn-Williams, 'The Use of Thyratrons for High

Speed Automatic Counting of Physical Phenomena' (see endnote 1 to this chapter, above).

4. (p. 40) According to Brian Randell, *The Colossus*, report 90, University of Newcastle upon Tyne Computing Laboratory, 1976, this was a Tom Gifford, of TRE, about whom we know nothing else.

5. (p. 40) The *Report* usually uses Arabic numerals to designate the various Colossi, and only occasionally Roman ones. We regularize to the Arabic form.

6. (p. 40) Donald Michie was one of the authors of the present *Report*. For a biographical note, see p.ciii.

7. (p. 40) 'Wren'= member of Women's Royal Naval Service.

Chapter 21: Some probability techniques

1. (p. 43) Sections **(a)**–**(f)**, **(k)**, **(l)**, **(n)** and **(p)** would have seemed unexceptional to a mathematical statistician in 1945, but sections **(g)** through **(j)** would have seemed novel and possibly controversial and section **(o)** almost certainly controversial. The main innovations here are the logarithmic form of the odds ratio, the *deciban* of **(g)**, and the proportional bulge of **(j)**, which is perhaps more clearly defined in **22E(a)**.

2. (p. 43) This is the ordinary inclusive or: $A \vee B$ means A or B or both. That is, at least one of A and B is the case.

3. (p. 44) Bayes' theorem, named after the Rev. Thomas Bayes (1702–1761), the author of 'An Essay Towards Solving a Problem in the Doctrine of Chances', *Philosophical Transactions of the Royal Society of London*, 53 (1763), pp. 370–418, which first introduced a version of the result stated here. The result gives (in 19th- and early 20th-century terminology) a formula for calculating 'inverse probabilities', that is, probabilities of possible causes for what has been observed. In late 20th-century terminology, this means calculating conditional probabilities of competing hypotheses, given observed data. Although Pierre Simon Laplace, (1749–1827) made extensive use of inverse probability methods for statistical inference, a variety of objections had brought them into disrepute in Britain by the 1930's. Although Bayesian methods become respectable again in the last quarter of the 20th century, they were not so regarded by the mathematical statistical community in Britain during the period covered by the *Report*. See Stephen M. Stigler, 'Laplace's 1774 Memoir on Inverse Probability', *Statistical Science*, 1 (1986), pp. 359–378, especially chapter 3, 'Inverse probability' for Laplace's use of the concept, and S. L. Zabell, 'Statistics at Bletchley Park', this volume, pp. lxxv–ci., esp. pp. lxxv–lxxviii.

4. (p. 45) Hut 8 housed the Naval Section cryptanalysts working on Enigma, where I. J. Good worked with A. M. Turing and C. H. O'D. Alexander (1909–1974) before he joined the Newmanry.

The *Report* is inconsistent in its abbreviation of 'deciban'. In this chapter, **21**, it uses 'd.b.', but in its glossary, chapter **71**, it uses 'db'. We have silently regularized to the latter form, for both singular and plural uses. This is precisely the same abbreviation used for the electrical engineers' term, 'decibel', which does not occur in the *Report*. Since deciban was coined by analogy with decibel, and since in fact it can be understood as a 'decibel of odds ratios', no serious harm will follow from this ambiguity. Indeed, I. J. Good, one of the *Report*'s authors, writing in 1950, uses 'decibel' as a synonym for 'deciban', presumably to help preserve the secrecy of GCCS's wartime activities. (I. J. Good, *Probability and the Weighing of Evidence* (London: Griffin, 1950), p. 63.)

5. (p. 45) The unstated calculation is that $\log_{10} 2 \approx .30103$, so $10 \log_{10} 2 \approx 3$.

6. (p. 46) This concept is spelled out much more clearly in Good, *Probability and the Weighing of Evidence* (see endnote 4 to this chapter, above), p. 68, and by example, in the third and fourth paragraphs of **22Y**. See also the discussion by S. L. Zabell, 'Statistics at Bletchley Park', this volume, pp. lxxv–ci, esp. pp. xcv–xcvi. In the notation of Good, *Probability and the Weighing of Evidence* (see endnote 4 to this chapter, above) one has a hypothesis, H, with sub-hypotheses H_i, and evidence E. The sub-hypotheses are assumed disjoint, and their disjunction (or union) is assumed equal to H. The overall Bayes factor for H is $f = P(E|H)/P(E|\overline{H})$, the probability of H_i given H is $p_i = P(H_i|H)$, where the partial factor given H_i is $f_i = P(E|H_i)/P(E|\overline{H})$. The identity $f = \sum p_i f_i$ then follows from **21(f)**.

The precise connection between these various versions of the 'weighted average of factors' is unclear. Presumably the author of **21(i)** (almost certainly I. J. Good) had some way of interpreting the scenario of **21(i)** in terms of that of **22Y** and of Good, *Probability and the Weighing of Evidence* (see endnote 4 to this chapter, above), or vice versa, but the description in **21(i)** is too sketchy for us to reconstruct it with certainty.

7. (p. 46) This is the probability that an even number of witnesses should lie.

The reference to a 'chain of witnesses' harkens back to an extensive literature in the 18th and 19th century that used mathematical probability to model the fidelity of information transmission by a succession of witnesses. The 'theorem of the chain of witnesses' was in fact known to Laplace, and appears in his *Théorie analytique des probabilités*, 3rd ed. (Paris: Courcier, 1820), Book 2, chapter 11, § 58. (But not in the first, 1812, edition.) Laplace's formula, which did not use bulges, is algebraically equivalent to the one above. See also Siméon Denis Poisson, *Recherches sur la probabilité des jugements en matière criminelle et matière civile* (Paris, 1837), pp. 108–112, who gives more mathematical details than Laplace.

This result first appears in P. Prevost and S. A. J. Lhuilier, 'Mémoire sur l'application du calcul des probabilités à la valeur du témoignage', *Mémoires de l'Académie Royale des sciences et belles-lettres* [Berlin] (1797), pp. 120–152, on p. 133, in the special case when the p_i are all equal. Prevost states (p. 130) that the model of a double falsehood resulting in truth (which the formula presupposes) first appears to the best of his knowledge in his 1794 lecture notes. Prior to that the model was effectively that once an error is made at any point in the chain, a report at any subsequent point in the chain remains erroneous. The probabilistic analysis of the transmission of testimony by a chain of witnesses goes back to John Craig (1663–1731); see Stephen M. Stigler, *Statistics on the Table: The History of Statistical Concepts and Methods* (Cambridge, Mass.: Harvard University Press, 1999), chapter 13.

8. (p. 47) The reference **R1** is to one of the Research Logs described in the *Report*'s 'Preface', **01**, p. 3 of this edition.

9. (p. 47) This last assertion is problematic. The standard result is that the approximation is good if a is large and the number of successes minus a is not large compared with $\sqrt{a}$.

10. (p. 47) Here the factorial of $\frac{1}{2}$ is understood to be $\Gamma(3/2)$, where

$$\Gamma(z) = \int_0^\infty x^{z-1} e^{-x}\, dx$$

is Euler's Gamma function, generalizing the factorial function: $n! = \Gamma(n+1)$. Then $\frac{1}{2}! = \Gamma(3/2)$ works out to $\sqrt{\pi}/2 \approx .8862$.

11. (p. 48) That is to say, if x and y are the probabilities of the propositions P and Q, respectively, then

$$4xy - 1 = (2x-1)(2y-1) + (2x-1) + (2y-1).$$

According to **21(j)** the proportional bulge of an event is defined relative to a 'wrong case' or 'random case' value of a probability, symbolized by p. In this instance, the wrong case p for the proposition $P.Q$ is $1/4$ but for the propositions P and Q it is $1/2$.

12. (p. 48) In this example, the unstated wrong case probability for the disjunction (union) of $P_1, \ldots, P_k$ is k times the common wrong case probability of the individual terms.

13. (p. 48) A mistake in the formula makes the sense of this passage unclear. The following seems to be what is meant. The tapes are regarded as having a fixed composition of letters, arranged randomly: the one with exactly Np_i copies of letter i, the other with exactly Nq_i copies of letter i, for letter values $i = 0, 1, \ldots, r$. Say the two tapes *match* at a given position if the letters on the two tapes at that position have the same value *and* that common value is not 0. Let ν be the number of positions where the two tapes match. For instance, if $r = 1$, the one tape has $N(1-p)$ zeroes and Np ones, etc., and ν counts the number of positions where both tapes show a 1. (For example, if the one tape has 000111 and the other has 001100, then $\nu = 1$: the shared prefix 00 does not count in ν because of the non-zero proviso.) This is a sampling-without-replacement result about exchangeable sequences. The 'characteristic functions' of **R4**, 105–108 are presumably what probabilists call 'indicator variables', which indeed yield the formulae as corrected, if all the summations extend over the range $1 \leq i \leq r$, excluding the $i = 0$ case.

14. (p. 48) The 'school of statisticians' that is under attack was headed by R. A. Fisher (1890–1962), who since 1933 had been Professor of Eugenics at University College, London. The example relating to testing a new fertiliser is probably intended as a reference to Fisher's involvement in agricultural research at Rothamsted (1919–1933). For further details see the introductory essay above by S. L. Zabell, 'Statistics at Bletchley Park', this volume, pp. lxxv–ci, esp. pp. lxxvii–lxxvii.

15. (p. 49) Anticipating the discussion in **22** somewhat, for a given link with given plain text language characteristics and given dottage d, the probability that $\Delta D_{12} = \bullet$ has some known value $p > 1/2$. Given a message of length N, one has 1271 scores X_i, and 1271 hypotheses H_i. According to H_i, the score X_i is a sample from the binomial distribution $\text{Bi}(N, p)$ and all the other scores, X_j, for $j \neq i$ are independent samples from the $\text{Bi}(N, 1/2)$ distribution. Thus, the probability of the observations under H_i is

$$P(X_1, \ldots, X_{1271} | H_i) = \prod_{j \neq i} \binom{N}{X_j} (1/2)^{X_j} (1/2)^{N-X_j} \times \binom{N}{X_i} p^{X_i} q^{N-X_i},$$

where $q = 1 - p$. Then the posterior probability of H_i given all the scores is $P(H_i | X_1, \ldots, X_{1271}) = (p/q)^{X_i} / \sum_j (p/q)^{X_j}$. It is easy to find, by Monte-Carlo experiments, in the particular case $N = 1000$ and $p = .55$, that when the correct X_i value is conditioned to equal 563, that is, to be 4σ above its expectation under the complement of H_i, the chance that the correct H_i's posterior odds ratio exceeds 2.3 is only about $1/2$, and that it exceeds 3 is only about $1/4$. This choice of parameter values is important: $p = .55$ represents a typical case arising in Tunny breaking (exhibited, for example, in the letter count given in figure **12(II)**, p. 21; this edition, p. 28), and $N = 1000$ is a message length that the classical, non-Bayesian, approach predicts should suffice for setting. But according to the discussion in **12C(d)**, cipher data with letter distributions as in figure **12(II)** would need a larger value of N. In cases like this, then, the results of applying the classical and Bayesian analyses differ considerably: according to the classical approach the setting problem in this case should be easy, with an obvious stand-out solution, but according to the Bayesian approach the setting problem is difficult, and the correct solution is not certain to stand out over its competitors. See the more detailed discussion in the introductory essay, S. L. Zabell, 'Statistics at Bletchley Park', this volume, pp. lxxv–ci, esp. lxxxix.

Chapter 22: Statistical foundations

1. (p. 50) The gap in the series of section names is announced in the *Report*'s 'Preface', **01**, p. 3 in this edition. Sections **22W** and so on 'cover advanced theoretical aspects' and involve more mathematics.

2. (p. 50) This chapter describes, from a theoretical point of view, the statistical biases in Tunny key and plain text that enabled the cipher to be solved. That is, the calculations and formulae given here are not necessarily carried out as operational steps in breaking particular Tunny wheels or setting particular messages; rather, they describe the reasons underlying the success of the solution procedures described in chapters **23–27**, and to a lesser extent, **28**.

3. (p. 51) Note that the formula for ΔU is defined as the sum of U and its following value, $\underline{U}$, instead of the more natural seeming difference $\Delta U = \underline{U} - U$. Modulo 2 the two are the same.

4. (p. 51) See also entry 'Donald's Theorem' in **71** and corresponding endnote 7 on p. 619.

5. (p. 52) The entries in the right-most column are evidently estimated from empirical data and not from the (fairly accurate) approximation $.63 \times$ Length nor from theoretical averages determined by an analogue of the method of **25X**. If all legal wheels were equally likely, the average number of crosses in $\Delta^2\chi$ would be 24.37, 18.20, 17.42, 15.32, and 13.57, respectively.

6. (p. 53) The original's usage 'is comprised of' is unexpected here. Although common in America, and later in Britain, in the 1940's the phrase 'is comprised of' was regarded as a solecism by Britons with public school or university backgrounds. We have accordingly corrected it as if it were a mistyping of 'is composed of'.

7. (p. 54) The restriction $ab = \frac{1}{2}$ makes the numbers of dots and crosses as nearly equal as possible, in each impulse. The five impulses are independent of each other, so all 32 possibilities are approximately equally likely.

8. (p. 55) Here the mathematical fiction of the 'sixth impulse' appears for the first time. It reappears later in **22H** and in chapters **24**, **25**, and **26**.

9. (p. 57) The streams U and V are assumed independent. The usual modern English equivalent of the German term *Faltung* is its translation, 'convolution'. It names a widely used concept in many branches of mathematics, including as here, probability theory. The probability law of the sum of two independent random variables is the convolution of their individual probability laws. Starting in about 1950 the earlier term gradually fell in popularity, but is occasionally still seen.

10. (p. 59) Portions of a Tunny message might be pecked out by hand at the keyboard, with corresponding erratic tempo detectable by the slip readers, but the bulk of the message would be

read automatically from a pre-punched paper plain text message tape, and hence at an even speed. See **11D(b)**, 'Transmissions', p. 18 in this edition.

11. (p. 59) Here again, ΔP is taken as the sum of two plain text letters, instead of their difference. See note 3 above.

12. (p. 60) Absurd as this seems, it may not have been completely unreasonable. The main German premise was that Tunny was secure. If no other means could be had to supply wheel patterns to a remote Tunny station, sending tomorrow's wheel patterns under the protection of today's makes a kind of sense; this logic must have been occasionally persuasive to the people in charge of the day-to-day operations of the teleprinter network. The authorities who mandated daily wheel pattern changes (after August, 1944; see **11E(c)**) probably did not know about this misuse of Tunny. Presumably the daily changes were intended to protect against a lingering chance that Tunny might not be perfectly secure after all, in which case sending future wheel patterns via Tunny would be imprudent.

This situation is covered by the German armed forces instructions governing cipher teleprinter operations. Clause 95 of the version taking effect in 1 December 1942 states (in a 41-page U.S. Army typescript translation) that 'The transmission by wire or radio of the teleprinter basic keys and teleprinter wheel keys, in whole or in part, is forbidden to the teleprinter personnel. Violation of this prohibition is to be punished as a serious offence against an order pertaining to the service, if court martial proceedings are not entailed.' This prohibition is immediately followed by a loophole: 'Exceptions are to be ordered by an officer or official of superior or high grade and are to be permissible only in urgent cases. A message of such nature is to be handled as a GKdos. telegram, and may accordingly, pursuant to par. 37, be transmitted only with the SFM in the type of operation "Enciphered." Should this be impossible because, for instance, the station being worked is not in possession of the necessary teleprinter cipher keys, then the message must be enciphered as *Geheime Kommandosache* by a hand or machine system, pursuant to par. 38.' (Here SFM = *Schlüsselfernschreibmaschine* = cipher teleprinter, and GKdos = *Geheime Kommandosache* = top secret.) (English translation of *Schlüsselfernschreibvorschrift (SFV), Gültig für die Wehrmacht v. 1. 12. 42*, NARA HCC 950:2186.)

13. (p. 66) The figure at the bottom of the column labelled ΔP is in error. It should read 1670 instead of 1821. The former is the count of instances where $\Delta P_{12} = \bullet$, the latter is the count of instances where $\Delta P_{34} = \bullet$, presumably mistranscribed from a tabulation like fig. **22 (X)**.

14. (p. 67) The notations JB, GDB, C2Z and JP presumably refer to the Berlin end of Jellyfish, the Berlin end of Gurnard, the Zagreb end of Codfish, and the Paris end of Jellyfish.

15. (p. 67) The righthand-most column of fig. **22 (IX)** adds up to 3211, not 3200 as it should.

16. (p. 68) The row labelled $\Delta P_2 = \bullet$ should be labelled $\Delta P_2 = \mathbf{x}$. Contrary to what is stated in the text, is clear that fig. **22(X)** lists counts and not bulges. Of the 3200 letters in the A sample, 1543 have $P_1 = \bullet$, and therefore 1657 have $P_1 = \mathbf{x}$. The corresponding proportional bulge is thus $(1543 - 1657)/3200 = -.035625$, and so on.

17. (p. 70) Here the mathematical fiction of a 6-impulse letter defined in **22D(g)** is used again.

18. (p. 70) This arduous-in-practice computation, like all the computations described in this chapter, is not part of the Tunny-breaking process. It is intended to help illustrate the statistical basis for the attack, that is, to make clear what statistical regularities the attack exploits.

This paragraph was possibly written after the authors found the job of preparing the tables **22 (VI)**, **(VII)**, and **(VIII)** more tedious than expected. The distribution of ΔD can be worked out theoretically from those of ΔP and $\Delta\psi'$ by using the convolution formula (H2) in **22H(a)** 'straight', but that would involve 32 multiplications for each of 32 letters Θ, 1024 multiplications in all, with about as many additions, by hand or by adding machine; this may have prompted the authors to think of ways of using Colossus or Robinson to tabulate the empirical ΔD count instead.

In fact there is a way of computing the desired convolution more cheaply, by using 'Yates's algorithm' (a form of the 'Fast Fourier Transform' algorithm, or FFT, specialized to the case of mod 2 addition), with 32 multiplications and a few hundred additions and subtractions, but there is no evidence that the authors of the *Report* knew about the Yates algorithm in 1945. (This algorithm was first described in F. Yates, *The Design and Analysis of Factorial Experiments* (Harpenden (Herts): Imperial Bureau of Soil Science, 1937). Interestingly enough, in I. J. Good, 'The Interaction Algorithm and Practical Fourier Analysis', *Jour. Roy. Statist. Soc. B*, 20 (1958), pp. 361–372, one of the *Report*'s authors generalizes the Yates algorithm to what is now known as the 'prime factor' FFT, a predecessor of the FFT algorithm described by J. W. Cooley and J. Tukey, 'An Algorithm for the Machine Calculation of Complex Fourier Series', *Mathematics of Computation*, 19 (1965), pp. 297–301.)

The algebra in **22X(d)** shows that the *Report* authors *did* know the theoretical relevance of Fourier transforms to computation of convolutions, but in 1945 seem not to have known the efficient Yates algorithm for computing them in practice.

19. (p. 72) As our footnote indicates, the 'PB' seems to have an illegible subscript. But a subscript does not make sense in this context, so more likely, the 'subscript' is really a blemish in the photostat.

There is no equation (E4); presumably the last equation in **22E(c)** is meant.

The *Report* does not give an explicit definition for the notation π_{ij}. Context makes it clear that this denotes the proportional bulge of $\Delta P_{ij} = \bullet$, that is, $\pi_{ij} = 2P(\Delta P_i + \Delta P_j = \bullet) - 1$. The logical place to have given this definition is **22G(e)**. The notation is used later in **22H(f)** and again in **24Y(a)**. Analogous uses of π with other subscripts are defined in **22E(c)**, **71**, and **72** and used in **25E** and **25Y**, including π_{1+2} to mean the same thing as this section's π_{ij} in the case $i = 1, j = 2$.

20. (p. 72) $\underline{\delta}_{\bullet\bullet}$, $\overline{\delta}_{\bullet\bullet}$, and $\boldsymbol{\delta}_{\bullet\bullet}$ are *not* special cases of $\underline{\delta}_{ij}$, etc., for the values $i, j = \bullet, \bullet$.

21. (p. 72) The middle four equations in fig. **22 (XII)** are in error. They should read

$\overline{\delta}_{\bullet\bullet}$	$\frac{\beta}{2}\{+(\pi_{\bullet\bullet} - \pi_{xx}) + (2-\beta)(\pi_{\bullet\bullet} + \pi_{xx})\}$
$\overline{\delta}_{xx}$	$\frac{\beta}{2}\{-(\pi_{\bullet\bullet} - \pi_{xx}) + (2-\beta)(\pi_{\bullet\bullet} + \pi_{xx})\}$
$\overline{\delta}_{x\bullet}$	$\frac{\beta}{2}\{+(\pi_{x\bullet} - \pi_{\bullet x}) - (2-\beta)(\pi_{\bullet\bullet} + \pi_{xx})\}$
$\overline{\delta}_{\bullet x}$	$\frac{\beta}{2}\{-(\pi_{x\bullet} - \pi_{\bullet x}) - (2-\beta)(\pi_{\bullet\bullet} + \pi_{xx})\}$.

22. (p. 73) The reference to equation (H6) should presumably be to (H8). The quantity π_{ij} is not defined in the *Report*: see endnote 19 to this section, p. 582 above.

23. (p. 74) The *Report* refers to equations (6a) and (6c) when the context makes it clear that

equations (F1) and (F3) are meant. This is possibly evidence of an imperfectly carried-out numbering change from a draft of the *Report*.

24. (p. 75) Room 41 in the Testery is described in **14B(c)** and chapters **36** to **39**.

25. (p. 76) See **22D(g)** for the interpretation of $\Delta\psi_6'$ as limitation plus **x**.

26. (p. 76) According to a personal communication to JAR from a Newmanry veteran, 28 Feb. 2008, the algebra of proportional bulges was invented by Shaun Wylie.

27. (p. 77) 'L.C.' = letter count.

28. (p. 77) According to a personal communication to JAR from I. J. Good, 14 December 2006 and confirmed in an email 29 May 2007, he and Alan Turing had discussed the metamathematical question of knowing why a theorem was *really* true, as opposed to merely verifying the step-by-step logic of a possibly un-illuminating proof. To make things concrete, Good asked Turing what was the real reason the formula for the inverse of a Fourier transform was almost identical to that of the transform itself. Turing suggested consideration of what has come to be known as the discrete mod N Fourier transform (i.e., the transform of a numerical function defined on a finite cyclic group of order N) where the similarity of formulae also holds, but where all analytic problems concerning convergence of integrals are avoided. (This much of the story repeats the evidence in a printed interview, David L. Banks, 'A Conversation with I. J. Good', *Statistical Science*, 11 (1996), pp. 1–19, esp. p. 10.) Good had at some point suggested that such mod N transforms might be useful in cryptanalysis, and then pointed out that for Tunny work N would have to be 2. Newman then suggested that was really wanted was the 5 dimensional mod 2 Fourier transform, which is what was used. See the following note for use here of the term 'Fourier transform' in a slightly anachronistic sense.

29. (p. 77) The Fourier transform is named after J. Joseph Fourier (1768–1830), inventor of the Fourier series. Between 1935 and 1945 the term 'Fourier transform' was used in mathematical publications exclusively for expressions involving integrals, like

$$\widehat{f}(y) = \int_{-\infty}^{\infty} f(x)e^{iyx}\,dx, \tag{1}$$

especially for square-integrable functions f. So the use of the term in the *Report* represents a departure from then-standard terminology, and a mathematical reader in 1945 might have expected an explanation at this point. (This explanation might have been available in the extended *Research Log* discussion cited in **22X(c)**, and is implicit in the story related in the preceding note.) The usage in the *Report* might have been based only on an informal but suggestive analogy with (1). Or it might have been coined by someone acquainted with the then-new theory of harmonic analysis of functions on groups. According to this theory, each commutative group has its own kind of Fourier analysis: for the additive group of real numbers, the classical Fourier transform (1); for the teleprinter group, the formula of **22X(d)**, and so on. Even though the then-available expositions of the new theory (listed below) did not use the term 'Fourier transform' in this generalized sense, they do make the analogy obvious and in effect give a kind of warrant for the terminology change. Indeed, the extended sense of the term became common in the 1950's and 1960's, so in this sense the *Report*'s authors were trend setters to use the term in its current sense somewhat before the rest of the world did.

The modern theory of harmonic analysis is based on the notions of group representations and group characters, as worked out at the end of the 19th century, notably by F. G. Frobenius (1849–1917). The details for the special case covering the teleprinter group are trivial, and seen in isolation (as presented, say, in H. Weber, *Lehrbuch der Algebra* (Braunschweig: F. Vieweg, 1912; reprinted New York: Chelsea, n.d. [*c.*1950]) are not recognisable as being connected with classical Fourier analysis. According to G. W. Mackey, *The Scope and History of Commutative and Noncommutative Harmonic Analysis* (Providence, RI: American Mathematical Society, 1992), 'That characters and group representations might have something to do with Fourier analysis seems to have been first recognised by Hermann Weyl (1885–1955) in 1927'. (See also K. I. Gross, 'On the Evolution of Noncommutative Harmonic Analysis', *American Mathematical Monthly*, 85 (1978), pp. 525–548.) Landmarks in the development and exposition of this theory were the 1927 paper F. Peter and H. Weyl, 'Die Vollständigkeit der primitiven Darstellungen einer geschlossenen Kontinuierlichen Gruppe', *Mathematische Annalen*, 97 (1927), pp. 737–755, the English translation L. Pontriagin, *Topological Groups*, trans. by E. Lehmer (Princeton: Princeton University Press, 1939), A. Weil, *L'Intégration dans les Groupes Topologiques et ses Applications* (Paris: Hermann, 1940) and H. Weyl, *Group Theory and Quantum Mechanics*, trans. by H. P. Robertson, trans. of 2nd German edition (London: Methuen, 1931; reprinted New York: Dover, 1949).

There were many ways by which the Newmanry, with its high level of mathematical culture, might have become aware of these developments. It is even possible M. H. A. Newman heard about them from H. Weyl himself, when Newman spent the academic years 1928–29 and 1937–39 at Princeton University. (According to Newman's son, Weyl was a personal friend of Newman's. See Christopher Newman, 'Max Newman — Mathematician, Codebreaker, and Computer Pioneer' in Copeland, *Colossus* (see endnote 18 to Chapter **11**, above), pp. 176–188, esp. p. 180.)

Interestingly, one of the *Report*'s authors, I. J. Good, seems to have been the first user in print of the applied mathematician's term 'discrete Fourier transform' (for the same concept, for arbitrary finite Abelian groups) in I. J. Good, 'Random Motion on a Finite Abelian Group', *Proc. Camb. Phil. Soc.*, 47 (1951), pp. 756–762, esp. p. 758. In that paper the term receives a comment, with a discussion of the connection between group characters and Fourier analysis, and a citation to page 165 of Weyl, *Group Theory and Quantum Mechanics*.

30. (p. 78) Presumably the left-hand side should be $\mathrm{P.B.}^{*}\,\Delta P(\mathrm{E})$.

31. (p. 79) Although the formulae are identical, the interpretation of the 'theorem of weighted averages' stated in **22(i)** does not fit the current application as well as the version stated in Good, *Probability and the Weighing of Evidence* (see endnote 4 to Chapter **21**, above), p. 68 does. (See endnote 6 to **21(i)**, p. 578 above.) The former is couched in terms of witnesses, only one of which has seen the evidence. The later refers to a collection of hypotheses, only one of which is correct. In the present application the hypotheses refer to the different possible plain text language characteristics, and it seems hard to construe them as witnesses, one of which has seen the evidence.

32. (p. 79) This is the usual Pearson χ^2 test of mathematical statistics.

33. (p. 79) Ten times the common (base 10) logarithm of x is the logarithm of x to the base $\sqrt[10]{10}$. Thus, decibans (introduced in **21(g)**) can be understood as logarithms to this apparently strange base.

34. (p. 79) 'Seedy' here presumably means 'implausible'.

Chapter 23: Machine setting

1. (p. 80) Here again, with the modulo 2 (or binary) arithmetic applying to Z, D, χ, and ψ, addition is the same as subtraction.

2. (p. 80) This multiplication is in error. In fact, $41 \times 31 \times 29 \times 26 \times 23 = 22{,}041{,}682$. The author of this passage seems to have made two mistakes: replacing the factor 29 with an extra copy of the factor 31 and then making a carry-digit error in working out $41 \times 31 \times 31 \times 26 \times 23 = 23{,}561{,}798$.

3. (p. 81) A run is a run on a counting machine, either Robinson or Colossus. For each setting of a specified set of wheels (usually one or two, but possibly three or even four), the counter tabulates the number of places in the cipher text where a given Boolean condition is satisfied.

In modern terminology, the counting machine executes a nested loop. The outer loop ranges over all settings (i.e., initial settings) for the wheels in question. For each such setting, the inner loop passes over the length of the cipher text, stepping the wheels forward from their setting, counting instances where the Boolean condition is met, possibly ignoring certain ranges of the cipher text by using 'spanning'.

At the end of the inner loop, if the count exceeds a threshold (the 'set total'), it is printed, along with the corresponding outer loop setting. At the end of the outer loop, the setting with the largest count will, in the most favourable situation, be the correct setting.

The Boolean condition is specified by a notation like '1+2' or '5=/1=2=4, U', as in the 'simple tree' of **23B(c)**. Notes (ii) and (iii) in **23(c)** specify, as well as anywhere in the *Report*, how these run code notations are to be understood. For instance, '1+2' means to count, for each combination of settings for the χ_1 and χ_2 wheels, the number of instances in the cipher text where $\Delta D_1 + \Delta D_2 = \bullet$. The more elaborate code '5=/1=2=4, U' means, for each setting of χ_5 (and only of χ_5 because of the position of the conditioning stroke /), to count instances in the cipher text where either $\Delta D_5 = \Delta D_1 = \Delta D_2 = \Delta D_4$ or $\Delta D = \mathrm{U}$ or both.

4. (p. 81) These trees are essentially 'decision trees', 'flow diagrams', or 'flow charts', specifying the sequence of solution steps to be undertaken by the Colossus operators. Topologically, their shapes are 'directed acyclic graphs', not 'trees', as their branching paths can sometimes merge. (The topological sense of 'tree' is apparently due to Arthur Cayley (1821–1895): Arthur Cayley, 'On the Theory of the Analytical Forms Called Trees', *Philosophical Magazine*, 4th ser., 13 (1857), pp. 172–176. The term was in common use by early 20th-century topologists, appearing (for instance) in R. L. Brooks, C. A. B. Smith, A. H. Stone and W. T. Tutte, 'The Dissection of Rectangles into Squares', *Duke Mathematical Journal*, 7 (1940), pp. 312–340.) We do not know when the term 'decision tree' was introduced; it seems to have become common after the publication of Howard Raiffa and Robert Schlaifer, *Applied Statistical Decision Theory* (Boston: Harvard Business School, 1961). This term does not appear in the *Report*, but does appear in postwar accounts by both Good and Michie of their Tunny work.

5. (p. 83) A copy of this table, labelled 'Sigma statistics on X setting runs', is included in an enclosure to Annex A of liaison report G-5 sent by Albert W. Small (1910–1966) to SSA on 12 December 1944, in NARA HCC 699:1704. That copy of the table bears the caption 'Figures indicate sigmage of run; first run on left, second on right. Long runs are two wheel runs, short runs one wheel. Blanks indicate no other run needed. Runs referred to are two independent runs which

agree as to the setting of a given X wheel; then if the sigmages are in the combinations shown, the setting may be classified "certain" or "good."' (Note the spelling 'sigmage', presumably reflecting a two-syllable pronunciation of the word; the *Report* consistently uses 'sigma-age' corresponding to a three syllable pronunciation. According to a personal communication to JAR from D. Michie, 8 Dec. 2004, 'Usage varied. It started as a three-syllable word, but idiosyncrasies developed. Jack Good used to delight in mispronouncing it 'sigmidge'! I think I personally used three syllables. But it was hard for the ear to detect much difference at normal rates of speech.')

6. (p. 83) Separately, the long run 3+4**x**/1**x**2**x** and the short run 3**x**/1**x**2• need sigma-ages of 4.0 and 3.2. But when combined, according to the next-to-last entry in the 'Certain, long, short' column of the table, the pair of individual sigma-ages 3.9, 2.3 suffices.

7. (p. 83) In the displayed equation, the second expression for the expected sigma-age is wrong. It should be $p\xi N/\sqrt{p(1-p)N}$.

8. (p. 84) The illustrations exhibited here are of Colossus output slips, produced by its printer. (See **53G(k)**.) The printing on a slip is a combination of what the operator typed and of what Colossus typed automatically. Most of the slips illustrated in this section start and end with operator typed data; Colossus calculated data is typically the tabular data in the middle. Some of the slips bear the operators' names.

9. (p. 85) 'C3' is a conventional shorthand name for the run 4=5=/1=2. See glossary entry for 'C1, C2, C3, C4', chapter **71**; other such shorthand names might have existed but we do not know of them.

10. (p. 86) P.M.H. is 'print main heading'; see **53G(g)**.

11. (p. 86) 'DO' = Duty Officer; see **71**.

12. (p. 88) The snippet of the plain text shown at the bottom of exhibit 23D/7, when translated out of teleprinterese, reads '*Böse Feind erst da* + KR –'. The first four words are Quatsch, probably a quotation from the Nazi song 'Das Lied von den Lügenlords' (the 'Lay of the Lords of the Lies') apparently written in 1940. (*Quatsch* (see **43A** and entry in **71**) was meaningless text inserted at the beginning of messages to defeat plain text guessing. The term means 'nonsense'. The official German name for such nonsense text was *Wahlwörter* (literally, 'arbitrary words'); we do not know if *Quatsch* was used in this specialized sense by the Germans or only by GCCS.) This song, excoriating the British politicians Churchill, Eden, Halifax, and Duff Cooper, starts with *In England wohnt ein kleiner Mann / der nie die Wahrheit sagen kann...* and ends with the lines

> Wenn der deutsche Michel naht, bleibt kein Auge trocken.
> Denn ist der böse Feind erst da,
> Zu spät ist's dann für Kanada.
> Dann, Lügen-Churchill, fähre well,
> Samt deiner Clique in die Höll!

('In England lives a little man who can never tell the truth... When the German [angel] Michael approaches no eye will remain dry. When the angry enemy arrives, it'll be too late for [fleeing to] Canada; then, lying Churchill fare well, together with your gang in hell!' The phrase *böse Feind* can mean, figuratively, the Devil, but in this context it does not.) The words to this song are reprinted in Volker Kühn, *Kleinkunststücke*, 5 vols. (Weinheim and Berlin: Quadriga, 1987–94), vol. 3 and (with slight variation) on a picture postcard, images of which are on the internet.

('Historische Bildpostkarten — 17.3 Bildpostkarten/Das Lied von den Lügenlords', Universität Osnabrück — Sammlung Prof. Dr. S. Giesbrecht, URL: `http://www.bildpostkarten.uni-osnabrueck.de/displayimage.php?pos=-2868` (visited on 07/06/2014).) According to Kühn, the song was performed by Wilhelm Strienz (1900–1987) accompanied by the band of Willi Rudek, and issued as a phonograph record. Kühn does not know who wrote the song. The postcard gives a credit line: *Entnommen dem 2. Heft der Liedersammlung des Großdeutschen Rundfunks "Lieder der Front".*

Following the Quatsch is '+ KR-'. According to the sources listed in endnote 23 to **28E**, p. 596 below, the plus sign indicates the beginning of the message, and the KR is a message priority sign.

13. (p. 89) This might seem surprising, since Colossus is usually thought of as having been a more capable machine than Robinson, not sharing the weakness of the latter described in **52(f)**, in addition to being faster and more reliable. But the run $1{\times}2{\times}\overline{\chi}_2{\times}$ OR $1{\bullet}2{\bullet}\overline{\chi}_2{\bullet}$ was not doable on Colossus because the corresponding Boolean predicate (which can be reexpressed as the AND of the two conditions $Z_1 = Z_2$ and $Z_2 = \overline{\chi}_2$) is simply not in Colossus's repertoire. It is not a function of any possible Q specifiable by the Q selection switches described in **53J(a)**, as it depends non-trivially on both Z_2 and on χ_2, and not on either of them separately or on their mod 2 sum alone, as required by **53J(a)**. Hence the Q panel cannot be used for this run. The only other means of enforcing a Boolean condition is via the plug panel described in **56K**. But it lacked AND jacks, so it too could not implement the condition in question. As suggested by the *Report*, this condition was easy to implement on Robinson; the 'Footnote' in **54D(h)** hints, and the examples in **54E(b)** show, how this could be done.

Shortly after the war it was found that Robinson could be used to help solve non-Tunny ciphers. In an exchange of cables in the summer of 1945, GCCS and SSA discussed the exchange, repatriation and disposal of cryptanalytic machinery. Cable GCCS 10930 of 26 Aug. 1945, from GCCS to SSA, reads 'GCCS would like to suggest trading the ROBINSON for two pre-sensing gang punches which they would prefer to slide run or camel. Refer GCCS 10113. Versatility of ROBINSON becoming constantly apparent. Use has been envisioned for such different jobs as enigma dudbusting and solution of JBN. Latter devised by LEVENSON [Arthur J. Levenson (1914–2007), American member of the Newmanry]. Will send details.' (TNA HW 57/1.) We do not know whether the proposed exchange occurred, nor what 'JBN' was (it is possibly the minor Japanese code mentioned in 'W.W. II Japanese Translation at Arlington Hall Station', *Cryptolog*, 6.1 (Jan. 1979), NSA DOCID: 4019659, pp. 13–16, URL: `http://www.nsa.gov/public_info/_files/cryptologs/cryptolog_49.pdf` (visited on 07/06/2014), esp. p. 16); of interest to us here is the statement of versatility of Robinson.

14. (p. 90) 'QTQ' = German Q code for limitation. See **71**.

15. (p. 91) C3 means the run 1=2=4=5; see entry 'C1, C2, C3, C4' in **71**.

16. (p. 92) The 'upper switches' are the stepping switches of **53D(c)**.

17. (p. 96) The 'triggers' were the circuitry on Colossus representing the wheel patterns. See our endnote 1 to chapter **53**, p. 606 below.

18. (p. 97) Here there is a hint that Colossus's counting was not considered completely reliable.

19. (p. 100) Here the vertical bar is used to mean the same thing that the conditioning stroke / means in **23B(c)** and everywhere else in the *Report*; see endnote 3 to **23B(b)**, p. 585 above. That

is, the motor run usually counts the number of instances where BM $= \bullet$, among places where ΔD's value lies in some specified set $\mathscr{C}$ of values, or among places where ΔD lies in $\mathscr{C}$ and also $\overline{\chi}_2 = \times$.

20. (p. 100) The run loops over all $37 \times 61 = 2257$ settings for μ_{37} and μ_{61}; the raw tape speed of 5,000 letters per second would give one second per setting, but by using multiple testing (see **53L**) Colossus ran five times as fast. This gives an estimate of $2257/5 = 450$ seconds, or 7 1/2 minutes. But there is some unavoidable wastage: the message tape must be a bit longer than 5,000 letters, and since 5 does not divide 37 evenly, the multiple testing takes a little longer, too.

21. (p. 102) The count of the letters /34 in undifferenced plain language, discussed in the last two paragraphs of **23M(b)**, is done on Colossus; a failure of the /34 test, as discussed in the last paragraph, might be due to Colossus being out of order.

22. (p. 102) The term 'theory' in this context is a little confusing. To each hypothesized setting, i.e., initial wheel position, there corresponds the resulting sequence, or trajectory, of successive positions following from the initial setting as the machine steps along. Because of the irregular stepping of the ψ wheels, two trajectories with differing initial settings, it turns out, can merge or coalesce; after a certain number of steps, the machine ends up at the same state.

23. (p. 103) Perhaps what is meant here is 'The phenomenon of coalescence also occurs with $\overline{\chi}_2\overline{\overline{P}}_5$ limitation. In this case ψ_5 corruption is liable to interfere with the coalescence.'

24. (p. 105) This is a loose quotation from J. V. Uspensky, *Introduction to Mathematical Probability* (New York: McGraw-Hill, 1937), pp. 154, 158. (J.V. Uspensky (1883–1947) was a Russian probabilist who emigrated to the United States in the 1920's, becoming Professor of Mathematics at Stanford University. His mathematically demanding book was the standard text on probability theory in his adopted country until the appearance of William Feller, *Introduction to Probability Theory and Its Applications* (New York: Wiley, 1950). It was the main exposition in English of the so-called 'St. Petersburg' school of analytical probability associated with such figures as A. A. Markov (1857–1922).) On page 154 Uspensky writes:

> **Problem 4.** Players A and B agree to play not more than n games, the probabilities of winning a single game being p and q, respectively. Assuming that the fortunes of A and B amount to a and b single stakes which are equal for both, find the probability for A to be ruined in the course of n games.
> **Solution.** Let $z_{x,t}$ be the probability for the player A to be ruined when his fortune is x (and that of his adversary $a+b-x$) and he can play only t games...

On page 158 the answer is given as formula (20):

$$z_{a,n} = \frac{q^a(p^b - q^b)}{p^{a+b} - q^{a+b}} - \frac{(2\sqrt{pq})^{n+1}(qp^{-1})^{\frac{1}{2}a}}{a+b} \sum_{h=1}^{a+b-1} \frac{\sin\frac{\pi h}{a+b}}{1 - 2\sqrt{pq}\cos\frac{\pi h}{a+b}} \sin\frac{\pi a h}{a+b}\left(\cos\frac{\pi h}{a+b}\right)^n.$$

Two lines later on page 158 is the sentence

> The first term in (20) naturally must be replaced by $\frac{b}{a+b}$ if $p = q = \frac{1}{2}$.

At least one copy of Uspensky's textbook was available in the Newmanry, that owned by I. J. Good, described in his essay Good, 'Enigma and Fish' (see endnote 5 to Chapter **11**, above), p. 160. According to Good the book was presented to him in Oct. 1943 as a belated farewell gift from the Hut 8 members of the Naval Section at GCCS: the gift was delayed because the book was unobtainable in Britain and had to be shipped from America. In a cable dated 16 Mar. 1944, an American liaison officer at GCCS, Capt. W. J. Fried, asks the commander of the SSA at Arlington Hall, Col. W. P. Corderman (1904–1998), for another copy of the same book: 'FISH section anxious to obtain Uspensky on Probability. Not available here. Lieutenant Dumey [A. I. Dumey, (1906–1995)] has a copy. If he will lend it please send by bag.' (TNA HW 57/1, cable BJC 3295.)

25. (p. 105) That is, a run for examples of repeats or antirepeats was ....

26. (p. 106) Possible paraphrase: 'The importance of checks at every stage, including those of making two tapes, of hand checks, and of exact numerical checks.'

27. (p. 107) See our endnote 4 to **13**, p. 573 above.

28. (p. 107) The *Report* uses different spellings for the solvent for the commercial adhesive Bostik, which used to stick Robinson tapes into loops. In this paragraph the spelling 'benzene' is used twice, as it is in **35D(a)**. But the entries for 'BOSTIK' and 'FIRE, THE' in **71** use the spelling 'benzine', once apiece. The *Report*'s authors or typists might have been unaware that these words name distinct substances. Benzene, a coal tar distillate, C_6H_6, is an aromatic hydrocarbon, after which the benzene ring is named. Benzine, a petroleum distillate, is a mixture of aliphatic or straight-chain hydrocarbons, such as pentane (C_5H_{12}) and hexane (C_6H_{14}). According to Roger Dulac, *Industrial Cold Adhesives; A Practical Handbook for the Maker and User*, trans. by Joseph L. Rosenbaum (London: Griffin, 1937), p. 175 'Rubber is soluble in aromatic hydrocarbons (benzene, toluene, xylene, solvent naphtha, etc.), aliphatic hydrocarbons (petrol, petroleum ether and benzine), ... In practice, benzene is the solvent usually employed owing to its price and to its universal availability. It is a true *solvent* for rubber.' (We are indebted to Elsa Atson of the Chemical Heritage Society, Philadelphia, for finding this passage.)

We do not know which of benzene or benzine was actually used with Robinson tapes, but the above quotation makes benzene seem somewhat more likely.

'Rubbers' are erasers, usually for pencil.

29. (p. 109) The last decode in the 23Z/1.2 exhibit shows Quatsch, reading *fuchsrote Knaben* (chestnut-haired boys). Following the Quatsch is '22 KR B', which is a little puzzling. From the discussion in endnote 23 to **28E**, p. 596 below, one would expect '+ KR...', indicating the end of Quatsch, the start of the actual message, and a priority sign.

Chapter 24: Rectangling

1. (p. 110) Throughout **24** the term 'wheel' is used elliptically, meaning 'differenced wheel pattern', in the sense of **11C(b)**. Thus, in the last sentence of **24A**, where it states 'wheels $\Delta\chi_1$, $\Delta\chi_2$ are found', what is meant is 'differenced wheel patterns $\Delta\chi_1$, $\Delta\chi_2$ are found', and so on. The essence of 'Turingery' is that ΔD is not perfectly random, and the essence of 'Tutte's method' is that this fact can lead to the recovery of $\Delta\chi$ wheels, via rectangling. Once the $\Delta\chi$ wheels have

been obtained, the recovery of the χ wheels themselves by integration is straightforward.

2. (p. 110) That is, positive numbers (such as 3) were entered circled, as (3), but negative numbers (such as -3) were entered uncircled and without the minus sign, as 3.

3. (p. 114) That is, the four-digit counter is split into a two-digit mod 41 counter and a two-digit mod 31 counter.

4. (p. 115) 'Cords' here means plug cords, used with a plug panel, as in **54D**. See also entry 'Plug' in **71**.

5. (p. 115) '...a set of places on the cipher' means '...a set of places in the cipher', or (almost equivalently) '...a set of places on the cipher tape'.

6. (p. 115) Although the *Report* does not mention it, passages such as this one create the impression that there was a standard format for specifying Colossus rectangling runs, perhaps given by a printed sheet with blanks filled in by the cryptanalyst.

7. (p. 117) But see endnote 15 to this chapter, p. 590 below.

8. (p. 117) 'Computer' here means human computer.

9. (p. 117) Skeleton: a numerically rounded-off version of the rectangle, intended to make the arithmetic of flagging less laborious. See entry in **71**.

10. (p. 118) Jacobs flagging; see our endnote 19 to this chapter, p. 591 below.

11. (p. 118) That is, to calculate all 31 choose 2 entries of the flag, comparing all pairs of rows of the rectangle.

12. (p. 122) Here the mathematical fiction of the 'sixth impulse' is used again.

13. (p. 123) Section **24W(a)** consistently uses the notation $\varepsilon_{j'}$ instead of the seemingly more natural ε'_j. The following few paragraphs make it clear that the index in the expression $\varepsilon_{j'}$ is j, not j' as suggested by the notation.

14. (p. 124) '1p2 score': a variant notation for '1+2 score'.

15. (p. 124) As the *Report* makes clear, the score values X eventually stop changing, but to conclude from this that the sign patterns stop changing, too, is slightly more complicated than indicated. Suppose that at a given stage of iteration the patterns are (ε_i) on the left and (δ_j) on the right, and that at the next stage of iteration the pattern on the left is (γ_i), and also suppose that the scores at these stages have reached their ultimate maximal value X:

$$X = \sum_{ij} \theta_{ij}\varepsilon_i\delta_j = \sum_{ij} \theta_{ij}\gamma_i\delta_j. \tag{2}$$

Then, as in the *Report*, defining $x_i = \sum_j \theta_{ij}\delta_j$, we have $X = \sum_i \varepsilon_i x_i = \sum_i \gamma_i x_i$, where the iteration rule makes $\gamma_i = +1, -1$, or 0 according to whether $x_i > 0, < 0$, or $= 0$. This means that $\varepsilon_i x_i \leq |x_i| = \gamma_i x_i$, hence (2) implies $\varepsilon_i x_i = \gamma_i x_i$, for all i. If x_i is non-zero, this implies $\varepsilon_i = \gamma_i$; but if $x_i = 0$, it is possible that $\varepsilon_i = \pm 1$ even though $\gamma_i = 0$. In this case the γ pattern agrees with the ε pattern except it might have more 0 entries. There can only be finitely many such iteration steps where extra 0 entries are gained; thereafter the sign patterns remain the same.

16. (p. 126) An 'American tournament' is, in British English, a sporting tournament in which each

competitor (or team) plays all the others in turn; in American English, a 'round robin tournament'. A Tunny flag (such as the one shown in fig. **26 (III)** p. 187) resembled the score sheet of such a tournament.

17. (p. 126) 'Hagelin machine' refers the C-38 or related cipher machines invented by Boris C. W. Hagelin (1892–1983), which, like Tunny, had a number of wheels of varying sizes, each with a pattern of active and inactive pegs. A general description of this family of machines, and of the life of their inventor, is given in David Kahn, *The Codebreakers: The Story of Secret Writing* (New York: Macmillan, 1967), pp. 426–434. The U.S. Army used a model of this machine, as did the Italian Navy.

It is possible that G. H. Vergine was the author of a 13-page SSA technical paper, 'A statistical method for analyzing certain types of flags applicable to Tunny and Hagelin systems', dated March, 1944 (NARA HCC 950:2811), which derives formulae equivalent to those of **22W(a)** involving $f(k,l)$. According to **01**, the cited research log reference (**R2**, p. 79) was written in May, 1944.

18. (p. 127) 'This' presumably refers to the accurate score of x pips compared with y pips.

19. (p. 127) The 'Jacobs' Flag' is presumably named after W. W. Jacobs (1914–1982), U.S. Army, who spent about six months in the Newmanry. The reference to **R2**, p. 101, puts the date of the invention of this quick-and-dirty approximate method of flagging in June 1944; the chronology of **74** lists its use starting in November 1944.

20. (p. 128) According to **44B**, autoclave (in the form of $\chi_2\overline{\overline{P}}_5$ limitation) was generally introduced in December 1943; this is borne out by the entry for that month in the chronology of **74**.

21. (p. 128) Black file: see Vergine quotation in endnote 5 to Preface **01**, p. 561 above, and endnote 2 to chapter **73**, p. 621 below.

22. (p. 128) See **44B(f)** for a discussion of early rectangling in the Research Section.

23. (p. 130) Here the symbol χ^2 refers not to a chi wheel but to the chi-squared distribution of mathematical statistics, which was introduced in **21(l)**.

24. (p. 135) Here K is the controversial k mentioned in **24E(d)**.

25. (p. 136) The quantity π_{12} in this formula, like π_{45} lower down in this subsection, is a special case of π_{ij} discussed in our endnote 19 to **22H(f)**, p. 582 above. Subscriptless π in this paragraph is a shorthand for π_{12}.

26. (p. 137) Possible paraphrase: 'Incidentally this shows 4+5 rectangles need less text to be barely significant than 1+2 rectangles do, if. . . '

Chapter 25: Chi-breaking from cipher

1. (p. 144) In colloquial British English, to 'knock off' can mean to reduce somewhat, as for example a price or a stated age.

2. (p. 144) These five-letter notations with dashes for omitted letters can be seen at the left sides of the wheel sheets for $\Delta\chi_4$ and $\Delta\chi_5$, figures **25G (V)** and **(VI)**, p. 172 in this edition.

3. (p. 148) The rules for legality for a χ wheel are set out in **22B**: the numbers of dots and crosses on the wheel should differ by no more than 1, and similarly for the differenced wheel, and the wheel should not have five consecutive dots or five consecutive crosses.

4. (p. 148) Obtaining a wheel from its Δ, so named, presumably, by the analogy between the finite difference operator Δ and the derivative in calculus. As in calculus, an integration constant must be assumed; the effect of choosing the wrong constant is to recover the wheel 'inside out', with all dots replaced with crosses, and vice versa.

5. (p. 148) Freeborn counts were counts made by the department at GCCS under Frederick Freeborn, by using punched card (Hollerith) equipment.

6. (p. 149) Room 41 in the Testery is described in **14B(c)** and chapters **36** to **39**.

7. (p. 150) A motor cross letter, as in **23L**, is a letter enciphered when the motor = **×**, that is, when the ψ wheels move.

8. (p. 150) The value 51 does not appear in the sequence of scores for $\Delta\chi_2$ given here. Presumably it occurred later on the worksheet from which the scores were copied. The discussion later in the paragraph makes it likely that the last listed score, 2, should have been circled: ⓶.

9. (p. 151) '**22H9**' is a reference to equation (H9) in section **22H**.

10. (p. 151) '**25Y4**' is a reference to equation (Y4) in section **25Y**.

11. (p. 152) '**25Y1**' is a reference to equation (Y1) in section **25Y**.

12. (p. 152) The parenthetical phrase '(ch **24**)' is a reference to chapter **24**, on Rectangling.

13. (p. 182) 'Previously' refers to **25W(a)**.

14. (p. 183) 'Legal wheel' is defined in **11C(a)** and **22B**.

Chapter 26: Wheel-breaking from key

1. (p. 185) Throughout this chapter, the term 'key' can mean a stretch of consecutive letters of the K stream, deduced from cribs or from depths.

2. (p. 186) The term 'non $\overline{\chi}_2$ keys' here refers to key stretches produced by the SZ 42 A with autoclave or by the SZ 42 B, that is, with any of the limitation schemes $\overline{\chi}_2\overline{\psi}'_1$, $\overline{\chi}_2\overline{\overline{P}}_5$, or $\overline{\chi}_2\overline{\psi}'_1\overline{\overline{P}}_5$, but not with plain $\overline{\chi}_2$.

3. (p. 187) Here 'modular sum' means the sum of the moduli or absolute values.

4. (p. 188) WB = 'wheel-breaking'.

5. (p. 189) Here 'keys' means stretches of key.

6. (p. 190) It is not clear precisely what 'to lack rigidity' means here. The phrase is reused in **43D(b)(ii)** where its meaning is equally unclear.

7. (p. 191) That is, whether in the $\Delta\chi$'s (and hence in the $\Delta\psi'$'s) the characters • and × are interchanged.

8. (p. 194) According to the fiction of the 'sixth impulse' (see entry in **71**), $\Delta\chi_6$ is another name for the complement of the limitation. Since **26E** treats the case where the limitation is $\overline{\chi}_2$, we have $\Delta\chi_6 = \tilde{\overline{\chi}}_2$, and the sense of the text is '...aim is to obtain $\Delta\chi_6$ signs (which is to say $\tilde{\overline{\chi}}_2$ signs) as well...'.

9. (p. 195) Here 'keys' is used somewhat ambiguously, to mean either stretches of key letters obtained from depths or cribs, or the wheel patterns in effect in particular days in particular links. See our Supplementary Glossary entry for 'key', p. 544 above.

10. (p. 197) Here 'Tunny' refers to the British Tunny machine, sense (4) of the term as listed in our Supplementary Glossary, p. 545 above.

11. (p. 213) 'Errors in both wheels' refers to mistakes in the recovered wheels.

12. (p. 214) The total score x defined here is referred to as X in the remainder of **26X(a)**.

13. (p. 214) ${}^5C_r$ in equations (X2) and (X3) denotes the binomial coefficient $\binom{5}{r}$, '5 choose r'.

14. (p. 217) At the time of writing (2015), the report of Major Tester's section has not been declassified. See our endnote 1 to **01**, p. 561 above.

15. (p. 218) This is an extension of the notation of **26C**, where $L_{n,m}$ is the generic name for any letter with n dots and m crosses. Here a third subscript is added, expressing a condition on $\Delta\psi'_{26}$, so that, for example, $L_{n,m},{}^{\times}$ denotes the occurrence of any letter with n dots and m crosses, when $\Delta\psi'_{26} = \times$ also holds. We follow the *Report*'s odd practice (limited to this paragraph) of placing this third subscript raised above the other two subscripts, so that the symbol is written $L_{n,m},{}^{\times}$ instead of the somewhat more natural-seeming $L_{n,m,\times}$ listed in chapter **72**.

Chapter 27: Cribs

1. (p. 220) 'OKH' = *Oberkommando des Heeres* = Army High Command.

2. (p. 220) In **27**, 'routine' is used as a noun, short for 'routine message'. Elsewhere in the *Report*, and in **27F(g)**, it refers to standardised Tunny-breaking procedures.

3. (p. 220) *Kriegsmarine Kurzlage* = Navy Short Report. *Lagebericht West* = Situation Report, West. *OKH Lagebericht* = Army High Command Situation Report. 'OBSW' = *Oberbefehlshaber Süd-West*; *OBSW Tagesmeldung* = Commander-in-chief (South-West[ern Theatre]) message of the day. The link listed as 'Cod' is almost certainly the same as 'Codfish'.

4. (p. 220) The suggestion is that routine messages were always sent, but not always by the radio teleprinter links intercepted at Knockholt.

5. (p. 221) That is, the available P was usually longer than the longest pause-free stretch of Z,

but occasionally was not.

6. (p. 222) Here 'clicks' refers to the last two digits of the internal serial number of a message, as described in the previous section, **27B(c)**, transmitted to the sender by the recipient of the message.

7. (p. 222) *Roem III,A*: *Roem* = abbreviation for *römisch* = 'Roman [numeral]'. An example of the use of this abbreviation in a German teleprinter message can be seen in the frontispiece of Roger Hesketh, *Fortitude: the D-day Deception Campaign* (London: St. Ermin's, 1999; reprinted Woodstock, NY: Overlook, 2000) which reproduces a 9 June 1944 Wehrmacht teleprinter message sent unencrypted by land line from HZPH (Zossen) to WFST (then in Berlin).

8. (p. 223) Paraphrase: '... identifying messages with known serial number and other characteristics in other links was easier than predicting them from log evidence alone'.

9. (p. 223) See the discussion of tape procedures in **33A**.

10. (p. 224) An insert machine was a tape copying machine with simple facilities for entering corrections by hand. See **56C**.

11. (p. 226) Here again, with the modulo 2 (or binary) arithmetic applying to Z, P, and K, addition is the same as subtraction. Hence the equation $Z+P=K$ is equivalent to $Z=P+K$. See **11B(i)**.

12. (p. 234) '**22Y3**' is a reference to equation (Y3) in section **22Y**.

Chapter 28: Language methods

1. (p. 237) This chapter describes Testery methods, including the basic procedures of depth-reading, ψ- and motor-breaking, as well as a miscellany of techniques for dealing with specialized problems. The methods described in this chapter rely on the cryptanalysts' puzzle-solving ability and knowledge of the plain text language to a greater extent than those described in chapters **22–26**.

2. (p. 237) The 'legs' of a depth are the messages which are enciphered by the same key. This is the earliest instance of the written use of the word in this specialized cryptanalytic sense that we are aware of. It does not appear, for instance, in the 1944 GCCS cryptographic dictionary (TNA HW 25/33 and NARA HCC 1413:4559; a transcription of which is on the internet at 'Cryptographic Dictionary', URL: `http://www.codesandciphers.org.uk/documents/cryptdict` (visited on 07/06/2014); nor in the 1947 American *Descriptive Dictionary of Cryptologic Terms* (reprinted United States Army Security Agency, *Descriptive Dictionary of Cryptologic Terms, Including Foreign Terms*, A Cryptographic Series 77, Reprint of Feb. 1947 issue by ASA (Laguna Hills, Calif.: Aegean Park Press, n.d. [*c.*1998])), nor in the 1942 GCCS textbook, *S.I. Course* (copies of which are in NARA HCC 833:2446, and 973:2969, reprinted as Government Code and Cypher School, *A Course in Cryptanalysis: S.I. Course, Revised and Enlarged, June, 1942*, 2 vols., A Cryptographic Series 33–34 (Laguna Hills, Calif.: Aegean Park Press, n.d. [*c.*1983]). But, informants tell us, this term was in common use among American and British code-breakers as early as 1952.

3. (p. 237) QSN and QEP are examples of Q-codes, described in our Supplementary Glossary entry 'Q-code', p. 544 above. The particular codes QSN and QEP were used to specify wheel

settings for the immediately following cipher message. Thus, 'QEP 11' would mean the following: use the 11th wheel setting listed in the current list of settings.

4. (p. 237) That is, the first of three messages was sent with 'QEP 34', the second without a QEP, and the third with a 'QEP 35', all in short succession. The inference is, the second message might well be in depth with the first, or with the third.

5. (p. 237) A memorandum of a meeting about non-Morse transmissions on 16 July 1942 (TNA HW 14/40) states plans to immediately install multiple teleprinter connections between Knockholt and Bletchley Park, and more yet within a month's time. Knockholt was equipped with teleprinters by 11 Jan. 1943, as is clear from a letter of that date from H. C. Kenworthy at Knockholt to Col. H. B. Sayer (TNA HW 14/64). We do not know if they had a direct connection to the Testery or if they terminated elsewhere at Bletchley Park. According to the Chronology (chapter **74** below), there was a direct teleprinter link between Knockholt and Block F in January 1944.

6. (p. 238) This is formula (A3) of **11B(i)**, a trivial consequence of the fundamental formula (A2) of **11B(i)**, that is, $Z = P + K$.

7. (p. 238) Here 'frequency' means relative frequency of occurrence. The displayed formula carelessly uses subscripted p to mean two different things on the left and on the right of the equals sign. A more careful version might assert that

$$q_\Theta = \sum_\Phi p_\Phi p_{\Theta+\Phi},$$

where q_Θ denotes the relative frequency of Θ in $P_a + P_b$, and p_Φ the relative frequency of Φ in P_a or P_b.

8. (p. 238) Here, as in **71**, it seems a 'click' is a matching letter in two streams of letters, that is, a / in the difference of two letter streams.

9. (p. 239) The use of the pronoun 'I' in this sentence suggests this passage was copied from another document, possibly from one of the Research Logs. It is only used here and in **91**: see endnote 2 to **91**, p. 622 below.

10. (p. 240) 'L.C.' is an abbreviation for 'letter count'.

11. (p. 240) 'D.O.' is an abbreviation for 'Duty Officer'.

12. (p. 242) At the time of writing, this document has not been declassified. See our endnote 1 to **01**, p. 561 above.

13. (p. 243) Both formulae are wrong. The correct versions are

$$(1-a)^2 + 2a(1-a)(1-b)^5 + a^2\left(b^2 + \overline{1-b}^2\right)^5$$

and

$$2(1-a)(ab^5) + a^2\{2b(1-b)\}^5,$$

respectively; they follow from **22D(e)**, equation (D6).

14. (p. 243) A 'click' is letter matching in two streams, that is, a / in their difference, as in **71**. An 'anticlick' is an 8 in their difference. These two letters are especially prominent in the sum of two $\Delta\psi'$ streams.

15. (p. 243) The theory here is that at the correct overlap, the ΔP of the broken de-χ differs from the ΔD of the unbroken de-χ by $\Delta\psi'$, which is recognisable by its excess of /'s, that is, by the clicks between the broken ΔP and the unbroken ΔD.

16. (p. 243) 'Rod' is a loan-word from Enigma work, where the permutations effected by each of the 26 rotational positions of a rotor (i.e., drum or *Walze*) were termed rods, the equivalent of figure **11 (I)** being termed a rod square. See entries for 'rod' and related terms in the 'Cryptographic Dictionary', TNA HW 25/33 and NARA HCC 1413:4559, and in **71**.

17. (p. 246) The '37 wheel' is the motor wheel μ_{37}.

18. (p. 246) 'It' refers to the chart in **22D(c)**.

19. (p. 246) BM is an abbreviation for 'Basic Motor', defined in **11B(f)**.

20. (p. 247) 'Cipher' here means the text of the cipher message.

21. (p. 247) TM is an abbreviation for 'Total Motor', defined in **11B(f)**.

22. (p. 247) The logic of this sentence is hard to follow. It might be a mistyped version of something like 'The larger the number of dots in μ_{37} the greater the proportion of changes of sign in ψ, and hence the smaller the amount of anagramming required.' The first assertion follows from the algebra of **11C(d)** and **(e)**, or from fig. **22 (II)**: the proportion of crosses in a $\Delta\psi$ stream is the proportion of changes in sign in ψ, which is (assuming $ab = 1/2$) given by $b = 37/(74-d)$, where d is the dottage of μ_{37}. The bigger d is, the bigger b is. The second assertion, that less anagramming is required when b is big, might reflect the fact that the inference from $\Delta\psi = /$ to $\text{TM} = \bullet$ is more reliable, that is, the conditional probability $P(\text{TM} = \bullet|\Delta\psi = /)$ is larger.

23. (p. 256) This was produced by the GCCS Tunny machine, which printed 9 (meaning SPACE) as full stop and printed + and - (meaning shift into and out of FIG mode) instead of 5 and 8.

The proper format for teleprinter messages is spelled out in the German armed forces service regulations for teleprinter usage, *Fernschreibbetriebs-Vorschrift* (a copy of the edition of 1 March 1944 is in NARA HCC 70:311), and for cipher teleprinter usage, *Schlüsselfernschreibbetriebs-Vorschrift*, (a copy of a 1944 translation into English of the 1 December 1942 edition is in NARA HCC 950:2816). In this 1943 message the typist seems to follow a somewhat different set of conventions than those specified in the 1944 regulations, but this does not prevent us from understanding the message.

Throughout the message the typist followed the regulations in using `NN` to indicate a correction to what had just been typed, so in the second line of the message as shown in fig. **28 (IX)**, for instance, `HAVD NN HAVXD` means `HAVXD`. Accepting his corrections, and following the shifts in and out of FIG mode, and rendering spaces as spaces, the raw plain text reads:

```
HBZCHORNSTEINFEGER ANNA/FF NR. 661 7.3.43 == (( ANN/FF NR. 661
7.4.43==)) HAVXD 18264 5.3. 1430 ==(( HAVXD 718 264 5.3. 1430
==)) WN ART. KDR. % BEIM PZ. AOK 1,( £.  GR. SUED ==(( AN ART
KDR. % FEIM PZ. AOK. 1, H. GR. SUED ==))  2 SCHW. ART. ABT. 7%5
((2 SCHW. ART. ABT. 7%5)) MUSZTE DREI ZWOFLTONNER ZUGMASCHINEN
MIT GENEHMIGUNG HOFH. ART. KDR.%08 (( HOEH. ARTM KDR. 308)) ZUR
4. PZ. DIV. (( 4. PZ. DIV.)) ASSTEKLEN. ALLE BEMUEHUNGEN DES
BATTR. CHEFS (( BATT. CHEFS)) ZUGASHCINEN ZURUECKZUBEKOMMEN,
```

```
SIND GESCHEITERT. BATTR. (( BATTR.)) BITTET UEBER DIE H. GR. ((
H. GR. )) DIE 4. PZ. DIV. (( 4.  PZ. DIV. )) ZUR HER USGABE ZU
VERANLASSEN, DA VERLADUNG IN ETWA 6 (( 6)) TAGEN ERFOLGEN SOLL.
ERBITTET BATTR. ((BATTR.)) MITTEILUNG, OB SIE DIE RUECKGABE DER
ZUGMASCHINEN SO RECHTZEITIG EWWARTEN KANN, DASZ SIE MIT TRSP.
DER BATTR. (( TRSP. DER BATTR.)) ABROLLEN KOENNEN. BATTR. ((
BATTR.)) ISTHZU ERREICHEN UEBER AOK 2 (( AOK 2)) AUFFAGSTAB
618; ROMNY [??]  FANGSTAB [??]  618, ROM [??].==)) DIENSTSTELLE
FPN [??]  201 [??]  HGFZ. IUSCHR.++ (( DIANSTSTELLE FPNR. 32
621 C GFZ. [??]  SCHR.++ )) BERICHTIGUNG : ZUGMASCHINEN VGL.
ZUGMASCHINEN QXA 800== QXA 8000==++ KAFFEH NUN WIEDER [??]  MAL
EIN E LKLAEINE PAUSE VE
```

(Here sequences of garbled letters are marked with `[??]`.) The message starts with 'Quatsch' or nonsense, a garbled form of the word *Schornsteinfeger* (= chimney sweep). The typist seems to use a convention not described in the 1944 version of the regulations, namely, of sometimes following a passage with a repeated copy set out in double parentheses. The regulations do specify using double dashes to set out underlined text (so `--Kirsch--` means <u>`Kirsch`</u>); the typist's use of repetitions here might indicate the same thing.

The regulations specify that message parts are separated by = signs, which seem to have been doubled in this example. The required message parts are: the head, the address or addresses, the message contents, and the signature. The head is supposed to start with a + sign to indicate the very beginning of the actual message, followed by a priority sign, followed by the name of the sending teleprinter office, the sending office's message serial number, the filing date and time of the message, and possibly the transmission time in parentheses, as in the example

```
+SSD WENE 254 24/5 0810 (0815)
```

given on p. 32 of the teleprinter service regulations. SSD is usually interpreted as *sehr sehr dringend*, 'very very urgent', but it indicated a relatively low priority. The teleprinter service regulations (on p. 34, and again in a chart on p. 80) give the various teleprinter message priorities. Lowest for the army in the field was S, then SSD and variants SSD-Trsp. and SSD-Mun. for transport and munitions supply, then KR, then KR Blitz, then KR-RM for messages from Göring, and finally FRR for messages from Hitler or his headquarters. This system of message priorities in fact is only an elaboration of that used in the end of the 19th century by the German civil telegraph service. According to Hans-Georg Kampe, *Nachrichtentruppe des Heeres und deutsche Reichspost: militärliches und staatliches Nachrichtenwesen in Deutschland 1830 bis 1945* (Waldesrsruh bei Berlin, 1999), p. 90, the priority markings for telegrams in 1892 were (in increasing order) none (for ordinary private telegrams), D for urgent (*dringend*) private telegrams, A for service telegrams (that is, telegraph network management messages), SS for government or military telegrams (*Staats- oder Militär-Telegramme*; presumably SS is a contraction of *Staats*), and Kr for the highest priority messages. In 1898 the new category of urgent military telegram was introduced, with a priority marking of SSd, presumably simply a concatenation of the existing marks SS and D. It thus seems likely that the interpretation of SSD as *sehr sehr dringend* is a 'backronym', an ex post facto invented meaning for SSD as an acronym.

In our message we have the header

```
ANNA/FF NR. 661 7.3.43,
```

where the typist omitted the +, the priority sign, and the filing time. The sending teleprinter office is ANNA/FF, the radio teleprinter office attached to exchange ANNA, which served the Army high command near Königsberg, as explained in endnote 2 to chapter **61**, p. 615 below. The message is evidently a forwarded message, whose original head appears as the next message part,

`HAVXD 718264 5.3 1430,`

for a message sent two days earlier. This is followed by the address, which uses ordinary German military abbreviations. The signature ends with a + sign, as it should. Then follows a spelling correction, in the regulation format, also ending with a + sign. Finally, the last few garbled words, *Kaffeh nun wieder mal eine kleine Pause ve...* ('Coffee, now another little break...'), which are either Quatsch or the operator chatting with his opposite number; these are worked out in fig. **28 (VII)**.

Some of the spelling mistakes are probably due to garbles: a single bit error probably converted `DIENSTSTELLE` into `DIANSTSTELLE`. Others, such as `ARTM`, are due to the typist failing to put punctuation marks in FIG mode.

Stripping off the Quatsch and the chatter, correcting obvious typos, interpreting the double parentheses as mark-up for underlining, taking double (instead of single) equals signs as the message-part separator, and taking the figure-shift meaning of the letter `F` as `/` (instead of `%`, as suggested by the teleprinter alphabet chart in **11A**) we arrive at the following approximation to what the intended recipient might have seen after the message was typed up neatly:

```
ANNA/FF Nr. 661 7.3.43

HAVXD 718 264 5.3. 1430

An Art. Kdr / beim Pz. AOK 1, H. Gr. Süd

2 schw. Art. Abt. 7/5 mußte drei zwolftonner Zugmaschinen mit
Genehmigung hoeh. Art. Kdr. 308 zur 4. Pz. Div. assteklen.
Alle Bemühungen des Battr. Chefs Zugmaschinen zurükzubekommen,
sind gescheitert.  Batt. bittet über die H. Gr. die 4. Pz. Div.
zur Herausgabe zu veranlassen, da Verladung in etwa 6 Tagen
erfolgen soll.  Erbittet Battr. Mitteilungen, ob sie die
Rückgabe der Zugmaschinen so rechtzeitig erwarten kann, daß sie
mit Trsp. der Battr. abrollen können.  Battr. ist zuerreichen
über AOK 2 Auffangstab 618,V

Dienststelle FPN. 32 261. [??]  HGFZ [??]  Schr

Berichtigung :  Zugmaschinen vgl. Zugmaschinen

QXA 100

QXA 1000
```

The signature is too garbled to make out, but FPN means *Feldpostnummer*, army post office number. QXA means 'letter count', but the message in fact is about 1,400 letters long. (The meaning and use of QXA is not given in the edition of the teleprinter regulations we have seen, but is given in a 6-page Sixta report, *Non Morse Army Q code*, GCCS serial number ULTRA/ZIP/NMS 15, dated 28 November 1944, a copy of which is included in Small Report F-122 of 29 November 1944, in NARA HCC 950:2821.)

A rough translation, guessing that *assteklen* is a typo for *abstellen* (which can mean 'detach') and that *Auffangstab* means [straggler] collection staff, is as follows:

From ANNA/FF, Message number 661, 7 March 1943

Forwarded from HAVXD, Message number 718 264, 5 March 1430

To Artillery Commander, Pz. Army 1, Army Group South

Battery 2 of heavy artillery battalion 7/5 had to detach, with the concurrence of senior artillery commander 308, three twelve-ton tractors to the 4th Panzer division. All attempts of the battery commander for the return of the tractors have failed. Battery requests through Army Group that 4th Panzer division announce delivery, as loading is to take place in about 6 days. Battery requests notification they can expect the return of the tractors in a timely fashion, so that they can roll off in the movement of the battery. Battery is reachable through 2nd Army HQ, Collection Staff 618,V.

Another sample Tunny decrypt, evidently in the possession of GCHQ, is reproduced in Gannon, *Colossus* (see endnote 2 to Chapter **11**, above), illus. 21 and transcribed in his Appendix O, pp. 480–483. Fragments of a decode of a Whiting message, WB 6773, sent from Berlin to H. Gr. Kurland on 14 Feb. 1945, are in the possession of the National Cryptologic Museum, National Security Agency, Ft. Meade, Maryland, illustrated on the web page Bob Lord, 'Decrypt Fragments', URL: `http://www.ilord.com/bp-decrypts.html` (visited on 26/02/2015).

Chapter 31: Mr Newman's section

1. (p. 260) If the *Report*'s photostat copy of this plan is true to scale, the supporting pillars in the machine room and along the outer walls of H block were spaced approximately 6 feet (183 cm) apart. The lettering for room 2, above the large word 'Block' in the legend, is unclear in the original. It seems to read 'Mr Maile'. Jackie L. Maile, according to a personal communication to JAR from F. Weierud, 10 April 2014, was a GPO civilian who worked in the Newmanry 1944–45. He was the supervisor of the GPO staff there.

2. (p. 262) These log books are operational log books, not the Research Logs referred to in the Preface **01** and discussed in our endnote 5 to **01**, p. 561 above.

3. (p. 263) W. G. Welchman (1906–1985), assistant deputy director for mechanization at GCCS from September 1943. See entry in Biographical Notes, p. 559. Prior to then he had been the head of Hut 6, in charge of cryptanalysis of German Army and Air Force Enigma traffic. His memoir, *The Hut Six Story* (New York: McGraw-Hill, 1982), p. 177, indicates he was not heavily engaged with this committee, or that its work did not stick in his memory.

4. (p. 263) Writing in 1958, a Newmanry veteran listed the cryptographic, i.e. cryptanalytic, staff in order of appearance (with Americans in italics): Max Newman, Donald Michie, Jack Good, Shaun Wylie, John Herivel, David Rees, Henry Whitehead FRS, *George Vergine*, Arthur Chamberlain, Joe Gillis, Walter Sharp, Michael Ashcroft, Michael Crum, Michael Sampford, Gordon Preston, *Tim Moilen* [*sic*, should be Moilien], Philip Watson, Oliver Atkin, Bill Tipler, *Howard Campaigne*, Sandy Green, Geoffrey Timms, Ken Le Couteur, Harry Peake, Leslie Chown, John Marriott, *Walter Jacobs*, Tom Eddleston, Brian Stratford. Part-time members: William Tutte, Peter Hilton, Peter Benenson, *Arthur Levenson*, *John Seaman*, Roy Jenkins, Kevin O'Neill, and Tom Colvill. (This list obtained by a discretionary release of retained material by GCHQ historian; ©Crown Copyright. Used with permission of Director GCHQ.) It is not clear whether 'part-time members' means members for a short time only, or members who divided their time between the

Newmanry and elsewhere, perhaps in the role of 'Mr X' or 'Mr Y', a Testery member lent to the Newmanry for a week, as described in **71**.

5. (p. 264) The breakdown of cryptographers (that is, cryptanalysts) by age in the left column only adds up to 12 (instead of 13), so there must be a mistake.

6. (p. 264) See endnote 21 to **71**, p. 620 below.

7. (p. 264) 'Certificate' here refers to school leaving examinations. Passage of the ordinary exams (which later became the 'O Levels') led to a 'School Certificate'; passage of the more rigorous exams (which later became the 'A Levels') led to a 'Higher Certificate'. Very approximate American equivalents are good scores in the 'SAT' and 'AP' exams, respectively.

8. (p. 266) See the list of screeds given in our endnote 1 to **73**, p. 620 below.

Chapter 32: Organisation of the Testery

1. (p. 267) The first reference is to the 'Testery Report', TNA HW 25/28, not released for public inspection. The other document is unknown; it might be the same as TNA HW 50/63, *History of the Fish Section*.

Chapter 33: Knockholt

1. (p. 268) The twenty-page March 1946 report, 'The Interception of German Teleprinter Communications by Foreign Office Station, Knockholt', TNA HW 3/63 and TNA HW 50/79, supplies much detail lacking in this skimpy chapter.

2. (p. 268)

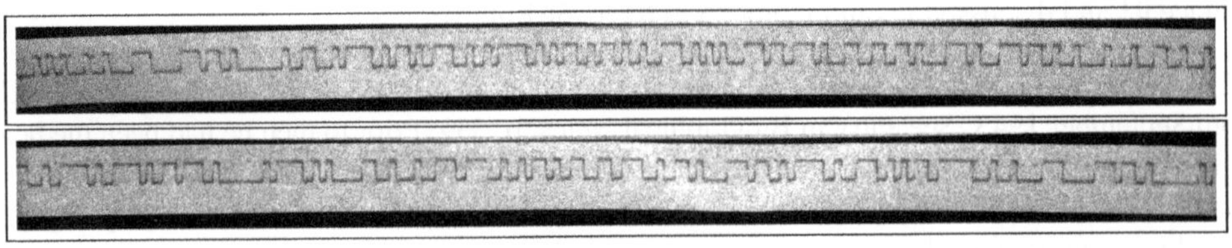

Figure 1. Undulator tape produced by refurbished wartime equipment in a demonstration of interception techniques used at Knockholt. The demonstration formed part of the display at the opening of the new Tunny gallery at the National Museum of the History of Computing, at Bletchley Park, on 26 May 2011. The actual width of the tape is about 12 mm.

See our Appendix B, 'Activities at Knockholt', this volume, pp. 503–524 above. The *Report*, especially Chapter **27**, makes extensive reference to 'undulator tapes'. These tapes, also referred to as 'slips', were graphical traces of the intercepted teleprinter signal, produced by a 'siphon recorder' or 'undulator' on long paper ribbons. According to Newcomb Carlton, 'Telegraph' in *Encyclopedia Britannica* (London, 1929), 'The recoder is a galvanometer with an ink syphon attached to the moving coil. The syphon rests against a moving tape, drawing a continuous line which is undulated above or below the centre by deflections of the galvanometer...' (vol. 21,

p. 885). Invented in 1858 by Lord Kelvin (William Thomson, 1824–1907), they were used to record incoming Morse code symbols on submarine cables (that is, trans-ocean telegraph cables), as part of normal operations. They were not typically used with teleprinter operations, and their use at Knockholt represents an adaptation of a familiar (and even old fashioned) technology to a new problem.

3. (p. 268) See our endnote 9 to **01**, p. 562 above.

Chapter 34: Registration and circulation

1. (p. 269) RF = Red Form; DR = dispatch rider = motorcycle messenger.

2. (p. 269) The 'A' tapes were presumably the long tapes used with the 'A procedure' described in **33B**.

Chapter 35: Tapemaking and checking

1. (p. 272) Here 'IBM' refers to an 'insert machine', described in **56C**.

2. (p. 272) The diagram shows the tape in the same orientation as in the illustration in **11A(b)**, with the punches for the 1st impulse near the top edge of the tape. The 'start' punch is positioned half way between the positions of the punches for the 3rd and 4th impulses; the 'stop' sign half way between the punches for the 4th and 5th impulses. The sprocket holes are between the punches for the 2nd and 3d impulses.

Since the holes were spaced about 1/10th of an inch apart, the amount of overlap at the join was about 1/5 of an inch, or 5 mm. The tape for a 1,000-letter message was 100 inches (8 feet, or 2.5 metres) long; one for a 10,000 letter message ten times as long. Since Colossus read the tape at 5,000 letters per second, the tape had to move 500 inches (about 42 feet or 12.7 m) per second, that is, about 28 mph or 46 kph.

3. (p. 272) R = **•x•x•** and Y = **x•x•x**, so a tape punched with repeated RYRY... will show an easy-to-notice chequerboard pattern.

Chapter 36: Chi-breaking from cipher

1. (p. 275) See **33A** for an explanation of the terminology of A and B procedure tapes. These were the tapes used for breaking a day's wheels, so if they had mistakes that day's traffic might not be readable.

2. (p. 275) This is the only explicit reference to Bletchley in the text of the *Report*. Elsewhere the cover term 'Station X' is used.

3. (p. 275) This refers to the rectangling gadget's cyclometers, which as a rectangle was calculated, counted how many of its cells contained particular numerical values. See **53M(g)**.

Chapter 37: Machine setting organisation

1. (p. 278) Only the first Robinson was called 'Heath Robinson'. The intended sense is that of '...the first Robinson ("Heath" Robinson) was replaced by 2 production models...'.

2. (p. 278) See **33A** for an explanation of the terminology of the various procedures for ordering traffic from Knockholt. The C.O. was the Control Officer, in charge of all contacts between the Newmanry or Testery on the one hand and Knockholt or Hut 3 on the other. See also **14B(a)**.

3. (p. 279) 'Wheel day' presumably refers to the period of time a given set of patterns was in effect. The patterns might not have been broken on the same day as they were first used.

4. (p. 279) E.S. means 'expected score', as defined in **23L**.

5. (p. 279) As explained in the Editors' Introduction, pp. xxv–lxxiv above, Hut 3 was the section to which decoded German Army Enigma and Tunny messages were sent. There they were translated, indexed, annotated, and assessed in the context of knowledge of current military plans and operations as revealed, in part, by other German Army messages. Information relevant to Allied plans and operations was forwarded to the appropriate Allied military authorities. In modern terminology, Hut 3 produced intelligence. According to **14A(a)**, the Naval Section and ISOS similarly received German Navy and intelligence services messages, respectively, where they received analogous treatment. The bulk of decoded Tunny messages, however, were Army messages and so went to Hut 3.

6. (p. 279) A four-wheel run involved trying out all possible initial settings for four wheels on Colossus. Section **23H(c)** mentions the four-wheel run 1=2=4=5/, which tries out all $41 \times 31 \times 26 \times 23 = 760058$ possible starting positions for χ_1, χ_2, χ_4, and χ_5. With multiple testing five starting positions could be considered per revolution of the message tape. If the message tape were 1000 letters long, running at a speed of 5,000 letters per second, such a job would take about 30,000 seconds, that is, almost 9 hours. Almost as effective is a 1=2 run followed by a 4=5/1=2, which involves examining the 1271 possible starting positions for χ_1 and χ_2 followed by 598 starting positions for χ_4 and χ_5. These would take about 2 minutes on the same problem.

Chapter 38: Wheel-breaking from key, organisation

1. (p. 280) A.T.S. = [a member of the] Auxiliary Territorial Service, the women's branch of the British Army.

2. (p. 281) This appendix is chapter **95**.

Chapter 39: Language methods

1. (p. 283) That is, according to **14A(a)**, route the decodes to Hut 3, which handled German Army messages, to the Naval Section, which handled German Navy messages, and to ISOS (also known as 'Mr Page's Section'; see our endnote 3 to **14A(a)**, p. 574 above), which handled German

Intelligence Service messages. For the activity of Hut 3, the main recipient of Tunny messages, see the Editors' Introduction, pp. xxv–lxxiv above, and our endnote 5 to **37**, p. 602 above.

2. (p. 283) That is, ISOS; see endnote 3 to **14A(a)**, p. 574 above.

Chapter 41: The first break

1. (p. 284) The German invasion of Russia started on 22 June 1941. This chapter describes work done in the second half of 1941 and the first few months of 1942. The reference to Vienna could be taken to mean either that the original termini of the Tunny link were Vienna and Athens, or that the messages studied originated in Vienna and Athens, passing by land line between Vienna and wherever the *Reich*-end of the link was located. There is a statement in Hinsley, Thomas, Ransom and Knight, *British Intelligence* (see endnote 2 to Chapter **11**, above), vol. 3 part I, p. 477, to the effect that the former case holds: the link termini were Vienna and Athens. But we do not regard this as completely decisive, as it is probably based on second-hand accounts similar to the one found in **41**, or the account **41** was based on, and likewise capable of being read two ways.

2. (p. 284) This correspondence matches the ITA 2 teleprinter alphabet and the English-language typewriter keyboard layout it was derived from, but not the standard German keyboard layout; see endnote 6 to **11A(a)**, p. 565 above.

3. (p. 285) 'Letter subtractor' was the standard Bletchley Park term for a cipher system using additive key. The term makes good sense in the case of the C-38 cipher addressed in G. W. Morgan's 1941 *Theory and Analysis of a Letter Subtractor Machine*, where the enciphering equation is $Z = K - P \pmod{26}$, and a kind of sense with ciphers for which $Z = K + P$ because then P is obtained from Z by subtracting K. (A copy of Morgan's paper is in NARA HCC 185:862.) Since the Research Section had just completed its analysis of the C-38 before tackling Tunny, its use of this terminology is understandable.

4. (p. 286) The Research Section was headed by Maj. G. W. Morgan.

5. (p. 286) This hypothesis is, essentially, that Tunny was a minor variant of the cipher machine invented by Parker Hitt, discussed in endnote 19 to **11B(j)**, p. 567 above. It had been offered for sale to the U.S. Department of State by the I.T.T. Corporation in 1931, but after study by the U.S. Army cryptanalysts was rejected as insufficiently secure. (See Frank B. Rowlett, *The Story of Magic: Memoirs of an American Cryptologic Pioneer* (Laguna Hills, Calif.: Aegean Park Press, 1998), pp. 70–74 and Cragon, *From Fish to Colossus* (see endnote 19 to Chapter **11**, above), especially Appendix C.) As described in endnote 19 to **11B(j)**, p. 567 above, a very similar machine, possibly developed from the Hitt machine, had been used as a predecessor model of the SZ 40, and was judged insecure by the German cipher authorities.

The guess that Tunny worked like the Hitt machine would, then, have been the simplest starting point for the diagnosis. It seems likely that the cryptanalysts either knew about this machine or hypothesized a similar one. (The same principle of regularly stepping wheels of differing sizes was also familiar from the recently solved C-38 cipher machine used by the Italian Navy. See Hinsley, Thomas, Ransom and Knight, *British Intelligence* (see endnote 2 to Chapter **11**, above), vol. 2, p. 22 and footnote, and also the minutes of the directing sub-committee for the Research Section, GCCS, 23 June 1941 (TNA HW 14/16), in which Col. Tiltman reported that the section had successfully attacked the Hagelin Machine, that is, the C-38. This is corroborated in a postwar reminiscence, William T. Tutte, 'At Bletchley Park', 6 May 2002, URL: `http://math.uwaterloo.ca/combinatorics-and-optimization/sites/ca.combinatorics-and-optimization/files/uploads/files/atbletchley.pdf` (visited on 07/06/2014), pp. 3–5.) It was implausible that the Germans were using something simpler and less secure than the Hitt machine, but it would be foolish not to check that, by some blunder, they were using something similar.

From this point of view the criticism in **41D(a)** seems a little harsh.

Chapter 42: Early hand methods

1. (p. 291) The reference to 'Section IV' is unclear. It might be to a section of the *Testery Report* or to part of an earlier draft of this chapter.

2. (p. 293) *Dritter Teil des Spruches, zwoter Teil des Spruches* = third part of the message, second part of the message.

3. (p. 293) Here 'screed' presumably refers to a document written in the Research Section, describing its Tunny work. It does not seem to be mentioned in the *Report*'s bibliography, Chapter **73**.

4. (p. 294) A memorandum from Travis of 10 May 1942 marks a bureaucratic milestone: henceforth the cipher is to be known as Tunny, Cdr. M. G. Saunders is to be the GCCS representative for all Tunny work done outside Bletchley Park, especially that concerned with interception, and Col. Tiltman is to deal with all Tunny matters inside Bletchley Park, including the construction of the new decoding machine, known as 'Mr Heil's decoding machine' (TNA HW 14/36).

Chapter 43: Testery methods 1942–44

1. (p. 298) This statement is false if the term 'information' is taken in its modern, Shannon-theoretic, sense: according to Theorem 7 in C. E. Shannon, 'A Mathematical Theory of Communication', *Bell System Technical Journal*, 27 (1948), pp. 379–423, 623–656, since the ΔK stream is derived from the K stream, there cannot be more information in it than in the K stream. But this sense of the term did not exist when the *Report* was written. What is meant here is that certain patterns are easier to recognise or easier to analyse in the ΔK stream than in the K stream, especially when one looks at the monographic (or marginal) distributions of the two streams.

2. (p. 299) Not shown in our redrawing of the cage diagram is a slightly off-centre dot in the third cell of the 18th column, which we believe to be a blemish in the photostat. If it were genuinely there, the number of agreements should be $\binom{3}{2} = 3$, not the figure $\binom{2}{2} = 1$ actually listed.

3. (p. 299) 'fig. **(I)**' presumably refers to the χ_3 cage illustrated (without caption) on p. 299.

4. (p. 301) *Zwoter Teil* = second part.

5. (p. 302) It is not clear precisely what 'to lack rigidity' means here. The phrase is also used in

26B(d) where its meaning is equally unclear.

Chapter 44: Hand statistical methods

1. (p. 305) The reference to 'Section VI' is unclear; possibly to **44E(f)**, or possibly to a section of the *Testery Report*.

2. (p. 306) `+++MAA8889` is a full stop followed by two dashes followed by a space, the full stop preceded by three figure-shifts and the dashes followed by three letter-shifts.

3. (p. 307) The reference to 'Part I' is unclear. Possibly it refers to chapters **11** to **15**, and possibly to the *Testery Report*.

Chapter 51: Introductory

1. (p. 309) This technical account by the Post Office engineers seems not to have been written.

2. (p. 311) A list of Newmanry equipment in March, 1944, almost exactly half way between the two temporal endpoints given in this chart, is contained in cable VIS 15 of 19 Mar. 1944 (in TNA HW 57/1). M.H.A. Newman at GCCS wrote to W.G. Welchman, then visiting SSA, describing the equipment on hand and expected soon: 3 single Robinsons, 1 coupled Robinson, 5 straight Tunnies (presumably 'decoding machines'), 2 special Tunnies for setting, 2 Mrs. Miles, 1 Garbo, 1 copy unit, 2 hand perforators. Colossus 1 nearly complete ('chis working, motor and psis on the way'), and there is a timetable for more equipment: 3 coupled Robinsons in 0, 3, and 6 weeks, Colossus 2 to be operative by 1st June, Colossus 3 one month later, one special Tunny any day, and 3 straight Tunnies [the] first [due] in six weeks. See our endnote 3 to **56F**, p. 610 below on Mrs. Miles.

Ten days later, in a 29 March 1944 letter to W. G. Radley at Dollis Hill, Nigel de Grey gives the predicted dates of arrival of Colossus 2 (1 June), Colossus 3 (1 July), and Colossus 4 (August). Tester's section seems to have had 4 decoding machines on hand on 29 March and was expecting a hand-me-down of another from the Newmanry when its replacement (possibly not a decoding machine but a British Tunny), which was scheduled to arrive at the Newmanry that day, had been installed. Then, of course, the Testery would have 5. Tester's section would need another decoding machine by 1 May (to keep up with Colossus 1 and the double bedstead Robinson) and another 2 with each new Colossus thereafter, that is, 7 more than the 5 it would have soon. (TNA HW 62/6; copy of letter courtesy R. Erskine.)

An inventory of cryptographic machinery at GCCS dated 28 February 1945 lists 12 Colossi, 4 Mrs. Miles, 3 Garbos, 16 Tunnys, 4 Robinsons, and 3 Dragons (1 from USA, 2 under construction). (NARA HCC 1126:3620.) With one exception the discrepancies between this inventory and the chart in **51(k)** of the *Report* are minor. The *Report* mentions Miles A through D, but lists only 3 Miles machines in **51(k)**; the inventory lists 4. The *Report* lists 2 Robinsons plus 2 nearly complete, the inventory 4. But the *Report* is very clear that there were 10 Colossi, with the 11th being only partly assembled when the war ended; and again shows the locations of the Colossi in the floor plans in **31**: Colossi 1–4 in Block F, and 5–10 in Block H, with space for just one more. This contradicts the inventory, which lists 12 Colossi. In this matter we think the *Report* is correct and the is inventory incorrect. The authors of the *Report* had daily first-hand contact with the Colossi, while the inventory was probably compiled from a variety of construction projection estimates, and not from a direct count of machines in place. (The inventory lists 2 Dragons under construction on 28 February but according to the *History of the Fish Section* (TNA HW 50/63, p. 12) Dragon 2 had been delivered on 4 January.)

Chapter 53: Colossus

1. (p. 318) For unknown reasons, the *Report* uses the term 'trigger' to refer to the circuitry used to represent a wheel pattern, implemented by an array of connectors or of switches. The present rotational state of a wheel of (say) size 31 was represented on Colossus by the presence of an arc between cathode and anode of precisely one of the 31 thyratrons in a ring, the anodes of which lead to the connector array. Current flows through the arc of the excited thyratron to the corresponding member of the connector array, which, depending how it is set, either passes the current on or sends it to ground. The output of the connector array thus represents the present wheel character, dot or cross. When the wheel is to step, a controlling signal (a voltage pulse on the grid) causes the quenching of the arc of the presently excited thyratron and the striking of a new arc in the neighbouring thyratron. The usual term for the controlling signal of a thyratron is 'trigger', and thus the *Report*'s usage of the term is a misnomer. The glossary entry 'triggers' in **71** makes it clear that this misnomer was resented by the engineers.

2. (p. 328) The explanation of multiple testing given in the *Report*, and in particular in **53L**, does not match statements given by Flowers in his reminiscence, T. H. Flowers, 'The Design of Colossus', *Annals of the History of Computing*, 5 (1983), pp. 239–252, esp. pp. 239–252, or descriptions of Colossus derived from Flowers's, such as those appearing in Copeland, *Colossus* (see endnote 18 to Chapter **11**, above). According to **13B(a)**, the Colossus tape reader ran at 5,000 letters per second but the effective speed was increased fivefold by use of multiple testing. According to Flowers, the same basic speed of 5,000 letters per second was effectively increased fivefold by use of a shift register (each of whose stages was presumably 5 bits wide) which stored the most recently read 6 letters of the message tape to enable computation of the most recent 5 letters of ΔZ; these time-delayed versions of Z and ΔZ were then distributed to five separate copies of the counting logic.

Although it does not give construction details, a close reading of **53L(b)** and **(c)** suggests that multiple testing was implemented with one shift register (referred to as the memory device in **53L(b)**) with 5 stages, each holding a single bit, representing recent values not of Z but rather of the bit stream from the wheel 'on multiple test' (or its Δ). If the stages of this shift register are named S_1 through S_5, with S_1 holding the current (or newest) value of the multiple test stream, and S_5 the value 4 back, and if m names the bit level which is on multiple test, then the multiple test versions of Q_m, the mth level of Q, can be obtained by $R_1 = Q_m$, $R_2 = Q_m + S_1 + S_2$, $R_3 = Q_m + S_1 + S_3$, $R_4 = Q_m + S_1 + S_4$, and $R_5 = Q_m + S_1 + S_5$. (This at the cost of 5 bits of shift register memory and 8 bit adds, instead of 25 bits of shift register memory and a fivefold increase in all the digital counting logic, as implied by Flowers's account.) Our understanding of how multiple testing was implemented corresponds schematically to that given in Cragon, *From Fish to Colossus* (see endnote 19 to Chapter **11**, above), fig. 8.5, but we do not believe there were two shift registers for multiple testing as he shows in his figures 8.6 and 8.7. The account in **53L** is corroborated to a certain extent by a U.S. Navy document, 'Report on British

Attack on "Fish" ', Communications Intelligence Technical Paper TS 47, May 1945, NARA HCC 607:1596. (Although this document carries no mark of authorship, it was almost certainly written by H. H. Campaigne, the only U.S. Navy member of the Newmanry.) The contradiction between Flower's account and the account of multiple testing in **53L** is noted on page 136 of Benjamin Wells, 'The PC-User's Guide to Colossus' in Copeland, *Colossus* (see endnote 18 to Chapter **11**, above), pp. 116–138.

The gist of the difference between the two explanations is this. Was the 5- or 6-stage shift register (as Flowers describes it) next to the photocells, and used to store recently read cipher letters, or was it (as we believe **53L** describes) somewhere between the wheel triggers and the *Q* and *R* circuits, and used to store recent values from the wheel on multiple test?

Which account to trust more is a delicate question. Chapter **51** of the *Report* begins with a disclaimer: the account in chapter **53** is that of a user of Colossus, and details of construction are omitted or made vague. Still, the authors of the *Report* were expert users of Colossus, who wrote their account when the details were fresh in their minds; they had participated in the specification of what Colossus was supposed to do. Flowers, of course, writes with the authority of the man who designed and built Colossus, and his article is filled with circumstantial detail, but the lecture his article was based on was given in 1981, about 37 years after the event, when he was about 75 years old. Flowers, too, has a disclaimer (on p. 252): 'The events recounted happened so long ago that when I came to write this paper I found I had forgotten many of the details. The happy result was that the inquiries I had to make caused me to contact many of the people who took part at the time. . . '.

It is our belief that in this matter Flowers's memory, or that of his informants, was slightly unreliable. In particular, his passage (on page pp. 245–246)

> . . . thus prompting the thought that the effective speed could be increased by parallel processing. By using five processors in parallel, all operating on the same program but with different input data from the tape, an effective speed of 25,000 characters per second was obtained and was enough. Five separate processors presented little difficulty. A photoelectric reader to supply them with data would have to read six lines of tape simultaneously, however, and would be very difficult to construct. Six lines were needed so that two consecutive but different lines could be presented to each of the five processors. This difficulty was solved by shift registers invented for the purpose. Data read from the tape were read into six-bit shift registers, which meant that six consecutive characters from the message tape were available for processing using a tape reader that had to read only one line at a time and was thus simplified compared with the readers first used with the Robinson machines.

seems to conflate three separate features of Colossus. The first is that Colossus's photocells read one line of holes, and the output fed into a shift register with 2 cells, each 5 bits wide, to calculate the current ΔZ, which was superior to the method used on Robinson with regards reliability and simplicity. The second is the presence of 5 separate counters, each (as explained in **53J**) counting occurrences of a different Boolean expression involving the current Z and ΔZ. The third is multiple testing and the 5-stage shift register needed to implement it. It also seems possible to us that an earlier candidate design for Colossus 2 had a 5- or 6-stage shift register for the most recent letters read from the tape, as described by Flowers, but that this design was replaced in the end by the multiple testing arrangement described in **53L**. This is an attractive hypothesis, as the candidate design is at once conceptually simpler, and needs more valves, than the design we believe is described in the *Report*. A process of optimization applied to the simpler design, finding how to achieve the same end effect with fewer valves, might well have ended with the design found in **53L**.

3. (p. 330) The upward-pointing switch in the bottom row is the TM test switch, mentioned in **53L(h)**. If set up, it restricts the count to places where TM = •; if down, to places where TM = ×. The neutral position (as in all the other examples in this chapter) imposes no TM restriction.

Chapter 54: Robinson

1. (p. 340) In fact there is no such diagram at the end of the volume.

2. (p. 344) In all the examples in **54J**, the row of letters at the tops of the diagrams label the start and stop switches of **54C(d)**. In all cases here, the start and stop signs are taken from tape *A*. None of the plugging examples show the use of the & + switch described in **54B(d)**.

In **54J(a)** the effect of the plugging is that $Q_1 = Q_6 = B_1$, that $Q_2 = Q_7 = B_2$, and that $Q_5 = Q_{10} = A_1 + \overline{A}_1 + A_2 + \overline{A}_2$. Here the 'red switch' described in **54F(a)** is thrown, so the aa and bb counts are split, that is, kept separately. The aa count is of instances where $B_1 = \times$, $B_2 = \bullet$, and $A_1 + \overline{A}_1 + A_2 + \overline{A}_2 = \bullet$. The bb count is of instances where $B_1 = \times$, $B_2 = \bullet$, and $A_1 + \overline{A}_1 + A_2 + \overline{A}_2 = \times$.

In **54J(b)**, $Q_1 = B_1$, $Q_2 = B_2$, and $Q_5 = Q_{10} = A_2 + \overline{A}_2$. The red switch is thrown, so the aa count (for $B_1 = \bullet$, $B_2 = \times$, and $A_2 + \overline{A}_2 = \bullet$) is kept separately from the bb count (for $B_1 = \bullet$, $B_2 = \times$, and $A_2 + \overline{A}_2 = \times$).

In **54J(c)**, $Q_1 = Q_6 = A_2$, $Q_2 = Q_7 = B_2$, and $Q_5 = Q_{10} = A_5 + B_5$. Here aa counts the number of occurrences of $A_2 = B_2 = \times$ and $A_5 + B_5 = \bullet$ and bb counts the number of occurrences of $A_2 = B_2 = \times$ and $A_5 + B_5 = \times$.

In **54J(d)**, $Q_1 = Q_6 = A_1$, $Q_2 = Q_7 = B_2$, $Q_8 = B_3$, $Q_9 = B_4$, and $Q_{10} = B_5$. The red switch is not thrown, and the count is for instances of $A = 9$.

Chapter 55: Specialized counting machines

1. (p. 346) This chapter describes machines used in the Testery, which were simpler than those in the Newmanry. Since the authors of the *Report* were more familiar with Newmanry machines, the account is sketchier than those of Newmanry machines in chapters **53** and **54**.

2. (p. 346) Dragon 1 was designed and built in America, Dragons 2 and 3 in Britain.

This note summarises the fuller story told in J. A. Reeds, 'American Dragon', *Cryptologia*, 35.1 (2011), pp. 22–41:

In late November 1943, the SSA proposed to GCCS that SSA build a cribbing machine for psi setting. GCCS agreed, and by mid-December the project was underway at SSA. (TNA HW 14/92, 28 Nov. 1943; NARA HCC 998:3043.) The machine was designed by Capt. E. L.

George of the SSA and was built by the Western Electric company in Cicero, Illinois. Final assembly and testing was done by SSA at Arlington Hall, Virginia, in August 1944, by which time the machine had acquired the name 'Dragon'. It was sent to GCCS in October, accompanied by its maintenance technician, Sgt. Thomas L. Collins. (NARA HCC 998:3043; Thomas L. Collins, 'My Reminiscences of World War II', n.d. [*c.*2003], private typescript memoir, supplied by author, 2009; TNA HW 57/1, 24 Aug. 1944.) It began operations 9 October, and soon after GCCS decided it needed more copies, first asking SSA if more were forthcoming from America, and then ordering the construction of two more Dragons by Dollis Hill on 28 October. (Dragon activity report covering 9 Oct. 1944 – Jan. 1945 enclosed in A. W. Small, liaison report G-25, 17 January 1945, NARA HCC 1009:3179; enquiry to SSA about further Dragons, TNA HW 57/1; request to Dollis Hill, TNA HW 62/6.)

These British Dragons, Dragons 2 and 3, were to be completed in February and March of 1945, respectively. Although Dragon 2 was finished on schedule, Dragon 3 was not finished by the end of the war. (Expected completion dates: W. J. Fried liaison report F-108 of 1 November 1944, NARA HCC 950:2821; arrival of Dragon 2: A. W. Small G-25 cited above, and *History of the Fish Section*, TNA HW 50/63, p. 12. and *Report*, **51(k)**.)

Dragon Reports 19 through 27, covering 23 February – 26 April 1945, not available when Reeds, 'American Dragon' was written, show Dragon 1 active throughout that period, getting 36 successes out of 102 runs, and Dragon 2 active during 2 March – 26 April, getting 53 successes out of 125 runs. (These are contained in liaison reports sent by Albert W. Small and William P. Bundy, NSA Small G-44, G-47, G-52, G-61, G-63, and G-66, obtained by FOIA request by Ralph Erskine.) Paragraph 5 of report G-44 (Albert W. Small, 'Small Report G-44', 8 Mar. 1945, FOIA release of liaison report, NSA DOCID: 3524259) (with two redacted phrases, 9 and 8 typewriter letters long, marked with square brackets below) describes a change of division of labour between the Newmanry and Testery that had an effect on Dragon work:

> Due to the increase [. . .] in Fish, a heavy burden has been thrown on Testery. It has therefore been decided to make the Newmanry responsible in the first instance for setting known motor and psi wheels. This was put into effect this week. Testery solves messages [. . .] and *breaks* psi's and motors from dechis but does not set pin or motors.

The implications are spelled out in paragraph 3 of report G-52 (William P. Bundy, 'Small Report G-52', 21 Mar. 1945, FOIA release of liaison report, NSA DOCID: 3524214).

> In general the Testery are finding the new division of labor described in G-44 a success. The chief purpose of this change was to enable the specialists of the Testery to concentrate on depths and thus to break more currently. This was thwarted at first by a falling off in the number of depths, but in the last two weeks the situation has been restored, and the experts have their hands full with depths and motor recovery. An unfortunate result of the new scheme is that the Dragon machines are almost squeezed out of work, as Annex C, the weekly Dragon report, reveals clearly.

And on 2 April, Bundy reports 'The Dragon report emphasizes again that the use of Colossus to set Psis has removed Dragon's most profitable material.' (William P. Bundy, 'Small Report G-57', 2 Apr. 1945, FOIA release of liaison report, NSA DOCID: 3524187, para. 4.)

According to the Dragon activity reports mentioned above, Dragon 1 continued with its operations into April 1945, by which time it had successfully set at least 179 messages out of 483 attempted.

This account contradicts many of the details given in Gil Hayward, 'The British Tunny Machine' in Copeland, *Colossus* (see endnote 18 to Chapter **11**, above), pp. 291–296, and to a lesser extent, in Gil Hayward, 'Operation Tunny' in Hinsley and Stripp, *Codebreakers* (see endnote 2 to Chapter **11**, above), pp. 175–192.

3. (p. 346) Dragon's tape reader was an ordinary electromechanical tape reader of the sort used in commercial teleprinter equipment (a Teletype model 14 tape transmitter), not a high-speed photoelectric reader like Robinson's or Colossus's. It is clearly visible in a photograph in NARA HCC 998:3043.

4. (p. 347) Even though Proteus used two tapes, its overall architecture was more like that of Colossus than that of Robinson. Like Colossus, it executed a nested loop, the inner one of which was implemented with a Colossus-style closed loop of punched tape — the dictionary tape $P^{(2)}$ — presumably read photoelectrically. The outer loop was stepped by an ordinary electromechanical tape reader, which read successive letters from the V tape, scrolling them into a 7 long shift register. Digital logic detected a hit between the current position of the V tape, the dictionary tape, and a crib set up by plugging. At the end of the V tape the job was done.

5. (p. 348) Here 'click' means not just a single stroke in the difference between two streams, as in **28** and **71**, but a sequence of such.

Chapter 56: Copying machines

1. (p. 350) This chapter describes the punched tape handling equipment needed to prepare tapes for Robinson or Colossus, or to help produce plain text once the wheels had been broken and set. None of them carry out cryptanalytic operations on their own.

Sections **56A** through **56C** describe machines which conceivably might have been found in an ordinary teleprinter office. Sections **56D** through **56H** describe machines which would not be found in an ordinary teleprinter office, because they carry out functions only of use in Tunny breaking. Their construction, however, would have been obvious to any teleprinter engineer. The machines of sections **56J** through **56L**, the various British functional equivalents of the German Tunny machines, would (because of their use of thyratron rings instead of mechanical wheels) have been very surprising to a German Tunny operator.

2. (p. 350) The figure shows 10 special keys even though the text here refers to 9.

3. (p. 352) The 'Miles' machines (occasionlly called 'Mrs Miles') were named after family of the first surviving British quadruplets, Ann, Ernest, Paul and Michael, born 28 November 1935 in St Neots (Cambridgeshire). This class of machines read one or more punched paper tapes, did simple tranformations of the data read from them and punched the results on one or more output tapes. Miles A, described in **56H**, in theory could simultaneously read six tapes and write three. Chapters **27** and **95** describe some of these machines' uses.

Chapter 57: Simple machines

1. (p. 361) The 'Plus Adder' was a commercial adding machine made by the Bell Punch Company of London (whose name derives from their main business, making bus ticket machines), introduced in the late 1930's. 'Comptometer' was the proprietary name for the Fell & Tarrant company of Chicago's line of adding machines; in popular usage it was applied to all similar machines, including the Bell Plus. These machines were key driven: the force of the depression of a key moved the corresponding digit wheel the indicated number of notches forward, a pawl mechanism taking care of the digit carries; they were in effect keyboard-operated versions of the calculator Blaise Pascal (1623–1662) designed in 1642. A peculiarity of the Bell Plus was the absence of keys for the digits 6 – 9, whose effect was achieved by multiple strokes on lesser keys. (Paradoxically, this meant for faster operation as the operator's hand did not have to move to reach the higher digits.) To add the number 87 into the total, the operator could depress the 4 key in the tens' position twice, and the 3 and 4 keys in the ones' position once each, to add $40+40+4+3=87$. The current value of the total was read from a row of windows. See the web site Nigel Tout, 'Bell Punch Company & Anita Calculators', URL: `http://www.vintagecalculat%20ors.com/BellPunch` (visited on 07/06/2014) for further details.

2. (p. 361) '£.s.d.' = Pounds, shillings, pence; that is, the units of traditional (non-decimal) British currency in use until 1971.

3. (p. 361) Heated to speed the evaporation of the solvent, benzene (or benzine; see endnote 28 to **23Z**, p. 589 above), used with Bostik.

Chapter 61: Raw materials — production, with plans of Tunny links

1. (p. 381) The numbers in this table agree, roughly, with those in a chart in the *History of the Fish Section*, TNA HW 50/63, Annex III. (This 20-page unsigned typed document is a month-by-month chronology of staffing and production matters in the Testery, and of the Testery's interactions with the Newmanry and with Knockholt.) We reproduce that chart in a slightly changed format below (on p. 612). That chart breaks down the statistics by month, and presents data in eleven columns, some of which are explained in footnotes. The first two columns, A and B, are labelled 'Intercepted' and 'Received', presumably meaning 'Intercepted by Knockholt, and 'Received at Bletchley Park from Knockholt', respectively. Until May 1944 Knockholt sent all its intercepted messages to Bletchley Park, but thereafter only ones likely to be useful.

The first column in the *Report*'s table corresponds to column B of the Annex III chart, and so its column head should be 'Transmissions received from Knockholt' not 'at Knockholt'. (This explains the apparent drop in quantity of intercept early in 1944.) The second and third columns in the table, which refer to the Newmanry alone, do not correspond to any column in the chart. They measure the input and output of the Newmanry's χ setting processes, which in the last year of the war seems to have worked in one case out of two or three. The analogous columns in the chart are columns C and D, representing the Testery's input and output respectively. As the chart's footnote indicates, C aggregates de-χ'd tapes (column 3 of the table) with tapes of messages in depths; these kinds of tapes were processed differently. The fourth and fifth columns in the table correspond to the columns D and E of the chart, indicating the total volume of plain text produced.

	A	B	C	D	E	F	G	H			
mm/yy								R	D	C	T
11/42	5980	5980	520	431	2146	2	2	–	2	–	2
12/42	6200	6200	540	441	2321	2	2	–	2	–	2
1/43	3854	3854	948	379	1138	3	2	–	2	–	2
2/43	3721	3721	872	352	1019	3	2	–	2	–	2
3/43	9040	9040	618	260	1229	5	5	–	6	–	6
4/43	10100	10100	464	192	570	5	5	–	5	–	5
5/43	7090	7090	962	428	1411	6	6	–	6	–	6
6/43	6780	6780	828	345	1082	5	4	–	5	–	5
7/43	5980	5980	560	226	971	8	5	–	5	–	5
8/43	7250	7250	711	281	1170	10	7	–	8	–	8
9/43	8320	8320	552	238	906	–	7	–	6	–	6
10/43	11040	11040	578	241	1186	–	7	–	7	–	7
11/43	12900	12900	574	236	984	–	9	–	6	–	6
12/43	10800	10800	747	256	975	–	6	–	6	–	6
1/44	10100	10100	363	242	1051	–	4	1	3	–	4
2/44	9500	9500	490	102	473	–	4				4
3/44	8400	8400	552	336	1665	–	5				5
4/44	?	2080	622	167	897	–	6				6
5/44	?	2047	1021	401	1868	–	4				5
6/44	15056	2088	903	476	1930	17	6				8
7/44	17220	1645	803	339	2129	21	6				13
8/44	22305	1826	856	404	2310	24	9				31
9/44	23786	1739	739	396	2421	25	7	19	11	6	36
10/44	22339	1887	1052	533	3123	28	10	30	12	5	47
11/44	26586	2850	1462	831	3852	23	9	45	12	8	65
12/44	25981	2185	1094	497	2632	29	11	33	21	1	55
1/45	26422	2029	1234	759	4313	26	9	49	17	2	68
2/45	23788	2599	1402	969	5028	24	13	57	33	7	97
3/45	22303	3127	1508	1425	6037	32	13	65	29	6	100
4/45	17989	3246	1558	1130	5219	24	18	59	37	8	104
5/45	1638	1324	400	195	1375	12	5	2	3	–	5
	–	–	–	13508	63431	–	–	–	–	–	721

Statistics (Nov. 1942 – May 1945) (Annex III, TNA HW 50/63)

Explanation of headings: Columns A–D are in numbers of transmissions. A = 'Intercepted', B = 'Received', C = 'Crypto. Poss. for Testery', D = 'Issued'. Column E = 'Letters Decoded', in thousands of letters. Columns F and G are counts of links: F = 'Heard', G = 'Broken'. Column H is in number of keys, with sub columns R = 'Rect.', D = 'Depth', C = 'Crib', and T = 'Total'.

Footnotes explain that column B agrees with column A until the period May 1944 onwards when 'we "ordered" traffic we wanted and could deal with'; that column C is the number of messages received in depth, plus Newmanry output; and that column H 'has been subdivided into method where reliable information is available. The total figure is sound.'

The table's last column corresponds to the chart's last column, with some small discrepancies. The column total in the table is 718, in the chart it is 721. For March, April, and May 1943, the chart lists 5, 6, and 5 keys broken, but the table lists 15. The chart lists 7, 6, and 6 keys broken in the last three months of 1943, but the table lists 18.

The system of daggers and double daggers in the table's last column, along with the breakdown of the chart's column H into keys recovered from rectangles, depths and cribs, make it clear that the Newmanry, in the last year of the war, was 'responsible' for about half of the Tunny keys recovered. This last statement, however, should not obscure the fact that the efforts of both sections were needed to process essentially every Tunny message: even if the Testery had recovered one key's χ wheels from a depth, they still needed the Newmanry to set those wheels on other messages using that key; similarly, even if the Newmanry had recovered all the wheels for a given key, they still needed the Testery to actually decode the message and pass it on to (say) Hut 3. (In fact, although the Newmanry regularly recovered χ wheels from cipher, it did not discover a method for statistically recovering μ and ψ wheels until the war had ended in Europe: see **28C(b)**.)

This table and the chart in *The History of the Fish Section* do not give direct answers to the natural questions: What fraction of Tunny messages were read? And with what delays after transmission?

The answers to these questions are different for the three time periods described in **11E**: the experimental period, the period of expansion, and the period of flux.

The answers also differ according to what one understands the 'fraction of Tunny messages' to be: the fraction of all Tunny messages sent, the fraction of those on links that GCCS wished to intercept, the fraction of messages actually intercepted, or the fraction of good intercepts sent from Knockholt to Bletchley Park. The documentary evidence becomes better as one progresses through this list, even if to a non-specialist the intrinsic interest of the answer might decrease.

(The matter is made more complicated by changing criteria for what to intercept or for which intercepts to forward to Bletchly Park. The August 1944 entry in the *History of the Fish Section* (TNA HW 50/63, p. 10) describes one such adjustment: 'In order to prevent unneccessary work at Knockholt, a new plan was introduced as from 1st August by which Knockholt refrained from working on messages of length suitable for setting until they were ordered. On days when wheel patterns were recovered, Knockholt had to account for every message intercepted on that link.' Fried's liaison report F-101 of 14 October 1944 states (on p. 2) that in September Knockholt had intercepted 40 million letters of presumably Tunny traffic, of which 2 1/2 million were decoded by the Testery. Of the 5835 transmission intercepted in the week ending 1 October, 4799 were shorter than 2000 letters, but 'except in rare instances nothing whatever is done with transmissions of under 2000 letters'. (NARA HCC 950:2821.)

In the experimental period, which lasted to the end of October 1942, during which the χ and ψ wheel patterns changed at most monthly, and during which the indicator of each message was a thinly enciphered version of its wheel settings, the answers must be: a very high fraction of all intercepted messages were read, but with what must have seemed a strange pattern of solution delays. The main solution techniques then current (exploiting depths and using the 'indicator method') would, if they succeeded, give the χ and ψ wheel patterns for the whole month, but this would happen only part way through the month. On each subsequent day the μ wheels would have to be recovered, but this was done comparatively quickly, so subsequent messages were deciphered with little delay. But messages sent before the χ and ψ patterns had been recovered would be delayed by at least whatever the calendar implied: if the χ and ψ recovery occurred on the 12th of the month, a message sent on the 2nd of the month would suffer at least a 10-day deciphering delay. The overall effect for consumers of decrypted messages is that they generally flowed in near real time, except for monthly blockages of several days' or weeks' duration.

Five Tunny messages, listed in Erskine, 'Tunny Reveals *B-Dienst* Successes Against the "Convoy Code"' (see endnote 3 to Chapter **14**, above), Table 1, p. 874, have known deciphering delays: 0, 3, 1, 5, and 5 days. A tabulation of the delays of all the 1942 Tunny decodes in the tranche of naval decodes found by Erskine gives these results:

number	delay (in days)
105	0–4
25	5–9
12	10–14
13	15–19
19	20 or more.

(Based on data supplied by Erskine in a personal communication to JAR, 26 April 2014.)

During the period of expansion, from November 1942 into the summer of 1944, indicators were not sent, settings being taken from QEP lists instead. (See TNA HW 50/63, p. 2, and **43C(a)**.) Hence, even if the wheel patterns had been recovered, each message had to be set if it was to be read. The variety of techniques described in **23**, and the variety of ways they could be tried in sequence, is testimony to the difficulty of message setting. According to the source (TNA HW 3/92) given in endnote 5 to **12**, p. 572 above, it succeeded with only about half of the long messages. The same overall pattern of deciphering delays seen in the experimental period could be expected to hold, but with only half as many messages ever being deciphered.

The period of flux was marked by daily wheel changes on all links. (This started link by link in June 1944 and was in effect everywhere by August; the available documents do not show exactly when the change-over occurred for each link.) This had the effect of increasing the wheel-breaking load 30-fold. It also had the effect of lowering the success rate of Newmanry wheel-breaking. The higher the μ_{37} dottage, the easier are the tasks of breaking and setting. Previously one set of χ and ψ wheels was used with a month's worth of different μ wheels, one of which might have a particularly favourable dottage. But now χ and ψ wheels used on low dottage days were not approachable this way. Annex II to the *History of the Fish Section* (TNA HW 50/63) shows the effect of this. Two important links in late 1944 were Jellyfish and Bream, connecting Berlin with O.B. West and with O.B. Süd West, that is, with the theatre commanders in France and in Italy; it is presumed GCCS would have assigned high priority to reading those links. The following is tabulated from Annex II:

month		Bream	Jellyfish
August	1944	6	5
September	"	7	0
October	"	6	7
November	"	15	4
December	"	11	9
total		45	25

Thus Bream keys were recovered for 45 out of the 153 days in that period, and Jellyfish keys for

25 days. Long messages sent on those days had a 50% chance of being set, so for that period, about 15% of long Bream messages received at Bletchley Park could be read, and about 8% of Jellyfish ones. But when readable, the delays would have been modest: there was no backlog of early-month messages waiting for the month's key to be broken. (Figs. **61 (II)–(IV)** show links Bream (or Bream 1) and Bream 2 active from mid-1944, so there might have been 306 Bream keys for that period, not 153. If so, about 8% of long Bream messages would have been readable. The *History of the Fish Section* (TNA HW 50/63) only mentions one Bream link.)

It is not known when daily wheel changes started on Bream, but it cannot have been before June 1944. Annex II shows a Bream key recovery for each of the first five months of 1944. Thus, there was a Bream key available for each of the 152 days of that part of the year, so perhaps 50% of long Bream messages sent in that period might have been read. The entry for May 1944 in the *History of the Fish Section* (TNA HW 50/63, p. 6) states 'At this time the section was decoding on the average 15 Jellyfish and 60 Bream transmissions each week, out of an average number of suitable transmissions intercepted of 78 Jellyfish and 180 Bream, i.e. 20% Jellyfish and 33% Bream.'

2. (p. 382) No attempt was made to preserve the exact proportions and positions of the elements of figs. **61 (I)** to **(V)**, or the exact punctuation of the labelling. The following changes have been made: In fig. **61 (II)**, the umlaut has been supplied to 'DÄNEMARK'. In the original, the names of the two central nodes in fig. **61 (IV)** are styled as 'ODO′FF' and 'HZPH′FF′2', rendered here as 'ODO/FF' and 'HZPH/FF/2' to be in conformity with fig. **61 (III)**.

The TNA copy of fig. **61 (I)** bears numerous pencilled notations. These may well have been made in the process of redrawing the figure for inclusion in Hinsley, Thomas, Ransom and Knight, *British Intelligence* (see endnote 2 to Chapter **11**, above), vol. 3 part I, facing p. 482. Arguing for Hinsley copying fig. **61 (I)** is the fact that one of the items on the diagram, 'Pz AOK 5' has been misannotated as 'P2 AOK 5'; the same mistake shows up in the diagram in Hinsley. Again, another item is labelled 'H. GRE' in fig. **61 (I)** but more correctly 'H. Gr. E' on figs. **61 (II)–(V)** (for *Heeresgruppe* E, Army Group E); the form 'H. GRE' appears in Hinsley. And the geometric layout of the lines connecting the boxes in the diagram is identical. Arguing against is a difference in title: Hinsley's diagram is labelled 'Tunny cross country links, German Army November 22 – July 1944', and for several links' starting dates not present in fig. **61 (I)**.

Figs. **61 (I)–(V)** are laid out roughly as maps of Europe, with Berlin in the centre, north at the top, etc., and show only those portions, to the extent known by GCCS, of the German military teleprinter network that used Tunny and were transmitted by radio. They do not show the entire teleprinter network. The boxes, variously labelled with military unit designations, place names and teleprinter office names, represent teleprinter offices. The links between them bear several kinds of annotations. Unbracketed dates in date ranges show first and last dates of interception for the link. Dates in brackets show dates at which either or both of the ends of the link changed. Thus, fig. **61 (I)** shows Dace connecting HOSF and ANNA with the date range 'November 43 – (July 44)' and connecting HZPH and ANNA with range '(July 44) – December 44', meaning Dace was intercepted continuously between November 1943 and December 1944, and in July 1944 the western end of Dace moved from HOSF to HZPH. 'Unclassified' links (such as 'Unc 11' connecting Pz AOK 15 with H. Gr. B in fig. **61 (III)** and 'UNCLD 45' connecting GEB AOK 20 with H. Gr. Kurland in fig. **61 (V)**) were on the air a short time only and were never assigned Fish cover names. (This explanation of link annotations is derived from the *Sixta Report* by a discretionary release of retained material by GCHQ historian.)

As with the civilian telegraph network or the ordinary postal service, or even the early 21st-century electronic mail network, messages sent on the German military teleprinter network were forwarded to their end destinations over routes the end users might not have been aware of. Thus, in 1942, if Naval headquarters in Berlin issued a secret circular teleprinter message to various Naval units, one of which was in Greece, a copy would be sent over the Army's Berlin to Athens Tunny link, because that was the only route to Greece on the military teleprinter network allowed to carry traffic of the given security level. (Almost all of the German message traffic described in Erskine, 'Tunny Reveals *B-Dienst* Successes Against the "Convoy Code" ' (see endnote 3 to Chapter **14**, above), fits this description.) Similarly, messages sent between relatively low-ranking communicants might pass over a Tunny link (as with the sample Tunny message illustrated in fig. **28 (IX)** and discussed in our endnote 23 to chapter **22**, p. 596 above).

Rather than dispersing teleprinter machines into the work spaces of their end users, as telephones and fax machines were usually placed in late-20th-century offices, the German Army concentrated them in special teleprinter offices, which, when connected together, formed the military teleprinter network. These teleprinter offices, *Fernschreibstellen*, each serving a headquarters unit, ministerial office, or other establishment, were run by special detachments of signals troops. Each teleprinter office had a name (*Fernschreibrufname*) used in addressing and routing messages. Although these names were usually referred to as 'teleprinter callsigns' by GCCS, they are *not* call signs in the strict technical sense. (Temporary enciphered radio call signs taken from frequently changing lists were used when setting up a radio teleprinter connection, but these — unlike teleprinter office names — were not visible to the users of the teleprinter network.)

As the war progressed, the Germans used an increasingly elaborate naming scheme for their teleprinter offices. When the war began, names were typically 3 or 4 letters long, but towards the end of the war 5 letter names were common. The first letter indicated the branch of the armed forces served by the teleprinter office: W, H, M, and L for armed forces (*Wehrmacht*), army (*Heer*), navy (*Marine*), and air force (*Luftwaffe*), respectively. The second letter of an H name indicated the military administrative region (*Wehrkreis*) if in the ranges A through N or P through Z. An O (as in HOKW or HOSF) indicated the office was attached to a branch of army headquarters (OKH, *Oberkommando des Heeres*). Subsequent letters sometimes indicated a geographical place name, and suffixes were used to distinguish between offices serving different sections of the same headquarters. Thus, as illustrated in a GCCS document, *German teleprinter call signs as a source of intelligence*, GCCS serial number CX/MSS/S.73, dated 30 August 1944 (NARA HCC 1382:4373), Army Group E, with teleprinter exchange HMYX had teleprinter offices with names HMYX/Fue., HMYX/Qu., HMYX/FF, for the operations, quartermaster, and signals staffs at Army Group E headquarters. The German service instructions for teleprinter usage, *Fernschreibbetriebs-Vorschrift, H. Dv. 424/4, M. Dv. Nr. 924, L. Dv. 704/3a* of 1 March 1944 (NARA HCC 70:311), lists (on p. 24) thirteen such suffixes. Of these, the ones corresponding to the three listed in the GCCS document are FU = *Führungsabteilung* (command section), QU = *Generalquartiermeister, Oberquartiermeister* (quartermaster), and FF = *Funkfernschreibstelle* (radio teleprinter office). The FF suffix appears in figs. **61 (III)** and **(IV)** and in the sample plain text illustrated in fig. **28 (IX)**, which is discussed in endnote 23 to **28E(b)**, p. 596 above. Both documents give a wealth of other information on the names of teleprinter offices; the German document gives details of the operation of a teleprinter office. An official German list of Armed Forces headquarters (*Oberkommando der Wehrmacht* (OKW)) teleprinter office names (*Fernschreibrufnamen der Fernschreibstellen des OKW*, 1 July 1942, NARA HCC 21:185) survives, but we have not been able to locate a corresponding list for OKH or for army field commands.

Teleprinter office names reflected the locations of the offices within the German military hierarchy, not necessarily their geographical locations. When a unit relocated, it took its teleprinter office name with it. The layout of figs. **61 (I)–(V)** is based in part on direction-finding evidence (which gives an indication of geographical location), and in part upon the identification of the units served by the teleprinter offices, which in turn was based on deductions based on reading the plain texts. Outlying nodes in the network are labelled with military unit names, as the identification of the name of a unit and its serving teleprinter office is easy: messages sent by HMYX, say, can only have come from Army Group E. The identification of users in the more ramified military hierarchy in Berlin with Berlin-area teleprinter offices is not as precise. Hence the compilers of the diagrams have used station names and occasionally place names to label central nodes, rather than organisation names as with the peripheral nodes.

In spite of the military-hierarchical and non-geographical meaning of the teleprinter office names, it is possible to detect vestiges of toponymy in some of them: e.g. WFRL at Freilassing, ANNA at Angerburg, HZPH at Zossen. The *German teleprinter call signs* document cited above lists some other examples.

The organisational names and abbreviations used to label the peripheral nodes in figs. **61 (I)–(V)** are: AOK = *Armeeoberkommando* = Army Headquarters; W. Bfh Dänemark = *Wehrmacht Befehlshaber Dänemark* = Commander [German] Armed Forces [in] Denmark; H. Gr. = *Heeresgruppe* = Army Group; O.B. = *Oberbefehlshaber* = Commander-in-chief; OBSO = *Oberbefehlshaber Süd Ost* = Commander-in-chief, South-east[ern Theatre]; WFSt = *Wehrmacht Führungsstab* = Armed Forces Operational Staff; Pz. AOK 5 = *Panzerarmee-Oberkommando 5* = Headquarters, Fifth Panzer Army; Geb. AOK 20 = *Gebirgs Armeeoberkommando 20* = Headquarters, Twentieth Mountain Army; H. Gr. Kurland = Army Group Courland; H. Gr. Weichsel = Army Group Vistula; D.H.M. RUM = *Deutsche Heeresmission in Rumänien* = German military mission to Romania. These are all standard German military abbreviations.

The nodes listed by teleprinter office names are as follows.

ANNA (whose initial letter does not follow the usual pattern for office names) was the teleprinter office of the OKH headquarters complex at Angerburg in East Prussia (now Wegorzewo in Poland), near Hitler's *Wolfsschanze* (wolf's lair) headquarters in Rastenburg (now Ketrzyn, in Poland), about 100 km from Königsberg (now Kaliningrad, in Russia) where the *Report* locates it. We see the usage ANNA/FF in the sample plain text discussed in endnote 23 to **28E(b)**, p. 596 above.

The precise location of ODO (another breaker of the initial letter rule) is something of a mystery. It was in Thuringia, not far from the 'OLGA' communications bunker near Ohrdruf, which had been built in 1937 as a spare trunk exchange, but apparently not used until late in the war. (According to **11E(c)** is was in Erfurt; according to a discretionary release of retained material by the GCHQ historian, the *Sixta Report* places less precisely it 'in the Erfurt area'.) Personal communications from H. G. Kampe and F. Weierud, Jan. 2013, state that OLGA itself did not have radio equipment, and ODO in effect served as its radioteleprinter outstation. Fig. **61 (IV)** shows the usage ODO/FF, and that it was in operation between 28 February and 17 April 1945.

The *German teleprinter call signs* document cited above states that HOSF was the teleprinter office of the *Chef, Heeres-Rüstung und Befehlshaber des Ersatzheeres* (Chief of Army Equipment and Commander of the Replacement Army) at OKH (as opposed to branches at other locations); the *Report* locates it at Strausberg (but spells it Straussberg; see endnote 27 to **11D(a)**, p. 570 above). The O of HOSF evidently indicated it was part of OKH. The German army signals organisation was administratively under the Chief of Army Equipment, so it seems possible that the earliest Tunny link ends in the Berlin area could have been in this teleprinter office. But this logic would place HOSF in Berlin or Zossen, not Strausberg. A possible resolution is that HOSF's was connected by land line to its radio equipment in Strausberg but its teleprinters and Tunny machines were in Berlin or Zossen, convenient to the offices of the Chief of Army Equipment.

That there was a radio station at Strausberg is implied by an account of the lead-up to the 20 July 1944 plot against Hitler. In a conversation on 22 November 1942, one of the plotters listed various places in the Berlin area to be guarded in the event of internal disturbances, listing '*das Haupttelegraphenamt, die Funkstellen in Nauen, Strausberg, auf dem Flugplatz Rangsdorf und die verlagerten Dienstellen in Berlin*' (the main telegraph office, the radio stations at Nauen, Strausberg, at the Rangsdorf airfield, and at various relocated installations). (See Hans-Georg Kampe, *Handbuch zur Geschichte des militärichen Fernmeldwesens, Teil IV: Das militärische Fernmeldewesen Deutschlands im Zweiten Weltkrieg 1939-1945* (Berlin: Erwin Meißler, 2008), pp. 459, 473 and Peter Hoffmann, *The History of the German Resistance, 1933–1945* (Montreal and Buffalo: McGill-Queen's University Press, 1996), p. 346. Hoffmann's note 29 on p. 640 to the cited passage casts doubt on the date, suggesting early 1943 or even late 1943. But of course this does change the point that an important radio station existed at Strausberg.) According to a personal communication by H. G. Kampe, Jan. 2013 to JAR, there was a military radio installation at Kagel during the war, several kilometres south of Strausberg, at a site later used by the East German *Nationale Volksarmee* (National People's Army) for a large telecommunications bunker.

HZPH was the main Army trunk teleprinter exchange, at the OKH headquarters complex at Zossen-Wünschdorf, in the 'Zeppelin' communications bunker. (The *German teleprinter call signs* document places it at 'Berlin, Zeppelin-Wiese', but this is probably a mistake of the authors, a confusion of the Zeppelin bunker in Zossen-Wünschdorf with the Zeppelin Wiese parade ground in Nürnberg, the site of the notorious annual Nazi party rallies.) We see the usages HZPH/FF1 and HZPH/FF2 in figs. **61 (III)** and **(IV)**.

WFRL was at Freilassing, near Salzburg, serving the portion of the WFSt that relocated to the south shortly before the war ended.

A different kind of indication of the extent of the teleprinter network is given by a POW interrogation report from the [British] Combined Services Detailed Interrogation Centre, *Notes on the German Army teleprinter network.* ('C.S.D.I.C. (UK) S.I.R. 1503', dated 28 February 1944, in NARA HCC 1338:4030.) According to the informant, there were two main teleprinter networks, the operational net, controlled from the Zeppelin exchange of OKH in Zossen (HZPH), and the static net controlled from the OKW exchange in Berlin. When he visited it in 1941, the army section of the OKW exchange had at its disposal in one room eight secret teleprinters and in an adjacent room eighty ordinary teleprinters. The report summarises a shortage of cipher teleprinters: 'The T 52 D secret teleprinter was available for use as far down as Army. Below that level formations fortunate enough to be allowed a secret teleprinter had to be content with the T 52 C. Divisions were rarely allotted secret teleprinters.'

In addition to the sources listed above, sporadic details are given in: Georg Glünder and Paul Whitaker, 'Wireless and "Geheimschreiber" Operator in the War, 1941–1945', *Cryptologia*, 26.2 (2002), pp. 81–96; Albert Praun, *Soldat in der Telegraphen- und Nachrichtentruppe* (Würzburg, 1965); Hans-Georg Kampe, *Die Heeres-Nachrichtentruppe der Wehrmacht, 1935–1945* (Wölfersheim-Berstadt: Podzun-Pallas, 1994); and Kampe, *Nachrichtentruppe des Heeres und deutsche Reichspost: militärliches und staatliches Nachrichtenwesen in Deutschland 1830 bis 1945* (see endnote 23 to Chapter **28**, above).

Chapter 71: Glossary and index

1. (p. 387) The reference **74** Mar'42 is to the entry for March 1942 in the chronological chart of chapter **74**.

2. (p. 388) This sense of 'anagram' is peculiar to Fish work. The entry for 'anagram' in the GCCS *Cryptographic Dictionary* of 20 July 1944 (TNA HW 25/33 and NARA HCC 1413:4559) lists as sense 3: '(misused for). To break any part of a letter subtractor, esp. machine-cipher, depth of two or more messages by differencing and stencil-search or virtual stencil search.'

3. (p. 388) Presumably named after A. Oliver L. Atkin (1925–2008). See entry in Biographical Notes, p. 547.

4. (p. 391) In **28** a 'click' is a single letter match between two streams; in **55** it is a run of such matches. See endnote 6 to **27D(c)**, p. 594 above, for a different sense of the term, occuring only in **27D**.

5. (p. 392) In the notation of **22X(d)**, a combination count is the count of all letters Θ for which $\Theta.\Phi = 0$, for some fixed given letter Φ. Thus, the count of all letters Θ for which $\Theta_1 + \Theta_2 + \Theta_4 = \bullet$ is the combination count corresponding to $\Phi = \mathrm{J} = \mathbf{\times\times\bullet\times\bullet}$.

6. (p. 395) See endnote 4 to chapter **21**, p. 577 above.

7. (p. 397) 'Donald' is presumably D. Michie, co-author of the *Report*. The result is an easy consequence of a standard result of É. Lucas: for prime p (in our case, $p = 2$), if $a = \sum a_j p^j$ and $b = \sum b_j p^j$, then

$$\binom{a}{b} \equiv \binom{a_0}{b_0}\binom{a_1}{b_1}\cdots \quad (\mathrm{mod}\ p).$$

(É. Lucas, 'Sur les congruences des nombres eulériens et les coefficients différentiels des fonctions trigonométriques, suivant un module premier', *Bulletin de la Société Mathématique de France*, 6 (1878), pp. 49–54, esp. pp. 51–52.)

Here, and in a few other entries in **71**, the authors of the *Report* smuggle in the personal name of a Newmanry member. Others are I. J. Good, M. H. A. Newman, A. M. Turing, and J. H. C. Whitehead (who have entries of their own, Newman's being MHAN), Leslie N. Chown and Tilmar Moilien under their initials, LC and TM.

8. (p. 398) Usually referred to as the Drunkard's Walk problem.

9. (p. 401) But there is no entry for 'Convergence, Five Dimensional'.

10. (p. 402) Entry 'HC' refers to non-existent entry 'Checks, Hand'.

11. (p. 405) LEC was both the name of the letter count switch on Colossus and (as here) the abbreviation for letter count used in annotating Colossus output slips.

12. (p. 407) Tate and Lyle is the name of a major British sugar firm. Perhaps the choice of names was influenced by the fact that sugar was rationed during the war.

13. (p. 408) See our endnote 3 to **56F**, p. 610 above.

14. (p. 408) According to a personal communication to JAR from I. J. Good, the perpetrator was

Oliver Atkin.

15. (p. 409) See our endnote 3 to **56F**, p. 610 above.

16. (p. 410) This recipe tells how to translate between the GCCS theory of what active cams meant on Tunny and German wheel pattern specifications. On the German Tunny machine Nocke always meant active. The discrepancy is explained in endnote 36 to **11E(III)**, p. 571 above.

17. (p. 416) *Quatsch* = nonsense. *Wahlwörter* = arbitrary words, nulls. The official term is *Wahlwörter*; *Quatsch* is slang.

18. (p. 419) *Rolle* = roll.

19. (p. 421) Probably named after Shaun Wylie, (1913–2009). See entry in Biographical Notes, p. 559.)

20. (p. 423) But there are no entries for 'Crib Re Slip' and 'Crib Slips' in **71**. There are entries for 'Crib Retransmission Slips' and 'Retransmission Slips'.

21. (p. 427) The name Tea Party may be derived from the series of Saturday afternoon seminars, called 'tea parties', organised by the famous geometer H. F. Baker (1866–1956) when he was Lowndean Professor at Cambridge, 1914 – 36. Like Newman, Baker was a Fellow of St John's College. In England regular academic meetings for students were an innovation at the time. It seems that a similar 'tea time' had been instituted by Lord Rayleigh (1842–1919) at the Cavendish Laboratory, Cambridge, when he was director there (1880–1884) and the practice was continued by his successor, J. J. Thomson (1856–1940). (See Dong-Won Kim, *Leadership and Creativity: A History of the Cavendish Laboratory, 1871–1919* (Dortrecht: Kluwer Academic Publishers, 2002), pp. 48, 92, 100.)

22. (p. 428) Tim Moilien is T/3 Tilmar Moilien, U.S. Army. See entry in Biographical Notes, p. 553.

23. (p. 428) Tone transmission = carrier telegraphy, the representation of the dot and cross by audio tones or combinations of tones. See Appendix A, 'Transmission of Teleprinter Signals', this volume, pp. 495–499 for details.

24. (p. 430) Professor John Henry Constantine Whitehead (1904–1960). See entry in Biographical Notes, p. 559.

25. (p. 431) The index entry for δ_0 which points to **24Y(a)** appears to be mistaken.

26. (p. 433) The text says 'An empirical distribution' but the referred-to passage in **24X(e)** (in the discussion of significance test IV) says and means 'the prior probability distribution of δ'.

Chapter 73: Bibliography

1. (p. 441) See our endnote 5 to **01**, p. 561 above, for a discussion of these Research Logs. A number of items listed in **73B** and **73E** are in TNA HW 25/34. Items mentioned in **73B** include: *Elementary Screed on ΔD counts and Colossus runs*: 10 pages + 2-page appendix dated 24/7/44; *Sigmas and Decibans*: 15 pages; *Checks and Tests*: 3 pages; *Wheel Slides and Message Slides*: 7

pages. Items mentioned in **73E** include the *'Good Certain' Chart*, the *Centiban Table*, the *Ratio of EB/σ...*, and the *Wheel Sliding Table.* A copy of the *Elementary Screed on ΔD counts and Colossus runs* is an annex to 'Fried Report F-71', of 3 August 1944, sent by Capt. Walter J. Fried to Arlington Hall. NARA HCC 1009:3179.

2. (p. 441) The 'black file' is referred to several times in chapter **24**. Almost certainly identical with the 'Black Book' mentioned by Vergine in the passage quoted in endnote 5 to **01**, p. 561 above, it seems to have been a separate collection of research ideas.

3. (p. 441) Copies of all three of these essays, which apparently are the three chapters of *Wheel-breaking by Rectangles*, are included as 'Annex A' to 'Fried Report F-91', of 12 September 1944, sent by Capt. Walter J. Fried to Arlington Hall. A copy of this report is in NARA HCC 1009:3179; another copy in Box 880, Item 2612, Folder 2612B. Part I, the *Theory of Rectangles*, is 9 pages long. Part II, *The practice of rectangle-making*, is 15 pages long. Part III, *What to do when a significant rectangle is obtained*, is 12 pages long. These essays must have been written before 3 August 1944, as they are mentioned in Fried Report F-71 of that date.

Chapter 74: Chronology

1. (p. 444) The *History of the Fish Section*, TNA HW 50/63, is an analogous chronology for the Testery. Its Annex II, 'Links Broken', gives a month-by-month tabulation of all Tunny keys broken.

2. (p. 449) A letter of 29 March 1944 from Nigel de Grey to W. G. Radley of Dollis Hill addresses the anticipated need for more decoding machines for the Testery: 'When the machine which is due to arrive [in the Newmanry] to-day has been erected and the one which it replaces has been re-errected in Tester's Section he [Tester] will have five machines in all.' Colossus 2 is expected on 1 June, Colossus 3 on 1 July, and Colossus 4 in August. The output of Colossus 1 and the double bedstead Robinson meant the Testery needed another decoding machine by 1 May, and with each new Colossus thereafter, two new decoding machines to handle the added output. (TNA HW 62/6; copy of letter courtesy R. Erskine.)

Almost the same anticipated Colossus delivery schedule had been stated in a 19 March 1944 cable from Newman to Welchman (then on a liaison trip to Arlington Hall): four Robinsons had been completed, Colossus 1 was almost finished (the χ wheels worked but the μ and ψ wheels did not yet), three more Robinsons were expected in the next six weeks, Colossus 2 was expected 1 June and Colossus 3 a month later. (TNA HW 57/1)

3. (p. 450) Golssen is a small town in Brandenburg, about 50 km south of Berlin.

4. (p. 450) The entry for 'Invasion of Europe' under July 1944 is odd. The invasion itself occurred on 6 June 1944, but the ensuing Battle of Normandy lasted two months.

It is possible that the practice of daily wheel changes in August 1944 was introduced as an indirect consequence of the 20 July 1944 bomb attempt against Hitler's life. One of the executed conspirators, General Erich Fellgiebel (1886–1944), had been the head of the German Army's signal corps and thus in charge of running the Tunny network. In consequence, the loyalty of the signal corps, and in particular of the Tunny operators, must have been suspect, and Fellgiebel's successor (Albert Praun (1894–1975), commander of the signal corps from 11 August 1944 to the end of the war) must have been eager to demonstrate his zeal by tightening cipher security practices. Echoes of this can be seen in Glünder and Whitaker, 'Wireless and "Geheimschreiber" Operator in the War, 1941–1945' (see endnote 2 to Chapter **61**, above).

Chapter 81: Conclusions

1. (p. 453) PAX = Private Automatic Exchange; PAX telephones = telephones connected only by an internal network.

2. (p. 454) 'Principle of inverse probability' = Bayes' theorem. In effect, the *Report* says here, the 'theory of probability' (that is, Bayesian statistics) is better for Tunny cryptanalysis than 'statistics' (that is, non-Bayesian statistics).

3. (p. 455) 'Rubbers' = erasers, usually for pencil.

4. (p. 455) See endnote 1 to chapter **15A(b)**, p. 575 above.

Chapter 91: The 5202 machine

1. (p. 459) We have been unable to locate this *Reference Manual for 5202 Equipment.* It is not identical with a 61-page document titled *5202* (NARA HCC 942:2748), dated 20 August 1945. This, an end-of-war project summary document, which is roughly an American equivalent of **91**, also cites the *Reference Manual for 5202 Equipment.* The American project summary's conclusion (on p. 61), that the 'effectiveness of the 5202 in its attack on the German cipher teletypewriter is as great as that of the Colossus', is difficult to reconcile with that given at the end of chapter **91** without considering the respective authors' motives. Here we have the final report by the American managers of a project to develop a piece of complicated and expensive machinery which in the end saw little or no practical application. One would expect such a report to stress the potential capabilities of the equipment, or of the technology embodied in the equipment, and not to mention disparaging operational practicalities of the sort found in **91C(ii)**. In contrast, the British author of **91** was most interested in how the 5202 equipment would have fit into the routine of Tunny-breaking as evolved at GCCS and, possibly to some extent, in finding something complimentary to say about their junior partners' efforts.

2. (p. 466) The use of the pronoun 'I' is unusual in the *Report*: the only other occurrence is in **28**: see endnote 9 to **28**, p. 595 above. The author of chapter **91** was D. Rees reporting work done by himself and S. Wylie. In a personal communication to JAR, 27 Feb. 2008, Wylie stated that he now believed his and Rees' 1945 examination of the 5202 machine had been perfunctory and did not explore its full potential.

Chapter 92: Recovery of motor patterns from de-chi

1. (p. 471) This chapter makes extensive use of the terms 'slide' and 'slide of columns' to refer to features in the motor rectangle. This is a special case of sense (4) for 'slide' given in our

Supplementary Glossary, p. 544, above.

Chapter 93: Thrasher

1. (p. 482) '*Rolle*' = roll, spool.

Chapter 94: Research into the QEP system

1. (p. 486) *Heeresgruppe Nord* = Army Group North; *Blatt* = sheet.

Bibliography

Archival Sources

Kew, Surrey
The National Archives of the UK (TNA)

The National Archives of the United Kingdom (TNA), (formerly the Public Record Office (PRO)), Kew, Surrey. All the documents we use are in the 'HW' collection of records created or inherited by the Government Communications Headquarters.

We use notations like TNA HW 14/36 to refer to documents in this collection.

HW 3/81. Metropolitan Police Sigint unit at Denmark Hill: correspondence 1926-1932 from head of police Sigint . . . (Includes 10-page typed 'A Brief History of Events Relating to the Growth of the 'Y' Service', by H. C. Kenworthy.) (Cited on pp. xxx, xl, xlvi, xlvii, 552.)

HW 3/92. History of UK Military Sigint, bound volume: includes relations and contacts with GCCS. (Not seen. Copy of excerpt courtesy R. Erskine.) (Cited on pp. 529, 572, 614.)

HW 3/163. History of interception of German teleprinter communications (FISH) by Foreign Office station, Knockholt, by HC Kenworthy, GCCS. (Twenty three-page typed report, with title 'The Interception of German Teleprinter Communications by Foreign Office Station, Knockholt', March 1946. Another copy: TNA HW 50/79.) (Cited on pp. xl, xlvi, xlvii, lxii, 512, 526, 625.)

HW 14. GCCS: Directorate: Second World War Policy Papers. This is a series of chronological files of in- and out-going correspondence and technical memoranda passing through the office of the head of GCCS, spread across many files, throughout the course of the war. Individual files we use are as follows; the descriptions are of particular items in them that we cite.

HW 14/14. Two-page typed minutes of 1 April 1941 meeting of Research Section Directing Sub-Committee, dated 11 April 1941. (Cited on p. 554.)

HW 14/16. Three-page typed minutes of 23 June 1941 meeting of Research Section Directing Sub-Committee, dated 8 July 1941. (Cited on pp. 563, 603.)

HW 14/36. One-page typed memorandum, by Travis, 10 May 1942. (Cited on p. 604.)

HW 14/38. One-page telephone directory of senior GCCS staff, late May 1942. (Cited on p. 570.)

HW 14/40. One-page letter from Travis to Chief, Secret Intelligence Service, 15 June 1942. Two-page hectographed minute of meeting about German non-Morse transmissions, 16 June 1942. (Cited on pp. 574, 595.)

HW 14/62. Two-page typed message from Travis to Tiltman, 28 Dec. 1942. (Cited on p. 576.)

HW 14/64. Two-page typed minute from Kenworthy to Sayer, 11 Jan. 1943. (Cited on p. 595.)

HW 14/66. One-page typed 'D.D. (S) Serial Order No. 80' by Travis of 1 Feb. 1943. (Cited on p. 537.)

HW 14/70. Two-page handwritten minute from Newman to Travis, 12 Mar. 1943. (Cited on p. 537.)

HW 14/87. One-page typed 'D.D. (S) Serial Order No. 117' by Travis of 10 Sept. 1943. (Cited on p. 537.)

HW 14/92. Eight-page typed 'Fish Traffic' report, by Lt. Col. Pritchard 24 Nov. 1943; two-page typed letter from Newman to Travis, 29 Nov. 1943.) (Cited on pp. xxxvi, 570, 608.)

HW 25/3. Mathematical theory of ENIGMA machine by A.M. Turing. (Cited on p. xxix.)

HW 25/4, 25/5. General Report on Tunny, With Emphasis on Statistical Methods, 1945. (Record Opening Date: 28 Sept 2000.) (HW 25/4 cited on pp. xiv, xxi, xxxiii–xxxv, xl, xlviii–li, liv–lviii, lxiii, lxv, lxix, lxx, lxxv, lxxx, lxxxii, lxxxiii, lxxxv–xciii, xcv–xcvii, 1–21, 257, 495, 497, 526, 538–540, 561–599, 601, 602, 604–606, 619–621. HW 25/5 cited on pp. xii, xiv, xxi, xxxi–xxxiii, xxxv, xxxvii, xl, xliii, xlv, xlvi, xlix, l, lii, liv, lvi, lvii, lix–lxviii, lxxxvii, 258, 362, 494, 503, 533, 537, 540, 566, 570–577, 580, 582, 583, 586–595, 599–623.)

HW 25/24. A Technical Description of Colossus I, by D. C. Horwood, 1971. (Cited on pp. xxii, xli, xlii, lxiv, 548.)

HW 25/26. Miscellaneous photographs of ENIGMA, TUNNY and COLOSSUS. (Cited on pp. 362, 372, 374, 375, 540.)

HW 25/28. Solution of German Teleprinter Cyphers (Testery) Linguistic Methods. (Not seen. Listed in the catalogue as being 'retained by Department', that is, not available for public inspection.) (Cited on pp. xl, 561, 600.)

HW 25/33. Chief Cryptographer [Brigadier Tiltman]. Miscellaneous cryptological papers. (Includes many records of the Cryptographic Co-ordination and Records Section, GCCS, including a copy of the Cryptographic Dictionary.) (Cited on pp. 566, 594, 596, 619, 629, 634.)

HW 25/34. Colossus Working Aids, 1945. (Cited on p. 620.)

HW 25/37. Report on the applications of probability to cryptography by A M Turing. (Cited on pp. xxxiv, xxxv, xliii, lix, lxxx.)

HW 25/38. Paper on statistics of repetitions by A M Turing. (Cited on pp. xxxiv, xliii.)

HW 43/63. GC&CS Sixta History. (Not seen. Listed in the catalogue as being 'retained by Department'.) (Cited on pp. xl, 562.)

HW 43/82–93. GC&CS Sixta History. (Not seen. Listed in the catalogue as being 'retained by Department'.) (Cited on p. xl.)

HW 50/63. *History of the Fish Section.* (Cited on pp. xxxii, xl, xliii–xlv, xlvii, xlviii, liv, lvi, lvii, 524, 600, 605, 609, 611, 613–615, 621.)

HW 50/79. The interception of German Teleprinter Communications at Foreign Office Station Knockholt. A description by Kenworthy, who was GC&CS's main technical officer for interception of new radio transmissions, dealing with the interception of German encyphered teleprinter transmissions (covername FISH)... (Duplicate of TNA HW 3/163. Copy courtesy R. Erskine.) (Cited on pp. xxxi, xl, xlvi, xlvii, li, lxii, lxviii, 500, 512, 526, 600, 624.)

HW 55/1. Foreign Office Intercept (Y) Station Knockholt, Kent: Equipment, Works and Buildings. (Cited on p. lxii.)

HW 57/1. Exchange of European cryptographic information between Bletchley Park and the Signal Security Agency (SSA), Washington. (In- and out- file of GCCS correspondence with SSA, with British liaison officers attached to SSA, and with GCCS visitors to SSA.) (Cited on pp. 533, 587, 588, 605, 608, 621.)

HW 62/5. GC&CS miscellaneous papers: Equipment — Machinery, Volume II 1943. (In- and out- file of correspondence between GCCS and various equipment suppliers.) (Cited on pp. xxvii, xxxvi.)

HW 62/6. GC&CS miscellaneous papers: Equipment — Machinery, Volume III 1944–1945. (In- and out- file of correspondence between GCCS and various equipment suppliers.) (Cited on pp. lxviii, 532, 605, 608, 621.)

HW 64/59. Correspondence concerning various machines and equipment including the transfer of Colossi from Bletchley Park to Manchester University. (Cited on p. xxxvi.)

Cambridge
Library of St John's College

Library of St John's College, Cambridge. M. H. A. Newman papers. Digitally scanned versions available at David P. Anderson, 'Newman Digital Archive', URL: `http://www.cdpa.co.uk/Newman` (visited on 07/06/2014).

3/1/7. Autograph letter from F. L. Lucas to M. H. A. Newman, 27 July 1942. (Cited on p. xxxvii.)

3/1/15. Typed letter from A. R. Binshaw to M. H. A. Newman, 19 Aug. 1942. (Cited on p. xxxiii.)

3/2/3. 'Exp. values, Set totals, & necessary lengths'. Twelve-page manuscript paper, with annotations possibly by I. J. Good. (Cited on p. 572.)

3/2/4. '$\Delta\chi$-method'. Eleven-page manuscript paper. (Cited on p. 572.)

College Park, Maryland
United States National Archives and Records Administration

U. S. National Archives and Records Administration II (NARA), College Park, Maryland. All the documents we use are in Record Group 457 (RG 457), 'Records of the National Security Agency/Central Security Service'. (Summary description at United States National Archives and Records Administration, 'Records of the National Security Agency/Central Security Service', URL: `http://www.archives.gov/research/guide-fed-records/groups/457.html` (visited on 07/06/2014).) Most of the documents we use are in the 'Historic Cryptographic Collection — Pre-World War I through World War II', which form Entry 9032 under RG 457, and a few are in the 'Archival and Historian's Source Files, 1952? – ca. 2007', which form Entry P 11 under RG 457.

These documents were not necessarily created by NSA or its predecssor organisations, but rather were once in its possession. A version of the NARA finding aid for the Historic Cryptographic Collection has been reprinted as *NSA Cryptologic Documents*, A Cryptographic Series 83 (Laguna Hills, Calif.: Aegean Park Press, n.d. [*c.*2000]). An online version of this finding aid is

Historic Naval Ships Association, 'National Security Agency Historic Cryptographic Collection', URL: `http://www.hnsa.org/doc/nara/nsaopendoor.htm` (visited on 07/06/2014).

Each item below lists first, the entry name, box and item number within RG 457, then in brackets the item's National Archives Identifier number, then the description of the item contents as found in the NARA finding aid, then in parentheses, our own additional description of the item contents, and then (if needed) a more precise specification of the particular sub-items in the item that we cite. (Individual items in RG 457, Entry 9032 often contain several documents; there are typically no box, item, or folder-contents lists. Most items occupy a single folder, but some consist of several folders or even boxes of folders.)

We use notations like NARA HCC 15:139 to refer to RG 457, Entry 9032, Box 15, Item 139. For items not in RG 457, Entry 9032 we use a longer form, such as 'NARA RG 457, Entry P 11, Box 45, Item number 6558'.

Entry 9032, Box 15, Item 139 [NAI 2806251]. German Communications Officer's Guide to Telephone and Teletype Technique. (German Army *Dienstvorschrift 794/1: Merkblatt Fernsprech- und Fernschreibtechnik für den Nachrichtenoffizier*, 1 April 1942. Printed; vi+144 pages.) (Cited on pp. 497, 499, 565.)

Entry 9032, Box 15, Item 140 [NAI 2806252].. Description of specifications for the perforated tape machine LS36. (Lorenz company pamphlet, *Beschreibung und Einstellvorschrift des Lochenstreifensenders LS 36*. (Literally, 'Description, and installation instructions for the perforated tape transmitter LS 36'.)) (Cited on p. 499.)

Entry 9032, Box 17, Item 154 [NAI 6266736]. German instructions and diagrams for teletypewriter Lo 15. (Instructional pamphlet of 17 schematic drawings. *Arbeitsunterlagen für den nachrichtentechnischen Unterricht. Fachgebiet CS XI: Fernschreibgerätelehre. Der Blattfernschreiber Lo 15*.) (Cited on p. 563.)

Entry 9032, Box 21, Item 185 [NAI 2806298]. Teletype callsigns used by German Army. (Photostat of *Fernschreibstellen des OKW*, Berlin, 1 July 1942.) (Cited on p. 616.)

Entry 9032, Box 70, Item 311 [NAI 2806436]. Teletype operating manual. (German Armed Forces service regulations for teleprinter operation: *Fernschreibbetriebs-Vorschrift, M. Dv. Nr. 924, L. Dv. 704/3a*, of 1 March 1944. Printed, 129 pages.) (Cited on pp. 596, 616.)

Entry 9032, Box 185, Item 862 [NAI 2807004]. Theory and Analysis of a Letter Subtractor Machine. (Mimeographed pamphlet, 20 pp. plus 4 pages errata. GCCS didactic exposition of techniques of solution of C-38 machine cipher, by G. W. Morgan. Main part undated but the last page of the errata bears the date 11/41. Probably written after April 1941; certainly not before June 1940.) (Cited on pp. 563, 603.)

Entry 9032, Box 607, Item 1596 [NAI 2808037]. Report of British Attack on Fish. (U.S. Navy Communications Intelligence Technical Paper TS 47, May 1945, 'Report on British Attack on "Fish" ', 94 pp. Another copy in Box 579, Item 1407. Almost certainly written by Lt. Cdr. Howard Campaigne.) (Cited on p. 606.)

Entry 9032, Box 699, Item 1704 [NAI 2808216]. Fish Notes. (Carbon copy of liaison report G-5, A. W. Small to SSA, 12 Dec. 1944.) Two pages, plus 4 pages of enclosures, including 'Dragon Report No. 7' for the week beginning 1 Dec. 1944, by Capt. A. McIntosh.) (Cited on p. 585.)

Entry 9032, Box 808, Item 2336 [NAI 2808867]. British Communications Intelligence. Typed list of U.S. Navy Liaison Officers at GCCS, with date ranges. Not seen; copy of one page courtesy R. Erskine. (Cited on p. 525.)

Entry 9032, Box 880, Item 2612 [NAI 2809159]. Capt. Walter J. Fried Reports/SSA Liaison with GCCS. (Another copy of the Fried report file. Duplicates many items also in Box 950, Item 2821; has unique copy of report F-114.) Carbon copy of liaison report F-114 from A. W. Small to SSA, 13 Nov. 1944, 2 pages, with enclosure of 'Dragon Report 3' for the week beginning 3 Nov. 1944, signed by Angus McIntosh, one-page carbon copy. (Cited on p. 621.)

Entry 9032, Box 942, Item 2748 [NAI 2809332]. 5202. ([4]+64+[5] page dittographed SSA project report *The 5202*, 20 August 1945, plus 3 wiring diagrams.) (Cited on pp. 533, 622.)

Entry 9032, Box 950, Item 2811 [NAI 2809396]. Statistical Method for Analyzing Certain Types of Flags applicable to Tunny and Hagelin Systems. (SSA Technical paper, March 1944.) (Cited on p. 591.)

Entry 9032, Box 950, Item 2816 [NAI 2809401]. Cipher Teleprinter Regulations for the Wehrmacht after 1 December 1942. (Carbon paper 41-page typescript of 20 Nov. 1944 U.S. Army translation of *Schlüsselfernschreibvorschrift (SFV), Gültig für die Wehrmacht v. 1. 12. 42.*) (Cited on pp. 571, 596.)

Entry 9032, Box 950, Item 2821 [NAI 2809406]. Fish Notes: Capt. Walter J. Fried. (File carbon copies of selected letters and enclosures from W. J. Fried to SSA, 1944, numbered F-101 of 14 Oct. 1944 through F-123 of 29 Nov. 1944; lacking F-114 of 13 Nov. 1944, which was by A. W. Small and is in Box 880, Item 2612.) F-101 of 14 Oct. 1944, 4 pages. F-105 of 25 Oct. 1944, 2 pages, with copy of report *Non-Morse operating procedure* and cover page, from Ensign Milton Gaschk, USN, to Op-20-G, 16 Oct. 1944, 9 pages. F-108 of 1 Nov. 1944, 1 page. F-111 of 7 Nov. 1944, 1 page, with 'Dragon Report No. 1', for the week beginning 20 Oct. 1944 (1 page) and 'Dragon Report No. 2', for the week beginning 27 Oct. 1944 (2 pages). F-118 of 21 Nov. 1944, 3 pages, with 'Dragon Report No. 4', for the week beginning 10 Nov. 1944, by A. McIntosh, 2 pages, and a copy of Sixta document *Log procedures relating to the use of 'limitation' on non-Morse army links*, 19 Nov. 1944, marked 'ULTRA/ZIP/NMS.14'. F-122 of 29 Nov. 1944, 1 page, with 'Dragon Report No. 5' for the week beginning 17 Nov. 1944 and a copy of a Sixta document 'Non-Morse army Q code', 28 Nov. 1944, marked 'ULTRA/ZIP/NMS 15'. (Cited on pp. 505, 598, 609, 613.)

Entry 9032, Box 970, Item 2941 [NAI 2809529]. Technical History of the 6813th Signal Security Detachment. 20 October 1945, (by Captain James K. Lively et al. [5]+26 typescript pages. Transcription available on the web: 'American 6813 Division History October 1945', [sic], URL: `http://www.codesandciphers.org.uk/documents/a6813his/us6813.pdf` (visited on 07/06/2014).) (Cited on pp. xxi, 553, 562, 633.)

Entry 9032, Box 973, Item 2969 [NAI 2809557]. S.I. Course, Vol–1 Explanatory text and short exercises; Vol II–Figures and cipher texts, 1942. (GCCS document. 'Revised and enlarged, June 1942.' There is also a photostat copy in NARA HCC 833:2446. Reprinted as Government Code and Cypher School, *A Course in Cryptanalysis: S.I. Course, Revised and Enlarged, June, 1942*, 2 vols., A Cryptographic Series 33–34 (Laguna Hills, Calif.: Aegean Park Press, n.d. [*c.*1983]).) (Cited on p. 594.)

Entry 9032, Box 998, Item 3043 [NAI 2809640]. Crib Tester for Geheimschreiber. (File of miscellaneous ASA documents about Dragon, including an undated 4-page marked-up typescript draft project narrative *Crib tester for Geheimschreiber (Dragon) — F Branch Project 1026*, negative photostats of two pages of routing and work sheets, 3–8 Dec. 1943, negative photostats of a one-page memorandum for file, dated 11 Dec. 1943, two pages of a mimeographed questionnaire filled in by hand, undated but evidently written after 15 Sept. 1945, two copies each of four glossy photographic prints of Dragon, and wiring diagrams.) (Cited on pp. 608, 610.)

Entry 9032, Box 1009, Item 3179 [NAI 2809776]. Fish Notes. (Collection of liaison reports from Capt. W. J. Fried and A. W. Small to SSA, 1944, and enclosures.) Fried reports: F-43 of 27 May 1944, F-71 of 3 Aug. 1944, F-91 of 12 Sep. 1944. Small reports: G-11, 20 Dec. 1944, 2 pages, with 1-page carbon copy 'Dragon Report No. 8' for the week of 8 Dec. 1944, signed by A. McIntosh. Report G-14, 27 Dec. 1944, 1 page, with 1-page carbon copy 'Dragon Report No. 9' for the week beginning 15 Dec. 1944, signed by A. McIntosh. Report G-18, 2 Jan. 1945, 1 page, with 1-page carbon copy 'Dragon Report No. 10' for the week beginning 22 Dec. 1944. Report G-25, 17 Jan. 1945, 1 page, with 1-page carbon copy 'Report on Dragon I — Work preformed 9th October, 1944 to 6th January, 1945', and GCCS mimeographed document 'Setting on Colossus — Elementary Openings', 14 Dec. 1944, 6 pages. (Cited on pp. 504, 608, 620, 621.)

Entry 9032, Box 1033, Item 3315 [NAI 2809914]. Ram File, 1944. (Not seen. Includes liaison reports by John N. Seaman. Copy of one-page 3 November 1943 report by Seaman to Arlington Hall supplied by R. Erskine.) (Cited on pp. 551, 555.)

Entry 9032, Box 1114, Item 3568 [NAI 2810185]. B-III Weekly Reports, January 1943 – October 1943, General Cryptanalytic Section. (Weekly Report, B-III, 9 July 1943, 4 pages, and Organization Chart — B-III, 1 Oct. 1943, 1 page. Copy courtesy Frode Weierud.) (Cited on p. 533.)

Entry 9032, Box 1126, Item 3620 [NAI 2810239]. E Operations of the GC & CS at Bletchley Park. (Collection of papers about Enigma work at GCCS.) One-page typed inventory 'Cryptographic machinery', 28 February 1945. Copy courtesy Ralph Erskine.) (Cited on p. 605.)

Entry 9032, Box 1338, Item 4030 [NAI 2810790]. Notes on the German Army teleprinter network. (Combined Services Detailed Interrogation Centre interrogation report of a POW, 28 Feb. 1944: C.S.D.I.C. (UK) S.I.R. 1503; mimeographed, 3 pp.) (Cited on p. 618.)

Entry 9032, Box 1382, Item 4373 [NAI 2811133]. German teleprinter callsigns as a source of intelligence. (GCCS serial number CX/MSS/S.73, 30 Aug. 1944. Mimeographed, 10 pp.) (Cited on p. 616.)

Entry 9032, Boxes 1405–1409, Item 4541 [NAI 2811302–06]. Codes and ciphers: Germany: German cryptanalytic documents. (Prints — many illegible — of microfilms of documents of the German Army's signal security agency, OKH/Ins 7/IV, captured at the end of the war. Five boxes, 18 folders. NARA HCC 1430:4737 is in effect a finding aid for these documents, listing them in sequence by title and date.) Box 1408, folder 13 contains studies of *Eigene SFM* ('our own cipher teleprinters'). (Cited on pp. 563, 567–569.)

Entry 9032, Box 1413, Item 4559 [NAI 2811324]. Cryptographic Dictionary — Cryptographic Co-ordination and Records Section, G.C. & C.S. 20 July 1944. (Foolscap mimeograph, [3]+95 pages. A distribution list names 36 copies: 17 to GCCS, 2 to the U.S. Army, and 17 to the U.S. Navy. Another copy in TNA HW 25/33. Transcription available on the web: 'Cryptographic Dictionary', URL: `http://www.codesandciphers.org.uk/documents/cryptdict` (visited on 07/06/2014).) (Cited on pp. 566, 594, 596, 619.)

Entry 9032, Box 1417, Item 4628 [NAI 2811393]. Special Fish Report. Albert W. Small. 1 December 1944. (112-page survey of Tunny breaking techniques. Transcription available on the web:Albert W. Small, 'Special Fish Report', URL: `http://www.codesandciphers.org.uk/documents/small/smallix.htm` (visited on 07/06/2014).) (Cited on pp. xxi, 642.)

Entry 9032, Box 1424, Item 4682 [NAI 2811446]. Knockholt Intercept Station. (Liaison report G-12, 23 Dec. 1944, from Albert W. Small to Maj. J. Seaman, SSA. Two-page typescript, plus

3-page typescript carbon copy enclosure *Brief notes for instructors who are required to teach the reading of teleprinter signals from undulator tape.*) (Cited on p. 511.)

Entry 9032, Box 1430, Item 4737 [NAI 2811501]. German Army high command (OKH) documents. (In fact a list of titles and dates of a collection of documents of the German Army's signal security agency, "OKH In 7/IV", seized at the end of the war, arranged by topic; 16 pages, dittographed. Headed: 'PART II / IF 272-TAB "D" / Arranged by Sections, and within Sections as transmitted to Army Security Agency, Europe from Military Intelligence Service, Austria.' Since the ASA came into being on 15 Sept. 1945, this document was written after that date. The listed documents were microfilmed, presumably at the same time Item 4737 was compiled, in the same order as listed in Item 4737, which thus serves as a finding aid for them.) (Cited on pp. 567, 629.)

Entry P 11, Box 45, Item 6858 [NAI 7420402]. PAJ Jellyfish Demonstration TICOM/M-5. (Two-page typewritten report, with title 'Demonstration of Kesselring "Fish Train" ', 8 July 1945. Online copy at `http://www.ticomarchive.com/iv-case-studies/geheimschreiber-t-52`, visited on 15/04/2014.) (Copy courtesy of Randy Rezabek.) (Cited on p. 501.)

Entry P 11, Box 46, Item 6897 [NAI 7420418]. PAJ Report Written by Vierling. (Fifteen-page typewritten report, TICOM I-43, 20 July 1945. Online copy at `https://docs.google.com/file/d/0B7sNVKDp-yiJZG1ZQmZ4Q1NIMXc/edit` visited on 15/04/2014.) (Copy courtesy of Randy Rezabek.) (Cited on p. 528.)

Entry P 11, Box 114, Item 10248 [NAI 7421059]. Final Report of TICOM Team I. ([2]+47-page typewritten report, dated 16 June 1945. Evidently identical with 'TICOM IF-15, 'Final Report of TICOM Team 1 on the exploitation of Kautbeuren and the Berchtesgaden area" mentioned in NSA European Axis SIGINT, vol III, p. 118. Online copy at `http://www.ticomarchive.com/the-teams/team-1`, visited on 15/04/2014.) (Copy courtesy of Randy Rezabek.) (Cited on p. 501.)

Fort Meade, Maryland
National Security Agency

United States National Security Agency (NSA). We use a number of electronic forms of partially redacted documents released by NSA under the Freedom of Information Act (FOIA). Each of these redacted documents bears a 'DOCID' serial number, presumably assigned at the time of the document's release. These documents were not necessarily created by NSA or its predecssor organisations, but rather are in its possession. Copies of many of these documents are held by the National Cryptologic Museum at Ft. Meade. Copies of some of them appear on the internet. We do not know what, if any, shelf mark symbols NSA uses for its archives, so we have supplied symbols of our own.

NSA European Axis SIGINT. United States Army Security Agency, *European Axis Signal Intelligence in World War II as Revealed by 'TICOM' Investigations and by other Prisoner of War Interrogations and Captured Material, Principally German*, FOIA release of 9-volume typescript report (Washington, D.C., 1946), URL: `http://www.nsa.gov/public_info/declass/european_axis_sigint.shtml` (visited on 07/06/2014). The nine volumes of this report bear DOCIDs 3560861, 3560816, 3560827, 3486746, 3560829, 3486663, 3486670, 3560798, and 3633965, respectively. (Copy courtesy René Stein.) (Cited on pp. xxii, lxxxvi, 567, 568.)

NSA Magic. Colin Burke, *It Wasn't All Magic: The Early Struggle to Automate Cryptanalysis, 1930s – 1960s* (Ft. Meade, Maryland: National Security Agency, 2002), URL: `http://www.nsa.`

gov/public_info/_files/cryptologic_histories/magic.pdf (visited on 07/06/2014), FOIA release of Center for Cryptologic History study CCH-E05-02-01, NSA DOCID: 4057009 (Cited on p. 530.)

NSA Mowry. David P. Mowry, *The Cryptology of the German Intelligence Services* (Ft. Meade, Maryland: National Security Agency, 1989), URL: http://www.nsa.gov/public_info/_files/cryptologic_histories/cryptology_of_gis.pdf (visited on 07/06/2014), Release of NSA Office of Archives and History, United States Cryptologic History, Series IV, Volume 4, NSA DOCID: 3525898 (Cited on p. 574.)

NSA Small G-34. Albert W. Small, 'Small Report G-34', 10 Feb. 1945, FOIA release of liaison report, NSA DOCID: 3524356 [Two-page typescript liaison report from Albert W. Small at GCCS to SSA. Lightly redacted. Missing Annexes A (13 pages, 1 diagram), B (2 pages), C (5 photographs), D (envelope).] (Copy courtesy Ralph Erskine.) (Cited on p. 609.)

NSA Small G-44. Albert W. Small, 'Small Report G-44', 8 Mar. 1945, FOIA release of liaison report, NSA DOCID: 3524259. [Two-page typescript liaison report from Albert W. Small at GCCS to SSA. Lightly redacted. Missing Annexes A (17 pages) and B (16 pages). Includes one-page 'Dragon Report 19: week beginning Friday 23rd February 1945', signed by Angus McIntosh, as Annex C.] (Copy courtesy Ralph Erskine.) (Cited on p. 609.)

NSA Small G-47. Albert W. Small, 'Small Report G-47', 17 Mar. 1945, FOIA release of liaison report, NSA DOCID: 3524231. [Second digit of day of month obscured. One-page typescript liaison report from Albert W. Small at GCCS to SSA. Unredacted. Includes one-page 'Dragon Report 20: week beginning Friday 2d March 1945', signed by Angus McIntosh, as Annex A. Missing Annexes B (20 pages) and C (a bundle of notes and wiring diagrams).] (Copy courtesy Ralph Erskine.) (Cited on p. 609.)

NSA Small G-52. William P. Bundy, 'Small Report G-52', 21 Mar. 1945, FOIA release of liaison report, NSA DOCID: 3524214. [One-page typescript liaison report signed by Bundy for A.W. Small, at GCCS to SSA. Unredacted. Missing Annexes A (20 pages) and B (a folder, a chart, and clipped papers). Includes one-page 'Dragon Report 21: week beginning Friday 9th March 1945', signed by Angus McIntosh, as Annex C.] (Copy courtesy Ralph Erskine.) (Cited on p. 609.)

NSA Small G-57. William P. Bundy, 'Small Report G-57', 2 Apr. 1945, FOIA release of liaison report, NSA DOCID: 3524187. [One-page typescript liaison report signed by Bundy for A.W. Small, at GCCS to SSA. Moderately redacted. Missing Annexes A (26 pages) and B (22 pages). Includes one-page 'Dragon Report 22: week beginning Friday 16th March 1945', signed by Angus McIntosh, as Annex C.] (Copy courtesy Ralph Erskine.) (Cited on p. 609.)

NSA Small G-61. William P. Bundy, 'Small Report G-61', 14 Apr. 1945, FOIA release of liaison report, NSA DOCID: 3524170. [One-page typescript liaison report signed by Bundy for A.W. Small, at GCCS to SSA. Unredacted. Missing Annexes A (26 pages) and B (a folder). Includes one-page 'Dragon Report 23: week beginning Friday, 23d March 1945', signed by Angus McIntosh, as Annex C.] (Copy courtesy Ralph Erskine.) (Cited on p. 609.)

NSA Small G-63. Albert W. Small, 'Small Report G-63', 21 Apr. 1945, FOIA release of liaison report, NSA DOCID: 3524135. [One-page typescript liaison report from Albert Small at GCCS to SSA. Moderately redacted. Missing Annexes A (24 pages) and B (32 pages). Includes one-page 'Dragon Report 24: week beginning Friday, 30th March 1945', and one-page 'Dragon Report 25: week beginning Friday 6 April 1945', both signed by Angus McIntosh as Annex C.] (Copy courtesy Ralph Erskine.) (Cited on p. 609.)

NSA Small G-66. Albert W. Small, 'Small Report G-66', 29 Apr. 1945, FOIA release of liaison report, NSA DOCID: 3524493. [Two-page typescript liaison report from Albert Small at GCCS to SSA. Unredacted. Missing Annexes A (28 pages) and C (10 pages). Includes one-page 'Dragon Report 26: week beginning Friday 13th April 1945', signed by Angus McIntosh, and one-page 'Dragon Report 27: week beginning Friday 20th April 1945', signed by D. E. Oswald as Annex B.] (Copy courtesy Ralph Erskine.) (Cited on pp. 532, 609.)

NSA TICOM I-45. Dr. Erich Hüttenhain and Sonderführer Dr. Walther Fricke, 'OKW/Chi Cryptanalytic Research on Enigma, Hagelin and Cypher Teleprinter Machines', 1 Aug. 1945, URL: `https://sites.google.com/site/ticomarchive/the-targets/okw-chi/related-reports` (visited on 07/06/2014), FOIA release of TICOM document I-45, NSA DOCID: 3422500 [19-page typescript plus 8 pages of diagrams, presumably translated from an essay written by Oberregierungsrat Hüttenhain and Sonderführer Fricke as part of their interrogation by the British and U.S. Target Intelligence Committee (TICOM) in its postwar investigation of Axis cryptographic activities.] (Copy courtesy Frode Weierud.) (Cited on pp. 563, 567.)

NSA TICOM I-57. 'Enciphering Devices worked on by Dr. LIEBKNECHT at Wa Pruef 7', 2 Aug. 1945, URL: `https://sites.google.com/site/ticomarchive/the-targets/okw-chi/related-reports` (visited on 07/06/2014), FOIA release of TICOM document I-57, NSA DOCID: 3541302 [15-page typescript TICOM interrogation report of Dr. Werner Liebknecht.] (Copy courtesy Frode Weierud.) (Cited on p. 568.)

Berlin, Germany
Politische Archiv des Auswärtigen Amts

Politisches Archiv des Auswärtigen Amts, Berlin. We use a number of documents held by the Political Archive of the German Foreign Office, in their collection of returned TICOM documents, the 'Bestand Rückgabe TICOM'. We use notations like PAAA T-1437 to refer to them.

PAAA T-687. *Der 1 kW Sender b (1 kW S.b)*, Berlin, 1942. [32-page printed pamphlet, with illustrations and circuit diagrams.] (Copy courtesy F. Weierud.) (Cited on p. 501.)

PAAA T-688. Untitled collection of equipment receipts. [TICOM's description, dated 26 July 1945: 2 booklets describing equipment of mobile teleprinter van, dated 1940. Receipts for teleprinter parts, 1945.] (Copy courtesy F. Weierud.) (Cited on p. 501.)

PAAA T-1437. *Schlüsselfernschreibvorschrift (SFV) vom 1.5.1945. Geheim.* TICOM Document T-1437, Box 75. [56 page printed pamphlet. 'H. Dv. g 422, M. Dv. Nr. 924a, L. Dv. 704/3b'.] (Copy courtesy F. Weierud.) (Cited on p. 571.)

PAAA T-3376. *Fernschreib-Grundschlüssel SZ 42 Nr. 1012 Prf.Nr. 1.* TICOM Document T3376, Box 166. [Collection of 31 daily wheel pattern sheets, stapled together with a cover sheet.] (Copy courtesy F. Weierud.) (Cited on p. 571.)

Printed Works

A History of Engineering and Science in the Bell System, [vol. 1:] The Early Years (1875–1925), ed. by M. D. Fagen (New York: Bell Telephone Laboratories, 1975).

A History of Engineering and Science in the Bell System, [vol. 7:] Transmission Technology (1925–1975), ed. by E. F. O'Neill (New York: AT&T Bell Telephone Laboratories, 1985).

Adams, J. F., 'Maxwell Herman Alexander Newman, 7 Febuary 1897 – 22 February 1984', *Biographical Memoirs of Fellows of the Royal Society*, 31 (Nov. 1985), pp. 436–452.

'American 6813 Division History October 1945', [sic], (transcript of NARA HCC 970:2941), URL: `http://www.codesandciphers.org.uk/documents/a6813his/us6813.pdf` (visited on 07/06/2014).

Anderson, David P., 'Newman Digital Archive', URL: `http://www.cdpa.co.uk/Newman` (visited on 07/06/2014).

—— 'The Contribution of M. H. A. Newman and his Mathematicians to the Creation of the Manchester "Baby"', *BSHM Bulletin: Journal of the British Society for the History of Mathematics*, 24 (2009), pp. 27–39.

—— 'Was the Manchester Baby Conceived at Bletchley Park?', British Computer Society: Electronic Workshops in Computing, Nov. 2007, URL: `http://www.bcs.org/upload/pdf/ewic_tur04_paper3.pdf` (visited on 07/06/2014).

'Archiv für technische Dokumente 1900–1945', URL: `http://www.superborg.de/d1050.htm` (visited on 07/06/2014).

Aspray, William, 'An Interview with Arnold Dumey', 9 Oct. 1989, URL: `http://conservancy.umn.edu/bitstream/11299/107760/1/oh088ad.pdf` (visited on 07/06/2014).

Banks, David L., 'A Conversation with I. J. Good', *Statistical Science*, 11 (1996), pp. 1–19.

Barrow-Green, June, ''A Corrective to the Spirit of Too Exclusively Pure Mathematics': Robert Smith (1689–1768) and his Prizes at Cambridge University', *Annals of Science*, 56 (1999), pp. 271–316.

Bauer, Arthur O., Ralph Erskine and Klaus Herold, *Funkpeilung als alliierte Waffe gegen deutsche U-Boote 1939–1945: Wie Schwächen und Versäumnisse bei der Funkführung der U-Boote zum Ausgang der 'Schlacht im Atlantik' beigetragen haben* (Rheinberg: Liebig Funk, 1997).

Bauer, Friedrich L., 'Erich Hüttenhain: Entzifferung 1939–1945', *Informatik Spektrum*, 31 (2008), pp. 249–261.

—— 'Origins of the Fish Cypher Machines', Appendix 12 in Copeland, B. Jack, ed., *Colossus: The Secrets of Bletchley Park's Codebreaking Computers* (Oxford: Oxford University Press, 2006), pp. 411–417.

Bayes, Thomas, 'An Essay Towards Solving a Problem in the Doctrine of Chances', *Philosophical Transactions of the Royal Society of London*, 53 (1763), pp. 370–418.

Beauchamp, K. G., *History of Telegraphy* (London: Institution of Electrical Engineers, 2001).

Bennett, Ralph, 'The Duty Officer, Hut 3' in Hinsley, F. H. and Alan Stripp, eds., *Codebreakers: The Inside Story of Bletchley Park* (Oxford: Oxford University Press, 1993), pp. 20–40.

Birch, Frank, *The official history of British Sigint, 1914-1945 / by Frank Birch*, ed. by John Jackson (Milton Keynes: Military Press, 2004).

Biswas, N., *Principles of Telegraphy* (London: Asia Publishing, 1964).

Boole, George, *A Treatise on the Calculus of Finite Differences*, 2nd ed. (London: MacMillan, 1872; reprinted New York: Chelsea, 1957).

Box, Joan Fisher, *R. A. Fisher: The Life of a Scientist* (New York: Wiley, 1978).

Briggs, Asa, *Secret Days: Code-Breaking in Bletchley Park* (London: Frontline Books, 2011).

Brooks, R. L., C. A. B. Smith, A. H. Stone and W. T. Tutte, 'The Dissection of Rectangles into Squares', *Duke Mathematical Journal*, 7 (1940), pp. 312–340.

Budiansky, Stephen, *Battle of Wits: The Complete Story of Codebreaking in World War II* (New York: Free Press, 2000).

Burke, Colin, *Information and Secrecy: Vannevar Bush, Ultra, and the Other Memex* (Metutchen, New Jersey: Scarecrow, 1994).

—— *It Wasn't All Magic: The Early Struggle to Automate Cryptanalysis, 1930s – 1960s* (Ft. Meade, Maryland: National Security Agency, 2002), URL: `http://www.nsa.gov/public_info/_files/cryptologic_histories/magic.pdf` (visited on 07/06/2014), FOIA release of Center for Cryptologic History study CCH-E05-02-01, NSA DOCID: 4057009.

Campbell, John, *Roy Jenkins: A Well-Rounded Life* (London: Jonathan Cape, 2014).

Carlton, Newcomb, 'Telegraph' in *Encyclopedia Britannica* (London, 1929).

Cayley, Arthur, 'On the Theory of the Analytical Forms Called Trees', *Philosophical Magazine*, 4th ser., 13 (1857), pp. 172–176.

Chadwick, John, 'A Biographical Fragment: 1942–3' in Smith, Michael and Ralph Erskine, eds., *Action This Day* (London: Bantam Press, 2001), pp. 110–26.

—— *The Decipherment of Linear B* (Cambridge: Cambridge University Press, 1958).

Chadwick, John and Michael Ventris, *Documents in Mycenaean Greek* (Cambridge: Cambridge University Press, 1956).

Collins, Thomas L., 'My Reminiscences of World War II', n.d. [*c.*2003], private typescript memoir, supplied by author, 2009.

Comte, Auguste, *Cours de philosophie positive*, 4th ed., 4 vols. (Paris: Baillère, 1877).

Cooley, J. W. and J. Tukey, 'An Algorithm for the Machine Calculation of Complex Fourier Series', *Mathematics of Computation*, 19 (1965), pp. 297–301.

Cooley, James W., 'How the FFT Gained Acceptance', *IEEE SP Magazine* (Jan. 1992), pp. 10–13.

Copeland, B. Jack, ed., *Colossus: The Secrets of Bletchley Park's Codebreaking Computers* (Oxford: Oxford University Press, 2006).

—— 'The German Tunny Machine' in Copeland, B. Jack, ed., *Colossus: The Secrets of Bletchley Park's Codebreaking Computers* (Oxford: Oxford University Press, 2006), pp. 36–51.

Copeland, B. Jack et al., 'Dollis Hill at War' in Copeland, B. Jack, ed., *Colossus: The Secrets of Bletchley Park's Codebreaking Computers* (Oxford: Oxford University Press, 2006), pp. 281–290.

Cormack, R. M., '[Obituary of Michael Robert Sampford]', *Biometrics*, 39.4 (1983), pp. 1109–1110.

Cragon, Harvey C., *From Fish to Colossus: How the German Lorenz Cipher Was Broken at Bletchley Park* (Dallas: Cragon, 2003).

Crawford, David J. and Phillip E. Fox, 'The Autoscritcher and the Superscritcher: Aids to Cryptanalysis of the German Enigma Cipher Machine, 1944–1946', *IEEE Annals of the History of Computing*, 14.3 (1992), pp. 9–22.

'Cryptographic Dictionary', transcription of item in TNA HW 25/33 and NARA HCC 1415:4559, URL: `http://www.codesandciphers.org.uk/documents/cryptdict` (visited on 07/06/2014).

David, F. N., Review of I. J. Good, *Probability and the Weighing of Evidence* (London, 1950), *Biometrika*, 38 (1951), p. 485.

Davies, D. W., 'New Information on the History of the Siemens and Halske T52 Cipher Machine', *Cryptologia*, 18.2 (1994), pp. 141–146.

—— 'The Early Models of the Siemens and Halske T52 Cipher Machine', *Cryptologia*, 7.3 (1983), pp. 235–253.

—— 'The Lorenz Cipher Machine SZ42', *Cryptologia*, 19.1 (1995), pp. 39–61.

Deming, W. E. and F. F. Stephan, 'On a Least Squares Adjustment of a Sampled Frequency Table when the Expected Marginal Totals Are Known', *Ann. Math. Statist.*, 11 (1940), pp. 427–444.

Dulac, Roger, *Industrial Cold Adhesives; A Practical Handbook for the Maker and User*, trans. by Joseph L. Rosenbaum (London: Griffin, 1937).

Edge, W. L., 'Geoffrey Timms, O.B.E., Ph.D., F.R.S.E.', Obituary, *Proceedings of the Edinburgh Mathematical Society*, 26 (1983), pp. 393–394.

Edwards, A. W. F., *Likelihood; An Account of the Statistical Concept of Likelihood and its Application to Scientific Inference*, rev. ed. Baltimore, 1992 (London: Cambridge University Press, 1972).

Erskine, Ralph, 'Kriegsmarine Short Signals Systems — and How Bletchley Park Exploited Them', *Cryptologia*, 23.1 (1999), pp. 65–92.

—— 'Tunny Reveals *B-Dienst* Successes Against the "Convoy Code"', *Intelligence and National Security*, 28.6 (2013), pp. 868–889, URL: `http:dx.doi.org/10.1080/02684527.2012.746414` (visited on 07/06/2014).

Erskine, Ralph and Michael Smith, eds., *Action This Day* (London: Bantam Press, 2001).

Farley, R. D., 'Oral History Interview OH-40-80 with Arthur J. Levenson', interview transcript, 25 Nov. 1980, URL: `http://www.nsa.gov/public_info/_files/oral_history_interviews/nsa_oh_40_08_levenson.pdf` (visited on 07/06/2014).

Farley, R. D. and H. F. Schorreck, 'Oral History Interview OH-17-82 with Dr. Solomon Kullback', interview transcript, 26 Aug. 1984, URL: `http://www.nsa.gov/public_info/_files/oral_history_interviews/nsa_oh_17_82_kullback.pdf` (visited on 07/06/2014).

Feller, William, *Introduction to Probability Theory and Its Applications* (New York: Wiley, 1950).

Ferris, John, 'The British Enigma: Britain, Signals Security and Cipher Machines, 1906–1953', Chapter 4 in *Intelligence and Strategy: Selected Essays* (London, 2005), pp. 138–180.

Field, J. V., 'Sigint and Automation', *IEEE Annals of the History of Computing*, 25.1 (Jan. 2003), pp. 65–66.

Fischer, Eric, 'The Evolution of Character Codes, 1874–1968', unpublished paper, 2001, URL: `http://www2.units.it/hirema/didattica/materiali/charset/ASCII/ascii.pdf` (visited on 07/06/2014).

Fisher, R. A., *Contributions to Mathematical Statistics* (New York: Chapman & Hall, 1950).

—— 'On the Mathematical Foundations of Theoretical Statistics', *Philos. Trans. Roy. Soc. London A*, 222 (1922), pp. 309–368.

—— 'On the "Probable Error" of a Coefficient of Correlation Deduced from a Small Sample', *Metron*, 1 (1921), pp. 3–32.

'Flight' Directory of British Aviation (Kingston upon Thames: Kelly's Directories, 1981).

Flowers, T. H., 'The Design of Colossus', *Annals of the History of Computing*, 5 (1983), pp. 239–252.

Freebody, J. W., *Telegraphy* (London: Pitman, 1958).

Friedman, W. F., *The Index of Coincidence and its Applications in Cryptography*, Riverbank Laboratories, 1922.

Fyske, Helge, 'Fu.H.E.c FunkHorcEmpfänger - c / Monitoring Receiver', URL: `http://www.laud.no/ww2/fuhec/index.htm` (visited on 07/06/2014).

Gaines, Helen Fouché, *Elementary Cryptanalysis — A Study of Ciphers and Their Solution* (Boston: American Photographic Publishing Company, 1939); reprinted as *Cryptanalysis* (New York: Dover, n.d. [*c.*1950]).

Gannon, Paul, *Colossus: Bletchley Park's Greatest Secret* (London: Atlantic Books, 2006).

Gillispie, C. C., *Pierre-Simon Laplace 1749-1827: A Life in Exact Science* (Princeton: Princeton University Press, 1997).

Girshick, M. A., Review of M. J. Moroney, *Facts from Figures* (Baltimore, 1951), *Journal of the American Statistical Association*, 58 (1953), pp. 645–647.

Givierge, M., *Cours de Cryptographie* (Paris: Berger-Levrault, 1925).

Glünder, Georg and Paul Whitaker, 'Wireless and "Geheimschreiber" Operator in the War, 1941–1945', *Cryptologia*, 26.2 (2002), pp. 81–96.

Good, I. J., 'Analogues of Poisson's Summation Formula', *Amer. Math. Monthly*, 69 (1962), pp. 259–266.

—— *Early Work on Computers at Bletchley*, 82, National Physical Laboratory Report Com. Sci., Sept. 1976.

—— 'Early Work on Computers at Bletchley', *Annals of the History of Computing*, 1.1 (1979), pp. 38–48.

—— 'Enigma and Fish' in Hinsley, F. H. and Alan Stripp, eds., *Codebreakers: The Inside Story of Bletchley Park* (Oxford: Oxford University Press, 1993), pp. 149–166.

—— 'From Hut 8 to the Newmanry' in Copeland, B. Jack, ed., *Colossus: The Secrets of Bletchley Park's Codebreaking Computers* (Oxford: Oxford University Press, 2006), pp. 204–222.

—— *Good Thinking: The Foundations of Probability and Its Applications* (Minneapolis: University of Minnesota Press, 1983).

—— 'Introductory Remarks for the Article in *Biometrika* 66 (1979), "A. M. Turing's Statistical Work in World War II"' in Britton, J. L., ed., *Collected Works of A. M. Turing...*, vol. 2 (Amsterdam: Elsevier, 2001), pp. 211–223.

—— 'Pioneering Work on Computers at Bletchley' in Metropolis, N., J. Howlett and Gian-Carlo Rota, eds., *A History of Computing in the Twentieth Century: A Collection of Essays* (New York: Academic, 1980), pp. 31–45.

—— *Probability and the Weighing of Evidence* (London: Griffin, 1950).

—— 'Random Motion on a Finite Abelian Group', *Proc. Camb. Phil. Soc.*, 47 (1951), pp. 756–762.

—— 'Studies in the History of Probability and Statistics. XXXVII: A. M. Turing's Statistical Work in World War II', *Biometrika*, 66 (1979), pp. 393–396.

—— 'The Contributions of Jeffreys to Bayesian Statistics' in Zellner, A., ed., *Bayesian Analysis in Econometrics and Statistics: Essays in Honor of Harold Jeffreys* (Amsterdam: North-Holland, 1980), pp. 21–34.

—— *The Estimation of Probabilities: An Essay on Modern Bayesian Methods* (Cambridge, Mass.: MIT Press, 1965).

—— 'The Fractional Dimensional Theory of Continued Fractions', *Proc. Camb. Phil. Soc.*, 37 (1941), pp. 199–228.

—— 'The Interaction Algorithm and Practical Fourier Analysis', *Jour. Roy. Statist. Soc. B*, 20 (1958), pp. 361–372.

—— 'The Interface between Statistics and Philosophy of Science', *Statistical Science*, 3 (1988), pp. 386–397.

—— 'The Joint Probability Generating Function for Run-Lengths in Regenerative Binary Markov Chains, with Applications', *Annals of Statistics*, 1 (1973), pp. 933–939.

—— 'The Population Frequencies of Species and the Estimation of Population Parameters', *Biometrika*, 40 (1953), pp. 237–264.

—— 'Turing's Anticipation of Empirical Bayes in Connection with the Cryptanalysis of the Naval Enigma', *J. Statist. Comput. & Simul.*, 66 (2000): *Special Issue*, pp. 101–111.

—— 'Weight of Evidence, Causality, and False-alarm Probabilities' in Cherry, Colin, ed., *Papers read at a Symposium on 'Information Theory' held at the Royal Institution, London, August 29th to September 2nd 1960* (London: Butterworths, 1961), pp. 125–136.

Good, I. J. and Donald Michie, 'Motorless Tunny', Appendix 11 in Copeland, B. Jack, ed., *Colossus: The Secrets of Bletchley Park's Codebreaking Computers* (Oxford: Oxford University Press, 2006), pp. 409–410.

Good, I. J., Donald Michie and Geoffrey Timms, 'The Motor-Wheels and Limitations', Appendix 10 in Copeland, B. Jack, ed., *Colossus: The Secrets of Bletchley Park's Codebreaking Computers* (Oxford: Oxford University Press, 2006), pp. 406–408.

Good, I. J. and G. H. Toulmin, 'The Number of new Species, and the Increase of Population Coverage, when a Sample is Increased', *Biometrika*, 43 (1956), pp. 45–63.

Government Code and Cypher School, *A Course in Cryptanalysis: S.I. Course, Revised and Enlarged, June, 1942*, 2 vols., A Cryptographic Series 33–34 (Laguna Hills, Calif.: Aegean Park Press, n.d. [*c.*1983]).

Grey, Christopher, *Decoding Organization: Bletchley Park, Codebreaking and Organization Studies* (Cambridge: Cambridge University Press, 2012).

Gross, K. I., 'On the Evolution of Noncommutative Harmonic Analysis', *American Mathematical Monthly*, 85 (1978), pp. 525–548.

Hacking, Ian, *Logic of Statistical Inference* (Cambridge, 1965).

—— *The Emergence of Probability* (Cambridge: Cambridge University Press, 1975).

Hald, Anders, *A History of Mathematical Statistics from 1750 to 1930* (New York: Wiley, 1995).

Hannah, Theodore M., 'Frank B. Rowlett — A Personal Profile', *Cryptologic Spectrum* (Spring 1981), pp. 6–21, URL: `http://www.nsa.gov/public_info/_files/cryptologic_spectrum/frank_rowlett.pdf` (visited on 07/06/2014).

Hardy, G. H., *A Mathematician's Apology* (Cambridge: Cambridge University Press, 1941).

Harper, John, 'It's Complete', *Bletchley Park Times*, 4 (Autumn 2006).

Hayward, Gil, 'Operation Tunny' in Hinsley, F. H. and Alan Stripp, eds., *Codebreakers: The Inside Story of Bletchley Park* (Oxford: Oxford University Press, 1993), pp. 175–192.

—— 'The British Tunny Machine' in Copeland, B. Jack, ed., *Colossus: The Secrets of Bletchley Park's Codebreaking Computers* (Oxford: Oxford University Press, 2006), pp. 291–296.

Heidman, Michael T., Don H. Johnson and C. Sidney Burrus, 'Gauss and the History of the Fast Fourier Transform', *IEEE ASSP Magazine*, 1.3 (1984), pp. 14–21.

Hell, Rudolf, 'Die Entwicklung des Hell-Schreibers', *Hell Technische Mitteilungen: Gerätentwicklungen aus den Jahren 1929–1939* (Heft 1, 1940), pp. 2–11, URL: `http://www.cdvandt.org/Hell%20Mitteilungen.pdf` (visited on 07/06/2014).

Herivel, John, *Herivelismus and the German Military Enigma* (Kidderminster: M.&M. Baldwin, 2008).

Hesketh, Roger, *Fortitude: the D-day Deception Campaign* (London: St. Ermin's, 1999; reprinted Woodstock, NY: Overlook, 2000).

Hilton, Peter, 'Living with Fish: Breaking Tunny in the Newmanry and Testery' in Copeland, B. Jack, ed., *Colossus: The Secrets of Bletchley Park's Codebreaking Computers* (Oxford: Oxford University Press, 2006), pp. 189–203.

Hinsley, F. H. and Alan Stripp, eds., *Codebreakers: The Inside Story of Bletchley Park* (Oxford: Oxford University Press, 1993; paperback repr. with corrections, 1994).

Hinsley, F. H., E. E. Thomas, C. F. G. Ransom and R. C. Knight, *British Intelligence in the Second World War: Its Influence on Strategy and Operations*, 5 vols. (New York: Cambridge University Press, 1979).

Historic Naval Ships Association, 'National Security Agency Historic Cryptographic Collection', URL: `http://www.hnsa.org/doc/nara/nsaopendoor.htm` (visited on 07/06/2014).

'Historische Bildpostkarten — 17.3 Bildpostkarten/Das Lied von den Lügenlords', Universität Osnabrück — Sammlung Prof. Dr. S. Giesbrecht, URL: `http://www.bildpostkarten.uni-osnabrueck.de/displayimage.php?pos=-2868` (visited on 07/06/2014).

Hodges, Andrew, *Alan Turing: The Enigma* (New York: Simon and Schuster, 1983; reprinted London: Vintage, 1992).

Hoffmann, Karl Otto, *Ln–. Die Geschichte der Luftnachrichtentruppe* (Neckargemünd: Kurt Vowinckel, 1973).

Hoffmann, Peter, *The History of the German Resistance, 1933–1945* (Montreal and Buffalo: McGill-Queen's University Press, 1996).

International Telegraph Union, *Règlement Télégraphique (Revision du Caire, 1938) Annexé à la Convention Internationale des Télécommunications (Madrid, 1932): Protocole Final audit Règlement* (Berne: Bureau de l'Union Internationale des Télécommunications, 1938).

Jeffreys, Harold, *Theory of Probability* (Oxford: Oxford University Press, 1939).

Kahn, David, *Seizing the Enigma: The Race to Break the U-Boat Codes* (London: Arrow, 1996).

—— *The Codebreakers: The Story of Secret Writing* (New York: Macmillan, 1967).

Kampe, Hans-Georg, *Die Heeres-Nachrichtentruppe der Wehrmacht, 1935–1945* (Wölfersheim-Berstadt: Podzun-Pallas, 1994).

—— *Handbuch zur Geschichte des militärichen Fernmeldwesens, Teil IV: Das militärische Fernmeldewesen Deutschlands im Zweiten Weltkrieg 1939-1945* (Berlin: Erwin Meißler, 2008).

—— *Nachrichtentruppe des Heeres und deutsche Reichspost: militärliches und staatliches Nachrichtenwesen in Deutschland 1830 bis 1945* (Waldesrsruh bei Berlin, 1999).

Kempe, H. R., 'Telegraph' in *Encyclopedia Britannica*, 11th ed. (Cambridge: Cambridge University Press, 1911).

Keynes, John Maynard, *Treatise on Probability* (London: Macmillan and Co., 1921).

Kim, Dong-Won, *Leadership and Creativity: A History of the Cavendish Laboratory, 1871–1919* (Dortrecht: Kluwer Academic Publishers, 2002).

Knuth, D. E., *The Art of Computer Programming, Volume 4A: Combinatorial Algorithms, Part 1* (Upper Saddle River, New Jersey: Addison-Wesley, 2011).

Kühn, Volker, *Kleinkunststücke*, 5 vols. (Weinheim and Berlin: Quadriga, 1987–94).

Kullback, S. and R. A. Leibler, 'On Information and Sufficiency', *Ann. Math. Statist.*, 22 (1951), pp. 79–86.

Kullback, Solomon, *Statistical Methods in Cryptanalysis*, United States Army Signal Corps, 1935.

Laplace, Pierre Simon, 'Mémoire sur la probabilité des causes par les évènemens', *Mémoires de mathématique et de physique, présentés à l'Académie royale des sciences, par divers sçavans, & lûs dans ses assemblées*, 6 (1774), pp. 621–656.

—— 'Mémoire sur les approximations des formules qui sont fonctions de très grands nombres', *Mémoires de mathématique et de physique, présentés à l'Académie royale des sciences, par divers sçavans, & lûs dans ses assemblées* (1783/1786), pp. 423–467.

—— *Œeuvres complètes de Laplace*, 14 vols. (Paris: Gauthier-Villars, 1878–1912).

—— *Théorie analytique des probabilités* (Paris: Courcier, 1812).

—— *Théorie analytique des probabilités*, 3rd ed. (Paris: Courcier, 1820).

Lavington, Simon, 'In the Footsteps of Colossus: A Description of Oedipus', *IEEE Annals of the History of Computing*, 28.2 (2006), pp. 44–55.

Lee, John A. N. and Golde Holtzman, '50 Years after Breaking the Codes: Interviews with two of the Bletchley Park Scientists', *IEEE Annals of the History of Computing*, 17 (1995), pp. 32–43.

Lehmer, D. H., 'A History of the Sieve Process' in Metropolis, N., J. Howlett and Gian-Carlo Rota, eds., *A History of Computing in the Twentieth Century: A Collection of Essays* (New York: Academic, 1980), pp. 445–456.

—— 'A Photo-electric Number Sieve', *American Mathematical Monthly*, 40 (1933), pp. 401–406.

Lord, Bob, 'Decrypt Fragments', URL: `http://www.ilord.com/bp-decrypts.html` (visited on 26/02/2015).

'Lorenz cipher', Wikipedia article, URL: `http://en.wikipedia.org/wiki/Lorenz_cipher` (visited on 07/06/2014).

Lucas, É., 'Sur les congruences des nombres eulériens et les coefficients différentiels des fonctions trigonométriques, suivant un module premier', *Bulletin de la Société Mathématique de France*, 6 (1878), pp. 49–54.

Lucas, Frank Laurence, *Style* (London: Cassell, 1955).

Luxembourg, Grand Duchy of, 'Loi du 14 avril 1934 portant approbation de la Convention Internationale des Télécommications de Madrid du 9 décembre 1932 et des Règlements télégraphique et téléphonique y annexés', *Mémorial du Grand-Duché de Luxembourg*, 24 (23 Apr. 1934), pp. 415–533, URL: `http://www.legilux.public.lu/leg/a/archives/1934/0024/a024.pdf` (visited on 28/02/2015).

Maas, F. J., 'Der Stand der Funkfernschreibtechnik in Deutschland bis 1944', 15 Feb. 1946.

Mackey, G. W., *The Scope and History of Commutative and Noncommutative Harmonic Analysis* (Providence, RI: American Mathematical Society, 1992).

Marschner, Rolf, 'Lorenz Lo 200 L36 bis Lo 500 FK41: "Ehrenmal"-Sender', URL: `http://www.seefunknetz.de/laboe.htm` (visited on 07/06/2014).

Metropolis, N., J. Howlett and Gian-Carlo Rota, eds., *A History of Computing in the Twentieth Century: A Collection of Essays* (New York: Academic, 1980).

Michie, Donald, 'Codebreaking and Colossus' in Copeland, B. Jack, ed., *Colossus: The Secrets of Bletchley Park's Codebreaking Computers* (Oxford: Oxford University Press, 2006), pp. 223–246.

—— 'Colossus and the Breaking of the Wartime "Fish" Codes', *Cryptologia*, 26.1 (2002), pp. 17–58.

Michie, James Crain, *The Odes of Horace* (London: Rupert Hart-Davis, 1964; reprinted London: Penguin, 1967).

Mill, John Stuart, *A System of Logic, Ratiocinative and Inductive*, 4th ed. (London: John W. Parker, 1846).

Millward, William, 'Life In and Out of Hut 3' in Hinsley, F. H. and Alan Stripp, eds., *Codebreakers: The Inside Story of Bletchley Park* (Oxford: Oxford University Press, 1993), pp. 17–29.

Ministry of Information, *What Britain has done, 1939–1945: A Selection of Outstanding Facts and Figures*, reprinted, with an introduction by Richard Overy (London: Atlantic, 2007).

Mises, R. von and H. Pollaczek-Geiringer, 'Praktische Verfahren der Gleichungsauflösung', *ZAMM — Zeitschrift für Angewandte Mathematik und Mechanik*, 9 (1929), pp. 152–164.

Mowry, David P., *The Cryptology of the German Intelligence Services* (Ft. Meade, Maryland: National Security Agency, 1989), URL: `http://www.nsa.gov/public_info/_files/cryptologic_histories/cryptology_of_gis.pdf` (visited on 07/06/2014), Release of NSA Office of Archives and History, United States Cryptologic History, Series IV, Volume 4, NSA DOCID: 3525898.

New Hart's Rules: the Handbook of Style for Writers and Editors (Oxford: Oxford University Press, 2005).

Newman, Christopher, 'Max Newman — Mathematician, Codebreaker, and Computer Pioneer' in Copeland, B. Jack, ed., *Colossus: The Secrets of Bletchley Park's Codebreaking Computers* (Oxford: Oxford University Press, 2006), pp. 176–188.

Neyman, Jerzy, 'Outline of a Theory of Statistical Estimation Based on the Classical Theory of Probability', *Philos. Trans. Roy. Soc. London A*, 236 (1937), pp. 333–380.

NSA Cryptologic Documents, A Cryptographic Series 83 (Laguna Hills, Calif.: Aegean Park Press, n.d. [*c.*2000]).

'[Obituary of Tilmar Moilien]', University of Iowa Statistics and Actuarial Science Department newsletter, 2003.

Oxford Dictionary of National Biography: In Association with the British Academy: From the Earliest Times to the Year 2000, ed. by H.C.G. Matthew and Brian Harrison (London: Oxford University Press, 2004), URL: `http://www.oxforddnb.com/subscribed/` (visited on 07/06/2014).

Pearson, Egon and Jerzy Neyman, 'On the Problem of the Most Efficient Tests of Statistical Hypotheses', *Philos. Trans. Roy. Soc. London A*, 231 (1933), pp. 289–337.

—— 'On the Use and Interpretation of Certain Test Criteria for Purposes of Statistical Inference', *Biometrika*, 20 (1928), pp. 175–240, 263–294.

Peter, F. and H. Weyl, 'Die Vollständigkeit der primitiven Darstellungen einer geschlossenen Kontinuierlichen Gruppe', *Mathematische Annalen*, 97 (1927), pp. 737–755.

Poisson, Siméon Denis, *Recherches sur la probabilité des jugements en matière criminelle et matière civile* (Paris, 1837).

Pontriagin, L., *Topological Groups*, trans. by E. Lehmer (Princeton: Princeton University Press, 1939).

Pratt, Fletcher, *Secret and Urgent — The Story of Codes and Ciphers* (Indianapolis: Bobbs-Merrill, 1939).

Praun, Albert, *Soldat in der Telegraphen- und Nachrichtentruppe* (Würzburg, 1965).

Preston, G. B., 'Oxford in the forties', *Magdalen College Record* (2008), pp. 105–111.

—— 'Personal reminiscences of the early history of semigroups' in Hall, Thomas Eric, P. R. Jones and J. C. Meakin, eds., *Monash Conference on Semigroup Theory, in Honour of G. B. Preston; Clayton, Australia, 11-13 July 1990* (Singapore: World Scientific, 1991), pp. 16–30.

Prevost, P. and S. A. J. Lhuilier, 'Mémoire sur l'application du calcul des probabilités à la valeur du témoignage', *Mémoires de l'Académie Royale des sciences et belles-lettres* [Berlin] (1797), pp. 120–152.

Price, Alfred, *Instruments of Darkness* (London: William Kimber, 1967).

Raiffa, Howard and Robert Schlaifer, *Applied Statistical Decision Theory* (Boston: Harvard Business School, 1961).

'Ralph Tester', Wikipedia article, URL: `http://en.wikipedia.org/wiki/Ralph_Tester` (visited on 07/06/2014).

Randell, Brian, 'The COLOSSUS' in Metropolis, N., J. Howlett and Gian-Carlo Rota, eds., *A History of Computing in the Twentieth Century: A Collection of Essays* (New York: Academic, 1980), pp. 47–92.

—— *The Colossus*, report 90, University of Newcastle upon Tyne Computing Laboratory, 1976.

Ratcliff, R. A., *Delusions of Intelligence: Enigma, Ultra, and the End of Secure Ciphers* (Cambridge: Cambridge University Press, 2006).

Reeds, J. A., 'American Dragon', *Cryptologia*, 35.1 (2011), pp. 22–41.

Rossberg, E. A. and H. E. Korta, *Teleprinter Switching* (Princeton: Van Nostrand, 1960).

Rowlett, Frank B., *The Story of Magic: Memoirs of an American Cryptologic Pioneer* (Laguna Hills, Calif.: Aegean Park Press, 1998).

Runciman, Brian, 'It's a Bouncing Baby Bombe', *ITNOW, A Journal of the British Computer Society*, 49.1 (Jan. 2007), URL: `http://www.bcs.org/upload/pdf/jan07.pdf` (visited on 07/06/2014).

Sampford, Michael Robert, *An Introduction to Sampling Theory, with Applications to Agriculture* (Edinburgh and London: Oliver & Boyd, 1962).

—— *Conscience of a Statistician* (Liverpool: Liverpool University Press, 1967).

Savage, Leonard J., *The Foundations of Statistics* (New York, 1954).

Schiweck, Fritz, *Fernschreibtechnik* (Prien (Bavaria): C.F. Winter, 1962).

Sebag-Montefiori, Hugh, *Enigma: The Battle for the Code* (London: Phoenix, 2004).

Shannon, C. E., 'A Mathematical Theory of Communication', *Bell System Technical Journal*, 27 (1948), pp. 379–423, 623–656.

Shorter Oxford English Dictionary (Oxford: Oxford University Press, 1944).

Simon, H., 'Bedeutung und Grundlagen der modernen Telegraphieverbindungen', *Funktechnische Monatshefte für Rundfunk / Hochfrequenztechnik und Grenzgebiete*, 5 (May 1942), pp. 61–76, URL: `http://www.cdvandt.org/FTM%201942%20H5%20telex.pdf` (visited on 07/06/2014).

Small, Albert W., 'Special Fish Report', (transcript of NARA HCC 1417:4628), URL: `http://www.codesandciphers.org.uk/documents/small/smallix.htm` (visited on 07/06/2014).

Smith, Michael, 'The Government Code and Cypher School and the First Cold War' in Smith, Michael and Ralph Erskine, eds., *Action This Day* (London: Bantam Press, 2001), pp. 15–40.

Smoot, Betsy Rohaly, 'Pioneers of U.S. Military Cryptology: Colonel Parker Hitt and His Wife, Genevieve Young Hitt', *Federal History Journal* (Issue 4, 2012), pp. 87–100, URL: `http://shfg.org/shfg/wp-content/uploads/2012/12/6-Smoot-Web-final.pdf` (visited on 07/06/2014).

Soutou, Georges-Henri, 'French Intelligence about the East during the Fourth Republic: Pedestrian but Sensible', a paper given at a conference 'Keeping Secrets: How Important was Intelligence to the Conduct of International Relations from 1914 to 1989?' held at the German Historical Institute, London, Apr. 2008.

—— 'La mécanisation du chiffre au Quai d'Orsay, ou les aléas d'un système technique (1948–1958)' in Merger, Michèle and Dominique Barjot, eds., *Les entreprises et leurs réseaux: hommes, capitaux, techniques et pouvoirs XIXe – XXe siècles* (Paris: Presses de l'Université de Paris-Sorbonne, 1998), pp. 697–710.

Stigler, Stephen M., 'Laplace's 1774 Memoir on Inverse Probability', *Statistical Science*, 1 (1986), pp. 359–378.

—— *Statistics on the Table: The History of Statistical Concepts and Methods* (Cambridge, Mass.: Harvard University Press, 1999).

Terman, F. E., *Radio Engineering* (New York: McGraw-Hill, 1937).

Thomas, Edward, 'A Naval Officer in Hut 3' in Hinsley, F. H. and Alan Stripp, eds., *Codebreakers: The Inside Story of Bletchley Park* (Oxford: Oxford University Press, 1993), pp. 41–49.

Timms, Geoffrey, 'On the Highest Space in which a Non-ruled Surface of Given Order Can Lie', *Proceedings of the Edinburgh Mathematical Society*, 2nd ser., 6.3 (Aug. 1940), pp. 149–150.

—— 'The Nodal Cubic Surfaces and the Surfaces from Which They Are Derived by Projection', *Proc. Roy. Soc. London A*, 119 (1928), pp. 213–248.

Tout, Nigel, 'Bell Punch Company & Anita Calculators', URL: `http://www.vintagecalculat%20ors.com/BellPunch` (visited on 07/06/2014).

Turing, A. M., *Collected Works of A. M. Turing*, 4 vols., ed. J. L. Britton (Amsterdam: Elsevier, 2001).

—— 'Computing Machinery and Intelligence', *Mind*, 59 (1950), pp. 433–460.

—— 'On Computable Numbers, with an Application to the *Entscheidungsproblem*', *Proc. London Math. Soc.*, 42 (1936), pp. 230–265.

—— 'On Computable Numbers, with an Application to the *Entscheidungsproblem*: A Correction', *Proc. London Math. Soc.*, 44 (1937), pp. 544–546.

Turing, A. M. and D. Bayley, 'Report on Speech Secrecy System DELILAH, a Technical Description Compiled by A. M. Turing and Lieutenant D. Bayley REME, 1945–1946', *Cryptologia*, 36.4 (2012), pp. 295–340.

Tutte, William T., 'At Bletchley Park', 6 May 2002, URL: http://math.uwaterloo.ca/combinatorics-and-optimization/sites/ca.combinatorics-and-optimization/files/uploads/files/atbletchley.pdf (visited on 07/06/2014).

—— 'Fish and I' in Joyner, W. D., ed., *Coding Theory and Cryptography: From Enigma and Geheimschreiber to Quantum Theory* (Berlin: Springer, 2000), pp. 9–17, URL: http://math.uwaterloo.ca/combinatorics-and-optimization/sites/ca.combinatorics-and-optimization/files/uploads/files/corr98-39.pdf (visited on 07/06/2014).

—— 'My Work at Bletchley Park', Appendix 4 in Copeland, B. Jack, ed., *Colossus: The Secrets of Bletchley Park's Codebreaking Computers* (Oxford: Oxford University Press, 2006), pp. 352–369.

United States Army Security Agency, *Descriptive Dictionary of Cryptologic Terms, Including Foreign Terms*, A Cryptographic Series 77, Reprint of Feb. 1947 issue by ASA (Laguna Hills, Calif.: Aegean Park Press, n.d. [*c.*1998]).

—— *European Axis Signal Intelligence in World War II as Revealed by 'TICOM' Investigations and by other Prisoner of War Interrogations and Captured Material, Principally German*, FOIA release of 9-volume typescript report (Washington, D.C., 1946), URL: http://www.nsa.gov/public_info/declass/european_axis_sigint.shtml (visited on 07/06/2014).

United States Delegation to the International Telecommunications Conferences, Cairo, 1938, *Report to the Secretary of State by the Chairman of the American Delegation, with appended documents* (Washington, D.C.: USGPO, 1939).

United States National Archives and Records Administration, 'Records of the National Security Agency/Central Security Service', URL: http://www.archives.gov/research/guide-fed-records/groups/457.html (visited on 07/06/2014).

United States War Department, *War Department Technical Manual TM 11-889, Diversity Receiving Equipment (RCA Model DR-89)* (Washington, D.C.: USGPO, 1945).

Uspensky, J. V., *Introduction to Mathematical Probability* (New York: McGraw-Hill, 1937).

Venn, John, *The Logic of Chance*, 2nd ed. (London: Macmillan, 1876; reprinted New York: Chelsea, 1957).

Vernam, Gilbert S., 'Secret Signaling System', US Patent 1,310,719, issued 22 July 1919.

Vigenère, Blaise de, *Traicté des chiffres, ou secretes manieres d'escrire* (Paris: Abel L'Angelier, 1586).

Weber, H., *Lehrbuch der Algebra* (Braunschweig: F. Vieweg, 1912; reprinted New York: Chelsea, n.d. [*c.*1950]).

Weierud, Frode, 'Bletchley Park's Sturgeon — The Fish that Laid No Eggs', *The Rutherford Journal: The New Zealand Journal for the History and Philosophy of Science and Technology*, 1 (Dec. 2005), URL: http://www.rutherfordjournal.org/article010106.html (visited on 07/06/2014).

—— 'Bletchley Park's Sturgeon — the Fish that Laid No Eggs' in Copeland, B. Jack, ed., *Colossus: The Secrets of Bletchley Park's Codebreaking Computers* (Oxford: Oxford University Press, 2006), pp. 307–327.

—— 'Sturgeon, The Fish BP Never Really Caught' in Joyner, W. D., ed., *Coding Theory and Cryptography: From Enigma and Geheimschreiber to Quantum Theory* (Berlin: Springer, 2000), pp. 18–52, URL: http://link.springer.com/chapter/10.1007/978-3-642-59663-6_3#page-1 (visited on 07/06/2014).

Weil, A., *L'Intégration dans les Groupes Topologiques et ses Applications* (Paris: Hermann, 1940).

Welchman, Gordon, *The Hut Six Story* (New York: McGraw-Hill, 1982).

Wells, Benjamin, 'The PC-User's Guide to Colossus' in Copeland, B. Jack, ed., *Colossus: The Secrets of Bletchley Park's Codebreaking Computers* (Oxford: Oxford University Press, 2006), pp. 116–138.

Weyl, H., *Group Theory and Quantum Mechanics*, trans. by H. P. Robertson, trans. of 2nd German edition (London: Methuen, 1931; reprinted New York: Dover, 1949).

Whittaker, Edmund and G. Robinson, *The Calculus of Observations, a Treatise on Numerical Mathematics* (London, Glasgow: Blackie, 1927).

Whitworth, William Allen, *Choice and Chance* (Cambridge: Deighton, Bell, 1867).

Wiesner, Lothar, *Telegraph and Data Transmission over Shortwave Radio Links* (London: Heyden & Son, 1977).

Wilkinson, Patrick, 'Italian Naval Decrypts' in Hinsley, F. H. and Alan Stripp, eds., *Codebreakers: The Inside Story of Bletchley Park* (Oxford: Oxford University Press, 1993), pp. 61–67.

Wrinch, D. and H. Jeffreys, 'On Certain Fundamental Principles of Scientific Inquiry', *Philosophical Magazine*, 6th ser., 42 (1921), pp. 369–390.

Wynn-Williams, C. E., 'The Use of Thyratrons for High Speed Automatic Counting of Physical Phenomena', *Proc. Roy. Soc. A*, 132 (1931), pp. 295–310.

Yates, F., *The Design and Analysis of Factorial Experiments* (Harpenden (Herts): Imperial Bureau of Soil Science, 1937).

Zabell, S. L., 'Alan Turing and the Central Limit Theorem', *American Mathematical Monthly*, 102 (1995), pp. 483–494.

—— 'Commentary on Alan M. Turing: The Applications of Probability to Cryptography', *Cryptologia*, 36.3 (2012), pp. 191–214.

Index

This index covers both the original text of the *Report*, which spans pages 1–493, and our added editorial matter. Page references printed in **bold** type point to defining entries in chapters **71** and **72**, or to our List of Abbreviations, or to our Supplementary Glossary. The alphabetization scheme is that used in chapters **71** and **72**, with mathematical symbols alphabetized together with the other terms. Greek-letter symbols are sorted in Greek alphabetical order *after* the end of the Roman alphabet.

Printed and bound by CPI Group (UK) Ltd, Croydon, CR0 4YY
18/09/2026
14965004-0003